Conceiving the Inconceivable

Other Books by Ashish Dalela:

The Science of God
Time and Consciousness
The Balanced Organization
The Yellow Pill
Cosmic Theogony
Emotion
Mystic Universe
Moral Materialism
Signs of Life
Uncommon Wisdom
Gödel's Mistake
Quantum Meaning
Sāṅkhya and Science
Is the Apple Really Red?
Six Causes

Conceiving the Inconceivable

A Scientific Commentary on the Vedānta Sūtra

Original Text Composed by
Sage Vyāsa

Ashish Dalela

Conceiving the Inconceivable—A Scientific Commentary on the Vedānta Sūtra
by Ashish Dalela
www.shabda.co

Interior Design: Ciprian Begu

Published by Shabda Press
www.press.shabda.co
ISBN 978-93-85384-24-0
v1.2(06/2021)

SHABDA
PRESS

"We have to explain what is meant by Vedānta. Veda means knowledge and anta means end; we have already explained. So, everyone is searching after knowledge, inquisitiveness. The science is also the same process. Science is trying to find out the ultimate cause, starting point. Is it not? That is scientific research. So, we have our departments of knowledge. He can study even a flower. Go on studying, you can come to the seed, the potential. This is scientific research. To find out the ultimate cause. So, there are so many departments of knowledge. Department of science, department of art. Vedānta means the Ultimate knowledge, the Original. That is called brahma-jijñāsā. ... [it] means this human form of life is specially meant for enquiring Absolute Truth. If the human being does not enquire about it then he's animal. You have to prove it logically, scientifically. This is first sūtra. So, you write on upon one sūtra, then I give you next sūtra. Every one of you can write according to understanding, athātho-brahma-jijñāsā. Now, this is the life for enquiring about the Ultimate goal, Absolute Truth."

— His Divine Grace A.C. Bhaktivedānta Swami Prabhupāda
From a recording by H.H. Bhaktisvarūpa Dāmodara Swami

We should always be enthusiastic to try for capturing the rhinoceros. That way, if we fail, everyone will say, "Never mind, nobody can catch a rhinoceros anyway," and if we succeed, then everyone will say, "Just see what a wonderful thing they have done!"

— His Divine Grace A.C. Bhaktivedānta Swami Prabhupāda
Quoted in "Chasing Rhinos with the Swami" by Syāmasundar Das

Contents

Series Preface

At present, the Vedic philosophical system suffers from many misconceptions—(a) the Vedic texts comprise many disparate or conflicting doctrines that don't form a coherent system, (b) these texts advocate the worship of different deities so the Vedic system must be polytheistic, (c) due to the differences between the various Vedic texts, they must have been authored by different people so they cannot be of divine origin, and (d) the texts produced by various human minds must have originated at different ages and times in history.

Those who want to correct these misconceptions are also making many mistakes. First, they defend the history as being a few thousand years older than modern estimates (when the Vedic tradition is sanātana or eternal). Second, they accept impersonalism as a solution to the supposed polytheism of the Vedas (even though it is solemnly rejected by the Vedic texts). Third, they apologize for the diversity of texts as the intellectual virtue of plural viewpoints (when plurality is different perspectives on a single understanding of reality). Fourth, they visualize Vedic knowledge through the mundane lens of geographical contiguity and genetic resemblances confusing the correction of mistakes with pedestrian ideals of nationalism, political unity, cultural pride, etc., and the true spiritual foundations under which all material identities of body, gender, society, and nation are rejected as a waste of time, are ignored.

This series of books differs from the above-mentioned goals and aspirations. This may potentially reduce the reader list to a smaller number of people who are truly interested in the truth, not a race, nationality, language, etc. But that risk must be taken in the interest of truth, and broader objectives of Vedic knowledge. The sacrifice of immediate interests is hence a necessary evil.

The primary goal of this series of books is to establish that the Vedas constitute a coherent description of reality, which has to be understood from multiple perspectives to grasp its true nature. This understanding can be broadly classified into the following categories—(a) the study of matter as concepts and qualities, (b) the understanding of the soul and its relation to God, (c) the practices by which this nature of the soul and God are practically realized and experienced, and (d) the system of reasoning and logic that is used to explain it to anyone who might be interested. The study of the nature of the soul and God is theology. The practice by which this nature is realized is religion. The description of matter as categories and qualities is philosophy. And the system of reasoning and logic used to explain it to those who are interested is science.

Each perspective can be, in principle, described and understood without the others. For example, we can practice religious mysticism without perfectly knowing theology. We can know the philosophy of reality without religion or theology. And we can understand the science without practicing mysticism.

Nevertheless, the Vedic texts do not put these into separate boxes. Every text discusses all the subjects—science, philosophy, religion, and theology—but with different relative emphases. Some texts are more focused on science, others more on theology and religion, while others more on philosophy. This unifying tendency in the Vedic system is the antithesis of the modern tendency to compartmentalize, separate one issue from another, focus on narrow problems, and create the illusion of progress by going round and round in circles.

The Vedic system looks at all inquiries holistically and their answers to one question cannot contradict the answers to any other potential question. If you progress in philosophy, then you also progress in religion, theology, and science. Scientific progress is not contrary to ethics and morality; spiritual development is not contrary to the necessities of life. The Vedic system is not divided into physics, chemistry, mathematics, sociology, economics, psychology, cosmology, theology, and so on, as its purpose is to create wise people—who know everything—rather than professional academics whose solutions are conceived within the narrow ambits of their primary expertise, rather than broadly concerned with several aspects of the problem needed for a wise person.

The understanding of the knowledge and its application to various areas of human knowledge should be the primary goal because by achieving that goal, the other goals can be achieved automatically. If the knowledge is useful and true, then each path meant to attain it can be useful for people with different abilities and interests. If the Vedic texts describe reality correctly, then the timelessness of the knowledge would be more important than the age of the text. If the philosophy is consistent and complete, then even plural authorship of the texts would indicate a multitude of mutually coherent viewpoints. If the personalistic and aspected nature of reality is understood correctly, then the myriad personalities would not be contradictory to a single person of God. And the universal applicability and the non-sectarian nature of knowledge would make any national, social, cultural, and political pride completely redundant.

Even as the Vedas are divine knowledge, and many times described as the word of God and transmitted through the creator of the universe—Brahma—nobody has to accept their divinity a priori. Vedas recommend faith in the teachers because no student approaches a teacher without some faith. But blind faith—as the antithesis of reason and experience—is rejected. The philosophy of the Vedas is meant to be studied, debated, and discussed by all qualified people (the restriction of the Vedas to a certain class is the restriction of qualification). And the knowledge of the Vedas is beyond race, nation, and society. In all these ways, the Vedas constitute a "secular science"—not atheistic, but secular—as they are amenable to reason and experience, open to sincere inquiry and discussion, and not to be conflated with narrow political objectives.

The primary aim of this series of books is to help the readers understand the knowledge. If the truth of the Vedic texts is known, then we can talk about their history. If the unity of Vedic philosophy is known, then we can talk about whether they had different authors. If by learning this philosophy, we can master every subject, then we can talk about its divine and eternal nature. And if all these are achieved, then we can speak of the intellectual, cultural, and social superiority of the people who have preserved, advanced, and propagated this knowledge selflessly. In fact, by establishing the truth, all other questions about history, authorship, and divinity will become moot—we will accept them without an argument, based on their superiority. Without proving the consistency, completeness, pervasive usefulness, and the empirical truth of this knowledge, there is no point in talking about history, authorship, divinity, geographical heritage, and socio-cultural identities. Without understanding the nature of reality, pride in ancient history makes no difference to the present. And without putting that knowledge into practice, all claims remain the subject of endless subjective opinions and pointless debates. If instead, we focus on the truth in the Vedas, then even the temporaneous goals can also be achieved naturally.

The Vedas in fact describe the history of their appearance, but because people don't believe in the Vedic truth, therefore, they don't accept the history. Because the academics have become accustomed to numerous mythological texts in the West, which were repeatedly modified and curated by religious institutions to suit their political objectives, they think that the Vedas too must be myths. But where is the evidence for the doctoring of the Vedas? We can find that evidence in the case of the Bible and the Koran for instance, where books have been revised many times, and the ideas of the doctors were inserted into the books. But the Vedic tradition gives us no such evidence. Instead, there is clear evidence of the separation of the texts from the commentaries on the texts. The texts are always separate from the commentaries by various authors. Therefore, if we rely on the Vedic texts, we can also understand their own history.

To understand the Six Systems of Philosophy, we need to take note of their historical appearance. The Vedas state that their knowledge has existed since time immemorial, and originated in the four Vedas compiled by Brahma—the creator of the universe—after being inspired in the heart by Lord Viṣṇu. Brahma imparted this knowledge to his sons—the seven sages, Manu, the four Kumaras, and others. These disciples and their successors then produced a broader oral tradition, which was called the "Vedic system"—because it was based on the original four Vedas that were narrated by Brahma to others. This oral tradition was significantly larger than what we know as the Vedic texts today.

Vedic cosmology divides time into cycles of yugas, which are further divided into four sub-ages called Satya-yuga, Treta-yuga, Dvapara-yuga, and Kali-yuga. The Kali-yuga is the smallest age and is 432,000 years. Dvapara is twice that of Kali-yuga, Treta is three times of Kali-yuga, and Satya is four times Kali-yuga. The present age is Kali-yuga. In the bygone ages—Satya, Treta, and Dvapara—which amounts to 3,888,000 solar years, the Vedas existed as an oral tradition, because the people following the system had a great memory.

At the beginning of Kali-yuga, these texts were scribed by Vyāsa, who is also sometimes called Bādarāyana. This is when the oral tradition became a written one. Vyāsa performed a selection from the oral tradition, and the texts he produced by scribing the oral tradition were a subset of the oral tradition.

Vyāsa also divided the oral tradition into many parts, which are today known as Saṃhita, Upaniśad, Tantra, Purāna, Itihāsa, etc. Each of these classes is further divided into many sub-classes and texts. For instance, there are 108 Upaniśad and 18 Purāna. He then also *composed* the Vedānta Sūtra after *compiling* the other Vedic texts. There is a subtle difference between compiling and composing. A compilation is the selective scribing of the oral tradition. But the composition is solely attributable to Bādarāyana (although he often quotes other sages even in this text). Quite simply, Vedānta Sūtra is Bādarāyana's summary of the oral tradition, after the selective scribing of the oral tradition.

While dividing, scribing, and compiling the Vedic texts, Vyāsa referred to the philosophies of some of the Six Systems such as Sāñkhya and Yoga and included them into the Vedic texts. He left out some of the philosophies such as Nyāya, Vaiśeṣika, and Mīmāṃsā as they were, and still are, considered supplementary. We might wonder why. And the answer is that Nyāya is a system of logic, Mīmāṃsā is the use of reason for semantic analysis, and Vaiśeṣika is the application of semantic analysis to the study of material nature. These are, strictly speaking, the applications of Vedic philosophy, which are of great interest to the experts, but not of primary interest to the general population. This exclusion of some philosophies from the primary Vedic texts means that logic, semantic analysis, and its applications to the study of nature, were considered to be not of interest to the people primarily interested in the conclusions.

The selective inclusions and exclusions of some philosophies do not mean that they weren't part of the Vedic tradition. For example, practically everyone undergoing scientific education at present uses logic and mathematics, but the foundations of logic and mathematics are studied only by experts. Similarly, practically everyone masters some language, but the foundations of linguistics are outside the scope for everyone except the experts. The doctors who treat patients learn medicine, but they don't study biochemistry because that is too much unnecessary detail that is not of primary interest to their needs.

Therefore, the inclusion of philosophies of Sāñkhya and Yoga should be viewed as based on the fact that these were considered general information for everyone's use, while the exclusion of philosophies like Nyāya, Vaiśeṣika, and Mīmāṃsā should be viewed as something that was needed only for experts.

Quite separately, complete systems of philosophy existed as the Sūtra texts that this series is about. They were authored by other sages (Sāñkhya by Kapila, Yoga by Patanjali, Nyāya by Gautama, Vaiśeṣika by Kanāda, and Mīmāṃsā by Jaimini). These other systems of philosophy are also based on the oral Vedic tradition, which preceded Bādarāyana's selected scribing of the tradition, although Nyāya, Vaiśeṣika, and Mīmāṃsā were not included in the scribing. They too existed as an oral tradition and were scribed by their tradition followers, but their names are not known at present because (a) the texts are relatively small compared to the texts that Vyāsa scribed, and (b) there was no selection performed in the scribing of these texts; they were presented as they were. In that light, we can view Vyāsa as an editor of the Vedic tradition, while the other systems of philosophy had scribes that did not try to edit the Sūtra texts.

The result of this difference between Bādarāyana's selected scribing, and the texts of the other five systems, is that we can sometimes find it hard to cite the claims in the philosophies of Sāñkhya, Yoga, Nyāya, Vaiśeṣika, and Mīmāṃsā from the Saṃhita, Upaniśad, Tantra, Purāna, and Itihāsa. This inability to find direct references for one system in another one should not be taken to mean that they are at variance, or that they are not Vedic, or that they were created after the scribing of Vedic texts by other philosophers who did not agree with Bādarāyana's view. We must rather understand that all the Six Systems are based on the oral tradition. Specifically, Sāñkhya, Yoga, Vaiśeṣika, Nyāya, and Mīmāṃsā had their oral tradition before Bādarāyana scribing a select portion of the oral tradition, followed by composing the Vedānta Sūtra. As far as the historical dates of composing are concerned, Vedānta Sūtra is later. It is for this reason that it is sometimes called Uttara Mīmāṃsā (later analysis).

When we study the Six Systems of philosophy, in one sense, we are studying the much older oral tradition—as it was understood by six different sages. And when we study the Saṃhita, Upaniśad, Tantra, Purāna, and Itihāsa, we are studying the Vedic system as it was selectively scribed by Bādarāyana. The differences in these systems do not indicate a contradiction, but the fact that the oral tradition was bigger than the combinations of all the texts at present.

The point is this: The Six Systems are Vedic because they are all based on the oral tradition. They are also Vedic because Bādarāyana's texts directly reference Sāñkhya and Yoga, which are also referenced by Nyāya, Vaiśeṣika, and Mīmāṃsā. Then, several doctrines about the nature of the soul and God are common across the Six Systems and can be found in Bādarāyana's texts. Therefore, the Six Systems are not divergent philosophies, but different streams within the oral tradition that emphasized different aspects, and were thereby encoded as the Sūtra texts, that came to be studied by different students, and that inherited method of teacher-disciple succession created many schools.

And yet, there is widespread perception at present that the Six Systems of Philosophy are divergent, or even contradictory. This perception of divergence is not entirely fictional; it is indeed based on fact. But its appearance is relatively recent. Such deviations appear in the age of Kali-yuga, where people tend to replace understanding with argument, and incommensurate ideas that deviate from the Vedic philosophy appear. To support their contentions, they also reject many essential aspects of the cohesive system of philosophy.

To understand this divergence, we need to consider the last few thousand years of history, in which three philosophies—materialism, voidism, and impersonalism—have dominated. Each of the Six Systems of Philosophy rejects these doctrines. The world, in Vedic philosophy, reflects the properties of God like a mirror reflects a person's image. The mirror is real, and hence, matter is real. The form in the mirror is objective—the image in the mirror is real. Similarly, the reflection in the mirror is not a creation of the mirror, or an illusion, because there is a person outside the mirror. Since there is a transcendent person, therefore, the mirror and the reflection in it are not the only reality; there is also a transcendent reality. By acknowledging a transcendent reality, materialism is rejected. By acknowledging that this transcendent reality is a person, impersonalism is rejected. And by recognizing that the person exists even if not reflected in the mirror—i.e., if the world doesn't exist—voidism is rejected.

The Six Systems texts delve into the details of why materialism, voidism, and impersonalism are false. They describe why God desires to see His reflection—namely, that it is a process of self-awareness and self-cognition. They describe how God is reflected in the mirror—the mirror is also a person, not an impersonal thing; the reflection in the mirror is the mirror "knowing" God; the mirror is then identified as God's energy or Śakti, and two realities—one masculine and the other feminine—are seen as the basis of the world. The immense variety in the reflection is attributed to the myriad aspects of God, which are integrated in God but separated in the Śakti. Thus, the created world is called *duality* whereas God is described as *non-duality*. The separation of the integrated reality is then understood as a mechanism by which God knows Himself—quite like a person looking into a mirror to see his varied features.

Each of the Six Systems of Vedic philosophy goes over these themes in different orders, emphasizing different aspects of this ideology, dwelling more on some things and less on others. Each philosophy refutes impersonalism, voidism, and materialism as these doctrines are contrary to the Vedic system.

In the modern context, the criticism of materialism can be equated to the rejection of modern science, and the ideas that underpin it. The Six Systems texts provide alternative descriptions of matter too, unparalleled by any other system in the past or present in its breadth and cohesiveness. The methods of realizing the truth of this description—i.e., the methods for practical and empirical confirmations—are also presented. The alternative to materialism is hence also rational and empirical, and without changing the definition of science—i.e., empirical, and rational truth—the reality is presented differently. It is rather the change of the doctrine of matter, with far wider empiricism, that covers the experiences of the senses, mind, intellect, ego, and the moral sense. The criticism of materialism therefore also constitutes an alternative science.

Similarly, in the modern context, the criticism of voidism can be equated to the rejection of Buddhism and allied traditions, which reject the reality of the soul and God. This rejection, similar to the rejection of materialism, is relatively easier, and the Six Systems of Philosophy don't dwell upon it as much.

The greatest focus in these systems—apart from the description of their position on the nature of reality—is to distinguish it from impersonalism because impersonalism uses more Vedic terminology than voidism. All over the Six Systems texts, we can find the rejection of all the contentions of impersonalism, namely—(a) that nature is a deluding agency, (b) that nature is inert, (c) that Oneness is the ultimate reality instead of diversity, (d) that this Oneness is formless, (e) that the desire and individuality of the soul are temporary.

All the followers of the Vedic tradition easily accept the rejections of materialism and voidism, but the rejection of impersonalism has become contentious because impersonalism used to be a non-Vedic system until Shankaracharya authored a commentary on the Vedānta Sūtra, to establish that impersonalism was Vedic. This commentary replaced the void of the Buddhists with two realities—called Brahman and māyā—with Brahman being an undivided consciousness, and māyā being inert matter (sort of like the Cartesian mind-body dualism). Since Brahman is undivided, therefore, the analogy of a person reflected in a mirror is modified to say that the mirror—i.e., māyā—creates an illusory picture of the formless. Since māyā is originally formless, and Brahman is always formless, this doctrine runs into difficulties in explaining the origin of forms. Calling something an illusion doesn't make it go away. The doctrine might also sometimes say that even māyā is a conscious entity, which deliberately tries to mislead Brahman into an illusion. This is also problematic, because if māyā is a deluding agency, then everything in the world—including the Vedic scriptures—must be illusory, as they are byproducts of māyā. The evil nature of māyā would entail that Brahman can never be liberated out of māyā because even the supposed sources of enlightenment are merely delusions.

The fact is that Vedānta does not support such an interpretation, because there are explicit statements about devotion to the Lord, the difference between the soul and God, and the divine relationship between God and His Sakti. Hence, Shankaracharya's commentary was an ill-conceived misrepresentation. His position was, in fact, subsequently criticized by other Vedānta views, and owing to these successive interpretations, the Vedānta system is popular today.

The Vedic practitioners of that time could have protested Shankaracharya's commentary, but they welcomed it on pragmatic grounds—they saw Indian society afflicted by Buddhism and considered that to be a bigger and more urgent problem. In voidism, every book is a delusion, because the whole world is unreal. Therefore, even the Vedas must be a delusion. Shankaracharya argued against that idea, and his key contribution was to explain why the Vedic texts are not delusions. But he married an un-Vedic doctrine of impersonalism to the acceptance of the Vedic texts as divine knowledge and divine authority.

To support his impersonal doctrine, Shankaracharya also created a schism between the Six Systems, rejecting the other five systems in his Vedānta commentary. Shankaracharya could not comment on Vedānta alone, if the integrity of the other five systems of philosophy—namely, Sāñkhya, Mīmāṃsā, Nyāya, Vaiśeṣika, and Yoga—wasn't challenged. Historically, these six systems had always supported each other and used each other's doctrines. The schism between the Six Systems of philosophy owes to the criticism of the other five systems by Shankaracharya. Since that time, people began to consider the Six Systems as divergent and inconsistent philosophies, and their teachers began to grow apart, instead of being considered a part of a single coherent system.

Even as later Ācharyas tried to correct this problem by commenting again on Vedānta Sūtra, the results were less than desirable. Three specific problems arose quickly out of these successive commentaries. First, the commentaries of Rāmanujāchārya, Mādhavāchārya, and others, emphasized the worship of Lord Viṣṇu, instead of Lord Shiva, thus creating a schism between Vaishnavism and Shaivism. Second, they restricted themselves to the discussion of the soul and God, neglecting His Śakti. Third, the study of material nature and Śakti was embraced by the Tantra system, and the Vedic system split again into the third sect of Shaktism, which seemed different from Shaivism and Vaishnavism.

The specific outcome of Shankaracharya's commentary was the schism between the Six Systems, and the specific outcome of the later commentaries was the schism between Vaishnavism, Shaivism, and Shaktism. Once these two types of schisms were created, the unity in the Vedic system was effectively lost. The Vaishnavas and Shaivas focused on Vedānta, and the Shaktas took a greater interest in the other five systems of philosophy. Over time, each of these three systems was further split into many subsects, each based on different Vedic texts, but each of them neglecting the principles presented in the other texts. To the outsider, this reinforced the belief that the Vedic system is not just diverse but also disparate; that it is a collection of many contradictory ideologies.

These schisms continue to play havoc on the understanding of the Vedic system even today. For instance, Sāñkhya is included in all Puranas, but practically everyone who reads these Puranas glosses over Sāñkhya and proceeds into the stories because the teachers of the Puranas are mostly Vaishnavas and they deemphasize everything other than select aspects of Vedānta. Similarly, the discussion of Yoga forms a core aspect of all the Upanishads, but the teachers of these Upanishads, who are mostly Shaivas, gloss over Yoga philosophy because they are focused on Vedānta. When outsiders look at these discrepancies, they find it justifiable to create even more discrepancies. For instance, the Yoga Sūtra doesn't speak about the Kundalini, although Tantra does. There is no discussion about Chakras in the Yoga Sūtra, although it is present in the Tantras. The Yoga Sūtra speaks of only one Asana or meditative posture, while Tantras speak of 8,400,000 such postures. While Tantra practitioners indulge in sexual practices, the Yoga Sūtra speaks of celibacy. While Yoga Sūtra rejects the pursuit of mystical powers, the Tantra system advocates it. The modern practitioners of Yoga have therefore effectively transformed it into Tantra. This means that even more people who are interested in the transcendental nature of the Six Systems of Philosophy, are repelled from it, as it is now Tantric.

The schisms between the various systems are also exacerbated because the Vedānta school emphasizes the urgency of liberation from the material world, while other systems discuss the nature of the material world. If you think of the material world as a raging firestorm, then Vedānta says that you must quickly get out of it. Sāñkhya explains how the fire started. Yoga explains how to get out of the firestorm. Nyāya explains how that fire is a logical outcome of the incompatibility between soul and matter. Vaiśeṣika explains how the fire burns. And Mīmāṃsā discusses the protections while trying to get out of the firestorm. Now, it is up to the reader to decide—Do you want to treat the methods of protecting yourself against the fire as a recommendation for permanently living in the fire, or a method to defend yourself while you are trying to escape? Do you want to consider the description of fire and how it burns just an intellectual curiosity or urgent information that matches the urge to escape the fire?

The divergences in the Six Systems are exacerbated when their position in the larger scheme of things is not understood. Then, a method for protection against the burning fire is treated as a recommendation to stay in the fire. Or, information about the fire's burning is used just for intellectual curiosity. This recommendation then is seen as a contrast against the exhortation to escape the fire, and, lo and behold, a contradiction between the texts is produced.

To avoid such misinterpretations, one must study all the Six Systems, because that gives one the conviction that there is a fire (in case you don't believe it), there is a reason why it was started (in case you are looking for a rational justification), there is a method to escape it, and there are methods to avoid its harmful effects while you are trying to run out of the firestorm. Wearing a mask is not contradictory to running out; understanding that the fire will not die on its own is not contradictory to deciding that one must run out of the fire. In this way, the Six Systems of philosophy are consistent and coherent, despite their diverging emphases. By studying them, we obtain a view into the larger oral tradition, how this tradition was adapted for different purposes, and why all the systems of philosophy are important for different aspects of the problem. These books are the manuals for life—useful for different kinds of issues.

Finally, a few words must be said about the prevalent commentaries, and how the present commentaries differ. The prevalent commentaries today fall into two broad categories. First, experts in one system, trained by their tradition, comment on only one system of philosophy. Second, academics not trained in any system by the tradition, but having some expertise in the Sanskrit language, comment on multiple systems; they produce false interpretations of things that they don't understand because the context in which the text is written completely escapes them. Both these classes seem interesting to historians, but they mean little to most people because their ideas are not compared to modern thinking. The experts are restricted to one system; the non-experts are misleading; and neither experts nor non-experts demonstrate the relevance of an ancient system in a modern world—when so much around has changed.

These commentaries aim to carry out an unthinkable marriage between (a) the text, (b) the broader Vedic context, (c) demonstrate how this knowledge is relevant today, and (d) make it assimilable to people who know little about Vedic philosophy (or even about Western philosophy and modern science).

This series of books is subtitled "Scientific Commentaries", by which I mean reason and experience—something that can be rationally explained, put into practice, and confirmed by experience. I also mean a contrast or similarity to modern science, Western philosophy, and other prevalent systems of thinking. The former is meant to demonstrate that this is not based on "faith"—although enough faith is needed to read the books, put some of it in practice, and realize the truth. The latter is meant to assist the understanding of the modern mind which is accustomed to almost everything other than Vedic doctrines.

We progress from what we know to what we don't. If what we know is true, then it must be confirmed. If what we know is false, then it must be rejected by reason and evidence. The books are meant to provide adequate background to help people understand. This is a different approach to commentaries than those that have been done in the past: The past commentators relied exclusively on referencing other Vedic texts, and that was acceptable in a society where the Vedic texts were popular and their tenets were accepted. It is not useful for a global audience, or those who are educated in modern science but know very little about Vedic texts. They need an alternative, and these books can help.

From an academic viewpoint, the purpose of writing scientific commentaries is also to transform the discussion of Vedic texts from one of history, linguistics, and religious studies to one about science, philosophy, and empirical merit. Unless Vedic texts are seen as technical information, rather than poetry and literature, their content cannot be truly evaluated and appreciated.

Any ambitious project is hard, and anything hard is likely to have flaws. But it is said that thoroughly honest people enjoy and appreciate reading about the truth even if imperfectly composed. I sincerely hope that you will too.

Book Preface

Science, by the common definition, is the study of reality through reason and experience, as opposed to faith. In Vedic epistemology, observation, reason, and faith are called pratyakśa, anumāna, and śabda, and the last method (which rests on the authority of the Vedas) is given greater importance over the first two. By this distinction, however, faith is emphasized, whereas reason and experience are not. Hence, in what way can the knowledge of God be "scientific", if the legitimacy of observation and reason is rejected? The answer to this question is that we need to redefine the nature of reason and experience.

The Vedic doctrine of experience is that it comprises three aspects. In the material world, these are called sattva, rajas, and tamas. In the description of a conscious person (e.g., soul and God), they are called sat, chit, and ānanda. These are also described as sambanda, abhidheya, and prayojana. In my earlier books, I have termed these relation, cognition, and emotion. In Greek philosophy, these were called ethos, logos, and pathos. We can understand them as the three criteria employed while judging and choosing: right, truth, and good. And there are other names by which these are described in different places.

All of these components are necessary for experience, but each of them is sufficient to cause experience (the other two). This leads to the doctrine that each of these three modes is sometimes dominant and sometimes subordinate. When the mode is dominant, then it is the cause, and at that time, it is sufficient to cause experience. But the effect (experience) requires all the three modes.

Thus, the variety of experience is constructed by the innumerable combinations of the modes, and it is described as an inverted tree whose root is the 'balanced' state of the three modes in which they are inseparable, but which then 'expands' into three 'branches', each of which then divides successively by the three modes creating infinite variety which is called the manifest world.

This description of reality however creates three problems. First, context determines which mode is dominant and in different contexts, different things are superior. Second, the superior is understood as the whole which is then divided into its parts; however, due to the modes, the whole in one situation becomes the part in another. Third, the cause in one context becomes the effect in another. The result is that this inverted tree-like structure involves infinite contradictions. The same thing is a cause and an effect; the same thing is the whole and the part; the same thing is considered dominant and subordinate.

Commentaries on Vedānta Sutra have tried to address these contradictions. To resolve one contradiction, we can remove one branch, twig, or leaf in the tree, and the tree is now incomplete. But if the branch, twig, or leaf is restored, then the contradiction returns. This is the basis of the problem—now well known in modern mathematics—that knowledge is either inconsistent or incomplete. The problem also exists in Vedānta Sutra commentaries: (1) if everything is described, then there are many contradictions, and (2) as contradictions reduce, more aspects of reality are rejected, as they are incompatible with other aspects. A consistent description is also the description of nothingness.

The Acintyabhedābheda doctrine says that the complete description is 'inconceivable' as the same thing is a cause and effect, whole and part, dominant and subordinate. That leads to the collapse of rationality. But this is not a problem unique to Vedānta. Any scientific theory that tries to be complete, will be ridden with contradictions; fewer contradictions mean more incompleteness; that is, a consistent theory will describe fewer aspects of our experience.

The doctrine of the three modes, with their dominant-subordinate, whole-part, and cause-effect relations, addresses this central problem of knowledge through experience. However, to formulate a scientific understanding, we must now update our understanding of the meaning of rationality or logic.

The problem with logic is that it describes universal truth—logical truth is true in all possible worlds. For example, $2 + 2 = 4$ is universally true. Logic is hence incapable of dealing with contextual truth. To solve this problem of universal truth, we must define what we mean by contextual truth: it is the answer to a question; if the question is changed, then the answer is changed.

Logic, therefore, must now be redefined not as the pair of premises and conclusions, but as the triad of the premise, question, and answer. Each premise gives rise to some questions, which then gives rise to an answer. The answer is not universal, because the question is contextual. And yet, it is true—in relation to the question, when the question is posed. The original premise, which leads to all questions and answers, is called the Absolute Truth. But all subsequent emanations from this truth are Relative Truths. The relative truth is not falsity. But it is true only in a context. It is one of the many branches of the tree.

The Absolute Truth is the primordial premise which creates everything else, by giving rise to questions and problems—which are termed as the 'desire' in the Absolute Truth. Due to this desire, the Absolute Truth is a person, and the premise doesn't exist merely as an idea. Once these questions and problems are created, then the answer to these are also created. The answer is a part of the premise, and it is connected to the premise through a question. However, since the premise becomes a question, and then becomes an answer, therefore, the same thing is alternately known as a premise, a problem, and an answer.

'Truth' must thus be defined as the relation between a question and an answer. If an answer solves a problem, then, it is true. But many answers can address a problem. Therefore, aside from the 'truth', we must also judge the 'good' and 'right'. If surgery is successful but the patient dies, then the surgery is not 'good'. A surgery performed by an unqualified person is not 'right'. Thus, the connection between solutions and problems is judged in three ways: (a) it solves a problem, (b) the solution increases happiness, and (c) we are permitted to it. By this definition, the 'Absolute Truth' is the answer to all questions, increases happiness in all situations, and everyone is permitted to use the solution.

With the redefinition of experience (as the combination of the three modes), causality (as one of the three modes), reality (as the tree of all mode combinations), and reason (as the choice of one of the tree branches), we meet the rational criterion for knowledge—it must be consistent and complete. The tests of truth, right, and good constitute the empirical criteria for knowledge. When rational and empirical criteria are met, then the knowledge is 'scientific'. Since these criteria are met, therefore, the knowledge of the Absolute Truth is 'scientific', i.e., rational and empirical. It need not necessarily be accepted on faith, although if it were accepted on faith, it will still be true, right, and good.

This interpretation shows how the above understanding is presented in the Vedānta Sutra. Vedānta has progressed over centuries through Advaita, Śuddhādvaita, Viśiṣṭādvaita, Dvaita, Bhedābheda, and Acintyabhedābheda. As the doctrines have become more complete, they have also become more inconsistent. The Advaita doctrine describes the soul, without matter and God. As successive doctrines add more aspects of reality, more contradictions are created. The Bhedābheda doctrine says that God, matter, and the soul are at once different and identical. And the Acintyabhedābheda doctrine acknowledges the failure of physical ideas of identity and difference. The next step in the progression of Vedānta is to make the complete understanding of reality also rational. And this rationality requires us to revisit the nature of whole and parts.

If wholes and parts are physical, then we are led to reductionism. For example, if the whole is an ocean, and the part is a drop, then removing a drop reduces the ocean. Indeed, there is no ocean apart from the drops. All physical analogies of whole and part have failed to correctly describe the Vedānta doctrine. Hence, this interpretation redefines the wholes and parts as ideas.

For example, a 'mammal' is the whole, and a 'cow' is the part. We can say: a cow is a mammal, but we cannot say that a mammal is a cow. The mammal exists independent of the cow, but the cow doesn't exist independent of the mammal. If cows ceased to exist, the definition of mammal would not change. But if the mammal ceased to exist, then cows will cease to exist as well.

The use of concepts as wholes and parts breaks the principles of modern logic. Since cows are mammals, but mammals are not cows, therefore, the principle of identity is broken (A is B, but B is not A). Similarly, the principle of mutual exclusion is broken (something is either A or not-A) because a mammal is neither a cow nor a tiger. Likewise, the principle of non-contradiction is broken (something cannot be A and not-A) because both cows and tigers are mammals. The failure of modern logic is pervasive, but it is not understood because we view the world physically. If the notion of whole and part is changed, then the principles of modern logic are rejected, and a new logic is needed.

This new logic is based on the hierarchy of concepts, and because the conventional separation and identity is rejected while understanding this hierarchy, therefore, we can say that the reality is Bhedābheda—i.e., neither different nor identical. Since conventional logic cannot be used with the hierarchy of concepts, therefore, we can say that reality is Achintya or inconceivable. But because everything can be understood through an alternative conception of reality as concepts, and its associated logic, therefore, the reality is conceivable.

As a result, every past doctrine about Vedānta is considered true, although from a certain perspective, i.e., that doctrine becomes a form of contextual truth.

The Acintyabhedābheda doctrine describes the Absolute Truth, but within current logic. And the present interpretation transcends the current logic.

The summary of Vedānta is that the Absolute Truth has a masculine and a feminine aspect. In different contexts, they are called superior to each other, equal to each other, different from each other, inseparable from each other, the cause of each other, and the effect of each other. The soul is sometimes called a part of the masculine, sometimes of the feminine, sometimes their child, sometimes similar to the whole, and sometimes dissimilar from the whole. The material world is sometimes called a part of God, sometimes separate from God, sometimes an expression of God, and sometimes God is said to be immanent in the world, and yet, the world is not considered identical to God. Every position is considered, debated, rejected in one sense, and accepted in another.

Vedānta is therefore not for the faint-hearted. Those who want to think of reality in terms of absolutely true and false claims are likely to be perplexed by these descriptions. Similarly, those who come to religion hoping to find an absolute set of unchanging ideas, are likely to be baffled. Vedānta is for the advanced student of Vedic philosophy, and it explains how seemingly contradictory positions are true, although they are not true universally. There is a sense in which one position is true, and another sense in which the opposite position is true. To employ these meanings, we must acknowledge that reality is itself meaning. Otherwise, these meanings and their truth would be attributed only to our minds, not to reality, and philosophy would be mere speculation.

The novelty of this interpretation is two-fold. First, it advocates a novel understanding of reality, which is semantic rather than physical. Second, it describes how every other Vedānta position becomes simultaneously true if such a view is adopted. The different Vedānta doctrines are therefore not false or contradictory. They are all true, and the study of Vedānta is the study of from different perspectives. The unity of Vedic philosophy exists even within Vedānta, even though the doctrines have ostensibly seemed contradictory.

INTRODUCTION

Background Information

The Problem of Knowledge

Commentaries on Vedānta Sūtra have been written once every few centuries, and only when there was something new to be said. This is one such commentary. It is not that the passing of time has made it inevitable. It is that there are some unsolved problems in Vedānta, and this commentary presents the solution. The central problem is that of the consistency and completeness of knowledge. Completeness means that everything can be known, and consistency means that it is known without contradictions. Regrettably, this goal of knowledge has seemed to be impossible. We now know—through many attempts in Western logic and mathematics, as well through previous attempts to solve this problem in Vedic philosophy—that no rational description is both consistent and complete. We are therefore compelled to sacrifice either consistency or completeness. The sacrifice of completeness is unsatisfactory, as it entails that everything cannot be known. The alternative seems appealing: everything can be known, but the knowledge will have contradictions. However, any contradiction also makes the truth of the entire system seem suspect.

There are many ways to understand such contradictions. Philosophies like Buddhism believe that reality is itself inconsistent and therefore consistent knowledge of reality cannot exist. Others like Advaita take the view that reality is consistent, but our language and experience produce inconsistencies in knowledge; therefore, we must reject experience and language. Then, there are Vaishnava doctrines that indicate that our experience can be consistent, however, our language is never consistent; therefore, the complete truth can be experienced although not described. And some philosophies aren't even aware of the problem, or even if they are aware, they do not try to find a solution.

There are two main sources of the problem, and both arise when we consider meanings as a part of reality. The first issue is that meanings are always defined through opposites such as hot vs. cold, bitter vs. sweet, big vs. small. In this world, these opposites exist in different things—i.e., something is either hot or cold—but the origin of everything must have both. Due to the coexistence of opposites, the source of everything becomes self-contradictory. However, if one side of the opposition is discarded, then the source becomes incomplete.

The second issue with meanings is that they exist in three modes—universal, individual, and contextual. For example, there is a universal idea of a circle, there are individual circles, and something not perfectly circular may be called a 'circle' sometimes. If we use the word 'circle', are we referring to the universal idea, the individual things, or the contextual use? It turns out that we need each of the three modes to obtain completeness, however, their coexistence creates contradictions if we are not careful to distinguish between the three modes. For example, if we call an imperfect round a 'circle' and treat that designation as the universal idea of a circle, then perfect circles would no longer be circles. Likewise, if an individual thing is circular and black, and we do not distinguish between the individual and the universal, then blackness becomes a part of the definition of a circle, and circles that are not black can no longer be circles.

The source of the consistency vs. completeness debate in Indian philosophy rests on the contradictories such as hot vs. cold, while the source of the same debate in Western philosophy lies in the existence of modalities. Naturally, if we combine them—and we must—then, the problem is bigger. However, there is also a bright side to this dilemma: By combining the contradictories with the modalities, we can open the doors to a solution. On the other hand, there is no solution to the problem of contradictories without modalities or vice versa. The solution with modalities must say that even the opposites are modalities; therefore, they are not simultaneously experienced, although they exist at once.

The Problem of Modalities

But even before we set out to solve any of these problems, we need a very profound change: We must give up the idea that the world is physical because in a physical world knowledge is impossible. For example, when you see a cow, there is a symbol of the cow in your mind. The external cow is also a symbol of the idea of a cow. The difference between the two is that the external symbol elucidates the idea in greater detail—and is hence 'bigger'—than the internal symbol. This means that even the external cow is not a physical object. It is as much a symbol of an idea as an internal symbol. Similarly, our minds are the symbols of the universal concept of mind. When the idea of cow exists in our minds, both of which are symbols, then the symbol of cow exists within a symbol of mind. Consequently, the symbol of the cow is a symbol within a symbol. Thus, the external cow, our minds, and the knowledge in our minds are all symbols. There is factually nothing physical in this world; everything must be treated as a symbol of some idea. Hence, when we speak of the modalities of reality, they pertain to the symbols. Each symbol has a universal, individual, and contextual modality. The universal modality is the idea in the symbol; the individual modality is that the symbol is an instance of the idea, and the contextual modality is that this symbol is related to other kinds of symbols.

These relations between the symbols also come in three modalities—each idea in a symbol is a part of a more abstract idea, the idea is distinct from other ideas that are also part of the more abstract idea and yet not this particular idea, and that there are potentially other symbolic instances of the same idea. Let us consider these three types of relations between the symbols one by one.

First, when you say that something is a cow, you also accept that it is a mammal. Now, most people today don't accept this claim. They say that ideas like mammal and animal are simply in our minds and that there is nothing objectively mammalian about the cow. That should also imply that we stop using the terms mammals and animals in relation to the cow. But we cannot do that either. Removing words such as mammal and animal from our vocabulary would create new problems—e.g., we would not be able to put horses and cows in the same category. Therefore, some philosophers like to live in the doublethink in which the cow is not objectively a mammal (as the mammal is in the mind), but use the word mammal in relation to the cow (otherwise, we will lose the capacity to group other animals together). In this doublethink, we don't accept that there is a symbolic representation of mammals in a cow. Owing to physical thinking, if a mammal were inside the cow, then it could not exist in other species such as tigers, horses, cats, and dogs. This is because something can only be inside the cow, and not outside, or vice versa. The physicalist in fact insists that a mammal is neither inside nor outside. It is only in our minds.

Second, when you say that something is a cow, you also mean that it is not a horse, cat, dog, tiger, etc. If you don't adopt this way of thinking, then saying that something is a cow would not be contradictory to stating that the same thing is a tiger. But how does the assertion that something is a cow entail that it is not a tiger? The short answer is that the negations of all other species must exist inside the symbol of a cow symbolically. Most people today don't accept this idea. They say that the claim that something is a cow, and the claim that it is not a tiger, are just claims in our minds. But if this idea were taken all the way, then we must also reject the use of logical oppositions—i.e., that a cow is not a tiger—in relation to the external world. We cannot do that, because it will lead to almost a complete collapse of logic and language. Thus, we keep saying that the cow is not a tiger, but there is nothing objective about it. Hence, we don't recognize that the negation of tigers must objectively exist in the cow.

Third, when you speak about a specific cow, you also implicitly assume that it is different from other cows. This means that a symbolic representation of other cows must exist in each cow. This is the only way you can say that a claim about this cow cannot be applied to that cow because this cow is different from that cow. However, again, due to physicalist thinking, we refuse to accept that what a thing is not, cannot be part of the definition of that thing. Hence, the doctrine of each thing existing in and of itself arises, because how that thing is different from the other things (or just like those things) is in our minds.

The problem of meaning is that it involves the universal and the individual modes at a minimum—a cow is an instance of the cow. However, the universal and the individual are then defined through distinctions to mammals, tigers, and other cows. Therefore, we get three modalities of universal, individual, and contextual, and each such mode again has three further modalities. For instance, after you have distinguished a cow from a tiger and dog (which involves the contextual modality), you must say that cows, tigers, and dogs are mammals. Thus, within the symbolic representation of a cow not being a dog, there must be the idea that even a dog is a mammal. By the universal modality of a mammal, cows and dogs are identical, but by the contextual modality, they are distinct. Likewise, the distinction of a cow from other cows is the individual modality in the contextual modality. Thus, there are three modes, but each of them enters the other modes, qualifies them, and creates infinite modes.

Therefore, when we adopt non-physical thinking, then we see how contradictions can exist within the same thing, although in different modes—e.g., that the tiger is within the cow, however, the cow is asserted, and the tiger is negated. We can also see how things much bigger than the cow exist within the cow—since to know the cow, we must know that it is a mammal, animal, etc. Other individuals also exist in an individual, but in each individual, the other individuals must be present as a negation, since we somehow know that one individual is different from the other individuals. The presence of other things within each thing leads to logical contradictions unless we accept modes.

However, if we try to avoid these contradictions, then we run into a different problem. When we say that "this is not a cow", it could entail— (1) this is not a mammal, (2) this is a mammal, but it could be a tiger, horse, cat, dog, etc., and (3) something else is a cow. Which of these outcomes follow the claim that "this is not a cow"? Each of the above outcomes is possible, but because we cannot say which of them is implied, our knowledge is incomplete. Therefore, in physicalist thinking, knowledge is always either inconsistent or incomplete. It is incomplete because the negations of statements produce many possible alternatives, and we cannot determine which alternative is implied. But if we add other things within a thing, then the result of the addition is inconsistency.

All philosophies—in the West or East—are victims of these conundrums. We might say that we haven't yet understood why and how logic works, but that would be an understatement. We haven't factually realized that the existence of anything contradicts physical thinking and its associated logic. My attempt in this commentary is to transcend these limitations of physical thinking, its associated logic, and its problematic conclusions. If we have traced the source of inconsistency and incompleteness, then we can hope to solve it.

The Evolution of Vedānta

With this background, we can briefly discuss the historical evolution of Vedānta, why varied types of attempts have failed previously, and what remedies can be used. Our story begins with the question: How can opposites exist in something without creating a self-contradiction? This question arises because the world is comprised of opposites, and if these opposites have emerged from a single source, then the source must be self-contradictory. The initial answer in Vedānta to this problem is that these opposites are not always manifest. They rather exist in an unmanifest state of possibilities. But, when they are manifest, they are also separated as different places, times, and personalities. Thus, the source of everything is not everything, but the *possibility* of everything. All the contentions in Vedānta are about the nature of this undifferentiated possibility. The personalist philosopher says that the origin of everything must be a form because the formless cannot be the cause of manifest forms. The impersonalist philosopher instead makes the counterclaim that if the Absolute Truth had a form, then the various parts of this form—e.g., head and toe—would constitute many truths, and that would defeat the purpose of seeking a singular truth.

Of course, it is one thing to criticize the opponent's view, and quite another to address the issues raised by the opponent's criticism. The problem with the impersonalist view is that it cannot explain the origin of forms, while also saying that the origin is formless. In fact, Buddhism battled with this problem and concluded that because the forms are mutually contradictory, therefore, their reconciliation must lead to nothingness. Therefore, the goal of a singular truth as the original source of all forms must be abandoned. The impersonalist now says: Let's accept that there are two realities. The first reality, called Brahman, is undifferentiated and can be called the singular truth, although it is not the origin of forms. The second reality, called māyā, is differentiated and is the source of all numerous truths, or the forms observed in space and time.

The personalist responds to this conclusion by saying that two is better than nothing, but one is better than two. Therefore, we cannot accept the separation of Brahman and māyā as singular and numerous truths. We must rather say that māyā is a part of Brahman, and differentiation exists within the oneness. This diversity within oneness is conceived as the body of God: God's body parts are the diversity and God is the unity. But you might ask: What is God if not for the collection of the body parts? The answer is that God is an object, and the parts of God's body are the properties of that object. Just like a material particle has numerous properties such as mass, charge, energy, momentum, etc. which are different aspects of the particle, similarly, the singular truth has many aspects or properties. The particle is their unity, and the properties are the diversity. This doctrine, which associates numerous properties with an object is called Viśiṣṭādvaita; the object is Advaita, and the properties are Viśiṣṭa.

This conclusion, however, produces a new problem: If the various qualities of God are distinct from God, then God must be without any quality. Specifically, He cannot have a form of hands, legs, face, and torso, because these must be the qualities of God, not God. Just as the particle is devoid of all its properties like mass and energy, similarly, God must be devoid of all the qualities. This then leads to the same conclusion as Advaita: God is Brahman and His body is māyā. Whatever we call the "form of God" is māyā, not God. In fact, the form of God exists only if māyā has covered the Brahman to produce a form.

To avoid this problem, the personalist provides a counter: There are two kinds of properties—matter and soul. Brahman is the individual soul, and it is covered by matter. However, God—the object of all these properties—is never thus covered. While this solves the problem of God having a body of souls (where God is the Supreme Soul), it also creates a new problem: If the soul is the body of the Supreme Soul, then the soul's suffering must also be God's suffering. After all, the individual soul is the body of the Supreme Soul. Therefore, God may not be directly covered by māyā, but even an indirect covering is problematic since it transforms the soul's suffering into God's suffering.

To counter this challenge, the personalist now says that the individual soul and the Supreme Soul are eternally separate and different realities. This doctrine of the eternal separation of the Supreme Soul and soul is called Dvaita. That claim, however, leads to the plurality of realities, and the rejection of the singular truth—the One from which many have expanded as His parts. The pluralism leads to questions of why these different realities must interact with each other, and why the soul must be dependent upon God. In fact, if the soul is eternally separate from God, then why is devotion to God required?

The personalist philosopher now makes a very bold move. To solve the problem of why the parts of the body of God are not separate from God, He says: Each part contains all the other parts, although in a hidden form. Therefore, the numerous truths are a part of the singular truth, and the singular truth is a part of each of the numerous truths. For example, the eyes of the singular truth are His part, just like His tongue. But the tongue is hidden within the eye, and the eye is hidden within the tongue. Since every aspect is hidden in every other aspect, hence, you cannot ask what they are aspects of. After all, the thing that they are an aspect of, is within that thing. This resolves the problem of object-property separation because the object is in each property, and the properties are in the object. Now, the form of God is not māyā because the whole truth is within each of the parts. Indeed, God is not different from God's body.

Thus, you cannot say that the eyes of God are not His tongue—implying that He cannot eat with His eyes. And you cannot say that His eyes are His tongue—implying that He has only tongue and no eyes. You must rather make two conflicting claims—the eyes are the tongue and not the tongue—but this conflict is not a self-contradiction, because the eyes and the tongue are in different places, and the eyes become the tongue (or vice versa) at different times. Thus, because God has both eyes and tongue, therefore, He can both see and taste. Similarly, His eyes can manifest the tongue property and the tongue can manifest the eye property, therefore, there is no necessity to suppose that God is different from the many body parts of God's body. These aspects of God's body are manifest simultaneously as different parts of His body, and each of these body parts can transform into any other body part one after another.

The rejection of the identity of eyes and tongue is called bheda and the rejection of their separation is called abheda. These two are combined into the doctrine called Bhedābheda. Now, we can say that the soul is part of God, and God is present within the soul. Due to bheda, when the soul falls into māyā, God is not fallen. But due to abheda, the soul is not separated from God. Thus, both soul and māyā are parts of God, and yet, God is separate from both.

This resolution of the problem, however, creates a new one. The doctrine rests on the idea that the whole is inside each part, but how the whole exists inside the part is never explained. Certainly, no physical theory can explain this. But since alternative ideas about reality are absent, therefore, the Bhedābheda doctrine remains inexplicable. One way to understand the doctrine is to say that the entire body is human, and each part of the body is also human. For instance, if you see a human hand, you can deduce that it is a part of a human body, since humanness is not just the whole body, but also in the individual hand.

The impersonalist, however, exploits this analogy. He says: If the whole is present in each part, then according to the claim of soul and matter being parts of God, it follows that God is present in matter and soul too (remember that separating soul and matter from God undermines the goal of knowing a singular truth). Furthermore, if we say that the presence of God in each part of God makes those parts God, then by extension, God's presence in soul and matter must make each soul and material object God. Therefore, God cannot be considered a Supreme Person because all souls and material objects are God.

If we try to solve this problem by saying that the soul and matter are not part of God, then we end up with many separate realities, which is worse than the Oneness of the impersonalist. If instead, we say that the whole is not present in each part, then these parts become different from the singular truth, and we must now say that the individual soul and the individual material objects are māyā, not the singular truth. Whichever doctrine is employed, we either end up with impersonalism or something much inferior to impersonalism.

Impersonalism is also problematic, because if there is only one Being, then how can we be individually liberated or fallen into the material world? We can either be collectively liberated or collectively fallen. If we are collectively fallen, then we must also be collectively liberated. Therefore, I cannot be individually liberated by my effort if everyone else is not getting liberated at once. In short, there is no value in individual effort, because there is no individuality.

Seeing these difficulties, Sri Chaitanya articulated the Acintyabhedābheda doctrine which states that the singular truth must be inconceivable. This was in recognition of the fact that all doctrines had some or another issue. The issue is that we are required to make three incomprehensible statements at once: (1) the parts are in the whole, (2) the whole is in the parts, (3) the whole in the part makes some parts the whole, but other parts do not become the whole.

Each of these is a hard problem. For example, to say that the parts are in the whole, we must have some idea about the whole, but we don't. What is an ocean, if not the mere collection of the drops? Isn't the ocean merely a word used to indicate the plurality of drops by a singular noun, as if it were a singular entity? In short, isn't the ocean merely a linguistic construct when in fact there are many drops? The second claim complicates the issue further. You could say that the drops are in the ocean, but how do you say that the ocean is in the drops? That immanence of the ocean within each drop defies all intuition. Finally, how do say that some drops are the full ocean, while other drops are not the full ocean? Even if the immanence of the whole within the parts were accepted, why should it be applied selectively? Naturally, the problems magnify at each successive stage. The problem is not just that we are unable to make all these claims collectively, but that we are unable to make them individually.

The Semantic Conception of Reality

This commentary tries to solve each of the above problems individually and collectively. The cornerstone of the commentary is the change in the conception of reality from physical to semantic. For example, we should not think of the whole and part in terms of an ocean and the drops in it. We should rather think of reality in terms of concepts like cows and mammals. The mammal is the whole and the cow is its part. However, if you see a cow, you also say that it is a mammal, although you cannot reduce the mammal to the cow. Therefore, the mammal exists in the cow, and the cow exists in the mammal. However, the mammal is not equal to the cow. This is expressed by saying that— (1) the cow is a mammal, and (2) the mammal is not a cow. This is possible only if reality is described as concepts—e.g., mammal and cow. It solves the problem of why some parts (i.e., matter and the soul) contain the whole but are not the whole. They are parts of the whole, just like the cow is a part of the mammal. Since the mammal exists in the cow, therefore, the whole is not merely the collection and hence not merely a word. It is rather present within each type of mammal.

The reverse problem of why the presence of the whole in each part (in the case of God) makes the parts equal to the whole, still needs to be addressed. To solve this problem, recall how each part is defined through a distinction to the other parts. This distinction, however, can exist in three modalities—of space, time, and person. We can apply these modalities to our bodies and understand their implications. In the person modality, we would say that my hand has a 'mind' of its own. In the space modality, we would say that my hand is not my leg, but there is a leg elsewhere. In the time modality, we would say that my hand is not my leg right now, but it can become the leg. In our body, only the spatial modality is prominently found. Only occasionally, our hands are not in our control—so we say that they have their own mind. Extremely rarely can a person perform the work of the hands using the legs. But in God's body, all these modalities are simultaneously manifest. Thus, each part of God's body has a mind of its own. Each part can become the other parts. But, by distinction to the other parts, each part is also defined by what the other part is not.

The difference between the soul and God is that places, times, and personalities are 'compressed' in God—this compression is achieved through semantic abstraction—but these are 'expanded' in the world. Due to this expansion, the soul is always in a specific place and time, and this place then limits the things its body parts can do. Since the soul can move from one body to another, therefore, a distinction between soul and body is made in the case of the soul. However, since God is all the space and time, therefore, He doesn't change His body. And yet, His body is all that is possible in all places, times, and personalities. Therefore, we can say that every part of God's body is God, but we cannot make the same claim about the soul. Quite simply, the soul is localized in space and time and is, therefore, an individual. God is also an individual, but all space and time and the other souls, are merely the parts of the Supreme Person. Since the soul and God are individual persons, therefore, there is a distinction between the soul and God. But since the soul is a part of God, therefore, the soul is not *independent* of God. God, however, is *independent* of all the souls.

The whole-part relation between God and the soul can be easily understood if we say that God is the object, whereas the soul is a property of that object. The object can exist without the property, but the property cannot exist without the object. For example, you can remove some mass from a particle, and the particle is undiminished. But you cannot remove the particle from the mass. The whole-part relationship now also becomes the object-property relation.

Apart from these properties, God also exists as a purpose. This purpose exists in God, but the same purpose can also exist in each soul, without equating the soul to God. Thereby, we can say that God is 'inside' everything—as its purpose. And yet, those individual things do not become God by this immanence. Therefore, we can say that God is partially present in each of the parts, but as the whole, He is separate from each of the parts. The immanence of purpose in each thing leads us to the conclusion that God exists in everything, but everything is not God. This is because God is immanent through His purposes in different souls and material objects. Hence, the presence of God in His body parts makes all these body parts God, but the same isn't true of the soul.

The immanence of purpose, and the separation of the properties, is resolved by relations. God is the whole purpose, each thing fulfills the purpose partially, therefore, the partial purpose is related to the whole purpose, like a part to the whole. This is not a relation between two equals. It is rather the relation of an object to its properties, or the relation between the whole and the part.

The above three modalities—purpose, property, and relation—are identified in the Vedas as the aspects of existence—ānanda, *chit*, and *sat*. Hence, after we say that the singular truth must be known semantically, we must distinguish between three types of semanticism—the purpose, property, and relation.

Once we understand this simple scheme of three aspects, then we can understand how these modalities are combined infinitely. The combinations occur by dividing each mode by each of the three modes. For example, we have discussed above how the property of being a cow entails that it is a mammal, it is not a tiger, and it is not other cows. Likewise, when we speak of our purpose, we can also talk about a higher purpose, what our purpose is not, and the same purpose in the other individuals. Finally, in the context of relations, we can talk about relations that are higher than our relations, those to whom we are not related, and others who have the same relation as us. These modes are in addition to what a thing is in three modes—a universal, and individual, and relation to other individuals instantiating a universal. Through the successive divisions of modalities, infinite such modalities are produced. And these modalities then form a hierarchical tree-like structure in which there are higher, lower, and peer nodes. The higher purpose, the higher concept, and the higher relation are 'above', and constitute the wholes. The 'peer' concepts, purposes, and relations are different from a node. And the 'lower' concepts, purposes, and relations, are the parts of the 'higher' nodes. This tree-like structure is a simplified vision of reality, in which everything expands from a root through the three modalities. But the construction of this tree, how this tree violates classical logic, and yet, with modalities, how it leads to completeness, is very complicated.

This tree can expand—through new combinations. It can contract—by removing some combinations. And it can evolve—by changing the combinations. If the existence of the tree is complex, then we can imagine that the expansion, contraction, and evolution of this tree is more incomprehensible. The creation of the material world is the expansion of this tree, and its annihilation is the contraction of the tree back into its root. While the tree exists, it also evolves, and that evolution constitutes the scientific study of the material world.

With these three kinds of modalities, all the issues in Vedānta philosophy are overcome. The singular truth now has a form and is not formless. This is because the singular truth is also a concept, a purpose, and a relation. The parts exist in the whole, and the whole exists in all the parts, and this mutual innateness is due to their semantic nature. Despite this mutual innateness, the soul can fall into the material world, but by that fall, God isn't fallen; the soul's suffering is not God's suffering. Each part of God's body is fully God, so, there is no distinction between soul and body in God. Therefore, God's body cannot be called the byproduct of māyā. God is innately present in tables and chairs as their purpose, however, this innate presence of God in tables and chairs doesn't make tables and chairs God. On the other hand, certain things like deities, names of God, or books on God, embody all of God's qualities so they are God; they just seem to be material parts, but by their qualities they are whole.

All these claims have been made at different points in the evolution of Vedānta, but there is no Vedānta Sūtra doctrine currently that supports them simultaneously. In fact, when a Vedānta Sūtra doctrine makes one of these true, it also makes some other claim(s) false. If they are simultaneously accepted to be true, then the Absolute Truth becomes inconceivable due to inner contradictions. The need for a new commentary on Vedānta Sūtra arises from this problem. This commentary shows how all these claims are true at once, that truth doesn't come at the expense of other claims, and all these claims can be made collectively and individually without producing inner contradictions.

I might caution the reader that this book is not easy reading. But remember that this is not an easy problem. It has existed for thousands of years and remains unsolved. The solution is also beyond conventional models of reasoning, so don't be surprised by the existence of contradictions in a classical sense. The problem is not the philosophy or its presentation. The problem is the very nature of knowledge. As we have seen, no known scheme makes knowledge both consistent and complete. A novel approach—complicated as it seems—is necessary to address this problem. If you can grasp the problem, then the solution becomes necessary and inevitable and the journey becomes extremely rewarding. I have made attempts to simplify this for the newcomer. The following sections discuss at length the nature of the problem, the varied previously attempted solutions, and their problems, before describing the proposal. I shall examine this proposal from numerous angles—scientific, philosophical, and religious. If you can be convinced of where this book is going to take us, then the subsequent arguments that validate this description can be undertaken.

Technical Overview

Scientific Background

One of the most intriguing ideas in Vedānta is the description of reality in terms of a whole-part theory. Other systems of Vedic philosophy take a different approach to solve the same problem. Sāñkhya philosophy, for example, describes matter as objects and their properties, the senses by which these properties are observed, the mind which understands the meaning, the intellect which judges the truth, the ego which formulates intentions, and the moral sense which perceives values. And this complicated description of matter is only one of the five ontologies in Sāñkhya—the others being the soul, God, time, and karma. With multiple ontologies, the complexity arising out of their interaction explodes. How can we reduce this complexity to a much simpler idea—namely the relation between a whole and a part? Doesn't this represent an oversimplification? If so, how could it be the conclusion of all knowledge?

When I thought about this problem, I was reminded of similar attempts in modern mathematics to reduce all kinds of mathematical objects to set theory. Set theory is also a whole-part theory, in which the set is the whole, and its members—objects or sets—are the parts. Set theory is simpler compared to many advanced mathematical topics. And yet, set theory is the foundation of modern mathematics, because other mathematical objects reduce to sets.

With set theory in mind, it seems that Vedānta was doing philosophy like mathematicians do mathematics today. There are very few parallels to this style of philosophy in the West. However, this realization gave me an initial glimpse into how the parallel between the whole-part doctrines in Vedānta and set theory as the foundation of all mathematics wasn't merely serendipity. Rather, the system could be made as rigorous as set theory, logic, and mathematics.

There are, however, serious problems in mathematical set theory. The central problem is that words in a language (which can be converted into numbers) exist in multiple *modes*—such as universal and individual. For instance, the word 'barber' can denote a class of people (universal) or a specific member of the class (individual). When we try to admit both these modes in language, we end up with contradictions. Therefore, the current set theory limits itself to just one mode—the mode of individuals. Now, if this set theory is used to construct a theory of numbers, then we get incompleteness because to count three objects, we must have the concept 'three' prior, and that necessitates the universals. Therefore, we have a fundamental problem: If we use more than one mode, then we get inconsistency. If instead, we use only one mode, then we get incompleteness. This tradeoff has been shown many times in mathematics, but none more ostensibly than by Gödel's proof that number theory is necessarily incomplete because the only alternative is that the theory is inconsistent.

Now, one could imagine that perhaps set theory is a bad choice for mathematical foundations. Maybe we should seek alternative foundations for mathematics. Since set theory arose because sets were a mathematical representation of concepts, perhaps, there are other ways to conceive of concepts. But, if the same type of foundation is also employed in Vedānta, the problem must lie elsewhere. Naturally, I suspected that the problem lay with modalities. The problem wasn't the whole-part nature of reality, but the fact that this reality can be simultaneously understood in different incompatible modes. And since the root of all these problems is the existence of multiple modalities, the only solution to these problems was to step outside conventional forms of logic.

The problems of mathematical set theory convinced me that such problems would arise in Vedānta too—unless a system of modal reasoning was being used, they would necessarily lead to contradictions. If set theory is riddled with paradoxes, then there cannot be a non-modal Vedānta doctrine that is consistent and complete. So, if we find problems of contradictions in Vedānta, we need to trace them to modalities, and not spend any time trying to solve them—because there is factually no solution to the problem within current logic. Sometimes knowing what not to do, can itself be an advancement. In this case, mathematical set theory helped me understand that all systems of Vedānta—if they try to be complete—must necessarily be inconsistent in current logic.

Philosophical Problems

I had previously encountered logical contradictions in Vedānta. For example, the Bhedābheda doctrine says that the whole and part are simultaneously different and non-different. And the Acintyabhedābheda doctrine says that this simultaneous difference and non-difference is inconceivable because it cannot be logically formulated. In short, the problems of mathematical set theory, how they lead to contradictions (if multiple modes are used) have been well-known in the Vedānta system. The difference between Vedānta and mathematical set theory is one of relative emphasis. The Vedānta system is unprepared to sacrifice completeness but is prepared to admit logical inconsistencies and inconceivability. Mathematicians instead prefer incompleteness over inconsistencies; they are prepared to reject modalities if that helps avoid contradictions.

The problems of logical inconsistencies have also been shown in other traditional philosophies, such as Buddhism. One such problem concerns the logical impossibility of the concept "I". For example, if you form a set of "friends" and "non-friends", then it is not clear whether "I" am my friend (which is not possible because friends are different from me) or a non-friend (because that would entail that I'm my enemy). There are variations of this problem in other parts of Indian philosophy. For example, when we speak about self-awareness, the self-aware state comes about when we desire self-awareness. In that desire, there is a difference between the knower and the known—after all, you could not desire something that you already have. To fulfill this desire, we establish a relation between the knower and the known, which means that there is again a difference between the knower and the known, although the two are related rather than disjointed. Finally, when the knower obtains knowledge of the known, the two are non-different. Now, the difference between the knower and the known, and the relation between the two are straightforward problems, because they are involved in all perceptions. The problem arises in the final stage of self-awareness where the knower and the known are non-different.

To accommodate these contradictory ideas, the difference and non-difference of the knower and the known in knowledge, non-difference must be added, since the difference is already understood. But how can two things be both different and non-different? This is impossible in classical logic as it violates the principle of mutual exclusion: Two things must either be different or non-different. Thus, "I" becomes self-contradictory as it breaks logical principles. Here, we aren't even using set theory or a whole-part doctrine. We are only employing two modes—i.e., the knower and the known—of the same "I". We are used to thinking of each thing as one kind of thing—e.g., a knower or a known. When the same thing must be understood in many modes, our classical forms of logic don't work. When the logic doesn't work, we tend to discard the modes (in modern mathematics) and we reject logic (in Vedānta philosophy).

Neither solution is fundamentally better; they are merely preferences.

The problem both in mathematical set theory and Vedānta philosophy is fundamentally one of the modalities, and how they lead to contradictions. The reality is one thing, but it must be described through mutually exclusive modes. Thus, a cow is both an individual and a universal. An observer is both a knower and the known. Everything is both a possibility and a purpose. Existence and truth are complementary modes. Truth, right, and good are different modes. How a thing looks like, and how it is used are different modalities. In a drama, an actor and a character are different modes. If we reject modes, then we can know only through one mode, and the knowledge is incomplete. If we add modes into our knowledge, then the knowledge turns self-contradictory.

The greater the number of modalities, the greater are the contradictions. And, the fewer the modalities, the more limited is the knowledge. Thus, we can envision a spectrum of philosophical positions that range from no modalities to infinite modalities. Buddhism rejects all modalities, and it ends up with nothingness—the maximum incompleteness. Advaita accepts three modes—it can describe the soul outside matter, but not the soul in matter. Viśiṣṭādvaita adds the modality of properties to the Advaita modality of the soul, and the soul can be described both in and out of matter. But this leads to the idea that the soul must be incomplete only being the property and not an object. Similarly, God must be incomplete because He is only an object and not a property. God and the soul must therefore be mutually dependent, as they are both incomplete. Dvaita recognizes that soul and matter are different realities, so they can exist in both object and property modes. But when they know each other, then God is within the soul, and the soul is within God. Thus, knowledge breaks the doctrine of their separation. Bhedābheda says that we can accept that the soul and God are within each other, but this leads to the problem that if God is within the soul, then the soul must be God. In Acintyabhedābheda, the Absolute Truth is inconceivable, but since concepts are expressed in words, therefore, inconceivability entails the end of all words, or at least speech would never be coherent. That entails that we must also stop talking about God and the soul.

The system of zero modalities is the most incomplete because nothing at all exists. Knowledge grows as we add modalities. But each such addition in knowledge brings an ever-growing number of internal contradictions.

Since this problem is so pervasive, it must have a universal solution. That solution will not be philosophy, science, mathematics, or religion. It will be all of them, and yet none of them. It will essentially be an understanding of how knowledge can be complete with many modes, without contradictions. This idea frames the problem of a 'Scientific Interpretation of Vedānta Sūtra'. It is not regurgitating a previous idea in a new language—e.g., English. It is not using modern science to understand Vedānta philosophy. And it is not a religious philosophy. It is fundamentally solving a thus far unsolved problem. Whatever comes out as a solution must be novel, so in some sense must go past what has previously been stated—in science, philosophy, mathematics, or religion. It is for this reason that a new commentary on Vedānta Sūtra is required, not merely the translation of the previous commentaries into English. It is also for this reason that the new commentary must differ from the earlier commentaries.

Three Basic Modalities

If you have followed the argument thus far, then we can begin understanding the solution. The cornerstone of the solution is that everything in Vedic philosophy is a soul, and souls exist in three modes—*sat*, *chit*, and *ānanda*. Some soul is the whole—and is called the Supreme Soul—while other souls are parts. But every soul comprises these three modes. What are these modes? Let's understand them through the example of the problem of "I" seen previously.

"I" exists in three modes—the knower, the known, and the relation between the two. The knower is ānanda; it is the potentiality for desire. But since desire doesn't always exist, therefore, the soul can exist without knowing itself. Enjoyment requires something other than the enjoyer. Therefore, if the desire for enjoyment is manifest, then a schism in the soul is created—the difference between knower and known. You miss yourself, and to overcome this missing, you relate to yourself. This relation is called *sat* or awareness. It is the connection between the knower and the known. Once this connection is established, then the knower enters the known, and the known enters the knower. We call this 'knowledge', and the Vedas call it *chit*. When you see an object, the object is inside you, and yet it is outside you. Similarly, you are inside that object, and yet you are outside that object. All these modes are beyond current logic. For instance, to say that the knower and the known are identical in the ānanda stage, and yet to enjoy, they must separate, is logically contradictory. Likewise, how can the self be related to itself? Finally, when we postulate a difference between the knower and the known, how can the knower be inside the known, and the known be inside the knower? The problem is that our logic is based on physical thinking, but the soul is not physical. In physical thinking, two things are either identical or different; if they are identical, then they cannot be separated; but if they have separated, then they cannot exist within each other.

The soul defies these limitations of physical thinking. Since everything in Vedic philosophy is a soul, therefore, everything—including matter—defies this logic. To understand anything, we must begin with the nature of the soul, which means understand the three modes in which it exists and the nature of each mode. For the simplicity of our further discussion, I will call these modes emotion, relation, and cognition. Don't worry about what these words mean in English. This is a technical nomenclature, that uses English words. For those who don't know Sanskrit, it is better than *ānanda-sat-chit*. But that doesn't mean we are dealing with the mundane understanding of these words.

You can see that there is a progression in the modes—from emotion to relation to cognition. This is because emotion exists first, it leads to a relation, and then to a cognition. If there was no experience, then this gradual progression creates experience. But you can also see that in the final cognitive experience, all three modes are combined. That is, when you have a cognition, you also have a relation, and you experience an emotion. However, if you have an emotion, you need not have a relation or a cognition. This brings us to the main point: Knowledge is cognition, and it depends on a relation and an emotion. If you have no desire to know, you cannot know. If you have a desire to know, but you don't relate to the known object, again, you cannot know. So, after you have a desire, and you establish a relation, you must enter the known (to grasp the nature of the known), and the known must enter you (to represent the nature of the known). This mutual penetration is knowledge. Since cognition comes from relation and emotion, therefore, it is the fullness of the three modes. Likewise, a relation needs two modes; and emotion is only one mode. Therefore, knowledge must be described as a combination of the three modes.

Each of these three modes involves a difference and non-difference. The ānanda mode is non-difference when the potential for desire exists, but it is difference if the desire is manifest. The *sat* mode is relation between the knower and the known, but since they are the same, there is non-difference (because they are not separable) and difference (because there is a relation between the two). The *chit* mode is the knower inside the known, and the known inside the knower; due to this mutual penetration, they are neither separable nor identical. The term 'non-difference' can therefore be used for these three modes, but it doesn't mean one thing. There are factually three kinds of non-difference.

We discussed earlier that with three modes, knowledge is self-contradictory. But we can now see that even with a single mode, there is self-contradiction because each mode exists in a state of non-difference. This additional complication is due to the existence of oppositions: Everything is defined through an opposition. Thus, the knower cannot exist without a known. When the emotion, relation, and cognition are absent, then the knower and known are merged into a state of potentiality, without knowledge. But as they are separated, then knower, known, and knowledge are created collectively. As a result, we cannot speak of abstract knowledge, without a person who knows. Hence, it is possible to speak about the unmanifest state of reality in which the knower, known, and knowledge are not separated, as pure potentiality. However, this state cannot be called either the knower, or the known, or the knowledge. Neither words, nor experience, nor a reality different from the knower exists in this stage. Hence, this stage of existence cannot be known or described in words. And yet, we can postulate its existence as the basis from with everything springs.

Vedānta worsens the problem that we knew of from set theory. In set theory, a single mode will give you incomplete knowledge, but at least it won't be self-contradictory. But in Vedānta, every mode is self-contradictory. Therefore, we must distinguish between two kinds of inconsistencies—those that exist within the modes, and those that arise from their mutual combination.

The problem gets much worse when we see that there are varieties or types of each of these three modes, and these types are mutually contradictory. For example, in cognition, you have opposite types such as hot and cold, big and small, rough and smooth, bitter and sweet, etc. Normally, we keep these types separate, and say that something is either hot or cold, either bitter or sweet, etc. But the problem is that they are defined through their mutual opposition; you cannot define hot, except in distinction to cold. Hence, a new type of non-difference arises: Hot and cold are different, and yet not completely separable.

Thus, the problem of modalities gets increasingly complex upon deeper investigation: (1) the three modes of the soul are mutually contradictory, (2) each mode is self-contradictory, and (3) types of these modes are mutually contradictory, although these contradictories are also defined by each other. Since there is no respite from such contradictions, we cannot hope to solve the problem of contradictions in classical logic. We need a generic solution to these contradictions, and, therefore, let's now turn toward that generic solution.

Dominant-Subordinate

The generic solution in Vedic philosophy is that these modes go dominant and subordinate. Sometimes we observe the individuals through sense perception, without classifying them into concepts. At other times, we focus on the classification and identify the universals by defocusing from sense perception. Sometimes we decipher the meaning and sometimes we judge whether this meaning is true. Sometimes we judge if some action is right, and then we judge if it is also good. Sometimes we understand a play based on actors and sometimes based on characters. Sometimes we suppress our emotions to prioritize our duties. At other times, we prioritize cognition and suppress emotions. The modes are ever-present. But they are not equally dominant all the time.

Due to changing priorities of these modes through dominant-subordinate relationships, the conflict between the modes is resolved—the dominant mode 'rules over' the subordinate mode and suppresses its nature. The flaw in modern thinking is that we give equal priority to all these modes simultaneously. Thus, for instance, we say that if we are seeing the individual, then we cannot know the universal, because the same thing cannot both be a universal and an individual. This is a flawed argument because it assumes that individuals and universals are simultaneously perceived. They are not. While our perception is focused on sensation, it is defocused from the meaning. But when it is focused on the meaning, then it is defocused from sensation. The modes flip rapidly, so we don't realize that the priorities are changing, but the modes are never simultaneous. Our experience is consistent because of the changing priorities. Our language or reasoning is inconsistent because we don't use priorities.

The mode flipping produces change, which is experienced as time; every moment is a different mode priority. However, there are many kinds of times. The deterministic evolution of the world—i.e., what is going to happen—is the universal description of the world and constitutes the universal time; it is also identified with the God-mode description of the world. The subjective evolution of the world—i.e., who is doing what—is identified with the soul-mode description of the same world. It constitutes the soul-mode time or the personal experience of time. Finally, how things are happening—i.e., the causal mechanism—is identified as the matter-mode description of the same world. It constitutes the objective description of time. In one sense, matter-, soul-, and God- modes are mutually exclusive. In another sense, since these modes are simultaneously possible, therefore, God, matter, and soul are three descriptions of the world. And yet, what will happen is prior to who will do it, which is prior to how it will be done. Therefore, God-mode is superior to soul-mode, which is superior to the matter-mode. Someone might say that while studying matter we don't see soul or God. That's just because we are stuck in a single modality—of how things happen. If we asked other questions—i.e., who will do what, and what will happen—then we will begin seeing soul and God within a theory. The questions of what, how, and who constitute complementary modalities. Their answers also constitute different modes of God, matter, and soul.

The Absolute Truth (which is a term I will use often, and it means the singular truth) is the collection of all the modes. The innumerable modes are produced by the combination of three modes, and the three modes spring from a primordial state in which the modes are undifferentiated. Thus, a oneness divides into three, which then creates infinite variety. This variety is due to the dominant-subordinate relations between the modes. Even the material world, for instance, is described as the dominant-subordinate structure of the three modes. These modes are called *sattva*, *rajas*, and *tamas* in Sāñkhya philosophy. What we call the 'mind' dominates in sattva; what we call the 'body' dominates in tamas; and the connection between mind and body dominates in rajas. We can simplify this terminology by saying that the body is an object, the mind is the purpose of that object, and the connection between mind and body is the control that engages the object toward a purpose. Likewise, the purpose too can be divided into three modes. The purpose in sattva is driven toward higher achievements, the purpose in rajas is driven toward the control of other living entities, and the purpose in tamas is driven toward the body's survival. In this way, all variety in Sāñkhya philosophy is first reduced to three modes, and then these three modes are reduced to a primordial state called Pradhāna in which the distinction between the modes is unmanifest. Thus, again, even in the case of matter, one divides into three, and three then produces infinite variety.

The three modes of material nature are reflections of the three modes of the soul that we have discussed earlier. Hence, if we understand the soul, then we can understand the nature of matter as well. The doctrines of soul, matter, and God are hence constructed in the same way. God, matter, and soul are three modes of the same reality. Each mode is in turn comprised of three modes, and the division by three continues indefinitely to create separate descriptions. As a result, we cannot say that God, soul, and matter are completely separate, just as we cannot say that they are identical. Due to modes, we must say that God, soul, and matter are non-different—as three modes of reality they are not identical, but as the modalities of the same reality, they are not different. Two things that are neither identical nor different create classical contradictions. But if we describe these things as the modes, then the contradictions cease to exist.

Alternative Philosophies

Materialism

Materialism dispenses with multiple modes by removing all concepts from the nature of reality. Without concepts, the mind cannot exist. If concepts and the mind don't exist, then knowledge cannot exist, because all knowledge involves concepts. If knowledge cannot exist, then we don't need books to understand the nature of reality. This is the position of the *nāśtika* or the atheistic school of materialism in Indian philosophy. The main proponent of this philosophy—Chārvāka—argued that the pursuit of knowledge is futile because concepts don't exist. There are only individual things, and we cannot classify them into groups, categories, or classes. A concept is something that spans across multiple objects; for example, the concept 'cow' spans across many cows. But we don't see anything that spans across many cows. What we cannot see, we cannot assume exists. Hence, there is no such thing as the idea of 'cow'. There are just individual objects, and we have invented some language to describe these things similarly, but all such descriptions are our constructions. There is no reality to such concepts, and without concepts, there is no knowledge.

It is worth noting that the materialism of modern science is somewhat different. It postulates three modalities—objects, properties, and values. The same object can have many properties, the same properties can exist in other objects, and the same values can exist in different properties. Objects, properties, and values, therefore, underdetermine each other. But since they are required in a scientific theory, they must also be separate modes. Examples of objects are particles and waves. Examples of properties are kinetic, potential, and thermal energy. And examples of values are the quantities associated with a property (numbers such as real numbers, natural numbers, complex numbers, etc.). Owing to multiple modes, the description of nature can never be complete.

An example of such incompleteness is that when two particles collide, the outcome of the collision is uncertain—the particles can split and join. The properties too can be converted from one to another—e.g., energy can transform from kinetic, to potential, to thermal. Since kinetic energy can be converted into potential energy, therefore, other properties like momentum and angular momentum are not conserved. In fact, we also know that energy can be converted into mass, and vice versa, so they are only collectively conserved. In so far as a unified theory of mass and charge doesn't exist, charge is supposed to be conserved, but if a unified theory existed, then charge and energy would be interconvertible. Finally, the total value of any of these properties may be distributed between multiple particles and multiple properties in many ways. Because the number of particles is uncertain, therefore, the particles are not conserved. Since the total number of properties is uncertain, therefore, the number of properties is not conserved. The only certainty in science is that the total value is conserved. For instance, the total amount of energy is conserved, although it can be distributed across many types, distributed over numerous particles. This creates incompleteness—we cannot predict how the total energy will be distributed into multiple particles, or even how many such particles will exist.

Thus, while objects, properties, and values are used as three modes in science, only one mode—i.e., the total values of properties—is objective. Whatever is not conserved cannot be called real; reality is that which is conserved. Thus, even as theories employ three modes, only the value mode is objective. This science is necessarily incomplete because it has been made consistent.

There is another kind of materialism encountered in atomic theory, which is not well understood at present because we don't understand how nature is multimodal. In this materialism, reality exists in mutually orthogonal and complementary modes. Unlike classical physics, where you could measure all the particles simultaneously, you cannot measure all the modes at once. Thus, one mode becomes dominant at a time, and the other modes remain subordinate. Quantum theory cannot predict which mode will be dominant when, but it statistically predicts the occurrence of modes. The statistical prediction is possible due to the hierarchy in the modes. We don't get equal probabilities for each possibility, and some possibilities have a zero probability (as they lie 'in between' the orthogonal modes). In classical materialism, we could not predict the total number of particles and their properties; we just knew the total value. In quantum materialism, we know the total number of particles, their properties, and their values. But we cannot know them at once as they are different modes, which become real one after another. If we changed our view of atomic theory—from particles to modalities—then we could say that objects, properties, and values are simultaneously real, so this theory is more complete than classical physics. However, because we cannot know all the modes at once, therefore, this theory *seems* incomplete. We need a description of how the modalities manifest one by one, and then the theory would also be complete.

Idealism

Idealism takes the opposite approach to materialism. It says: Let's forget about the individuals of this world. Let's only focus on the universals, because our goal is knowledge, and we need to know this knowledge as concepts. That's a viable goal, but it means that you and I cannot separately have knowledge, because that would mean that there are two separate instances of knowledge, and we already began by saying that we cannot include individuals. This position, therefore, leads to the conclusion of solipsism: Only I exist, the world is simply my idea, and even when I see others, they are ideas within me. Due to the rejection of other things besides me, there are no individuals. There is only me, and because there is only me, we can discard the individual modality.

But there is still a problem. You can perceive two instances of red, which would require you to have two modalities—universal and individual. That would still be problematic. So, to be consistent, we must say that there aren't two instances of red; there are just two sensations, and we cannot call them red or black or yellow or anything. They are just two things, without a commonality. Philosophers call this idea "dustbowl empiricism" because your experience is a collection of data points—like particles of dust—which are not tied together into a conception of some external reality; hence there is no knowledge.

Many Western philosophers—such as Berkeley and Hume—have gone on to take these radical empiricist positions and argue that knowledge is impossible because you only have sensations, which cannot be organized into properties and objects. Without properties and objects, there can be no scientific laws. And without such laws, there can be no knowledge. Therefore, we just have experiences, but we can never convert these experiences into knowledge.

Immanuel Kant wanted to turn this problem around, and he said that the other modalities—such as properties and objects—come from *us*. The world only gives us sensations, but we add concepts (like properties and objects). But there is a problem. Since we are providing these concepts, therefore, everyone can provide their ideas in whichever way they choose. Only the sensations will be scientific, their explanations using objects and properties would be our creation. That would mean that science is possible, but it is always a personal interpretation of the world. Of course, Kant argued that to save ourselves from this subjectivity, we must say that properties and objects are universal. But that idea reinjects the universals, which are different from the individuals. The existence of universals and individuals wasn't the only problem of course. Since each observer is a separate individual, there were many 'copies' of the universal in each observer. Why should these copies of the universal be identical? Don't we have individual freedoms to interpret reality in different ways? So, Kantian universality compromised the individual freedom, and the resurrection of freedom must similarly compromise universality. Again, we can have only one of them; having both is contradictory. However, removing one of them leads to incompleteness. For instance, if there is individual freedom, then there is no universality—we cannot talk about objective knowledge. If instead there is universality, then there cannot be individual freedom. Either alternative becomes incomplete. Therefore, in practice, both modes were used by constantly revising the universals. For instance, scientists continuously invent new properties and object-types and use them in new theories, and each such theory is called a 'universal theory' until it turns out to be merely an individual perspective.

Some philosophers after Kant—e.g., Edmund Husserl—tried to solve this problem by saying that we must 'bracket' all that's coming from the external world. In short, we try to understand ourselves, because that understanding will give us the universals innate in us. In short, you pursue the object and property modalities, but you get rid of the value modality. You still cannot tell which object must have which property, so even your inner investigation of the self must remain incomplete. And by 'bracketing' the external world, you have lost the ability to test whether our innate ideas are also useful. In short, you can no longer be certain if you should be here, whether you and the world are compatible if knowledge can be acquired, and what that knowledge is good for. Martin Heidegger called this purposeless existence *dasein*— "being there". It is incomplete because there is no method to confirm whether the discovery of the dasein is actually true, and potentially everyone can make a different discovery. Now, you can get radical individuality, but there is just no universality.

There was another kind of idealism prevalent in Greek times. It argued that there exists a perfect world of ideas, called the Platonic world, and the ideas from this perfect world are reflected in this world. This meant that there was a perfect definition of a man, and some men reflected this idea perfectly, while others did not. The problem was in defining this perfect man. Greeks did not define ideality as the perfection of moral character. Instead, they reduced perfection to shape, size, and color. Therefore, tall, well-built, white men were perfect, and everyone else wasn't. The non-ideal men had to be subordinated to the ideal, which means that people with different skin tones could be enslaved.

Then, the superiority of false ideals was used to propagate enslavement. This is a clear illustration of how universals negate the existence of individuals. If only tall, white, and well-built men are ideal men, then everyone else is not.

Western society continued with such false ideals for nearly two thousand years, until the dawn of Postmodernism, which rejects the pursuit of all ideals: there is no one better or worse. The rejection is correct if it is taken to mean the rejection of the false ideals of shape, size, and color. But it is flawed because it also discards the traditional moral virtues—based upon the acceptance of a higher purpose in the present life—along with the false traditional ideals. Thus, the right-wing politicians speak about the ideals, but their idealism rejects the individuality of different ideals. The left-wing politicians reject the ideals and speak about gender, race, and color diversity. They are both wrong rejecting all ideals, or applying a universal ideal onto everybody are equally useless.

Vedic philosophy also speaks of ideals, but they are identified as moral values. Those with such moral values are considered superior. However, these ideals have to be adapted to individuals and their priorities must be changed in different contexts. Therefore, when Idealism is used in Vedic philosophy, it is neither blanket universalism, nor random individualism, nor free contextual customization by everyone. The conclusion is far more nuanced—there are universal ideals, that have to be adapted to the individual's nature, which have to be adjusted based on different contexts. The domination of these three modes is variable because each of the three modes can be legitimately dominant.

Buddhism

While materialism and idealism struggle with the problem of multiple modes and the contradictions resulting from them, Buddhism says that each of these modes is self-contradictory. Thus, even if you are interested in ideas, and are prepared to reject the individuals, there is still no hope because all these ideas are defined through mutual opposites. For instance, if you say that something is a table, you mean that it is *not* a chair, house, car, bed, etc. According to Buddhism, it is fundamentally impossible to define the idea of a 'table' except through a distinction to every other idea—e.g., table, bed, house, etc. Therefore, either all these ideas are collectively defined, or nothing is defined at all. As an illustration, if you picked up a dictionary of word-meanings, you would find that words are defined by using other words. You cannot define any word by itself—i.e., there is no self-evident word. But if all the words are defined through such mutual distinctions and oppositions, then either the multitude of words exists simultaneously, or nothing at all exists. When this multitude of words exists, they exist as opposites—hot and cold, bitter and sweet, rough and smooth, etc. They are logical contraries, so you cannot call this consistent knowledge. The only consistent state is if you dissolve everything; all these contraries disappear, the contradictions go away, and nothing at all exists.

Thus, in Materialism and Idealism, there is some hope for knowledge, if you employ only one of the modes, although the knowledge will be incomplete. But in Buddhism, there is no hope for knowledge because every mode is self-contradictory. You don't just avoid contradictions by rejecting multiple modes.

You must also reject even a single modality because of the contraries.

You could say that the flaw in the Buddhist argument is that even though there are opposites such as hot and cold, the same thing is never both hot and cold. So, yes, as dictionary definitions of universals, both contraries must exist simultaneously, but this doesn't mean that the same object is simultaneously those opposites. However, the Buddhist will say that you are assuming that the individual thing you are referring to as the basis for resolving this contradiction is not itself contradictory. As we have discussed earlier, the 'self' or 'I' is also self-contradictory because it is comprised of three contradictory modes.

Thus, according to Buddhism, even your claim of self-awareness is defined by an opposition between the knower and known. If you remove the known, then the knower doesn't know itself, and hence it doesn't exist. Dissolving one side of the distinction dissolves both. If the 'self' is contradictory, the individuals have the same fate as the universals—they are both mutually opposed contraries. Thus, we cannot use the separation of individuals to solve the problem of universals; you must begin by solving the problem of the individuals!

The crux of the issue in Buddhism is that there is nothing self-evident; everything is defined through opposition to something else. If we look at Western philosophy, this problem was never grasped. For instance, Descartes said that I could distrust everything in my perception, but I could not distrust my own existence. Therefore, at least my existence is completely certain to me. I am therefore not defined by a relational opposition to others. I am defined by myself. But this is because Descartes did not deconstruct the nature of the self. He merely took self-awareness as the self-evident indication of the self. When Buddhists refute this self-evident nature of the self, they conclude that there is factually no self. What we call the 'self' is the combination of two opposites, and it is as much a material construct as every other mutual opposition. The only solution is that we discard these contradictions and arrive at nothingness.

Monotheism

The journey from the material world to nothingness seems viable, but the journey from nothingness to the material world seems implausible. What causes nothingness to split into opposites? Monotheistic religions offer a solution to this problem, in which the world is created *ex-nihilo*—i.e., nothingness precedes the world and God splits this nothingness into mutual opposites.

Of course, Abrahamic religions don't have a sophisticated notion of the world as logical opposites. But in principle, that problem could be solved if Buddhist ideas were combined with Monotheism as a solution to the problems of nothingness. However, the Buddhist will still argue: The notion of 'self' or soul is self-contradictory. So, the idea of God must also be self-contradictory. How are you going to solve this problem? Unless you solve the problem, the claim that God created the world from nothing would not be acceptable, because God Himself would be defined by the existence of mutual opposites. In fact, one could argue that this opposition already exists as God and Satan.

To reinstate the existence of God, one could say that matter is not defined by mutual opposites. These opposites are semantic categories like hot and cold.

But we can reject these categories and just talk about temperature as a physical property. So, the adoption of modern science becomes a solution to the problem of Buddhism because the world is no longer described by oppositions. However, if you reject these conceptual categories, then you cannot have concepts and minds, and you cannot explain conceptual knowledge. Furthermore, by rejecting these semantic categories, you have lost the ability to rationalize nothingness as the combination of opposites. So, if you say that God created the world *ex nihilo* then it follows that God created an infinite amount of energy because the world did not exist prior to God creating it. But how did God create energy from nothing? Isn't that a case of something coming out of nothing? The Monotheist can argue that God is supernatural, but this supernatural being violates the conservation of energy because He creates matter and energy. Since matter and energy are not eternal, therefore, God's existence is contrary to natural laws. Now, all religion becomes contrary to everything in science.

The problem could in principle be avoided if Monotheism discarded the *ex-nihilo* doctrine, and said that energy preexisted in God, and it was converted into the world. But postulating such a mechanism would mean that since energy in God is transformed into this world, therefore, God after creation must be reduced in energy. Just like a billiard ball transfers its energy to another billiard ball, similarly, upon creation, God must either cease to exist or even if He exists, He must be considerably diminished upon this creation. A God that is diminished by His actions of creation would not truly be called God. So, this solution is never applied, and that simply means that God's existence is contrary to the laws of nature (such as the law of conservation of energy). The *ex-nihilo* doctrine becomes the basis of conflicts between God and science.

Pantheism

The pantheistic approach tries to address the problem of conflict between God and science. It says that conservation of energy is true, and God was this energy before creation. However, when this world is created, then God simply becomes the world as all the energy is transformed from God into the world. Thus, He ceases to have a separate existence, and the world again becomes God when everything is destroyed. In other words, there is either God or the world, and these are merely two different states of energy—concentrated in God or distributed in the world. Supernatural ideas are not needed, because conservation of energy is upheld. And yet, right now, because the world is manifest, therefore, God doesn't exist. Your worship of God must be false right now.

There is still a nagging problem. How does God become the world, and how does the world become God? Clearly, there needs to be some free will or volition involved in these changes. If God has volition before creation, but then He becomes the world, then the volition must also be gone. Once the volition is gone, then the world cannot convert back to God. So, the creation of the world must be a one-time activity, and after that God doesn't exist forever. And yet, if that is indeed the case, then the worship of God becomes even more unnecessary. Earlier, God did not exist now but could exist in the future. In the new doctrine, God existed in the past but never in the present or any future.

While all this may pose some theological problems, there is no rational or logical problem in saying that this indeed happened. The new problem is that there is only energy, hence there cannot be ideas, mind, or knowledge. The addition of the mind would require a new modality, and that will create logical contradictions, and all the logical beauty of this doctrine would disappear.

Schools of Vedānta

Advaita

Advaita has a position like that of pantheism although it postulates two categories—Brahman and māyā—both of which are eternal, but their combination is not eternal. Due to the eternity of māyā, conservation of energy is true. And due to the eternity of Brahman, free will or volition also remains eternal. The living entity in this material world is said to be the combination of Brahman and māyā, and the liberated living entity is said to be Brahman without māyā. As these two are separated, māyā doesn't cease to exist. However, the experience of this māyā comes to an end. Since māyā is eternal, therefore, energy is eternally conserved, and there is no contradiction between religion and science. Since Brahman is separate from māyā, therefore, God doesn't become the world (if we say that God is Brahman), and the creation is not *ex-nihilo* (because the creation is from māyā). But you can ask: What about knowledge? We have been concerned about the nature of knowledge, and it was deemed impossible. How does the separation of Brahman and māyā address that problem? The Advaita response to this problem is that there are two kinds of knowledge. The first type of knowledge is the knowledge of this world. This knowledge is contradictory because māyā is contradictories, and these contradictories are dissolved leaving a state of nothingness. Hence, when Buddhism speaks about nothingness, it is referring to māyā and not to Brahman. The second type of knowledge is the knowledge of Brahman, and this knowledge is not self-contradictory if we dissolve the notion of "I". Recall that the problem of contradictories is extended into the self by Buddhism. But if we dissolve the self, then contradictories don't exist. But this 'solution' raises many other questions. If there is no "I", then there is also no self-awareness, because "I" means is self-awareness. If we say that Brahman is without self-awareness because there is no "I", then how do we know that Brahman even exists? How different is Advaita, simply by postulating the existence of Brahman, when the conclusion is that there is no "I"?

Buddhism and Advaita are nearly identical doctrines because in both the doctrines the world is contradictories, and consistency is achieved when these contradictories are dissolved to produce nothingness. Similarly, in both doctrines, there is no self or "I" because "I" involves contradictories. The difference is simply that Advaita postulates that there is a Brahman beyond māyā which has the potential to become self-aware. When this self-awareness doesn't exist, then the "I" is dissolved into Brahman. And when Brahman becomes self-aware, then "I" is produced. And once this "I" is produced, then, the "I" also become ensnared in the contradictories of māyā. Hence, Advaita is slightly better in terms of being able to explain how the present world is produced.

Now, you can ask: How does Brahman become self-aware? The answer is modalities. Brahman exists as *sat*, *chit*, and ānanda, which are simply potentials or possibilities. The ānanda mode is the sense in which Brahman is different from itself—i.e., it can become different individuals or knowers. The *chit* mode is the sense in which the soul is non-different from itself—i.e., the different individuals being known. And the *sat* mode is the sense in which the knowers are connected to other knowns to create the material experience. However, since these are simply potentials, therefore, in Brahman the distinction between the different knowers, the different knowns, and the relation between these knowers and knowns doesn't exist; only the potential for such distinction exists.

Thus far, everything is good. The problem begins when we ask: How does unmanifest become manifest? If the three modes are simply possibilities, then to convert them into a reality we need a choice. This choice needs a personality, which means there must be an "I" outside Brahman. Since Advaita has already rejected any "I" outside Brahman, it is compelled to say that the cause of the manifestation is māyā. In short, māyā causes the Brahman to divide into many selves, and then ensnares them into the material world. However, if māyā is the cause of the division of Brahman, then it must also be the cause of return to Brahman. The net result of this doctrine is that Brahman has no causality. Since we are Brahman, we have no free will to either be entangled or liberated. Both entanglement and liberation are thus dependent on the agency of māyā.

But how can māyā have any agency? And what kind of agency is that? If we say that māyā has free will and individuality, then we cannot assert that it is different from Brahman. If we say that māyā has no free will and individuality, then upon fall into matter we cannot get liberated, and if we are liberated then we cannot fall into matter. Since we are fallen right now, we cannot get liberated. After all, whatever desire for liberation we acquire is simply a desire. How can the succession of these desires lead to a desireless state? The production of desireless from desire would itself be called self-contradictory.

Thus, we can see how Advaita goes very far in addressing the issues with the other doctrines and is hence superior to them. Certainly, Materialism, Idealism, Monotheism, or Pantheism come nowhere close to Advaita. Advaita has many similarities to Buddhism, but the one difference it posits between Brahman and māyā fails to hold up to scrutiny. It only makes Brahman causeless and māyā as the origin of causality. The net result of this limitation is that Advaita cannot accurately describe the cause of the soul's fall and liberation.

Viśiṣṭādvaita

Viśiṣṭādvaita sets out to address the problem of fall and liberation. The solution is through the doctrine of God. God is also a soul, and hence, like in Advaita, He too has three modalities. But God is defined as an object, while soul and matter are His properties. Just as a particle has properties like mass, energy, momentum, etc. similarly God is an object with innumerable properties. Viśiṣṭādvaita gives the analogy of body and soul; just like the body is a property of the soul, similarly, the soul is the 'body' of God. Just as the parts of the body serve the soul, similarly, as properties of God, the soul must serve God. However, the soul may choose not to serve God, and enjoy independently. Thus, the soul falls into matter. He acquires a material body and tries to be like God—i.e., the object who then has subsidiary properties. The soul gets liberated when he gives up this mentality to be the object and remains as God's property.

Since the nature of matter is not changed in Viśiṣṭādvaita, like Advaita, it doesn't contradict the duality of matter. Likewise, since the three modes of the soul and matter are acknowledged, therefore, Viśiṣṭādvaita can explain how the "I" emerges from an unmanifest state. Thus, liberation into Brahman is not denied, however, that liberation doesn't entail the dissolution of the identity of the soul. All souls hence remain eternally individual. However, if the three modes enter an unmanifest state, then the *experience* of individuality is lost, although the individuality is not lost. Since individuality is eternal, therefore, external causes of the soul's fall into the material world are not needed. The soul can fall into matter when individuality develops, and the soul considers itself an object. Likewise, the soul can be liberated into Brahman if it dissolves its individuality. Finally, the soul can be liberated through a relation to God if it gives up the mindset of being an object and prefers to remain a property. Also, since God is a soul, hence, God is not subject to the dualities of māyā.

The term Viśiṣṭa denotes qualities or properties, and Advaita denotes the *unity* rather than *oneness*. The purpose of this unity is to connect all the diversities. God as the object of all properties is the unity, and His properties are the diversities. Therefore, Viśiṣṭādvaita means the properties of the Unity

There is, however, one serious problem in Viśiṣṭādvaita. The problem is that when the soul enters the material world, he acts like an object rather than a property. If the soul can act as an object, then there must at least be the potential of being an object, even if this objectivity is not always visible in the liberated state. Owing to this problem, we cannot say that the soul is only a property. We must rather say that the soul can be both a property and an object. In the spiritual world, the soul is present as a property, and in the material world, a soul is an object. As an object, the soul combines with material properties (such as hot and cold, bitter and sweet, big and small) which then become the soul's properties. And as a property, the soul describes the nature of God. But if the soul can be both object and property, but only one of them is seen in the spiritual and material worlds, then the spiritual world must be as incomplete as the material world. In both worlds, the soul incompletely realizes its potential—the soul is either a property or an object and can never be both. Since both potentials can be realized, but they are only realized alternately, therefore, object and property are modalities of the soul, and they cannot be simultaneously true. It follows that if the soul has been liberated as a property of God, then it must fall as an object into matter. And if the soul has fallen as an object into matter, then it must be liberated as a property of God. Thus, neither fall nor liberation is eternal, and both situations must be experienced alternately. This is because, in each kind of world, one type of incompleteness is bargained for another.

Dvaita

The problem in Viśiṣṭādvaita can be solved if we say that the soul is not merely a property but also an object. And the property and object modalities of the soul are eternally manifest. To make this argument, we would have to change the analogy of soul and body in Viśiṣṭādvaita. We would no longer say that the soul is the body of the Supreme Soul. We would rather say that the soul is like the part of the body. To make this analogy work, we could say that God is the head of the body, whereas the soul is like the hands and legs of the body. Each part of the body—e.g., hand and leg—can be treated as an object, which then also has properties like color, shape, size, etc. And if the soul is these parts, then it exists in both object and property modes, so it doesn't have to fall into matter to realize its object modality, and the liberated state is complete.

However, now a new problem arises. If the soul is like the hand, while God is like the head, then if the soul leaves the association of God, then God must be diminished—it is as if God's hand was cut off. If, on the other hand, we say that the soul never leaves God's body, then God is never diminished, but when the soul suffers in this world, then God too must be suffering—it is as if the hand is being burnt so the pain must also be experienced by the head. This problem doesn't arise when we say that the soul is God's property because God is the object. If we remove a property from an object, the object is not changed. For example, if you take away some energy from a particle, the particle is unchanged. The problem arises if we say that we are cutting off a part of the particle. In that case, the particle would be divided into two particles. Therefore, if we say that the soul is God's property, then the object and property modes cause a problem because they make liberation temporary. If, on the other hand, we say that the soul is both object and property, then, due to the object mode, removing the soul from God would entail that God is reduced. If instead, we don't remove the part, then the soul's suffering entails God's suffering.

The Dvaita system sets out to solve this problem by saying that the soul and God are different individuals, and the soul is not part of God. Therefore, if the soul leaves God, then God is not reduced. And because the soul can leave God's association, when the soul suffers, God is not suffering with him. Similarly, matter is separate from God, and therefore, God is transcendent to matter. Now, if the soul is different from God, then, why does it need to devote itself to God? Can it not just live and enjoy independently of God? To answer this quandary, Dvaita states that God is omnipotent while the soul is not. Due to omnipotence, God is the soul's controller, and the soul is the controlled. In some sense, the soul must surrender to God because God subdues the soul by His power. Now, lest you think that God is the tyrant who rules the world by His power, Dvaita also says that even though God is omnipotent, He is also benevolent. So, His use of power is not like that of a tyrant, but like that of a benevolent ruler.

However, there is one problem in Dvaita, which is that both matter and the soul are separate from God. This contradicts Vedic statements such as *janma ādi asya yatah* which means that God is the source of everything, implying that even matter and souls have emanated from God, and both are eternal but not separate from God. He is also called *sarva kāraṇa kāraṇam* or the cause of all causes. If we say that the soul and matter are separate from Him, then God could not be the cause of matter and the soul. Finally, there are statements such as *pūrnasya purnam ādaya* which indicate that the whole is taken out of the whole, and the emanating whole refers to the material and spiritual worlds, whereas the cause of that emanation is God. If we say that matter is separate from God, then the world cannot be an emanation from God. Even as the Dvaita system solves the problem of God's suffering, it becomes inconsistent with Vedic statements because it postulates an eternal difference between the soul, matter, and God. All claims of God being the source must be discarded.

While Advaita says that there is only one reality, and Viśiṣṭādvaita says that there is a unity in diversity, Dvaita says that there are many realities without a unity. The unity is established by God's omnipotence and benevolence. Just like a king rules over others to create a cohesive society, but he is not the source of the citizens or the land on which he rules, similarly, the land and the people God rules upon are eternally real. He is just the prominent ruler. The problem here is that Vedānta is supposed to describe a singular origin. If the origin is God, then God cannot be diminished by creation. Hence, God is not just the ruler of creation, but also the original cause of the creation. His rulership of the world is established not just by His power, but by His being the creator. If you create something, then you are entitled to rule over it. In the Dvaita system, God is the ruler of the creation, but not its creator. This is because the soul and matter are eternally real, and eternally separate from Him. The ontological pluralism of Dvaita is incompatible with the Vedic claims of God being the single origin of everything, and hence it violates a fundamental principle of Vedānta.

Bhedābheda

Viśiṣṭādvaita and Dvaita set the tone for future interpretations because there are problems associated with the soul being a property of God, a part of God, and not being a property and a part of God. Regardless of which position is adopted, different kinds of problems are encountered. If the soul is a property of God, then the soul remains incomplete because he is not an object. If the soul is a part of God, then when the soul suffers, God must also suffer. If the soul is separate from God, then God cannot be the cause of the soul's origin. Given these problems, the conclusion is that the soul must be a part of God, and yet not a part of God. This simple idea is called Bhedābheda. Bheda means that the soul and God are different. Abheda means that they are non-different. This non-difference is a new logical category because it is neither different nor identical. Due to the rejection of identity, the Advaita position is rejected. And due to the rejection of absolute Dvaita, the separation of God and the soul is rejected.

Now, the contentious issue is what do we mean by different and non-different? The stock example in Bhedābheda is the whole-part relation. One such example is that of fire and spark. Bhedābheda states that because the spark came out of the fire, therefore, it was part of fire; and yet, it is now separate from it. Therefore, the spark is part of the fire, and yet not its part. The trouble with all such examples is the physicalist conception. If a spark came out of the fire, then some energy was lost by the fire. Therefore, the fire must have reduced in its intensity, and it cannot be called the same fire that existed before the spark being emitted. If fire constantly emits sparks, then it will eventually die out. So, as God creates the world, He must constantly be reduced by this creation.

Similarly, another example says that the part is like a drop of water in an ocean; the ocean is not equal to the drop, but the drop is not separate from the ocean. Again, if you remove the drop from the ocean, the ocean will reduce. Ultimately, all physical analogies of whole-part doctrine result in reductionism. The whole is nothing other than the collection of the parts. Therefore, as the parts are removed, the whole is continuously diminished in the process.

My view of this problem is that the doctrine of Bhedābheda is correct, but the examples used to illustrate this doctrine are not. The correct examples are not those of the physical whole-part relations, but *semantic* whole-part relations. Think for the moment about a mammal and a cow. A cow is a part of a mammal. But if you remove the cow from the set of mammals, then the definition of a mammal isn't changed. You can remove every type of mammal—e.g., cows, tigers, goats, horses, etc.—from the mammal, and yet, it would not change the definition of mammal. Therefore, we can see how the first problem concerning the diminishing of the whole by removing the parts is solved. If fire sparks leave the fire, then fire is reduced. But if cows are not part of mammal, then mammal is not redefined. Furthermore, we can say that a cow is a mammal, but a mammal isn't a cow. Since the cow is a mammal, therefore the two are non-different. But since the mammal isn't a cow, therefore, the two are different. So, now we get both properties needed for Bhedābheda because we changed the analogy of the whole-part doctrine from objects to concepts.

What does this mean? It means that we should stop thinking of reality in terms of objects. We must rather think of this reality as concepts. God is an idea—the original idea of knowledge. There are many parts of this knowledge, such as physics, chemistry, biology, mathematics, economics, etc. Each of these parts can be called 'knowledge' and yet they are not complete knowledge. Therefore, it would be wrong to say that biology is not knowledge. And it would also be wrong if you said that biology is complete knowledge.

Now we can apply this understanding to both Viśiṣṭādvaita and Dvaita. The idea cow is not just a part of the idea mammal, but it is produced by dividing the idea mammal into different types of mammals. Therefore, the idea cow would not exist if the mammal did not exist. In that sense, the idea cow is dependent on the idea mammal. However, the idea mammal isn't dependent on the cow. Even if all the types of mammals did not exist, the idea of mammal will still exist. Similarly, the soul is a part of God and depends on God. But God doesn't depend on the soul. Therefore, if the soul leaves God's association, it becomes incomplete, although God is not diminished by this departure. Then when the soul returns to the association of God, it regains its completeness, however, God is not enhanced. Likewise, God is the origin of all the parts, but even after emanating all the parts, God is not reduced by the emanation.

Since all concepts can be organized in a hierarchy, we can envision this like a tree, whose root is God, and its leaves are the souls. If we look at this tree from the perspective of the root, then the root is the object, and all the leaves are properties of that object. However, if we see the intermediate branches, then these are both objects and properties—properties from the perspective of the root, and objects from the perspective of the leaves connected to them.

Therefore, we can adopt both object and properties modes alternately. Since a branch is a property of the root, therefore, Viśiṣṭādvaita is true. But since the branches are also objects, therefore, Dvaita is true. Since both Viśiṣṭādvaita and Dvaita can be simultaneously true, therefore, the Bhedābheda doctrine is true. However, neither of these doctrines works in a physical sense. They only work if we use a semantic approach. But someone can say: You are using the tree analogy, which is a physical analogy. Yes, it is different from fire and ocean analogies, but it is still physical. The short answer to this problem is that this tree analogy is incomplete, and the reason is that you can say that the branches and leaves came out of the root, but you cannot say that the root is present in the leaves or branches. A better analogy would be that of a seed and fruit. The fruit comes out of the seed, but the fruit is again contained within the seed.

So, does that mean this physical analogy will now work for the doctrine? Yes and no. To make it work, we must say that the soul came out of God as the fruit came out of the seed. But then God is present inside the soul like a seed is present inside the fruit. Now you get another problem: if God is present as a seed inside the fruit, then the soul must be able to create the entire universe, just like God (as the seed) previously created all the fruits. In fact, the soul can now be the cause of the entire material creation, infinite other souls, etc. This is when this physical analogy fails, but the semantic analogy still works. When the mammal is present in a cow, the cow doesn't produce all kinds of mammals—i.e., dogs, horses, tigers, etc. Likewise, even if we say that God is present in the soul, this seed cannot be the cause of the entire creation yet again.

Acintyabhedābheda

The central problem with physical analogies is the claim that a 'cow is a mammal'. It indicates that every time we see a cow, we also see a mammal, and therefore, the mammal must be inside the cow. But how could that be, if the mammal not only transcends the individual cows but also tigers, horses, cats, etc.? Furthermore, there is also an animal inside the mammal, and a living being inside the animal, etc. All these concepts are organized hierarchically, and therefore, the higher concept transcends the lower concept. And yet, the higher concept is also immanent in each of the lower concepts. Due to transcendence, we say that a mammal is not a cow. Due to immanence, we say that a cow is a mammal. How can both ideas be true simultaneously when they are clearly contradictory? Of course, we can say that transcendence and immanence are two modes of existence, but we need a deeper understanding of this issue.

The Acintyabhedābheda doctrine clarifies the Bhedābheda doctrine. This clarification is a tripartite modality in the Absolute Truth, which are called

Brahman, Paramātma, and Bhagavān. Bhagavān is transcendent; we can compare Bhagavān to the concept of mammal. Brahman is part of Bhagavān; we can compare such parts to the various types of mammals such as cows, tigers, goats, etc. Within each type of mammal, there is an immanent form of mammal, called Paramātma. Bhagavān is the whole truth, which is also transcendent; Brahman is parts of this truth, and Paramātma is the whole truth immanent in each of the parts. Since Brahman is inside Bhagavān, the diversity is inside the unity. Since Paramātma is inside diversified Brahman, unity is inside diversity. Due to these three entities, there is diversity inside unity, and unity inside diversity.

This idea is immensely important for the following reason. Suppose that the whole truth was only transcendental to all the manifest parts. To know this truth, you will have to first know all the parts and after knowing all the diversity, you could know the unity. In practice, this is impossible because none of us can know everything, and if knowing everything was the precondition to knowing the origin of everything, then the origin could never be known. Now consider the converse proposition—the whole truth is inside every part, so to know the whole truth you just must know *one* part correctly. That one part could be *you*—the knower—and if self-knowledge was obtained completely, then the origin of everything would also be automatically known. But we must remember that this knowledge of the self is not merely the self; it is the understanding of how the whole truth—i.e., Paramātma—is in the self. It is worth reminding ourselves that we are long past physical ideas of containment; the Paramātma is not *physically* in the soul; He is semantically immanent. In simple terms, knowing the self is knowing the meaning of our existence, and while this meaning is immanent in us, the meaning is not us; the meaning is immanent as Paramātma, and the meaning is transcendentally existing as Bhagavān.

The three modalities of the Absolute Truth are existence, meaning, and purpose. Many things exist; they have become manifest from a common source, but this manifestation is not a complete understanding. The fuller understanding is that the common source is the purpose immanent in the different things. Creation has a purpose immanent in each part manifested from the whole. Thus, the soul has a purpose, just as material objects have a purpose; the purpose is the same for both, so the doctrine of immanence and transcendence is not limited to the understanding of the soul; it is also the understanding of matter. Paramātma, for instance, is not just in the soul, He is also in all the material atoms because these atoms are as purposeful as the soul is purposeful. The purpose is immanent, but the purpose points to something transcendent.

This problem can also be framed in familiar terms as the problem of perception. If you are looking at an apple, then there is an apple in your mind, but the apple is also outside your mind. The apple in your mind is the picture of the apple outside, and yet this picture of the apple is a representation of the apple, not the apple itself. Because the apple is represented in our minds, it is 'inside' our mind. But because closing our eyes stops the mental picture, but doesn't destroy the apple, therefore, the apple is 'outside' the mind. The picture of the apple in the mind can be as detailed as we like—e.g., it can include shape, color, size, taste, smell, etc. So, in all practical ways, the picture in the mind can be made equivalent to the real apple outside. And yet, this picture is a projection into our minds, created by the real apple. Due to this projection, we think that what we are seeing in our mind is transparently the thing that is outside.

In the same way, the Paramātma is a *representation* of Bhagavān, like a picture of an apple is represented in our minds. The representation has all the properties of the object. And yet, it is not the object. The understanding of the Bhedābheda doctrine given by Acintyabhedābheda is that the whole divides into parts and then enters these parts as a representation. The whole is Bhagavān, the parts are Brahman, and the internal representation is Paramātma.

When this idea is applied to the soul, we can say that the soul is a symbol of meaning that was spoken by God, and this speech had a purpose. It is not enough to say that the soul is eternally existent. We must also speak about the eternal purpose of the soul's existence, and this purpose must come from God who produces the soul as His expression. The purpose is immanent in the soul, but it is also transcendent to the soul. This is just like when we say, 'the sky is blue', there is meaning in the sentence, but the sky is outside the sentence.

The problem is that our logic can deal only with physical things, and no physical thing can be both inside and outside. Therefore, this description is called inconceivable. But it is conceivable if we treat reality as meanings because the meanings can inside and outside. Thus, we say that a cow is a mammal (because a mammal is inside the cow) and a mammal is not a cow (because a mammal is outside the cow). This conceivability means that the whole, the part, and the whole in the part are three modes of existence. They are also successive stages of dividing the whole into parts and the whole entering the parts.

With a semantic conception of reality, we can speak of modes, and reality is conceivable. However, if we use the physical analogies, then the whole cannot be inside the parts, and the whole reduces to the parts. Then, only the parts are real, and the whole is an illusion. With this conclusion, knowledge is also impossible. Acintyabhedābheda indicates that reality is inconceivable under a physical whole-part doctrine. But, is that a claim that reality is inconceivable? Or is it an indictment of physical conceptions? Acintyabhedābheda can be understood in two ways—as the claim that reality is inconceivable, or as the claim that reality is not physical. In the former case rejection of inconceivability would seem to be a rejection of Acintyabhedābheda. But in the latter case, the rejection of inconceivability would be the acceptance of the reason why reality is called Acintyabhedābheda and then transcending that reason to fix the inconceivability. We can call the latter to be the project of conceiving the inconceivable.

Conceiving the Inconceivable

The Doctrine of Matter

You may have noticed that the previous interpretations of Vedānta try to solve the problem of what the soul is, how it falls into matter, and then how it gets liberated. But the soul is not the only reality; matter is also real. What is matter? In Advaita, māyā is separate from Brahman. Since Brahman is the conscious entity, māyā is unconscious, and the world is created by the combination of conscious and unconscious existence. But in subsequent interpretations of Vedānta, māyā and God are not separate. They are related as an object and its property in Viśiṣṭādvaita. They are separate objects in Dvaita, but this separation is not like that in Advaita (i.e., conscious vs. inert)—both matter and the soul are personalities. God is predominant, and matter is the predominated person. They are both separate and inseparable as in Bhedābheda, just as a part is different from the whole, and yet, the part is non-different from the whole. In short, after solving the problem of the soul's fall and liberation, these Vedānta doctrines extend the understanding of the soul to matter as well. Matter is then treated as a property, as a predominated person, or an inseparable part.

But are such extensions correct? The doctrine of the soul arises from the soul's fall and liberation. But matter never falls and is never liberated. In Advaita, matter is inert, and there is no question of fall and liberation. In other interpretations, matter is a property, a dominated person, or an inseparable part, but unlike the soul, matter is forever liberated. Thus, the doctrine of the soul cannot be extended without explaining why matter is never fallen.

Other systems of Vedic philosophy explain this by an example: God is the father, matter is the mother, and the soul is the child. The child can leave the mother and father, but the mother never leaves the father. But this example, while illustrative, doesn't clarify whether the mother is God's property, a subordinated individual, or an inseparable part. Different systems of philosophy adopt these ideas either simultaneously, or in different places alternatively.

Given the problems in Viśiṣṭādvaita and Dvaita regarding the soul's fall and liberation, it is prudent to extend the Bhedābheda doctrine even in the case of matter, rather than trying to understand matter within the Viśiṣṭādvaita and Dvaita doctrines. However, given the difference between matter and the soul, the Bhedābheda doctrine must be modified to illustrate a different kind of difference and non-difference, which is not the soul's whole-part relation.

This new doctrine is found in many places in Vedic texts, and it identifies God as Puruṣa and matter as Prakriti or Śakti. Puruṣa means the enjoyer or one who has desire and will. Prakriti is the power to fulfill this will or desire. But are these separate or inseparable? If will and power were separate, then some will could never be satisfied, and some power would never be utilized. Conversely, if they were identical, then every time there is power, the will must be present. In short, the power shall control the will, rather than being controlled by the will. Both alternatives are denied. All will can be satisfied, and all power can be utilized. So, these are not completely distinct. And yet, power can exist unutilized, but the will can never exist unfulfilled. Therefore, will is superior to power because every time there is will, the power is utilized. However, every time there is power, the will to use might not be there. In short, power serves the will, but the will doesn't serve the power. This is still a Bhedābheda doctrine, but it is not a whole-part doctrine. Rather, there are two complementary entities, which are simultaneously different and non-different. The power is feminine, and She is subordinate to the will or masculine. But this subordination is not like that of the soul which is subordinate because it is a part of God.

Therefore, we must distinguish between three flavors of Bhedābheda:

- The Puruṣa and Prakriti are different and non-different,
- The soul and the Puruṣa are different and non-different,
- The Paramātma and Bhagavān are different and non-different.

The Doctrine of Spirit

The essence of the doctrine of matter is that will may or may not be manifest; when it withdraws, the power is also withdrawn, and the creation is unmanifest. But if that were indeed the case, then why is the spiritual world always manifest? Doesn't will ever withdraw from the power? If so, this power and will must be different from the material will and power which can be withdrawn. To explain the eternity of the spiritual world and the temporariness of the material world, we either need two separate doctrines (one for matter and the other for spirit), or we must modify the will-power doctrine, in a way that explains both the spiritual eternity and the material temporariness. Naturally, a single doctrine for both matter and spirit is better than two doctrines.

Let's first consider the use of a different doctrine for the spiritual world. We could say that in the case of the spiritual world, the separation of will and power is not needed; it is needed only for the material world. If we collapse their difference and say that the will is power, and the power is will, then the eternity of the spiritual world can be explained. However, this solution would imply that the spiritual world is also static or unchanging. Everything possible would always be manifest due to will, because will and possibility are identical. This would now become the Platonic world of static universals. But this leads to the question: If the spiritual world is static, then how does this world produce pleasure? If everything is eternal, then all will is fulfilled. There is nothing left to be achieved and without the constant production of will and its fulfillment, there can be no pleasure. This state is intellectually satisfying but you cannot exist in this state eternally. You need a question, a problem, a challenge, a purpose. Problems are bad when they cannot be solved. However, the end of all problems would mean the end of life. We need a problematic life, but those problems must be solvable. In fact, ideally, one problem must lead to another problem, and the succession of problems must never end. But since every problem is solved, hence, life is an eternal process of discovery and adventure.

This is a philosophy of life, not the philosophy of knowledge or reality. And this philosophy entails that the separation of will and power is necessary not only to explain the creation and dissolution of the universe; it is also necessary to produce an eternal life of happiness. Therefore, the separation of will and power is not a defect—that causes the dissolution and creation of the universe. It is also the perfection of what we mean by living—as something that leads to happiness. Knowledge is only a means to happiness; it is not happiness itself. Happiness is the succession of solvable problems. The material world presents us with unsolved and unsolvable problems by taking from us the abilities, opportunities, and desires to solve the problems. The impersonalist hence states that we should dissolve all the problems and the quest for their solutions. The transcendentalist however says that the eternal world also has problems, however, they are successively solved, something new is discovered, which then leads to new problems. Thus, an alternative view of spiritual reality is needed. This alternative view must redefine both material and spiritual doctrines.

The alternative is that the will is a problem, and the power is its solution. Every time a problem is solved by power, a new problem is created. The problem in fact exists within the solution. Thus, the cause is present inside the effect, and the effect is present inside the cause. When the cause is a problem, then the effect of a solution is produced by the problem. When the cause is the solution, then the effect of a problem is produced by the solution. We cannot truly separate cause and effect because the cause is within the effect, and the effect is within the cause. As a result, will is the cause of power being manifest, and the manifestation of the power is the cause of the will being manifest. Every problem produces a solution, and every solution produces a new problem. Therefore, power and will are mutually the causes of each other. We can extend this idea to both material and spiritual worlds, but the joint solution would not explain why the material world is temporary while the spiritual world is not.

Matter-Spirit Combined Doctrine

This is where a modification is required. Although a solution leads to a problem, and a problem leads to a solution, these two are not *deterministically* produced. There is still a choice, which can provide different solutions to the same problem, and the solution can then be interpreted in different ways to create new problems. The difference between the material and the spiritual worlds lies in the choice of the solution to a problem, and the choice of the problem that follows the solution. Let's understand this difference in choices.

The fundamental problem with the material world is that most problems result in impractical solutions. For example, if you ask the wrong teacher for a spiritual path, he might say: You should quit everything in this world, go to the jungle and mediate. The solution may be valid, but you won't be able to execute it. Why? Because the ability and opportunity to execute the solution are absent. The ability is missing because we cannot tolerate hardships, and the opportunity is missing because we cannot find the jungles where we can survive. Even if we find such a jungle, our minds and senses are always restless. Therefore, solutions that don't account for our abilities and opportunities become useless. Since you cannot solve the problem in this way, you give up the desire to solve the problem. This is a very practical method by which desires are forced in this world: You give a solution to a problem that can never be applied. Or you provide a solution but confuse the recipient by telling them that numerous problems will arise from using the solution. Then, nobody can blame you for not providing a solution. And yet, because the solution cannot be applied, or its application will lead to additional problems, it will prevent you from using the solution. Without a solution, you will be forced to change your desires.

Now, suppose that every desire is frustrated in this way. You realize that every solution produces an unsolvable problem; or, even if some of these problems are solved, eventually you end with unsolvable problems. Once you realize that all endeavors are futile, you give up all kinds of desires. This is the nature of the material world. You try to fulfill your desires and seek answers. Material nature will mostly give you impractical answers—i.e., those for which you lack the ability and opportunity. Even if there are some practical solutions, ultimately most of them will lead you to a dead end. You attempt the solution for a while and believe in your progress, but you eventually hit a wall. The purpose of material nature is to frustrate your desires while pretending to fulfill them. Material nature is like that person who will give you 'solutions' that can never be implemented, or they will lead to more problems even if they were implemented. Ultimately, you must give up all desires. But the rejection of desires is temporary. You just feel frustrated with your failures and falsely pretend to be renounced. After some time—when you have become frustrated with the so-called renunciation—you try to engage with nature again.

The spiritual nature is different. It gives solutions that can be applied because the ability and opportunity to apply the solutions are eternal. And when these solutions are applied, whatever new problems are created are also solvable—again because the ability and opportunity to solve them is present.

Thus, material nature is described in two ways. The first description says that nature is temporary—i.e., the ability and opportunity to apply the solutions is sometimes present and sometimes absent. The second description says that the purpose of the material nature is to frustrate all our desires and make us turn toward the spiritual reality. Of these two descriptions, the purpose of frustrating our desires is a better answer, because in every situation there are good and bad answers. The good answer is that which can be applied to fulfill our desires, and the bad answer is that which will lead to frustrations. The difference is merely a choice—which question must be given which answer.

With this understanding of material nature, the distinction with spiritual nature is diminished. What is called 'material nature' is simply the frustrating answers to questions. And what is called 'spiritual nature' is satisfying answers to the questions. Even if good answers are possible, material nature will provide only frustrating answers, because it is trying to change our desires. Conversely, even if bad answers are possible in spiritual nature, they will guide you toward good answers. Thus, it becomes very hard to remain happy in the material world, and it is very hard to become unhappy in the spiritual world. Hence, one view about spiritual and material nature is that they are not different. The mechanism is simply choosing the answer to a question. If your desires are averse to the Lord, then nature will give you bad answers. But if the desires are inclined toward the Lord, then nature will give you the good answers.

But, before we say that there is no difference with spiritual nature, along with this non-difference, there is also a difference. The difference is that in the material world, the abilities and opportunities factually appear and disappear. A few hundred years ago you could not drive a car or fly an airplane. You could enjoy horse rides and walk in a garden, which is slowly becoming impossible. Similarly, the human body and mind had much better immunity, strength, and sharpness; those abilities are now disappearing and being replaced by new kinds of abilities—e.g., to play video games on computers. The nature of the material world is that the abilities and opportunities evolve with time. The nature of the spiritual world is that the abilities and opportunities are eternal.

Thus, material and spiritual natures are non-different in the sense that the basic mechanism is the sequence of questions and answers. These two natures are different because material nature produces frustrating answers to questions and forces us to change the questions. Spiritual nature produces meaningful answers to questions and thereby produces satisfying questions and answers. For the devotee in the material world, nature only produces satisfying answers and questions, although the abilities and opportunities keep changing. Thus, the material nature will find the best answer to a problem that a devotee needs to serve the Lord. But the same nature will frustrate the non-devotees.

Thus, even though material and spiritual natures are described as Puruṣa and Prakriti, these are of two kinds. The Puruṣa in the spiritual world is factually an enjoyer, and He enjoys fulfilling His desires. The Puruṣa in the material world is also an enjoyer, but His enjoyment is austerities or self-abnegation. By this self-abnegation, the Puruṣa sets the example for others to renounce the material world. Those who don't renounce it, are bewildered by His Śakti. Thus, the Śakti and Puruṣa play complementary roles in this world: the Śakti bewilders and frustrates the soul, and the Puruṣa teaches renunciation of the world. Ultimately, both Puruṣas have a common purpose—the spiritual Puruṣa attracts the soul toward spiritual enjoyment, while the material Puruṣa pushes the soul away from material enjoyment; The former is attraction, while the latter is repulsion. Thus, they are non-different (because of the common purpose), and they are different (due to the different ways of achieving the purpose).

The Masculine-Feminine Doctrine

Thus, the doctrine of matter is revised when the doctrine of spirit is propounded. The revision is that the will and the power can be mutual causes of each other. Therefore, it is not true that the will always controls power. To the extent that the power generates a problem, it also causes the will. By changing the answers to the questions, the questions themselves are changed. Therefore, power is not a slave to will, nor is power the unconscious and acausal māyā, waiting only to be used by Brahman, as in the case of impersonalism. Her personality, individuality, choice, and control are reflected in Her ability to give different answers to a question, which then causes a change in the questions. Likewise, the masculine is a person, and His choice, personality, individuality, and control are the ability to change His questions based on the answers.

Thus, masculine and feminine are both persons. They represent questions and answers, and their choice is to ask a different question based on the answer or to answer a question in different ways. They can control each other because questions are determined by previous answers, and answers are determined by previous questions. But this mutual causality is not devoid of choice. Hence, we cannot collapse the distinction between masculine and feminine. We also cannot call one a person and the other impersonal or consider them both to be impersonal. We cannot say that one person is a slave and the other person is a master. And we cannot claim that they are independent of each other.

Once this mutual dependence and independence of the masculine and the feminine is understood, then it is modified yet again. The modification is that if the masculine and feminine are separated, then the masculine always initiates the reunion in the material creation. Similarly, when they are united, the masculine initiates the separation in the material world. Thus, in the material world, it is said that the Lord glances at His Śakti and by that glance, He expresses His desire to reunite with the Śakti. The feminine has been waiting expectantly, and She agrees with the desire. Likewise, when the masculine is fulfilled, He withdraws from the feminine, and the feminine then waits expectantly. Therefore, after stating the mutual dependence and independence of the Puruṣa and Śakti, it is further said that the masculine is superior because He initiates the separation and reunion. But the situation is reversed in the spiritual world, where the Puruṣa waits expectantly for the Śakti to initiate their union. Hence, the Lord appears if the devotee desires, and the Lord disappears if the devotee doesn't desire. In the material world, the feminine loves the fact that the masculine is independent. But in the spiritual world, the masculine loves the fact that the feminine is independent. Feminism is hence a doctrine of the spiritual world, although it is not a doctrine of the material world. When the soul enters the material world, then in the masculine body, he tries to become dominant just like the Lord of the material world. Meanwhile, the soul in the feminine body tries to become dominant just like the feminine in the spiritual world.

The Puruṣa in the material world exhibits His dominant nature. But the Puruṣa in the spiritual world exhibits His subordinate nature. For example, when Kṛṣṇa appears in this world, He plays the flute and invites the gopis to dance, but when they arrive, He acts detached and asks them to return. The gopis feel heartbroken and beg Kṛṣṇa for His love. But in the spiritual world, the dance is arranged by the gopis, and if Kṛṣṇa arrives, the gopis tell Him that He cannot participate. Kṛṣṇa then begs the gopis for participation. However, the dominant and subordinate positions of the Puruṣa in the material and spiritual world are not absolute. For example, even in the material world, where the Puruṣa is mostly dominant, some forms of Śakti—e.g., Kāli—are said to be dominant and portrayed as standing on the chest of Lord Śiva. Likewise, in the spiritual world, the Puruṣa also acts dominant by selecting to enjoy with different gopis. However, by and large, the Puruṣa is dominant in the material world, and the Śakti is dominant in the spiritual world. And yet, dominant and subordinate doesn't mean mastery and slavery. It is a role-play for enjoyment. Both masculine and feminine enjoy being dominant and subordinate alternately.

Once the equality of masculine and feminine is understood, followed by the dominant positions of masculine and feminine in the material and spiritual worlds, the doctrine is modified for the last time. The final modification says that in a primordial state, when the masculine and feminine are not separated as interdependent persons, then the combined state is Puruṣa. In this state, the Śakti remains a part of the Puruṣa as His power. However, the Puruṣa is then agitated by the Śakti from within, and as a result, Śakti separates from the Puruṣa. The doctrine is even harder, because the feminine is a part of the masculine, and yet, the feminine is the cause of the activity in the masculine. Since the Śakti is a part of Puruṣa, therefore, the Puruṣa is called superior. But since the Śakti is the cause of activity in the Puruṣa, therefore, the Śakti is called superior. If we know the nuances in these doctrines, then they are not contradictory. However, mundane ideas about domination make them confusing.

The Nature of Absolute Truth

Thus, all the problems in previous doctrines are addressed. The problem of māyā being inert and Brahman being active are rejected and accepted. The rejection is that māyā is a person and so not inert. The acceptance is that māyā is feminine, and not the efficient cause of creation or annihilation, and hence inert. The doctrine of Viśiṣṭādvaita is also accepted and rejected. The acceptance is that the Śakti is the power of the powerful and serves at the will of the powerful. Hence, She is His property. But the doctrine is rejected because the feminine is a person and remains a controller of the Puruṣa. The Doctrine of Dvaita is also accepted and rejected. The acceptance is that the masculine and the feminine are different individuals. The rejection is that because they serve each other's purpose in the spiritual world, therefore, they are not truly separable. The Bhedābheda doctrine is also rejected and accepted. The rejection is that the Śakti is not a part of the whole as the soul; She is a complementary counterpart of the Lord. The acceptance is that the Śakti is distinct and yet inseparable from the Lord. The Acintyabhedābheda is articulated in two ways. One version says that the primordial state is Puruṣa and Śakti is His part. And the other version says that the Puruṣa is activated by the Śakti—from within and not outside.

Acintyabhedābheda is therefore not yet another doctrine. When looked at through the lens of the soul, it is merely a minor extension of the Bhedābheda doctrine. But this is not the primary purpose of the doctrine. Unlike the previous doctrines which deal in the difference and non-difference between the soul, the main purpose of Acintyabhedābheda is to describe the difference and the non-difference between the Lord and His Śakti. In the process, the soul-God Acintyabhedābheda is different from the God-Śakti Acintyabhedābheda. The limitation in Acintyabhedābheda is the inconceivability, which arises because reality is not described through modalities. Without modalities, all doctrines are treated as universal claims. And this universality then leads to contradictions, which leads to the conclusion that the ultimate truth is inconceivable. If modalities were adopted, then Acintyabhedābheda is also conceivable.

The conceivability is that in the primordial state, the ability to answer questions exists, just as the questions exist. However, the ability to answer the questions is not used to answer the questions. The impersonalist says that this primordial state is an answer, but the personalist says that it is a question. The reasoning for these two systems is different. The impersonalist claims that the primordial state is achieved when the answers are obtained. The problem is this: If you got the answer, then why should there be any more questions? In short, why should the world be created and destroyed again and again? If the answer exists, then how it gives rise to a question is very hard to explain. The personalist says: The primordial state is always a question. These questions can remain unanswered, but there is an internal impetus to answer them. If the question exists, then how it produces an answer is much easier. Therefore, the personalist explanation is that the Puruṣa—as the question—creates the world as an answer. The purpose of the world is to answer the question in the Puruṣa; the creation cannot become a question to be answered by the Puruṣa. Hence, the creation is always subordinate to the Puruṣa, but to the extent that the Puruṣa is impelled from within to seek an answer, the Śakti is superior.

Advaita in Vaishnavism

The conflict between Advaita and Vaishnava doctrines is very subtle. And this conflict is not absolutely upheld in all situations. There are subtle ways in which Advaita is incorporated into the Vaishnava doctrines. We can illustrate the incorporation of Advaita in Vaishnavism through the different types of experiences had by devotees. The devotee sometimes misses the Lord, and in this situation, he knows that he is different from the Lord—this is Dvaita. Then, he sometimes sees the Lord and understands he is simply a part and property of the Lord—this is Viśiṣṭādvaita. And finally, sometimes the devotee is so overwhelmed by the devotion to the Lord that he loses his self-identity and starts acting just like the Lord—this is Advaita. Similarly, the Lord sometimes misses His devotee, and then He knows that the devotee is different from Him—this is Dvaita. Then, when He sees the devotee, He knows that the devotee is a part and a property of Him—this is Viśiṣṭādvaita. And finally, sometimes when He is overwhelmed with love, He acts just like the devotee—this is Advaita.

The understanding of Advaita thus far has been limited to that of Brahman; it is said that the soul merges into Brahman and becomes undifferentiated. Subsequent Acharyas go beyond Brahman, illustrating the nature of Vaikuṇṭha as a realm that lies beyond Brahman, and in the process, they reject the identity of the soul and the Lord. At the least, Advaita is said to be an inferior understanding of the Absolute Truth. But this is not the only understanding of Advaita. A more sophisticated view is that the soul and the Lord can take on each other's roles and moods. Normally, each actor is tied to a character. For example, the soul acts like a devotee, and the Lord acts as the master. But the actors can take on different characters. Thus, a devotee overwhelmed by the love of the Lord, forgets that he is a devotee. He starts acting just like the Lord. Similarly, the Lord, overwhelmed by the love of the devotee, forgets that He is the Lord. He takes on the role and the mood of the devotee and behaves just like the devotee. The Dvaita conception of the difference between the Lord and the devotee, the Viśiṣṭādvaita conception of the devotee as a property of the Lord, and the Bhedābheda conception of the devotee as a part of the Lord are simultaneously emasculated by one person taking on another's role. The understanding of this love revives Advaita in which the soul and the Lord are identical—in their role and mood. But they are still not to be considered identical individuals!

This new kind of Bhedābheda was demonstrated in the pastimes of Lord Chaitanya, who is Kṛṣṇa, but He takes on the role and mood of devotees. As we have discussed, the Lord has three modes of existence—role, ability, and mood. When the Lord takes on the role and mood of the devotee, then the ability to behave like the Lord is suppressed, and His opulence is not demonstrated; He just exhibits the humility and helplessness of a devotee and dances before the Lord in ecstasy. When the Lord takes on the role of a devotee, but the mood is of the Lord, then He discards His humility and helplessness; He now becomes the most fearsome critic of atheism, impersonalism, and voidism, and destroys them like He otherwise kills demons; since He isn't actually in the role of the Lord, but only in His mood, He doesn't kill those demons; He only refutes their ideologies. When the Lord is in the mood of a devotee, but the role is of the Lord, then He accepts worship from the devotees, just like a teacher is worshipped as the Lord, thinking that the Lord is being worshipped thereby.

With this new kind of Bhedābheda, a new definition of God is obtained—He is the *chit* or the ability to be the Lord. But He may not necessarily be in the mood of the Lord (the ānanda) or the role of the Lord (the *sat*). In fact, since the mood and role can dominate the ability, even though He is the Lord, His opulence may be invisible. But since that opulence is subordinated, it can be manifest sometimes. Thus, by becoming the devotee, the Lord doesn't lose His lordship. He remains the Lord but feels and acts like a devotee. Lord Chaitanya did not teach this understanding of Himself, but because He demonstrated all these things, His followers teach them as such. The devotees also recognize that they can take on the mood and role of the Lord. When they are in the mood of the Lord, they act fearsomely against the atheists, destroying their philosophies. They don't accept humility and submissiveness; rather, just like the Lord, they consider it their job to destroy the demons. Then, when they are in the role of the Lord, they accept worship from other devotees, just like the Lord. But even as they are worshipped, they don't confuse themselves to be the Lord. But most often, they only remain as the humble servants of the Lord, constantly feeling separated from Him, considering themselves His part, and not Himself.

Since we are now splitting the modalities of the Lord into separate aspects, the devotee and the Lord can be different and non-different—although in a completely new sense. This is also Advaita, but it doesn't mean 'oneness' (because all three aspects are not identical); it rather means non-difference (because in one or more ways, the Lord and the devotee are indistinguishable). In short, the term Advaita doesn't mean *identity*. It only means *indistinguishability*.

The problem of Advaita is quite like the problem of Abheda. Most people mistake Advaita and Abheda as 'oneness'. This follows from the dualistic logical system in which if something is not Duality, then it must be Oneness. Both Dvaita and Bheda mean the same thing: There are two different things, and they must be known as different things. Dvaita is an ontological and Bheda is an epistemological claim: If there are two things, then we must know them as two things. Then, if twoness is denied in Advaita and Abheda, under the dualistic logical assumptions (arising from a physicalist worldview), non-duality is taken to mean 'oneness'. Now, Advaita becomes an ontological commitment to a single reality, and Abheda becomes an epistemological claim that we must know everything as oneness. However, this dualistic reasoning doesn't account for the difference between modalities—e.g., Being and Becoming. I can Become one thing and still Be another thing. This is possible in semantic reasoning.

The Lord can Be the Lord, and yet Become a devotee. Just like actors on a stage are one person but they act and feel like another person. This acting and feeling can make them forget that they are another person otherwise. But this is not a permanent illusion about one's identity. There is a difference between the actor and the character, and yet you cannot separate them sometimes. The distinction between the actor and the character, and yet, the inseparability of the actor and the character, is Advaita and Abheda. Such differences are impossible in physicalist thinking because in physics you cannot distinguish between an object and its role. An actor feels being himself and becoming someone else. They are neither the same nor are they separable. If you watch a performance, you can see how the actor brings his persona to the character, but it would be a mistake to apply the character back to the actor or equate the actor to the character. Thus, with a semantic view, Advaita and Abheda lose their conventional oneness claim: They both mean non-difference. Advaita is still an ontological commitment to the reality being non-different, and Abheda is still an epistemological commitment to knowing this non-different reality non-differently.

The Doctrine of Brahman

As we have seen, the Vedic system recognizes three primordial modes—*sat*, *chit*, and ānanda. We have previously called them the modes of relation, cognition, and emotion, and contextuality, universality, and individuality. Our cognition obtains universals—such as color, shape, size, taste, smell, meanings, etc. Our emotions individuate us from other individuals. And contextuality means giving new meanings to the universals in different contexts. Infinite variety is thus created from the three modes as the modes enter each other. Hence, creation is the process in which the universal becomes an individual and enters the instance individual of another mode. The individual then also has contextual relations to other modes. But since the mode is a universal, it is not separate from the original state of the mode. Therefore, annihilation is a process in which the mode goes from the individual and contextual state to the universal state—i.e., it 'merges' into the original state and simply exists as a universal.

Through the successive penetration of the modes within each other, a hierarchical structure is produced; in this hierarchy, the 'higher' level mode is the dominant mode, and the 'lower' level mode is the subordinate mode. Likewise, hierarchy is collapsed when the subordinate mode exits the domination of the dominant mode and goes back into the universal state. Remember that universal, individual, and contextual are simply modalities of existence. Thus, infinite instances of these three modes are just the three modes in the universal modality. This universal is also an individual, and it exists in the context of Itself. That is, the Absolute Truth is knowledge, He is a person, who knows Himself. However, this knowledge is simply what God is, not what He is not. The absence of the negative conception of knowledge means the whole exists, but the parts—and how the whole is defined in relation to these parts—do not exist.

This primordial state is called Param Brahman. However, this is not the Brahman of Advaita. This is because Śakti is within the Param Brahman, however, according to Advaita, māyā is separate from Brahman. Once the Param

Brahman enters the manifest state, it divides into three personalities—Kṛṣṇa, Balarāma, and Hara. Since Kṛṣṇa is the enjoyer and the ānanda mode of Param Brahman, He represents the question to be answered. In the Param Brahman stage, the question is: "Who am I?" and the answer is "I am Kṛṣṇa—the all-attractive". In this stage, however, Kṛṣṇa is not known in relation to what He is not—i.e., His Śakti and the souls. When Param Brahman divides, then Kṛṣṇa manifests the souls, Hara manifests as His Śakti, and Balarāma as God.

If the Advaita philosopher chants the mantra OM, he refers to Brahman. But when the Vaishnava philosopher chants the mantra OM, he refers to Param Brahman. All Vedic texts and mantras employ OM. The Advaita philosopher takes this to mean that Brahman is the primordial reality, and forms of God are manifest from Brahman. Since Brahman is separate from māyā, therefore, these forms must be the combination of Brahman and māyā. Thus, the Advaita philosopher says that the incarnations of God are Saguna Brahman—the combination of māyā and Brahman. However, the Vaishnava philosopher says that OM refers to the Param Brahman, and māyā is a part of the Absolute Truth. Therefore, when God manifests in the material world, He manifests along with His Śakti, but the form of God is not the combination of Brahman and māyā. Rather, māyā is a part of the Param Brahman and all His incarnations. Similarly, when the Vedānta Sūtra speaks about Brahman being the source of everything, the Advaita philosopher says that it is the origin of the soul, but not the origin of māyā. The Vaishnava philosopher, however, says that the origin of everything is Param Brahman; māyā or Śakti are all part of Brahman. This fundamental misunderstanding between Brahman and Param Brahman is the origin of all the problems in Vedānta. If Śaṅkarācārya had spoken about Param Brahman, and not equated it to Brahman, then successive philosophies of Viśiṣṭādvaita, Dvaita, Bhedābheda, and Acintyabhedābheda would be unnecessary. All contradictions would be reconciled in the doctrine of Param Brahman. So, in one sense, Vedānta has only progressed from Brahman to Param Brahman, passing through Viśiṣṭādvaita, Dvaita, Bhedābheda, and Acintyabhedābheda.

Aside from the confusion between Brahman and Param Brahman, Advaita also creates confusion between Brahman and Puruṣa. Factually, Brahman is that state of Puruṣa in which the Puruṣa knows Himself, but not His parts. Conversely, when the will is manifest, then Puruṣa knows Himself and His parts. Thus, we can say that in the unmanifest state, Puruṣa is Brahman—the only existent. But in the manifest state, Brahman is Puruṣa—the source of numerous other existents. The definition of Puruṣa changes from being the only existent to the source of infinitely many existents. But this change is the development of a new experience, rather than the creation of a new reality. Hence, we cannot say that Puruṣa did not exist previously, but we can say that Puruṣa did not know Himself completely, and He expands to complete His knowledge.

Once these confusions are clarified, then one can still ask: Given that the same thing can exist in a manifest or an unmanifest state, which of these states is better? Should we say that the unmanifest state is better because it is primordial? Or should we say that the manifest state is better because there is cognition, relation, and emotion—not merely the potentiality for these things?

The answer to this question is nuanced. The recombined state includes the uncombined state, but the uncombined state doesn't include the recombined state. Just because there are individual cows, you don't say that the idea cow has ceased to exist. However, it is possible that the idea cow exists, but the individual cows don't. Therefore, since the recombined includes the uncombined, therefore, it is fuller and superior to the uncombined. But this superior reality is not the primordial reality; the primordial reality is still uncombined. Thus, the central problem in Vedānta interpretation has been the confusion between the primordial reality and the superior reality. The uncombined is primordial, but it is also considered incomplete. The recombined is not primordial but it is superior and complete. We can say that the primordial reality strives toward greater completion—by desiring to know itself and this attempt at self-knowledge produces everything else. While the self-unaware state is primordial, the self-aware state is superior. Therefore, even though Brahman and Param Brahman are primordial, we still prefer the manifest personalities.

Expansions of the Absolute Truth

The Chatuśpāda Doctrine

In many places in the Vedānta Sūtra, we find a doctrine called Chatuśpāda. The term *pāda* has many meanings; in the simplest case, it means parts, but it also means aspects. The term *pada* (instead of pāda) also means words or symbols. Since we see the terms pada and pāda being used interchangeably, therefore, we nuance the meaning—there are four parts or aspects, and they are symbols of the whole. Thus, when you see a part or aspect, you don't say that it is partial. And yet, you don't say that it is the whole. When you see a drama, you don't say that the actor is not the character; but you don't say that the actor is the character. A nuanced understanding is used—the actor is the full person, but in a role, he exhibits the full personality in a certain limited way. That limited expression is partial, but it is an expression of the full actor. The actor is not partially present in the character, and yet the character is not the full actor.

The Chatuśpāda doctrine is used in many ways in Vedic philosophy. In one way, the manifest reality is divided into four parts, aspects, or symbols. These four parts are Matter, Brahman, Vaikuṇṭha, and Goloka. Within each of these parts, there are four such aspects. The first part is the combined state of the three modalities. In the spiritual world, this primordial reality is Param Brahman and has three manifest parts—Kṛṣṇa, Balarāma, and Hara. In the material world, this primordial reality is called Param Śiva, and He has three manifest parts—Mahesh (ānanda), Viṣṇu (sat), and Śakti (chit). The Mahesh mode becomes God; the Śakti mode becomes matter, and the Viṣṇu mode becomes the soul. In Param Śiva, the God, matter, and soul modes are not manifest. They are manifest when the three aspects of Param Śiva are separated. Once these modes of God, soul, and matter are manifest, then each mode divides into three parts.

The original soul-mode manifestation is Vāsudeva. He is the Universal Soul. But since the soul also has three aspects, therefore, Vāsudeva, manifests three other forms called Kāraṇodakaśāyī (Saṅkarṣaṇa), Garbhodakaśāyi (Pradyumna), and Kṣīrodakaśāyī (Aniruddha). These three forms predominate in the three modalities of the soul. Kāraṇodakaśāyī Viṣṇu is *sat* or awareness; it is said that Kāraṇodakaśāyī "divides Himself by Himself" to create the awareness of the soul. Garbhodakaśāyi Viṣṇu is the *chit* or cognition, and He becomes the original speaker of Vedic knowledge to Brahma. Finally, Kṣīrodakaśāyī Viṣṇu is ānanda or purpose, and He exists inside everything as their purpose.

The original God-mode manifestation in the material world is Mahesh. He represents Universal Time. As a soul, He has three aspects, therefore, Mahesh manifests into three further forms called Sankar, Rudra, and Bhairava.

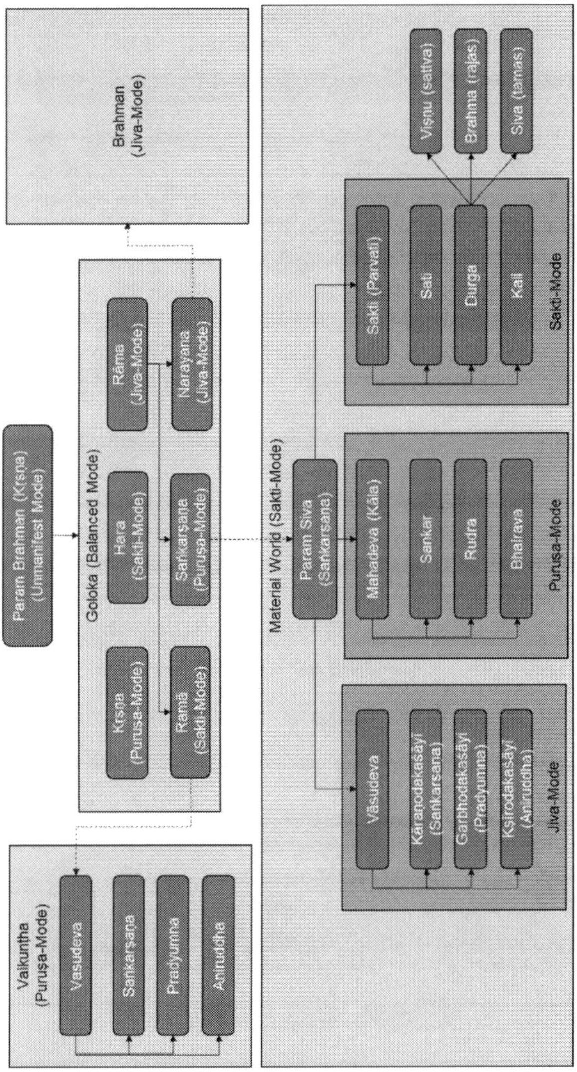

The original matter-mode manifestation is Śakti. She represents Universal Space. But, as She is also a soul, and has three aspects, therefore, Śakti manifests into three further aspects called Sati, Durga, and Kāli. Sati dominates in the universal mode, Durga in the individual mode, and Kāli in the relational mode. From Durga—who is in the individual mode—three types of universals are created: Viṣṇu, Brahma, and Śiva, and they become the sources of the three modes of nature called sattva, rajas, and tamas. And from these universals, many relational subordinates are produced. These servants of the modes (Brahma, Viṣṇu and Śiva), Who are themselves aspects of the individual (Durga), Who is as an aspect of the unmanifest (Param Śiva)—are called Āditya, Vasu, and Rudra. They constitute the 33 demigods controlling the universe. But Durga is the ultimate source of matter; Viṣṇu, Śiva, and Brahma are the intermediate sources of matter; the Āditya, Vasu, and Rudra are lower-level sources of matter.

Since Param Śiva manifests Viṣṇu and Śakti, therefore, He is called the supreme reality and is considered superior to Viṣṇu and Śakti. Since Brahma, Viṣṇu, and Śiva—as the controllers of three modes of nature—are manifest from Śakti, therefore, it is said that Śakti is the supreme reality and Śiva and Viṣṇu are subordinate to Her. Since the soul is manifest from Viṣṇu, therefore, scriptures say Viṣṇu is the only master of the soul. Finally, because Kṛṣṇa exists in the transcendent world of Goloka, it is said that He is the cause of all causes. Depending on which text you are reading, you can see these conflicting claims: sometimes Śiva is supreme, sometimes Viṣṇu is supreme, and sometimes Śakti is supreme. And those who don't understand the modal nature of reality make this 'supremacy' universal. There is indeed a supreme reality called Param Brahman or Kṛṣṇa. But because this reality is modal, and the modes enter each other and become subordinate, therefore, everything is dominant or subordinate in some or other situation. These are not contradictory doctrines. Everything becomes clear if we understand the modalities of the Absolute Truth.

In the material world, since Lord Viṣṇu is the source of the soul, therefore, the liberation of the soul is described in relation to Lord Viṣṇu. However, since Viṣṇu, Mahesh, and Śakti are manifest from Param Śiva, therefore, one could say that the soul is also originated from Param Śiva. Therefore, two descriptions of the soul's destiny are given in different Vedic texts. In the Vaishnava texts, it is said that the soul merges into Kāraṇodakaśāyī Viṣṇu. And in the Shaiva texts, it is said that the soul merges into Param Śiva. These two statements are the basis of the conflict between the Vaishnava and Shaiva systems. There is factually no contradiction between these doctrines if we understand that Kāraṇodakaśāyī Viṣṇu is a partial manifestation from the person of Param Śiva.

However, if we go deeper into other Vedic texts, we also find that there are many Viṣṇu forms manifest from Balarāma Who are transcendental to the material world. They reside in Vaikuṇṭha and are different from Kāraṇodakaśāyī Viṣṇu. Vaishnava texts clearly distinguish between Kāraṇodakaśāyī Viṣṇu who manifests the soul in the material world, Kṛṣṇa who manifests the soul in the spiritual world, and the transcendental Viṣṇu forms to whom the soul can be devoted in the Vaikuṇṭha planets. However, this distinction doesn't come out clearly in the Vaishnava philosophies. The transcendental Viṣṇu forms are present in different planets of Vaikuṇṭha and the soul can 'travel' from one planet to another because the soul is not 'bound' to any of the Viṣṇu forms. If one of these Viṣṇu forms was indeed the origin of the soul, then the soul could never go to another planet in Vaikuṇṭha. However, because the soul originates from Kṛṣṇa, he obtains the freedom to roam to all the parts of the spiritual world.

Now, based on this understanding of four aspects or Chatuśpāda, we can say that Vaikuṇṭha, Brahman, and the material world are three aspects of Goloka. From Param Brahman—which is the unmanifest stage—the first manifestation is Goloka. But this Goloka manifestation has three aspects, which are successively manifest, and these are Vaikuṇṭha, Brahman, and the material world. Vaikuṇṭha is the God aspect of Param Brahman, Brahman is the soul aspect of the same Param Brahman, and material world is the Śakti aspect of the same Param Brahman. All these aspects are alternately dominant in Goloka, but they are permanently dominant in the other aspects. Thus, in Vaikuṇṭha, the God aspect of Param Brahman is permanently dominant. In Brahman, the soul aspect of Param Brahman is permanently dominant. And in the material world, the Śakti aspect of Param Brahman is permanently dominant. Due to the permanent dominance property, they are considered relatively incomplete with respect to Goloka, where all these three modes are alternately dominant.

Thus, in Goloka, sometimes God dominates, sometimes the soul dominates, and sometimes the Śakti dominates. God often serves the devotee or acts like a devotee. God similarly serves the Śakti and acts like the Śakti. The soul and the Śakti sometimes act like God, sometimes act like each other, and sometimes serve each other. The situations in which God, soul, and Śakti act like they are God, soul, and Śakti, are hence a part of the whole truth. There are always situations in which they take each other's roles and moods and act contrary to their position. They are different, but because they take on each other's roles and moods, they are non-different. This non-difference is Advaita, but it is not oneness because there is a difference between God, soul, and Śakti as well.

Thus, Kṛṣṇa is the whole truth, Kṛṣṇa is a part of the whole truth, Kṛṣṇa has parts which are His servants, and Kṛṣṇa is also a servant of the parts. Similarly, Kṛṣṇa is transcendent to all the parts, Kṛṣṇa is the source of all parts, Kṛṣṇa is different from the parts, but the parts are not different from Him, and Kṛṣṇa is immanent in all the parts. All these positions are true, and yet, due to modalities, they are alternately true. If you deny any position, you will get contradictions. We can only assert that all these positions are true. And yet, because the universalist view of simultaneous truth also leads to contradictions, therefore, we employ a modal description. Hence, we need to avoid two kinds of pitfalls in thinking— (1) you cannot say that any of these positions are false, and (2) you cannot say that all of them are simultaneously true. Both views will create contradictions. The Acintyabhedābheda doctrine is that no position is false. But since everyone concludes that these positions must be simultaneously true, which leads to a contradiction, therefore, the result is inconceivability. Conversely, if we deny the simultaneous truth of all the positions—without making any position false—then we achieve the position of Cintyabhedābheda.

The Pañcatattva Doctrine

There are many places in the Vedic texts, where the Chatuśpāda doctrine (the doctrine of four aspects) is updated to the Pañcatattva doctrine (the doctrine of five essences). The addition of the fifth aspect or essence is in between the unmanifest stage—called Param Brahman—and the three manifest aspects (e.g., Kṛṣṇa, Balarāma, and Hara). The doctrine goes as follows. The Param Brahman is the unmanifest; He is merely the possibility of the three aspects. However, since it is only a possibility, therefore, the self is unknown. There is no emotion, no relation, and no cognition, although the possibility of emotion, relation, and cognition exists. From this unmanifest stage, the first manifestation is the self-aware state. There is hence desire to know oneself, relation to oneself, and knowledge of oneself. In this stage, one is in love with oneself, aware of oneself, and serves oneself. This stage corresponds to the "I" that we discussed earlier; it springs from the self-unaware stage. However, in this state of "I", there is nothing other than "I". Sometimes, it is said that in this state, the three modes exist in a balanced state which means that no mode is dominant or subordinate. When the modes go dominant and subordinate, then the "I" divides into three aspects—e.g., Kṛṣṇa, Hara, and Rāma. Since Param Brahman is called Kṛṣṇa in the unmanifest stage, this manifest stage of "I" is also identified as Kṛṣṇa. And finally, the separated enjoyer aspect is also known as Kṛṣṇa. There are hence three forms of Kṛṣṇa—the unmanifest Param Brahman, the balanced manifest "I", and the "I" imbued with desires other than "I". Along with such desires, there are also things other than the self, and the power to connect the desire to things other than the self. These things to be known, and the power to know them, are manifest along with the desire to know these things. Kṛṣṇa is the desire for knowing, Balarāma is the creator for all the different things to be known, and Hara is the power that connects the desire to those things.

Thus, along with Param Brahman, and the three manifest aspects, the addition of "I" in between the unmanifest and the fully manifest leads us to the doctrine of Pañcatattva. Unlike in the Chatuśpāda doctrine, where everything was being divided into four aspects, now the division is into five aspects.

There are many illustrations of the Pañcatattva doctrine found all over Vedic texts. For example, to the four aspects of Vasudeva, Saṅkarṣaṇa, Pradyumna, and Aniruddha, a fifth aspect—called Nārāyana—is added. While the previous four are called Chaturvyūha, these five are called Pañcatattva.

Similarly, in Shaivism, Param Śiva is sometimes understood as the unmanifest individual, and then also sometimes as the original "I" that creates the material universe. The "I" stage of the unmanifest Param Śiva is also called Param Śiva, but they are distinct, in the sense that when the material universe is annihilated, then the Param Śiva goes into the unmanifest mode. However, if the material universe exists, then Param Śiva also exists in the "I" mode.

Likewise, in Shaktism, Śakti has five aspects: revelation, hiding, creation, annihilation, and maintenance. The 'hiding' is the unmanifest stage of Śakti; the 'revelation' is the manifest self-aware state, which hasn't divided into further aspects; following this, the "I" state of the Śakti is divided into creation, maintenance, and annihilation as the three modes of rajas, sattva, and tamas.

In the "I" state, Param Śiva combines Puruṣa, Śakti, and soul. There are thus depictions in Shaiva and Shakta systems of an androgynous personality who is simultaneously masculine and feminine. This is the basis for the idea that the feminine was previously a part of the masculine and is created from Him.

In some depictions of Nārāyana, He is shown alone. And in other depictions of Nārāyana, He is shown along with three other aspects—Lakshmi, Seśa, and Brahma. Lakshmi is Nārāyana's Śakti-mode existence, Seśa is Nārāyana's Puruṣa-mode existence, and Brahma is Nārāyana's soul-mode existence. When He is shown alone, then He is just the "I". When Lakshmi, Seśa, and Brahma are depicted alongside, then there is "I" that is manifest in three aspects. These are not just pictures for us to see. These are scientific descriptions of reality. The entire reality is simply summarized in a picture for our understanding. But these are not physical pictures. We need philosophy to understand them.

This five-fold description of reality is employed in Gaudīya Vaishnavism, and these five aspects are called Chaitanya, Nityānanda, Advaita, Gadādhar, and Srivās. Sri Chaitanya is Param Brahman without a distinction between desire, the power to fulfill the desire, and the objects of desire. The desire, object, and power are all one. Nityānanda is the manifest stage of Param Brahman and exists as the "I". Once this "I" divides, there are three manifest aspects—Advaita is Puruṣa-mode, Gadādhar is Śakti-mode, and Srivās is soul-mode. Gaudīya Vaishnavas thus worship the Absolute Truth in five essences.

Pañcatattva in Sāñkhya and Yoga

Such descriptions also abound in Sāñkhya and Yoga philosophies. For example, the Yoga system describes the body as comprising of five sheaths, called ānanda-maya, vijñāna-maya, mano-maya, prāṇa-maya, and anna-maya.

In Shaiva philosophy, the ānanda-maya is further classified into five parts—rāga, vidya, kalā, kāla, and niyati. Rāga means that I can only like a few things; I cannot like everything. Vidya means I can only know a few subjects; I cannot know everything. Kalā means I am only capable of certain types of activities; I cannot perform every type of action. Kāla means I exist in a specific age and time; since I am a product of some specific age, therefore, I must live according to that age. Niyati means that I was born in a certain nation or society; since I am a product of some nation and society, therefore, I must abide by the ideologies and principles of my nationality, society, or the place of living. Thus, ānanda-maya creates our limited personality. It is the ways in which we create our material identity based on likes, abilities, knowledge, place, and time. It is a sense of "I", but it is not self-awareness; it is rather one's personality.

There is also a hierarchy within these aspects of personality. The full personality is all that you can desire. A subset of what you can desire manifests at a given time. To fulfill that temporal desire, you desire that place that can fulfill the desire. After you desire the place at a given time, then you desire to know a subset of things at that place. And once this subset of things is desired, then you desire to use a smaller subset of things in your actions. For instance, you can desire to eat Indian food, which is one of the many possible desires, but that desire manifests at a given time. Once the desire has manifest, the desire for eating becomes the desire for an Indian restaurant. Once you reach the restaurant, your desire changes and you ask for the menu. Upon seeing the menu, your desire again changes and you ask for a specific dish from the menu. Thus, from your unmanifest personality, the desire to eat manifests, which then becomes the desire for a restaurant, then it becomes the desire for the menu, and then it becomes a desire for a specific dish in the menu. Thus, the personality of desires progressively manifests into time, place, knowing, and action.

Then, vijñāna-maya is also divided into five parts. These are called Pradhāna, Prakriti, Mahattattva, Ahaṃkāra, and Buddhi. The term vijñāna means judgment, and there are five stages of judging. The fifth stage of Buddhi is the judgment of truth. The fourth stage of Ahaṃkāra is judgment is good. The third stage of Mahattattva is the judgment of right. The Prakriti stage is the formulation of preferences about truth, right, and good, based on which later judgments can be done—e.g., I will value equality over justice, or vice versa; I will value knowledge over beauty, or vice versa; I will value my job over my family, or vice versa. Once these axioms are formed, everything is judged based on these preferences. And these preferences are called Prakriti. Finally, the original stage of Pradhāna is the possibility of all such preferences; we haven't chosen them yet, but we must know the possibilities to make a choice. For example, if you did not know that equality was an option, you could not value it over justice. All these kinds of judgments are "I", but they the sense of "I" that judges.

The mano-maya represents the mind which cognizes the meanings. These meanings are also divided into five parts, which are then called thinking, feeling, willing, knowing, and acting. For example, you can say that a shooter shot an innocent person. Then, in the knowing mode, you say that the shooter was tall or short, white or black, ugly or beautiful. Then, in the thinking mode, you say that the shooter was a professional or an amateur. In the feeling mode, you say that the shooter hated, loved, or was simply careless. And in the willing mode, you judge a person's intentions—the shooter had premeditated the action, or it was an accident. These five kinds of meanings complete the understanding of any observation, and the understanding thus has five parts. This is also a sense of "I", but the self is a thinker, feeler, intender, knower, and doer. By interpreting the world as meaning, we define the self accordingly.

Then prāṇa-maya represents the power to do things. This power is also divided into five parts—called prāṇa, apāna, udāna, vyāna, and samāna. These are understood as the power of ingestion, digestion, assimilation, circulation, and excretion. A system's behavior can be explained by these five types. This is also a sense of "I", but it identifies the soul as a type of living system.

Finally, the anna-maya represents the body of 'food'. This 'food' is divided into five elements—called Earth, Water, Fire, Air, and Ether. The element called Ether is the unmanifest stage of the five elements. In the stage called Air, this Ether has manifested energy. This energy is then divided into three parts—Fire, Water, and Earth. The Fire mode of Air is called 'energy'. The Earth mode is called 'object'. And the Water mode is the 'relation' between the two. Thus, energy is not randomly distributed to every object. Rather, there are objects, a specific object is selected to receive the energy, and then energy is transferred.

Then, to measure all these things, we need some properties, these properties must have standards, and there must be an observer who applies these standards to measurement, and then observes them. The observer is divided into five parts as the five senses or jñāna-indriya. Each such indriya measures five properties—e.g., the sense of sight measures color, shape, size, distance, and direction. And each such property has its own standards. The senses are the mere possibilities of every type of perception. In this stage, they remain unmanifest. The manifestation of the sense is when a standard is selected. If your senses have selected 'big' standards, then they cannot see 'small' things, and vice versa. In the unmanifest stage, the senses of all the living entities are the same. But in the "I" stage, these senses have standards. Now, each soul has acquired a different type of sense, which can see different kinds of things.

Now, if you look at a standard—e.g., a kilogram or a meter—then it has three aspects. First, it has a property—e.g., weight or length. Second, it has a value—the value in all standards is 1. Third, the standard is also an individual object. In the same way, when senses become standards, then they divide into three aspects—objects, values, and properties. To understand this description, one should think of dreams rather than the waking experience. In a dream, experiences are produced by the senses, and each person sees different kinds of dreams. This is because they have different kinds of senses. Essentially, the sense—as a standard—divides into objects, properties, and their values. This division of the sense into three aspects causes our dreaming experience.

Once the dreaming experience is understood, then the waking experience is described in the same way. The primordial reality is created as a standard. These standards are just numbers or identities of different objects. From this identity, three further things are produced—object, value, and property. Thus, we can say that the 10th object is a table, which has the properties of shape and color, and the shape is square while the color is black. The table is the object, shape, and color are the properties, and square and black are their values. But before these objects, properties, and values, there is simply a number. Whatever originates from this number can also be described as a number. Hence, objects, properties, and values can also be understood as numbers. This description of reality as numbers (which exist in many modalities) is called Sāñkhya.

Similarly, there are five karma-indriya or the senses of actions. Each of these five indriya can do five types of things, each of these five types have their standards, objects, and values. This description is not elaborately found in the Vedic texts, but it can be gleaned and extended from the previous descriptions.

The jñāna-indriya, karma-indriya, and bhūta exist in three modes of nature—*sattva*, *rajas*, and *tamas*. Then there is a balanced state of these three modes which is called tāmasic ahamkara or "I-ness in the object mode". This is also a sense of "I", although after the previous notions of "I"—as a personality, a chooser, a knower, and a living entity—we get the identity as a body. Although the body is comprised of hands and legs, if one of these were absent, the 'body' still exists. Whatever is absent from the body (e.g., if the hand was cut-off) goes into the state of potentiality, while the other parts of the body are present. The evidence of the whole body being present is that if a part is cut-off, then the other parts continue their functions. We can contrast this to a team comprised of people; if one person leaves the team, the others share the work between them. But if your hand and legs are cut-off, then the lungs, heart, and stomach don't start doing the work of the hands or legs. This is because the missing body part still exists, although in an unmanifest state. It is as if the person has not completely left the team, but merely gone on a vacation.

A well-known illustration of this problem is the existence of 'phantom limbs'—many soldiers who return from a battle with their limbs amputated, continue to feel pain in those limbs. The reason is that the limb exists in three modes—purpose, function, and object. When the limb is amputated, the purpose and function exist; only the object-mode reality is absent. This is like a person on a team who has gone on vacation. The role and purpose exist, but the body performing that role and fulfilling the purpose is absent. But since the function and purpose exist, therefore, the other body parts don't fulfill the function and purpose of the missing part. And since the function and purpose exist, therefore, the limbs can be replaced. Sometimes even without this replacement, the limb performs its function and purpose, and hence feels the pain.

Beyond this 'body' is another body that exists in an unmanifest state. This body is a collection of successive bodies—e.g., child body, a youth body, old body, etc. All these bodies are potentialities, but different potentialities are manifest one after another. Therefore, due to this unmanifest body, we can say that the same body was a child, then become young, and then became old. Then again, since these are only potentials, we can also say that we are changing bodies, and the child body is not the same as the youth body or the old body.

Thus, we can see how our existence is divided into five sheaths, each of which is then divided into five parts, and in many cases—such as the division of the gross body—there are further five-fold subdivisions of the gross body. This is a generic method or principle of division and manifestation, and it can therefore be applied to the body, to the entire universe, and to the Absolute Truth. Therefore, Pañcatattva is a generic doctrine about five modalities.

The ānanda-maya is known as the 'unconscious' in Western psychology. The vijñāna-maya is the beginning of the conscious experience, and it is further divided into mano-maya, prāṇa-maya, and anna-maya, which are also sometimes called manas, prāṇa, and vāk, as three modes of *sattva*, *rajas*, and *tamas*. The 'unconscious' is the unmanifest stage of matter. The vijñāna-maya is the beginning of the manifestation when the person obtains a sense of conscious identity. Then, this identity is further divided into three aspects or modes.

Other Uses of Pañcatattva

This doctrine is sometimes employed in the Pañcopāsanā system as well, when five deities—Śiva, Śakti, Viṣṇu, Surya, and Iśta—are worshipped. Śiva, Śakti, and Viṣṇu are representations of God, matter, and soul. Surya represents the balanced combination of these three—the Sun god is Viṣṇu, the sunlight is Śakti, and Sun's rotation is time or Śiva. Factually, what we call the sun-globe doesn't exist as an object. It is merely a collection of potentialities. From this collection, one by one the various potentialities are selected, and these are called the aspects of the sun, represented by the 12 zodiac signs, and their succession is time. However, since these properties can be applied to every single planet—e.g., Moon or Jupiter—since they are also persons, energies, and phases, therefore, in principle, Surya is optional in the worship of five deities and could be replaced by any other planet. Nevertheless, the Sun is not replaced, and the reason is that he is considered the perfect balanced combination of Śiva, Viṣṇu, and Śakti. If one wants to worship another personality, then the fifth deity called Iśta is treated as the person being worshipped *through* the Sun. In short, you make your offering to the Sun—because he is manifest—but this offering is in turn delivered to the Iśta or the deity of your choice through the Sun. For example, those who worship Ganeśa must do so through the Sun god.

In Vedic astrology, all other planets are considered simply aspects of the Sun. Unlike the Sun in which these three aspects of Śiva, Śakti, and Viṣṇu are balanced, in other planets, these modalities are dominant and subordinate. Thus, owing to the dominant-subordinate structures, there are six other planets—Jupiter, Saturn, Mercury, Venus, Mars, and Moon—in which the modes go dominant and subordinate (6 = 3 x 2 x 1). Hence, there are six aspects of the Sun, and together with the Sun, there are seven primary planets. Then, because the properties of these planets are further divided into dualities (such as hot and cold), therefore, two other planets—Rahu and Ketu—are added to the list. Thus, the same Pañcatattva doctrine also leads to other kinds of descriptions. In some of these descriptions, there are six aspects of a balanced reality. Then together with the balanced reality, there are seven aspects collectively. Then there are also nine aspects if we combine the dualities of the material world. Then because the Sun is the combination of Viṣṇu, Śiva, and Śakti, and Viṣṇu divides into 12 or 24 aspects, Śiva divides into 15 aspects, and Śakti divides into 8 aspects, therefore, even more complex systems of division are employed.

Vedic cosmology also describes the universe as a five-fold covering. The first such covering is the ānanda-maya, which is divided into an unmanifest, which is called the kārana, and a balanced manifest which is called mahattattva (this mahattattva is different from the same term used in other contexts). The balanced manifest then divides into six further aspects. Unlike the five-fold division in the Pañcatattva doctrine, the division, in this case, has eight parts—the unmanifest, the balanced manifest, and its six different aspects (just like the balanced manifest of the Sun has six different aspects). It might seem that this division is fundamentally different, but it is not. The first two stages are the same, and the next six stages are a variation from the three separated modes to six separated but combined modes (in dominant-subordinate states). The balanced manifest and its six imbalanced aspects constitute the seven coverings of a universe, and the unmanifest is common to all the universes. The balanced manifest is the universe's "I" state, and it springs from the common unmanifest state. Thus, all the universes are merged into the kārana unmanifest state. From this state, each of the varied universes springs out as a unique "I". This "I" can be viewed as the balanced state of three modes of "I". It can also be understood as the combination of the six separated states that are imbalanced in the three modes. And finally, it can be divided into five aspects of ānanda-maya. The ānanda-maya is like the personality of the universe—there are different kinds of desires, knowledge, abilities, places, and times within each universe.

Once this ānanda-maya is produced, then there are vijñāna-maya, mano-maya, prāṇa-maya, and anna-maya divisions of the universe. All the forms of the Supreme Lord in the universe are vijñāna-maya. These forms are described variously as one, two, three, four, five, six, seven, eight, or even more. The universe is then divided into three subparts—the planets of demigods, of demons, and the hellish planets. Each of these is then divided into seven subparts. The Vedānta Sūtra speaks of these three-fold and seven-fold divisions. The planets of the demigods are in the mode of sattva, those of demons are in the mode of rajas, and the hellish planets are in the mode of tamas. They can also be called mano-maya, prāṇa-maya, and anna-maya. And yet, these are simply three aspects of the vijñāna-maya. Since these are only aspects of the Supreme Lord, therefore, the whole cosmos is understood as a Cosmic Man and the Vedānta Sūtra describes how the Lord can be understood through a cosmic form.

It is impossible to capture all the varied systems of modalities here, and I don't aim to do that. For the interested reader, I will refer you to my book *Cosmic Theogony*, which discusses this topic at greater length. My goal in the present book is to primarily illustrate how all these systems are created from a primordial unmanifest, comprising of three fundamental modalities. And this system then gives us a template of how to construct more complex modal descriptions. Even without going into further details, we can see how this modal description brings together numerous thus far disparate descriptions. These are not truly disparate; they are just developments of an unmanifest reality.

The Unity of Vedic Philosophy

When we adopt the semantic view, in one sense, we change the doctrine of Vedānta Sūtra from *achintya* to *chintya*. In another sense, this is not yet another doctrine that merely differs from the previous doctrines (or worse, contradicts them). This is a doctrine that makes every other doctrine equally true. Thus, Advaita is true because the Lord and the devotee can take on each other's moods and roles. Viśiṣṭādvaita is true because the devotee is a property that describes the object. Dvaita is true because even if the soul falls, the Lord is not fallen. Bhedābheda is true because the soul is a part of the Lord, and His Śakti is a complement of the Lord. Acintyabhedābheda is true because all these approaches cannot be reconciled in the physical view of things. And the *chintya* doctrine is true because they can be reconciled in the semantic viewpoint.

The modal view of reality helps us see how Vaishnavism, Shaivism, and Shaktism are three aspects of the same truth. In the material world, Vaishnavism is the soul-mode description of reality; Shaivism is the God-mode description of the same reality; and Shaktism is the Śakti-mode description of the same reality. As we have discussed, the God-mode defines *what* will happen, the soul-mode defines *who* will do what, and the Śakti-mode defines *how* things will happen. What, who, and how are complementary explanations of reality. The who-mode is also the *why*-mode because the soul's choices are the explanation of the soul's bondage. The Śakti-mode is also the *where*-mode since Śakti creates the variety of the material world, which is the universal space. Finally, the God-mode is also the *when*-mode because God (as Time in the material world) controls the world. Thus, if we understand these three modalities, then we get the answer to six questions—what, who, how, when, why, and where. In one sense, there are six different explanations of the same reality. In another sense, there is just one reality, which exists in three distinct modalities.

The modal description simply says that you can never answer these six questions simultaneously. You can, however, answer them alternately. If you remain fixed in the matter-mode, then soul-mode and God-mode descriptions will never be seen. If you try to add all three modes simultaneously, then you will get contradictions. Due to these problems, you either get incompleteness (you can't have all three modes simultaneously), or you get contradictions (if you use all three modes at once). If we want to get past the incompleteness and inconsistency problems, then the modal solution says that these six questions can be answered alternately, but not simultaneously. This is because the soul alternates between these modes and hence language too must alternate.

This understanding of Vedānta can also reconcile the other five systems of philosophy—i.e., Sāñkhya, Yoga, Vaiśeṣika, Nyāya, and Mīmāṃsā. Sāñkhya is the description of the world as mathematics, numbers, and the process of counting. Vedānta, on the other hand, is the reduction of Sāñkhya—or number theory (and all of mathematics)—to the whole-part doctrine (i.e., set theory).

Given that there are many whole-part doctrines, therefore, we end up with many models of logic. For example, in Materialism, the whole reduces to the parts, so we get the non-contradiction and mutual exclusion of modern mathematical set theory. In Buddhism, the opposites are mutually defined, so, we must reject both non-contradiction and mutual exclusion, but we can say that these opposites combine to make the whole nothing. In Idealism, the parts are not mutually contradictory, so they can be combined in a hierarchy to produce a universalist conception of truth; however, to make this combination, oppositions must not exist; therefore, the existence of all falsities must be rejected, and nobody can ever be illusioned or have any alternative viewpoint. In Monotheism, this universal truth creates many diversities from the universal truth, but because this creation violates natural principles, therefore, the principles of non-contradiction and mutual exclusion apply to the creation, but not to God. In Advaita, non-contradiction and mutual exclusion apply to Brahman, but not to matter. They apply to Brahman because there is only one thing. And they don't apply to māyā because there are opposites in māyā. In Viśiṣṭādvaita, non-contradiction and mutual exclusion don't apply to the object, because He has contradictory properties. And they don't apply to the parts because the parts always exist in three modalities which contradict the principles of universal truth. In Dvaita, the whole and the part are different, but because each entity has modalities, therefore, each entity is self-contradictory, but collectively they are consistent. In Bhedābheda, the new category is non-difference which violates classical logic. And in Acintyabhedābheda, there are many Bhedābheda, so classical logical principles break down in numerous ways. Each of these views of reality brings a different model of reasoning. Therefore, Nyāya is contingent upon the doctrine of reality. If the notion of reality is modified, then, the attendant method of reasoning about that reality must also be changed.

Once the logic is revised, then the whole-part theory should lead to the understanding of 'atoms' in Vaiśeṣika which constitute the logical limit to the division of the whole into parts (this type of atomism is sometimes called 'logical atomism' in Western philosophy). The union of the parts with the whole forms the essence of Yoga and the analysis of the whole into parts is the essence of Mīmāṃsā. Mīmāṃsā is the description of how the whole divides into parts, and Yoga is the explanation of how despite this division the parts remain connected to the whole. If the whole-part theory is constructed correctly, then, the other five systems (Nyāya, Vaiśeṣika, Sāñkhya, Yoga, and Mīmāṃsā) become natural corollaries of Vedānta. A problem in this construction, however, makes the six systems of Vedic philosophy seem divergent and conflicting with each other. A test for the correctness of the Vedānta system is that it also makes every other philosophical system true and reconciles their apparent contradictions.

If one looks at earlier Vedānta commentaries, the doctrine of Vedānta often comes at the expense of the other five systems of philosophy, as other systems are refuted to establish a Vedānta doctrine. Since these other systems are also based on the Vedic texts—they are all considered *āstika* or theistic—the refutation of these systems entails that they cannot be considered the final truth because they contradict other Vedic texts. For example, the Sāñkhya and Yoga systems are pervasive across both śrutī and smriti. The Bhagavad-Gita describes both systems in a summary form. If a Vedānta Sūtra commentary rejects these systems, then it also rejects the Bhagavad-Gita. Similarly, other Vedic texts discuss atomism and its relation to the entire cosmos—the smallest part depends on the definition of the largest part; if we change the definition of the whole, then we must change the definition of the parts. If these ideas are rejected—by discarding Vaiśeṣika and Mīmāṃsā—then the scientific study of nature (e.g., as atomism and cosmology) becomes impossible. Similarly, just because the whole-part doctrine is contradictory to current logic, the conclusion cannot be that reality is not amenable to rational inquiry. Therefore, Vedānta doctrine cannot in principle reject the Nyāya system. Its goal should rather be to formulate the correct Nyāya, compatible with the Vedānta doctrine.

My conclusion is simple—any doctrine that rejects the other five systems cannot be considered the true Vedānta. The unity of Vedic philosophy is unquestionable. If we bring into question some part of the Vedic texts, then every other part becomes doubtful. The purpose of Vedānta Sūtra commentaries should be to establish the primacy of the whole-part theory, and how these parts exist in the modalities of will and power, without rejecting the truth of the other five systems. If this primary goal is not met, it doesn't matter what other goals are satisfied in the process. The Vedānta Sūtra states that knowledge should be acquired in such a way that the contradictions between the different texts are resolved. How can we abide by Vedānta Sūtra, if we reject the other five systems of philosophy? Therefore, the evolution of Vedānta doctrines must also endeavor to reconcile the apparent contradictions with other systems.

I'm offering these diverse examples to make a singular point—the diverse schools of philosophy are not truly disjointed. They uphold a single philosophy, which is misunderstood due to the modal nature of reality. If we adopt a semantic view of nature, then all these modalities become amenable. This modal view unites Vedānta, Sāñkhya, Mīmāṃsā, Nyāya, Vaiśeṣika, and Yoga. It reconciles diverse Vedānta doctrines and entails that none of them is false. It may not mean that they are true simultaneously. However, they can all be true alternately. There is no contradiction between the yoga systems because the devotee performs actions without the desire for results (which is karma-yoga), his actions are performed with perfect knowledge of the Absolute Truth (which is jñāna-yoga), he sees the Lord in his heart (which is aśtānga-yoga), and the purpose of his life is the service to the Lord (which is bhakti-yoga). Similarly, the Vaishnava, Shaiva, and Shakta traditions are aspects of a single system.

Science Without Materialism

The caveat is one—we reject physicalist, materialistic thinking in all forms. It is fundamentally opposed to Vedic philosophy; it is called *nāstika* or atheistic, and it has no place in the Vedic system. This simple caveat of rejecting all forms of physicalist, materialistic thinking segregates Vedic philosophy from modern thinking. Every other claim holds true if materialism has been rejected.

Thus, there can be an alternative non-materialistic description of matter. For example, when you desire an apple, then you are different from the apple. When you obtain an apple, then you have a relation to the apple. But when you eat the apple, you are non-different from the apple. The difference is Dvaita, the relation is Viśiṣṭādvaita, and the non-difference is Advaita. Since all three can be true, the term Bhedābheda can be applied to matter—i.e., something is simultaneously different, non-different, and related. But since we don't presently distinguish between these three modalities—that involve difference, non-difference, and relation—we end up with logical contradictions. The doctrine is now advanced to Acintyabhedābheda to say that all these three are equally true, but we cannot say so within current universalist logic. However, if we shifted the description to modalities, then the understanding is non-contradictory.

Desiring, obtaining, and eating don't happen simultaneously. They rather happen one after another, so one mode goes dominant, while the other mode goes subordinate. You desire an apple, bring it closer to your mouth, and then take a bite. Then, you desire again, bring the apple closer to the mouth and take another bite. All these are contradictory modes, but by their flipping, you desire, obtain, and eat, one by one. If we want to understand how we desire an apple, obtain an apple, and finally eat the apple, then we must revise our scientific theories to such modal forms of existence. This philosophy about the soul, God, matter, and their interrelations thus applies even to material reality.

The Structure of Vedānta Sūtra

Time and Logic

The mode-flipping produces a peculiar model of change or progression, which then changes our understanding of logic and time. The progression goes from a premise to the problem it produces, to an answer that solves the problem and becomes the new premise. This model of reasoning is not the *linear progression* from premises to a conclusion as in current logic. It is the *alternating progression* from premises to questions to answers. Thus, an answer exists, which we can call the 'premise'. But it doesn't automatically lead to a conclusion. It first gives rise to a question. The question conflicts with the premise, following which the conflict is resolved by a new answer. This new answer addresses the previous conflict, but it leads to a new problem, question, or conflict, which is then resolved again. Thus, I can say that "I exist", which is the premise. But it can lead to the question: "Why do I exist?" This question has sent philosophers in search of the meaning of life in all ages. But there is a choice in the generation of questions from answers. For instance, after I say, "I exist", the next question may be: "How can I continue to exist or survive?" The progression from an answer to a question is not *deterministic*. In fact, because contradictory questions can arise from the same premise, therefore, it should be possible to produce answers that respond to the contradictory questions.

So, there is a fundamental difference between the current idea that logic is about *consistency* with premises and our everyday notion about 'reasoning' which alternates between answers and questions, and the basic mechanism of its progression is *conflict*. If I'm a rich man, I can ask myself different questions: "How do I become richer?" or "How do I spend my riches most effectively?" Both questions produce conflict, and I cannot just sit idle staying rich. I will rather move to answer the emerging question. The conflict is, therefore, the cause of change. Since these questions do not deterministically follow the premises, there is a choice involved in the creation of the question from the answer. And because these questions can be contradictory, and they can lead to contradictory answers, therefore, contradicting answers must be *logically* allowed; the existence of contradictions between the answers cannot be considered a *logical contradiction* because they arose in response to contradicting questions. If such contradictions are possible, then the possibility can be used to make meanings (which are defined through mutual oppositions) a reality. And since either side of the opposition can be chosen, it necessitates a role for choice. In short, an alternative view of logic enables a role for both meanings and choices.

Furthermore, because the contradictory questions take us in different 'directions', and the answers thus produced are logical opposites of other answers, we are naturally led to the conception of a 'space' in which contradictions cannot exist in the same 'place'—as that would be called self-contradiction. Two people possessing conflicting questions can, therefore, move in opposite directions, chasing conflicting answers, and this process leads naturally to a novel understanding of 'distance' and 'direction'—both must be viewed semantically rather than physically. If 'space' were defined as the domain of all possible questions and answers, then motion would be defined as the change of position in this space. Similarly, 'time' must be defined as the succession of questions and answers, or the causality that converts an answer to a question. In short, an alternative conception of logic naturally produces alternative notions of space, time, causality, and motion, in which opposite ideas are opposite 'locations' and 'directions' in space, and the movement in this space is governed by conflicting types of choices. And all this is simply a consequence of mode-flipping.

The Nature of Logical Progression

The wonder of Vedānta Sūtra is not just that it describes the process of this progression, but that it also demonstrates it through its progression from premises to questions to conclusions. Vedānta Sūtra is called nyāya-prasthāna or a logical treatise. But it is not Nyāya or logic in the sense of premise to conclusion. It is rather Nyāya in the sense of a premise to a question to a conclusion. It is therefore rationality, although it is not the Western sense of rationalism.

If we view Vedānta Sūtra through the lens of Vedānta philosophy, then we also must revise the methodology of commenting on the text. One such modification is that the text only lists the answers, but not the questions. These questions must therefore be inserted by the commentator to interpret the text correctly. Furthermore, the questions can never be repeated, such that the different answers could never contradict each other. Just as in a mathematical proof, it is acceptable to use the previously arrived conclusions as premises, but we cannot try to reprove the premise, or contradict the premise, similarly, the text must progress without repetition. Just as in a mathematical proof we cannot make leaps of inference, but must proceed step-by-step, without leaving gaps, similarly, the discussion cannot jump discontinuously from one claim to another, violating the condition of 'logical' progress. These requirements on interpretation mandate that the questions before a sūtra flow from the previous answers, without producing discontinuities, and the same conclusions cannot be proved repeatedly to avoid redundancies. This can be much harder than it seems.

The reason is that the same answer can be understood differently if the question preceding it is altered. As an illustration, the single word answer of "no" can be taken to deny any number of questions, and the meaning of "no" (i.e., what it is denying) is not apparent unless we know the question itself. So, when a conversation proceeds dialectically, the meanings become subject to the context—e.g., what was said previously, and the objection to that answer. We often find that the next question is based on not just the previous answer, but also what has been said in the entire sequence. Each sūtra is not independent of the previous sūtras. It is necessarily an incremental logical progression.

Now you might argue: Since there is a choice in inserting a question before a sūtra, therefore, such an interpretation is a personal choice. How can you call this a valid interpretation if you are inserting questions in it? The answer to this problem is that if you fix the sequence of answers, then the sequence of questions must also be fixed. The choices in interpretation begin to disappear rapidly as we elongate the sequence of questions and answers—remember that the same question and answer can never reappear, there can be no overlaps or gaps in the succession. But you might still argue: We can see that the choices in interpretations dramatically reduce as we progress, but isn't it possible that the entire sequence of questions could be changed to fit the answers differently? My response to that problem is: Yes, in principle they can be changed. However, ultimately, the interpretation must produce something consistent and complete. If this condition is not satisfied, then Vedānta Sūtra would be yet another incomplete philosophy—much like the numerous prevalent philosophies. On the other hand, if this condition is met, then even if we have alternative interpretations, their conclusion would still be the same—i.e., how do we get an alternative conception of reality that is both consistent and complete?

Therefore, the meaning of the text is not simply to be known by its textual interpretation. It must also follow from a unique methodology of logic, and the criterion of consistency and completeness. These latter imply that— (1) the six systems of Vedic philosophy must be reconciled, (2) all interpretations of Vedānta must be upheld, and (3) diverse schools of the Vedic system, such as Vaishnavism, Shaivism, and Shaktism must be simultaneously true. In short, the meaning of Vedānta—as the conclusion of all Vedic knowledge—must be compatible with the meaning of Veda (i.e., the diversified descriptions of reality). We cannot call something Vedānta if it is contradictory to Veda. If this goal is satisfied, even different interpretations of the sūtras are not a problem.

Hence, I want to refrain from the 'academic' definitions of textual interpretation, which look at a text in isolation. They only focus on Sanskrit grammar and linguistics. But, in this case, two more criteria must be added— (1) logical progression, and (2) the consistency and completeness of knowledge.

If a sūtra can be interpreted in many ways—because many interpretations are consistent with the rest of Vedic philosophy, and consistent with the Sanskrit grammar and linguistics, one such interpretation can be chosen based on the criterion that (a) the question and answer aren't repeated, (b) the question and answers don't take leaps and produce discontinuities. At the level of each sūtra, the differences thus arising can often seem rather small. But the differences accumulate and produce visible divergences over a succession of sūtras. This divergence is essential if it takes us through different modalities—e.g., how the same two things are different, non-different, and related. To deal with this one modality you need three statements that restate three different views. Then you need multiple other statements that reconcile the resulting contradictions. The divergence has a purpose—it must produce the requisite completeness.

Hierarchical vs. Cyclical

The nature of logical progression through modalities entails that you can never describe reality fully at once. You state one view and draw its conclusions. But then you find that the conclusions either conflict with previous conclusions or are necessarily incomplete. To overcome these problems, you revise the doctrine again, which is then evaluated against other inconsistencies and incompleteness yet again. This produces a cyclic type of argument because the same topics are covered, again and again, each time in a different way. This cyclic nature of the argument contradicts the book's hierarchical structure.

By a hierarchical structure, I mean that the book is divided into chapters, sections, topics, and sūtras. If we treat Vedānta Sūtra like any other text, then each chapter, section, topic, and sūtra must be devoted to a unique question or problem. Once that question or problem has been discussed, it should never be revisited, although it can be employed for subsequent arguments. Vedānta

Sūtra doesn't follow this principle. Although there are four chapters, each of which has four sections, each section has a varying number of topics, and each topic has a varying number of sūtras, the argument of the text is cyclical. It discusses the same topics iteratively, constantly nuancing its position.

For example, initially, it is said that one must inquire into the nature of Brahman because it is the source of everything; later it is said that the Brahman itself originates from the Supreme Lord, as light emanates from a candle. Initially, it is said that one must aspire for liberation from the material modes, and later it is said that the devotees don't even aspire for liberation as they only aspire to please the Lord. In the beginning, it is said that the Lord is transcendent to material nature, and later it is said that He is also immanent. At first, it is said that revelation is the source of true knowledge, and later it is said that the Absolute Truth can also be directly perceived and understood rationally. In the beginning, it is said that the soul is separate from the Lord, then it is said that the soul is a part of the Lord. Initially, the Lord is distinguished from the material world, and later the material world is called His property, inseparable from Him. At some point, it is said that the Lord and the soul are qualitatively similar but quantitatively different, and later it is said the soul is both qualitatively and quantitatively different from the Lord. Initially, the Absolute Truth is described impersonally; then the same Absolute Truth is described as a masculine person; finally, the same Absolute Truth is described as masculine and feminine persons and their union. At some point, it is said that social duties must not be discarded, but later, it is said that the devotees can reject social duties if they are pleasing to the Lord. At many places, it is said that the diverse paths to spiritual progress must be rejected in favor of the devotional path, and later it is said that all these paths must be combined for attaining perfection. Initially, it is said that one must focus on the conclusion of all knowledge, and later it is said that many disciplines are important to understanding the Absolute Truth. I can go on and on with examples, but I think you understand the point.

The point is this: when we hear that X is true, then we conclude that not-X is false. We take a claim to mean that its opposite is automatically denied. But the Vedānta Sūtra doesn't take this view. It constantly revises its position to incorporate opposite ideas and reconciles them with a nuanced explanation. The previous claims are never rejected, but their opposites are accepted later. And yet, as you progress through the text, you don't find it contradictory, because the subsequent claims reconcile both the previous and the new claims. There is constant back and forth for nuancing the position to incorporate opposites. Thus, I must advise the reader: Don't conclude anything unless you have read the full text. Whatever has been said now, is likely to be updated later. If you are thinking that something is being rejected, wait until it is accepted.

If one needed a metaphor for the structure of Vedānta Sūtra, then it is like a spiral that goes outward to inward through incremental steps. At each successive step, you think you are moving one step forward, so the structure seems to be linear. This is the microstructure of the book. Over a longer interval, you see that you are going cyclically because the position is constantly revised. This is the intermediate structure of the text. And eventually, you see how the conversation goes deeper toward the center of the spiral. This inward movement is the hierarchical and macroscopic structure of the book. You find that every claim and counterclaim has been argued and reconciled, and the Absolute Truth is therefore understood as the source of every kind of contradictory idea. The successive chapters, sections, topics, and sūtras therefore can be divided into four stages—each successively more reconciled than the previous ones.

By the time you finish reading the book, you will see what I mean by logic—it is linear, cyclical, and hierarchical. This logic is also the process of life if one wants to progress toward the perfect understanding of the truth. If one has the Supreme Lord as the goal, then each stage of life is one step forward. But over time, you find yourself revisiting the same questions and problems. Finally, as you iterate over these issues and get a deeper understanding, you understand the Supreme Lord, who is the source of everything but reconciles them.

There is nothing comparable to this structure in the world today. However, this literary structure implies that the reader cannot take the hierarchical structure in the text too seriously. One should rather read the sūtras and understand the logical flow, but a chapter or section doesn't deal with exclusive topics. As we progress, the same topics will be revisited but based on the previous discussion, each time the understanding of that topic would be nuanced and enhanced. Until you finish the book, you don't know if you really have the final truth. If nothing else, this tells you to read the book from start to finish! A cursory glance at chapters or selectively picking a sūtra without the context can be erroneous. All that is said only exists as a part of this helical progression.

CHAPTER 1

This chapter deals with the relation between the soul, God, and nature, how the soul is entangled in matter due to its rejection of God, and how it can be liberated by devotion to God. Many methods of reviving this devotion are also described such as the meditation on the Lord in the heart, the study of the Vedic scriptures, and the understanding of the Universal Form of the Lord.

Section 1: This section begins with the prescription that the purpose of human life is to inquire into the nature of Brahman. It then prescribes the study of the scriptures as the primary method for the acquisition of the knowledge of Brahman. It describes Brahman as that which expands from itself and merges into itself. The expansion of Brahman divides the One into many, without the cessation of the One, and the cause of this expansion is the desire for pleasure. Thus, the soul is expanded from Brahman, and it is said to be different from the One, and yet never separated from the One. However, in the material existence, the soul is caught in the three modes of material nature, due to which it considers itself different from the One. To restore the connection to the One, the section prescribes liberation from the influence of matter by developing the devotion to the Absolute Truth. This constitutes the overview of the entire text, and the same themes are revisited, evaluated, and nuanced over and over.

Section 2: The discussion of the process of liberation is taken up in this section, and it is stated that the form of the Supreme Lord exists along with each soul as the Paramātma. This form of the Lord aids the liberation of the soul from material existence. The Paramātma is said to be the controller of the world, including the various demigods who control the delivery of the various kinds of karma. While the material world is different from the Paramātma, it is stated to be an expression of the Lord, like an author may express his ideas in a text. Furthermore, this expression is also said to be His property, in the sense that the Lord owns the material creation, and the creation reflects His nature. Then the text states that since the creation reflects the properties of the Paramātma, therefore, it can also be used to understand His nature. One such method of knowing the Lord is described to be the study of the universe as the Universal Form of the Lord which is not sense-perceivable but can be meditated upon. Thus, even if the soul cannot find the Lord in the heart, he can still understand the Lord through the study of His expansion as the cosmic manifestation.

Section 3: This section moves beyond the material world into the discussion of the transcendental world. This world is described as comprising many forms of the Lord, which are manifest to fulfill the different desires in the soul as well as the Lord to enjoy with the soul. The conversation then moves into how this transcendental world can be attained, and the prescription is to take the shelter of a qualified guru. Following the discussion about the qualifications of the guru, a discussion is taken up about the qualifications of the disciple. In this discussion, it is stated that those without a good moral upbringing and faith in the Lord are forbidden from the study of the scriptures. A remedy for such people is however prescribed—namely, the chanting of the names of the Lord. How the chanting of the names leads to gradual purification is then discussed.

Section 4: This section discusses how the transcendental forms of the Lord, which exist eternally in the spiritual world, incarnate in the material world. And yet, despite their presence in the material world, they are not bound by the laws of material nature. Since the Lord looks just like the other people in this world, the text states that He is identified as the Lord due to the great deeds He performs. Since the demigods also have greatness, the discussion moves into why their greatness reflects the greatness in the Lord, and hence why they must not be worshipped. A method is now prescribed for those who want to progress in the spiritual life, but do not possess devotion to the Lord: It is said that such people can study Vedic texts and elevate their understanding by reconciling the contradictions across many scriptures. As this study is perfected, then one naturally develops an attraction to the Lord, and devotion naturally springs as the byproduct of perfected knowledge. Finally, the text elaborates on how the Absolute Truth comprises the interrelated masculine and feminine aspects.

SECTION 1

Topic 1

QUESTION

What should I do?

Everyone is seeking guidance about what they must do in their lives, the purpose of their existence, and how they can achieve it. This is a natural question that arises in everyone's life, and it is the beginning of Vedānta Sūtra as well. The question emerges from the acknowledged fact of our existence.

1.1.1 (1)

अथातो ब्रह्मजिज्ञासा

athāto brahmajijñāsā

atha—now; ataḥ—therefore; brahmajijñāsā—an inquiry into Brahman.

TRANSLATION

Now, therefore, an inquiry into Brahman.

COMMENTARY

The terms 'now' and 'therefore' can be interpreted in many ways. They can refer to the fact that the reader is now in a human form of life, and therefore he must inquire into Brahman because in other species of life this inquiry is not possible. It can refer to the fact that the Vedānta Sūtra are the conclusions of the Upaniśad, and were authored after them, so now (having read and understood the Upaniśad) one must have concluded that Brahman is the ultimate reality, so one must inquire into its nature. It can also mean that now since you have met enlightened souls, you must begin an inquiry into Brahman. Finally, it can mean that now that you are reading the conclusion of all knowledge—namely, the Vedānta Sūtra—you must endeavor to inquire into the nature of Brahman (as opposed to other Vedic scriptures where other topics are discussed).

Topic 2

QUESTION

But why should I inquire into Brahman?

The previous sūtra stated that one should inquire into Brahman, so a skeptic can ask: Why? In other words, why is this inquiry important over the other things that I can do? Why should I focus on Brahman instead of other things?

1.1.2 (2)

जन्मादयस्य यतः

janmādyasya yataḥ

janmādi—the birth source; asya—of this (world); yataḥ—from which.

TRANSLATION

Brahman is the birth source of this (world) from which (the world sprung).

COMMENTARY

This sūtra is exhorting the reader that the inquiry into Brahman is important because it is the birth source of everything. The term ādi can be interpreted in two ways— (1) as the origin, and (2) as one of many things (etc.). In the latter case, we would include the maintenance and dissolution of the world into the reason for the study of Brahman. I prefer to use the term ādi to denote 'original' because dissolution and maintenance will be discussed later (although including maintenance and dissolution would not be technically incorrect). The use of the term 'original' also has significance here, because there are secondary sources of the creation. For instance, Brahma is a secondary creator of the material world, who creates many kinds of life forms, after the universe of the material elements has already been formed. However, Brahma is created by the primal source. Thus, we are not interested in the secondary sources, but in the primary or original source from which the secondary sources have emanated. The purpose of Vedānta Sūtra is that primal source of everything.

Topic 3

QUESTION

How should I inquire into Brahman?

Now that the previous sūtra states that we should inquire into Brahman because it is the origin of everything, the question is: How can I know the nature of the thing from which everything originates? What methods must I use?

1.1.3 (3)

शास्त्रयोनत्वात्

śāstrayonitvāt

śastra—the scripture; yonitvāt—from being the mother (of knowledge).

TRANSLATION

From the scripture, which is the mother (of the knowledge of Brahman).

COMMENTARY

It's noteworthy that methods such as empirical observation and logical inference are not mentioned here. We will see later that this position will be revised. For now, we can say that empirical observation and logical inference employ the senses and the mind, and the origin of everything is also the origin of the senses the mind. One of the problems in scientific causality is that the cause determines the effect, but the effect doesn't determine the cause. For example, if you push a billiard ball using a cue, then you can say that the ball will move. However, if the ball is moving, then you cannot say that it was pushed by the cue; it may as well have been pushed by another ball, which was then pushed by a cue, or by a ball, which was pushed by another ball, which was pushed by the cue. In this way, there are infinite plausible explanations of an effect. This problem is known as the underdetermination of cause from the effect in Western philosophy. It implies that if the senses and the mind are effects, then we cannot know their cause from these effects. Hence, revealed knowledge given by the Vedic scriptures is the only means of knowing the original cause.

The problem of underdetermination entails that there are many possible explanations of any observation. Each explanation postulates a different cause. Given that the senses and the mind are effects, they underdetermine the cause, and many potential causes could be speculated. To avoid such speculation, and to arrive at the definitive cause, one must accept the scripture. If this cause is known, then the effects of this cause can be derived. Therefore, the origin of everything becomes the hypothesis based on which we study everything. When reason and experience are applied to this hypothesis, and everything else is explained based on the hypothesis, then reason and experience become the methods for confirming the hypothesis. The knowledge received from scripture, therefore, doesn't eliminate the use of reason and experience, except that its use is restricted to the verification of knowledge, rather than its discovery.

Topic 4

QUESTION

How can you say that by studying the scripture I will know Brahman?

The Vedic scriptures deal in many topics, such as the worship of demigods, the rituals of daily life, the narrations of the material world including cosmology, the histories of the past kingdoms, how the universe was created, the various types of species, the cycle of birth and death, etc. Therefore, how can we preclude all these topics and focus exclusively on Brahman? A related objection is that the scriptures often make seemingly contradictory claims, meant for different times, places, contexts, and persons. Which claim applies to which time, place, situation, or person is not always evident from the scripture. Therefore, one can argue that since the scripture deals with such diversities, therefore, it cannot tell us about unity. Since the scriptures cover the duality of this world and are therefore often contradictory, how do we know the Absolute Truth?

1.1.4 (4)

तत् तु समन्वयात्

tat tu samanvayāt

tat—that; tu—but; samanvayāt—on account of agreement or harmony.

TRANSLATION

But that (Brahman is known only from the scriptures), because (the understanding of Brahman) brings agreement or harmony (in the diversity).

COMMENTARY

This sūtra answers the doubt about why the study of scripture leads us to the knowledge of Brahman. The answer is that although the scriptures deal with many topics, they have a common goal, namely the understanding of Brahman. In this regard, we can envision the scriptures as a tree of knowledge. The tree has many trunks, branches, twigs, and leaves. But the tree has only one root. The leaves, branches, and trunks represent the duality and diversity of this world; however, the root from which diversity emerges is non-dual or singular. In short, the scriptures are dealing with both duality and the non-dual. However, non-dual unity is the cause of the duality and reconciles it. However, this also means that we cannot treat everything in the scripture as Absolute Truth. Some statements of scriptures are indeed like the leaves, branches, and trunks; while we accept them as true, they are not be considered the Absolute Truth. There is hence a distinction between relative and absolute truth; the latter being defined as that which reconciles the diversity and duality of the other descriptions. The progress in knowledge, therefore, represents the path from the leaves through the twigs and trunks to the root of the tree. That root is identified as Brahman: It is both the origin of the tree as well as the destination of knowledge, although the destination is to be attained by understanding the reconciliation of the diversity. Brahman is that which harmonizes the contradictions.

Topic 5

QUESTION

You state that Brahman reconciles the oppositions and contradictions. But when you combine the oppositions and contradictions, they must mutually negate each other, and the ultimate result of reconciliation must be nothingness. How can we say that the reconciliation of contradictions and duality results in the knowledge of Absolute Truth if their combination creates nothingness?

This argument is employed in Buddhism. The argument states that the world is opposites, but to know the Absolute Truth, we must negate both oppositions. This process is also sometimes called neti-neti or not this and not that. In classical logic, the principle of mutual exclusion states that either one of the opposites must be true. Thus, if X is false, then not-X must be true. But what if both X and not-X are simultaneously true in different contexts? Since the Absolute Truth is the origin of both X and not-X, their combination must negate both X and not-X and we must end up with nothingness. If the origin of everything is nothingness, then how can this nothingness be known? After all, isn't it impossible to conceive of something that is neither X and not-X? By the fact that it reconciles the opposites, the Absolute Truth also becomes unknowable!

This point is also asserted as the claim that the source of everything cannot be grasped by words because words employ oppositions (such as hot and cold, black and white), and the source of duality must be beyond such opposites. Since the source reconciles all oppositions, and the words are representations of the opposites, therefore, the primal source cannot be expressed in terms of these oppositions. Therefore, we cannot use any word to describe Brahman, and even if some such word was employed it would just mean nothingness.

In another alternative form, the argument is presented as the distinction between forms and the formless. The forms of this world—which include the words used to describe the world—are representations of either side of duality. When this duality is reconciled, the result would be formless. Since everything has emanated from Brahman, therefore, language must have emanated from Brahman. Just as the reconciliation of words would result in something formless, similarly, the reconciliation of all duality must result in formlessness. Brahman must, therefore, be something formless, and hence it cannot be described by words, which are forms. Since the scripture is expressed in words, therefore, the descriptions must also be inadequate in describing Brahman.

1.1.5 (5)

ईक्षतेर्न अशब्दम्

īkṣaterna aśabdam

īkṣateḥ—seeing (thinking); na—not; aśabdam—that which cannot be expressed through words, or that which can't be spoken of (i.e., formless).

TRANSLATION

We cannot see or know that which is formless.

COMMENTARY

This sūtra accepts the argument that the formless cannot be known—and yet refutes it by providing a counterargument that if the Absolute Truth cannot be known then knowledge would be impossible. If knowledge is impossible, then the origin of everything cannot be known, and if the purpose of life is to know the origin, then this purpose cannot be fulfilled. This leads to nihilism, such that the ultimate meaning cannot be sought because there is no ultimate meaning. Or, that ultimately, the meaning is nothingness. This is indeed the path of Buddhism where ultimate reality is nothingness. Buddhism also says that reality cannot be grasped by words—which are forms—therefore there is no point in reading scripture that describes the truth in words. Buddhism also prescribes that the goal of life is to empty the mind and silence the senses.

This is the rejection of all knowledge that comes as forms. If we take away forms, then we cannot hear, see, or perceive anything. Similarly, this process applies to thought as well. Even ideas have forms. Therefore, if we remove the forms, then we cannot think either. Emptiness, nothingness, and nihilism are alternatives, but this sūtra doesn't advocate them. It just says that if we reject forms, then it would be impossible to know anything. Indirectly, this is a prelude to the subsequent conclusion that the non-dual Absolute Truth must also have a form. If we start with the premise that the Absolute Truth must be known, and then we conclude that it cannot be known, then we have ended up in a self-contradiction. This sūtra simply highlights that self-contradiction.

QUESTION

You are stating two mutually contradictory things. First, that the Absolute Truth reconciles the oppositions of this world. Second, this reconciliation of oppositions can be expressed through words, which are implicitly understood as forms and must be subject to duality. How do you reconcile this conflict?

In the previous sūtra, a proof by contradiction was presented, which is not totally satisfying. One still wants to know how the Absolute Truth can be the reconciliation of contradictions without these forms canceling each other.

1.1.6 (6)

गौणश्चेत् न आत्मशब्दात्

gauṇaścet na ātmaśabdāt

gauṇaḥ—the three gunas; cet—know; na—not; ātmaśabdāt—from the words used to describe the ātmā, i.e., the soul.

TRANSLATION

Know that the three gunas are not the words for the soul.

COMMENTARY

The previous sūtra proved the impossibility of claiming knowledge of Absolute Truth if this truth is formless. But the reader asks: How can we know something transcendent? This sūtra offers the example of the soul. The soul is beyond the material guna (modes of nature) and yet it can be known. If the material modes were canceling each other, then, anything beyond these material modes would be nothingness. But the soul is not nothingness. This is illustrative because Buddhism indeed takes the argument of nothingness all the way and says that there is no soul or God. Once the dualities are dissolved, even the self is dissolved, and there is, hence, no eternal self. This sūtra distinguishes the Vedānta doctrine from that of Buddhism by asserting that the soul is beyond the three modes of nature, and yet this transcendence is not nothingness.

Now, one can argue: Whatever you call the soul, is not beyond the three modes. That individual is only a product of the three modes of nature. So, it is important to understand what the three modes are, and how the soul is beyond these modes. The central problem is that the three modes describe the qualities, such as short or tall, dark or fair, young or old, male or female, beautiful or ugly, rich or poor, etc. But a rich person can become poor, a young person becomes old, someone beautiful can become ugly, etc. Through all these attribute transformations, the self remains unchanged, because we also claim that the *same* person who was previously rich is now poor; the same person who was previously young is now old; the same person who was previously beautiful has now become ugly. Thus, through the changing attributes ascribed to the person, the person remains unchanged. The term ātmā or 'self' pertains to this unchanging identity of the person to whom many changing attributes can be applied.

The distinction between the ātmā and the modes of nature is quite like that between an *object* and a *property*, which is often made in modern science. For example, a ball is an object and the speed of the ball is its property. The ball can move faster or slower, and the properties of the ball can change. But through this change in property, we say that the *same* ball changed its speed. The transcendence of the soul can therefore be established even within the world of the material modes—not necessarily by transcending this world. The three modes are the properties, and the object to which the properties are applied is the ātmā. These properties change over time, but the object remains unchanged.

We can extend this analogy and say that Brahman can be different from the duality of this world, and yet it can be ascribed these dual properties. In effect, Brahman is the object and the properties ascribed to this object are distinct from the object. To know Brahman, we must transcend the material attributes.

In the Bhagavad-Gita (chapter 2, verse 45), Lord Kṛṣṇa says:

trai-guṇya-viṣayā vedā
nistrai-guṇyo bhavārjuna
nirdvandvo nitya-sattva-stho
niryoga-kṣema ātmavān

> The Vedas mainly deal with the subject of the three modes of material nature. Rise above these modes, O Arjuna. Be transcendental to all of them. Be free from all dualities and from all anxieties for gain and safety and be established in the Self.

The above verse recognizes that the Vedas contain information that is colored by the three modes of nature, but they also contain transcendental information. The goal of knowledge is to rise above these modes and know the self and Brahman which are transcendental. In this regard, we can note that this sūtra introduces a third category called the ātmā or the individual soul, which is different from the previous two categories—Brahman and the three guna. The impersonal interpretations reject the individuality of the ātmā. They claim that there is only one object—Brahman—and by the attachment of attributes, Brahman is perceived as the ātmā. But if that were true, then the ātmā could not be transcendental; it would be a byproduct of the three modes. The fact that it is called transcendental here means that it is not a product of three modes.

QUESTION

You have earlier referred to Brahman, and the three modes, and now you are also saying that the ātmā is transcendental to the three modes. But your statement implies that the ātmā is caught in the control of the modes. If that is the case, then how the ātmā become liberated from the three modes?

1.1.7 (7)

तन्निष्ठस्य मोक्षोपदेशात्

tanniṣṭhasya mokṣopadeśāt

tat—to that; niṣṭhasya—of the devoted; mokṣopadeśāt—from the teaching of salvation.

TRANSLATION

From the teaching of salvation of the devoted to that (Brahman).

COMMENTARY

This sūtra states that if one wants to extricate oneself from the duality of this material world, then faith in the Absolute Truth is needed. The existence of this faith entails a distinction between the ātmā and the Absolute Truth. In the Bhagavad-Gita 7.14, Lord Kṛṣṇa makes a similar assertion as follows:

daivī hy eṣā guṇa-mayī
mama māyā duratyayā
mām eva ye prapadyante
māyām etām taranti te

> This divine energy of Mine, consisting of the three modes of material nature, is difficult to overcome. But those who have surrendered unto Me can easily cross beyond it.

The previous sūtra asserted that the ātmā is beyond the three modes of nature. If the ātmā is real, then there are numerous individuals. Once we recognize that there are numerous ātmā then neither of these can be the Absolute Truth. Rather, the Absolute Truth must be separate from the ātmā. Thus, by distinguishing the ātmā from the three modes of nature, we naturally establish the distinction between the ātmā and the Absolute Truth or Brahman. This contrasts with the impersonal interpretations of Vedānta Sūtra where there are only two realities—the three modes of nature and Brahman. This sūtra alludes to the distinction between the ātmā and Brahman and states that freedom from the three modes of nature is attained for those who have faith in the Brahman.

From the previous sūtras we can see how three categories—namely, ātmā, Brahman, and guna are recognized. The ātmā was stated to be transcendental to guna, and this sūtra says that it can be liberated by devotion to Brahman. Thus, in a very few sūtras, the conclusion of Vedānta has been summarized. This devotion between ātmā and Brahman means that the term Brahman is not used here in an impersonal sense. It is rather a reference to the Supreme Lord. This will also become amply clear in the subsequent sūtras which speak about how the Lord expands into diversity and then merges it back into Himself.

QUESTION

If liberation is obtained for those who have faith in the Absolute Truth, does it mean that everyone who is without this faith does not obtain liberation?

In Vedas, four kinds of endeavors are described. These are called dharma, artha, kāma, and moksha. The first three pertain to the performance of one's mundane duties, the accumulation of wealth, and the enjoyment of life using this wealth. The Vedas state that the fourth endeavor—namely moksha or salvation from the material entanglement—is the ultimate purpose of life. The previous sūtra asserted that this salvation requires us to disentangle ourselves from the three modes of nature, but that goal cannot be achieved without faith in the Absolute Truth. Therefore, while the pursuit of dharma, artha, and kāma is described in various Vedic texts, the fourth endeavor of moksha is not possible with the knowledge of these three endeavors. Rather, since it is the fourth pursuit, its achievement would require the rejection of the first three and the acquisition of something that yields moksha. The reader is now curious: Since salvation is not achieved by the performance of the first three endeavors, should one reject the portions of Vedic texts that deal in the first three endeavors?

1.1.8 (8)

हेयत्वावचनाच्च

heyatvāvacanācca

heyatva—inferiority; avachanāt—from not being stated (by the scriptures as leading to the salvation of the soul from matter); ca—also.

TRANSLATION

From not being stated (by the scriptures as leading to the salvation of the soul), they (i.e., all other statements of the Vedas) are also considered inferior.

COMMENTARY

This sūtra confirms the claim of the question, asserting that while Vedas deal in dharma, artha, kāma, and moksha, the inquiry into Brahman pertains to moksha. It is a summary rejection of significant portions of the Vedic texts. In most religions of this world, all texts are given equal importance. But this is not the case for Vedic scriptures. Even though there are texts that describe how to live in this world, by describing marriage procedures, the rules of governing a nation, the nature of matter as created by the three modes of nature, etc., these are considered aparā vidya or inferior knowledge and must be rejected in comparison to those portions of the Veda that deal solely in transcendence.

This sūtra gives insights into how to distinguish between different scriptures. It exhorts us to neglect those scriptures that are dealing with material well-being, ascendency to higher planetary systems, different kinds of material enjoyments, the acquisition of wealth and improving life in the present world, while focusing on those scriptures where salvation is being recommended. Scriptures that deal with dharma, artha, and kāma will also keep us bound to the material world. But the scriptures about the Absolute Truth will lead us toward salvation. Therefore, a distinction between mundane and transcendental knowledge is made here. The transcendental scriptures lead to salvation, while the mundane scriptures keep a person bound to the modes of nature.

QUESTION

I understand the difference between inferior and superior knowledge, but I'm only well-versed in the inferior knowledge—i.e., the knowledge of this material world (dharma, artha, kāma). What is the nature of transcendence?

By drawing a distinction between the knowledge important for dharma, artha, and kāma vs. the knowledge necessary for moksha, the reader has understood that everything in the Vedic texts is not to be considered at the same level. He is now inquisitive about the nature of the Absolute Truth. This line of questioning implies a rejection of the mundane parts of knowledge, namely, those concerned with the material well-being and enjoyment of this world.

1.1.9 (9)

स्वाप्ययात्

svāpyayāt

svāpyayāt—from merging in one's self.

TRANSLATION

(The Brahman is known) from that which merges in itself.

COMMENTARY

To understand this sūtra, we need to discuss the process of creation and dissolution. Creation is like the emanation of trunks, branches, and leaves from a root, and dissolution is the retraction of the manifested leaves, branches, and trunks into the root. During dissolution, the element of Earth merges into Water, Water merges into Fire, Fire merges into Air, and Air merges into Ether. The Ether then merges into the mind, which then merges into the intellect, which then merges into the ego, which then merges into the mahattattva, which then merges into pradhāna. During creation, pradhāna manifests into mahattattva, which then manifests into the ego, from which other elements such as the intellect, mind, senses, besides the elements such as Ether, Air, Fire, Water, and Earth, and expand. In this hierarchy of element manifestation, the source is called sūkshma or subtle while the product is called sthūla or gross. Every sthūla element manifests from a sūkshma element. And, every sthūla element merges into something sūkshma. If this process were used indefinitely, then there must always be a higher element from which the previous element manifests. That would, in turn, lead to an infinite cascade of material elements.

This sūtra states that this process of expansion and dissolution has a natural end in the Absolute Truth. Everything expands from this Truth and merges back into this Truth; however, the Absolute Truth has not expanded from anything else. It is rather self-expanding and self-contracting. Therefore, unlike the material elements which have an origin in another element, the Absolute Truth has no such origin, as it expanded out of itself. So, here, a distinction is drawn between matter and God, namely, that the material elements have expanded from a higher element, but the Absolute Truth is self-expanding. By studying matter, we can understand how the lower element has expanded from a higher element, but to find the Absolute Truth, we must find that element that expands from itself and contracts into itself. When the Absolute Truth rests within itself, there is no world. The world is created from the Absolute Truth expanding itself. And upon dissolution, everything goes back into the Absolute Truth.

Critics of religion sometimes ask: If God created everything, then who created God? The question is rhetorical because it can be posed for any kind of theory of origin. For example, we can ask: If Big Bang created the universe, then what created the Big Bang? The answer generally offered to this kind of question is that before the Big Bang there was a Big Crunch; that there is no origin of the universe, and the universe merely expands and contracts. A similar type of claim is made in this sūtra—there is no origin to the Absolute Truth. Rather, everything expands from this Absolute Truth and collapses back into it. The two explanations differ only in one respect—namely, that God is a person, and the Big Bang is impersonal. The expansion of the person is based on His will, but the expansion of the Big Bang has thus far no known explanation.

QUESTION

You have earlier stated that Brahman is the origin of everything. You are now stating that Brahman is also the thing that manifests from itself, and therefore has no other prior origin. So, in what state was the world before it was manifest from the Absolute Truth? Where was it before it was manifest?

There is a subtle distinction between the ideas of *creation* (as found in other religious texts, where God creates the world) and that of *manifestation* which is found in Vedic texts. The problem of creation necessitates the existence of some 'stuff' from which God must create the universe. But in the idea of manifestation, God is the 'stuff' from which everything manifests. But what happens when the world is not manifest? In what shape or form does it exist? Clearly, if it is being manifest—rather than being created—it must exist eternally. But if it exists eternally, why is it sometimes manifest and sometimes unmanifest?

1.1.10 (10)

गतिसामान्यात्

gatisāmānyāt

gati—movement; sāmānyāt—from the universal undifferentiated.

TRANSLATION

From the movement of the universal undifferentiated (diversity is caused).

COMMENTARY

This sūtra states that diversity is produced from the universal and undifferentiated. The universality indicates a singular cause, and the undifferentiated indicates that it was previously undivided or One. Similarly, once the world has dissolved, it rests in the Absolute Truth. There is hence Oneness of the Absolute Truth, and the diversity rests *within* that Oneness. Oneness and diversity are therefore not mutually opposed ideas. Rather, the diversity manifests from the Oneness due to its movement and then returns to Oneness.

Therefore, even when the world disappears, it doesn't cease to exist. It remains within the Absolute Truth as a potential to manifest again. There is hence a difference between the temporariness of the phenomenal world vs. the eternity of matter. The impersonalist claims that as the phenomenal world appears and disappears, therefore, it must be an illusion; this argument is not false. The problem arises if this illusion of the phenomenal world is extended to matter. If matter is unreal, then what causes the illusion to appear or disappear?

The difference between illusion and reality is now simply this—all illusion is created by reality, but the illusion is occasionally produced although that reality is eternal. In short, we see that reality occasionally and hence call it an 'illusion'. If something is eternal, but not seen always, then how do we understand its existence? The answer is that it always exists as a possibility but is sometimes visible as a phenomenon. If it is visible, it is not 'created'. If it is invisible, it is not 'destroyed'. It is simply manifest and then unmanifest. The unmanifest state exists in the Absolute Truth, as many kinds of potentiality.

QUESTION

The śrutī primarily speaks about the Oneness of Brahman. But you are insisting that there is diversity within Brahman. This would imply that Brahman is not formless; rather just like the body has front and back, head and toe, left and right, similarly, the Brahman would have a form with many aspects. How can you justify this stance when the śrutī mainly speaks about the Oneness?

1.1.11 (11)

श्रुतत्वाच्च

śrutatvācca

śrutatvāt—from being declared by the śrutī; ca—also.

TRANSLATION

(That Brahman comprises diversity) from being declared by śrutī also.

COMMENTARY

This sūtra acknowledges that Brahman has a form; there is Oneness, and diversity manifests from that Oneness. But that diversity rests in that Oneness. Unlike the seed from which the tree manifests on the supplication of soil, air, and water, there is nothing external to the Absolute Truth. However, this eternal reality is not always visible. The creation of the universe is not something coming into existence. It is something that exists eternally becoming visible.

The novelty of this sūtra is that it accepts that the Absolute Truth is not just Oneness, but that diversity exists inside that Oneness. The implication is that Absolute Truth has a form in which diversity exists within the unity. The sūtra points out that while śrutī speaks about the Oneness, it also sometimes refers to the diversity inside the unity. In short, the śrutī is not describing a formless Oneness. It is describing a Oneness that has form and the manifest diversities are the aspects of this form. The emphasis in śrutī is primarily on Oneness, which is why the sūtra states that the śrutī 'also' speak about the diversity.

Thus, this sūtra accepts both unity and diversity in Brahman—yes, the śrutī talks about Oneness, but it also talks about the diversity inside the unity. So, we don't have to take the statements about Oneness in isolation. We must rather consider them along with the statements where the Oneness is described as a form. With that form, the Oneness naturally becomes comprised of diversity.

Topic 6

QUESTION

If the Brahman is already Oneness, why does it expand into diverse forms? Since diversity is produced by the expansion of the Oneness into the many, what causes this expansion, and how should the diversity be explained?

1.1.12 (12)

आनन्दमयोऽभ्यासात्

ānandamayo'bhyāsāt

ānandamayaḥ—consists of bliss; abhyāsāt—because of habit or practice.

TRANSLATION

Because of habit or practice (of enjoyment), Brahman consists of bliss.

COMMENTARY

Here an answer to the question—how One becomes many—is given. The answer is pleasure. The cause for expansion of Brahman from One to many is the enjoyment of pleasure. The One has many aspects, but awareness of each aspect produces a different pleasure. The One is habituated to pleasure, and the aspects are separated by the desire for happiness. To obtain happiness, one must have an experience, and that experience involves a distinction between a knower and a known. Therefore, if only Oneness existed, then there cannot be happiness. Even self-experience involves a distinction between the knower and the known, although they are the same individual. Therefore, separation from Oneness is essential to produce happiness. If Brahman is accustomed to the pursuit of happiness, then it cannot exist as Oneness; it must also separate.

In sūtra 1.1.7 (7) a distinction between the Absolute Truth and the ātmā was made. This distinction can be understood as being caused by the desire for pleasure. The One—which is Brahman—divides itself into many, and those many include the ātmā; the division creates the distinction between the knower and the known. The different knowers have different desires to know. Thus, the choice to view the known in different ways and aspects manifests. The desire for pleasure creates diverse ātmā and the diverse aspects of the Oneness.

In one sense, the One is enjoying with Itself, because there is nothing other than that One. In another sense, the One has divided into many parts—the knower and the known—by the desire for enjoyment. The diversity in the One is therefore ultimately a production of the diversity in choice and pleasure. Unless the pleasure in each aspect was different, there would be no diversity.

The diverse visions of the Oneness are a property of the ātmā, not of the Absolute Truth. The Absolute Truth is the combination of all the aspects but in the vision of each ātmā, the Oneness is perceived differently. Consider the example of a person who is a father, a husband, a friend, a brother, a son, and an employee in different relations. The person is the same, but through different relations, a different aspect of the person is revealed. The feature of being a father is not manifest in the friend relation, and the feature of being an employee is not manifest in the husband relation. Just as the person is manifest in different ways for different knowers, similarly, the One is manifest in different forms in the vision of different ātmā—who perceive the One through different relationships. This diversity attributed to the One is in the ātmā and it is also in Brahman. But in Brahman, the diversity is invisible, and in the ātmā it is visible.

It is implied here that the state of Oneness is not pleasurable because pleasure is created only by interaction with others. Since in the state of Oneness there is nothing other than One, the One expands into many to enjoy. We can infer from here that the One is not a social entity, but the many are social entities. However, these many are also expanded from the One to create society.

QUESTION

If the bliss of Brahman is attained through the division of the One into the many, then should we not say that this divided state of the Oneness is a modification of the One? In other words, the many parts of the One must come into existence when the One seeks bliss, but otherwise, it remains Oneness.

Here an argument can be made that Oneness is the fundamental state of Brahman, and the diversity is the occasional emergence of bliss. The argument would imply that diversity is not eternal but an accident of the creation of desire, resulting in the division. Of course, the argument would then beg the question—How does Brahman develop the desire for pleasure? And the answer to that question would then have to say that the desire for pleasure is a vikāra or modification of Brahman. The term vikāra can be understood as a random fluctuation, like a wave in an ocean. If the desire for happiness is a vikāra in the Brahman, then we would conclude that the One may divide into many, but this change is temporary. Whatever is temporary would become unreal, therefore, the expansions would be unreal. This argument is the extension of a similar idea in yoga philosophy where the chitta or the consciousness of the ātmā is described as an ocean in which desires emerge as occasional waves. The purpose of yoga is then said to be the termination of the vritti or modifications of the chitta. If this idea is extended to Brahman, then we must say that the desire for pleasure is a vritti or vikāra of Brahman—quite like a wave emerging in a calm ocean. We might say that the natural state of the ocean is to be calm, and without the vritti or vikāra of waves, Brahman is Oneness. Consequently, the division of the One into many must be temporary, and indeed termination of these desires (and hence the division of the One into many) must be the primordial state of Brahman. It would follow that these divisions of the One into the many must not be considered fundamental because the desires are temporary.

1.1.13 (13)

विकारशब्दान्नेति चेत् न प्राचुर्यात्

vikāraśabdānneti cet na prācuryāt

vikāraśabdāt—from the statements of vikāra or modification; na—not; iti—thus; cet—if; na—not so; prācuryāt—from the abundance.

TRANSLATION

If it is said that from the statements of the impossibility of modification in Brahman we cannot (say that Brahman is bliss), (we say) not so, from the abundance (of bliss in Brahman).

COMMENTARY

This sūtra refutes the idea that bliss arises as a modification or vikāra in Brahman. The term ānandamayaḥ of the last sūtra cannot be interpreted as an occasional modification, because (as this sūtra clarifies), the pleasure is prachur or abundant. Abundance implies that some part of Oneness remains undivided. However, that doesn't mean that division is an aberration. Hence, the desire for pleasure is not pervasive and Oneness exists; but the desire for pleasure is also not occasional such that the division of the Oneness is incidental. Brahman can exist in an undivided form, but Brahman also exists in a differentiated form. Therefore, both the differentiated and undifferentiated forms are eternal.

If the effect is small—like the small waves in a massive ocean—then we can say that the natural state of the ocean is to be without waves. However, if the nature of the ocean is such that there are always some waves, then we cannot insist that the natural state of the ocean is to remain calm. The argument depends on the extent to which waves are found in the ocean. In this sūtra a similar argument is made—the waves of differentiation are not occasional; they are abundant. This doesn't mean that the entire ocean is turbulent. However, it means that the emergence of waves is also a natural property of the ocean.

This sūtra rejects the universality of Oneness, without completely denying that Oneness can indeed exist. Therefore, both Oneness (without differentiation) and differentiation (caused by the desire for pleasure) are permanent features of the Brahman. In fact, a more extensive argument about the fundamental nature of desire can be made as follows: If the desire for pleasure is natural, then the suspension of that desire is also a possibility. However, if the desire for pleasure is unnatural, then its emergence is problematic. So, even if we accept that the desire for pleasure is a vikāra, we would still be straddled with the problem of explaining how this modification emerges suddenly. However, if the desire for pleasure is eternal, then the suspension of this desire would be merely an aspect of desire: To not make a choice is also a choice. The suspension of choice is not the negation of choice; it is the choice of not dividing and therefore not selecting one of the divisions. Therefore, the suspension of choice is one of the applications of choice, however, the emergence of choice (if choice and differentiation are denied as being fundamental) is deeply problematic.

This nuanced understanding of choice entails that by and large there is differentiation and individuality indicated by the fact that the desire for pleasure is abundant. However, this desire is not a universal fact, and it is possible to suspend the desire and thereby dissolve the differentiation into Oneness.

QUESTION

Even if the One had pleasure originally, which then resulted in the division into many, does it not mean that now I have acquired the desire for pleasure and can, therefore, pursue my happiness without the Absolute Truth?

Here an argument about the independence of the living entity is made. The argument says that if happiness is all-pervasive, then everyone is responsible for their happiness. Therefore, each living entity doesn't have to be subordinate to the happiness of the Absolute Truth, which caused the original division. That is, everyone can pursue their happiness, and they don't have to serve the happiness of the Absolute Truth. So, the Absolute Truth created the individual beings to enjoy, but because these are now individuals, they have become free of the Absolute Truth. Due to the pervasiveness of happiness in each soul, these souls must now be entitled to pursue their separate joys and pleasures.

The individual pursuit of happiness is considered a fundamental right in modern times. Due to this, everyone becomes selfish: They think that they have a right to pursue their happiness, regardless of the happiness of others. If, however, we insist that we must please someone else in order to be happy, then the conclusion is that we must be their servants. Under this servitude, the pleasure of the master decides the pleasure of the servant. Factually, nobody wants this servitude; everyone wants to be free to pursue their happiness without having to please anyone else. Since everyone is pursuing their happiness, nobody is concerned about whether someone else is happy. Now, it depends on the individual's capacity to acquire the means for this happiness, and everyone may not be equally capable. Ideally, we expect that people achieve happiness by making others happy. But the notion that we shall become happy by pleasing others can seem very improbable: What if the other person is selfish, and they accept the happiness that we provide to them and do not reciprocate? The fear of being cheated in the process of pleasing others makes everyone wary of serving others. This then reinforces the idea that everyone is only responsible for their own happiness, and if the happiness of others were forced upon us—as the means to become happy—then our fundamental right to happiness would itself be denied (due to the possibility of being deceived in the process).

1.1.14 (14)

तद्धेतुव्यपदेशाच्च

taddhetuvyapadeśācca

tat—that (pleasure of the Brahman); hetu—the purpose, vyapa—pervasive; deśāt—from being in all the places; ca—and.

TRANSLATION

From being in all the places, that (pleasure of Brahman) is also the pervasive purpose (of everything).

COMMENTARY

This sūtra refutes the claim that everyone can pursue their separate happiness because the Absolute Truth is not only the cause of their individuality but also the purpose of their existence. In short, because the individual soul was created due to the desire for happiness in the Absolute Truth, the fulfillment of this desire is the purpose of the individual ātmā. This purpose—for which the ātmā has been created—must become the purpose of the individual and the ātmā can be happy only if this purpose is fulfilled. Thus, no ātmā can become happy by itself; it can become happy only in relation to the Absolute Truth. Therefore, ātmā's happiness must be obtained by making the Absolute Truth happy. If the ātmā is not making the Absolute Truth happy, then it is not fulfilling its purpose, and the ātmā cannot, therefore, become happy on its own. Thus, although the ātmā is an individual, its individuality is dependent on the fulfillment of its purpose—and that purpose is the happiness of the One.

Now, you could also argue that maybe some individuals may serve the Absolute Truth, while others may become independent of the Absolute Truth. To counter this argument, the word 'pervasive' and 'in all places' is used. That is, you cannot go anywhere to seek independent happiness. The Absolute Truth is the cause of happiness or bliss in all places, and there is no place where He is not the cause. It also follows from the pervasiveness of the cause that you can be anywhere and still be blissful, in connection to the Absolute Truth, because no place is devoid of the influence of that Absolute Truth in creating the experience of bliss. Thus, nowhere is bliss possible without the Absolute Truth's bliss. And everywhere bliss is possible from the bliss of the Absolute Truth.

QUESTION

How can the individual soul become the cause of the happiness of the Absolute Truth when the Absolute Truth is the greatest while the soul is incredibly small? How can such a small entity create an effect of bliss in the greatest?

Here an argument about the incapacity of the soul is made. In the previous sūtra, it has been asserted that the ātmā is not independent and must serve the happiness of the Absolute Truth. The reader now wonders how he can serve the Absolute Truth when he's so small and incapable of making a difference to the Absolute Truth, which is the original cause of everything. Therefore, the project of fulfilling the happiness of the Absolute Truth seems unachievable.

1.1.15 (15)

मान्त्रवर्णिकमेव च गीयते

māntravarṇikameva ca gīyate

māntravarṇikam—the letters of mantras; eva—certainly; ca—also; gīyate—in singing or glorifying.

TRANSLATION

Certainly, the letters of mantras are also in the glory (of Brahman).

COMMENTARY

The answer to the question of how the individual soul can please the Absolute Truth is given here. The answer is that the soul can glorify the Absolute Truth using mantras. Since the word giyate or songs is used here, we can infer that this sūtra refers to the Sāmaveda, which comprises songs of glorification of the Absolute Truth. The Absolute Truth is infinite. However, the same Absolute Truth is represented through the symbols of the songs and names. These symbols can be grasped and known by the individual soul. Just like the universe is infinite, but the word 'universe' is finite. And this word encompasses the infinity of the universe into a finite word, similarly, the Absolute Truth is infinite, but the same Absolute Truth is finite when represented through symbols.

Implicit in this description is the idea that the Absolute Truth is both meaning and existence. The existence of the Absolute Truth cannot fit inside the soul. But the meaning of the Absolute Truth can fit within the soul. When we use the word 'universe', we haven't understood everything in the universe. And yet, by the word 'universe' we refer to the same thing. Semantically these two are identical, but physically they are different. Thus, the claim that the infinite cannot be captured by the finite is refuted. Yes, the infinite is not physically captured by the finite; but the infinite is semantically captured by the words.

QUESTION

Can we not consider these mantras as referring to the glorification of ātmā instead of the Absolute Truth? Why would we prefer the Absolute Truth?

This is a variation of the earlier question where the ātmā seeks its separate happiness rather than the happiness of the Absolute Truth. In the previous sūtra, it was stated that the Absolute Truth should be pleased by the mantra. But we can ask: Why not consider the chanting of these mantras as the source of one's liberation, rather than the pleasure of the Absolute Truth? Many mantras lead to the peacefulness of the mind, so why should we not consider the purpose of their chanting the liberation of the mind from material troubles?

1.1.16 (16)

नेतरोऽनुपपत्तेः

netaro'nupapatteḥ

na—not; itaraḥ—the other, i.e., the jīvā; anupapatteḥ—because of the unreasonableness (or an invalid, illogical conclusion).

TRANSLATION

(The Brahman and) not the other (i.e., the individual souls are indicated here) on account of the unreasonableness (of the latter assumption).

COMMENTARY

This sūtra asserts that the mantras to be sung are not meant for the satisfaction of the ātmā. In many New Age religions, the chanting of mantras is said to quieten the mind. Indeed, the meaning of 'mantra' is itself the freedom of the mind (manah trayate iti mantra—that which frees the mind is called mantra). So, one can argue that the purpose of the mantra is the freedom of the mind from the incessant flow of thoughts and feelings, the resulting peace of mind can be considered the purpose of the mantra chanting. However, this sūtra negates such an interpretation of the mantra as being meant for the happiness and satisfaction of the self. One can then ask: But by chanting the mantra we can see that the self is satisfied. So, how can we deny this effect of mantra chanting and claim that its purpose is not the satisfaction of the self when it is practically observed? The answer is that the satisfaction from the chanting of the mantra is due to the satisfaction of the Absolute Truth and since the ātmā is a part of the Absolute Truth, the satisfaction of the Absolute Truth creates self-satisfaction. Like watering the root of the tree waters the trunks, branches, and leaves, similarly, the fact that the chanting of mantras results in the satisfaction of the self doesn't mean that the purpose of these mantras is the satisfaction of the self.

New Age religions claim that the idea of spirituality is the rediscovery of the spiritual nature of the self as different from matter. There is no dearth of people who seem to be opposed to the existence of a Supreme Being or God as the person who must be satisfied for a person to become happy. Instead of glorifying the Lord, the New Age religions assert that religion must be freed from the conception of God, and the spiritual entity replacing God is the individual soul. Thus, spiritual practices are meant not for the satisfaction of the Absolute Truth, but the attainment of peace and satisfaction of the individual self.

This sūtra, however, states that such an endeavor is futile. If the mantras are not sung to satisfy the Absolute Truth, then words are uttered but the references of these words are incorrect. When we speak a sentence, there are two types of meanings. First, there is the conceptual meaning, or what the word or sentence states. Second, there is also a reference to the object, which the sentence describes. For instance, if we say that "John is tall", the cognitive meaning is that someone is tall, but the reference is John—a person or individual who is referred to by that statement. The *referential* component of Vedic mantras is the Absolute Truth, and the names used in glorification refer to it. If we retain the cognitive meaning, but we don't understand the reference, then the statements of glorification are false. For instance, if John is replaced by "I" in the statement, then the claims of the statement would refer to the self; but the self may not be tall. So, although the words are uttered, and their meanings are clearly understood, the statement becomes false. Salvation cannot be expected through the chanting of false utterances. The sūtra states that the glorification of the Absolute Truth cannot be applied to the individual soul. So, even if you chant the Vedic mantras thinking that they are meant for self-satisfaction, ultimately, the utterances are false because the mental intention or reference is misplaced.

Thus, it is not enough to chant the mantras. It is also necessary to mentally refer to the individual being described and glorified through the mantra. There can be some cognitive satisfaction simply by chanting the true statements; however, the truth is not just the conceptual meaning but also the reference. If the reference is missing or is misplaced toward the self, then the utterances are false. Since the meaning of the mantra cannot be truthfully applied to the self, the sūtra says that the view that the mantra refers to the self is illogical.

QUESTION

But we have previously stated that the ātmā was differentiated from the Brahman by the desire for pleasure. Once this differentiation has occurred, then the different ātmā are just like the drops of water separated from the ocean of water. If something is said about the water in the ocean, then it must also apply to the drops of water in the ocean. Then, why can't the statements about the Absolute Truth not apply to the ātmā if the ātmā is a part of the Absolute Truth?

1.1.17 (17)

भेदव्यपदेशाच्च

bhedavyapadeśācca

bheda—difference; vyapadeśāt—because of the declaration; ca—and.

TRANSLATION

And on account of the declaration of the difference (in ātmā and Brahman).

COMMENTARY

It is true that many assertions about Brahman are also true about the ātmā. For example, the Absolute Truth is the capacity for consciousness, knowledge, and pleasure (also called sat, chit, and ānanda). The same is true of the ātmā as well. However, there are other statements about the Absolute Truth that do not apply to the ātmā. For instance, the Absolute Truth is omniscient, but the ātmā is not. The consciousness of the ātmā can be directed toward one thing at a time, but the consciousness of the Absolute Truth can be directed toward everything at once. Thus, the pleasure of the ātmā is limited to that derived from a limited awareness and knowledge at any moment, but the pleasure of the Absolute Truth is unlimited. Therefore, the ātmā and Brahman are *qualitatively* similar as they have the same capacity for awareness, knowledge, and pleasure. But the ātmā and the Absolute Truth are *quantitatively* different because the latter is omniscient and omnipotent while the former only has a limited capacity for knowledge and power. Thus, some statements about the Absolute Truth can also be applied to the ātmā; but not every statement can be used thus.

While we can say that the water in the ocean and the water in the drop have many qualitative similarities, there are also statements about the ocean—such as the "ocean is vast"—which cannot be applied to the drop of water. This similarity and difference between ātmā and Brahman have been the basis of many Vedānta Sūtra interpretations. Of special significance here is the sūtra asserting that they are not identical in all respects. Of course, the ātmā is a part of the Absolute Truth, but the part cannot be equated to the whole in all respects.

QUESTION

If the chanting of mantra must be directed to the pleasure of the Absolute Truth, aren't there other methods by which I can attain my happiness? For example, can I not detach myself from the modes of material nature using reasoning, the cultivation of knowledge, and other methods, such as austerities?

Individualism and independence are deep-seated desires in each person. We trust in our powers of sensation and reason, but we don't have faith in surrender to something other than the self. This question is prominent in today's world where people want to rely on their personal experience and mental prowess to attain their objectives. They don't want to place their faith and trust in someone or something else. There are two main reasons for this. First, there is an individual pride in each person which tells them they are self-sufficient and don't need anything else to attain their goals; surrender to something else would necessitate humility—I'm not capable of attaining my goals on my own and therefore I need to surrender. Second, there is a deep distrust of others, especially in the statements of scriptures. If the scripture says that one must chant the mantra for happiness, what guarantee exists that this process will yield the results that I'm aspiring for? Maybe this is all a fanciful imagination of some people which I must examine skeptically. The combination of pride and skepticism makes one distrust any spiritual process that demands that we put faith in something other than our powers of experience and reason. Therefore, if the scripture states that this faith is needed, then the seeker would typically make every possible attempt to avoid this reliance on faith and surrender.

1.1.18 (18)

कामाच्च नानुमानापेक्षा

kāmācca nānumānāpekṣā

kāmāt—from desiring; ca—also; na—not; anumāna—the imagination or speculative knowledge; apekṣā—expectation.

TRANSLATION

From desiring also, the imagined (thing) cannot be expected. Or, from desiring and speculation we cannot expect (to attain the Absolute Truth).

COMMENTARY

There are two possible translations of this sūtra, which are noted above. The first of these translations is quite straightforward. Why can't we attain a perfect life without pleasing Brahman? The answer is: Just by desiring, we cannot achieve the goals. We have to follow the process indicated in the Vedic texts. The second possible translation indicates that we cannot get to the Absolute Truth by speculation. Why? Because innate to that speculation is the idea that the soul is independent of the Absolute Truth, and when logical inference is based on false assumptions, then the conclusions of inference are also false.

All reasoning is based on assumptions or axioms. This is a famous critique of rationalism in Western philosophy where reason only expands upon what has already been assumed in the axioms. For example, Euclid's geometry makes five main assumptions, based on which numerous theorems can be derived; the collection of all these theorems is called Euclidean Geometry. However, these axioms are not necessarily sacrosanct. In 20th century mathematics, Euclid's fifth postulate (namely, that the shortest path between two points is a straight line) was challenged resulting in non-Euclidean geometry. While Euclid's geometry works in most practical day-to-day scenarios on Earth, there are cosmological problems where space must be considered curved—i.e., the shortest path between two points is not a straight line—to explain the bending of light. The existence of non-Euclidean geometry, however, doesn't disprove the theorems of Euclidean geometry, because these proofs are always relative to the axioms.

Mathematics is famous for formulating theories based on different axioms. Whether these theories are useful or not doesn't concern the rationalists. They aim to make assumptions and derive conclusions from them. Whether those assumptions themselves are true or not is beyond reason. Some philosophers of science then argue that these assumptions can be tested empirically. However, the issue is that the testing is relative to the domain in which you apply the theory—e.g., terrestrial vs. celestial problems for geometry. Just as Euclidean geometry is adequate for most terrestrial problems, similarly, unless we find those problems where its assumptions are invalidated, the theory would stand vindicated. The main point is that axioms or assumptions are not true or false; they are simply useful or useless relative to the problem we are trying to solve; if you are trying to build a bicycle, Newton's mechanics works fine; but if you are trying to build an atom bomb, then quantum mechanics is necessary.

Now we come to the main question that concerns us here: How do you choose the problems that are to be solved? What should you consider an important problem that has to be attacked and solved through rationality?

There is no rational prescription for picking problems. What you consider an important problem may be worthless for others. Some people are trying to solve the economic problems of a nation, while others consider earning their day-to-day livelihood an important problem. Some people wonder about the workings of nature, while others only worry about raising a happy family. In short, the problems are our *choices*. We choose a problem, and we make assumptions or axioms that are suitable to solve the chosen problem. Reason operates only when the assumptions have been made. If the chosen assumptions fail to solve the problem, we might go back to the drawing board and make new or different assumptions. Assumptions are thus never true or false; they are only good or bad relative to a chosen problem. The same assumption may be good for one problem but bad for another. Just because the assumption works in one case doesn't make it true; it must work in all cases for it to be true.

Now, we can understand this sūtra, namely, to know the Absolute Truth through reason, we must be trying to solve the ultimate problems of life. Our goal cannot be bicycles, steam engines, economic theories, or atom bombs. The goal must be to know who I am, the purpose of my existence, and the method by which it can be fulfilled. This purpose has been explained previously—i.e., satisfying the Absolute Truth. If we disregard this understanding, then we might frame some false axioms, and the result will also be false conclusions.

The implied criticism is that most people who want to know the Absolute Truth through reason, start with the wrong problem of trying to build a better mousetrap. They frame their axioms suitable to solve the better mousetrap problem. And if the mousetrap is improved, then we call the underlying assumptions as truth. Conditioned by such assumptions we now try to make inferences about the Absolute Truth. We are unprepared to change our axioms because they worked for the better mousetrap. We fail to see that to formulate new axioms, we must fundamentally change the problem. We cannot use the better mousetrap assumptions to solve fundamentally different problems. Hence, before we try to use reasoning to know the Absolute Truth, we must change our desires toward the Absolute Truth. We must be eager to solve the ultimate problems of life, and then axioms can be rationally applied. Based on our desires we choose different problems and make different assumptions.

QUESTION

You stated at the beginning that now we must inquire into the nature of Brahman. You then distinguished Brahman from ātmā and stated that this distinction arises due to the desire for pleasure. You then further said that

the ātmā can attain freedom from the modes of nature by pleasing Brahman. What happened to the goal of knowing Brahman in this process? Haven't we shifted the goal from knowing Brahman to pleasing Brahman, and the goal of knowing has been lost in the process? How can knowing be associated with pleasing?

In the Vedic tradition, there is a contentious issue between the pursuits of knowledge and devotion. The proponents of knowledge or jñāna assert the superiority of the intellect and claim that devotion is inferior. This is due to the recognition that, in this material world, emotions (including desires) are the cause of the bondage of the ātmā to this world. By intelligence, we must learn to control the desires of the mind, and detach the mind from the world. But if we reject reason and inference as a process for attaining Brahman, then how can we ever hope to attain the original goal of knowing the Absolute Truth?

1.1.19 (19)

अस्मिन्नस्य च तद्योगं शास्ति

asminnasya ca tadyogaṃ śāsti

asmin—in Him; asya—of the jīvā; ca—also; tat—that; yogaṃ—union; śāsti—(śrutī) teaches.

TRANSLATION

And moreover, the scripture, teaches that the joining of this (the individual soul), with that (i.e., consisting of bliss—Brahman) results in knowledge.

COMMENTARY

This sūtra uses the term yogam or union between the ātmā and the Absolute Truth. When the ātmā is joined to the Absolute Truth, then knowledge of the Absolute Truth is attained. Therefore, after stating that the Absolute Truth must be glorified using mantras and rejecting the intellectual process of knowing the Absolute Truth, the sūtra states that the goal of knowing the Absolute Truth is not rejected by rejecting the intellectual process. Rather, by the union of the soul with the Absolute Truth, the knowledge of the Absolute Truth is attained. This represents the inversion of the process in which first we know the Absolute Truth and then we become devoted to that Absolute Truth. The previous sūtra stated that it is unreasonable to expect the knowledge of the Absolute Truth to arise without devotion. This sūtra then asserts that if devotion exists, then knowledge naturally arises. Thus, knowledge follows devotion.

Topic 7

QUESTION

To join to the Absolute Truth, I must know what the Absolute Truth is. What does this union truly mean? How to join with the Absolute Truth?

In the previous sūtra, the term yoga was used for the union with the

Absolute Truth. However, before we can unite, we must know the object to be united with. This creates a circular problem—to know Absolute Truth, we must unite with Him; but, to unite, we must know the Absolute Truth. Note that this problem doesn't arise in the case of the intellectual process because if we can know the Absolute Truth by reasoning, then we can subsequently unite with it, form a relationship to the knowledge, and meditate upon it. The previous sūtra and the one before that, however, refuted this idea of being able to know the Absolute Truth without uniting, meditating, or via a relationship. So, this creates a curiosity in the seeker: Where should I find Absolute Truth to unite with?

1.1.20 (20)

अन्तस्तद्धर्मोपदेशात्

antastaddharmopadeśāt

antaḥ—within; tat dharma—His nature; upadeśāt—from the teaching.

TRANSLATION

From the teaching of that essential nature being present within.

COMMENTARY

One possible interpretation of this sūtra is that the ātmā present within (the heart) is the Absolute Truth; indeed, this the interpretation of impersonalism. While this confusion will be clarified in the next sūtra where the distinction between two souls inhabiting the heart is described, even in this sūtra we can see that the term 'tat' indicating 'that' is used. The context reveals that this must denote the Absolute Truth because the previous sūtra spoke about union with the Absolute Truth. So, 'tat dharma' should not be interpreted as referring to the ātmā. Now, 'antah tat dharma' means that the presence of Absolute Truth as the characteristics by which the Absolute Truth is identified. It doesn't entail that the Absolute Truth is itself present, otherwise, the use of the term 'tat dharma' (or that nature) would be unnecessary. We would just state that the Absolute Truth is *in* the self. The implication is that the Absolute Truth is not present in the self, however, its distinguishing characteristics are manifest. For example, the fire spreads its influence, and by this spreading, its presence can be known everywhere, even though the fire is localized. Similarly, the presence of the Absolute Truth can be felt in the heart—like the spreading of heat from fire—although the Absolute Truth is not in the heart. So, the use of "that nature" has a nuanced use in this sūtra that cannot be equated to direct presence. As a result, this presence cannot be conveniently equated to the presence of ātmā.

QUESTION

But we can interpret the above statement to refer to the ātmā if we say that the ātmā is not truly present in the heart, but only visible by its effects. As you have already stated, the ātmā is transcendental to the three modes of

nature, and the body is comprised of these three modes. So, to say that the ātmā is present in the heart would entail that the ātmā is somehow physically inside matter, and therefore not transcendental. Would it not be more accurate to say that the ātmā is transcendental to matter but only by its effects (like the effect of heat due to fire) its presence is visible in the heart? That would imply that that which is inside—and which you are referring to as Brahman—is indeed the ātmā.

In many parts of Vedic literature, it is said that the yogi must withdraw their senses from the external world and focus it upon the heart. Since consciousness spreads to the external world through the senses, it can mean that by withdrawing the senses, consciousness merges within its source. The merger is 'self-knowledge', and the yogi is atmarāma or one who enjoys within oneself. Notably, the property of consciousness is that it is aware of itself and in all forms of awareness of the world, the awareness of the self is always present. So, self-awareness precedes the awareness of the other, but if we withdraw from the awareness of the other then the other ceases to exist. We could now argue that the division of the world into knower and known is the result of the outward movement of consciousness—produced by defocusing on the self and seeking pleasure in something other than itself. If this line of reasoning is extended, one could argue that the world is manifest out of this outward movement of consciousness and it doesn't truly exist 'outside' the self. It is simply a projection of the ātmā like a movie projector projects images outwardly. If therefore, the light of the projector was turned inwardly, then the projection out of the ātmā would also cease to exist, and the distinction between the knower and the known—produced by the outward movement—would cease.

One could now say that by yoga we simply mean the cessation of the distinctions between the knower and the known; when the knower collapses into the known, that union can itself be called yoga. Thus, drawing the consciousness inward, defocusing on the projections, and concentrating on the self would entail detachment from the body and hence liberation from the modes of nature. The term 'tat dharma' in the previous sūtra would now be interpreted as the consciousness of the ātmā—namely, that the ātmā is not present within the heart, however, its effect (like the heat of the fire) as consciousness is seen.

1.1.21 (21)

भेदव्यपदेशाच्चान्यः

bhedavyapadeśāccānyaḥ

bheda—difference; vyapadeśāt—because of the declaration; ca—and, also; anyaḥ—is different, another, other than the jīvā or the individual soul.

TRANSLATION

And there is another one (i.e., the Lord who is different from the individual ātmā animating the body) on account of the declaration of distinction.

COMMENTARY

To refute the argument that yoga is the focusing of the consciousness on the self, this sūtra states directly that which was said indirectly in the previous sūtra—namely, the yoga is not the union with the self; it is rather with another individual who is present in the heart. This second person is generally referred to as Paramātma in the Vedic literature; He is said to be One and yet all-pervasive. The Bhagavad-Gita 13.23 describes this personality in greater clarity:

upadraṣṭānumantā ca
bhartā bhoktā maheśvaraḥ
paramātmeti cāpy ukto
dehe 'smin puruṣaḥ paraḥ

Yet in this body, there is another, a transcendental enjoyer who is the Lord, the supreme proprietor, who exists as the overseer and permitter, and who is known as the Supersoul.

This is further confirmed in the Bhagavad-Gita verse 9.4 as follows:

mayā tatam idaṁ sarvaṁ
jagad avyakta-mūrtinā
mat-sthāni sarva-bhūtāni
na cāhaṁ teṣv avasthitaḥ

By Me, in My unmanifested form, this entire universe is pervaded. All beings are in Me, but I am not in them.

This verse is important for two reasons. First, it states that the Lord pervades everything. Second, it also states that the Lord is not in those things. This is a paradoxical statement, but it can be used to understand the meaning of 'tat dharma' in the previous sūtra. Just as heat spreads from the fire and can be found in many places, but the fire is not directly present everywhere, similarly, the Lord can be One and yet spread to many different things. In fact, the standard analogy of the impersonalist—called pratibimba-vāda, or the argument of reflection—can be directly applied in this case: Just as the sun is one and yet its reflection is indicated in every pot of water, but if you break the pot, then the sun is not destroyed, similarly, the Lord is present in every heart by His qualities, although He is not in the heart. He is present by His distinguishing characteristics—e.g., heat is the characteristic of fire. The presence of the sun heats the pot, even though the sun is not within the pot of water; similarly, the presence of the Lord affects the heart, although He is not confined to the heart.

The implication is that yoga doesn't mean a merger with the self because the self is not the Absolute Truth. As already indicated, there is a difference between the ātmā and the Lord. However, if further confusion exists, then it can be stated that there are two kinds of kṣetrajña or "knowers of the field" (the term 'field' refers to the space of the body). The ātmā is the knower of the body or limited portions of the field. However, the Paramātma knows the entire field, including the fields known by the different individual ātmā. Thus, the ātmā is a limited knower of one field, whereas the Paramātma is also omniscient.

Topic 8

QUESTION

Why should a distinction between ātmā and Paramātma be made? Can we not say that Paramātma is the all-pervasive consciousness, and ātmā is simply the experience of individuality of this consciousness? We could say that the all-pervading entity is the space in which everything exists. And the things within that space would be the experiences of consciousness. We could also say that a consciousness creates its experience and consciousness is One, but experiences are diverse. Then, by dissolving the experience, ātmā and Paramātma can become one entity—in that One, there is consciousness without experience.

Some New Age philosophers suggest that the universe is self-aware, and it is created by the production of experience within a 'field' of consciousness, but this field has no origin. It is like light, but that light doesn't emanate from a source like the sun. The ātmā can now be called an *experience* of consciousness; it exists within the universal field or space, but it is a creation of consciousness and therefore has no reality. Thus, Paramātma is the field, and ātmā is a creation of an experience in the field, and there is no origin of the field itself. Some New Age philosophers say that this 'field' can be equated to a vacuum from which objects pop out as individuals and then pop back in as energy. Thus, the all-pervading energy field transforms automatically, which manifests objects, and when the transformation is reversed then the objects disappear. This appearance and disappearance of objects can be analogically used to explain not just the creation and destruction of the universe, but also ordinary changes.

This view simplifies the ontology (the things that exist) for several reasons. First, we don't have to postulate the existence of a source—i.e., God—who manifests the field; the field is eternal. Second, we don't have to separate matter from consciousness because the field is consciousness and matter is the objects manifest within this field; hence, the problem of matter-consciousness interaction or the distinction between matter and consciousness (which in Vedic parlance we would call the distinction between ātmā and the three modes of nature) doesn't have to exist. Third, once the distinction between matter and consciousness is collapsed, then the distinction between the different individual ātmā can also be collapsed: We can say that when the experience is created, a limited notion of the knower is produced in the process, which appears to us as an individual observer. Therefore, in one swoop, we can dissolve the distinction between God, the soul, and matter, and just call it Oneness or Brahman.

1.1.22 (22)

आकाशस्तल्लिङ्गात्

ākāśastalliṅgāt

ākāśaḥ—space; tat—that Absolute Truth; liṅgāt—from procreative organ.

TRANSLATION

From the procreative organ of the Absolute Truth, the space is manifest.

COMMENTARY

This sūtra refutes the existence of light without a source of light. It asserts that the space in which everything exists is Brahman. However, this Brahman is manifest from a form or a deity. This form or deity is like the sun or fire, and Brahman is the light expanding from the sun or fire. The idea that there is all-pervading light without a sun or fire is therefore rejected. In short, we accept that there is an all-pervading space. However, we also assert that this space has an *origin* as the source of the space, and space expands from this origin.

The term liṅga can be understood as the male organ of procreation. So, this deity from which Brahman emanates as light is like the father who expands His existence like a father produces children; the source is the father, and the expanding light is His children. The Bhagavad-Gita 14.4 states this as follows:

sarva-yoniṣu kaunteya
mūrtayaḥ sambhavanti yāḥ
tāsāṁ brahma mahad yonir
ahaṁ bīja-pradaḥ pitā

> It should be understood that all species of life, O son of Kunti, are made possible by birth in this material nature, and that I am the seed giving father.

In the above verse, the use of mahad-yoni is significant. Just as the term linga denotes the male procreative organ, the term yoni indicates the female procreative organ. Mahad-yoni indicates the material nature into which the seed-giving father imparts the ātmā—the 'seed' in this case is the ātmā. Notably, since the father imparts the seed, the seed previously existed inside the father, and therefore the ātmā was originally part of the seed-giving father. However, since the seed is imparted into the mahad-yoni, the seed is also separated from the father and embedded into the material nature. The material nature is inert prior to the imparting of this seed, and it expands into the world with this seed. So, the mahad-yoni (the greatest feminine sexual organ) is the kṣetra or the 'field', and the ātmā becomes the kṣetrajña or the knower of the field.

One might argue that once the ātmā has entered the material nature, and has become the kṣetrajña, it is the only kṣetrajña and hence the only one present in the heart as consciousness. This would contradict the previous sūtra which said that there is another knower—Who is omniscient—whereas the ātmā is a limited knower of the part of the field. To understand the two sūtras together, we must say that the seed-giving father not only imparts the seed but also enters the kṣetra along with the seed, as the omniscient and all-pervading entity—He is called the Paramātma or the Supreme Soul, as opposed to the ātmā. The term yoga then applies to the union between the ātmā and the Paramātma.

Hence, the all-pervading entity is Brahman, which is like light emanating from a source of light—the sun or fire. However, this light is also divided into particles—the ātmā. Notably, all three premises of the impersonal philosopher noted above are refuted in the process. First, because there is a difference between the *bīja* or seed and the *pitā* or the father—namely, the light and the source of light—hence, there is a distinction between the soul and God. Second, because the seed is imparted into the mahad-yoni or matter, therefore, there is a difference between the ātmā and material nature. Third, since there is a difference between the father and the mother, God is different from matter.

There is a difference between the all-pervading space and the points in this space. Since the ātmā is always accompanied by the Paramātma, therefore, the points in the space can be individuated. Similarly, since the space expands from an origin, therefore, the origin can be distinguished from the rest of the points in space. There is hence no 'field of consciousness'. The 'field' is in fact comprised of points. The term ākāśa or space refers to the collection of individual points; it is not a continuum without individual ātmā. It is just collectively called the undivided Brahman, like we use the term 'space' to indicate all the locations collectively. This space of individual points has an origin, from which all the locations emanate. They were previously contained inside that origin, but they emerge from that origin. This is the significance of saying that the pitā or father distributes His seed. Therefore, although there is an all-pervading field comprised of individual points, there is an origin of the space, which constitutes the *absolute reference frame* in terms of which we measure the points.

Those familiar with relativistic conceptions of space will realize that the observer is considered different from the space: The observer becomes the origin in relation to which space is mapped. There is, however, a preexisting space as well because the conceptions of near and far are preexisting in space, not because there is an observer. The observer only adds a reference frame or the origin and the dimensional vectors to this space. Now, if we collapse the distinction between the space and the observer, then space itself must have an origin. So, there cannot be an all-pervading entity that has no origin and is without dimensional vectors because that would not be considered 'space'. In short, the idea that there is an all-pervading space brings with it the notion that there must be an origin because without that origin space itself loses meaning.

Topic 9

QUESTION

If the ātmā is injected into matter, and then becomes the kṣetrajña, then it must also be disconnected from its source—the father imparting the seed. So, why is yoga needed when the ātmā has separated? Once separated, the ātmā must be independent of its source. Just like if a light particle has emerged from the sun, it is no longer bound to the sun. It can move independently.

Yes, it can be absorbed into matter, but even if it is absorbed, it is free of its source! What would be the point of returning or maintaining a connection to the source?

We have earlier stated that Brahman is comprised of points. But if these points are independent, then the *distance* between them would become meaningless because nothing joins these points. If there is no distance between the points—i.e., a path that connects one point to another—then there cannot be space. What we call space would be a disjointed set of locations and one could not go from one location to another. Effectively, each point in space would be an island unto itself from which one cannot reach the other islands. Motion or communication would be impossible in such a space as these points are disconnected from each other, and nothing can move from one point to another.

If the points in space were ātmā, then it would follow that no ātmā can know any other ātmā. Similarly, the ātmā cannot move in this space or change its relation to other ātmā. Finally, the ātmā cannot know the source from which it emanated, as there would be no connection to this source. Each ātmā can only be considered an island unto itself, disconnected from other ātmā and the source of all ātmā. Once disconnected, the justification for yoga disappears.

In scientific terms, when we postulate the existence of space, we hypothesize two things— (1) a set of points, and (2) the metric or distance that connects these points. Once these two have been hypothesized, then we also add an observer which provides the origin and dimensional vectors for space. For the present, let us consider the metric which gives the space a structure as the proximity and distance from the origin. If the metric doesn't exist, then space has no structure, because no point is either closer or farther. We cannot order or count points in space because for ordering or counting there must be a sequence—before and after. This sequence requires a metric. If the metric doesn't exist, then there may be some points, but there is no way to know how many points there are. The metric between the points acts as the connection to the origin.

If we say that the Brahman is simply a collection of points, and if there is no connection between these points (because the points are independent), then we could not speak about the connection to the origin or the distance from the origin. In fact, we could not even speak about the path from one point to another, including the path to the source, because these points have been separated. Once we say that the separation has occurred, then the mutual knowledge of the different ātmā would be impossible, as there would be no path from one point to reach another point. If this path is voided, then no ātmā can know another ātmā or the source of their emanation. Once this knowledge has become impossible, then yoga or establishing a connection to the source—i.e., between ātmā and Paramātma—would also become impossible.

1.1.23 (23)

अत एव प्राणः

ata eva prāṇaḥ

ata eva—therefore; praṇaḥ—the prāṇa (is necessary or refers to Brahman).

TRANSLATION

Therefore, the prāṇa (is necessary or refers to Brahman).

COMMENTARY

This sūtra clarifies that even though Brahman is a collection of points—and is hence not an all-pervasive unitary oneness—there is still a connection between these individual points through the prāṇa. This prāṇa is like the path or distance between the many points, including the source from which they originate. Therefore, even if the particle of light has emanated from the sun, this particle cannot be considered independent of the sun, and the reason is that this particle is still connected to the sun through the agency called the prāṇa.

For those familiar with atomic theory, the idea that light moves from one point to another is itself a fallacy of classical mechanical thinking because the atomic particles transition from one state to another. For example, if an electron moves from one atom to another, it doesn't move between the atoms—i.e., passing through the positions in the 'space' between the atoms; the atom is at one moment in one atom and at the next moment in the other atom. So, the idea that atomic particles 'move' in space is a classical caricature of change, that has failed in atomic theory. However, a new notion of change hasn't yet emerged, and so we continue to employ the classical caricatures, even if they are incorrect.

The new notion of change is indicated here: The particles don't move to push and pull each other (called locality in modern science). Rather, the particle remotely causes a change. This agency for remote change is prāṇa; for it to cause change, there is must be a path or connection; in short, prāṇa must be able to reach the destination which has to be changed, and the path to the destination is itself the cause of change. However, nothing moves on this path; the path or connection to the other thing is itself the cause of changes. These changes can be called knowledge and action, depending on which direction we consider the path (the path that goes from A to B also goes from B to A, but the directions are different—so, there are two directions, although on the same path).

Thus, the connection between the ātmā and the Paramātma or the seed-giving father is never lost, even if the seed has been separated from the father. There is always a connection—which we can call the path to the source—which keeps the two connected. This path creates the 'distance' between the origin and the other points in space. The distance between the points and the source of space is not fixed, so the ātmā can move closer to or farther from the source. The main purpose of prāṇa is to enable the changes to the relative positions to the origin and can, therefore, be called the 'freedom' of the ātmā. Unlike the points in material space which have fixed locations, the points in Brahman are free, and that freedom is simply that these points can move in relation to the origin. By enabling this motion, prāṇa represents choice. By this choice, the soul can control its experience. In short, whether in relation to the material space or in relation to the points in the Brahman—the cause of motion is prāṇa.

And yet, regardless of how far the ātmā moves from the source, it never loses the path to the source. This path keeps the space joined together and the very reason that we can call it an all-pervading entity that doesn't have 'holes' in between.

If we delve deeper into Vedic philosophy, this structure between the source and the other points is like an inverted tree. The source of the tree is the root, and other points in space are like the trunks, branches, and leaves. The prāṇa connects the locations on the tree and therefore forms the path between the many points. Due to the existence of such paths, it is possible for one ātmā to know another ātmā and for the ātmā to know the source of all ātmā. Similarly, by changing this prāṇa, one can move closer or farther to the source. However, in no situation is the connection to the source or origin of space is lost. In short, space doesn't break apart into mutually disjointed islands, such that you can never go from one island to another. If that were the case, then each ātmā could become an island unto itself and would thereafter never need to maintain a relation to the source of ātmā. It would rather be totally independent.

Herein lies the germ of the idea in yoga philosophy that by manipulating prāṇa one can attain union with the Paramātma. The tree noted above is inverted, with the root upwards, and the leaves downward. The soul can change its distance from the source by manipulating the prāṇa; in short, it can move up or down this tree—coming nearer to the source or going farther away. The upward movement of the prāṇa takes one closer to the source, and the downward movement takes the soul farther away from the source. So, the basis of the yoga practice is the manipulation of prāṇa to move closer to the source. But even if the soul doesn't come closer, the connection to the source is never lost. Therefore, the possibility of the soul moving closer to the source is always open. There is never a point at which the soul gets disconnected from its original source.

Now, when we supplement the idea that Brahman is the space, with the idea here, that these points are joined to the source through prāṇa, we get a nuanced understanding of this space: There are many points, but the *locations* of these points relative to the source are not fixed. The points can move closer or farther from the source, so what we call 'space' doesn't have a fixed *structure*. Due to the closer or farther movement of the points, space is a dynamic entity. This is unlike the modern idea of space in which points in space have a fixed location; a point closer to the origin can never become farther, or vice versa. This is, however, not the case with Brahman. It is comprised of points that can change their relative positions, establish new paths, or destroy older paths. Through the making and breaking of paths—the creation and destruction of metric distance—the knowledge of other individuals is created or destroyed.

In the Tantra, it is said that the universes are manifest when Kāraṇodakaśāyī Viṣṇu *breathes out*—i.e., ejects the soul from His body into matter. Similarly, the destruction of the universes is compared to Kāraṇodakaśāyī Viṣṇu breathing in when the souls are absorbed back into His body. So, the soul is part of Lord Viṣṇu, but there is a difference between the whole and the part. Lord Viṣṇu is the whole and the jīvā is the part, and they are joined mutually through the prāṇa of Lord Viṣṇu. This prāṇa must be understood as the śakti of Lord Viṣṇu, which at once divides Him into many parts, and yet keeps the parts connected to the whole. In short, even though the whole is divided into parts, the parts don't get separated from the whole, because they are always connected to the whole through His śakti. Therefore, when we speak about Brahman, we must understand that it is comprised of two things—the individual jīvā and the śakti that joins this jīvā to the source. Because of the existence of this śakti which joins the jīvā to the source, Brahman is also called prāṇa in this sūtra.

Topic 10

QUESTION

You have been describing the nature of Brahman in two different ways—(a) the all-pervading whole comprising of atomic parts or ātmā, and (b) the source from which everything (i.e., these parts) emanates. You explicitly drew a distinction between the space as Brahman and the origin of this space in the previous sūtra and compared this to the emanating light and the source of that light. This implies that Brahman is not everything; there is also a source apart from it. If Brahman is not everything then what else exists apart from it?

1.1.24 (24)

ज्योतश्चिरणाभिधानात्

jyotiścaraṇābhidhānāt

jyotiḥ—the light; caraṇa—feet; abhidhānāt—from the manifestations.

TRANSLATION

From the manifestations, the light is one of the feet (of all that exists).

COMMENTARY

To understand this sūtra, we need to look at the following statements from the Chāndogya Upaniśad 3.12.5-6 which mention the feet (pada):

Chandogya Upaniśad 3.12-5

saiṣā catuṣpadā ṣaḍvidhā gāyatrī tadetadṛcābhyanūktam

Word-for-word meanings

Sā eṣā gāyatrī catuṣpadā—this gāyatrī has four feet [i.e., quarters]; ṣaṣvidhā—each of them sixfold; tat etat ṛcā abhyanūktam—this is stated in a Ṛk mantra.

Translation

The Gāyatri has four quarters, each being six-fold. This is what is stated in a Ṛk mantra.

Chandogya Upaniśad 3.12-6
tāvānasya mahimā tato jyāyāṃśca pūruṣaḥ
pādo'sya sarvā bhūtāni tripādasyāmṛtaṃ divīti

Word-for-word meanings

Tāvān—like this; asya mahimā—its glory; tataḥ jyāyān ca puruṣaḥ—that [i.e., the glory] of the puruṣa is still greater; pādaḥ asya sarvā [i.e., sarvāṇi] bhūtāni—all the created entities constitute one foot [or, quarter] of him; tripād asya—[the remaining] three feet [or, quarters] of him; amṛtam divi—are in the place devoid of death.

Translation

Its glory is like this. But the glory of the puruṣa is still greater. All the created living entities (bhutani) constitute one-quarter of him. The remaining three quarters comprise the place that is devoid of death (or repeated birth and death).

The context for this śrutī is that the Gāyatri mantra is compared to the body of the living entity. The Gāyatri meter has 24 syllables, and in the above śrutī, it is said to be divided into 4 parts comprising 6 parts each. The nature of these 24 parts and what they represent in Gāyatri is an involved topic, but briefly, Gāyatri is the worship of the sun. The initial terms *bhū*, *bhuvar*, and *svar* represent the three upper planetary systems in Vedic cosmology to which the light of the sun reaches. There are 4 other planetary systems above these three (*jana*, *tapa*, *mahar*, and *satya*) that are not illuminated by the sun's light. Similarly, there are 7 planetary systems below the *bhū-loka* which are also not illuminated by the sun's light. Therefore, Gāyatri is specifically focused on the glorification of the sun, and the mantra points this out clearly. Since the sun illuminates these three planetary systems, it is sometimes referred to as Surya-Narāyanā or the incarnation of Lord Viṣṇu in the material world. The Ādityas beginning with Surya are also said to be representations of Lord Viṣṇu. The orbit of the sun is sometimes divided into 12 parts (the months) and at other times into 24 parts (the fortnights). For a discussion of the significance of these 12- and 24-fold divisions, I would refer the interested reader to my book *Cosmic Theogony*.

The main point is now made in the next śrutī which states that even this Gāyatri (representing the sun god and hence the material world) is only one-fourth of all that exists; the remaining three-quarters of existence comprises of the place that is *amrtam* or devoid of death (*mrta* represents death). In short, the place of birth and death (the material world) is one-fourth of the total existence. Also, the śrutī mentions the puruṣa and glorifies Him as someone greater than this material world, and the material world is precisely one-fourth of His full expansion; the remaining three-fourth is a realm beyond birth and death.

A brief description of the three-fourths of the existence is in order here. Throughout the Vedic texts, the living entity is described as having three aspects—*sat*, *chit*, and ānanda. The term *sat* represents consciousness or how we become connected or related to something other than the self. The term *chit* denotes cognition and conation—which follows the connection to something. Finally, ānanda denotes pleasure derived from cognition and conation. Hence, there is a progression from consciousness to knowledge and action to pleasure. The three parts transcendent to the material world are the domains in which these three aspects of the soul are dominant (the other two become subordinate). In the realm of Goloka, pleasure or ānanda dominates. In the realm of Vaikuṇṭha, the *chit* or the cognitive capacity and the concepts cognized by this capacity predominates. And in Brahman, the *sat* (consciousness) is dominant. Apart from these three, where there is no birth and death, is the material world, where birth and death recur. Thus, Brahman is one-fourth of the existence; another half is beyond Brahman, and one-fourth of the existence is material.

In three parts of this existence (excluding Brahman), the living entities are distinct due to the desire for pleasure. Since they are originally differentiated from Brahman, in one sense they are originally part of Brahman such that Brahman is the origin of everything. In another sense, once the differentiation has occurred, the remaining undifferentiated part is Brahman and hence it is one-fourth of the existence. Since the desire for pleasure is abundant, the differentiation is not considered temporary; otherwise, the living entities in Goloka and Vaikuṇṭha would not be considered *amrta* or beyond birth and death.

The living entities with material desire collectively constitute the form called Narāyanā when they are present within His body. He is the father of the materially embodied souls who undergo birth and death. However, because the material creation is not eternal, sometimes the ātmā exists within Narāyanā (when He breathes in), and sometimes the same living entity is embodied in matter (when He breathes out). Even within the body of Narāyanā, the living entity still has the desire for enjoyment, but enjoyment doesn't exist. Therefore, even though the soul is within Narāyanā, it is not considered liberated. In the strictest of senses, Brahman is that realm of souls liberated from matter which has transcended the body of Narāyanā and has become undifferentiated.

Finally, a few words might be said regarding the use of the term 'light' in this sūtra. Concerning Brahman, it is the agency that illuminates matter. What we mean by illumination is *differentiation*. To know something is to distinguish it from the other things. For example, in a dark room, we cannot differentiate things from one another, and hence there is no knowledge. The presence of Brahman in matter causes matter to be differentiated into *objects*. The material elements are eternal, but they are merged into the higher elements (as already discussed in the purport for 1.1.9 (9). Under the presence of the soul, these elements begin expanding from subtle to gross. This separation can be called illumination because we can know the difference between the elements. Since the presence of Brahman causes this separation, hence it can be called "light".

However, given the sūtra's context—a verse from Chāndogya Upaniśad is mentioned referring to Gāyatri, which celebrates the sun god—and the reference to the sun god (in the material world) is then called one-fourth of all that exists, the more likely interpretation should be that "light" refers to the sun. Factually, whether we call the sun a materially embodied being who powers the universe, or we consider it the spiritual entity which helps us discriminate the things in this world, there is no contradiction in understanding. These can be regarded as different points of emphasis in relation to the same sūtra.

QUESTION

You have said that the liberation for the soul is obtained due to faith in Brahman, and by the chanting of the mantra. But now you have said that the most important of these mantras—the Gāyatri—refers to one-fourth of the existence, which is the material creation. So, previously you said that the chanting of mantra leads to liberation, but now you have said that the mantra refers to the beings in the material world. How can these mantras be suitable for liberation from the modes of nature when they pertain to the material world?

This problem was seen earlier where the reader questioned the idea that if the material world comprises the three modes of nature, then even the mantra would be these modes, as they are in the material world. How can we consider them to be the causes of liberation? To that question, the Vedānta Sūtra had responded that many parts of the Vedic scripture pertain to the three modes, but some do not. It is these parts that are considered the source of liberation.

However, now that Gāyatri has been implicated (due to reference from Chāndogya Upaniśad) as referring to the sun in the material world, the question can be raised again—if the most important mantra is referencing the sun god, then how can we expect that other mantra will lead to transcendence?

1.1.25 (25)

छन्दोऽभिधानान्नेति चेत् न तथा चेतोऽर्पणनिगदात् तथा हि दर्शनम्

chando'bhidhānānneti cet na tathā ceto'rpaṇanigadāt tathā hi darśanam

chhandas—meters like Gāyatri; abhidhānāt—from manifestations; na—not; iti—thus; cet—if; na—not; tathā—thus; ceto'rpaṇa—offering of the mind; nigadāt—from that which has left (i.e., the source of the manifestation); tathā—in the same way; hi—certainly; darśanam—it is seen.

TRANSLATION

If it is said that Brahman is not denoted by the mantra (such as Gāyatri), we reply not so, because thus i.e., by means of the meter, the offering of the mind on that—from which the manifestation has emerged (i.e., the Lord)—is stated. In the same way, the certainly it is seen (that soul dedicates to the Lord).

COMMENTARY

The impersonalist argues that everything in the material world is comprised of modes, so there cannot be a representation of transcendence in this world. But this line of argument is not without its flaws. For instance, we can now ask: If everything is material, then even the scripture being read is also material. How can the knowledge in the scripture be considered transcendent, or leading to liberation into Brahman, if everything in the world is tainted by the three modes? The argument is therefore fallacious because it denies even the validity of the scripture, and hence the source of all knowledge. Ultimately, it decries even the validity of impersonal philosophy and leads to voidism: Everything is duality and illusory, so freeing oneself from all experience must be liberation. Śri Śankarācārya battled against voidism, with the primary aim to establish the authority of the Vedic texts. In short, he aimed to say that everything else may be material, but the scripture is not material. The Vedic texts are thus said to be *apauruṣeya* or not of human origin. As the sounds are spoken by the Lord Himself, they are considered different from material nature.

However, now, one might object that not all portions of Vedic texts are transcendental. And since we have already rejected those statements, then does Gāyatri also fall into the same category? It has also been stated earlier that anything that doesn't lead to liberation from the material world must be rejected. So, this sūtra answers the question by saying that by chanting this mantra it is observed that one obtains liberation from the material world. In short, even though Gāyatri is described as praising the sun, it is not to be considered a material portion of the Vedas. The reason for this discrimination is not explained here, but in other texts such as the Śrīmad Bhāgavatam, the sun-god is called Sūrya-N*ā*r*ā*yana. Like Lord Nārāyana glances over material nature, and thereby experience is created, in the same way, Surya glances over the material world and makes it visible to everyone else. So, his role in the material world is like that of Nārāyana in relation to material energy (outside the universe).

QUESTION

You have said that the entirety of existence is divided into four parts, which were originally manifest from Brahman. This manifestation also includes the material world in which the souls are injected by the Lord. Thus, aren't you implying that the material world is also differentiated from Brahman? Since Brahman is all that exists, and the material world is differentiated from this Brahman, shouldn't the material world be considered a part of Brahman?

1.1.26 (26)

भूतादिपादव्यपदेशोपपत्तेश्चैवम्

bhūtādipādavyapadeśopapatteścaivam

bhūtādi—the origin of living entities; pada—foot, part; vyapadeśa—declaration or expression; upapatteḥ—due to the proof; ca—also; evam—thus.

TRANSLATION

And thus, also the origin of the materially embodied living entities (*bhūta* = the embodied living entity, ādi = the origin of these living entities) or the existence of all material elements (*bhūta* = Earth, Water, Fire, Air, and Ether, ādi = etc. or other such material elements of the material universe) are one foot because such a declaration can also be proven thus (using the above statements).

COMMENTARY

There can be confusion in the translation of this sūtra because *bhūtādi* has two possible interpretations. First, the term *bhūta* is used to refer to material elements such as Earth, Water, Fire, Air, and Ether; they are distinguished from the *tanmātra* and the *indriya*, and from the mind, intellect, ego, and *mahattattva*. The term ādi can now refer to 'etc.' indicating that there are many such elements. Therefore, the term *bhūtādi* would now refer to the collection of all material elements. Second, the term *bhūta* is also used to refer to the 'embodied', meaning that there is a soul which has taken birth in the material world and will eventually discard this body and take rebirth. The term ādi will now refer to the origin of these living entities. Thus, the term *bhūtādi* will refer to the origin of all the materially embodied living entities. If we take the first interpretation, then the implication is that the material world is a *pada* or part of the entire existence. If, however, we take the second interpretation, then the origin of the living entities (i.e., Brahman from where the living entity has fallen into the material existence) is one part of the entire existence from which the material world expands. In the former case, we would say that the material world is one-fourth of existence and in the latter case, we would assert that Brahman is one-fourth of all the existence. While they assert different claims, ultimately, both claims are true, because Brahman is one-fourth (after the material world and Goloka and Vaikuṇṭha are separated), and the material world is one-fourth (as already stated in the statement of Chāndogya Upaniśad).

Of these two possible interpretations, the claim of the first was already made in 1.1.24 (24) where it was said that the material world is one-fourth of all the existence. If we take the interpretation that *bhūtādi* refers to the material elements, this sūtra would repeat the claim made previously. If instead, we take the second interpretation, the claim that Brahman is one-fourth of all the existence would be new (recall that the śrutī of Chāndogya Upaniśad merely stated that there are three parts beyond the material world; it wasn't clearly asserted that Brahman is one part; while we had explained that Brahman which dominates in the *sat* is one part, this wasn't obvious either from the sūtra or from the śrutī of Chāndogya Upaniśad). Therefore, while both interpretations are true, we prefer the second interpretation (namely that Brahman is one-fourth of the existence) because of its novelty (the principle of logical progression due to the Vedānta Sūtra being *nyāya-prasthāna*). Therefore, if there are two interpretations, we reject one of those interpretations on the grounds of novelty.

The implication of this sūtra is that Brahman is not the only transcendent destination. While this was previously asserted (that there are three regions beyond the realm of birth and death), this sūtra states that Brahman is only one of those regions. The novelty in the earlier sūtra was that there are three regions beyond the material world. The novelty in this sūtra is that Brahman is one of those three regions. While the position of the impersonal philosopher isn't entirely incorrect—in the sense that there is an undifferentiated region beyond the material differentiation—it is ultimately false in asserting that *all* differentiation is material because there are non-material regions of differentiation too.

QUESTION

In the beginning, you said that Brahman is the source of everything. Now you are saying that Brahman is only one-fourth of everything. Previously, everything was part of Brahman. Now, Brahman is also called a part (of something which is so far unstated). Should we consider Brahman as being separate from the other three parts, or should we regard it as the source of everything?

1.1.27 (27)

उपदेशभेदान्नेतिचेन् नोभयस्मिन्न् अप्य् अविरोधात्

upadeśabhedānneti cet na ubhayasminnapyavirodhāt

upadeśa—teaching; bhedāt—from the difference; na—not; iti cet—if it be said; ca—also; ena—of this; na—no; ubhayasmin—in both; api—even; avirodhāt—due to there being no contradiction.

TRANSLATION

If it be said that this is different from the teaching (i.e., that Brahman is everything) we say not so. Also, of this (i.e., that which was stated in the last sūtra—namely, that Brahman is one-fourth is not different from the teaching). In both cases (of Brahman being whole and one-fourth), there is no contradiction.

COMMENTARY

One of the sources of confusion in the Vedānta sūtra is the presence of many apparently contradictory statements, and unless they are taken collectively, there is scope for confusion. For instance, in 1.1.2 (2), it was stated that Brahman is the origin of everything. Then, in 1.1.12 (12), it was stated that this Oneness divides into many individuals because of the desire for pleasure. Now, this could be taken to mean that once the division has occurred, the Oneness no longer exists. But this assertion is refuted in 1.1.13 (13) which says that the desire for pleasure is *prachur* or abundant, but it is not absolute, which means that the undivided Oneness still exists if there is no desire for pleasure. Then, in 1.1.6 (6) it has been stated that the soul is beyond the three modes of nature, indicating that it can fall into material influence. Hence, the position in Brahman is not absolute because—(a) there are souls in the three-fourth realm which are not in Brahman, and (b) there are souls in material nature which are not in Brahman. The impersonal philosopher considers the latter of these two alternatives and he might cite 1.1.7 (7) to say that the soul can be liberated into Brahman. But in the process, he neglects other statements—such as, (a) 1.1.21 (21) which states that the ātmā is different from the Paramātma, and (b) 1.1.22 (22) which states that Paramātma is the source of ātmā and expands from there into matter. The correct understanding is that which treats all the statements as being true.

With these clarifications, we can answer the doubt—namely, whether Brahman is the origin of everything (as stated in 1.1.2 (2)) or whether Brahman is only a part (as stated in 1.1.26 (26)). The answer is that both statements are true, based on the context. As the original Oneness from which differentiation occurred due to desire, Brahman is the cause of everything. However, when the differentiation has occurred, then the undifferentiated part is one-fourth. If Brahman refers to the original Oneness, then it is the cause of everything. However, if Brahman refers to the state devoid of the desire for pleasure, then it remains as one of the four parts that are not differentiated into individuals. This resolves the contention between two conflicting ideas, namely, whether Brahman is the source of everything or whether Brahman is a part of the entire existence. Both statements are correct, based on the context—i.e., whether we look at reality before differentiation or after the differentiation has occurred.

Topic 11

QUESTION

You have stated previously that ākāśa or material space originates in a procreating organ, and this space is differentiated into many points, which are connected to the source through prāṇa. In short, that light and the source of light are never separated, even when light has emanated from the source. But this was in the context of the material creation. What does it mean for the soul?

1.1.28 (28)

प्राणस्तथानुगमात्

prāṇastathānugamāt

prāṇaḥ—the prāṇa; tathā—in the same way; anugamāt—from servitude.

TRANSLATION

In the same way, from the servitude of prāṇa (the soul is a servant).

COMMENTARY

We might recall, that a similar claim (*ata eva pranah*) was made in 1.1.23 (23), indicating that the living entity is a particle of light connected to its source through prāṇa. That statement is being referred to in this sūtra through the term *tatha* which indicates "in the same way". But we might wonder, why the same claim is made again when it has been made previously? The reason is that the previous assertion was made in the context of the material creation, wherein 1.1.22 (22) it was said that ākāśa (indicating the substrate on which the material world is sustained) is produced from a *linga* or an organ of procreation. This then led to the question of why the ātmā is not considered separated once it has been created, and the response to that was that despite being present in the material nature, the origin of space and the different points in this space are to be considered connected by prāṇa. This sūtra is, however, talking about Brahman, rather than the soul injected into material nature. And yet, it is stating that just as in the case of material nature the ātmā was connected to its source through prāṇa, similarly, even in Brahman, it is connected in the same way. Indeed, it goes on to say that the ātmā even in Brahman is a subordinate follower or servant. What is it subordinate to? That is not clarified in this sūtra. However, because of the comparison to the previous sūtra, we can infer that there is a similar connection to the source, of which Brahman is a collective emanation.

This sūtra assumes importance as the impersonal philosopher argues that because there is no differentiation in Brahman, therefore, the distinction between the ātmā and the Paramātma disappears. This sūtra refutes that claim, although in a nuanced manner. It doesn't say that there is differentiation *inside* Brahman. It rather says that Brahman (as a whole) is subordinate to the Absolute Truth (the latter is implied due to the comparison with the previous sūtra). So, the claim that because there is no differentiation in Brahman, therefore, the ātmā and the Absolute Truth have become identical is rejected, because the difference is *in between* Brahman and the Absolute Truth, and the former is a subordinate follower of the latter. Not only are they distinct, but they are also not equal (if one doubted that they could be separate domains, and the domain in which the Absolute Truth is dominant is separate from that of Brahman).

QUESTION

If prāṇa is the life force and the ātmā is the living entity, doesn't this living entity possess its separate life force independent of the Absolute Truth? Why is the life force connected to the Absolute Truth (in the material world and in Brahman)? What is the point of calling something 'living' if it doesn't have its separate life force? Without that life force, shouldn't it be considered dead?

The situation of the living entity being described here is like that of a child connected to its mother through an umbilical cord—the prāṇa being that cord. Just as the child is dependent on the mother for nutrients and life force through this umbilical cord, similarly, the soul is dependent on the Absolute Truth for its life. The term *anugamat* in the previous sūtra indicates that because of this connection, the ātmā remains subordinate to the Absolute Truth. In short, if the umbilical cord is cut, then the ātmā would be lifeless. Now, this raises the question: In what sense is the ātmā a living entity if it doesn't even have an independent life force? Just as a machine is lifeless without the power supply, shouldn't we consider the ātmā lifeless without the life force energizing it?

1.1.29 (29)

न वक्तुरात्मोपदेशादिति चेत् अध्यात्मसबन्धभूमा ह्यस्मिन्

na vakturātmopadeśāditi cet
adhyātmasambandhabhūmā hyasmin

na—not; vaktuḥ—the statement; ātmā—the self; upadeśā—teaching; iti—thus; cet—if; adhyātma—spiritual or soul; sambandha—connection, relation; bhūmā—the numerous; hi—certainly; asmin—in this (way).

TRANSLATION

If it is said that the teaching (of prāṇa) is not a statement about the self, (then we say) that the soul's connection to the numerous is certainly in this (way).

COMMENTARY

To understand this sūtra, we need to understand the role of prāṇa. The ātmā is well-known to be sat-chit-ānanda, which means it has the capacity for awareness, cognition, and pleasure. However, to create an experience, these three capacities must be combined. As an example, by directing our awareness to an apple, we can have diverse types of cognitions—such as color, smell, form, taste, etc. Similarly, corresponding to each such cognition, there can be varieties of pleasure—e.g., we can particularly enjoy the smell, tolerate the color, and dislike the shape. Likewise, each such type of pleasure, resulting from likes and dislikes, can emerge out of many different cognitions (e.g., we can enjoy clothes, books, houses, etc.) by directing our awareness to different things. What we call 'experience' is thus a combination of awareness, cognition, and pleasure.

However, each type of awareness, cognition, and pleasure *underdetermines* each other. The awareness can be directed to many different things. Following this, each such thing can be cognized in many ways. Subsequently, such cognition can lead to a variety of pleasures. To create an experience, awareness must be directed to something specific. Following this, a certain kind of cognition (e.g., taste or smell) must be selected. Following this, our desires and attitudes must be brought to bear upon that cognition. Therefore, an experience combines a specific type of awareness, a specific type of cognition, and a specific kind of pleasure. Since each aspect of experience underdetermines each other, there is a choice (of awareness, cognition, and pleasure) in the combination.

The 'field' or *kṣetra* to be known comprises many properties, to which we can relate in different ways, with different attitudes. Thus, the experience cannot be determined only by the property. For instance, we cannot say—look at John—and the rest would be automatically decided. You also must know the relation to John—e.g., whether you are looking at him as your father, son, friend, spouse, employee, etc. Similarly, you have the nature of likes and dislikes about certain types of cognition (e.g., race, height, facial features, clothes, etc.), which will decide whether you enjoy or suffer or remain neutral. The key point is that in addition to the thing being known, there is also the nature of the knower and the relationship between the knower and the known. Each of these three plays an equally important role in the construction of experience. We can call these the subjective, objective, and intersubjective components of the experience. Since they don't determine each other, their combination is a *choice*.

Prāṇa is the power of choice—or the power to combine the subjective, objective, and intersubjective—to create an experience. While the ātmā is the possibility for experience, this possibility cannot become experience without the power of choice. This sūtra (and the previous one where ātmā is said to be connected to the Absolute Truth) states that the power of choice doesn't belong to the ātmā. It belongs to the Absolute Truth and by this power the Absolute Truth places the ātmā into a combination of objective, subjective, and intersubjective, thus creating its experience. Factually, the experience of the ātmā is subordinate, because the primary *kṣetrajña* is the Absolute Truth. He knows all combinations of the above three ingredients, due to which He is omniscient and omnipresent. However, the ātmā knows a part or a specific combination of the three ingredients, which places it at a certain position in the *kṣetra*. In the material world, the *kṣetra* comprises the objective, subjective, and intersubjective, and the ātmā can roam on this field. This roaming is due to the change in prāṇa. Factually, the ātmā is not moving; the movement is of the prāṇa. The ātmā is only connected to the *kṣetra* by prāṇa—giving it a 'position' in the *kṣetra*—creating an experience. Thus, it is said that the prāṇa 'carries' the ātmā from one place to another. The ātmā is the possibility of experience, but it depends on the prāṇa to convert that possibility into an experience. In the material world, the combination comprises objects, relations to those objects, and the material desires which create pleasure, and prāṇa combines them into an experience.

When the soul is liberated, the material experience (produced from material objects, relations to these objects, and the material likes and dislikes) ceases. However, this cessation is not the end of the experience. The ātmā can still have an experience, even though it is liberated from the material world. Since the material world is missing, and the ātmā hasn't yet entered a world of differentiated living entities (i.e., Goloka and Vaikuṇṭha), the ātmā has self-experience, and this state is called Brahman. By this self-experience, the ātmā knows that it exists eternally, and its consciousness or awareness is directed toward itself. The ātmā's cognition is the cognition of the self. And its pleasure is the pleasure of enjoying oneself. This *atmarāma* state is liberation into Brahman. However, as has been noted earlier (in the description of Brahman as 'space'), even in this *atmarāma* state, the ātmā is connected to the Absolute Truth through prāṇa. Thus, there is self-knowledge, but also a relation to the Absolute Truth.

It is evident from this sūtra that the prāṇa of the Absolute Truth spreads throughout the *kṣetra* or the field to be known, thus producing experience. Just like in our body, the soul is situated in the heart, but its experience spreads in the body due to the spreading of prāṇa through the nerves and veins, similarly, the Absolute Truth is situated in one place, but due to prāṇa spreading throughout the existence, He knows everything. The ātmā can then be understood as participating in the experience of one such vein or nerve. The implication is that the ātmā is a part of the Absolute Truth for two reasons. First, the primary experiencer is the Absolute Truth and the ātmā experiences due to the Absolute Truth's experience. Second, the power to creates this experience (by combining awareness, cognition, and pleasure) is controlled by the Absolute Truth.

The use of *bhūmā* indicates that there is a multitude or a collection of such individuals even in Brahman. However, because each ātmā is focused on self-enjoyment, it remains unaware of the existence of other ātmā and hence doesn't relate to them. This self-focused experience is advised in many scriptures where the ātmā withdraws its consciousness inward—away from the objects of the external world—and focuses it upon itself. Ideally, this focus must be upon the Absolute Truth, however, it is possible to focus it on the self. Once the awareness has been withdrawn from other individuals, they practically cease to exist for the ātmā—as far their *experience* is concerned. They haven't ceased to exist factually, but for all practical purposes, their unawareness of each other's existence entails that the differentiation between the self and the other has ceased; they consider themselves to be both knower and known. Once the knower and the known have become identical, the differentiation is experientially lost. Thus, the self-focused consciousness is said to be *undifferentiated;* it is not a factual unification of all ātmā, but a lack of observed difference. By closing our eyes the world ceases to exist in experience, similarly, by withdrawing our consciousness, the difference between the knower and the known ceases.

Since the lack of differentiation pertains to the awareness of the ātmā, not a factual Oneness of all the ātmā, the term *bhūmā* (indicating a multitude or collection) is used in this sūtra. Each ātmā is still different from the Absolute Truth and has a 'location' in the space expanded from the Absolute Truth. Thus, Brahman is sometimes called the liberated state of ātmā and at other times identified with the prāṇa (of the Absolute Truth by which He knows the ātmā).

QUESTION

You are saying that as the individual ātmā is expanded from the Absolute Truth, similarly, the individual prāṇa is expanded from the prāṇa of the Absolute Truth. What is this collective prāṇa that expands the individual prāṇa?

From the previous sūtra, the relation between ātmā and prāṇa has been explicated. The relation between ātmā and the Absolute Truth has also been explicated. We have seen that the Absolute Truth is omniscient but the ātmā is a limited knower. With such distinctions between the possibility of experience and the power of experience, it seems obvious that to be omniscient, the Absolute Truth must possess greater power than the ātmā. So, the next question becomes: What is this power of experience, which subsequently expands?

1.1.30 (30)

शास्त्रदृष्ट्या तूपदेशो वामदेववत्

śāstradṛṣṭyā tūpadeśo vāmadevavat

śāstradṛṣṭyā—through insight based on scripture or as attested by śrutī; tu—but; upadeśaḥ—instruction; vāmadevavat—like that of Vāmadeva.

TRANSLATION

The declaration (about prāṇa) is possible due to such attestations by śrutī, as in the case of Vāmadeva.

COMMENTARY

In the Tantra, Lord Śiva is said to have five faces; one of these faces is called Vāmadeva who is the representation of prāṇa. The following asserts this:

Aitareya Aranyaka 2.1.5:

> The Devas (speech, etc.) said to him (the breath): 'He is to be loved by all of us.' Because the Devas said of him, that he was to be loved (vāma) by all of them, therefore there is (the poet of the fourth Mandala of the Rig-veda, called) Vāmadeva. Therefore, people call him who is really Prāṇa (breath), Vāmadeva.

The previous sūtra asserted that prāṇa is not owned by the ātmā. This was in the context of verses that described the Brahman as prāṇa. Now, this sūtra gives another example in the context of the material world. However, there is a difference between these two descriptions. In 1.1.23 (23), it was said that the relation between ātmā and the Absolute Truth is through prāṇa because He is the seed-giving father, and by this connection, the ātmā could know the Absolute Truth. In this sūtra, the knowledge of the material world is being described and the prāṇa is a form of Lord Śiva. Thus, we must understand that the same term prāṇa is used in many ways, depending on the type of experience. It always represents the combination of the three aspects of experience. However, these three aspects could pertain to the self-experience of the ātmā, the experience of the Absolute Truth, and finally, the experience of the material world.

Since Lord Śiva is the controller of the material energy, in this sūtra, prāṇa refers to the combination of the three aspects in matter, regardless of which ātmā experiences this combination. This is still called prāṇa; however, it is a material energy that produces material experience, which the soul can obtain if it applies its prāṇa given to it by Paramātma. Therefore, there are two types of combinations—(a) the combination of three aspects of matter to create an experienceable entity, and (b) the attachment of the ātmā to this entity. The former must be considered material, and the latter must be considered spiritual, although this spiritual energy has been directed toward a material combination. The former is a material choice to combine the material ingredients comprising relation, cognition, and emotion. The latter is a spiritual choice to direct the power of experience in the ātmā toward this material combination. Therefore, even though prāṇa is referred to in relation to the Absolute Truth and Vāmadeva, these two types of prāṇa factually refer to different things.

QUESTION

You are saying that the agency by which the ātmā creates its experience is not under its control; this control rests with the Absolute Truth and with Vāmadeva. But, if I'm not in control of my experience, then how can I accept or reject any spiritual process that might liberate me from the material existence? My liberation would depend on the will of the controllers of prāṇa. It would then follow that I cannot liberate myself; I must just rely on their grace.

From several sūtras, the relation between ātmā and prāṇa has been explicated and it has become clear that while the ātmā has the potentiality of experience, to have any experience, the ātmā must rely on prāṇa, which was originally described as the connection to the Absolute Truth and then as Vāmadeva. With these descriptions, it seems obvious that the ātmā is helpless in producing its own experience because the choice by which experience is created is under the control of the Absolute Truth or Vāmadeva. If the ātmā has no choice, then it is legitimate to ask how it can be held responsible for its actions? In fact, how can we say that the ātmā fell from the association of the Absolute Truth into the material world, and how can it liberate itself from the modes of nature? Since the power rests in the hands of the Absolute Truth, only He can liberate the ātmā from the clutches of material nature; the ātmā cannot do anything. This position in fact seems a straightforward denial of the free will of the soul.

1.1.31 (31)

जीवमुख्यप्राणलिङ्गान्नेति चेत् न उपासात्रैविध्यात् आश्रितित्वात् इह तद्योगात्

jīvamukhyaprāṇaliṅgānneti cet na upāsātraividhyāt āśritatvāt iha tadyogāt

jīvā—the ātmā; mukhya—the leader or controller; prāṇa—prāṇa; liṅgāt—that came from the progenitor; na—not; iti—thus; cet—if; na—not; upāsa—worship, meditation; traividhyāt—from the three knowledge; āśrita—taking shelter; tvāt—of Him; iha—in this way; tadyogāt—from the union with Him.

TRANSLATION

If it is said that the ātmā is not the controller of prāṇa because it came from the progenitor (the Absolute Truth), then we say no. Worship arising from the three knowledge (the three Vedas called Rig, Yajur, and Sāma), taking shelter of Him in this way, and from the union with Him (is in the soul's control).

COMMENTARY

We have discussed how the ātmā has the three potentialities for awareness, cognition, and pleasure. Of these three, the potentiality for pleasure is the controlling agency, and (generally) drives the other two. For instance, if you desire to eat tasty food, then by your awareness you will first find the relevant type of food, and then by your cognition, you will taste that food, following which the desire for pleasure will be fulfilled. The potentiality for pleasure is the ability to have desires. The fulfillment of that desire is a pleasure. Therefore, on its own, the ātmā can have desires, but these cannot be fulfilled without the power of prāṇa. The ānanda aspect of the ātmā exists as the production of desires, and the same aspect also exists as pleasure or enjoyment in the fulfilled state.

Unless the ātmā is forced by circumstances (called good or bad *karma*), it pursues its desires through its ability for awareness and cognition. However, even if the ātmā is thus forced, the desire for pleasure always exists. For instance, you might not receive tasty food due to circumstances, and you may be forced to taste unpalatable food, but the *desire* for tasty food can still exist. Thus, the ātmā doesn't have the power to acquire tasty food on its own because the fulfillment of desires requires the combination of the three agencies—i.e., the acquisition of tasty food followed by the ability (the tongue) to acquire the cognition—and this combination depends on prāṇa, which is under the control of the Absolute Truth. However, the desire for tasty food is independent of whether the tasty food can be acquired, or the tongue is capable of tasting.

Hence, there is a subtle difference between a *choice*, which as we previously noted is the power to combine the three potentialities to create an experience, and the *desire* for that experience without its fulfillment. In general, the desire arises, following which there must be the power to fulfill the desire. But even if the desire is unfulfilled, it can continue to exist in the ātmā in a latent form. With this distinction between *choice* and *desire*, we can say that the ātmā isn't free to fulfill its desires, but it is free to desire. Therefore, even if the prāṇa—or the power for fulfilling desires—is not in its control, the desire is in its control.

With this distinction, we can understand this sūtra, which denies that the soul lacks free will. The denial is that the ātmā can desire, and if by that desire it takes shelter of the Absolute Truth and develops the urges to follow the methods prescribed in the three Vedas, then it can perform yoga. It has previously been mentioned that the ātmā is liberated from the material modes by yoga. The practice of yoga requires some effort, which then needs the power of prāṇa under the control of the Absolute Truth. So, what can the ātmā do to obtain this power, to practice yoga? The answer is simply desiring. Just as the Absolute Truth is fulfilling other desires of the ātmā—in the material world—He can similarly fulfill the desire for relation to Himself if it so arises. Implicit here is the understanding that the Absolute Truth fulfills the desire of the ātmā.

In the Bhagavad-Gita 7.14, Lord Kṛṣṇa states the following:

daivī hy eṣā guṇa-mayī
mama māyā duratyayā
mām eva ye prapadyante
māyām etāṁ taranti te

> This divine energy of Mine, consisting of the three modes of material nature, is difficult to overcome. But those who have surrendered unto Me can easily cross beyond it.

Similarly, in Bhagavad-Gita 10.10, Lord Kṛṣṇa states the following:

teṣāṁ satata-yuktānāṁ
bhajatāṁ prīti-pūrvakam
dadāmi buddhi-yogaṁ taṁ
yena mām upayānti te

> To those who are constantly devoted and worship Me with love, I give the understanding by which they can come to Me.

BG 10.10 indicates that simply by devotion, the Lord provides the intelligence by which He can be attained. The use of *dadāmi* indicates that "I provide"; this means that the power to attain Him is not because of one's personal capacity to attain Him; rather, the power to attain Him is provided by Him. Furthermore, it is provided if someone is devotionally *yukta* or associated.

Similarly, in BG 7.14, it is indicated that overcoming the material nature is very hard; however, those who are devoted to Kṛṣṇa can easily cross beyond it.

God is well-known in all religions as omniscient and omnipotent. However, whether He is also benevolent is sometimes debated—especially because the ātmā suffers in the material world as many of its desires are unfulfilled. The existence of evil leads many people to argue that God is not benevolent. However, in the above sūtras, it has been clarified that even those engaged in evil are doing so using the power of the Absolute Truth, based on His approval. This approval is based on two things—whether the ātmā desires and whether it deserves. If these two conditions are satisfied, then the Absolute Truth delegates His power. A similar kind of fulfillment is possible even in the case of yoga—provided we desire, and we become deserving. By desiring, we obtain the power to practice yoga and by the perfection of this yoga, we become deserving. Therefore, liberation from material existence would follow the same process as that which is used for the fulfillment of other (material) desires.

It is said that "man proposes, and God disposes". This sūtra also asserts the same, with one difference: The man who proposes must also be deserving for God to fulfill the man's desires. While desiring is the start, one must use this desire to become deserving of the result. The act of deserving is explained here using the term *traividya;* it indicates that one must follow the processes prescribed in the Vedas to become qualified. One cannot whimsically invent the method of transcendence. Desiring is good, and God will provide the intelligence to understand His nature and the process to attain Him, but obedience to the revealed knowledge in the Vedas is also a mandatory precondition.

SECTION 2

Topic 1

QUESTION

You are describing the path of bhakti-yoga or surrender to God. But there are other recognized systems of yoga. Since the previous sūtra said that by following the three Vedas, we perform yoga, then how can taking shelter of God be considered the primary method? Isn't there aśtānga-yoga, karma-yoga, jñāna-yoga, etc.? In fact, the study of the Vedic literature is considered jñāna-yoga. So, how can you assert the validity of bhakti-yoga above all else?

It is understood that books are a source of knowledge. Knowledge requires reason and logic, often argument and counterargument, and upon a long and careful analysis of the subject matter one can arrive at some reasonable conclusions. The Vedic texts themselves describe Brahman which is well-known to be the impersonal reality into which the ātmā is supposed to merge. Especially the impersonal philosophers vociferously argue that the primary method of attainment of Brahman is jñāna-yoga. How can bhakti-yoga suddenly replace it?

1.2.1 (32)

सर्वत्र प्रसिद्धोपदेशात्

sarvatra prasiddhopadeśāt

sarvatra—everywhere, in every Vedantic passage i.e., in all Upaniśad; prasiddha—the well-known; upadeśāt—from the teaching.

TRANSLATION

From the teaching being well-known or famous everywhere.

COMMENTARY

The impersonalist assumes that bhakti-yoga is inferior to jñāna-yoga. He believes that by their intellect they can grasp the nature of ultimate reality. But if the sūtras in the previous section have been understood, then it has been amply clarified that the power to think—and indeed the understanding—only comes to one if they have taken the shelter of the Lord. The assumption that the ātmā has the power to think, act, and understand is itself rejected earlier, and this is not just true for transcendence but even for material desires. The ātmā is helpless; it is entirely dependent on the grace of the Lord even in this world. Therefore, to think that one can obtain the understanding by their effort is false. Rather, the shelter of the Lord is needed to obtain intelligence. Therefore, even if one is trying to understand the meaning of the Vedas, or the understanding of Brahman—and thereby merge into the Oneness—one must still take the shelter of the Lord, because only by His grace will he get the understanding.

This is not merely an obscure or isolated aspect of the Vedānta doctrine. As this sūtra asserts, this is to be found everywhere, and is, therefore 'famous'. In short, it should be considered the purport of the Upaniśad and Vedānta.

QUESTION

It has previously been stated that Brahman is beyond the material guna or the qualities of material nature. This is sometimes called Nirguna-Brahman. You are talking about a personal form of Brahman which would indicate that it is imbued with qualities (and should be called Saguna-Brahman). Shouldn't these qualities be considered material, and therefore not transcendental?

1.2.2 (33)

वविक्षतिगुणोपपत्तेश्च

vivakṣitaguṇopapatteśca

vivakṣita—one who is desirous to enter; guṇa—qualities; upapatteḥ—because of the reasonableness; ca—and, moreover.

TRANSLATION

Moreover, this method is reasonable or suitable for one who is desirous to enter the realm of (spiritual) guna (the domain of eternal differentiation).

COMMENTARY

The root *viv* in the above sūtra means differentiation. When joined with *ikṣhita* it means those desirous of this differentiation. We might recall from the previous section that existence has been divided into four quarters, of which three quarters are considered beyond the realm of birth and death. Of these three, Brahman is one of the quarters where differentiation doesn't exist; however, the other two—Goloka and Vaikuṇṭha—are places with differentiation. So, the argument that only Brahman is transcendence because it is beyond the material guna has already been refuted earlier. This sūtra further asserts that the method of bhakti-yoga is especially suitable for those who are desirous of entering these differentiated realms beyond the undifferentiated Brahman.

The use of guna is contentious. It can be used as a general noun to indicate 'qualities' or as a particular noun to indicate the three modes of nature. If we take the latter meaning, then the sūtra would mean "those who are desirous of entering the material world perform bhakti-yoga", which would contradict the previous sūtra. Hence, we must translate guna as the general noun 'qualities' rather than the specific noun indicating three modes of material nature.

This raises the question that if there are qualities beyond the material world, what are those? The Vaiṣṇava Tantra describes these qualities as being six-fold: knowledge, beauty, power, wealth, heroism, and renunciation. These qualities are present even in the material world; however, they are only manifest partially. For instance, there is a knowledge of architecture, a knowledge of medicine, a knowledge of chemistry, etc., but we cannot find *knowledge itself*. Similarly, there is beauty in art, beauty in music, beauty in poetry, etc., but we cannot find *beauty itself*. And yet, despite our inability to find anything corresponding to these words, we still use the terms 'knowledge' or 'beauty' in ordinary language. What do they mean? If we say that nothing corresponds to knowledge itself and beauty itself then these words become meaningless.

If the six words mentioned above are meaningless, then we cannot use them even in the material world. Thus, it is appropriate to say that while the material world doesn't have these qualities in fullness, they are present partly, and we don't know what their fullness is. But, if someone is desirous of being acquainted with these six qualities in their fullness, he must go beyond the material world, and that quest is indicated here by the term *vivikṣhita guna*, namely, those desirous of entering the realm of qualities in their original form.

QUESTION

But why can't these qualities be attained in the present world? After all, even in this world, everyone is searching for knowledge and beauty, everyone wants to be rich, powerful, and famous, and some people renounce the world. So, if they are desiring these things, why can't they attain them here? What would be the point of transcending this world if these can be attained here?

1.2.3 (34)

अनुपपत्तेस्तु न शारीरः

anupapattestu na śārīraḥ

anupapatteḥ—not being justifiable, because of the impossibility, because of the unreasonableness, because they are not appropriate; tu—but on the other hand; na—not; śārīraḥ—the embodied, the jīvā or the soul in the material world.

TRANSLATION

On the other hand, (those qualities) are not possible (in) the embodied.

COMMENTARY

The material world is described as an inverted tree in many places in Vedic literature. The root of this tree is the fullness of everything, but the trunks, branches, and leaves are parts of this fullness. Due to the duality of material nature, these qualities also become mutually opposed. For example, there is some beauty in the forest and some beauty in the mountain; but these are different kinds of beauties. We can combine these beauties if there were a mountain with a forest on top, but that would leave out other kinds of beauties—such as that of rivers, oceans, and cities. We can conceive that some of these beauties could be combined—e.g., that there can be a small river flowing on top of the mountain, but we cannot combine a mountain with a large river or a big city. Similarly, there is some pleasure in cold and some pleasure in heat, but we cannot combine their pleasures because they will negate each other. So, we can alternately enjoy the weather of heat and then enjoy the weather of cold, but we cannot enjoy them simultaneously. This is the reason that the origin of the material world—also called Pradhāna—is described as a state in which the three modes of nature are not differentiated. In other words, the entire universe exists, but the diversities have canceled each other out. When the material world is manifest, the diversities are spread into different locations. This means that if we combine the diversities, they cancel each other, and we cannot find any diversity. On the other hand, if we see diversity, they are already in disparate or different things. So, we cannot find one thing that has all the diversity; we can only find the cancellation of all diversity or distributed differences.

As we look around this world, we find mutually irreconcilable qualities because the material world is differentiated in a way that conflicting types of properties are found in different things and cannot be combined. The combination, in fact, would produce a self-contradiction: something would have to be simultaneously large and small, hot and cold, bitter and sweet, empty and full, etc. If these things were simultaneously combined, they would cancel each other, and the combination would be nothingness. Hence, it is impossible in the material world to find something that has all the beauty, all the knowledge, all the power, all the wealth, all the fame, and all the renunciation. These must be necessarily distributed because they come in mutually opposed diversities.

Of course, the same problem exists in the case of the transcendental world as well; there are contradictory qualities. However, God is described as the person Who has all these qualities as His *aspects*. He is, for example, simultaneously the largest and the smallest, but we can perceive only one aspect of these qualities at any one time. The reason is the nature of *our* cognition: we cannot perceive something that is simultaneously the largest and the smallest. To see something very small, we must look at it very closely, but to see something very large, we must be far away from it. Since we cannot be simultaneously near and far, therefore, it is impossible for us to know if the same thing is both the smallest and the largest. To possess this knowledge, we would have to be omniscient and omnipresent, such that we can perceive all the aspects simultaneously.

So, the reason that it is impossible for the ātmā to attain these properties in the material world (or any other world) is that it is localized. It can perceive one aspect, and therefore even in relation to God, the ātmā knows God in a specific manner—e.g., as the largest or the smallest—at any given time. Indeed, the different ātmā may even disagree with each other regarding their perception—e.g., one may insist that God is the smallest and the other may claim that He is the largest. There is no way to reconcile these contradictions except if the ātmā shifts its perspective and understands the other aspect. The limited nature of the jīvā ensures that it cannot know or acquire all these properties at once.

So, there are two reasons why jīvā cannot become like God. First, in the material world, the qualities are distributed in different locations and the jīvā can only be present in one place. Second, in the spiritual world, the qualities are combined in God, however, the jīvā is still limited to observe only one aspect of this infinite diversity. In both cases, the jīvā must be omniscient to attain the fullness of the six qualities, and that is something that it can never become.

QUESTION

We see that people become knowledgeable, powerful, rich, and famous for their work. Similarly, in the Vedic texts, it is described that one can ascend to heavenly planets through austerities. Why can't that be possible for acquiring the position of God? In short, why can't we become God by our effort?

Since the world is an inverted tree, there are descriptions of how the living entity can ascend this tree, rising to higher and higher positions where they acquire greater knowledge, beauty, power, fame, wealth, and renunciation. As one rises upward, the contradictions between the diversities are reconciled, as one ascends to a position from which they can observe multiple perspectives simultaneously. If the world were flat, then one could not observe multiple aspects simultaneously, because by being in one place one could not be in other places. But, if the world is an inverted tree, then by rising upward, the diversities are incrementally reconciled. So, the question becomes: If we can ascend this inverted tree to greater and greater heights, why can't we reach the root from where everything has diversified? Then we can also become God.

1.2.4 (35)

कर्मकर्तृव्यपदेशाच्च

karmakartṛvyapadeśācca

karma—action; kartṛ—agent; vyapadeśāt—due to the teaching; ca—and.

TRANSLATION

Also, due to the teaching of action and agent (distinction).

COMMENTARY

This sūtra explains that even those who rise higher in the material world haven't acquired perfection as their *native qualities*. These qualities are due to their *karma* and there is a distinction between the actor and the result of their activities. Due to the result of activities, one obtains a higher position temporarily, but because there is a difference between the actor and the result of actions, these acquisitions are not considered permanent, as the *karma* eventually ends, and the soul falls from its previously acquired position. God is in a different position; He is called Achyuta or One who never falls from His position. Therefore, while the soul can acquire a high position by his deeds, these are necessarily temporary, and because the soul falls it cannot be compared to God.

The implication is that God did not attain His position due to hard work.

His actions are not the cause of His Godliness. Rather, He acts because He is already in that position. For the soul, his higher position is due to his actions. These actions can help him rise, but by this rise, he cannot become the source of his own existence. His existence is assumed before his actions are performed. Likewise, God's existence is assumed before His actions are considered.

QUESTION

But you are accepting that one can ascend a high position by one's karma. Does this mean that we can become God temporarily by our actions?

While many people may be deterred by the idea that a position of power is temporary and would be followed by a fall from power, not everyone may be dissuaded in this way. A person might decide to enjoy these temporary pleasures, fall from that position, and then work again to regain that position. In short, there can be people who alternate between working and enjoying, and the temporariness of the position doesn't dissuade them. Even the temporary attainment of the position of God may be considered sufficiently good. After all, if they can attain it once, then they can attain it again. Like the president or a prime minister of a country can ascend to a powerful position, and then lose in the next term, only to come back again into power, similarly, one can imagine the possibility where they become God, lose it, and then acquire the position again. In short, God would not be a *person*. God would rather be a position, which anyone can attain if they have worked for it sufficiently. This is the extension of the idea of power and position in the present world where nothing is permanent; kings can lose their kingdom and win it back again. So, if God was the king of the whole world, maybe it is possible to win and lose that position based on one's effort. It might be temporary, but it would still be a fair system in which the person who works the hardest acquires the position of God.

1.2.5 (36)

शब्दविशेषात्

śabdaviśeṣāt

śabda—they are called; viśeṣāt—because of adjectives or properties.

TRANSLATION

Because (qualities obtained by effort) are called adjectives or properties.

COMMENTARY

In this sūtra, a distinction between an object and its properties is drawn. For example, if you paint a chair red, it acquires the property of redness. However, this paint is a covering or an attribute of the object, and the object is different from that property. Similarly, if you heat water, it acquires the property of heat, but there is a difference between the heat and the water. In the same way, there is a difference between the ātmā and the qualities it acquires in the material world. This difference is described by a distinction between the soul and its body and mind. The body can be rich, powerful, famous, and beautiful, while the mind can be knowledgeable and renounced. However, since the body and the mind are the 'coverings' of the soul, they are not considered *native* properties of the soul. This difference is confirmed by the fact that the body and the mind change, and whoever is rich and powerful will either eventually die or become poor and powerless. But if one is not deterred by this proposition of losing their position and would like to acquire the position of God temporarily, this sūtra indicates that God is that person who has no distinction between the soul, the body, and the mind. The qualities being referred to are the native qualities of God. Since God is eternal, therefore, these qualities are never lost. So, not only are the qualities eternal, but they are not distinct from God. Therefore, we will not call these qualities *adjectives* of a noun; we won't say that there is a chair with the property of redness. Rather, redness is innate to that chair.

In the material world, there is a distinction between the nouns and the adjectives, and when the soul ascends to a higher position, the noun (i.e., the soul) is the same, but it acquires adjectives—e.g., power, fame, wealth, knowledge, beauty, renunciation, etc. So, we say that such and such has become powerful or famous or knowledgeable. But this use of language—i.e., associating the person with a quality—still involves a distinction between the person and the quality. The distinction is illustrated by the fact that we say that so and so *has* wealth; we don't say that so and so *is* wealth. Or, so and so *has* knowledge; we don't say that so and so *is* knowledge. The use of 'has' rather than 'is', indicates that we are distinguishing between the object and its property; the property is possessed by that object, but that object is still different from the property. In the case of God, however, the attribute 'has' is not applied. Thus, we must not say that God has knowledge; we must rather say that God is knowledge.

In short, there is no difference between God and His qualities, unlike the jīvā who can acquire these qualities but is always different from them. This is another way of saying that these qualities are the body and the mind of the jīvā and while they are attached to the jīvā as its properties, they are not the jīvā itself. On the other hand, there is no difference between God and His properties. Hence, there is no such thing as God as a soul and His body and mind. That body and mind are God. So, He is knowledge, beauty, power, fame, etc.

In the previous sūtra, it was stated that God hasn't acquired His qualities through hard work; He natively possesses these qualities. But in this sūtra, even the idea of possession is being rejected, because one could argue that even if the qualities could be possessed (and then lost) one could possess them again by hard work. God is being defined as that person Who is those qualities. Thus, a distinction between the jīvā and God is drawn here; the jīvā isn't those qualities although it can acquire them. God, on the other hand, is all those qualities.

QUESTION

But such qualities aren't mentioned in the śrutī or the Upaniśad. If Vedānta Sūtra is the conclusion of these Upaniśad, then how can we accept that the Supreme Person has these qualities? We only know about material qualities.

This counterexample is frequently offered by the impersonalist. The impersonalist claims that the Vedas and their divisions, such as the Upaniśad, are the original texts, and other literature—such as the Vaiṣṇava Tantra we noted above—are later additions to the Vedic system. Most Indologists, in fact, try to date these scriptures and claim that the four Vedas are the original texts, and other things—such as the worship of Lord Viṣṇu—came much later. Since these qualities are ascribed to personal forms of God, which are then considered to be later additions to the Vedic system, therefore, it is argued that they cannot be considered as authoritative as the original texts. Since the original texts are providing descriptions of such qualities and the impersonal description is dominant in these scriptures, therefore, it must be considered secondary.

1.2.6 (37)

स्मृतेश्च

smṛteśca

smṛteḥ—from the smriti; ca—and, also.

TRANSLATION

From the smriti also (we know the qualities of God).

COMMENTARY

By referring to the smriti—i.e., the Purāna and Tantra—the Vedānta Sūtra clarifies that the knowledge in the śrutī is not the only source of all knowledge. If Vedānta Sūtra is considered śrutī, its reference to smriti must be considered an indication that these texts did not come 'later' as many academics currently claim. If the smriti did not exist earlier, then they could not be referenced. Factually, the entire Vedic system is considered eternal by the true practitioners, although it is divided into many aspects for differently inclined people.

In the Śrīmad Bhāgavatam, it is noted that the Vedānta Sūtra was composed after the composition of Upaniśad, Purāna, and Mahabharata. Bādarāyana who converted the oral tradition into a written one, however, was not satisfied after the composition of these works of literature as they did not explicitly glorify the personality of God and the deepest mysteries of amorous love between the soul and God were left unexplained. His guru Nārada then instructed Bādarāyana to compose the Śrīmad Bhāgavatam; since it was composed after Vedānta Sūtra, Śrīla Jīvā Goswami offers extensive justifications in the Tattva Sandarbha about why the Śrīmad Bhāgavatam must be considered a natural commentary or explanation of the Vedānta Sūtra. However, for the skeptics, who might not accept these arguments, this sūtra itself provides a reference to the smriti texts.

QUESTION

But you have previously stated that the Paramātma is also present in the heart and is a kṣetrajña like the jīvā. Doesn't His presence in the heart indicate that He has fallen into the material world and is therefore just like the jīvā?

As we can see from the previous sūtra, there is a discussion on the difference between God and the soul. This conversation has emerged especially after the previous section ended by stating that the soul must surrender and take shelter of God. The questions have therefore also shifted from the nature of Brahman or absolute reality to the difference between the soul and God. Here, the seeker is asserting that God must be considered fallen into the material nature because He is also present in the heart, just like the jīvā. If the jīvā can be considered fallen, then why can't God be considered fallen in the same way?

1.2.7 (38)

अर्भकौकस्त्वात् तद्व्यपदेशाच्च नेति चेत् न निचाय्यत्वादेवं व्योमवच्च

arbhakaukastvāt tadyapadeśācca neti cet na nicāyyatvādevaṃ vyomavacca

arbhak—very small; kastvāt—from going; tadyapadeśāt—a false description; ca—and also; na—not; iti—therefore; cet—if; na—not; nicāyya—the multitude or many; tvāt—Him; evaṃ—thus, so; vyomavat—like the ether; ca—and.

TRANSLATION

If it is said that He (the Paramātma) is going inside a very small place (the heart) and therefore a false description (is given—that He is Supreme) we say no because He is in a multitude of places just like the all-pervasive ether.

COMMENTARY

The Lord is described as both transcendent and immanent. It is important to understand how both are true simultaneously. Consider the use of an ordinary concept such as 'cow'. The concept is transcendent to each individual cow, and it will exist even if no cow exists. However, when the cows exist, the concept 'cow' exists in each of them because of which we call them cows. Notably, if the concept did not enter each individual cow, then we could not call them cows. However, if we reduced the concept to an individual cow, then we could not call other cows by the term 'cow'. Therefore, the idea 'cow' is transcendent and immanent; as transcendent we can say that it exists when none of the cows exist; in this sense, the concept is eternal and imperishable. However, when the cows are manifest, then the concept also exists in each cow; by this incarnation of the concept inside each cow, the concept becomes immanent. The problem of transcendence and immanence is not unique to God; it is pervasive in the use of all concepts. Therefore, to understand how Paramātma is pervasive in all places, we need not focus on this as a unique theological idea; we can also examine the immanence of concepts in things to understand the problem.

This problem is that of the instantiation of a concept. There is a universal concept called 'cow', and this concept instantiates into many individual cows. Just as there is a difference between the concept 'barber' and an individual barber, similarly, there is a difference between the concept and the instance of that concept. Generally, when we start understanding concepts, we look at each individual instance; for example, if a child were to be taught about cows, then the parent will point to an instance of a cow and say— "that is a cow". It doesn't reduce the concept of 'cow' to that individual cow; however, this is how we learn about concepts: we see the instances one after another and then we generalize and start perceiving the general concept across the many instances.

So, to understand how Paramātma is in each heart, we must understand two things. First, there is a transcendent form of God called Bhagavān; He is like the concept of 'cow'. Second, this concept instantiates into each thing, when those things are created; this instantiation is Paramātma. The Bhagavān form is transcendent, and the Paramātma form is immanent. However, if all the instances were wound up—e.g., if the material world ceased to exist—then the instantiation of Bhagavān into Paramātma would cease to exist. This is quite like the fact that if dinosaurs cease to exist, then the concept 'dinosaur' still exists, however, there is no instantiation of that idea into an individual.

With this background about transcendence and immanence, we can understand this sūtra. The purport is that Bhagavān instantiates into individual things, and hence there are many instances of Paramātma, and He is present everywhere. However, the jīvā is not instantiating into more than one thing at any time; therefore, there is only one instance of each jīvā at any time. The reason for this difference is that Bhagavān is a general concept—He is like the idea of 'cow' which can have numerous instances. However, the jīvā is a very contingent or specific concept, which can only be instantiated into one thing. As a result, Bhagavān can expand into numerous forms, with different aspects; He can also instantiate into many individuals of the same form (an example is the many deities of the Lord which are all instances of the same form). However, the jīvā cannot be present in many bodies at the same time (although it is said that by mystic perfection, a yogi can simultaneously expand into 8 bodies, but not more than that, unlike Paramātma who can have infinite expansions).

The ātmā can be likened to specific concepts, such as the Taj Mahal, the Eiffel Tower, the Pacific Ocean, or the Sistine Chapel. We call all these *proper nouns* as opposed to a cow, which is a *common noun*. There are many instances of the common noun, but there is only one instance of the proper noun. They are, however, both *nouns* that identify individuals. The difference between God and the soul is like that between common and proper nouns. The former incarnates into many forms but the latter has one instance. Hence while they are both individuals, there is a difference between the nature of these two nouns. This difference is the foundation of the distinction between the soul and God.

QUESTION

Even if we say that the ātmā is in one place and Paramātma is in many places, when the Paramātma has entered these many places, He must be enjoying or suffering like the jīvā. If the jīvā is enjoying and suffering in one place, then the Paramātma must be enjoying and suffering in many places simultaneously. The enjoyment and suffering in the world are the problems of material bondage. So, if the Paramātma is in many places, and thus subject to enjoyment and suffering in many places, then He cannot be considered liberated.

1.2.8 (39)
संभोगप्राप्तिरिति चेत् न वैशेष्यात्
saṃbhogaprāptiriti cet na vaiśeṣyāt

saṃbhogaprāpti—that it has experience of pleasure and pain; iti—thus; cet—if; na—not; vaiśeṣyāt—from the specific nature (of the Paramātma).

TRANSLATION

If it is said that (being connected with the hearts of all the individual souls due to Paramātma's omnipresence), it would also have experience of pleasure and pain, we say no, based on the specific nature of the (Paramātma).

COMMENTARY

The soul in the material world is enjoying or suffering due to material desires; if these desires are fulfilled, then pleasure is created; if they are not fulfilled, then suffering is produced. But if the desire ceases to exist, then the soul becomes equanimous to all outcomes; there is neither suffering nor enjoyment. There is still cognitive experience, but there is no emotive result because there is no desire. The soul enters the material world due to the desire for enjoyment and is hence forced to suffer when the desire is unfulfilled. However, the Paramātma doesn't enter the world for enjoyment. When the soul is spiritually advanced, then he perceives everything cognitively, but he doesn't feel sad or happy. Similarly, the Lord can perceive all that is happening, but He is not enjoying or suffering. This is because emotion is cut off from cognition. This separation between cognition and emotion is practiced by the yogis. They subject themselves to extreme austerities which produce intense suffering. But this suffering also produces the necessity to separate cognition from emotion.

Our experience arises due to a combination of outside-in and inside-out causes. The inside-out cause is desire, and the outside-in cause is karma. If desires cease to exist, then the inside-out cause ends and the generation of emotion, pleasure, and pain ceases. Then, the outside-in cause also terminates.

The position of Paramātma is like that person who has no material desires. Therefore, He doesn't enjoy or suffer, unlike the jīvā who is enjoying or suffering. Of course, by the cessation of material desires, the jīvā can also stop enjoying or suffering. By attaining this stage, the jīvā would have a similar type of experience as that of Paramātma, however, due to the previously mentioned reasons (e.g., that Paramātma is everywhere while the soul is localized) it would never become identical to Paramātma. Therefore, the claim that because the jīvā is suffering in this material world must entail that Paramātma must also suffer because they are both situated in the heart is a wrong understanding. The jīvā is influenced by material desire, but Paramātma is not thus influenced.

Topic 2

QUESTION

In many places, the Lord is described as the enjoyer of the material world. In Bhagavad-Gita 5.29, Kṛṣṇa calls Himself the enjoyer of all yajñá and austerities (bhoktāram yajñá-tapasam). In yajñá, offerings are made to the Lord for His pleasure. But you have stated that the Lord is not enjoying or suffering in this world, which would entail that He cannot be the enjoyer of yajñá and austerity. If He is not the enjoyer, then why should any yajñá be performed for Him?

1.2.9 (40)

अत्ता चराचरग्रहणात्

attā carācaragrahaṇāt

attā—the eater; carācara—the movable and immovable (i.e., the whole universe); grahaṇāt—from the acceptance (as His food or as an offering to Him).

TRANSLATION

The Lord is the eater of the movable and immovable from the acceptance of these things (if they are offered to Him).

COMMENTARY

In the Bhagavad-Gita 9.26, the Lord states that if offered with love, He accepts the offerings. Similarly, when the Lord states that He is the *bhokta* of *yajñá* and *tapasyā*, the reference is to the offerings being made by the practitioners.

patram puspam phalam toyam
yo me bhaktya prayacchati
tad aham bhakty-upahrtam
asnami prayatatmanah

> If one offers Me with love and devotion a leaf, a flower, fruit a water, I will accept it.

The implication is that the Lord is not normally enjoying or suffering in the material world because He is free of material desires and has no goal to be attained. However, if He is offered something with devotion, He accepts it. The importance here must be attached to devotion; one cannot offer miseries to the Lord. Just as a person loving another person gives them those things that will please them, similarly, the meaning of loving devotion is that the offering is meant to please the Lord. Thus, those things that are displeasing to the Lord will not be accepted by Him. The acceptance or refusal rests with the Lord; He cannot be forced to accept something, unlike the living entity who is compelled by the circumstances—because he is placed in those circumstances—which may be against his desires. Thus, the jīvā is forced to accept things although he may be unwilling, and the result is displeasure. But the Lord accepts only the pleasing things, if they are offered with the intent to pleasing Him, and with the understanding of what pleases Him. If either of these conditions is not fulfilled, then the offering is not accepted by the Lord. Thus, He is not compelled to accept things; however, He does accept if something is offered devotionally.

QUESTION

You are stating that the Lord accepts if something is offered with devotion but neglects other things. But how can He selectively enjoy some offer when everything is said to be based on His approval and His supervision? How can we say that He sometimes accepts certain things (when offered with devotion) and doesn't accept (when they are evil) but still approves them anyway?

1.2.10 (41)

प्रकरणाच्च

prakaraṇācca

prakaraṇāt—from the context or the episodes; ca—also, and.

TRANSLATION

From the context (or based on the episodes) we can determine.

COMMENTARY

There is a subtle difference between approving something and wanting something. For example, children often do things that please their parents; but in many cases, they also insist on doing things that the parent doesn't approve. The parent still allows those things to happen. If the child gets hurt or unhappy because of those independent actions, the parents cannot be said to get hurt; in fact, the parent will generally say: "I told you so". In the same way, there are things that the jīvā can do for the pleasure of the Lord, and the Lord not only allows it but also accepts and enjoys it. In other cases, the jīvā does things that are independent (and not meant for the pleasure of the Lord) and the Lord still allows it (subject to the *karma* or deserving of the jīvā) but He doesn't enjoy it. This doesn't mean He is suffering because the jīvā has become disobedient.

The distinction between the two forms the attitude of the Paramātma, because in one case He approves and enjoys, and in another case, He approves (based on the *karma*) but doesn't suffer (neither does He enjoy). The distinction is that in one case He is happy, and in the other case He is neutral. While the neutral position is not as good as the one where He enjoys, it also cannot be called His suffering, because suffering would mean that it is out of His control and happening against His will. To uncover these distinctions, we must look at the emotional state of the Lord in different contexts, rather than universal statements about this state. There is a range of emotions between the extremes where the Lord is happy to when He is neutral and allows things to happen in order to fulfill the jīvā's desire. One must note in this context that if the Lord did not allow the jīvā the free will to ignore His instructions, then the love between the ātmā and Paramātma would be considered forced: We would say that the ātmā has no option other than to do what the Paramātma wants. And if there is no choice, then there can be no responsibility. Yes, there can be a perfect world in which everything is perfectly in order, but without free will. That, in turn, would entail that the ātmā cannot have its separate desires and that ultimately it is not an individual. So, the denial of free will collapses individuality; as we have noted, Oneness separates into many because of desires. If these desires are eliminated, then individuality is also lost. However, when individuality exists, all individuals are responsible for their actions. So, neither is the Lord evil because He permits the existence of free will nor is He powerless because things are happening against His will. Both types of claims are incorrect, and the distinction needs to be made based on the context, or a case-by-case basis.

Topic 3

QUESTION

If the Paramātma allows the soul to do what it desires (subject to its karma) then why does He even exist in the heart? He could stay outside, appear externally if the soul is devoted, but remain absent otherwise, and allow the soul freedom that it desires. Why should the Paramātma co-exist with the soul?

1.2.11 (42)

गुहां प्रविष्टावात्मानौ हि तद्दर्शनात्

guhāṃ praviṣṭāvātmānau hi taddarśanāt

guhāṃ—in the cavity (of the heart) praviṣṭau—the two who have entered; ātmānau—are the two souls (individual soul and the Supreme Soul); hi—indeed; taddarśanāt—to make that (the knowledge of the truth) visible.

TRANSLATION

The two who have entered the cavity (of the heart) are indeed the individual soul and the Supreme Soul, to make that (the knowledge) visible.

COMMENTARY

We have noted in 1.2.7 (38) that the Lord expands into an individual just as the concept 'cow' incarnates into each individual cow. Why doesn't this constitute a sufficient explanation of Paramātma's existence in the heart? Why would a seeker inquire more about the same question? The answer is that when we seek the explanation of some event, then there are several types of explanations to be offered; I will divide these into three categories—causes, reasons, and justifications. For instance, if someone with a gun shoots a person, and he is asked: "How did the person get shot?", he might say: "because the trigger of the gun was pressed". This is the cause of the shot. But if he is asked further:

"But why did *you* shoot the person?", he might say: "because I had the intention to kill". However, this still doesn't justify killing. So, if the same question is asked again, seeking to justify his action, he might say: "I was ordered to do so." In short, there are three kinds of explanations for any kind of action: objective, subjective, and intersubjective. All these three kinds of explanations can be offered.

The explanation in 1.2.7 (38) is objective: the Paramātma enters the body as it is an instance of the pure concept of a body or form—i.e., that of God's body. To this explanation, several counterarguments (such as why God doesn't suffer like the soul?) were asked and answered. But if the seeker presses for a response, a deeper reason—namely the subjective explanation—can be offered. The answer is that God wants to come along with the soul. You may ask why? The answer is given in this sūtra: The Lord comes to enlighten the soul, to give it knowledge about 'that' (meaning something beyond this world; the use of the word 'this' would have meant to provide the knowledge of the present world). The explanation indicates that the Lord has compassion for the soul; He comes as He wants to liberate the soul from the clutches of material existence.

The situation is akin to that of a child playing with fire; since the child is defiant, the mother may allow the child to do so, and doesn't need to watch (if the mother did not care for the outcome). But the mother is also compassionate; she allows the child to play with fire, and even assists the child by giving him implements to start the fire, but also keeps a close watch over the child in case he goes too far, gets burnt, and then remembers or cries for the mother to help. The mother is just nearby to immediately rescue the child if so needed.

QUESTION

Since the Paramātma is guiding the soul in both cases—i.e., when we want to enjoy the material world, and when we want to be liberated—how can we know which guidance is for which purpose? This guidance comes to us as ideas. But how can we distinguish between the idea that can liberate us from the material world and the one that is going to bind us to the material world?

This question arises in the life of all spiritual practitioners. The Paramātma simply gives us ideas to fulfill our desires. Therefore, even if we have the desire to kill somebody, Paramātma will still give us the intelligence on *how* to kill effectively (since we don't want to be caught in the act). This means that the Paramātma is supporting both good and evil desires. Now, this poses the question: How do we know which guidance is good or evil? Isn't it possible that the idea given by Paramātma is going to bind me to the material world?

1.2.12 (43)

वशिषणाच्च

viśeṣaṇācca

viśeṣaṇāt—from the distinctive qualities; ca—and.

TRANSLATION

Also from the distinctive qualities.

COMMENTARY

There are difficulties in understanding this sūtra because the meaning of 'distinctive qualities' is not apparent. We have discussed the many ways in which the ātmā and Paramātma are different; so, it is illogical to suppose that 'distinctive qualities' refers to this difference. We have also spoken about the difference between the ātmā and prakriti or the three modes of nature, and the goal of the entire text is liberation from matter; so, it is imprudent to suppose that 'distinctive qualities' refer to the difference between matter and the soul. We have also spoken about the difference between material and transcendental qualities—namely, that the transcendental qualities are knowledge, beauty, power, wealth, fame, and renunciation itself, and they are mutually reconciled in God's person, while the material qualities are just parts of these qualities and they cannot be reconciled; hence, the difference cannot refer to the distinction between God's qualities and the material qualities. We have also spoken about the differences in God's attitude toward the devotee and the non-devotee: He remains neutral to the non-devotee and favorably accepts the offerings of the devotee; He is inclined toward the devotee but not biased against the non-devotee (as He fulfills the desires of even the non-devotees). Therefore, the term 'distinctive qualities' also cannot refer to the different moods of the Lord.

If we remove all the above interpretations, because they have already been indicated previously, and don't have to be repeated (bear in mind that the Vedānta Sūtra is nyāya-prasthāna and must proceed logically), then we are compelled to use another interpretation of the term 'distinctive qualities'.

One possible understanding is that the term 'distinctive qualities' refers to the attitudes of the jīvā itself. The previous sūtra mentioned that the Lord comes with the soul to save Him. But He doesn't always save Him from danger or from material entanglement. Therefore, the distinction between when He saves and when He doesn't save must be attributed to the distinctive qualities in the soul—i.e., it depends on the soul's inclination and desire. In the previous sūtra, it was mentioned that the Lord accepts if something is offered to Him lovingly. At the end of the previous section, it was also explained that even though Paramātma controls everything, the jīvā can liberate Himself by taking shelter of the Paramātma. All these actions require an act of will on the part of the jīvā—i.e., the jīvā must endeavor by desiring the help of Paramātma. In the sūtra 1.2.10 (41) we have discussed the importance of free will, namely, that the Lord will approve even if something is dangerous to the soul. So, the Lord cannot be accused of non-compassion, because forcing the best outcome becomes contrary to the existence of free will. The implication again is that the prerogative of taking the help from Paramātma rests with the jīvā, not the Paramātma.

So, the interpretation of 'distinctive qualities' can be that the jīvā has different desires and attitudes; sometimes it desires surrender (when he is suffering) and then independence (especially when he is enjoying). The inspirations from the Paramātma are accordingly different. Therefore, if one wanted to truly know if the Paramātma is giving transcendental advice or simply fulfilling one's material desire, then, one can also look at one's attitudes. Am I desiring something pure and transcendental, or am I asking for material enjoyment? Is the guiding motivation underlying my desires material or spiritual?

This sūtra points towards a reflective state of the mind in which to know the truth, we don't look outward—e.g., whether some facts will confirm or deny the truth of my ideas, or whether these ideas can be proved or disproved. We rather look at our attitudes. Do I have the right attitude? Because the ideas that are coming to me may or may not be rationally or empirically confirmed; their confirmation doesn't indicate that they are spiritual, and their disconfirmation doesn't indicate that they are material (or even vice versa). The real test is the purity of the inclination or intention with which I seek answers. If my intentions are pure and transcendental, then the answers provided by Paramātma will lead me to transcendence. If they are impure, they will bind me to the material world, and I have nobody other than myself to blame. for the outcome.

Topic 4

QUESTION

Parents may sometimes abandon their children if they are consistently defiant. In such cases, even if we consider the parents of the child to be compassionate, this compassion seems to have limits. Doesn't the compassion of God have limits? Doesn't He abandon the defiant child under any circumstance?

While practicing spiritual life, a person can become dejected due to lack of progress, or very slow progress. He might realize that he hasn't entirely been dedicated to the Lord or being devoted to Him. A doubt then arises in his mind: Since I haven't been totally devoted, the Lord must have abandoned me. Since I have performed many sinful activities (sometimes called aparādha—such as by offending other devotees) the Lord has finally decided that I am irredeemable and therefore left me helpless. Now I have no hope because I have no guidance from within on how to achieve the transcendental purpose of life. I'm lost. The seeker is asking such a question: What if I'm indeed very sinful? Does that mean that the Lord will abandon me such that I have no scope for redemption?

1.2.13 (44)

अन्तर उपपत्तेः

antara upapatteḥ

antaraḥ—inside, the being inside; upapatteḥ—due to justification.

TRANSLATION

The Lord stays within because this is the justified action.

COMMENTARY

We earlier cited three explanations for a question—causes, reasons, and justifications; causes are objective, reasons are subjective, and justifications are intersubjective. The objective and subjective explanations of the Lord's presence in the heart have already been offered. We said that the Lord appears in the heart since the jīvā is an instance of the Supreme Person. Then we said that the Lord appears because He is compassionate and wants to free the soul from the clutches of material existence. But if someone insists on the same question, the third argument—the *justification*—can also be offered. Given the repeating nature of the similar statement—namely, that the Lord exists in the heart—we are compelled to ask ourselves: Why is the same thing being repeated in the same way? The answer is that different explanations are being offered.

The answer is that the Lord is duty-bound to be present in the heart. Even if the soul commits many offenses—e.g., hurting other devotees or consistently defying the instructions of the spiritual master—the Lord never abandons the soul. His compassion has a limit, and His love is not infinite; in particular, the Lord is indeed offended if other devotees and the spiritual master are offended. To hurt someone who is devoted to the Lord is indeed offensive and invites the anger of the Lord. He is not merely a passive observer; He has feelings too. But despite His feelings of anger at a defiant soul, He doesn't abandon the soul because He considers it His duty to rescue the soul. This just means that the Lord may not provide spiritual guidance to the soul, but He is ever-present lest there is a moment of repentance and realization that a change needs to be made.

This idea is important considering that in other religions the soul is eternally condemned to hell. This and the previous sūtras have been asserting that the Lord never abandons the soul. This one particularly says that the Lord is ever-present in the heart because He is duty-bound to do so. Just like we are duty-bound to protect all the parts of our body, and we never consider any part of the body a burden—even if it gives us pain—similarly, the Lord considers the soul as part of His existence, and even though He may be disenchanted with the scope for progress, He stands a watch just in case the soul changes his desire. This statement can be considered the ultimate answer to the problem of spiritual abandonment due to offenses against the Lord or His devotees. While these are real problems, the Paramātma still doesn't abandon the soul.

QUESTION

If the Paramātma is present in all living entities, why can't we worship all these living entities as if they were God? We could say that even dogs and cats have Paramātma in them, so by feeding them, we are feeding the Paramātma. In short, why can't we worship God through the other living entities?

Many people are fond of saying that "service to man is service to God". Missionary organizations, therefore, have made it a practice to provide food, clothes, education, hospitals, etc. as a method of serving God. There are of course in many cases hidden agendas underlying the missionary services: Some of them may use such offerings to 'convert' the person to a certain religion, as a way of increasing the following of that religion, etc. These conversions may then be used for political purposes or social engineering. However, even if such ulterior purposes did not exist—and 'conversion' for political or social reasons wasn't being employed—you could still say that the service of the poor and destitute was service to God because ultimately God is present in everyone.

1.2.14 (45)
स्थानादिव्यपदेशाच्च
sthānādivyapadeśācca

sthānādi—all places; vyapadeśāt—from concealments (of the object); ca—and.

TRANSLATION

And all the places (i.e., objects) are from concealments of the real object.

COMMENTARY

The contentious part of this sūtra is the use of vyapadeśāt. In other sūtras, we have translated it as 'due to the statement' or 'due to the claim'. If we apply that translation here, then the sūtra would say: "and because of the statement in all places". In reference to the previous sūtra, where the Paramātma's existence within has been justified, this sūtra would state precious little. We have expended this entire section discussing the Paramātma's existence within, how He differs from the soul, and three explanations of why He exists within. So, why should we repeat the same by asserting that "it is also said in all places". Of course, this is not an invalid translation; it would just be redundant.

Therefore, we translate vyapadeśa as the concealment of the real object. In nātya-sāśtra, or the scripture on the performance of drama, this term is used to denote one of the twelve ways of expression: "to speak with the purpose of deception, is called pretext or vyapadeśa". In some contexts, the term can be used to denote 'fraud' or 'dishonesty'. What we see, is not what reality is. The implication is that even though God is everywhere, those places are the covering, a symbolic representation, or the deception of the real thing. Now, one can say that this contradicts all that we have discussed previously, so some clarification is required; we can understand the meaning by Bhagavad Gita 9.4:

mayā tatam idaṁ sarvaṁ
jagad avyakta-mūrtinā
mat-sthāni sarva-bhūtāni
na cāhaṁ teṣv avasthitaḥ

By Me, in My unmanifested form, this entire universe is pervaded. All beings are in Me, but I am not situated in them.

Two things are important here. First, the term *avyakta-mūrtinā* which means the 'unmanifest form'; it is a form, so it is not impersonal. But it is not manifest.

Now one might say: If He is not manifest, then in what way can we say that He exists? This question is answered in Bhagavad-Gita 9.29:

samo 'haṁ sarva-bhūteṣu
na me dveṣyo 'sti na priyaḥ
ye bhajanti tu māṁ bhaktyā
mayi te teṣu cāpy aham

I envy no one, nor am I partial to anyone. I am equal to all. But whoever renders service unto Me in devotion, I am also present inside them.

In short, the Lord is present everywhere, but He is not *manifest* to our vision unless there is a devotional attitude. His 'equality' toward everyone is explained by the fact that He is present everywhere, but His disposition to manifest is toward those who are devoted to Him. Therefore, all beings—such as cats and dogs—or even other humans, cannot be worshipped as God, unless they are devotees, because God is not manifest in their hearts, although He exists in an unmanifest form. He cannot accept the offering made to such beings unless He is manifest; therefore, such offerings are only to the 'covering' that hides His unmanifest form. In short, the bodies of different living entities cannot be worshipped as if they were God. This is clearly stated in Bhagavad-Gita 9.25:

yānti deva-vratā devān
pitṝn yānti pitṛ-vratāḥ
bhūtāni yānti bhūtejyā
yānti mad-yājino 'pi mām

> Those who worship the demigods will take birth among the demigods; those who worship ghosts and spirits will take birth among such beings; those who worship ancestors go to the ancestors; and those who worship Me will live with Me.

This is a repudiation of the idea that if God exists everywhere, the worship of all beings must produce the same result and can be called service to God. The worship of demigods, ghosts, spirits, ancestors—and by extension, the worship of humans, animals, trees, etc.—cannot be considered God's worship.

We have explained this previously in a different way when we cited the example of the concept of cow instantiating into an individual cow. The perception of an individual cow requires us to bring to the mind the concept of cow and realize that this is an instance of that concept. But if we don't use the correct concept, then we will not see a cow. Of course, that will be a wrong perception, but it is a perception we can have. The cowness in a cow is a possibility; it can manifest itself if we perceive it correctly. But we may not perceive it correctly. In the same way, Paramātma's presence is a possibility; He exists, but He is not manifest. To convert that possibility into a reality, we need a devotional attitude. We must have a strong desire to perceive His existence. The service of those individuals where such a devotional attitude already exists can be considered the worship of God; accordingly, the service to the pure devotees of the Lord is considered the service of the Lord, because the Lord is manifest in their heart. But it cannot be extended to all beings where He is not manifest.

QUESTION

If the manifestation of the Lord in the heart is the outcome of our devotion, then how will we know where He is manifest and where He is unmanifest? In short, whose worship and service should be considered as service of God?

In the previous purport, it was said that the Lord is hidden, and the body is a deceptive covering of His existence. But if that is the case, then how can we identify in whose heart He is manifest, and where He is not manifest? This is an important practical question for those seeking self-realized devotees. How can such devotees be identified, if the body is merely a deceptive covering?

1.2.15 (46)

सुखविशिष्टाभिधानादेव च

sukhaviśiṣṭābhidhānādeva ca

sukha—bliss; viśiṣṭa—the qualities, the symptoms, the distinguishing characteristics; abhidhānāt—on account of the wealth; eva—certainly; ca—and.

TRANSLATION

And because the distinguishing characteristics of bliss are certainly manifest because of the wealth (of the presence of Paramātma in the heart).

COMMENTARY

Many people pretend to be spiritually advanced. They might speak well; they may be great scholars or have large followings. However, these are not the symptoms by which a spiritually advanced person is to be identified. A simple prescription of this advancement is described here: the existence of bliss in the heart is also manifest externally. These symptoms are sometimes called *asta-sattvika-vikara* or eight modifications of the body. These are: being stunned, perspiration, standing of the bodily hairs on end, faltering of the voice, trembling, fading of the body's color, tears, and devastation. As has already been indicated previously, the spiritually advanced soul is one who has the perception of God; it is not merely the acquisition of theoretical knowledge, but the realization of this knowledge as the Original Form. Since this realization requires devotion, the symptoms of advancements are also the development of an internal bliss due to the perception of the Lord in the heart. This perception then manifests through the mind and eventually through the body. Those who cannot perceive the spiritual state, or the mind can still distinguish the spiritually advanced persons through the presence of the *aśta-sāttvika-vikāra*.

QUESTION

You have said that the Lord is seen by a devotional attitude. But what

does a person do if he doesn't have the attitude? Can one acquire an attitude?

At the end of the last section, the surrender to the Lord was prescribed. Through the current section thus far, the nature of the Lord, His existence in the heart, and why He is present and yet absent until devotion is manifest has been described. However, the process of developing this devotion hasn't been spoken about. The seeker is now asking about the method for acquiring devotion.

1.2.16 (47)

श्रुतोपनिषत्कगत्यभिधानाच्च

śrutopaniṣatkagatyabhidhānācca

śruta—heard; upaniṣatka—Upaniśads; gati—way, or process, or method; abhidhānāt—because of the wealth; ca—and.

TRANSLATION

And the process (of acquiring devotion) is the hearing of the Upaniśad because they provide the wealth (of information about the Lord and the devotion toward Him; both these types of information can be considered wealth).

COMMENTARY

This sūtra indicates that if one doesn't possess the devotional attitude, then he must hear the Upaniśad where the Lord is described. By hearing this knowledge, a devotional attitude can be developed. We must recall that the guidance to acquire the knowledge of Brahman through the study of Vedic scripture was provided in 1.1.3 (3). Subsequently, the text also discussed how the scripture discusses various topics, but their goal is to understand the nature of the Absolute Truth. Therefore, one might wonder: why is the study of Upaniśad being prescribed again when it has already been stated at the very beginning of Vedānta Sūtra? The short answer to that is the context of this sūtra is different from that of the previous statements. Earlier, the guidance was based on the general inquiry of how one can know about Brahman. However, now, through the previous sūtras, the devotion to Paramātma has been discussed. This sūtra should, therefore, be understood not merely as a repetition of what has previously been stated, but as a further statement that the devotion to the Lord is acquired through repeated hearing from the scriptures.

Many academics study the Upaniśad and analyze its meaning; they claim to be scholars of texts. But we cannot find the symptoms of bliss on their body, as we discussed in the previous sūtra. The meaning of this sūtra is uncovered in the context of the mention of that bliss and how it is acquired. It means that if someone hasn't developed the bliss, then he hasn't understood the Upaniśad. They may not have a devotional attitude, or they may simply be progressing on the devotional path, although they may not have perfected it. Either way, true knowledge is understood to have been gained only if that bliss is present. This sets the benchmark for who can be considered knowledgeable in the Upaniśad: they must have acquired the internal bliss by the perception of the Lord.

QUESTION

If we repeatedly dwell on something, we develop an attraction toward it. How can this repeated hearing not be considered indoctrination into an ideology? By repeated hearing, we change the way we look at the world. Once our mind has been altered, we are naturally bound to see the world in terms of that ideology. So, how can this repeated hearing of Upaniśad not be considered the creation of perceptual bias, that leads to the outcome that we desire to see?

The problem of indoctrination resulting in perceptual bias is real. If we repeatedly hear about something, we begin to believe it, no matter how false it may be. This is the basis of propaganda—a lie repeated sufficiently enough times begins to be accepted as truth, just because it has been heard repeatedly. If the prescription of the process to develop devotion is to repeatedly hear about the Lord, isn't this process like the propaganda that relies on repetition?

1.2.17 (48)

अनवस्थितिरसंभवाच्च नेतरः

anavasthiterasaṃbhavācca netaraḥ

anavasthiteḥ—not existing always; asaṃbhavāt—from the impossibility; ca—and; na—not; itaraḥ—any other.

TRANSLATION

From the impossibility also, it cannot be any other as they are not always existing.

COMMENTARY

You can fool all people some of the time, and some of the people all the time, but not all people all the time. The same holds true of indoctrination and propaganda. It can be used to deceive many people, but eventually, most people will come to their senses. This is because all false propaganda and indoctrination have an end; it ends when facts and truths contradict their existence.

The narrations of the Lord, however, are not indoctrination because He is established in the heart, then the bliss is incomparable to anything else. The experience of bliss causes the devotee to abandon all other focuses, and the perception of the Lord becomes continuous. The experience of bliss and the persistent focus are impossible for anything else; those other things may be established in our mind and can become the lenses through which we perceive the world, however, their perception doesn't create bliss. Though stringently abiding by such beliefs, the soul is never happy; he keeps seeking something better, although he stridently claims the truth of what he believes in. In fact, if challenged about his beliefs, the person becomes angry—if this idea, which I have painfully acquired were to be taken away from me, then I would be left in utter confusion; I would have no other rock to anchor my life onto. To avoid that devastating outcome, one aggressively fights the opponents to convince himself. However, despite showing signs of external aggression and belief, such a person remains dissatisfied with their beliefs because they do not produce happiness. The perception of the Lord is not like that. It leads to bliss, the destruction of all confusion, the overcoming of anger and fear because of which the soul is completely convinced of the Lord's existence even if he is surrounded by those who may not have the same beliefs; similarly, the soul overcomes all boredom—the cause of constant distractions; he is situated in bliss. The combination of all such outcomes is impossible for anything other than the Lord.

Topic 5

QUESTION

I can understand that such attainment would be ideal. However, the process seems difficult. In the meanwhile, I have many practical problems in day-to-day life. It is said that the different demigods control the different aspects of material life—such as Kubera for wealth, Kāmadeva for marital happiness, Chandra for a peaceful mind, Surya for a strong body and health, etc. Shouldn't we worship the Lord alongside these demigods for all-round happiness of the body, mind, and soul? Your prescriptions are only meant for the soul.

1.2.18 (49)

अन्तर्यामी अधिदैवादिषु तद्धर्मव्यपदेशात्

taddharmavyapadesat antaryāmī adhidaivādiṣu taddharmavyapadeśāt

antaryāmī—the dweller within; adhidaivādiṣu—the origin of the demigods; tat—His; dharma—attributes; vyapadeśāt—being pervasively present.

TRANSLATION

The internal dweller (the Paramātma) is the origin of the demigods; His attributes and qualities are pervasively present (as the demigod's qualities).

COMMENTARY

The three modes of material nature—called sattva, rajas, and tamas—are also said to manifest into three parts called ādidaivika, ādibhautika, and ādiatmika. The ādiatmika represents the body and the mind of a person. The ādibhautika represents the other living entities with whom a person's body and mind interact. However, this interaction is controlled; it is not that anybody can interact with anybody else. These controllers—who decide who will interact with whom (or what)—are called the ādidaivika or the demigods. For example, your body is ādiatmika, food is ādibhautika, and the demigod who controls the body's access to food is ādidaivika. Therefore, the body and the mind are the subjects, the things with which we interact externally are the objects, and the demigods decide if some subject can be permitted to interact with other objects.

These interactions are based on two things—our desiring and our deserving. Sometimes, the deserving overrides the desiring and delivers things that we may not desire; we may be pleasantly or unpleasantly surprised by this automatic encounter with desirable or undesirable interactions. At other times, the desiring overrides the deserving and we can choose one out of many pleasant or unpleasant outcomes. In either case, the demigods are controlling the fulfillment of desires. This sūtra further states that the Paramātma is the origin of the demigods who partially manifest His power over different things. For example, there is a controller of rain (Indra), the mind (Chandra), the body (Surya), etc. The power of their control is a partial manifestation of the Paramātma.

The implication is that even if one is worried about their mental and physical difficulties, it is best to worship the Paramātma because the demigods work under His supervision and manifest His power of control. The Paramātma has delegated these powers—as a king delegates work to ministers, but the ministers still work under the instructions and order of the king. Therefore, if the king is pleased, then the ministers will automatically do his bidding. In the Bhagavad Gita 7.16, it is stated that four kinds of pious people worship the Lord: these are called the distressed, the desirous, the curious, and the knowledgeable. Therefore, even one distressed or desirous should still worship the Lord.

catur-vidhā bhajante māṁ
janāḥ su-kṛtino 'rjuna
ārto jijñāsur arthārthī
jñānī ca bharatarṣabha

> O best among the Bharatas, four kinds of pious men render devotional service unto Me—the distressed, the desirer of wealth, the inquisitive, and he who is searching for knowledge of the Absolute.

The sūtra indicates that the well-being of the soul—through the worship of the Paramātma takes care of the well-being of the body and mind as well.

QUESTION

But the smārta (a tradition of ritual worship prevalent in ancient India) indicates that one must perform different kinds of rituals and that is the only dharma. They are also opposed to the Upaniśad as being the source of truth. How do we reconcile this contradiction in the different approaches?

The smārta tradition is also called Pūrva-Mīmāṃsā as it deals with the "earlier" Vedic texts, which prescribe the performance of rituals; however, it doesn't consider the existence of gods or God, the primary knowledge. It considers the Upaniśad as "later" texts and secondary in nature. As a result, the Vedānta system (propounded through this text) came to be also known as Uttara- Mīmāṃsā. For the Mīmāṃsā school, dharma is rituals, and social duties are of primary importance. Any philosophical doctrine of reality is secondary.

1.2.19 (50)

न च स्मार्तम् अतद्धर्माभिलापात्

na ca smārtam ataddharmābhilāpāt

na—neither; ca—also, and; smārtam—that taught by smārta brahmanas; ataddharmābhilāpāt—from qualities contrary to its nature being mentioned.

TRANSLATION

And (the Paramātma is) not that which is taught in smārta system because qualities contrary to its nature are mentioned (here).

COMMENTARY

The distinction between Mīmāṃsā and Vedānta can be illustrated through the example of *realist* and *instrumentalist* views in the philosophy of modern science. The realist believes that when an action is performed (the cause), a result (the effect) is produced. However, the connection between the cause and the effect is mediated by a law described in a theory that generally invokes many metaphysical concepts. For example, the gravitational theory postulates the existence of metaphysical ideas like mass and a gravitational force to explain the observed motion. The realist takes this causal mechanism seriously and considers it real. However, many philosophers of science—beginning with David Hume and George Berkeley—challenged these assumptions. Hume, for instance, argued that causality involves necessity (that every time the cause occurs, the effect will naturally follow), but scientific theories cannot prove necessity as they have not been tested in all possible scenarios. This problem was further established as science provided newer explanations for older phenomena. It was now realized that if older theories could be falsified, then a similar fate was imminent even for current theories. But this problem was not taken very seriously as long as there was a causal explanation. A far more damaging problem was encountered in atomic theory where one could make probabilistic predictions although there were no explanations. Many scientists now adopted an instrumentalist doctrine—that science is not about the nature of reality; it is simply an instrument that can be employed to make some predictions; these need not be all the predictions, and since the theory wasn't about the nature of reality, it could also be revised in future. The theory was simply a convenient tool to be used to build successful technologies, waiting to be changed later.

In a similar vein, the Mīmāṃsā philosopher states that the essence of life is the performance of actions; these actions produce effects, and that is enough. How the cause connects to the effects—e.g., that the actions produce results because there are demigods controlled by the Paramātma—are irrelevant to the performance of rituals and the results thus obtained. We just focus on the actions and ensure that they are performed correctly. The results will automatically follow; it is not our job to analyze why the results follow the actions, because we have no empirical method to observe what happens "behind the scenes". The Mīmāṃsā philosopher is an instrumentalist. He treats the rituals as useful methods to obtain the desired results but doesn't worry about the mechanisms that connect causes to effects. They, of course, may not deny that such causal mechanisms can exist; they are just not interested in them.

The Vedānta philosopher is, on the other hand, a realist. He is interested in how the world originated, what existed before this origination, how the soul is caught in the cause-and-effect of material nature, how it can be liberated from the cycle of birth and death, and the reality beyond this world. Owing to this focus on the nature of reality—which lies "behind the scenes"—the Vedānta system is least interested in the appearances—i.e., the performance of rituals and the obtainment of these results. He considers them temporary because all effects are eventually lost, and the actions must be performed again. He is primarily interested in the nature of reality, or that which is eternally existent.

While we might see a contradiction between Mīmāṃsā and Vedānta philosophies, they are not logically contradictory. The former is focused on action and result, while the latter on the mechanisms behind this cause and effect. Owing to this difference, the prescription of Mīmāṃsā to just be an instrumentalist and forget about the reality behind change, is rejected in Vedānta. Vedānta rejects this instrumentalist view and claims that we haven't understood the world simply because by actions we get results; we ought to know the nature of reality that underlies the phenomena because that is the eventual goal.

In that vein, the sūtra asserts that the qualities pursued by Mīmāṃsā—i.e., the action and its results—are different from those which we are discussing here. Their goal is a practical technology for solving day-to-day problems, and our interest at present is the science that makes this technology possible. Whether the Vedas described the technology before science is irrelevant to us. Ultimately, if we know the science, we can also build the technology. But, if we just know the technology, we cannot understand the science. Therefore, the pursuit of Mīmāṃsā—while practically useful—is ultimately incomplete.

QUESTION

However, you have earlier mentioned that hearing of the Upaniśad is the path to attaining devotion. So, you are also prescribing a process, which can be called dharma. In the same way, the smārta practitioners also consider the chanting of the Vedic mantra as dharma. How can these be different?

A legitimate doubt is being raised here, namely, that the smārta Brahmins are chanting the mantra from the 'previous' sections of the Vedas, while the Vedānta system is prescribing the chanting of the verses from the 'subsequent' sections of the Vedas. Now, one may say that one is an instrumentalist and the other a realist. But for the practitioner, what difference does it make? Even the chanting of mantra by the smārta produces results. So, even if the smārta doesn't believe in the underlying realist causality, he must ultimately get the result. Vedānta may believe in the reality that causes the effects. However, ultimately, both are chanting mantras and hence both are getting their results. How can we discriminate between the Mīmāṃsā and the Vedānta if we are only looking at the outcomes of chanting instead of the phenomena vs. the reality?

1.2.20 (51)

शरीरश्च उभयेऽपि हि भेदेनैनमधीयते

śarīraśca ubhaye'pi hi bhedenainamadhīyate

śarīraḥ—the body; ca—also; ubhaye—both (ātmā and Paramātma); api—even; hi—certainly; bhedena—by way of difference; enam—these (the matter referred in the previous sūtra—namely rituals); adhīyate—bind or tie.

TRANSLATION

Even though both (the ātmā and Paramātma) are certainly different from the body, these (rituals) also increase the bondage to the body.

COMMENTARY

There is a problem here: Why should *ubhaye* be used, when it suffices to say that the ātmā is different from the body? The answer lies in Mīmāṃsā where the ātmā is considered eternal (and hence real), however, the system rejects (or is unconcerned) with the reality of any gods or God. By implication, the existence of Paramātma is also not accepted. By noting that even the Paramātma is different from the soul and the body, indirectly, two separate statements are being made in sūtra: (1) the bondage resulting from the performance of rituals, and (2) that there are two eternal entities in Vedānta whereas there is only one entity (the ātmā) in Mīmāṃsā. This difference is pertinent to the entire context because the purpose of yoga as described earlier is the devotion between the ātmā and Paramātma; it is not merely the performance of worldly duties.

With this clarification, we can try to understand this sūtra. The previous sūtra mentioned that the qualities of Paramātma are different than those presumed by the *smarta*; we further clarified that the goal of the *smarta* is an empirical success while the goal of the Vedānta is the pursuit of reality. However, one can argue that regardless of whether a person is a realist or not, ultimately, the results matter—e.g., salvation from the material world. If one system is chanting the 'previous' texts while the other is chanting the 'subsequent' texts, they are both chanting, and they will therefore obtain the result—i.e., salvation. So, how does the belief in some reality make a difference to the outcome?

This sūtra clarifies that the actions of the Pūrva Mīmāṃsā philosopher will bind them to the material existence. Most people work only because there is a result. This attachment to results, and performance of work under that expectation, is contrary to karma-yoga, where an aspirant is instructed to act without expectation. This detachment is necessary—while we need things for the body, the ātmā is different from the body; attachment to results doesn't lead to the realization that the ātmā is different from the body; in fact, it binds it more.

The goal of Vedānta is liberation from the cycle of action and consequence. So, there is a difference between dharma or the duties of the material world (which produce the outcomes because those outcomes must be reaped) and the dharma performed for liberation from the material world. If one keeps performing these actions, one is continuously in the cycle of action and reaction. How can that cycle be considered salvation from the material existence? The goal of Vedānta is not the pursuit of material duties, but the understanding of the transcendent reality. The mantras pertaining to this transcendent reality—i.e., the Upaniśad—take one out of the cycle of action and reaction, and lead to salvation. Therefore, we cannot consider the 'previous' and 'subsequent' sections of the Vedas on the same level or producing the same kind of outcomes (e.g., salvation). Although both are chanted, the former pertains to the cycle of action and reaction of this world, while the latter yields freedom from this cycle.

The distinction between Mīmāṃsā and Vedānta isn't simply that one pertains to 'previous' texts while the other one to 'later' texts. The difference is not just that the former is instrumentalist while the latter is realist. The prominent difference is that the former keeps one bound to the material world through the cycle of action and reaction while the latter results in salvation from this cycle. Therefore, both are chanting the Vedas, but one is creating bondage to the cycle of cause and effect, while the other is yielding freedom from this cycle.

Topic 6

QUESTION

But how can we believe that such transcendent reality exists? It is easier to trust that which we can perceive (by our senses). The Mīmāṃsā system deals with what we can perceive—the actions and their results. On the other hand, you are describing an invisible reality. How can we believe that any such reality exists 'behind' the perceptions when perceptions are all that we can have?

This is a famous argument in Western philosophy, originally formulated by George Berkeley against the distinction between primary and secondary properties. The proponents of science claimed that certain properties (such as length, mass, speed, time, etc.—called primary properties) are real, whereas other properties (such as color, taste, smell, touch, etc.—called secondary properties) are unreal. This argument rests on the claim that the secondary properties depend on the observer, but the world must be independent of the observer. Berkeley, however, argued that the so-called primary properties are only objectification of our sensations. For example, the primary property of 'weight' is the objectification of the perceptual experience of 'heaviness'. The primary property of 'temperature' is the objectification of the perception of 'heat'. Therefore, only our perceptions are direct and real, and everything—supposedly 'behind' these perceptions—is only our theoretical construction. A similar type of argument was also advanced during Greek times by Socrates through the example of cavemen who look at shadows on the walls of the cave, but these shadows are cast by something that is behind them (they cannot see the source). How can they know that the figure of a man is created by a real man or by the hands of a shadowgraphist creating the false impression of a man? In the same vein, we can argue that Mīmāṃsā is dealing with what we can observe, while Vedānta is talking about this reality which lies behind the observation and hence remains invisible; how can we believe this reality indeed exists?

1.2.21 (52)
अदृश्यत्वादिगुणको धर्मोक्तेः
adṛśyatvādiguṇako dharmokteḥ

adṛśyatvādi—invisibility; adi—the origin; guṇako—one who possesses the quality; dharmokteḥ—because of the manifestation of observable qualities.

TRANSLATION

The invisible is the origin and possessor of all the observable qualities.

COMMENTARY

All scientific theories draw a distinction between an *object* and its *property*. The property can be position or mass or speed, while the object is a particle. The particle is always invisible; however, we postulate the existence of such an invisible entity to give a realist interpretation to science—namely that there is something to which the properties are bound; this particle is the 'possessor' of the properties; thus, for instance, we say that the particle has mass or speed or position. In classical physics, two such types of objects are used, namely, particle and field. The main difference is that the particle has a definite position (i.e., is in one location) while the field doesn't have a position (because it is spread everywhere). We could talk about the position within a field, but we could not attach a position to the field itself. Therefore, it was understood that certain types of objects can only have certain types of properties. This fact has created many problems in atomic theory because the atoms—which we like to think are particles—seem to be simultaneously present in more than one place, thus exhibiting the property that we would normally associate with fields. However, there cannot be two objects underlying the same property because then we could not say that the object is the possessor of the property. The point is that of the distinction between an object and a property; the object is the invisible entity to which the visible properties are attached, as nouns and adjectives.

So, if we argue that since the object is invisible, and its existence is therefore suspect, and only the visible properties must be considered, then the result is the collapse of realism because we would be preoccupied with the study of properties, and not know what lies 'behind' these properties, which ties them together. Once we lose the reality of the object, then how the properties hang together would also be lost. We could still speak about 'property atoms'—e.g., a unit of mass or speed—but we could not tie these two properties together because the agency of the object that tied them doesn't exist. This idea is sometimes called 'dustbowl empiricism' where the universe is the dustbowl of properties; there are merely atoms of properties, but nothing ties them together, and therefore this 'dust' doesn't accumulate into objects. There is also a more serious issue, namely, that we cannot formulate the laws of change if we take away the objects. For instance, we could not say that the particle is moving *because* it has mass. After all, the speed of motion and the mass are two unrelated properties as the object which tied them together no longer exists. So, the rejection of the invisible leads to a complete collapse of science. This might be news to many people, who think that science deals only in what can be observed; this is not true. Science also postulates the existence of invisible things—e.g., particles—which tie all the visible properties together and it is due to the postulate about the invisible that we are even able to formulate predictive natural laws.

Returning to the sūtra, a similar point is made here: The invisible objects (the ātmā and Paramātma) tie together the material properties. They are akin to the 'objects' of science, which possess material properties. As a result, we can say that the ātmā 'has' a body, or the ātmā 'has' thoughts, etc. If these objects are taken out of the equation—as the Mīmāṃsā philosopher argues—then we are left with 'dustbowl empiricism'; we will have properties, but we cannot tie them together. Without the agency that binds these properties, we cannot explain why some taste is tied to some smell or some color is tied to some form; once we lose this property binding, all predictive causality would be lost.

Another distinctive point in this sūtra is that the objects tying the properties together are ātmā or the Paramātma. There is no 'particle' or 'wave' as in the case of material science. This is a rejection of material 'objects' that tie the properties together. The claim is that there are material properties, but they come together because of the soul. This is very important because it entails that all the material properties such as taste, smell, touch, form, color, etc. are not 'together' into an object because of some material object (such as a particle or a wave). These are together due to the existence of the invisible objects of ātmā and Paramātma. There is hence a subtle but important difference between the notion of invisible objects in the case of modern science and Vedānta: Science postulates the invisible material objects, e.g., particle and wave. Vedānta Sūtra instead states that there are no such material objects; the object in question is the ātmā or the Paramātma. If these don't exist, then material properties cannot come together to form bodies; the world would be a dustbowl of properties.

Now, we can answer the question of whether the object that ties together these properties is ātmā or Paramātma. This question should be answered from the perspective of the Mīmāṃsā philosopher, who accepts the ātmā, but not the Paramātma. The context also indicates that the difference between the performance of material duties and transcendence is in regard to the Paramātma. The 'invisible' should, therefore, be understood as the Paramātma; He is called avyakta-murti or the invisible form. We can also say that for the ātmā the existence of the self is not in doubt; this could also be asserted based on the Cartesian dictum that "I think therefore I am". When we talk about 'invisible' in material science, the question is different than for someone who accepts the ātmā.

Therefore, the implication is that the Paramātma binds the properties together. Vedic texts describe the Paramātma as a manifestation of the mode of sattva-guna (unlike Brahma who represents rajo-guna and Śiva who represents tamo-guna). Furthermore, the Paramātma 'maintains' the world, Brahma 'creates' it, and Śiva 'destroys' it. These descriptions can be understood through this sūtra. The creation, maintenance, and destruction pertain to the body. The material properties are eternal; however, they are instantiated, combined or dissociated. While they are associated, the Paramātma is the 'maintainer' Who keeps everything together. In short, the fact that I have a body is because the Paramātma is the object who is holding the material properties together.

However, this raises a difficult issue: If the Paramātma is holding the world together, and He is the object underlying the phenomena, then the laws of nature must also apply to the Paramātma. In short, He would become implicated in the process of our actions. This is where we must invoke the understanding of the previous sūtra where the Paramātma is holding things together on behalf of the soul; He accompanies the soul to fulfill its desires. Therefore, if the body is like a chariot, then the seat, wheels, axle, reins, etc. of the chariot are held together by the Paramātma, and the soul becomes the passenger in the chariot. The Paramātma drives this chariot according to the desiring and the deserving, and therefore only the ātmā is implicated in the cycle of cause and effect.

The main takeaway from this sūtra is that we cannot claim that the gods or God—in this case the Paramātma—don't exist because we cannot observe them. If this view is adopted, then the object that holds things together will disappear. If the ātmā is the cause of this binding, then the implication would be that the ātmā is well-versed in the understanding of material nature because it is orchestrating the body. This is obviously not true, because most of us are not aware of how the body works. The only reasonable position is that someone else is orchestrating this machine on which the ātmā is only a temporary passenger.

QUESTION

It was quite acceptable when you said that the Paramātma is the *kṣetra-jña* or knower of the *kṣetra* or the field because there was an implicit difference between the knower and the known. Owing to this difference, we could say that the Paramātma is transcendent to the matter. However, by saying that the Paramātma is the object that binds together the material properties, you have broken that distinction. It now seems that the Lord has acquired material properties. How can we consider the Lord transcendental when He is being attached to material properties? Wasn't the purpose of Vedānta Sūtra to describe how the Lord is different from the material properties or transcendent to them?

In modern science, the distinction between an object and a property is *logical*. There is no mechanism by which we 'connect' an object to a property. Therefore, if we say that an object has a property, it is implied that the object and the property are connected, however, because the nature of this connection is not clarified, it is natural to suppose that if an object has a material property, then it has become material. In earlier sūtras, the difference between the Lord and the material guna was described, and it was stated that the Lord has no material guna. However, now, we have stated that the Lord possesses these material gunas. This produces a contradiction between the two statements.

1.2.22 (53)

विशेषणभेदव्यपदेशाभ्यां नेतरौ

viśeṣaṇabhedavyapadeśābhyāṃ netarau

viśeṣaṇa—adjectives or qualities; bheda—difference; vyapadeśābhyāṃ—on account of the hiding or covering; na—not; itarau—the other two.

TRANSLATION

The other two (the ātmā and Paramātma) are different from the adjectives or qualities (of the object) because (the latter) are coverings (of the former).

COMMENTARY

There are two distinct ways in which the word 'property' is used: (a) in the scientific sense, the property controls the object, and (b) in the ordinary sense the object controls the property. Take for example the claim that I own this house, this house is mine, and therefore I control the house. The house is my *property* and I am not controlled by the house; rather, I am the controller of the house. However, in the scientific sense, when we ascribe a property to an object, the property becomes the object's controller. For example, a particle moves in a gravitational field due to its mass. The mass is the property, and the particle is the object. But the object is not in control of the mass: i.e., the object cannot decide whether the mass should exert a force or not. The mass acts independently of the particle, according to the laws of gravitation, and that force then pushes the particle. In short, the mass drives the particle's dynamics. If the same situation was applied to the ordinary ownership of properties, then we would say that the acquisition or ownership of the house is forcing me to do things (that I would not otherwise do). That would, however, bring to question the premise of ownership: Do I possess the house, or does the house possess me?

It is true that the Lord is the *kṣetrajña* or the knower of the *kṣetra* or the field. It is also true that the *kṣetra* is a property of the *kṣetrajña*. However, unlike the scientific properties, which control the object, in this case, the object controls the properties. In scientific theories, the causality of motion is in the property (such as mass) and the particle is causally inert. In the case of Vedānta, the material properties are inert, and the object has the causality of motion. In short, the world is moving not because there is some mass that is attracted by other masses due to gravitational force, and the objects (e.g., particles) are dragged by this force. The world is moving because the observable properties (like taste, touch, smell, sound, sight) are inert, but they are pushed by the will of the Lord. The claim that matter is a property of the Lord presents a problem if matter drags the Lord. But it doesn't present a problem if the Lord drags matter.

With this understanding, we can say that this sūtra reiterates the difference between the Paramātma and matter, *after* we have asserted that matter is His property. We cited the fact that the Lord holds the world like a particle that holds diverse properties such as speed, mass, energy, momentum, etc. This was necessary to explicate the idea that there are no 'material objects'; that the world doesn't hang together due to matter itself; it rather hangs together because of the presence of the Paramātma. He is, therefore, the object underlying the properties. But this also invokes the counter-image of the object being controlled by the property. We should thus understand that the term 'property' can be used in two ways—I can possess the house, or I can be possessed by the house.

The Lord has been called the possessor (of the material qualities) previously; if its true meaning wasn't clear before, it has been clarified here. As an illustration, if you go to meet a friend at his house, you can see that he lives inside a house. However, because the house covers the friend doesn't mean it controls him, or that he is bound by the house. The friend can walk out of the house if he wants, and he would still be the owner of the house and the house would still be his property. The problem arises if we think in physical terms—the house is large, and the friend is small. Since he is living inside the house, therefore, he must have come under its control. This idea of the covering controlling the covered is prominent in material science—where the covering (e.g., mass) controls the covered (e.g., the particle). This idea is also prominent in the case of the ātmā—the soul comes under the control over the material covering. However, if the term property is understood in a different sense, the problem doesn't arise. The owner is different from the house; the owner possesses the house as his personal property, but the house doesn't possess the owner.

In this case, both ātmā and Paramātma are different from matter. However, Paramātma controls matter while the ātmā is controlled by matter. The Lord indirectly controls the ātmā through the material energy: He controls matter, which controls the ātmā. The liberation from this control has been noted earlier: devotion to the Lord frees one from material control. On a related note, this sūtra could have been translated as: "The two (ātmā and Paramātma) are different because the material qualities cover (the ātmā)". The covering of the ātmā by the material modes and the transcendence of the Lord have been stated previously. However, positing this transcendence also entails that matter must be working independently because the soul and Paramātma are transcendent. To solve that problem, we must say that the soul and Paramātma are the objects, which control the properties. However, the soul can also be controlled by the properties. Just like mass is the controller of particles, similarly, under the material influence, the soul becomes just like a material particle controlled by the material properties. Its liberation is when it comes out of this control.

QUESTION

You have said that the Lord controls matter, although He is different from matter. This presents the classic mind-body problem in the case of God, where God and matter seem to be different like the 'mind' and 'body', and yet the mind somehow controls the body. How should we understand this interaction and control by God? How does the Lord cause the material energy to work?

1.2.23 (54)

रूपोपन्यासाच्च

rūpopanyāsācca

rūpa—form; upanyāsāt—from a fictional reality; ca—and, also.

TRANSLATION

(The Paramātma) gives the world a form, from a fictional reality.

COMMENTARY

A contentious term here is *upanyāsāt*. Generally, fictional literature—such as novels, dramas, stories, etc.—are called *upanyāsa*. However, the word could also mean "as has been narrated". The latter translation would bring to question: Where has it been narrated? Clearly, the control of the material world by the Lord has not been described previously. However, it is possible to invoke statements from other Upaniśad to describe this control. I have preferred the 'fictional' translation here because of two reasons. First, it doesn't require us to invoke other texts, and we can rely on the present text itself. Second, there is indeed real meaning to the term 'fictional' here, as will become apparent shortly. Notably, the fiction exists, but its meaning is imaginary. It is, therefore, a concoction and hence it is not true; and yet, its existence is factual. The claim is therefore that the Lord is orchestrating a fictional story by His control.

Presently, let's turn to the word rūpa which means form or structure. Again, there are two possible interpretations of this term. First, we can say that the material world is a formless substance, and the Lord gives it form. Second, we can say that the material ingredients themselves have form, although the Lord provides an additional form to these ingredients. The primordial material reality is called Pradhāna in Sāñkhya philosophy and it is indeed formless. However, this formlessness arises because the three modes of nature—sattva, rajas, and tamas—are in a 'balanced' state. Diversity begins when these modes are separated, and then one mode becomes dominant over the other modes. All variety follows from this dominant-subordinate structure between the modes because sattva can subordinate the mode rajas, but rajas can also then subordinate (another instance) of sattva. This dominant-subordinate pattern produces a tree-like structure in which the root is formless, but by distinction, it produces three trunks of sattva, rajas, and tamas, which then divide into three parts, and the process continues indefinitely. This leads to the question: What are the three modes? And how are the many instances of these modes produced?

To answer these questions, we must distinguish between the universals and the individuals. The three modes are universals, but there are only three of them. Since these modes proliferate in many things, the modes must also be replicated many times, to produce the dominant-subordinate structure. The universals are described in Sāñkhya as 24 elements—5 gross elements, 5 tanmātra, 5 knowledge senses, 5 working senses, mind, intellect, ego, and mahattattva. Once these universals are created, numerous instances of these universals must be combined to produce individual objects. For instance, the purple color can be produced by a combination of the instances of red and blue.

Once the individuals are created, then they can also be collected into systems and societies where each individual interacts with some other individuals.

Accordingly, rūpa or form can be seen in three ways. First, it can pertain to the 24 elements of Sāñkhya. Second, it can pertain to the instantiation and combination of these elements into individual things. Third, many types of instances of the universals enter causal relations with each other to produce different structures. Due to the first two, rūpa is individual things that we can perceive and conceive by the senses and the mind. Due to the third, rūpa is the creation of roles in a society into which the individual objects participate.

The Lord's control of matter can then be described as these three processes. The first process is the creation of the universals, which is called Śakti. The second process is the combination of these universals into individual objects, which is caused by three forms of Lord Viṣṇu—(1) Kāraṇodakaśāyī Viṣṇu creates the individual desires, (2) Garbhodakaśāyi Viṣṇu creates the individual roles, and (3) Kṣīrodakaśāyī Viṣṇu creates the individual bodies. The third process is that Śiva creates the universal society in which the individual bodies and roles are combined. Together, these constitute five kinds of rūpa. The universals are rūpa as they are pure concepts. The individuals are rūpa because the universals are combined in a particular manner to create a form. The roles are rūpa because they organize different individuals into a social order. The evolution of this society is also rūpa because it follows a cyclical and hierarchical pattern. As the creator of all these forms, the Lord is the controller of the world.

Now, one might argue: If the Lord is the creator of everything, and the Lord is eternal, why is His creation called fictional? The short answer is that the universals, individuals, roles, society, and the resulting drama are not fictional. The same types of things are produced again and again. The same kinds of roles are created over and over. Due to this repetition, they are eternal; they only become manifest and unmanifest. The fictional aspect is that a certain soul becomes a certain type of individual, then plays a certain role, at a certain place and time. This mapping of the soul to the body to the role to the place and to the time is not eternal. Hence the universe is called an upanyāsa or fictional story.

The term 'real' pertains to the eternally existent, although it may be manifest or unmanifest. The bodies, roles, places, and times are eternal and real in this sense. But their combination with a soul is not eternal. The difference with the spiritual world is simply that this mapping between the soul, body, role, place, and time is eternal in the spiritual world. Thus, a different actor can play the same character in this world, so actors are not tied to characters. However, each actor is a different character in the spiritual world. If the actor and the character are tightly connected, then we don't consider their behavior a 'drama'. What they do is their eternal role, not just a temporary role upon a stage. Thus, both the soul and the forms are eternal. However, the forms of the soul are not eternal in the material world. These forms are eternal in the spiritual world.

Topic 7

QUESTION

You have said earlier that the Paramātma is invisible, and yet He is the object underlying the material properties. Then, in the previous sūtra, you said that He gives the world its form. Does this suggest that since this visible form is produced by Him, we could consider this form as His representation?

We are inclined toward the things that we can see. If we cannot see the Paramātma, it is much harder to understand Him. In such a situation, can the understanding of the external world—which can be observed and analyzed—be considered a suitable substitute for loving devotion to Paramātma?

1.2.24 (55)

वैश्वानरःसाधारणशब्दविशेषात्

vaiśvānaraḥ sādhāraṇaśabdaviśeṣāt

vaiśvānaraḥ—Cosmic Man; sādhāraṇa śabda—common word; viśeṣāt—because of the qualities.

TRANSLATION

Because of its qualities, the ordinary word for (the universe) is Vaiśvānara.

COMMENTARY

Etymologically, Vaiśvānara is comprised of two parts—*visva*, meaning the universe or the creation, and *nara*, meaning the man. Therefore, Vaiśvānara can be translated as the Cosmic Man. The sūtra confirms that if one is unable to meditate on the Paramātma within, then he can understand the nature of the Lord by the study of the external world—provided, through this study, we can conceive of the universe as a body. This form is sometimes called the Virāta Rūpa or the Gigantic Form in the Purāna. The different parts of His body comprise the different Loka or planetary systems; the head is the place of Brahma while the feet are the hellish planets. Now, one might ask: What would be the point of such an understanding? The short answer is that it makes you see the universe as an interconnected whole in which the different parts are not independent of each other. Just like the hand feeds the stomach, and the stomach gives strength to the hands, similarly, there is interdependence between all the parts. This interdependence is described in the Bhagavad-Gita where the demigods and the humans are interdependent—the humans by offering sacrifices to the demigods, and the demigods by providing the daily necessities such as water, sunshine, air, etc. to the humans. By seeing the universe as a body, we begin to understand that we are just parts of the whole (which is quite evident even now), but these parts also must work cohesively (which is not very apparent right now). The cohesion among the different parts—which we might call 'cooperation' within the material universe—can curtail the evil that bedevils everyone: Namely, the tendency to be envious, selfish, and uncooperative. One realizes that their existence depends on serving someone else because they too are being served; without this mutual service, their existence is impossible. Ultimately, one must serve the Lord, but if one finds that the Lord is invisible, even the understanding that one must serve the demigods (which have been described as the manifestations of the Lord previously) can be progress.

In this ongoing discussion, many methods to attain transcendence are being successively described. At the beginning of Vedānta Sūtra, it was stated that the study of the scriptures—provided they are devoid of the three modes of nature—is the process for transcendence. The previous section ended by stating that surrender to the Paramātma is the method for transcendence. Then the chanting of the Upaniśad was prescribed, along with a distinction between Mīmāṃsā and Vedānta (i.e., the worship of demigods was rejected). Now, if the seeker is feeling helpless in all these ways, then, another method is being permitted—namely, that of meditating on the Universal Form of the Lord (and thereby indirectly meditating on the presence of demigods in this world).

Modern science also studies the cosmos, although it can only understand the visible part—which is now said to be only 4% of all that exists. The invisible parts are called 'dark', although the nature of this 'darkness' is hypothesized in contrary ways—the 'dark energy' causes expansion, and the 'dark matter' causes contraction. In Vedic cosmology, this 'darkness' is ascribed to the fact that our vision is confined to a limited part of *bhū-loka*, some parts of *svarga-loka* (e.g., the planets such as the sun and the moon, although planets like Rahu and Ketu are not visible), going up to the *Dhruva Loka* or the polestar. The four planetary systems above this—namely, the *jana*, *tapa*, *mahar*, and *satya-loka*—are not visible to us. Similarly, the lower seven planetary systems, and below which like the 27 hells, are also invisible. Large parts of *bhu-loka*, including the other parts of *Jambudvīpa*, and the other six 'islands', are also invisible.

If we compare what is visible vs. invisible in Vedic cosmology, the visible part is much less than 4%. In short, we don't know the structure of the universe if we rely on the visible part. But by adopting the understanding of the Universal Form, we can obtain a fuller understanding of the creation, and how each part of this universe is interdependent on the other parts. Finally, we must also understand that certain places in the material universe—such as *Sveta-Dvīpa*—are described to be the residence of Paramātma, and they are included as part of the Universal Form. So, not only are we observing the existence of higher and lower beings, but also understanding how they are under Paramātma's control. This true picture of the cosmos, therefore, also leads to cosmic theism.

There is a growing interest in Vedic cosmology among people today. Counterarguments against this study say—our goal is to transcend the world, and everything produced from the three modes of nature. How can the study of cosmology be considered a route to transcendence? By implication, how can it be regarded as being of any relevance to the person aiming for transcendence? The answer to this question is provided in this sūtra, and the answer is that it is very hard to understand the Lord because He is invisible. In fact, as we discussed earlier because He is invisible, it is even harder to trust that He exists. However, the universe—at least some parts of it—are still visible to us. Based on this visibility, we can gain some trust in the existence of the other parts, which we cannot see. If faith is reposed in these descriptions, and the person meditates on this Universal Form, the process can lead to transcendence.

QUESTION

My question is only partially answered by the previous response. Since we have previously talked about the surrender and devotion to the Lord, does this study or meditation on the cosmos constitute an adequate substitute for that devotion to the Lord? Can the scientific study of the world be considered a substitute for the devotion to the Lord, which was described previously?

As described in the Bhagavad-Gita, Lord Kṛṣṇa displayed the Universal Form to Arjuna, but he did not like it very much; he requested Kṛṣṇa to return to His normal human form with which Arjuna was more acquainted. However, Kṛṣṇa had to display this form to convince Arjuna that He is indeed the lord and master of the universe. This immense display of power is often required to convince an ordinary person about the greatness of God. Since the form of the Lord looks just like our forms, many people may underestimate His nature, or even disbelieve His existence. Therefore, an ostensible display of power changes the seeker's perspective: He can see that the Lord is not an ordinary mortal. It can be a preparation for surrender—after all, we are naturally inclined to surrender only when we see the other person is extremely powerful. But does this preparation also constitute a substitute for the devotion to the Lord?

1.2.25 (56)

स्मर्यमाणमनुमानं स्यादिति

smaryamāṇamanumānaṃ syāditi

smaryamāṇaṃ—meditation; anumānaṃ—imaginary, indicatory, or something from which we can draw an inference; syāt—perhaps; iti—because, thus.

TRANSLATION

Because that (cosmic form of the Lord) is only an imaginary or indicatory mark, one may perhaps meditate upon it (but it is not the conclusion).

COMMENTARY

Here it is clarified that the meditation on the Universal Form is neither necessary nor sufficient. But to the extent that the alternatives can seem harder to some people, this meditation is not decried or rejected as a useless process.

The Vedas progress gradually toward the conclusion. For instance, in the Bhagavad-Gita, Lord Kṛṣṇa initially gives a materialistic argument to Arjuna—"if you win this battle, you will enjoy the earth; but if you lose the battle, you will still enjoy in the heavenly planets". It is only gradually that the discussion proceeds into many forms of yoga, including karma-yoga and jñāna-yoga, before the final instruction of surrender to Kṛṣṇa. In the same vein, we have discussed how the 'earlier' portions of Vedas deal with rituals, and the later portions of the Vedas are the conclusion of the Vedas. Likewise, in the Purāna, such as the Śrīmad Bhāgavatam, the initial goal of devotion is described, but subsequently, the text moves into the discussion of material nature (in the 3rd

Canto), followed by the discussion of cosmology (in the 5th canto). It is only later that Kṛṣṇa's pastimes with the gopis—which are considered the pinnacle of the love of God—are described. The Ācāryas have therefore recommended gradual step-by-step progress, rather than 'jumping' to the conclusion quickly.

This sūtra should, therefore, be looked at pragmatically. In principle, the love of God is supreme. However, in practice, to attain that love of God, one must progress slowly. Those who have progressed in earlier lives can skip the meditation on the Universal Form. But for the new initiates, such a process can be useful. Therefore, the prescription is not definitive; this is indicated using the term *syat*, which means 'perhaps' or 'maybe'. The decision is finally left to the practitioner, hoping that he can estimate his state of progress correctly.

The reason for this ambivalence is also described in this sūtra; the Universal Form is called 'imaginary' or 'indicative' or 'something from which we can draw inferences'. To understand this predilection, we can draw parallels from how society is compared to an organism, which is described as having four parts—the Brahmanas are the head, the Kshatriyas are the hands, the Vaishyas are the belly, and the Sudras are the legs—but this 'body' or 'organism' is not a living person. Society is ruled by powerful people, who can organize and structure it. But this structure is only an indication of the intent in the controller or ruler. The societal structure doesn't become a conscious being by this process. In the same vein, organizations and institutions today are widely viewed as organisms and persons—with rights and duties—although they are not conscious beings. The meditation on the Universal Form should be viewed in the same light; the Paramātma is the controller, however, He is invisible. And yet, if we can understand the cosmic structure, and give the Paramātma a 'position' in this structure, at least we can see that He is the supreme controller in relation to the other beings. We may not have a face-to-face encounter with the Lord; however, at least we have understood His 'position' regarding other beings.

For example, if you understand an organizational structure in which the CEO is at the top, different department heads are under his supervision, and so on, then you can attribute many actions to the people you don't see. Thus, you could say— "the department head ordered this work to be done". You may have never met the department head, but you can still know that he exists. Organizational structures are not conscious beings; however, the different parts of the structure are interdependent like parts of the body. In that sense, they are collectively compared to an 'organism' even though they are nonconscious. The universe is similarly a large organization with many layers of governance. It is, collectively speaking, a diverse society comprised of many types of living entities. This society or organization is the Universal Form. Its parts constitute the living places or occupations in the universe. The individuals occupying these roles are controlled by Paramātma, but the Universal Form is not alive.

QUESTION

By calling the Universal Form 'imaginary' aren't you delegitimizing the meditation on this form? The world has already been called 'fictional' in a previous sūtra. All these descriptions seem to indicate that we must only consider meditation upon the true Lord to be the One established within the heart.

The proponents of many religions are often seen arguing with each other about whose method is superior. The proponents of jñāna-yoga claim that bhakti-yoga is inferior because it involves 'emotion' which is inferior to 'reason'. The practitioners of bhakti-yoga might claim that the Vedic knowledge has a divine origin, and to have faith in this knowledge, one must have faith in the teacher—i.e., the Lord—who provided this knowledge. Such arguments are generally pointless. Just like to reach a destination you might first walk, then catch a taxi to a train station, then take a train to the airport, and then catch a flight that takes you to the destination, similarly, different methods can and must be employed at different stages of the spiritual journey. Yes, the airplane may take one to the destination, but to reach the airport, one needs to walk, take a taxi, and then catch a train. Therefore, just because the final leg of the journey involves catching a flight doesn't mean that other steps aren't needed. However, if one says that the preliminary steps are not going to take you to the destination, then, a natural doubt arises: Are we rejecting this process?

1.2.26 (57)

शब्दादिभ्योऽन्तःप्रतिष्ठानाच्च नेति चेत् न तथा
दृष्ट्युपदेशात् असंभवात् पुरुषमपि चैनमधीयते

śabdādibhyo'ntaḥ pratiṣṭhānācca neti cet na tathā
dṛṣṭyupadeśāt asaṃbhavāt puruṣamapi cainamadhīyate

śabdādibhyaḥ—many descriptions; antaḥ—within; pratiṣṭhānāt—from the established (i.e., the Lord who is situated within the heart); ca—and; na—not; iti cet—if it is said; na—not so; tathā—in the same way; dṛṣṭyupadeśāt—based on the instructions to see; asaṃbhavāt—from the impossibility; puruṣam—the person; api—even; ca—and; inam—in this way; adhīyate—in remembering.

TRANSLATION

If it is said that by many descriptions or words, that which is established within is not known, (we say) not so. In the same way, based on the instructions to see, even though the Puruṣa is impossible to see, in this way also is seen.

COMMENTARY

One of the specialties of Vedānta Sūtra is that it defies a simple interpretation. We have seen many examples of this before: The Brahman is Oneness, but it is also comprised of the individual ātmā; the ātmā is part of the Paramātma and yet he is to be considered separate from the Lord; the Vedas are a source of truth, however, not everything in the Vedas can be considered Absolute Truth; matter is originally formless and is then given a form by the Lord but we cannot consider the form produced by the Lord as He Himself, etc. As we proceed through the discussion, we always find that the answer is very subtle: it is neither of the two extremes that deny the opposites, but something more nuanced. In this case, the contentious issue is whether the Puruṣa is inside or also the Universal Form, and the answer is that neither position can be rejected.

They must rather be understood as different stages of the same understanding.

QUESTION

The term 'Puruṣa' is generally taken to mean not just a person, but also a controller. The Universal Form seems to possess a form like a person, but He cannot be called the controller of the universe because you have previously said that the Paramātma is the origin of the ādidaivika or the controllers. So, in what way should the Universal Form be considered a Puruṣa if He is not a controller?

The term Puruṣa has many meanings; it can represent 'male' or 'man', and it also means 'dominator' or 'controller'. We have discussed previously that the controller is Paramātma who is hidden in the heart; He is also the source of all the demigods. The Universal Form cannot, therefore, be called the controller. And yet, if He not called a controller, then how can we consider Him a Puruṣa?

1.2.27 (58)

अत एव न देवता भूतं च

ata eva na devatā bhūtaṃ ca

ata eva—for the same reasons; na—(is) not; devatā—the controller; bhūtaṃ—the living entities or the embodied souls; ca—and.

TRANSLATION

And for this reason (the Universal Form) is not the controller of the soul.

COMMENTARY

The sūtra accepts that the Universal Form is not the controller. But this view must also be nuanced with details. In this regard, we can compare the Universal Form to the idea of a Vāstu Puruṣa prominently employed in Vedic systems of architecture. The land, and the construction upon it, are compared to a person, with head, hands, legs, belly, etc. The properties of these parts of the body become the defining method for placing different functional parts of the house in different parts of the Vāstu Puruṣa body. For example, some parts dominate in the element fire, so, the kitchen must be kept in that part. In the same way, time is also divided into different phases and has different characteristics. Thus, the musical ragas are suited for certain times. So, the place and time are 'rulers' as they have functional properties—they prescribe what type of activity must be performed at which place and time. Similarly, the Vāstu Puruṣa is a controller—different parts of His body represent the places in which different types of activities are performed. There is hence a place for the sun, the moon, the other planets, the stars, the demigods, the demons, the humans, etc. The Universal Form is the functional design of the universe, and it is neither fictional nor arbitrary. But in another sense, the design is different from the designer.

When a car is manufactured, the design constitutes the system architecture for the car—e.g., how long and wide it will be, whether the engine will be in the front or the back, whether the car is a two-seater or a four-seater, the space for luggage or goods that must be provided, etc. This architecture is not random or whimsical; it is produced by a designer's intention to produce a certain type of car. In fact, once the system architecture has been produced, it dictates where people will sit, and how many of them can sit, how much luggage can be carried, etc. So, the architecture itself 'controls' many things. But the architecture is not the person who designed the car. In the same way, there is a person who designs the car, and then there is a design that controls the other things.

Similarly, the Universal Form is and is not a controller. He is a controller because different parts of the universe are meant for different kinds of roles, pleasures, cognitions, and activities; the places in the universe determine what is possible or impossible at that place, and the universe is not *uniform*. Because of the design, the Universal Form can be called a controller. But because the design is not the designer, the Universal Form is not the controller. The structure of the universe is like a body, but the Lord is the soul of that body. We cannot say that this body is our creation, or that it doesn't exist, or that any part of the body can do anything. On the other hand, we also cannot say that the body is identical to the soul. The body exists because of the soul; so, it is a representation of the qualities of the soul; however, it is not the soul itself.

QUESTION

The idea that the Universal Form is itself a representation of the Lord is like that of Pantheism, which identifies God with the universe. Pantheism rejects a transcendental God who created the universe but stands apart from it. By supporting such an idea, aren't you delegitimizing a transcendental God?

If we only accept the transcendental form of the Lord, then we can be accused of delegitimizing the meditation on the Universal Form. However, if we accept the Universal Form, we can be accused of supporting pantheism and rejecting a transcendental Lord. The question about the first delegitimization has been asked before; the seeker is now asking about the second problem.

1.2.28 (59)

साक्षादप्यविरोधं जैमिनिः

sākṣādapyavirodhaṃ jaiminiḥ

sākṣāt—the visible; api—also; avirodhaṃ—no difficulty; jaiminiḥ—(so says) Jaimini.

TRANSLATION

Jaimini (says that there is) no difficulty in also (accepting) the visible (as a form of God as opposed to the invisible or the transcendental form of the Lord).

COMMENTARY

The sage Jaimini was a disciple of Bādarāyana and the founder of the Mīmāṃsā school. He is well-known for his treatise entitled the Pūrva Mīmāṃsā

Sutras, also called Karma-Mīmāṃsā. We have already discussed the differences between Mīmāṃsā and Vedānta; in particular, both accept the eternality of the soul; however, Mīmāṃsā rejects the existence of the invisible gods or God. The focus of Mīmāṃsā was on what can be sensually perceived and practically used. The sūtra mentions his name and quotes him saying that the Universal Form is apparent (sākṣāt) because it represents the structure of the universe. This should not be considered the delegitimization of a transcendental Lord; it can rather be used by those who cannot accept a transcendental Lord and would be more comfortable in accepting the universe itself as the form of God. This is an indirect reference to atheists who don't accept a transcendental form of God or a God who creates the universe but stands apart from it. Jaimini has been quoted here because the Mīmāṃsā system doesn't accept the existence of God, although they still accept that we can think of God as the Universal Form.

QUESTION

However, the main problem remains; you have said that the Universe is controlled and given form by the Lord. Yes, we can study this form, and we are indirectly understanding the creation of the Lord. However, the Pantheists will still say that there is no separate God apart from the universe. There is God, but He transforms into the universe. So, once the universe is manifest, there is no separate God. And God, therefore, exists only when there is no universe. How will you address the resulting problem that God did not *create* the universe, but God *became* the universe—which eventually results in Pantheism?

We have previously said that the Universal Form is the *design* and the Paramātma is the *designer*. However, the pantheist can argue that there is no designer separate from the design; rather the designer itself became the design. We can compare this to the existence of a seed from which a tree grows; once the tree has grown, the seed ceases to exist. In fact, since the tree may produce other seeds, we can say that the original seed produced many designers, which remain in potential form but eventually convert themselves into a tree. So, this cycle of the designer becoming the design repeats itself many times, and hence a single seed can then lead to the production of many seeds—i.e., different living entities—who are constantly transforming themselves into the trees (namely, the mind and body), and there is no seed left once the tree has grown.

1.2.29 (60)

अभिव्यक्तेरित्याश्मरथ्यः

abhivyakterityasmarathyah

abhivyakteḥ—due to expression; iti—so; āśmarathyaḥ—Āśmarathya.

TRANSLATION

On account of the expression, so says Āśmarathya.

COMMENTARY

This sūtra states that the universe is the *abhivyakti* or expression of the Lord. Like thoughts can exist in our minds, and we express them into words, similarly, the universe exists inside the Lord and is then expressed outwardly. We cannot say that the speaker becomes the speech, and this example of the seed becoming the tree (and disappearing thereafter) is unsustainable due to the eternality of the soul. The same soul reincarnates into multiple bodies. So, we cannot say that the seed manifests into the tree, and then it ceases to exist. We must rather say that the seed manifests into a tree, and it remains; in fact, it can manifest into different trees one after another. The seed is therefore never destroyed. In the same way, the universe is an expression of the Lord, but it cannot be equated or identified with the Lord. This can be understood based on the similarity between the ātmā and the Paramātma; the ātmā undergoes reincarnation and manifests different bodies as its expression. Since it is not destroyed by the expression, the Paramātma is also not reduced to the creation.

Thus, the designer can never be the design because the same designer can produce many designs. We have compared the universe to a house owned by the person who lives in it. The person inside the house is different from the house, and yet, the house represents his qualities. For instance, the house of a devotee would be decorated by pictures of the Lord, but the house of a materialist would be decorated by portraits of himself, his family, or ancestors. The house of a poor man may be spartan, but that of a rich man would be opulent and full of many assets. The house of an academic would contain books, that of a musician musical instruments, and that of a sportsperson sports gear. A person with classical tastes will live in an ornately designed house, whereas one with modern tastes will live in a house with simple functional designs. So, we can understand the person from their expressions. These things are a 'reflection' of the person who owns and creates them, but those things are not the owner.

In the same way, the sage Āśmarathya is being quoted as saying that the universe is the *abhivyakti*—the articulation of thoughts into words—of the Lord. Yes, the words are separate from the person who speaks them. However, by hearing those words, we can know the person's thoughts. In the same way, the Lord can be understood by this external manifestation of His person.

QUESTION

If we call the universe an expression (abhivyakti) of the Lord, as you have compared it to the expression of the mind into speech, doesn't it follow that we would be preoccupied with the perception of the senses? We have discussed that many parts of the universe are not perceivable by the senses. So, on one hand, we cannot perceive the Universal Form by our senses, and on the other hand, it is an expression of the Lord. How do we reconcile these positions?

1.2.30 (61)

अनुस्मृतेर्बादरिः

anusmṛterbādariḥ

anusmṛteḥ—for the sake of meditation; bādariḥ—(so says) the sage Bādari.

TRANSLATION

The sage Bādari says that (Vaiśvānara) is for meditation.

COMMENTARY

Since in the previous sūtra the Universal Form was compared to a verbal expression of the thoughts in the mind, one might conclude that the Universal Form must be seen through the senses—after all, the words are heard by the ear. This sūtra rejects this idea. It quotes sage Bādri as saying that this Universal Form is for meditation or mental remembrance. It is an indirect statement that we cannot observe the Universal Form by senses. This is also directly confirmed by the fact that many parts of the Universal Form (such as the lower planetary systems, the many parts of *Jambudvīpa*, many of the higher planetary systems above the polestar) are not sense perceivable. Therefore, even though there is a difference between the designer and the design, we cannot assume that this design is completely sense perceivable. The use of *abhivyakti* or expression in the previous sūtra is meant to indicate a difference between a design and a designer; it is not meant to indicate that the expression (or the design) is entirely sense perceivable (like it would be if that expression was audible speech).

This sūtra also confirms that this design can be understood mentally. In short, to meditate upon the Universal Form, we need to employ the mind, rather than the senses. This fact is illustrative for those who draw 'models' of the Vedic universe and having constructed the model, they think that it represents the universe in its sense perceivable form. They neglect the fact that many parts of the universe cannot be perceived by the senses. So, how can a model in which we perceive these parts by our senses be a representation of those parts? A classic example of such confusion is to treat the flatness of the bhū-mandala as the literal flatness of the earth, thereby producing contradictions with observations. This sūtra answers this point—we must see the form mentally, rather than sensually. It is thus a *mental model* of the universe, not a *sensual model*.

Let's understand this idea through an example from modern science. Take the Standard Model of particle physics for illustration. It is typically drawn as a set of 16 boxes stacked on top of each other into four rows. There are 6 quarks, 6 leptons, and 4 bosons. The picture of the Standard Model is a mental model; it is how we organize things in our minds, but it doesn't represent any facts about the perceivable world. There are no boxes with 6 quarks, 6 leptons, and 4 bosons in the real world. Similarly, take the Periodic Table of chemical elements as another example. It is a classification method that divides elements into alkali, alkaline, lanthanides, actinides, metals, metalloids, noble gases, etc. This is also a mental model of the world of chemical elements. However, you will not find a stacking of a hundred-odd boxes representing elements anywhere. And yet, we consider the periodic table very 'real'. It is 'real' if you use the periodic table for understanding; it is unreal if you use it for sense perception. In such mental models, something is 'above' and something is 'below'. Something is to the 'left' and something is to the 'right'. This above, below, left, and right has nothing to do with sense perception. Just because Hydrogen and Helium are shown to be at the same 'level' in the periodic table doesn't mean that we will observe Hydrogen and Helium at the same height if we perceive sensually.

In the same way, the Universal Form is for mental understanding. It is not a description of the sensual world, but a conceptual description of reality. Therefore, it should not be confused with empirical measurements of modern science (e.g., that the bhū-mandala is not sensually flat—just like Hydrogen and Helium at the same level in the mental model doesn't mean that they are at the same 'height'). It follows that the Lord's expression of the universe is in the form of a mental model; it should not be confused with sense perception.

QUESTION

But previously we compared the creation to the design of a designer and said that the designer is different from the design. In the case of ordinary designs—e.g., the design of a car—we can understand the design through sense perception. Are we now suggesting that there are many types of designs, some of which are sense perceivable while others may not be sense perceivable?

1.2.31 (62)

संपत्तेरिति जैमिनिःतथा हि दर्शयति

saṃpatteriti jaiminiḥ tathā hi darśayati

saṃpatteḥ—because of the changing nature; iti—thus, so; jaiminiḥ—(says) Jaimini; tathā—in this way; hi—because; darśayati—can be seen.

TRANSLATION

Because of the changing nature (of the visible world), one must (mentally) perceive (the Universal Form of the Lord)—so says the sage Jaimini.

COMMENTARY

We have compared the Universal Form to society as an organism. When society is compared to an organism, the Brahmanas are higher than the Kshatriyas, who are higher than the Vaisyas, who are higher than the Sudras. But if we see with our eyes, we will not find the Brahmanas standing at a greater height than the Kshatriyas. This point has been illustrated in the previous sūtra where we spoke about mental models. The present sūtra makes another point: that from a sense perception view, things are always changing. For instance, particles are created, destroyed, or moved. But from the perspective of the mental model, they are fixed in a position (in the model). Thus, the Kshatriya may climb a mountain and be present at a greater height than the Brahmana; but by changing his location in this way, the Kshatriya doesn't become a 'higher' role than the Brahmana. So, if we see society by our senses, then we will observe people moving around, doing their work, etc. but we will never see the hands, the legs, the belly, or the mouth of the society. This means that there is a difference between mental models and sense perception, as we have said before.

Now, one may argue that in some cases, we don't see such a difference. For example, there is a similarity between the design of a house comprising a kitchen, bedroom, dining room, living room, study, toilets, etc., and the physical structure of the house. Similarly, there is a correspondence between the design of the car and the structure of the car. Normally when we understand models, we view them as pictures of the physical world—or physical models. But there are also mental models where no such correspondence can be found. So, how can we understand the difference between these two kinds of models?

Underlying the two types of models, are different notions about space. In the physical space—where we draw physical models— 'height' has a physical meaning. But there is another space in which we draw the mental models; in this model, there can be many kinds of distances. For example, if we draw the tree of life, and show tigers and jaguars close by, we are not indicating that they are always found close to each other; we are rather indicating that they belong to the cat family. Likewise, if we draw an organizational structure, and show that the CEO is above the department heads, it doesn't mean that the department heads cannot walk up in a building and the CEO cannot walk down; this hierarchy represents a functional structure. We can speak about emotional proximity: e.g., that someone is 'close' because we are emotionally attached to them, whereas some other people are emotionally 'distant' from others.

The tigers and jaguars can run around, but the conceptual distance doesn't change. The CEO and the department heads can walk up and down, but it doesn't change their position in the organization. The emotionally close ones can go to another country, without changing their emotional proximity. While the world keeps changing in many ways, the models persist. To depict this persistence—in the face of a changing world—we need alternative notions of space. The models drawn in these spaces have nothing to do with the physical space in which things seem to move and change. So, if someone is wondering why we need such mental models, the answer is that we want to understand a changing world in an unchanging way. We might note in this regard that even the heavenly bodies are moving; and yet, the Universal Form is fixed. This sūtra states that we are picturing a changing world using an unchanging model.

In modern science, only the laws of nature are unchanging. Thus, as time passes, the bodies move, but the laws governing that motion don't change. But in this case, we are introducing a new category of reality—namely, many types of mental models—which are also unchanging. There is considerable similarity between the scientific theories or laws and such mental models. The difference is that we don't treat such laws as things that exist; they are just formulae that govern and control the world, but they are nowhere to be found. In the case of the Universal Form, however, we are stating that the mental models are real.

They are expressions of the Lord; however, we should not confuse them with physical designs—e.g., the architecture of a house or the design of a car. While the house and car design represent the physical models and can be called the expressions of the creator, we are speaking about a more sophisticated idea.

QUESTION

Your proposals seem quite like the difference between phenomena and reality in Western philosophy. The phenomena are what is apparent to us (which you have called the 'physical' world) but there is an underlying reality (of which we draw mental models). You are suggesting that the Universal Form is reality rather than phenomena, even though it is to be considered material and imaginary (because it not truly a person). Would you agree with this?

1.2.32 (63)

आमनन्ति चैनमस्मिन्

āmananti cainamasmin

āmananti—(they) teach; ca—also, and; enam—this; asmin—in this.

TRANSLATION

Also, they (the scriptures) teach this (the Universal Form) in this (way).

COMMENTARY

As we come to the end of this section, the description of the Vaiśvānara is being summarized by saying that the scriptural references to the Universal Form (i.e., the descriptions of Vedic cosmology) are to be understood as mental models upon which we can meditate upon, but cannot sensually perceive.

The distinction between phenomena and reality is illustrative. The indication is that the phenomena are not 'real'—as they are changing. The transcendental form of the Paramātma is eternal and unchanging. In between the eternal but transcendental form of the Paramātma, and the changing world of phenomena, there is something unchanging—namely the nature of material reality from which these phenomena are constructed, and which we understand through science and philosophy by drawing mental models for our understanding. Just as in science we say that the laws of nature are unchanging, similarly, there is a 'form' of the world produced by the Paramātma that is unchanging. The descriptions of cosmology should be understood as that unchanging reality. Even though it is material, it is quasi-eternal (in so far as the universe is temporary and is repeatedly created and destroyed). This type of meditation is not the loving devotion to the Lord and is not a substitute for it. But to the extent that we find it hard to understand the form of the Lord relative to the moving bodies of the present world, the unchanging material reality can be a stepping stone toward that deeper understanding. Specifically, the scriptural descriptions should not be confused with the sensual perception of the world. It is rather a mental model by which the universe can be understood.

It can be meditated upon because simply the distinction between the material phenomena and the material reality can be quite illustrative before we speak about the transcendental reality (and the transcendental phenomena arising from that reality).

SECTION 3

Topic 1

QUESTION

You have thus far spoken about the origin of the soul (from the Supreme Lord), the difference between ātmā and Paramātma, and that the ātmā, Brahman, and Paramātma are beyond the material world. You have also said that the Paramātma is the controller of the material world through the demigods. I would now like to know about the origin of the material world.

1.3.1 (64)

दयुभ्वाद्यायतनं स्वशब्दात्

dyubhvādyāyatanaṃ svaśabdāt

dyu—space, sky; bhu—earth, or the entire universe; ādi—the origin; ayatanaṃ—the abode or the resting place; sva—own; śabdāt—from the saying.

TRANSLATION

From the saying, the origin and resting place of space and the universe is His abode.

COMMENTARY

This verse can be translated in two ways, one of which is given above. The other translation can be: "The heaven, the earth, etc. are considered His own abode". Such a translation would be inconsistent with the previous statements where the Lord's abode has been said to transcend the material world, and with the subsequent verses where only the liberated (from the material world) can attain this abode, and many methods of making advancement (which are valid methods of moving within the material world) are rejected as being capable of yielding such a possibility. Even if we say that there is a form of the Lord within this universe, and the place is called Sveta-Dvīpa, it is still a specific place; it cannot be identified with heaven, earth, or other places in the universe. We could also say that since the Lord is in the heart of each living entity—as Paramātma—thus He can also be found in all places, including heaven, earth, and all the other places where the living entities are found; however, such a statement would be redundant because His pervasiveness in this form has been noted many times before; what would be the point of repeating it again?

Therefore, the translations which identify heaven, earth, etc. as the abode of the Lord should be rejected given all the problems that follow from it. Now that we eliminate the alternative translation, we can try to understand this sūtra.

We have previously discussed that the material world is one-quarter of the entire existence; even in this quarter, the Lord injects the soul into the material energy, and the soul remains connected to the Lord even in the material world—both due to prāṇa as well as due to the presence of Paramātma. In fact, the very notion that the jīvā has 'fallen' into the material world when understood physically—as if he has 'entered' the body like a person is inside a house—is misleading because the jīvā is always transcendent to the material nature. The 'fall' into the material existence should be understood as the change of its experience: its *focus* has been diverted into the material nature. The expansion of the material world is, therefore, the expansion of the substrate of the material experience, and the consciousness of the jīvā is directed to this substrate by the influence of a material prāṇa (different from the prāṇa that connects the jīvā to the Lord). The soul is said to be 'carried' to different bodies by this prāṇa; however, this should not be understood as physical transport. It should be seen as the changing focus or awareness of the soul. In short, we can say that a material prāṇa 'connects' the jīvā to the material substrate. If this connection changes, then without movement, the jīvā's experience changes.

In the same way, the material substrate must also be seen as expanding from the Lord's abode. This expansion is sometimes called māyā, or that which is *not*. We have noted previously that the Oneness differentiates to become many due to desire. The expansion of the material world should also be understood as the expansion due to a certain type of desire—which we can call the 'material desire'. The term 'māyā' should be understood as being defined in relation to the Lord; the material world is all that the Lord is *not*. The negations, however, don't have an independent existence. Even to say that something is 'not red', we must postulate the existence of 'red'. If we say something is 'not a table', we must assume that there is something called 'table'. Thus, we can understand that the material world is the negation of the Lord, but these negations are possible only when the assertion already exists; if some assertion did not exist, then the negation would also not be possible. Hence, the material world, as the negation of the Lord, has a root in the Lord. Unlike the jīvā which has emerged out of His body, the material energy is separated from the Lord; and yet, the material energy is completely dependent on the Lord, just as the negation depends on the assertion. Therefore, the material world has no independent existence. And yet, the Lord stands apart from the material world.

However, we must distinguish between two distinct concepts of origin. First, we use the term 'origin' in a substantive sense: The Lord originated the world, so the world was previously existing within the Lord; since other types of origins are from within His person, this origin must also be from within His self. Second, we can use the term 'origin' in a scientific sense: the material world is all that the Lord is not, but since the negations must have an 'origin' in the assertions, therefore, the Lord is the origin of the material world. Since the material energy is His negation, therefore, it is called *aparā* or inferior when the Lord is called *parā* or superior. This is because the negation depends on the assertion. However, these two concepts about origin present contradictions. For example, if the material energy is a negation of the Lord by the second concept, then how can it exist within the Lord by the first concept? Doesn't the existence of the negation of the Lord within the Lord present a self-contradiction?

The answer is that the Lord is the original qualities of knowledge, beauty, power, wealth, fame, and renunciation, but these are not mutually contradictory. Their subdivisions, however, can be mutually contradictory. For example, if color is the whole, then black and white are its parts. Black and white exist inside color, but in this state, they do not create a contradiction. It is only when color is divided into black and white, a mutual contradiction is produced. But this division also produces a space in which black and white are in distinct locations. They are like the branches of a tree whose root is color. Since color is not self-contradictory, therefore, the origin is not self-contradictory. Since black and white are in different locations, therefore, they are not self-contradictory. Thus, contradictions are resolved in many ways. First, contradictory concepts are reconciled into a more abstract concept (just like black and white are reconciled in color). Second, if they are not reconciled, they exist in different locations. Third, if they exist in the same location, they are separated by time.

The material and spiritual worlds are present different possibilities in different regions of space. The Lord advents in different forms—with different desires—to control these worlds. In the material world, this form is called Param Śiva (also called Shambhu), and the Brahma Samhita compares this form to milk turning into yogurt. The forms of the Lord in the spiritual world are engaged in the enjoyment of pleasure, but the form in the material world is engaged in austerity. There is pleasure in austerity too—you can enjoy exercising, working, etc. So, the Lord is not suffering in the material world. However, His pleasure takes an opposite form than the pleasure in the spiritual world. This austerity is said to cause the Lord to 'sweat', and the material energy exits His body through the pores on the skin; then it forms the Kārana Ocean, or the Causal Ocean, in which the Lord lies; He then glances at this material energy, and the jīvā is injected into the Causal Ocean through His glance. In short, the material energy has exited His body through the pores on His body, and the jīvā has entered the material energy—not physically—but simply by getting absorbed in the perception of this energy through His glance. Therefore, the Lord is both the substantive cause of the material world—because the material energy exits His body as His sweat resulting from austerity. And He is also the seed-giving father, although the soul doesn't physically exit His body (like the material energy). The soul is only absorbed in the perception of the material energy.

The process by which the senses perceive the world is described in the Bhagavad-Gita, where it is said that the yogi withdraws His senses like the tortoise draws its limbs inwards. This means that while perceiving the world, the senses are drawn outwardly. In modern science, we think that light enters our eyes and creates an impression in the brain. However, in Sāñkhya and Yoga philosophy, the senses are moving outward. Due to this outward movement, it is possible to control the senses and choose to not see something. Such control is impossible in the scientific description because, by the time you see, the light has already entered the senses. In the same way, the perception of the material energy—through the Lord's glance—must be considered the outward movement of the Lord's senses, rather than a physical detachment of the sense from the Lord's body. The injection of the soul into the material energy is like the senses moving outward into the perceived objects. Therefore, the jīvā—like the glance of the Lord—is never truly 'detached' from the Lord. And yet, its awareness is focused on the experience of the material energy produced by austerity.

Therefore, the Lord is the origin of the material world in both the substantive and the scientific sense: the material energy is His negations, which have emerged out of His own body. As negations, the energy is 'separated' from the Lord, and yet since the negation has no independent existence, the Lord is still the resting ground for them. Likewise, the energy has separated from His body when the Lord changed His nature from enjoyment to austerity, therefore, the Lord can also be called the substantive origin of the material world.

QUESTION

If the Lord is the origin of the material world, and the jīvā has entered the material energy by the agency of the Lord, then how can the jīvā return to the abode of the Lord? Would that return not be contrary to the Lord's will?

1.3.2 (65)

मुक्तोपसृप्यव्यपदेशात्

muktopasṛpyavyapadeśāt

mukta-upasṛpya—to be attained by the liberated; vyapadeśāt—because of the material covering, or because of the declaration.

TRANSLATION

Because of the declaration (in the scriptures) or because of the material covering (of consciousness), (His abode) is attained by the liberated.

COMMENTARY

The sūtra states that even though the Lord has created the material world, and the soul is in the material world due to this creation, the soul can still return to the abode of the Lord, and this return would not be contrary to the Lord's will. This return is called mukti or liberation. The contentious issue is what mukti really means, because it must explain why the soul entered the material world, to begin with. Since the Lord is the cause of the material world, the soul is not the sole cause of his entry into the world. At the least, the Lord is the creator of the material opportunity, and the soul uses this opportunity. Similarly, since opportunity exists even if an individual soul is liberated, therefore, the individual soul is not the complete cause of the opportunity. Rather, we must consider the desires of the other souls as well. But ultimately, each soul's material journey is caused only by their desire, not the Lord's will.

The next problem is the point at which the soul is considered liberated. For example, if some soul develops the desire to be liberated, does it mean he is immediately liberated? Or, must he wait for death before liberation? If the soul is liberated without leaving the material body, then presence in the material world isn't bondage. In many religions, liberation only comes at the point of death, but in Vedic texts, a person in the material body can also be liberated. Such a person is called jivanmukta, and even Śri Śankarācārya, who otherwise taught liberation as merger into Brahman (which only happens when the bodily individuality is lost) accepted liberation during one's lifetime. This presents a contradiction in the impersonal view, because if liberation is the dissolution of the material identity, then as long as the soul is in the material body, the identity is not dissolved. So, how can a person be called jivanmukta with the body?

The correct answer to this problem is that the soul's fall is due to his desire, and the liberation is also due to a change in his desire. However, this liberation is not a desireless state, because that would entail the dissolution of the body, and would be possible only after death. For someone to be liberated in this body, liberation must be understood as a change in desire—which creates individuality, and therefore entails a body—and yet that desire is not material.

If the jīvā has developed loving devotion toward the Lord, then he is considered jivanmukta and 'mukti' is freedom from material desire rather than from the material world. In Gaudīya Vaiṣṇavism, the aspiration for mukti as the merger into Brahman, or the liberation from the cycle of birth and death, are both rejected. The aspiration is only to turn one's consciousness toward the Lord. Thus, Śri Chaitanya emphasizes the following in His Śikṣāṣṭakam:

na dhanam na janam na sundarim
kavitam va jagad-isha kamaye
mama janmani janmanishvare
bhavatad bhaktir ahaituki twayi

> O, almighty Lord, I have no desire to accumulate wealth, nor do I desire beautiful women, nor do I want any number of followers. I only want Your causeless devotional service birth after birth.

The rejection of wealth and beautiful women must be understood as the rejection of the material pleasures of the gross material body. The rejection of many followers must be understood as the rejection of the pleasures of the subtle body (mind, intellect, ego, and mahattattva). Finally, the statement about 'birth after birth' entails that there is also a rejection of the liberation from the cycle of birth and death. The devotee is only desirous of the 'causeless devotional service'. The meaning of 'causeless' is that it springs naturally from the soul's ānanda potency, and it desires nothing but the happiness of the Lord (excluding even liberation from the cycle of birth and death—which entails that material suffering is acceptable). This is a radical concept of liberation, that goes beyond the concept of jivanmukta which is liberation within the present body, without scope for rebirth; the jivanmukta is not expected to be reborn. In Śri Chaitanya's description, even rebirth is acceptable if there is devotion.

The soul's fall into material nature is not physical. The soul is still with the Lord; as the Lord glances at the material energy, the soul's consciousness is diverted into material nature. But just like the Lord's eyes don't get detached from His body due to this glance, similarly, the soul doesn't get detached from the Lord. The soul's fall is the misunderstanding about the purpose of the material world—the soul thinks that this world is for his enjoyment when the fact is that it is meant to be Param Śiva's austerity. The world can also be the pleasure of the Lord—in the transcendental sense. But it is never the pleasure of the soul. If this understanding of purpose is revised, then the soul is liberated. The soul doesn't have to forego the material experience, only the misunderstanding that the world is meant for his enjoyment. Thus, we can distinguish between two kinds of liberation. First, it is the entry into the spiritual world, which the Lord has created for His pleasure; the soul also enjoys in this spiritual world. Second, it is a development of the same devotion in the material world by which the devotee engages everything in the material world in the service of the Lord.

Entry into the abode of the Lord has no relation to the exit from the material world, the discarding of the material body, or the freedom from the cycle of birth and death. Yes, in many cases, the jīvā who has developed a devotion to the Lord will never be born again. But that would also entail that the jīvā is not in the Lord's abode while in the body; He can only attain the Lord's abode after the death of this body. In the deepest conception about this attainment, the soul can exist in the Lord's abode even if he is living in the material world.

QUESTION

You are saying that the soul's fall is due to his desire. But others say that the soul's fall is due to ignorance. The desire is an emotive state, and ignorance is a cognitive state. Accordingly, the proponent of 'desire is the cause of fall' can argue for liberation by devotion. However, the proponent of 'ignorance is the cause of fall' argues that knowledge is the cause of liberation. You have yourself said that the study of Vedic scriptures leads us to liberation. Therefore, it seems that you support both the fall by ignorance and fall by desire. Which of these two positions must be considered the real cause of the soul's fall?

1.3.3 (66)

नानुमानम् अतच्छब्दात्

nānumānam atacchabdāt

na—not; anumānam—what is imagined or inferred; atat-śabdāt—not from the scriptures.

TRANSLATION

Not (attained) by imagination (or) even the study of scriptures.

COMMENTARY

In 1.1.3 (3) it was stated that the śāstra or the scriptures are the right sources of knowledge about the Absolute Truth. This sūtra, however, states that the study of the śāstra itself doesn't lead to entry into the Lord's abode. In this regard, we might reference the following statement by Śri Śankarācārya:

bhaja govindaṁ bhaja govindaṁ
govindaṁ bhaja mūḍha-mate
samprāpte sannihite kāle
nahi nahi rakṣati ḍukṛṅkaraṇe

Worship Govinda, worship Govinda,
Worship Govinda, oh fool!
At the time of your death,
Rules of grammar will not save you.

As a classic example, many Indologists and Western scholars have studied the scriptures and translated them into English and other languages. However, despite this study, they have no faith in the truth of the scriptures, and they haven't developed devotion to the Lord. Therefore, despite studying the scriptures, they cannot be liberated. If the qualification for liberation was merely the study of the scriptures, then Indologists and Western scholars who have no devotion to the Lord would automatically be considered liberated from material existence, and hence qualified to enter the abode of the Lord. This is not an admonishment of the study of scriptures; it is only a statement that theoretical understanding residing in the mind and intellect is not enough. To enter the Lord's abode, one must also develop devotion to the Lord. If the scholar of Vedic texts is averse to the Lord—which most of the Indologists and Western scholars are—their study of scripture is a veritable waste of effort and time.

Yes, once we understand, we may begin to like it. But understanding may not lead to liking. Many people go to colleges to study courses; they may even do well in the exams and obtain good grades, but they hate the subject they are studying and dislike the educational process. They have naturally developed a good understanding of the subject under study, but they have not developed a liking for the subject. On the other hand, many people may have a natural like for some subject, and even if they are unable to go to college, they may study the subject on their own, and obtain a good understanding. Therefore, we can accept that understanding doesn't always lead to liking but liking always leads to understanding (given enough time and opportunity). In that sense, the study of the scripture is inadequate, because one may not develop the devotion.

QUESTION

You have said that the jīvā and the Lord are connected by the prāṇa. Thus, yogis state that by controlling the prāṇa one can transcend the material world and enter the Lord's abode. The practice of yoga and prāṇayāma are quite popular. They are presented as secular practices, which can be adopted by a person of any religion. Are these the appropriate methods of transcendence?

1.3.4 (67)

प्राणभृच्च

prāṇabhṛcca

prāṇa—the five airs; bhṛta—carried (by prāṇa); ca—also (na—not).

TRANSLATION

(Nor) by the support of the prāṇa (i.e., the practice of prāṇayāma).

COMMENTARY

There can be some contentions in the translation of this sūtra because the meaning of *pranābhṛta* is "carried by the prāṇa". This term can be treated as a noun or a verb. If it is treated as a noun, then it represents the soul (as the soul's consciousness is carried from one body to another due to prāṇa). However, if it is treated as a verb, it represents a process by which one can enter the abode of the Lord. Suppose we treat *pranābhṛta* as the noun; the sūtra would then state, "the soul also cannot enter the abode of the Lord", which would make the entire Vedānta Sūtra doctrine pointless. Therefore, I have treated it as a verb. Under this translation, the sūtra reads: "the soul cannot enter the abode of the Lord by the effect of prāṇa". This is not problematic, but it must be understood.

We have previously noted that the attention of the soul is diverted from one part of the material world to another due to prāṇa. By controlling prāṇa, one may also divert their attention toward other things. However, this method is rejected for entry into the Lord's abode. The reason is that the prāṇa by which we control the body and the mind is also material in nature. It is not the prāṇa by which the soul is connected to the Lord. Therefore, even though the process of prāṇa manipulation is useful in advancing to better bodies in this world, this method is not enough for entry into the Lord's abode. This should, however, not be considered a rejection of the aśtānga-yoga system, because the system comprises of eight stages, and control of prāṇa—called prāṇayāma—is the 4th stage. The 4th stage is control of the material prāṇa. Following this, the crucial 7th stage of dhāraṇā or fixation of the attention on the Lord must follow. The 7th stage involves the prāṇa that connects the jīvā to the Paramātma; it is a different kind of prāṇa which exists in the spiritual world, and indeed in Brahman, as we have discussed previously. Therefore, merely the control of the material prāṇa is inadequate; it can help control the mind and the body and prepare it for focus on the Lord. But despite this control, the Lord is not easily found even in the heart of the yogis. The cessation of thoughts and enjoyment doesn't entail the development of devotion to the Lord. Vedic texts describe many yogis who have succumbed to material enjoyment after thousands of years of such practice—when they are enticed by heavenly damsels for sex. Such yogis have obtained mastery of the material body and the mind, but they haven't developed devotion to the Lord. Hence, despite their control of the body and the mind, their consciousness is still not diverted toward the Lord. Since it is still focused toward matter, the yogis may fall when the opportunity presents itself.

Many people say that yoga is secular, and it has hence become an alternative to other religious practices—which explicitly accept a transcendental God. Secularism merely indicates that there are many ways to approach God, and the soul may adopt one of the many methods. However, ultimately, the purpose of any spiritual practice is to develop devotion to the Supreme Lord. If yoga is practiced with the aim to develop loving devotion, as is recommended in the Bhagavad-Gita, where the ascetic withdraws the senses inwards and focuses the awareness on the Paramātma in the heart, the process is legitimate. However, if the process is without loving devotion to the Lord, then it must be considered atheistic—although more advanced than current materialism. Atheism is the aversion to the Lord, and everyone who practices yoga without devotion to the Lord is atheistic. Āsana and prāṇayāma are not spiritual processes; they are mechanical changes to the gross and subtle bodies. The key to spiritualism is the change in the consciousness that connects the jīvā to the Lord.

We noted above a difference between the prāṇa by which the soul controls the body and the mind, and the prāṇa that connects the jīvā to the Lord. In general, prāṇa is the connection between the knower and the known. If the Lord is the known, the connection is still called 'prāṇa' even though the nature of this connection and the process of observation (of the Lord) are different from that of matter. The prāṇa that carries the jīvā's consciousness in the material world is controlled by other types of material agencies, such as guna, karma, and time. Even when the soul moves to another body, the previous body and mind are left behind, but the guna and karma move with the soul caused by time.

In this regard, we must understand that there are many kinds of material prāṇa. There is a type of prāṇa that works under the control of guna and karma. Due to this prāṇa, the body continues to work even when we don't exercise volition. Then there is a prāṇa by which the soul accepts or rejects the desires automatically created due to guna. Then there is another prāṇa by which the demigods and ultimately the Paramātma control the delivery of karma. In short, there is a prāṇa which is inferior to guna and karma, and there is a prāṇa that is superior to guna and karma but under the control of different entities—the prāṇa superior to guna is in control of the jīvā and the prāṇa superior to karma is in the control of the Paramātma (as well as the demigods). Finally, there is a prāṇa which directs our consciousness toward the Lord. This prāṇa works under the control of the devotional energy of the Lord and without such devotion, this prāṇa cannot be activated. This sūtra only refers to the inferior forms of prāṇa—which are used to control the gross, subtle, and causal bodies—and the spiritual prāṇa under the devotional practice isn't referenced.

QUESTION

It seems from your statements that no process—either involving the discipline of the body or the mind—is adequate for attaining the abode of the Lord. These processes are merely an adjustment of the mind, senses, or the prāṇa. The true cause of change must happen in the desires of the soul. However, how can we be led to such changes if none of the practices can lead one toward it?

1.3.5 (68)

भेदव्यपदेशात्

bhedavyapadeśāt

bheda—the difference; vyapadeśāt—from the covering of vision.

TRANSLATION

From the covering of vision (of the Lord), the difference (of the jīvā).

COMMENTARY

Both terms—*bheda* and *vyapadeśāt*—are contentious here. The term *bheda* means difference, but the difference between which two things? Does this difference refer to that between the jīvā and the Lord? If so, it has already been stated many times earlier. Does it refer to the difference between jīvā and the three modes of nature? That too has been stated earlier. Does it refer to the difference between Prakriti and the Lord? That too has been noted earlier (the Lord is transcendental to the three modes of nature). If all these differences have already been noted, and cannot be repeated, then what does *bheda* refer to?

To understand this sūtra, we need to carefully analyze the origin of the jīvā's entry into the material world. In 1.1.12 (12) we discussed that the Oneness becomes differentiated due to desire for pleasure. We have discussed earlier that the ānanda aspect of the jīvā is the capacity to enjoy; the capacity always exists; however, the pleasure may not always exist. Enjoyment is preceded by desire, and it is the fulfillment of desire. If things go according to our desire, then we enjoy; if they are against our desires, then we suffer. The root cause of differentiation of the jīvā from the Oneness is desire; in the case of the material world, it must be understood as material desire. But, what do we mean by material desire? How is it different from other kinds of desires? Since the desire of devotion to the Lord has been noted as yielding liberation from the material world, we can surmise that 'material desire' is the opposite of devotion.

The jīvā has also been described as always being connected to the Lord through the prāṇa; by this connection, we described how the jīvā must be understood as a part of His body. Just like in our present body, the prāṇa flows from the heart to the different parts of the body, and this expansion of the prāṇa then makes us conscious of the entire body, in the same way, if the Lord is understood as the Supreme Soul, then jīvā can be described as a part of the Lord's body; the Supreme Soul can be considered the 'heart' and the jīvā is then the different parts of the body connected to the heart through the prāṇa. The entire body is spiritual; however, the Supreme Soul is the 'heart' while the individual souls are the different parts of the spiritual body connected to the heart through prāṇa; this prāṇa makes the Lord aware of the existence of the soul. And yet, the soul cannot be identified with the Lord because of the difference between the body's heart and the other parts of the body connected to the heart.

The different parts of the body serve each other—e.g., the hand feeds the stomach, and the stomach energizes the hands—and they ultimately serve the soul. In the same way, the jīvā must serve the other jīvā, but ultimately the Supreme Soul. It has previously been described that the Absolute Truth reconciles the diversities and we compared this to the root of the tree. The Supreme Soul is the root, from which the prāṇa expands like many branches of the tree—stretching over the body and covering all the parts—connecting the body to the soul. In this case, the jīvā and the Supreme Soul are simultaneously connected and yet different. By service to each other, and ultimately by service to the Supreme Soul, the jīvā is liberated from material existence and is situated as part of the Oneness, which has many parts (like in the body). This process of liberation achieved through devotion to the Lord has been described previously.

So, now, we have two facts to consider. First, the soul is always connected to the Supreme Soul. Second, it has entered the material world because of something called 'material desire', which must be understood as being opposed to devotion. By putting these two facts together, we can understand what we mean by 'material desire': It is the desire to be independent of the Lord; rather than being situated as part of the Oneness, it is the need to be a separate individual; rather than serving as part of the Oneness, and the heart of that Oneness, it is the need to be independent and different from parts and from the heart.

However, we have also discussed how the jīvā is simply the potentiality of enjoyment; it can have desires, but it cannot fulfill the desires on its own. As we noted in the previous sūtra, the soul can control the prāṇa that controls the guna. However, it cannot control the prāṇa that controls the karma. Therefore, Paramātma facilitates the fulfillment of the desire in the material world. However, if the desire is to become independent of the Lord, it can never be fulfilled because the jīvā doesn't have its own power of fulfillment—it must always rely on the prāṇa that delivers *karma* which is under the control of the Paramātma. Thus, the attainment of independence is ultimately futile; the jīvā must realize that it depends on the Supreme Soul's goodwill to even fulfill its material desires of enjoyment, but the desire for independence cannot be fulfilled. To the extent that the jīvā harbors this desire, it must exist in the material world where the *illusion* of independence is created when the Lord becomes invisible to the soul. Because the Lord is invisible to the jīvā, the jīvā can imagine that the Lord doesn't exist and that it is free to enjoy independently, rather than serve others, and ultimately serve the Lord. When the explicit desire to see the Lord is developed, the desire for independence must be given up; the jīvā can be liberated from the cultures of material existence if the material desire is overcome.

In 1.3.1 (64) we discussed how the material world is the negation of the Lord. But we had described this negation cognitively ("not red", "not table", etc.). We can now describe the same negation emotively: the jīvā develops a 'distance' to the Lord by becoming averse to Him; the 'distance' here is 'emotional distance'. Both ordinary and scientific uses of the term 'origin' can be understood in this context. Substantively, the 'origin' represents the thing we are averse to (i.e., the Lord), and māyā represents this emotional rejection of devotion to the Lord. Scientifically, we also use the term 'origin' to measure the distance from a chosen center (of some coordinate system). In this case, the Lord is described as the origin, and both types of meanings can be applied. There is a sense in which the jīvā emotionally negates the Lord, and there is a sense in which the jīvā moves 'away' from the Lord; the 'distance' between the jīvā and the Lord grows. The cause of distancing is the desire for independence.

The emotional distancing is the primary source of the separation—as has been noted in 1.1.12 (12). Thus, when the material world originates in the Lord, we must understand this origination primarily in the emotional sense, and secondarily in the material sense. As space is defined by the distance from the origin, similarly, the material space is to be primordially understood as the distance from the Lord. Thus, the term *bheda* used in this sūtra must be understood as the difference between the jīvā and the Lord; however, this difference has already been noted. What wasn't described is that this difference is unbridgeable due to which any process of spiritual progress—such as jñāna-yoga or aśtānga-yoga—doesn't take one into the Lord's abode unless the emotional attitude is changed. Therefore, even if one is studying scriptures, one must do it devotionally. Even if one is performing meditation, one must focus on the Lord. The term *bheda* hence refers to the aversion toward the service of the Lord. It points to the aspiration to become free of His control, or equal to Him, and not to be devoted to Him. This desire makes every other effort futile.

Similarly, the term *vyapadeśāt* is contentious. We have previously translated it as— (1) statement, claim, or declaration, (2) the covering, hiding, or misrepresentation. Both translations are appropriate here. Based on the first, we can say that "it is declared that the jīvā has aversion to the Lord". Alternatively, *vyapadeśāt* can also mean that "the jīvā's aversion hides the Lord (from its vision)". The Lord doesn't appear before the jīvā, and the jīvā cannot forcefully enter the Lord's abode if there is an aversion in the jīvā. The Lord is present everywhere; He is not absent even from this world. However, He is still invisible due to the presence of material desire in the soul. No process of transcendence—whether the reading of scripture, analysis, and discussion, or meditative practices—can deliver the results if this aversion remains unchanged.

Even though the reading of scriptures and chanting of its mantras has been advised previously, we must distinguish between the cognitive and the emotional aspects of the soul. The cognitive aspect is called *chit*, and it represents the capacity to understand and do things. However, it is different from the emotional aspect called ānanda, which represents the desire and capacity to enjoy. If we read the scriptures without faith and devotion or chant the mantra without such devotion, the processes don't have an effect. On the other hand, the reading of scripture is not necessary. The gopis of Vṛndāvana, for example, did not study scriptures; when Uddhava approached them with the philosophical understanding of the Absolute Truth, they rejected it, and only desired to know about the Lord's well-being. Thus, every process can work when devotion is employed, and no process will work without the presence of devotion.

QUESTION

But what is the guarantee that the jīvā will aspire for devotion to the Lord and will be able to enter His abode? How can we trust this process?

There is natural skepticism in everyone because we have been cheated in love in this life or in our previous lives. The idea that love is reciprocated is touted in romantic novels, but true love is very hard to find. On the other hand, the process of love involves many sacrifices—e.g., to develop an attachment to the Lord, one must give up attachment to this world. In short, one would have to sacrifice the worldly possibility of love, in order to develop the love of the Lord. So, the seeker may question the process itself: What if I'm cheated in the process of love, and I sacrifice everything, and yet do not obtain the result?

1.3.6 (69)
प्रकरणात्
prakaraṇāt

prakaraṇāt—from the episodes, descriptions, pastimes (in the scriptures).

TRANSLATION

From the many episodes and pastimes (of devotees in the scriptures).

COMMENTARY

There is no panacea for doubt when it comes to devotion. Doubts can pertain to the nature of reality, and they can be discussed rationally or empirically. Devotion doesn't come under this category. We can explain the nature of the Absolute Truth through philosophical argument. But we cannot make anyone *like* the Absolute Truth by arguments. Such liking may automatically develop in some when the understanding is gained. But it may also not develop in others even with an understanding. Also, it is said that the progress in understanding depends on devotion; with devotion, the understanding advances; without devotion, the understanding remains preliminary. In short, reason can destroy doubts about what the Absolute Truth is. But the destruction of doubts is not devotion. One may know that the Lord is the origin of everything, but that doesn't mean that one will necessarily love the Lord or have trust in the Lord.

The panacea for such doubts is assurances given in the scriptures. For example, in the Bhagavad-Gita 18.66, Lord Kṛṣṇa assures Arjuna that He should not worry (*mā śucaḥ*) that surrender to Him will lead to any suffering.

sarva-dharmān parityajya
mām ekaṁ śaraṇaṁ vraja
ahaṁ tvāṁ sarva-pāpebhyo
mokṣayiṣyāmi mā śucaḥ

Abandon all varieties of religion and just surrender unto Me. I shall deliver you from all sinful reactions. Do not fear.

The best panacea for doubts is the association of pure devotees because this devotion is infectious. They have surrendered to the Lord and found bliss in their devotion. If one is unable to find such devotees, then the pastimes of the devotees described in the scriptures can be used to understand the nature of devotion. Such pastimes often contain elaborate prayers to the Lord, where His glories are sung, and His affection toward the devotees is described. Devotion can only be acquired by experiencing the devotion; it cannot be acquired by logic and reasoning. However, to the extent that rational doubts prevent us from developing devotion, a philosophical understanding is necessary.

QUESTION

But why can't the Lord become kind to the soul and appear before it? Since the Lord is said to be magnanimous, He can demonstrate this magnanimity and appear before the jīvā despite its doubts or aversion. Just like a mother or father forcibly love the child, why can't the Lord do the same with the averse jīvā?

1.3.7 (70)

स्थित्यदनाभ्याम् च

sthityadanābhyām ca

sthiti—fixed; adana—food, act of eating; abhyām—the two; ca—also.

TRANSLATION

(The Lord is already present with the soul) on account of the two (living entities) one of which silently observes even as the other eats (enjoys).

COMMENTARY

Many people practicing spiritual life become frustrated with the process. They claim that they have been studying the scriptures, following rules and regulations, controlling the body and the mind, etc. And yet, they don't seem to find the bliss that must come with the devotion to the Lord. Then they blame the Lord for being too discerning or unkind, for not appearing before them, showing them some 'signs' of His presence, or demonstrating kindness in other ways. As we have discussed in the previous sūtra, the processes of reading, understanding, or even practicing (by the body and mind) are not adequate. They are merely cognitive and conative changes, and they cannot produce the ultimate result unless one develops devotion. This devotion cannot be acquired by any process; however, if the devotion exists, then all processes help its advancement. Factually, even though many people perform spiritual processes, they harbor alternative material aspirations, rather than unconditional love to the Lord. Their main aim may be to become happy in this life, to improve the condition of the world, to initiate many disciples and be known as a spiritual leader, etc. All these desires are hindrances to spiritual progress; every process will work if there is a latent desire to unconditionally love the Lord. Similarly, no process—even the reading of scripture and chanting of mantra—will work if the desire is to pursue alternative goals rather than the devotion to the Lord. Lord Kṛṣṇa states in the Bhagavad-Gita 4.11 His reciprocal approach to love.

ye yathā māṁ prapadyante
tāṁs tathaiva bhajāmy aham

As they surrender to me, I am devoted to them in the same way.

The term *prapadyante* means 'surrender', and the term *bhajāmy aham* indicates the Lord 'worships' the jīvā in the same way. The root *bhaj* indicates devotion, and the Lord ascribes to Himself that devotional reciprocation in accordance with the way in which the soul surrenders to the Lord. The cause of the Lord not appearing is thus the lack of devotional attitude in the soul.

But, if one goes further, and argues that the Lord should be the bigger person in the devotional relationship, and must initiate the devotional inclination, then this has already been confirmed by the presence of the Paramātma in the heart. As we have discussed earlier, the Lord comes with the soul due to three motives—causes, reasons, and justifications. The cause of the Lord's presence is that He delivers the good and bad results of his actions, the reason is that the Lord is attached to the soul, and the justification is that He considers it His duty to liberate the soul. The magnanimity of the Lord is not in question because He is already present in the heart as the silent observer and approver of the soul's desires for independent enjoyment. The desire for independence can only be fulfilled if the soul had the power to create a world for himself; in short, he should become a creator just like the Lord. The soul aspires for such independence where it creates its own world and becomes its master. This illusory type of enjoyment is facilitated by the Lord. So, He cannot be faulted for lack of progress in the spiritual life; the responsibility rests entirely with the soul.

Topic 2

QUESTION

You have stated that the Lord is the origin and the basis of the material world. He has been called transcendent to the material world. What is the nature of this transcendence, and how does it differ from material existence?

1.3.8 (71)

भूमा संप्रसादादध्युपदेशात्

bhūmā saṃprasādādadhyupadeśāt

bhūmā—the multitude, collection, assembly, world; saṃprasādāt-adhi—from beyond the state of deep sleep; upadeśāt—from of the teaching.

TRANSLATION

From the teaching, the bhūmā is from beyond the state of deep sleep.

COMMENTARY

The term bhūmā represents the plurality of individuals. It is not merely the Supreme Person we call "God" but a 'world' that exists in relation to God. We can call it 'Godhead'. This is also evident from the previous topic, which stated that the abode of the Lord is the origin of the material world. This sūtra continues the discussion and calls this 'abode' bhūmā or a world in which God exists with His devotees. In relation to the material world, it is described as being beyond the state of deep sleep; in the Yoga philosophy, there are four states of conscious experience— (1) vaikharī or waking state, (2) madhyamā or dreaming state, (3) paśyanti or deep sleep state, and (4) parā or transcendent state. The bhūmā or the transcendent reality is here described as the fourth state.

During the waking state, the soul acquires experiences of the five gross elements—namely, Earth, Water, Fire, Air, and Ether. When these elements interact, they produce a representation of the world, which the senses, the mind, the intellect, and the ego interact with to create an experience. During the dreaming state, this bodily interaction with the world is absent; however, the senses, the mind, the intellect, and the ego are still active. These senses and the mind are not just perceivers of the world; they can also create this world. During the waking experience, the perception of the world is dominant, and therefore, the waking state is identified with the five gross elements. It is not that the subtle elements are absent; it is just that these five elements are the dominant cause of the experience. However, when we enter the dreaming stage, the senses and the mind become creators of the experience. In this state, we can understand the mind and senses better than during the waking experience, and hence the dreaming stage is identified with the working of the senses, the mind, the intellect, the ego, and morality. The dreaming state is said to be superior to the waking state because during dreaming we can realize that experience is not limited to the gross body. Therefore, if one was identifying with this body, then dreaming indicates that this body is not the cause of experience, because such experiences can also exist during dreaming. The movement of the senses, the mind, the intellect, the and ego stops during the deep sleep state, but the unconscious—called the kārana sarīra—remains active. This activity involves the integration of the waking and dreaming experience into the formation of deep-seated beliefs, fears, wishes, and relationships. It is sometimes said that what we learn during the waking state needs deep sleep to be assimilated.

Beyond these three kinds of activities, there is also the activity of the soul. This activity originates in the automatic springing of desire for enjoyment. While the previous three are described as material, the fourth state—namely, the activity of the soul—is considered transcendental to matter. This sūtra states that the abode of the Lord also involves activities, but they are in the fourth state of experience—i.e., they are produced by the soul, and not by matter.

QUESTION

By calling transcendence the fourth state of consciousness, you are only distinguishing it from different types of matter. It can also be construed as a negative definition—the transcendent state is *not* these three states. But how do we understand the transcendent state in a positive sense—what it is?

1.3.9 (72)
धर्मोपपत्तेश्च
dharmopapatteśca

dharma—nature; upapatteḥ—cause, justification, evidence; ca—and.

TRANSLATION

And (its) nature is (self)-causation, (self)-justification, (self)-evidence.

COMMENTARY

In logic, *upapatti* is used in various ways to indicate causation, evidence, justification, substantiation, and the rationale underlying a law. The transcendent state is here described as something whose very nature is causation, justification, and rationale. This can be understood in contrast to the previous sūtra where the previous three types of material experiences were noted; all these experiences involve matter. The material elements such as Earth, Water, Fire, Air, Ether, mind, intellect, ego, and morality are not automatically activated; they are activated by the presence of prāṇa. The prāṇa is also not automatically active in the material world; it is animated by guna and karma. Finally, guna and karma are also not automatically causal; they are activated by the influence of time. This time—which causes all changes—is the representation of the Lord, called Saṅkarṣaṇa. Time automatically animates the material world, however, the jīvā can reject the animations of guna. The jīvā cannot reject the animations caused by karma. Thus, we cannot control what will happen to us, but we can control how we respond to it. This 'response' to the automatic animation due to time is the ability in the jīvā to reject the automatically arising desires. For instance, if someone slaps you, your mind would automatically develop a fight or flight response. This inclination is automatically produced by one's guna (some people may want to fight while others will try to escape) under the influence of time. The jīvā can reject such automatically created impulses.

But we must now ask: What is the cause of the jīvā making a certain type of choice? And the answer is that there is no external cause. The nature or dharma of the transcendent reality is that it is self-caused, or spontaneous. Therefore, as we seek deeper forms of causality, we progress from the body to the senses, to the mind, intellect, ego, and morality, into the unconscious guna and karma, which are animated by time, and finally to the jīvā who chooses a response. This choice cannot be pushed further back to anything other than the soul; the choice is self-caused, self-justified, and the jīvā is the only cause of such a choice.

So, the transcendent reality is the ultimate *upapatti*—the cause, reason, and justification—for all experiences. Within this self-justified and self-initiated causation, the Lord has greater power to control, greater capacity to enjoy, and greater ability for cognition, compared to the jīvā. Hence, the jīvā is subordinate to the Lord. However, both the jīvā and Lord have self-causation. In short, both the soul and the Lord have free will by which they can change things. The transcendent reality is being described as that which has self-causation; in contrast, the material reality is without self-causation or spontaneous action and must, therefore, be animated by either the will of the soul or that of the Lord.

Topic 3

QUESTION

You have previously said that the Lord is the origin of the material world. Now, we have also talked about the Lord's abode, and you described it as bhūmā, entailing that there are many living entities. Is the Lord also the origin of these liberated living entities, like in the case of the material world?

The impersonalist philosophers sometimes accept the Lord's worship as a stepping stone into the impersonal Brahman; they call the forms of the Lord Saguna-Brahman as opposed to the Nirguna-Brahman; the implication is that the Saguna feature of the Lord is temporary in this material world: He appears in a form to liberate the living entity, but thereafter merges into Brahman. The seeker is asking whether this differentiation (as previously indicated by bhūmā) must also be considered another 'world', just like the material world?

1.3.10 (73)

अक्षरमम्बरान्तधृतेः

akṣaramambarāntadhṛteḥ

akṣaram—the Imperishable; ambara-anta—to the end of space; dhṛteḥ—supports.

TRANSLATION

The Imperishable supports (everything) till the end of space.

COMMENTARY

We have earlier discussed the four quarters of existence. All these collectively constitute everything that exists, although they are divided into different domains. In this sūtra, by using the term *ambara-anta*, or the end of space, an indirect reference to the hierarchy between these domains is being made. The material world is at the bottom of this hierarchy; Brahman is above the material world; the Vaikuṇṭha planets are above the Brahman, and Goloka is above the Vaikuṇṭha planets. Each of these places is differentiated into individuals, and accordingly, each of these places involves a 'distance' between the Lord and the jīvā; if this distance did not exist, the jīvā would be identical to the Lord.

We have previously discussed how the jīvā is averse to the Lord, and its 'distance' from the Lord is based on the emotional aloofness produced by aversion. But in the three-quarters of liberated realms, the jīvā are not averse to the Lord. So, how are they still different from the Lord, rather than identical with Him? To understand the differentiation, we must distinguish between different kinds of desires. There is a type of desire in which the jīvā loves the Lord and wants to serve Him personally. Due to the attitude of service, the jīvā considers himself different from the Lord, and yet he wants to see Him face to face. This desire is devotion but accompanied by a *boldness*—I'm qualified to serve the Lord. To serve, I must be different from Him, and yet close to Him. There is another kind of desire in which the jīvā loves the Lord but is shy; he keeps a distance from the Lord since he considers himself unqualified to meet the Lord face-to-face. Such a soul prefers to serve the other devotees of the Lord. This 'distance' to the Lord is however only cognitive; the jīvā stays out of sight, and this cognitive separation intensifies the emotional separation and brings him emotionally closer to the Lord. In fact, the shy devotee is emotionally dearer to the Lord than the bold devotee. There is also a third type of desire in which the jīvā recognizes that the Lord is Supreme, and He is not averse to the Lord, but His appreciation is silent and distant. The jīvā doesn't want to be independent but he also doesn't want to come close to the Lord. In this case, the jīvā is both cognitively and emotionally distant, although not averse to the Lord.

These three types of desires correspond to the three-quarters of existence that we have discussed previously. The devotion conditioned by shyness constitutes the place called Goloka. The devotion conditioned by boldness constitutes the place called Vaikuṇṭha. The devotion of silent appreciation is called Brahman. And apart from these three—the fourth quarter of existence—the material world, is the place where the jīvā has the desire for independence.

In Goloka, the jīvā has the greatest emotional connection to the Lord, exacerbated by the cognitive distance (in this world, distance makes the hearts go fonder). In Vaikuṇṭha, the jīvā is cognitively close, but the emotional connect is reduced (in this world, familiarity breeds contempt). In Brahman, both cognitive and emotional distances are greater, as the jīvā doesn't want to serve the Lord personally, and he doesn't miss the Lord because of not serving Him. The jīvā is content appreciating the Lord from a distance. And in the material world, the jīvā is averse to the Lord. Therefore, based on the emotional distancing, we can construct the space of the four quarters of existence: Goloka is closest in emotional distance, Vaikuṇṭha is slightly farther, Brahman is even farther, and the material world is the farthest. In this sūtra, it is stated that the Lord supports everything up to the farthest end of space. This 'farthest end' should be understood as the material existence, and it is most detached from the Lord.

The main point is that even the transcendent realm is differentiated like the material realm. It can be described as multiple 'worlds' in which the same Lord is the Supreme Person, although based on the cognitive and emotional distancing, He is understood in different ways. Thus, we should not think that the material world is differentiated, and transcendence is undifferentiated. The statements about Oneness should rather be understood as the unity in purpose, being parts of a Whole, and being interrelated rather than independent.

QUESTION

You have previously said that the Lord is the controller of the material world, and the demigods are subordinate to Him. Does this kind of rulership or control of the other living entities exist even in the transcendent world?

Everyone in the material world resents having a boss, but everybody wants to be the boss. The impersonal viewpoint envisions the dissolution of this boss mentality by suggesting that we are all one, so there is no boss because there is no difference between us. But if we get past that idea, and acknowledge the existence of individuals, there is also the conception of an egalitarian society in which people live in a communion comprised of equals where nobody is anyone else's boss. Modern ideas of democracy have emerged from the attempt to dismantle the permanence of bosses; however, given that there would be anarchy in the material world if there were no boss, we still envision the existence of a temporary boss—e.g., a democratically elected leader—who can be replaced by someone else if he acted too bossy. So, one can surmise that the existence of bosses was a necessary evil in this material world, and a transcendent world must therefore be perfectly egalitarian—because everyone is well-behaved, so there is no need for a boss. In short, if we cannot merge with God to become God, then at least we can still aspire to become equal to God. God may remain the first among equals, but he could not wield power over the others.

1.3.11 (74)

सा च प्रशासनात्

sā ca praśāsanāt

sā—this (the previous sūtra); ca—and, also; praśāsanāt—from rulership.

TRANSLATION

From the rulership, also this (the Lord is the origin and supporter).

COMMENTARY

The sūtra rejects all egalitarian ideas—which often follow when the impersonal oneness is rejected. It states that the Lord is the ruler apart from being the origin and the supporter of all existence. The term *praśāsana* means 'administration'. It has been noted that in the material world, the Lord has administrators in the demigods—each responsible for various departments of the worldly control—and the Lord presides over them. Accordingly, there is a hierarchy in this control structure: there isn't one ruler who controls everything. Rather, He delegates the power of control successively through a hierarchy of controllers. Now, if one thought that this was unique to the material world, the implication here is that the hierarchy applies even to the spiritual world. In short, not only is there one Supreme Controller, there are also subordinate controllers under the supervision of the Supreme Controller. The souls, therefore, work under the supervision of 'senior' or 'superior' souls, and the society isn't egalitarian.

QUESTION

What is the necessity for supervision or rulership when everyone is liberated? Since the jīvā is freed from aversion to the Lord, and hence aversion to other living entities, they would naturally cooperate with each other. With this natural cooperation, there should be no need for a supervisor or ruler.

1.3.12 (75)
अन्यभावव्यावृत्तेश्च
anyabhāvavyāvṛtteśca

anya—another; bhāva—nature; vyāvṛtteḥ—due to diversity; ca—and.

TRANSLATION

Due to diversity (of opinions) and different natures (of the souls).

COMMENTARY

The emergence of a cooperative mindset doesn't entail the dissolution of variety and diverse opinions. Just because everyone is liberated doesn't mean they will perfectly agree with each other on everything. They may maintain diverse viewpoints, and still, one viewpoint must win over the others. The hierarchy enables the existence of diversity, and yet a choice among the diverse viewpoints can be made. The cooperation is simply that those individuals whose viewpoints were overruled will not harbor resentment. They will rather respect the opinion of a superior living entity, even if they disagree with it.

Topic 4

QUESTION

Why should different liberated souls have different opinions and natures? Aren't we discussing the nature of the Absolute Truth which must be considered universal, and hence its perception must also be the cognition of the universal? How could we regard such diverse opinions of the Absolute Truth?

1.3.13 (76)
ईक्षतिकर्मव्यपदेशात् सः
īkṣatikarmavyapadeśāt saḥ

īkṣati—seeing; karma—acting; vyapadeśāt—because of the appearance, or because of the description, or because of representation; saḥ—He.

TRANSLATION

Because He is seen and acts in many ways (in relation to different jīvā).

COMMENTARY

We have discussed earlier how all the quarters of existence are substantively expanded from the Lord. We have also seen how the jīvā adopts different emotional attitudes toward the Lord (here we are discussing only the favorable attitudes). Finally, we have noted that the 'space' of the different domains of existence is defined in relation to the 'origin' in the Lord—i.e., different positions in the creation are different places in relation to Him. Accordingly, from the viewpoint of each jīvā, the same Absolute Truth is perceived differently.

Topic 5

QUESTION

You earlier stated that the Absolute Truth is Oneness, which reconciles the diversity. The diversity was the parts of the whole, like the branches of the trees. Now, you are also stating that whole or the root itself—which was earlier said to be Oneness—can be understood in diverse ways. Then, why would we consider this diversity as Oneness, when it presents itself in diverse ways?

1.3.14 (77)

दहर उत्तरेभ्यः

dahara uttarebhyaḥ

daharaḥ—child or small; uttarebhyaḥ—due to being subsequent.

TRANSLATION

Due to being subsequent, (the soul) is small or the child (of the One).

COMMENTARY

In the previous sūtra, it was stated that the Lord is seen and acts in different ways in relation to the different jīvā. This leads to the doubt that even the Absolute Truth is not the *universal truth,* because each jīvā can have a different conception of the Absolute Truth. This doubt rests on the notion that the universal truth is an idea, and everyone must have the same idea. In Vedic philosophy, however, the Absolute Truth is a person, and everyone can know the same person differently. If the Absolute Truth is only an idea, then the knowledge of this Absolute Truth must also be the universal truth. If on the other hand, the Absolute Truth is a person, then this person can be known by different individuals in different ways. This is not to say that the Absolute Truth is not an idea; He is also the original ideas of knowledge, beauty, power, wealth, fame, and renunciation. But everyone need not have a perfect understanding of all these principles. For example, many devotees of the Lord may not see His power; they may merely see His beauty. Likewise, they may not consider the Lord as the completeness of all knowledge; they may think of Him merely as a child, or a handsome young man. Thus, everyone is allowed a different conception of the Absolute Truth, if they all pertain to the same Absolute Truth.

This problem comes up frequently in the clashes between different religions. The monotheist says that there is only one God, and under the notion of Absolute Truth being the universal truth, he asserts that everyone must have a common conception of God. The Vedic system rejects this idea. There is an

Absolute Truth, which is also an idea, however, that idea may be partially or fully understood by different souls. The full understanding is better, but even a partial understanding is not bad if it pertains to the Personality of God. Thus, even the demons who think of the Lord's qualities in an angry mood attain liberation. You just need to be a sufficiently angry demon to always think of the Lord.

This sūtra says that the individual jīvā is subsequent to the Lord. With each jīvā, there is a different idea of God, but the idea has a common *reference*. Just as one person might say that John is a father, while the other person says that John is an employee, similarly, different jīvā can describe the Lord in different ways, but there is no fault if they refer to the Absolute Truth. The many forms of the Lord don't entail many Gods, but the personalized understanding of each soul. Across these souls, the Absolute Truth isn't the universal truth. There are individual truths in each jīvā which are partial understandings of the Absolute Truth. They are not considered *falsity* if they refer to the Absolute Truth.

Thus, you can say that God is kind, and you can say that God is cruel. You can say that He is the oldest, and you can say that He is just born. He can be called most loving, or the most fearsome. He can be attached or detached. Whatever we can think of, God can be assigned that quality. This is the meaning of Absolute Truth—He is the origin of all words and hence all ideas. Each soul can worship the Lord based on a different idea of the Absolute Truth. They create personalized and relativized truths, but because they are all attributed to the Absolute Truth, they constitute a partial understanding of the whole. This understanding is not false, and it is also not the whole truth. If there were no diversity, then there would be no difference between the soul knowing God, and God knowing Himself. But if there was no unity, then we could never say that we know the truth. Thus, there are two notions about truth—the reference and the meaning. Monotheists confuse these two; they believe that if there is one God, then He must be understood in the same way. The Vedic system accepts the universality of the reference but rejects the universality of meaning.

QUESTION

In our earlier discussion, it was implied that there are many individual jīvā. However, the jīvā was also described as the potentiality for sat, chit, and ānanda, and it followed that the soul can desire, perceive, and form relations. But now we are explicitly stating that these individuals are also different from each other—they have different viewpoints and desires. So, they aren't merely different individuals of the same type, but different types of individuals.

Things in the world are distinguished based on many modalities. For example, you can say that two things are different because one is a table and the other is a chair. Or, you can say that two things are different because they are two separate instances of a chair. The preliminary understanding of individuality is that there are different things. But a more advanced understanding is that some of these things are also different or similar types of things. This leads to the question: Should we say that all souls are basically similar types of persons? Or, should we say that they are different types of individuals?

1.3.15 (78)
गतशिब्दाभ्यां तथा हि दृष्टं लङि्गं च
gatiśabdābhyāṃ tathā hi dṛṣṭaṃ liṅgaṃ ca

gati—view, conception; śabdābhyām—from the statements; tathā hi—likewise; dṛṣṭaṃ—it is seen; liṅgam—the forms; ca—and.

TRANSLATION

Just like different meanings can be derived from the same statement, similarly, the different forms are seen (from the same Absolute Truth).

COMMENTARY

Here a comparison is being made to the relation between statements and their meanings. The same statement can be interpreted in many ways. A well-known example of such interpretation is the statement: "I saw a man on a hill with a telescope". This statement has at least four different meanings:

- I saw a man using a telescope. The man was on a hill.
- I saw a man. I was on the hill, looking through a telescope.
- I saw a man. The man was on a hill and had a telescope.
- I was on the hill. I saw a man. The man had a telescope.

Meanings are determined in three different ways. First, they depend on the words themselves—a different set of words would constitute a different statement and therefore a different meaning. Second, the meaning is decided by the context—the place, time, and the roles of the people who are exchanging these words. Third, the meaning is decided by the intention of the person speaking it. In this process, the intention is the highest: we begin by the desire to say something. The context comes next: we judge which context requires the meaning to be expressed in which way. Finally, the combination of the intention and the context is converted into words. When the listener hears these words, he can obviously perceive the words (provided he can hear). He can also—in most cases—understand the context if enough information about the context is available. This context requires us to know what was said before and after, the place in which it was said, and the relation between the speaker and the listener. The words are objective, and the context is intersubjective. But the intention is subjective and depends on a person's goals and objectives. Many people take this to imply that the real meaning underlying a statement is unknowable.

Intentions are knowable by the perception of emotions—normally through tones and pitches. For example, the statement "I hate you" can mean many things based on the tone: (1) if said quietly, the statement means the person indeed hates the other person, (2) if said angrily, the statement entails that there is actually love, but it is not being fulfilled, (3) if said jokingly, the statement entails that there is no hate, but the speaker has been embarrassed and since they are unable to respond appropriately, they jokingly state their hatred.

This sūtra states that the fact that the Absolute Truth is interpreted differently is based on the relation to the jīvā and the jīvā's emotional state. In one sense, all the souls are the same because they are capable of emotion, relation, and cognition. In another sense, they have different desires, relations, and viewpoints. Factually, there is no contradiction in these two statements. Normally, the preliminary understanding is of the capacity, and the advanced understanding is due to the outcomes of that capacity. The fact that the jīvā is differentiated from Oneness due to desire, entails that everyone has a different desire. So, they see the Lord in a different way because they want to see Him differently. This perception of the Lord is a subjective interpretation of the jīvā.

QUESTION

If you say that the different perception of the Lord is their subjective experience, then doesn't it follow that these subjective perceptions are like hallucinations, and there is no objective existence to them? It would mean that the diverse forms and activities of the Lord are merely in my experience?

There is a prominent school of philosophy—called Idealism—which is contrasted against Realism. Idealism emerged out of the problems of interpretation. Given that everyone can have a different view of the world, philosophers claimed that there is no objective reality. This leads to the ridiculous position of solipsism in which only I exist, and everyone else is just my idea. To do a little better than solipsism, the Idealist philosopher says that there is an objective but meaningless world, to which we attribute meaning and purpose. In short, the existence of the world is objective, but the meaning and purpose are subjective. If you accept either of these positions, you are dangerously close to claiming that everyone has their own personalized hallucinations, and your truth is no better than mine. It then follows that nobody can claim to know the truth.

1.3.16 (79)

धृतेश्च महिम्नोऽस्यास्मिन्नुपलब्धेः

dhṛteśca mahimno'syāsminnupalabdheḥ

dhṛteḥ—supporting; ca—moreover; asya mahimnaḥ—of His greatness or diversity; asmin—in the Lord; upalabdheḥ—being seen.

TRANSLATION

Moreover, His greatness (i.e., diversity) is seen to be supported in the Lord.

COMMENTARY

This sūtra can be understood through an example. A man reveals his romantic side in relation to his wife, his compassionate side toward his children, his bossy side toward his servants, and his friendly side toward his compatriots. When a friend meets the man, he doesn't say that I met a 'part' of the man; the man is fully there; and yet, the friend will not see his romantic side or the bossy side. All these aspects of a person are simply potentialities. They are present, but they are not always revealed. The potentiality is converted into a vision and action through a relation. If the relation changes, the same person is seen differently, and he acts differently. In the same way, the Lord is innumerable potentialities, aspects, and personalities. However, in different relationships, He manifests a different side of His person. Therefore, when we see the Lord as Kṛṣṇa we should not say that Rāma is not present in this form. We must understand that Rāma is also a potentiality that is latent in Him; however, based on the relationship, the Rāma aspect of the Absolute Truth is not manifest.

The situation can be contrasted with the idea of five blind men seeing different parts of the elephant. They don't know that they are seeing an elephant. They just claim to see a trunk, a tail, a stomach, ears, or legs. And they think that these parts are the whole truth. The correction for the blind men is simply that these are aspects of the elephant. The difference between the ignorant and the enlightened soul is that the ignorant soul thinks that different visions are different things, and the enlightened soul knows that there is only one thing to be known, which has innumerable aspects. The ignorant soul thinks that the many forms of God must be different persons. But the enlightened soul knows that they are the same person, although manifesting only a certain aspect.

The difference between meaning and reference is relevant here. The five blind men think that the legs, the tail, the trunk, the belly, and the ears are both the meaning and the reference. But the man with vision knows that the reference is the elephant while the meanings are the legs, tail, trunk, belly, and ears. The souls with diverse opinions about the Lord are not like blind men seeing parts of the elephant, who think that these are factually different things. They are rather like the wife, child, friend, and employee of a person, who see the same person, and yet, only an aspect of their full personality is revealed.

Now, in some relationships, many aspects of a person can be revealed. For instance, married couples can have many types of diverse relations; they can have romantic love for each other; they can be friends; they can pamper each other like a parent pampers a child, and sometimes they may even boss over each other (with the other person happily accepting their bossiness). Based on this example, we can distinguish between relations in which many aspects of a person are revealed vs. those relations where only one aspect may be revealed. Accordingly, there is a relation in which the complete form of the Lord is known—i.e., all His aspects are understood. There are also relations in which fewer or only one aspect of the Lord may be seen. These various forms are called Bhagavān-svayam (God in fullness), aṁsa (part of the full), kalā (part of the part), and puruṣa (part of the part of the part). So, when we speak about diverse relations, we must understand that some relations are *superior* to others because they reveal more personality aspects of a person than the others.

Therefore, the argument that if we have diverse opinions then we cannot be talking about the Absolute Truth is wrong. It is a caricature extended from the perception of the five blind men to the spiritual realm. This type of understanding should be rejected. We must rather say that whether the Lord appears as Vāmana or Narsimha or Kṛṣṇa, the exact same Absolute Truth has appeared, although only a certain aspect of the Absolute Truth is manifest. Therefore, there aren't many Gods. There are simply many descriptions of the same God relativized to the person who interacts with the Lord in a different way.

The description of reality as potentiality applies even to the material world and is found in atomic theory. However, atomic theory is not well understood because we look at the world like blind men seeing an elephant. For example, when we observe the atoms, we think that they are like the leg, the tail, the belly, the trunk, and the ears of the elephant, which is correct. The problem is that the blind men think that these are independent individual things, rather than *aspects* of the elephant. In short, you see parts, and you think that there is no whole other than the parts. Since we don't understand the whole, we don't even think that when we see the legs of the elephant, we are seeing the elephant, although in a certain limited way. The correct conception of reality is that the part of the whole is an *aspect* of the whole, not separate from the whole. The aspect is not equal to the whole, and it is not separated from the whole.

When reality is described through aspects, then we find many kinds of aspects. The legs, the seat, the backrest, and the armrest are some of the aspects of a chair. Similarly, the 'garden chair' and the 'study chair' are different aspects of the same thing. Likewise, shape, size, and color are different aspects of the chair. These aspects constitute the different modalities of perceiving the chair. You can enter the physical modality and see the chair as the aspects of legs, seat, backrest, armrest, etc. Then you can enter the sensual modality and see the same chair as color, shape, size, etc. And then you can enter the mental modality and see the same thing as a garden chair or a study chair. Then you can enter the intellectual mentality and see this as a hallucination or reality. There are many such modalities in our perception, and each modality is comprised of many sub- and sub-sub-modalities. All these modalities are aspects of the whole, but they are not at the same level. The physical modality is lower than the sensual modality, the sensual modality is lower than the mental modality, which is lower than the intellectual modality, etc. The hierarchy between the modalities is the key differentiator from the physicalist view. In the physicalist view, a part of the whole is like a leg or a backrest of the chair, but in the hierarchical viewpoint, these parts are many different types of aspects of the whole. The first step in knowing reality is to transition from blind men to men who can see. Then transition to thinking, judging, intending, moralizing, and so forth.

Each modality is a partial understanding of the Lord. However, as we rise in the hierarchy, the understanding gets better. Thus, the Lord's toes are a modality of the Lord, just like His hands. But the full Lord is also modal, and He appears as a child, father, friend, master, lover, etc. The blind man thinks that these are different, but the enlightened soul understands that the same Lord manifests Himself in different aspects through different kinds of relations.

Now, if someone says that these modes are simply our hallucinatory perception, then this sūtra denies that claim. The feet and hands are aspects of the Lord; they can exist in our perception, but they also exist in the Lord. Likewise, the father and the child aspects of the Lord can also exist in our perception and in the Lord. So, the claim that these perceptions are hallucinations is rejected.

QUESTION

You previously noted that the different understandings of the Absolute Truth are like the different meanings of a sentence. That led to the view that

these meanings are private conceptions of the Lord held by the jīvā and don't have an objective existence. But now you are saying that these meanings of the sentence are within the sentence itself. In fact, you are saying that these meanings are parts of the sentence or partial understandings of the sentence.

1.3.17 (80)
प्रसद्धिेश्च
prasiddheśca

prasiddheḥ—due to being well-known or famous; ca—also

TRANSLATION

And (the diverse forms of the Lord are) due to His being famous.

COMMENTARY

We have earlier discussed the six qualities of the Lord, namely, knowledge, beauty, renunciation, power, wealth, and fame. The Lord is knowledge itself, the original idea. The idea, however, is only one aspect of the Lord. The other aspect is that He is a person. When the idea and the individual are combined, we say that the Lord is the embodiment of the idea or a symbol of the idea. The idea is, in fact, not separate from the symbol. These two aspects are the śabda-brahman and artha-brahman, or word and meaning, aspects of the same thing. The artha is the meaning, and the śabda is the instance of that meaning.

The Absolute Truth is also beautiful, and this beauty has two aspects: the symbol is beautiful, and the meaning is beautiful. The Lord looks beautiful and His thoughts are beautiful. The meaning and the symbol are cognitive, and the beauty is emotive. So, knowledge and beauty are related and yet distinct.

As the original idea, the Absolute Truth is self-evident and independent. He doesn't need anything to rationalize, justify, explain, or cause His existence. This self-evidentiary nature of the Absolute Truth is also a modality, due to which we say that the Lord is not just a person, but also the Original Person. As a result, we make three claims about the Lord—(1) there is the idea of knowledge, (2) there is a symbol of this idea, and (3) this symbol and idea are the original thing from which everything else has expanded or manifest.

As He expands into other things, this creation becomes His wealth. All the creation in the four quarters is His property or wealth, and He is the object underlying that property. We have earlier discussed the attribute and ownership meanings of property; these two meanings are also the modalities of the Lord's creation. Due to the attribute mode, we can say that the creation is simply an attribute of the Lord, like weight or size is an attribute of a table, and the two cannot be separated. However, due to the ownership mode, we can say that the property is different from the Lord, and the Lord owns the creation. Thus, when the creation ends, the Lord is not minimized. However, when the creation exists, knowing the creation is tantamount to knowing aspects of the Lord.

Once the wealth of the creation has expanded from the Lord, He also exercises control over His wealth. This control is called His power. Finally, He also enters this creation in many forms to enjoy it, like one may live in one's house, drive one's car, wear one's clothes, etc. This entry into the creation is called His fame. If we think of the creation as His ownership, then we can say that to enjoy different kinds of owned properties, He takes many different forms. However, when we say that these properties are simply His attributes—like mass is an attribute of a particle—the understanding is more nuanced: the mass was previously in the particle, and now the particle is present within the mass. Thus, by knowing anything, we can know the source from which it emanated.

The Lord's renunciation aspect is that He is outside of everything. And His fame aspect is that He is present inside everything. He also has the controller aspect, all the things are simply His aspects, the source of this diversity is the individual who embodies the idea of knowledge, which is also beautiful. Thus, to know the Lord as these six attributes is to know the entire existence.

The jīvā is also a manifestation of the Lord, and the Lord enters the jīvā. Since the Lord is knowledge, therefore, by this entry the jīvā acquires an understanding of the Lord. However, since the jīvā is a part or aspect of the Lord, the understanding of the Lord is different in each jīvā. Thus, the part is inside the whole, and a partial understanding of the whole is inside each part. This partial understanding is the Lord's fame. However, this partial knowledge is also a part of the full knowledge. So, it is not merely a hallucination in the jīvā. It is also present in the Lord. The difference is in the reference of this partial understanding. In the material world, the parts are considered independent things. And under spiritual realization, these parts are aspects of the Lord. The understanding may be partial, but the reference of that understanding is full.

QUESTION

So, the implication seems to be that the diverse perceptions of the Lord are not merely subjective interpretations of the Lord by the jīvā. They are also objectively present, and hence they cannot be treated as personal creations. Why couldn't the Lord allow the jīvā to create its own subjective creations?

It is possible to make arguments for and against subjectivity. If the argument is for subjectivity, then it might say that due to subjectivity I'm seeing a hallucination that doesn't really exist. If the argument is against subjectivity, then it might say that if I'm not free to interpret reality as I like, then I have no free will. The former argument was previously made. The latter is made here.

1.3.18 (81)

इतरपरामर्शात् स इति चेत् न असमभवात्

itaraparāmarśāt sa iti cet na asambhavāt

itara—the other, or the individual soul; parāmarśāt—because of the judgment, or the opinion, or the viewpoint, or the reference; saḥ—He (the Lord); iti cet—if it be said; na—no; asambhavāt—on account of impossibility.

TRANSLATION

If it is said that the Lord is simply the opinion or judgment or viewpoint of the individual soul, (we say) no, on account of the impossibility.

COMMENTARY

We have discussed earlier that the jīvā is only a potentiality. It has the capacity to desire, relate, know, and act, but it cannot fulfill its desires. This means that the jīvā has senses to perceive and act, but it depends on the Lord to obtain the objects of sensation and action. Thus, when the jīvā obtains an experience, that experience is not his creation. The experience is always the result of the Lord fulfilling the desire of the jīvā. In the same way, when the soul desires to perceive the Lord, the Lord appears by His grace. This experience is not the creation of the jīvā. It is the soul's desire being fulfilled by the Lord.

This constitutes the resolution of two contradictory arguments—for and against free will. If the Lord is objectively present, then someone can say that there is no free will: The Lord is forcing a vision upon us. If, on the other hand, we freely create an understanding of the Lord, then one can argue that this understanding is a subjective opinion and not objective truth. However, if the soul can only desire (and not create the opinion) and the Lord appears to fulfill that desire, then both arguments can be simultaneously refuted: The Lord is objectively present and not a subjective creation, and yet, He has appeared in a form that was previously desired by the jīvā. So, there is free will, and yet there is objectivity. The object appears based on the desire, to fulfill the desire.

The 'impossibility' refers to the inability in the jīvā to fulfill its desires. This is true in the material world, and it is true in the realm of liberated souls as well. In both cases, the Lord fulfills the jīvā's desires. In the material realm, this fulfillment is subject to a condition—namely, that the jīvā deserves fulfillment based on its karma. However, in the realm of the liberated soul, this requirement of deserving is removed; there is only desire and its fulfillment.

QUESTION

You have previously said that the jīvā is subsequent to the Lord. You have also now said that the Lord appears in many forms (objectively) to fulfill the jīvā's desires. Therefore, it would follow that these different forms of the Lord are also subsequent to the Original Form? In short, the various forms of the Lord would not be eternal, but they would appear based on the changing desires of the soul. So, if a soul develops a new desire, then the Lord will also manifest in a new form to fulfill that desire, which did not exist earlier.

1.3.19 (82)

उत्तराच्चेत् आविर्भूतस्वरूपस्तु

uttarāccet āvirbhūtasvarūpastu

uttarāt—from the subsequence; cet—although; āvirbhūta—manifest; svarūpaḥ—the form; astu—present.

TRANSLATION

Although manifest subsequently, these forms are eternally present.

COMMENTARY

In the previous sūtra, it was said that the Lord fulfills the soul's desires. Therefore, one can argue that the Lord's forms that fulfill these desires are created after the soul's desires, and these forms could not be preexisting. This sūtra rejects this contention. Yes, the Lord appears in a different form to fulfill the jīvā's desire, but these forms are preexisting. To understand this better, let's consider the example of a hallucination when we see a rope as a snake. The association of the snake with the rope is a hallucination. However, that doesn't mean that the idea of a snake is a creation of the person hallucinating. Factually, the idea preexisted our perception, and therefore, the experience of the snake is real. However, the reference of experience—namely, that *this* thing is a snake—is false. Therefore, even when the soul is hallucinating, the experience is real, and only the reference of that experience is false. Now, we can extend this argument to diversified notions about God. All these notions are preexisting, and the soul is not the creator of these notions. Its free will is simply in choosing a notion. When God fulfills the soul's desire, the Lord's form is not created.

It has already been said that the Lord is objectively present (and not merely a subjective hallucination). However, it may now be argued that this objective presence is temporary, and the Lord merely appears in a certain form to fulfill the jīvā's desire, and if that desire disappears then the Lord's form also disappears. Such a situation would amount to the Lord taking on a temporary role to fulfill the jīvā's desire, which would be akin to serving the jīvā for his happiness. Buddhists have a notion called Pratītyasamutpāda which means an apparent codependent arising. It states that the subject and the object are co-created, so if the observer disappears then the observed also disappears. If this idea were applied to the Lord, then it would follow that the Lord takes on a form only when the jīvā desires, and then gives up that form when the jīvā doesn't desire. This sūtra refutes this idea and states that all the forms are always manifest.

However, it was previously said that the jīvā is subsequent to the Lord, and the other forms of the Lord—beyond the Original One—are also subsequent. So, one can wrongly interpret this idea to say that the different perceptions are created just-in-time for the soul's experience. The correct way to understand these forms is that they present opportunities for the jīvā to serve the Lord. The opportunities are eternal, but the desire may not be eternal. In short, the Lord has manifested in all the ways in which the jīvā can ever desire. There is no possibility of pleasure that cannot be fulfilled. So, we shouldn't think that there is some desire that was previously not considered by the Lord as a possibility, and when this desire arises the Lord comes to the jīvā to supply it. Rather, we must understand that all the desires have previously been anticipated and the method of fulfilling them is already existing. The jīvā doesn't create a form of the Lord; however, the jīvā can approach a certain form of the Lord.

QUESTION

If all the forms of the Lord are already manifest, and the jīvā has the desire for a different form, how does the jīvā attain the vision of that form?

1.3.20 (83)

अन्यार्थश्च परामर्शः

anyārthaśca parāmarśaḥ

anyārthaḥ—for a different purpose; ca—and; parāmarśaḥ—pulling, drawing, seizing.

TRANSLATION

And (the soul) can pull, draw, or seize (a form) for a different purpose.

COMMENTARY

The different forms of the Lord are eternally situated in their own planets in the space beyond the material world. These planets and their ruling forms are never created or destroyed. But the jīvā can enter one of these planets if it so desires. It has already been stated that the jīvā enters the Lord's abode based on loving devotion. So, if the nature of the jīvā's devotion changes, it can enter a different planet, and see a different form of the Lord and serve Him differently. This is effectively the jīvā roaming through the spiritual world.

The main purport of this sūtra is that free will doesn't end when the jīvā enters the spiritual realm. This free will is the basis on which the jīvā is differentiated from the Lord. But the implication of such differentiation is also that the 'distance' between the Lord and the jīvā is not fixed. The jīvā can come closer or move farther; it can also go back to the material world after being liberated, although the chance of such a thing happening is extremely remote (due to which it is said that once liberated the jīvā 'never' falls). However, more importantly, the implication of free will is that the jīvā can change its liking or how it wants to enjoy. The Lord is simultaneously enjoying in all the possible ways, and the jīvā can enjoy with the Lord in different forms one after another. Another implication is that there can be natural curiosity in the jīvā to know the different forms of the Lord and he may want to see the different pastimes of the Lord. To entertain such possibilities, the jīvā must roam in the spiritual world. If the jīvā has decided that he prefers a certain form of the Lord and would like to serve Him exclusively, then his position would be fixed. If such a decision hasn't been made, it can be made after reaching the spiritual world. Finally, it also means that spiritual development doesn't end with the exit from the material world. The jīvā can constantly develop spiritually—i.e., change the extent of its devotion toward the Lord. In all these ways, the spiritual world is just like the material world—i.e., one can see different visions and act differently.

QUESTION

But what happens if the jīvā is not able to decide which form he prefers? You have described that there are as many forms as there are possible

desires, and all these forms are eternally existent. So, should we not study all the forms before we decide which of the forms we prefer? But if the forms are infinite, then how can we ever make an informed choice about a specific form?

Some people have a problem with choice. After all, there are infinite options to choose from. How can we decide which alternative to choose unless we understand all the options? If we are hasty and we choose without understanding all the alternatives, then won't there be doubts in our heart that we may not have made a perfect choice? With such doubts, how can we devote ourselves to the Lord? On the other hand, the alternatives are so huge that we cannot hope to know everything—in this case all the forms of the Lord. So, given this limitation, how can we choose a specific form of the Lord over the others?

1.3.21 (84)
अल्पश्रुतेरिति चेत् तदुक्तम्
alpaśruteriti cet taduktam

alpa—smallness; śruteḥ—because it is heard, or because the śrutī states; iti cet—if it be said; tat—that; uktam—has been explained (in the last sūtra).

TRANSLATION

If it is said that on account of the scriptural declaration of the smallness (of the jīvā) (we cannot decide) (we say that) has already been explained.

COMMENTARY

If someone considers choice a burden, and fears that he might choose the wrong alternative, then the answer to that has been given in the last sūtra where it was stated that the jīvā can choose a different alternative. The problem can seem real to some people because in the impersonal philosophy the choice is simple—remain entangled in the material world or attain liberation from the material world. When the choice is presented in this binary way, it seems that liberation would be preferred. However, if liberation leads to entry into three-quarters of existence, as opposed to one-quarter of the entire material existence (which comprises innumerable universes), then the problem of choice becomes worse with liberation. If we could not fathom the entirety of the material creation (or even the entirety of a single universe), then how can we fathom the realm of the liberated living entities which is three times bigger? And if we cannot fathom the entirety of the spiritual creation, then how do we choose?

In Western philosophy, this is called the problem of Buridan's Ass. The story goes that there was an ass who had hay and water before it but could not decide whether to chew the hay or drink the water first. Unable to decide, the ass remained both hungry and thirsty. If we were like Buridan's Ass, then if we go to a grocery store looking for cereal, and we find hundreds of brands of cereal (which we cannot perfectly compare), we don't try to compare them. We pick the first one that satisfies our needs, although there may be other brands that could satisfy us more. Unless we are dissatisfied with a cereal brand, we keep picking the same brand every time—because it has worked before.

In the same way, there may be infinite possibilities, but we don't analyze everything before we make a choice. We rather pick the one that satisfies us, and we settle with that choice. Unless there is dissatisfaction with the choice, there will never be a change. So, this problem of infinite choice, resulting in decision paralysis, is not a real problem. Every living entity has a natural desire toward some form of the Lord. This preference is not based on an analysis of every other form—maybe that one is better than this one. It is an intuitive desire by which the jīvā chooses a form of the Lord and serves Him eternally because there is no dissatisfaction. If, however, one is still insistent that he may want to change his mind later on, and if the possibility was eliminated after the first choice then the person would feel 'stuck' forever, the answer has already been given—you can change the choice; this is not a type of bondage or captivity.

Topic 6

QUESTION

I am still not convinced. If you say that there is an intuitive desire for a specific form of the Lord, then I don't have any intuition. I'm in the material world, and I have little understanding of what transcendence is. If I cannot choose a form of the Lord, then what will I meditate upon? And without such a choice, how will I develop devotion by which I can enter the Lord's abode?

1.3.22 (85)

अनुकृतेस्तस्य च

anukṛtestasya ca

anukṛteḥ—due to acting according to instruction; tasya—them; ca—also.

TRANSLATION

(You can) also (develop devotion to a form of the Lord) by following their (the pure devotees of the Lord) instructions.

COMMENTARY

We have discussed in the earlier sūtra that devotion to the Lord is not attained by theoretical knowledge, reading of scriptures, or even bodily and mental exercises, although if these things are performed with devotion they lead to advancement. But this begs the question: How will I develop devotion if not for these processes? We briefly discussed the method for this earlier—the association with the devotees who can impart this devotion. However, this sūtra states something different—it is by following the instructions of such devotees.

One might wonder how following the instructions of a devotee leads to devotion. The answer is that devotion is an emotional state, and it is acquired from a devotee when we become emotionally attached to the devotee. For example, if we associate with an angry person, we also become anxious. If we are with a happy person, the association gradually makes us happy. Similarly, if we associate with a devotee, we can also acquire their mood. These moods are infectious, but they are not transferred cognitively as the words are. The transfer of moods happens only when we are emotionally attached to a person. Thus, for example, a doctor in a hospital sees so many people suffering but he or she may not become sad by their suffering, because they are not emotionally attached to them. On the other hand, we are easily affected by the sadness or happiness of those whom we love. In the same way, a deep emotional attachment to the spiritual master makes a person qualified to receive a devotional attitude. Now, one may ask: How do you get emotionally attached to the devotee? The answer to that question is stated in this sūtra—namely, *anukriti*, or doing and acting as instructed. Thus, by following the instructions of the advanced devotee, one develops an attachment to them. Through that attachment, we acquire a devotional attitude. And with that devotional attitude, we can see the Lord.

The 'acceptance' of a guru is called 'initiation'. Many people confuse this process with a ritual. However, in the Chaitanya Charitāmṛta, this process is called the acquisition of a bhakti-lata-bīja or the 'seed' of the devotional creeper, which is obtained by the grace of the guru or the spiritual master. The 'initiation' is not a ritual; far from it, it is the development of an emotional attachment by which one begins following the instructions. So, the 'acceptance' of a guru is implicit in obeying the instructions of the spiritual master. However, one must be careful in distinguishing between ordinary people—who can speak the knowledge but have no devotion—and a genuine guru who has devotion. The qualification for devotion is not academic learning, the ability to chant mantras, the number of followers, or his standing in the material world. There is simply one qualification—he does everything with a devotional mood. If one obeys the instructions of an ordinary person, they may get attached to such a 'guru', but they cannot impart the devotional mood, because they don't have it themselves. So, the qualification of being a guru is the possession of pure devotion. The term *tasya* refers to such devotees; not the ordinary charlatan so-called 'guru'.

QUESTION

But how will I identify a genuine devotee? What are the symptoms of such devotees? How can we distinguish a devotee from other non-devotees?

1.3.23 (86)

अपि च स्मर्यते

api ca smaryate

api ca—moreover; smaryate—in the smriti.

TRANSLATION

Moreover, (the symptoms of pure devotees) are described in smriti.

COMMENTARY

The sūtra doesn't go into details about the qualifications of the guru but merely states that one must consult the smriti. Herein, we can understand the importance of smriti in addition to the śrutī—the śrutī gives information about the Absolute Truth, but the processes of attaining this (such as the surrender to a guru, the qualifications of guru, etc.) are described in the smriti. Therefore, the śrutī provides knowledge of the Absolute Truth, and the smriti describes the practical processes and methods for the realization of this knowledge.

Topic 7

QUESTION

But despite the description of the qualifications in the smriti, there are still many difficulties in identifying a guru. The reason for such difficulties is that we can only observe a person's actions but not understand the extent of their spiritual realization. We may see that a person is austere, pious, renounced, etc. But how can we know that such a person is also a devotee of the Lord?

1.3.24 (87)

शब्दादेव प्रमितिः

śabdādeva pramitaḥ

śabdāt—from the word; eva—certainly; pramitaḥ—measured.

TRANSLATION

(We can) measure (the guru) certainly based on the words.

COMMENTARY

We have earlier discussed three kinds of meanings used for understanding: objective, intersubjective, and subjective. The objective meaning is evident from the words and the grammar. The intersubjective meaning depends on the context between the speaker and the listener, the sequence of questions and answers, etc. And the subjective meaning comes to us from the mood, style, or the way it is spoken. When the spoken words are converted into written text, the words remain intact, and the context may also be preserved (unless something is taken out of context). However, the mood, style, and the way it is spoken are lost. Therefore, the written text is never as accurate as the spoken word.

Owing to this fact, most people prefer to see a person talking live, rather than reading a book. The power in a speech contains not just the words, but also the emotions behind it. The intonation or emphasis on different sounds can often change the meaning. We can go back to any number of powerful speeches and try to read them in their edited form; you can see that these two are just not the same. Therefore, considerable emphasis has been laid in the Vedic system on 'hearing' from the right person. It is not merely the objective meaning arising out of words and grammar; it is also not merely the context in which these things are spoken; it is also the way of speaking that delivers meaning.

Many people can memorize the sūtra and statements from the scriptures; they may also present them scholarly. But unless the speaker is convinced through realization, and by putting that teaching into practice in their own life, they cannot change anyone's life. The conviction is not apart from the words, but it is present only in the words of a person who has realized that knowledge. Of course, a person who only knows the truth theoretically is better than one who doesn't know the truth or is convinced of falsities. Thus, speaking convincingly is not a substitute for speaking the truth. Scriptures do not begin with the qualification of a guru. They begin with the nature of the Absolute Truth. Once that question is settled, and what is to be said is decided, the next question is about who is convinced of this truth vs. who just knows it theoretically. The questions of Absolute Truth have been settled previously, and this sūtra is only speaking about the qualification of the person who has realized this truth.

QUESTION

But what if a person is unable to find a suitable spiritual master or guru who can guide him toward spiritual progress? Should the person just keep waiting for the guru to come around? Or should one do something else?

This question is prominent today due to a shortage of spiritually advanced people. Many who claim to be gurus have been corrupted by greed, power, lust, and fame. They are often involved in illicit sexual activities, drug abuse, the accumulation of wealth, improper use of power, lying, cheating, and other more heinous crimes such as murder. So, someone who seemed spiritually advanced may later be revealed to be a cheater. As many cheaters are exposed, people lose faith in the spiritual path. Even those who continue the process, suffer from the trauma of having been cheated and find it harder to believe that the process might work for them. Can we get out of this destructive stage?

1.3.25 (88)

हृदयपेक्षया तु मनुष्याधिकारत्वात्

hṛdyapekṣayā tu manuṣyādhikāratvāt

hṛdi—in the heart; apekṣayā—in comparison to; tu—but; manuṣya—the human being; adhikāratvāt—from having the entitlement.

TRANSLATION

But in comparison to (the problems) one can take shelter of (the Lord) in the heart, (because spirituality) is the entitlement of every human being.

COMMENTARY

In this sūtra, the term *manuṣyādhikāratvāt* is used, which means "due to human rights". The United Nations defines human rights as follows: "Human rights include the right to life and liberty, freedom from slavery and torture, freedom of opinion and expression, the right to work and education, and many more. Everyone is entitled to these rights, without discrimination." This declaration of human rights doesn't mean they are going to be fulfilled. For example, we can say that we have a right to work and education, but so many people are jobless and uneducated. The governments may try to reduce joblessness and improve education, but they cannot guarantee these "rights". A fundamental right is one that can never be denied. The encounter with a suitable guru doesn't count as one of the fundamental rights. In fact, it is said that one meets a suitable guru only due to great fortune, as a result of pious activities. So, if one hasn't performed these pious activities, their encounter with a suitable guru is unlikely. In fact, because of one's impiety, one may meet a cheating guru.

What is one supposed to do if they haven't been pious, or have met cheating gurus, or cannot find a suitable guru despite their efforts (subject to the judgment by the words as was prescribed in the previous sūtra)? This sūtra recommends that one must take shelter of the Lord and seek His guidance. Specifically, the guidance is to be sought from the Lord situated in the heart. The ability to take shelter of the Lord in the heart is every human's birthright, because it can never be denied, regardless of one's personal situation, the ability to find the right guru, etc. So, life and liberty, education and work, freedom of opinion and expression, freedom from slavery and torture, are not "rights" guaranteed by nature and the Lord. These are merely human concoctions, which we believe will help us form a just and equitable society. And yet, nobody can guarantee these rights because a person's life is controlled by their past karma. Under such a situation, one must focus on "duties" rather than "rights". If there is confusion about what my duty is, then we have a "right" to consult the Lord in the heart. This is the only fundamental and inalienable right that we can claim.

In this regard, we can also note that this sūtra talks about "human rights", which means taking shelter of the Lord as a guru in the heart is unique to humans. The animals don't seek a guru. So, there is no question of how to identify the right guru, and what to do when the right guru is not found. The animals might consult the Lord in the heart to save their life and limb. But that is not the purpose of the guru. In the same way, those humans who take shelter of the Lord to save their life and limb are not considered 'humans' here. This is a specific comment about what to do if one is unable to find a suitable guru. This means previous efforts to find and learn from a guru have been made.

The encounter with a suitable guru is a matter of *bhāgya* or good fortune produced by good actions in the past. Therefore, not everyone is entitled to a guru, at least not a good one. Many are also entitled to cheating gurus. However, the soul's surrender to the Lord in the heart is not subject to good fortune. The surrender to the Lord in the heart for spiritual guidance is an inalienable right in the human body. We should use this "right" to consult the Lord.

Topic 8

QUESTION

Does this mean that only humans can make spiritual progress, and this progress is impossible in any other form of life? I'm asking this because it seems possible that one's spiritual journey may remain incomplete in one life. How can a person keep progressing in spiritual endeavors in other bodies?

1.3.26 (89)

तदुपर्यपि बादरायणःसंभवात्

taduparyapi bādarāyaṇaḥ saṃbhavāt

tadupari—above them, i.e., living beings higher than humans; api—also; bādarāyaṇaḥ—Bādarāyana opines; saṃbhavāt—because (it is) possible.

TRANSLATION

Also (beings) above them (the humans) (are entitled for surrender to the Lord) on account of the possibility (of it) according to Bādarāyana.

COMMENTARY

In Vedic cosmology, human beings are described to exist on the bhū-loka; notably, there are many kinds of humans—some more advanced than the others. However, all of them have been stated as having the "right" to surrender. Above the bhū-loka, are six other planetary systems, namely, bhuvar, svarga, jana, tapa, and satya. The living entities in svarga are called ādidaivika and they have been earlier described as being expansions of the Paramātma. The Lord entrusts them with important responsibilities to manage the universe given that they are obedient to the Lord. In the realms beyond svarga are ascetics and sages, who are naturally inclined toward the worship of the Lord. In fact, in Vedic cosmology, the bhū, bhuvar, and svarga-loka are periodically destroyed, but the upper four planetary systems—and the living entities in them—remain. In this sūtra, all these living entities above the humans are said to be qualified to surrender to the Lord. In short, if one has progressed from a lower planetary system to a higher one, due to the dint of their pious activities, but hasn't yet completed the process of spiritual advancement, they can continue it from their new positions. Notably, this hasn't been stated about the lower planetary systems; therefore, implicitly, spiritual progress has been denied to them.

This sūtra quotes the possibility of even the higher living entities advancing in the spiritual life to Bādarāyana, who is the author of Vedānta Sūtra. One might wonder: Why is Bādarāyana referring to himself in the third person by saying that "this is the opinion of Bādarāyana"? The other statements by him are not being referenced in this way. So, why this one? One answer is that Bādarāyana appears at the end of every Dvapara-yuga and divides the Vedas into four parts. In a day of Brahma, there are 1000 chatur-yugī, so Bādarāyana appears 1000 times in a day of Brahma. The person appearing as Bādarāyana is different each time, but he is always performing the same duty of dividing the Vedas and is hence referred to as Veda Vyas or Bādarāyana. It is possible that the name 'Bādarāyana' used here refers to a person from a previous age.

QUESTION

But isn't it said that the demigods are engaged in material enjoyments of heaven? And these enjoyments are contrary to spiritual advancement?

1.3.27 (90)

वरिोधःकर्मणीतिचेत् न अनेकप्रतपित्तेर्दर्शनात् ॥ २७ ॥

virodhaḥ karmaṇīti cet na anekapratipatterdarśanāt || 27 ||

virodhaḥ—contradiction; karmaṇi—to actions; iti cet—if it is said; na—not; aneka—many; pratipatteḥ—statements; darśanāt—from the philosophies.

TRANSLATION

If it is said that the actions (of the demigods) are contrary (to the surrender to the Lord), (we say) no because we find many statements from philosophies (which permit a process of gradual progression from lower to higher).

COMMENTARY

In the Bhagavad-Gita 7.16, Lord Kṛṣṇa states the following:

catur-vidhā bhajante māṁ
janāḥ su-kṛtino 'rjuna
ārto jijñāsur arthārthī
jñānī ca bharatarṣabha

O best among the Bhāratas, four kinds of pious men render devotional service unto Me – the distressed, the desirous of wealth, the inquisitive, and those searching for knowledge of the Absolute.

Generally, most people come to religion due to suffering—mental or physical. The poor and destitute are suffering physically and they worship the Lord for relief. Many rich and powerful also turn to religion due to suffering—although the suffering may be mental. However, those who are situated in a position that is relatively free of bodily and mental suffering are generally not inclined toward devotion to the Lord. Therefore, in general, it is understood that the practice of devotion is harder in other planetary systems because there are many incentives for enjoyment. The demigods are especially in a situation of great power, and their enjoyment generally prevents them from surrender to the Lord; they are not disobedient to the Lord, but they are busy enjoying their position of power and the luxuries of the heavens. Therefore, if someone argues that their position is not suitable for spiritual advancement it is correct.

However, we must note that the previous sūtra used the term *saṃbhavāt* indicating the possibility of seeking the Lord as one's guru or spiritual master. The sūtra did not say that the higher beings are necessarily devoted to the Lord in this way. Indeed, it is often stated that the guru of the demigods is Brihaspati. He is also identified with the planet Jupiter, and its positive influence indicates the inclination toward knowledge. However, this may or may not be spiritual knowledge of the kind being discussed here—namely transcendence from the material world. Thus, just like humans have a possibility of surrendering to the Lord in the heart, and seeking His guidance as a guru, similarly, the possibility also exists for the demigods. The demigods are after all very pious, and favorable to Lord Viṣṇu, so they can accept surrender to the Paramātma. On the other hand, the animals are too ignorant, and the demons in the lower planetary systems are explicitly averse to Lord Viṣṇu, which makes this surrender impossible. Therefore, we must distinguish between the suitability of the heavens for spiritual progress and the possibility of such progress. The heavens are not suitable, but it is still possible for a person to advance spiritually as opposed to animals or the demons for whom even such a possibility doesn't exist.

Similarly, this sūtra also indicates the existence of many philosophical positions about spiritual progress. One can, for instance, perform karma-yoga in which the actions of mundane duties are performed, but the results of this action are offered to the Lord. Similarly, one can pursue jñāna-yoga with the understanding that there are many stages of knowledge and the top-most stage is the understanding of the Lord. The aśtānga-yoga system can be practiced with the aim that once the preliminary stages of āsana and prāṇayāma have been crossed, one will turn one's consciousness toward the Paramātma in the heart. These are described as jñāna-karma-miśra bhakti or devotion "mixed" with the processes of jñāna and karma. The possibility of such mixing entails that these processes are not mutually exclusive. Notably, the sūtra is not recommending such an approach, but just pointing to the possibility of its existence.

So, the allurements for enjoyments make the devotion to the Lord difficult; nevertheless, the possibility of such devotion always exists. This sūtra should be understood in the context of the previous sūtras where it was said that one generally approaches a guru but if one is unable to find a guru then the Lord in the heart can be a guru. This is a possibility for humans and demigods.

QUESTION

But you have previously stated that for enlightenment one must listen to the words of the advanced devotees. You have also stated at the beginning that the scripture must be considered the source of Absolute Truth, implying that other methods—such as jñāna or speculation and karma or activities followed by their results—are unsuitable as the source of the Absolute Truth. However, now you are saying that all processes can be mixed as they are described in the scriptures, and therefore they should all be considered valid. How do we reconcile the contradiction between the previous and the present statements?

1.3.28 (91)

शब्द इतिचेत् न अतःप्रभवात् प्रत्यक्षानुमानाभ्याम्

śabda iti cet na ataḥ prabhavāt pratyakṣānumānābhyām

śabde—in regard to the words (Vedic texts); iti cet—if it be said; na—no; ataḥ—from these (words); prabhavāt—because of the creation; pratyakṣa-anumānābhyām—the methods of direct perception and reasoning.

TRANSLATION

If it is said that (only the) words (of devotees and scriptures are valid), (then we say) no because from these words have emerged the methods of direct perception and inference (or empirical and rational knowledge).

COMMENTARY

In the previous sūtra, the term *darśanāt* was employed, indicating many philosophical positions. However, etymologically, the term indicates "seeing". When taken together with śabda or scripture, used in this sūtra, we can understand this as "seeing through the lens of the scripture". Specifically, this sūtra states that the processes of jñāna and karma are not contrary to the process of bhakti, and we should not consider them as being mutually exclusive. Rather, these processes can be combined or mixed (as was stated in the previous sūtra). This sūtra also asserts that the methods of direct perception and inference (which constitute the basis of karma and jñāna) should be understood as having emerged or manifested or being created from the śabda or scriptures. This is a very profound statement, and to understand it we need to digress a little.

Perception involves the acts of distinguishing and ordering. By distinguishing I mean there is more than one thing, and by ordering, we mean that something is more important or preferred over the other. For example, if you see a cow grazing in a field, you must be able to distinguish the cow from the field; without such distinction, there is no ability to identify that there is an individual cow separate from the field. To make such distinctions, one must possess the concepts of 'cow' and 'field' a priori. If we don't have these concepts, then our visual field will only have colors. To aggregate these colors into objects, we must have the concepts of cow and field. In fact, we must also have the concept of color, white, green, shape, etc. Otherwise, we will not be able to say that there are some properties (color and shape) with values (white and round), which belong to a 'cow' or a 'field'. The perception of a cow in a field arises when one already has a certain number of concepts. If you have never seen a computer before, and you are asked to search for a computer, you will not be able to identify such a thing even if it was right in front of you because you don't have the concept of a 'computer'. Therefore, to perceive things, we need concepts.

If a distinction between a cow and a field has been made, there must also be an ordering of these objects—e.g., that the cow is foreground and the field is background (or vice versa, based on what you are focusing on). This ordering is a function of our choices: we can focus upon either the cow or the field.

Similarly, reasoning also needs preexisting concepts. We call these assumptions or axioms which we take for granted as being true. Using these concepts, we can construct more sophisticated concepts through combination. In fact, logic in some forms is understood trivially as the ability to mutate the simplest of concepts to arrive at more complex concepts; therefore, from the premise of accepted axioms, we can use logic to prove more complex theorems.

Therefore, to use reasoning and observation, one must have some basic ideas. From these ideas, we can acquire more ideas. The child, therefore, cannot be born a 'blank slate', as John Locke claimed (suggesting that the world is objective properties). As George Berkeley argued, the so-called 'primary' physical properties are mere objectifications of subjective experience. Therefore, according to Berkeley, there is no objective reality apart from subjective experience. Then, David Hume took this a step further to say that doing science necessitated laws, and in forming a law we had to invoke a necessity—namely, that the effect necessarily followed the cause—and this necessity could never be established because we had no way of knowing what's happening in reality. Immanuel Kant, in his *Critique of Pure Reason*, claims that he was "woken from his slumber" by Hume's critique of science, and went on to argue that we don't acquire ideas from the external world in order to create science, laws, an objective reality, etc. Rather, all these ideas are innately present within us.

This notion of preexisting ideas is explained in Sāñkhya philosophy as the superiority of the mind and intellect over the senses and the objects, not just because the mind controls the senses and their objects but also because the senses and their objects 'emerge' from the mind. The mind itself emerges from the intellect, which comes from the ego, which follows from the mahattattva. The 25 elements of Sāñkhya are then equated to the 25 consonants of Sanskrit in many Tantra texts. The 16 vowels and 8 semi-vowels are similarly compared to deeper forms of material energy (which are different from the Sāñkhya elements). These 49 letters, along with three other conjunct consonants (क्ष्, त्र्, ज्ञ्) which are separated representations of the three modes of nature and are to be combined as Prakriti, constitute the 50 alphabets of Sanskrit. The separation of material energy into these forms is attributed to a sound representation of eternal reality—called Śabda Brahman. The Śabda Brahman symbolizes the primordial concepts that we can know, use, enjoy, and relate to, and the world takes a form pursuant to the native capacities of the soul to relate, know, act, and enjoy. Thus, matter is modeled after the nature of the soul or consciousness.

Hence, we can understand the claim that "from these words have emerged the methods of direct perception and inference" in two ways. First, based on the analysis of ordinary experience—which has been carried out in Western philosophy—we can note that some primordial ideas must exist before we can even perceive. Second, based on the descriptions in Sāñkhya and Tantra, we can elucidate this hierarchy from the most primordial ideas to the manifest world that we can relate to, perceive, use, and enjoy. These primordial ideas are the śabda or the eternal truths about the nature of the soul and God; they represent a detailing of what we mean by soul and God in terms of the myriad abilities to perceive, conceive, judge, act, connect and enjoy. The term śabda also denotes the 'scripture' as the explanation of a transcendental reality. These two uses of the term śabda—namely, the primordial symbolic representation of Brahman and the scripture which explains the nature of this Brahman—are closely related in the sense that both explain the nature of the soul and God. The Śabda Brahman is the more fundamental reality and the scriptures are verbose and detailed descriptions of the same reality. This sūtra emphasizes the first meaning—namely, that even our direct perception and imagination or inference have ultimately emerged from the primordial reality. Therefore, if we keep the understanding of the scriptures in view, then this manifest world of thoughts and perceptions can be seen through the lens of the scripture.

We must emphasize here that direct perception and inference are not taken as independent methods of attaining knowledge. Rather, the claim is subtler—*if* you take the śabda for granted, then you can use it to confirm the understanding by observation and reasoning. In short, reasoning and observation are used to validate and confirm the śabda, rather than to discover the nature of reality. There is a subtle but important difference between 'discovery' and 'verification'. Faith in the śabda is needed for discovery, but reason and observation can be used for verification. So, there is no fundamental contradiction between reason, observation, and scriptures, provided scriptures have been accepted. If one has understood the scriptural knowledge, then its application to day-to-day life (through reason and observation) will only confirm the scriptural truth. Hence, even those who engage in other methods—such as karma and jñāna—are still to be considered progressing in their spiritual understanding, although this understanding comes through confirmation by reason and observation.

Implicit faith in the Lord as the source of knowledge is essential, otherwise, one would never put their faith in the scriptures. The faith in scripture is itself the faith in the Lord: only if you trust a teacher, would you trust their books. If trust is placed in the books, implicit trust is placed in the teacher as well. In fact, many times to understand the books, a spiritual aspirant can approach a guru. If such a guru is unavailable, one can approach the Lord in the heart. So, by this sūtra we can see why faith and devotion in the Lord are not contrary to the practices of jñāna and karma—provided faith is reposed in the Lord.

QUESTION

However, by allowing the possibility of jñāna and karma along with devotion to the Lord, aren't we compromising the exclusivity of devotion itself? By saying that bhakti can be mixed with other processes—as these have been described in the scriptures—aren't we saying that purity of devotion (and the rejection of the other processes such as jñāna and karma) is unnecessary?

Many devotees argue that if we are relying on reason and observation, then in some sense we are trying to confirm the knowledge of the scripture by our senses and the mind, and therefore our faith in the Lord is not perfect because we are unable to accept the truth of the scripture as they are. Our need to confirm the truth by other methods—experience and reason—indicates our lack of faith. So, this mixing of jñāna and karma with bhakti can be construed as lacking faith in the scripture or the words of the Lord. In short, if we were perfect devotees, free of jñāna and karma, then we must blindly accept the scripture.

1.3.29 (92)
अत एव च नित्यत्वम्
ata eva ca nityatvam

ata-eva—from this very reason; ca—also; nityatvam—the persistence.

TRANSLATION

From this ability (to mix karma and jñāna with bhakti) also follows the persistence (of the devotion in the scripture and toward the Lord).

COMMENTARY

In the previous sūtra, we discussed that when faith in the scripture and devotion in the Lord has been reposed (by acceptance of scriptures and the Lord as the teacher in the heart), then there is no contradiction between reason, observation, and scripture. However, one may argue that this continuous process of asking questions, and the need to understand things based on reasoning indicates a lack of faith. This sūtra refutes this argument and states that our continuous inquiries from the scriptures, guru, and the Lord in the heart, are an indication that our faith in these methods of getting knowledge is intact.

The term *nityatvam* can be understood in many ways; it can indicate eternity; it can also indicate continuity or persistence. The latter meaning clarifies this sūtra much better than the former, given the context of previous sūtras. The claim is that even if we ask repeated questions, expressing our doubts, and seeking clarification, we should not be considered a non-devotee. Similarly, if we learn something from the scripture, the guru, or the Lord, and we put it to test by applying it in day-to-day life, it is not the rejection of faith. Implicitly, a distinction is drawn between 'faith' and 'blind faith'. Blind faith is the uncritical acceptance of whatever is said or taught. Under it, we listen to something, but we don't ask further questions, and we don't try to test its truth. On the other hand, faith means that we try to examine the teaching using observation and reason, and every time a doubt arises, we will go back to scripture, the guru, and the Lord to overcome the doubt. So, one who is testing the teaching should not be considered unfaithful, and his devotion should not be doubted. In short, we reject the blind acceptance of the teaching and encourage rational and empirical verification; these are not symptoms of lacking faith in the Lord.

In this regard, we must note that Vaiṣṇava Ācāryas have indeed rejected bhakti mixed with jñāna and karma. Śri Rupa Goswami writes in the Bhakti-rasāmṛta-sindhu, that bhakti free from jñāna and karma is the highest.

anyabhilasita-sunyam jñāna-karmadyanavrtam
anukulyena krsnanusilanam bhaktir-uttama

That which is free from other desires, that which is not covered by jñāna and karma, and that which is the favorable following of Lord Kṛṣṇa is called supreme (or superior) bhakti.

However, such bhakti is attained after the destruction of all doubts when perfect knowledge has been realized through direct experience, and there is no more need for testing the teachings of the scripture or the inspiration of the Lord. We should not confuse the rejection of testing after realization with the progressive stage of bhakti where the soul is still developing an understanding. Yes, in the ultimate state, when all doubts are destroyed, the tests of knowledge end. However, while doubts exist, and tests are being performed, they should not be considered unfaithfulness in the guru, the Lord, or the scripture.

QUESTION

But you have earlier said that the transcendent realm is the three quarters beyond the world of birth and death, and the material world is the place of repeated birth and death. On this basis, a distinction between the material and the transcendent realms was drawn. But now you are saying that the transcendent truth can also be confirmed or verified in the world of birth and death?

1.3.30 (93)

समाननामरूपत्वाच्चावृत्तावप्यविरोधो दर्शनात् स्मृतेश्च

samānanāmarūpatvāccāvṛttāvapyavirodho darśanāt smṛteśca

samāna-nāmarūpatvāt—because of the similar names and forms; ca—and; āvṛttau—in the revolving of the world cycles; api—even; avirodhaḥ—no contradiction; darśanāt—from the śrutī; smṛteḥ—the smriti; ca—and.

TRANSLATION

And on account of the sameness of names and forms in every fresh cycle, there is no contradiction (to the confirmation of eternal knowledge) even in the revolving of the world cycles, as is seen from the śrutī and the smriti.

COMMENTARY

Here, the terms *nāma* and *rūpa* are used; they respectively mean names and forms. Rūpa indicates the bodily forms or species of life, such as cow, horse, lion, dog, cat, etc. These species are not always manifest. Of late, due to environmental degradation, millions of species are becoming extinct. However, this sūtra states that they will appear again with the cycles of time. In short, the idea of the species is eternal, but its manifestation as an individual of that species is temporary. In the same way, nāma indicates the name by which we identify someone. These names can pertain to an individual or to the role of a person. For instance, we call the same person 'John' or the 'President'. Notably, John may not be President in every cycle of time, but the President will still appear. In this regard, we can note that the names of demigods such as Indra, Surya, Chandra, Yama, etc. are quite like we call someone "Mr. President". The person who occupies this role can, however, change. Since these roles are recreated, therefore, they are conceptually eternal; nobody occupies the position of Indra permanently. However, the meaning of the term Indra—i.e., the duties that this role is expected to perform—remains intact. So, because these names and forms reappear, again and again, we must consider them conceptually eternal.

We have previously spoken about three components of our experience—subjective, objective, and intersubjective. The rūpa or bodies are objective. The nāma or roles are intersubjective. However, the person occupying the body and the role is subjective. The person who takes a body and roles doesn't repeat the same body and role in the different cycles; if this were the case, then the soul could never be liberated from the cycle of birth and death. So, there is a temporary aspect to the world—namely, that the soul changes its body and role. And there is a permanent aspect to the world—namely, the bodies and the roles reappear. This reappearance entails that the body and the role are conceptual.

The implication of this eternity is that the species we find in the material world (cats, dogs, fishes, birds, etc.) exist in the spiritual world as well. Similarly, the roles of this world such as Indra, Chandra, Surya, etc. exist even in the spiritual world (they may be called by different names). Due to the absence of the time cycles, however, these are never created and destroyed. Their conceptual eternity is therefore also their existential eternity. Similarly, because there is no birth and death, once a person has occupied a role and a body, they never have to change that role and body. So, the eternity of the role and the body is indirectly implied by the lack of birth and death. In short, the diversity in this world is conceptually eternal and is also manifest in the eternal realm. This diversity appears and disappears in this world, but due to the repeating cycle of appearance and disappearance, the roles and the species are conceptually eternal. This eternity is similar but not identical to that in the spiritual realm.

The contention of this sūtra is that this conceptual eternity is itself the eternal transcendental knowledge. So, just because the soul is changing bodies doesn't entail that everything in the material world is temporary. This world is also reflecting the eternity through the reappearance of names and forms in every cycle of time. Therefore, it should not be supposed that the eternal truth cannot be understood from the temporary world. If we limit our focus to certain periods of time and specific places, then the cycles of time indicate change. But if we broaden the understanding through scriptures, then the same roles and species are eternal. So, the focus on the testing of knowledge obtained through scriptures or the Lord in this world is legitimate and such tests should not be considered contrary to scriptures because we are obtaining the concepts to understand from these scriptures and checking if these concepts are true.

QUESTION

But if the demigods have such powerful positions, and a life relatively free of difficulties, then why aren't they advancing in spiritual life? Why is it said that the demigods fall from their position and are born again on earth?

1.3.31 (94)

मध्वादिष्विसम्भवादनधिकारं जैमनिः

madhvādiṣvasambhavādanadhikāraṃ jaiminiḥ

madhvādiṣu—In Madhu Vidya etc.; asambhavāt—on account of the impossibility; anadhikāraṃ—disqualification; jaiminiḥ—Jaimini (is of opinion).

TRANSLATION

On account of being in Madhu Vidya, the demigods are disqualified (from spiritual life) because of the impossibility (of practicing Madhu Vidya and spiritual life simultaneously), such is the opinion of the sage Jaimini.

COMMENTARY

Madhu Vidya refers to the drinking of the intoxicant called Soma. The nature of any intoxicant is that it makes you fearless, daring, and confident. Intoxicants also give rise to a higher level of creativity. At the level of the body, this creativity manifests in elaborate sexual activity. At the level of the mind, the same creativity manifests in fantastic visions resulting from auditory and visual stimulations, and these stimulations then get mixed in various ways. It is said that upon drinking Soma one feels so confident that he considers himself as powerful as ten thousand elephants. In this regard, we can note that the body can be made extremely strong and powerful, provided the person is emotionally strong. Most illnesses arise due to emotional weakness, which damages the immune system and brings other diseases. So, if one becomes emotionally strong and is freed from fear, then their body automatically becomes stronger. Therefore, Soma is also said to be something that nourishes the body and makes it stronger. But the cause of this strength is not that Soma is an exemplary type of nutrient. The real cause is that it destroys the fear within a person.

All of us are gripped by fear within; even the demigods are afraid that they will one day be replaced by someone else. This fear is exacerbated due to circumstances incompatible with our emotional nature. For instance, a naturally peaceful person will avoid conflicting situations, but if he is thrown into conflicting situations, he would become naturally fearful. On the other hand, the person who enjoys conflict will become morose if he is unable to engage in aggression with others; such people will get naturally excited and energized by the possibility of conflict. So, there is a natural fear in the heart, and it gets exacerbated by the situation. People take intoxicants to overcome this fear.

The devotee of the Lord is also often gripped by this fear in the material world, but he takes shelter of the Lord and seeks His protection from within the heart. As soon as the love of the Lord appears in the heart, one feels fearless. The love of the Lord is therefore the most powerful type of intoxicant.

Thus, there are two methods by which to overcome fear—the use of intoxicants which make one feel very powerful, and the devotion to the Lord. If one is accustomed to intoxicants, then the love of the Lord takes a backseat. The disqualification of the demigods is their drinking of Soma, which makes it impossible for them to love the Lord because fear is being mitigated by the intoxicant. So, even though there is a possibility they can surrender to the Lord and seek

His shelter, they generally do not do so. They rather use Soma to feel strong. It is only when they lose battles against the demons, they seek help from Lord Viṣṇu, but once having regained their position they go back to enjoying. This is quite like a person who worships the Lord when in difficulty but forgets the Lord as soon as the difficulty is mitigated and starts enjoying again.

The demigods are being portrayed in a bad light here. One could conclude from this that the demigods are no better than us. After all, they are just enjoying an intoxicant! We must caution against this hasty conclusion, because this view is attributed to Jaimini—who, as we have seen, disregarded the existence of demigods and God. If someone argued against Mīmāṃsā by citing other Vedic scriptures where the demigods are said to be in a superior position, their counterargument would be— "Oh, their superiority is just due to drinking Soma". This is not truly the position of Vedānta Sūtra, which will become clearer in the subsequent sūtras. This is the explanation of why the demigods are not being liberated from the material world despite their superior position, and this somewhat derogatory view of demigods is attributed to Jaimini.

QUESTION

So according to Jaimini, the demigods are no better than human beings. As we are conditioned to forget the Lord, likewise the demigods are prone to neglect the Lord. Hence, they are not exemplars of devotion to the Lord?

1.3.32 (95)
ज्योतिषि भावाच्च
jyotiṣi bhāvācca

jyotiṣi—as mere spheres of light, or as mere astrological entities; bhāvāt—because (they are used) in the sense; ca—also.

TRANSLATION

(Jaimini further states that the demigods are) mere spheres of light or astrological entities; after all, (their names are) also used in this sense.

COMMENTARY

The view of Jaimini is continued in this sūtra. According to him, the demigods simply don't exist. The world is controlled by the movement of planets or the spheres of light, and we have artificially personalized nature by calling these spheres of light demigods like Surya, Chandra, Brihaspati, etc. But since nobody can see these demigods, all such demigods don't exist. Again, we shouldn't get carried away by this viewpoint, because the next sūtra refutes it, and because this view is attributed to the atheistic philosophy of Jaimini.

Now, a question arises: Why discuss the demigods at all, if they must be portrayed in a poor light? The answer is that the demigods were introduced into the discussion by the question of whether any beings other than humans are qualified to pursue a spiritual life. The answer to that question is that there are indeed beings who have performed austerities and situated in sattva-guna as opposed to humans who are largely in rajo-guna and the demons below who are largely in tamo-guna. So, from a material perspective, the demigods are higher. They are also higher because sattva-guna is closer to transcendence than rajo-guna and tamo-guna. However, this material superiority shouldn't be taken to imply spiritual superiority. Normally when we see people in positions of greater power, we are inclined to respect them. A devotee of the Lord may be poor and destitute, and he would not be as much respected according to social customs. The position of demigods is also similar—they have performed austerities and practiced sense control due to which they have superior positions in the administration of the universe. According to social customs, they are respectable. But this respect for demigods in society should be taken with a pinch of salt when discussing the extent of their spiritual advancement. This is not to say that the demigods are atheistic or opposed to the Lord like demons. However, it is also not to be presumed that their superior material position automatically entails that they are also spiritually advanced. So, the discussion about their intoxication is simply to reveal the other perspective, so that one can form a balanced opinion about their position. A derogatory view of the demigods has been presented—but it is a view from a spiritual viewpoint.

QUESTION

However, you have previously said that the demigods are ādidaivika and work under the supervision of the Paramātma. If we accept Jaimini's opinion that the demigods simply don't exist, then how shall we reconcile it with your previous statements about them being the controllers of the material world?

1.3.33 (96)

भावं तु वादरायणःअस्तिहि

bhāvaṃ tu vādarāyaṇaḥ asti hi

bhāvaṃ—the existence (of demigods); tu—but; vādarāyaṇaḥ—Badarayana (maintains); asti—does exist; hi—because.

TRANSLATION

But Bādarāyana accepts the existence (of demigods) because they exist.

COMMENTARY

The controversy created by the previous two sūtras is finally put to rest by saying that even though Jaimini believes that the demigods don't exist because we cannot observe them, Bādarāyana maintains that their existence is real.

In 1.3.30 (93) it was stated that the transcendent reality of names and forms is also visible in the material world in the different cycles of time, and we had identified these names as Indra, Chandra, Surya, etc. But the Mīmāṃsā philosopher could argue: if you are claiming that a transcendent reality can be confirmed in this world by reason and observation, then I cannot see such demigods through my senses. So, your claim that a transcendent reality exists, and can be confirmed by our observation to reaffirm our faith in its existence, must be rejected. And since we cannot confirm the existence of such a reality through reason and experience, then any attempt to ask repeated questions or test the knowledge through practical application must also be rejected. The only recourse for the transcendentalist is blind faith in such claims, and if someone wants to have such blind faith, then why even engage in a discussion? After all, the discussion is supposed to be carried out using reason and observation, and if the claims cannot be confirmed by reason and experience, then there is no point in any discussion. Your belief in gods or God is simply blind faith.

We have seen how the Mīmāṃsā philosopher is an instrumentalist rather than a realist. Modern science is very close to the Mīmāṃsā position although it doesn't accept the existence of a soul, karma, or even choice. But it is quite possible to turn modern science in a New Age movement, which accepts the existence of a soul, karma, and choice, and yet remains atheistic. This is an important point because many people are enamored by the onset of such New Age movements, which advocate the existence of a soul, choice, and even karma, and they think that this is significant progress toward a spiritual understanding. They may not realize how dangerously close it is to blatant atheism. A person involved in gross materialistic activities, who accepts the reality of demigods and God, should be considered far superior to the New Age movements. The worship of demigods is not the ultimate destination, but one who worships the demigods recognizes the existence of a higher authority even in this world. Their devotion to the demigods is superior to one who believes that such demigods and God don't exist, although he accepts the soul, choice, and karma.

Topic 9

QUESTION

You have earlier stated that humans are qualified to take shelter of the Lord in the heart (in case they cannot find a suitable guru). But some so many people are guided by their material desires, even when they claim to be guided by the Lord. Similarly, if the real guru is to be judged by their words (conviction), but many humans may not be so perceptive to understand the real meaning. So, in what way are all humans qualified for spiritual progress if they don't have the qualification to either find a real guru or accept Lord's guidance in the heart?

1.3.34 (97)

शुगस्य तदनादरश्रवणात् तदाद्रवणात् सूच्यते हि

śugasya tadanādaraśravaṇāt tadādravaṇāt sūcyate hi

śuk—grief; asya—his; tat-anādaraśravaṇāt—from hearing the insult; tat—that (about him); ādravaṇāt—owing to his approaching in a not humble manner (ādrava—not liquid or melted); sūcyate—is referred to; hi—because.

TRANSLATION

He was in grief on hearing insulting words about him because he did not approach in a humble manner—this can be referred to (as a counterexample).

COMMENTARY

In the earlier sections, the qualifications of a guru were discussed. In this section, the qualifications of the disciple are being discussed. In Bhagavad-Gita 4.34, Lord Kṛṣṇa states the qualification of a disciple approaching a guru:

tad viddhi praṇipātena
paripraśnena sevayā
upadekṣyanti te jñānaṁ
jñāninas tattva-darśinaḥ

> To know that (the Absolute Truth) fall before (a spiritual master), ask him questions submissively, and render him service. They can teach the knowledge because they have seen the truth.

The first such qualification is that one must be extremely humble; one must ask questions submissively, and one must render service to the guru. If these conditions are not satisfied, then the guru is not obliged to teach the knowledge. Therefore, not every human is qualified to learn from a guru; they must be submissive and deeply inquisitive, and prepared to serve the guru to learn.

This sūtra cites a counterexample from Chāndogya Upaniśad where King Janasruti approached a teacher Raivaka in a not so humble manner. The specific term used here is ādrava which means in a non-liquid or non-melted manner. It can be contrasted to Lord Kṛṣṇa's use of *pranipatena* in relation to the guru which means prostration at someone's feet in a very humble manner. Instead of offering his humility, the King offered Raivaka some material goods—a necklace, a chariot, and some cows—and asked him to impart spiritual knowledge. Looking at his arrogant attitude, Raivaka was greatly displeased and called the King a "Sūdra" or a man unqualified for spiritual knowledge. Raivaka returned all the gifts the King had brought and refused to impart him knowledge.

QUESTION

What did the King then do? Did he approach the Lord in his heart? Did he approach another spiritual master? Was he able to obtain knowledge?

1.3.35 (98)

क्षत्रयित्वगतेश्चोत्तरत्र चैत्ररथेन लिङ्गात्

kṣatriyatvagateścottaratra caitrarathena liṅgāt

kṣatriyatva-gateḥ—having the nature of a Kshatriya; ca—and; uttaratra—

subsequently; caitrarathena liṅgāt—by exhibiting signs like Chaitraratha.

TRANSLATION

(Despite him) having the nature of a Kshatriya (i.e., pride and arrogance), subsequently (he) exhibited the signs like that of Chaitraratha (i.e., humility).

COMMENTARY

The story of King Janaśruti continues from the previous sūtra. The Kshatriyas are naturally very proud and do not submit to anyone easily. Yet, despite this natural pride in him, and the insult that caused him grief, the Chāndogya Upaniśad describes that the King came back a second time to Raivaka. This time, he was much humbler and offered his daughter in marriage to Raivaka. A daughter is especially very dear to a father, so if a father is offering his daughter in marriage, his seriousness should be accepted. Looking at the King's changed attitude, Raivaka agreed to impart the knowledge to the King. In this context, a comparison between Janaśruti and Chaitraratha is made. Chaitraratha was a Gandharva, who demonstrated great arrogance to Arjuna, considering him to be a mere human. Then, Arjuna defeated Chaitraratha in a battle and was about to behead him. Chaitraratha and his wife begged Arjuna to spare his life, and Arjuna demonstrating his compassion let Chaitraratha go free. The comparison with Chaitraratha is appropriate as he was initially proud and arrogant and fought against Arjuna and later begged for his mercy. The implication of the previous sūtra was that if a person is arrogant, then the guru must reject him. But if he becomes humble, he should be imparted knowledge.

QUESTION

In the story of Janaśruti and Raivaka, since Raivaka calls Janaśruti a "Sūdra", and then rejects him as a disciple, does it mean that the Sūdra cannot be accepted as disciples? You have earlier said that spiritual knowledge is appropriate for all human beings. But now you are saying that it may not be meant for the Sūdra. Doesn't this create a contradiction with the earlier claim?

1.3.36 (99)

संस्कारपरामर्शात् तदभावाभिलापाच्च

saṃskāraparāmarśāt tadabhāvābhilāpācca

saṃskāra-parāmarśāt—from purificatory ceremonies and morality being mentioned; tat-abhāva-abhilāpāt—from its absence being declared; ca—and.

TRANSLATION

Because purificatory ceremonies and moral character are mentioned (in the twice-born) and because their absence is declared (in the case of the Sūdra).

COMMENTARY

There are two meanings of saṃskāra, one generic and the other specific. The generic meaning is that while growing up, a child is taught moral values, good behavior, dignity and respect toward others, cultivation of the mind, cleanliness, pure habits, regulated living, the importance of austerity, etc. In this generic meaning, saṃskāra indicates the latent impressions on the psyche that are formed during childhood. Childhood is a formative time during which the mind, intellect, and body are developed. Whatever happens during childhood leaves a lasting impression. Thus, the generic meaning of saṃskāra is ethical and moral upbringing". The children are impressionable; they gather ideas quickly from their surroundings. These are typically obtained from parents, teachers, and friends. Therefore, a good family upbringing and association are important during childhood. These leave impressions which last a lifetime.

The second, more specific, meaning of saṃskāra is the performance of a ritual. In the Vedic custom, a pūjā is performed invoking the Lord's blessings before beginning anything important. This pūjā has two purposes—(1) remembering the Lord before starting anything new, and (2) seeking His blessings to remove any defects that remain in our actions despite our best efforts. Such rituals include the ceremony of marriage, the ritual of impregnation, childbirth, the beginning of solid food by the child (different from mother's milk), the first introduction to reading and writing, the beginning of formal education, and the completion of education whereby the guru grants a sanctified thread to be worn by the disciple used for chanting the Gāyatri mantra three times a day.

Take the example of Garbhādhāna or the impregnation ceremony. The husband and wife are not expected to engage in indiscriminate sex for enjoyment. Sex is primarily meant for conceiving the child. And if the husband and wife desire to have a child, they perform a ceremony and seek the blessings of the Lord. The entire family is invited to this ceremony, and through it, everyone comes to know that the couple will now engage in sex. Sex is therefore not a private matter or something that two people do, unknown to everyone else. It is rather publicly declared that a couple is now seeking a child, and hence they will indulge in sex. If one wants to have more children, this ceremony is performed for every child. Therefore, every instance of sex is preceded by a ceremony of conception, and through such ceremonies, life is regulated.

In this degraded age, a moral upbringing, seeking the shelter of the Lord, and asking for His blessings to remove any remaining defects despite our best efforts, have mostly disappeared. There is still in some cases a residual sacrament of wearing a thread, even if these people don't chant the Gāyatri mantra three times a day. It is just a physical adornment used by some people to call themselves "Brahmana" as opposed to those who don't wear such threads. As a result, the term saṃskāra has come to symbolize those with a thread.

We should, however, understand saṃskāra in a broader sense—beginning with a moral upbringing and seeking the benediction of the Lord at every stage of life, along with the purificatory ceremonies that are performed to regulate enjoyment in life. The thread comes at the culmination of the education, but there is much more that precedes and follows the wearing of the thread.

With this background, the Sūdra are those people who do not abide by this system. They don't have a good moral upbringing, and they don't invoke the Lord's blessings at important stages in their life. Thus, a person who has sex without declaring the intention of conception is to be considered a Sūdra. Similarly, those who have sex with contraception are to be considered Sūdra.

In an earlier sūtra, Raivaka insults Janaśruti as Sūdra because he did not show the respect that a disciple must toward the guru. There are many such Sūdra spiritualists at present who despite their ignorance about the truth, a misfortune which distances them from good teachers, and laziness to study books, remain extremely arrogant. When a genuine teacher approaches them despite their misfortune, instead of showing humility and gratitude, they simply challenge and criticize the teacher. Their hubris indicates a lack of moral upbringing, and such people are not considered civilized in the Vedic system.

Raivaka could see that Janaśruti was a king. After all, who but a king can offer such wealth? But the fact that the king thought that he can buy knowledge in exchange for some of his wealth indicated his depraved mindset. It is an indirect statement that even the kings can behave like Sūdra and they should, therefore, be considered Sūdra. Conversely, when his behavior changed, and he returned humbly, Raivaka granted him knowledge, which again indicates that correct behavior and mindset are the basis of deciding who a Sūdra is.

The essence of this sūtra is that not all humans can be granted spiritual knowledge. There is a basic threshold of moral character and faith in the Lord that is a prerequisite for this knowledge. Furthermore, the prospective disciple must also demonstrate humility instead of arrogance. Those lacking in all these basic qualifications should not be granted spiritual knowledge. The upper three classes in society, namely, the Brahmana, Kshatriya, and Vaisya are expected to have these qualities to varying degrees, with the Brahmana possessing them to the highest level. Similarly, the Sūdra are those who don't possess such qualities. Therefore, they are disqualified from being taught Vedic knowledge.

QUESTION

You are stating that a guru cannot blindly accept disciples. Rather, the guru must evaluate the suitability of a person based on their moral character and faith in the Lord before deciding to impart them spiritual knowledge?

1.3.37 (100)

तदभावनिर्धारणे च प्रवृत्तेः

tadabhāvanirdhāraṇe ca pravṛtteḥ

tadabhāva—the absence of that (namely, the qualities of a Sūdra); nirdhāraṇe—in the ascertainment; ca—and; pravṛtteḥ—from inclination.

TRANSLATION

In the ascertainment of the absence of that (the existence of good qualities and lack of faith in the Lord—i.e., the qualities of a Sūdra) and based on their inclinations (a guru can impart knowledge to a prospective disciple).

COMMENTARY

In the previous sūtra, the action of Raivaka was clarified and justified—namely, why he called Janaśruti a Sūdra and later accepted him as his disciple. This position is now being generalized for all the prospective teachers and their disciples. In the process, the sūtra states that not only must one not have the qualities of the Sūdra, but one must also have the *pravritti* or inclination and tendency toward this knowledge. What do inclination and tendency mean? It indicates that a person—once having acquired such knowledge—will not abandon it. He has a natural inclination and tendency toward practicing this knowledge, and the guru is assured that the disciple will not acquire this knowledge and then either misuse it, or abandon it, and thereby become a bad example for others who might be seeking such knowledge in the future.

Many people join spiritual practices and take initiation from a guru. But it may often be done on the spur of the moment. As time passes, their natural disinclination becomes obvious. The person now abandons the spiritual path and takes to other activities that are totally counterproductive to this path. They may also try to use this knowledge for their own material advancement. Or, sometimes, they may totally abandon the path and engage in activities that prompt others to wonder—If this man could do such things after so many years of spiritual practice, then is there something wrong with the practice itself?

The sūtra holds the guru responsible for preventing such outcomes. He is expected to judge the disciple not only from the present demonstration of good qualities such as humility and submissive inquiry, but also the long-term prospect of a person being able to continue the practice in such a path. This further constrains the process of spiritual initiation—One should not initiate just because a person is demonstrating good qualities right now. Rather, the guru must also judge a person's nature and estimate whether he would be able to sustain this practice over his lifetime. Sometimes people approach a guru because they are distressed; their temporary suffering draws them toward a guru, but their real inclination is quite different. So, the reasons for which someone approaches a guru must be judged by the guru and a decision must be made as to their suitability to impart the knowledge based on their true inclinations.

QUESTION

It is sometimes said that the śrutī—e.g., the Upaniśad—are harder to understand for the common people, and they are therefore recommended or allowed only for the most advanced people. It is also said that the smriti—such as the Ramayana, Mahabharata, and the Purāna—can be studied even by the less intelligent or less qualified people. So, when you speak about the disqualification of a disciple, does it pertain only to the śrutī or also to the smriti?

1.3.38 (101)

श्रवणाध्ययनार्थप्रतिषेधात् स्मृतेश्च

śravaṇādhyayanārthapratiṣedhāt smṛteśca

śravaṇa-adhyayana-artha-pratiṣedhāt—because of the prohibition of hearing, studying, and interpreting; smṛteḥ—the smriti; ca—also.

TRANSLATION

Because of the prohibition from hearing, studying, and interpreting the smriti (those lacking in moral character and faith in the Lord) as well.

COMMENTARY

The distinction between śrutī and smriti is not as hard and fast as is sometimes made out to be. For example, the Bhagavad-Gita is a Upaniśad and can, therefore, be called śrutī. However, because Bhagavad-Gita is a part of Mahabharata, and the latter is considered smriti, therefore, the Bhagavad-Gita is also called smriti. In the same vein, it is argued that śrutī is what was heard from the Lord, while smriti is produced by enlightened souls. If we take that distinction, then the above description of Raivaka and Janaśruti cannot be considered the speech of the Lord; it is clearly a narration of events like those in the Purāna. By that measure, Chāndogya Upaniśad must be considered a smriti rather than śrutī. Owing to these objections, sometimes the Upaniśads are treated as smriti rather than śrutī. But the problem is not limited to the Upaniśad. There are numerous conversations between the Lord and His devotees found all over the Vedic literature; The Bhagavad-Gita is an example of Lord Kṛṣṇa instructing Arjuna; since it is spoken by the Lord, it must be considered śrutī. Likewise, there are many such conversations between the Lord and His devotees in the Purāna and the Tantra. So, by the claim that śrutī is spoken by the Lord, the Tantra and Purāna must also be classified as śrutī and the scope of smriti is practically limited. A classic example of this problem is that Sāñkhya philosophy is spoken by Lord Kapila to mother Devahūti in the Śrīmad Bhāgavatam. As an incarnation of Lord Viṣṇu, His words must be considered śrutī, and Sāñkhya philosophy (which is classified as one of the six schools of philosophy under the smriti category) must now be considered śrutī instead of smriti.

Now, some historians say that only the four Vedas are śrutī. But Vedic texts describe how the four Vedas are created from the four heads of Brahma. If śrutī is only spoken by the Lord, then the four Vedas are spoken by Brahma. So, by that measure, the four Vedas cannot be called śrutī. Furthermore, the division of the Veda into four parts is a creation of Brahma, after he received the knowledge from Lord Viṣṇu. So, the four-fold division of knowledge is due to Brahma, and not due to the Lord who spoke the knowledge to Brahma. If śrutī is only Lord's speech, then we cannot consider even the four Vedas śrutī.

The bottom line is that no definition of śrutī and smriti works correctly. Words of the Lord are found in the smriti, and narrations of advanced preceptors are found in the śrutī. Any method of classification based on history, grouping, and literary style is useless. The terms śrutī and smriti are used heuristically, which means by and large the śrutī will contain direct information from the Lord, and smriti will contain its understanding and interpretation by the advanced preceptors. However, these are not mutually exclusive categories. Ultimately, the term 'Veda' means knowledge or to know. It comprises several types of knowledge, some of which are mundane, and others are transcendental. The 'earlier' parts of the Veda, which comprise the mantras for the worship of demigods, and which formed the basis of Pūrva Mīmāṃsā, are generally mundane knowledge. Conversely, the 'later' part of the Vedas, such as the Vedānta Sūtra, constitute transcendental knowledge. So, even if we look at the accepted chronology of the texts, the progression isn't always from the transcendental to mundane; is it often also in the reverse order. Given all these difficulties, we must not consider śrutī and smriti as being fundamentally different. The Mahabharata for example describes the Purāna as the fifth Veda. We must rather view them as taking a seeker to different levels of spiritual advancement. The context reveals which scripture is meant for which purpose.

With the inability to clearly separate śrutī and smriti, it is no surprise that this sūtra states that those without a good moral character, faith in the Lord, and the long-term inclination to pursue and practice this knowledge, should also not be taught the smriti. In short, there are some prerequisites for all disciples, and those not meeting the qualification should not be imparted this knowledge. This sūtra explicitly forbids hearing, studying, and interpreting. These are progressive stages—one begins by hearing, then studies them himself, and then may author an interpretation. The implication is that if one can hear, then he will start studying, and eventually author an interpretation. As interpretations by the unqualified proliferate, it would become impossible to distinguish between the true understanding and the concocted ideologies. The knowledge will therefore eventually get corrupted and misunderstood.

We can understand from here that such corruptions have occurred many times in history, so this statement is made with the benefit of hindsight. As Lord Kṛṣṇa states in the Bhagavad-Gita, He appears in every age to re-establish the knowledge when it has declined, and we should assume that despite this forbidding of hearing, studying, and interpreting by the unqualified, such things happen; as a result, the understanding declines, and the Lord then appears again to reestablish it. So, even as this sūtra cautions against teaching the knowledge to the unqualified, we can assume that such things happen anyway.

Topic 10

QUESTION

You have sent me into a great dilemma by stating that those without a good moral character and faith in the Lord should not be imparted spiritual knowledge, because most people would be disqualified by this predilection. Especially in today's time, most people don't have a good moral character and they don't have faith in the Lord. The implication for them is that they are all disqualified from this knowledge. If that is so, then how can they become qualified if we close the doors to real knowledge for them? The only hope for liberating such a person is to have them acquire this knowledge, although they may still reject it due to their nature. But if we close the doors to this knowledge by precluding them, then what hope exists for such unfortunate people?

1.3.39 (102)
कम्पनात्
kampanāt

kampanāt—from the vibrations.

TRANSLATION

(Spiritual knowledge can be obtained) from the vibrations.

COMMENTARY

To understand this sūtra, we can recall the life story of Sage Valmiki who was a hunter in a forest prior to becoming a sage. Once, upon a chance meeting with Nārada Muni, he was advised to give up his hunting and purify himself of his sinful actions. But due to the accumulated effects of his actions, he had lost all good moral character and faith in the Lord. He could not even chant the names of the Lord. So, Nārada advised him to chant "Marā" instead of "Rāma". "Marā" means "to kill" and given Valmiki's proclivities at that time, he could easily chant this word. When "Marā" is repeated again and again, it produces the same sound as "Rāma". So, even though the mental state of the chanter is to utter "Marā", over the course of time the sound purified him, and he became the great sage Valmiki who composed the epic Ramayana, which is considered a smriti. This sūtra similarly suggests that even if someone is unqualified to hear, study, and interpret, they can still just utter the sounds as "vibrations".

The Śrīmad Bhāgavatam narrates a similar story about Ajāmila, who was born a Brahmana but then abandoned all his good qualities, including his wife, and started living with a prostitute. Once some sages came to Ajāmila's house and seeing the prostitute pregnant with Ajāmila's child, asked Ajāmila to name the child Nārāyana. When this child was born, Ajāmila became deeply attached to his son, and would constantly call him "Nārāyana". At the time of death, the servants of Yama came to take him to hell, and out of fear and desperation, Ajāmila again called out for his son "Nārāyana". No sooner than this name was uttered, the servants of Lord Nārāyana arrived on the scene and saved Ajāmila from going to hell; he was in fact taken to Vaikuṇṭha. Ajāmila had no understanding of the meaning of Nārāyana; he wasn't calling out for Lord Nārāyana, but the sound vibration was enough to save him from the gravest danger.

In the previous sūtra the hearing, studying, and interpreting of scriptures has been forbidden for unfaithful or sinful people. All these activities involve the mind. Hearing involves the attempt to understand, which means giving the sound an interpretation. Studying involves the correlation of the acquired meaning with the ideas previously acquired, checking if they are consistent or inconsistent, and in case of inconsistencies, seek alternative meanings. Finally, interpretations are the reconciliation of some apparent contradictions and clarifying the understanding of each scripture by explaining the meaning.

The unfaithful regard the scripture with disdain, and never even try to understand them. If they happen to study something, any encounter with a contradiction reinforces their disdain. Hence, they never progress into the study phase where these contradictions are reconciled. Then, without such reconciliation, people begin authoring commentaries based on their limited understanding. Such misrepresentations abound today due to the reading, studying, and interpreting by scholars and academics who had no faith in the scripture or the Lord. In short, the unqualified are forbidden from using their minds.

Then, in this sūtra, such unqualified people are permitted to engage in "vibrations". Notably, we need not use our minds to understand these vibrations. We can simply listen to these sounds attentively, and there is no need to understand what they mean. This can make an unqualified person qualified.

The normal course prescribed for a spiritual aspirant is that they acquire knowledge, and then put that knowledge into practice. But if the aspirant is disqualified from acquiring knowledge, then this sūtra states that they can still "vibrate" some sounds. What are these sounds? In the above examples of Valmiki and Ajāmila, they are the sounds of the names of the Lord. The difference is that in the case of scripture, one needs to grasp the meaning, but in the case of chanting the names of the Lord, the understanding of meaning is unnecessary. Without understanding the meaning, one can still reap the benefits. In this regard, we can note that the Kali-Santārana Upaniśad mentions that the chanting of the names of Hari is the only process for transcendence in Kali-yuga where most people have little faith in the scripture and the Lord and don't have a good moral character. If one is sincere about chanting the names of the Lord, then they can eventually come to the point of developing an understanding.

Topic 11

QUESTION

You previously said that one must worship the Lord in devotion and surrender to Him. For this surrender, one must have some knowledge, which we discussed can be tested through reason and observation, and upon such confirmation, we can repose faith in the Lord and then surrender to Him. But if knowledge itself is being precluded for such a person, then how can vibrating the names of the Lord lead to the ability to acquire the knowledge? Should it not be considered the uttering of some mumbo-jumbo, which we ourselves don't understand? How can mumbo-jumbo lead to perfect knowledge?

1.3.40 (103)

ज्योतिर्दर्शनात्

jyotirdarśanāt

jyotiḥ—light; darśanāt—from seeing.

TRANSLATION

From seeing the light (by the performance of vibrations).

COMMENTARY

The previous sūtra said that if someone chants the names of the Lord then they will become qualified for receiving spiritual knowledge. And this sūtra reinforces that understanding—the changing of the names of the Lord is light. When the names of the Lord are heard, then attentive hearing is the reception of light, by which the nature of the self is understood. Similarly, when the names of the Lord are uttered attentively, then those names become the light by which everything else is demystified. The utterance of the names is now like a torch that illuminates things in a dark room. As the saying, 'knowledge is light, ignorance is darkness', this sūtra indicates that by the chanting of the Lord's names we get enlightened in two ways: (a) to see the nature of the self, and (b) to perceive the nature of reality. But we have to chant to experience this.

We earlier noted that to see a 'cow', we must possess the concept of 'cow', because only then can we discriminate the cow from the field it is grazing in. We had concluded that there must be some basic set of innate concepts using which we must acquire new concepts, but we ended the discussion on the note that this indicated concepts must be logically prior to the external things. Now we are faced with a different question: How do I acquire a concept of which I have no understanding yet? I need this concept to discriminate it from other things, and if I don't have it then even if I see those things right in front of me, I would still not be able to understand their presence. Just like a person who doesn't know what a cow is, won't see a cow even if it were in front of him. In the same way, without the understanding of the Lord in some form, we cannot understand the scriptures. Books use words, but the meaning of these words has to be realized by experience. If these meanings are wrong, then all subsequent understanding is also incorrect. This sūtra recommends that such an understanding can be obtained through sound vibrations; as an example, those trying to understand the nature of Brahman are advised to vibrate the sound 'OM'. This sound is the *name* by which Brahman is called, and by repeating the sound, we get the meaning. Using those meanings, we understand scriptures. In short, if you don't know the meaning, don't go consulting a dictionary! Rather, chant the names of the Lord, and then those meanings will be seen.

In this regard, we can recall that all concepts are universals, but they are also instantiated as individuals. So, an individual cow is an instance of the universal concept 'cow', and to create this instance, the individual must associate with the universal. Once the concept is instantiated, it exists both inside the instance (as the immanent meaning) and outside (as the transcendent concept). In the same way, if we chant the name 'Kṛṣṇa', then Kṛṣṇa is both outside and inside the name. The name contains the meaning like the individual cow contains the concept cow. If we repeat this name, the mind can acquire the meaning. If the meaning is acquired, then it becomes the 'light' by which we can discriminate. Just like knowing the meaning of 'cow' helps us see the 'cow', similarly, by knowing the meaning of 'Kṛṣṇa' we can see Kṛṣṇa. Without this meaning, even if Kṛṣṇa was right in front of us, we won't be able to see Him.

So, 'light' means the concepts by which we discriminate, distinguish, organize, etc. It is called 'light' in comparison to ordinary light for the ocular vision, which helps us distinguish things. The claim of the previous sūtra was that by chanting some sounds, we can acquire the meaning. The claim of this sūtra is that by acquiring these meanings we can begin to understand the scriptures—the word is now understood. With even a preliminary understanding, we can start reading the scripture, and follow the rest of the process of analyzing, testing, accepting a guru or seeking the Lord's guidance. If one has no faith in the Lord, because he has no understanding of the Lord, then reading scriptures would not help, because these scriptures will merely refer to Him by a name. To understand the meaning of that name, we must repeat that name, and by this repetition, we will also acquire the meaning automatically, and once such a meaning has been acquired, it will then enable us to read scriptures.

Topic 12

QUESTION

If the meaning is already in the sound, then a single utterance must reveal the meaning to us. Why do we have to repeat this sound again and again? Also, if this process were extended to the rest of the language, then why would anyone ever need a dictionary or translation? We can just hear the sounds, and since they contain the meanings, we should have no problem in understanding the spoken words. In fact, if such meanings were innate, then even by reading the scriptures we will automatically acquire the meanings the first time, and we would never be disqualified due to our moral character or lack of faith. So, how you reconcile the immanence of meaning with the repeated chanting?

1.3.41 (104)

आकाशोऽर्थान्तरत्वादिव्यपदेशात्

ākāśo'rthāntaratvādivyapadeśāt

ākāśaḥ—the space (whose property is sound); artha—the meaning; antaratva—because it is different; ādi—the origin; vyapadeśāt—from the hiding.

TRANSLATION

From the hiding of the origin, a difference between sound and meaning.

COMMENTARY

To understand this sūtra, we need to recall our previous discussion about the universals and individuals. My body has hands, legs, head, chest, belly, fingers, etc. and all of these are universals because your body has them too. These universals are organized in a hierarchy. For example, the higher-level universal for us is 'human'. Inside this universal, a lower-level universal is the 'hand'. Inside this is another lower-level universal, the 'finger', inside which is another lower-level universal of 'nail'. But, when an individual body is created, all these universals are instantiated. Thus, we acquire a personal hand, leg, belly, head, chest, fingers, etc. The instantiation is rooted in the soul, but from this soul—who is an individual—the individuality expands to instantiate the different parts of the body. As we have discussed earlier, this individuality originates in the ānanda potency of the soul and is understood as 'desire'. Just like there is a hierarchical tree of universals, similarly, there is a hierarchy of desires, which expand from the soul into the subtle body and then into the gross body, and then from this gross body into products of this body such as speech. Every part of our body, therefore, has desire; it's not that desire only exists in the heart or the mind; it is expanded all over the body. Thus, our tongue, skin, eyes, genitals, legs, and hands, all have desires. The mind can control these senses because the mind has a higher-level desire, and the soul can control the mind as it has an even higher-level desire. Thus, in summary, the body and its products (such as speech) are the combinations of the cognitive and the emotional—the cognitive is the universal, and emotional desires create an individual instance.

Now, when we chant the name of the Lord, we are creating an instance of the universal, and this instantiation involves a desire. However, this instantiation can occur at many levels—from the deepest level of the soul's desire to an intellectual, mental, sensual, or gross material level. A person without devotion to the Lord doesn't have the higher-level desires of the soul, intellect, or mind. So, he has no attraction for chanting. Nevertheless, if he chants, there is an instance as a gross sound, due to some desire. If there were no desire to chant, even this gross sound would not be produced. So, for one who has no deeper level desires, the chanting is recommended because at least we can instantiate the name of the Lord using the lowest level desire of the body. If this process is continued, then the desires rise—from the body to the senses, to the mind, to the intellect, and eventually to the soul. Accordingly, the same universal—i.e., the Lord—can be perceived at many levels. The grossest perception of the Lord is the sound vibrated by the tongue, but this doesn't lead to a sensual or mental understanding. The sensual understanding comes when the desire expands from the body to the senses. Now, the tongue can 'vibrate' the sound without producing anything audible. Similarly, when the desire expands from the senses to the mind, then one can chant in the mind, without the tongue. So, the meaning appears in the mind because the desire expands into the mind.

Ultimately, the universal is very subtle; as we have discussed earlier, the universal is the combination of knowledge, beauty, power, wealth, fame, and renunciation. By our senses, we can hear words, but we cannot understand the meaning. By our mind, we can grasp some meaning, but we don't know if it is knowledge. By the intellect we judge something to be true—and hence knowledge—but it is in a specific field, such as physics, psychology, economics, etc. We have no clue about what 'knowledge itself' means. This can only be grasped by the soul. Therefore, even though the universal manifests as the sound which we can hear, the universal is not the gross material vibration.

This sūtra states that the sound—which manifests in the ether—is different from the meaning. Why? Because the universal is innate in the sound, but we cannot perceive that innateness, even though it is present within the sound. But if we persist with the chanting, then the innateness is also perceived. This is because the perception depends on the acquisition of the concepts: If we don't have the concept, then we cannot perceive it. Thus, through desire, we chant, and by chanting we acquire the ability to perceive, and then a greater desire. This cyclical process of desiring, chanting, and perceiving leads to perfection.

Topic 13

QUESTION

You seem to be indicating that there isn't one kind of meaning—e.g., that we understand through the mind. Rather, this meaning deepens through the development of desire, and while the ultimate meaning is transcendent, it can appear, manifest, or be represented (as through sound) even at the gross material level. How many such levels of understandings can be obtained? You have indicated the gross material sound and the understanding at the level of the mind or intellect by which we can understand the scriptures if the desire develops from the gross body into the mind. Are there deeper forms of understanding the Lord, that go beyond the representations of the body and mind?

1.3.42 (105)

सुषुप्त्युत्क्रान्त्योर्भेदेन

suṣuptyutkrāntyorbhedena

suṣupti—deep sleep; utkrāntyoḥ—death; bhedena—there is a difference.

TRANSLATION

There is a difference between deep sleep and death (or transcendence).

COMMENTARY

In the previous sūtra, a difference between the gross material sound (as the property of ether) and the meaning (which resides in the mind) was made. In this sūtra, a further distinction between the deep sleep and transcendent states is being made. Collectively, these are called vaikharī, madhyamā, paśyanti, and parā. The gross material sound is vaikharī; the mental and sensual meaning is madhyamā, the deep sleep state is called paśyanti, and the soul is parā. These are also identified as waking, dreaming, deep sleep, and transcendent states of experience. Since the distinction between word and meaning (i.e., vaikharī and madhyamā was drawn in the previous sūtra), this sūtra states a further difference between the states of deep sleep (paśyanti) and transcendence (parā).

Each of these four states is described in Vedic texts as a 'space' that possesses 'sound'. However, the nature of the space and the sound changes successively. At the level of vaikharī, the 'sound' is objective information; at the level of madhyamā, the sound is meaning, judgments, intentions, and morals. At the causal material level of paśyanti, the sound is the unconscious material identity or personality. And at the spiritual level of parā, the sound indicates the nature of the Lord, relation to the Lord, and devotion to the Lord. The implication is that there is a process of purification by which first the body is purified, followed by the sensations, thoughts, judgments, intentions, and morals, followed by the unconscious material personality, following which the soul perceives the Lord through its spiritual cognitive, emotional, and relational abilities. If there is some purification of the mind and the senses (which have been called a 'good moral character' or saṃskāra earlier), and if there is some faith in the Lord (which exists at the unconscious level, called the deep sleep state here), then the aspirant is entitled to scriptural study, and acquiring spiritual knowledge. If deeper imprints are missing, then one can chant such that the body, the senses, the mind, the intellect, and the unconscious can be gradually purified.

QUESTION

But the Lord is the Absolute Truth, and the origin of everything else, and the sound of His name is just one of the parts of the material manifestation. How can the whole truth be represented by a name in the universe? Doesn't this create a contradiction where the whole is represented inside the whole?

1.3.43 (106)

पत्यादशिब्देभ्यः

patyādiśabdebhyaḥ

pat—falls, descends; adi—the origin; sabdebhyah—by the sound.

TRANSLATION

The original form of the Lord descends or incarnates by the sound.

COMMENTARY

There are some difficulties in translating this sūtra which arise when we try to dissect the word *patyādi*. One possible dissection is *pati* + *adi* which would render this sūtra as indicating "He is called by names such as *pati* or husband". The other possible dissection is *pat* indicating a fall or descent, *adi* indicating from the origin, and *sabdebhyah* now indicates "as sound". This would render the sūtra as "the original form of the Lord descends as sound". Which of these two translations must be used for understanding this sūtra?

If we interpret this sūtra based on *pati* + *adi* then the inference would be that *pati* is a name of the Lord, which can lead to spiritual understanding. But a closer look at the prevalent names of the Lord in the scriptures reveals that the name *pati* is never used in isolation as a name of the Lord. The Lord has names such as Lakshmīpati (the husband of Lakshmi), Umāpati (the husband of Uma), Dwarakapati (the ruler of Dwaraka), Bhūpati (the Lord of the earth), Kailaśpati (the ruler of Kailash), Pashupati (the ruler of all animals), Kamalāpati (the husband of Kamala or Lakshmi), Prajapati (the ruler of all the population), etc. The Lord is indeed the *pati* or master. However, He is never called *pati* in isolation; whenever the husband or master is spoken of, the wife or the servant is necessarily mentioned, and the Lord takes a form suitable for that role.

Therefore, we translate this sūtra as "the Lord incarnates as His name". We have earlier said that the name is a 'sound representation' of the Lord; the Lord is immanent in the sound, and yet transcendent to the sound. His appearance in His creation is like the word 'universe' is a part of the universe, and yet represents the entire universe. The sound is a part and yet the meaning is the whole. Thus, He is physically a part, but semantically the whole. Here it is noted that the name of the Lord is an incarnation of the Lord within the creation.

SECTION 4

Topic 1

QUESTION

You have stated that the Lord incarnates or descends as His name and by vibrating this name we can purify our senses and our mind. However, in our previous discussion, you had said that the material world was related to the Lord as the house is related to an owner, or the design is related to the designer. You explicitly forbade the idea that the designer becomes the design. And yet, now, you are saying that a part of the design is the designer because the sound vibration is a material entity, and we consider this an incarnation of the Lord. How do we reconcile the contradiction between the material world being a separate entity from the Lord, and yet the Lord incarnating in this world? In fact, since the Lord is said not to have a material body, His incarnations in the material world are sometimes called forms only meant for our imagination.

1.4.1 (107)

आनुमानिकमप्येकेषामिति चेत् न शरीररूपकविन्यस्तगृहीतेःदर्शयति च

ānumānikamapyekeṣāmiti cet na śarīrarūpakavinyastagṛhīteḥ darśayati ca

ānumānikam—that which is imagined; api—also; ekeṣām—as an individual; iti cet—if it be said; na—no; śarīra-rūpaka—in the form of a body; vinyasta—has descended; gṛhīteḥ—for capturing; darśayati—seeing; ca—and.

TRANSLATION

If it is said that what appears as an individual is also imagination, (then we say) no; (the Lord) descends in a bodily form for our capturing and seeing.

COMMENTARY

There is a subtle difference between saying that the Lord is reflected in His creation like an artist's personality is seen in his works and the idea that the art is itself the artist. When we spoke about the connection between the Lord and the material energy, we treated this energy as His property. Like the owner lives in the house, but doesn't become the house, similarly, the Lord remains separate from the material energy. However, in the previous few sūtras, we shifted our position by saying that the Lord incarnates as His sound vibration.

This question is part of a larger problem of religious symbolism in the philosophy of religion. Although we grant that the material world is comprised of three modes, and these modes must be transcended, it is also recognized that certain things in this world—e.g., the process by which transcendence must be attained, which involves the use of material ingredients—must be transcendent. If the process of transcendence—e.g., the chanting of mantra—is tainted by the material modes, then there would be no hope for attaining transcendence.

Now, we have discussed this problem earlier in the context of the Vedas. We noted that if everything in this world is material, then even the Vedas must be material. After all, they are printed using ink and paper, and although prior to this printing, they existed in an oral form, even that sound is material. If these sounds are considered mundane, then they cannot lead to transcendence. We also discussed how Śri Śankarācārya established the divinity of the Vedas—stating that there is at least one thing (i.e., the Vedas) that is transcendental (with respect to those parts which lead to liberation). He, therefore, opened the door to religious symbolism in which religious texts are symbols of truth. But he did not cross the chasm: If Vedic scriptures can represent truth, then why can't other things—e.g., deities and names of the Lord—also represent this truth? What is so sacrosanct about the words written on paper with ink that the same meaning cannot be embodied in other ways? Why should we consider the scripture to have a divine origin, and other things such as deities or pictures or names of the Lord—which are also described in the scriptures—to not be of divine origin? The problem lay in the rejection of demigod worship in Śri Śankarācārya's philosophy. If these forms are rejected for transcendence, then all forms—including those of the transcendent Lord—must be rejected.

Śri Śankarācārya did not distinguish between the demigods and God. His philosophy accepted the divinity of Vedic texts but rejected all other forms. But we can see that even scripture is a form—and is often worshipped on par with the deities. By drawing a distinction between scripture and deities, which is artificial, and then not making a distinction between demigods and God, he condoned the idea that the incarnations of the Lord must also be just like the demigods—they appear to teach us knowledge, but they are not transcendent. With the introduction of the Lord's names as His incarnation, the door opens to treating many such names and forms as the Lord's incarnations as well.

This distinction requires us to induct the ability of an artist to draw his self-portraits, in addition to other things (such as landscapes) that he might paint. The self-portrait is also an expression of the artist, and therefore on par with the other works of art. And yet, the self-portrait is also a complete representation of the artist. Therefore, there is no contradiction in saying that the world is an artist's expression, and the idea that the artist is in that creation—provided we admit the ability of the artist to draw his self-portraits as works of art. Of course, the artist is in the painting even when a landscape is painted, but the artist is hidden in the painting. He or she becomes visible in a self-portrait. Hence, there is a distinction between worldly landscapes and self-portraits. The form of the self-portrait resembles the form of the artist even without a deeper look.

In so far as we admit the reality of everything else that is perceived, such self-portraits must also be real. Just as the landscape is not imaginary, similarly the self-portrait is also not imaginary. We have only augmented our previous notion of the Lord as the artist by saying that He can also paint His self-portrait. So, the claim that such forms of the Lord are imaginary is automatically rejected based on the reality of other works of art that are considered real. It does, however, lead to the question of why the artist would paint a self-portrait. The answer to this question is given in this sūtra—for those who can only see the works of art and not the artist, the self-portrait is a vision of the artist.

QUESTION

But we can argue that if the Lord has become visible or perceivable to our senses, then His body must be comprised of the five material elements such as Earth, Water, Fire, Air, and Ether. If the Lord takes on a material body, then how can He be considered transcendental to the nature of material reality?

1.4.2 (108)

सूक्ष्मं तु तदर्हत्वात्

sūkṣmaṃ tu tadarhatvāt

sūkṣmaṃ—subtle; tu—but; tat—that (He, the Lord); arhatvāt—from being deserving, celebrated, or praised.

TRANSLATION

But He (the Lord) is celebrated as the subtle (cause) (of the visible).

COMMENTARY

In 1.2.29 (60), the material world was called Lord's *abhivyakti*, or expression, like a person expresses thoughts in their mind. The speech objectifies the meanings in the mind so that others can perceive them (using their senses). This objectification is called 'sound' in the ether; it is the reality that exists before we perceive sound. Similarly, the other elements such as Air, Fire, Water, and Earth are the objectification of touch, sight, taste, and smell; they are the reality that exists before our senses interact with them to produce the sensations of touch, sight, taste, and smell. However, this is only one aspect of objectification; if this all that existed, then we could not say that a book objectifies knowledge, that a painting or musical composition objectifies beauty, that a person represents the idea of power, etc. After all, we are only seeing taste, touch, sight, sound, and smell; how could we perceive 'knowledge', 'beauty', 'power', etc. in the same representation? The answer is that there are many layers of gross and subtle realities in every representation. However, they are perceived through separate types of senses: The gross reality is perceived by the five senses, and the subtle reality by the mind. Thus, the mind is decoding knowledge, beauty, power, etc., just as the five senses are decoding taste, touch, smell, sight, and sound.

The term sthūla indicates 'gross' and the term sūkshma indicates 'subtle'.

They are related as words and meanings. The meaning is present in the words, but it is only perceived by the mind. Furthermore, we don't speak the word and then worry about the meaning. We rather determine the meaning, and then use the word to express it. Therefore, the meaning is the cause of the word. In the same way, the sound of the Lord's name is caused by the Lord (meaning).

The fact that the pure and transcendental meanings can be expressed in this world produces a conundrum. When the Lord incarnates in this world, His presence is temporary—He is visible for some time, and invisible after that. This prompts people to think that because the Lord disappears from the world, and because truth can never cease to exist, therefore, this form must be false. This confusion is a byproduct of two distinct meanings of *sat* and *asat*. The term asat means that which is (1) temporary and (2) false. Conversely, sat means that which is (1) eternal and (2) true. Since the Lord's incarnations are not eternally manifest (in this world), should we say that they are temporary or false?

We can compare this problem to the existence of Vedic knowledge. The knowledge of the Vedas is true, but it is not always manifest. In the present age, for example, several Vedic scriptures have been lost. Lord Kṛṣṇa states that He appears repeatedly (as incarnations) to resurrect this knowledge. So, we must distinguish between *truth* and *eternity*. The distinction is that the meaning is eternal, but its manifestation can be occasional or temporary. Therefore, what we call sat should pertain to the meaning, rather than to the expression. Just because some portions of the Vedas are now lost, doesn't mean they have become asat or false. They are still eternally true, but they are invisible now.

A fiction book exists for a few years, and its meanings are false. The Vedic texts can also exist temporarily, but their meanings are true and eternal. Therefore, if we apply *sat* to meaning, then eternity is truth and truth is eternal, and the two meanings of *sat* are identical. However, if we apply *sat* to the expression of meaning, then the two meanings of *sat*—i.e., eternity and truth—are not identical because the truth is only expressed temporarily through a book. The Lord's appearance in this world must be understood in the same way—He manifests temporarily although the meaning being manifest is eternal. The temporariness refers to the manifestation and not to the meaning. The meaning is still true and eternal; however, the meaning's manifestation is temporary, but not false.

This requires us to distinguish between *existence* and *truth*. In modern logic, truth is proven if existence is proven. The proof of existence, therefore, becomes the proof of truth, and proof and truth are equated. This is, however, a misleading premise of modern logic. If I think that "the sky is green", then the thought exists in my mind, but it is false. So, false things can exist, just like true things can exist. Since they can exist, their existence can be proven. And yet this proof doesn't indicate their truth. So, the term *asat* indicates temporary existence. It doesn't necessarily indicate falsity. Under this temporary existence, there can be fictions that are false and knowledge that is true. So, both the truth and the false can be temporarily manifest; regarding the form of the Lord, the terms *sat* can be applied because the meaning is true, and the term *asat* can be applied because the meaning is temporarily manifest in our vision. The fact that the world exists temporarily should not be interpreted as indicating everything is false; it should rather indicate that everything is temporary. However, underlying this temporary expression, there can sometimes be eternal truth.

This sūtra states that the Lord is the *sūkshma* cause of the visible. In short, He is the eternal meaning, which is temporarily expressed through words. The Lord is the eternal form of knowledge, beauty, power, wealth, fame, and renunciation. This form can become visible to our senses if the Lord manifests.

QUESTION

When the soul accepts a material body, he is said to be caught in the material world. Why should that entanglement in matter not be applied to the Lord when He accepts a body just like the other beings? After all, there are some laws of nature, which must apply to anybody present in this world. And if these laws start applying to the Lord, must He not also be under nature's control?

1.4.3 (109)

तदधीनत्वादर्थवत्

tadadhīnatvādarthavat

tat—His (the Lord); adhīnatvāt—from being dependent; arthavat—just like meaning.

TRANSLATION

From being manifest from the Lord, the manifestation is dependent on the Lord just like meaning (is dependent on the speaker of that meaning).

COMMENTARY

The soul is caught in the material body due to guna and karma. The guna are the soul's desires, which need to be fulfilled by the body; to the extent that the body fulfills these desires, the soul remains attached to the body, and doesn't want to leave it. But even if the soul wanted to leave the body, he cannot until he has reaped all the consequences of past karma. These two conditions of the soul's bondage don't apply to the Lord. The Lord is innately blissful, and He doesn't need a material body to fulfill His desires. Similarly, the actions of the Lord do not produce any consequences or karma. Therefore, unlike the soul who is bound due to guna and karma, the Lord is not bound in either way.

But one might still say: If I mix sugar with milk, then I will get sweet milk, rather than salty milk. To the extent that these are laws of nature, the Lord also cannot produce salty milk by mixing milk and sugar, so He must be bound by the laws of nature. This is indeed true; the Lord cannot produce salty milk by mixing sugar and milk. However, this is not bondage. Unlike the soul, whose access to sweet milk is restricted by their guna and karma, the Lord is not restricted in this way. We may not enjoy sweet milk, or we may not have access to the ingredients to produce sweet milk. The Lord is not restricted in either of these two ways. This doesn't mean that the Lord violates the laws of nature; He still follows the natural law according to which the mixing of milk and sugar produces sweet milk. But He cannot be prevented from drinking sweet milk due to karma, and He cannot be compelled to drink sweet milk due to guna.

There is a difference between descriptive and prescriptive laws. The descriptive laws pertain to the production of sweet milk by mixing milk and sugar. The prescriptive laws pertain to the consequences of actions or karma and the near impossibility to control desires caused by one's guna. The Lord is bound by descriptive laws, but He is not bound by the prescriptive laws.

The previous sūtra used the term *arhat* and this sūtra uses the term *artha*; the former indicates transcendence and the latter indicates the meaning. The Lord is both *artha* and *arhat*: He is the meaning, which is also transcendent.

QUESTION

But if the Lord is not compelled to come to the world, then why does He appear? You have stated that He is independent of the world, He is the meaning and purpose of its existence, and He is not bound by nature's laws. You have also said that the material world is unlike His nature, and the living entities here are averse to Him. So, why does He take the trouble of manifesting if there is no compelling force that is pushing Him towards manifesting Himself?

1.4.4 (110)

ज्ञेयत्वावचनाच्च

jñeyatvāvacanācca

jñeyatvā—knowability; vacanāt—through the words; ca—and.

TRANSLATION

And (the Lord appears) so that He can be known by His words.

COMMENTARY

In the Bhagavad-Gita, Lord Kṛṣṇa states that whenever there is a decline of religion and a rise in irreligion, He manifests to reestablish the principles of religion, protect the devotees, and destroy the demonic living entities. His actions of protecting the devotees and destroying the demonic living entities involve the display of His heroism or 'greatness'. This will come up for discussion shortly in a subsequent sūtra. In this sūtra, only the purpose of reestablishing the principles of religion is noted. It is further noted that He speaks so that He can be known through His words; in short, He speaks about Himself.

QUESTION

But isn't it said that the Vedas are His speech? If He has already explained His nature through the Vedas, then shouldn't we just study the Vedas? Why does the Lord appear when His words are already recorded in the Vedas?

1.4.5 (111)

वदतीति चेत् न प्राज्ञो हि प्रकरणात्

vadatīti cet na prājño hi prakaraṇāt

vadati—(someone) says; iti cet—if in this way; na—no; prājñaḥ—intelligent; hi—for; prakaraṇāt—from the treatise, books, passages.

TRANSLATION

If it is said that (the Lord) is already known from the Vedic texts, then (we say) no (because these texts) are meant only for the most intelligent.

COMMENTARY

The question arises: Why should the Lord speak about the nature of religion by appearing again and again when the Vedic texts are already present? The short answer is that the existence of these texts is not always enough; there must also be intelligent people who can understand and present the true essence of Vedic knowledge. This essence is preserved through the guru-disciple succession. But if this succession is broken, then false conceptions of religion are produced. In fact, demonic people now use religion for political, economic, and sociological aims. He appears to establish the essence, purpose, and the core ideas around which all other ideas must be organized and understood.

Knowledge has an innate hierarchy—from core to context. But what is core and what is context keeps changing with time. During a spiritual era, the core idea of human life is to attain transcendence from material existence, and God becomes the center around which everything else is organized. During a materialistic era, the core idea is to obtain unrestricted enjoyment, and sense enjoyment becomes the center around which everything else is organized. The Vedic system comprises many texts with different cores and contexts. The texts on medicine, for example, focus on the body, with some references to the mind, little attention to the soul, and almost no reference to demigods or God. If you are looking at the veins on a leaf, you cannot see the whole tree, let alone the forest. This focus on different areas is deliberate—sometimes you need to see the leaf instead of the full forest. But these differing areas of emphasis can also produce confusions—maybe the leaf is more important than the forest?

The existence of various texts doesn't tell us how they must be organized—from most important to less important to least important. The intellect produces this hierarchy, and whatever is ordered first becomes the basis on which the importance of the subsequent things is judged. So, the decline of intelligence means that we lose the ability to understand the difference between core and context; different people start treating the context as the core, and they might even consider the core irrelevant or false. So, the Lord appears to establish the difference between the core and the context of knowledge within the Vedas.

QUESTION

But if the main problem is that people are less intelligent to understand which part of the Veda is more important, then could this not be established by some intelligent person? Why would the Lord need to appear Himself?

1.4.6 (112)

त्रयाणामेव चैवमुपन्यासःप्रश्नश्च

trayāṇāmeva caivamupanyāsaḥ praśnaśca

trayāṇām—of three; eva—really; ca—and; evaṃ—thus; upanyāsaḥ—introduction or hint or stories; praśnaḥ—question, doubt; ca—and;

TRANSLATION

And (the Lord appears) really to display the pastimes of the three (quarters of existence) (for those) who might have doubts (about its existence).

COMMENTARY

After saying that the Lord appears to speak about Himself, and then stating that the Lord defines the core and the context of knowledge, this sūtra establishes the final point, namely, that ultimately the Lord appears to display (within the material world) the nature of the three-quarters of existence beyond the material world. The Vedas contain theoretical knowledge of the nature of Absolute Truth, exhorting the living entity to transcend the material world. But unless we say what the transcendental world looks like, how will people be attracted? Freedom from material suffering may not be an adequate justification for many people to pursue transcendence. Furthermore, many people may cynically believe that the present life here is all that is ever possible, and whether we like it or not, there is no better type of life. So, the Lord's appearance is also to provide a hint or indication of the nature of transcendence. These hints are available through the Lord's pastimes with His devotees in the world.

QUESTION

But His pastimes seem like ordinary human activities in many cases. How can anyone understand that He is also the Supreme Being by such pastimes?

1.4.7 (113)

महद्वच्च

mahadvacca

mahadvat—like greatness; ca—and.

TRANSLATION

(He) also (acts in) great ways or demonstrates (His) greatness.

COMMENTARY

Many people might argue that the pastimes the Lord displays in a human-like form indicate that He is just a human. To counter this argument, this sūtra states that the Lord also demonstrates His greatness to convince people that He is not a mere mortal. In the Bhagavad-Gita, for example, Lord Kṛṣṇa displays

His universal form to convince Arjuna of His greatness. We earlier noted that the Lord also protects the devotees and destroys the demonic. This constitutes His heroism and shows that He is not merely a mortal. His pastimes are often imbued with the sweetness of love, affection, and personal relationships. But that should not mislead anyone to think that He is an ordinary mortal. We should look at the other side of His pastimes which are humanly impossible. For instance, Lord Kṛṣṇa lifted the Govardhan mountain even as a child, which is an activity humanly impossible for anyone to perform. By demonstrating such activities, the Lord not only protects the devotees and destroys the demons, but for those who might have doubts, He clarifies His greatness.

Topic 2

QUESTION

It is sometimes said that "God is great". However, greatness can also be found in this world. There are many people who have attained great things in this world. So, if greatness is the measure by which we detect the presence of God (because His pastimes seem like those of an ordinary mortal), then by that measure, should we not consider other great people as incarnations of God?

1.4.8 (114)

चमसवदविशेषात्

camasavadaviśeṣāt

camasavat—like a spoon; aviśeṣāt—from nothing special (about them).

TRANSLATION

(Others are) like spoons; from there being nothing special (about them)

COMMENTARY

The term *camasvat* in this sūtra follows the term *mahadvat* in the previous sūtra. Since *mahadvat* is "like greatness", *chamasvat* should be understood as "like insignificant". If we make a contrast to greatness, we must ask: What is greatness? Greatness is often measured by the magnitude of what one achieves, and how difficult it was to achieve; thus, for instance, walking is not very difficult, so if someone is able to walk a mile, we would not consider it great. However, if someone walks the entire earth, then the action would be called 'great'. But, if one has lost their legs, then winning a walking race for the physically challenged would be considered great. Greatness is, therefore, relative to the difficulty. If one is born in a poor family and has no access to wealth or education, but still manages to achieve success, then their achievement is considered great. All stories of heroism are based on the basic theme that a hero overcomes difficulties and comes out victorious against them. The stories of heroes, therefore, become inspirational narrations for common people—they motivate us to overcome the obstacles in life and come out victorious by such struggle.

However, nothing is difficult for the Lord. He has no challenges and He doesn't become a hero by overcoming obstacles. The idea that "God is great" is a materialistic conception of God. When He demonstrates His greatness, by performing deeds that would be impossible for others, He isn't the hero who has overcome difficulties. These deeds are considered great from our perspective; they are ordinary for the Lord. But to the extent that we are impressed by such things, the Lord performs them, to convince us that He is not a mortal.

For example, when Lord Rama constructed a bridge to Lanka over the ocean, ordinary people might consider this action great, and they may then compare it to modern engineering marvels where humans have also constructed long bridges over the sea. But the Lord's greatness doesn't lie in the construction of the bridge; it lies in the fact that the stones from which the bridge was made were floating in the water simply by writing His name on the stones. So, people can make great bridges across the ocean, but they cannot match the greatness of the Lord who has the mystical power to have large boulders float in water simply by the power of His name. Similarly, after the bridge was constructed, the Lord gave credit to the monkeys who wrote His name and threw the boulders into the ocean. So, the Lord is not impressed by such feats.

Likewise, some people lift weights to demonstrate their strength, and we see them huffing and puffing as they lift the weights for a few moments. But Lord Kṛṣṇa held the Govardhan mountain on His little finger continuously for seven days without huffing and puffing. After He put the mountain down, He gave the credit for this lifting to the cowherd boys supporting the mountain by their cattle staffs! The Lord's greatness is not just that He performs deeds that nobody else can, but also that He is not enamored by these great acts. Any ordinary mortal would feel proud of their achievements and brag about them. But the Lord does far greater things, and yet He is not impressed by them. Therefore, the Lord's deeds should not be compared to those of the ordinary heroes; in this sūtra, the deeds of other heroes are dismissed as "just like spoons".

QUESTION

But it is sometimes said that everything great in this world is the Lord Himself. For example, in the Bhagavad-Gita, the Lord states that He is the taste of water, the light of the sun and the moon, the power in men, etc. So, doesn't this indicate that everything we consider great can be worshipped as the Lord? In effect, we would not need to chant the names or the Lord or worship His incarnations, if we only consider all such heroic greatness as the Lord Himself.

1.4.9 (115)

ज्योतिरुपक्रमा तु तथा ह्यधीयत एके

jyotirupakramā tu tathā hyadhīyata eke

jyotirupa—heavenly bodies like the sun and the moon; kramā—method or simile; tu—but; tathā—so; hi—because; adhīyata—remembering; eke—by some.

TRANSLATION

Heavenly bodies (like the sun and the moon) (are not the Lord) but it is said so because (they are) similes or methods (for) remembering by some.

COMMENTARY

The world is an expansion of the Lord and previously existed within Him. Since it has expanded from the Lord, therefore, everything is His part. However, it has been described previously that these parts are the properties or the wealth of the Lord. Certain things in the world—such as the light of the sun and the moon, or the power in men, etc.—are attributed to the Lord, not because the Lord is those things but because by thinking in this way, we can always remember the Lord. For instance, every time we drink water and relish its sweet pure taste, we can remember the Lord as that sweetness. Likewise, when we see powerful people, we can think of the Lord and consider His presence in their power. In this way, the presence of great things in this world can be a reminder of the Lord, and meditating in this way can be considered a method of remembering the Lord. However, all the powerful people, or light and water, should not be considered the Lord Himself. The use of the term *tu* (but) indicates that heavenly bodies are not the Lord. Similarly, the use of *tatha* (in this way) indicates that they are spoken of as the Lord. Finally, the use of *hi* (because) indicates that there is a reason for speaking in this way, which is then clarified using *krama* (method) and *adhīyata* (for remembering) and *eke* (by some people).

QUESTION

So, you are supporting those who think of the Lord in terms of the greatness manifest in this world, even though this greatness is not the Lord?

1.4.10 (116)

कल्पनोपदेशाच्च मध्वादिवदविरोधः

kalpanopadeśācca madhvādivadavirodhaḥ

kalpanopadeśāt—from the instruction for imagination; ca—and; madhvādivat—just like honey etc.; avirodhaḥ—no incongruity.

TRANSLATION

And from the instruction for imagination, there is no incongruity (if one consider them great), just like honey (is seen as a representation of the moon).

COMMENTARY

When someone is wealthy, we say that he has Lakshmi (the goddess of wealth). A powerful king is sometimes called Bhagavān (the Supreme Lord, who possesses everything). Fruits and vegetables are sometimes called soma or the moon because they give strength and nourishment. And fire is sometimes worshipped as the sun. This doesn't mean that coins are themselves Lakshmi, or the king is the Supreme Lord, or that fruits and vegetables are the moon, or that the fire is the sun. It only means that they have some of the qualities that are fully present in the deities. Just like biology may be called 'knowledge' although it is not knowledge itself (because there are other areas of knowledge), similarly, there are partial representations of qualities in different things, and by these qualities, we can think of the origin which has these qualities in full. The partial presence is helpful because it spiritualizes our thinking. For instance, if we call money Lakshmi, we will be careful not to waste it. We will also not be proud of owning money; we will consider it the grace of Lakshmi. So, there are many advantages in this type of thinking because it makes us treat the world around us with respect, as it has originated in the Lord. The greatness of this world can remind us of the Lord, and it is hence a method of meditation. This sūtra states that if we think of the Lord while seeing the greatness in this world—e.g., knowledge, beauty, power, wealth, fame, renunciation—there is no incongruity in such meditation, as it reminds us of the Lord's presence.

Topic 3

QUESTION

Once we start thinking of the great things in this world as deserving of our respect, we also start worshipping them. For example, even if vegetables and fruits are not the moon, by worshiping the moon we can obtain vegetables and fruits. Even if the intellect is not the sun, by worshiping the sun we can obtain intellect. Since you have indicated that all such great things are manifestations of the Lord, is it appropriate to worship all these great things themselves?

1.4.11 (117)

न संख्योपसंग्रहादपि नानाभावादतिरेकाच्च

na saṃkhyopasaṃgrahādapi nānābhāvādatirekācca

na—not; sāñkhya—the elements of Sāñkhya philosophy; upasaṃ—worship; grahād—the planets; api—even if; nānā—many; abhāvāt—on account of the absence; atirekāt—on account of doubtful excess; ca—and.

TRANSLATION

Do not worship the planets (for obtaining) the elements of Sāñkhya, even if there are many kinds of absence or if the abundance seems doubtful.

COMMENTARY

The 24 elements of Sāñkhya philosophy form our gross and subtle bodies. Due to karma delivered by the planets, which are studied in astrology, the gross and subtle bodies are hurt or benefitted. If one is undergoing difficult times in their life, astrologers often advise their clients to worship these planets for alleviating the suffering. Similarly, even if someone has abundant pleasure, due to greed, they may worship these planets to expand that pleasure. Many people think that these planets and their demigods are the causes of the various kinds of material well-being, and since these planets are the representations of the Lord by which we can think of Him, it is alright to worship these planets.

In the previous sūtra, we noted that the material world around us should be treated with respect because it is a manifestation of the Lord. However, the previous sūtra also clarified that this respect is only for our thinking about the Lord or meditation upon Him. Now, one can argue that if we are thinking of these planets as the greatness of God in this world, then why not worship these planets because they are delivering us greatness through such worship?

This sūtra clarifies this confusion by stating that these representations of greatness in the material world should not be worshipped because they are not the Lord Himself. In this regard, we can recall our previous comparison with the artist and the work of art. If we respect the artist, then we treat his works of art with respect. We may even praise the work of art, with the understanding that it has been created by the artist, and such praise reminds us of the artist through the work of art. However, we should not worship the work of art; the work of art is only a reminder of the greatness of the artist. Similarly, material nature is not to be worshipped, although it manifests the Lord's greatness.

The previous sūtra stated that there is no incongruity in treating the greatness of the material world as a representation of the Lord. But in this sūtra, the worship of the representations of greatness is rejected. We say that a cow is a mammal, but the mammal isn't a cow. The cow can help us understand the nature of the mammal, but that doesn't reduce the mammal to the cow. Similarly, everything in the world can help us understand the nature of the Lord. But all these things are not the Lord. People worship the demigods either when they are suffering or when they are greedy. Hence this sūtra notes two conditions—"due to absence" and "when abundance is doubtful"—and rejects both cases.

QUESTION

But the same type of argument could be advanced in relation to the soul and the body—if the soul is rejuvenated, then the body and the mind don't need a separate rejuvenation. However, in practice, we do feed the body and lead a healthy lifestyle, nourish the mind by knowledge and loving relationships, apart from making spiritual advancement for the soul. So, even if the demigods are subordinates to the Lord and feeding the root feed the trunks and branches, in practice, we do feed the body and mind apart from the soul. By this practical application, doesn't it entail that we can worship the demigods even with the understanding that they are for the body and mind, and not for the soul?

1.4.12 (118)

प्राणादयो वाक्यशेषात्

prāṇādayo vākyaśeṣāt

prāṇa—the vital force; adayaḥ—the origin; vāk—the sound or words; aśeṣāt—not the residue, or completely.

TRANSLATION

The prāṇa is the complete cause or origin of the sound or words.

COMMENTARY

There are several interpretive difficulties in understanding this sūtra. First, should the term *adayah* be interpreted as "the origin" or as "etc."? Second, should *vākyaśeṣāt* be dissected as *vāk* + aśeṣāt or as *vākya* + *śeṣāt*? The first dissection would mean "the complete sound" and the second dissection would mean "the statement about the residue". Accordingly, we can enumerate the following four potential translations based on the above two alternatives:

- The vital force etc. are the residue of the words
- The vital force etc. are the complete word
- The vital force is the origin of the residue of the words
- The vital force is the complete origin of the words

To choose between these translations, I will use the tripartite distinction between *manas, prāṇa,* and *vāk,* found at numerous places in the Vedic texts. The term manas represents the meaning or the mind. The term vāk represents the sound representation of this meaning or the expression of meaning into words. And prāṇa is the agency by which meaning is converted into words.

The residue of words can refer to manas rather than prāṇa. For instance, even if do not remember the exact words spoken by someone, we can remember the meanings of those words. But, if we remember the words, then we also remember the meaning. Therefore, if the words are present, then the meaning is also present. But if the words are absent, then the meanings can still be present. Therefore, the meaning is the residue of the sound. If we attach 'residue' to prāṇa, then we will produce a contradiction with ordinary experience.

Then, we can discuss whether *adayah* refers to "the origin" or "etc.". By treating *adayah* as "etc." we get "the vital force etc. are the complete word", which is patently false because the prāṇa can exist even when the words are not expressed. When the soul moves to a new body, it is carried by prāṇa, even as the gross body is left behind. The power to speak exists, but the speech doesn't exist; the prāṇa is the power by which we can speak, and the words are the outcome of that power. Therefore, we can eliminate three of the four alternatives. We are now left with: "the prāṇa is the complete origin of the words".

This translation is consistent with the distinction between manas, prāṇa, and vāk, where the power of prāṇa causes the expression of manas or meaning into vāk or words. Thus, if the prāṇa is weak, the mind may have thoughts, but we cannot speak or express our thoughts in proper words. If the prāṇa is disturbed, then we may have thoughts, but their expression would be garbled, and people won't be able to understand what we are saying. In this way, we can distinguish between prāṇa or power and vāk or the use of that power.

The tripartite distinction between manas, prāṇa, and vāk, is a generic template for constructing a hierarchy. Thus, when you hear someone speak, the sound is converted into meaning. But once you have understood what is being said, you also want to know if it is true. The judgment of truth is a deeper level of meaning, for which the meaning in the mind is the 'sound'. Then, to judge the person's intentions behind telling the truth or lying, the truth or falsity are the 'sound' and the intention or purpose behind it are the meaning. Likewise, to understand one's values from their intentions, one needs another layer of meaning; now, the intention is the word, and the value is the meaning.

The elements of Sāñkhya form a hierarchy, with many levels of meaning. Each of these levels is vāk relative to the higher level, and manas relative to the lower level of meaning. Thus, for instance, the 'meaning' of being evil expands into the 'word' that deception is justified because it is in my self-interest, and becomes a new level of meaning, which then expands into a lower level 'word' of developing an intention to cheat others, which then expands into a careful crafting of an argument that seems logical and consistent but is aimed to deceive others, this argument is then expressed into mental meanings, which are then expressed into words. At each level, there is some 'sound', which is a symbolic expression of the deeper level 'meaning'. This expansion of meaning into words is caused by prāṇa—as the power of expression. Similarly, the words are converted into deeper meanings by prāṇa—as the power of assimilation.

The hierarchy of words/meanings constitutes a tree, in which the nodes at the various levels of the hierarchy are connected to each other due to prāṇa. Owing to prāṇa, this tree expands during expression, and contracts during assimilation. If prāṇa disappears, then expression and assimilation end.

Now, with this background, we can understand the meaning of this sūtra, which is that the elements of Sāñkhya are expanded due to prāṇa. So, the greatness we see in this world is the expression, but the power underlying this greatness is prāṇa. We have previously noted that there are many kinds of prāṇa of which two are most important in this context. The first prāṇa helps the soul to reject the automatically arising desires. And the second prāṇa is used by the Paramātma to deliver the results of actions, or karma. By the first prāṇa, we can desire. But this desire cannot be fulfilled unless Paramātma uses His power. This is indicated in Bhagavad-Gita 7.8 when Lord Kṛṣṇa says that He is *pauruṣaṁ nṛṣu* or the power in men, and in 7.10 that He is *tejas tejasvinām* or the strength in the strong. So, the elements of Sāñkhya are the perceivable appearances of greatness—e.g., that someone has a sharp mind or intellect, someone has a strong and beautiful body, etc.—but, ultimately, all this is a result of Paramātma delegating His power to fulfill the desires of the jīvā. Therefore, we should not attribute the display of power to the demigods, because such attribution would be false; the real attribution is to the Lord who controls prāṇa by which karma is delivered and the person seems powerful and great.

The role of prāṇa and its control by Paramātma has been noted earlier. So, we can ask: Why is that being repeated here? The short answer is that the explicit connection between the symbols of greatness and the power that creates that symbol wasn't made earlier. Therefore, one can be confused that if someone is demonstrating power, then he must also have the power, and can be considered the greater person. The demigods are not just subordinate to the Lord, and not just displaying a part of the greatness that the Lord can display. They are rather helpless without the support of the Lord. Their only qualification is that they have good karma and they have the desire or guna to enjoy in a certain way. They don't have the power to even fulfill their own desires, so how can they fulfill our desires (if the goal of worship is to fulfill some desires)? They are mere passengers in a chariot that moves very gloriously and gives the illusion that the person sitting in the chariot is the cause of that movement when the fact is that the Lord is moving that chariot by deploying His power.

QUESTION

If the Lord is the all-powerful controller and deploys His power to create the appearance of the powerful, then why do some people worship the demigods? Shouldn't they realize that the power underlying the appearance of the powerful is owned by someone else that they cannot see in this greatness?

This is an argument from popularity: If many people accept something to be true, then it must be true. One such example is the prestige of modern science. Although there are many conceptual, logical, and experimental problems in modern science, its prestige—and wide acceptance by many people—leads to the question: If science was wrong then why would so many people accept it? The seeker here is asking the same type of question—if demigod worship is so bad, then why are so many people doing it? Shouldn't the wide prevalence of such rituals and worship indicate that there is indeed some truth in it?

1.4.13 (119)

ज्योतिषिकेषामसत्यन्ने

jyotiṣaikeṣāmasatyanne

jyotiṣ—astrology, the luminaries; ekeṣām—of some; asati—unchaste or unfaithful (wife); anne—for food.

TRANSLATION

Some unchaste or unfaithful (people) (worship) the luminaries for food.

COMMENTARY

The conjunct *asatyanne* used in this sūtra can be dissected in two ways—(1) *asatya + anne*, or (2) *asati + anne*. The former would mean "false food" or "false enjoyment", if *asatya* or falsehood is attached to food or enjoyment. This translation would indicate that the food or enjoyment is itself false or doesn't exist. It takes us toward the notion that the things that we eat, or the pleasure we enjoy in this world, aren't real. It is a short step from here to say that the world is an illusion. To avoid this conclusion, we have noted earlier that *sat* can indicate both truth and eternity. Food and pleasure are not false, although they are fleeting. So, if we use *asatya + anne*, the sūtra would translate as "some (people) worship the luminaries for temporary food (or pleasure)". This kind of resigned agreement to the actions of common people doesn't befit the speaker of the Vedānta Sūtra. Therefore, we prefer to use *asati* + *anne*, and apply the term *asati* to *ekesam*, which then means "some unchaste men".

In all legitimate worships of demigods in the Vedic system, Lord Viṣṇu is worshipped. A mound of rice may be placed at the center, and through a mantra, the presence of Lord Viṣṇu is invoked. The other demigods may be represented by mounds of rice surrounding the center, and mantras are chanted to invoke the presence of these demigods. In other cases, Lord Viṣṇu may be substituted by Lord Śiva as the controller of the material energy. In the Śrīmad Bhāgavatam, it is described that King Daksha performed a yajñá but did not deliberately make an offering to Lord Śiva to insult Him. Sati, Lord Śiva's wife, and the daughter of Daksha was present in that yajñá and pained by the humiliation of Her husband, immolated Herself. Lord Śiva then ordered the destruction of the yajñá because the demigods are never worshipped without the presence of either Lord Śiva or Lord Viṣṇu or both. In this sūtra, people who worship the demigods alone are called *asati*. This has a two-fold meaning. First, it means 'unchaste', and second, it also means someone who is unlike Sati. The term 'unchaste' indicates a wife who has a husband but desires other men. We can conclude that such offerings are never legitimate Vedic sacrifices.

Topic 4

QUESTION

I understand that most people worship the demigods to get something from them. But can't we worship them simply because they are glorious? We may not ask them for benedictions to improve our lives, and by not desiring any benefits, we can remain unselfish. But could we still worship them because they are glorious individuals, not because we want something from them?

This is a sophisticated argument for demigod worship that equates devotion to the Lord with the devotion to demigods. An impersonalist can argue that the goal of life is liberation from material existence, so there is no point in getting entangled in various types of rituals which then lead to karma and then rebirth. Therefore, worshipping demigods to get a good material life is pointless. However, to the extent that these demigods are representing the qualities of greatness in this world (even if partially), they can be worshipped as the path to liberation. In fact, one could argue that any demigod can be worshipped because there is no fundamental difference between the worship of the Lord and those of the demigods. This type of impersonalism applies the principle of *bhakti* to the demigods and states that the forms of God and demigods are equally good because we are not asking them for benedictions anyway. We are just worshipping them for their qualities, and that unselfish devotion, when applied to the demigods, is as good as when it is for the Supreme Lord.

1.4.14 (120)

कारणत्वेन चाकाशादिषु यथाव्यपदिष्टोक्तेः

kāraṇatvena cākāśādiṣu yathāvyapadiṣṭokteḥ

kāraṇatvena—as the cause; ca—and; ākāśādiṣu—the origin of space; yathā—just as; vyapa—pervading; diṣ—directions; ukteḥ—it is stated.

TRANSLATION

Just as He is the cause and origin of space, similarly, it is stated that (He) pervades in all the directions.

COMMENTARY

The previous sūtra rejected the principle of selfish worship—e.g., for obtaining food. But if someone argues that the demigods can be worshiped unselfishly, quite like we glorify the Lord for His qualities (rather than asking Him for benedictions), then the counterargument would have to say that the Lord is the creator of the qualities that we consider glorious in the demigods. Since all these glories are encompassed in the 24 elements of Sāñkhya, the Lord should be described as the creator of these elements, and hence all the greatness. This is what this sūtra does, although the meaning is not immediately evident unless we understand the precise nature of 'space', 'place' and 'direction'. So, before concluding that this sūtra refutes the unselfish bhakti to demigods, let's understand why the Lord is the creator of all the glories attributed to demigods.

The contentious term in this sūtra is *vyapadiṣ*. Readers can recall that we have translated *vyapadeśa* in three ways earlier—(a) a statement, (b) the hiding or covering of the truth, and (c) as pervading in all places. There is an important difference between *vyapadiṣ* and *vyapadeśa,* but we will return to this difference shortly. Let's apply the above three possible translations of *vyapadeśa* to this sūtra and understand the meanings that result from their application.

Suppose we say that *vyapadeśa* refers to "the hiding of the object". The sūtra will then say that "the cause or origin of space is hidden". This conclusion was noted in 1.2.14 (45): "And all the places (i.e., objects) are concealments of the real object". Suppose we say that *vyapadeśa* refers to a true statement or assertion. Then the sūtra will say that "it is stated that He is the cause or origin of space". This too was previously stated in 1.3.1 (64): "It is said that the origin and resting place of the space and the universe is His abode". This translation would also produce a duplication of meaning between *vyapadeśa* and *ukteh;* the former means "statement", and the latter "saying", and their combination would produce a meaningless repetition "statement is stated". If we apply the third meaning of "pervading in all places", then this too has is noted in 1.1.14 (14): "And because He is the cause of it (i.e., of bliss) and it is pervasive in all places". By the criterion of not duplicating claims, we reject these translations.

Now, we can note the difference between *vyapadeśa* and *vyapadiṣ*. The term *deśa* means a 'place', and the term *diṣ* indicates a 'direction'. This difference would cause no change to the first two meanings, namely, "a true statement", or "the hidden object". But it will result in a difference in the third meaning. Like *vyapadeśa* indicates "pervading in all places", *vyapadiṣ* would indicate "pervading in all directions". This is unique and has not been said before, so from a logical viewpoint, it can be acceptable. However, we may still wonder: if "all the places" are noted earlier, doesn't this include "all the directions"? The resolution to this problem is that the previous application of "all the places" in 1.1.14 (14) was in relation to the individuality that emerges from the desire for pleasure. The Lord accompanies the soul everywhere, so as the cause of all bliss, and by accompanying the soul, He can be said to be all-pervading. The term *vyapadiṣ* must, therefore, refer to something other than the soul. In this context, the only other thing that we can speak of in terms of place and direction is the material world, so *vyapadiṣ* must pertain to the 'directions' in space.

We have spoken of three kinds of spaces—universals, individuals, and relations. The universal 'cow' combines with an individual to create an individual cow. Similarly, the universal 'field' combines with an individual to create an individual field. The individual cow and the individual field are then placed in mutual relation to say that "the cow is grazing in the field". The relation between the cow and the field is established by the demigods owing to karma—the cow gets to eat the grass because of its karma. The power for delivering the karma is under the control of the Paramātma, and the demigods are subordinate departments which deliver different kinds of karma, which has been discussed previously. Therefore, the space of directions can refer either to the space of universals or of individuals (and not to the space of relations).

From a logical standpoint, we must speak about the universals before the individuals. After all, there is no sense in talking about an individual cow, if we don't know what 'cow' means. Therefore, because the individuals follow the universals, universals must be spoken of first, and this sūtra must be understood as indicating the directions of space when these pertain to the universals. Moreover, we will see the description of the individuals in the next sūtra.

Now, we can see what "pervading in all directions" means. We are speaking about a conceptual space, which is organized like an inverted tree from root to leaves. The root represents the highest-level or the most abstract concept, while the branches and leaves constitute parts of the root and the lower-level concepts. As an example, tigers and leopards belong to the cat family; the cat family belongs to mammals; the mammals belong to the animal family; and the animals are one branch of all forms of life (trees, birds, fishes, being separate). Thus, a tiger is both a lower-level concept and a part of the highest-level concept. In the tree structure, everything is both a dimension and a value—it is a dimension when we look 'downward' (from the root toward the leaves), and it is a value when we look 'upward' (from the leaves toward the root). Thus, all trunks, branches, twigs, and leaves of this tree are dimensions; it is an infinite-dimensional space because the concepts are practically infinite. The concepts of animal, mammal, and cat are present even within the tiger. So, as these branches are diversified from the root, the source becomes all-pervading. Thus, "pervading in all directions" refers to the root being present in all the leaves.

Once these universals are created, they can also be instantiated into individuals. The demigods are perfect or ideal instances of these concepts. Relative to them, lower individuals are imperfect or non-ideal instances of such concepts. However, as we saw above, before we speak about the ideal or non-ideal instance, we must speak about the concept or universal, which is then instantiated into an individual. Thus, someone can say that I created the perfect computer. But before this perfect computer was created, the idea of computing—e.g., as a Turing Machine—was theoretically constructed. Before steam locomotives were created, the theoretical model of a steam engine was produced.

The perfect instance of an idea embodies all the elements or aspects of that idea. An imperfect idea, on the other hand, implements that idea partially. So, the credit of a person who instantiates this idea perfectly lies in copying the idea completely, perfectly, and honestly. In the same way, the Lord is the creator of all the elements, and the credit of the demigods is that they are representing these elements perfectly, without removing anything or contaminating them in any way. They can be called 'pure' in this sense, but it is only an instance of the purity that was created by the Lord. Just as the disciple who perfectly repeats the words of his spiritual master can be credited for not changing the knowledge imparted by the guru, but he cannot be credited for the knowledge itself, in the same way, the Lord must get the credit for the greatness.

This sūtra says that just as the Lord is the origin, He is also the expansion in many directions. As the origin, He is the highest-level idea, and we have discussed this before—the Lord is ideas of knowledge, beauty, power, wealth, fame, and renunciation. There are many subparts of these higher-level ideas, which pervade this world. The demigods are instances of these parts. So, each demigod only embodies one type of idea, whereas the Lord embodies all the ideas together. Nevertheless, if someone was to argue that we can worship these ideas one by one, rather than all in the combined form, then this sūtra states that the Lord is not just the original idea, but the cause of all the ideas, whereas each demigod is the perfect instance of one of these ideas. Therefore, whether we want to see all these ideas in combination, or whether we want to understand them separately, their greatness only belongs to the Lord.

QUESTION

But I can only understand these great qualities by looking at their great instantiations. For example, if I have never seen an individual cow, how can understand the concept of 'cowness'? Similarly, if I have not seen cats and dogs, then how can I understand that a 'mammal' is a higher-level concept? In the same way, before I understand the highest-level idea, should I not understand lower-level ideas? How can we understand the highest-level idea if we don't gradually proceed upwards passing through all the lower-level ideas?

We can see a progression from worshiping demigods for material benefits, to worshiping demigods unselfishly because they represent some form of greatness, to now arguing helplessness to understand the Lord without worshiping the demigods, as demigod worship may be easier on our understanding.

1.4.15 (121)

समाकर्षात्

samākarṣāt

sama—similar; ākrṣāt—from the attraction.

TRANSLATION

From the attraction of the similar.

COMMENTARY

The author of Vedānta Sūtra has offered counterarguments against the worship of demigods on matters of principle—e.g., that they are not powerful, that they are not the origins of the greatness or the glory you seek, and that such worship will entangle you in the cycle of birth and death. But if someone claims that they are helpless in understanding the Supreme Lord, and find it is easier to understand the demigods, the author can at best be resigned to the seeker's tendency and say that—"similar things attract each other"—indicating that if you are expressing helplessness in understanding the Lord and find the understanding of the demigods much easier, then this attraction to the demigods cannot be justified on principle, although it can be attributed to your nature.

It is an indirect rejection of the seeker's question by saying that he is not attracted to the Lord, because if he were, then he would seek Him. If he changes his nature, then by the principle of similar things attracting each other, he would be attracted to the Lord. The process of such advancement has also been noted earlier—namely, that if you are not qualified to understand the scripture, then you can still chant the names of the Lord. In Bhagavad-Gita, Lord Kṛṣṇa states that those who worship the demigods go to the planet of the demigods. And in 1.3.31 (94), it was said that the demigods are disqualified from spiritual pursuits due to their intoxicating habits. So, the gradual upliftment from human life to the life of demigods in the onward journey toward the Lord's abode has been rejected previously. But if the seeker still expresses helplessness in pursuing the direct path, then the teacher can only express their resignation.

However, this resignation is also an indication of a path forward. The indication is that we don't have to pass through a theoretical or conceptual understanding of greatness, one step at a time. We can rather leapfrog this hierarchy and jump to the highest level—if we develop an attraction for it. Now, one can argue: How can I be attracted to something if I don't know what it is? In this argument, the intellectual understanding precedes the devotion. But even if we were to know something, the attempt at knowledge is long and difficult. How would one persist on such a path unless they had a strong desire for achieving the goal? That strong desire to know the Lord is indication of one's devotion to the Lord. If this devotion doesn't exist, then knowledge is never obtained because the seeker quickly abandons the path due to difficulties. On the other hand, if the seeker persists through the difficulties, their persistence purifies the soul of materialistic desires, and the truth is now seen uncontaminated by our desires for the truth to be something. Therefore, devotion must exist to acquire knowledge, and sincerity is essential to succeed even in the path of knowledge. Ultimately, devotion leads to persistence, purification, and knowledge. Therefore, the Absolute Truth is not known other than through pure devotion.

The claim that "similar things attract each other" needs some explanation. In this case, we are not speaking about the universals, but the individuals. Specifically, a person's individual nature attracts them to similar other things. To understand this idea better, we need to go beyond Sāñkhya, which deals with the universals and consider the Vaiśeṣika system which deals in the individuals. The individual instances of the Sāñkhya elements are called 'atoms'. For example, there is a universal called the 'element' of 'earth' which indicates a class of things, and then there are individual 'atoms' of earth, which are members of this class. In modern science, the term 'atom' and 'element' are used interchangeably—the element Hydrogen, for example, is an atom of Hydrogen. In the Vedic system, however, there is a demarcation between the atoms or individuals and the elements or the universals. This system of demarcating the universals from the individuals carried forward into Greek metaphysics, which identified four elements—Earth, Water, Fire, and Air—as 'substances', and for a while, there was no conception of atoms. Atomism was introduced in Greek philosophy by Democritus, and after that, the atoms of Earth, Water, Fire, and Air, were spoken of. The distinction between the element and the atom was however dropped in physical sciences subsequently due to the rejection of universals as materially real things. Thus, only individuals were recognized, and universals remained non-material (although theoretical) entities. This is part of the larger project to banish the reality of the mind from physical sciences.

Once we understand that the universals are different from the individuals, we need to ask: How are these individuals created? We have seen that the soul differentiates itself from Brahman due to desire. A similar principle is employed for material individuation as well; the desire is also called guna and constitutes the causal body of the soul. Based on this causal body, the subtle and gross bodies are produced by instantiating the universals into the individuals.

Thus, every atom of an element is produced due to some desire, and it is because of this desire that the elements are attracted to each other. For example, each of us has an atom of the universal element called ghrāna or the sense of smell. Similarly, there are atoms of the element earth. These two atoms are attracted to each other—if the guna or the desire in them are compatible or 'similar'. Thus, the senses of smell in different people are attracted to different kinds of smells, and this attraction is the cause of their interaction. As a result of this interaction, a sensation of smell is produced, which then fulfills the desire of smell. Whether the sense of smell deserves to interact with the objects of smell is due to karma, but whether the sense of smell will desire that smell is due to guna. Similarly, the enjoyment or suffering after interaction is due to guna.

So, to know the Lord, our past karma can bring us in contact with teachers who can impart this knowledge. There are also compassionate teachers who take the trouble to educate people who might otherwise be undeserving of this knowledge due to their bad karma. Thus, the problem of bad karma can be overcome by a teacher's compassion. However, eventually, one must have the guna or desire toward the Lord to undertake the journey of understanding. The fact is that most people are not just unfortunate to not get good teachers, but also lazy to not pursue this understanding even if the teacher is prepared. This laziness is not due to karma, but due to guna. If we have the appropriate guna, then we will be naturally attracted toward the understanding of the Absolute Truth. This is the meaning of "similar things attract each other"—we must become similar to the Lord to desire Him. This is the only goal of human life.

Topic 5

QUESTION

I understand your point about knowledge not being achievable without devotion. Since you have earlier noted that this devotion is itself developed through the chanting of the names of the Lord, I want to understand this better. Why the emphasis on chanting? Aren't there other methods for devotion such as deity worship, which have been practiced for ages in the Vedic system?

1.4.16 (122)

जगद्वाचित्वात्

jagadvācitvāt

jagat—the world, or all that is visible; vācitvāt—from the speech-like.

TRANSLATION

The world or all that has become visible is from the speech-like.

COMMENTARY

Western philosophers have argued that when we perceive the world—e.g., a red apple—then the redness, sweetness, and roundness of the apple is only in our senses and the mind. The world itself is not red, round, and sweet. It is comprised of primary properties—such as length, mass, charge, momentum, energy, etc.—which are completely unlike our sense perception. This then gives rise to the question of how these properties become sense perceptions, thoughts, judgments, intentions, morals, and desires. This problem has come to be known as the mind-body divide in Western philosophy, and so far, it has no resolution. While we can identify certain parts of the body and brain, which, when stimulated, produce sensations and thoughts, we cannot explain how the physical properties of the world are creating subjective experiences.

In Vedic philosophy, this problem is addressed by describing the world as word and meaning; the meaning is logically prior, and the word embodies this meaning and expands from that meaning. The distinction between word and meaning is a template, which recurs over several levels in a hierarchy. Thus, if the external world is words, then the senses are the meaning; if the sensations are the word, then thoughts are the meaning; if thoughts are the words, then judgments are the meaning; if judgments are the word, then the intention is the meaning; and if intentions are the word, then moral values are the meaning.

Thus, everything is treated both as a word and a meaning, depending on which tier in the hierarchy it is being spoken of. For example, when the apple is seen as red, round, and sweet, then the external world is the symbol of these ideas. These symbols are objective, and therefore red, round, and sweet is also objective—hence, you can claim that the 'apple is red' is a true statement (not merely our imagination or hallucination). However, to understand the symbol, we need an interpreter, which in this case are the senses. Therefore, the senses interact with the symbols of red, round, and sweet, and produce the sensations corresponding to these words. Thus, everything from our body to our senses, mind, intellect, ego, and moral sense are 'vibrations' that encode meanings. We have earlier discussed three broad classifications of this meaning into gross, subtle, and causal bodies, and how the soul is beyond these bodies. We can also say that the soul is the meaning of these three bodies. The soul is also a symbol whose meaning is God. God, however, is His own symbol and meaning, and the distinction between words and meanings ceases to exist within God.

This sūtra summarizes this understanding by stating that the entire *jagat* or the reality that can be perceived (by the senses, mind, intellect, etc.) is like sound. Therefore, whether we are thinking about the Lord, or whether we are doing deity worship, or whether we are chanting the Lord's names, ultimately, everything is a sound or a symbol of meaning. The Lord can be worshipped by offering Him a fruit, flower, water, or leaf (Bhagavad-Gita 9.26), and these are also symbols. Just because they are different from the words we speak and hear shouldn't confuse us about what we mean by 'sound' or *vāk*. Sometimes, *vāk* is used to just indicate the spoken word. But in the ultimate sense, everything is sound. When we hear the names of the Lord, we hear the meaning of our existence. Therefore, the chanting of the names of the Lord is the simplest *complete* method of realizing our own nature. It doesn't require regulations, unlike deity worship where cleanliness is important. One cannot do deity worship while eating, bathing, walking, or working; but one can always chant the names of the Lord during any type of activity. Therefore, the chanting is recommended. It is not a rejection of deity worship, but a preference for chanting.

QUESTION

Many people might argue that by chanting the names, and meditating on the sound, one *becomes* the meaning denoted by the sound. Thus, for example, it is argued that by chanting the mantra OM, one becomes Brahman. In the same way, by chanting the names of the Lord, does one become the Lord?

In the Vedic texts, five kinds of liberation are described, beyond the liberation of Brahman. These are called *sālokya* (on the same planet), *sārūpya* (having the same form), *sāyujya* (merger into the Lord's form), *sāmīpya* (similarity and proximity to God), and *sārsti* (having the same opulence as God). In these forms of liberation, the jīvā becomes very similar to the Lord, and because the jīvā can be like the Lord, many people confuse this with the notion that the jīvā has become the Lord. Thus, they might practice devotion to become the Lord.

1.4.17 (123)
जीवमुख्यप्राणलिङ्गान्नेति चेत् तद्व्याख्यातम्
jīvamukhyaprāṇaliṅgānneti cet tadvyākhyātam

jīva-mukhyaprāṇa-liṅgāt—from the jīvā being the master of the body of prāṇa; na—not; iti cet—if it is said; tat—that; vyākhyātam—has already been explained.

TRANSLATION

If it is said that (liberation is obtained) from the jīvā being the master of the body of prāṇa, (then) we say no, (because) that has already been explained.

COMMENTARY

Sometimes the child of a king may want to sit on the king's throne to just experience how it feels like to sit on the throne. The king is not envious of his child and allows him to sit on the throne. In the same way, sometimes the jīvā might think: "How does the Lord feel to have so much power, wealth, knowledge, beauty, fame, and renunciation?" When such a desire arises, then the Lord is kind enough to give the jīvā an understanding of His own nature, by giving him a form, power, knowledge, wealth, etc. just like He has it. But just as a child wanting to sit on his father's throne is doing so playfully, and doesn't want to displace the king, similarly, the Lord grants this position because the child is devoted to the Lord and is free from the desire to replace Him. By sitting on the king's throne, the child doesn't become the king, although he playfully pretends to be just like the king, and this playfulness between the Lord and His devotees is called liberation in the various forms. There is an implicit understanding in the child that he is not the king but is occupying the throne because the king loves his child and would give anything to him.

In the same way, the jīvā in the liberated state understands that he is acting just like the Lord, by the grace of the Lord. This sūtra states that even if one attains a position like the Lord, the real power behind the position is still under the Lord's control. This is true not only in the material universe but also in the spiritual world. Even if the jīvā occupies a position just like the Lord, there is still a difference between the jīvā and the Lord, because the jīvā is desiring and the Lord is fulfilling the jīvā's desire. This fulfillment doesn't mean that the jīvā has become the Lord. Rather, the jīvā has desired to be like the Lord, and due to his devotion, the Lord has fulfilled that desire. The greatness exhibited by the forms of the jīvā acting as the Lord cannot be attributed to the jīvā. The greatness is rather like that which is exhibited by the demigods in which the Lord fulfills the desire of the demigods based on their karma. The difference in the case of liberation is that the Lord grants such desires due to the jīvā's devotion.

So, as one chants the names of the Lord, and becomes devoted to Him, he may develop the curiosity—I can understand what the Lord is, but I want to have the first-hand experience of what the Lord feels to be the Lord. If this desire is present without envy of the Lord and is intended only playfully, the Lord can even fulfill the jīvā's desire to be just like Him. This fulfillment should not be confused with the idea that "I have become God". One should rather understand that the Lord is kind enough to fulfill my desire to be like Him, and the real power that enables this position is the power of the Lord, not mine.

QUESTION

So, what happens to a person who has no devotion to the Lord, but may have some (intellectual type of) interest in transcendence or spirituality?

1.4.18 (124)

अन्यार्थं तु जैमिनिः प्रश्नव्याख्यानाभ्यामपि चैवमेके

anyārthaṃ tu jaiminiḥ praśnavyākhyānābhyāmapi caivameke

anyārthaṃ—for another goal (different from the devotion to the Lord); tu—but; jaiminiḥ—Jaimini; praśnavyākhyānābhyām—because of the question and elucidation; api ca—moreover; evam—thus; eke—some.

TRANSLATION

Some (people), like Jaimini, with other goals (not devotion to the Lord), (believe that transcendence) can also be achieved by questions and answers.

COMMENTARY

We have discussed earlier that the Mīmāṃsā philosophers did not believe in the existence of God or demigods, although they treated the soul as an eternal entity, and considered the Vedas to be true. This truth was predicated on the claim that the instructions for the performance of rituals work. If something works, then it must be considered true, unless someone else can come up with another description of how things work. The Mīmāṃsā philosophers also believed that the meaning of each text is self-evident because the meaning is in the sound itself. The Sanskrit language in their view is not an ordinary spoken language where the connection between the word and the meaning is made largely by speaker and listener conventions. The Mīmāṃsā philosophers held that the sounds of letters in the Sanskrit language is itself meaningful. This idea has been confirmed through phonosemantic studies in languages such as English, which show that sound is itself the denotation of meaning. For example, the sound 'str' as found in words like strip, strap, street, straight, etc. denotes something thin and elongated. Empirical studies on dictionaries have classified the words based on these phonemes and found that each phoneme has a couple of different meanings, but the association between the phoneme and the meaning is not arbitrary. So, the claim is that the meaning of the text is in the sound or how it is spoken, and if we want to find the complete truth in the Vedas, then we must discover this meaning through the analysis of the sound.

But how do we find the relation between sound and meaning? Mīmāṃsā philosophers provided rules for interpreting the texts, but ultimately, the criterion for truth is practical—it must work. So, if we are confused by what something means, then we can test whether it works. The act of testing involves asking a question, and the result of that testing provides an answer. This method can be applied to the verification of ritual practices—e.g., perform them and see if you get the results. If you get the results, then you have understood the meaning of the text. Over time, as we develop a deeper understanding of texts, we can also formulate rules by which texts must be interpreted. But these rules are gleaned by the study of many texts, seeing what works, and then formulating the rules by which we can show that the meaning is indeed verifiable.

Jaimini has been quoted here because he did not believe in the existence of God, and correspondingly rejected devotion to the Lord. But he still accepted the authority of the Vedas. So, if there are people who believe in the truth of the Vedas, but don't want to devote themselves to the Lord, then they can try to glean the truth of the Vedas by linguistic analysis or empirical testing. This view is attributed to Jaimini, not explicitly endorsed by the author, nor is it rejected by the author. We can recall that at the beginning of the Vedānta Sūtra, the scriptures were described as the source of knowledge, and reason and observation (as methods of discovery) were rejected. But we also noted that scriptures are open to rational analysis and empirical confirmation, and anyone who asks questions and seeks answers should not be considered faithless if they are prepared to accept the source of knowledge. The Mīmāṃsā philosopher is one who considers the Vedas to be true, and yet not spoken by the Lord. In one sense, he has faith in the scripture, and yet, he doesn't have faith in the Lord speaking it. The knowledge of Absolute Truth is therefore in the Vedas, although this truth is not provided by a person. If you reject the existence of a person, then you are left with impersonal semantics and you can analyze these meanings by asking questions and answers until you think you have arrived at the truth.

It is sometimes said that Bhagavān takes many forms, and the books about Him are also representations of His person. So, if one has faith in the book, but doesn't consider these books a 'revelation' by the Lord, then he can simply study the books, analyze their meanings, and test their truth. This is a scientific literary-semantic analysis to obtain an understanding of the Absolute Truth. Indologists also carry out such study of Vedic texts. However, they do not believe that these texts are true. They don't make an attempt to understand the descriptions as they are found across different texts—instead of accepting that the same knowledge is presented in different ways in different texts, they claim that this knowledge has evolved over time, and they try to date these texts. If the truth of these texts is not accepted, they are never put into practice or tested. They simply remain things of historical and archeological interest. Such study of texts is, therefore, worse than the Mīmāṃsā approach, which accepts the texts as true, tries to understand their meaning, and puts them into practice.

Topic 6

QUESTION

But we have discussed that the different Vedic texts may not always be consistent, or one text may not provide the complete information about a subject. How does one deal with the problem of inconsistency (of various texts) and the incompleteness (of individual texts) to obtain complete truth?

1.4.19 (125)
वाक्यान्वयात्
vākyānvayāt

vākya-anvayāt—from the logical connection of passages.

TRANSLATION

(Vedic texts should be understood) from their logical connections.

COMMENTARY

This sūtra should be understood as indicating that the different Vedic texts are not contradictory, although each text may be individually incomplete. The differences between the texts may be due to the differences in the questions of the seekers—as in the previous sūtra the phrase 'question-and-answer' was employed. They may be different based on the context of the presentation, the place, or the time. If we do not find the complete truth in one place, then we can consult other texts. But as we consult other texts, we may start coming across differences or contradictions. And yet, these differences are still logically connected because they are answers in response to different questions. The truth lies in the reconciliation of these apparently contradictory claims. In the beginning of the Vedānta Sūtra, it was discussed that the Vedic texts are contradictory, and it was advised that we should consider only those parts of the texts which are pertaining to transcendence (and neglect others). It was also said that the Absolute Truth is that which reconciles the diversity, whereupon that unification was described, and faith in that Absolute Truth led to liberation. If, however, one wants to return to the study of the texts, without explicit devotion to the Lord, this sūtra states that you must now study the texts in a way that the inconsistency and incompleteness of individual texts is resolved. In short, if you see an inconsistency, understand that a deeper level of truth will reconcile this conflict. And if you find something incomplete, look at other texts until you find the corresponding information that completes it. The texts are logically connected to each other, so they must also be understood collectively.

QUESTION

But how will we know that we have obtained the truth by this study?

A standard problem in all empirical and rational approaches to knowledge is that we never know if we have obtained the complete truth. Even if our knowledge works in many cases, we don't know if it will work in all the cases. Owing to this fact, the empirical and rational methods are known to be forever incomplete—the ideas can be falsified in the future, but they cannot be confirmed to be true (as potential falsifiability always exists). Similarly, if we take to analyzing texts and understanding their meaning, what is the guarantee that we have obtained the complete truth? Isn't it entirely possible that what we know now may be an incomplete understanding, which could be updated later?

1.4.20 (126)

प्रतिज्ञासिद्धेर्लिङ्गमाश्मरथ्यः

pratijñāsiddherliṅgamāśmarathyaḥ

pratijñā—knowledge of everything, or certain knowledge; siddheḥ—on the fulfillment; liṅgam—indicatory mark; āśmarathyaḥ—Āsmarathya.

TRANSLATION

On knowing everything indicatory marks (appear), (says) Āsmarathya.

COMMENTARY

The term *pratijñā* has many meanings. In the simplest form, it should be considered as a 'promise'. But if we dissect *pratijñā* = *prati* + *jñā*, *prati* can mean 'toward' or 'in relation to' such as in *pratispardhā* or competition. And sometimes, *pratijñā* is also used to indicate 'certain knowledge'. For instance, in Bhagavad-Gita 9.31, Lord Kṛṣṇa says to Arjuna: *kaunteya pratijānīhi na me bhaktaḥ praṇaśyati* which means "O son of Kunti, know with certainty that my devotee is never vanquished". The interpretation of *pratijñā* as 'promise' is inappropriate in this context because the sūtra would be translated as "on fulfillment of the promise indicatory marks are visible" and no promise has been referred to thus far. It is possible to translate *prati* as "in relation to knowledge" or "toward knowledge", but the sūtra would then be translated as "as one approaches knowledge or tries to learn, indicatory marks appear". This translation is consistent with Sanskrit, but such a claim has no confirmation in the Vedic texts. Therefore, I have preferred to translate *pratijñā* as "certain knowledge".

This sūtra sidesteps traditional methods of knowledge by empirical and rational methods—which seek confirmation in the external world. It states that the confirmation lies in the knower, and when certain knowledge is attained, the indicatory marks appear in the knower. What are these marks? They are not described in this sūtra, but it is assumed that the listener already knows.

The basic indicatory mark of knowledge is freedom from fear and hope—resulting in detachment. This is an emotional state, rather than an intellectual state. If we are not sure that our knowledge is true, then there will be fear in the heart—we are unsure if something is true and could be falsified later. On the other hand, if it has been falsified, then we search for truth under the hope that it will be confirmed. But even if it is confirmed, the fear remains because it could be falsified in the future. Thus, one oscillates between fear and hope—the hope arises from the excitement that we may find the full truth and the fear from the despair that we may not find the full truth, and whatever seems true right now may be demonstrated to be false at a later time. However, this sūtra states that if truth has been obtained, then these hopes and fears will be destroyed. This confirmation is not based on empirical and rational demonstrations. Rather, when the truth has been obtained, a new emotional state of peace, satisfaction, contentment, along with freedom from fear and hope is established.

So, even though the Mīmāṃsā philosophers are not devotees, they are not complete materialists either. They understand that the purpose of knowledge is freedom from the suffering in this world, caused by hope leading to hard work, which then becomes futile, leading to despair, and the seeker then goes in search of another truth under hope. If one wants to be free from the cycle of hope and fear—which we can call 'liberation' or 'salvation'—then the symptoms of knowledge must appear in us rather than in empirical confirmation in the external world, or rational agreement through argument and discussion. It is an introspective view of the knowledge by which one obtains salvation.

QUESTION

If we allow this intrinsic confirmation of the truth, then everyone will likely pretend or claim to know the truth. They might feign contentment, satisfaction, etc. How can one know that this method will naturally lead to the truth?

1.4.21 (127)

उत्क्रमिष्यत एवंभावादित्यौडुलोमिः

utkramiṣyata evaṃbhāvādityauḍulomiḥ

utkram—automatically arising or springing; iṣyataḥ—desires; evaṃ bhāvāt—such emotional states; iti—thus; auḍulomiḥ—(the sage) Audulomi.

TRANSLATION

Such emotional states (e.g., of contentment, satisfaction) automatically arise like desires (are automatically created), thus says the sage Audulomi.

COMMENTARY

The term *utkramiṣyataḥ* is significant in this sūtra. The meaning of *utkram* is random, unpredictable, impulsive, etc. The meaning of *iṣyataḥ* is desires. The sūtra states that just like desires automatically arise in the heart, similarly, the symptoms of having perfect knowledge—namely, the emotional states of contentment and satisfaction also arise automatically. So, there is a difference between a person feigning the satisfaction, and the person in whom these arise automatically. The difference is that the pretender tries to look contented, while the person who has truly attained the knowledge is naturally contented. Those who feign such contentment, however, cannot always remain satisfied. They will eventually become dissatisfied, which would be seen in their pursuits.

Spiritual advancement is different from mental or intellectual development because when something is known mentally or intellectually, it doesn't exist permanently. We keep forgetting it, and then we must keep reminding ourselves about its truth. However, when something has been perfectly realized, then the soul never forgets about it and doesn't need to be reminded of its truth. All doubts are therefore destroyed by the perfect realization. And thereafter, the recollection of knowledge automatically springs in the heart. Therefore, in the Bhakti-rasāmṛta-sindhu (1.2.234) we find the following statement:

ataḥ śrī-kṛṣṇa-nāmādi
na bhaved grāhyam indriyaiḥ
sevonmukhe hi jihvādau
svayam eva sphuraty adaḥ

> Therefore, the names etc. of Śri Kṛṣṇa cannot be grasped by the senses. But certainly, as one becomes inclined to serve with the tongue, these (i.e., the names etc.) automatically spring.

The relevant term here is *sphurati* which means springing forth with a quivering, vibration, etc. A similar term *utkram* is used here, which indicates automatically arising or springing without an effort, and the comparison to desires is drawn, indicating that the springing forth is just like the arising of desires. The main point is that as we start the process of learning, we try to understand and assimilate the knowledge, and we need to constantly remind ourselves of its truth. But, as one reaches perfection, the truth automatically springs in the heart. The knowledge is innate in the soul, but the soul must be awakened. Like a diamond when polished naturally starts shining, similarly, when the soul is purified of the contamination of ignorance, it becomes a spout of truth.

QUESTION

But how can someone—who hasn't reached such a state—know if a person claiming to have reached such a state has indeed attained perfection in knowledge? Many teachers may look peaceful and content, but it is not clear if that is just an acquired habit, or deceitful presentation, or something that is deeply internal, which is springing forth naturally and automatically. In short, how can someone distinguish between a realized soul and a charlatan?

1.4.22 (128)
अवस्थितेरिति काशकृत्स्नः
avasthiteriti kāśakṛtsnaḥ

avasthiteḥ—firm, fixed; iti—thus; kāśakṛtsnaḥ—Kāśakritsna.

TRANSLATION

Because they are firm and fixed, so says Kāśakritsna.

COMMENTARY

A similar question was asked previously in the context of the selection of a guru but that was in the context of knowing whether a person has become a devotee of the Lord. The answer to that question was that a self-realized person can be known from his words; these words are not merely flowery speech, but something that will transform your life by germinating the seed of God's love in the heart. In this sūtra, we are not speaking about the devotees of the Lord. We are rather considering those people who study the scriptures and analyze their meaning. Their conviction is naturally much less than those of the devotees because the happiness, contentment, and conviction in a devotee are much higher. However, even those who don't have an infallible conviction can still be highly convinced. Their words may not convince others, but we can see that at least they are themselves fixed in their pursuit and path. When the understanding reaches a point of maturity, a person will not fall back into the states of ignorance indicated by fear and hope. Such a person is technically said to be situated in the mode of undeviating *sattva-guna* or the mode of goodness. He may not have an experiential vision, but he has progressed in his knowledge to a point where he is fully convinced of its truth and will never deviate.

Topic 7

QUESTION

But it is hard to detect if someone is going to deviate. So many times, we trust a person who seems fixed in their knowledge, but we eventually find that they have deviated. Isn't there a better criterion for judging such a person?

1.4.23 (129)

प्रकृतिश्च प्रतिज्ञादृष्टान्तानुपरोधात्

prakṛtiśca pratijñādṛṣṭāntānuparodhāt

prakṛtiḥ—material nature; ca—also; pratijñā—full knowledge; dṛṣṭānta—illustration; anuparodhāt—not injuring or being contradictory.

TRANSLATION

(They) also have full knowledge of the material nature and can illustrate and demonstrate it (for you) without producing any contradiction.

COMMENTARY

Most of us tend to think that a person advanced in religion knows about the transcendental world. Since we don't have direct experience of that world, many people are frequently cheated in the process, as they start trusting a person who fakes their advancement. While there are methods to detect such impersonation, such as checking if a person is fixed in the path or not, or whether they display symptoms of inner bliss, or whether their words are transforming our lives, many of these are subject to deception as well. This sūtra, therefore, guides the seeker to check a claimant's understanding of the material world. This is not to say that one who has perfect knowledge of the material world would necessarily have a perfect understanding of the spiritual world as well. It is to say that one who understands the spiritual world will also understand the material world. Therefore, material knowledge doesn't entail spiritual knowledge. But spiritual knowledge entails perfect material knowledge.

This criterion can be applied both to individuals and to religious systems. Anyone who claims to be spiritually advanced but cannot explain the material world is a pretender. Similarly, any religion that cannot explain the material world, or provides false explanations, should be rejected. So, this sūtra is prescribing a sniff test, in which one doesn't have to accept a religion as indicating the truth if they do not have a full understanding of the material world.

QUESTION

But how can the perfection of knowledge of the material world be related to the understanding of the transcendental world? We have spoken of how the material world reflects the Lord, like a painting is expressed by an artist. We also spoke of how the Lord incarnates in this world. We have spoken about the Universal Form of the Lord as something suitable for meditation. But all these were meant to glean the understanding of the Lord from material nature, not indicate expertise in the study of material nature. Now you are saying that a spiritualist is also advanced in material knowledge and that this expertise is a test of their advancement. How do we reconcile these varying viewpoints?

1.4.24 (130)

अभिध्योपदेशाच्च

abhidhyopadeśācca

abhidhya—longing for; upadeśāt—on account of the teaching; ca—also.

TRANSLATION

The teaching (of the material world) also leads to longing for (the Lord).

COMMENTARY

The study of material nature through modern science has made many people atheists. But science is itself deeply flawed. First, there is no explanation of perception, or how we experience color, taste, smell, touch, etc. which arises because modern science draws a distinction between the physical properties and the perceived qualities. Second, if such qualities are rejected, then the concepts are also rejected; in fact, both sensations and concepts are merely in the mind, and therefore unreal, and hence meanings become unreal. If meanings cannot be understood, then how can science explain the existence of meaningful objects—e.g., books, music, works of art, or even claim the possibility of knowledge—which is always expressed through symbols of meaning?

Third, if we cannot understand meanings, then how will we judge? These judgments come to us in three ways—like truth, right, and good. The existence of a sentence doesn't tell us its truth (in modern science truth is judged by existence). So, even truth cannot be judged without meanings. Then, we also incorporate judgments of good (e.g., what is pleasing or displeasing) and right (i.e., something that is my duty or not, based upon my roles and responsibilities). If we cannot judge the truth, then the judgments of right and good are also excluded. Therefore, we can never formulate laws of choice and consequence, because we fundamentally don't have a conception of right and good. No action can be called right or wrong because it is just the motion of particles. Likewise, no such motion can be good or bad, because we cannot explain the difference between enjoyment and suffering based upon such particle motions.

The atheism of modern science is founded on ignorance. It is not just ignorance about the soul and God. It is also the ignorance about sense perception, the understanding of meaning, and the abilities to judge truth, right, and good. The real understanding of nature is that which allows us to incorporate sensations, meanings, and judgments of truth, right, and good. On the other hand, if sensations, meanings, and judgments are understood, then we can understand choices, and how the choices should ideally be made (because the non-ideal choices reduce the freedom to make choices). That scientific understanding of reality would not be contrary to the existence of the soul and God.

The Bhagavad-Gita states that the process by which the body changes at death is the same as the process by which it is changing right now. So, the body is not 'growing' (from childhood to youth) and not 'declining' (from youth to old age). Rather, the connection between the soul and the body is changing every moment. Just as one can wear different clothes, and then abandon them, similarly, the change of the body is the soul picking different kinds of clothes. Thus, the change of body must be described as the selection of a dress, rather than one dress evolving into another dress. If you remove the shirt and pants and wear denim and t-shirts, the shirt and pants haven't evolved into denim and t-shirt. Rather, the person has changed his clothes. This view of change entails that the wardrobe of clothes preexists the selection of a dress. The clothes are not created or destroyed. Rather, when something is worn, it is visible, and when it is removed, it goes back into the wardrobe and remains invisible. Even this invisible piece of clothing, however, exists as a *possibility*. What we call 'matter' is, therefore, a possibility hidden in a wardrobe. The laws of science should be able to describe how this possibility becomes an experience.

The key point is that theism is not a superimposition of the ideas of the soul and God on the unchanged substrate of atheistic scientific ideas. Rather, theism entails a change to all scientific notions about the nature of matter, causality, and laws. If the paradigm of change is the motion of billiard balls, then the laws of nature are deterministic. But if the paradigm of change is wearing and discarding of clothes, then the causality of this change will involve many new ideas—e.g., that we desire certain clothes and we deserve certain clothes. This desiring and deserving leads to the selection of some clothes, and the laws of nature should explain how this causal mechanism of desiring and deserving evolves. This kind of description, in turn, requires us to introduce several things that have been left out of modern science—from perception to concepts to judgments of truth, right, and good—and the laws of nature would now be based on these judgments. For instance, the right action leads to happiness, and the wrong action leads to suffering. To define right and wrong, we must have a 'role' in addition to a body, and to define good and bad, we must introduce an individual whose desires result in the experience of pleasure and pain.

Meanings necessitate a change in our conceptions about space—from a box to a tree. The conversion of meanings into things requires a distinction between universals and individuals. Their combination enters roles, which define right and wrong. If we understand that the cycle of birth and death is due to our right and wrong actions, then we can speak of transcendence. Once we understand that our suffering or enjoyment is dependent on the demigods delivering the results of our past actions—under the supervision of the Paramātma—then we can see that nature is administered by personalities and it is not impersonal. With the foundations of personalism, we can speak about transcendental persons, who are not compelled to change their dress due to natural laws.

Thus, material knowledge doesn't lead to atheism. Modern science is atheistic because it is false. It studies parts of our experience and neglects the senses, mind, intellect, happiness, and the relation between choice and consequence. Based on a limited investigation, it formulates a false understanding of space, time, causality, and laws of nature. And due to its economic power arising from modern technology, it pushes atheism by destroying all dissenting voices. If these ideas are corrected, then the knowledge of the material world would naturally lead to the understanding of the Supreme Person beyond this world.

This viewpoint is confirmed in this sūtra by stating that the understanding of material nature leads to a longing for the Lord. In numerous Vedic texts, such as the Śrīmad Bhāgavatam, and other Purāna, the material world and the cosmic structure are described alongside the devotion to the Lord. Thus, the idea that knowledge of the material world is opposed to transcendental understanding is false. A true understanding of matter leads to devotion to God.

QUESTION

If the study of scriptures without devotion leads to devotion, then can the reverse be said—i.e., that those who are devotees, also understand the material world (even if they have not spent extensive efforts in the scriptural study)?

1.4.25 (131)

साक्षाच्चोभयाम्नानात्

sākṣāccobhayāmnānāt

sākṣāt—direct; ca—and; ubhayām—both; nānāt—the diversities.

TRANSLATION

(The devotees) obtain direct experience of both (spiritual and material worlds) and the many kinds of diversities (present in these kinds of worlds).

COMMENTARY

The term *sākṣāt* indicates 'directly'. It is different from *pratyakṣa* which means phenomena. The meaning of *sākṣāt* is the understanding of reality as it is different from phenomena. All phenomena are mediated by the senses, mind, intellect, etc. But *sākṣāt* indicates perception by the soul or knowing things as they are. The term *ubhayām* indicates both the material and the spiritual worlds, and along with *sākṣāt* it means the direct (and unmediated by the senses, mind, or the intellect) perception of both material and spiritual reality. Finally, the term *nānāt* indicates that both material and spiritual worlds are diverse. The impersonalist believes that the material world is diverse, but the spiritual reality must be undivided. This is a wrong understanding as indicated in this sūtra. The existence of unity doesn't imply the absence of diversity. The Lord is the unity and the different parts expanded from this unity are the diversity. If one has understood the unity, then the nature of the diversity is also understood because we can see that the unity has a form of knowledge, beauty, fame, wealth, power, and renunciation; the unity also has a desire and the capacity for relationships. Due to His desire, the unity expands into diversity, His qualities are divided into their parts, and He relates to all these parts.

The study of diversity perplexes us about the nature of unity—we wonder how all this diversity can expand from one thing. And a naïve and simplistic view of this unity is that all the diversity must be destroyed when the unity is attained. The correct understanding is that all this diversity exists within the unity; the unity is knowledge, and the diversity is the many kinds of knowledge; the unity is beauty, and the diversity is the many types of beauty. It is not easy to understand unity since it is comprised of all contradictory qualities. But if one can understand the unity, then the understanding of the diversity is automatic. Therefore, one who has understood the Supreme Lord understands both material and spiritual diversity manifested from the Lord.

QUESTION

You have mentioned that the devotees know both the spiritual and the material worlds. What is their understanding of how these are produced?

1.4.26 (132)

आत्मकृतेःपरिणामात्

ātmakṛteḥ pariṇāmāt

ātmakṛteḥ—done by the self, on the self; pariṇāmāt—as results.

TRANSLATION

(The worlds are produced) as the results of the Self acting on the Self.

COMMENTARY

The Absolute Truth is the combination of two things—the will and the power to fulfill that will. If He was only will, He could desire, but those desires would never be fulfilled without the power. If He was only power, it will lie inert, and never produce anything, because there is no will to use the power. These two aspects of the Absolute Truth—namely, will and the power—are identified as masculine and feminine aspects of the same reality. The will is called Puruṣa and the power is called Śakti. These are two aspects of the same reality, and yet they are neither separable nor are they identical. They are simply two complementary ways of understanding the Absolute Truth.

When there is power, the possessor of the power is enticed to use it, and that enticement is will. The presence of power thus creates the will. And once the will is created, then the power which produced the will is used by the will. Thus, the feminine aspect of the Absolute Truth agitates the masculine aspect to create a will in the masculine aspect. The masculine aspect then uses the feminine aspect as its power to fulfill the will. The feminine aspect is both the cause of the creation of the will and the agency that fulfills the will. And yet, because the power serves under the control of the will, the masculine is said to be superior. Factually, these considerations about which is superior to the other are pointless. The feminine is superior because She agitates the masculine. And the masculine is superior because He uses the feminine to fulfill His desires.

The term ātmakṛteḥ or Self acting on the Self refers to this dynamic between the two aspects of the Absolute Truth. When the feminine Self agitates the masculine Self, She acts on Him to create a desire. Then, when the masculine Self is agitated, He uses the feminine Self to fulfill that desire. The fulfillment of the desire produces pleasure, and the creation is the process by which the desire is fulfilled. The fulfillment of desire requires the combination of will and power, and the combination creates the world as a byproduct, as indicated by the term *pariṇāmāt*. Thus, two aspects of the Absolute Truth, which are inseparable, act upon each other as if they were separate. Then they unite to produce an effect, which becomes the agency by which enjoyment is produced. This separation and union of the two aspects of the Absolute Truth produce the world as a result. The situation is loosely compared to the mating of a male and a female, who then produce a child as a result. The creation is the child of this Absolute Truth because it has expanded out of the Absolute Truth. However, this creation was previously within the Absolute Truth, so even though it has emerged from the Absolute Truth, it remains a part of that Absolute Truth. This is unlike the products of worldly sexual activity, in which the children are separated from their parents. Therefore, the divine masculine-feminine intercourse should not be confused with the materialistic male-female sexual activity.

This process can also be understood as the interaction between possibility and choice. If you go to a shopping mall, and you see some goods to buy, you naturally get the desire to buy them. The goods exist as a possibility for enjoyment, and they create a desire in the buyer to procure these goods. But as soon as this desire is fulfilled, the desire automatically expands to explore more possibilities. With the expansion of desire, the possibility also expands, which then leads to more desire, more possibility, and the process continues indefinitely. The initial cause of the desire is the feminine, which entices the masculine with a desire. But once that desire has been triggered, it not only seeks the feminine but also expands in new ways, which then causes the feminine to expand. In an earlier sūtra, it was noted that the cause of the One becoming many is a desire for pleasure. This sūtra develops that understanding and states that the many are produced due to the expansion of the One when It acts upon Itself.

In the case of the material creation, the desire is triggered by the feminine energy of the Lord, and the Lord then enjoys with this energy. But after a long period, the desire for enjoyment contracts, and the feminine energy also contracts accordingly, until the entire creation collapses back into the Absolute Truth. In this collapsed state, there is the potential for desire, and the potential to fulfill that desire, but both potentials remain dormant. They are activated again when the desire is produced, and the universe expands again. This expansion and contraction produce a cyclic change of creation, sustenance, and annihilation of the material universes, and while the Absolute Truth is eternal, the manifest universes are temporary. The material world is therefore sometimes considered non-different from the Absolute Truth, and sometimes called an illusion. In the case of the spiritual world, the desire for enjoyment never contracts, and the masculine never disengages with the feminine, and the feminine never stops agitating the masculine. The spiritual world is thus eternal, and unlike the material creation, it is neither created nor annihilated. Owing to this, the spiritual world is always described as being non-different from the Absolute Truth, and never termed as an illusion (like the material universe).

QUESTION

If the creation is the result of the separation and union of the masculine and feminine aspects of the Absolute Truth, then what is the nature of the soul? Should the soul be described as masculine desire, or the feminine power to fulfill the desire? Is the soul known as the enjoyer puruṣa or the enjoyed śakti?

1.4.27 (133)

योनिश्च हि गीयते

yoniśca hi gīyate

yoniḥ—the feminine; ca—and; hi—because; gīyate—sings in praise.

TRANSLATION

(The soul) is also feminine because (she) sings in praise (of the Lord).

COMMENTARY

In an earlier sūtra, it was stated that the Lord is the *linga* or the masculine genital that injects the soul into material nature; from that claim we would tend to think that the soul is part of the masculine but gets injected in the feminine. In this sūtra, the soul is described as feminine because she is devoted to the Lord. By that devotion, the soul attracts the Lord, and the Lord then uses the soul for His pleasure, and the soul enjoys being used for the Lord's pleasure. These two sūtras create confusion—is the soul masculine or feminine?

The answer to this question lies in the process by which the masculine and the feminine expand. As we have noted in the purport of the last sūtra, the feminine agitates the masculine to produce a desire in the masculine. The soul is this agitation in the masculine and is created as a desire in Him. But this desire enters the feminine, and the desire to enjoy in the masculine becomes the desire to fulfill the desire in the feminine. The entry of the masculine's desire into the feminine is called the masculine injecting the feminine with His 'seed' or *bīja*. This 'seed' is the soul. In a simple sense, the masculine is the father and the feminine is the mother. And the soul produced out of their interaction is neither the mother nor the father. The soul is not the father, because it cannot create more children. And the soul is not the mother because the soul cannot agitate the masculine to create more children. Therefore, before we answer the question of whether the soul is masculine and feminine, we must understand that the soul is neither the mother nor the father. And yet, because the soul originates in the masculine, he is sometimes called masculine. Similarly, since the soul is the desire to fulfill the masculine as part of the mother, so she is feminine.

Even though the soul originates in the father, it cannot become the enjoyer of the mother, imagining that it was created as the desire to enjoy with the mother. Likewise, even though the soul enters the mother with the desire to fulfill the masculine, the soul is not the mother to enjoy with the father.

Therefore, in one sense, the soul is both masculine and feminine—the soul originates as the desire in the masculine and enters the feminine to fulfill that desire. And yet, in another sense, the soul is neither the father nor the mother. So, even if the soul takes a male or female form, it is incapable of creating a soul—which the real father and mother are. Finally, even after the soul is created as a desire, it has no capacity to fulfill the desire. Since the soul cannot fulfill its own desires, therefore, it must serve the masculine's desires, as part of the feminine. If the soul accepts this position, then it becomes the enjoyer who enjoys by fulfilling the feminine who is trying to fulfill the masculine. Thus, by serving the feminine in this way, the soul is satisfied, the feminine is satisfied, and the masculine is satisfied. The satisfaction of the masculine fulfills the purpose of the soul's existence because the original desire is being fulfilled.

The separation of the soul from the masculine doesn't entail that the soul is an independent enjoyer. However, when the soul develops the illusion of being an enjoyer—as a father or a mother—then it falls into the material world. Even in this world, the soul cannot fulfill its own desires. But the soul develops the illusion that the real father doesn't exist, and therefore an incestuous relation to the mother is possible. The mother is not interested in incest. Therefore, she treats the soul as Her child, and this makes the soul very angry and frustrated. The soul tries to obtain power over material nature, trying to impress the mother to be its consort. But all such attempts are always frustrated, because the mother always steals this power and makes the soul a helpless child.

Topic 8

QUESTION

The description of the Absolute Truth as will and the power to fulfill

that will—which you have called masculine and feminine—explains how the Absolute Truth is simultaneously one and yet expands into many by its action upon itself. I can now understand how the One becomes many due to desire for pleasure, and how the soul is simultaneously a part of the masculine and yet considered feminine. Is this the supreme understanding of the Absolute Truth?

1.4.28 (134)

एतेन सर्वे व्याख्याता व्याख्याताः

etena sarve vyākhyātā vyākhyātāḥ

etena—thus; sarve—all; vyākhyātā—explainer; vyākhyātāḥ—explains.

TRANSLATION

In this way, the explainer explains everything.

COMMENTARY

Here, the term *vyākhyātā* or the explainer should be understood as the Supreme Lord, and the *vyākhyātāḥ* or the explanation should be understood as the expansion from the Supreme Lord. The explanation is the combination of the Lord's will and His power, so the explanation is both masculine and feminine. However, this explanation is the manifestation by the Absolute Truth acting upon itself. The Vedas are said to be the Lord's speech, and the material manifestation has been called His 'expression'. So, why does the Lord speak, and why does He expand from One to many? The answer is that He as the explainer explains Himself, and that explanation is the manifest world. The explanation has expanded from the explainer, and it describes the explainer. The explainer is the cause, and the explanation is the effect, but the effect describes or explains the cause. So, by this explanation, we can understand the explainer, provided it is understood that the explanation came from an explainer.

If one begins with the explainer, then one can easily understand the explanation. But even if one begins with the explanation, one can find the explainer, because the explanation is about the explainer. So, the explanation and the explainer are not identical, and yet, one can be known from the other. The explanation of everything is that the Absolute Truth is One but has masculine and feminine aspects; the masculine is the will, and the feminine is the power to satisfy that will. The power and the powerful cannot be separated, and yet they are also distinct. By this distinction, the Absolute Truth acts upon Itself and the One becomes many. The simultaneous unity and the distinctness of the masculine and feminine principles is the explanation of all other explanations.

The many interpretations of Vedānta Sūtra, such as Advaita, Dvaita, Viśiṣṭādvaita, Bhedābheda, etc. all deal with the relation between the soul and God. The Advaita system says that the soul and God are identical. The Viśiṣṭādvaita school states that diversity is part of the unity. The Dvaita system states that the Lord and the soul are distinct. The Bhedābheda system says that the soul is separate from the Lord but also dependent on the Lord; due to this dependence, it cannot be considered separate (i.e., independent); and yet because the soul is not identical to the Lord, therefore they are separate.

All these interpretations take off from the fundamental problem that Śri Śankarācārya created by identifying the soul with Brahman; this is a problem because we could not explain how that One divides into many. The impersonal doctrine that māyā covers the soul has been explicitly rejected above because the Self acts upon the Self. It is not māyā that is acting upon the soul. It is rather the desire in the soul, which māyā fulfills. Therefore, māyā is not responsible for the soul's fall into matter. It is rather the soul who desires the fall, and māyā fulfills it. For the soul to have a desire, it must have personality. The fall into māyā entails the preexistence of a person, and if there is a preexisting person, then how individuality was produced from Oneness becomes a problem. The personalist interpretations of Vedānta Sūtra are a solution to that problem.

Śri Chaitanya's philosophy differs from all previous Ācāryas in one significant respect—it is not preoccupied with the relation between the soul and God. It is rather preoccupied with the nature of the Absolute Truth as comprised of masculine and feminine aspects, which are simultaneously different and yet inseparable. This description of the oneness and difference in the Absolute Truth is called Acintyabhedābheda. The non-difference in Bhedābheda is about the relation between soul and God, and not the aspects of the Absolute Truth.

This grand shift in Vedānta is not understood if Acintyabhedābheda is presented as the relation between the soul and God when it is the relation between the two aspects of the Absolute Truth. The addition of inconceivability to the preexisting doctrine of Bhedābheda doesn't produce new clarity; in fact, it leads to more confusion—if it is inconceivable, then how do we understand it, and how can something inconceivable be considered a view on Vedānta Sūtra which is supposed to be clarifying the nature of reality through logic?

To understand Śri Chaitanya's philosophy, we need to sidestep the relation between the soul and God, and look at the Purāna, Itihāsa, and Tantra scriptures, where there are pervasive descriptions of couples, such as Lakshmi-Nārāyana, Sita-Rama, Radha-Kṛṣṇa, Śakti-Śiva, etc. They are one, and yet they are different. The soul is always subordinate to these couples, and emphasis should, therefore, be laid on the understanding of these couples rather than the relation between the soul and the Lord. The doctrine of Acintyabhedābheda pertains to the unity and distinction in the couple, rather than to the relation between God and the soul. Once this type of Bhedābheda is understood, then the relation between the soul and God is automatically clarified as a corollary. The soul originates in the father, so he is part of the father, but then the soul becomes part of the mother, and hence separate from the father. But since the mother is inseparable from the father, the soul is not totally detached from the father. And yet, he is also not identical to the father. So, a new kind of Bhedābheda doctrine related to the soul results from the focus on the Bhedābheda in the Divine Couple. This understanding of Vedānta Sūtra dissolves the distinction between śrutī and smriti. Whereas in śrutī that One Absolute Truth is emphasized, in the smriti the same Absolute Truth is described as comprising of two inseparable aspects. The Vedānta Sūtra, when understood in this way, becomes the doctrine of unity across diverse Vedic scriptures.

CHAPTER 2

Having undertaken an overview of the summary of the Vedas, this chapter starts addressing many common philosophical objections to these descriptions. These include the discussion of the problem of evil, the cause of the soul's fall in the world, how the soul creates karma by choosing evil over good, and how these choices arise due to the envious nature of the soul. The simultaneous existence of good and evil entails that classical logic is inadequate to understand the Absolute Truth, but when they are combined in the Lord, they enhance the sweetness of His nature, which is then relished by the Lord's devotees.

Section 1: This section discusses the nature of the soul, why the soul falls into the material world, how the responsibility of the fall rests on the soul (rather than the Lord), and yet despite this fall, the soul's original purpose of serving the Lord is never lost even when the soul is fallen. The connection between the soul and the Lord comes up yet again. Especially important is the fact that the soul is a part of the Lord, however, when the soul falls into matter, the Lord is not considered fallen. Although the soul falls due to his own desires, he might often attribute the fall to the Lord's will (in what is called the problem of 'evil'). The section discusses how evil is also created by the Lord, but evil is not prescribed by the Lord. Therefore, the responsibility of choosing the evil rests with the soul. Finally, the section discusses how evil exists in the Lord, but it makes the goodness of the Lord sweeter. Thus, lying, stealing, and deception are part of the Absolute Truth, but they enhance the Lord's goodness.

Section 2: This section discusses the nature of dharma or duties and how the neglect of duties produces karma. As one goes through different stages of good and bad karma, the section advises one to remain detached from the results of previous actions and continue performing one's duties. The fall of the soul is again discussed and attributed to the enviousness in the soul against the greatness of the Lord, and his attempt to try to become just like the Lord. How the negation of the Lord leads to conflicts and competition in society is discussed. These conflicts lead to suffering and make society unstable. However, when the Lord's supremacy is recognized, then competition is replaced by cooperation, and society becomes stable again. This leads to the understanding that the soul falls into the material world due to its selfishness of prioritizing himself and seeking his interest over the collective happiness of all beings.

Section 3: This section discusses how the understanding of the Absolute Truth violates the conditions of classical logic such as non-contradiction and mutual exclusion. For example, things are supposed to be either hot or cold, but the Absolute Truth must contain both these alternatives simultaneously as the source of these contrarian opposites. Similarly, because the Absolute Truth contains the opposites, therefore, the principle of mutual exclusion cannot be applied to Him. However, the violation of these logical principles doesn't entail the impossibility of understanding the Absolute Truth because these opposites manifest one by one, or if they are manifest at once, then one of these qualities remains dominant while the other qualities are subordinated. The section then discusses several ways in which a person can become qualified for spiritual emancipation. Finally, the section discusses many ways in which a person becomes disqualified for spiritual emancipation—e.g., by neglecting the basic rules of living associated with the body. Many forms of deceptive religious activities are discussed and rejected as being unfavorable to transcendence.

Section 4: This section discusses how the practices of jñāna-yoga and aśtānga-yoga can be employed in conjunction with bhakti-yoga, although without devotion these methods do not lead to liberation. An extensive discussion about the nature of matter and how it is controlled by prāṇa follows, which then leads to the discussion of how demigods deliver the consequences of actions, or karma. While the worship of demigods was previously rejected—as the means for obtaining better results for enjoyment—the worship of demigods that improves a person's ability to perform their duties or dharma is recommended. Thus, the power of demigods as the providers of good and bad results is distinguished from the power that makes a person more capable of handling the situations being produced due to the good and bad results. While the former disqualifies a person for transcendence, the latter becomes an assistance.

SECTION 1

Topic 1

QUESTION

In many smriti the Lord is known as the Supreme Person, and His Śakti is subordinate to Him. If we now say that the Śakti is inseparable from Him (although not identical to Him) don't we create a contradiction with the claim that the Lord is supreme and His Śakti is subordinate to the Supreme Person?

In most Vaiṣṇava and Shaiva scriptures, Lord Viṣṇu or Lord Śiva are described as the Supreme Person (of the spiritual and material worlds).

2.1.1 (135)

स्मृत्यनवकाशदोषप्रसङ्ग इति चेत् न अन्यस्मृत्यनवकाशदोषप्रसङ्गात्

smṛtyanavakāśadoṣaprasaṅga iti cet na anyasmṛtyanavakāśadoṣaprasaṅgāt

smṛti-anavakāśa-doṣaprasaṅgaḥ—the defect of having no scope for (some) smriti; iti cet—if it be said; na—no; anyasmṛti-anavakāśa-doṣaprasaṅgāt—from the defect of leaving no scope for other smritis.

TRANSLATION

If it be said that (by calling the Lord and His energy inseparable) there would be a defect of leaving no scope for some smriti (which describe the masculine as the supreme), we say no, (on the contrary, the rejection of this separation will) create the defect of leaving no scope for other smriti (which describe the masculine and feminine as two aspects of the same Absolute Truth).

COMMENTARY

Apart from the Vaiṣṇava and Shaiva scriptures, there are also scriptures on the supremacy of the Śakti. Together, these three constitute the three main types of personalism—Vaishnavism, Shaivism, and Shaktism. Therefore, the masculine forms of the Lord are accepted alongside the feminine forms as being supreme. Furthermore, even in Vaiṣṇava scriptures, the names of the Lord are almost always preceded using Śri which indicates His energy. Thus, Vaishnavism doesn't speak about Lord Viṣṇu alone. He is rather referenced as Sri Viṣṇu. The different descriptions are differences of emphasis. As noted earlier, the feminine is supreme because She agitates the masculine to enjoy. And the masculine is supreme because He uses the feminine to enjoy. The feminine is the cause of desire in the masculine, and the masculine is the cause of activity in the feminine. Due to this mutual causality, both masculine and feminine are controllers of the other, and in different contexts they are said to be supreme. There is no discrepancy in these descriptions if the context is understood.

QUESTION

Isn't the doctrine of a single universal Brahman better than the doctrine of that Absolute Truth comprising of a masculine and a feminine aspect?

The doctrine of two distinct but inseparable aspects of the Absolute Truth is certainly more complex than the one that posits an undivided Brahman. This separation but inseparability is hard to understand although we can see that there is a distinction between the will and the power of fulfilling the will. Could there not be a third doctrine that makes this conclusion simpler? On the other hand, if there isn't a third doctrine, doesn't the doctrine of Oneness seem to be superior to the doctrine where that Oneness has two distinct aspects?

2.1.2 (136)

इतरेषां चानुपलब्धेः

itareṣāṃ cānupalabdheḥ

itareṣāṃ—of the others; ca—also; anupalabdheḥ—non-perception.

TRANSLATION

Anything else also cannot be known, perceived, or is non-existent.

COMMENTARY

The use of *itareṣāṃ* can be understood either as referring to the Oneness of the Brahman, or some third doctrine (which hasn't been mentioned). If it refers to a third doctrine, then *anupalabdheḥ* would simply indicate that no such thing has been mentioned in the scriptures, or that it is never known, etc. If, however, *itareṣāṃ* refers to the Oneness, then *anupalabdheḥ* would indicate that this Oneness cannot be known or perceived. We have explained the reason for this before—the masculine is the potential for desire, and the feminine is the potential for activity. When they are united, there is the potential for desire but there is no desire. Similarly, there is potential for activity but there is no activity. Without desire and activity, the Oneness must remain unknowable. Even self-knowledge involves the union of the desire to know the self and the power by which the self can be known. The Self acting on the Self produces this self-knowledge and it activates both the desire and the power simultaneously. If these are not activated, the Oneness exists as an unknowable possibility.

Topic 2

QUESTION

But haven't we spoken about yoga as the union between the jīvā and the Lord, indicating that they are somehow combined or unified. In the same way, can we not say that the masculine and the feminine are united into Oneness?

2.1.3 (137)

एतेन योगःप्रत्युक्तः

etena yogaḥ pratyuktaḥ

etena—by this; yogaḥ—yoga philosophy; pratyuktaḥ—is (also) refuted.

TRANSLATION

By this (claim of Oneness), the yoga philosophy is also refuted.

COMMENTARY

The impersonal philosophers claim that yoga is the union of the ātmā and Paramātma. The assumption in this claim is that the jīvā has its own power and capacity to know, and when it knows itself, then the distinction between the self and the other is understood as being illusory, and the individuality of the ātmā is thereby lost. One now realizes that he is identical to Paramātma.

But what if the jīvā has the will to know but no power to know? And the distinction between will and power itself entails that even if one knows oneself, it is only with the power that is coming from somewhere else? When the power of knowledge belongs to the Lord, then the correct use of that power is knowing the Lord. When the jīvā is absorbed in the consciousness of the Lord, then it loses even self-consciousness, just like a person absorbed in the perception of an attractive external object loses the sense of one's present condition. It is not to say that the individual merges into the object of perception; it is only to say that one's awareness is directed from self-interest to the nature of the observed object. If the Lord is that object of observation, and He remains aware of Himself, while the soul becomes absorbed in the awareness of the Lord, then their awareness is united—they are both perceiving the same thing. There can be an identity of awareness and purpose, without the identity of the individuals. If two people have the same beliefs, knowledge, purpose, and thoughts, then their experiences are identical, but they are not identical. The meaning of yoga is using the Lord's power to understand the Lord. The power acts under the will, and if the will is directed toward the Lord, then it is identical to the Lord's will.

Yoga involves experience. It is not the cessation of all experience. The jīvā only has the power to know itself, but this self is one of the numerous selves. As a result, the self-knowledge of the jīvā is also incomplete knowledge, because in knowing oneself, the jīvā only knows a small fraction of everything that exists. However, if the jīvā seeks the purpose of its existence, and connects this purpose to the Lord, then by this union, the diversity is connected to that unity, without dissolving the diversity into the unity. The impersonalist argues that the soul is a drop of ocean, and it should merge back into the ocean, without explaining how the drop of the ocean came out of the ocean in the first place. The cause of the soul's separateness is the desire in the Lord to enjoy. So, when the soul wants to merge into the Lord, his desire is opposed to the Lord's desire, and it defeats the reason why they were separated for seeking pleasure.

Topic 3

QUESTION

But haven't you said that the Lord is transcendent to material nature, which implies that there is a difference between the Lord and material nature? Doesn't that seem contrary to the claim that the Lord and His power are inseparable? How does this inseparability compare to the Lord being different from material nature? How will we reconcile these two seemingly contradictory claims?

2.1.4 (138)

न वलिक्षणत्वादस्य तथात्वं च शब्दात्

na vilakṣaṇatvādasya tathātvaṃ ca śabdāt

na—not; vilakṣaṇatvāt—from contrary nature; asya—of this (world); tathā—in the same way; tvaṃ—you (the soul); ca—also; śabdāt—it is said.

TRANSLATION

(The Lord) is not from the contrary nature of this world; in the same way, you are also (not of a contrary nature to the Lord); so it is stated.

COMMENTARY

The transcendence of the Lord doesn't entail the separateness of the Lord from material nature. The meaning of transcendence is that the Lord is never bound by the laws of material nature—i.e., action and consequence—which cause repeated birth and death. Since the soul is bound by these laws, to motivate his liberation it is said that the soul is transcendent to matter. Most people take this to mean that the soul must get out of the material body, and therefore death must be the precondition to liberation. However, that view of transcendence would also mean that a liberated person cannot exist in the material world, or if the Lord appeared in this world, then He would also be bound by the laws of choice and consequence. The notion of transcendence where one must get out of the material world to be liberated from the laws of matter is false.

Within the material world, there are two kinds of causality—material causality and efficient causality—and both have separate laws. A law of material causality is that salt can be dissolved in water. A law of efficient causality is whether I will be dissolving salt into water. The laws of material causation can remain true, but they may not apply to us. Thus, salt will still dissolve into water, but I may not be the one dissolving salt into water. In simple terms, my choices are not forced by my previous actions. When the Lord appears in the material world, the laws of material causation remain true, but the laws of efficient causation are not. Similarly, the soul can also exist in the material world, and not be affected by the laws of choice and consequence. Thus, the separation of the soul and the Lord is not necessary to say that they are transcendent.

This distinction between the Lord and the soul arises because the soul is acting contrary to the Lord's will, while material energy is still acting according to the Lord's will. Therefore, there is a perfect union between the Lord and material nature. However, because the soul's will is contrary to the Lord's will, therefore, the soul is contrary to material nature as well. Material nature is still serving the Lord, but the soul is trying to satisfy itself. The Lord has allowed the soul to satisfy itself, within the constraints of previously created karma. If the soul's will is identical to the Lord's will, then karma is never produced. And without karma, the soul is never impeded by the laws of efficient causality. Thus, the terms 'bondage' and 'liberation' are applied to the soul when the soul is disobedient to the Lord's desires. The Lord is never bound in this way. Ultimately, both the soul and the Lord are transcendent to matter, but they don't need to be separated from matter to demonstrate their transcendence.

QUESTION

If material nature is working according to the will of the Lord, why isn't it obvious to the soul? Why does the soul consider itself the doer? For example, when I eat food, I believe that I am the cause of my eating; I do not consider the Lord to be the cause of my eating. Therefore, in all such practical ways, the Lord's actions are hidden from the soul. Why should they be so hidden?

2.1.5 (139)

अभिमानिव्यपदेशस्तु वशिेषानुगतभि्याम्

abhimānivyapadeśastu viśeṣānugatibhyām

abhimānivyapadeśaḥ—due to the covering of arrogance or pride; tu—but; viśeṣa—the property; anugatibhyām—being an obedient follower.

TRANSLATION

Because of the covering of pride or arrogance, (the soul) gets the property of being a follower (of material nature, i.e., comes under its full control).

COMMENTARY

In Bhagavad-Gita 3.27, Lord Kṛṣṇa states the following:

prakṛteḥ kriyamāṇāni
guṇaiḥ karmāṇi sarvaśaḥ
ahaṅkāra-vimūḍhātmā
kartāham iti manyate

The spirit soul bewildered by the false ego thinks himself the doer (of its actions) when (in fact) these actions are enacted by prakriti (or material nature) due to the collective guna and karma.

The term *ahaṅkāra* used in the above verse and the term *abhimāna* used in this sūtra indicate the same thing—the false pride of "I am the doer".

The Bhagavad-Gita, however, goes a step further in calling this causation the result of collective guna and karma. Let's consider the example of a buyer purchasing some fruits from a vendor. The buyer has the desire or guna to eat fruits, so this desire to eat fruits is the cause of the purchase. Likewise, the vendor also has a desire or guna to sell fruits, so the vendor's desire is also a cause. Then, the buyer has some money due to their karma, so this karma is also a cause. Finally, the vendor has some karma due to which he has acquired fruits to sell, so his karma is also a cause. Thus, two pairs of guna and karma are involved in each transaction. Sometimes, a buyer may be forced to buy against his wishes, and a vendor may be forced to sell against his wishes. But what is force? Each person will do unpleasant things to avoid a greater unpleasantness. That preference for one unpleasantness over another is guna. Thus, even if it seems that we are doing something against our desire, there is desire which is causing it. Hence, there is no action without a pair of guna and karma.

This is a simple example, but it quickly gets very complicated if we realize that the fruit seller exists only because there is a large market of buyers of fruits. And this market exists because there is a choice of many types of fruits, so there must be many sellers. In short, the guna and karma of the souls are fulfilled collectively by creating a market of buyers and sellers. Their guna and karma are their individual material qualities, but their fulfillment is collective.

The prakriti or material nature is described here as the cause of this collective fulfillment. It is not the causality of modern science in which one particle pushes another without any desiring or deserving. But, the introduction of desiring and deserving can lead to a misunderstanding that because I am desiring, therefore, I am the cause of my actions. This notion of "I am the doer" is rejected here. The desires in us are automatically produced by the guna. We don't have control over the production of these desires, but we can reject these automatically created desires. When we reject them, the desires cease to exist, and in that case, we can say that we prevented something from happening. But we can still not say that we were the cause or the doer of anything. The prakriti is still the cause of when things happen, but we can refuse to take part in them. By that refusal we retain our free will, but we are not the doer of the actions.

The desires are different from the soul, but all desires produce the experience of absence—desire means that someone is missing something. That someone can be me, or it may not be me. When the soul rejects these desires, he says—I am not missing this, so it cannot be my desire. On the other hand, when the soul accepts these desires, then he agrees—I am indeed missing this. Thus, the desire is a negative identity of the soul: It represents what I am not.

When this negative identity is created, it must be compensated by a positive identity. That positive identity is called 'pride' or *ahaṅkāra*. If we lose our pride, then we also lose our desire. For example, if a woman insults a man, then he will stop desiring her. This is not because the desire is gone, but because the desire is a negative identity, and it cannot exist without a positive identity. When a person undergoes depression or anxiety, their pride is undermined, and since the positive material identity ceases to exist, therefore, desires also disappear. Whatever seemed pleasing previously seems tasteless now. However, depression and anxiety are not due to freedom from desires. They are rather situations in which a person's pride, ego, or self-respect is destroyed.

Ahaṅkāra is necessary for any desire to exist, and it exists even for the devotee. The devotee feels great pride in being the servant of the Lord. Due to this pride, he accepts all the desires to serve the Lord. And then he also thinks—I am the servant of the Lord, and I am serving the Lord, and he feels happy due to this pride. Factually, even while serving the Lord, the soul is not the cause of his actions. Those actions are still carried out by the Lord's Śakti. However, since *ahaṅkāra* must exist for desire to exist, therefore, even the devotee must have an *ahaṅkāra* or pride. It is just that the nature of pride is different.

This sūtra uses the term *anugatibhyām,* which means being the obedient servant or follower. When the pride is in one's being a master, then the soul becomes a servant of the material nature. But when the pride is in being the servant of the Lord, then the soul not only fulfills the desire of being a servant but out of this servitude to the Lord, it often acts as the Lord's master. Thus, if one pursues the pride of mastery, then the desires are frustrated. But if one pursues the pride of servitude, then both mastery and servitude are fulfilled.

QUESTION

Many people say that this material world is a dream. Just like in a bad dream we might feel that we have been imprisoned by some enemies and we are being tortured, and we might suffer, but factually we haven't been imprisoned. In the same way, the soul is not truly bound by the material world.

In the previous sūtra, it was said that the idea that the soul is the doer of all the actions is an illusion because these actions are carried out by the material nature. The skeptics like to take this idea further and claim that if the idea that I'm a doer is an illusion, then the entire experience must be an illusion.

2.1.6 (140)

दृश्यते तु

dṛśyate tu

dṛśyate—is seen; tu—but.

TRANSLATION

(Even if you call it a dream) it is still experienced.

COMMENTARY

This sūtra doesn't confirm or deny whether the world is an illusion. It just says—even if you think it is an illusion, you are still experiencing it. So, you are suffering and enjoying in a way that is beyond your control. You cannot deny that you are suffering or enjoying, because even in a dream you suffer and enjoy. And because you are suffering, you cannot claim that you are in control (because you do not want to suffer). So, if your suffering is out of your control, then how can you say that I'm the cause of my pleasure? Wouldn't it be more appropriate to say that both pleasure and suffering are out of my control?

It is a commonly seen fact that when people enjoy their lives, or are successful, then they claim to be the doers. Only when they start suffering, fail in their lives, or lose control over what they can and cannot do, then they claim that the world must be an illusion. So, this is a sour grapes mentality: If I cannot get what I want, then it must be that even getting something is illusory. However, these claims about illusion or not don't change anything in the real world, because you keep suffering, and it remains out of your control. Calling something illusory only works if you can get out of the illusion. So, if this world were an illusion, then why can't the person calling it an illusion wake up? Why can't he just put an end to his suffering by realizing that everything is an illusion? Since this is practically undoable, these claims are armchair philosophizing.

QUESTION

But the point of calling it a dream is to then say that it is self-created, and the suffering is self-inflicted. Just like a spider might emanate a web from itself, and then feel that it is caught inside that web. In the same way, the world we see is a projection from within, like the web of a spider. So, then we can say that the material world is not dragging us like a menial servant. Rather, we have created the web of hallucinations in which we have now become caught.

2.1.7 (141)

असदिति चेत् न प्रतिषेधमात्रत्वात्

asaditi cet na pratiṣedhamātratvāt

asat—non-existent; iti cet—if it be said; na—no; pratiṣedhamātratvāt—from it being merely a restraint.

TRANSLATION

If it is said that (the world) doesn't exist (as it is self-created), (we say) no; (after all, even in the example of a spider), there is restraint (e.g., the web).

COMMENTARY

The main problem in calling the world a dream or hallucination is still the same as when it is considered real: Why isn't this dream or hallucination perfect and pleasing? If we are creating our dream or hallucination, then we must have created it perfectly, such that we were always enjoying this dream, rather than suffering in it. Why would we create a dream and suffer because of it? Since we don't want to suffer, but we are forced to suffer, we cannot claim that we are creating this suffering; if it acts against our will, then it is not caused by us.

The term *pratiṣedha* has many meanings. It can mean a restriction that is preventing us to attain our goals. It can mean something that is forbidden (due to laws or regulations). Basically, *siddhi* means attainment, and if *prati* precedes *siddhi* then it is something that prevents that attainment. Everyone wants to attain enjoyment and pleasure; so, this pleasure is the goal that we would like to attain. But the material world is preventing this attainment. So, there is no point in the semantics of whether the world is cognitively an illusion, and whether it is created by the self. These cognitive positions about the reality of the world don't change the fact that we want to enjoy, and we are suffering.

QUESTION

I don't deny that we are suffering, or that it is against or will. However, if the world is produced as the web of a spider from the spider itself, then the spider can potentially withdraw the web and then become free of the web.

2.1.8 (142)

अपीतौ तद्वत्प्रसङ्गादसमञ्जसम्

apītau tadvatprasaṅgādasamañjasam

apītau—by deflating or absorbing; tadvat—like that (it was previously created); prasaṅgāt—the episodic world of events; asamañjasam—creates a doubt.

TRANSLATION

(The claim that we can become free of the world) by deflating or absorbing the episodic world of events just like (it was previously created) creates a doubt (about why it was produced to cause the soul's suffering in the first place).

COMMENTARY

Just as the seeker is persisting on the argument that the world is an illusion or hallucination produced by the soul, the author of the Vedānta Sūtra is also persisting on his original argument that you cannot claim yourself to be the creator of the world if you are caught in the web and suffering because of it. In this sūtra, the specific claim that if we call this world a self-created illusion, then we can also withdraw it ourselves, begs the question of why this illusion was created in the first place. Why would anyone tie themselves into ropes? Moreover, why would anyone make this argument and not merely withdraw the web of illusions? After all, if the world is an illusion, then the argument about the world being an illusion must also be an illusion. Why perpetuate the illusion by making such arguments if you can simply withdraw the illusion? Arguments about illusion must end in the claimant shutting up permanently.

QUESTION

We can say that this emanation of the world from ourselves was a mistake. We did not know that we will be caught in the web created by ourselves, and by mistake we created it. Now we want to correct this mistake

by withdrawing it back. Can we not be prone to mistakes and then aspire to correct them?

2.1.9 (143)
न तु दृष्टान्तभावात्
na tu dṛṣṭāntabhāvāt

na—not; tu—but; dṛṣṭānta-bhāvāt—the feelings caused by the events.

TRANSLATION

But you cannot (explain) the feelings caused by the events.

COMMENTARY

The argument about a person making a mistake rests on their ignorance about the nature of reality. A child can play with fire, and then say that he did not know that the fire will burn him and that ignorance about the nature of the fire caused the burn. However, this argument is acceptable only if the child isn't the creator of the fire. If the child created the fire out of himself, then he must have known what it can do. Whatever exists in the effect, must exist in the cause. So, the fact that the fire will burn the child would have existed as the intention to self-burn, if the child is the self-creator of the fire that burns him. So, the argument from ignorance or mistake cannot be applied if we also keep calling the world our self-creation. If we create something, we know its nature, and we also know how to control it. We cannot claim to create a monster out of ourselves and then say that we did not know that it would be a monster that swallows the creator. The act of self-creation entails a full understanding of the action.

The term *bhāvāt* has many potential meanings. It can mean 'existence', in which case the purport of this sūtra would be that "you cannot explain the fact that the existence of events (which cause your suffering) is based on a mistake when you are the creator of the world". It can also mean 'nature', in which case, the purport of this sūtra would be that "you cannot explain the nature of the events of this world (i.e., that they cause suffering) based on a mistake when you are the creator of the world". Finally, it can also mean 'feelings' or 'emotions' such as pain and suffering, which would make the same meaning even more direct, and there would be no need to import the notion of suffering from the previous sūtra. Owing to this directness, I have preferred this translation.

QUESTION

But in many religions of this world, the fall of the soul into the material world is attributed to his own mistake. For example, Adam and Eve fall from heaven because of a mistake, and if they correct the mistake then they can return to heaven. Isn't this path of self-correction open in your viewpoint?

2.1.10 (144)

स्वपक्षदोषाच्च

svapakṣadoṣācca

svapakṣa-doṣāt—due to faults in one's view; ca—also.

TRANSLATION

(The fall into material world is) also due to faults in one's view.

COMMENTARY

The existence of the fault in the soul is not denied; in fact, this sūtra accepts that the fall is due to the faults in the soul. However, the use of *ca* indicates that this is not the only cause. In particular, the soul cannot say that he made a mistake, and due to that mistake, he created a world out of himself, in which he was then caught, and now wants to be liberated. The mistake entails that the soul is not the creator or the controller of the world, nor does he have full knowledge of the world. He thought that he could enjoy in the world, and his mistake arose out of a misunderstanding of the true nature of the world.

If the soul is not the creator, then the world must be created by someone else—i.e., the Lord. So, its existence cannot be called a hallucination or imagination. Such a world must truly exist objectively, and hence the events of the world must be objective, and the suffering caused by them must be real too. So, by saying that the fault in the soul is *also* the cause, it is implied that it is only one of the causes; the Lord is the other cause of the creation; in fact, He is the creator and the controller, and therefore fully knows the nature of the material world. He may advise—as in some religions—to avoid committing the mistakes that can lead to a fall. But if the soul ignores this advice, then the world is not created by this neglect; only the fall into the world is due to this neglect.

QUESTION

If you are accepting that the soul has fallen due to a mistake of his own, then how did this mistake arise? If we say that the mistake is always innate, then the soul cannot get liberated. If on the other hand, we say that the mistake was caused by an external source, then why should the soul suffer for it?

If one says that the evil is in the soul, and he falls due to his own mistake, and God is only fulfilling the wishes of the soul, then we are led to the question: If the evil is in the soul, and the soul is eternal, then evil must also be eternal. If the soul is eternally evil, then how can he get liberated from this world?

2.1.11 (145)

तर्काप्रतिष्ठानादपि; अन्यथानुमेयमिति चेत् एवमप्यनिर्मोक्षप्रसङ्गः

tarkāpratiṣṭhānādapi; anyathānumeyamiti cet evamapyanirmokṣaprasaṅgaḥ

tarka-pratiṣṭhānāt—by reasoning we cannot establish; api—also; anyathā—otherwise; anumeyam—should be inferred; iti cet—if it be said; evam—so;

api—even; anirmokṣa-prasaṅgaḥ—there will be outcome of no liberation.

TRANSLATION

If it be said that we should be able to infer (the cause of fall down) otherwise we also (cannot practice the process of liberation) (we say that) by reasoning we cannot establish (the cause for the fall down), and even (if we tried to do) so, that will not lead us to liberation (from material existence).

COMMENTARY

It has been stated in the previous sūtra that the fault lies in the soul, although the soul alone isn't the cause of material experience. The desire of fall is attributed to the soul, but the facilitation and fulfillment of this desire is due to the Lord and His Śakti. And yet, none of these causes are permanent. If the fall was due to God, then why will God try to liberate the soul after the fall? Similarly, if the soul was inherently and eternally evil, then its liberation would be impossible. Thus, after placing the responsibility of the fall with the soul, the sūtra states that the origin of the fall cannot be traced, and moreover, such questions do not lead to liberation. The focus should be on liberation rather than figuring out what might have led to the fall. By trying to guess the cause of the fall we will never come to any conclusion, and the time that could be spent in the process of liberation would be wasted in a meaningless investigation. In short, there should be no attempt to rationalize or justify or explain the fall.

Topic 4

QUESTION

Some people say that the evil stands apart from God, almost on an equal footing as God, and has the power to delude the soul. This evil is sometimes called Satan. So, God and Satan are pulling the soul in different directions.

2.1.12 (146)

एतेन शष्टिापरग्रिहा अपि व्याख्याताः

etena śiṣṭāparigrahā api vyākhyātāḥ

etena—by this (i.e., holding the soul responsible for his fall); śiṣṭāparigrahāḥ—not accepted by the wise; api—also; vyākhyātāḥ—are explained.

TRANSLATION

In this way (i.e., holding the soul responsible for his fall) (other ideas which are) not accepted by the wise are also explained.

COMMENTARY

In some religions, such as Christianity, the problem of fall is partially attributed to the existence of Satan, who deludes the soul. Satan is considered a fallen angel and can never be liberated from this evil. However, the soul can be liberated if he becomes obedient to God. By postulating the existence of Satan, the problem of evil is confined into *one* individual: The evil exists in Satan, and by that, it can spread to others, but others are not inherently evil; they are rather tempted and deluded by Satan. But that again begs the question: If Satan is deluding the soul, then why is the soul suffering rather than Satan who deluded the soul? Why is God punishing the soul instead of Satan? Moreover, if Satan is a fallen angel, then how did he fall, and why can't he ever be liberated?

This sūtra states that such ideas—which attribute a fall to someone other than the soul, in trying to partially reduce the soul's responsibility—are not accepted by the wise. However, if one insists that the soul can get deluded by the influence of others, they too are fallen in the same way as the other souls. There is no eternally fallen agent like Satan who causes the fall because that doesn't minimize the soul's responsibility of being tempted by Satan. On the other hand, the postulates of a fallen soul who can never be liberated are not accepted by the wise. Liberation is open to everyone if only they are interested in it.

Topic 5

QUESTION

You have previously said that even if the soul enters the world, he doesn't lose the connection to the Lord. So, it is sometimes said that the soul is never truly separated from the Lord and hence should not be considered 'fallen' into the world. This fall is only the experience of enjoyment or suffering of this world when the consciousness of the soul is directed toward the world.

2.1.13 (147)

भोक्त्रापत्तेरविभागश्चेत् स्याल्लोकवत्

bhoktrāpatteravibhāgaścet syāllokavat

bhoktrāpatteḥ—the fault of being the enjoyer; avibhāgaḥ—non-distinction; cet—if it be said; syāt—possible; lokavat—just like in this world.

TRANSLATION

If it is said that the fault of being the enjoyer is non-distinction (from the Lord—as He is also enjoying), (we say), that is possible as in this world.

COMMENTARY

There are two prominent theories of causation—local and non-local. The local theory of causation states that two objects must be in close proximity to each other in order for an object to affect another object. A classic example of such causation is the collision of two billiard balls, in which the balls must contact each other before either ball pushes or is pushed. In the non-local theory of causation, two objects can be far apart and yet can exert an influence on each other; a classic example of such causation is the idea of a gravitational force.

In the same vein, one can say that the soul is 'fallen' into the material world and has therefore contacted it like a billiard ball contacting another such ball. We can also say that the soul is not physically 'fallen' into the world but is remotely connected to the world just as in the case of gravitational force.

In the previous sūtra, we have said that the soul is connected to the Lord through prāṇa. We also said that the soul connects to the material world through prāṇa. When the soul moves to a different body, the prāṇa 'carries' the soul to that body, thereby establishing a connection to a new body. We also described that when the Lord glances over the material energy to inject the soul, the glance is like the senses moving outward to perceive an object, but the senses don't get disconnected to the Lord through such a glance. Therefore, the soul is always connected to the Lord even in this material world. Only the consciousness of the soul is directed toward the material world, just as in the case of remote causation, in which an object contacts another object remotely.

But should we say that this turning of consciousness away from the Lord into the material energy is not a 'fall'? Factually, both positions can be argued for. Because the soul turns his consciousness away from the Lord into the material energy, he can be called 'fallen'. And because the soul hasn't lost the connection to the Lord, therefore, he can be called 'not fallen'. If we understand how the soul is connected to both the Lord and the material energy simultaneously, either the connection to the material energy can be used to call it a 'fall', or the connection to the Lord can be employed to call it 'not a fall'. It doesn't change the fact that the soul is entangled in the laws of material nature, even though the soul is transcendent to material nature. This entanglement is essentially the consciousness of the soul evolving from one experience to another.

Therefore, this sūtra uses the term *syat* or possibility of saying that the soul is not fallen, even though it has been clearly stated earlier that the soul is entangled in the material world. Depending on whether the connection to the material world or the Lord is emphasized, either position can be argued for.

Topic 6

QUESTION

If the soul is always connected to the Lord, then why is the fall of the soul into the material world not considered the fall of the Lord? Shouldn't we say that a part of the Lord has fallen therefore the Lord must also be fallen?

2.1.14 (148)

तदनन्यत्वमारम्भणशब्दादिभ्यः

tadananyatvamārambhaṇaśabdādibhyaḥ

tad—its (the soul's); ananyatvam—non-difference; ārambhaṇa—origin or beginning; śabdādibhyaḥ—just like the origination of words.

TRANSLATION

The non-difference of the soul (from the Lord is asserted) due to origination or beginning, just like the words (are spoken by a speaker).

COMMENTARY

The material world has previously been called the Lord's 'expression' and compared to speech. In this sūtra, the soul is also compared to the Lord's speech. The speech is separate from the speaker, and yet, it is always connected to the speaker because the speaker is the cause, origin, or beginning of speech. We have earlier spoken of the triad of *manas-prāṇa-vāk*, in which *manas* is the meaning, *vāk* is the speech, and *prāṇa* is the connection between the two. Very simply, the meaning resides in the speaker, and through prāṇa, it is expressed as speech. Once the speech has been expressed, the spoken words can be twisted or interpreted in many ways. But these twisted meanings are not the real explanation of why the speaker spoke those words. To understand the meaning, we must reference the speaker's intentions because those intentions were the cause of the speech. In the same way, the soul is an expression of the Lord, and the Lord created that expression for a certain purpose or intention. However, once the expression was created, it is open to misinterpretation. When such misinterpretations are applied, then because of the difference between the intended meaning and the interpreted meaning, the soul and the Lord become separate. However, despite such misinterpretation, the origin of the speech is still the Lord, so the speech must always be attributed to Him.

In short, the disconnection between the soul and the Lord is due to the disparity in the intended and interpreted meanings. The Lord intended the soul for a certain purpose, but the soul interpreted its existence differently. As the speaker of the word, the Lord is still connected to the word. But because the meaning has been altered, the Lord has become disconnected from the soul. Therefore, the fall of the soul must not be attributed to the Lord; this fall is like the misinterpretation of the meaning of the word, and its variance from the intended meaning is due to the soul's free will, not the Lord's intention.

QUESTION

When the words are separated from the speaker, can we ever truly know the meaning that the speaker intended? On the other hand, if the meaning is never available after the words are separated, then how can one know what the meaning was, or should be, since the words have already been separated?

2.1.15 (149)

भावे चोपलब्धेः

bhāve copalabdheḥ

bhāve—in the intentions, meanings, purpose, or desires; ca—also; upalabdheḥ—are available, present, experienceable, or obtainable.

TRANSLATION

(The meaning is) also perceivable in the intentions (of the words).

COMMENTARY

When we hear a sentence, our ears only process the sounds of the words. But the mind is capable of understanding three kinds of meanings—(1) the dictionary meanings and grammatical structures, (2) the nature of the context in which these words are spoken, and (3) the intention of speaking based on the understanding of the speaker. The sounds are universal—i.e., the same for everyone. The dictionary meanings and grammar structures are native to the speakers of a certain language. The context of speaking is further limited to a few people who might have been in that situation. And the intention or personality of the speaker is unique to that speaker. Thus, to understand meanings, we go from the universal, to the social-cultural, to the contextual, and finally to the individual. Each such transition is not easy, but such transitions are possible. The bigger question is: are these transitions simply our interpretations? This sūtra refutes this claim. It says that the meaning is present in the words.

We have discussed this idea before while considering the three modalities of nature. When we see an individual cow, which is a symbol of the idea of cow, the idea cow is present in the individual cow. Likewise, the words are expressions of the meanings, and meanings are present within them. All these arguments are being made to establish a simple idea—that the soul is a symbol, this symbol can be interpreted, but the symbol also has an innate meaning.

The expression of meaning begins with an intention, which is then used to produce a structure, which is then populated by individual words. This three-tier model of meaning expression can be seen in the process of making a chair. The chair's designer begins with the intention to make a chair; the intention leads to a design; and finally, the design is converted into an object using pieces of wood. We can see the pieces of wood. If we move our attention away from the individual pieces and look at the collection of these pieces, we can also see the structure or interrelations between the parts. However, we don't conclude that something is a chair unless we believe that it was meant to be a chair.

Materialists abhor the idea of design in nature. They claim that given enough time, even a monkey hitting the keys of a typewriter can produce the complete works of Shakespeare. And the debate then shifts to asking how fast the monkey is typing, and how long has the monkey been typing. There are no clear answers to this problem because the rate of typing can change with time, and the duration for which the monkey has been typing is only knowable when something meaningful starts to come out of that typing. Materialists neglect the fact that for something to be called living, it must be able to perceive and understand its environment, and that involves representing the outside world within. That representation entails that some molecules within a living entity are symbols of the external world. If *some* molecules could be symbols, why not all molecules? In short, why would some nature be meaningful, and the rest of nature be meaningless? There is no other way to explain this problem unless we say that all nature is meaningful. And if there is meaning, then there must be purpose, because that meaning and purpose causes the expression.

Thus, material objects like books, art, music, scientific theories, legal documents, etc. have both a meaning and a purpose. Even tables and chairs are symbols of ideas. So, why should we not consider atoms and molecules to also be symbols of ideas? The atomic particles are phonemes, they are combined into complex sentences using grammatical structures, and this structure has an underlying intention. The world is not meaningless, and not purposeless.

This sūtra claims that the intended meaning exists in the spoken words objectively, not merely in the mind of the speaker. The mind is a 'sense', which is capable of producing and absorbing meanings; when the words are spoken, even the meanings are objectified along with the words. However, to understand these objective meanings, the minds of the speaker and the listener must be similar. If the speaker and the listener have very different minds, then the listener will not grasp the objectively present meaning. He will then try to *interpret* the words according to his own mind and arrive at a different meaning. So, the claim that once the words have become separated from the speaker then we cannot know the true intended meaning of the speaker is rejected here.

QUESTION

But why does the soul misinterpret the intended meaning? What is the cause of its turning away from the true meaning toward a false meaning?

2.1.16 (150)

सत्त्वाच्चापरस्य

sattvāccāparasya

sattvāt—from the truth; ca—also; aparasya—aversion, inferiority.

TRANSLATION

Also (the fall is) from the aversion to the truth.

COMMENTARY

It is not easy to live in the presence of greatness, because that greatness makes us feel inferior. The devotees of the Lord see the Lord's greatness and they feel protected by this greatness; they are naturally inclined to serve the Lord because He is so great. However, the soul can also develop a sense of inferiority looking at the greatness of the Lord. We have discussed previously how every desire is accompanied by pride. The pride can be that I am a servant of the Lord, or it can be that I am myself the enjoyer. If there is pride in being the servant of the Lord, His greatness reinforces the devotee's pride. But if the pride in being the Lord's servant is lost, then the soul develops an aversion to the Lord due to his own sense of inferiority. When this aversion develops, then the soul reinterprets his existence, creating his own purpose as the pursuit of superiority. This false interpretation 'covers' the original meaning; the original meaning is hidden, and the false interpretation is accepted as the truth.

We can see many common occurrences of this type of phenomenon in the present day. When we contact a person far superior to us, there is a natural tendency in many people to challenge their superiority. Unable to accept that someone is better than us, we try to put them down, insult them, humiliate them, or point out their faults. We also try to demonstrate our superiority by arguments or achievements. This outward projection of our greatness is caused by an innate sense of inferiority. The greater the sense of inferiority and self-loathing in a person, the greater is the outward projection. Thus, people who feel innately inferior try to project their power, wealth, beauty, knowledge, etc. seeking the attention of others. The slightest of inconveniences in demonstration makes such a person angry and the feeling of self-loathing returns.

The true devotee of the Lord is free from the sense of inferiority. He takes pride in the fact that he is a servant of the Lord. But many spiritualists don't have this sense of pride in being a servant. They may be seeking salvation, but they don't like to call themselves the servants of the Lord. They rather use terms like 'spiritual but not religious' or a 'seeker' instead of calling themselves servants of the Lord. These are symptoms of an inferiority within the person, and an aversion to the Lord. So long as it exists, there can be no salvation.

QUESTION

Some philosophers say that a sentence doesn't have an objective meaning. Rather, the meaning must be derived from the context in which that sentence is being used. The same sentence used in a different context can, therefore, have a different meaning. In the same way, if the soul is like the speech of the Lord, then we cannot say that it has an original intended purpose. Rather, we must say that this purpose changes from one context to another, just like the same words being used in different contexts have different intended meanings.

2.1.17 (151)

असद्व्यपदेशान्नेति चेत् न धर्मान्तरेण वाक्यशेषात्

asadvyapadeśānneti cet na dharmāntareṇa vākyaśeṣāt

asat-vyapadeśāt—due to covering by false (ideas, pride); na—not; iti cet—if it be said; na—no; dharmāntareṇa—by change in the person's duties; vākyaśeṣāt—(the original meaning) from the sentence that remains.

TRANSLATION

If it is said that (the fall of the soul is) not due to a false covering (of the original intention), (we say) no (because) by changing the contextual duties (the original meaning) of the sentence can be known from that which remains.

COMMENTARY

The intended purpose of a kitchen knife is to cut vegetables. However, the knife can also sometimes be used as a weapon. The use as a weapon doesn't undermine the fact that the knife was originally produced for cutting vegetables. In the same way, the original intended purpose of the soul is to serve the

Lord. This service is always performed through a relationship with the Lord. But when the soul enters the material world, he also enters other temporary relationships such as father, mother, son, daughter, wife, husband, friend etc. in relation to other persons. In these relations he performs his duties quite like the knife may sometimes be used as a weapon. These duties are called dharma, but they are different from the sanātana-dharma or the eternal duty in relation to the Lord. This sūtra asserts that just because one's duties change (*dharmāntaran*) in this world, doesn't mean that the original duty ceases to exist.

Some philosophers of language claim that the words don't have intrinsic meaning because the same words could be used in different contexts to indicate different things. It is true that the words underdetermine the meaning. But it has also been asserted that the words won't come into existence unless there was a meaning. So, even though the same word may be used in different contexts, in each such context there is also a different intended meaning. The contextual use of words doesn't take away the fact that the speaker intends to say something to a listener. The context rather determines what is appropriate or right and can be justified based on a person's roles and duties. So, the intentions underlying the words always exist, although some of these intentions may be wrong—e.g., meant to cheat or lie—and incompatible with one's duties.

Whether the speech is right or wrong is a separate question from what is being meant in that speech. Only when we can determine the meaning, can we decide whether it is right or wrong. So, by rejecting the existence of inherent meaning, and then using the context to decide what is being meant, we remove the possibility of determining whether the thing being said is right or wrong, whether it should have been said or not, and whether it was a person's duty to say such things or not. Instrumentalists have had such a view of language and they think that speech is meant to get a job done. Thus, speech may be used to command, instruct, cajole, insult, inquire, or answer, and that gets some work done. The meaning of the words is the work that gets done; this liberates the quest for meaning from the pursuit of intentions and reduces meaning to the observation of facts and changes that result from getting some work done. But what if someone disobeys the command or instruction, and does something contrary to what was intended? By the criterion of measuring the meaning by the effects it produces, we would say that the meaning was the effects. In short, we will lose the ability to judge whether the words were true or false, right or wrong, and good or bad. Words would become akin to billiard balls that push some objects to produce some effects, and just like the billiard ball carries no meaning but can produce some effects, similarly, words too will be judged by their effects. This would entail the collapse of meaning and judgment.

Therefore, the context should not be used to decipher the meaning. It should rather be used to determine whether the actions are right or wrong.

QUESTION

You are saying that the use of the same word in different ways in different contexts is an aberration? By the example of a kitchen knife being used for cutting vegetables, you are indicating that each thing has a unique

intended purpose and, thus, any other type of usage must be regarded as an aberration?

2.1.18 (152)

युक्तेःशब्दान्तराच्च

yukteḥ śabdāntarācca

yukteḥ—to be used (plural, indicating many different uses); śabdāntarāt—from the differences in the words; ca—and.

TRANSLATION

Different words (should) also (be put to) different uses.

COMMENTARY

A chair can sometimes be used as a table, and at other times as a ladder. Yes, such a usage gets a job done, but we would typically use the chair as a table or a ladder only if we did not have the table or a ladder. If we had the ladder, we would *prefer* to use the ladder rather than a chair. Similarly, we might also use a chair as a ladder if we don't need a ladder frequently. If we needed to use a ladder more frequently, we will acquire a ladder because it is more suited for the job. Thus, an expert workman would have many types of tools in his toolbox ideally suited for different kinds of activities. An amateur, on the other hand, may try to get the same things done inefficiently with fewer tools. But if the amateur needs to do expert work, then he must procure the best tools.

This sūtra is therefore prescriptive—it is saying that ideally, you need to have different tools for different jobs. Each tool is meant for producing a different effect, and it should be employed for that purpose. While other tools may seem to also get the job done in many cases, they are inefficient for the purpose, and may also not get the job done perfectly. The implication is that each person is suited for a certain type of activity, and they should ideally be engaged in that type of work. They might be able to do other things imperfectly because they haven't been crafted for that purpose. Just like the chair will ideally work as a chair, but non-ideally can substitute an ideal ladder, in the same way, each soul has a unique purpose in relation to the Lord. When it is employed in other ways, it does the job imperfectly and can therefore never be satisfied.

QUESTION

But many philosophers say that all souls are identical to each other; they have the same capacity for cognition, emotion, and relation. They are compared to drops of water in an ocean of water. But you are saying that each soul is different—not only as an individual drop of water—but also that this drop must be put to a different use because it is ideally meant to be used so?

2.1.19 (153)

पटवच्च

paṭavacca

paṭavat—like cloth; ca—and.

TRANSLATION

(You can) also (think of the soul) as cloth.

COMMENTARY

Sometimes all it takes to change our understanding is the change in the analogy. If we think of the soul as a drop of water, then all the souls seem identical. But if we think of the soul as cloth, then we can also see that it can be crafted into different types of clothes—such as shirts, trousers, hats, socks, underwear, etc. As a cloth, all the souls are identical. But as different clothes they are different. So, we should not think of the different souls as mere pieces of cloth which can alternately be used as a shirt, trousers, underwear, etc. We should rather think that this piece of cloth has already been crafted into a specific type of garment and hence it is meant for a different kind of purpose. Yes, the shirt can sometimes be wrapped around the waist, and trouser can also be used to cover the chest. But these are not the ideal purposes of the shirt and the trouser. The shirt and the trousers have been created for different purposes.

We can, therefore, make a distinction between two kinds of individualities. The first individuality refers to a different identity—like a different drop of water. The second individuality refers to a different type of object—like a different kind of garment. In the previous sūtra, the first type of individuality has been indicated—namely, that the soul is an individual, and this individuality emerges because of the desire for enjoyment. In this sūtra, a further distinction is made by stating that each such individual is also a different type of individual. In short, they are not merely different persons, but they also have different *personalities*. Each such personality is ideally suited for a different kind of role and purpose, and this personality, therefore, constitutes its intended purpose.

QUESTION

You seem to be indicating that the soul's personality is innate and eternal. If each soul has a unique personality, then how is this personality created?

2.1.20 (154)

यथा च प्राणादिः

yathā ca prāṇādiḥ

yathā—just as; ca—also; prāṇādiḥ—the origin in the prāṇa.

TRANSLATION

Just as (the soul) has its origin (in the Lord) through prāṇa, also (the personality of the soul is created in the same way).

COMMENTARY

In 1.1.22 (22) it was stated that Brahman is to be identified as a 'space' and the Lord is its origin. Then in 1.1.23 (23) it was stated that Brahman is also called prāṇa. Then in 1.1.24 (24), Brahman was compared to light. In the purports, we noted that these three sūtras taken together indicate that locations in the space called Brahman are the different individual souls, while prāṇa is the connection from the origin to each individual soul, which can also be called the 'distance' from the origin to different points in the 'space' called Brahman. This idea is understood by stating that Brahman is like the rays of light emanating from the source of light—i.e., the Lord. Brahman is hence also called Brahmajyoti. This Jyoti or light is not without a source; in short, there is a source of light in the Lord, and the soul is the particle of light that emanates from this source.

These sūtras are being referred again by the term *yatha prāṇādiḥ*, indicating 'just as the soul is connected to the source via prāṇa'. The use of the term *ca* or 'also' indicates that the unique personality referred to in the previous sūtra (by comparing each soul to a garment crafted from cloth) is also due to the same reason. In short, the different locations in Brahman are not just individual persons, but also different types with unique personalities. Just as in the body, the prāṇa spreads to many parts of the body such as hands, legs, stomach, head, etc. and each of these has a different function and a type, similarly, the souls emanating from the Lord (and connected to Him via prāṇa) have different personalities. The identity of the soul is not merely a unique individuality but also a different personality. As individuals, these souls are unique persons. But as differing personalities, they are also different from the other persons. Just like a chair and a table are not just two different things, but also two different *types* of things, and each such thing is ideally suited for a different kind of purpose, similarly, the unique purpose of the soul is based on its unique persona.

We have noted earlier that 'space' in Vedic philosophy is semantic. There is a type of space in which individual locations are different concepts. There is another type of space in which different locations are different roles. And there is another space in which different locations are different emotions. These three types of spaces constitute the three aspects of the soul, namely, *sat* (the role), *chit* (the concept), and ānanda (the pleasure). The role defines the duties of the person; the concept describes how those duties are fulfilled, and the pleasure describes how the fulfillment of duties results in different types of happiness. We have also discussed how the three aspects of the soul often conflict: what you desire may be incompatible with what you are capable of, and what you are capable of may not be available in your present role. And yet, the experience is the combination of these three components. When there is a conflict between three aspects, and yet the three must be combined, the combination is produced by creating a dominant-subordinate structure. For instance, some people will remain focused on fulfilling their desires, and if they don't have the ability and opportunity, they will try to attain those first to fulfill their desires. Others may just accept whatever is possible within the current ability and role. As these three potentialities can be organized in a hierarchy, the dominant-subordinate structure produces many kinds of personalities. Prāṇa is the choice of creating such combinations by producing a dominant-subordinate hierarchy.

Therefore, prāṇa is described as both a connection to the origin, as well as the cause of the individual personality. The individual particles of 'light' are not identical to each other, nor are they 'merged' into a single 'field'. They remain, individuals because they have an inner form caused due to the prāṇa. The prāṇa being spoken of here should be considered spiritual rather than material. It is the agency by which a soul can create his experiences (including the experience of self-existence). This agency has been given to the soul by the Lord, and it was intended to produce a certain type of experience—i.e., a specific dominant-subordinate structure—which would then create a unique personality. So, the personality of the soul is God-given, and it cannot be changed. However, this same personality can be adapted to different situations just like a chair may also be used as a ladder. Such uses, however, don't fulfill the soul, as they are contrary to his innate and predefined nature, and the soul remains unhappy. It is only when the native personality is reinvigorated that the soul becomes happy.

Topic 7

QUESTION

It would have been easier to understand the fall if the soul did not have an innate personality. Now that you are saying that the soul has an innate personality, by which is it meant to be devoted to the Lord, how does he go against his innate nature? Doesn't this make the cause of the fall harder to understand?

2.1.21 (155)

इतरव्यपदेशाद्धिताकरणादिदोषप्रसक्तिः

itaravyapadeśāddhitākaraṇādidoṣaprasaktiḥ

itara—the other (the Lord); vyapadeśāt—from the covering; dhita—bestowed; akaraṇādi—causeless origin; doṣa-prasaktiḥ—imbued with faults.

TRANSLATION

Due to the covering of the Lord, which has a causeless origin, the soul becomes bestowed (into material nature) and imbued with many faults.

COMMENTARY

The question of fall is again brought up, this time in the context of the claim that the soul has an innate personality. If a fall occurs, then the soul must go against his own nature. It is not because of extraneous factors, and therefore the responsibility of the fall still rests on the soul (as has been asserted before). However, one is again perplexed: Why would someone go against their own nature? The sūtra repeats the previous answer—namely, that we cannot find the origin because it is causeless (i.e., not caused by external factors). However, it augments that answer by the claim that the fall is because the soul turns away from the Lord. Just as we might have a natural love for someone, but we might occasionally turn away to look at other people, similarly, the soul too has a love for the Lord, but due to unexplainable reasons, he sometimes looks away. The moment he looks away, and forgets the Lord even for a moment, he falls.

Devotion to the Lord is exclusive and continuous. One cannot maintain multiple simultaneous affections that cause us to forget the love of the Lord. Even if we love others, that love is due to their attachment to the Lord. So, even in the love of others, the Lord is constantly remembered. The moment one starts loving someone else directly—and forgets that this love is due to the connection to the Lord—the Lord exits our consciousness and we become focused on the other person. This forgetfulness of the Lord then results in the fall. The implication is that the devotees in the spiritual world do not forget the Lord even for a moment. Their remembrance is continuous and unwavering. But even if the soul forgets the Lord and falls, the Lord still remembers to rescue him.

QUESTION

Doesn't it sound excessive that a moment's fault of forgetting the Lord leads to the fall? It entails that the soul is not allowed to commit mistakes, or the consequences of that mistake are dire. Why can't the situation be more permissive where the soul can occasionally either love or forget the Lord?

2.1.22 (156)

अधिकं तु भेदनिर्देशात्

adhikaṃ tu bhedanirdeśāt

adhikaṃ—excessive; tu—but; bheda-nirdeśāt—on account of the instructions about the difference (between matter and spirit, or soul the Lord).

TRANSLATION

(The situation may be called) excessive, but, the difference (between matter and spirit, or soul and the Lord) has already been instructed (and known).

COMMENTARY

Here a simple definition of matter and spirit is being provided: The spirit is the remembrance of the Lord, and matter is the forgetfulness of the Lord. The spiritual world is called yoga-māyā or the idea that "I am not the Lord, but I'm His servant, I'm connected to Him". The material world is called mahā-māyā or the idea that "There is no Lord, and I am independent". In both cases, the term māyā means "that which is not". In the spiritual world, the soul realizes that he is not the Lord, but is connected to the Lord. In the material world, the soul forgets the existence of the Lord and considers himself independent. When matter and spirit are demarcated in this way, then a moment's forgetfulness of the Lord naturally entails material existence. We may call this 'excessive', but the difference between matter and spirit is clearly described in this way.

The qualification of entry into the spiritual world is described here. It is not membership of an institution, taking initiation from some guru, or even some service to the Lord. If a moment's forgetfulness leads to falling into the material world, then the qualification of entry into the spiritual world is unceasing remembrance of the Lord. In fact, the moment we remember the Lord, we are already in the spiritual world. And the moment we forget the Lord we are immediately in the material world. As we have said previously, the soul doesn't physically fall into matter. Only its consciousness is directed toward matter. Similarly, consciousness can also be directed toward the Lord. The moment it is directed toward the Lord, the soul is in the spiritual realm, and the moment it is directed toward its own enjoyment, the soul is in the material realm.

QUESTION

But some people might call the Lord hard-hearted because He banishes the soul from the spiritual world just because the soul has forgotten the Lord.

2.1.23 (157)

अश्मादविच्च तदनुपपत्तिः

aśmādivacca tadanupapattiḥ

aśmādivat—like stone etc.; ca—also; tadanupapattiḥ—its untenability.

TRANSLATION

(The claim that the Lord is) like a stone is also untenable.

COMMENTARY

There is a saying: Heads I win, tails you lose. If the Lord was to never allow the soul to leave the spiritual world and let him enjoy his independence, the Lord would be called hard-hearted as He doesn't give the soul freedom. If, on the other hand, the Lord allows the soul to immediately leave the world as soon as he desires independence, the Lord may again be called hard-hearted. Such arguments are untenable because the Lord is not 'punishing' the soul by abandoning him. He accompanies the soul and waits for the soul to turn toward Him. Many people turn toward God when they are suffering and ask for His grace. But as soon as the suffering is over, they again forget the Lord. This is an indication that despite suffering, the soul is not inclined to return to the Lord. Despite seeing how everyone is suffering in this world and experiencing such suffering directly, the soul still thinks that he can enjoy independently. Even if this enjoyment comes along with some suffering, if there is some enjoyment, people are prepared to tolerate a lot of suffering. This continued neglect of the Lord indicates that the soul indeed carries a desire for independence. So, not allowing the soul independence as soon as he develops such a desire would be tyrannical, rather than immediately allowing him the freedom and waiting for his return. If the Lord was hard-hearted, He would not accompany the soul in the material world as Paramātma in the heart who enables the enjoyment.

Topic 8

QUESTION

You say that the Lord is very kind, and He appears in the material world to take the soul back to the spiritual world. But isn't He also very powerful, who can forcibly change the circumstances in a way that the soul can return to His place? We have seen that kind and compassionate parents sometimes force the child against his wishes to do what is right and avoid what will hurt him. So, why can't the Lord forcibly take the soul to the spiritual world? The Lord can show some miracles to the soul to attract Him if He wants the soul to return.

2.1.24 (158)

उपसंहारदर्शनान्नेति चेत् न क्षीरवद्धि

upasaṃhāradarśanānneti cet na kṣīravaddhi

upasaṃhāra—the act of drawing closer; darśanāt—from being seen; na—not; iti cet—if it be said; na—not; kṣīravat—like milk; hi—since.

TRANSLATION

If it is said that the Lord is not drawing the soul closer by becoming visible to him (e.g., through miracles etc.) (we say) no, because (He is) just like milk.

COMMENTARY

The problem of evil generates much debate in the philosophy of religion. This problem has been indirectly brought up previously. For instance, earlier it was asked about why the Lord accepts things offered with devotion, but doesn't accept other things (which are not offered with devotion) although they are still done under His supervision? And the answer was that there is a difference between wanting something and approving something (reluctantly). The Lord accepts what He wants, but He approves other things (if the soul wants). Subsequently, it was asked: If the soul has evil in this world, and the Lord created the soul, then the evil must be in the soul. To that, the answer was that the Lord created the soul to serve Him, but the soul felt inferior in this position and wanted to become independent of the Lord's service to overcome this inferiority. In the previous sūtra, there was an attack on the kindness of the Lord by stating that since He allows the soul to enter the material world, He is unkind; the response to that was that the Lord also comes along to save the soul. Now, a different kind of critique is offered: If the Lord is this kind, then why doesn't He demonstrate His presence to the soul by becoming visible to the soul?

To counter this argument, the author compares the Lord to milk, which is the source for innumerable kinds of foods—cream, buttermilk, yogurt, cheese, butter, clarified butter, cottage cheese, etc. Sometimes, the material world is compared to yogurt, while the spiritual world is compared to milk. Now, the point is that when we see varied transformations of milk, we don't see the milk, although these are transformations of milk. We think that the milk has disappeared, and a transformation has appeared. In the same way, even the material creation is an emanation from the Lord, but it has been transformed. The capacity to transform the milk into many kinds of preparations means that the Lord behaves in relation to the soul just as the soul wants to relate to the Lord.

If the soul wants to be devoted to the Lord, then the Lord becomes sweet. But if the soul wants to compete with the Lord's greatness, then the Lord is prepared to compete. We cannot compete with a greater person and then expect them to be defeated by us despite their greatness. Therefore, the Lord's transformation into a competitor means that the soul will always be defeated. This is not a fault in the Lord. It is based on the soul's desire to compete.

We can also say that milk is sweet, while yogurt is sour. The sweetness is love, and sourness is competition. It leads to disunity, disharmony, clashes, and conflict. The unity that was previously present in milk is now missing. The lack of unity, however, arises because we have rejected the unifying entity—the Lord. However, if the Lord is understood as the unifying agency, then the same world can be transformed back into milk, and oppositions will not entail contradictions; they will simply indicate two complementary sides of the same thing. Just like a coin has head and tail, and yet these are simply two sides of the same coin, in the same way, there are opposites, but there can be unity if each side is viewed as denoting a complementary aspect of the same reality.

Therefore, the argument should not be that the Lord has disappeared from our vision, and He is not appearing in our vision to attract us back to the spiritual reality. The argument should rather be that *we* have decided to reject the presence of the Lord, thereby creating disunity and disharmony, which then leads to conflict and suffering. This suffering is our creation, not the Lord's.

QUESTION

Does the presence of conflict and disharmony in this world indicate that the Lord is absent from this world, or is He present even in this world?

2.1.25 (159)

देवादिवदपि लोके

devādivadapi loke

devādivat—like the demigods and higher living beings; api—also; loke—in their respective planets or places in the world.

TRANSLATION

Like the demigods and other higher living beings who are situated in higher planetary systems, (the Lord) also (is situated in His place).

COMMENTARY

In the normal course of things, yogurt doesn't transform back into milk. However, in this case, the material world can become the spiritual world if the presence of the Lord is acknowledged. This sūtra states that the Lord exists even in this world, although we compete for superiority. Despite the conflict in the material world, the world doesn't fall apart, and it won't fall apart, because the Lord is keeping it composed and organized in His role as a *maintainer*. In short, there is conflict and disharmony due to the soul's desire for superiority. However, there is no anarchy because the Lord still preserves the universe. Conflicts, therefore, do not entail the absence of the Lord. On the other hand, we should see why the conflicts do not result in the complete destruction of the universe. In this sūtra, the Lord's presence in the universe is compared to the presence of the many demigods. Each demigod occupies a different planet, and the Lord too has His own planet within the universe, which is called Śveta-dvīpa. This planet is said to be the residence of the Paramātma or Kṣīroda-kaśāyī Viṣṇu.

Even though the existence of the Lord in the heart has been stated earlier, most people are not inward-looking. They like to think that if God exists, then there must be a place of His residence. If the residence is beyond the material world, then His existence is suspect. So, both answers are dissatisfying in some respect— (1) that God exists beyond the world and is therefore invisible, and (2) God exists in each person's heart but is still invisible to most of the people. Since we cannot see the Lord beyond the world or in the heart, someone can say that the Lord doesn't exist in the world. This type of question is being answered here by saying that the Lord is not just existing beyond the material world, and not just in each person's heart. He is also present on a planet within the material universe, just like the planets of the other demigods. While the other demigods perform the administration of the different departments in the universe, the Lord prevents the world from falling apart. We might note in this regard that the different departments in a government or a company compete for power. The head of the government or the CEO in a government resolves their conflicts by balancing their respective powers. If the head of the government or the CEO of the company is absent, the government and the company will fall apart due to internal competition between the departments. Similarly, the Lord gives greater and lesser powers to different demigods to balance them. He also punishes the tyrants and rewards the cooperative. Through all these actions, the Lord maintains and preserves the world of competitors, although this competition is never eliminated due to the tendencies in the soul.

Topic 9

QUESTION

You have earlier indicated that the duality of this world must be rejected, and only the unity must be accepted. You are now stating that this duality need not be rejected because it is complementary aspects of the Lord, which seem to be conflicting due to our vision lacking the unifying cause. How should we understand the rejection of duality and the acceptance of complementarity?

2.1.26 (160)

कृत्स्नप्रसक्तिर्निरवयवत्वशब्दकोपोवा

kṛtsnaprasaktirniravayavatvaśabdakopovā

kṛtsna-prasaktiḥ—devotion to the whole; niravayava—without parts; tvaśabda—many scriptural statements; kopovā—against the prevalent.

TRANSLATION

The devotion to a whole without parts is against the scriptural statements.

COMMENTARY

In the previous sūtras, it has been argued that the suffering of the material world is our creation, and it exists despite the Lord's attempts at unification. It has also been stated that these so-called conflicts of this world are factually non-existent. Just like a coin has a head and tail, or a person has a back and front, similarly, these opposites are reconciled in the Lord. However, if we don't see the Lord, then we think that these oppositions are irreconcilable, and hence one side of the opposition must be true. Then, we compete in ensuring that one side of the coin wins, but the fact is that it cannot exist without the other side. The Lord ensures that the balance between the sides is restored, but as each side occasionally wins or loses, we tend to consider the material world as a place of suffering because we are not constantly winning. The cause of this distress is that we are capable of being one side only; only the Lord is capable of being opposites. So, when we compare the world to ourselves, we think that only one side of the coin must be real or true, while the other side must be unreal or false. The devotee instead compares the world to the Lord, not to themselves. He can see that these opposites are simply different facets of the Lord, and they seem opposed to each other because of our comparing the world to ourselves.

This sūtra goes on to state that there is no point in thinking of a coin by rejecting the head and tail of the coin. There is no point in thinking of a person who doesn't have a front and a back, head and feet, a left and a right, etc. We must rather understand both the unity and the diversity. The diversity cannot be rejected, although the unity must be prioritized. The earlier rejection of the duality is merely to indicate that there is a unity beyond this diversity. Once we understand that, then we can understand how this diversity is parts of the unity. Like the head and the tail are parts of a coin, or the head and the feet are parts of the body, similarly, the duality is aspects and parts of the Lord. So, simply the study of unity is not enough. We must also see how the diversity is part of that unity, has expanded from it, and is also reconciled within it.

QUESTION

The simultaneous study of unity and diversity is interesting because you previously rejected the importance of diversity in favor of unity. Since we had said that we should reject the scriptures that deal in duality, and only focus on those scriptures that deal with the unity, does it mean that we can go back to studying all the scriptures—even those that are dealing in the duality?

2.1.27 (161)

श्रुतेस्तु शब्दमूलत्वात्

śrutestu śabdamūlatvāt

śruteḥ—the scriptural texts; tu—but; śabdamūlatvāt—on account of the sound having a common root (in the Lord).

TRANSLATION

The diverse scriptures (both dealing in the study of duality and non-duality) are but (the diverse manifestations of) a common root (in the Lord).

COMMENTARY

The term *mūla* means a 'root', and the term *mūlatvāt* means 'from just like a root'. When the speaker of the scriptures—i.e., the Lord—is the root, then the scriptures are like shoots. Some of these scriptures may make conflicting statements, and followers of these scriptures may sometimes argue with each other claiming the superiority of their scripture or their viewpoint. Previously it was said that we must reject the scriptures that are dealing in duality, and only focus on the transcendent unity. But now it is also being stated that these scriptures—which can seem mutually contradictory—must be understood as words of the Lord. They are diversified just like shoots are diversified from the root. The ultimate goal of all the scriptures is to reach the root, the shoots must not be understood as being false; they too are of divine origin and parts of the Lord.

This claim is important because Vedic philosophy is often accused of presenting conflicting points of view. For instance, there are personalist and impersonalist views. Within personalism, there are differences between Shaivism, Shaktism, and Vaishnavism. The personalist and impersonalist views are only interpretations of Vedānta—one of the six schools of theistic philosophy; schools like Mīmāṃsā don't accept the existence of a God or demigods. Meanwhile, other schools such as Sāñkhya deal with the nature of the material universals, Vaiśeṣika deals with the nature of material individuals or atoms, Nyāya deals with the process by which the world of individuals evolves (e.g., through a succession of questions and answers), and Yoga deals with the understanding of how this diversity can be understood as being related to a single unity.

Owing to the multitude of doctrines, most modern academic students conclude that all these ideas must have existed at various times and these scriptures must have been written at different times. They date the written copies of these texts or examine the points in time at which one philosophy dominated over the others, thereby concluding that these have indeed evolved over time. But in this sūtra such attempts have been rejected. All these philosophies are branches of a common root; they can aid in the understanding of the root, and they are reconciled if the root is understood. Just as the understanding of head and tail helps us understand the coin better—i.e., something that has opposite sides—similarly, these scriptures should be viewed as leading us to the root.

QUESTION

But why create so many scriptures when only one truth is important? Yes, we can say that the diversity expands from the unity, and both must be studied. But doesn't the explication of this diversity create numerous confusions? In particular, as you have said, they can bind the soul into the material world unless the transcendent portions of these texts are emphasized. So, why even create those Vedic texts that can then mislead the soul into meaningless pursuits?

2.1.28 (162)

आत्मनि चैवं विचित्राश्च हि

ātmani caivaṃ vicitrāśca hi

ātmani—in the individual soul; ca—also; evaṃ—thus; vicitrāḥ—diverse; ca—also; hi—because.

TRANSLATION

The diversities are also found in the individual soul in the same way because (they exist in the Lord) also.

COMMENTARY

Although the goal of the Vedic texts is attaining the understanding of the root from which everything has emanated, not everyone is interested in the conclusion. We find people interested in mathematics, physics, economics, psychology, etc. although everyone seeks to find the meaning of their lives. Even the study of diverse subjects is ultimately the quest for oneself through these diverse subjects; if we understand these subjects, we think we have partly understood ourselves. So, in one sense, there are many partial and diverse ways of understanding the self, and in another sense, there is a complete understanding of the self. All these partial and complete types of pursuits are present in the different souls because the souls are also diverse with material and spiritual personalities. This sūtra states that all these diversities are created for people with diverse interests, such that they can gradually progress from the shoots to the root. Each scripture may emphasize one aspect of reality, but they do not reject the truth of other realities. For instance, even scriptures devoted to Vaishnavism mention Lord Śiva and His Śakti as the masters of the material world. This was earlier indicated in the sūtra 1.4.19 (125) by the 'connected nature of the scriptural passages' implying that even if one sees apparent conflicts, one should only accept the interpretation that resolves their apparent conflict.

One might wonder: What is the need to propound theories about the material world if such theories can be created by humans? Shouldn't the scripture be exclusively devoted to the transcendence that we cannot perceive? The short answer to that question is that the theories produced through our speculation are not guaranteed to converge into a coherent understanding. At the present, not only are there diverse irreconcilable theories within each department of knowledge (e.g., physics), but most of the departments (such as physics, psychology, and philosophy) don't even read each other's works or attempt to formulate a shared understanding of the truth. They are quite content working in isolation, making conflicting claims. A system that doesn't even aim for unity cannot hope to achieve the goal of unity and explain how that unity expanded into the observable diversity. The Vedic descriptions are substitutes for these endeavors since the reader can progress from one aspect to another and obtain greater levels of unity in their knowledge. In short, you traverse from the leaves to the twigs, to the branches, to the trunks, and finally to the root. Your interest in the leaves is not contradictory to the understanding of the root, although limiting oneself to that leaf is not recommended. By stating that the scriptures have a common root, it is implied that one can find the unity by studying them. Meanwhile, those who are directly interested in the diversity, rather than the unity, can still study these scriptures according to their differing natures. Such studies will not be futile in the quest for the nature of the complete reality.

QUESTION

Many people claim that the diverse fields of inquiry can never be reconciled. They are necessarily limited models of reality that have been created for our own understanding and we should not even demand their consistency. Accordingly, we should not aim for the quest of the ultimate truth, as there is no guaranteed method for attaining such a truth by attempts of reconciliation.

2.1.29 (163)

स्वपक्षदोषाच्च

svapakṣadoṣācca

svapakṣa—one's own opinion; doṣāt—on account of the faults; ca—also.

TRANSLATION

On account of faults in one's own opinion also (should be rejected).

COMMENTARY

All modern attempts at knowledge are beset with the dilemma between consistency and completeness. This dilemma arises due to duality, which is then presented as contradictions between the opposites. Owing to this duality, if you study one side of the opposition, you can have consistency within your viewpoint, but your views will necessarily be incomplete because they do not incorporate the other side of the opposition. If, on the other hand, you try to reconcile these opposites without the understanding of the Lord in whom these opposites are reconciled, then your attempts at reconciliation will fail—i.e., they will lead to contradictions. If we avoid the contradictions, then our understanding is always incomplete. So, due to duality, the pursuit of consistency results in incompleteness, and the pursuit of completeness results in inconsistency. The person who argues against the attempt to unify the diverse areas of study has understood that they are indeed dealing in dualities, and they are prepared to sacrifice completeness in favor of some internal consistencies within their fields. They are worried that if they tried to unify, they would have to throw away the assumptions that contradict the other fields, leaving them with nothing.

But we must also realize that any incomplete description is also necessarily false. For instance, in physics, light was initially described by Newton as corpuscles, which turned out to be false when interference phenomena were detected and led to the idea that light is a wave. This wave theory was also found false with the discovery of black-body radiation which entails that light is absorbed or emitted as particles. Today, two incongruous ideas—namely, wave and particle—are employed to describe the nature of light, which means that unless you induct both your theory is incomplete, and if you use only one, then your theory is necessarily false (i.e., incompatible with the facts). The point is that you cannot claim the truth of a theory unless you have reconciled these contradictions, and all seemingly consistent theories are all potentially false.

So, the person who argues for keeping separate fields of consistency must face not just the problem of incompleteness, but also the problem of potential falsity. Similarly, the person who argues for completeness must face the problem of inconsistencies between the dualities. The solution to the latter problem has been described—if you use the scriptures to study the diverse fields, you will find the unity in the diversity. You will not only understand the diversities but also how they exist inside the unity. Therefore, the argument of the person who rejects such unification is also rejected here on the grounds that their approach will neither lead to completeness nor even to an incomplete truth.

Topic 10

QUESTION

But even if we study the diverse scriptures, we may keep seeing the contradictions in them, and we may never be able to resolve these contradictions. What is the guarantee that we will come to a complete understanding? Isn't it possible that we are forever lost in conflictual ideas in diverse scriptures?

2.1.30 (164)

सर्वोपेता च तद्दर्शनात्

sarvopetā ca taddarśanāt

sarvopetā—having everything; ca—also; tat-darśanāt—from seeing that.

TRANSLATION

(Full knowledge is) also (attained) from seeing that which has everything.

COMMENTARY

Every area of scientific inquiry is based on the formulation of models. For example, the motion of planets in the solar system is based on the model of a stone tied to a rope being rotated around a center. Similarly, the model of light is based on the idea of vibrating strings or water waves. Each area of human inquiry creates an understanding of the world based on a model, and these models are often conflicting, which leads to conflict between the theories. To reconcile these contradictions, we need a model that contains all the diversities.

This sūtra asserts that the Absolute Truth is that model. What does this mean in a practical sense? It means that we must think of everything as persons, which exist in complementary ways. Material nature is therefore not impersonal. It should also be understood as a person. But what do we mean by a person? The answer is that a person has three aspects—cognition, relation, and emotion—and material nature should also be described in terms of these three modes. Then, because the Absolute Truth can expand, similarly, material nature also expands from a root into trunks, branches, and leaves. Thus, matter is also organized as a hierarchy of relations, cognitions, and emotions. Then, each of these relations, cognitions, and emotions comes in various flavors. For instance, cognition has six aspects of knowledge, beauty, power, wealth, fame, and renunciation. Thus, all the expansions also have all these qualities. Finally, the cause of all these changes is that the feminine creates a desire in the masculine, and the masculine then uses the power of the feminine to fulfill the desire.

So, by the model, we mean that nature is not moving linearly; it is rather a dialectical movement from questions to answers to questions. This dialectic involves three aspects of a person, each of which is organized into a hierarchy, and this hierarchy is produced by the mixing of the three aspects. Thus, clues about the nature of the Absolute Truth give us the model by which we can understand how diversity is created, and how it can be reconciled. We cannot speculate our way to such an answer; we must rather understand the nature of the Absolute Truth, which can then result in the unifying understanding.

QUESTION

The central problem seems to be that most people like to think of the Absolute Truth impersonally, rather than personally. Thus, for instance, the world must be governed by laws, rather than by a person. The origin for everything must be something without will or consciousness, and the world must exist without a purpose. Or, that life arises late in the evolution of the material world. You are saying that we must begin in understanding personalities and their interactions and that the material world would be explained in the same way?

2.1.31 (165)

विकिरणत्वान्नेति चेत् तदुक्तम्

vikaraṇatvānneti cet taduktam

vikaraṇatvāt—as if from something devoid of instruments (of perception and action); na—not; iti cet—if it be said; tat—that; uktam—has been explained.

TRANSLATION

If it is said that (everything is produced) as if from something devoid of instruments (i.e., senses), (we say) no, and that has already been explained.

COMMENTARY

This sūtra is the summary rejection of impersonalism and voidism. In voidism, the ultimate truth is the reconciliation of opposites, and that reconciliation leads to nothingness, because the opposites cancel each other. In impersonalism, the opposites are not present in the Absolute Truth; they are instead the attributes of material energy, which can either be regarded as real or as illusory, but since the opposites are missing from the Absolute Truth, ultimately (even if we regard the material energy as being real), all the opposites are unreal.

This sūtra says that we should not think of the Absolute Truth in terms of impersonalism and voidism. We should rather think of the Absolute Truth as a person with senses. When there are senses, there is a cognitive capacity and a desire for pleasure. To fulfill this desire, there must be diversity, and the senses are used to create the diversity and then enjoy with the diversity. And since the diversity is created by a personality, that person is also the Supreme Being.

Of course, this understanding has been stated at the end of the first chapter. So why is it being repeated? The answer is that the previous description pertained to *everything* and the present description pertains to *anything*. Impersonalism and voidism reject personalism when it comes to the ultimate reality, and if personalities are rejected in an absolute sense, they must also be rejected in a relative sense. For instance, the world must be governed by impersonal laws rather than personal administration. The personalist acknowledges the reality of personalities in an absolute sense. But with that acceptance, we should also acknowledge the reality of personalities in a relative sense. For instance, we must now say that the world is controlled by persons; the lawfulness in nature is because these persons behave in a regulated manner, rather than randomly. The judgment of right and wrong, the delivery of results of pleasure or suffering, are all under the supervision of persons. The understanding of the laws of nature simply means understanding the person who implements the orderly behavior that we consider a law. This orderly nature is the personality of the person and the law prevails because a soul administers the law.

So, personalism is not merely a theory about the nature of the absolute reality. It also entails a different understanding of how ordinary phenomena must be modeled in terms personalism. Every time we face problems in understanding something, we can resolve them by thinking in terms of persons.

For example, the wave-particle duality in atomic theory can be understood if we say that the 'particle' is a symbol of meaning, with contextual relations to other particles which we call the 'field'. The complete description of a cow involves saying two things—(1) that there is a particle called cow, and (2) there is a field that defines how this cow is not a tiger, it is a mammal, and it is not other cows. In classical physics, each physical particle could exist by itself. But now, because reality is symbols, therefore, the symbols are only defined through a distinction to other symbols. The field entails the inseparability of the cow from everything else. So, the quantum is observed as a particle, and it is indeed an individual thing. However, this individual thing is not a classical particle; it is rather a symbol of meaning defined in relation to other such symbols. Finally, something being a cow, and not being a tiger are complementary descriptions of the same thing; therefore, they cannot be applied simultaneously. Indeed, we might sometimes contrast the cow to a tiger, and say that the cow is gentle, and the tiger is fierce. Then we may contrast the cow to the horse, and say that the cow is slow, and the horse is fast. Then we may contrast the cow to a goat, and say that the cow's milk is thick, while the goat's milk is thinner. In this way, different properties of the cow are revealed in contrast to other animals. However, since all these contrasts are not simultaneous, therefore, all the properties of the cow are not known at once. We rather know the same thing in different ways—one after another—because these qualities are *modes* of the cow.

The remaining question is—what is the order of these contrasts? Do we know the cow in contrast to the horse before we know the cow in contrast to the goat? The answer to that question is that these contrasts are sequenced due to our desiring and deserving. The properties of the cow in relation to the goat, horse, tiger, etc. constitute the *chit*. The desiring constitutes the ānanda, and the deserving constitutes the *sat*. Current physics describes the *chit* or cognition as meaningless particles. If we enhanced this understanding as cognition and conation, then the same world would be known as symbols of meaning. And then we can talk about how these symbols are sequenced through desiring and deserving. Thus, if we model the atomic world using the principles of persons, then we can solve one of the most perplexing problems of modern time.

The same principle can be applied to any area of inquiry, such as biology, psychology, sociology, economics, etc. We can use the understanding of the Absolute Truth to understand anything else. Thus, when everything or the Absolute Truth is known, then anything or the individual relative truths are automatically known. These are not two separate kinds of knowledge. Only those who do not know the Absolute Truth find a difference between the Absolute and the Relative truths. If the Absolute Truth is known, everything is known. In fact, everything is known consistently and through the same model.

Topic 11

QUESTION

Whenever we speak about senses (of perception and action), we also speak about the objects of these senses. For example, for the sense of smell, the smell is an object. The senses are drawn toward their objects, and the purpose of these senses is to interact with these objects. In the case of the Lord, who is described to have senses, where are the objects of these senses—i.e., their purposes?

2.1.32 (166)

न प्रयोजनवत्त्वात्

na prayojanavattvāt

na—not; prayojanavattvāt—as if on account of having needs or wants.

TRANSLATION

(The senses of the Lord) are not as if driven by needs or wants.

COMMENTARY

If you are unhappy, then you want your friends because they can make you happy. You expect them to lift you up, say cheerful things, so that the enjoyment will dissipate your unhappiness. But if you are already happy, when you meet a friend, you share your happiness, and try to make them happy. You are not expecting anything from them; you are rather expressing your happiness. There is hence a difference between needing and sharing. Our senses are needy; they contact the material objects to overcome the incompleteness. But the Lord's senses are not needy; and yet, they are used to express His happiness. Thus, in the material world, we use our power to acquire objects of the senses so that the unhappiness of desiring can be overcome. However, in the spiritual world, the power is used to express or expand a person's happiness. This expression makes others happier, and they then express their delight, producing an unending cycle of happiness and its expression. In the material world, everyone is needy, and when they take some objects of happiness, then someone else becomes unhappy. So, our quest for the objects of the senses to find happiness should not be compared to the expression of objects due to happiness. The search for happiness in the external world is the *prayojana* or the purpose of material causality and it drives our senses towards their objects. But the expression of inner happiness is the *prayojana* or the purpose of spiritual causality and it produces the objects of the senses for the happiness of the Lord.

QUESTION

Since you are distinguishing between material and spiritual causality, in both cases the senses are being employed, but for different purposes. Does this mean that the spiritual world is in some ways quite like the material world in that in both places there are senses, objects, and their mutual interactions?

2.1.33 (167)

लोकवत्तु लीलाकैवल्यम्

lokavattu līlākaivalyam

lokavat—as in this world; tu—but; līlākaivalyam—liberated pastimes.

TRANSLATION

(The spiritual world is) just like this world, but it is liberated pastimes.

COMMENTARY

After denouncing impersonalism and voidism, this sūtra clearly states that the transcendent world is just like this world—i.e., there are persons with desires, they have senses, which then interact with the sense objects. The use of the term *tu* or 'but' followed by *līlākaivalyam* or 'liberated pastimes' indicates a difference between the present world and the spiritual world. The use of *kaivalyam* or liberation means that we are free from the hankering of material desire, which is produced from an inner unhappiness and sense of incompleteness, and to overcome that unhappiness we try to use others for our happiness. When this hankering of desire arising from inner incompleteness is overcome, then a new type of desire is produced, which *expresses* the inner happiness. Now, the soul becomes interested in making others happy rather than becoming happy. Since everyone is trying to please everyone else, and nobody is in need for happiness arising from internal distress, the result is unending joy. The activities of this spiritual world are *līlā* or pastimes just like the social interactions in this world. However, they are not caused by selfishness to satisfy one's own senses. Rather, the senses are satisfied through satisfying others' senses.

Topic 12

QUESTION

You seem to be implying that even the material world is a *līlā* or pastime of the Lord. Isn't it harsh and cruel to say that the world in which the souls are suffering life after life is merely an enjoyable pastime for the Supreme Lord?

2.1.34 (168)

वैषम्यनैर्घृण्ये न सापेक्षत्वात् तथा हि दर्शयति

vaiṣamyanairghṛṇye na sāpekṣatvāt tathā hi darśayati

aiṣamyanairghṛṇye—partiality and cruelty; na—not; sāpekṣatvāt—on account of the selfish view; tathā—so; hi—indeed; darśayati—perceives.

TRANSLATION

(The Lord's pastime in this world is) not on account of partiality and cruelty, (but) on account of the selfish viewpoint (the soul) indeed perceives it so.

COMMENTARY

In 2.1.23 (157) the claim that the Lord is just like stone or hard-hearted because He banishes the soul from the spiritual world was rejected. It was explained that the soul turns away from the Lord, but the Lord still accompanies Him into the material world as Paramātma to bring the soul back. However, one can still argue: while I'm suffering, the Lord is not suffering, so He must be cruel. Implicit in this argument is the demand that the Lord must also suffer when the soul is suffering; after all, the soul won't complain that the Lord is not enjoying when the soul is enjoying. The intent of coming to the material world was due to the inferiority relative to the Lord, and the desire to be like Him. But if the soul is unable to attain the same position as the Lord, then he can complain that the Lord is cruel that He makes us suffer while He continues enjoying.

This sūtra rejects the conclusion that the Lord is cruel but acknowledges that due to the soul's selfish attitude he indeed sees the Lord as cruel.

Psychologists recognize a Narcissistic Personality Disorder in which a person humiliates others in order to feel superior to them; however, when they are shown to be in the wrong, they refuse to accept responsibility for their actions, while arguing and fighting with the person who pointed out their faults, ultimately trying to turn the tables in order to prove that their accuser is at fault. Their basic inner insecurity prevents them from accepting that they are ever wrong. They always try to shift the blame to someone else. Most often, these blames are shifted to the people who are kindest and gentlest toward them. A narcissist believes that such people who are caring for them will not be able to retaliate, and their attempts at shifting the blame would be successful. Their inner crisis is so severe that they consider any criticism as fundamentally undermining their self-love, and they are unable to accept their mistakes.

The soul who considers the Lord unkind and cruel is a prime example of a person suffering from a Narcissistic Personality Disorder. This narcissism, or the need to love oneself unconditionally, while refusing to accept any fault and then blaming others for one's unhappiness, is referred to here as *sāpekṣatvāt* (being situated on one's own side, or considering only one's own viewpoint). Acceptance of mistakes leads to guilt, which then leads to corrections. But if the person is so weak that they cannot accept the mistake, then they inevitably resort to blaming the people who are kindest and gentlest towards them. Such blaming doesn't solve any problem; it just pushes the kind and gentle people away, leaving no one to blame. In the same way, by blaming the Lord, the soul increases his distance to the Lord, and gradually becomes atheistic. When the Lord no longer exists for the soul, the soul is left with no one to blame. Ultimately, by pushing the Lord away, the soul is forced to accept responsibility. So, the right approach would be to accept responsibility from the start.

QUESTION

But many people ask: Why do bad things happen to good people? They say that they have been good all their life and done all their duties. They even have faith in the Lord. And yet, bad things have happened to them. If these bad things are happening, then what is the point of being good or doing good deeds? The world seems not to care about our good or bad natures. And if there is no morality in this world, then how can we repose our faith in the Lord?

2.1.35 (169)

न कर्मावभिागादतिि चेत् न अनादत्विात्

na karmāvibhāgāditi cet na anāditvāt

na—not; karma—actions; avibhāgāt—due to lack of distinction; iti cet—if it be said; na—no; anāditvāt—because of (karma) being without a beginning.

TRANSLATION

If it is said that there is no distinction between (good and bad) actions, (we say) no, because karma is going on since time immemorial.

COMMENTARY

While we have indicated the role of karma in the purports to the previous sūtra, this is first instance of the use of this term in Vedānta Sūtra. Karma is responsible for what happens to us; how we react to it is based on our guna. Everyone is situated in some role in their life, which demands the performance of duties, which are called dharma. Ideally, one must perform their duties without expectation of results; "doing as a matter of duty" is called karma-yoga because by such performance one does not produce karma. However, in this material world, we always perform our duties expecting some results. When dharma is performed with the desire for happiness, then good karma is created. But what is 'good'? It is whatever we like. If a person is lazy, then good karma will allow him to live a lazy life. If, however, a person is hardworking, then good karma will give him many opportunities to work. So, karma doesn't have an absolute meaning; the meaning of karma—i.e., good or bad—is relative to our guna. When our duties go against our nature or guna, then we tend to neglect them, or perform them reluctantly, or perform them with bitterness. This negative intentional state then produces bad karma. Accordingly, the actions of a person are classified into three categories—*sukarma* or good karma, *vikarma* or bad karma, and *akarma* or no karma. Once sukarma and vikarma have been created, they lie latent or unmanifest; they gradually become manifest through the course of one's life, and indeed, over the course of numerous lives.

The time of birth fixes the type of karma that will manifest over our lifetime. This is the basis of astrology, by which we can predict what will happen to us; however, we still cannot predict how we will react to it. Even though a person has guna or a material nature, which predetermines one's reactions to situations, the guna can be controlled by the soul if it rejects the automatically produced reactions due to guna. The time of birth that fixes the karma that will manifest over our lifetime is called *prārabdha*. As time passes in this life, both good and bad karma are manifest according to the dashā of planets. The karma that is manifesting right now is called *kriyamāna*. And the karma that is still in store for future lifetimes is called *sañcita*. So, if you have performed good or bad deeds, the results are not immediately seen, because the karma of the lifetime was fixed at the time of birth—called prārabdha. Similarly, if you perform bad deeds, the results will not manifest immediately; you can keep enjoying the results of prārabdha even as you perform bad deeds. The results of our actions are stored in the repository called sañcita. Based on a person's guna, one gets a certain type of body—e.g., human, dog, cow, bird, tree, fish, etc. And a small part of the sañcita then becomes the prārabdha for a given lifetime.

Once we understand this science of action and consequence, then we can see how doing good things may not immediately lead to good outcomes; it is because of previous bad actions, that in turn defined the prārabdha, that our life may continue to be full of difficulties. However, this doesn't mean that there is no consequence of our actions. All these actions are getting accumulated in the sañcita and will produce their effects over successive lifetimes. Nature has a perfect system of morality, and every action produces a consequence. But we must understand the science of this action and consequence, and not assume that good actions must immediately produce good outcomes. This sūtra specifically states that the cycle of action and reaction has no beginning. The karma we are reaping right now could have come from any of the previous lives. So, instead of thinking that there is no consequence of our actions, we must understand that our suffering is due to bad karma produced in earlier lives.

QUESTION

But many people will say that they are not willingly doing bad actions; rather, circumstances are forcing them to do so. For example, if a man is born very poor, is abandoned by his parents, and then falls into bad company, which then indoctrinates him into crime, should we not blame the circumstances? If these circumstances are produced due to previous bad karma, and the bad circumstances then lead him into further bad action, then he is perpetually caught in the cycle of bad action, bad consequence, and then more bad action. It seems that bad action then predestines him to eternal suffering due to karma.

2.1.36 (170)

उपपद्यते चाप्युपलभ्यते च

upapadyate cāpyupalabhyate ca

upapadyate—is produced; ca—and; api—also; upalabhyate—is reaped; ca—also.

TRANSLATION

(The consequences of actions, or karma) are being produced just as they are being reaped (the same action both produces and reaps karma).

COMMENTARY

The sūtra refutes the claim that one must necessarily be caught in an eternal cycle of bad actions leading to bad circumstances which then lead to more bad actions. Every bad circumstance offers us an opportunity to act in an appropriate way; it may not be the best thing we want, and it is also possible that we may not be able to do the ideal thing. But if it is the best thing that could be done in that situation, then performing those actions will lead to good karma.

Dharma or duty is not universal; it is always contextual. We cannot change what happens to us, but we can change how we respond to it. So, even if we are in a bad situation, we still have the choice to change our response to it. It may not be easy, but who can we blame for a bad situation if we are creating these situations through our actions? Every action is partially governed by the situation and partially governed by our response to the situation. The situation is due to the reaping of past karma, and the response creates new karma.

Topic 13

QUESTION

So how can a person become free of the suffering caused due to karma?

2.1.37 (171)

सर्वधर्मोपपत्तेश्च

sarvadharmopapatteśca

sarva-dharma-upapatteḥ—caused by the doing of all duties; ca—also.

TRANSLATION

(The freedom from karma) can also be gotten by doing all our duties.

COMMENTARY

In the previous sūtra it was stated that karma is simultaneously being reaped and created, and in this sūtra, the reason for the creation of karma is being explained. The reason is that we don't perform all our duties. Why? Because there is always contention between different duties. Sometimes we neglect our family because we are driven by the greed to earn more money at the workplace, and sometimes we neglect the workplace because we are too attached to enjoying with the family. Contentions between different duties drag us in different directions, and to prioritize one duty over another we ask ourselves: What type of work will produce better results for me? We don't realize that karma entails a destiny about what will come to us, and by greater or lesser effort we cannot change that outcome. We rather become enamored by the possibility of better results by the performance of one type of activity and we neglect other duties. If we realize that karma fixes what results we will get, then we will perform our duties in a detached manner, and the side effect of that detachment is that we will perform all our duties. Of course, sometimes some duty takes precedence over others, and that is part of understanding dharma. So, the ask is not to perform all the duties simultaneously (because that isn't possible). The ask is not to neglect a duty, by balancing different duties. And the cause of karma is that we are driven by greed and neglect some duties.

The performance of duties without the expectation of results, and the performance of all the duties, are just two ways of expressing the same idea. To perform all the duties, we must be detached from the results—e.g., that I'm spending time away from some work, which might produce better outcomes for me. And by getting detached we can perform all the duties. The detachment from the expectation of results is called karma-yoga, and the same idea is explained here differently—performance of all duties is also karma-yoga.

Note the use of *ca* or 'also' in this sūtra. The performance of all the duties is not the only way for obtaining freedom from karma. Specifically, how can a person become detached from the results of our actions unless they realize that they are not this body, and the present life is one of many lives lived before and after? The cultivation of knowledge or jñāna-yoga helps in detachment, and therefore, the performance of all the duties. Similarly, even if we cultivate knowledge, there are latent unconscious tendencies, which force a person to behave in predetermined ways. How does one gain control over the mind and make it free of these unconscious productions of desires? This is where the practice of aśtānga-yoga can be useful, which teaches one to control the body followed by the mind, and then focus one's consciousness in the heart. But how can one keep oneself focused on one thing unless he is enjoying the experience? Ultimately the desire for enjoyment will drag the person somewhere else. Thus, the practice of bhakti-yoga is important to make life pleasurable so that the mind can be detached from other mundane desires and their push-pull. Thus, the implication is that karma-yoga is one of the ways, and it doesn't stand alone. To properly practice karma-yoga, one must have cultivated detachment which comes due to the acquisition of knowledge. This knowledge is made practical by the control of the body and mind. And this control is persistent only through devotion to the Lord. If this devotion exists, then all other things—i.e., control of the body and mind, the realization of knowledge, and the detached performance of duties become automatic. On the other hand, if one doesn't have devotion, then a person can begin by doing all the duties to gradually develop detachment, which will then assist in knowledge, which will then lead to control over the body and the mind, which will then lead to devotion.

SECTION 2

Topic 1

QUESTION

But how do we know what all the duties we need to perform are? Most of the duties we perform seem to be artificially created by social circumstances, and they change from one culture and society to another. For example, the laws of behavior are different in different countries. Thus, many people argue that these so-called duties are mere social constructions; there is nothing fundamental about them, and we can create whatever duties we deem fit for us.

2.2.1 (172)

रचनानुपपत्तेश्च नानुमान

racanānupapatteśca nānumānam

racanānupapatteḥ—due to the absurdity of fabrication; ca—and; na—not; anumānam—that which is imagined.

TRANSLATION

It is absurd to say that our duties are fabricated, and (we must know) that these duties cannot be (concocted) based on our imagination (or inference).

COMMENTARY

When materialism is born, meaning, choice, and morality die. The materialist in physical sciences claims that meanings don't exist; then the materialist in the mind sciences claims that choice is an illusion; and finally, the materialist in the social sciences claims that morality is our creation. But all three claims are false. Our bodies are symbols of meaning: the meaning is a universal type or concept. These symbols are instantiated from the universal idea due to our choices or desires. And these symbols are then placed in different roles, contexts, situations, or circumstances due to karma, where we can reap the results of good or bad actions in the past. These situations create our roles, and each role comes with a different duty, responsibility, and morality. The violation of that morality produces karma, which then changes our circumstances.

The materialist claims that we are randomly born rich or poor, that our birth in a specific society or to a specific type of mother and father is random, and that we can collectively concoct our duties based on what we like. The fundamental question that the materialist never answers is this: Why is someone rich while another person is poor? Why is someone healthy while the other person is sick? Why is someone enjoying, while others are suffering? Even most religions are unable to answer these questions correctly because they don't realize that we are enjoying or suffering due to the results of our past actions. These results are produced because there was a duty and responsibility that we fulfilled or neglected. And these duties are defined by our role in society. We may not see this role as an object, because it exists as relationships, and the causality of choice and consequence operates based on these relationships. So, the claim that our duties are simply our imaginative constructions is rejected here.

QUESTION

But aren't there practical difficulties in deciding our roles and duties? How do we know or decide what type of role and duty one must accept?

2.2.2 (173)

प्रवृत्तेश्च

pravṛtteśca

pravṛtteḥ—based on the tendency; ca—also.

TRANSLATION

(The duties can) also (be decided) based on (a person's) tendencies.

COMMENTARY

It has been noted above that a person must perform all their duties. But what if those duties are very hard to perform? What if the person is simply not inclined toward certain types of duties, or is incapable of doing them? For example, to become a philosopher, one must have the necessary intellect for analyzing things, must have the patience to not be disturbed by arguments and counterarguments, and must be able to think about not just what is true, but also what is right and good. A soldier cannot be expected to indulge in intellectual arguments; he must rather get the opportunity to engage in physical contact, aggression, and engagement of chivalry for a greater good. Those who are physically and mentally weak and cannot endure the hardships of battle or the rigor of intellectual discussion, but can still build strong human relationships, can engage in business and trade. And those who are incapable in all these ways can position themselves as workers who assist the other types of people.

This classification of people based on their respective tendencies is called the Varna System of social organization. The type of role accepted by a person is not based on their birth into a certain class or to certain types of parents. It is determined by their own ability to perform all the expected duties, because the non-performance of such duties leads to adverse karma and one cannot cite their inability or disinclination as the causes of this neglect. For example, a person who is emotionally weak should not become a ruler or leader in society.

The basic qualification for a leader is that they are fearless and can do what is right regardless of the adverse consequences that follow—even including their death. Unfortunately, at present people become leaders even if their hearts and minds are gripped by fear and insecurity about their position. They aim not to do the right thing; they aim to protect their position of leadership or power. By neglecting their duties, they are constantly producing bad karma, which will then lead to suffering in their future lives. This sūtra advises people to accept only those roles and responsibilities that are compatible with their tendencies—i.e., their abilities to do what is required, and their inclination to do it.

So, if one wants to become free of the effects of bad karma, then one must not accept roles in society that they cannot fulfill completely. Their acceptance of such roles not only creates problems for others, but for themselves too.

QUESTION

You say that one's roles and duties should be defined by their ability and inclination, but we can see that so many people who are qualified by their ability and inclination don't get the appropriate roles in society. On the other hand, the unqualified people often ascend the roles that they are unqualified for. We can understand that the unqualified people will incur bad karma, but what about those people who are qualified but don't get appropriate roles? Isn't the principle that one gets the role if they are qualified inapplicable here?

2.2.3 (174)

पयोऽम्बुवच्चेत् तत्रापि

payo'mbuvaccet tatrāpi

payo'mbuvat—like milk and water; cet—if it be said; tatra—there; api—even.

TRANSLATION

If it is said (that a person doesn't get a role according to their tendencies), even there (one must be) like (the mixture of) milk and water.

COMMENTARY

The three aspects of the soul—emotion, cognition, and relation—manifest into desire, ability in the body, and opportunities. The soul is only born with desires, but due to opportunities afforded by their circumstances, they develop the body of abilities. Therefore, the body is a consequence of both guna and karma—we develop the abilities based on what we like to do, and what we can do (under the circumstances). However, since karma can be both good or bad, sometimes due to good karma (and guna) we obtain good abilities, but due to bad karma we don't get the appropriate opportunities. Conversely, due to bad karma (or guna) we don't obtain the necessary abilities, but due to good karma we get opportunities we aren't suited for. All these discrepancies are produced because guna and karma don't work in lockstep. The ideal situation is that the unqualified must not accept the roles for which they are unqualified.

When a conflict between our ability, desire, and opportunity is produced, there are two ways in which we can respond. First, we can get frustrated and angry that we are qualified and yet not receiving our due; under this anger and frustration, we would tend to neglect even the duties that are currently available to us, and that would then result in adverse karma. Second, we can accept our fate, and use our abilities to the best extent possible under the given circumstances; in short, we don't become angry and frustrated by the situation and don't neglect the responsibilities that are presently available to us. We can continue to perform our duties in whatever role we have received, even if it is not appropriate for our abilities, and inconsistent with our tendencies.

The term 'milk' represents our desires or pleasure. And the term 'water' represents the dilution of the milk. The mixture of milk and water represents the unfulfilled or partially fulfilled desires. If there is a little bit of milk and a lot of water, the mixture will taste like water—i.e., something that we don't want. If there is a lot of milk and a little bit of water, then the mixture will taste like milk—i.e., we will be mostly satisfied with the outcome. The mixture represents a compromise; if we cannot get the perfect thing we want, we can work with whatever we have received, but also control our emotions—i.e., not get angry and frustrated with the situation, and not neglect the current duties. If our duties are performed in this detached manner, then gradually the bad karma will come to an end, and no bad karma would have been created in this time. Thus, by being patient in difficult times, we can transcend the effects of karma.

QUESTION

It is so difficult to live like this; how can a person remain in a situation that is contrary to his nature, where he is unable to act according to his nature?

2.2.4 (175)

व्यतिरेकानवस्थितेश्चानपेक्षत्वात्

vyatirekānavasthiteścānapekṣatvāt

vyatireka—separation; na—not; avasthiteḥ—being situated; ca—and; anapekṣatvāt—due to becoming impartial (toward the good or bad of this world).

TRANSLATION

Be situated (in the understanding of being) non-separate (from the Lord) due to becoming impartial (toward the good and bad of the present world).

COMMENTARY

Many things have been said in the previous sūtras one by one. First, it was said that one's suffering is because of one's bad karma. Second, it was said that bad karma is created due to neglect of duties. Third, if one objects that this neglect arises because the duties are contrary to one's nature, it was said that one can choose their duties based on their nature so that they can avoid bad karma. Fourth, if one argues that I'm not able to find the duty compatible to my nature despite my best efforts, the previous sūtra stated that one must learn to compromise. Finally, if one expresses their helplessness is practicing this compromise with the material world, this sūtra states that one must consider himself non-separate from the Lord because by this a person can be impartial or neutral (i.e., neither averse nor attached) to the events occurring in this world.

This is an indication that karma-yoga is very difficult to practice because as we face adversities in this world, it is very difficult to remain detached. If one reacts impulsively and neglects their duties or does something not allowed by their duties, then they are further implicated in the consequences of karma. So, after propounding the theory of karma, material entanglement, and possible ways to get disentangled, the Vedānta Sūtra arrives at the original conclusion of remaining devoted to the Lord and considering oneself non-separate from Him. Non-separate means: (1) we are not identical to the Lord, and (2) we are not separated from Him. We are rather the parts—which are neither equal to the whole nor are they separate from the whole. When one is situated in this understanding, then he automatically becomes detached from this world. Therefore, karma-yoga cannot be practiced without devotion to the Lord.

QUESTION

What are the symptoms of a person who has obtained detachment from this world due to developing devotion and attachment to the Lord?

2.2.5 (176)

अन्यत्राभावाच्च न तृणादिवत्

anyatrābhāvācca na tṛṇādivat

anyatra—elsewhere; abhāvāt—because of absence; ca—and; na—not; tṛṇādivat—even as grass etc.

TRANSLATION

(Such a person doesn't go) elsewhere due the absence (of luxuries) and (he is) not (disturbed) even if (he is treated) like grass etc. (i.e., stepped upon).

COMMENTARY

Previously the symptoms of devotees have been described by stating several things: (1) they develop bodily symptoms of divine happiness, (2) by their words they can change the life of other materialistically inclined people. In this sūtra, another such symptom is described: such devotees are undisturbed by worldly difficulties; they don't run away from a situation even if there are difficulties, and they are not deterred even if they are mistreated by others. In short, they are emotionally resilient to difficulties and humiliation. They are free from fear, and remain steadfast in their duties, performing them to the best of their abilities, and considering themselves the servants of the Lord.

Many people think that devotion to the Lord is very easy. They claim that the devotees abandon their worldly duties, they do not take the trouble of acquiring knowledge, they don't perform the austerities necessary for purification, etc. Their quick acceptance of the Lord's shelter entails that they are emotionally weak. This sūtra refutes such misconceptions. It states that contrary to these ideas of weakness, the devotees of the Lord are stronger than everyone else in the face of difficulties. Even sages who have practiced yoga for thousands of years are unable to handle humiliation; if treated badly, they become angry and curse others. Intellectuals are especially arrogant; they consider themselves superior as they have thought through things much more than others. However, this knowledge also makes them incapable of handling difficulties. They live in their cocoon of ideas, where they feel superior to everyone else by imagining that they have conquered the mysteries of the world by their mind. But what if someone doesn't care about their learning and erudition? Similarly, people who are righteous about their duties cannot accept mistreatment after having performed their duties; they expect to be respected for doing their job. If society rejects them with disrespect—after they have performed their duties—they tend to become extremely unhappy and perhaps rebellious. This sūtra states that the devotees of the Lord are so strong that they are not disturbed even if treated like blades of grasses—stepped upon by others.

We have discussed earlier how living entities in this world are suffering from fear and shame. This shame is then covered by false pride and one projects this false pride outward to overcome the innate sense of inferiority. The practices of karma, jñāna, and yoga help one progress in the control of the mind and senses, but they are often the avenues for expressing pride that covers the inferiority. Thus, people who perform great deeds, acquire a great deal of knowledge, or mystical powers due to yoga, seem happy because the pride covers their inferiority. But these achievements are not everlasting. As soon as the achievements are gone or ineffective, the pride is shattered, and the innate sense of fear and insecurity rears its ugly head again. Only the devotees of the Lord can overcome the deepest levels of fear and insecurity, and while they may seem externally meek and obliging, they are internally free from all fears.

QUESTION

But why should one tolerate disrespect at the hands of others—e.g., being treated as blades of grass and trampled upon? Isn't it our fundamental right to protect our dignity? How can you justify meekness against mistreatment?

2.2.6 (177)

अभ्युपगमेऽप्यरथाभावात्

abhyupagame'pyarthābhāvāt

abhyupagame—accepting; api—even; arthābhāvāt—because of the absence of any purpose.

TRANSLATION

Even though (it is a duty of ordinary people to defend their dignity) (the devotees) accept (the material suffering) because (the principles of defending one's dignity do not apply to those) devoid of (mundane) aspirations.

COMMENTARY

Defending our dignity, or leading a life of dignity, are often stated to be fundamental rights of a person. Tolerating injustice, on the other hand, is considered a weakness, and one is urged to retaliate against any oppression. But this sūtra states that all these conceptions of dignity and fundamental rights are based on mundane aspirations or goals. The fact is that due to karma, one's rights and aspirations may be frequently stepped on anyway, despite our best efforts. Since many 'fundamental rights' are violated due to karma, we cannot consider them inviolable rights. But to the extent that normal people fight to defend their rights is because they are attached to their bodies and positions in society and seek enjoyment. The devotee has no such aspirations. He is satisfied in the devotion to the Lord, and he understands that both material suffering and pleasure are fleeting. If a person is so devoid of material aspirations, even the commonly stated rights and conceptions of justice do not apply to them.

QUESTION

But if someone is so meek and helpless, then how can he defend the position of the Lord or of His devotees? Materialistic people will consider him foolish as he tolerates all difficulties, so won't he condone the attacks on the Lord and His devotees because he has accepted a meek position in society?

2.2.7 (178)

पुरुषाश्मवदिति चेत् तथापि

puruṣāśmavaditi cet tathāpi

puruṣa-aśma-vat—like a rock; iti cet—if it be said; tathāpi—even though.

TRANSLATION

If it is said (that a meek person would tolerate insults to the Lord) (we say) even though (they tolerate personal insults) (they become) just like men made up of stone (if there is any insult to the Lord or His devotees).

COMMENTARY

The meekness of the devotee of the Lord should not be considered his weakness. While he is prepared to tolerate all kinds of personal difficulties and insults, he becomes just like a stone or a rock when the Lord is attacked. The devotee is meek like a sheep on account of personal difficulties, but he is also ferocious like a lion on account of the devotees and the Lord. They may not stand up for their personal rights or against personal injury, but they will always defend the Lord and His devotees like a stone is used to injure others. This shows that they are factually not weak or helpless. They just tolerate the material difficulties as they don't want to waste their time trying to correct others when it comes to their personal well-being. Their lack of goals pertains to this mundane world, not to the devotion toward the Lord or His devotees.

Many people accuse devotees of insulting atheists or materialists; they say that a spiritualist must remain polite and humble. This politeness and humility is a standard practice in academic circles where atheists constantly attack devotion to the Lord, and devotees are—owing to their humility—not expected to attack them. This sūtra rejects such humility; the devotee is humble, but he is not spineless. He is devoted to the Lord, and like a servant protects his master, similarly, the devotee fights on behalf of the Lord. Of course, the Lord is not in need of such defense. His material energy can easily punish the atheists. But the devotee out of love behaves as if the Lord needs protection like a helpless child. These are not symptoms of a devotee trying to win a mundane battle to establish his own superiority. They are rather the symptoms of the love of the Lord. When the devotee becomes ferocious in defending the Lord, the Lord also relishes the mood of a helpless child being defended by a protective parent. Therefore, hidden under the façade of external aggression, there is no personal ambition. There is only unflinching love toward the Lord, and the devotee doesn't shy from aggression on the pretext that devotees must be tolerant.

QUESTION

But even the atheists are souls, and as such they are parts of the Lord. Shouldn't the devotee consider them as parts of the Lord's body and thereby not attack them? By such attacks, isn't the devotee attacking the Lord?

2.2.8 (179)

अङ्गित्वानुपपत्तेश्च

aṅgitvānupapatteśca

aṅgitva—the position of (the soul) being a part (of the Lord); anupapatteḥ—owing to the inapplicability or an illogical conclusion; ca—and.

TRANSLATION

(The use of the argument that) the soul is part of the Lord (so any punishment to the soul must also be a punishment to the Lord) is illogical.

COMMENTARY

A kitchen knife may be intended for cutting vegetables, but if it is being used as a weapon, then it must be considered a weapon. The intended use of an object cannot be considered the reason for treating it as such when it is not being used in that way. In the same way, the soul is intended to be a servant of the Lord, and that intended use always remains a possibility (like a kitchen knife can always be used to cut vegetables). But if the soul takes an alternative course, then we cannot make the argument that since the intended purpose was to be a part of the Lord, therefore, the soul should be treated *as if* he is part of the Lord. The intention and the ability don't exhaust the free will of the soul. When the soul changes the intention and engages in another possibility, then the intended possibility is subordinated, and the soul is technically not a part of the Lord.

In short, we should clarify that the soul is not physically a part of the Lord. He carries a portion of the properties of the Lord (the capacity for knowledge, beauty, power, wealth, fame, and renunciation). The soul has a portion of the desires the Lord has (i.e., to express one's happiness and become happy by the happiness of others). And the soul is a part of the system or organization supervised by the Lord—whether in the spiritual or the material worlds. But if the capacities of the soul are employed for another purpose (e.g., his own enjoyment) then the soul is intentionally detached from the Lord, although he continues to have the potential to return to the service of the Lord. In this regard, we can note that every object reveals different properties in relation to different things. The same person behaves differently as a boss, husband, father, subordinate, child, etc. When the soul contacts the material energy, his behavior as the controller of this energy is markedly different from the behavior as the child of the Lord. Just because the soul is supposed to be a child of the Lord doesn't entail that he should be treated as a child even if he is acting like a boss. In particular, the child disowns responsibility for his actions, being subordinate to the parents, and the parents assume responsibility for the child. But this is not true for the boss; the boss must assume responsibility for his actions. Hence, this sūtra asserts that this logic of the soul being a part of the Lord when he is not acting according to the nature of the part is illogical and inapplicable.

QUESTION

But the Lord is also said to be omniscient because He is present everywhere as Paramātma. You have previously said (in sūtra 1.2.8 (39)) that the Paramātma doesn't suffer along with the soul because He has a different nature—i.e., He doesn't desire material enjoyment, so His consciousness is drawn away from the material world. Doesn't this imply that the Lord is not omniscient because He doesn't know about the type of suffering the soul undergoes? If on the other hand, He knows the suffering, shouldn't He also be suffering?

2.2.9 (180)

अन्यथानुमितौ च ज्ञशक्तिवियोगात्

anyathānumitau ca jñaśaktiviyogāt

anyathā—otherwise; anumitau—if it be inferred; ca—even; jñaśakti-viyogāt—owing to the absence of the power of knowledge.

TRANSLATION

Even if it is inferred otherwise (that the Lord is omnipresent, so He must be suffering) (we say no) due to the absence of the knowledge energy.

COMMENTARY

In sūtra 1.2.8 (39) the objection was brought up that since the Paramātma is present everywhere He must be suffering just like the soul; in fact, the soul is only in one place but the Paramātma is everywhere; so He must be suffering far more than the soul. The response to that question was that Paramātma has a different nature—i.e., He doesn't have desires about the material world, so He doesn't suffer or enjoy, because His consciousness is withdrawn. The same point is repeated here but also elaborated to counter the argument that if the Lord doesn't suffer like the soul, then He must also not be omniscient.

To understand this elaboration, we must note that the Lord is said to have three kinds of energies, which are described in Śvetāśvatara Upaniśad 6.8.

parāsya śaktir vividhaiva śrūyate
svābhāvikī jñāna-bala-kriyā ca

> The energies of the Lord are said to be numerous; they can be classified into three categories called jñāna, bala, and kriyā.

The *bala* of the Lord is the energy that creates desire in the Lord; as we have seen previously, the Lord's Śakti agitates Him and produces a desire. This agitation is called *bala* or the power of will. Once this will is created, the *kriyā-śakti* fulfills the Lord's desires by creating what He has willed. Finally, with the *jñāna-śakti* the Lord knows what has been created; this knowing fulfills the previously created desire, and that fulfillment produces the pleasure in Him.

This sūtra makes a technical point that the jñāna-śakti is missing in the material world. However, the bala and the kriyā-śakti are still active. Therefore, the world is working according to the will of the Lord, and all the actions of the kriyā-śakti are performed under this will. However, the Lord is not observing this world like the soul due to the absence of the jñāna-śakti. So, He wills, and things happen according to the will, but because He never observes the results produced due to this desire, His desire doesn't produce pleasure or pain. He is still omniscient because He has willed, and this will is never violated. So, He doesn't have to double-check through the jñāna-śakti whether the will has been fulfilled. In fact, He is not interested in the material world, so He keeps His consciousness or the jñāna-śakti away from the observation of the world.

It has also been said earlier that there are two birds in each body: one bird (the soul) eats the fruits, while the other bird (the Paramātma) watches. We might wonder: What is He watching? The short answer is that the Paramātma watches the soul who is eating, but He doesn't eat Himself. As we have noted earlier, the soul and Paramātma are connected through prāṇa. The soul and material energy are also connected through another prāṇa. But the Lord is not connected to the material energy by this prāṇa. In short, there are two different kinds of jñāna-śakti involved here. The soul's jñāna-śakti is attached to the material energy, but the Lord's jñāna-śakti is attached to the soul. So, the Lord knows what is happening to the soul, but He is not experiencing the material energy, because His jñāna-śakti in relation to the material world is absent. He can see that the soul is suffering, but He is not suffering just like the soul.

QUESTION

If the Lord doesn't observe the world because of the absence of jñāna-śakti, then why can't the soul do the same? Can he not withdraw his consciousness

when there is suffering, and then use it again when there is enjoyment? That way, he can selectively enjoy the pleasures but avoid all the suffering.

2.2.10 (181)

विप्रतिषेधाच्चासमञ्जसम्

vipratiṣedhāccāsamañjasam

vipratiṣedhāt—due to conflicts; ca—also; asamañjasam—being disturbed.

TRANSLATION

(The soul is) also disturbed by conflicts.

COMMENTARY

Whenever we are faced with conflicts, there is a natural fight-or-flight response. When a person's courage dominates, then there is a tendency to fight. But when fear dominates, then there is a tendency for flight. The confusion is whether to fight or to flight. If one flies away from a situation, he naturally feels inferior, and he cannot keep escaping without hating himself. Sometimes, to restore self-confidence, the person also fights. There is always hope in a person that if he fights, he will win, and then prove himself to be superior. But there is also fear in the person that if they fight, they might be vanquished. So, even a person who flies away from a situation hopes to come back and fight again. And even a person who is fighting is always gripped by the fear that they may be vanquished. The soul is gripped by the tendencies of hope and fear.

The fear is caused by tamo-guna and hope is caused rajo-guna. The mode of sattva-guna represents detachment—i.e., freedom from both fight and flight—which gives one the ability to endure difficulties without fear, and without hope for winning and becoming dominant again. If one becomes detached, then he can withdraw his jñāna-śakti. The yogi is advised to withdraw their senses from the world just like a tortoise draws its limbs inward into its shell. The cessation of jñāna-śakti represents this withdrawal of the senses. But if the person is gripped by fight or flight, then he cannot withdraw the senses. He must remain on high alert—either due to hope or due to fear. In this state of high alert, the senses and the jñāna-śakti are always drawn outwardly.

Scientists describe our nervous systems as being comprised of the sympathetic and parasympathetic systems; the sympathetic system represents the fight-or-flight response, which is conditioned by rajo-guna and tamo-guna. The parasympathetic system represents the relaxation and is conditioned by sattva-guna. The yogi activates their parasympathetic nervous system and becomes relaxed from the tendency of fight and flight by the control of breath. This is a mechanical process by which one gets situated into sattva-guna and free from rajo-guna and tamo-guna. The suffering of the soul is due to the fight and flight tendencies, which keep the soul anxious and disturbed. Under their influence, the soul cannot relax and hence cannot become detached from the world.

Topic 2

QUESTION

But what is the root cause of these conflicts? Why can't the soul get out of these conflicts, become detached, and then become free of suffering?

2.2.11 (182)

महदद्दीर्घवद्वा ह्रस्वपरिमण्डलाभ्याम्

mahaddīrghavadvā hrasvaparimaṇḍalābhyām

mahat-dīrgha-vat—just like greatness and bigness; vā—moving; hrasva—atomic; parimaṇḍalābhyām—by surrounding or engulfing it.

TRANSLATION

Just like something big surrounds something small and makes it move.

COMMENTARY

The term *vipratiṣedhāt* used in the previous sūtra can also be translated as "due to restrictions or bondage". In this sūtra, *parimaṇḍalābhyām* can be understood as that restriction or bondage that surrounds the soul. However, all these are somewhat superficial meanings, because it isn't clear what is small and what is big, why the big surrounds the small, and causes it to move. Are these metaphors or is there a deeper meaning underlying these sūtras?

Let's begin by asking: what is big and small? In modern science, we think that the universe is big, and the atoms are small. But big and small in Vedic philosophy have a different meaning: they indicate the biggest and the smallest things we can conceive of. Atomism is not based on what we can perceive by the senses, but what we can conceive. Thus, if you can mentally analyze something into smaller and smaller parts, then the smallest thing you can conceive is called the 'atom'. It is not an infinitesimal point; it must be the idea that you can understand. Similarly, the entire material creation is called mahattattva and is the biggest material thing we can conceive of. However, mahattattva isn't physical bigness. It is rather the principles of greatness. These big and small conceptions cover the soul. Under the conception of bigness, the soul conceives of the greatest personality that he can be, and under the idea of smallness, the soul conceives the smallest personality that he can be. We have discussed earlier how the soul enters the material world under the influence of inferiority relative to the Lord. The Lord's devotee knows that he is very small and insignificant, but he feels delighted by the greatness of the Lord. The non-devotee, on the other hand, realizes that he is small, but feels angry at the greatness of the Lord. So, the origin of the material existence is the sense of smallness (which is present even within the devotee) compounded by jealousy and fear of the big.

This sense of smallness, coupled with the jealousy and fear, is called māyā or that which is *not*. The soul is covered by the sense that he is not beautiful, knowledgeable, powerful, famous, wealthy, or renounced. But immediately from this sense of inferiority springs the idea of greatness—namely, that even though I am not great, I *want* to be great. This idea of greatness is called mahattattva. It covers our inferiority and gives rise to ideas about how we can be great. But even if we developed some ideas of greatness, we will not be able to do anything if we keep thinking that I'm not even great enough to pursue greatness. To overcome this problem, from mahattattva springs ahamkāra or false pride: I don't just have ideas of greatness, but I'm also great (in terms of one or more of the ideas of greatness). At least, I'm entitled and deserving of this greatness. So, I may not have this greatness in full, but I'm great enough to pursue greatness. Once this sense of greatness or entitlement arises, then the intellect or buddhi springs from the false pride: since I'm entitled, I'm now going to construct plans and methods for becoming great. From this buddhi springs the mind, which starts conceiving of all the external things that will imply our greatness. From this mind spring the senses, which add sense perceptions to the meanings by the mind. From these sense perceptions spring the objective world. This process of gradual development of material nature from the innate sense of insecurity and smallness to the external world is called Sāñkhya.

The conflict described in the previous sūtra is between the innate smallness and the superficial covering of greatness that arises from the smallness. No matter how great we become, the inferiority never goes away; the more you achieve, the more you want to achieve because you never stop feeling small despite your achievements. The desire to achieve more leads to fear (as it reinforces the idea that we are incomplete) and hope (because we believe that if we have come so far in greatness then we can hope to become even greater).

With this understanding, we can see that the different ideas, namely—(1) the soul is caught in conflicts, (2) the soul is covered by the idea of greatness, (3) the soul is itself conditioned by the idea of smallness, (4) the conflict is between inferiority and greatness, and (5) this conflict keeps the soul engaged in the world, are all deeply intertwined. The hope and fear we spoke of in the previous sūtra are connected to the greatness and smallness in this sūtra.

Topic 3

QUESTION

But just a few sūtras ago you stated that the cause of suffering is karma, and you confirmed that this karma is going on since time immemorial. I had understood that the fall of the soul in the material world happens because of the soul's aversion to the Lord, but the suffering was only due to karma, which arose due to neglect of duties. Now you are stating that the soul is always suffering because there is a conflict between the sense of bigness and smallness? Which of these two things should be considered the cause of suffering?

2.2.12 (183)

उभयथापि न कर्मातस्तदभावः

ubhayathāpi na karmātastadabhāvaḥ

ubhayathāpi—in either case; na—is not; karma—activity; ataḥ—therefore; tat-abhāvaḥ—negation of that.

TRANSLATION

In either case (whether you consider the cause of suffering as karma or not), it is (ultimately) not karma; therefore, it is the negation of that (the Lord).

COMMENTARY

There are two causes of suffering—one external and the other internal. The external cause of suffering is due to karma because it puts us in situations contrary to our desires. But the internal cause of suffering is the incessant desires which can never be fulfilled. In fact, even the neglect of duties arises because we have desires, which are produced because we are trying to overcome the sense of inferiority in us. Therefore, it is not wrong to say that karma is the external cause of suffering. But ultimately, even this karma is produced due to internal desires. So, after stating that the soul is suffering incessantly due to karma (in response to the question about why bad things happen to good people), this sūtra says that karma is not the ultimate cause. Rather, the negation of that (i.e., the Lord and His service) is the ultimate cause of suffering. As we have discussed earlier, this negation appears as māyā or the idea that "I am not that". This māyā is also referred to here as *tat-abhāvaḥ* or the absence of "that".

QUESTION

How does the absence of the Lord lead to suffering in this world?

2.2.13 (184)

समवायाभ्युपगमाच्च साम्याद् अनवस्थितेः

samavāyābhyupagamācca sāmyād anavasthiteḥ

samavāya—collection; abhyupagamāt—from the agreement; ca—also; sāmyāt—harmony or stability; anavasthiteḥ—in the unstable.

TRANSLATION

Because (the Lord's presence brings) agreement or cooperation in a collection (of individuals), also (the Lord's presence brings) stability in instability.

COMMENTARY

Several times before we have spoken of the Lord as being the unity in the diversity. There are three such kinds of unity—of purpose, of origin, and of control. The unity of purpose arises due to the Lord's ānanda: when He is the person to be pleased, there is unity of purpose. The unity of origin arises due to the Lord's *chit*: when He is the origin, all diversities of this world are reconciled in the singular origin. The unity of control arises due to the Lord's *sat*: when the Lord is the ruler or controller, everyone is subordinated to His control. The unity spoken of earlier was prominently in the sense of *chit*: The Lord is the common origin from which the diversity springs, and this has been expressed in various ways by stating that Brahman is beyond the diversity, the world is the expression of the Lord, and even the soul is compared to the Lord's speech. In this sūtra, the unities due to ānanda and *sat* are being referred to.

The unity of ānanda is the unity of purpose. When this unity is present, then there is cooperation between the different individuals; everyone has a common goal—namely, the pleasure of the Lord—and nobody has an individual goal (namely, their own satisfaction). When the individual goals are dissolved, and a common goal is established, then cooperation between individuals naturally follows. Similarly, the unity of *sat* is the unity of control. When this unity is present, then there is a central command authority under whose supervision everything is done. Just like societies have kings, and organizations have CEOs, and these leadership roles bring about unity in the society, similarly, the presence of the Lord and obedience to His command brings about unity.

When the unity of purpose and control are removed, we are just left with the unity of origin. We can speak about the fact that all this diversity has originated from a common source, but it doesn't help to bring a unity, because we can still claim to have different purposes and refuse to accept any control authority. Then, everyone would work for themselves, and society would be engulfed by anarchy. To create cooperation, rulers and politicians have used religion since time immemorial: the king was supposed to be the representation of God on earth; similarly, the acceptance of a common God was the incentive to bring about political unity in disturbed times. This is not to rationalize the wars of religion, or how kings have misused religion to establish their rule. It is only to say that the principle of unity exists only when there is a common control and a shared purpose. If this unity is removed in principle—by dissolving the existence of God—then the world would be thrown into chaos; everyone will fight with the other person considering themselves independent and autonomous, neglecting the collective interest. To avoid such outcomes, some societies collectivize by claiming that everyone must work for the government, although the government is not itself under a moral or spiritual principle. That then leads to even greater atrocities and chaos than acknowledging individuality. The real answer to these problems is the recognition that society has a common purpose and control. When this purpose and control is established, then competition gives way to cooperation, and instability gives way to stability. Similarly, when the Lord is removed from the picture, then suffering ensues because everybody acts in their interest; they don't acknowledge their duties, and by the neglect of duties adverse karma is produced, which then leads to constant suffering. Likewise, when nobody is cooperating, then everyone's desires will remain unfulfilled. These unfulfilled desires will then exacerbate our inner insecurities, and thereby lead to greater unhappiness in society. So, everything hinges on the presence of unity as it brings cooperation and stability in the world.

QUESTION

It is seen that when there is cooperation and stability in a society, the society also becomes long-lived. On the other hand, competition and lack of central control lead to instability, which then leads to temporariness. Does this mean that the eternity of the spiritual world is due to the presence of the Lord?

2.2.14 (185)

नित्यमेव च भावात्

nityameva ca bhāvāt

nityam-eva—certainly eternal; ca—also; bhāvāt—because of the existence (of the Lord).

TRANSLATION

The existence of the Lord also makes the (spiritual world) eternal.

COMMENTARY

The soul and the Lord have already been said to be eternal. Similarly, the material energy is also eternal, being a consort of the Lord. However, the material world created by this energy—namely, bodies, planets, universes—are temporary, while the spiritual world is eternal. This difference is now attributed to the presence of the Lord as the common purpose and controller of existence. History shows that civilizations continue to exist if there is a powerful ruler who brings order in society, and the people have a sense of affiliation to that nation, society, and ruler. If the ruler becomes weak or corrupt or goes missing, alternative rulers spring up, and the society loses its affiliation to that country or civilization. The longevity of a society therefore depends on the effectiveness of the ruler, under whose command the rest of society operates. If this ruler is eternal, and everyone is devoted to the ruler, the society also will become eternal. Thus, the spiritual world is eternal because of the Lord's presence.

QUESTION

But in modern society it is believed that while the universe has a common material origin, there cannot be a common purpose and central control. Everybody is different, and they want to be able to choose their purpose and ruler according to their nature. The argument goes that given that there cannot be a common purpose, a common control will inevitably lead to conflicts. So, allowing different purposes and controllers is the method of getting stability.

2.2.15 (186)

रूपादिमत्त्वाच्च विपर्ययो दर्शनात्

rūpādimattvācca viparyayo darśanāt

rūpādi—form etc.; mat—(differing) opinions or beliefs; tvāt—from just like; ca—also; viparyayaḥ—conflicts or oppositions; darśanāt—as it is seen.

TRANSLATION

From the existence of multiple opinions or beliefs just like diversified forms also (arise) conflicts and oppositions as it is seen (in the world).

COMMENTARY

People may organize themselves into groups, organizations, societies, cultures, or religions, based on a shared purpose and control, but they will continue to fight with other groups, organizations, societies, cultures, and religions based on their differing opinions. The diversity of this world naturally leads to oppositions and conflicts—unless there is a shared purpose and control. If there is a shared purpose, then we can understand that all the diversity can be employed for a common goal—i.e., serving the Supreme Lord. But even with a shared purpose, unless the Lord is considered the ruler and controller of the world, many different leaders will spring up and claim that there should be a common purpose, but *their* purpose is that common purpose. The Lord should thus be considered the common origin of diversity, the common purpose to be served by the diversity, and the common controller who creates order.

In this sūtra, the different opinions or beliefs are compared to forms etc. (including things like color, size, etc.). Thus, ideas too have the properties perceived by the senses, which is why we identify ideological positions by colors such as red, blue, and green; we say that thinking is sharp or dull; we attribute lightness and darkness to ideas; ideas are called big and small, etc. These are not merely metaphorical ways of speaking; the ideas too have shapes, colors, sizes, besides sensations such as hard and soft, hot and color, bitter and sweet. The meanings in our mind are classified into six categories—knowledge, beauty, power, wealth, fame, and renunciation—and each of these is further divided into different forms of knowledge, beauty, etc. These forms have different shapes, sizes, colors, taste, hardness, etc. For instance, mathematics and physics are called 'hard sciences', and in our minds, we think of them as having angular shapes. Likewise, economics and sociology are considered 'soft sciences', and in our minds, we think of them as having oblong shapes.

Since ideas have different forms, they are incompatible with other such ideas, unless we know how to fit them together in complementary ways just like filling up the pieces of a jigsaw puzzle. To complete this jigsaw puzzle, two things are essential—(1) we must be convinced that this diversity is actually parts of a single larger picture and must be used to construct that picture, and (2) there must be somebody who puts the pieces together into that picture. If everyone believes that there isn't a single picture, or if there is nobody to put the pieces together, then the pieces of the puzzle remain incompatible.

QUESTION

The impersonalist argues that this world is temporary, and because it is comprised of duality, we can expect clashes and conflicts. To get away from these conflicts, we must dissolve the individuality of separate purposes, and

the existence of a central controller who organizes a diversified society. By removing the need for a shared purpose and common control, all the diversity will be ultimately collapsed into a common origin—the Brahman—and this Brahman can be considered the origin of the temporary material diversity.

2.2.16 (187)

उभयथा च दोषात्

ubhayathā ca doṣāt

ubhayathā—because of the two; ca—also; doṣāt—from existence of faults.

TRANSLATION

Because of the two (the rejection of a common control and shared purpose) from the existence of faults (the impersonalist viewpoint is also faulty).

COMMENTARY

Here the impersonalist view is criticized on the ground that it recognizes a common origin in Brahman but doesn't consider that Brahman to be the shared purpose of existence, and the central controller of diversity. To avoid acknowledging the shared purpose and common control, the impersonalist dissolves the diversity into a unity, and the existence of a world comprised of diversified qualities, different individuals, who perform different roles, also disappears. By considering this to be the ultimate reality, the impersonalist is ignorant of a transcendental world in which the Lord is not merely the origin, but also the purpose and controller. There is a stable, cooperative, and eternal society due to the presence and recognition of the Lord. Of course, the Lord also exists in the material world, but His presence is not accepted by everyone. So, everyone considers themselves free to do whatever they want, competing with others, disregarding their responsibilities, and breaking laws. The impersonalist thinks that the solution to the problems of the material world is dissolving all the diversity. No doubt, this is *a* solution, but it is not the *only* solution.

QUESTION

Are you rejecting the impersonalist viewpoint as a legitimate solution?

2.2.17 (188)

अपरिग्रहाच्चात्यन्तमनपेक्षा

aparigrahāccātyantamanapekṣā

aparigrahāt—because it is not accepted (by the devotees); ca—also; atyantam—in the ultimate analysis; anapekṣā—cannot be used for comparison.

TRANSLATION

Also, because it is not accepted (by the devotees), in the ultimate analysis (the impersonalist's viewpoint) cannot be used for comparison.

COMMENTARY

The previous sūtra said that impersonalist view is faulty but did not completely reject it because the undivided Brahman indeed exists. So, in this sūtra, it is said that in the ultimate analysis—after analyzing all the pros and cons—we can reject the impersonal viewpoint. The Absolute Truth has three aspects—*sat*, *chit*, and ānanda. The *chit* creates different objects, bodies, planets, etc. which are diversified from a root. The *sat* creates the roles in which these objects are organized into a hierarchical structure, at the root of which lies a ruler who controls the world. And ānanda creates diverse kinds of pleasures, desires, and wills, which are all subparts of the pleasure, desire, and will of the source of diversity. The impersonalist negates the roles of individuals organized in a hierarchy, and how these individuals serve at the pleasure of the common source, the Lord. Having gotten rid of a common ruler and a shared purpose, he then collapses the diverse objects into a single unified existence devoid of diversity. And when this diversity has been rejected, the impersonalist calls this the ultimate truth. This raises a fundamental question: Why should *sat* and ānanda exist if they must be rejected? And why should *chit* be capable of producing diversity when all this diversity must be rejected? The impersonalist incorrectly attributes the problem to diversity, rather than the absence of common control and shared purpose. With a shared purpose and common control, the same diversity is the cause of an eternal, stable, peaceful, and delightful society.

The rejection of impersonalism is not the rejection of Brahman. Most people tend to incorrectly equate these two ideas. As has been discussed earlier, even Brahman is particles of light originating from a source of light. The flaw in impersonalism is recognizing this light and rejecting the source of light. As light seems diffused and you cannot see small particles of light, similarly, the impersonalist supposes that the light is the ultimate undivided reality. If, instead, it was recognized that even Brahman is small particles of light, then we would have to accept that this light has an origin. Once that origin is recognized, then we can see that He is also the purpose because the diversity emerges from Him due to His desire for pleasure. And since He is the creator of this diversity, He becomes its controller, using the creation for His enjoyment. All these conclusions follow naturally when we realize that light is not an undivided unity; it is rather comprised of small particles of light that seem undifferentiated.

So, the impersonalist view is a limited caricature of the whole truth; the devotees of the Lord don't accept it because it rejects the source of light, the reason why the source emits this light, and how the source then controls the manifestation. The Vedānta Sūtra recommends the rejection of this view.

Topic 4

QUESTION

You have said that without a shared purpose and a common controller

there will be clashes and conflicts in society, which will lead to instability. But the materialist doesn't consider this a problem. He rather claims that conflicts between individuals lead to natural selection in which the unfit are eliminated, and the fit survive. Therefore, conflict and clash are not a bad thing for the materialist. They would claim that it is the very means for making progress.

2.2.18 (189)

समुदाय उभयहेतुकेऽपि तदप्राप्तिः

samudāya ubhayahetuke'pi tadaprāptiḥ

samudāye—in the collection; ubhaya-hetuke—in both reasons; api—even; tat-aprāptiḥ—that is not achieved.

TRANSLATION

Even in the collection, that (unity) is not achieved in both reasons.

COMMENTARY

Groups of people are formed only when there is a shared purpose and a visionary leader. If there is no shared purpose, and if there is no leader, people will not even come together. Sometimes, people may come together because of a shared purpose, although a leader has not yet emerged; the leader is selected later. Similarly, sometimes, there can be a visionary leader who then defines a purpose, that is adopted by everyone. Thus, if there is a vision but not a leader, a group can still be created. Similarly, if there is a leader, but not a vision, the group can be formed. The missing components are added subsequently. However, if both a shared mission and a common leader are missing, the group is never formed. This sūtra asserts that if both the shared purpose and a common leader are missing, we cannot even speak about the formation of a group. Unless a group is formed, we cannot speak about selection and evolution.

Modern science studies the world as material objects and claims that these objects aggregate to form complex systems due to natural forces. However, every such interaction due to natural forces is indeterministic. Take for example the collision of two billiard balls. The laws of physics say that the total energy and momentum remain conserved before and after the collision. However, this conservation of energy and momentum is achievable in innumerable ways: (1) all the energy can be transferred to ball A or ball B, (2) the energy can be distributed in many ways between the two balls, and (3) each of the balls can be blown into smaller pieces, each possessing a different amount of energy. The total number of possibilities resulting from the same laws is so vast that we can never predict what will happen. Now, we have three possible alternatives. First, we can say that our laws are complete, but nature is indeterministic. Second, we can say that our laws are incomplete, although nature is not indeterministic. Third, we can say that our laws are wrong as they cannot predict the outcomes. Scientists today take the first route; they say that nature is indeterministic, thus allowing 'random mutations' which cause objects to aggregate.

The right answer is that the laws are incomplete and wrong. Specifically, our notion that matter aggregates due to forces of nature is itself flawed.

In Vedic philosophy, three causes of material aggregation are recognized. First, there are the objects or particles which aggregate. Second, the aggregation is due to a structure, in which each object is accorded a different role in the collection. Third, this structure is created due to a purpose or goal. For example, if you are constructing a chair, the construction begins with the purpose. It is then exemplified into a structure, which we call the design of the chair. And finally, this design is then converted into an actual chair by using wood blocks. The wood blocks don't aggregate without a preexisting structure. And the structure cannot exist unless there is a purpose. So, what scientists call 'random collections' are not random; they are occurring because of the existence of deeper forms of reality, which we refuse to acknowledge. What scientists call force fields are not forces at all; they are forms of space in which objects are organized. And these forms are produced due to an objective intention.

In everyday life, this structure is visible through the functional divisions in society—e.g., that an organization has many functional parts, or a government is divided into functional departments, etc. And this functional division appears because there is a purpose—e.g., people aggregate into an organization due to a shared purpose, and then they organize themselves into various functional departments. If there is no purpose, then there can be no structure, and without this structure, there cannot be aggregation of individual parts. The functional structure is the mechanism of control, and the goal to be fulfilled by that functional organization is the purpose for which the structure exists.

If we take out the purpose and the structure, then there cannot be any aggregation of parts. This is what the sūtra states. There must be some purpose, which then leads to some structure, to organize the world. It is quite possible that the purpose is not shared, and according to different purposes, different structures are created, which then compete and clash with each other leading to conflicts. But the claim that nature is without purpose and without controller entails that there will be never be a stable arrangement of bodies, societies, ecosystems, and organizations. So, the claim that nature randomly aggregates into larger systems is a flawed idea because the laws on the basis of which we arrive at this conclusion are predictively incomplete, but rather than accepting that our theories and laws are flawed, we transfer the randomness to nature. These are shortcomings of our understanding of nature, not of nature itself.

QUESTION

Some philosophers accept the reality of structure, without acknowledging the existence of a shared purpose and a central controller. For example, Buddhists advocate the idea of Pratītyasamutpāda or co-dependent origination in which two opposites simultaneously manifest from nothingness as mutual opposites. Each opposite becomes the reason or the justification for the other, so they are mutually justified, but we cannot trace this origin to a First Cause. As these opposites appear, structure is created, but there is no central controller or a shared purpose for its causation. Therefore, Buddhists don't accept the existence of a God or a soul, but they thus explain the order in nature naturally.

2.2.19 (190)

इतरेतरप्रत्ययत्वादिति चेत् न उत्पत्तिमात्रनिमित्तत्वात्

itaretarapratyayatvāditi cet na utpattimātranimittatvāt

itaretara—mutual; pratyayatvāt—from as if proof, definition; iti cet—if it be said; na—no; utpatta-mātra—merely produced; nimittatvāt—from being symptoms.

TRANSLATION

If it is said that from as if mutual proofs or justifications (of opposites) (we say) no (because) they are merely produced as symptoms (of the real cause).

COMMENTARY

A classic illustration of the thesis of Pratītyasamutpāda is the yin-yang duality, which is depicted by two parts of a circle—one black and another white—with a part of the black being white, and a part of the white being black. Each part, therefore, contains its own opposite, even as the opposites are said to be complementary. If these opposites are collapsed, then their mutual opposition results in nothingness. Hence, they are said to spring from nothingness and can dissolve back into nothingness. When they exist, they justify the existence of their opposite, and hence the opposites emerge and dissolve simultaneously. This idea is not entirely new; it exists in the Vedic description of the world as duality: the world is comprised of opposites such as hot and cold, bitter and sweet, rough and smooth, and these opposites are defined mutually. However, this mutuality of the opposites is only a partial description of nature. For instance, hot and cold are opposites within the sensation of touch; bitter and sweet are opposites within the sensation of taste, etc. We can normally perceive the existence of hot vs. cold, bitter vs. sweet, but we don't perceive the existence of touch or smell, or taste. We just use them as invisible concepts that cannot be perceived, although they are properties in terms of which we perceive.

These properties are both transcendent and immanent. For example, black and white are both colors, so color is immanent in both black and white. However, since there are other colors—e.g., red, green, blue—therefore, color is beyond black and white. Thus, color exists in both black and white, and yet, color is neither black nor white. Since color is inside black, and white is a type of color, therefore, white is also inside black. Similarly, since color is inside white, and black is a type of color, therefore, black is also inside white. If the transcendent property of color did not exist, then black and white will also not exist. And if the immanent property of color (within black and white) did not exist, then black and white would remain logical opposites, but not definitionally interrelated because the common property of color—which is immanent in both—would not exist. Therefore, the claim that two opposites are mutually defined is only a superficial understanding. The deeper reason for this mutuality is that properties such as color are both transcendent and immanent.

Now, by the above argument, we would say that the property of color is immanent in shades of color, but not in flavors of taste. Similarly, the property of taste would be immanent in flavors of taste but not in the colors. This is factually wrong. Some colors produce sensations of sweetness—e.g., lavender. Likewise, other colors produce the sensation of bitterness—e.g., brown.

This is the point at which we must recognize that these concepts are arranged in a hierarchy, and emanate from a root like trunks, branches, twigs, and leaves. The root of this tree is the Original Idea which exists as the form of knowledge, beauty, power, wealth, fame, and renunciation. This form is sometimes called Bhagavān in Vedic philosophy, because He is full of all the qualities (i.e., everything is in Him), and He is transcendent to everything. Similarly, the immanent form of these properties is called Paramātma, and it exists inside everything. Thus, the Lord is both immanent and transcendent; inside everything and outside everything. Due to the immanence of the Lord, everything is inside everything else, because the whole truth exists inside all partial truths.

These partial truths are visible to us, but the complete immanent truth remains invisible. Lord Kṛṣṇa calls this invisible form avyakta-mūrti. But from this invisible form, anything can be manifest, so nothing is truly separated from anything else. Thus, tastes can appear within colors, and colors can appear within tastes. The Buddhist claim that the structure in this world is visible as mutual oppositions is true. However, the claim that these opposites are mutually defined on their own is incorrect. The reason for this interrelatedness is the immanent form of the Lord. As the transcendent form, He manifests all the opposites, and as the immanent form, He interconnects everything. Thus, it is said that everything is inside the Lord, and the Lord is inside everything. This inside and outside is not a unique property of the Lord; it is rather a pervasive property of all concepts. It's just that ordinary concepts are immanent only in a few objects, but the Original Idea is immanent in everything. Therefore, when we speak about conceptual oppositions, we can relate colors like black and white, tastes like bitter and sweet, but we cannot connect everything to everything, unless we say that there is an original idea which is immanent in everything, because everything is a partial manifestation of the transcendent Being.

QUESTION

If everything is inside everything, then why isn't this visible? When we see a table, we don't see a chair in the same thing. Due to the mutual exclusion of these things, we believe that these are separate material objects. But you are saying that because the Lord is immanent in everything, everything is inside everything else. And yet, why don't see everything inside everything else?

2.2.20 (191)

उत्तरोत्पादे च पूर्वनिरोधात्

uttarotpāde ca pūrvanirodhāt

uttarotpāde—in the time of the production of the subsequent thing; ca—also; purva-nirodhāt—because the antecedent one has been forbidden.

TRANSLATION

Because in the time of the production of the subsequent thing, the previous thing has also been forbidden.

COMMENTARY

All things in the material world are built out of the three modes of nature—sattva, rajas, and tamas. In the primordial state of prakriti, these modes are said to be in 'balance', and this state is called śuddha-sattva. As an example, the mode of tamas represents inertia, the mode of rajas represents activity, and the mode of sattva represents knowledge. When tamas or rajas are present, then knowledge is absent, and whether one is lazy or active, both are under ignorance. The lazy person remains inert under ignorance, and the active person works very hard under ignorance. The lazy person produces no results, while the active person produces adverse results. When sattva is present, then knowledge is gained, but there is no activity. So, knowledge is not being applied to produce something useful. The balanced combination of these modes represents knowledge that leads to activity, but without losing stability. The person is not hyperactive or endeavoring very hard. At the same time, he is also not lazy. Everything is done with understanding, deliberately, and at due pace. The combination of the three modes doesn't result in nothingness; it rather results in a pure state that is devoid of the separated influence of the three modes.

So, what is separation? When the soul is injected into the material energy, based on the soul's choices, the three modes become dominant and subordinate. For example, when tamas dominates, and sattva is subordinated, and rajas is further subordinated, then due to tamas the person remains lazy, due to subordinate sattva he indulges in armchair philosophy, and due to rajas, he produces books on this armchair philosophy. Similarly, if sattva dominates, and tamas is subordinate, and rajas is further subordinate, then due to sattva there is pursuit of knowledge, but due to tamas this pursuit describes nature as being dull and meaningless particles, and due to rajas, these particles will be moved by some force. If the order of rajas and tamas is flipped, then a philosopher will say that there is only change and particles are the epiphenomena of this change. Thus, we can psychoanalyze the author from the theories they have produced.

The variety of the world is due to the repeating dominant-subordinate structure of the three modes, and it exists in a tree-like structure—the root is śuddha-sattva, the three modes are the trunks, each of these trunks is divided into three parts by each mode, and this process continues indefinitely. If we count the instances of sattva, rajas and tamas in anything, by and large, everything has the combination of the three modes in equal proportion. The objects are different only due to the hierarchy or the dominant-subordinate structure of the three modes. Therefore, to change one thing into another, we don't need new material 'stuff'. We just need to change the hierarchy of the modes.

The modes organized in one specific hierarchy constitute one branch of the tree; other hierarchies represent other branches. In one sense, each branch is merely a transformation of another branch in which the components of a branch are rearranged in a different order. In another sense, each of these branches are unique, individual things. Due to the first reason, everything is inside everything else in a potential form—you could transform it into anything else if you changed the hierarchy of the modes. But as soon as you make that transformation, the present thing will become unmanifest and rest as a potential.

This is what this sūtra states succinctly: everything exists in everything else, but the moment one thing manifests, the other thing is hidden. This hidden form is the world resting in a potential state, so, we cannot perceive it because it is indeed not manifest. But if we understand the science of material transformation, then we can convert anything to anything else. While material scientists may be excited by the possibility of creating gold out of sand, this knowledge has been previously used for transforming oneself into a better person.

QUESTION

Generally, we say that if something exists, then it must be observable. But you are saying that even the possibilities—which cannot be observed—are existing. And everything is inside everything else as a potential or possibility. How can we justify a stance in which the non-observable is considered real?

2.2.21 (192)

असतिप्रतिज्ञोपरोधो यौगपद्यमन्यथा

asati pratijñoparodho yaugapadyamanyathā

asati—in the non-existence; pratijña-uparodhaḥ—obstruction of the possibility; yaugapadyam—simultaneity; anyathā—otherwise.

TRANSLATION

In the non-existence there is obstruction of possibility. Otherwise, we must say that (all possibilities) must exist simultaneously.

COMMENTARY

There can be some contention regarding the translation of *pratijña* used here. The root *jña* means knowledge or to know. The root *prati* indicates towards or against. Thus, in combination, *pratijña* has many meanings, based on the context. It can mean a 'promise' which is toward a reality (fulfilled by the promise) and not yet a reality (because it is still a promise). It can mean a 'possibility', which is toward a reality and not yet a reality. It can also mean a 'claim' which hasn't yet been proven, so it is toward a reality and not yet a reality. It can mean 'the thing to be known, which is not yet known'. I have translated *pratijña* as possibility here, based on the context of the previous discussion.

There are two ways to measure reality. First, we can say that the thing that exists is all that we can see. Second, we can also say that the thing that exists is produced by the negation of all the other things that it could have been. Generally, when we measure the world as matter, we employ the first method—we measure the properties of an object and we say that such and such exists. However, if we measure the world as information, we employ the second method—we say that the total information contained in something is equal to the number of choices that had to be made to eliminate all the alternative possibilities. The second method of measuring existence is now standard practice in many areas of modern science in the last couple of centuries, starting with the introduction of the statistical mechanical description of thermodynamic phenomena. In classical mechanics, reality is described as everything it is. In thermodynamics, the opposite method—i.e., everything it is not—was found to be suitable.

To describe the information contained in a system, we construe all the possible states of the system, which is called its 'entropy'. The information in the system is then said to be inversely proportional to the entropy—i.e., if the possibilities are too many, then the information encoded in the system must have had to remove all these alternatives to create something definite; the larger the number of possibilities to eliminate, the greater the information needed. Therefore, if we only describe the world as material things, then reality would be all that we can see. But if we describe the same world as information, then reality would be all that is possible, and what we can observe would be created by the elimination of all except one potentiality to create something definite.

In Indian philosophy, the Vaiśeṣika system is known to have introduced abhāva or absence as a category of knowledge. For example, when you conclude something is a cow, you also conclude that it is not a dog, not a horse, not a tiger, etc. In Western philosophy, the negative method of proof has been called reductio ad absurdum, or that the contrary postulate leads to a contradiction. But despite these prevalent methods, the underlying metaphysics for why this method is so useful isn't understood, because we tend to think that parts are the primordial reality and the whole is constructed from the combination of the parts. If we invert this idea and say that the whole is the reality, and the parts are produced by negating portions of the whole, then the part would be defined only after we consider the whole. In short, we would have to first consider all the possibilities, and then how they are eliminated to create an observation.

The Vedic metaphysics follows this inverted system, in which the root is the whole truth, and the parts are produced from this whole (as branches emanating from the root) through successive but partial negations of the whole. The process of this negation is called māyā or that which is not. Māyā 'covers' the Absolute Truth (in the vision of the soul, not in the vision of the Lord) and creates partial truths. Therefore, we cannot understand a table just by looking at its observable properties. We must understand this object in relation to the complete set of possibilities—i.e., the whole truth—and how it fits as a part of that whole. Just because we don't see the whole truth doesn't entail it doesn't exist. In fact, this invisible reality is the basis on which to understand the visible. Thus, every part must be understood only in relation to the full truth.

This point is made in this sūtra by asserting that if we claim that the alternative possibilities don't exist, then we would have to conclude that they are impossible. On the other hand, if we say that they exist, then we would have to acknowledge that all the possibilities are eternally and simultaneously true.

QUESTION

Since you are saying that the whole truth exists inside all the partial truths, can we not just negate all these partial truths and we will get the whole truth? After all, these partial truths are negations of the whole truth, so by negating the negation, we will obtain the whole truth. Many philosophers call this the method of negation—that by denying everything we obtain the truth.

2.2.22 (193)

प्रतिसंख्याप्रतिसंख्यानिरोधाप्राप्तिःअविच्छेदात्

pratisaṃkhyāpratisaṃkhyānirodhāprāptiḥ avicchedāt

pratisaṃkhyā—the countable; apratisaṃkhyā—the uncountable; nirodha-aprāptiḥ—not obtainable by negation; avicchedāt—owing to inseparability.

TRANSLATION

The uncountable cannot be obtained by negating the countable, because (the countable) is inseparable (from the uncountable).

COMMENTARY

To understand this sūtra, we must understand what we mean by countable and uncountable. Countable means all those things that can be numbered as 1, 2, 3, 4, etc. This numbering is infinite, but it is still possible to individually count them; hence, in mathematics, this is called a countable infinity. The universe is comprised of such countably infinite things, if we look at the universe at any given moment of time; i.e., if we take a snapshot of the universe at any given moment, then we can enumerate the things in the universe one by one. However, because the universe is changing continuously, the things that appear at any given time, may not appear at another moment in time. The things that appear in the universe at a moment in time are a subset of all the possible things that could appear. Therefore, if the set of all possible things is N, then the manifest things at a moment would be a subset of N. In fact, as time elapses, each moment would create a different subset of all the possibilities. This set of all subsets (of the set of all the possibilities) is exponentially larger than N—and denoted as 2N. It is also sometimes called uncountable infinity, which represents all the states of the universe through time. Thus, there are two kinds of space—(1) the countably infinite space of all possibilities, and (2) an uncountably infinite space of all the subsets of all the possibilities, as they appear in time.

The significance of the uncountably infinite space is that we can draw the evolution of the universe as a trajectory in this space. Each point on this trajectory would represent the state of the entire universe at a given moment. And, in principle, the trajectory would cover the entire space over the lifetime of the universe. With these two spaces, we would say that the universe is uncountably infinite, however, at any given moment, it appears to us as countably infinite. This countable infinity is all the manifest things, but the uncountable infinity is all those things that the universe could be but is not at the present moment. The uncountably infinite space would constitute the 'entropy' of the universe, and the information encoded in the universe at any moment in time would be defined relative to all the states that the universe hasn't taken currently.

If we count all the currently existing objects, we will get a countably infinite reality. But that isn't the reality. The reality is that which can be observed any time in the past, present, or future. This reality—as we said—is uncountably infinite. So, the method of negating what we currently see to understand reality is flawed, because reality is exponentially larger than this negated observation. The fact that both these realities are infinite shouldn't entail that they are similar because the uncountable reality is qualitatively different than the countable reality. The uncountable reality is what the universe can ever be, and the countable reality is all that the universe is presently. The countable reality is created by negating the information in the uncountable reality. We can say that time chooses one point in the uncountable space to create the universe at any moment, but the universe is factually the entire space, not just a point.

This understanding of countable and uncountable can help us understand this sūtra. The countable is a point in the uncountable space, so by negating that countable we will only obtain a point in the uncountable space, not the entire space. If, however, this is wrongly taken to mean that the countable and uncountable are different things, then, that conclusion is also rejected by stating that these two are inseparable. Essentially, what is visible at any given time is not separate from that which exists timelessly. And yet, what exists timelessly manifests what is visible in time. To understand that timeless reality, we must observe all that will manifest over time. The method of negation must be rejected because it doesn't give us that timeless truth. Only the method of seeing everything over the duration of the universe gives us the timeless reality.

The conclusion is that if we see an object right now, it is not merely defined in relation to the other objects that we can see right now. Instead, everything that can be presently seen, is defined in relation to those things that have been visible in the past and will exist in the future. Just as we cannot separate a specific state in space from the other states, similarly, we cannot separate all these states collectively from the states at any time in the past or the future. It is hard enough to know all the states at present to fully know the state of an individual object. If these states are collectively defined in relation to past and future states, then the problem is much worse. However, this much worse problem also gives us an insight into how the universe evolves. It is not due to the actions in the individual objects; it is rather the collective state selection of the entire universe. Thus, the evolution of the universe is independent of any individual actor. This evolution is deterministic, because of the order of states in the uncountable space, and the ordering of states within each such state (from the uncountable space) creates a predetermined sequence of events. However, this determinism is different from that in classical physics, where when a state is visible, the previous states are gone. In the determinism described here, every state exists in relation to every other state, and each state is created by negation of other states. There are two kinds of negations—of distinct locations in space and time.

Apart from the space and time distinctions, there is also the distinction of observers. The observer is not predetermined, even though the events in space and time are determined. Therefore, what will happen—in space and time—is fixed, but who will do it is not fixed. As a result, we get three kinds of complementary descriptions—of space, of time, and of persons. As we have discussed earlier, these are the Śakti-mode, the God-mode, and the soul-mode descriptions of the same observation; they constitute the how, the what, and the who. The determinism of the universe is predictively complete, but it is explanatorily incomplete. That explanation requires the observers. Thus, two modes of space and time suffice to say what will happen, but the third mode of persons is necessary to explain who will do what. These three modes provide the complete prediction and explanation of everything—which is the goal of science.

QUESTION

You are saying that the material world can never be completely known. What is then the point of this knowledge if it takes the lifetime of the universe to know everything? How can anyone exist for such a long period of time?

2.2.23 (194)

उभयथा च दोषात्

ubhayathā ca doṣāt

ubhayathā—in either case; ca—also; doṣāt—because of faults.

TRANSLATION

In either case (you can) also see faults.

COMMENTARY

If the world was completely knowable in an instant, then the universe would be static, and nothing would ever change. One would argue: What is the point in living in this world when we know everything in the future? Then, there would be no point in any action because actions would not change anything. If, on the other hand, the world is known only when it is lived through experience, then someone can argue: If the world is never fully known in finite time, then what is the point of even attempting to know anything? Either way, one can claim there is a fault, so there is no point in explaining either alternative. The argument against change is the argument against the existence of time. There is a timeless reality called Brahman in which only the self is known. Nobody ever knows anyone else, the different things that they are capable of, or what the others are capable of. Neither space nor time exists in the Brahman. Although there are many individual persons, they are never known. Only the self—as devoid of all space and time distinctions—is known. This knowledge of the self is eternal, and yet, it is incomplete. On the other hand, the complete truth is all that is ever possible, and it is completely known over time. It can mean I never know everything since it manifests over time. But it can also mean that life is a constant process of discovery of novelties. If this process of discovery is pleasurable, then there should be no problem with the novelty.

QUESTION

You have earlier said that the Lord is the origin of space, from which the rest of space expands. You are now saying that the Lord is also the whole space in which all the possibilities pre-exist as potentials to be known. How can we reconcile these two ideas about the origin and the complete space?

2.2.24 (195)

आकाशे चाविशेषात्

ākāśe cāviśeṣāt

ākāśe—in case of space; ca—and; aviśeṣāt—due to being no difference.

TRANSLATION

Also due to there being no difference between (the origin) and the space.

COMMENTARY

The difference between origin and the rest of the space arises in a physical conception of space, in which the origin is only one point in space. But, if we view space as a domain of concepts organized hierarchically as a tree, then the higher concepts contain the lower concepts. For example, Alsatians and Pomeranians are breeds of dogs, which are part of mammals, which are part of animals. When space is understood conceptually, then the trunks, branches, twigs, and leaves are all emanations from the root, and they are contained inside the root, although they may not always be visible. The expansion of the root into the visible tree is making the possibility manifest, and this manifestation requires higher-level concepts to be manifest before the lower-level concepts. For instance, the idea of a dog must be manifest before the Alsatian or the Pomeranian are manifest. So, the root is the collection of all the possibilities in unmanifest form, and the tree is the same possibilities in a manifest form. Hence, there is no difference between the origin and the rest of space—if we are speaking about the possibilities that preexisted their manifestation because the origin contains everything as a potential from which the manifest world expands.

QUESTION

If everything already exists in the Lord, then why is it not manifest simultaneously? Why are different aspects being revealed at different times?

2.2.25 (196)

अनुस्मृतेश्च

anusmṛteśca

anusmṛteḥ—the memory of a small part; ca—also.

TRANSLATION

(You can understand this) also as the recollection of parts of memory.

COMMENTARY

The Lord is the fullness of all possibilities, but even He doesn't know everything about Himself all the time. Rather, all these possibilities are like long-term memory which are recollected one by one; when they are recollected, they are manifest in His experience, and that manifestation then becomes the world. More accurately, His capacity for desire is infinite, and His Śakti fulfills that desire. However, the Lord doesn't desire everything simultaneously. His desires are sequenced, and that sequence appears as time; as these desires are fulfilled by the Lord's Śakti, the world is manifest and unmanifest. By comparing this process of manifestation to recollection of memories, two questions are being addressed here. First, the existence of all possibilities is compared to memory; even though we have memories, we aren't always remembering them; and yet, just because we don't recall something right now doesn't mean we don't know. Therefore, the fact that the Lord remembers one thing at a time doesn't entail that He is not omniscient; He knows everything because it exists as His memory, and yet He isn't conscious of everything simultaneously. Second, when the memory is recalled, a new experience is created, and the succession of these experiences constitutes time. The awareness of the Lord therefore simply scans His memories and that recollection becomes His experience.

This analogy is slightly misleading because memory is different from the soul. The memory is unconscious, and the experience is conscious. This is where we can recall the discussion about each part being defined in relation to all the other parts—including those parts in the future and the past. Therefore, in one sense, knowing something right now is knowing the past and the future, because the past and the future are embedded in the present by a negation. In another sense, knowing something right now is not knowing what is in the past and the future. If only the latter meaning is adopted, it seems that God is not omniscient about the past and the future. If, to overcome this problem, we say that everything is known at once, then it entails an eternal but static world. The knowledge by distinction to past and future solves both these problems. The Lord is fully omniscient because in knowing the present, He also knows the past and the future, although the past and the future are currently unmanifest. Thus, His experience is evolving, and yet His knowledge is eternal. The knowledge is knowing everything that is everywhere and everywhen. But experience is here and now. These claims are not contradictory because the experience here and now is not knowledge; the knowledge is its relation to everything else including all the past and future experiences, and all parts of these experiences.

The use of the term *anusmṛteḥ* is significant here because it comprises of two parts—*anu* or atomic, and *smriti* or memory. As we have discussed, the space of all possibilities is uncountable, and what manifests at a given time is a point in that space. This point is the 'atom' of recollection out of the entire space of *smriti* or memory. Thus, for us, the universe seems infinite, but for the Lord it is only an atom. These atoms are uncountable which means that there is no limit or end to the memories of the Lord, and hence time never ceases.

QUESTION

Does that mean that even if something is not visible to us, it continues to exist in the Lord as a pre-existing memory which can be later recalled?

2.2.26 (197)

नासतोऽदृष्टत्वात्

nāsataḥ adṛṣṭatvāt

na—not; asataḥ—non-existent; adṛṣṭatvāt—from not being seen.

TRANSLATION

(Something) from not being visible has not become non-existent.

COMMENTARY

The universe is temporary for us, but it is eternal for the Lord. Impersonalist philosophy is based on the idea that because the world is temporary, therefore it has no reality; it just appears as an illusion to us. This sūtra directly contradicts this belief by stating that even if something is destroyed, it hasn't become non-existent. It has just gone out of our vision because this vision was created by the Lord's recollection of His memory. The world seems temporal and changing because the Lord's awareness moves through His memory, and this movement makes the world manifest or unmanifest. This awareness is called *sat* but the substrate on which it moves is called *chit*. The cause of this movement is His desire for pleasure or ānanda. Thus, the Lord recollects or understands Himself driven by His desire for self-knowledge resulting in pleasure. As His consciousness scans His memory, the world is manifest. When the consciousness moves to another memory, the experience corresponding to the previous memory disappears, but the memory is not destroyed. The impersonalist claims that because bodies, societies, and civilizations are created and destroyed, therefore, everything is unreal as it ceases to exist eventually. Reality must only be that which exists eternally, and Brahman is thus real because it is eternal. In this sūtra, it is stated that even the material world is eternal.

Therefore, although the world appears and disappears it doesn't become non-existent. Brahman is the knower and it never appears or disappears, in the sense that one never ceases to be aware of one's own existence. But going in and out of awareness is not the criterion for measuring reality. If I turn my head away from something and stop seeing it, the fact that my experience of that thing has ended doesn't entail that the thing has ceased to exist. In the same way, the changes we see are the effects of the Lord's moving awareness.

QUESTION

If the material world is eternal, then there should be no reason for happiness when something is created, or lamentation when it is destroyed. Then, why are people becoming happy on seeing, and lamenting on destruction?

2.2.27 (198)

उदासीनानाम् अपि चैवं सद्धिः

udāsīnānām api caivaṃ siddhiḥ

udāsīnānām—those who are detached or indifferent (to this world); api—even; ca—and; evam—thus; siddhiḥ—attainment of perfection.

TRANSLATION

Even those who are detached or indifferent (to this world) can also attain perfection (liberation from the laws of matter) by this understanding.

COMMENTARY

Most people are excited by the achievement of things that they haven't seen before, and they lament the loss of things they have achieved. They may not realize that the things we have achieved have been previously achieved by innumerable people, which were subsequently lost, and then achieved again. There is no novelty in this material world; we have been rich and poor, beautiful and ugly, powerful and weak, intelligent and stupid, and respected and ill-treated innumerable times. Whatever is achieved is lost, and whatever is lost is achieved again. If one understands that this cycle of loss and achievement repeats innumerable times, then one becomes detached. For example, we might think that the creation of modern technology such as airplanes, telephones, televisions, etc. are great advancements of our time, which did not exist before. And we get enamored by the progress of technology as it seems to bring new things. But one who is knowledgeable realizes that all this has existed before; it periodically manifests and unmanifests; if we are seeing something today, it will certainly be lost; and if something has been lost, it will certainly be achieved again. So, there is no permanent gain and no permanent loss. One who has attained this realization becomes detached from the events of this world. He is neither delighted on an achievement nor suffers due to a loss. Such a person, who has transcended the effects of material gain and loss is said to have achieved perfection because he loses all desire for material achievements.

Topic 5

QUESTION

But if both material and spiritual worlds are eternal realities, and they are both manifested by the Lord, then what is the harm in being attached to

the material world? How can we prefer the spiritual reality over the material reality, when both realities are eternal, and both are created by the Lord?

2.2.28 (199)
नाभावःउपलब्धेः
nābhāvaḥ upalabdheḥ

na—not; abhāvaḥ—unmanifest; upalabdheḥ—experienceable.

TRANSLATION

The unmanifest is not experienceable.

COMMENTARY

In the spiritual world, there is night and day; the Lord wakes up in the morning and goes to play with His friends, grazing His cows. In the evening He returns home and talks about His escapades during the day with His father and mother. But in the night, He escapes from the home of His parents to dance with His girlfriends. Due to the passing of day and night, we say that the Lord's experiences are manifest and unmanifest—sometimes He is playing with His friends, then talking to His parents, and then dancing with His girlfriends. However, this doesn't mean that when He is not talking to His parents, friends, or girlfriends, they must disappear. They exist simultaneously, but they meet the Lord one after another. This meeting and separation constitute the evolution in time. However, this spiritual time is different from material time in which people die such that you cannot talk to them the next morning like you were doing previously. The eternity of the spiritual world is not static. It essentially means that nobody dies, and nobody is born. The evolution of the material world is birth and death. So, we cannot equate these two kinds of times.

The previous sūtras said that even in the material world, if something has been destroyed, the potentiality for that thing has not ceased, and it is manifest again and again. In short, the dinosaurs disappear, and the dinosaurs appear. The disappearance of dinosaurs from our experience doesn't mean that the species did not exist previously or would not exist in the future. So, the material world is eternal in that sense. However, this eternity of the material world is different from the eternity of the spiritual world because in the spiritual world nothing ever dies. Hence, this sūtra says that what has become unmanifest has gone out of our experience. The reverse is not necessarily true. For instance, something that has gone out of our experience is not necessarily unmanifest. Thus, even in this world, we can stop reading a book, and that doesn't mean that the book has disappeared. However, if the book is burnt, then we must necessarily stop reading it. In the spiritual world, all change is because of choice—just like we stop reading a book. In the material world, changes are both due to our choices and forced due to time—i.e., the book can be burnt, and we can stop reading the book. In this sūtra, the burning of the book is referred to. The content of the book—i.e., the ideas in it—are not burnt when the book is burnt. That content will again manifest, but it is not visible right now.

QUESTION

But someone can argue that even if the dinosaurs are not visible right now, we could still experience them during dreams. Since these things become visible during dreams, they are testimony not only to the fact that they are eternal but also the fact that they can be manifest to us at any point in time. How then can we say that certain things are not available to us at certain times?

2.2.29 (200)

वैधर्म्याच्च न स्वप्नादिवत्

vaidharmyācca na svapnādivat

vaidharmyāt—due to the difference of (material and spiritual) nature; ca—and; na—is not; svapnādivat—just like dreams etc.

TRANSLATION

There is a difference between (material and spiritual) natures, and (the spiritual world) is not like the dreaming state (in the material world).

COMMENTARY

The dreaming state is considered superior to the waking state because in the dreaming state we can see things that we will not see during the waking state. How do we see such things? Are they merely 'creations' of the mind? All perception in Vedic philosophy is perception of a preexisting reality. It may exist as our memory, or it may exist as an external possibility, or even a manifest reality. Our mind and the senses merely 'roam' in this space of possibilities, and through this contact experience is created. So, the cause of experience is the roaming of the senses and the mind. But what causes the roaming? As we have seen earlier, there are two causes—guna or desiring, and karma or deserving. Sometimes when we have an intense desire to solve a problem, we might see a solution to the problem in our dreams, although we could not see it during waking. Similarly, due to karma, we might have good or bad experiences during dreams. The guna and the karma themselves manifest under the influence of time. So, the dreaming experience is as much subject to the influence of time as the waking experience. Just because we can see dinosaurs in dreams should not mean that we can see anything or everything that is possible. Just as waking experiences are subject to the influence of time, similarly, the dreams are too. The difference is that dreaming enables us with a much wider contact with possibilities because our senses and the mind directly contact the possibilities, unmediated by the body. While the body is present in one place—e.g., sleeping on the bed—the mind and the senses can roam far and wide. In one sense, this shows how we are not bound to the body, and the understanding of dreams can lead to spiritual progress. But in another sense, the laws of converting the possibility to reality are the same whether in the case of waking or dreaming.

In simple terms, if our karma doesn't allow it, then we cannot enter heavenly planets during dreams, and enjoy just like demigods. So, even in dreams, we are bound by our karma. The spiritual world is not like that because there is no bondage of karma. Thus, we are not forced to have bad experiences, like we are forced to have bad dreams in this world. And we are not prevented from having good experiences—e.g., that of entry into heavenly planets—like we are prevented due to karma in this lifetime. In the spiritual world, everything is always accessible, everything is always pleasing, and nothing is forced. Therefore, the spiritual world cannot be compared to the materialistic dreams.

QUESTION

If we can see things during dreams that we cannot see during waking, and you are acknowledging that material reality is eternal like spiritual reality, then what is the main difference between the material and the spiritual realities?

2.2.30 (201)

न भावःउनुपलब्धेः

na bhāvaḥ anupalabdheḥ

na—not; bhāvaḥ—existence; anupalabdheḥ—not experienced.

TRANSLATION

All that exists (i.e., is possible) is never inexperienceable.

COMMENTARY

In the last but one sūtra it was stated: *nābhāvaḥ upalabdheḥ*, or that which doesn't exist cannot be experienced. In sūtra, the reverse statement is being made: *na bhāvaḥ anupalabdheḥ*, or that which exists can never be inaccessible to experience. The former statement pertained to the material world, and the present statement is about the spiritual world. The sūtra indicates that everything in the spiritual world is always knowable. It doesn't mean that everyone knows everything in the spiritual world. It only means that anyone can know anything if they so desire. The *upalabdhi* is availability and is not forced.

The existence of this possibility also entails that someone always knows something that others do not know, and collectively all individuals know everything. One only needs to develop the right type of relationship to the Lord to know His various aspects. The Lord is always revealed to different devotees in different ways, and one who has the desire and the suitable relation to the Lord can know Him in that manner. This point has also been made a little differently earlier where it was said that there are innumerable forms of the Lord according to desire and relationship of the soul to the Lord. In this sūtra, the converse point is also made, namely, that every aspect of the Lord is always manifest to some devotee. The situation is thus incomparable to the material world.

QUESTION

But the same argument could also be applied to dreams, namely, that different people can dream different mutually exclusive things, and therefore, we can say that even the material reality is always manifest to someone.

2.2.31 (202)

क्षणिकत्वाच्च

kṣaṇikatvācca

kṣaṇikatvāt—on account of the momentariness; ca—also.

TRANSLATION

(We cannot say that the spiritual reality is like a dream) also because (the dreams) are momentary (and the spiritual experience is not momentary).

COMMENTARY

The material world is produced due to the combination of guna or desiring, and karma or deserving. We may desire good things to happen to us, but they may not happen due to bad karma. Similarly, we do not desire bad things to happen to us, but they will happen due to bad karma. Even if our desires are stable, our karma is temporary, and since our experiences are caused by karma, all these experiences are temporary. Even if we are enjoying a dream, it will not continue permanently. And even if we have something good during waking experience, it will not continue to exist permanently due to karma. So, even though the material energy is eternal, our karma is not eternal. The temporariness of karma creates temporary experiences. If this karma is dissolved, then we are just left with guna or desires. Now, karma doesn't restrain what we can or cannot experience. As soon as we desire something, there is no inhibition in achieving it. So, if our desire remains stable, then the experience also remains stable. We cannot be forced out of some experience due to bad karma. Thus, the material and the spiritual worlds are both eternal, but the material experience is not eternal. The spiritual experience, on the other hand, can always be eternal.

QUESTION

Are you saying that temporariness is the main problem of the material world because we are compelled to change our position due to karma?

2.2.32 (203)

सर्वथानुपपत्तेश्च

sarvathānupapatteśca

sarvathā—in every possible way; anupapatteḥ—inappropriate; ca—and.

TRANSLATION

And (the comparison of the spiritual world to material dreams) is inappropriate in every possible way.

COMMENTARY

Multiple arguments refuting the comparison of the spiritual world to materialistic dreams have been made in the previous sūtras. First, we are forced to suffer even in dreams due to our karma. Second, we are restricted from pleasures during dreams in the material world. Third, whatever pleasure is obtained in the material world through dreams is temporary. Conversely, in the spiritual world, the soul is not forced to suffer; the soul is not restricted from any pleasure; and whatever is obtained can be obtained eternally. Thus, it is not one argument against this comparison; there are multiple arguments against it.

Topic 6

QUESTION

You have said that the Absolute Truth is all the possibilities that will manifest in the world. What if someone has a desire that is outside this possibility? Since the Absolute Truth doesn't have this possibility, it can never be fulfilled. So, how can we say that freedom from material world leads to happiness?

2.2.33 (204)

नैकस्मिन्न् असंभवात्

naikasminn asaṃbhavāt

na—not; ekasmin—in one; asaṃbhavāt—on account of the impossibility.

TRANSLATION

Nothing is impossible in the One (the Absolute Truth).

COMMENTARY

It is one thing to say that the Absolute Truth is all the possibilities that will manifest. It is quite another to say that nothing is impossible in Absolute Truth. One can argue that I'm not satisfied with everything possible; I want something that is impossible, or outside the collection of all possibilities. If I develop such a desire, how can that be fulfilled if the Absolute Truth is only the possible things? This sūtra states that whatever you can desire is already there in the Absolute Truth. The Absolute Truth is not just all the possibilities that can be realized, but nothing is impossible in the Absolute Truth. Essentially, by 'possibility' we don't mean a realm restricted by laws or conditions. For example, a scientist can say that anything is possible if it doesn't violate the laws of logic, mathematics, and physics. But what if someone has a desire for something that violates these laws? You might want a car that runs without fuel, or a time-machine that takes you into the past, etc. Are these in the realm of possibility or not? The sūtra states that nothing is impossible in the Absolute Truth.

QUESTION

If everything that can be desired is also possible in the Absolute Truth, does that mean that every soul can desire any of these possibilities?

2.2.34 (205)

एवं चात्माकार्त्स्न्यम्

evaṃ cātmākārtsnyam

evam—thus; ca—also; ātmā—the soul; akārtsnyam—incompleteness, or non-fullness.

TRANSLATION

(Just as the fullness of the Absolute Truth implies the existence of all possibilities) in the same way the incompleteness of the soul also (implies that the soul cannot desire everything that is possible in the Absolute Truth).

COMMENTARY

Everything in the Lord can be liked by someone, but everything in the Lord will not be liked by everyone. Just as there are opposite kinds of smells, tastes, colors, forms, etc. similarly there are also opposite kinds of likes and dislikes. If the soul desires, then he can experience the opposite natures of the Lord. But that doesn't mean that soul will desire all such opposite natures. Thus, for instance, some devotees are attracted to the childhood pastimes of the Lord, but they don't like the fearsome, commanding, and intimidating features of the Lord. Conversely, some like the Lord to be powerful and fearsome, and don't like His pastimes as a child where He remains dependent on His parents. Every soul is attracted in a different way to the Lord, and while the Lord can fulfill all desires, it doesn't mean that every soul is attracted to all aspects of the Lord. The existence of desire entails the existence of a personality that chooses or prefers some aspects over others. Since the soul is small and incomplete, it will always be attracted only to some aspects of the Lord, not to all His aspects. Thus, the varied forms of the Lord are not opposed to monotheism. Rather, monotheism is restrictive as it says that the Lord is always known in one way. We should understand that the soul wants to know one of the many personality features of the Lord and prefers to be involved only in some pastimes.

QUESTION

If the soul cannot desire every possibility, does that mean he is bound to always live in a certain limited understanding of the Absolute Truth?

2.2.35 (206)

न च पर्यायादप्यविरोधःविकारादिभ्यः

na ca paryāyādapyavirodhaḥ vikārādibhyaḥ

na ca—neither; paryāyāt—approach from (a different view); api—even; avirodhaḥ—no hindrance; vikārādibhyaḥ—on account of change etc.

TRANSLATION

Neither is an alternative approach (always occurring); (nor) even is there a hindrance to (a soul) changing (their understanding of the Lord).

COMMENTARY

We have previously discussed that the soul has an innate nature based on how it was intended to serve the Lord. And yet, the soul sometimes foregoes this intended nature of serving the Lord and tries to become independent. This independence indicates that there is always potential for change even in the spiritual world, because whether in the spiritual or the material worlds, the soul retains its free will. But such changes are not frequent because the soul has an innate nature, and although it can change its nature, this is a rare event. So, the intended nature of the soul should not be considered as being contrary to the existence of free will—i.e., that the soul is permanently bound to have a fixed personality. Conversely, we should also not assume that because such changes can occur due to the soul's free will, they must be occurring frequently. In short, the existence of free will does not entail whimsical experimentation.

QUESTION

So, can we say that by and large, the soul and the Lord are situated in a fixed relationship that is typically not expected to change, although in principle it can change if the soul develops an alternative desire toward the Lord?

2.2.36 (207)

अन्त्यावस्थितेश्चोभयनित्यत्वादविशेषः

antyāvasthiteścobhayanityatvādaviśeṣaḥ

antya-avasthiteḥ—ultimately situated; ca—and; ubhaya-nityatvāt—from the two in an eternal (relationship); aviśeṣaḥ—due to inseparability.

TRANSLATION

From the two (the soul and the Lord) being ultimately situated in an eternal relationship due to their inseparability.

COMMENTARY

There are many relationships in this world, but they are temporary. The relationship between the soul and the Lord is eternal, and this eternity is attributed to their inseparability—the Lord is the whole and the soul is the part. The part can never be separated from the whole, and yet the part is never equal to the whole. Therefore, the soul can never become the Lord, but even if it tries to pretend to have become the Lord, the relationship between the soul and the Lord is never broken. This is the reason that the term *antya-avasthiteḥ* is used in this sūtra, which indicates the ultimate position. And this ultimate position is also described as being *nityavat* and *aviśeṣaḥ* or eternal and inseparable. We might wonder why this claim is being made again, when the same types of claims have been made previously. The reason is the context, where the seeker was asking the question about whether the soul can change its relation to the Lord and know the Lord in one of many possible ways. Such a change was not forbidden, and yet it wasn't considered typical. In that context, we can again say that the soul and the Lord are in a mutual and eternal relationship.

Topic 7

QUESTION

If the soul is situated in such an eternal relationship to the Lord, can he fall into the material world? Can this relationship be forgotten or suspended?

2.2.37 (208)

पत्युःअसामञ्जस्यात्

patyuḥ asāmañjasyāt

patyuḥ—the fall; asāmañjasyāt—from being very doubtful or unlikely.

TRANSLATION

(If the soul is situated in an eternal relationship to the Lord) the fall (into the material world) is very doubtful or unlikely or unconventional.

COMMENTARY

The relationship between the soul and the Lord is so sweet that the fall into the material world is very unlikely. The basis of love is that each person is seeking the happiness of the loved one. Under such a situation, both sides—the soul and the Lord—willingly compromise and bend to each other's desires. Due to this loving relationship, the discrepancy in their relation is very unlikely.

QUESTION

But you are not completely ruling out the possibility of the soul's fall? You are saying that this is very unconventional, but there is still a possibility?

2.2.38 (209)

संबन्धानुपपत्तेश्च

saṃbandhānupapatteśca

saṃbandha-anupapatteḥ—adversity in the relation; ca—also.

TRANSLATION

Adversity in the relationship also (can result in a fall).

COMMENTARY

This sūtra affirms that the fall is always a possibility; the relation between the soul and the Lord is based on love, but love can never be forced. Even though the fall has been called unconventional in the last sūtra, this sūtra states that any insufficiency or adversity in the relationship can result in a fall.

QUESTION

But what can lead to such an adversity that the soul leaves the Lord?

2.2.39 (210)

अधषि्ठानानुपपत्तेश्च

adhiṣṭhānānupapatteśca

adhiṣṭhāna-anupapatteḥ—rulership being impossible; ca—and.

TRANSLATION

(The fall can occur when the soul tries to be the Lord) because rulership (of the soul over the Lord) is impossible.

COMMENTARY

In several previous purports we have noted the sense of inferiority in the soul, and how the soul tries to overcome this inferiority by trying to become the Lord. This is the first sūtra, however, where this desire in the soul to become the Lord—rather than remain a servant—is explicitly noted. We have discussed how the soul has the power of will but doesn't have the power to fulfill the will. Thus, the soul depends on the Lord's Śakti to fulfill his desires. The Lord's Śakti, however, is only serving the Lord, so it cannot become the Śakti for the soul, especially if the soul is trying to be a competitor to the Lord. Thus, the soul's attempt at rulership (over the Lord or His Śakti) is deemed impossible.

Nevertheless, if the desire for rulership arises, then the soul falls into the material world. He is granted independence, but that independence comes with a responsibility. Accordingly, the laws of choice and responsibility are framed, and if the soul follows these laws, then he enjoys independently. However, the nature of the material world is that the soul easily forgets that he is bound by these laws. While enjoying, he thinks that he has become the master, and the laws of choice and responsibility do not apply to him. That in turn leads to suffering. In contrast, in the spiritual world, there is only choice and no responsibility. Whatever is done in devotion to the Lord has no consequence. Thus, the soul doesn't love the Lord so that the Lord will love him. And the Lord doesn't love the soul because the soul is loving Him. These cause-and-effect relations cease to exist. The soul spontaneously loves the Lord, and the Lord spontaneously loves the soul. The material world is different—everything is based on cause and effect. Therefore, if you have loved, then you will be loved. If you have not loved, then you will not be loved. Hence, independence comes at the cost of responsibility, but independence is also possible. Except that this is not domination or control over the Lord. That domination is rejected here.

QUESTION

But can't such discrepancies in the mutual relationship arise due to inadvertent circumstances? The soul may be just trying to serve the Lord, but he may fail in serving appropriately. How can such discrepancies result in a fall?

2.2.40 (211)

करणवच्चेत् न भोगादिभ्यः

karaṇavaccet na bhogādibhyaḥ

karaṇavat—as an instrument; cet—if it be said; na—no; bhogādibhyaḥ—because of the desire for enjoyment.

TRANSLATION

If it is said that (the fall is due to discrepancy) as an instrument (i.e., mistake in serving the Lord) (we say) no; (the fall is) because of the desire for enjoyment (by becoming the master or ruler, as already stated in the previous sūtra).

COMMENTARY

Here, the fall is attributed not to a mistake but an aversion toward the Lord, which leads to the desire for independent mastery and enjoyment.

The soul has three aspects—cognition, emotion, and relation. The cognition is achieved through the mind, senses, and the body, and these are the *karana* or the instruments. The senses of action, the intellect, and morality are also the instruments. But there is a difference between a *karana* and a *kārana*—the former is the instrumental cause, and the latter is the intentional cause. Sometimes we might make mistakes even though we have good intentions. If the *kārana* or the emotional state is not flawed—e.g., due to revulsion to the Lord—then the mistakes of *karana* or the instrumental cause are disregarded. The Lord is extremely forgiving of mistakes made by the soul if the intentional and emotional state is devotional, and the soul is trying to serve the Lord rather than pretending to be His master. The rules and regulations of devotional life are not hard and fast. They are prescribed to overcome pride, disrespect, disregard, and laziness. Those who are already devoted need not follow such rules. But even those who are following such rules may make mistakes despite their best intentions. The Lord is sāra-grāhī or the seeker of the essences. He doesn't consider the mistakes of the *karana* seriously because He understands the *kārana*. This sūtra states that any discrepancy in the actions of the soul do not lead to a fall. It is only the emotional state, which, if changed, can result into a fall.

This sūtra hints at the possibility of mistakes even in the spiritual world. These mistakes can arise if the devotee doesn't read the mood of the Lord correctly. For example, the Lord might say: "I love you so much, that I cannot live without you", and He is expecting a banter in response: "Is that so? All your promises in the past have been broken. So, why don't you prove your love?". That response will be a segue into a pastime where the Lord will beg incessantly for forgiveness and concessions, while the devotee will pretend to be abstruse. But after much begging, the mood of the Lord can change, and He then wants to be accepted. In that situation, the devotee should also acquiesce. However, the devotee may not read the Lord's mood correctly, and stay abstruse. This is a discrepancy in the loving exchange. However, this is a discrepancy in understanding the Lord's mood, and not enviousness to become the Lord's master. While such mistakes can occur, these are not the cause of the soul's fall.

Advancement in spiritual life is not just knowing the Lord philosophically; of course, one must know the philosophy. But advancement means being able to grasp the changing moods of the Lord. An advanced devotee reads the Lord's moods correctly, and that ability to understand the Lord leads to intimate relationships. If that understanding is limited, then the Lord also keeps a distance from the devotee, saying what He means, rather than saying things that are contrary to what He intends. But in advanced stages, the discrepancies between words and meanings become prominent. These discrepancies between what is said and what is meant can lead to misunderstandings. However, such mistakes are tolerated by both parties, and not the cause of a break in their love.

QUESTION

But how can we know the difference between aversion and mistakes? After all, a discrepancy can be attributed to a deliberate neglect or to an inadvertent mistake. How can we say that it was indeed a deliberate neglect?

2.2.41 (212)

अन्तवत्त्वमसर्वज्ञता वा

antavattvamsarvajñatā vā

antavat—being limited; tvam—you; sarvajñatā—omniscience; vā—the revered one.

TRANSLATION

You are limited, but the revered one (the Lord) is omniscient.

COMMENTARY

We normally associate knowledge with cognition, but our emotional state can also be known. Common examples of the emotional manifestation include the rising of the blood pressure on anger, the calming of the body on happiness, etc. But, in general, decoding the emotional state is harder than decoding the cognitive state. For example, to understand the anger from a person's speech is harder than understanding the meaning of the words. Thus, one can argue that some bad action is caused due to a sincere mistake rather than a deliberate dereliction of duty. But this difficulty pertains to ordinary people who see the body and try to infer the mental and the intentional state. The problem doesn't apply to the Lord who can perceive all the levels of reality from gross to subtle. In this regard, we must note that even emotions have forms. When the soul has a different desire or intention, it changes form. Under different kinds of emotional states, the soul's form changes. We may not perceive these subtle forms because we are conditioned only to sense perception, and even mental forms are not easily perceived by us, then what to speak about the spiritual forms.

The Lord is, however, not limited in this way. He can see when the soul has changed its form due to a different desire. The notion that certain things are 'private' to us is ultimately false; there is nothing private; everything is deciphered from the forms, but externally, these forms are *known* and internally these forms are *experienced*. There is hence a difference between being angry and knowing that someone is angry. But it is always possible to know the emotional state. The omniscience of the Lord pertains to this ability to know everyone's emotional state from the change in their forms. Even in this world, the ability to read people's emotions through their body language is considered an art and not easily understood by most people. Even those who can decipher emotions from bodily forms may not always be correct in their determination. Such faults are thus outcomes of our limited understanding of the relation between emotion and forms. The Lord is not constrained by such limitations; He is not prone to make mistakes in understanding the soul's real intentions.

Topic 8

QUESTION

Does the aversion to the Lord suddenly arise out of nowhere even within a devotee? Can we say that someone suddenly becomes a non-devotee?

2.2.42 (213)

उत्पत्त्यसंभवात्

utpattyasaṃbhavāt

utpatti-asaṃbhavāt—owing to the impossibility of genesis.

TRANSLATION

It is impossible to postulate a genesis (out of no previous existence).

COMMENTARY

Throughout Vedic philosophy we can find the idea that everything that exists in a manifest form previously existed in an unmanifest form. We never find the notion of genesis out of nothingness. Even when the Lord creates the universe, it is an expansion out of Himself, not ex nihilo creation. Therefore, if something is emerging within the soul, it must preexist in the soul.

Accordingly, even the aversion toward the Lord must have a preexistence in the soul. We cannot claim that this aversion suddenly springs out of nothing. Such a claim would in fact support ex nihilo creation. Thus, by rejecting the notion of genesis, the sūtra indicates that the aversion doesn't emerge out of nothingness.

We have extensively discussed the theory of modes, which exist in dominant and subordinate states. Aversion to the Lord exists innately in all souls, but it becomes dominant in some souls and remains subordinate in others. When it becomes dominant, we cannot say that it emerged out of nothing. And when it is subordinated, we cannot say that it has disappeared permanently. Thus, a soul who has been liberated hasn't lost the ability to fall again. And the soul who has fallen has not lost the ability to be liberated. The aversion to the self also exists within the Lord. This self-averse form of the Lord is known as Param Śiva and He indulges in self-abnegation. Similarly, if the soul becomes averse to the Lord, he falls into the material world ruled by Param Śiva.

Thus, the rejection of the Lord is within each soul because self-rejection is also within the Lord. The Lord is not always enjoying. He is also sometimes guilty about that enjoyment. That guilty form of the Lord is Param Śiva. He indulges in austerities and denies Himself pleasure. The difference between the soul and the Lord is simply that the soul can alternate between different modes of self-enjoyment, self-abnegation, and serving the Lord. The Lord, however, is simultaneously in all these modes. Thus, when the soul becomes averse to the Lord, then he enters a realm in which the Lord is averse to Himself. In this state too, the soul is only serving the Lord, although in a different mood. Thus, the soul never goes out of the Lord's service. However, in the material world, the soul must undergo austerities if he wants to enjoy. While performing these austerities, the soul is directly a part of Param Śiva by acting just like Him. And while enjoying, the soul serves Param Śiva by becoming His negation. Thus, many souls, who enjoy austerities, can permanently remain servants of Param Śiva, and that state of austerity is also considered to be their liberation. Other souls, who don't like austerity, tend to suffer because they desire pleasure, however, this pleasure cannot be obtained unless austerities are performed.

Thus, the so-called 'evil' exists in everything because it also exists in the Lord. It appears as Lord's self-abnegation. Thus, the Lord is not just an enjoyer. He is also austere, where He denies His own pleasure and enjoys that austerity. Finally, the Lord is also self-satisfied, where He is neither enjoying nor performing austerities. These states of enjoyment, austerity, and satisfaction are different moods of the Lord. In the Goloka realm, the Lord is the enjoyer. In the Vaikuṇṭha, He is satisfied. And in the material world, He is austere. These are simply different moods of the Lord. Nevertheless, the enjoying state of the Lord is considered superior to His satisfied state, which is considered superior to His austere state. Accordingly, the soul also participates in these varied moods of the Lord by enjoying with Him, being satisfied with Him, or assisting His austerity. In no situation is the soul contrary to the Lord. The soul is factually always the Lord's servant. But the soul may be serving austerity when he wants to enjoy. And this discrepancy leads to suffering in the material world.

QUESTION

Since the Lord is said to be the cause of all causes, can we say that this aversion is in some way created by the Lord's actions or by an agency?

2.2.43 (214)

न च कर्तुःकरणम्

na ca kartuḥ karaṇam

na ca—nor; kartuḥ—from the action; karaṇam—the instrument.

TRANSLATION

Nor (is the aversion) created by an action or instrument.

COMMENTARY

While the previous sūtra clarified that the soul's rejection of the Lord is caused by the soul itself, the seeker is still asking the same question by presenting alternative mechanisms of such fall. Maybe the rejection of the Lord is caused due to an action (of either the Lord or a soul) or something other than these two (e.g., the energy of the Lord, which acts as His instrument)? It was previously said that some mistakes can occur in our actions, and maybe once these mistakes occur, then the Lord becomes unhappy even though the soul did not intend to make Him unhappy, and seeing this unfavorable response to the soul's sincerity, maybe the soul also becomes averse to the Lord? Similarly, since the Lord's energy fulfills the soul's desires, perhaps some shortfall in this fulfillment creates an aversion? Finally, the energy also creates desires in the soul, thus, maybe the Lord's energy is the cause of the soul's aversion?

This sūtra rejects all such alternative mechanisms for the fall. It says that no action or instrument is the cause of this fall. Coupled with the previous sūtra, which said that the cause of the fall is within the soul, this is a rejection of any external causation. In short, the fall must be attributed to the soul alone. Even though the Lord has the mood for self-abnegation, and correspondingly His Śakti also aids in this self-abnegation by creating a world where the soul enjoys by forgetting the Lord's pleasure, the existence of the Lord's moods and His Śakti's assistance of that mood are not the causes of the soul's rejection.

People sometimes argue that if the soul has evil, and God created the soul, then the evil must originate in God. Then, why should the soul be considered responsible if God created this evil in the soul? If, on the other hand, God is not the creator of the evil, then how can evil exist in the world? In monotheistic philosophies, this problem is solved by postulating a Satan opposed to God, who tempts the soul and creates evil in him. This hardly solves the problem, because Satan is created by God, and is a 'fallen angel'. If Satan could fall and then cause others to fall, then the cause of all that fall must be in God who created an angel who then had the tendency to fall. Thus, the problem is only one step removed from God by the postulate of Satan, not truly solved by it.

The answer to that problem is that what we call evil is not truly evil in the Lord. The Lord's self-abnegation is the Lord's austerity. He is not punishing others; He is punishing Himself. In fact, as Param Śiva performs austerities, He also sets the example of how one must live austerely. Nevertheless, the Lord created the soul with the ability to reject Him. If this ability were not created, then free will would lose its meaning. The Lord would be called a master who created the soul as His slave. The slave has no choice whether to serve or leave the master. By creating the ability to reject the Lord, the Lord created not a slave, but a person with free will. The existence of free will, however, doesn't entail that the Lord supports or causes its misuse. The soul is entitled to reject the Lord due to its free will, but the soul is not entitled to interfere with the free will of others. In fact, even the Lord does not consider Himself entitled to interfere with the other's free will. Then, how can the soul be entitled to this interference?

The problem of evil is simply this—both the soul and the Lord have free will, the Lord created this free will in the soul, but the Lord doesn't misuse His free will and yet the soul does. The Lord cannot be faulted for free will in the soul, so how can He be faulted for the soul's misuse of that free will? The misuse of free will arises if the soul compares himself to the Lord, finds himself lacking, and tries to overcome this inferiority by dominating others. The Lord doesn't force anybody to love Him, and yet, the Lord's devotees love the Lord out of their own free will. Since the soul is not loved in the same way by other souls, his envy causes him to try to force that love out of others. In short, the soul tries to bend others to his will. Once free will is misused in this way, it creates karma, and the person is entrapped in the recurring cycle of suffering. At that point he again says: God made me perform all this evil, but that is not true.

QUESTION

But you have said that the enlightened soul already has perfect knowledge about the material and the spiritual worlds, so he must know the nature of the material world. Doesn't this knowledge control his negative attitudes?

2.2.44 (215)

वज्ञिानादभिावे वा तदप्रतषिेधः

vijñānādibhāve vā tadapratiṣedhaḥ

vijñānādibhāve—in the existence of the realized knowledge etc.; vā—moving or going; tat-apratiṣedhaḥ—no restrictions due to that.

TRANSLATION

In the existence of realized knowledge etc., there are no restriction of moving or going (against the Lord).

COMMENTARY

The impersonalists make an argument about ignorance, claiming that the soul falls because he comes under the influence of māyā. In this sūtra, this claim is rejected. The soul is fully enlightened at the time of fall; ignorance doesn't come before the fall; ignorance is the consequence of the fall. The fall is rather a deliberate desire in the soul, which has no external cause, is not influenced by the will of the Lord, and cannot be said to be sprouting out of nowhere.

The only legitimate argument is that God did not make me God, so that I could be capable of creating souls, who would then be subordinate to me. But even if God had made the souls as god, who could then create more souls, those souls who are created by the second-order god, would have the same complaint! They would now say: God was compassionate in creating second-order gods. But these second-order gods did not create souls equal to themselves. Then the problem of evil would propagate back to God—namely, that He did not create second-order gods such that they would in turn create third-order gods, and everyone would eventually be god. But even if God created other gods capable of creating more such gods, then every new generation of god would complain: what good is being god if we have no subordinate souls? We are simply god in name, and we have no rulership over anyone else!

So, the argument that God did not make the soul god, is ultimately nonsense. If some of these souls are god, then God still receives the blame of partiality. If each one of these souls are god, then everyone complains incessantly. And both these situations are no better than just one God. The conclusion is that there is no situation better than the one that we are presently in. The only alternative is: I don't mind if God is unfair, if only He is unfair in my favor.

QUESTION

You are rejecting many potential causes of the fall—external circumstances, the will of the Lord or His agency, spontaneous generation, and the unsolicited covering of ignorance. Then what is the true cause for the soul's fall? How can he go from being a devotee to suddenly having an aversion to the Lord?

2.2.45 (216)

वप्रितषिधाच्च

vipratiṣedhācca

vipratiṣedhāt—because of contradictions; ca—also.

TRANSLATION

(The fall) is also caused by the presence of contradictions (in the soul).

COMMENTARY

The soul has three aspects—*sat*, *chit*, and *ānanda*. In the material world, these manifest as opportunities, abilities, and desires, and they are generally contradictory. Thus, we might desire something, but we don't have an opportunity to get it. Or, we may get an opportunity, but we don't have the ability to use that opportunity. Conversely, the opportunities presented to us are contrary to our desires. Or, the opportunities may be contrary to our abilities. In all these ways, the soul suffers due to contradictions between ability, opportunity, and desire. These contradictions also lead to compromises. For example, if our desire is not fulfilled in the current opportunities, then we may change our desires to enjoy whatever is available in the present opportunity. Or, if we don't have the ability to get what we want, then we try to get what we can. Conversely, if our desire is very strong, then we will keep seeking the opportunity that can fulfill our desires. Or, if we don't have the necessary abilities right now, we might try to enhance our abilities to get what we deeply desire. Thus, sometimes, desires subordinate the opportunity and ability and push the person toward obtaining the appropriate opportunity and ability. At other times, the opportunity or ability may subordinate the desire, and force us to like what we can get. Thus, due to the contradiction between ability, desire, and opportunity, there is a constant tussle between the three factors that create experience about which goes dominant, and which others are subordinated. Each such dominant-subordinate relation represents a *choice* as well as a *compromise*. Basically, the soul resolves the conflicts in his experience by making some compromise. Once that compromise has been made, the soul feels peaceful again, until the next conflict arises, which then necessitates a new compromise, and so forth.

However, when the soul enters the spiritual world, these conflicts or contradiction between ability, desire, and opportunity ends. The soul is perfectly capable of doing what he desires, and he gets the opportunity to use those abilities. Everything is driven by desires, and the ability and opportunity are fulfilled according to those desires. There is hence no need for compromises. The nature of choice is now altered—from making compromises to desiring.

But, if you could desire anything, what would you desire? Remember that desiring also involves prioritizing: If I'm both hungry and thirsty, should I eat before I drink, or should I drink before I eat? The end of conflict between ability, opportunity, and desire, doesn't mean the end of conflicts themselves; these conflicts now appear within the desires themselves. In the material world, the locus for all decisions is the self: we decide based on what we like, or what will be good for us. In the spiritual world, the Lord is the locus for all decisions: the soul decides what is good based on what the Lord will like. There can be discrepancies in this understanding—one might think that the Lord will like something, but He might not. But that doesn't cause a fall because this is not a discrepancy of love, but a shortfall in understanding the Lord's nature. The fall is caused if the locus of decision-making shifts from the Lord to the soul: the soul starts deciding what is good for him, rather than what is the Lord's liking.

The conflict is within the soul—should I prioritize myself or the Lord? And there is a range of responses to this question ranging from always thinking of the Lord to sometimes thinking of oneself and sometimes thinking of the Lord, to always thinking of oneself. Depending on the type of response, the soul can be in the different spiritual realms or the different material existences. The devotees of the Lord, therefore, reject the aspiration of liberation from the material world because it involves some level of thinking about oneself. They are rather content with staying in the material world life after life *if* that pleases the Lord. Not everyone in the spiritual world is necessarily always thinking of the Lord; they are sometimes also thinking about their welfare. The material world is just the limiting extreme where the soul rarely remembers the Lord, and even if he does remember the Lord, it is only for getting a better life for himself.

Modern thinking has been developed upon the idea that change follows logical reasoning, and logical reasoning follows the principles of consistency. Thus, even the soul is understood in some religions as a rational being. He has some premises—which could be internal or external—and he arrives at the conclusions. This line of thinking doesn't recognize that in the material world, the internal and external premises are not always consistent, and giving one premise priority over another itself requires a compromise. But even if there was no conflict externally, there are always internal conflicts—we too have many desires, and they cannot be fulfilled at once. To fulfill each of them, we must prioritize and compromise—e.g., let's do this one first before we do others. Therefore, conflict is the basic principle of reasoning. It is not that consistent reasoning is impossible; however, that consistent reasoning depends on premises being consistent. If the premises are contradictory, then reasoning cannot lead to a conclusion. Therefore, the initial step in reasoning is resolving conflicts. The focus of any problem solving is conflict resolution through compromises.

The soul also has innate desires for love of the Lord and independence from the Lord. Each of these desires can be dominant or subordinate. This dominant-subordinate pattern of desires is the soul's choice. The Lord has created the soul to be able to choose. But the Lord doesn't choose for the soul. And the soul is conflicted. If the soul could only desire one thing, then the Lord would be accused of limiting the soul to one desire. If the soul is capable of many desires, then it must make choices and compromises. Thus, these inner conflicts in the soul are described to be the cause of the soul's fall in this sūtra.

SECTION 3

Topic 1

QUESTION

If the conflict is within the soul, then why doesn't the soul split apart into different individuals? Doesn't the existence of inner contradictions imply something that is logically contradictory and cannot be self-consistent? For example, hot and cold cannot exist in the same place due to self-contradiction. Then, why should the soul remain self-contradictory due to conflicting desires?

2.3.1 (217)

न वयित् अश्रुतेः

na viyat aśruteḥ

na—not; viyat—going apart; aśruteḥ—not stated by śrutī.

TRANSLATION

(The soul) does not split apart, as this is not accepted by śrutī.

COMMENTARY

The idea that objects in this world must only have one kind of property is an illusion of the physical world. All material objects have many properties—often contradictory—which are manifest in different situations. For example, we can say that a cow is normally gentle, but she can be aggressive if her calf is in danger. So, the properties of being gentle and aggressive are in the cow, but they are visible in different situations. It is pointless to say that since the cow is gentle, her aggression should split the cow into two parts: one gentle and the other aggressive. Both properties exist in the cow, but they are manifest alternately. We cannot collapse these differences to create a self-contradiction since these properties are manifest in different places, times, and situations.

In the same way, the soul is capable of contradictory desires—sometimes being active, and at other times being inactive, sometimes being gregarious and at other times being silent, sometimes being bold and at other times being shy. Each person is capable of all such desires, but their relative proportions vary. Thus, the cow is mostly gentle and only occasionally aggressive. The tiger, on the other hand, is mostly aggressive and occasionally gentle. That doesn't entail the absence of aggression in the cow or the absence of gentleness in the tiger. All such properties exist in contrast to their opposites. However, the gentleness can subordinate aggression or vice versa. That subordination makes some qualities invisible, but they are not absent. Thus, contradictions exist in everything, and this creates inner contradictions, which then lead to dominant-subordinate conditions. The soul makes a choice of what is dominant or subordinate.

QUESTION

But then you are accepting that the soul cannot be understood logically because it can have mutually contradictory desires, at least one after another?

2.3.2 (218)

अस्ति तु

asti tu

asti—there is; tu—but, of course.

TRANSLATION

But, of course, such is the case (the soul not being logically consistent).

COMMENTARY

Classical notions of logic entail that given a premise there must be only one conclusion, or at least, the conclusions must be mutually consistent. The premise of the existence of the soul, however, doesn't entail such consistency because contradictory desires can be produced from the same premise. We have noted this problem at the beginning where we said that the premise of my existence can lead to diverse questions: "Why do I exist?" or "How can I continue to exist?" Troubled by the problems of life, some people develop a stronger desire to fight their problems while others resign to end their lives. Thus, the same premise leads to mutually inconsistent conclusions. Hence, the soul cannot be studied using logical consistency. We have seen earlier how "I" is riddled with problems of mutual exclusion and non-contradiction. For instance, if we classify all the individuals into two groups—friends and non-friends—then it is not clear whether I'm my friend (because friends must be different from me) or non-friend (because how could I be my enemy?). Regarding the self, we are compelled to conclude that I am neither my friend nor my non-friend.

Thus, due to the production of conflicting desires, we must say that the soul is *both* these desires. And due to being separate from the material opposites (such as friends and non-friends) we must say that it is *neither* of these opposites. The use of both and neither is contrary to classical conceptions of logic because if something is not-X then it must be X, and it cannot both be X and not-X. The soul cannot be studied using classical logical categories.

QUESTION

Shouldn't we say that this inner contradiction is due to the influence of

the material modes? The reason is that the material world is the experience of conflict and contradiction. If we say that the soul is itself contradictory, then aren't we imputing the contradictions of this world back onto the soul itself?

2.3.3 (219)
गौणी असंभवात्
gauṇī asaṃbhavāt

gauṇī—mixed up with guna; asaṃbhavāt—due to the impossibility.

TRANSLATION

(The conclusion of being) mixed up with guna is impossible.

COMMENTARY

Material nature exists in three modes of sattva, rajas, and tamas. But the soul also exists in the three modes of sat, chit, and ānanda. Just as the three modes mix over and over to produce a tree-like hierarchical structure, similarly, the modes of the soul also mix over and over to create his personality of desires, a body of senses, mind, intellect, ego, and morality, and diverse types of relations in which the soul is superior in some roles and inferior in other roles.

Therefore, the claim that if there are some contradictions, then they must be due to material modes is ignorant of the fact that the soul is also in three modes. The material nature is the Lord's Śakti, and a person. The three modes of sattva, rajas, and tamas are reflections of the sat-chit-ānanda in the Lord's Śakti. The problem in impersonalism is that it considers the soul to be living and material energy to be dead. Thus, Brahman is alive and māyā is dead. This is an utterly false caricature because material nature is the Lord's Śakti.

The three modes of nature are universal, individual, and relational. In the spiritual world, the universal mode dominates over the relational mode, which dominates over the individual mode. Therefore, the Absolute Truth is dominant, everything is defined in relation to Him, and the individual soul remains subordinate. In the material world this prioritization is inverted. Now, the individual mode dominates, the relational mode is subordinate, and the universal mode is further subordinate. Therefore, every soul thinks that he is the master of the universe, everything is defined in relation to him, and whatever universal truth exists—e.g., in case of modern science—must be used in his service.

The problem is not the qualities of nature, but their prioritization or the dominant-subordinate structure. Thus, the material world becomes the spiritual world for the devotees, and the spiritual world becomes the material world for the materialist. The qualities in both worlds are the same. But the ordering of these qualities is completely opposed in these two worlds. Therefore, the claim that the qualities are only due to the material world is false. Qualities exist in the spiritual world too, but their hierarchy is inverted in matter.

QUESTION

We don't see a rational and logical person saying self-contradictory things. How can we say that a soul, purified of material influences, is conflicted?

2.3.4 (220)

शब्दाच्च

śabdācca

śabdāt—from their words; ca—also.

TRANSLATION

(We can know the conflicts in a soul) from their words as well (i.e., they will say contradictory things).

COMMENTARY

The Vedas are the primary examples of conflicting ideas, as there are many mutually contradictory ideas described in the Vedas. Thus, the Lord is both transcendent and immanent, the material world is His part and yet separate from Him, and the Lord exists in many moods, forms, and relationships.

The term śabdāt can refer both to the words of spiritually realized souls, or to the Vedic scriptures. Since these scriptures are spoken by the Lord and His devotees, the contradictions exist in the Lord Himself, but they manifest in different times, places, and contexts. The soul is similarly capable of many kinds of desires, and different levels of advancement. Thus, the different kinds of scriptures are meant for people with different mentalities and desires. For those who desire material enjoyment, a restricted form of enjoyment through rituals is prescribed. For those who want to renounce these enjoyments, the path of knowledge and detachment is prescribed. Those who want to change the quality of their enjoyment are advised in modifying their minds and bodies. And those who want to enjoy in the association of the Lord are prescribed devotion.

The unity underlying this diversity is that each of these processes uplifts the soul toward devotion to the Lord, but the stages of this upliftment may be mutually contradictory. Thus, the Vedas describe both *pravritti* and *nivritti*, which encourage practitioners to engage in their duties or renounce their duties. A self-realized teacher may advise one disciple to go out and work, take care of their family, perform their social duties, etc. because he is not yet prepared for renunciation; even if he was advised to sit in one place and meditate, he would keep thinking about what he is missing. Only a person who has indulged in these activities and realized their futility can be advised renunciation because he can then withdraw the mind and senses from worldly engagements. A person who cannot control his sexual urges may be advised to have multiple marriages, while a person who has transcended such urges may be advised to renounce. The conflicting statements are meant to achieve the same purpose, ultimately, although they are intended for people who have different levels of spiritual progress, and hence prescribe different paths of progress for them.

The Lord Himself has contradictory desires—in Goloka He desire to enjoy with others, in Vaikuṇṭha He remains self-satisfied, and in the material world He engages in austerity. Some forms of the Lord are angry, while other forms are humorous. These are simply manifestation of the different desires in the Lord, and He enjoys in innumerable ways by fulfilling His desires. Thus, contradictions appear in the Lord, and they appear in all the souls. The extent of contradictions in us is nowhere near the extent of contradictions in the Lord because we are limited to a few places, times, and situations. Since the Lord is manifest in everything, therefore, the variety is both contradictory, and yet it has a single source. If we can understand the existence of contradictions within us, then by extension we can imagine their existence in the Lord as well.

QUESTION

We can understand that when a single truth manifests into many individuals, and they are placed in different situations or contexts, then different paths may be prescribed, and contradictory statements can be made. But shouldn't the Absolute Truth from which everything originates be logically consistent? How can we understand an Absolute Truth that is also self-contradictory?

2.3.5 (221)

स्याच्चैकस्य ब्रह्मशब्दवत्

syāccaikasya brahmaśabdavat

syāt—is possible; ca—and; ekasya—of the same; brahmaśabdavat—like śabda-brahman (manifests conflicting meanings).

TRANSLATION

Just like śabda-brahman is manifest (as conflicting meanings) from the same source, (similarly), it is possible (for a pure soul to say conflicting things).

COMMENTARY

The ideas of self-consistency are based on physical notions of reality. When we think about concepts, however, both cows and tigers are part of mammals. The cow is gentle, and the tiger is aggressive, and yet, they are both mammals, and they are part of mammals. Since they are parts of mammal, therefore, contradictory things come out of the same truth. But someone might say that we only know about cows and tigers, never about mammals. For such people we can say that the mammal is also within the cow and the tiger. Thus, there is diversity inside the unity, and unity inside the diversity. There are opposites, but because they are not manifest simultaneously, there is no contradiction. These contradictory opposites are potentialities in the Absolute Truth, and then are manifested as partial expressions of this Absolute Truth. When they are manifest, we think they are opposites and don't see their unitary source.

This sūtra gives the example of śabda-brahmān, which is a sound representation of Brahman. Since it is the origin of all words, therefore, many contradictory words are produced from Brahman. Thus, śabda-brahmān is not without contradictions because it is the origin of all the words, whose meanings are mutually contradictory. The words are also not formless; therefore, the source of all words cannot be formless. Each word is a unique form, and the origin of these forms is the speaker of these words. The speaker must have an organ of speech, which can also represent the knowledge of all the parts of His body. Thus, śabda- brahmān is all the words, and the speaker of śabda-brahmān provides the description of Himself. Therefore, śabda- brahmān is a representation of the Lord. This representation is all the mutually contradictory words. Therefore, the source or the speaker of śabda- brahmān must have these contradictions. Therefore, we cannot understand the source using logical consistency.

We might note here in addition that these forms are semantic, rather than physical. Left and right, top and bottom, front and back, are not merely physical sides; they are also conflicting meanings, and this conflict is illustrated by the fact that if something doesn't have a top, then it also won't have a bottom. If something doesn't have a front, then it also won't have a back. These are mutually opposed, and they are only defined in the presence of the other. The Absolute Truth combines these opposites, so it is outside conventional logic.

QUESTION

You keep saying that the Absolute Truth is outside conventional logic, but how are we to understand this new type of logic? What new logical principles must be adopted, and which older logical principles must be discarded?

2.3.6 (222)

प्रतज्ञिाहानरिव्यतरिकाच्छब्देभ्यः

pratijñāhāniravyatirekācchabdebhyaḥ

pratijñā-ahāniḥ—non-contradiction; avyatirekāt—from the non-exclusion; śabdebhyaḥ—the words.

TRANSLATION

From the non-exclusion of the words, there is no contradiction.

COMMENTARY

Our conventional understanding of the world is based on the idea that X and not-X are non-contradictory and mutually exclusive. So, if X is true, then not-X must be false, and at least one of these must be true. This sūtra accepts non-contradiction but rejects mutual exclusion. In fact, mutual exclusion is replaced by *avyatirekā* or non-exclusion. To understand this position, think of the head and the tail of a coin. Only one head will be seen at any time. However, the mere presence of a head entails the existence of a tail, although both are not seen simultaneously. Therefore, since either head or tail are seen, therefore, there is non-contradiction. However, since the existence of either entails the existence of the opposite, therefore, there is non-exclusion. The non-contradiction pertains to our experience, and the non-exclusion pertains to existence. Hence, both opposites exist and are mutually defined, but only one of them is seen at any given moment, in a specific situation. The basic point is that all reality has a form, and we can see only one aspect of the form. Just like we see one of the two faces of the coin, or one of the six faces of a die, similarly, the existence of forms entails that everything is not seen at once. However, seeing any aspect entails the existence of the other aspects as these are mutually defined.

Thus, when the scriptures or the advanced souls speak of different aspects at different times or in different contexts, we should not presume contradiction. We should rather say that when one claim was made, the opposite one automatically entailed—just like seeing the head of the coin entails that the tail also exists. In short, assertions don't entail the negation of their opposites. Rather, the assertion entails that the opposite is true but in a different context.

Mutual exclusion is commonly used in *reductio ad absurdum* proofs, where, the mere truth of X entails the falsity of not-X. This problem arises because logic doesn't have the distinction of space, time, and persons, and logical truth is supposed to be Universal Truth. The Vedic conception of truth is not universalist; it is rather absolutist. What is the difference? When we speak about Universal Truth, then relative truth is not true; it is just what you and I think and because you and I think differently, therefore, at least one of us must be thinking falsities. It is possible that both of us are under illusion; but at least, one of us must be under illusion. Now, the problem with logic is that whatever is false also cannot exist. Thus, if the sky is blue, then a red sky cannot exist. This leads to a serious problem—the person who is thinking falsities cannot exist—if only true things exist. So, if someone says that the sky is red, he must not exist. But, of course, we can see the existence of those who don't agree with us. By the universalist notion of logic, only one of us must exist. Since I cannot deny my existence, therefore, I must say that whoever disagrees with me cannot exist. Thus, universalist conceptions of truth lead to obvious problems.

However, when we speak about the Absolute Truth, then relative truth is not false; it is only a *part* of the whole truth. Each such partial truth also has three further aspects—objective, subjective, and relational. For example, in seeing a snake, there is an objective snake, I must be there to see the snake, and I must see it correctly as snake. Relative truth is when the objective, subjective, and relational are consistent. That is, there is a snake, I am present near the snake to see it, and I see it as a snake. Relative falsity is when either there is no snake, or I am not present to see the snake, or I don't see it as a snake. However, seeing the snake—when it is seen perfectly (i.e., there is a snake, I was there to see it, and I saw it correctly)—is not Absolute Truth. It is only relative truth. The relative truth is different from relative falsity; relative truth is not falsity.

Thus, in the universalist conception of truth, all relative knowledge is false. But in the absolutist conception of truth, all relative knowledge is partial.

The implication of this partial knowledge is that it doesn't exclude its opposites. Thus, if I see a snake, then someone else can see a rope. I may see the snake and the rope at different places or times. And two people can see snake and rope simultaneously at different places. If one of these—the time, place, or person—is different, then there is no contradiction in different seeing. And the absence of such contradiction precludes mutual exclusion in the universalist sense; we can say that seeing a rope doesn't exclude the seeing of a snake, and this seeing of the snake is not a falsity if seeing the rope is true. Since all these truths emerge from the Absolute Truth, the existence of such contradictory knowledge is not actually contradictory because perception involves the distinctions of place, time, and person, and the Absolute Truth is all the perception, but that perception is divided across many places, times, and persons.

As we have discussed earlier, the Absolute Truth exists in three modes—place, time, and person; the Śakti-mode is the place-mode; the God-mode is the time-mode, and the soul-mode is the person mode. Through the combination of these modes, infinite relative truths are created. But when they are uncombined, then the same truth is called Absolute Truth. The uncombined is the whole truth, and the combinations are the parts of the whole truth. Hence, partial, or relative truth is created with the Absolute Truth as diversity. This diversity is non-contradictory due to different place, time, and person. But it is also non-exclusive because one place, time, and person entails others.

Impersonal philosophers misinterpret this diversity by saying that since all such truths are possible, therefore, whatever anyone sees must be truth. This is again a wrong position. There are both relative truths and relative falsities. The Absolute Truth is never false, and the Universal Truth is always false. So, the recognition of the falsity of Universal Truth doesn't entail that every relative experience now becomes truth. You can see a snake when there is a rope. That seeing is relative falsity, not relative truth, and certainly not Absolute Truth. Thus, the rejection of Universal Truth is not the rejection of Absolute Truth, and the rejection of Universal Truth doesn't make every relative lie a truth.

QUESTION

Won't the rejection of mutual exclusion as a logical principle lead to many faults? For example, we say that "you can't have your cake and eat it too" because eating the cake and having it are mutually exclusive alternatives.

2.3.7 (223)
यावद्विकारं तु विभागो लोकवत्
yāvadvikāraṃ tu vibhāgo lokavat

yāvat-vikāraṃ—whatever faults; tu—but; vibhāgaḥ—separateness; loka-vat—as in the world.

TRANSLATION

Whatever faults (we impute on these words) are but due to the (idea of) separateness (of opposite claims) just as in the material world.

COMMENTARY

The previous sūtra rejected the application of mutual exclusion to the Absolute Truth, but this sūtra accepts its application to the material world. The result of this principle is change: if you are given some cake, and you eat it, then the cake no longer exists. In short, eating the cake would entail a change as the cake ceases to exist. In contrast, we can envision the spiritual world as a place where you can eat the cake and the cake also remains intact. Your eating therefore doesn't end the existence of the cake, and hence everything is eternal.

There are two kinds of eternity we can envision. First, everything remains static and unchanged, and in this state, there are no activities—e.g., you cannot eat anything. Second, you can envision a world where there are continuous activities—e.g., you can eat cakes—and yet everything is eternal. The impersonalist argues for the first type of eternity, and the personalist for the second type of eternity. The first type of eternity is static, and it implies the absence of change because change would—under the material world logic—entail birth and death. The second type of eternity is dynamic, and activities are constantly being performed, their results are being enjoyed, and yet the world is eternal. This eternity is impossible with mutual exclusion, but it is possible if we agree upon non-exclusion as the logical principle—as stated in the last sūtra.

In this world, change occurs when a cause becomes an effect, and then ceases to exist. That cessation of the cause, after the effect has been created, is called mutual exclusion. This mutual exclusion is false in many cases. For example, we can use a block of wood as a chair or as a table; while using it as a table, we can say that the table exists, but we cannot say that the chair doesn't exist. Rather, the same thing can be used as table and chair one after another. However, there are situations in this world when things are *destroyed,* and they cannot be said to exist anymore. The eating of the cake is its destruction. If you burn wood, then the wood ceases to exist and is replaced by ash. From this ash you cannot get the wood immediately, although over time, the ash will mix into soil, will be consumed by a seed, become a tree, and then wood again.

This so-called irreversible change is different from the reversible change. For instance, I can act as a father at home and employee at work, and such changes are reversible. But when I die, the change is irreversible. If all changes were reversible—as in the spiritual world—then non-exclusion would hold, and mutual exclusion would always be false. If some changes are reversible, as in the case of me shuttling between father and employee roles, then sometimes non-exclusion is true, and sometimes mutual-exclusion is true. But whenever the change is irreversible, then mutual exclusion is true and non-exclusion is false. This sūtra says whatever cases of mutual exclusion we see are unique to the material world. By this, the phenomenon of birth and death is indicated.

It is not truly mutual exclusion, because those who have died will be born again, and they could be born in the same species, in the same gender, and even potentially at the same place. Even if they are born in another species, gender, or place, they can return to the same species, gender, and place later. Thus, birth and death can be reversible, as the soul goes through 8,400,000 species. As he passes through these species, he cannot say that being in a dog body excludes his being in a cat body. However, these changes are not obtained at will. Thus, I can go to work and come back at home at will. But I cannot become cat and dog at will. That gives rise to the idea of irreversibility, but over a longer time, it is not. If the soul is in the material world, and undergoing cyclic changes, everything is reversible, although not at our will. Only liberation from the material existence is irreversible, but as we have seen earlier, a liberated soul can also fall into the material world, so it is also not considered irreversible.

Thus, we can ask: Is there anything irreversible and mutually exclusive? The short answer is no. Everything is always possible, and hence always reversible. This reversibility entails non-exclusion. The difference is simply that in the spiritual world, this reversibility is obtained at will, and in the material world, it is not obtained at will. The absence of change at will makes us think that the world is irreversible—e.g., that time goes linearly forward—but that is not true. Therefore, the apparent lack of reversibility is an outcome of our inability to control our lives with our will, and to the extent that we can control it things are reversible, and when we can't control it seems irreversible. This irreversibility is an apparent phenomenon observable in the material world.

Topic 2

QUESTION

You have said earlier that the possibilities are eternal, and that the possibilities are also contradictory. Above, you have also said that these contradictory possibilities cannot be realized at once, which means that the possibilities are manifest one by one. What is the process of this manifestation?

2.3.8 (224)

एतेन मातरिश्वा व्याख्यातः

etena mātariśvā vyākhyātaḥ

etena—by this; mātariśvā—air; vyākhyātaḥ—is explained.

TRANSLATION

By this (conflicting separations) (the emergence of) air is explained.

COMMENTARY

Beginning with this sūtra, the emergence of successive realities will be explained one by one. The existence of possibilities defines a 'space' which is also called ā*k*āśa or ether. This ether is a tree-like structure, which means that locations in this space are like branches of a tree. From every branch, twigs and leaves can grow. The emanation of these twigs and branches is the successive elements such as air, fire, water, and earth which manifest one by one. Notably, all these elements are present in the ether, just as a cow is present in mammal. And yet, the cow is invisible in the meaning of mammal. The manifestation of the cow from the mammal involves the subdivision of the mammal into parts. When the subdivision has occurred, then the mammal is also inside the cow. In the same way, the ether contains all the elements, and when an element manifests from the ether, then it also contains the ether. Therefore, space is the container of everything, and space is inside everything. The first such element is described here—it is called 'air'. The property of air is touch, which leads to the sensations of pressure, heat, roughness, etc. The property of ether is sound, which leads to tone, pitch, form, etc. The successive elements carry the property of the previous element and they also modify these properties by adding new properties. Thus, for instance, everything that can be touched can also be heard. However, everything that can be heard is not necessarily touchable. This simply means that the possibility of a thing exists as a sound, but when it begins to manifest into perceivable things, the first such perception is touch. If you can talk about the possibility, it has already manifest partially—i.e., as a sound. If you can feel the effect of that possibility as heat, roughness, or pressure, then it has manifest as air. The manifestation of vision or sight follows next.

Topic 3

QUESTION

But I can talk about anything, and yet it doesn't become manifest as touch. What explains the fact that the possibilities do not always become real?

2.3.9 (225)
असंभवस्तु सतःअनुपपत्तेः
asaṃbhavastu sataḥ anupapatteḥ

asaṃbhavaḥ—that which has not become possible; tu—but; sataḥ—eternal; anupapatteḥ—as it not attainable.

TRANSLATION

That which is not possible is also eternal, but it is not (always) attainable.

COMMENTARY

All the possibilities are not always manifest due to the nature of time. Time in Vedic philosophy is classified into several *yuga* or ages, and different kinds of phenomena manifest during these ages. This doesn't mean that these possibilities are temporary; they are still considered eternal, but a distinction between unmanifest, about to manifest, and manifest is made to describe how the world transitions from unmanifest to about to manifest and certain things become possible at that time. For instance, the modern world of technology emerged out of the age of Enlightenment in Europe where the human powers of reasoning and observation were used to formulate laws of nature. The age of Enlightenment itself arose out of the Protestant movement, which then arose out of the disenchantment with the corruption of the Catholic Church.

The previous stage creates the conditions for the manifestation of the next stage, and these conditions are called the 'about to manifest' stage. From the about to manifest, emerges the manifest. History is studied as the succession of these manifests, but a closer inspection of history also indicates how the conditions that manifest subsequently were building up and preparing for the advent of the next stage. In many cases, we can see that everything that lies prior does not decide the future, and many such prior trends die or are weakened, and the stronger trend determines the future. The selection of which trend becomes stronger or weaker is the function of time. Time makes some trends stronger even if they were weak, and it weakens other trends even if they were strong. We can attribute these changes in the strength of trends to different actors, but the absence of such actors would not have prevented them; these actors would only have been replaced by other such actors. Thus, history or events is predetermined, but the actors and their participation in different trends is not. The manifestation of the unmanifest entails that the future exists in the past and is produced by the past, whereas the past exists in the present and hides it. There are many possible futures hidden in the present, but one such future would be selected by time, while others will remain hidden. Whatever remains hidden will eventually manifest, although at a different point in time.

The life of the universe is the realization of all the possibilities within the universe, and the size of the universe is all those possibilities. Thus, the size of the universe and the life of the universe are directly related to each other in the sense that in the lifetime of the universe, all possibilities must be manifest. As have noted earlier, the space of all possibilities is uncountable and the manifestation at a moment is countable. The countable emerges from the uncountable, and therefore everything manifest at one moment can be counted—although it is infinite. The succession of these countable states is itself uncountable. The term *asaṃbhavaḥ* or that which has not happened indicates that uncountable. Like the space of real numbers—which are uncountable—it is also eternal, but not always visible. Conversely, *anupatteḥ*—which is the countable—indicates the manifest. The discussion of countable and uncountable occurred earlier. So, why is the same topic of manifest and unmanifest being revisited now?

The answer is that we have now spoken of how the countable and the uncountable are defined mutually such that even if they are contradictory meanings, their successive existence is not contradictory, and their simultaneous existence is not excluded. Since successive existence is not contradictory, therefore, a society that was earlier barbaric can later become civilized. And since their simultaneous existence is not excluded, therefore, a civilized society may exist in conflict with another barbaric society. The meaning of non-exclusion is simply that it is not necessary for a civilized society to exist in a conflict with a barbaric society. And the meaning of non-contradiction is that there is no logical condition that prevents barbarians to become civilized. Thus, the evolution of the same thing and the conflict with another opposite thing are both possibilities—neither are these possibilities precluded, nor are the logically necessary. Generally, in the universalist logic, denying something means confirming its opposite. Both the preclusion and necessity of outcomes is rejected here. This goes to say that logic doesn't contradict choices. Logic is the enabling of choices. Logic also decides consequences of choices, but that is not discussed here. At the present, we are only discussing how logic can never preclude choices.

When civilization can emerge out of a barbaric society, then we must say that the seed of civilization existed within them but was not manifest. This seed of the future exists in everything, and the past exists in everything as a seed. We all have seeds of many kinds of futures; the question is simply: Which seed are we going to water? Logic allows the choice of watering different seeds.

Thus, although terms like countable and uncountable—which are found in modern mathematics too—we previously used, the temptation to say that these things about numbers being talked about in modern mathematics are the same as those in the past, are untenable. Current number theories uphold mutual exclusion, which means that if 2 were true, then -2 must be false. In short, a barbaric society cannot become civilized, because 2 cannot become -2. If you found a single theorem that demonstrated how a sequence of logical steps could convert 2 into -2, then everything in modern mathematics would collapse. To prevent that outcome, mathematicians choose consistency over completeness. They choose the impossibility of some barbarians becoming civilized.

Such transformations are modal in nature. The change begins with desire, which is a mode. The desire for change doesn't contradict the reality. This desire then leads to contact with the opposite—namely, those from whom civilization can be learned. Then after it is learned, then it is put into practice. That practice is the sequence of steps of reasoning. However, now we are dealing with two contradictions—the contradiction between desire and reality, and the contradiction between two realities (e.g., of barbarianism vs. civilization). The first contradiction pushes for a change, and the second one prevents a change. The person or society caught in these contradictions is also conflicted—which contradiction should be preferred? If the first contradiction is preferred, then barbarians become civilized due to logic—they are trying to overcome the first contradiction. Notably, they could have also preferred the second contradiction and remained uncivilized. Therefore, logic enables choices, rather than preclude them.

Here we can see a preliminary insight into how completeness can be obtained—it begins in the acceptance of non-exclusion. This acceptance forms the seed of the Bhedābheda doctrine, which is also called non-difference. Exclusion would have entailed a difference and non-exclusion is non-difference. This sūtra explains how non-difference comes about—the opposing things are not manifest in the same place, time, and person. If we combine this claim with those in the previous sūtras, then we can see how the existence of possibilities is so intimately tied to the problems of modern logic and mathematics.

Topic 4

QUESTION

You said that air manifests from space, and we can feel pressure, heat, roughness, etc. But we cannot still see the things that create such sensations? What is the cause of the world becoming visible as we experience the effects?

2.3.10 (226)

तेजोऽतःतथा ह्याह

tejo'taḥ tathā hyāha

tejaḥ—fire; ataḥ—therefore; tathā—so; hi—verily; āha—emerges.

TRANSLATION

The element fire therefore verily emerges from this (air).

COMMENTARY

Western science has believed that everything that exerts a pressure must be visible, but here it is described that we may not see those things which exert a pressure. This idea is important in modern cosmology where 'dark' energy and 'dark' matter are postulated to explain the pressure. They are 'dark' because they don't emit light, and we cannot see them. And yet, their presence exerts a pressure that can be measured. This dark reality is the element of air, which has not yet manifested into fire. Therefore, it cannot be seen, and yet it can exert pressure. Modern science struggles with a reality that can exert pressure but cannot be seen, so, we can infer that it is limited to the gross element of fire. This element of fire is described in atomic theory as electricity or electrons, and light or photons. When this light is present, then air is present intrinsically, therefore, with electricity we can push things—e.g., drive the machines. But the problem is that light and electricity are not the cause of motion. The motion is caused by air, and not by fire. But since we don't understand air, and air exists in fire, therefore, we assume that electricity must cause the fan to move. Factually, it is not electricity but the air present within that electricity. The electricity is the element of fire, and the cause of motion is the air in the electricity.

Another problem in atomic theory is that heat and light are combined into a single theory of radiation. This is a problem because heat is perceived by the sense of touch, and light is perceived by the sense of seeing. These are separate senses and separate elements, so there cannot be a common theory because sometimes heat may be present although light is absent. Similarly, sometimes, light may be present, but heat may be low. A practical example is that sometimes there is no sun, but the day is very hot because there is also no wind. If heat was caused by the sun, then the absence of the sun should entail a cool day. But that is not always true. We see is that a sunny day can be cool if there is wind. And a dark day can be hot if there is no wind. This is because heat and light are attributed to different elements of air and fire. Heat isn't light, although light can be heat. Modern physics combines these two assuming that since there is heat whenever there is light, therefore, heat must exist due to radiation.

A further problem in cosmology is the notion of Cosmic Background Radiation, which is said to be 40 K. What we measure is heat, but we interpret this to be radiation or light—because atomic theory equates heat with light. As more and more such equivalences are drawn, the confusions become endless.

Atomic theory has many conceptual problems about the nature of reality—namely, that reality is conceptual and not physical, that the meanings of conceptual reality are only defined through distinctions to other concepts, etc. However, all these conceptual problems are today accepted on the premise that the theory *works*. What is that working? Well, electricity can push fans and motor cars. Since it is working, therefore technology is possible, and so we accept the truth of the theory. Then, we face a new problem: this pushing is possible even when you cannot see the thing that is pushing. To explain that, we would have to modify the theory in a very practical sense—the push is not due to the electromagnetic forces postulated in atomic theory. The push is due to air, which cannot be seen, but its presence can be perceived due to pressure.

Hence, the theory is not just flawed in the sense of conceptual problems, but also in a practical sense that the things we see, and which are supposed to be pushing, are not actually pushing. The cause of that push is something that we haven't yet understood in atomic theory because it cannot be seen.

When most people come across the theory of five elements, they often roll their eyes. They think that modern science has changed the understanding of matter and all these ideas are false. On the contrary, science hasn't shown anything wrong with Vedic philosophy, but Vedic philosophy can show many things wrong in modern science. These mistakes are both conceptual and empirical, and hence these ideas remain important for scientific development.

Topic 5

QUESTION

What is the next manifestation after the manifestation of vision?

2.3.11 (227)

आपः

āpaḥ

āpaḥ—water.

TRANSLATION

(The next element emerging from fire is called) water.

COMMENTARY

The element of water brings the property of taste or flavor. Everything that can be tasted, can also be seen, can also be touched, and can also be spoken of. Thus, when water exists, the previous elements of fire, air, and ether also exist. The ordinary water that we drink is a combination of water, fire, air, and ether. For example, when we boil water, it becomes hot. However, this heat is not due to the water; it is due to the presence of air. Similarly, the fact that we can see water isn't because of water; it is due to the presence of fire. The element water should not be confused with ordinary water; the element is responsible only for taste, although ordinary water also can be seen, touched, and talked about.

Present day computers carry information through electricity and light. The computer works through electricity, but the information coming into the computer can be due to light. However, we cannot carry taste and smell through electricity or light. Therefore, if you are having a videoconference on a computer, then you can see others and hear them. With virtual reality techniques, you can also feel the push and pull. But you cannot get the taste and smell. According to modern atomic theory, taste and smell are due to the molecular structure, and this structure is caused due to the electromagnetic forces. If taste and smell were due to the molecular structure, then it should be possible to encode the information about this structure into light, transfer the light, and then convert the molecular structure back into smell and taste at the receiver. But this can never be achieved because the elements of water and earth—which carry taste and smell—are not just the element of fire. Water and earth emerge out of fire, however, in the fire element, water and earth are not manifest.

The problem with atomic theory is that it observes things that have taste and smell. But this observation is limited to the study of the molecular structure. Since everything that has taste and smell also has form, color, and structure, therefore, scientists infer that the taste and the smell must be due to the atomic structure. This is a false conclusion. Taste and smell are not perceivable in fire. Hence, we cannot conclude that molecular structure causes taste and smell. The practical result of this problem is that computers that run on electricity and light cannot transfer the taste and the smell, although we can see, touch, and hear.

We can conclude that present atomic theory is limited to the fire element. The more subtle elements such as Ether and Air are not understood because they cannot be seen. And the more gross elements of Earth and Water are not understood because fire doesn't manifest taste and smell. Modern Western science is highly visual—all its explanations are based on what we can *see*. But what we can see is not all that we can perceive. So, science attempts to reduce all perception to the models obtained by seeing. Thus, space is described as a box because that is what we see. The push and pull of air are attributed to the properties of fire—e.g., the 'charge' of particles—when it is due to air. The taste and the smell are not even explained. Thus, by reducing the properties of the five elements to the properties of one element—namely, fire—a hugely problematic theory is produced. And people enamored by modern science think that this explanation of matter is far superior to the theory of five elements.

It is commonly observed that even those who accept the authority of Vedic knowledge, are unable to understand these five elements. For example, they continue to think that space is a box. That the planets must be moving due to gravitational force. That light actually 'travels' in space, or that this movement is the cause of heat. They have carried forward numerous caricatures of reality in modern science and they try to interpret the Vedic descriptions according to these presuppositions. A little careful thought would show that these two systems cannot be reconciled. And it is because modern science is totally false. Science is a long way away from studying the five elements instead of one. Then it is even farther away from combining these five elements into a single theory rather than many disparate theories. This combination is possible only when we say that reality is symbolic. But acknowledging that symbolism entails throwing away conventional logic and mathematics. We have seen the problems of logic above, but as a result, all subsequent ideas like the nature of numbers and the notion of space and time in geometry must be changed.

Topic 6

QUESTION

What follows the manifestation of water (and its associated taste)?

2.3.12 (228)

पृथवि अधिकाररूपशब्दान्तरेभ्यः

pṛthivī adhikārarūpaśabdāntarebhyaḥ

pṛthivī—earth; adhikāra—position, office, section; rūpa—form, color, etc.; śabdāntarebhyaḥ—within the sound.

TRANSLATION

(The next element emerging from water is called) earth; it (was previously) situated (as a part) within sound, form, color, etc.

COMMENTARY

A fundamental aspect of the Vedic doctrine of causality is that everything that manifests as experience was previously present within the cause. Thus, even though air, fire, water, and earth manifest successively from ether, these are not 'creations' out of nothing; they were previously unmanifest or hidden inside the cause. In this sūtra, this claim is made explicitly by stating that earth was situated inside sound, form, color, etc. The property of earth is smell, and while everything that can be spoken of, or touched, or seen, or tasted, need not have smell, the smell is intrinsically hidden inside those things. The smell cannot be perceived, but we cannot say that it doesn't have the smell. Thus, when a person talks in a crude language, we say that his speech is "bitter". Even when you don't smell, you can say that "this person stinks". And without tasting, you can say that a person is "sweet". There is no sense perception corresponding to these claims, but the mind doesn't depend on the sense perceptions. The mind decodes these unmanifest realities even when the senses cannot. Therefore, the mind is the sense that is superior to all the five senses, because it can perform the job of all the five senses—although in understanding, not in sensation.

Likewise, it is seen that when you smell tasty food, then your mouth starts watering, and there is naturally a taste on the tongue. From this taste, there is naturally fire produced in the gastric system, and the body naturally warms up. Therefore, if someone was feeling cold, the mere smell of tasty food can make them feel warm. Likewise, someone's speech can make you feel cold, just as some speech can make you feel warm. How the subtle manifests into gross, and the gross carries the subtle is a very sophisticated science. But this science is available to all of us through ordinary perceptions and experiences. If we can analyze these experiences, we may be able to accept Vedic descriptions.

Much of the damage in the public perception of these theories was caused by the Greeks in the West and the Chinese in the East. The Greeks discarded the Ether, and only accepted Earth, Water, Fire, and Air as four elements. There was no understanding of how the grosser elements exist inside the subtler elements, and the subtler elements exist inside the grosser elements. There was no understanding of how these elements are related to the five sensations. And, there was no understanding of how the mind perceives all five of them. Thus, a caricature of this theory was presented, debated, and eventually rejected. The Chinese had some understanding of how one element can be created from another. But to fit the theory in their understanding, they modified the elements. Ether and Air—the two subtle elements which are hard to understand—were replaced by Wood and Metal, keeping only Fire, Water, and Earth. If we try to explain the Vedic descriptions, many people may start recalling the older Greek and Chinese ideas, which would be worse than modern science.

Topic 7

QUESTION

How does one element exist inside the other even as it is unmanifest?

2.3.13 (229)

तदभिध्यानादेव तु तल्लिङ्गात् सः

tadabhidhyānādeva tu tallingāt saḥ

tadat-abhidhyānāt—because of the purpose being reflected internally; eva—certainly; tu—but; tallingāt—from His senses; saḥ—He.

TRANSLATION

Because the purpose reflected internally (in the elements) is but certainly Him caused by His senses (from which the material elements emanate).

COMMENTARY

In the previous sūtra it was stated that the elements are inside the other elements. This sūtra states that this embedded nature of the elements is because the Lord is embedded inside the elements as their purpose, as this purpose has emanated from His senses. The elements are Prakriti and they exist as pure possibility. The Puruṣa is the will and activates this possibility to become reality. The body of the Puruṣa is the many types of desires, and His senses are the desires for sense enjoyment. Therefore, the purpose underlying the creation is the fulfillment of the Lord's desire. This Puruṣa or the will is the efficient cause of the creation while the Prakriti or the possibilities are the material cause; the created elements combine the possibility with the will to produce a reality.

If the will has manifested from the Lord's sense of hearing, then the manifested element is ether. If the will has manifested from the Lord's sense of touch, then the manifested element is air. Similarly, the wills manifested from the Lord's sense of sight, taste, and smell manifest the elements of fire, water, and earth. But each of the Lord's senses is capable of every other function. Thus, His sense of taste can produce the desire of sight; His sense of touch can have the desire for smell; and His sense of hearing can have the desire for seeing. The reason for this is that all desire arises in the mind, and depending on the type of desire, it is simply manifest through the senses. Thus, if a person can control their mind, then they can also control their senses. The desire in primordial form becomes the desiring for hearing, then it advances into touching, then it develops into seeing, then it progresses into tasting, and finally into smelling. Similarly, the elements also manifest from the subtle element due to the development of desire. But the possibility of everything exists in the ether; to see a specific property, the desire for that possibility must convert it into reality.

The desire created in the mind can transform into desire of any of the senses, and accordingly the element that fulfills that desire can also become the element corresponding to any of those senses. The progressive manifestation of the elements is simply the development of desire that converts one element into another. This is the seed of a material science in which anything can be created simply from space by the application of desire. We might think that space is empty, but it is the possibility of becoming anything we desire. Our desires are fulfilled due to the presence of karma, but one who understands this science can create anything out of space; it will seem magical to others, but it is not magical; this is also a science in which possibility develops due to desire.

Topic 8

QUESTION

If the Lord can create through desire, can He also destroy by desire?

2.3.14 (230)

वपिर्ययेण तु क्रमोऽतःउपपद्यते च

viparyayeṇa tu kramo'taḥ upapadyate ca

viparyayeṇa—in the reverse order; tu—indeed; kramaḥ—order; ataḥ—from that; upapadyate—in the order of creation; ca—and.

TRANSLATION

And (the destruction) occurs indeed in the reverse order from that in the creation (i.e., the elements dissolving back into previous elements).

COMMENTARY

An element exists in a certain form only if there is a purpose or desire to sustain it. If the desire is withdrawn, then it collapses back into the previous possibility. Thus, by withdrawing the desire for enjoyment, the Puruṣa also withdraws the Prakriti from the manifest into the unmanifest form. Thus, earth dissolves back into water, the water into fire, the fire into air, and everything goes back into ether. The ether itself goes back into the mind, the mind collapses into the capacity for judgment, which has three parts—the judgment of truth in the intellect, the judgment of good in the ego, and the judgment of right in the moral sense or mahattattva. These judgments then collapse back into the axioms or assumptions about truth, right, and good, which are called Prakriti.

Each person has a unique Prakriti, which means that they carry varied notions of truth, right, and good. In modern society, for example, the perceptions of the five senses are considered true; we may have different ideas and beliefs in the mind, but these are not considered true. Therefore, if you speak about something that people cannot perceive by the five senses, then they will say: "maybe that is your opinion, but it cannot be true". In modern science, even these opinions are considered unreal, because there are only molecules. Likewise, people think that goodness is only the enjoyment of the five senses. If you are giving people food, clothing, and shelter, then it is good. But if you are teaching people about the nature of the soul, then it is a delusion. Right and wrong are also based on the five senses, and it is believed that these only exist as social customs. Thus, each government is free to create laws of right and wrong, ignoring dharma and karma. Thus, eating cows is legal in some societies, but eating dogs is not. In other societies, eating anything is legal.

Ultimately, these ideas about truth, right, and good emerge from the Pradhāna which is the unmanifest reality. The meaning of unmanifest is that truth, right, and good are not separated. Therefore, truth is right, and right is good. In the manifest world, truth, right, and good are separated. Thus, truth is not required to lead to right action, and right action is not required to lead to happiness. Thus, a scientist can be immoral or unhappy, and his morality and happiness are not a criterion to decide if he knows the truth. This separation of truth, right, and good is called Prakriti, and it creates problematic ideas about how truth, right, and good must be judged—i.e., that these can be independent.

Modern society has been adopting such systems with vigor. At the dawn of the modern age, two such separations were carried out— (1) the separation of church and state, and (2) the separation of body and mind. The former separation says that right and good are separate things; the state will decide what is right, and the church can decide what is good. The latter separation says that scientists will decide what is true, but each person can decide what is good for them. This is a classic example of extreme separation of Prakriti. Formerly, there were separations, but modern society has taken them to extremes. Thus, as time elapses, sometimes Prakriti is more separated, and at other times it is less separated. The universe originates in the unseparated state of Pradhāna.

During creation, Pradhāna creates Prakriti, which creates mahattattva, ego, and intellect, which produce the mind, which manifests the senses, which produce the sensations, which create the five gross elements. Within these five elements, Earth comes from Water, Water from Fire, Fire from Air, and Air from Ether. During annihilation, they collapse back in the reverse order. Finally, everything rests in the unmanifest Pradhāna, which is the unseparated state.

Topic 9

QUESTION

In the material creation, we also spoke about the manifestation of the four aspects of the internal organs—namely, mind, intellect, ego, and mahattattva. Aren't these elements also being differentiated from the Lord's senses?

2.3.15 (231)

अन्तरा विज्ञानमनसी क्रमेण तल्लिङ्गादिति चेत् न अविशेषात्

antarā vijñānamanasī krameṇa talliṅgāditi cet na aviśeṣāt

antarā—the internal organs; vijñānamanasī—intellect and the mind; krameṇa—in the order; talliṅgāt—owing to separate senses for that; iti cet—if it be said; na—not so; aviśeṣāt—on account of non-difference.

TRANSLATION

If it is said that the internal organs such as the mind and intellect should manifest in order due to having separate sense organs for that, (then we say) no, (because) there is no difference (between these senses in the Lord).

COMMENTARY

The *antaha-karan* or the internal instrument is divided into four parts in the living entities according to both Sāñkhya and Yoga systems. These four parts are called manas or mind, buddhi or intellect, ahamkara or ego, and mahattattva or morality. The mind generates meanings, the intellect judges if these meanings are true, the ego judges if these meanings are good, and the morality judges if these meanings are right. Since the meanings generated by our mind can be false, bad, and wrong, therefore, there is a difference between these four senses. But if the mind is purified, then everything it thinks is always true, good, and right, and this separation of thinking from judgment becomes unnecessary. The Lord's mind is also purified in the sense that it is not subject to the judgments of truth, right, and good. Rather, whatever appears in His mind is the very definition of truth, right, and good. Thus, His thoughts are always true; His desires are always good; and His actions are always right. Therefore, the *antaha-karan* of ordinary living entities is divided into four parts, due to the separation of meaning, and its truth, rightness, and goodness. But as a person becomes spiritually advanced, these differences are dissolved. Ultimately, there is only the mind, and there is no need to judge if it also true, right, and good. The Lord is said to have such a pure mind; His *antaha-karan* is only one.

Therefore, the primordial reality should be understood as true meaning, the desire for this meaning, and the action of creating true meaning. This meaning has six forms, as we have discussed earlier—knowledge, beauty, power, wealth, fame, and renunciation. But, among these six categories, knowledge is the most fundamental, and other categories spring from knowledge. Thus, the Absolute Truth is sometimes also called *jnanam-advayam* or non-dual knowledge (our knowledge is imbued with dual opposites). Ultimately, the 'mind' of the Lord is inseparable from His intellect, ego, and morality, because the meanings, desires, and actions are always true, good, and right. This distinction is made in the material elements for the souls whose minds are contaminated by selfish desires, producing illusory thoughts, and engaging and unsuitable actions. The separation is a facility for the living entity to perform judgments about what they think, desire, and do, and these instruments of judgment are therefore pathways to understanding the Lord as truth, right, and good.

Topic 10

QUESTION

If the Lord manifests the world as truth, right, and good, then how does it become false, wrong, and bad? How can something good turn into evil? How can something true turn into falsity? How can right turn into wrong?

2.3.16 (232)

चराचरव्यपाश्रयस्तु स्यात् तदव्यपदेशो भाक्तःतद्भावभावित्वात्

carācaravyapāśrayastu syāt tadvyapadeśo bhāktaḥ tadbhāvabhāvitvāt

carācara—the moving and stationary; vyapāśrayaḥ—the shelter of the all-pervading; tu—but; syāt—may be; tadvyapadeśaḥ—pervading in all of that; bhāktaḥ—the enjoyer; tadbhāva-bhāvitvāt—it becomes due to the absence.

TRANSLATION

The Lord may be (the creator of) the moving and stationary, the shelter for the all-pervading (Brahman), present pervasively (as Paramātma), and their enjoyer (as Bhagavān), but (the world) manifests due to His absence.

COMMENTARY

We indulge in inappropriate actions due to selfish desires. Our conceptions of truth are impersonalized to detach truth from the Supreme Person. Our notions of right and wrong are socially constructed to avoid the idea that our actions are being judged by the Lord. Therefore, although the Lord creates the world through His mind, we think it is disconnected from the Lord. We forget that He is the shelter of Brahman as the light emanates from a source. We forget that He is the original meaning that incarnates inside every created thing. We forget that He has created the world for His enjoyment, and we consider that it exists for our pleasure. When our desires turn away from the Lord, the purpose underlying the creation is not seen. We then invent ourselves as the purpose of our existence, and we lie, cheat, deceive, and disown our duties because we don't see that the truth, right, and good are defined in relation to the Lord.

The truth, right, and good are three distinct realities but they have been mentioned as inseparable in the previous sūtra. This simply means that when the Lord creates the world, then everything that exists is true (falsities don't exist), every action is pure (wrongs don't exist), and all desires are based on love (selfishness doesn't exist). However, the living entity separates the inseparable reality and creates his conception of truth, right, and good, in relation to himself, rather than in relation to the Lord. The separation of truth, right, and good is the rejection that only the presence of the Lord unifies them; anything that is devoid of the understanding of the Lord may be partially true, partially right, or partially good; but it cannot be completely true, right, and good.

The separation of truth, right, and good is caused by māyā which stands for the rejection of the Lord's existence. When our vision is covered by this illusion, then we don't see how truth, right, and good cannot exist separately. A classic example of this separation in modern times is the differences between physical, social, and mind sciences. The physical sciences study the nature of truth, but they have no idea that this truth must be tied to morality. The social sciences speak of social roles and responsibilities, but they have no knowledge of how there are laws of choice and responsibility. Finally, the mind sciences aspire to create happiness, but they have no idea of how happiness is produced. Thus, because of māyā we tend to separate truth, right, and good, and everyone pursues their conception independently, while everyone rejects the Lord.

The cause of the separation of truth, right, and good is the absence of the Lord. He is not truly absent. But the soul thinks that He doesn't exist. The soul's Prakriti is a byproduct of the extent to which the soul thinks that the Lord is absent. Thus, some people will accept kindness, justice, equality as inviolable principles, but they may not accept their origin in God. Others may reject all these ideas and claim that might is right. In short, if you have the power, then you create your own definitions of what is right and wrong. As atheism grows, there are as many definitions of truth, right, and good as there are people. And since nobody can agree with anyone else, the atheists fight with each other.

This fighting, competition, enviousness, and hurting the others is the primary form of evil in this world. It is not created by the Lord. It is rather created by the soul under the delusion that the Lord—the principle of unity—doesn't exist. Thus, the Lord can't be accused of creating lies, wrongs, and suffering. These are rather created by the soul when he rejects the Lord's existence.

Topic 11

QUESTION

But you have earlier said the soul is not the creator of anything, that all creation is carried out by the Lord and His Śakti. So, how can we now attribute the creation of lies, evil, and wrongs to the soul? Even if we say that the evil is created by the separation, then the separation is not caused by the soul.

2.3.17 (233)

नात्मा आश्रुतेर्नित्यत्वाच्च ताभ्यः

nātmā āśruternityatvācca tābhyaḥ

na—not; ātmā—soul; āśruteḥ—not being (so) mentioned by scriptures; nityatvāt—from being eternal; ca—also; tābhyaḥ—practiced by them (souls).

TRANSLATION

The soul is not (the creator of evil) as it is not mentioned by scriptures; from (such things) being eternal also; the soul is accustomed to them (the evil).

COMMENTARY

If you cook food for someone, then you can say that they are the cause of the cooking, even though they are not the cooks. In the same way, the world is created by the Lord and His Śakti, but it remains about to manifest. The soul is the cause of the manifestation. Therefore, the soul is the cause of evil, and he is not the cause of evil. In the previous sūtra, it was said that the division of nature occurs due to the Lord's absence, but He is not factually absent. His absence is only in the soul's imagination. But we have also said earlier that the material world is created due to the Lord's self-abnegation. We can now draw a distinction between these two kinds of creations. The creation by the Lord is the unmanifest becoming about to manifest, but it is manifest by the soul. The conversion from about to manifest to manifest is due to karma and guna, which are controlled by the Lord. But these occur because the soul desires and has karma to be reaped as the consequences of actions due to his past desires. Therefore, ultimately, the Lord is the cook, but He cooks based on the souls' desires.

We have spoken about the separation of truth, right, and good, but this is not the only kind of separation. The separation occurs many times over. For example, truthfulness, kindness, cleanliness, and sacrifice are generally understood to be moral principles in every society. But they are reconciled only in the Lord. When the Lord is absent, then these principles are also separated.

The result of this separation is that we often see contradictions between these principles. For example, we can show kindness to others and sacrifice for them, but we may also demand kindness and sacrifice from them. We can say that criminals do not deserve kindness, because they treat others unkindly. Or, we can say that to correct the mistakes of criminals, they must be shown kindness. Thus, if we punish the criminals, then we are demonstrating the principle of truthfulness, but we are not showing kindness. Conversely, if we don't punish them, then we are showing kindness, but not demonstrating truthfulness. By the virtue of truth, a criminal must be punished, and by the virtue of kindness, he must not be punished. Which of these virtues must be upheld?

Thus, morality is simply virtues, which can be dominant or subordinate. One could argue that for a petty criminal, we can show more kindness than truthfulness because he has just begun his crimes, and he can be corrected. But the reverse argument can also be made—if we don't teach this guy a lesson right now, then he will grow into a more hardened criminal. Finally, one could say that such severe punishments are the main cause of hardening a criminal.

Thus, we can go on arguing endlessly because we don't know the nature of the person. Thus, the basic principle of morality in Vedic philosophy is tit-for-tat. No criminal goes unpunished, regardless of the severity of their actions. If they are further hardened by their crimes, then nature punishes them even more. However, compassion is also shown by educating the person in right and wrong.

The Lord sets the example of how truthfulness and kindness are resolved. He punishes the demons, but He also imparts the principles of dharma. Thus, compassion is applied to education, and truthfulness to the consequences of one's action. But when these principles are detached from the Lord, then how the Lord employs them is forgotten. We then think that these principles are universal, and that universality then produces conflicts and contradictions. The conclusion is that no doctrine based on principles or ideas works. It is only the person who embodies all these qualities that knows how to apply them. Therefore, to apply morality, we must study the Lord's actions via His pastimes.

Topic 12

QUESTION

If the soul is creating the separation between truth, right, and good, then how can the soul know what is simultaneously truth, right, and good?

2.3.18 (234)

ज्ञोऽत एव

jño'ta eva

jñaḥ—knowledge, or intelligence; ata eva—for this very reason.

TRANSLATION

Knowledge or intelligence is to be used for this very reason (i.e., understanding what is simultaneously true, right, and good).

COMMENTARY

In this sūtra, the symptoms of a truly intelligent and knowledgeable person are described. The symptom is that he is simultaneously able to judge what is truth, right, and good. We have previously said that the intellect judges the truth, the ego judges the good, and the moral sense judges the morality. These are collectively being called 'intelligence' here, which basically indicates the power of judgment. Every judgment must be performed *relative* to some assumptions. For instance, if you believe that the sky is blue, then anyone who makes the statement 'the sky is green' would be deemed false. Similarly, if you consider truthfulness as a moral virtue, any liar, no matter what his intentions are (good or bad) would be considered immoral. If you consider intoxication a form of suffering, then any intoxicated person would be considered unhappy.

In short, every judgment requires us to have preformed ideas, beliefs, or axioms. Therefore, intelligence, judgment, and knowledge are tightly interrelated ideas. Based on your beliefs—or what you accept to be true—you judge the truth, rightness, or goodness of other things. The act of drawing comparisons between your beliefs and the facts you are judging is intelligence. But intelligence is simply an instrument of determining truth, good, or right; it can produce results only if there are preformed beliefs. Within this context, we can see that to judge something that is true, right, and good, we must understand the Lord who is simultaneously true, right, and good. If we don't have such a belief about something that is true, right, and good, then we will have several fragmented and potentially incorrect judgments of truth, right and good. Thus, knowledge or intelligence simply entails an understanding of the Lord.

Topic 13

QUESTION

But what happens if we are unable to understand what is simultaneously true, right, and good, and we keep considering or viewing them separately?

2.3.19 (235)

उत्क्रान्तिगत्यागतीनाम्

utkrāntigatyāgatīnām

utkrānti-gati-āgatīnām—dying, going, and coming.

TRANSLATION

(The cycle of) dying, going (to another place), and coming (being born).

COMMENTARY

In every life we seek the nature of truth, right, and good, although the understanding of truth and right is most prominent in the human form of life. In the human life, we can also understand that there are several grades of happiness—e.g., from the sense pleasures, to mental and intellectual happiness, to the quest for eternal happiness, finally leading to the understanding of the self and the Lord. The pinnacle of this understanding is that there is something that is simultaneously true, right, and good, which reconciles all the contradictions. If we don't arrive at this understanding, our journey of discovery must continue. This journey is called repeated death, transport to another place, and rebirth into another body. Thus, the discovery of truth, right, and good isn't necessarily a single life endeavor. It is, in fact, the cause of birth and death, because if we have developed some misconceptions, then they can be corrected only by contrary experiences, and such experiences may require other types of bodies, environments, interactions, etc. The understanding of the Absolute Truth is the only purpose of repeated birth and death, and thus the Vedānta Sūtra began with the assertion that now, therefore, we must inquire into Brahman.

QUESTION

You said above that knowledge and intelligence can be used to understand what is true, right, and good simultaneously. Does that mean that the Absolute Truth can also be understood through theoretical knowledge and reasoning?

2.3.20 (236)

स्वात्मना चोत्तरयोः

svātmanā cottarayoḥ

svātmanā—one's own self; ca—and; uttarayoḥ—rise, deliver, north;

TRANSLATION

(The knowledge must) also arise or spring of its own accord.

COMMENTARY

The knowledge we acquire theoretically or philosophically rests in our memory, which can be recalled or even sometimes forgotten. This knowledge is accessible to the soul, but it is different from the soul. The content of the knowledge may be spiritual, but it is not considered realized knowledge. Until this realization is attained, mistakes are repeated, and these mistakes are then corrected by the faculty of judgment to obtain the truth, right, and good.

Thus, without the realization, the mind, the intellect, the ego, and the moral sense are distinct. The mind produces meanings, but they may not be true, right, or good. The intellect, ego, and moral sense then correct these meanings. However, when perfect realization is attained, then there is no need for the instruments of judgment, separate from the instrument of thinking. Rather, whatever is thought is always true, right, and good. Now, we must understand that the mind automatically gives rise to thoughts; these are said to arise in the mind like waves in an ocean. With our intellect, ego, and moral sense, we suppress these waves. But when the mind is perfectly purified, then there is no need to suppress anything, nor is there any necessity to produce only the true, right, and good thoughts mediated by the instruments of judgment. Therefore, the purification of the mind means that only the Absolute Truth appears in the mind, and this truth, right, and good doesn't need to be curtailed. This merger of the instruments of judgment into the mind, and the unceasing production of the thoughts in the mind is referred to here by the term *svātmanā* here.

QUESTION

Some people argue that because the knowledge of the infinite can exist in the soul, therefore, the soul too must be infinite. On the other hand, if the soul is itself finite, then how can he know the nature of the infinite? So, the realization of the Absolute Truth must entail the infinity of the soul's existence.

2.3.21 (237)

नाणुरतच्छ्रुतेर् इति चेत् न इतराधिकारात्

nāṇuratacchruter iti cet na itarādhikārāt

na aṇuḥ—not atomic; atat-śruteḥ—as the scriptures state; iti cet—if it be said; na—not so; itarā-dhikārāt—due to the other being its position.

TRANSLATION

If it is said that the soul is not atomic because the scriptures state (that he can attain the knowledge of the Absolute Truth which is also infinite), we say no; due to the other (being small rather than infinite) being its (real) position.

COMMENTARY

The impersonalist makes a mundane argument about the soul's size. Since the soul is small, and the Absolute Truth is big, therefore, the big cannot fit into the small. If, on the other hand, the big fits into the small, then the small must be as big. The impersonalist doesn't realize that knowledge is like a tree. The soul is the root of his knowledge tree, and this root can be atomic, but the tree doesn't have to be atomic. Therefore, the atomic soul can acquire the knowledge of the infinite because the tree is infinite, but the root is atomic. As a result, the argument about the infinite not 'fitting into' the atomic is unacceptable.

The real reason that the soul doesn't know the full truth is because this knowledge is acquired only in proportion to our service to the Lord. As the demand for service grows, the knowledge also grows. The impersonalist has no demand for serving the Lord. He only has a demand to become the Lord. But the Absolute Truth is never known in this way. He is known on a need-to-know basis. Why do you need to know? Well, you may want to serve the Absolute Truth, and some information is required. Our knowing is not based on *wanting* to know—e.g., I want to know everything! Curiosity isn't a sufficient reason for the Absolute Truth to be known. He is only known by the *need* to know.

Just like the chauffeur of a rich man doesn't need to know everything about the man he drives around. He just needs to know the schedule at which he must bring the car around. The chauffeur cannot ask his boss—tell me everything about yourself before I will drive you around. Unless I know everything about you, how can I drive the car for you? Just as silly as this sounds, it is equally silly to demand knowing the Absolute Truth before we start serving that truth. The conclusion is that one must not try to know the Absolute Truth. We must rather try to serve the Lord, and whatever is needed to serve the Lord will be automatically provided by the Lord based on our needs to serve Him.

However, those who aren't devoted to the Lord need the knowledge to develop the devotion. For example, a chauffeur will normally demand a salary from his boss, unless the boss was the president of a country. If the boss is the president of the country, then the chauffeur would feel privileged to drive the car, rather than asking the boss for a salary. In the same way, knowledge of the Absolute Truth invokes devotion. That knowledge however doesn't mean that the chauffeur knows the president intimately. He may however know the president intimately if he performs the service well. Thus, philosophy is needed to invoke devotion, and then devotion is needed to get intimate knowledge.

Many people confuse these two forms of knowledge. They argue: if the Lord is obtained by devotion, then why cultivate knowledge? The short answer is that real devotion doesn't spring without true knowledge. The devotees without the philosophical knowledge are like chauffeurs driving around ordinary people. The chauffeur may chat with the passengers, and this friendship is confused with devotion. But if the passenger refuses to pay, then the friendship disappears. In the same way, without philosophy, devotion is temporary. The so-called devotee loses all faith in the Lord the moment he encounters problems. But if philosophical knowledge is acquired, then the chauffeur knows that he is driving the president of the country, and even his own life is less important than the life of the president. The chauffeur will keep silent unless he is spoken to. So, there are no overt signs of devotion. But that is real devotion.

QUESTION

Are you saying that there is a difference between knowing the infinite and being infinite? That the soul can know the infinite, but that doesn't make him infinite? If so, what is the difference between knowing and being infinite?

2.3.22 (238)

स्वशब्दोन्मानाभ्यां च

svaśabdonmānābhyāṃ ca

svaśabda—His own words; unmānābhyām—from measurable; ca—and.

TRANSLATION

From being measurable by His words also.

COMMENTARY

When we look at a tree, there is a picture of the tree in our minds. To hold this picture, we don't have to be equal to or larger than the tree. Also, when we know the tree, we don't become the tree. This is because we have a representation of the tree, not the tree itself. Similarly, when we know the Lord, we have a representation of the Lord, which is in one sense the Lord and in another sense not the Lord. The tree projects itself into our minds, and the Lord—when known—projects Himself into our consciousness. Having this projection of representation of the Lord within us doesn't make us equal to or larger than the Lord, because there is a difference between the object and the symbol representing it. By the existence of symbolism, the Lord can have a name, which is a sound representation of the Lord. However, if we don't call the Lord's name, the Lord doesn't cease to exist. So, by symbolism, knowing is not being that thing; even if we know the Lord, we don't become God. Likewise, even though we are finite, we can still know the infinite by a symbol representation.

QUESTION

The impersonalist says that the problem of the finite knowing the infinite would not arise if the consciousness was present everywhere because then its omnipresence would lead to omniscience and dissolve the contradiction between being in one place and knowing many things simultaneously.

2.3.23 (239)

अवरोधश्चन्दनवत्

avirodhaścandanavat

avirodhaḥ—no contradiction; candanavat—like sandalwood.

TRANSLATION

There is no contradiction (between being situated in one place and knowing many things simultaneously) just like sandalwood (can be in one place and its smell can spread far and wide away from the sandalwood itself).

COMMENTARY

The distinction between being and knowing is again being asserted here. In the previous sūtra, it was said that these are different because the infinite can be known by the finite and yet this knowing doesn't entail that the knower has also become infinite. In this sūtra it is said that knowing many things is not contradictory to being in one place. If you are seeing an apple, then you are still in the same place, but your consciousness has spread to the apple. This spreading is not contradictory to being in one place because the soul exists in three modes. The soul's desire is still in the same place, but his consciousness has spread. Therefore, the soul is in one place, and yet he is in many places.

Here, the sūtra gives the example of the use of perfumes. You wear a drop of perfume, and everyone around you smells the perfume. Sandalwood has been used as a perfume for ages, and a little amount of sandalwood produces a faint aroma over a very large area. So, by analogy, the notion of being in one place, and spreading to many places—by its effect—is stated in this sūtra.

This problem in well-known in modern science as wave-particle duality. The particle is one place, but its effect—the field or the wave—the particle spreads everywhere. In classical physics, each field extends infinitely into space, but quantum fields are not like that; they spread by the emission of a particle, which is supposed to 'travel' to the destination, while a reverse particle (represented by the complex conjugate of the wave) travels in the opposite direction. This problem is called 'entanglement' because both forward and backward waves are moving simultaneously (one from source to destination, and the other from destination to the source). Even though a particle travels between two objects—which makes the interaction local—the concurrent propagation of forward and backward particles makes this interaction non-local.

When this model is applied to perception, we can say that our consciousness is 'reaching out' into the apple, and the apple is 'entering into' our consciousness. And yet, even as the apple and the self are interacting, they are not becoming unified (even with the non-locality of bidirectionality). This is because what we call consciousness or awareness is only one aspect of the soul. It is what we can call the 'relation' to the world, which defines the world in relation to us, and us in relation to the world. The focus of our awareness—i.e., which object it is directed toward—is under control of our will. For instance, in the yoga practice, we can withdraw the consciousness from the worldly objects, and then neither our consciousness enters the world, nor the world enters our consciousness. Even as consciousness spreads everywhere, the will that causes this spreading is situated in one place, which we can call the soul. Specifically, the non-local aspect of consciousness is called *sat*, the local aspect is called ānanda, and result of the local and non-local is cognition and action or *chit*. In short, we develop a will, which causes the consciousness to interact with something else, and the interaction then produces cognition and conation.

So, the claim that because my consciousness can spread to many places in order to know the external world and therefore the self is non-localized can be rejected by the simple analogy that the sandalwood tree is in one place but its effect of smell—like the spreading of consciousness—is everywhere. Thus, we reject the superficial contradiction between locality and non-locality; both locality and non-locality are real, the locality causes the non-locality because if this wasn't the case, then our consciousness would permanently be spread to everything in the world, and it could not be withdrawn by the use of choice.

QUESTION

The problem of consciousness spreading applies not just to the spreading into the external world, but also the spreading within the body. We are aware of the different parts of our body—such as hands and legs—so someone can argue that since consciousness spreads in the body, so it cannot be in one place. By extension, one could say that consciousness must also be non-local.

2.3.24 (240)

अवस्थितिवैशेष्यादिति चेत् न अभ्युपगमाद्धृदि हि

avasthitivaiśeṣyāditi cet na abhyupagamāddhṛdi hi

avasthiti—situated; vaiśeṣayat—in individuals; iti cet—if it be said; na—not; abhyupagamāt—from being engaged; hṛdi—in the heart; hi—certainly.

TRANSLATION

If it is said that (the soul is situated) in the individuals (i.e., all over the body due to awareness) (we say) no, from being engaged in the heart certainly (we can say that it is then spread all over the body).

COMMENTARY

Like the claim of the soul spreading all over the universe due to awareness was rejected in the previous sūtra, in this sūtra, the claim that the soul spreads all over the body due to awareness of the body is rejected in this sūtra. The soul is situated in the heart, as the root of the tree which is the body. Thus, a person can be brain dead, but not heart dead. If the heart has stopped working, then the person is considered dead. Similarly, spiritual bliss is experienced in the heart, but its effects—such as hair standing on end, the wavering of the voice, trembling of the body, etc.—are spread to the rest of the body. The bliss in the heart can be continuous, but the symptoms may sometimes not be manifest.

Thus, we distinguish happiness from pleasure. The body feels pleasure, but the heart feels happiness. If someone touches your hand, you can feel comforted or relaxed in the skin, but not happiness. The happiness arises in the heart, even for ordinary sensations. This is especially true for spiritual bliss, which is experienced in the center of the chest, not all over the body. The symptoms of this bliss can spread to all over the body—such as hairs standing on end or the body quivering, or tears coming out of eyes—but these are the symptoms of the bliss in the heart, not the bliss itself. The symptoms are cognitive and can be seen by others, but the bliss is personal and only experienced by the individual. The awareness is therefore non-local; however, the source of awareness is local.

QUESTION

If you are saying that the soul is situated in the heart, then what causes the movement of consciousness all over the body and all over the world?

2.3.25 (241)

गुणाद्वा लोकवत्

guṇādvā lokavat

guṇāt—owing to the guna; vā—movement; lokavat—as in the world.

TRANSLATION

(The) movement (of consciousness) all over the world is due to guna.

COMMENTARY

When we perceive the world, our consciousness moves out into the world, and the world moves into our consciousness, thus resulting in a bidirectional field propagation. The cause of this movement in our heart is desires, which are produced due to *guna* or material tendencies. Similarly, the objects (of the mind and the senses) have material tendencies to be attracted toward these desires. These tendencies are potentials and they generally lie dormant, but when the desire arises in the heart, the objects are attracted to the mind and the senses, and the senses and the mind are attracted to the objects. This mutual attraction is due to the innate tendencies and can be loosely called the 'force' of attraction (or repulsion—in case our desire is opposed to certain things). Then we seek these kinds of objects in the external world, trying to fulfill these desires. In simple words, the desire for an object contains the object in a subtle form because the desire refers to the object. In the same way, the objects contain the desires, or the intended purpose in subtle form, as the object exists for a purpose. When the purpose in our senses matches the purpose in the objects, the senses and the objects are mutually attracted due to this matching. This then results in the forces of attraction and repulsion driven by the guna.

In material science, we imagine that objects are naturally attracted to each other due to physical forces, which means that the attraction must spread everywhere and all the time. This view of attraction—which existed in classical physics—has failed in atomic theory because the so-called force of attraction requires the emission and absorption of a particle and these particles are not always emitted or absorbed. The point of emission and absorption is also not predictable, which means that the application of force (i.e., when the force is applied or not applied) is unpredictable. This unpredictability leads to the probabilistic nature of atomic theory. This sūtra offers a remedy to the problem—the cause of the force is not the mechanical attraction or repulsion; it is rather the potentials which exist in complementary forms in the object and in the senses; the potential in the senses and the mind is called 'desire' and the potential in the objects is called 'ability'. When the desire arises, it is naturally attracted to the ability; likewise, the ability is naturally attracted to the desire. This attraction between desire and ability is called 'entanglement' in modern science; when the objects are entangled, then the interaction occurs bidirectionally. And the cause of this entanglement is the guna that lead to desire in the heart.

Both desire and ability are called guna, but they are separated in Sāñkhya as senses and their objects. The desires become the senses, and the objects become the sensations. The conditioning due to guna means that some tongue likes spicy food, while another tongue likes sweet things. Some eyes desire green, while other eyes desire yellow. So, the guna create predispositions in the senses and the objects, and due to these predispositions, science can model them as probabilities. However, science can't explain how these predispositions get entangled, then attracted to each other, finally resulting in an interaction. The cause is time, which converts the predisposition in the mind and the senses into a desire. Unless time acts, desires don't arise, the attraction to the objects isn't created (although the predisposition exists), and experience isn't created. Thus, guna are the causes of attraction, and the movement of awareness.

QUESTION

But there are so many scenarios in which the desire is created by perception rather than perception caused by desire. Thus, for example, we might see tasty food, and then suddenly develop hunger even though we weren't hungry before seeing the food. How can we say that the cause of the movement of consciousness is guna when perceptions can also lead to desires within us?

2.3.26 (242)
व्यतिरेको गन्धवत्
vyatireko gandhavat

vyatirekaḥ—the mutual-exclusion (the object i.e., the soul, which constitutes the spreading of our awareness); gandhavat—like odor.

TRANSLATION

The mutual exclusion (the soul, or the spreading of consciousness from the soul) (can be caused by the perception of sensations) just like odor.

COMMENTARY

An analogy like that of a sandalwood tree is used here—in the sense that both speak about the spreading of smell—but there is a difference. In Sāñkhya philosophy, there is a difference between the objects and the sensations; the objects are called bhūta and the sensations are called tanmātra. These tanmātra include sabda, sparsha, rūpa, rasa, and gandha or sound, touch, form, taste, and smell. The use of gandha here indicates the existence of a tanmātra or a sensation, and the implication is that just like desires can attract us to objects, similarly, the perceptions can also result in the drawing out of consciousness.

In simple terms, object perception can lead to desire, just as desire can lead to object perception. The original claim that the cause of movement is guna is not affected by this clarification because the guna exist both in the senses as well as in the observer. As we noted above, there are two forms of these guna—namely, possibility and desire. The possibility is feminine, and the desire is masculine. While the overall material energy is feminine, a further distinction between masculine and feminine is made within this material energy. Just as the feminine can agitate the masculine into desire, similarly, the objects of the senses and the mind can agitate the mind and senses into desire. There isn't hence a strict causality from possibility to desire, or desire to possibility, because either possibility or desire can result in the creation of the other.

QUESTION

So, you are stating that experience is caused by the interaction of possibility and desire, and these are divisions within the material energy, and each of them can be the cause of the other, so should we not call it 'mutual causality'?

2.3.27 (243)

तथा च दर्शयति

tathā ca darśayati

tathā—thus; ca—also; darśayati—the experience is created, or the philosophy (of perception) states.

TRANSLATION

Thus (through the interaction of the guna present in the senses and the objects) the experience is created, or the philosophy of perception states.

COMMENTARY

Through the influence of modern science, we have become accustomed to linear models of causality in which a cause creates the effect, but the effect could not create the cause. Therefore, if we say that our desires in the mind are the cause of the bodily activity, then the body could not create desires. Conversely, if the body is the cause of the activity, then the mind must be causeless. These linear models of causality emerged from the understanding of objects, which can cause a change to another object only if they have the same properties. For instance, a billiard ball can push another billiard ball because they have the same properties of mass, momentum, energy, etc. This model fails when we start speaking about two different kinds of things—e.g., mind and body. The problem of mutual causality arises because the body can change the mind, and the mind can change the body. In fact, the same experience can be caused by either the body or the mind. Thus, we cannot say that the body or the mind are *necessary* and *sufficient* conditions for their reciprocal effects. Hence, if the cause is not necessary and sufficient, then it cannot be considered a cause.

These models of causation are inappropriate for understanding experience. Instead of billiard ball causality, if we begin with perception as the model of interaction, then we can extend this model to ordinary interactions as well. For instance, we can say that inherent in each thing is not just a possibility but also a purpose. Both possibility and purpose lie in an unmanifest state, and they are manifested by the other. Thus, possibilities can manifest a purpose, but it requires a purpose to exist in unmanifest form. Similarly, the purpose can make the possibility manifest, but there must be a possibility to begin with.

This sūtra gives us the clue that we must think in terms of mutuality and complementarity of possibility and purpose. If the possibility exists, then it can create a purpose. Similarly, purpose can activate the possibility. Thus, if you are looking for a weapon, a kitchen knife will be perceived as a weapon, and the possibility of being a weapon would be realized out of the many alternatives. Likewise, if you see the possibility of food, you can develop hunger for food. So, mind and body are mutually capable of causing the other and this becomes obvious when we understand these in terms of desires and possibilities.

The desire is still superior to the possibility because the mind cannot just control the body, but it can also control itself. If the body creates a desire in the mind, the mind can reject it. But if the mind has a desire, and the body can enact it, then the actions would be enacted. Therefore, the mutual causality between the mind and the body should not make the mind 'at the same level' as the body; the mutual causation doesn't entail the similarity of types in the two.

QUESTION

Whenever we speak of mutual causation, we are unable to separate the cause from the effect. In science, we call this inseparability non-linearity, due to which we can never speak of the self and the world as separate things. If we lose this separability, then we lose the sense of realism—i.e., that I exist independent of the world, or the world exists independent of me. Without such separability and realism, how can we say that we are choosing to see? The inseparability would entail an infinite causal chain in which the possibility created the desire, but that possibility was created by desire, and so on, ad infinitum.

2.3.28 (244)
पृथगुपदेशात्
pṛthagupadeśāt

pṛthak—separate; upadeśāt—on account of the teaching.

TRANSLATION

The (possibility and desire, or matter and mind) are said to be separate.

COMMENTARY

The philosophy of materialism recognizes an external reality but claims that the mind is also material; so, the desires are produced from matter. This matter, however, cannot exist in a state of possibility, because then there would be no desires. If matter doesn't exist in a state of possibility, then there is no free will, because we cannot choose what to experience and what to avoid. Specifically, we cannot withdraw our consciousness from the objects of perception. The philosophy of idealism, on the other hand, rejects the existence of an external reality, and claims that all that we see is merely a phantasm of the mind. It is produced by our desires, so it exists as our will. This, however, fails to explain why we are suffering in this world—if everything is a product of the mind, and is caused by our free will, then everything we experience should make us happy. After all, at every moment our desires are being fulfilled by experience!

The existence of an external reality enables our choice; thus, realism is necessary for free will. Similarly, the separation of the will from the external possibility is necessary to explain why we aren't happy—the external world is not always in accordance with our will. Hence, the separation of the will and the possibility is necessary to explain why we have will, and why it is sometimes not fulfilled. The claim that will causes possibility, which then causes will, thus producing an infinite cycle of causes doesn't come close to understanding the nature of the two. For instance, even though possibilities can cause our will, not every possibility will create a desire in us. In fact, we might look at certain things and be revulsed by them. So, even as a desire is created in us, there are certainly predispositions toward what we will like or hate. So, the creation of the desire is within the possibilities of desires, or innate tendencies of likes and dislikes. Similarly, even though our desires can manifest the possibilities, the external reality is still a definite set of possibilities from which we select. The mutual creation of will and possibility pertains to the activation of a preexisting dormant reality, rather than to the creation of something that doesn't exist. Hence, when we say that will was created due to possibility, the potential for that will preexisted in us, and was activated by the presence of possibility.

Since both will and possibility exist in such potential forms prior to being excited, therefore, they are mutually separate and individuals, even though their interaction can activate a dormant state into a reactivated one. The mutual causation doesn't collapse the distinction between will and possibility. As a result, we must reject both materialism and idealism; there is an objective external world, although it is not an object. There is similarly potential for enjoyment within us, although it might not always be manifest as desire or pleasure. The capacity for enjoyment and the ability to fulfill the desire are separate realities, and their mutual causation changes the causal model, not their separability.

This is a form of the Bhedābheda that we have seen in the masculine and feminine aspects of the Absolute Truth. The will and the possibility are separate, and yet they are identical because every will can be fulfilled, and every possibility can be desired. Due to the one-to-one mapping between the will and the possibility, we can say that they are non-different. And yet, they are still different because the will and the possibility can remain separate. (i.e., without experience). This distinction becomes unavoidable when we recognize that the will and the possibility in the material world are not one-to-one mapped: we might have desires that cannot be fulfilled, and we might have possibilities that we don't desire. And yet, we seek to fulfill the desires by using available possibilities, which entails that the two are separate and yet when the experience is produced, it is only through the combination of will and possibility, so at the point of experience we can say that the two have become non-different.

QUESTION

If the will and the possibility are separate, then how do they combine? What is the cause of their interaction, and what brings about their combination?

2.3.29 (245)

तद्गुणसारत्वात् तु तद्व्यपदेशःप्राज्ञवत्

tadguṇasāratvāt tu tadvyapadeśaḥ prājñavat

tadguṇa—its qualities; sāratvāt—due to the essence; tu—but; tadvyapadeśaḥ—that pervades; prājñavat—as awareness or consciousness.

TRANSLATION

(Each of the two) exist due to the essence of their qualities, but they intersect or enter each other as the awareness or consciousness (of the other).

COMMENTARY

The senses and the mind are said to be the manifestation of sattva-guna, which represents desire. The objects of the senses and the mind are manifestation of tamo-guna or the possibilities of fulfilling the desires. Their interaction is caused by a third entity called prāṇa which manifests due to rajo-guna. Each of these three guna are material representations of spiritual qualities in the soul. The desire is a representation of the ānanda potency. The objects are the manifestation of the *chit* potency. And the connection between the objects and the senses is created by the *sat* potency. Here, the term *sāratvāt* is used which indicates the 'essence', or 'in a primordial state'. This primordial state is the possibility for enjoyment or desire in the ānanda potency. It is the possibility for fulfilling the desire in *chit* potency. And it is the possibility of connecting the desire to its objects in the *sat* potency. We have also previously called them emotion, cognition, and relation, where emotion is the desire, cognition is the object, and relation is the connection between the desire and the objects that fulfill it.

The cause of the interaction between will and possibility is that in both there is a third ability to form relations. Thus, when the will excites the possibility, it is through a relation, which we can call consciousness or awareness. In matter, this 'awareness' has a material counterpart that we can call 'structure'. When structure is established, two entities start interacting; the structure also defines their mutual roles. This means that two material objects do not always interact, regardless of how physically close they are. They interact only after a relation is formed between them, and this relation—also being a potential—is activated. Hence, either the cognition, the emotion, or the relation can be causes of experience. For instance, we can have desire, which then drives our relation to the world to pick something that will fulfill our desire. There can be a potential for fulfilling the desire, which then drives the object into our awareness and produces a desire. Finally, a relation can sometimes be established without a prior desire or the ability to fulfill the desire, and both ability and desire may then be activated. In different situations, these three entities become dominant or subordinate; the dominant entity becomes the cause of the subordinate entities. That is, either emotion, relation, or cognition can give rise to the others.

QUESTION

If we can fulfill our desires just by directing our consciousness to the desired objects, then why are so many of our desires always unfulfilled?

2.3.30 (246)

यावदात्मभावित्वाच्च न दोषःतददर्शनात्

yāvadātmabhāvitvācca na doṣaḥ taddarśanāt

yāvat—as soon as; ātmabhāvitvāt—due to the desire in the soul; ca—also; na doṣaḥ—absence of defect; taddarśanāt—from that being seen.

TRANSLATION

As soon as desire arises in the soul, also that is seen (i.e., the desire is fulfilled as soon as the desire arises in the soul) in the absence of defect.

COMMENTARY

The term *doṣaḥ* used here should be contrasted with *guna* previously. In one sense, *guna* are qualities, but in another sense (contrasted to doṣaḥ), they are also 'good' qualities; the term doṣaḥ then means 'bad' qualities. All illnesses and diseases for instance are attributed to the presence of doṣaḥ instead of guna. But what is doṣaḥ? It is the state when the guna are either excessive or debilitated. For example, the debilitation of the senses can lead to loss of sensation or desire for sensation, while the guna in excess can cause hypersensitivity or excessive desire. The modes of nature are expected to remain in a 'balance', but when this balance is disturbed, then doṣaḥ are created. So, doṣaḥ is nothing but guna although in an excessive or debilitated state. When one mode goes out of balance, then the other modes either become dominant or debilitated. And this change in the normal balanced state creates illnesses and diseases. This sūtra asserts that all discrepancies in desire fulfillment can be called doṣaḥ.

The causes of this imbalance are not noted here, but they could be attributed to our senses, the objects of the senses, or the relation between the objects and the senses. Each of these is described according to the three modes. But the cause of this imbalance can either be our desires which become habits over time, or these could be due to the consequences of previous actions, or it could be exaggerated effects of the time, place, and circumstance a person is in (which are again caused due to conscious or unconscious memories). Here, only the general principle of 'good' qualities becoming 'bad' is being noted.

QUESTION

Some people say that if our desires are controlled, then they die slowly. Do our desires go away if we suppress them or they remain unfulfilled?

2.3.31 (247)

पुंस्त्वादवित् त्वस्य सतोऽभिव्यक्तियोगात्

puṃstvādivat tvasya sato'bhivyaktiyogāt

puṃstvādivat—like the origin of masculinity; tu—certainly; asya—its; sataḥ—eternally; abhivyaktiyogāt—from manifestation upon union or contact.

TRANSLATION

Just like the origin of masculinity (in the Supreme Lord), its (the soul's) (desires) are certainly eternal, and they are manifest from union or contact.

COMMENTARY

In this sūtra, the emergence of the desire in the soul is compared to the emergence of desires in the Lord. The term *puṃstva* indicates masculinity or virility. The Lord's desire to enjoy exists as a possibility in Him. But it can be activated by the Lord's energy when the feminine looks at the masculine, and the masculine is excited to enjoy with the feminine. The soul has the same potential for enjoyment, but his desires can be either like the Lord's (i.e., to enjoy by domination) or like the Lord's energy (i.e., to enjoy by serving the Lord).

Of course, the soul can give up both these kinds of desires and remain situated within Brahman, but the potential for enjoyment can never be destroyed. This potential is the essential innate property of the soul, and sense or mind control can restrain the soul's enjoyment but cannot destroy the potential for such enjoyment. This sūtra states indicates that desire for enjoyment can spring up any time in the soul when it contacts the material or the spiritual energy. Thus, the claim of the impersonalist that desire and enjoyment exist only in the material world is rejected by stating that the virility in the soul—and this virility can be masculine or feminine (although the term used here is masculine)—is eternally existent, and it springs into desire in contact with its objects.

QUESTION

I can understand how you are describing the separation of the Absolute Truth into masculine and feminine, and extending this to the emergence of desire in the soul, and how it enjoys with the Lord or with the material energy. But doesn't this separation between masculine and feminine complicate the philosophy of the Absolute Truth? Isn't a single reality much better in comparison instead of saying that there are two inseparable aspects of this reality?

2.3.32 (248)

नित्योपलब्ध्यनुपलब्धिप्रसङ्गोऽन्यतरनियमोवान्यथा

nityopalabdhyanupalabdhiprasaṅgo'nyataraniyamovānyathā

nityopalabdhi—perpetual perception; anupalabdhi—non-perception; prasaṅgaḥ—the incidents or outcomes or episodes; anyatara—either; niyamaḥ—limitation of the power; vā—or else; anyathā—otherwise.

TRANSLATION

(Without the philosophy of masculine and feminine), either of two outcomes would follow: perpetual perception (by the union of desire and possibility) or non-perception (by the separation of desire and possibility). In either of these two cases, there will be limitations on both (the will cannot withdraw from enjoyment, and the possibility cannot control the will's emergence).

COMMENTARY

This sūtra refutes two opposite claims simultaneously— (1) there is one Absolute Truth and it has no aspects such as feminine and masculine, and (2) there are two separated realities (masculine and feminine) such that their interaction is unnatural. The sūtra notes that if we take the first position, then there is no possibility of ending the experience, and if we take the second position then there is no possibility of starting the experience. Some impersonal philosophers take the first position and say that matter doesn't really exist. The material experience is an illusion created by the self within the self. The sūtra argues that if this were the case, then there would be no way to end the material experience because the soul is eternal and therefore the illusion would also become eternal. Other impersonal philosophers take the second position and say that the soul and the material energy are very different such that their combination is very unnatural. The sūtra argues that if the combination was unnatural, then it should not arise in the first place to even produce a material experience.

If either of these conditions is granted, then either the enjoyment cannot begin or if it has begun it cannot end. The beginning and end of the material experience entails that the soul has free will to engage or withdraw. Similarly, the material energy has the power to entice or hinder the enjoyment. By this enticement, the soul is allured to enjoy, but by the hindrances, the soul suffers and becomes detached from enjoyment. Its ability to be attracted or detached constitutes the soul's free will, and merging the soul with matter, or separating the soul from matter would not explain the phenomena (*prasaṅgaḥ*).

Topic 14

QUESTION

This description of mutual causation between the masculine and the feminine is unsatisfactory because it doesn't say why each side must act in the first place. If the feminine is the cause of the activation of the masculine, what causes the feminine to become activated? If we say the cause is masculine, then it leads to an infinite circularity of causality. How can you resolve this problem?

2.3.33 (249)

कर्ता शास्त्रार्थवत्त्वात्

kartā śāstrārthavattvāt

kartā—the actor; śāstrārthavattvāt—from just like engaging in a discussion between them (which is like a debate on the real meaning of the scriptures).

TRANSLATION

From the actors (masculine and feminine) being engaged in a mutual discussion (which is aimed to obtain a better understanding of each other).

COMMENTARY

The ideas of linear causation are based on a criterion in logic in which a premise leads to a conclusion, or a cause leads to an effect. According to this model of causation, either the feminine or the masculine must be the original cause; but since they are both potentials (of desire and the power to fulfill that desire), one of them must come first and cause the other. This is the point at which we need to alter our notions of logic as linear causation. We must rather defer to a dialectical model of causation in which a premise exists, but it doesn't lead to a conclusion automatically unless a question is asked. The question presents itself as a problem, and the pair of question and answer constitutes a contradiction. This contradiction is resolved when the premise expands into an answer—specifically to resolve the problem posed by the emerging question.

In this case, the feminine is the premise, and the masculine is the question. The premise can exist forever, but it doesn't lead to the creation of the world unless a question is asked. But when the question is asked, then the premise becomes the answer, and the question is satisfied. However, the answer will then lead to another question, which must be answered, and so on, ad infinitum. This process of questioning and answering is described in this sūtra as śāstrārtha. This term refers to a practice in ancient times in which two debaters will sit down for a debate, and one will ask the other questions. As the questions are answered, new questions are raised based on the previous answer. And this process continues until one of two conditions is satisfied— (1) there are no more questions to be answered, and the questioner is satisfied, or (2) some question is not answered, and the questioner is dissatisfied. This process of dialectical inquiry was used to check the consistency and completeness of a theory. For instance, if a theory is incomplete, then some question would remain unanswered. And if the theory is inconsistent, then the questioner can point out the contradictions in the answers which makes a new question—which of these two answers would you like to prefer? And if a choice is made, then the original question (which was answered by the rejected answer) returns to the fore. Ultimately, under a contradiction, some question must remain unanswered. Thus, every inconsistency eventually leads to some incompleteness (as we prefer not to answer some questions, rather than provide a conflicting answer).

The literal meaning of śāstrārtha is the 'interpretation of scriptures', and this interpretation is debatable because there are many ways to interpret. How do we know which of the interpretations are correct? The short remedy to this problem is consistency and completeness: all questions must be answered, and no answer must contradict the other answers. Therefore, the method of deciding the 'interpretation of scripture' was debate, discussion, and testing the hypothesis. It was understood that the scripture can be understood in many ways; while the text is eternal, its understanding can change. A superior interpretation is one that satisfies the twin conditions of consistency and completeness.

In this sūtra, the interaction between the masculine and the feminine is compared to such a discussion. The difference is only that such debates can be finite or infinite. In the case of the material world, the soul asks the questions to material nature, and material nature gives the answers. These answers update our understanding, but we are not free to create this understanding whimsically. We are free to ask any question we want, but the answers are decided by material nature. Therefore, we cannot come up with an understanding of nature by speculation; this understanding must be based on previously asked questions. Of course, when an answer is provided, the answer is itself subject to interpretation. To clarify which interpretation is correct, we can ask further questions. But since every answer is subject to interpretation, to converge on the right answer, we must remember the previously asked questions and answers. If we forget the previous questions and answers, then the process is infinite. Therefore, enlightenment is a difficult problem because we forget.

The Lord doesn't forget the answers given by His Śakti, but He is never satisfied by the answers. He keeps seeking clarifications—i.e., posing new questions—based on the previous answers. Since the process is dialectical, the Śakti can change the Lord's questions by giving different answers to the same question. If there are infinite questions and infinite correct answers to each question, then the process of questioning can never come to an end. However, this endless process doesn't indicate an ignorance; it is rather the endless quest for understanding. The masculine understands the feminine by Her answers, and the feminine understands the masculine by His questions. These are two complementary methods of understanding—we can know the other person by what they answer, just as we can know them by the type of questions they ask.

QUESTION

If this process of questioning and answering potentially never comes to an end, then what is the point of this sequence of questions and answers? Why should someone engage in an endless sequence of questions and answers?

2.3.34 (250)
वहिारोपदेशात्
vihāropadeśāt

vihāra-upadeśāt—due to the teaching of their playing, pleasure trip.

TRANSLATION

This is described as their play or pastime.

COMMENTARY

The purpose of the manifestation of the world is the enjoyment of pleasure. It is not a goal that ends, because pleasure can be enjoyed eternally. Therefore, we should not think of the process of questioning and answering as a finite sequence that comes to an end. Indeed, questions are asked only because we want to be happy. Answers to a question are accepted if they make us happy. If the process of discussion is itself the source of pleasure, why must it end? This sūtra states that there is no purpose in this process other than pleasure itself.

QUESTION

You are saying that the purpose of the masculine and the feminine is to know each other. But don't we speak about self-knowledge as the main goal?

2.3.35 (251)
उपादानात्
upādānāt

upādānāt—due to the appropriation (of meaning to the self).

TRANSLATION

(Self-knowledge is obtained) by appropriating (the other-knowledge).

COMMENTARY

The masculine and the feminine are different due to being will and possibility. But they are non-different because every will can be fulfilled, and every possibility is desirable. Thus, if you see some possibility, you know that it can be desired. Similarly, if you see some desire, you know that it can be fulfilled.

So, knowledge of the other is also non-different from self-knowledge. The impersonalist thinks that self-knowledge is the goal of existence, but as it has been noted in an earlier sūtra, if the knower and known are merged together, then there is no cessation of perception. It follows that everything must always be known, and there cannot be a sequence of questions and answers that lead to discovery, which then results in a new type of pleasure at every moment. When the process of self-knowledge only involves the self, then this knowledge is unchanging. But when it involves the self and the other, then it evolves. This evolution should not be confused with the material temporariness; it is an ever-deepening understanding of the same truth; what was previously known doesn't become false after you know something new; the previous knowledge is rather nuanced, complemented, and exemplified by the new discovery.

QUESTION

Are you indicating that self-knowledge is non-different from knowledge of the other because each side knows the other through their actions?

2.3.36 (252)

व्यपदेशाच्च क्रियायाम् न चेन्निर्देशविपर्ययः

vyapadeśācca kriyāyām na cennirdeśaviparyayaḥ

vyapadeśāt—on account of mention; ca—also; kriyāyām—in respect of action; na cet—if it were not so; nirdeśa-viparyayaḥ—the reference (would have been) of a different kind.

TRANSLATION

If it were not the case that the action (of one side) describes (the other side), then the reference (or purpose of each side) would be different.

COMMENTARY

In this sūtra, the nature of non-difference is being exemplified further. The masculine and the feminine are non-different not just because all the desires are possible, and all the possibilities are desirable. It is also because the desires and the possibilities are mutually referencing each other. In short, the desire exists because it is possible, and the possibility exists because it is desirable. Each side can be called the reason or purpose for the existence of the other. The sūtra also states that if this mutual justification or purpose wasn't there, then the mutual actions by which the other is mentioned would also not exist. Each side would be self-absorbed, and the will would never be fulfilled, while the possibility would never be realized. That would entail the end of all manifestation.

QUESTION

Can this sequence of questions and answers not come to an end? Doesn't this process have a limit that culminates in the completeness of knowledge?

2.3.37 (253)
उपलब्धिवदनियमः
upalabdhivadaniyamaḥ

upalabdhivat—just like perception; aniyamaḥ—no limitation.

TRANSLATION

Just like perception, (the process of discussion) has no end.

COMMENTARY

Most people today believe that if perfect knowledge were possible, then it will also have an end. That is, we will someday know everything there is to be known, and nothing would be known after that. Unless everything is known, we cannot call our knowledge perfect. If perfection is attained, life becomes boring after that because there is nothing more to be known. Therefore, we must choose between an ignorant life and a boring life. An ignorant life will be exciting because there is much to be known. And a boring life would be full of knowledge because there is nothing left to be known. Now perfection that leads to liberation must also lead to an endlessly boring existence. On the other hand, ignorance must be bliss—because there is so much yet to be known.

Many devotees too have a similar viewpoint. They think that whatever had to be known is already known, and it is now time to put it into practice. But since this practice doesn't reveal anything new, therefore, the person quickly loses interest in the practice too. By treating spiritual life as a practice, rather than a process of discovery, they lose both the discovery and the practice.

This sūtra indicates that perception and discussion are both infinite. Hence, we can never know the Absolute Truth completely. There will always be room for new things to be found, and for new things to be discussed. Does this entail that the spiritualist also doesn't know the truth? No. The ignorance in the material world is that the new knowledge repudiates the previous knowledge. The ignorance in the spiritual world is that the previous understanding is never falsified, but new information is endlessly added to the existing understanding. For example, we can look at a forest from a distance, and not see the trees. Then when we come closer, then we see the trees. Then we come even closer and we see the leaves. An even closer examination reveals that the leaves have veins in them. And we can then zoom out and look at another leaf, another branch, or another trunk, and then again zoom in and look closer at more details.

Does this mean that your knowledge of the forest was false? No. There is a forest, and it is not an ocean or a river or a mountain. That knowledge is correct, and if the forest was all that existed, then the knowledge is also complete. However, this knowledge is *abstract* rather than *detailed*. The soul is liberated when it obtains the abstract knowledge of the whole, because this is the whole truth. But the details are within that abstraction, and because they are infinite, they are never completely known. This doesn't they cannot be known. It just means that life is an infinite journey of constant discovery of the details. Those details do not refute the previous understanding of the whole truth, or of the previously discovered details. It just nuances and enhances that knowledge.

Thus, we can say that nobody knows everything. However, that ignorance is not the same as one possessing false beliefs. Thus, material and spiritual ignorance are different—in the former case you believe in falsities, and the in latter case you don't know all the truths, although you know the whole truth.

QUESTION

Even if the Lord is infinite, should we not suppose that this process can come to an end because the knowers are finite? After all, don't they ever become satisfied with knowing enough, and end the process of continual knowing?

2.3.38 (254)
शक्तविपिर्ययात्
śaktiviparyayāt

śaktiviparyayāt—due to being contrary to the nature of śakti.

TRANSLATION

(Being finite) is contrary to the nature of śakti.

COMMENTARY

While previous sūtras have accepted that the soul is finite and atomic, this sūtra states that even the soul's knowledge can be infinite, and this infinity is attributed to the Śakti. The finitude of the soul is that it can focus on one thing at a time, while the Lord can focus on everything at once. The infinity of the soul is that it has infinite capacity for memory, which comes from the Śakti.

At present we recall one thing from the past at any one time, but we have the capacity to recall numerous things. Similarly, in the spiritual world, the soul knows many things, but it remembers one thing at a time. On the other hand, the memories are destroyed in the material body, and many of the unpleasant memories are blocked. But in the spiritual world, the memory is eternal, and nothing previously experienced is ever forgotten. If the soul were finite, it could only remember a finite past. This doesn't happen because memory is afforded by the Śakti. If the soul is outside the Śakti, then it has no memory, and hence no past. If the soul is within Śakti, then the soul has a past, which can be recalled eternally. As the memories are destroyed in the material world, the 'size' of the universe—i.e., the information that needs to be stored in the universe—remains finite. But, since the past is remembered in the spiritual world, therefore, the spiritual world constantly expands, as the past events are never forgotten.

Effectively, the memory of the past is not in the soul, but in the Lord's Śakti. This idea has been previously described as the 'collective unconscious' in Jungian psychology, where our memory is not our individual property, but a property of the entire universe, although we get to access many parts of this memory, and our shared values and ideals include those that existed in the past that is long gone. The past is ever-present in the Śakti, but it is selectively recalled by the soul. Like we don't have to be infinite to access an infinite library of information, similarly, the soul doesn't have to be infinite to recall the past. The Śakti is the library of information, and She fulfills the soul's desires to know. Thus, when the finite takes shelter of the infinite, then the finite acquires some of the capacities of the infinite. The finite can still only read book at a time from the library, but he has access to the library of infinite information.

QUESTION

Your descriptions of the separation of the soul and the Lord, who are then engaged in constant mutual enjoyment, seem contrary to the concept of samadhi in which the distinction between the soul and the Lord is lost.

2.3.39 (255)
समाध्यभावाच्च
samādhyabhāvācca

samādhi-abhāvāt—due to the absence of samadhi; ca—also.

TRANSLATION

Due to the absence of samādhi also (the soul and the Lord enjoy).

COMMENTARY

The term *samādhi* is made up of two roots—*sama* (which means uniformity without a distinction) and *adhi* (situated at). Thus, *samādhi* refers to the soul merging into Brahman, which lacks diversity (*sama*). The soul has inner contradiction between its three modes, and one of the results of this conflict is that every answer produces a new question. However, in Brahman, the *sat*, *chit*, and ānanda, are not in conflict, because the soul has a relation to the self, fully knows the self, and because the soul is finite, there is nothing more to be known. This produces a static knowledge of the self—i.e., there is nothing new to discover about the self at every moment. Thus, in one sense, the desires of the soul come to an end, although the soul still has the potential for desire. This sūtra states that association with the Lord cannot be called *samādhi* because the soul is not self-absorbed; he is rather absorbed into the nature of the Lord.

Thus, a distinction is drawn between the dissolution of two separate identities (i.e., the soul and the Lord) and their union (yoga) through mutual knowledge. If you see an apple, your consciousness is merged with the understanding of the apple. And yet, you are not identical to the apple. You still know that you are different from the apple, and your knowledge is *about* the apple. In the same way, the soul is merged in the Lord because his consciousness is absorbed in the thoughts, sensations, and pleasure of the Lord. And yet, this merger of consciousness is not the dissolution of their separate identities.

QUESTION

If the soul decides to enter samadhi, and become self-absorbed rather than being absorbed in the knowledge of the Lord, does it mean that the

experience of the Lord and the interactions with Him no longer exist for the soul?

Topic 15

2.3.40 (256)
यथा च तक्षोभयथा
yathā ca takṣobhayathā

yathā—just as; ca—also; takṣa—cutting through; ubhayathā—both ways.

TRANSLATION

Just as (the soul withdraws from the Lord) also (the Lord withdraws from the soul); (the disconnection between soul and Lord) cuts both ways.

COMMENTARY

In the previous sūtra it was stated that the soul and the Lord enjoying with each other mutually are not in samādhi (i.e., they are different individuals). In this sūtra, the same point is made by stating that if the soul enters samādhi then the connection to the Lord (i.e., the consciousness and experience) are severed mutually. That is, if the soul is not engaged with the Lord, then the Lord is also not engaged with the soul. They exist as separate individuals, who have the potential to know each other, but that potential remains unrealized. The relationship to the Lord is therefore about mutual devotion and affection. If the soul wants to ignore the Lord, then the Lord doesn't force Himself upon the soul.

Topic 16

QUESTION

Does this severance of the relationship between the soul and the Lord permanently close the doors to a relationship in the future? Or is this absorption in Brahman a temporary state, which can also be altered in the future?

2.3.41 (257)
परात्तु तच्छ्रुतेः
parāttu tacchruteḥ

parāt—from the Supreme Lord; tu—but; tat—that (the soul); śruteḥ—so declares the śrutī.

TRANSLATION

The śrutī states that the soul has but emerged from the Lord (so there can never be a permanent disconnection between the soul and the Lord).

COMMENTARY

It has previously been noted that the soul is always connected to the Supreme Lord even in Brahman (through the agency of His prāṇa). This sūtra confirms that the soul can rise above Brahman and enter the pastimes of the Lord. The entry into Brahman is not a limitation to entry into the Lord's pastimes. In effect, what we call 'eternity' is not contrary to the possibility of change.

QUESTION

You have earlier said that the soul enters the Lord's association due to devotion. But how does he enter the undifferentiated state called Brahman?

2.3.42 (258)

कृतप्रयत्नापेक्षस्तु वहितिप्रतषिदि्धावैयर्थ्यादभि्यः

kṛtaprayatnāpekṣastu vihitapratiṣiddhāvaiyarthyādibhyaḥ

kṛtaprayatna—one who endeavors; apekṣaḥ—future prospect or expectation; tu—but; vihita—injunctions according to scriptures; pratiṣiddha—forbidden or prohibited; vaiyartha—uselessness; ādibhyaḥ—due to etc.

TRANSLATION

One who works according to scriptural injunctions, rejecting what is prohibited, and avoiding what is useless, etc. without expectation of future results (is entitled to enter the undifferentiated state called Brahman).

COMMENTARY

This sūtra describes the philosophy of karma-yoga and how it leads to Brahman realization. The cornerstone of karma-yoga is performing the prescribed duties, not indulging in sinful actions, avoiding all useless actions, but doing what needs to be done without the expectation of results (positive or negative). Generally, people over-endeavor in actions where they expect a positive result, and they neglect the actions where the outcomes are feared to be undesirable. Thus, the person creates good or bad karma, which entangles him in the cycle of repeated birth and death. Karma-yoga, however, liberates the soul from the cycle of birth and death, and leads to the Brahman state. As we have discussed before, the soul is bound to the material world due to guna and karma. When actions are performed without desire, then the guna or the ropes of desire are broken. And when the actions are performed in this way, then the cycle of karma is also broken. This liberation from the material world is the end of guna and karma, in which the soul is self-absorbed. But this self-absorption is incomplete because other souls, including the Supreme Soul, remain unknown.

Topic 17

QUESTION

The practice of karma-yoga is very difficult, because how can we act without thinking about the results of our actions? Is it possible that someone who is unable to practice karma-yoga can also attain the Brahman realization?

2.3.43 (259)

अंशो नानाव्यपदेशात् अन्यथा चापि दाशकितवादित्वमधीयत एके

aṃśo nānāvyapadeśāt anyathā cāpi dāśakitavāditvamadhīyata eke

aṃśaḥ—part; nānāvyapadeśāt—on account of the many descriptions; anyathā—otherwise; ca—and; api—also; dāśakitavāditvam—being cheating servants etc.; adhīyate—in the followers (of the Lord); eke—some.

TRANSLATION

Besides the parts (devotees) described in many ways (previously), in some cheating servants who follow the Lord additionally also (Brahman attained).

COMMENTARY

A cheating servant is one whose faith and commitment to the master are based on getting something in return. In this world, we can see that people bear loyalties to each other if they are rich and powerful, and those loyalties are broken if the master loses his power or wealth. The soul can similarly serve the Lord because the Lord is rich and powerful because by association, the soul obtains something in return. Since the Lord is always rich and powerful, therefore, this loyalty may never be broken, and it might seem that the soul is devoted to the Lord like others who are devoted without self-interest. But, such a servant, who is only devoted to his self-interest, and seems devoted to the Lord because he gets something in return, is called a 'cheating' servant here.

Such devotees accept that God is great because He supplies their necessities, but they are not interested in God. Their self-interest manifests in the desire for happiness, and the avoidance of suffering, which also manifests in the quest for liberation. Most devotees of Lord Śiva, for example, worship Him for liberation or sometimes material gain, because He grants boons easily. They may call themselves devotees of Lord Śiva, but their real devotion is to themselves. Thus, for example, they might chant the mantra *śivoham* or that "I am Śiva". Since Lord Śiva is detached from the material existence, by chanting this mantra, one may get liberated from the cycle of birth and death. This sūtra mentions that some (*eke*) souls are liberated by this process, which means that even if one has selfish interests, one must still have reverence toward the Lord. They must admire and respect the Lord, even if they are using Him for self-interest.

QUESTION

Even the practitioners of cheating religion expend much effort in worshiping the deities, offering them something in exchange for something else. If one is unable to do such worship, is there another way for getting liberated?

2.3.44 (260)
मन्त्रवर्णाच्च
mantravarṇācca

mantravarṇāt—due to the letters of the mantra; ca—also.

TRANSLATION

By the accurate pronunciation of Vedic mantras as well (one can get liberated from the material existence into the state called Brahman).

COMMENTARY

The Vedic mantras are manifestations of śabda-brahman or the sound representation of Brahman. For instance, the mantra OM, which is comprised of three letters—A, U, and M—is said to the origin of the varṇamāla or the garland of letters (there are 50 letters in the Sanskrit varṇamāla). These three letters represent the three primordial aspects of the soul—*sat*, *chit*, and ānanda—and by chanting this mantra, one can realize that one is eternal and can be situated in relation to oneself, that the external world is not necessary for self-awareness and self-knowledge, and that this self-awareness itself brings happiness. The mantra OM simply means "I am". Similarly, mantras such as ahaṃ brahmāsmī or "I am Brahman" means that I am beyond the material existence. The sound vibration of these mantra can liberate the soul from the bondage to the cycle of birth and death, and if one cannot worship the Lord, this sūtra suggests that one can chant such mantra if they want to be liberated from life and death.

QUESTION

The chanting of mantras generally requires a person to give up their material lives, sit in an isolated place, and meditate on the sound of the mantra. What if someone is not able to give up their material life for the changing of mantra in isolated places? Is there a path for liberation for such souls as well?

2.3.45 (261)
अपि च स्मर्यते
api ca smaryate

api—also; ca—and; smaryate—those who follow the sṃriti (such as Manu Sṃriti which prescribes the rules of living a regulated pious human life).

TRANSLATION

Even those who follow the principles of sṃriti (such as Manu Sṃriti).

COMMENTARY

The previous sūtra recommended the chanting of mantras from the śrutī, and this sūtra recommends that if one cannot follow the mantras of the śrutī, then even leading a regulated life as prescribed in the smriti is a practical way for getting liberated. We have earlier discussed how the terms śrutī and smriti are used loosely in the Vedic system. It is said that śrutī is words spoken by God, but Bhagavad-Gita, and many Purāṇa where the Lord speaks directly are termed as smriti. Meanwhile, even in the Upanishads, there are numerous narrations of conversations between self-realized souls instructing their disciples, not necessarily the words spoken by the Lord. The exact meaning of these terms is understood only based on the context, and in this case, the term smriti refers to the texts such as Manu Smriti which prescribe the four-fold classification of human society into Brahmana, Kshatriya, Vaisya, and Sudra, and their respective duties. The sūtra states that if one follows the prescriptions of Manu Smriti correctly, he can be liberated from the cycle of birth and death. In short, if society is organized properly according to the principles of Manu Smriti, just following the rules and regulations of social organization can lead us to Brahman.

QUESTION

If good social organization can lead us Brahman, then shouldn't the worship of demigods, such as Sun, Moon, stars, etc. also lead to liberation? You have rejected this process earlier, but would you recommend it now?

2.3.46 (262)

प्रकाशादिवन्नैवं परः

prakāśādivannaivaṃ paraḥ

prakāśādivat—like light etc.; na—is not suitable; evaṃ—for this; paraḥ—the path toward transcendence (i.e., the attainment of Brahman).

TRANSLATION

The worship of the luminaries (such as sun, moon, stars, etc.) is not suitable for this process of attaining transcendence (i.e., liberation into Brahman).

COMMENTARY

In the previous sūtra, the proper organization of society according to the principles of Manu Smriti was recommended as a path to liberation, but in this sūtra, the worship of demigods is rejected for the purpose. Thus, we can see how proper social organization has greater importance than the worship of demigods; many people think that they are on the same level, and because the worship of demigods is rejected, therefore, the principles of social organization can also be rejected. From the previous sequence, we can see that karma-yoga, the chanting of certain mantras (such as OM), and social organization are preferred over demigod worship. This assumes significance because the Mīmāṃsā system, which worshipped the demigods, was dominated by

Brahmanas. Buddhism rose as a reaction to the dominance of the Brahmanas, and it flattened society, removing the erstwhile class structure. Thus, two birds were hit with the same stone, but only one should have been hit. The rejection of demigod worship is not the rejection of the system of four classes according to this sūtra. The principles of Varṇāśrama have been slightly modified with time, such as rejecting the killing of animals by the Kshatriya, the consumption of intoxicants by the Sudra, and elevating the position of women who are qualified to lead society. But underlying all these changes is an understanding that there is a transcendental society where animals are not killed, intoxicants are not consumed, and women have equal or greater role in society as the men.

Therefore, both personalism and impersonalism accept a classful society, although they reject the worship of demigods. There is considerable false propaganda today that because we are all souls, and therefore children of God, and because we merge into oneness, therefore, everyone should be treated equally. The classful societies of the past had a superior role for kings and priests, who worshipped the demigods. As the demigod worship was demolished, the classful system also disappeared. But here the demigod worship is clearly separated from a classful society—the obedience of the rules of a classful society are said to lead to Brahman, whereas the demigod worship is explicitly rejected.

QUESTION

It has become very difficult to follow the rules of good social organization in modern times. We are forced to do things that we are not supposed to do, and we are often unable to do things that we are expected to do. For those who cannot follow the rules of a good social organization, what is the way?

2.3.47 (263)

स्मरन्तिच

smaranti ca

smaranti—those who remember (at the time of death); ca—and.

TRANSLATION

Even those who can remember (the Lord at the time of death) (can get liberated from the material existence and become situated in Brahman).

COMMENTARY

There are many reasons to remember the Lord at the time of death. First, when a person is sinful, they fear death because it is now the beginning of the repayment of the sins, and they might remember the Lord out of this fear. Second, a person might be suffering in the present life and is prepared to die to alleviate this suffering, but he is also looking for a better material body in the next life; they might remember the Lord to give them a better next life. Third, a person may be enjoying this life, and doesn't want to leave this body; since death entails separation from the body, wealth, and family, therefore, he might cry due to the incumbent separation, and he might pray to the Lord to prevent the death. Fourth, one might be detached from this world—neither sinful, nor suffering, nor enjoying, and may want to be liberated from the cycle of birth and death; they can remember the Lord to give them liberation from the cycle of birth and death. Fifth, a devotee will remember the Lord out of love, because he always remembers Him in good or bad times. The result of remembering the Lord depends upon the mood or intention underlying the remembrance.

In the progression of sūtras, we can see that the seeker is trying to find the minimal requirement for liberation. He first rejects the devotion to the Lord. Then he rejects karma-yoga, then the chanting of mantras, then the regulations of the social order. Due to the rejection of karma-yoga, the person is not aspiring for detachment and liberation. Due to the rejection of the chanting of mantras, he is not interested in spiritual endeavors. Due to the rejection of the restrictions of social order, he is not even interested in a responsible life. In short, the seeker is asking—what is the appropriate method for liberation for one who is not devoted to the Lord, isn't detached from the material world, doesn't want to undertake any spiritual activity, and doesn't like social rules and regulations? The only reason for such a person to remember the Lord at death is that they haven't done anything to deserve a better life, and they are about to lose their present life. Such a person only remembers the Lord unwillingly for a moment, just like an atheist in a state of shock and fear, might occasionally say: "Oh, my God".

This sūtra then says that even such a person can get liberated into Brahman due to their remembrance of the Lord at the time of death. However, the reality is that most people don't even remember the Lord despite such concessions. Most of our recall or memory works as part of the intellect. For example, when we see a cow, then the intellect recalls the images of the cows from the memory to say that "this is a cow". But under fear, the intellect stops working. Therefore, when we see death, our intellect doesn't say: "now I'm seeing the Lord". Therefore, the intellect cannot help us remember the Lord under great fear. This remembrance is possible if we have felt a more powerful emotion than the fear of death. The fear of death is the most powerful material emotion and to feel something other than this fear, one must feel an even more powerful emotion that conquers the fear. Therefore, the Lord's remembrance is easily achieved by devotees, but there are accidental cases in which it can be achieved by others.

QUESTION

What is considered sinful life due to which a person is cast repeatedly into the cycle of birth and death and is disqualified from liberation into Brahman?

2.3.48 (264)

अनुज्ञापरिहारौ देहसम्बन्धाज्ज्योतिरादिवत्

anujñāparihārau dehasambandhājjyotirādivat

anujñāparihārau—injunctions and prohibitions; dehasambandhāt—on account of the connection with the body; jyotirādi-vat—like light etc.

TRANSLATION

(Those who do not follow) the injunctions and prohibitions (even of) the body (such as cleanliness, eating, sex, etc.) and do not believe in the existence of the demigods (who deliver good and bad karma) (are disqualified).

COMMENTARY

Those aspiring for the Lord's devotion or liberation from matter don't worship the demigods, but they don't disregard their existence or role in the material world. For instance, they understand that the universe is governed by moral laws whose results (good or bad) are delivered by the demigods. They don't worship the demigods because these results are bound to come depending on our actions, and demigod worship cannot mitigate the good or bad results of our actions. Nevertheless, they don't reject the existence of the demigods precisely because that rejection would entail the rejection of good and bad karma, and once the law of karma is rejected, then people will descend into immoral activities. All morality comes down to the actions of the body, combined with a mental state. For instance, just thinking of harming someone does not entail sin unless an action by the body is performed. However, if the action is performed without the intention of harming, then the deed involves a reduced sin.

To save us from these sins, the scriptures provide many injunctions (of what to do) and prohibitions (of what not to do). In the last but one sūtra, the injunctions of social life were described—i.e., the things that one must do. And in this sūtra, the prohibitions of social life are referenced—i.e., the things that one must not do. These include regulations about eating, cleanliness of the body and the surroundings in which we live, sex regulations, what can and cannot be said, etc. The devotees of the Lord can do anything for the pleasure of the Lord, and they are not implicated by karma because their intentions are pure devotion to the Lord. But those who don't have such devotion have to follow rules and regulations related to the body. Liberation from material existence of course involves the purification of the mind. But if someone cannot even follow the purification of the body through regulations (and has an impure or uncontrolled mind) then he is disqualified from any type of transcendence.

QUESTION

Does this mean that only purification of the body is necessary? What about the actions of a person? Do they qualify or disqualify a person from liberation?

2.3.49 (265)

असन्ततेश्चाव्यतिकरः

asantateścāvyatikaraḥ

asantateḥ—discontinuous; ca—and; avyatikaraḥ—not acting reciprocally.

TRANSLATION

Those who neglect their reciprocal duties or perform them inconsistently (i.e., sometimes they do and sometimes they don't) (are forbidden).

COMMENTARY

In an earlier sūtra, a cheating religion was described as a system of worship in which the person serves the Lord only to obtain something in return. Practically everyone in this world works for selfish reasons. Thus, a laborer toils because he is paid a salary. People remain honest because they fear the punishments. But some people are even lower; they cannot perform the reciprocal duties, even to avoid punishment. This class of people believe in exploiting others and using them for their interest, but do not reciprocate the good they have received, or reciprocate inadequately (i.e., sometimes they reciprocate and at other times they don't). Maddened by their power, they feel invincible. These people are said to be disqualified from the pursuit of transcendence. As we have said, devotees are the most unselfish, as they serve the Lord and other souls without expecting returns. Those aspiring liberation are next, as they work for their own benefit, but they don't use others for their needs. Lower than those aspiring for liberation are those who engage in honest give-and-take transactions—i.e., they give and take reciprocally; they don't exploit, and they are not exploited. But the lowest of all these classes is those who exploit others.

Note that this sūtra follows the previous one where the rules and regulations of the body, such as regulated eating, sleeping, sex, cleanliness, etc. were prescribed. So, the implication is that there are people who follow all such bodily regulations—they lead a healthy lifestyle, refrain from intoxicants, regulate their sex-life, etc.—and yet their goal is only to keep a body and mind healthy enough to exploit others. Prime examples of such a class of people is present-day high-ranking members of society who use their wealth and power to extract more than they are giving back. They may come across as very clean, family-oriented, healthy, well-educated, and articulate people. And yet, their exploitative and deceitful activities disqualify them from any spiritual attainments.

QUESTION

There are many altruistic people who perform many kinds of charities. They are giving back more than they are taking from others. So, we can say that they are not exploitative, because they are performing more than their fair share of reciprocal duties. Are they qualified for the pursuit of transcendence?

2.3.50 (266)

आभास एव च

ābhāsa eva ca

ābhāsaḥ—an appearance or pretense; eva—only; ca—also.

TRANSLATION

(The performance of charities creates) the appearance or pretense (of religiosity) only; (such people are) also (disqualified from transcendence).

COMMENTARY

In former times, kings used to perform a great yajñá worshiping the demigods, and after the yajñá was complete, they would give away a lot of their wealth in charity. Such charities are meant to earn good karma, and the performance of yajñá elevates the person to heavenly planets. Therefore, they are materially good for the performer, but they are not considered spiritual activities for the simple reason that even if you perform some charity, you cannot give to anyone more than what they will otherwise get due to their own karma. The person receiving the wealth in charity is destined for this wealth due to his past pious activities, just like one might inherit wealth from their parents due to a good birth without having to work for it. The person who performs charity gains good karma but the person receiving it was entitled for it anyway. In modern times, for example, many people are either unqualified, uneducated, disabled, or simply unfortunate to not get a job. The government provides them with food and minimal shelter and medical care, which constitutes charity. But we should not suppose that these people receiving the charities are receiving something *ex gratia*. They are entitled by their karma to live a certain level of life, which means that they don't get the pleasure of working, earning, and being able to decide how they want to spend the earning; they are limited to a bare essential survival, because nature has ensured this fate for them.

When religion is mixed with such pious activities—such as by giving away free food, opening schools and colleges, or running low-cost medical facilities for the poor and incapable—an illusion or appearance of religiosity is created in which the main purpose of transcendence is forgotten and temporary purposes of serving the body, saving the environment, or helping people in their day-to-day materialistic lives passes off in the name of religiosity. Many people are greatly impressed by such activities because we have become so accustomed to exploitation that we equate any generosity and piety to transcendence. Of course, charity is better than exploitation for the person who indulges in such activities. However, from the perspective of the receiver, both outcomes are decided by their karma. Thus, whether you are being exploited by others or receiving charity from them, your actions are key determinants of these outcomes. The person who is performing such charity is pious, but not a transcendentalist. His piety is called a pretense or appearance of religion here.

QUESTION

There are many people situated in the renounced order of life. They follow all the rules and regulations of the body, they believe in the existence of demigods and the law of moral consequences, they don't exploit others and they stay away from unnecessary social and political engagements knowing that transcendence lies beyond this body. Does the renunciation of the material world by such people enough qualification for attaining transcendence?

2.3.51 (267)

अदृष्टानियमात्

adṛṣṭāniyamāt

adṛṣṭa-aniyamāt—cannot see that there are no rules or restrictions.

TRANSLATION

(The renunciates) cannot see that there are no rules or restrictions (for the practice of transcendence); (renunciation alone doesn't lead to transcendence).

COMMENTARY

In India, and in other cultures, there are traditions in which people become monks at an early age, renouncing mundane pleasures, detaching themselves from society, strictly following the rules and regulations of the body, and not indulging in any kind of exploitative or reciprocal business activities. This renunciation is good because it frees up time and energy for spiritual practices. But many of these renunciates don't perform any spiritual practices, such as chanting mantra or meditating on the Lord. They only believe in performing extreme forms of austerity, standing under the sun or rain, tolerating hot and cold, eating whatever nature provides, and torturing the body in various ways. But this renunciation doesn't achieve much because the accumulated pile of good karma is postponed, and the accumulated pile of bad karma is reaped by self-torture. Ultimately, the person is not liberated because even though the bad karma may be reduced or destroyed, good karma remains, and the person will be forced to take birth to enjoy this good karma. Thus, penance without a spiritual practice is merely the torture of the body and not transcendence.

In this sūtra, it is also noted that such people don't realize that transcendence is not restricted to renunciation; even those who are engaged in karma-yoga, or chanting the mantras from śrutī, or doing their Varṇāśrama duties, or worshiping the Lord asking for liberation, are better placed in the path of transcendence rather than those who are simply torturing the body. While rules and regulations of the body are necessary, this sūtra states that they are insufficient. One cannot be freed from the bondage of life and death by austerities, although one's sinful karma can be destroyed by such austerities. Formerly, austerities were prescribed for the destruction of bad karma, but the good karma is destroyed only when one develops a spiritual understanding of the self.

The soul is ānandamaya or having a natural inclination toward pleasure. So, how can austerity—which is contrary to pleasure—be considered a natural state? It can at best be a temporary provision for destroying sinful reactions. One cannot perform austerities forever because of the ānandamaya nature of the soul. So, unless the soul becomes situated in transcendental pleasure—either of the self or of the Lord—austerities will eventually end and the soul will fall back to material enjoyment, repeating the cycle of birth and death.

QUESTION

The Brahmins perform sandhyā-vandana three times a day. They say that

by this process the body and the mind are purified, and by the chanting of Gāyatri during this process, one can attain spiritual realization. Is this true?

2.3.52 (268)

अभसिन्ध्यादष्विपर्चैवम्

abhisandhyādiṣvapi caivam

abhisandhyādiṣu—in those regularly following Sandhya etc.; api—even; ca—and; evam—like this.

TRANSLATION

(The Brahman cannot be attained) even in those who are thus following the regular practice of Sandhya (the chanting of Gayatri three times a day).

COMMENTARY

The term Sandhya refers to three times in a day—sunrise, sunset, and mid-noon. These times have been used for chanting the Gayatri, which worships the sun. Just like the soul emanates from the body of the Lord as light, similarly, the energy of the sun is considered a material counterpart of the Lord from whose body the light illuminates the universe. Analogically, the sun is called Sūrya Nārāyana, because the soul emerges from the body of Lord Nārāyana at the time of creation and goes back into His body at the time of annihilation. However, the sun's worship is not considered transcendental because the words *bhu*, *bhuvar*, and *svarga* in the Gayatri refer to the three planetary systems in which the sun's light is manifest. The light of the sun doesn't reach the four upper planetary systems, nor does it reach the seven lower planetary systems, or the 28 hellish planets. Therefore, the Gayatri mantra is ineffective in all these places. The purpose of the Gayatri is to understand that our bodies and minds are sustained by the sun's light, and the connection between our body and the sun is established through prāṇa. The chanting of Gayatri can help a person maintain a strong body and mind, because the sun is the signifier of physical and mental health (the senses, the mind, and the intellect).

Therefore, even though the Brahmana chanted the Gayatri three times a day, the chanting did not define the qualification to be a Brahmana. The real definition of a Brahmana is one who is learned about the nature of Brahman—*brahma jānāti iti brahmana*. Just like humans may brush their teeth but brushing the teeth doesn't define our humanity; it is prevalent, but neither necessary nor sufficient. Similarly, Sandhya has been popular among the Brahmanas, although this practice does not define the essence of being a Brahmana. With the passing of time, such rituals have remained and become the defining characteristics of Brahmana. Thus, we can find many people today who wear the sacred thread, and chant the Gayatri three times a day, and yet have no understanding of Brahman. Thus, it is sometimes said that in the kali-yuga simply wearing a thread would identify someone as Brahmana. This sūtra rejects the practice of Sandhya as the sole qualification for the attainment of transcendence.

QUESTION

Many people believe that transcendence can be achieved simply by living in holy places, and if one dies in a holy place, one is automatically elevated to the spiritual world. This seems quite an easy way to attain transcendence.

2.3.53 (269)

प्रदेशादितिचेत् न अन्तर्भावात्

pradeśāditi cet na antarbhāvāt

pradeśāt—due to place; iti cet—if it be said; na—not so; antarbhāvāt—from the internal state.

TRANSLATION

If it is said that (one can attain transcendence simply) due to the place (of birth, death, or living) (we say) not so; it is based on the internal state.

COMMENTARY

All places in Vedic philosophy are not the same. Space is structured like a tree, which means that locations in this space are higher and lower. The higher places affect a greater number of aspects of our lives, and the lower places affect fewer aspects of our life. The spiritual world is the highest place, and a minor discrepancy in the spiritual world immediately leads to a fall. Within the material world too, there are higher and lower places, and good deeds in the higher places produce greater benefit, just as the sinful activities in these places produce greater suffering. Hence, it is said that we must perform good deeds in holy places, as any sinful deeds in those holy places produce greater sin.

Thus, there was a tradition to discuss spiritual topics in holy places to amplify the understanding. Many sacrifices were also performed in the holy places because they produce greater benefits. However, the holy places are not the only determinant of a person's spiritual standing. If that were so, then an advanced devotee of the Lord could not exist in the material world, because the material world is considered a fallen place. The ultimate determinant is a person's internal state, and the Lord's devotion can therefore exist everywhere.

However, as time passes, and the spiritual understanding declines, people start associating the place itself with holiness, rather than understanding that the place facilitates the results, but is not the sole cause of the results. Every religion identifies some holy places, and people visit these places frequently. This sūtra rejects the conception that birth, death, or living in a holy place is enough for transcendence. Even if the actions in a holy place produce greater benefits, ultimately it is the internal transformation that counts, not the place. The same transformation could also be attained in other places, although a person may have to endeavor harder for similar results. The holy places make spiritual transformation easier, but they are not substitutes for our efforts.

SECTION 4

Topic 1

QUESTION

You have earlier (in sūtra 1.3.4 (67)) rejected the use of prāṇa for attaining the Lord and said that this is only possible through devotion. Does this hold true for attaining the Brahman stage? Many yogis believe that they can attain Brahman by the practice of prāṇa control; since the soul is transported from one body to another by the influence of prāṇa, it is said that the prāṇa can also liberate the soul into Brahman. What is the conclusion on this understanding?

2.4.1 (270)

तथा प्राणाः

tathā prāṇāḥ

tathā—in the same way; prāṇāḥ—the five vital airs in the body.

TRANSLATION

In the same way (transcendence cannot be attained just by) prāṇa.

COMMENTARY

We have earlier distinguished between three types of prāṇa. The first type of prāṇa works under the control of guna and karma, which are in turn under the control of time; due to this prāṇa, we breathe without conscious effort, the blood circulates without our knowledge, the immune response works without our intervention, etc. Likewise, diseases appear without our inviting them. The second type of prāṇa works under the control of the soul, due to which the soul can reject the automatically created desires produced out of guna (under the influence of time), and the soul obtains mastery over the body and the mind. This prāṇa is responsible for the effects of free will translating into the body and the mind because by exercising this prāṇa we can control the body and the mind. The third type of prāṇa connects the soul to the Lord, due to which Brahman has been called prāṇa earlier. The attainment of Brahman requires the rejuvenation of this connection to the Supreme Lord, and it is activated only when the soul establishes its relation to the Lord, which is also called sambandha. Once this relation is established, typically, the soul also serves the

Lord, which is called abhidheya, leading to pleasure which is called prayojana. However, it is possible that after the soul has established a relation, the service and the concomitant pleasure are absent. This occurs when the relation is *śānta* or one of silent appreciation. The service to the Lord begins with the *dasya* (the relation of a master and servant). It progresses with *sakhya* (the relation of friendship), *vātsalya* (the parent-child relation), and *mādhurya* (amorous relation). In the *śānta* relation, the soul understands that God is great, and the soul is small. In this silent appreciation, the soul appreciates the Lord from a distance, just like we might admire a person in our heart, but not express that admiration through words of glorification, or actively participate in serving the person we admire.

The term prāṇa here refers to the material energy by which the soul controls his desires, and the yogis aspire for this control to obtain mastery over the mind and the body by the control of prāṇa (which is also called prāṇayāma). By controlling our breath, we can control our thoughts, and relax the body.

In the aśtānga-yoga system, prāṇayāma is the 4th step toward self-realization. Following this, the yogi practices *dhyāna* (establishing a relation to the Lord), *dhāraṇā* (full cognition of the Lord), and *samādhi* (being absorbed in the pleasure attained from the cognition of the Lord). These last three steps involve the use of the spiritual prāṇa that connects the soul to the Supreme Soul, and it is triggered only when the soul develops devotion toward the Lord, although the devotion is only developed only till the point of silent appreciation. The mere control of the material prāṇa thus doesn't lead even to Brahman.

QUESTION

But you have earlier said that the soul is bound to material nature due to guna and karma. If the guna are dissolved, then the karma will also be eventually dissolved, and the soul can get liberated from material existence. Since the soul has the capacity for controlling the desires emerging from guna, and it can reject these desires, can't the soul get liberated by controlling its desires?

2.4.2 (271)

गौण्यसंभवात्

gauṇyasaṃbhavāt

gauṇi—covered by the guna; asaṃbhavāt—from being impossible.

TRANSLATION

(Becoming free of guna) from being impossible for one covered by guna.

COMMENTARY

Suppressing our desires doesn't mean freedom from desires. The material prāṇa operates under the control of guna and karma, while the soul's prāṇa operates under the soul's control. By this control, the soul can suppress one's desires, but that suppression doesn't mean freedom from material desires.

Material guna represent our habits, desires, and proclivities. To be free of the guna means to change the purpose of our life, which requires a new purpose. Simply the rejection of the material purpose is insufficient, and the soul being extremely small, cannot make himself the purpose of its existence. Thus, the real method for liberation is to make the Lord the purpose of our existence. If this purpose doesn't appear, then no matter how much we try to reject the material purposes—in relation to this world—we cannot completely reject these purposes. This fact is seen in many meditators who don't become devotees of the Lord, and after long periods of meditation, they come back to material purposes—e.g., opening hospitals, schools, engaging in politics, etc. One such example of returning to material purpose is described in the life of Sage Viśvāmitra who became envious of Sage Vasiṣṭha (who was a devotee of Lord Rāma), and performed severe austerities for thousands of years, but could not free himself from sex desire, the hunger for power and superiority, etc.

Many people falsely presume that liberation is being free of all desires. However, to become free, you must have the desire to be free of desires, which is also a material desire. "I don't want this" is not a spiritual desire, because the mere reference to what we don't want can exist only if that thing exists. If we keep thinking about what we don't want, we keep that thing alive in our minds. The spiritual desire begins by wanting the self and becoming self-absorbed. By self-absorption, the world is automatically forgotten. But one cannot remain self-absorbed because the soul is the potential for relation, cognition, and emotion, but in self-absorption, these are not fulfilled. How can we be satisfied with seeing the unfulfilled potential? Can a musician be happy thinking that he can play music, without ever playing music? This is the cause of the soul's fall.

Thus, desires can never be completely overcome. They can be suppressed in the material world, and they can remain in a potential state in the soul. But ultimately, the suppression and elimination of desire fail. Freedom from material desire is not the rejection of all desire; it is the desiring of the Lord. Thus, anyone who wants to be freed from guna need only desire the Lord.

QUESTION

Can the material entanglement not be ended by knowledge? The practitioners of jñāna-yoga claim that liberation is obtained through knowledge.

2.4.3 (272)

प्रतज्ञिानुपरोधाच्च

pratijñānuparodhaccha

pratijñāna—toward knowledge; uparodha—interruption; ca—also.

TRANSLATION

As one progresses toward the knowledge (of the Supreme Absolute Truth), the material nature (of a person) is also interrupted (by knowledge).

COMMENTARY

This sūtra indicates that knowledge is helpful but is not the ultimate answer to the cycle of birth and death. As one acquires transcendental knowledge, one's material activities begin to cease, but they don't fully come to an end until devotion for the Lord is established in the heart. Regular hearing of the scriptures, for instance, destroys most of the material desires, but doesn't end them completely. This end is achieved only when the Lord is perceived. Therefore, liberation too is attained only through devotion, although spiritual knowledge can certainly arrest and interrupt the progression of material entanglement. With spiritual knowledge, a person realizes the value of human life, and starts endeavoring toward transcendence. But material attachments are not easily destroyed. No amount of knowledge can change a person's heart. Only when a superior kind of happiness is experienced are material desires destroyed.

QUESTION

But finding the Lord in the heart as Paramātma—as you have recommended earlier—is also not easy. Isn't there a way that a person can enter meditation while practicing prāṇa without seeking the Paramātma in the heart?

2.4.4 (273)

तत्प्राक्श्रुतेश्च

tatprākśruteśca

tat—that; prāk—first; śruteḥ—hearing; ca—also.

TRANSLATION

To do that (i.e., achieve transcendence without meditating on Paramātma), one must first hear (the names of the Lord) as well (as prāṇa control).

COMMENTARY

In the Śrīmad Bhāgavatam, a process that combines the yogic practices along with the chanting of mantras is described in the narration about Maharaja Dhruva, who was given this process by Sage Nārada. Dhruva stood on a single leg, controlled his breath, and began pratyahāra or reducing in eating; gradually he stopped eating, drinking, and even breathing; such was his mastery of the prāṇa that the breathing of the other living entities in the universe was curtailed because Maharaja Dhruva had controlled his breath. However, this wasn't the only practice he was following; he also continuously chanted the mantra *om namo bhagavate vāsudevāya.* With this meditation, the Lord automatically appeared in his heart, and he was able to meditate upon Him.

This sūtra refers to the mastery of prāṇa along with the hearing the sound of the mantras, thus meditating on the sound, by which the Lord automatically is revealed in the heart, a process previously prescribed by Sage Nārada.

QUESTION

The meditation on the Lord in the heart is performed silently. Should these mantras also be chanted silently in the mind along with breath control?

2.4.5 (274)

तत्पूर्वकत्वाद्वाचः

tatpūrvakatvādvācaḥ

vācaḥ—the speech; tatpūrvakatvāt—from being prior (to the hearing).

TRANSLATION

The speech (vocal utterance) from being prior (to the hearing).

COMMENTARY

The mind is the sense that perceives meanings of the words, just as the senses of hearing and speaking utter those words. When the meaning of the mantra is firmly established in the mind, then vocal utterances are not necessary. But for the beginner, vocal utterances are essential because only by meditating on the sound is one's mind purified to even understand the meaning. This sūtra recommends audible chanting of the mantra followed by the hearing (which was prescribed in the previous sūtra) along with breath control.

Topic 2

QUESTION

What is the role of prāṇa in chanting and hearing? How is the process of prāṇa control noted earlier related to the process of chanting and hearing?

2.4.6 (275)

सप्त गतेर्विशेषतित्वाच्च

sapta gaterviśeṣitatvācca

sapta—seven; gateḥ—centers, places of refuge; viśeṣitatva—the agency of instantiation or individuation; ucca—is called or described as.

TRANSLATION

(The prāṇa is) the agency of instantiation or individuation; it is described or said to have seven centers or places of refuge (called the chakra).

COMMENTARY

The prāṇa is the agency that divides the whole into parts and connects the parts to the whole. If the whole is the mammal, and the part is the cow, then the following three facts hold true about the division of the mammal into the cow: (1) the cow is an *instance* of mammal, (2) the cow is a *part* of mammal, and

(3) cow is a *detail* about mammals. These three properties of being an instance, a part, and a detail are ascribed by the term *viśeṣitatva*, which stands for 'more specific', 'more detailed', or 'individual'. The process of converting the abstract into contingent is said to proceed through seven levels, in which the whole—at the topmost level—is successively divided into parts through seven stages. These seven stages are noted in both Sāñkhya and Yoga philosophies.

In Sāñkhya, the stages are called objects, sensations, senses, mind, intellect, ego, and moral sense. In Yoga philosophy, these seven stages are identified with centers of prāṇa organized hierarchically and identified as chakras called Mulādhāra, Svādhiśthāna, Manipura, Anahata, Viśuddha, Ajna, and Sahasrāra. The spiritual aspirant is expected to raise themselves through these levels. One begins by the objects, or the uttering of the sound. Then one progresses into the sensation which is hearing. Over time, the senses are purified, and one develops an attachment to hearing. After this attachment, one realizes that the name of the Lord refers to the Lord; this realization occurs in the mind. Then by the intellect one realizes that the Lord is the Absolute Truth. By the ego, subsequently, the soul develops devotion to the Lord. And by the moral sense, one becomes a servant of the Lord. Once this servitude is attained, the cognition of the Lord and the pleasure of the Lord attained by that cognition are spiritual.

The ascent of the prāṇa under the control of the soul can take one to the point of establishing a relationship to the Lord. However, the soul doesn't have the power to see the Lord by this prāṇa. This seeing or revelation is due to the prāṇa controlled by the Lord, and He appears when He so desires. Thus, we can be situated in the relationship to the Lord, but we cannot force the Lord to appear. There is hence value in our effort—to bring us to the point of a relationship to the Lord. But after this, the Lord is only seen through His grace.

By practicing the control of prāṇa, the process of sensual, mental, intellectual, emotional, and moral purification can be accelerated, because there is a parallel between the ascent of prāṇa and the purification of the senses, mind, intellect, ego, and the moral sense. This doesn't mean that the Lord is controlled by our prāṇa, and that we 'attain' spiritual realization by our efforts. We have the power to establish a relationship to the Lord and to serve Him. But ultimately, the Lord will appear only when He sees devotion and love in us.

QUESTION

The prāṇa you are talking about is present all over the body, such as in hands and legs as well. Then what is so special about the chanting of mantras relative to this breath control? Can't the same breath control be practiced along with the activities of the other senses, such as those of the hands and legs?

2.4.7 (276)

हस्तादयस्तु स्थितेऽतो नैवम्

hastādayastu sthite'to naivam

hastādayaḥ—hands etc.; tu—but; sthite—being situated; ataḥ—therefore; na—not; evam—like this;

TRANSLATION

(The prāṇa is) but situated in the hands etc. and therefore this process is not (highly recommended, or not a suitable method of advancement).

COMMENTARY

The Lord can be served by all the senses of the body, not just the tongue and ears. The serving by hands or legs is neither superior nor inferior to the service by the tongue; ultimately, the quality of the service depends on how deep the realization of the person is—i.e., whether it just permeates the gross body, or even the senses, the mind, the intellect, the ego, and so on. When a yogi performs prāṇayāma, the body remains static, and only the ear and the tongue are involved in serving the Lord. To make progress in this path, one would have to remain situated in this state for long periods of time. In contrast, one who can serve the Lord through all the senses—e.g., the hands, legs, etc.—doesn't need to make these senses still and idle. He can keep serving the Lord through the entire body, and while it seems that the person's prāṇa is not being controlled, the fact is that the person is constantly being purified through this service. Therefore, if one insists on using prāṇa control, the previous sūtra recommended that one also chant the names of the Lord while doing such meditation. But since we know that prāṇa is not just activating the senses of hearing and chanting, but every other sense and the main cause of spiritual progress is the sound rather than the prāṇa itself, therefore, engaging the entire body into the Lord's service is a preferred method rather than the control of prāṇa itself.

Topic 3

QUESTION

If prāṇa is the agency for individuation, and these individuals become atoms, then shouldn't the cause of individuation be also considered atomic?

2.4.8 (277)

अणवश्च

aṇavaśca

aṇavaḥ—atomic; ca—also.

TRANSLATION

(The prāṇa is) is also atomic.

COMMENTARY

We have discussed how experience is created by the combination of three factors— ability, opportunity, and desire—through the power of prāṇa. In the previous sūtra, prāṇa was described as the agency that divides and expands the abstract ideas into contingent ideas. This division produces the three types of possibilities—abilities, opportunities, and desires—like the trunks, branches, and leaves expanding from a root. These expanded spaces constitute the 'unmanifest' world—i.e., something that is yet not experienced. Experience is then created by a *choice* that combines an ability, an opportunity, and a desire.

The 'atomism' of prāṇa is the indivisibility of choice. The spaces of ability, opportunity, and desire exist as atoms, and the choice that combines these atoms is also atomic, although it produces an experience. The choices occur in sequence; therefore, the atoms of choice are temporal: they are created and destroyed. While they exist, the experience is also sustained. Thus, we distinguish between the atoms of space (desire, possibility, and opportunity) and time (choices). Due to these atoms, experience has a spatiotemporal division.

The atoms of time—the smallest durations of experience—define the units of time. The smallest unit is called Truti, and it is approximately 1/3 microsecond. Thus, every second of experience involves millions of choices, and hence millions of atoms of prāṇa. This makes us think that the experience is continuous, rather than discrete. When a yogi slows the prāṇa, then time also slows, because a fewer number of choices are made. Thus, the mind, the senses, and the intellect remain still and steady, rather than fleeting and changing. By the control of prāṇa, the yogis can elongate their lifespan, and the underlying science for that longer life is that what we call 'time' is produced by choices, which are atomic. If we can slow down the succession of atoms, then we can slow down time. In this state, we can observe individual atoms of experience and how they are created from possibilities by the application of choice.

Topic 4

QUESTION

You have earlier said that the prāṇa transports the soul from one body to another, implying that the soul is being controlled by prāṇa. In the above sūtra, you are saying that the successive states of experience are choices, which I take to mean are being produced by the soul. So, in one case you are saying that the prāṇa is forcing the soul to move, and in another case, you are suggesting that the prāṇa is being controlled by the soul. Which of these is the case?

2.4.9 (278)

श्रेष्ठश्च

śreṣṭhaśca

śreṣṭhaḥ—being superior; ca—as well.

TRANSLATION

(The prāṇa can) also be the controller (just like the soul can be controller).

COMMENTARY

We have discussed how the three kinds of prāṇa work: (1) the material prāṇa is controlled by guna and karma, (2) the soul's prāṇa is controlled by the soul, and the Lord's prāṇa is controlled by the Lord. Due to the first prāṇa, the soul is dragged by prāṇa. Due to the second prāṇa, the soul controls the body and mind and can form a relationship to the Lord and perform loving service to Him. And due to the third prāṇa, the Lord controls even the soul. Hence, the soul can be controlled by matter, and the soul can control matter. Similarly, the Lord can be controlled by the soul, and the soul can control the Lord. These are not contradictory claims once the nature of prāṇa is completely understood.

Topic 5

QUESTION

So your main point seems to be that because devotion to the Lord is the development of desire, and this desire is ultimately in the control of the soul, rather than the control of prāṇa (or its antecedents like karma and Causal Time), therefore, prāṇa cannot be considered the cause of the soul's liberation?

2.4.10 (279)

न वायुक्रिये पृथगुपदेशात्

na vāyukriye pṛthagupadeśāt

na vāyukriye—not the action of the air; pṛthak—separately; upadeśāt—on account of its being mentioned.

TRANSLATION

(Devotion to the Lord) is not the (result of the) action of the prāṇa; it is always taught to be separate (and transcendental to the material elements).

COMMENTARY

After delving into details about the nature of prāṇa and explaining how prāṇa control helps to control the mind and the body, this sūtra states that the prāṇa is not the cause of devotion in the soul. Prāṇa can be used to control the mind and the body, and to the extent that the mind and the body impose needs and desires upon the soul, the control of prāṇa is useful in concentrating the mind and controlling the body. Prāṇa control is therefore not completely useless as it can be employed in meditation of the Lord by suppressing bodily and mental urges. But, once these urges have been suppressed, the prāṇa cannot lead to the development of devotion toward the Lord. Without that devotion, there is no happiness, and after some time, the need for enjoyment will give way to the urges of the body and the mind, and the effect of prāṇa control will be lost. Thus, prāṇa control is a useful method for stopping the noise generated by the body and the mind so that the soul can meditate on the Lord. But in this role of control, we cannot say that prāṇa is the cause of the devotion to the Lord.

QUESTION

Does that mean that when the devotion is developed, then the control of the body and the mind (through the agency of prāṇa) becomes unnecessary?

2.4.11 (280)

चक्षुरादिवत्तु तत्सहशिष्ट्यादिभ्यः

cakṣurādivattu tatsahaśiṣṭyādibhyaḥ

cakṣurādivat—like eyes etc.; tu—but; tat-saha-śiṣṭyādibhyaḥ—being controlled or disciplined along with that (the prāṇa that controls the senses).

TRANSLATION

(The senses) such as the eyes etc. are but disciplined along with that (the prāṇa, which is controlled by the development of the devotion to the Lord).

COMMENTARY

In the previous sūtra, it was said that the devotion to the Lord is not caused by prāṇa, although prāṇa can help control the body and the mind. This sūtra now goes a step further and states that if devotion to the Lord is developed, then the prāṇa is automatically controlled by that devotion. In short, the control of prāṇa is inadequate in producing devotion, and it is unnecessary after devotion is developed. It may be useful in mind-body control when devotion hasn't yet been developed, for the practice of developing such devotion. The term *tat-śiṣṭya* means the 'disciplining of that', which ultimately indicates the control of the prāṇa that then controls the senses and the mind. Thus, a cascading hierarchy of control—from the devotion to the Lord to the control of the prāṇa to the control of the mind, to the control of the senses—is indicated here. When devotion to the Lord develops, the mind is filled with emotions about the Lord, and the pleasure of the mind and the senses in relation to the world becomes insignificant. The pursuit of higher desires makes lower pursuits insignificant.

QUESTION

It was earlier said that the soul is connected to the Lord through prāṇa, and just as we control the parts of our body through prāṇa, similarly, the Lord can control the soul through the (spiritual) prāṇa. In short, this (spiritual) prāṇa was the instrument of control of the soul. But now you are saying that the devotion to the Lord is an innate property of the soul, and it cannot be forced by the prāṇa, so does this imply that the Lord doesn't force devotion on the soul?

2.4.12 (281)

अकरणत्वाच्च न दोषःतथाहि दर्शयति

akaraṇatvācca na doṣaḥ tathāhi darśayati

akaraṇatvāt—due to not being an instrument; ca—and; na—not; doṣaḥ—faults or discrepancies; tathā hi—because thus; darśayati—He is seen.

TRANSLATION

(Upon the development of devotion, the prāṇa) ceases to be the instrument of control (of the Lord), and this is not considered a fault or discrepancy because only through such (unforced devotion of the soul) is He (the Lord) seen.

COMMENTARY

The spiritual prāṇa is like a rope that binds the soul and the Lord. The Lord can use this rope to pull the soul towards Himself, but He doesn't do that, unless the soul pulls first. This is the nature of the Lord and His Śakti—the Śakti must pull the Lord first, and the Lord will then pull the Śakti. In the material world, the soul is controlled by karma, which is ultimately in the control of the Lord. But once the soul is free from karma, the Lord doesn't exert control over the soul. The soul is free to be devoted to the Lord or be a passive/silent observer of the world or remain self-absorbed. In that sense, the prāṇa ceases to be a *karana* or instrument of the Lord. And yet, this freedom of the soul to pursue its own goals is not considered a fault—e.g., that the Lord is no longer in control of the soul. In fact, the contrary is now stated, namely, that the soul can control the Lord by this prāṇa if he so desires. A symptom of that control is that the Lord now appears before the devotee, compelled by the devotee's love.

In this regard, we must note that all vision (even material vision) is caused through an interaction between two objects. As we discussed before, our senses have desires, and the material objects have purposes to be used for the senses. When the senses interact with the objects, the desire in the senses is created and the purpose in the objects is activated. This activation then results in a stronger interaction, which makes the desire and purpose even stronger. Thus, through an iterative process, the senses and their objects come 'close' to each other: this proximity is not physical; it is caused by their mutual interaction. The stronger the interaction, the greater is the perceived proximity. (This is the inverse of the modern scientific idea that greater proximity results in a stronger interaction). Similarly, when the devotion in the soul arises, the strength of that desire forces an interaction by which the Lord becomes visible to the soul—i.e., proximate. Proximity is therefore an *effect* of the interaction, not a *cause*. That is, the Lord doesn't come close to us before we see Him. We rather desire the Lord very strongly, and the desire results in an interaction by which proximity grows, and ultimately, we see the Lord. If we understand the process of material vision, then we can also understand the process of spiritual vision because both processes are caused by an interaction resulting in a proximity and when there is proximity, we get clarity of vision and we think we are 'seeing' the object.

Practicing devotees sometimes ask: Why can't the Lord come closer to me, become visible to me, or show signs of His existence to me, so that I can firm my faith in the Lord's existence? We must note that such kind of accidental appearance before us is caused by karma—e.g., due to good karma we can meet things, to which we get attracted and the karma then fulfills the desire. The Lord is, however, not controlled by karma. It is the strength of desire in us that evokes a desire in the Lord, and these two desires gradually become stronger due to mutual interaction. They then bring the soul and the Lord face to face.

QUESTION

If the Lord can be controlled by the spiritual prāṇa, does it mean that the spiritual prāṇa is also like material prāṇa, which controls material objects?

2.4.13 (282)

पञ्चवृत्तिर्मनोवद्व्यपदिश्यते

pañcavṛttirmanovadvyapadiśyate

pañcavṛttiḥ—having five natures; manovat—just like the mind (has five natures); vyapadiśyate—it pervades in all directions, or it is thus asserted.

TRANSLATION

(The material and spiritual prāṇa) have a five-fold nature, just like the mind (has a five-fold nature); by this nature, the prāṇa exists everywhere (i.e., wherever the consciousness of the soul or the Lord is directed by desire).

COMMENTARY

This sūtra gives further insights into the process by which an interaction occurs, and how things become visible (as was noted in the previous sūtra). This insight comes from the five-fold nature of the mind, which is said to proceed through five stages called thinking, feeling, willing, knowing, and acting. The thinking stage of the mind involves a cognitive understanding of an object, which we can call the picture of the object. It comes to us suddenly due to recollection, just as waves arise automatically in the ocean. When a memory suddenly arises, we either like it or dislike it. This like or dislike constitutes the feeling stage. If we dislike the idea, the picture is pushed out of our recollection. If, however, we like the idea, then the liking is subjected to a judgment—e.g., is the thing that we are desiring also true, right, and good? For instance, we might develop a craving for sugar, but we have been forbidden from eating sugar, then the judgment of true, right, and good will stop the desire immediately. If the judgment agrees to proceed further (or is overwhelmed by the desire), the mind proceeds into the willing stage—I have decided to get this object. To obtain the object, one must know how to obtain it; this is called the knowing stage which involves procedural knowledge of how to get the things we want. Finally, we must apply this knowledge and act upon it—which is called the acting stage—that converts procedural knowledge into actions. The result of these actions is that one comes closer to the destination. As one comes closer, another cycle of thinking, feeling, willing, knowing, and acting occurs. That is, at every step, we evaluate if we still want this object, if we will like to have it, if it is worth the effort we are putting in, if we should change the method of getting it, and if alternative methods will get us to the destination easier and faster.

The working of the prāṇa is compared in this sūtra to the cyclic process of thinking, feeling, willing, knowing, and acting. As we can see, each step of the process involves a decision or a choice. As we come closer to the results we are working toward, the thoughts of the object to be attained automatically arise in the mind, which then strengthen the desire, which then strengthen our resolve to pursue the goal, which clarify the process by which we can move further, and the clarity and resolve drive us to endeavor harder as we get closer. In short, the prāṇa is described as a reflection of the working of the mind.

In many places, the five-fold nature of the prāṇa is also called *prāṇa, samāna, apāna, vyāna* and *udāna*, which represent ingestion, digestion, excretion, assimilation, and production. This five-fold process can be applied to the mind in analogy to the body—e.g., the mind ingests ideas, breaks them down into simpler ideas that are already understood, which can be called 'digestion', excretes or rejects some ideas that don't fit our current understanding, then assimilates the accepted ideas with the rest of our conceptual worldview, and finally uses the newly acquired knowledge to produce new things.

The prāṇa is an intermediate level of reality between the mind and the body. Thus, the understanding of prāṇa can be modeled after the actions of the body—e.g., ingestion, digestion, assimilation, excretion, and production. Or, it can be modeled after the actions of the mind—e.g., thinking, feeling, willing, knowing, and acting. In this sūtra, the comparison is made to the working of the mind, rather than to the working of the body. Therefore, this sūtra should not be viewed as referring to *prāṇa, samana, apana, vyana* and *udana*, even though in most other contexts, a five-fold division will entail these five.

Topic 6

QUESTION

You have previously called the prāṇa as being atomic and described it as comprising choices. You are now stating that choices can further be divided into five parts—thinking, feeling, willing, knowing, and acting. Doesn't this entail that the atomism should be understood as five types of choices?

2.4.14 (283)

अणुश्च

aṇuśca

aṇuḥ—atomic; ca—as well.

TRANSLATION

(The five-fold division of the prāṇa and the mind, as noted in the previous sūtra, can be applied to) atomism as well.

COMMENTARY

Many people think that the existence of choice will not alter the understanding of matter; at best, the choices will select material possibilities. In this sūtra, this idea is challenged by suggesting that when an atom is a choice, and there are many kinds of choices, then there are many kinds of atoms. Atomism simply means indivisibility, which is characterized by a choice—a choice is a unit that can break into parts, but you don't necessarily break it apart. If your choices divide the things into smaller parts, then atomism can refer to the smallest division that can be performed by choice. But, if you don't use the choices to divide, then atomism can also represent the individual choice, which need not be picking something small. For instance, we can choose the Absolute Truth, and that 'atom' of choice will include everything that exists. There is hence a difference between the ideas that atoms are indivisible and the idea that the atoms are small things. In this case, the indivisible is not necessarily small. The Absolute Truth is therefore an 'atom' in the sense that it cannot be reduced to smaller things. And yet, many smaller things are part of that Absolute Truth. This type of atomism is understood only using concepts such as cow and mammal. The concept mammal cannot be reduced to its members—cows, dogs, cats, horses, etc. And yet, cows, dogs, horses, cats, etc. are part of mammal.

Since thinking, feeling, willing, knowing and acting all involve choices, therefore, the atomism can also be construed in multiple ways. The atom of thought, or an idea, is different from the atom of feeling or emotion. Similarly, the acquisition of a relation to a goal is different from the idea (after all we can have an idea, and not decide to make it a goal), or the feeling (after all, we can like or dislike something but not make it the mission of some pursuit). Procedural knowledge is also an atom, although different from descriptive knowledge. And actions that put these procedures into actions are also atoms. When we begin with a physical world, then atoms are the smallest things that exist. If instead we begin with the postulate that everything can be experienced, then the different categories of experience constitute different kinds of atoms.

Topic 7

QUESTION

If we classify the atoms according to our mental states, then don't we have the problem about the interaction of the mind with an objective world? Would it not entail that we can obtain anything in the world simply by our will?

2.4.15 (284)

ज्योतिराद्यधिष्ठानं तु तदामननात्

jyotirādyadhiṣṭhānaṃ tu tadāmananāt

jyotirādi-adhiṣṭhānaṃ—presiding over luminaries etc.; tu—but;

tat-āmananāt—on account of not thinking or understanding about that.

TRANSLATION

(The association of mental states to atomism doesn't create problem because) the demigods are presiding over the material elements and the luminaries, although we don't necessarily see them or understand their role (and that their mental states are involved in giving us the results of our actions).

COMMENTARY

Our experiences are the combination of ability, opportunity, and desire. To eat tasty food, I must desire tasty food, I must have the opportunity to get tasty food, and I should have the ability to eat. The mental states in the last sūtra referred to the combination of ability and desire, and this sūtra states that mental states are fulfilled by the presiding deities of elements who deliver karma. In Sāñkhya philosophy, there are 24 primary elements, and each element has its own presiding deity. Thus, for example, Brahma is the presiding deity of the moral sense, Rudra of the ego, Surya of the intellect, and Chandra of the mind. In the same way, five planets—Jupiter, Mercury, Mars, Venus, Saturn—are the presiding deities of the five gross elements. This simply means that these personalities arrange our encounter with the world at different levels.

We don't see the demigods, but we can see the effects of the demigods, which appears in the fact that some people are rich while others are poor, some enjoy prosperity while others live through poverty, some receive good moral upbringing during childhood while others are born in immoral families, some are lucky to find good teachers while others end up in bad schools, etc.

Atomism is personalized when we treat the mind also as comprised of atoms. But this atomism only consists of our abilities and the reflections of desire which lead to goal formation. Atomism is further personalized due to demigods when they are said to be delivering the results of our desires, and objects by which our abilities to sense and act are converted into sensations and actions. If we do not personalize atomic theory, then it will remain incomplete. This personalization is not subjectivity, because there are many modes in nature. The 'how' mode of explaining is impersonal, but 'who' and 'why' are personal. If science tries to explain 'how' we eat an apple, then, it can talk about the successive states of my body and the apple, and how they come to interact. But this is an incomplete explanation. Completeness is obtained only when we say 'who' gets to eat the apple, and 'why' they get to eat the apple instead of others.

The role of the demigods in delivering karma has been previously discussed. So, why is it being discussed again? The answer is that we are now getting into details about their role and connecting it to the nature of atoms. Modern science assumes that atoms are moving automatically—e.g., due to properties like mass and charge in them—but this idea is rejected here. The atoms are moving because the demigods are causing them to move. But the demigods are also not independent; they are only delivering the consequences of our actions. Therefore, in one sense, we are in control because we reap the consequences of our actions. In another sense, the demigods are in control since they decide which consequence is reaped when and where. Thus, what will happen where is not in our control. But whether it will happen to us, and whether it will be done by us, is within our control. Thus, some people will go hungry and there is nothing we can do about it. What we can do is two things—(1) if they are destined to receive food, then we can be involved in giving it to them, and (2) we can decide by our good actions that we will not have to go hungry.

By the consideration that a person can only change his own destiny, a person is selfish. But by the consideration that others' destiny can be fulfilled by us, we can be altruistic. This altruism doesn't mean that we are changing the world. It only means that within the scope of whatever is destined to happen, we can participate in the good outcomes and avoid the bad outcomes. The devotee of the Lord, however, goes beyond these conceptions of selfishness and altruism. He offers to others the representations of the Lord. These offerings are mainly in the form of knowledge of the Lord, but they can be in the form of food offered to the Lord, a chance to see the Lord in His deity form, etc.

QUESTION

If the objects of our senses are under the control of the demigods, then the demigods too have senses. If our senses are controlled by the demigods, then who controls the senses of the demigods? Alternately, who is the presiding deity of the elements for the demigods, if they are the presiding deities for us?

2.4.16 (285)

प्राणवता शब्दात्

prāṇavatā śabdāt

prāṇavatā—one possessing the prāṇa; śabdāt—from the scriptures.

TRANSLATION

The owner of the prāṇa (the Supreme Lord) is said (in the scriptures) (to be the final presiding deity or controller for everyone, including demigods).

COMMENTARY

In the previous sūtra, atomism was connected to the demigods. In earlier sūtras, material atoms were connected to the prāṇa. And now in this sūtra, the connection between atomism, demigods, and prāṇa is being made. If each of these have been understood individually in the past, then they are now being described collectively in this sūtra. This is the process of diversity leading to unity. There is also the reverse process of unity resulting in diversity. Thus, the argument goes from the root toward the leaves, and from the leaves toward the root. By employing the top-down process from root to leaves, we enunciate religion. But by using the bottom-up process from leaves to root, we describe science. Thus, there is no contradiction between religion and science, but there is a difference: religion goes top-down, and science goes bottom-up.

A demigod may provide us with the opportunity to enjoy a sense object.

In doing so, he is exercising his power and control, and that use of power also constitutes the demigod's enjoyment. The demigod's power is in turn enabled by a higher demigod, who is also enjoying in granting that opportunity to the lower-level demigod who then enables the enjoyment of the humans. In this way, everything we enjoy involves the enjoyment of many other higher beings. Ultimately, the Lord who controls all the demigods is the provider of opportunities for all the demigods, which enables their enjoyment. So, He is the ultimate presiding deity for every material element and enjoyment, and just as lower-level demigods deliver the karma for the humans, the higher-level demigods deliver the karma for the lower-level demigods. Ultimately, the Supreme Lord, delivers the karma for the highest-level demigod—Brahma—to create the opportunity for him to control the lower-level demigods, who then control the lower-level living entities. If the Supreme Lord did not create an opportunity for Brahma to exercise his will, and enjoy his karma, then the lower-level demigods and humans won't be able to exercise their wills either. Thus, in each enjoyment, there many levels of enjoyers exercising their power and karma.

The Supreme Lord, however, is not constrained by karma, because His power is His Śakti, who is always serving Him, and He doesn't need karma to obtain His power. The souls in the material world suffer from the fear of losing their power, but the Lord is fearless because He never loses His power. The enjoyment of the humans, demigods, and Brahma are finite, and they end with time. But the enjoyment of the Lord is eternally facilitated by His Śakti.

QUESTION

To become the presiding deity for a lower-level living entity, the higher-level living entity must have a longer lifetime, because only then can he control which living entity enters a specific type of body and life opportunity.

2.4.17 (286)

तस्य च नित्यत्वात्

tasya ca nityatvāt

tasya—His; ca—also; nityatvāt—on account of permanence.

TRANSLATION

(Ultimately this entails) the eternity of the Supreme Lord as well (because He is the presiding deity for all the other lower temporary demigods).

COMMENTARY

One of the amazing features of transcendental literatures is that they connect the knowledge of the material world to the Lord. Such literatures are not afraid to delve into the questions of space and time, matter and causality, or karma and rebirth. However, they deliver this knowledge by connecting it to the Lord. Thus, someone may ask about the body, the material elements, the mind, the process of perception and judgment, etc. and even as answers to these questions are given, the ultimate truth is also given. In fact, the former always implies the latter. This sūtra shows how after discussing atomism, prāṇa, the demigods, and how the Lord is the controller of the world, we now come to the transcendental truth—that the Lord is eternal. This is important because in each country there is a supreme ruler, under whose authority subordinate administrators do their work. But these rulers die and are replaced by other rulers. By extension, one could argue that the Lord is a ruler in so far as the material world exists. If the world ceased to exist, then the Lord would also cease to exist.

This sūtra eliminates that argument by saying that the Lord is not just temporarily supreme, but He is eternally supreme. Transcendence begins with eternity, and supremacy follows this eternity. This is because supremacy is needed if there are many individuals, one of whom is supreme. But if these individuals are within the One, then the supremacy is not demonstrated, although eternity is. Now, the impersonalist argues: the supremacy is temporary, and because the Lord is temporarily supreme, the notion of "God" is only temporary. If these individuals enter the Lord, then nobody is superior or inferior. Therefore, we don't have to worship the Lord since we can merge within the Lord. This merger is expected to dissolve the difference between God and the soul.

However, as we have discussed earlier, this kind of whole-part relation is construed on physical analogies, such as the ocean and the drop within it, and it rests upon the idea that the Lord and the soul are quantitatively different but qualitatively similar. This identity doesn't exist when the whole and the part are meanings, because now they are also qualitatively different. Thus, the mammal and the cow are both quantitatively and qualitatively dissimilar. Reality is known at many levels of detail and abstraction. The impersonalist thinks that the Lord knows all the facts, and the soul doesn't know them. Therefore, the Lord is quantitatively different from the soul, but ultimately all knowledge is merely facts. This is false. Knowledge is both facts and theories. The theories are deeper than the facts, and there are shallower and deeper theories. The knowledge of the Lord is not merely the facts, but also all the deeper explanations of these facts. He is therefore qualitatively different from the soul.

His supremacy is His qualitative difference from the soul. His supremacy as described in the previous sūtras, and the eternity of this supremacy is described in this sūtra. This means that the theories emerge before the facts. The explanation is the cause, and the cause then produces the effects. We can see some of these effects, but the Lord sees the effects and their explanations.

Vedic cosmology provides descriptions of the hierarchy of control in the material world, in which each living entity lives for 100 years, but the definition of a 'year' varies for each type of living entity. Thus, for instance, what constitutes a year for us, constitutes a day for the demigods (of which 6 months in the year are considered day, while the next 6 months are night). At successively higher levels of control, the controllers also have a much longer lifespan. Thus, a Manu—who has control for a period of a Manavantara and constitutes 72 cycles of four-ages (satya-yuga, tretā-yuga, dvāpara-yuga, and kali-yuga)—lives only for a fraction of Brahma's day as there are 14 Manus in a single day of Brahma. Brahma's lifetime adds up to approximately 311 trillion solar years. But the Supreme Lord is eternally situated in His abode to create and destroy the universes innumerable times, to create the opportunities for others to enjoy. His desire is part of every other fulfillment, so He is indirectly enjoying as everyone enjoys. His enjoyment is the control of nature for everyone's enjoyment.

Topic 8

QUESTION

The senses and the objects of the senses are present everywhere. How do the demigods control the interaction between the senses and their objects?

2.4.18 (287)

त इन्द्रयािणि तिद्व्यपदेशादन्यत्र श्रेष्ठात्

ta indriyāṇi tadvyapadeśādanyatra śreṣṭhāt

te—they; indriyāṇi—the senses; tadvyapadeśāt—from designated as that (i.e., the masters of the senses); anyatra śreṣṭhāt—from another superior place.

TRANSLATION

They (the demigods) from being designated (as the masters of) the senses (control the access of the objects for the senses) from another, superior place.

COMMENTARY

The causes of experience are divided into three parts in Sāñkhya philosophy: ādibhautika, *ādiatmika,* and ādidaivika, or the objects, the senses, and the demigods. In modern science, we think that objects are directly interacting with the senses, and there is nobody in control of our perception. But such a theory cannot explain why someone is rich while another person is poor, why someone is intelligent while another person is not, etc. The demigods are responsible for ensuring that everyone gets their due according to their karma. Thus, even the food that we eat every day is provided by the demigods due to karma. This food can come from many different sources—we can grow the food, we can purchase it from someone, someone can give us the food in charity, etc. Karma simply ensures that we will get the food, but the source of that food is not predetermined. This source is decided based on both guna and karma—e.g., someone has the requisite *karma* to give food, and they want to give the food. Sometimes, karma will override guna and a person will be forced to give even if he or she doesn't want to give. Sometimes, guna will override karma and a person will give to someone who he wants to give. These arrangements of provider and consumer are made by the demigods. The mechanism of this type of causality involves establishing a relation between a provider and a consumer.

At the advent of modern science, it was believed that every object exerts a force on every other object; so, for example, our bodies are exerting a gravitational force on the sun, just as the sun is exerting a gravitational force on us. This meant that everyone had access to everything in this world, which is patently false. Later developments in science have shown that objects occasionally interact with each other only when they have become 'entangled' with each other, and during an interaction the causality flows in both directions—from source to destination and from destination to source. There are not good explanations of this causal model in classical or modern science, because we are used to thinking of the interaction in terms of the interacting objects alone.

The fact is that these interactions are created by demigods who 'entangle' objects with each other such that they can interact. This entanglement is based on a combination of our desiring and our deserving, and by this entanglement we fulfill our desires and reap our karma. This entanglement is prior to the exchange of energy by which force is exerted, so we cannot attribute 'force' as the cause of entanglement. And without understanding the cause of this entanglement all other causal explanations become incomplete. The short answer to this problem is that objects don't get entangled; the objects enter different relations or roles which are mutually entangled. We call these roles by names such as 'consumer' and 'provider'; these are not objects, but roles of give and take. The demigods move the individuals into these roles based on their karma.

Scientists believe that to change an object a force must be applied on it. They may not realize that this force is exerted after a role is changed, and the changes to these roles are not due to forces. The causality in matter is conditional on the interaction: *if* you eat a medicine, then you will be cured or *if* you eat food, then your hunger will be satisfied. But that doesn't mean you automatically access the medicine or the food. So, the modern notions of material causality are incomplete: they say that something is possible but cannot predict which possibility becomes real for whom. The power of the demigods is to enable access to opportunities that can be utilized (by our desires). By wielding this power, the demigods are said to be in a 'superior position'; this superiority refers to their ability to exert control over our life, not necessarily to everyone else's life. The demigods, for instance, don't control the life in the lower planetary systems, nor do they control the living entities who are situated in positions above them. So, their control is also limited, and universal. Their position of power is also enabled and controlled by higher living entities, which means that their positions are not permanent. Only the position of the Supreme Lord is eternal.

Finally, the demigods are only said to be controllers of the senses in this sūtra. This means that all desires cannot be fulfilled, even if we have the karma. The objects of desiring—e.g., flying machines—are not created by demigods. They are produced due to time. If we desire, and the object is possible, and the karma is manifest at the present, then the person can fly. Thus, the causality has many causes—the soul, his guna and karma, matter and the effect of time.

QUESTION

The distinction between the Lord and the demigods seems to be based on the distinction between a person and a role. The Supreme Lord is eternally situated in His role as the supreme controller, but the roles of the other demigods are temporary. Why do we distinguish between the person and a role?

2.4.19 (288)

भेदश्रुतेः

bhedaśruteḥ

bheda—the difference; śruteḥ—as stated in the śrutī.

TRANSLATION

The scriptural texts differentiate between them.

COMMENTARY

Every organized system requires a hierarchy of controls, and this hierarchy requires a distinction between a person and the role played by the person. The 'person' here is represented by their desire and the role constitutes their deserving. These two must be distinguished because every desiring person cannot acquire a position unless they are also deserving. Similarly, every deserving person doesn't get to fulfill their desires immediately—they may need to wait for the right time to arrive for fulfilling their desires. The restrictions of deserving do not apply in the spiritual world, and experience is controlled only by desire. Therefore, the only qualification to see and serve the Lord is a desire. These desires are spiritual, and they automatically spring from the soul, due to which they are often called causeless. They are also always manifest to serve the Lord. Therefore, the devotee doesn't say—I desire to see the Lord, because I would be delighted by it. That kind of desire is not considered spiritual. But if a causeless desire springs in the soul, the Lord and His Śakti fulfill it.

QUESTION

But we can see that there are many people who acquire powerful positions due to their preexisting wealth or connections. They seem to have the good karma, they are obviously desirous of these positions, but they may not be qualified. Shouldn't we say that that karma and desire are insufficient to decide the most deserving person, as they must also be skilled in doing their job?

2.4.20 (289)

वैलक्षण्याच्च

vailakṣaṇyaccha

vailakṣaṇya—uniqueness, specialization; ca—also;

TRANSLATION

(In addition to good karma and desire, the person) must be qualified also.

COMMENTARY

The law of karma ensures justice for all the souls—you get what you deserve, and that deserving is decided by previous actions. However, it is possible that a person with good karma is incapable of fulfilling the demands of the role.

Hence, there are two types of qualification—the ability and the entitlement. The entitlement is fulfilled by karma, but many incapable people may also ascend powerful positions in society due to entitlement, not due to their ability.

Karma is like money, which can be spent to purchase the things that we want. But once we obtain these things due to karma, we may still not know how to use them. Nature allows such outcomes, and even unqualified people ascend powerful positions if they desire it, and if they have the karma, even if they don't have the ability. Thus, it is seen that even demigods commit mistakes. They might be envious of other demigods or even humans, and might compete with them, instead of focusing on their own roles and responsibilities. The demigods have the desires for power, and they have the karma for power, but they don't necessarily have all the abilities. Such abilities are obtained only by devotees. If a pure devotee of the Lord ascends a position of power, then he doesn't work by his own intellect. He rather works by the guidance of the Lord, and whatever he may be missing, the Lord supplies the necessities. Therefore, the devotees do not fail the duties of their position due to their inabilities.

If a person neglects their duties deliberately, the laws of nature produce a greater karma. If a person neglects their duties due to inability, the laws of nature still punish, although the punishment is lesser. Therefore, incapable people must not accept the roles they cannot fulfill—simply because they are offered such positions, and they would like to enjoy the position of power. One should rather understand their abilities against the demand for the position. If the demands exceed their abilities, then a person must renounce that position, and allow someone more qualified to accept the position. Even if there is no one more qualified, an unqualified person must not accept a position beyond his abilities—on the pretext of doing 'serving the greater good'. But if such a position has been accepted by mistake, it must be quickly renounced. That renunciation will save the unqualified person from subsequent suffering.

QUESTION

How can unqualified people ascend to positions of power, simply due to good karma? Shouldn't the laws of nature allow only those people who are both qualified (to play the role) and have the good karma (to obtain the role)?

2.4.21 (290)

संज्ञामूर्तक्लृप्तस्तु त्रिवृत्कुर्वत उपदेशात्

saṃjñāmurtiklṛptistu trivratakurvata upadeśāt

saṃjñā—designation or naming; murti—form or deity; klṛptiḥ—conforming; astu—in this way; trivrata—the vow of three times a day; kurvata—those who perform; upadeśāt—based upon the teaching.

TRANSLATION

(Qualifications can be obtained by those who) designate a deity based upon the teaching (of the scriptures) and perform the vows (of worshipping the designated deity) three times a day (again, according to the scriptures).

COMMENTARY

The worship of the demigods has been decried many times before, but in this sūtra, it is being recommended. To understand this recommendation, we must distinguish between the three aspects of experience we have discussed previously—desire, opportunity, and ability. We might have desires, but they remain unfulfilled unless we have the right karma. The opportunities to fulfill the desires are given to us by karma. But, if we have the desire, and get the opportunity, but don't have the ability, we will not be able to use the opportunity well. The demigod worship is recommended if one wants to obtain the ability to deal with the present opportunities. This doesn't entail a change in the situation or getting better opportunities, because the demigods cannot change our karma. However, the demigods can give us the power to deal with the present situation better. The result of this betterment is that our responses to the problems will be more effective and appropriate; instead of fumbling through the problems, we can provide correct and measured responses to them.

Therefore, whether we pray to the Lord or to the demigods, we should never ask for improving our situation. We should rather ask for giving us the ability to deal with the situation. This ability can mean a stronger body or mind, greater moral and emotional courage, and the strength to keep doing our duties even under adverse and difficult circumstances. The worship of demigods for getting a better life is futile. But the worship of the demigods for getting better abilities to deal with whatever life we are getting is still appropriate. The devotees of the Lord take shelter of the Lord and ask for His help in giving them strength, courage, patience, and tolerance to deal with difficult situations. They also beg the Lord for the power to spread His glories. It is said that by the mercy of the guru, a dumb man can speak, and a lame man can cross mountains. Thus, all kinds of worship—of the Lord, of the guru, or of the demigods—are only meant to obtain the abilities by which we handle the difficulties of life, even as we can use the same abilities for spreading the glorification of the Lord.

The devotees know how to engage powerful people in the Lord's service. They don't have to shy away from wealthy or powerful people, in the name of renunciation. The demigod worship is similarly accepted, after numerous previous rejections, provided it is sought not for enjoyment, but for betterment of our abilities to fulfill our duties. Thus, a person with a poor intellect can worship Sarasvati to understand the scriptures. A person with a disturbed mind can worship Chandra to perform their duties. And a warrior fighting the moral battle can worship Durga or Kali to obtain the power that can help them win these battles. Arjuna obtained weapons of various kinds before the battle of Mahabharata by worshipping the demigods. If the intention is the Lord's service or even the strength to perform one's mundane duties, then the demigod worship is accepted. Thus, everything described in the Vedic texts is ultimately for a single purpose—the service of the Lord. The soul conditioned by selfishness, however, falsely construes this knowledge to be meant for his enjoyment.

QUESTION

You earlier said that the demigods are delivering our karma by which our roles are decided. You are now also saying that the demigods can give us better abilities (of the body and the mind) making us more capable of dealing with circumstances. How are these abilities delivered to the living entities?

2.4.22 (291)

मांसादि भौमं यथाशब्दमितरयोश् च

māṃsādi bhaumaṃ yathāśabdamitarayoś ca

māṃsādi—flesh etc.; bhaumaṃ—from the earth; yatha—just as; śabdam—the sound; itarayoh—the other two (i.e., the guna and karma); ca—also.

TRANSLATION

Flesh etc. (the body of abilities) are formed from the earth, just as the sound (is formed) from the other two (i.e., guna and karma) as well.

COMMENTARY

We have earlier discussed the three modalities of existence—universal, individual, and contextual. The type of body—e.g., tiger, tree, bird, fish, etc.—are universals. The guna is the soul's desire, which differentiates the soul materially from other souls, and constitutes the individual mode. The universal and the individual combine, the soul gets a type of body (e.g., cat or dog or human) due to its guna. Now, the third mode—of contextuality—decides the environment in which this body is placed, and this contextual modality is due to karma.

This sūtra draws a comparison to speech. The meaning is the universal, and its expression as words are the individual instantiation of that meaning. However, those words are also spoken in some context—e.g., to some people.

This process is cyclic, which means that after we express some meaning, the other person also expresses other meanings. By this expression, our desires change, and we tap into different universals, and speak different words. We might also change the context, and speak to other people, or stop speaking to the person we were speaking to earlier. Thus, causality begins in our guna or desires when we obtain a type of body. Then by the interactions of this body with its environment, the body develops slowly—e.g., we eat some food, we acquire some knowledge, we develop some aspirations, and learn some values. This development then shapes the meanings, and their expressions.

The worship of demigods enhances this process as the demigods can give the person not just the things that they deserve due to their karma but also portions of their ability by which these things enhance their effects. For instance, if Sarasvati—the deity of knowledge—is worshipped, then the effort invested in learning will produce better knowledge with the assistance of Sarasvati. As we become better equipped with knowledge, strength, health, etc. we are better prepared for the good or bad situations that come naturally due to karma.

In Vedic philosophy, even the mind is sometimes included in the body, because both are considered the coverings of the soul. Thus, in this sūtra, a gross material example of bodily flesh being generated from the element earth is given, to make the point that the food we get to eat is fixed by our karma but the same food can build a stronger body by the grace of demigods. Of course, the abilities in the demigods are also provided by the grace of the Supreme Lord. So, one who worships the Lord is said to eventually develop all the great qualities of all the demigods—not just a specific demigod. This internal strength or ability in the mind and the body of a person is not a permanent quality; it can rather come and go; sometimes the mind and the body become very strong and we can do difficult things easily. Sometimes even simple things become very difficult because the mind and the body are weakened. The strength and weakness of the body and the mind can be obtained through the grace of the Lord (or the demigods) without being conditioned by karma. Thus, we can see descriptions in Vedic texts where people perform yajñá or austerities to get the benedictions from demigods that gives them strong bodies and minds.

QUESTION

You are saying that the health of the body and the mind can be improved by the grace of demigods. Since this health has many components, coming from the different elements of matter, is there a separate demigod for each such element that gives us not just the element but also the ability to consume it?

2.4.23 (292)

वैशेष्यात्तु तद्वादस्तद्वादः

vaiśeṣyāttu tadvādastadvādaḥ

vaiśeṣyāt—due to the specialization; tu—but; tad-vādas—they are called; tad-vādaḥ—by that name.

TRANSLATION

For each kind of material specialization, there is a demigod who is called by the same name (as the type of specialization that he or she represents).

COMMENTARY

There are innumerable kinds of talents, abilities, and specializations in this world. Some people are artists, others are musicians, writers, orators, philosophers, scientists, cooks, dancers, etc. Each such specialization has a personification in a demigod who specializes in that area. These demigods represent the parts of the ability, talent, and specialization in the Lord. Thus, the Lord is full of all talents, but each demigod only personifies one such type of talent.

When the ability of a demigod is present in a person, the demigod is said to have become immanent in that person. Otherwise, the demigod is always transcendent by the fact that he delivers the specific type of karma or objects. Thus, for instance, Sarasvati is delivering knowledge to everyone (according to their karma). But some of these people acquire an extraordinary ability to understand, assimilate, and transmit that knowledge. The goddess Sarasvati is said to be 'present' in them. In a previous sūtra, the term *anyatra śreṣṭhāt* was used to describe how the demigods control the world from another, superior place. In this sūtra, the power to give opportunities is contrasted to their power to deliver abilities by being present by their portion in a person's body.

The Vedic texts describe a form of incarnation called śakti-*āveśa avatār* in which the Lord appears as ability in the body and the mind of a soul. Veda Vyās, the author of Vedānta Sūtra, is, for instance, considered śakti-*āveśa avatār*. In every millennium, at the dawn of kali-yuga, a different soul appears as Veda Vyās, who converts the oral Vedic tradition into a written one. This conversion is entrusted to an empowered soul, who is called Veda Vyās. Veda Vyās, however, is not the Lord, and yet empowered with the Lord's powers.

When Śukadeva Goswami spoke the Śrīmad Bhāgavatam, his father (Veda Vyās), his grandfather (Parāśara), and his father's spiritual master (Nārada Muni) were present in audience. Even though Veda Vyās is an empowered incarnation, and the author of Śrīmad Bhāgavatam, he doesn't consider himself qualified to speak on the Śrīmad Bhāgavatam. Why? Why are the author, the author's father, and the author's guru in the audience, while the disciple and son speaks? The answer is that the devotee is superior to the empowered incarnation. If the devotee speaks, then even the Lord listens in rapt attention.

नाहं वसामि वैकुण्ठे योगिनां हृदये न च ।
मद्भक्ता यत्र गायन्ति तत्र तिष्ठामि नारद ॥

O Nārada, I do not reside in Vaikuṇṭha, nor do I dwell in the hearts of the yogis; I am firmly situated wherever my devotees are singing.

The description of the Lord by the devotees is superior to the Lord's description of Himself, or the description by an empowered incarnation of the Lord. The Lord describes Himself analytically by indicating His powers. But the devotees speak about the Lord's sweet nature, which the Lord doesn't speak of Himself. Thus, Vedānta Sūtra and the Śrīmad Bhāgavatam are both conclusions of the Vedas. The Śrīmad Bhāgavatam is called the ripened fruit of the tree of Vedic knowledge (*nigama-kalpa-taror galitaṁ phalaṁ*). The Vedānta Sūtra is also that ripened fruit, or the conclusion of all knowledge in the Vedas. However, the Śrīmad Bhāgavatam is made sweeter by the biting of the fruit by Śukadeva Goswami (śuka-mukhād amṛta-drava-saṁyutam), but the Vedānta Sūtra is not. The Śrīmad Bhāgavatam we read is not the Śrīmad Bhāgavatam that was written by Veda Vyās. It is rather Śukadeva Goswami's exposition of what Veda Vyās wrote. Expositions of the original text by the devotees are superior to those authored by the empowered incarnation of the Lord. If we understand the Vedānta Sūtra devotionally, then they are non-different.

The conclusion is that power is inferior to devotion. Many people call advanced devotees a śakti-*āveśa avatār*, thinking this to be a glorification of the devotee. But the Lord's devotee is superior to the empowered incarnation. Those enamored by power, magic, and mystical abilities, think of the devotees as possessing power. The devotee has no power. He is helplessly in love with the Lord. And the Lord provides whatever he needs. This is not an inferior position. It is rather superior to anyone possessing Lord's empowerment.

In summary, the demigods can be worshipped to obtain the strength to serve the Lord. But empowerment by the demigods, or even by the empowered incarnations of the Lord present as śakti-ā*veśa avat*ā*r*, are inferior to devotion. Hence, if possible, one must only remain devoted to the Supreme Lord.

Chapter 3

This is the longest chapter in the text, and it establishes the doctrine of difference and non-difference in many ways. First, it states that consistency of claims is not a goal because the soul moves through conflicts and its choices are made to resolve these conflicts. Second, it undertakes a detailed discussion about the difference and non-difference between various scriptures, various methods of spiritual upliftment, and how they are different and yet non-different. Third, it describes how even for the perfected soul, the difference between truth, right, good vs. false, wrong, and bad exists, and yet these are also reconciled in the Absolute Truth. Fourth, it describes how this process of difference and non-difference is the cause of the manifestation of the material and spiritual worlds and the scriptures. Fifth, it describes how freedom and regulations are intertwined: as people act more individualistically and independently, they are bound by a greater number of laws and regulations; but as they act more cooperatively and unselfishly, the laws and regulations are eliminated for them.

Section 1: This section introduces the idea of movement by inner conflict. It is said that the soul evolves by a succession of questions and answers, and the conflicts between them lead to progression. It also says that inner conflict is resolved by choices, which are controlled by prāṇa. It then answers questions about the soul's free will, which seems to be lost in the world, and how that free will is recovered upon the dissolution of karma. Then follows a detailed discussion around the nature of sin, why the soul must suffer the consequences of sin, the nature of hell, and the type of rebirth that occurs after enduring the results of karma in hell. A discussion about various kinds of species, and how they appear and disappear suddenly, is then undertaken. The text states that children need not have similarities to their parents, and new species can be created by a mother and father who are quite different from their children.

Section 2: This section discusses how the transcendental state is beyond the conventional opposites of attachment and renunciation, bondage and liberation, etc. It then describes that despite the dissolution of such opposites, the distinction between truth and false, good and bad, right and wrong doesn't disappear. Thus, the liberated soul exists in the world, makes a distinction between true and false, good and bad, right and wrong, and also remains equanimous to all such distinctions. Hence, the existence in the material world is not considered bondage, and liberation is not getting out of the material body. Rather, the devotee lives in the world for the Lord's pleasure and tolerates everything. Then the section propounds the whole-part doctrine of the

Lord being the whole and the soul being the part and explains how the whole divides into parts. This division is said to follow a logical or rational process. Thus, the world is created by a rational process, the production of karma or consequences of actions are also created rationally, and even scriptures are produced rationally. This sets up the motivation for the scientific study of the world and the scriptures.

Section 3: This section discusses the different processes of attaining the Absolute Truth. While earlier many methods had been rejected as unsuitable, they are now accepted as being useful complements aiding in the understanding of the Absolute Truth. Thus, many forms of yoga, the study of scriptures, and the pursuit of philosophical understanding are recognized as valid methods. And yet, it is established that all these methods work correctly when the devotion to the Lord is accepted as the supreme goal. It is also said that sometimes one path doesn't deliver the complete result, and the missing results can be obtained by the alternative paths. Thus, the hard and fast distinctions between the various paths are dissolved, and these paths are described as various methods available to the spiritual aspirant to overcome different problems in their journey. The understanding of the whole-part relation is modified, and it is said that just as the part is within the whole, similarly, the whole is within the part. This idea is now extended to the relation between the masculine and feminine aspects of the Absolute Truth, and they are described to be distinct, and yet inseparable. This further rejects the absolute separation of different methods, because each method is sufficient in one sense, and all the methods are collectively necessary in another sense. In this way, the doctrine of non-difference is established.

Section 4: This section takes the discussion of morality and compares it to the process of sacrifice in which a lower good must be sacrificed for a higher good, however, in this sacrifice, the least amount of good must be sacrificed. The text now discusses the three systems of social organization—egalitarian, hierarchical, and distributed. In the egalitarian system of society, everyone has the right to make the best decision of what can be sacrificed for which good. Since this system doesn't work unless the people are enlightened, a hierarchical system of organization is discussed in which the higher sections of society (determined by their higher morality) have greater freedom of choosing than the lower sections (determined by their lower morality). Then, when the upper sections of society go missing, then a distributed system of morality is described in which people are equally bound by rules and regulations and nobody has greater or lesser freedom. Finally, the nature of spiritual society is discussed in which nobody has any rights or duties, although everyone acts voluntarily.

SECTION 1

Topic 1

QUESTION

You are explaining the process of change through guna and karma, but the explanation is difficult to understand due to many inherent complexities. Is there a simpler and easier way to understand this process of change?

3.1.1 (293)

तदन्तरप्रतिपत्तौ रंहति संपरिष्वक्तः प्रश्ननिरूपणाभ्याम्

tadantarapratipattau raṃhati saṃpariṣvaktaḥ praśnanirūpaṇābhyām

tadantarapratipattau—upon a change toward a new conclusion; raṃhati—goes; saṃpariṣvaktaḥ—enveloped by many types of statements; praśnanirūpaṇābhyām—by the dual process of questioning and answering.

TRANSLATION

The (soul) enveloped by many kinds of statements goes upon a change toward a new conclusion by the dual process of questioning and answering.

COMMENTARY

This sūtra describes the evolution of the soul occurring by the same process as the evolution of knowledge. Knowledge is described as *saṃpariṣvaktaḥ* or the covering of many statements. These statements are the facts, axioms, beliefs, and convictions we carry at present. However, nobody is fully satisfied with their belief system because they know that something is missing. Unless perfect happiness is attained, the doubts about one's beliefs remain. And under these doubts, one naturally develops the tendency to ask questions. These questions appear as different kinds of desires, pursuits, and quests, and present themselves as problems to us. The problems created from the current belief system conflict with the beliefs—so long as something is missing from the beliefs—and this conflict then leads to the need for conflict resolution. Thus, the incompleteness of our beliefs leads to inconsistency between beliefs and questions.

In most modern thinking, we suppose that nature moves from premises to conclusion by recursively applying a certain type of logic to the premises. For example, in classical physics, the current state of a particle is the premise. The application of some natural laws (such as the law of gravitation) pushes the particle to a new state, which then becomes the new premise, to which the same logic (e.g., the mathematical law of gravitation) is reapplied, to get another conclusion. But this process of successive change begs a question: When did it begin? What was the primordial initial state of reality upon which the laws of nature were applied to obtain conclusions? In short, when and in what state did the universe begin? Aristotle during Greek times had formulated an 'Unmoved Mover' argument to illustrate the problem: if everything is moving because of being pushed by something else, then the original cause which got the universe rolling could not have itself been caused (because that would lead to infinite regress) and the movement is due to an 'Unmoved Mover'. The thesis of the 'Unmoved Mover' paralyzed Western thinking for two millennia because the mechanism of movement involved a contradiction—something that wasn't being pushed was the cause of the original push. And yet, this thesis was necessary to answer all fundamental questions of philosophy of that time: namely, that the world has an origin, that it was caused by an uncaused agent, and therefore, the meaning and purpose of this existence rested in that first cause.

Western science began when Newton discarded the idea of an Unmoved Mover. His first law of motion states: Things keep moving unless hindered by a force. In short, we don't have to ask how motion started; we just take it for granted and only study the changes to the motion. Implicit in this view of the world was the idea of logic as something that leads us from premises to conclusions. So, if motion is given as a premise, then the laws of motion (e.g., the theory of gravitation) are only needed to find a conclusion (i.e., the next state of motion) based on the premise. This logical conclusion then led to determinism: If you fix the initial state of a system, all subsequent states are logically fixed. There was hence no role for choice, which subsequently became the problems of morality, the responsibility for our actions, and why we even seek happiness.

Now, contrast this idea of change by the one being described here: we have several beliefs, axioms, or facts, which constitute the premises. However, premises don't lead to conclusions; they first give rise to a question, a problem, or a doubt. This doubt then creates a conflict with the premises, and a new conclusion must be drawn to resolve that conflict. The difference now is that these premises and conclusions aren't merely physical states; they can also be semantic states, such as ideas, theories, and data. So, reasoning doesn't merely move a particle to its new state. Rather, in the evolution of knowledge, our theories, premises, and axioms can change along with the observations of the world. Ideally, you want to be able to explain both the earlier and the new data. But in real life, we might discard the assumptions of our childhood as we grow into adulthood, because we may think that childhood is never coming back.

In we apply the Western model of inference to the development of new ideas, then the problem is that reasoning can never change the axioms. So, if we began with wrong assumptions, we will forever be restricted to conclusions that are consistent with our previous beliefs—an echo chamber of self-reinforcing ideas. The only way experience changes our assumptions is if it is not following the process of logical inference—i.e., presenting us with problems incongruous with our previous assumptions. This forces us to choose between two undesirable extremes: (1) nature is illogical, but we can improve our ideas by experience; we don't know what the destination is, because there are no logical-mathematical laws governing nature, or (2) nature is logical, there is no choice in improving our knowledge, so either we are already in perfect knowledge, or we can never obtain perfect knowledge even if there were infinite time.

This sūtra offers a resolution of this conundrum: there are perfect laws of nature, but the process of change alternates between solutions and problems. These problems can arise within us due to perceived inconsistencies in our axiom system, or they can arise because we are compelled to observe things inconsistent with our prior formed beliefs. The genesis of questions involves a choice: (1) you may not develop an internal problem if you don't want to rethink your assumptions, and (2) you may selectively process the data that fits your assumptions and ignore the rest of the data or interpret it differently. By and large, change is slow because we either reject the data incompatible with our assumptions or we try to explain it based on preexisting assumptions. It is rare that choice is involved, namely, when we must decide to stop ignoring the new data or trying to explain it away using the preexisting beliefs.

We can simplify this issue by saying our beliefs are the answer to the problem posed by the world, and these answers are used to solve the problems of the external world. These beliefs are changed only when they fail to solve the problems. The soul covered by beliefs is the internal world that tries to determine the answers to the externally posed questions. The soul can decide whether a problem needs a new premise or the reuse of a previous premise. This dialectical process of knowledge evolution is here generalized to define the evolution of the soul: the soul evolves through alternating questions and answers; the covering of beliefs changes to address the emerging questions.

QUESTION

You are saying that the soul evolves due to inner and outer conflicts. But how is that possible if the soul is one? How can the soul have conflicts?

3.1.2 (294)

त्र्यात्मकत्वात्तु भूयस्त्वात्

tryātmakatvāttu bhūyastvāt

tryātmakatvāt—due to having a three-fold nature of the self; tu—but; bhūyastvāt—on account of the preponderance of one of the aspects.

TRANSLATION

Owing to the soul having a three-fold nature (conflicts can develop) but due to the preponderance of one of the aspects (the conflict is resolved).

COMMENTARY

As discussed in previous chapters, the soul has three aspects, *sat*, *chit*, and ānanda. *Sat* is responsible for our relation to something (including ourselves), which we call consciousness or awareness (of the object). Following a relation there is a cognition (of the self or the object of awareness), which is called *chit*. Finally, the cognition either fulfills a desire or contradicts it; due to the satisfaction or dissatisfaction, there is ānanda or happiness and distress. This causal sequence from relation to cognition to emotion can also be reversed, when we begin with a desire for something (emotion), form a relation to something to fulfill that desire, and then cognizing that thing which fulfills the desire. Likewise, we can also begin in cognition—e.g., innate beliefs—and infer that these beliefs imply that some desires can be fulfilled through some relationships.

Of course, our desires can be incompatible with our cognition and relation—e.g., when we are not seeing what we want to see. This incompatibility between our cognition, emotion, and relation creates a conflict. The resolution of this conflict can involve a change to either of these three aspects. For instance, we can suppress our desires to comply with the current cognition and relation. Or, we can change our relation and cognition to comply to the desires. All conflict thus results in a resolution, and the resolution is that one of three aspects of the soul becomes dominant, while the other aspects are subordinated.

In this sūtra this dominance is called *bhūyastvāt* or the preponderance of an aspect. The preponderance can be a problem or a solution. If, for instance, our desires are constantly being suppressed to comply to the current relation and cognition, then the suppression of the desire produces a problem. The resolution of that problem is that relation and cognition are subordinated to emotion, and the force of emotion compels a change to the relation and cognition.

After stating that change occurs due to the conflict between the questions and answers in the previous sūtra, this sūtra states that both questions and answers can be modeled in the same way—i.e., as the dominant-subordinate structure of the three aspects. If some aspect is consistently dominant, then it presents a problem to be solved, and the solution is the reversal of the dominant-subordinate structure. The reversed structure is again temporary and becomes a problem after some time and must be reversed after a while. Thus, sometimes we work according to our desires, and sometimes we compromise our desires to adapt to the situation. Sometimes the situation creates a desire in us, and sometimes the generated desire causes a change to the present situation.

While we have discussed the effects of such dominant-subordinate structures in the previous purports, this the first time Vedānta Sūtra itself mentions this dynamic. I have employed this idea in earlier sūtras because we have noted at the outset that nature is self-contradictory, the soul is self-contradictory, and even God as the source of all contradictory ideas is self-contradictory. There is no universalist system of reasoning or logic that can explain how these contradictions co-exist. Such existence requires us to say that these contradictions are possibilities, which manifest in three modes. If they manifest at the same time, then they must manifest in different places. This manifestation can also be enjoyed by different persons. But if they are in the same person and place, then they must manifest one after another. Hence, the modalities of space, time, and persons resolve these contradictions. Even though everything is self-contradictory, these contradictions don't manifest at the same person, in the same place, at the same time. Each of these modalities prevents the contradiction.

But since one or more modalities can avoid these contradictions, one of the three modes must be the dominant reason for avoiding the contradiction, while other modes remain subordinate. The flipping of these modes allows us to say that the same person can exhibit different qualities at different places and times, and while these qualities are in the person as possibilities, their coexistence doesn't produce a contradiction. In short, we cannot do logic without space, time, and persons. The universal truth is simply a possibility. The experienced truth is always at some time, place, and for some person. The flipping of these modes constitutes the mechanism for change, evolution, and logical progression, but it is radically different from modern notions of change. The idea of the tripartite nature of the soul, which then reflects in the three modes of nature, and how both the modes and the self are often self-contradictory, and how this contradiction then results in change is central to understanding Vedānta.

QUESTION

But if there is a change in the preponderance of the three aspects, then what is the cause of this change? How do we decide which aspect has to be dominant or subordinate? Isn't there a choice involved in this change?

3.1.3 (295)
प्राणगतेश्च

prāṇagateśca

prāṇagateḥ—due to the movement of the prāṇa; ca—also.

TRANSLATION

(The selection of one of the three aspects of the soul, which constitutes a choice is) due to the movement of the prāṇa also (aside from the three aspects).

COMMENTARY

We discussed earlier how knowledge evolves through the accumulation of data if the data becomes incompatible with our understanding or beliefs. But this change in beliefs doesn't come about with the first encounter with a discrepancy. Rather, even as contradictory data accumulates, we try to explain away the discrepancies, until we reach a tipping point. At this tipping point, suddenly the data (and the discrepancies) become more important and the beliefs become subordinate to the data. This causes a change in our beliefs.

Thomas Kuhn—an American physicist and philosopher—described the process of scientific evolution as comprising two parts. He called large-scale changes a 'paradigm shift', when old ideas are suddenly discarded and replaced by radical new ideas. He also called the accumulation of small changes 'normal science', where the previous paradigm shift is validated and any inconsistencies are ignored. Kuhn's main argument was that science doesn't progress linearly—i.e., adapting our theories to every new emerging data. Rather, science tries to explain the new data using existing theories until the discrepancies between the data and the theory reach a tipping point and the process is reversed—we now use the data to change theories rather than theories to explain the data. Thus, according to Kuhn, the evolution of knowledge involves a distinction between 'normal science', which explains the emerging data based on current theories with little to no modification to the basic ideas (which Kuhn calls a 'paradigm'), and a 'scientific revolution' that involves the overturning of existing theories and beliefs (which he describes as 'paradigm shift').

Clearly, there is a role for the accumulated data in causing a paradigm shift. We cannot overthrow a belief system because of a few discrepancies, and the resistance to change creates some stability in knowledge. However, the stability is peppered by occasional drastic changes. The point at which we bring that change is a choice. We can choose to ignore the accumulated discrepancies because our beliefs work quite well for other things. This belief in the current powers of science is called 'scientism' and it claims that science is always right even if it cannot explain the accumulating discrepancies. Scientism stands for what Kuhn calls 'normal science' that ignores all the discrepancies. Under scientism, even alternative ideas, which satisfy the conditions of rational and empirical verification—but which violate the established dogmas—are rejected as 'pseudoscience'. The greater the accumulated discrepancies, the greater is the force of change, and the change—when it comes—causes serious disruptions to our thinking. Ideally, we don't want to accumulate many discrepancies because the resulting change would be enormously disruptive. In the interest of stability, we should aim to continuously evolve our beliefs to resolve the conflicts. But whether one makes continuous changes or is forced to adapt to disruptive changes is a choice. Choices are forced when discrepancies accumulate; but we can avoid this force by voluntarily changing while there is still time.

When this dynamic of knowledge evolution is applied to the evolution of the soul, then we can see a role for choice, apart from the three aspects. If one aspect is subordinated for a long time, a disruptive change will be forced, and that change will be caused by the subordinated aspect. But before such a drastic change is forced upon us, we can choose to voluntarily change gradually.

This process of gradual change is called prāṇa. It represents our choices by which we prevent the creation of serious imbalances, which eventually lead to disruptive and drastic changes. We rather evolve by balancing between the forces generated by the three aspects—each pulling in a different direction—allowing each aspect to dominate alternately to prevent the creation of serious imbalances. The action of prāṇa thus contrasts the ideas of 'normal science', which explains without changing itself, and 'paradigm shift' which creates drastic disruptions when the old belief system is replaced by a new one. The action of prāṇa is continuous change in which our theories and ideas co-evolve with the data. All living beings possess this ability for gradual evolution. Societies and organizations also have this ability for gradual evolution—if the people managing the society and organization are themselves prepared to evolve. However, since such evolution involves a conscious intervention into resolving a conflict, and becoming responsible for that choice, most people, societies, and organizations tend not to make the choice and own the responsibility. They wait for the situation itself to force a drastic and dramatic change. A person, society, or organization that delays the changes to avoid the responsibility emerging from that choice has surrendered their choice to the circumstances. They are effectively not living because they are not making the correct choices.

A non-living system will be naturally disrupted by the accumulating discrepancies. A living system can change itself to avoid the disruption. Thus, the term *ca* in this sūtra refers to the fact that evolution can be both conscious and non-conscious. Non-conscious evolution is forced by the accumulated discrepancies reaching a tipping point. Conscious evolution—caused by prāṇa—is the ability to prevent disruptive change and maintain the stability and longevity of the system through smaller, balanced, and incremental adaptive choices.

QUESTION

In the everyday world, we see changes occurring due to transfer of energy. For example, food gets cooked by fire, machines run by burning fuel, and even the human body generates heat as long as it is living. It is said that the sun powers this planet and the life on it. So, if change is seen when there is heat and energy, then why do we say that the soul's choices are the cause of change?

3.1.4 (296)

अग्न्यादिगतिश्रुतेरिति चेत् न भाक्तत्वात्

agnyādigatiśruteriti cet na bhāktatvāt

agnyādigatiḥ—due to the movement of fire etc.; śruteḥ—as it has been stated in the scriptures; iti cet—if it be said; na—not so; bhāktatvāt—because (notion of the movement of fire etc.) is only said in a secondary sense.

TRANSLATION

If it is said that the śrutī attributes the cause of motion to fire etc. (then we say) not so; such statements are only made in a secondary sense.

COMMENTARY

The term *bhāktatvāt* used in this sūtra has many meanings, apart from the secondary sense, which I have used here. All these meanings are relevant to this discussion. For instance, *bhāktatvāt* also means 'due to fit for eating', 'due to fed by something else', 'due to control of something else', the 'devoted', etc. To understand all these meanings, let's look at the different kinds of causes.

It is true that the world changes due to heat and light. But what causes the transfer of heat and light? We know from atomic theory that the emission and absorption of light is indeterministic—(a) we don't know when the light particle will be emitted, (b) we don't know which object will emit the light, and (c) once the light is emitted, we don't know where it will be absorbed. These three kinds of uncertainties in atomic theory correspond to the three modes of nature. We only know that matter exists as a possibility and its conversion into an observation requires another agency. This agency decides when a particle is emitted, where it is emitted, and where it is absorbed. The von Neumann interpretation of quantum theory calls this agency 'choice' or 'consciousness'.

In Vedic philosophy, the agency is called prāṇa. The prāṇa itself has five types, which are called ingestion, digestion, circulation, elimination, and expression. Therefore, the cause of change is not one. Sometimes, an atomic object moves because the destination of information wants to absorb it—this is called 'ingestion'. At other times the atomic object moves because it is adapting to its environment—this is called 'digestion'. Then sometimes the atomic object moves because it is unable to adapt within an environment—this is called 'elimination'. If the information has adapted in an environment, then it spreads within that environment—this spreading is called 'circulation'. And once it has spread within an environment, it crosses the boundaries of the environment—this crossover from one environment to another is called 'expression'.

The problem in modern science is the legacy of classical physics in which change was caused by a material force. In atomic theory we know that force is not always exerted toward everything. It is exerted sometimes, by some particles, toward some other particles. Therefore, there are three types of uncertainties. And yet, to fit this uncertain model of atomic into the certainty of classical physics, we say that the emission of light is uncertain, but the change resulting from this emission is deterministic. In short, even when choice is involved in the emission of the light, the effects are due to light, rather than choice. This too is false. The cause of emission can decide which particle emits light, and when it emits it. But it cannot decide where this light particle ends up eventually. To make the latter claim, we must say that the causality is bidirectional.

For instance, we can say that we are able to see because the sun is shining. But what causes the sun to shine? The short answer is that there is a person—the sun god—who controls the emission of light, and the sun globe is merely the possibility of that emission. But the sun may be shining, and yet its light may be covered by the clouds. Alternately, we may sit in a dark room and not receive the sun's light. Therefore, the causality is not merely in the sun; it is also in our desiring and deserving. We may desire not to receive the sun's light, and we can avoid it by desiring. But sometimes, we may be forced to receive the sun's light even though we desire to sit in a cool and shady place. Our desiring and deserving are also governed by the prāṇa as much the sun's light is.

Thus, the Vedic texts draw a distinction between the sun god, the sun globe, and the sun light. The sun-god represents the choice to emit light. This choice acts on the possibility of the emission of light represented by the sun globe. And the effect of the choice is the sun light. When we see sun's light, we attribute this seeing to the sun globe, and not to the person—i.e., the sun-god. Then, we claim that the sun has risen instead of saying that the sun-god has come.

In many Vedic texts, the sun god is worshipped via the sun globe; for example, the worshipper can offer water to the sun-god by looking in the direction of the sun globe. But this sūtra clarifies that anything attributed to the sun-globe—i.e., the ball of fire—is only in a secondary sense. The primary cause is the sun-god under whose supervision the sun globe emits the light. We have seen the rejection of impersonalism earlier where matter is itself the cause of changes in the world, and this is another clear example of this rejection. The impersonal reality is not rejected, and its causality is not denied. However, this causality is said to be the inferior or secondary type of cause, which we have called 'possibility' earlier. This possibility is described variously as 'something fit for eating', 'controlled by something else', etc. Therefore, all these meanings of *bhāktatvāt* are simultaneously true one we realize that the sun-globe is the material cause, and the sun-god is the efficient cause, while sun-light is the effect of the combination of the material and efficient causes. The nuclear reactions in the sun are not the sole cause of the sun-light, because all such nuclear reactions are only possibilities, which may never happen. The real cause is that the sun-god's prāṇa controls these nuclear reactions through a choice.

QUESTION

But what you call the appearance, or a secondary cause, is the first thing we perceive. And what you call the real cause remains invisible. We measure the world by the effects that we can perceive because we cannot see the cause itself. Isn't it natural to explain the world by the effects rather than causes?

3.1.5 (297)

प्रथमेऽश्रवणादितिचेत् न ता एव हि उपपत्तेः

prathame'śravaṇāditi cet na tā eva hi upapatteḥ

prathame—primary; aśravaṇāt—because not heard; iti cet—if it be said; na—not so; tāḥ eva—that only; hi—because; upapatteḥ—the conclusion.

TRANSLATION

If it is said that because (the prāṇa is) not heard to be primary (therefore it cannot be called primary) (then we say) not so; it is only because (the primary cause) is the derived conclusion (and not directly found from the effects).

COMMENTARY

This sūtra uses contrasting words to the previous sūtra—instead of the term 'secondary', this sūtra uses the term 'primary'. Instead of the term śrutī (or that which is heard authoritatively), this sūtra used the term śravaṇāt (or that which is heard commonly). Beyond these contrasting words, the point of the sūtra is that we never arrive at the cause by the effects, the *pratyakśa* or the observation because there are potentially numerous explanations of the same effect. Rather, the effect is derived from the cause, which is called *upapatti* or the inference of the cause into effect. In modern language, we can distinguish these two as *truth* and *proof*. The effect we perceive is the truth, but it is not the cause. The cause is the proof underlying the truth—because truth is arrived at via the proof.

This is a rejection of empirical truth as knowledge. At least, it is knowledge only in a secondary or inferior sense. The real knowledge pertains to the reality which creates the effect, and that effect can be proved logically from the premise or the reality. The claim is that what we observe is heat and light, but that is merely the truth. We must generate this truth using a proof, and that proof—e.g., why, when, and how a possibility becomes a reality—is the real cause.

The existence of prāṇa entails the existence of the soul, since prāṇa represents the choices. Thus, impersonalism arising from the idea that the cause of observations is light or heat is rejected here as only being as a secondary cause. The real causation is attributed to a person whose choices generate heat and light.

QUESTION

But many impersonalists argue that choice or free will is an illusion. They cite Bhagavad-Gita 3.27 (The bewildered spirit soul, under the influence of the three modes of material nature, thinks himself to be the doer of activities, which are in actuality carried out by nature) to suggest that the soul is not doing anything; it is merely caught in the observation of material changes, but falsely considers itself to be the doer or controller. In short, there is no choice, and things are moving automatically due to matter. So whatever personalism we attribute to nature—e.g., that nature is controlled by demigods—must factually be an illusion because nature is said to be the cause according to scriptures.

3.1.6 (298)

अश्रुतत्वादिति चेत् न इष्टादकारिणां प्रतीतेः

aśrutatvāditi cet na iṣṭādikāriṇāṃ pratīteḥ

aśrutatvāt—due to being against the claims made in śrutī; iti cet—if it be said; na—not so; iṣṭādikāriṇām—the numerous controllers (e.g., soul and God) in the śrutī; pratīteḥ—becoming merely imaginary entities.

TRANSLATION

If it is said that due to (the claims of personal causality being) against śrutī (we cannot accept them), (then we say) not so (such a conclusion will entail that) the numerous controllers (e.g., soul and God) in the śrutī are imaginary.

COMMENTARY

In the beginning of this chapter, it was stated that the progression of the soul is due to the succession of questions and answers, and this progression involves a choice. The seeker is now rallying against the existence of choice from a different viewpoint than before, arguing for the determinism of material nature. Note that the soul has been held responsible for its fall in earlier chapters, and any attempt to shift the blame for one's choices to God or the circumstances has been refuted. But one can attack the idea using a different argument: namely, that matter is working deterministically and hence I have no choice. If I have no choice, then the succession of questions and answers doesn't involve a choice, and if that is the case, then I'm not responsible for my evolution.

The sūtra however counterargues and says that we have already acknowledged the existence of ātmā and Paramātma as the secondary and primary controllers of material nature. So, now saying that material nature is working automatically—i.e., without the intervention of conscious choices—would result in a contradiction. To solve this contradiction, we would have to say that the ātmā and Paramātma are imaginary entities, concocted by us. And such a claim then goes against the grain of previous statements and śrutī in general.

We can note here that some philosophers such as Hegel have described a dialectical model of change that involved thesis, antithesis, and synthesis. The trouble with this doctrine is its determinism. If the thesis is defined, then antithesis is just its logical opposite. And once both thesis and antithesis are defined, then the synthesis is also predetermined. Yes, the generation of the antithesis may seem a little counterintuitive under the notions of classical logic—How can X become not-X?—but this doesn't change the fact that the evolution is deterministic. Under this determinism, we have no choice; we are simply driven by the historical flow of thesis and antithesis, and if the thesis was fixed to begin with, then everything subsequently is predetermined. In short, we can argue that this dialectical model of change in the sequence of question and answer eliminates choices, which then eliminates the personalism and leads to a new kind of impersonalism—which has come to be known as 'dialectical materialism'.

The key point of inflexion in this argument is that asking a question is not stating an antithesis. Yes, the question presents a conflict with the premise or the thesis, and the answer to that question resolves the conflict to present a new answer which then becomes the thesis. However, the generation of the question from the thesis is not predetermined like the generation of antithesis from the thesis. For instance, if the thesis is that "I'm rich", then the questions can be "How do I become richer?" or "How do I spend my riches?". The antithesis on the other hand would be that "I'm poor", which will then lead to the synthesis that "I am moderately rich—neither rich nor poor". The opposition to that claim would again be "I'm not moderately rich" which could be interpreted in two ways—"I'm extremely rich" or "I'm extremely poor". How do you decide which of these two types of interpretations constitute the antithesis? And unless we can make that decision, the subsequent evolution will come to a halt. Therefore, even if we stick to the thesis-antithesis-synthesis model, we cannot escape choices because the model—while presented as determinism—is not so.

If choices are inevitable, then personalism cannot be avoided even if we adopt a dialectical model of material change. If there are choices, then there must be judgments—i.e., how do decide between the alternatives? These decisions must be rational, and the rationality involves truth, right, and good. Due to rightness, the choices have consequences, and due to goodness, these consequences may be painful, forcing us to revise our judgments and choices.

One can ask: if there are choices, then why is nature said to be governed by prakriti rather than the soul? The short answer is that there is a difference between the doer and the approver. Material nature puts up a proposal for approval, and executes that proposal, provided it is approved by the soul. Nature is therefore doing the grunt work of creating proposals and executing them. And yet, the soul is still the executive decision-maker who accepts and rejects these proposals. The false ego of the soul is not just that it is the decision maker, but that it is the doer. This claim is false because when a person goes to sleep, the body is still working even though we are not making choices. So, if the body can work on its own, the soul's decisions are unnecessary for nature. And yet, just because nature can work independently doesn't mean that is always so.

As we have noted earlier, if we don't make a choice to bring about a change, changes will be forced upon us. Choices can precede these forces and can be used to make a change before the change is imminently forced. So, the determinism of nature is not contrary to our choices; nature gives us an opportunity to make the right decisions and forces a change if we remain inert. It rewards good decisions, and punishes bad ones, but is not dependent upon us to bring a change. Thus, nature can work automatically *if* we don't act. Due to this action, the world will evolve regardless of our choices. Our choices are simply opportunities by which we can act correctly or incorrectly and enjoy or suffer as a consequence of the right or wrong choices made in an opportunity.

QUESTION

But if the soul was indeed the controller of the material world, then why would it be forced to suffer against its choices? Why would it be bound to do things that it is not truly desirous of doing? Isn't that against free will?

3.1.7 (299)

भाक्तं वानात्मवित्त्वात् तथा हि दर्शयति

bhāktaṃ vānātmavittvāt tathā hi darśayati

bhāktaṃ—in a secondary sense; vā—but; anātmavittvāt—on account of lack of self-knowledge; tathā—so; hi—because; darśayati—so seen.

TRANSLATION

(The causality in material elements) is said to be secondary (to the causality in the soul) but due to the lack of self-knowledge (the soul is) thus (bound by the laws of matter) because it sees (itself as being covered up by matter).

COMMENTARY

The soul is the controller of the body (as stated above) but it comes under the control of the body due to lack of self-knowledge. What is self-knowledge? That the soul is full of pleasure, and it doesn't need the support of the body to be happy. But because the soul doesn't know that there is happiness within itself, he seeks happiness in the external world, through the body and the senses. Thus, the soul becomes dependent on the body for his happiness and starts serving the body's needs rather than being the controller of the body. If the body's necessities are not fulfilled, the soul considers itself unhappy. When the same necessities are fulfilled, then the soul considers itself very happy. So, the happiness of the body becomes the happiness of the soul, rather than the happiness of the soul becoming the happiness of the body. In short, the soul becomes the servant of the body, rather than being the master of the body.

Topic 2

QUESTION

Then how can the soul recover its free will and get freedom from matter?

3.1.8 (300)

कृतात्यये ऽनुशयवान् दृष्टस्मृतिभ्याम् यथेतमनेवं च

kṛtātyaye'nuśayavān dṛṣṭasmṛtibhyām yathetamanevaṃ ca

kṛta—acquired; atyaye—on the finishing; anuśayavān—possessed of the consequences of one's actions; dṛṣṭasmṛtibhyām—from the recollection or memory of the soul; yathā etam—just as it is; anevam—not so; ca—and.

TRANSLATION

Upon the finishing of the previously acquired consequences of one's actions that possess the soul, (the covering of matter is) also (finished) from the memory of the seer (the soul) just as if it was never there (to begin with).

COMMENTARY

Several important points are made in this sūtra. First, the consequences of one's past actions are compared to a smṛiti or memory. Normally, the term memory is reserved for the things that we can recollect from the past. We call this the 'conscious' memory. However, in addition to these facts—which are generally limited to the events of this life—there are also memories from the past lives, which remain unconscious. These unconscious memories have three parts—(a) the *chitta* or the unconscious imprints of past events, (b) the habits or proclivities of enjoyment, and (c) the consequences of previous actions.

First, the chitta creates thoughts in us. Due to the proclivities of the past, we like or dislike these thoughts and develop our plans for enjoyment. Due to the results of previous actions, these plans are fulfilled or disrupted. The unconscious constitutes our 'causal body' or *kārana sarīra* that covers the soul life after life, and the subtle and the gross bodies are developed from it. The subtle body constitutes our conscious memories, thoughts, moralities, etc. And the gross body comprises the senses of perception and the organs in the body. Often, we see things that we instantly recognize, although we cannot find a conscious memory in this life about encountering these things. This is because the chitta has these memories which remain unconscious and can be manifest into our experience either on their own or due to contact with the external world. Similarly, our desires or tendencies and consequences of previous actions are manifest from the unconscious. All these are manifest because of time.

Second, by the time karma is destroyed, the material desires and the impressions of the past are also destroyed. Of course, it is possible that some souls who have overcome the material desires and the impressions of past lives that create thoughts in us may still have some residual karma. As a result, some pure souls may also continue to suffer or enjoy in the material world, even though they have become enlightened. However, the reverse is generally false—i.e., by the time karma is destroyed, the soul becomes free of all desires and impressions. Thus, this sūtra states that the destruction of karma entails freedom from the material covering of desires and past impressions, which then lead to complete freedom both from the push exerted by the thoughts and desires, and the consequences one is compelled to face to fulfill these thoughts and desires. Thus, the freedom from karma entails the removal of material covering.

Third, once this material covering is removed, the soul loses all history of material existence. It is now said to be eternally liberated, because the history of past births and deaths, the experiences of many lifetimes, and the fulfilled or unfulfilled desires of the past are all destroyed. Even though the soul was previously born in a body, and may exist in a body at the present, such a soul is said to be *nitya-siddha* or eternally liberated. It is as if there was never a material birth or death, and the soul had never entered the material existence. Thus, upon liberation, there is no difference between those souls who had never entered material existence, and those who had entered and were liberated.

QUESTION

You are saying that freedom from karma leads to freedom from the material covering. Why not the reverse—i.e., freedom from the material covering leading to freedom from karma? Can we not say that if a person has developed good qualities and conduct, he should be free of the consequences of past actions? After all, he has now learned the lessons of life, and corrected himself?

3.1.9 (301)

चरणादिति चेत् न उपलक्षणार्थेति कार्ष्णाजिनिः

caraṇāditi cet na upalakṣaṇārtheti kārṣṇājiniḥ

caraṇāt—due to conduct; iti cet—if it be said; na—not so; upalakṣaṇārthā—for the purpose of secondary qualities of a person (also known as their roles or duties); iti—thus; kārṣṇājiniḥ—Kārṣṇājini (states).

TRANSLATION

If it is said that due to good conduct (a person can become free of karma) (then we say) not so (because) the secondary qualities of a person (the roles and responsibilities of past actions still must be borne); thus, says Kārṣṇājini.

COMMENTARY

There is a doctrine in modern law that states that a person sent to prison due to their misdeeds can be freed earlier if they exhibit good behavior. In this doctrine, the purpose of punishment is to correct a person, and if the person has been corrected, then there is no need for them to suffer. Thus, those exhibiting good behavior are let go earlier than their normal sentence. This sūtra refutes such doctrines. It states that if a person has committed crimes, there is due punishment regardless of their corrected behavior. If they haven't been corrected, then they will commit more crimes in the future, and there will be subsequent punishments for them. But just the fact that someone is behaving well now doesn't entail a reduction in their punishments. This is important because people often ask: Why do bad things happen to good people? Their assumption is that if people have become good, then their punishments must also be reduced or eliminated. This sūtra, however, cites Kārṣṇājini as saying that a person must suffer all the karma regardless of whether they have been purified or not. It also means that the consequences of good and bad actions don't cancel each other. So, we cannot perform good deeds and hope to nullify bad karma. The good and bad actions produce individual results which must be endured.

There can be a debate about the meaning of *upalakṣaṇārthā* in this sūtra. For instance, one can argue that it denotes "indirect meaning", "secondary meaning", "indirect purpose", etc. Based on this we can translate this sūtra as follows: "If it is said that due to good conduct (a person can become free of karma) (then we say) not so (because) the hidden/indirect/secondary purposes or meanings in a person; thus, says Kārṣṇājini". Such a translation would imply that unless a person has suffered the consequences of their deeds, they cannot be said to have fully learned their lessons. Since they have gotten off easily, they may believe that there are ways to escape the punishment of bad deeds—e.g., doing good deeds or exhibiting good behavior and thus it is all right to mix both good and bad deeds as these can cancel each other's effects. Such alternative meanings of *upalakṣaṇārthā* don't change the purport, namely, that a person must endure their previous karma regardless of good behavior. This endurance can be attributed to the fact that bad karma exists and cannot be nullified by good behavior. Or, it can be attributed to the notion that nullifying such karma due to good behavior would create the wrong conclusion—i.e., that good deeds can be used to cancel the outcomes of bad deeds—which is unacceptable. So, regardless of how we interpret *upalakṣaṇārthā*, the purport is the same.

QUESTION

But freedom from suffering is often an incentive for people to improve. If we say that good behavior doesn't cancel the bad deeds, then doesn't it take away the incentives for a person's improvement? Some people may not improve if they think that improvement doesn't reduce their present suffering.

3.1.10 (302)

आनर्थक्यमिति चेत् न तदपेक्षत्वात्

ānarthakyamiti cet na tadapekṣatvāt

ānarthakyam—resulting in counterproductive outcomes; iti cet—if it be said; na—not so; tadapekṣatvāt—due to in comparison/contrast to that.

TRANSLATION

If it is said that (good qualities don't immediately lead to freedom from suffering) will result in counterproductive outcomes (i.e., people not renouncing bad deeds) (we say) not so due to the comparison/contrast to that.

COMMENTARY

If you purchase something on a loan, and you start paying the premiums of those loans, your good behavior of repaying those premiums doesn't reduce the number of premiums you have to pay. If this were the case, nobody would buy anything by paying cash; everyone would purchase things on a loan, pay some premiums, and then ask for a reduction in the total payment. Karma, similarly, is a debt, which must be paid in full. If one argues that a person under debt will get an incentive to be debt-free if the lender forgave the debt, the counterargument is that if such debts were forgiven, more people would want to get into debts because they wouldn't have to pay the full price of things. They can just buy things on a loan, pay some premiums, and then ask for clemency. Thus, such an arrangement would not reduce the number of people under debt. In fact, it would increase their numbers, besides, of course, creating an unfavorable situation for those who pay the full cost of a thing upfront in cash. In fact, those who were paying their loans fully, might now argue: Why do I have to pay the loan fully when so many others are not paying their loans? This sūtra contrasts the two competing positions and states that the outcomes of forgiving are even more counterproductive than the outcomes of not forgiving.

QUESTION

This objective treatment of karma may lead people to say that natural laws on morality are not compassionate as they don't forgive a person's actions. Isn't that criticism justified given that you say that nature's laws are unforgiving?

3.1.11 (303)
सुकृतदुष्कृते एवेति तु बादरिः
sukṛtaduṣkṛte eveti tu bādariḥ

sukṛta—good activities; duṣkṛte—evil activities; eva—certainly; iti—thus; bādariḥ—says the sage Badari.

TRANSLATION

(This argument can be) certainly applied to both good and evil activities; thus, says the sage Bādari (i.e., if it were applied to good activities, then sometimes we may not get the good returns on the previous good activities).

COMMENTARY

If one argues that delivering the just punishment to one who has already suffered a lot is uncompassionate, then how about we reverse the argument and say that giving happiness to someone who's had a lot of it already is unjust? If too much of the outcome of evil actions is unjust, then too much of the outcome of good actions must also be unjust. So, by that measure, even if someone has performed several good deeds, nature should not deliver the good returns in proportion because giving too much good to one person would be unjust. The point of the sūtra is that people ask for a reduction in the bad outcomes but not a reduction in good outcomes. How can we accept one but not the other? If we started reducing the outcomes of bad actions, then we would also need to reduce the outcomes of good actions, which means that the evildoers will suffer less, and the good-doers will enjoy less. Would that be considered justice?

Topic 3

QUESTION

The scriptures are primarily devoted to the description of good deeds, including those that lead to salvation. How can a person know what sin is, and how to lead one's life, if the descriptions of sins are not very prominent?

3.1.12 (304)

अनष्टिादकिारणिामपि च श्रुतम्

aniṣṭādikāriṇāmapi ca śrutam

aniṣṭādikāriṇām—the descriptions of sinful activities; api—even; ca—also; śrutam—is declared by the śrutī.

TRANSLATION

Even the descriptions of sinful activities are also given in the śrutī.

COMMENTARY

While the knowledge of Vedas is eternal and encompassing, its presentations may vary in emphasis based on time, place, and the type of persons. For example, if a society is not incestuous, then the scripture may not forbid incest, because it is considered unnecessary. They may instead, based on the lack of incest, instruct the people to treat other people's wives like their mothers and sisters. On the other hand, if incest was prominent in a society, then scripture would forbid incest, and not recommend other women to be treated like mothers and sisters (because the idea then would be that if incest is possible in the family, then even other women—who are like one's daughters and mothers—can also be enjoyed since they are just like our mothers and daughters).

Thus, what is present or absent in scriptures often depends on the people f the scripture is meant for. The descriptions of sinful activities are limited in the śrutī because society was almost sinless. Texts like Rig Veda don't describe hells. Atharva Veda describes places of suffering for sinful people, but these descriptions are not detailed. Yajur Veda provides more substantive descriptions about hells. Thus, this sūtra states that there are descriptions of sinful activities in the śrutī. The use of *api* and *ca* indicates that these are "also described". It is accepted that the emphasis is not on such descriptions, but they are present indicatively for those who might be interested in such guidance.

QUESTION

But there are many people who don't accept the descriptions of sin in scriptures. How can they be corrected from the performance of sinful actions?

3.1.13 (305)

संयमने त्वनुभूयेतरेषामारोहावरोहौ तदगति दर्शनात्

saṃyamane tvanubhūyetareṣāmārohāvarohau tadgati darśanāt

saṃyamane—in the abode of Yama; tu—but; anubhūya—having experienced; atareṣām—of others; ārohāvarohau—the ascent and descent; tadgati—the result of the actions; darśanāt—from the observation.

TRANSLATION

(A person can be corrected from sinful activities) in the abode of Yama; but having experienced the ascent and descent of others, resulting from their previous actions, one can (also) be corrected from such observation (of others).

COMMENTARY

There are three prominent methods of knowledge—*pratyakśa, anumāna,* and śabda, or direct experience, inference from experience, and scriptural knowledge. If someone doesn't accept the word of the scriptures, they can obtain the same knowledge by direct experience or inference from experience. These two methods are referred in this sūtra. The direct experience is provided in the planets of Yamarāja who administers the results of sinful activities by punishing the sinner. Otherwise, we can also observe how other people are going up and down in the lives and understand that their enjoyment or suffering is due to their previous actions. This is knowledge by inference—namely that if other people are suffering or enjoying, then the distinction must be due to their past activities, and hence one must avoid sinful activities. In short, we should not consider suffering and enjoyment to be accidents of life. We must try to explain them, and the logical inference is that enjoyment and suffering are due to one's past actions. Thus, the preferred method of knowledge is scriptural descriptions, but if one doesn't accept that, then there is knowledge by inference obtained when one learns from the experience of others. If a person is still not convinced (and regards these as accidents) then there is direct experience. Thus, like all other knowledge, the knowledge of sins is available in many ways.

QUESTION

But don't you think a detailed description of hells and their respective sufferings is important if people are to avoid various kinds of sufferings?

3.1.14 (306)

स्मरन्तिच

smaranti ca

smaranti—the smritis declare; ca—also.

TRANSLATION

(Those interested in a detailed understanding of the hells) can also refer to the smṛiti (such as the Purāṇa, or texts such as the Manu Smṛiti).

COMMENTARY

Detailed descriptions of hells are found in several Purāṇa such as the Śrīmad Bhāgavatam and the Devi-Bhāgavata Purāṇa. They are also found in Manu Smṛiti. Here is another instance in which the Vedānta Sūtra treats the śrutī and smṛiti as a continuum of texts providing different kinds of information. If the description of hells is not prominently found in the śrutī—because these were meant for the almost sinless souls—they are prominently found in the smṛiti which are meant for the common population. Thus, we can see that the different descriptions are relative to the kind of people. The knowledge is universal, but its presentation changes emphasis depending on the audience. The sinless souls don't need descriptions of hells, as they are already disinterested in such things. The sinful souls—which may be found among the common population—can easily benefit from such descriptions. Still, the description of hells is less than 1% of the content of the smṛiti. It means that even those reading the smṛiti were expected to be mostly sinless.

QUESTION

Is the suffering for all kinds of sinful activities the same? Or are there differences in the type of suffering endured for different kinds of sinful acts?

3.1.15 (307)

अपि च सप्त

api ca sapta

api ca—moreover; sapta—seven.

TRANSLATION

(The sinful activities and the hells) are moreover seven (distinct types).

COMMENTARY

The conscious experience of the soul is divided in Sāñkhya into seven layers—morality, ego, intellect, mind, senses, properties, and objects. Based on this seven-fold layering of experience, the universe is divided into upper and lower halves, each with seven parts where the pleasure dominates in these seven layers of experience. The earth planetary system is the seventh in the upper half of the universe, and the primary pleasure here is derived from objects. In svarga, however, the senses themselves can create pleasure. In further higher planetary systems, pleasure is obtained through the actions of the mind, the intellect, the ego, and the moral sense. In all these seven planetary systems, there is morality tied to the existence of the Lord; that is, there is an understanding that the punishment of sinful activities is meant to uplift a person toward transcendence. But as one goes into lower planetary systems, this understanding gradually vanishes and is replaced by the fear of powerful authorities that govern these places. These lower realms are ruled by demons, and in this society the duties are performed not due to the desire for transcendence or spiritual upliftment but due to the fear of the rulers, government, etc. There is no inner desire for perfection; it is only the fear of punishment that controls the demonic.

Each of these fourteen planetary systems (seven above and seven below) are sometimes further divided into fourteen subparts. The bhūloka is, for instance, divided into seven 'islands' and 'oceans'. This method of division is often carried forward into subsequent subdivisions. Thus, depending on the level of detail, the same seven-fold method of division is employed many times. This method of division is referenced in this sūtra regarding the hells as well.

The Śrīmad Bhāgavatam and Devi-Bhāgavata Purāṇa describe the existence of 28 hells, mimicking the 28-fold division of the non-hellish regions. This sūtra shortens that description and refers only to a seven-fold division. We can infer that these divisions pertain to the suffering at various levels of experience ranging from the body, sensations, senses, mind, intellect, ego, and moral sense. A soul can suffer in many ways. For example, if someone doesn't receive justice in a society, the pain is experienced in their moral sense. The pain of being cheated is experienced through a person's ego. The pain of having accepted false information as true, is experienced in the intellect. The pain of misunderstanding is felt in the mind. The pain of ineptitude is felt in the senses. And the pain of hot and cold is felt through the sensations. Finally, the suffering of the body includes weakness, tiredness, and numerous kinds of illnesses. Everybody doesn't suffer in the same way. Depending on the source of their sinful actions, the results of sinful actions are also reaped in the same way.

QUESTION

When a person suffers a lot, he sometimes takes shelter of the Lord, begs for forgiveness, and promises a change in his attitude. Is this true for the hells, and can a person remember the Lord even in hell, just like the present life?

3.1.16 (308)

तत्रापि च तद्व्यापारादविरोधः

tatrāpi ca tadvyāpārādavirodhaḥ

tatra—there; api—even; ca—and; tat-vyāpārāt—due to the business of that (i.e., progressing in spiritual life); avirodhaḥ—is not impeded (by suffering).

TRANSLATION

Even there (in the hells) due to the business of that (i.e., progressing in spiritual life) not being impeded (by the suffering of the body and mind).

COMMENTARY

Abrahamic religions believe in an eternal hell; this idea is summarily rejected here. Not only is hell not eternal, but it doesn't forbid one from progressing in spiritual life. In fact, as people turn toward God during suffering, the soul can get purified of his sinful desires, even as he undergoes many types of suffering, thus preparing him for a better life after the hellish existence. Spiritual progress can never be impeded by any material circumstances—good or bad. When the situation is good, the spiritualist takes advantage of the comforts and diverts his attention toward spiritual practices. When the situation is bad, the spiritualist still takes advantage of the situation and learns to be detached from the material existence and focuses on transcendence. Thus, for the spiritualist, no situation is harmful, as all situations lead to spiritual progress.

QUESTION

How can a person who has seen hellish life (because they ignored the word of scriptures) prevent recurrence of this life? Also, how can one who wants to avoid going to hell prevent the occurrence of sinful activities in their life?

3.1.17 (309)

वद्याकर्मणोरिति तु प्रकृतत्वात्

vidyākarmaṇoriti tu prakṛtatvāt

vidyākarmaṇoḥ—the knowledge of actions (and consequences); iti—thus; tu—but; prakṛtatvāt—from producing or creating (the body and life).

TRANSLATION

From the knowledge of actions (and consequences) as noted earlier (i.e., in the śrutī and smriti) but (also the knowledge of) how actions create (new life).

COMMENTARY

It is impossible to list all kinds of sinful activities just as it is impossible to list all kinds of good deeds. A partial list of good and evil deeds is present in the scriptures, subject to the time, place, and the type of persons involved. If one wants to ensure that he is not performing sinful deeds, one must learn the science of how our actions create future lives. This science involves three parts. First, every action leaves behind a memory in the *chitta*, which can become a thought, which can become a desire and lead to sinful activities. Thus, the purification of the *chitta* is the primary means of avoiding sinful actions. Second, every action we perform becomes a liking and habit at an unconscious level; if we have done something once, we have formed a habit, which can recur. These habits will then make us believe that it is all right to do sinful actions again—after all, we have done them once; what's the harm in doing it again? These habits lead to a new body; for example, a meat-eater will be born in a species where meat-eating is a natural habit or tendency. Third, the consequences of the actions leave behind karma which then puts the soul into a new type of circumstances where the soul is forced to suffer or enjoy; for instance, due to good karma a tiger will get to hunt and eat deer, but due to bad karma, the same tiger will either have to stay hungry or eat the leftovers of other tigers.

Thus, if one understands the science of how the present body leads to a new body, then the quality of future lives decides what we do right now. For instance, if we want to be born again in a human body, then we should avoid the tendencies of animals who hunt, kill, and eat other animals. We don't even have to understand the prescriptions of the scriptures that killing is bad; we just must know that if we act like animals, then we will be reborn as animals. Likewise, if we understand that by cheating and deceiving others, we would also be cheated and deceived in the future, then the numerous ways of cheating and deceiving don't have to be found in the scriptures. If we understand that every action creates an impression and forms a habit, which then produces subsequent thoughts and behaviors, then we would be careful about what we think and what habits we form. The cause of suffering is the lack of understanding of how a new life is created by the actions of the present life. If this knowledge was acquired, then the person who knows this would avoid all sinful actions.

QUESTION

But so many people are incapable of understanding the laws of karma and how it creates the body. They may not want to neglect the word of scriptures or the process of reincarnation and karma. But they just don't understand it. What happens to people who are not intelligent and capable of knowledge?

3.1.18 (310)

न तृतीये तथोपलब्धेः

na tṛtīye tathopalabdheḥ

na—not; tṛtīye—in the third; tathā—so; upalabdheḥ—being found in.

TRANSLATION

(Those who are incapable of understanding the knowledge of karma and reincarnation) are not found in the third stage of existence (hellish planets).

COMMENTARY

The material universe is divided into three parts—heavenly planets, demonic planets, and the hellish planets. The entry into hellish planets is ascribed to those who are openly atheistic and disregardful of the scriptural injunctions. Those who are unintelligent, uneducated, or uninformed about these injunctions are treated just like animals who have no idea about morality, the purpose of human life, and how it is restricted by the laws of nature. Their ignorance is not punished by the experience of hellish planets according to this sūtra. They are just unfit to be humans, and they are hence reborn as animals. Animals too have some altruism, but that is not because of a moral sense of responsibility. It is only because of emotional attachment and kinship. Thus, many animals protect their own, not because of a sense of duty, but due to attachment. Animal society is not structured hierarchically in which the powerful are also aware of their responsibilities. Animal society is simply power without responsibility. Therefore, those who cannot understand responsibility are born as animals. If they have good karma, they also get power. If they have bad karma, they are born weak. They still suffer and enjoy, but they don't feel guilty about their bad actions, nor do they feel unhappy about the injustices by the powerful.

QUESTION

Many people may think of doing something bad but may not do it. Is the thought of sinful activities also punishable by the experience of hells?

3.1.19 (311)

स्मर्यतेऽपि च लोके

smaryate'pi ca loke

smaryate—thinking; api—also; ca—and; loke—in the world.

TRANSLATION

And those thinking (about sins) are also in the world (that is not hellish).

COMMENTARY

The succession of sūtras here is quite interesting because the previous sūtra asked if a person who performs actions unknowingly—i.e., has no conscious intention of being sinful—is sent to hell, and the answer was no. This sūtra responds to a different question—what if the person is consciously intending, but doesn't enact those intentions? The answer to that question is again no. In short, both the action and the intention are considered. If there is unintentional action, then there is some punishment, but it is not hell. Likewise, if there is intention without a corresponding action, then again there is no hell. However, a person who harbors evil thoughts is best suited to live a life where these thoughts may be fulfilled. This will be clarified in subsequent sūtras where people who possess sinful thoughts are born into lower forms of life. In short, those who harbor sinful thoughts, but don't act on them, are not sent to hell, but they don't continue in human life either. They are considered fit for animal life forms.

There is hence a distinction between guna and karma. Those who perform sinful actions produce adverse karma. But those who simply think sinful thoughts still create sinful guna. Such living entities change their bodies where they can fulfill their sinful desires, without incurring sin or hellish life.

Karma doesn't disable the mind, or the other subtle instruments such as intellect, ego, and morality. If karma disabled the mind, then one could claim that all subsequent misdeeds are caused by the mind not working properly, and one misdeed, therefore, leads to another misdeed, which then perpetuates an eternal cycle of misdeeds. However, if one constantly thinks of sinful activities, their morality, ego, intellect, mind, and senses become unfit for human life.

Such people may also perform sinful activities in this life. Thus, many people are too selfish to execute their responsibilities; they keep exploiting others but do not give in return on par with what they are taking from them. Some are extremely egoistic and insensitive to others. Some present false ideas as truth. And many are simply illusioned by the preponderance of false ideas. As one performs sins under various influences, the cause of the sin is traced back to the mind, the intellect, the ego, or the moral sense. Thus, if sinful reactions originate in a bad morality, then the punishment is also felt in the moral sense—e.g., others will behave selfishly with them. If the sins originate in the ego, then the punishment is also felt in the ego—e.g., they will be humiliated by others. If the sins originate in the intellect, then the punishment is also felt in the intellect—e.g., they will be cheated and deceived. If the sins originate in the mind, then the punishment is also felt in the mind—e.g., those who misinterpret others would be misinterpreted themselves. Thus, it must be understood that if things remain in the mind, the intellect, the ego, or the moral sense, then the soul simply changes the body appropriate for that type of mentality. But if the mental activity becomes the bodily activity, then the soul suffers not just bodily but is also hurt mentally, intellectually, emotionally, and morally. But this hurt doesn't disable the mind, the intellect, the ego, or the moral sense. Therefore, the working of karma is very nuanced and difficult to understand. There is no sin unless the body acts; if the body acts, then mental suffering is entailed by the sinful activity; and yet, despite this suffering, the mind can still prevent the recurrence of sinful activities and stop the cycle of action and reaction.

QUESTION

What about people who see criminal acts being performed but aren't doing those actions themselves? Does this silent observation lead one to hell?

3.1.20 (312)

दर्शनाच्च

darśanācca

darśanāt—on account of observation; ca—also.

TRANSLATION

On account of observation also (one doesn't go to hell).

COMMENTARY

Seeing a sinful activity is not the same as doing the sinful activity. This, however, holds true only when the person seeing these activities is not authorized to prevent its occurrence. For instance, leaders who are responsible for others' behavior cannot escape their responsibility by saying that I was only observing the sins, and I'm sinless because I did not perform the sins. Thus, the Kshatriya or the rulers are implicated if they neglect their duties silently. This statement applies only to those who are not expected to prevent others from sinful actions, and yet, they may be silent observers to others' sinful activities.

Inaction is also the action of endorsing the sinful actions when a person in authority is expected to prevent it. The person who is not in such a position to prevent the sinful actions cannot be said to be endorsing it. However, this doesn't mean that they go unpunished. There is still punishment, although the suffering is not as severe as those of the hellish planets. Conversely, those in the position of power, who do not prevent sinful actions, are destined to hell.

QUESTION

But many of these people—who watch the performance of sinful actions—may not protest them because they are enjoying their performance. They may not do such sins themselves, but they like to watch others do such sins. Doesn't karma punish them in some way? Or, are they considered totally sinless?

3.1.21 (313)

तृतीयशब्दावरोधःसंशोकजस्य

tṛtīyaśabdāvarodhaḥ saṃśokajasya

tṛtīya-śabda-avarodhaḥ—the third stage is said to be not advocated for them; saṃśokajasya—they are born into species that spring from sweat.

TRANSLATION

The third stage (the hellish planets) are said to be not advocated for them; they are born into species that spring from sweat (called *svedaja* species).

COMMENTARY

Vedic texts identify four kinds of births—*andaja* (born from eggs, like reptiles), *pindaja* (born from a womb, like humans), *svedaja* (born from sweat, like bacteria), *udbhija* (born from the seed, like plants). The *svedaja* body subsists on rotting materials. Among these four classes, they are the lowest type of birth, and this sūtra states that those living entities who enjoy watching the performance of sinful activities are born to subsist upon rotting materials. An example of such decadence is watching illicit sex, gambling, stealing, and murder in movies. People who watch such movies may not do these things as they know they are wrong. But they still like to watch others do it and perpetrate the performance of such activities in society by paying for such 'entertainment'.

The progression of these sūtras indicates successively greater types of sins, which are yet not sinful enough to take a person to hell. Thus, we first spoke about those who perform sins unknowingly. Then we spoke about people who know what is right and wrong, and they don't perform the sinful actions because of this knowledge, but they cannot stop thinking about doing these sins. Then we spoke about those who know the difference between right and wrong, but they might not have the courage to stop their occurrence even when they see it. Now we are speaking about those who don't perform such sins, but they still enjoy watching sinful actions and may pay others for doing them.

This decadent form of pleasure is condemned in this sūtra, and those enjoying such decadence are said to be born to subsist on rotting materials. They are not as sinful as those who perform such actions. But because of their tendencies to enjoy such decadent pleasure, they are born as bacteria and worms.

Topic 4

QUESTION

Are all sinful creatures reborn into the species produced from sweat?

3.1.22 (314)

तत्साभाव्यापत्तिःउपपत्तेः

tatsābhāvyāpattiḥ upapatteḥ

tat-sābhāvya—according to their nature; āpattiḥ—misfortune or calamity; upapatteḥ—being the reasonable conclusion.

TRANSLATION

According to their nature, and whatever is a reasonable conclusion (based upon their activities), a misfortune or calamity (is assigned to them).

COMMENTARY

The previous sūtra described the qualification for entering the *svedaja* body. But we have previously spoken of other types of sinful activities, such as doing sins unknowingly, thinking about doing sinful activities, and watching sinful activities uncomfortably but not preventing their occurrence. Those who enjoy seeing others do sinful activities are condemned to be born out of rotting materials, but this is not the fate of every other sinful type of person. This sūtra states that there are many grades of life and one goes to them according to their nature. All these species are called a calamity or misfortune. However, the level of misfortune is decided by assigning whatever is a reasonable response.

Topic 5

QUESTION

Is the soul stuck in these lower species of life for a very long time? Or does he get a chance to get back to the human form of life after a short while?

3.1.23 (315)
नातचिरिण वशिषात्
nāticireṇa viśeṣāt

na—not; aticireṇa—in a very long time; viśeṣāt—due to specialties.

TRANSLATION

(The soul) is not (in lower species of life) for a long time (if) there are special qualities (which entitle the soul to be reborn into the human form of life).

COMMENTARY

The entry into the animal species of life is contingent upon their guna. With this guna, they can enjoy or suffer their specific natures. Thus, some dogs remain street dogs, while other dogs get a comfortable home. Some cows are protected by their owners, while other cows are slaughtered by their owners. Enjoyment or suffering doesn't end even as the soul leaves one body and enters another. However, the nature of the enjoyment or suffering changes depending on the guna. Therefore, a soul who enters an animal body due to some animalistic qualities can come back to higher forms of life if their guna changes.

The animal form of life is obtained due to the dominance of tamo-guna. If the tamo-guna reduces, and rajo-guna increases, then the soul is reborn into the human life. This sūtra notes that life in the animal body is limited if tamo-guna is limited. Thus, one should not try to generalize all living entities born into a lower species as being equally sinful. Some of them are less sinful, and if their tendencies are corrected, then their existence in these species is shorter.

Topic 6

QUESTION

Can the soul be born without a mother or father from a species? In other words, can life be created out of material elements, without another life?

People often get tired of the difficulty in understanding the process of rebirth. There is a role for the body and the mind; when the mental activity manifests into the body, there is sin, but otherwise, there is simply change in the body. Whether or not there is sin, the suffering is not eternal. In fact, the soul can remember the Lord even in hell. And some bodies are long-lived while others are short-lived. Sometimes, the soul goes through many bodies before returning to human life. And sometimes the soul may return to human life after one animal birth. Troubled by these difficulties, some people have a knee-jerk reaction: Let's forget about all these complexities, and just say that all life is temporary; the birth into a specific type of species has no explanation, etc.

Such questions are found not just in atheists or materialists. Even many spiritual aspirants, who have practiced some form of spiritual process, can also fall into this trap if they are unable to understand the complex explanations. They now seek alternative explanations, including materialistic answers.

Even many religions are victims of such knee-jerk reactions. Faced with the difficulties in explaining rebirth, they claim that there are no demigods or demons, animals and trees have no life, the soul is born in a human life only once, and after this human life, there is eternal salvation or eternal hell.

3.1.24 (316)
अन्याधिष्ठिते पूर्ववत् अभिलापात्
anyādhiṣṭhite pūrvavat abhilāpāt

anya-adhiṣṭhite—into what is ruled by another; pūrvavat—as in the previous cases; abhilāpāt—due to the manifestation.

TRANSLATION

(A soul is born) into a body that is ruled by another (soul), just like the previous soul (was born into a body ruled by another soul). (This birth into different bodies is) due to the manifestation (of their guna and karma).

COMMENTARY

Material scientists like to believe that life is created from matter, but in this sūtra, this idea is rejected. Life is always created by a previously existing living body, and that life too was produced from a previously living entity. So, there is never a point in which the living being is produced from non-living matter. We have already discussed that matter exists as a possibility and therefore all species of life are eternally possible. They are, however, manifest occasionally, and this sūtra states that the birth into a species is according to the process of this manifestation. The process of manifestation is based on the soul's desires and the consequences of their previous actions. The desires determine the type of mind and body, and the consequences of previous actions decide the kind of environment this body is placed into. Thus, the soul can be born not just into different bodies but also into different environments. These two are sometimes called nature and nurture in modern times. The nature is the soul's desires or guna, while the nurture is caused by the soul's actions or their karma.

This sūtra is testimony to the fact that even after discussing the nature of the Absolute Truth, devotion to the Lord, the nature of the soul's bondage and suffering, one is still prone to falling back into the trap of materialistic thinking. When such questions arise, scientific knowledge of rebirth, guna, and karma become essential. Therefore, one must not prematurely consider oneself advanced in spiritual life unless they have understood the process of rebirth. Such questions can arise at any time in anyone's mind, and they destroy a person's spiritual endeavors if left unaddressed. Unless a soul is situated in perfect bliss through the realization of the Lord and has completely transcended the cycle of repeated birth and death, the scientific knowledge of birth and death never ceases to be relevant. One neglects the philosophy at their own peril.

QUESTION

This process seems imperfect because there are so many species that aren't manifest at any time, and so many new species are created at different times.

So, how can we say that a soul is born according to their desire and action?

The argument of the previous sūtra is continued here. Even though we have discussed the eternity of matter earlier, the same topics are revived again for a simple reason—the discussion of sin, death, rebirth, and entry into hell, generally makes a person atheistic. Who is God to judge my actions, and cause my repeated births, or punishment in hell? Everything that was learned previously is forgotten if we are assigned responsibility. Thus, we find many pseudo spiritualists who talk about happiness and liberation but never discuss sin and hell. They simply like to speak about all the good that can happen if someone follows some practice, but they don't like to discuss the fate of those who don't. But if these topics are somehow encountered, the pseudo spiritualist becomes a materialist. He starts saying: there is no hell or heaven; these are just our creations. All spiritual practices are then not for liberation from the cycle of birth and death; they are only to obtain greater peace and happiness in this life.

3.1.25 (317)
अशुद्धमिति चेत् न शब्दात्
aśuddhamiti cet, na, śabdāt

aśuddham—imperfect; iti cet—if it be said; na—not so; śabdāt—based on the statements in the scriptures (i.e., the descriptions of the various *yuga*).

TRANSLATION

If it is said that this process of manifestation is imperfect (because many species are not always present) (we say) not so; (these species are manifest in due course of time) based on the descriptions of the scriptures.

COMMENTARY

The manifestation of the possibilities involves two distinct tiers—cosmic and individual. Due to time, certain unmanifest things go into the 'about to manifest' state; what seemed impossible earlier becomes possible; this is the cosmic stage of manifestation. Subsequently, a living entity can convert this 'about to manifest' state of matter into a manifest state. The living entity enters a certain type of body based on their desires. And this body is placed in a certain kind of environment based on the consequences of their previous actions. Thus, even if a living entity wants to be born in a certain type of species, he must wait until the time for the manifestation of that species has arrived. Thus, the cosmic evolution of the species is predetermined by time, but the birth of a specific individual into that species is based on their desires and previous actions.

The influence of time is described in the scriptures as the cycles of *yuga* and *manavantara*. All things happen at their pre-appointed time, not before or after. The universe is completely deterministic in terms of what will happen when. However, the universe does not determine who will do what. Therefore, the soul's desires and actions determine their future body under the control of time. Due to time, not everything is possible at every moment. But due to the soul, not everybody will choose to be the instrument of every timely possibility.

QUESTION

But so many species are not present right now (such as dinosaurs). How can they be created if you insist that they are only created by living beings? How can these unmanifest species come into manifestation without parents?

The theory of evolution has become a standard doctrine for atheism. According to this doctrine, since some living bodies have ceased to exist, therefore, the species must be evolving. If the species are evolving, then we can say that even humans have evolved from other species. And if humans have evolved from previous species, then there was a time we did not exist. And if the human species is not eternal, therefore, the present life cannot be ascribed an eternal or transcendental purpose. If such eternity is not possible, then rebirth must also be an illusion. If rebirth is an illusion, then moral responsibility, eternal hell, or heaven, must be fictions of the human mind to enforce moral behavior on the humans. If people could create such fictions in the past, then we can also create another set of fictional moral principles—which evolve with time—now. Thus, we can be 'good' people without requiring God, but that good is either subjective, or collectively intersubjective. It cannot be defined in an eternal way.

3.1.26 (318)

रेतःसिग्योगोऽथ

retaḥ sigyogo'tha

retaḥ sika-yogo—union of male and female procreative fluids; atha—then.

TRANSLATION

By the mixing of the male and female procreative fluids.

COMMENTARY

The atheistic reasoning of the theory of evolution can be arrested at the very first step by answering the question: How do species appear and disappear at different times? The answer is that material bodies are combinations of three modes—the universal, the individual, and the contextual. The dinosaur is a universal. It sometimes becomes an individual and is then born in some contexts or environments. The same universal can appear as many individuals, in different contexts. Therefore, the universal is separate from the individual and the contextual. When we study the fossils of the dinosaurs, we see the individual and the contextual. But we don't see the universal. And without the universal, it seems that the appearance of a species must be the accident of the environment. If the environment changes, then the species must be destroyed.

This kind of thinking is borne out of materialism in which ideas don't exist. Or if they exist, then they are simply epiphenomena of chemical reactions. However, we also know that if we take out modalities from a scientific description, then the theory is always incomplete. Evolutionary theory is also incomplete for several reasons. The first reason is that all scientific theories must provide predictions, but evolutionary theory cannot make predictions. The second reason is that scientific theories must provide explanations that are necessary and sufficient, but evolutionary explanations are neither necessary nor sufficient. For instance, the mechanism of evolution is random mutation, but since there is no cause of the random mutation, therefore, the explanation is insufficient. Similarly, the adaptation by natural selection doesn't indicate which direction the evolution could go—should the species adapt to the environment, or does the environment adapt to the species? Since the theory cannot say which adaption is preferred, therefore, the explanation is not necessary. If we consider the theory of evolution as a scientific theory, then by the same measure, we must also consider every other doctrine that doesn't predict and doesn't provide an explanation that is necessary and sufficient, as a scientific theory! That should mark the end of all scientific questions and rational inquiries.

However, refuting the random mutation and adaptation mechanisms of evolution is not the explanation of how the universals are instantiated. This sūtra provides an answer, which is—consistent with the previous claim that every new life is born out of previous life—that there is always a mother and a father. Does this mean that dinosaurs are always born out of previously existing dinosaur parents? Not necessarily. The mother and the father can belong to another species, although there must always be a mother and a father.

This viewpoint calls into question a very fundamental assumption in modern biology—genetic inheritance. The claim is that the genes of the child must be like the genes of the parents, and children can only have minor differences with their parents. The similarity between parents and children is not accepted in the Vedic texts. We already know of numerous ways in which children can differ from their parents. The children can be much taller than their parents, far more intelligent than their parents, or have talents that their parents did not. But biologists claim that these are merely phenotypical rather than genotypical differences. In short, the children of a human will always be humans. If at all there is a possibility of variation, then, they must also occur very slowly.

However, the Vedic texts describe how non-human species are born from humans. An example is Kadru and Vinita—two wives of sage Kaśyapa—giving birth to snakes and to the bird Garuda, respectively. Similarly, the demigods and demons are created from the wombs of Aditi and Diti, respectively—also wives of Kaśyapa. While the process by which the children differ so significantly from their parents is not discussed here, the Vedic texts mention that Kaśyapa was empowered by Brahma to broaden the population and the types of species in the universe. This sūtra only states that new species are born by the mixing of the male and female procreative fluids. What is uncommon, however, is that the parents of one species can create children of another species. The creation by sages such as Kaśyapa is detailed in the subsequent sūtras.

QUESTION

Then a materialist can argue that if they are able to create the male and female procreative fluids as chemicals and combine them, then they can also create new species. Doesn't this contradict your previous statement that all life comes from previously existing life, rather than from non-living matter?

3.1.27 (319)
योनेःशरीरम्
yoneḥ śarīram

yoneḥ—from the womb; śarīram—body.

TRANSLATION

The body (of the new species) must be built in the womb (of a mother).

COMMENTARY

Scientists can isolate the genetic material of a male and a female as chemicals and mix them outside a living body. However, a living body doesn't develop unless this mixture of genetic material is implanted back into the body of a living mother. As we have discussed before, matter doesn't move by itself; it is always moved by the influence of prāṇa. Thus, for instance, food cannot reach a fertilized egg without the presence of prāṇa. It is prāṇa that causes the ingestion, digestion, circulation, and excretion. Similarly, processes like cell division, the specialization of a cell into different kinds of cells uniquely suited for different functions in the body, the formation of a functional structure, etc. are all dependent on the presence of prāṇa. Life is therefore not identified with the material elements; it is rather identified with the presence of prāṇa. And prāṇa is always associated with the presence of a soul. A mother's body feeds and builds the body of a child, or the mother produces an egg which is imbued with the life force that can produce a child. Although chemicals can be mixed outside a living body, the life force cannot be created by these mixtures. Therefore, a living mother is essential to produce life, and the idea that because we can mix the genetic material in a test tube, we can also create new life, is false. Yes, we can produce new kinds of genetic materials, but we can't create new life if there wasn't already a type of life that can convert the genes into a living body.

SECTION 2

Topic 1

QUESTION

You are saying that the species are created in due course of time by the combination of some appropriate mother and father, according to the cycles of time described in the scriptures. Do these creations happen all throughout the ages, or is there a certain phase in which the species are dominantly produced?

3.2.1 (320)

संध्ये सृष्टिराह हि

saṃdhye sṛṣṭirāha hi

saṃdhye—in the sandhi stage (between the various ages); sṛṣṭiḥ—(there is) creation (of the new species); āha—suddenly; hi—certainly.

TRANSLATION

(New species) are certainly suddenly produced during the *sandhi* (the joining between the different ages called the yuga and chatur-yugī).

COMMENTARY

Vedic cosmology describes time as comprising of cycles called *yuga*. These yuga are aggregated into cycles of four called a *chatur-yugī*. These chatur-yugī are aggregated into a cycle called *kalpa*, which are then aggregated into a cycle called *manavantara*. The periods between these successive yuga, chatur-yugī, kalpa, and manavantara are called *sandhi* (hyphenation or conjunction) or *sandhyā* (the evening of the previous phase of the cycle). The durations of these conjunctive periods vary depending on the type of cycle that is beginning or ending. Thus, longer cycles also have longer periods of sandhi, while shorter cycles have a shorter period of sandhi. All the sandhi, however, occur at predefined periods of time. This period of transition is said to destroy most of the previously existing life forms, in what seems like a partial annihilation. This sūtra states that the creation of most of the species also occurs during this stage. So, the period of sandhi destroys older species and creates new ones.

This idea goes against the notion of gradual evolution, where species are slowly created over a long period of time. This sūtra states that there is sudden creation of species (and elsewhere we can find descriptions of destruction at the end of each age). There is some empirical evidence of this sudden creation in what is today called the Cambrian Explosion where many species are known to have been suddenly manifest, counter to the notion of gradual evolution.

QUESTION

It is said in Vedic texts that Brahma is the creator of all the species, and so he should create all the species at the beginning of the universe. Then why are new species manifest at different stages (the sandhi) during the creation?

3.2.2 (321)

नरि्मातारं चैके पुत्रादयश् च

nirmātāraṃ caike putrādayaś ca

nirmāta—well instructed; itāraṃ—the others; ca—and; ike—some; putrā-dayaḥ—sons etc.; ca—also.

TRANSLATION

And well-instructed, the others are created by some of the sons as well.

COMMENTARY

The creation of the species is described in the Purāṇa, and it begins when Brahma creates four sons called the four Kumāra. He asks them to perform austerities before they begin producing further progeny. However, these four sons become enlightened by their austerities and refuse to engage in the process of sexual creation. In fact, to never be enamored by sex, they refuse to grow up beyond the age of four. Brahma then very angry at their refusal to obey his orders, and as a result Rudra—the 'crying one'—is born. Brahma doesn't consider Rudra suitable for creating further progeny and considering the futility of anger, Brahma then creates more sons, and is finally successful in expanding the population and filling the universe with various kinds of species. Kaśyapa, as discussed above, is one such son, who creates demigods and demons, birds and snakes, etc. Thus, Brahma is the creator of the sons, who create further species. Thus, the term *ike putra* or some sons is used because other sons (like the four Kumāra) did not create further progeny. Likewise, the term *itara* or the others is used to indicate that Brahma created some sons who then created other species. Thus, the creation is primarily attributed to Brahma, and secondarily to his sons. But not all his sons are the cause of the subsequent creations.

QUESTION

In what way is Brahma and his sons said to be the creators when the material energy is said to be the real creative energy? You have previously mentioned that the Lord injects the soul into the material energy, just like a father impregnates a mother. Then how are Brahma and his sons the creators?

3.2.3 (322)

मायामात्रं तु कार्त्स्न्येनानभिव्यक्तस्वरूपत्वात्

māyāmātraṃ tu kārtsnyenānabhivyaktasvarūpatvāt

māyā—the illusory covering; mātraṃ—only; tu—but; kārtsnyena—in entirety; anabhivyakta-svarūpatvāt—by the unmanifest state of forms.

TRANSLATION

But the illusory covering only produces the forms in their entirety by creating the unmanifest forms (which are manifest by Brahma and his sons).

COMMENTARY

The various types of minds and senses are manifestations of the *chit*. In Sāñkhya philosophy, the chit is moral sense, ego, intellect, mind, senses, their properties, and the different values of these properties. The root of all these elements is the unmanifest prakriti. Along with these elements constituting the chit, there is a parallel creation of various types of desires, which in the unmanifest stage is called māyā or 'that which is not'. As discussed before, māyā is an inferiority complex of the soul and all desires are produced to overcome this inferiority. Each creation of the prakriti is suited to fulfill some desires produced by māyā. Hence, Vedic texts distinguish between chit-śakti and māyā-śakti, as two different kinds of energies. Their creations, however, combine as each type of desire requires some instruments to fulfill the desire. The Lord injects the soul into māyā-śakti, and the soul acquires a personality of desires. To fulfill these desires, Brahma creates a body of instruments by employing the prakriti. Thus, chit-śakti is various body types and māyā-śakti is various desire types. Then, due to karma, these bodies are placed in different contexts.

If the soul thinks that "I am not knowledgeable" then knowledge becomes an ideal in the moral sense; then, the goal of acquiring knowledge using our own strength becomes a goal in the ego; then, some assumptions about this knowledge will be acquired or what constitutes knowledge are formulated as intellect; then based on these assumptions, speculative theories about the nature of the object of knowledge are produced in the mind; these speculations are then transformed into observational procedures in the senses; these procedures are then transformed into purported objective properties of reality; finally, these properties are converted into a world of material objects.

What we see is the objects and their properties. However, the observer, which employs senses, mind, intellect, ego, and a moral sense remains hidden. Even more hidden is the māyā or the inferiority complex of the soul. Thus, everyone pretends to be the Lord and master of the world, while suffering from the inferiority of not being able to become the Lord and master internally.

The creation of the elements of Sāñkhya is called the primary creation, and the creation of bodies from these elements is called the secondary creation. Lord Viṣṇu creates the elements as universals at the beginning of the universe. Lord Brahma then creates these body and mind types. These body types are subdivisions of the various elements. For instance, the original or pure mind is represented by the form called Aniruddha. However, this mind gradually gets modified and contaminated and becomes the mind of individual living entities. These modified varieties of minds are produced by Lord Brahma. When these diversified forms are absent, the original and pure mind exists. However, because the living entities are influenced by varieties of inferiorities, these inferiorities combine with the original mind and create partial ignorant minds. These partial ignorant bodies and minds are like the trunks, branches, twigs, leaves, and fruits manifested from a root: the root is complete and unmanifest, but the byproducts of this root are incomplete and manifest as material bodies.

QUESTION

You earlier said that māyā is the cause of the material existence. You are now saying that there are many kinds of māyā—and māyā is not one thing?

3.2.4 (323)

सूचकश्च हि श्रुतेःआचक्षते च तद्विदः

sūcakaśca hi śruteḥ ācakṣate ca tadvidaḥ

sūcakaḥ—the symptom; ca—also; hi—certainly; śruteḥ—from the śrutī; ācakṣate—say; ca—also; tadvidaḥ—those who are knowledgeable in that.

TRANSLATION

Also (the bodies and minds are) certainly the symbols or symptoms (of māyā); such is the opinion of the śrutī and those who know this subject.

COMMENTARY

If matter is viewed physically, then the parts are in the whole, but the whole is not in the parts. But if we understand the whole and part semantically, then the part is in the whole, and the whole is in the parts. The presence of the whole in the parts, makes these parts the symbols of the whole. Therefore, the various types of minds and senses are subdivisions of the whole as well as the symbols of the whole. Just as a cow is a subdivision of mammal, as well as a symbol of mammal, similarly, māyā also has subdivisions which are its symbols.

Māyā means aversion to the Lord. This basic desire for aversion divides into many parts, to create many kinds of aversions. But the whole—i.e., the māyā—is present in each part. Therefore, all these parts are symbols of māyā. In simple terms, we can find numerous kinds of desires in this world, but they are all symptoms or symbols of the aversion to the Lord. Anybody who has a desire to serve himself, his family, community, society, nation, etc. is expressing a portion of māyā, and that portion is the symbol of the aversion to the Lord.

The parts of chit, however, are not averse to the Lord. The chit that exists in this world is exactly like the chit in the spiritual world. This means that all that we can see, taste, smell, hear, or touch, all that we can think, judge, intend, or value, also exists in the spiritual world. The difference is simply that in the spiritual world, the chit is used to serve the Lord, and in the material world, it is used to fulfill the aversion to the Lord. Similarly, the relations in this world are exactly like those in the spiritual world. Thus, out of three components, two—the material bodies and their relations—are identical to their spiritual counterparts. Only the third—our desires—are averse to the Lord. For a devotee, therefore, the material and the spiritual worlds are not different because he doesn't see the material body and relations as being contrary to the Lord. He rather sees them as instruments and opportunities to satisfy the Lord's desires.

When desires are used to serve the Lord, the instruments and relations also become spiritual. Conversely, when the desires are averse to the Lord, the instruments and relations become material. Hence, the body of a devotee is spiritual, and the body of an atheist is material. The relationships of the devotee are spiritual, and the relationships of an atheist are material. All the knowledge, beauty, wealth, power, fame, and renunciation of this world are useless unless they are meant for serving the Lord, because they are all symbols of māyā. They are like a lot of 0's in which the first number is also a 0. When the first number is changed to 1, then all these 0's become collectively valuable. Similarly, when everything originates from māyā, then everything is worthless. And when the same māyā is transformed into devotion to the Lord, then it is valuable.

QUESTION

You have earlier said that by the meditation on the Supreme Lord māyā is destroyed, and the soul is liberated from material existence. But now you are indicating that the material world need not be considered bondage. How do we reconcile these opposites: Is the present world liberation or bondage?

3.2.5 (324)

पराभिध्यानात्तु तिरोहितम् ततो ह्यस्य बन्धविपर्ययौ

parābhidhyānāttu tirohitam tato hyasya bandhaviparyayau

parābhidhyānāt—by meditation on the Supreme Lord; tu—but; tirohitam—destroyed; tataḥ—thereafter; hi—certainly; asya—this; bandhaviparyayau—bondage and its opposite, i.e., liberation.

TRANSLATION

By meditation on the Supreme Lord (māyā) is certainly destroyed; but thereafter (one attains) a state beyond the opposites of bondage and liberation.

COMMENTARY

Liberation from the material world is taught as a preliminary idea, when we don't have a good understanding of matter and the nature of our bondage. The superficial cause of bondage is karma, but the deeper cause of bondage is our desires. The bodies and the relations used to fulfill these desires or karma are not material. Hence, the desire is the cause, and karma is the effect. And these two are the only material reality; everything else is spiritual. If the desires are corrected, then karma slowly dies out, and the soul is said to be liberated. Once the soul is liberated, he can choose to live in a body as long as he wants. He can choose to die whenever he so desires. He is neither forced to be born, nor forced to die. Both birth and death, and the bodies, become his choices.

As discussed previously, the manifested reality is divided into four parts, of which Brahman and the material world are just two parts. These are respectively the domains of liberation and bondage. Beyond these two realms are two further realms of Vaikuṇṭha and Goloka. In the realm of Vaikuṇṭha, the devotee associates with the Lord as His servant. But in the realm of Goloka, the devotee also associates with the Lord as His friend, elder, or lover. The bond of the friend, elder, or lover is stronger than the bond of the servant to the master. Thus, after the soul is liberated from material entanglement, the bondage doesn't go away; it rather increases further as one's love is deepened.

Therefore, 'beyond bondage and liberation' has many meanings. First, it can mean that the soul exists in this world but is not bound by the laws of birth and death. Second, it can mean that he transcends the material world and Brahman, which are the domains of bondage and liberation. Third, it can mean that the soul, even after liberation from this world, becomes bound again to the Lord in a relationship, but that bondage of love is neither painful nor temporary.

QUESTION

If liberation from this material body and mind is not the goal of meditation on the Supreme Lord, does it mean that the devotee of the Lord remains bound to the material body eternally? Or does he also get liberated from the body?

3.2.6 (325)

देहयोगाद्वा सोऽपि

dehayogādvā so'pi

dehayogāt—from its connection to the body; vā—moving or separated or detached; saḥ—that (the soul); api—also.

TRANSLATION

The soul is also detached from the connection to the body.

COMMENTARY

The non-devotees are always insecure, but the devotee has no insecurity because the Lord provides him with everything necessary. When the non-devotees compare themselves to the devotees and find them superior in some way, their insecurity manifests as enviousness. Instead of accepting that whatever the devotee has is only by the grace of the Lord, and it can never be taken away unless the Lord desires, the non-devotees mount their aggression on the devotee. When the devotee is troubled in this way, he may decide to leave. But whether the devotee stays or leaves, he is not bound to take rebirth. He may choose to be reborn to serve the Lord or may return to the Lord's abode.

Topic 2

QUESTION

You are saying that the devotee need not be freed from the material body, and yet he transcends the states of bondage and liberation. If he is said to be liberated while living in the body, what then happens to bodily maintenance?

3.2.7 (326)

तदभावो नाडीषु तच्छ्रुतेःआत्मनि च

tadabhāvo nāḍīṣu tacchruteḥ ātmani ca

tat-abhāvaḥ—the absence of that; nāḍīṣu—in the nerves; ātmani ca—and in the self-consciousness; tat-śruteḥ—upon hearing that (i.e., the Lord).

TRANSLATION

Upon hearing that (the names of the Lord), and feeling separated from that (the Lord), the devotee loses all consciousness of the body (obtained through the nerves) and even the sense of the self (i.e., concern about oneself).

COMMENTARY

Awareness of the material body is produced due to lust and fear. We are conscious of the body because we desire the enjoyment of the senses, or because we are afraid that we might lose this enjoyment and we act fervently through the body to protect the body and the things that give the body pleasure.

However, when the devotee becomes absorbed in the consciousness of the Lord, he simultaneously feels connected and separated from the Lord. This is the nature of love: it makes the heart ache, and it delights the heart. The aching is the separation from the Lord, and the delight is the union with the Lord. In the material world, union and separation are contrary: you are either united or you are separated. However, the transcendental experience is beyond this duality. In this experience, there is simultaneous union and separation. The separation is the cause of the wakefulness, and the union is the cause of the unconsciousness. Thus, in the state of wakefulness, the devotee anxiously searches for the Lord, and if the Lord is found (through the process of hearing His name), then the devotee loses his consciousness and becomes unaware of his self. Thus, wakefulness means that I exist, but I'm devoid of the Lord. And conscious ness means that I have found the Lord, and I have lost the sense of self. Through constant separation and meeting, the devotee loses consciousness again and again, only to wake up and search for the Lord almost like a madman.

QUESTION

If the devotee is losing consciousness of the body and the self, then how can this state be called the state of enlightenment, knowledge, self-awareness, etc.? Isn't self-realization contrary to the loss of awareness of the self?

3.2.8 (327)
अतःप्रबोधोऽस्मात्
ataḥ prabodho'smāt

ataḥ—thereafter; prabodhaḥ—full understanding; asmāt—from this.

TRANSLATION
From this (loss of the sense of self) follows the full understanding (of self).

COMMENTARY
We are constantly seeking the purpose of our existence. This purpose is the separation from the objective of our existence. When this purpose is found, we lose ourselves in fulfilling that purpose. But through this purpose, we also discover our true nature. So, finding the purpose means losing the self in that purpose and finding the true meaning of our existence. Finding the self and losing the self only seem to be contradictory ideas from a mundane perspective, and that is because we think that the self is the purpose of existence. Self-realization is thus touted to be full self-awareness. But what if we are not the purpose of our existence? In the material world, we are searching for mundane purposes, and even here we lose ourselves in these purposes, sometimes forgetting to take bath, eat food, sleep well, or take care of the near and dear ones. Since these purposes aren't completely fulfilling, we are frustrated, especially because by losing ourselves in these purposes we also destroy the sense of self. Then we go about seeking a new purpose of existence, where we can lose ourselves, and yet find ourselves through that purpose. When the Lord is the purpose of our existence, the goal is never frustrated. Thus, we lose ourselves in that purpose and forget the self-interest due to love. And yet, through this love of the Lord, we also find the real purpose of our existence. Thus, this sūtra states that the idea of finding the self by self-awareness is a flawed conception. The real self-discovery is the understanding of the purpose of existence that comes by losing the self in that purpose, and that loss is also the supreme gain.

Topic 3

QUESTION
If someone has not attained this supreme understanding of the self through the loss of the self into the purpose, what can he do to obtain it?

3.2.9 (328)
स एव तु कर्मानुस्मृतिशब्दविधिभ्यः
sa eva tu karmānusmṛti śabdavidhibhyaḥ

sa eva—Him certainly; tu—but; karma-anusmṛti—working and

remembering (the Lord); śabda-vidhibhyaḥ—following the scriptural processes.

TRANSLATION

The Lord is certainly (the purpose); but (He should be worshipped) by remembering through regular duties, as prescribed in the Vedic scriptures.

COMMENTARY

In Bhagavad-Gita 8.7, Lord Kṛṣṇa tells the following to Arjuna:

tasmat sarvesu kalesu
mam anusmara yudhya ca
mayy arpita-mano-buddhir
mam evaisyasy asamsayah

Therefore, Arjuna, you should always think of Me and at the same time carry out your prescribed duty of fighting. With your activities dedicated to Me and your mind and intelligence fixed on Me, you will attain Me without doubt.

When we perform our day-to-day activities, we keep thinking about the outcomes of these actions. For example, someone might think that they will get money out of their work, and the ways they will enjoy with that money. Or, they might think about their families and dear ones, and how this money would be used to make them happy, and their happiness will become our happiness. This meditation on the purpose, even as we do our day-to-day duties, is already present in everyone. This sūtra states that we should change this purpose to the Lord. By changing this purpose, we slowly become attached to the Lord.

A key symptom of this attachment is that all our choices only prioritize the Lord's happiness. For example, a person may be offered a job that gives him more money, but it will also take time away from the Lord's service. The non-devotee will choose the job over the Lord's service, and the devotee will choose the Lord's service over the job. Constantly remembering the Lord means that our choices at every moment are driven by what will please the Lord the most.

Topic 4

QUESTION

But if meditation on the Lord is the real purpose, then why do we even bother with material duties as prescribed in the Vedic scriptures? Why can't we renounce all such mundane duties and just focus upon the meditation?

3.2.10 (329)

मुग्धेऽर्धसंपत्तिःपरिशेषात्

mugdhe'rdhasaṃpattiḥ pariśeṣāt

mugdhe—being engrossed in delight; ardhasaṃpattiḥ—half wealth or possession; pariśeṣāt—due to the only thing left in the material world.

TRANSLATION

Being engrossed in delight (in remembering the Lord) (the devotee considers the material body and its possessions) half-wealth (and that engrossment and delight) due to (the Lord) being the only thing left in the material world.

COMMENTARY

In this section we can see that many false contradictions are being refuted one by one. First, the contradiction of whether māyā is one or many was refuted. Then the contradiction between bondage and liberation was refuted. Then the idea of losing oneself as being contradictory to finding oneself was refuted. Now, the contradiction between association and renunciation is being refuted. Through these refutations, a transcendent reality that goes beyond the apparent opposites of this world is being established. These contradictions are found in impersonalist philosophy, and by refuting them, impersonalism is refuted.

The impersonalist believes that the material world is false; that it doesn't exist, or it exists as an illusion. The devotee doesn't reject the existence of the world but rejects the *purpose* of this existence as being the self. In the impersonalist interpretation, māyā being the source of the world, and māyā being that which doesn't exist, is taken to imply that the world doesn't exist. In the personalist interpretation, māyā is the source of the world, and is that which doesn't exist, but this māyā is the purpose of existence, from which existence springs. Accordingly, freedom from māyā is the freedom from the false purpose, rather than the freedom from the material body. Once the false purpose is discarded, whether the material body exists or not becomes immaterial. Instead, even the material body can be used for the Lord's purposes. Thus, freedom from the material body—or what is called liberation—isn't the goal of life. The goal is to revive the true purpose of our existence—namely, the Lord.

Māyā is the emotional or intentional cause of the world. From this purpose, springs the prakriti or the material cause of the world. The impersonalist believes that there is only a material cause, but why this material cause covers the soul—i.e., what purposes are fulfilled by this covering—remains unanswered. The root cause is the envy in the soul, but this envy then develops into an inferiority complex; the envy is in the soul, and is real; however, the inferiority is material and is false. And yet, when the inferiority covers the soul, the soul starts feeling inadequate, incomplete, and insufficient. It forgets its true nature, and this forgetfulness is then identified as that which doesn't exist. The impersonalist now concludes that since the root of material existence is the material cause, therefore, liberation from matter is the primary goal of life. But this sūtra refutes this understanding. It states that renunciation of the world is not the real answer, because the world is not false; the purposes we attribute to this world—i.e., that this world is meant for my enjoyment—is false. The devotee isn't interested in discarding the world. He is only interested in changing the purpose of his existence. In other words, change lies within the soul, rather than in the rejection of the world. Once this change has occurred, then whether the body is temporary, or eternal, doesn't matter. The devotee simply tries to please the Lord through all his efforts, and the world is employed in this service.

This sūtra also says that engrossed in the thoughts about the Lord, the devotee considers everything else insignificant. Whether it is there or not, doesn't matter. Thus, all these things are called half-wealth in this sūtra. This means if they are there, then the devotee performs his duties as necessary. But if they are not there, then he is not disturbed. The real wealth is the unflinching devotion to the Lord. The materialistic wealth, family, fame, or love cease to be meaningful. The only meaningful thing in this world is remembrance of the Lord.

Topic 5

QUESTION

Some people say that this world is false, except for things like the holy places of worship, the scriptures describing the Lord, and the deities by which the Lord is worshipped. So, they don't reject the entire world, but they are also partially rejecting the world. Is their position acceptance or rejection?

3.2.11 (330)

न स्थानतोऽपि परस्योभयलिङ्गम् सर्वत्र हि

na sthānato'pi parasyobhayaliṅgam sarvatra hi

na—not; sthānataḥ—due to (the difference of) place; api—even; parasya—of the transcendental; ubhayaliṅgaṃ—the twofold deities; hi—because; sarvatra—present everywhere.

TRANSLATION

(For the devotee) it is not the differences of place, not even the twofold deities of the transcendent reality, because (the Lord is) present everywhere.

COMMENTARY

The neophyte devotees like to worship the deities, read the scriptures, and live in holy places. They might consider all other things, such as the performance of social duties, teaching the knowledge to others, or other kinds of services to the Lord—which seem to involve the material world—as inferior. The neophytes are prescribed these kinds of rules so that they don't get entangled in the material world and start using it for their enjoyment. Their life is limited in this way to help them advance in spiritual life. However, one who has advanced through such regulative practices, comes to the point where he sees that everything is meant for the satisfaction of the Lord. Everything is real, but the purposes for which we are using it may not necessarily be real. Such a devotee becomes qualified to engage everything in the service of the Lord, and the false dichotomy of material and spiritual, renunciation and attachment, etc. is destroyed. This sūtra states that such a devotee is not even attached to the holy places or the worship or the twofold deities (the masculine and feminine forms of the Absolute Truth) because he can see that these forms are everywhere.

This sūtra says that the Lord is everywhere. He is of course present in the deities, the scriptures, and the holy places. But He is not absent from the other places. In the deities, the scriptures, and the holy places, the Lord is more manifest, but only the devotees can see the Lord in these forms. The atheistic people consider scriptures 'mythology', deities as 'idols', and the holy places as being no different than any other place. Therefore, even to give greater regard to the holy places, scriptures, and deities, one must be a devotee. As this devotion advances, the Lord is seen everywhere. This 'everywhere' vision doesn't mean everything is the Lord. It only means that the Lord is the purpose of everything. The purpose exists in everything, but those things are not the purpose.

QUESTION

But if you say that the advanced devotees see the Lord present everywhere, does it mean that they lose the discrimination between good and bad, right and wrong, true and false? Because they see the Lord being present everywhere?

3.2.12 (331)

न भेदादिति चेत् न प्रत्येकमतद्वचनात्

na bhedāditi cet na pratyekamatadvacanāt

na—not; bhedāt—due to difference; iti cet—if it be said; na—not so; pratyekam—toward the One; atadvacanāt—due to the contrary declaration.

TRANSLATION

If it is said that (the devotees) cannot make the difference (between right and wrong, good and bad, true and false) (we say) not so; everything toward the One (is true, right, and good) since (non-discrimination is) rejected.

COMMENTARY

The impersonalist sometimes argues that since everything is Brahman, or the Lord is everywhere, so there is no high or low, nothing good or bad, nothing is right or wrong, etc. But this is a wrong idea because the meaning of the statement "the Lord is everywhere" is that the *purpose* of everything is the Lord. The Lord is in everything as its purpose; the purpose exists in everything, and it is the same purpose for everything—i.e., to serve the Lord. However, the purpose is also different from those individual things, and the Lord is hence also outside each of those things. Only the Lord is fully identical to Himself because He is His own purpose. He is also the purpose of everything else, and due to that purpose, He remains immanent in everything, even as He is transcendent to everything. If we don't distinguish between the existence and its purpose, then we equate the idea that "the Lord is everywhere" to existence, rather than purpose. Then we think that if the Lord is everywhere, then everything can be worshipped. This is a false claim. Everything cannot be worshipped, but everything can be used for worship. When this purpose of the existence is reestablished, then we can see that the Lord is present in everything as their purpose.

This sūtra states that the devotee knows how to judge things based on the purpose they are being used for. Elaborately cooked food that is not offered to the Lord is therefore inferior to uncooked fruits, flowers, leaves, or water, which are offered to the Lord. Elaborately cooked food can also be offered to the Lord, so there is potential for it to be superior. The devotee can see how everything can be used for the service of the Lord, but that doesn't mean everything is being used for the service of the Lord. The devotee thus discriminates between high and low, right and wrong, good and bad, true and false, in relation to the Lord. Everything that pleases the Lord is higher than things that don't please the Lord. Things that please Him more are superior to things that please Him less. Thus, the Lord is the single standard for all judgments, and the idea that if the Lord is everywhere then everything must be worshipped is rejected.

QUESTION

Does this mean that certain things that are considered wrong or bad or false from the mundane point of view (i.e., the viewpoint of the materially entangled souls) could also be considered spiritually superior by the Lord's devotees?

3.2.13 (332)
अपचिवमेके

apicaivameke

api ca—moreover; evam—thus; eke—some.

TRANSLATION

Moreover, by this criterion some (forbidden actions can be devotion too).

COMMENTARY

Living entities are prescribed dharma according to their social roles. Thus, a father must take of his children, a son must serve the parents, a citizen must defend the country, etc. But the service to the Lord takes precedence over various kinds of dharma and is called sanātana-dharma or eternal duty. When there is a contradiction between dharma and sanātana-dharma, then the latter takes precedence. However, such cases are generally rare, and the use of the term *eke* or some indicates that rarity. Quite often, when we reject dharma, thinking that we are performing sanātana-dharma, then we are in violation of both.

An example of such violation is the use of murder and mayhem to propagate religion. Innumerable crimes have been committed in the name of religion. All such actions are justified as sanātana-dharma (service of God) over dharma (moral principles such as peace, non-violence, and tolerance). Hence, a blind rejection of dharma to perform sanātana-dharma is a very treacherous path. The fact is that when people reject dharma, claiming to perform sanātana-dharma, most times they are in violation of both dharma and sanātana-dharma.

The general principle is that dharma must always be performed, and one must try to find all ways and means to do sanātana-dharma within their prescribed dharma. The rules and regulations of society have also been ordained by the Lord, as a countermeasure to religious upstarts using religion and God to create chaos. In general, if someone says that their religion requires changes to the basic principles of social organization, then their religion is wrong.

But this also means that we inquire into the nature of dharma. What is proper social organization? What are the correct principles of economy and government? What are the duties of citizens? How must different classes in society conduct themselves? Unless we know dharma, we will keep changing the ideas about society, economy, and government, and one dharma would be replaced by another. The study of dharma is a vast subject, and the basic principle of understanding dharma is karma—namely, that there are natural laws of morality, and social laws must be formulated to prevent sinful activities.

If dharma has been formulated by the understanding of karma, then there are only rare situations in which it can be superseded by sanātana-dharma.

What are those situations? These are situations in which dharma is itself not clear because there are contradictory principles at play. Such an example is provided in the Śrīmad Bhagavatam where King Bali is advised by his guru to ignore his promise to Lord Vāmana to donate three steps of land. This presents a dilemma: if King Bali broke his promise, he would have neglected dharma; similarly, if he rejected the order of his guru, he would have neglected dharma. When faced with such dilemmas, we can ask: which of these two principles would please the Lord? King Bali chose to reject his guru because he realized that Lord Vāmana was indeed the Lord Who had come to ask for his land. This principle is also enunciated in the Bhagavad-Gita where Arjuna is caught in a dilemma regarding his duty. He thinks that defending his honor is his duty. He also thinks that killing his relatives is against his duty. Since defending the honor contradicts the protection of his relatives, Arjuna is caught in a dilemma. He engages in a long discussion about the nature of dharma, but even as Lord Kṛṣṇa describes various paths, such as karma-yoga, jñāna-yoga, and dhyāna-yoga, they don't resolve the dilemma about whether he should fight or not. Either of these choices are equally consistent with all the above three paths. Therefore, Lord Kṛṣṇa provides the final answer: Do what pleases Me the most. This resolves the dilemma, and Arjuna fights because Lord Kṛṣṇa asks him to.

Therefore, we must always follow dharma unless there is a conflict in deciding what the dharma is. If a conflict in deciding dharma arises, then we must choose one dharma over another based on sanātana-dharma. If the law of karma is understood, then dharma is also understood, and the situations of dilemma are very rare. But when these dilemmas arise, and sanātana-dharma overrides dharma, it is not truly rejecting dharma. It is only preferring one kind of dharma over another. However, to the extent that one dharma may be rejected due to sanātana-dharma, it is noted here as *eke* or a rare situation. Finally, sanātana-dharma can be performed while performing dharma. As we have discussed above, one can remember the Lord, and wherever possible, make those choices that are suited for increasing our remembrance of the Lord.

QUESTION

But many people say that these social distinctions and duties that come with them only increase our entanglement to the world. We think we are father, mother, son, daughter, citizen, etc. and by these designations we get entangled. So, their recommendation is that we give up all these designations. Once these designations are discarded, then there is nothing higher or lower, nobody is superior or inferior. We are just spiritual particles who must give up our false identities. What would be your answer to this type of counterargument?

3.2.14 (333)

अरूपवदेव हि तत्प्रधानत्वात्

arūpavadeva hi tatpradhānatvāt

arūpavat—formless; eva—only; hi—certainly; tat-pradhānatvāt—from that being just like pradhāna (the unmanifest state of material nature).

TRANSLATION

Certainly (the attitude of giving up all kinds of designations), only leads to a formless state, just like from the primordial state of matter called pradhāna.

COMMENTARY

Brahman is a state in which the knower-known distinction is abolished. In this state, there is nothing other than the self, because the self is the only known. Thus, other individual souls are *believed* to not exist, because everyone is self-absorbed. From this self-absorbed state emerges pradhāna in which the soul can see that there are many other individuals, but they are of the same type as us. In Brahman, only "I" exist. In pradhāna, many "I" exist, but they are all the same type. This distinction indicates different kinds of impersonal philosophies. The spiritual impersonalist says that there is only one knower and that knower is the known, and hence all the individual knowers are illusions. The material impersonalist recognizes the individuality of different souls but says that we are all equal. The modern left-wing political ideology is derived from this material impersonalism, where society aims to drop all distinctions of gender, race, rich and poor, higher and lower, all in the name of 'equality'.

There is a charm in this ideology because it is in some sense anti-materialistic; it rejects superficial distinctions, gross materialism, and exploitation of others. But it has a mistaken idea about individuality; we are never the same type of individuals. We are all different, and the difference is qualitative. Some people have better qualities and they are expected to be higher; others have lower qualities and they are expected to be lower. The designations in society are supposed to be based on these qualities or guna. The problem of this material world is that people who don't have the right guna but have the right karma, get into powerful, influential, and affluent positions. They then exploit others and to avoid exploitation, society then conjures a state of equality.

The ideology in which we recognize many individuals but consider them to be of the same type is pradhāna. By pursuing this ideology, one cannot get liberated from the material existence. But one can still reach the primordial state of material reality of egalitarian equality. It is better than gross material existence but not as good as Brahman, and certainly not equal to personalistic transcendence where distinctions are based on a person's genuine qualities.

Karma is absent in the transcendent world, so an unqualified person can never become rich, powerful, famous, etc. Only people who have good qualities are in a superior position, and those with lesser qualities are in inferior positions. This is a stable situation because the distinctions of high and low remain, and yet everyone understands that this is a meritorious society. When merit is equated with karma rather than guna (as in the material world), then people with bad qualities also become powerful. This aberration of the material world is deliberate, and its rejection simply takes us to the primordial state of matter. To enter the transcendental world, we must distinguish by qualities, not karma.

QUESTION

But don't the Vedic scriptures say that the soul is sat-chit-ānanda and since all souls have this property, therefore, all the souls must be of the same type? They are only separate individuals, although they cannot be higher or lower? Some people say that we are all particles of effulgence, and this material body is simply a covering of these particles? Thus, if this material covering is discarded, then isn't what remains simply the sat-chit-ānanda nature of the soul?

3.2.15 (334)

प्रकाशवच्चावैयर्थ्यात्

prakāśavaccāvaiyathyārt

prakāśavat—like light; ca—also; avaiyatharyāt—due to not meaningless.

TRANSLATION

Due to not being meaningless, (the souls) are also like light.

COMMENTARY

The *sat-chit*-ānanda of the soul is simply a potential—the potential to relate to other individuals (*sat*), the potential to know those individuals (*chit*), and the potential to desire and enjoy with other individuals (ānanda). We can also call these the capacities for relation, cognition, and emotion. However, these capacities don't become experience unless there is an actual relation, cognition, and emotion. The conversion of the potentials of cognition, relation, and emotion into an actual experience requires a choice. This choice produces a meaning, namely, a specific type of relation, emotion, and cognition. Hence, this sūtra says that the soul is light, namely, the potential to enlighten. But that light must also fall on something to enlighten that thing. What does it fall upon? That is up to the soul's choice, and such choices are made to produce meaning. So, the fact that the soul exists as the potential for relation, cognition, and emotion, doesn't entail that there are no differences; the difference is their choices.

QUESTION

If you are saying that the soul is a potential, then it means that it is incomplete without the reality that converts the potential into an experience?

3.2.16 (335)

आह च तन्मात्रम्

āha ca tanmātram

āha—declares; ca—and; tanmātram—form only.

TRANSLATION

(It is) also said that (the soul) is just like tanmātra or form alone.

COMMENTARY

To understand this sūtra, we must understand the meaning of *tanmātra*. In Sāñkhya philosophy, the term tanmātra is used to denote properties such as form, color, taste, shape, smell, size, pitch, tone, roughness, heat, etc. Each of these properties then divides into many types called bhūta, which represent the values of these properties. For example, if the property is color, then the values are red, green, and blue; if the property is shape, then the values are square, round, and triangle; if the property is taste, then the values are sour, bitter, sweet, pungent, etc. In modern terminology, the properties are called *dimensions* and their values are called *values*, which are present on these dimensions. For instance, if weight is a dimension, then 5kg is a value on that dimension; if temperature is the dimension, then 50 0C is the value on that dimension.

So, tanmātra or property is a dimension. However, these dimensions are incomplete without the values. The values on these dimensions are different kinds of relations (father, mother, child, etc.), cognitions (table, chair, red, hot, bitter, etc.), and emotions (fear, desire, greed, anger, confusion, etc.). These dimensions and values constitute a 'space' in which the soul acquires a position. This position is a choice, and by obtaining the position, each soul becomes different from other souls—as each soul obtains a different position. The soul and the Lord are identical in terms of their dimensions—each has three dimensions of relation, cognition, and emotion. But the Lord and His Śakti are the origin of this space, from this origin the rest of space expands, and the soul obtains a position in that space. These three dimensionalities of the Lord, His Śakti, and the soul are mistakenly interpreted as the identity between the soul, the Lord, and His Śakti. The correct understanding is that the Lord and His Śakti define the three dimensions and the complete value as the origin of space, and while the soul has the same three dimensions, and it can make a choice about the position in space, it can never become the origin of this space. It can also never obtain the experience of the complete value of these dimensions.

The soul is pure tanmātra or dimensionality and the Lord's Śakti is pure values. The soul is always incomplete unless it obtains a position—i.e., the dimension gets a value. This value represents the experience of the soul, and the experience is produced due to a choice. The soul is capable of a choice, but the possibilities from which he must choose are produced by the Lord's Śakti.

QUESTION

The term tanmātra is used in relation to sense perception. But the soul also has mental, intellectual, and subtle emotional experiences like happiness (beyond the sense pleasures). Are these also gained from the external reality?

3.2.17 (336)

दर्शयति च अथो अपि स्मर्यते

darśayati ca atho api smaryate

darśayati—sees; ca—and; atho—then; api—also; smaryate—remembers.

TRANSLATION

(The term tanmātra) can be applied to sense perception and then also to remembrance (or thought processes occurring in the mind and intellect).

COMMENTARY

The distinction between dimension and value is not unique to sense perception. The capacity to think and judge is also a dimension, and the meanings and the judgments are values on dimensions. Due to this distinction, concepts and judgments are also objective, rather than subjective. Thus, they can exist outside an individual's mind and intellect and due to this objectivity, we can attribute objective meanings to a sentence. Similarly, we can say that some meaning is true or false. If these were not objective values, then the meaning and judgment would only exist in a person's mind, and we could not say that the world is objectively a table or a chair, or that meaning is true or false. The distinction between the capacity to think and judge and the concepts and judgments is essential to maintain the objectivity of meanings and judgments.

When space is understood as a tree, then every node on that tree is both a dimension and an object. For example, color is a space because it contains shades like yellow and green. But color is an object in the space of seeing. And color is a property in relation to other properties like shape, size, distance, direction, etc. This means that when we speak of 'color', we must use three modalities. In the space modality, we look downward, and see many shades of color. In the object modality we look upward and see color as a part of seeing. Finally, in the property modality we look sideways and understand how color is one of the many properties. Thus, by looking upward, downward, and sideways, in a space of concepts, we understand an idea in different ways.

Now, the main point is that color manifests from seeing, and yellow manifests from color. Similarly, thoughts manifest from the mind, and the judgments manifest from the intellect. So, the senses, the mind, the intellect, etc. are considered tanmātra or spaces (or dimensions) that produce objects (or values). Hence, the term tanmātra is not limited to sense perception. Once we understand what it means, then tanmātra can be extended to thoughts, judgments, intentions, and morals. The context delineates what we mean by tanmātra.

QUESTION

But due to the possibility of hallucination, we also distinguish between the perception and the object of perception. If the soul is associating with a perception and mental reality, then that reality must be understood as the image or representation of the world. And this image must be different from the world being perceived or thought of. Does this mean there is a relation between the object being perceived and the perceptions—both of which are objective?

3.2.18 (337)
अत एव चोपमा सूर्यकादिवत्
ata eva copamā sūryakādivat

ata eva—therefore; ca—also; upamā—comparison; sūryakādivat—like the images of the sun etc.

TRANSLATION

Therefore, we also draw a comparison to the images of the sun.

COMMENTARY

The image of the sun is different than the sun, and similarly, a distinction is drawn between a picture of the world in our senses and the mind as against the reality that is being pictured. Both the picture and the object being pictured are objective, but the picture also refers to its object. This reference may be true or false. For example, when a rope is perceived as a snake, then both the picture (of the snake) in the mind and the senses, as well as the object being perceived (the rope) are real. However, the referential connection between the picture and the object is false. Thus, the hallucination exists, but it is not considered true. The rejection doesn't reject the reality of a snake or a rope; both are real and eternal concepts. It just means that *this thing* that we are seeing is not a snake.

QUESTION

So, what happens when we close our eyes and stop perceiving the world?

Do we still have the capacity for perception, or is this capacity also lost?

3.2.19 (338)
अम्बुवदग्रहणात् तु न तथात्वम्
ambuvadagrahaṇāt tu na tathātvam

ambuvat—like water; agrahaṇāt—from not being in a house; tu—but; na—no; tathātvam—similarly them.

TRANSLATION

But just like water from not being in a house (a pot for water); (the perceiver or the senses) don't have a house (or border), and they exist in that state.

COMMENTARY

In Yoga philosophy, the mind and the senses are compared to an ocean, with thoughts and sensations arising as waves in this ocean. To understand these waves, think of a vibrating string. For a string to vibrate, it must be clamped at the two ends. If the string is not clamped, and you push it, it will simply be displaced from one position to another; it will not vibrate. If the string is clamped at one end, then any push will cause it to rotate, rather than vibrate. All vibration, therefore, arises when there is a boundary exerted on a string. In physics, these are also called 'boundary conditions'. The senses and the mind are also described as water here, that is not in a pot. When the restrictions of the pot are removed, then the mind and the senses are like a non-vibrating membrane. This is the basic principle of mind and sense control: remove the restrictions of the boundary conditions. Since the world exerts a boundary condition on the senses and the mind, they start vibrating, and that vibration is called sensation and thought. But if the boundary condition is removed, then the mind and the senses become silent. So, perception is due to these boundaries.

A lot of impersonalist philosophy is based on this idea of sense and mind control. It says that this world exerts a boundary on the consciousness, and these boundaries then produce an individual consciousness (which we call the soul), and once the individual soul is produced by exerting a boundary, then the consciousness starts producing waves. If we remove these boundaries, then there are no longer individual souls, and they will not vibrate. Hence, the removal of these boundaries removes all perception and individuality. The impersonalist, therefore, talks about *ghatākash* and *mahākasha*. The *ghatākash* is space inside a pot, and *mahākasha* is space without the pot boundary. The claim is that māyā is the pot, and it divides space into potted spaces. These potted spaces then vibrate, and these vibrations produce perceptions. If the pots of māyā are removed, then the individual space will merge into the universal space, and as the individuality is lost, the vibrations will also cease. Thus, by removing these boundaries, we become devoid of sensation and thought, and that freedom from all perception is the transcendental state of the soul.

There is however another way to understand this description. In this understanding, the vibration is not a problem; the problem is the meaning of this vibration. What we call the boundary—which creates the vibration—is not physical. This boundary is created by a meaning, and this meaning is the relation between the whole and the part. For example, if the idea of mammal is the *mahākasha* then the *ghatākash* of the cow is created from this *mahākasha* by expanding the idea of mammal into a cow. Now, we must note that the idea of cow already existed in the idea of a mammal. It is not an external imposition on the mind. It is rather *avyakta* inside the mammal and it becomes *vyakta*.

In the impersonal philosophy, the boundary or māyā is an external imposition on the consciousness, and by exerting these boundaries potted spaces are created. But what if the pot was inside the space—like a cow is inside a mammal—and it only comes out of the space? This requires a different understanding of space which enfolds the complexity within itself and unfolds it gradually. The impersonal understanding of space is that it is like an infinite box. The personalist understanding of space is that it is like tree—expanded from the root. The root is the origin, but as trunks, branches, and twigs are manifest from the root, the space also expands. This expansion is the subdivision of space, and by this subdivision, the *ghatākash* is created from the *mahākasha*. So, the impersonal understanding is based on a physical notion of space. If this idea of space were revised to a semantic understanding—in which the root is an idea, which then divides into smaller ideas—then māyā will cease to be an external imposition. It will rather spring out of the consciousness as its innate property.

If this understanding of space is clarified, then a distinction can be drawn between an externally imposed boundary, and an internally springing out boundary. The externally imposed boundary is called *bahiranga śakti* or external energy, and the internally springing out boundary is called *antaranga śakti* or internal energy. The contention of the impersonalist that all boundaries are externally imposed is thus rejected. Yes, the material boundaries are externally imposed, but there is another kind of boundary that springs from within.

When a pure devotee chants the names of the Lord, the mind and the senses vibrate. The impersonalist thinks that this vibration is an external imposition on the mind—a boundary that was applied to create a vibration. But the devotee understands that this vibration was enfolded in the soul, and it is just being unfolded. This vibration springs out of the soul like a tree grows out of a seed. Devotion is therefore compared to a *bīja* that gives rise to a creeper.

This philosophy about the natural springing of sound was also expounded by stalwarts of Sanskrit like Bhartṛhari who speak about language as a *sphota*—a bursting out or an explosion. Vaishnavas also say that when the consciousness is purified, then the sound springs out automatically—*svyameva sphurati adah*. These terms like *sphota* and *sphurati* indicate the same idea—the vibration is not due an external boundary. It is rather innate and immanent in the soul in an unmanifest form. It is only manifest when the soul is purified.

Thus, in the physical analogy of vibrations, the boundary is applied externally. But in the semantic understanding of vibrations, the boundary springs out of the soul. It is like a spider producing a web that binds the spider. The web is not an unnatural thing; it is rather immanent in the soul, and manifest from the soul. Of course, the spider can keep the web within itself. And that control of the consciousness is Brahman, where the soul is *avyakta*. It rests like a seed which hasn't manifested the tree of devotion from within itself. The soul in this seed form is not considered the full-blown consciousness. However, because it has the potential for full-blown consciousness, it is always an individual. The destruction of boundaries—that are externally imposed by the material nature—brings the soul to a non-vibrating state or liberation. Upon further progress, the vibrations come out of the self and are not externally imposed.

In this sūtra, the externally forced boundaries are being described, and it is said that if the pots are broken, then the senses and the mind become silent. Since this often leads to an impersonal misunderstanding about the transcendent state beyond the state of complete silence, we must understand the difference between the externally imposed and the internally created boundaries. If we changed the analogies, then we can see that even the external imposition is ultimately the fulfillment of the soul's desires: we want to be entangled in material nature, and material nature simply fulfills our desires. The desire for entanglement, however, sprang from within; the material energy simply fulfilled that desire by providing the boundaries that cause the mind and the senses to vibrate. So, māyā is not forcing itself upon us. We are asking māyā to come to us. If we give up material desires, then these boundaries on the mind and senses will end. But another kind of boundary will spring from within. This new boundary will create new kinds of vibrations and hence perceptions.

QUESTION

But factually we cannot close our eyes forever. We must perceive, think, judge, and intend—even if we want to pursue spiritual life. So, how can someone who is unable to break the pot boundary become spiritually realized?

3.2.20 (339)

वृद्धिह्रासभाक्त्वमन्तर्भावाद् उभयसामञ्जस्यादेवम्

vṛddhihrāsabhāktvamantarbhāvād ubhayasāmañjasyādevam

vṛddhi-hrāsa-bhāktvam—enjoying growth and decline; antarbhāvāt—from being within; ubhaya-sāmañjasyāt—from equanimity in both; evam—thus.

TRANSLATION

From being situated within, enjoying the growth and decline (i.e., the up and down of a vibration), being equanimous in both thus (leads to Brahman).

COMMENTARY

The root cause of material entanglement is material desire. Due to this desire, right or wrong actions are performed, and karma is produced. Even if we stop desiring, the fruits of the karma must be borne out. These fruits will automatically bring us in contact with the external world, and under this contact, the mind and the senses will start vibrating. This sūtra advises that when this happens, the soul must remain equanimous through the ups and downs. In short, end the process of liking and disliking of perception and bear out the fruits of the previously created karma. Once the karma has ended, and the soul has ceased in its desires, then the soul will automatically be liberated. The key, however, is remaining equanimous. How can we keep tolerating the pleasures and pains produced due to karma if there is nothing to look forward to? A simple praise makes us happy, and an insult makes us unhappy. A person can be equanimous only when there is innate happiness, and the happiness or sadness provided by the external world become insignificant in comparison. If the solution to the problem of entanglement asks us to become equanimous before we can become happy, then the solution is easily stated, but very difficult to practice. The converse solution where we become happy first, and that leads to equanimity is more practical. Therefore, this solution—while not impossible—is difficult to practice and often doesn't result in the intended outcomes.

QUESTION

But how can one become equanimous in this turbulent world? We are tossed by the waves of changes, and some make us happy, while others make us sad. It is very hard to maintain equanimity in the face of these changes.

3.2.21 (340)

दर्शनाच्च

darśanācca

darśanāt—due to seeing or philosophical understanding; ca—as well.

TRANSLATION

(Equanimity in the face of happiness and distress) can also be obtained by seeing the world through the lens of correct philosophical understanding.

COMMENTARY

Philosophical understanding is the beginning of spiritual realization, because it brings detachment—one can see that the happiness and suffering is caused by one's own actions in the past, and one must tolerate these perceptions because they are temporary. Eternal happiness lies beyond this material world when we transcend the material desires, and the fruits of past actions have been consumed. Unless one is detached, even the practice of devotion doesn't work, because one maintains materialistic goals, and devotion is used for fulfilling the materialistic desires. Thus, we see that many so-called religious people are extremely materialistic; they talk about God, but what they really want is material prosperity. This kind of devotion—which exists without a philosophical understanding—is useless. It is a pretentious religion, that doesn't lead one to any spiritual realization. The first step is a philosophical understanding of this material world—i.e., how and why we are entangled. With this understanding, one becomes detached from the suffering and enjoyment of this world. This equanimity then stops the further production of material desires and karma. Once this detachment to the material world is acquired, then devotional practices produce the real joy, as one performs devotion for the Lord's pleasure because the materialistic goals have ended, so every activity must be performed for a transcendent purpose. This is also called 'pure' devotional service. Without detachment, devotional practices are impure and imperfect. And without correct knowledge, the beginner doesn't acquire detachment or equanimity. Of course, one who has true devotion doesn't need the philosophical understanding; they are already situated in perfect bliss and the pleasure and suffering of the material world has become irrelevant to them. So, they don't need philosophy to become detached from the world. Thus, at some point, the philosophical understanding ceases to be important. However, for the beginner, it is the essential bedrock on which the practice of devotion itself must be erected.

Topic 6

QUESTION

You earlier said that everything can be used in the service of the Lord. Now you are saying that a person must be detached from this material world. How can we reconcile these two contradictory statements? Should we accept everything or reject everything? What is the correct path to transcendence?

3.2.22 (341)

प्रकृतैतावत्त्वं हि प्रतिषेधति ततो ब्रवीति च भूयः

prakṛtaitāvattvaṃ hi pratiṣedhati tato bravīti ca bhūyaḥ

prakṛta-etāvattvaṃ—all that has been created until now; pratiṣedhati—rejects; tato—then that; bravīti—says; ca—and; bhūyaḥ—that I exist.

TRANSLATION

When a person rejects all that has been created until now only then he says that "I exist" (i.e., that I am different from all that has been rejected).

COMMENTARY

The term *prakṛta* means something created. It also means one's nature. When these two meanings are combined, then we can see that what we consider our nature is both created and something that we consider to be ourselves. This *prakṛta* is comprised of three aspects—our roles in the world, our cognitions and experiences, and our desires or personality of likes and dislikes. This has been described to be 'external' to the soul, and yet the soul identifies with these things and considers them his true nature. Thus, we identify with the roles in society and say that "I'm a father", "I'm a mother", etc. We identify with our cognitions and abilities, and say that "I'm strong", "I'm intelligent", "I'm creative", etc. Then we identify with our emotions and say that "I'm loving", "I'm angry", "I'm happy", etc. There is an "I" or the self, and relations, cognitions, and emotions, are the properties of this self. The soul also has innate properties, which manifest from within as its internal energy, just like a cow manifests from a mammal. However, until these external creations and identifications have been discarded, the internal things remain unmanifest and invisible. Examples of such identifications are citizenship, gender, race, language, etc. People may talk about spiritual life, but they remain attached to these identifications. The sūtra states that unless we keep identifying with these external attributes, we will never realize who we are distinct from these material attributes. And if these attributes always keep changing, identifying with them will lead us to believe that we are also changing; in short, that an eternal "I" doesn't exist.

There is, however, no contradiction between renunciation and association, if the material energy is identified as the Lord's property, rather than our property. In short, just because we are currently situated in a nation, gender, race, or linguistic identity doesn't mean that's who we are. The devotee sees these as coverings of the soul and identifies them as the Lord's properties rather than his property or, worse still, himself. Thus, a rich devotee doesn't think "I'm rich". He rather says: this richness belongs to the Lord, I'm also the Lord's property, and hence one property (myself) is engaging another property (the riches) into the Lord's service. In short, both the soul and the riches are instruments. One instrument engages the other instrument in the Lord's service. However, we must also understand that this is an advanced stage of self-realization. The preliminary stage of realization is that I'm not this body and its associated attributes. Once we strip out all these attributes, then we come to ask: Who am I?

The answer to that question is: "I'm a servant of the Lord". Once this question is answered, then we can ask: "What are these things currently associated with me?" and the answer to that is also: "These are servants of the Lord". Then one servant engages another servant into the service of the Lord. If the first question—i.e., "Who am I?"—is not answered correctly, then the subsequent answers also remain incorrect. The answer to the first question also involves many components. The first component is that "I'm not this body". Following this answer, we can say that "I exist even if all the bodily attributes are changed". If our eternal existence is established, then we ask a further question: "What is the purpose of my existence?". Note that existence and purpose are quite different questions. I can exist eternally purposelessly. Or I can exist eternally with an eternal purpose. If the first question of my eternal existence is not answered properly, then the answer of eternal purpose is also wrong.

Hence, this sūtra states that first we must realize that we are not this body. And this is possible if we reject all the attributes associated with the body. The impersonalist states that our questions end with this one answer. But the devotees disagree. They say that after we have established our eternal existence, we must also ask about our eternal purpose. If I exist eternally, and a lot of other souls exist eternally, should we be involved in our self-interest? Or, is there a common interest that goes beyond the interests of the individual souls? So, the answer that "I exist" is incomplete. The further realization is "others exist too". And then a further realization is that there is a shared purpose. But, to progress in these successive realizations, one must first reject the bodily identity.

QUESTION

But if one rejects the body and the mind, then how can one think of the Lord? The soul, as you have clarified, is only the potentiality for relation, cognition, and emotion. How can this potentiality be converted into a reality without the body? How will the soul in the disembodied state think and perceive?

3.2.23 (342)

तदव्यक्तम् आह हि

tadavyaktam āha hi

tat—that; avyaktam—is not manifest; āha—says; hi—certainly.

TRANSLATION

That (body and mind by which the soul perceives and conceives the Lord) is certainly unmanifest (at the present) thus it is said (by the scriptures).

COMMENTARY

The impersonalist thinks that the body that covers the soul is always an external envelope of the soul, and when this envelope is discarded, there is no other body. This is, however, a false understanding. There is another kind of body that is unmanifest right now and will be manifest from *within* the soul. Just like a seed manifests into a tree, similarly, the soul can also manifest a body. This body is hidden inside the soul in an *avyakta* or unmanifest form, just like the tree exists inside the seed, and yet unless the seed is watered, the tree remains unmanifest. The water is external to the seed, but the tree is internal to the seed. When the material body is used to serve the Lord, that is like watering the seed. Under these conditions, the tree comes out of the seed automatically. The purpose of the material body is the developing of the spiritual body.

If we identify with this body, then we engage in materialistic activities and the seed is not watered. If we reject the body prematurely, then, we can see how the soul is separate from the material body, but the seed is not watered. Thus, both conditions of materialism (identifying with the body) and impersonalism (rejecting the body) culminate in the same result—the seed is not watered. And unless this seed is watered, the tree of the spiritual body is unmanifest.

QUESTION

Does this mean that the body manifest from the soul is just like this present body in the sense that it can also be used for perception and conception?

3.2.24 (343)

अपि च संराधने प्रत्यक्षानुमानाभ्याम्

api ca saṃrādhane pratyakṣānumānābhyām

api ca—and moreover; saṃrādhane—in perfect meditation (it is experienced); pratyakṣa-anumānābhyām—for direct perception and inference.

TRANSLATION

And moreover, in perfect meditation (on the Lord) (the body) can be used for direct perception and inference (about the Lord, just like this body).

COMMENTARY

A person might simultaneously exist in many roles such as father, employee, citizen, husband, etc. but they are not simultaneously manifest. In the same way, the spiritual body of the soul exists inside the soul in an unmanifest form. It is said that necessity is the mother of invention. That necessity is desire in the soul. When this desire is created, then a body suitable to fulfill that desire is produced. And once this body is produced, then it enters a relation to the Lord. If the soul's desires change, then it can manifest a different body, and using that body, the soul can enter a different relation to the Lord. Even in the material world, as we have discussed earlier, the chit-śakti or the body is manifest after the māyā-śakti. The Lord injects the soul into the māyā-śakti, and based on the desires, a suitable type of body for enjoyment is acquired.

An example of the desire in the soul is that it wants to eat tasty food. Then, māyā-śakti creates varieties of cuisines—e.g., Indian food, Mexican food, Chinese food, Mediterranean food, etc.—and the soul chooses one such flavor at one time. Once the soul accepts one such taste, then it develops into the desire for the place where this food is available. Once the soul reaches that place, then he develops a desire for a menu of dishes within a type of flavor. And then the soul picks up some dishes within that menu. Finally, the soul enjoys a certain type of food. The basic desire about "I want tasty food" thus successively manifests into the desire for a cuisine, a place that serves the cuisine, a menu about that cuisine, and a dish within that cuisine. The soul doesn't create all this variety, however, that doesn't mean that it doesn't have a desire for eating.

The impersonalist claims that if the māyā-śakti did not create varieties of cuisines, then the soul will not have a desire for taste. This is a false idea. If nothing is available, then the soul can remain content for some time, and this contentment is called Brahman. But when the desire for tasting develops, then the soul falls again into māyā-śakti, gets a desire, and then gets a body.

In the same way, when the soul develops a desire for the Lord, then he wants to see, hear, smell, touch, and taste the Lord. Again, māyā-śakti produces many kinds of desires, and the soul accepts them and acquires a body. Both spiritual and material bodies are produced from māyā-śakti, but they are described to be two different kinds of māyā: yoga-māyā and mahā-māyā. Under mahā-māyā, all the desires are devoid of the Lord; thus, the soul wants to see, taste, smell, hear, and touch, but those things must not be the Lord. Under yoga-māyā, the soul only wants to see, taste, touch, hear, and smell the Lord.

This sūtra says that with a spiritual body one acquires direct perception of the five senses. In this direct perception, we can hear sounds, but we must infer the meaning. We can see bodily expressions, but we must infer the emotions. We can see the actions, but we must infer the roles. This inference is performed by the mind. Therefore, the spiritual body also has mind and senses, and it can directly perceive taste, smell, sound, touch, and sight, and it can infer moods, roles, and meanings. The spiritual body is hence just like the material body. The difference is simply that the spiritual body can see, taste, touch, smell, and hear the Lord, but the material body cannot. Therefore, everything about the Lord is inaccessible through the material body, and the Lord hence appears in the form of a deity so we can see and touch, in the form of a scripture so we can hear, and as the remnants of His food that we can taste and smell. We can perceive and understand these things through the material body, and as we engage our senses and the mind in this activity, the soul develops attraction for the Lord. When that attraction is developed, then a spiritual body is acquired. Through the spiritual body, the soul can directly perceive and understand the Lord.

QUESTION

I can understand that the body is unmanifest presently, and is manifest from within the soul, but isn't there still a difference between the body and the soul? If so, how can the body be considered the nature of the soul itself?

3.2.25 (344)

प्रकाशादविच्चावैशेष्यं प्रकाशश्च कर्मणि अभ्यासात्

prakāśādivaccāvaiśeṣyaṃ prakāśaśca karmaṇi abhyāsāt

prakāśādivat—like light etc.; ca—and; avaiśeṣyaṃ—no difference; prakāśaḥ—the light; ca—and; karmaṇi—in the actions (or the effects of the light); abhyāsāt—on account of the work, practices, or the habits (of the soul).

TRANSLATION

And just like there is no difference between the light and the actions or the effects of the light (e.g., heat and illumination) (similarly, there is no difference between the soul and) the work, practices, or the habits (of the soul).

COMMENTARY

The body and the soul are different and non-different. They are different because the soul can accept different bodies; this acceptance comes in the form of having different moods, perceptions, and relations. They are also non-different because the part is inside the whole and the whole is inside the part. Thus, our body is a part of the soul because bodily awareness is one of the types of awareness of the soul, and the soul is present in each part through its consciousness. This mutual permeation is indicated by two factors— (1) the soul controls the body, and (2) the body serves the soul. The body springs from the desire for enjoyment, and this desire leads to control of the body. However, when the body is created, then the body parts serve the other body parts because they are serving the soul. This cow is different from the mammal, because even if the cow ceased to exist, then mammal would still exist. And yet, the mammal is present in the cow. Similarly, if the body ceased to exist, then the soul will still exist. And yet, while the body exists, the soul is present within the body.

This sūtra makes a profound point about the mutual presence of cause and effect within each other. The claim is that the cause and effect are different and non-different. Why? The effect existed inside the cause and was manifest from the cause. Similarly, once the effect is manifest, we can know the cause of that effect from the effect. If the effect wasn't in the cause, then the effect would appear from nothing—ex-nihilo creation. Likewise, if the cause wasn't in the effect, then we could not say which of the many causes created the effect.

Suppose you see a moving billiard ball. You know that its motion was caused by something that was moving, and hence, the effect of motion was produced by a cause in which the energy of motion previously existed. But the billiard ball could be moving because it was struck by another billiard ball or by a billiards cue. Which of these two are the real cause? In modern physics we say that we have no way of knowing whether the billiard ball or the cue caused the motion, unless we go back in time and see what caused it. But in this sūtra, it is indicated that we can know the cause simply by observing the effect. That means that the cause is immanent in the effect—as the cause of the effect.

As an example, the theists say that God created the world, which means that the world must have existed in some form in God prior to the creation. This is the effect existing inside the cause. However, once the effect is created, the theists draw a separation between matter and God, and the materialist now latches on to this separation and says: How do you know that God created the world? This creation is also consistent with a big bang! Since we cannot go back in time to know what caused the universe, we have no empirical way of knowing the universe's origin. Thus, both theists and atheists accept that effects are in the cause, but they don't accept that the cause is inside the effect. In monotheistic religions of the West, even the effect is not accepted to be in the cause; they, for instance, claim that God created the universe *ex nihilo*, which means an infinite amount of energy was created from nothing. If we don't take that position, then by the law of conservation of energy, God would be diminished upon creation. Thus, monotheism removes the effect from the cause, which materialism does not. But materialism removes the cause from the effect. Hence, monotheism and materialism posit different kinds of cause-effect notions.

By removing the effect from the cause, an unscientific doctrine is produced—because energy conservation is rejected. And by removing the cause from the effect, an incomplete science is produced—because the same effect can be explained by innumerable causes, so you cannot know the cause from the effect. The result of the first claim is that the cause is not necessary for an effect—because the effect comes out of nothing. The result of the second claim is that no cause is necessary as other causes can explain the effect, and therefore, no explanation can be considered a sufficient explanation of the effect. Once we take out necessity and sufficiency, then science itself becomes meaningless.

Therefore, we must understand that causes within the effect, and effects within the causes are required for necessity and sufficiency, which are in turn necessary for science. However, necessity and sufficiency come at the cost of conventional logic—namely, that the cause and effect are within each other. The problems of logical violations must now be addressed by modalities. There are two such modalities—possibility and will—which must now be accepted. The effect exists inside the cause as a possibility, and the cause exists inside the effect as a will. This means when we see an effect, we can say two things. First, this effect is manifested from the cause by a will, and the will is within the effect as the purpose of why the effect was manifest. If we know the purpose of things, then we know the cause that produced them. If we reject will and possibility, then our explanation is incomplete (or there is no explanation). If we accept both possibility and will, but we don't describe them as different modes of existence, then we have a self-contradictory explanation. Modal explanations are therefore necessary for any cause-effect explanation and the cornerstone of this modality is simply that the cause exists within the effect as its purpose.

The soul similarly exists in the body as the purpose of the body, and God exists in the world as the purpose of the world. That doesn't mean that the soul is the body, or that God is the world. They are different and non-different. Likewise, the body was previously within the soul, and the world was within God.

In modern science, when a photon is absorbed, we cannot say whether this photon came from the sun or the lamp. Likewise, from the perspective of the sun or the lamp, we cannot say whether the photon will illuminate the table or the chair. This is incompleteness of the theory, because we cannot tell the effect from the cause (i.e., whether the table or the chair will be illuminated) and we cannot tell the cause from the effect (if the illumination was due to the sun or the lamp). In classical physics we could say that if the source of light existed, then the destination will be illuminated, but in atomic physics we cannot even say that—because the emission of the photon is indeterministic. To solve these problems, we must say that the photon is a possibility in the source of light, and it is emitted by a will, and this will is immanent within the illumination.

In atomic theory we also say that light is emitted only when it can be absorbed. Therefore, the sun doesn't emit the light unless there is an atomic object whose present and subsequent state differences exactly match the energy in the photon. And in Vedic philosophy, we further say that the light is received at a destination due to karma—i.e., it is not merely purpose but also the receiver must be deserving of the light. Hence, the effect of illumination is not just the sun or the lamp; it is also the receiver being capable of receiving and deserving of the light. Thus, the explanation of light is extremely complicated, but all this complexity is necessary and sufficient for a complete theory of vision.

The impersonalist doesn't know how the cause and the effect mutually permeate each other. He simply says—the body is the effect, and the soul is the cause, but they are different as māyā and Brahman. He cannot explain how the soul falls into māyā, because the will of fall is within the soul, and that will is possible only when the soul is an individual person. The māyā serves this will but while māyā serves the will, the will is immanent in māyā. Therefore, the world is not moving automatically due to māyā. It is moving because there is a will, and that will is moving the māyā from within—due to immanence. Therefore, in one sense, we can say that māyā is itself moving because there is no external cause, and it would be true because the cause is within māyā. In another sense, we can say that the will emanated from the soul or God, so there is a transcendent cause of this will, which subsequently became immanent.

The position of the soul is described nicely in the Bhagavad-Gita by differentiating the passenger from the chariot. The passenger says: I want to go to place X. The chariot then drives the passenger to X. The causality in the passenger is simply about the intention, but the mechanism of the chariot is not controlled by the passenger. In short, *how* the chariot is moving is due to māyā, but *why* it is moving is due to the soul. Finally, *when* and *whether* the chariot moves—despite our will—is decided by the Lord. Thus, the soul, māyā, and God are collectively moving the chariot, and we cannot separate them, because if either one of them was absent, then the chariot would not move. But that doesn't mean that the questions of why, how, and when are identical. The questions are different, but the answers to these questions are combined in the effect.

QUESTION

If the spiritual body of the soul is non-different from the soul, then, does it mean that even the spiritual body of the Lord is non-different from the Lord?

3.2.26 (345)

अतोऽनन्तेन तथा हि लिङ्गम्

ato'nantena tathā hi liṅgam

atah—therefore; anantena—with the infinite; tathā—in the same way; hi—certainly; liṅgam—the form.

TRANSLATION

(Since the soul and its spiritual body are non-different), therefore, in the same way, a form (is associated) with the infinite (namely, the Lord).

COMMENTARY

This sūtra clearly refutes the impersonalist doctrine by stating that the infinite is also a form. This infinite has two components—will and power to fulfill that will. The form of the Supreme Lord is due to will; it is not a material form; the shape of the Lord's body is the form of will or desire for pleasure. The form of the Lord's Śakti is the form of the power that fulfills this desire for pleasure. Will and power are not formless, although if the will is unmanifest or the power is not being used, these forms remain invisible. The invisible state also has a form, although the form is only visible when it creates an effect. Just like if we don't see an apple, the apple remains a possibility of being seen. In this state, there is a form, although the form is unmanifest. When we observe the apple, the form becomes visible. The visible form is just like the invisible form, although, the invisible form is the cause, and the visible form is the effect.

The previous sūtra noted the example of light producing the effects of heat and illumination. If light is not manifest, then it exists in an invisible form. When it is manifest, then it becomes an effect of heat and illumination. So, when we see the light, we don't call it an illusion of our vision. We rather say that there was an objective reality which was previously in an unmanifest state.

Similarly, the Supreme Soul is the potential for all experiences. And when these potentials are realized, then the body of the Supreme Soul is the experiences. In different situations or contexts, different potentials are realized. As a result, the same Supreme Soul can manifest many kinds of bodies. It's not that the other bodies have disappeared; it is just that they are unmanifest. They continue to exist in the Supreme Soul as potentials or possibilities. Based on this manifestation, the Supreme Soul is identified by different names and forms. All these forms are the same Supreme Soul, but depending on the extent of manifestation, some of these forms are called 'superior' to the other forms.

QUESTION

You keep talking about manifest and unmanifest states. Why do these two states are being distinguished? Why can't we just have only one state? Also, if the unmanifest state is not observable, why do we recognize its reality?

3.2.27 (346)

उभयव्यपदेशात्त्वहिकुण्डलवत्

ubhayavyapadeśāttvahikuṇḍalavat

ubhayavyapadeśāt—due to both being stated; tu—but; ahikuṇḍalavat—just like a serpent that is coiled, or in straight and coiled serpent states.

TRANSLATION

Just like a serpent can exist in a coiled or straight state (similarly), (the manifest and unmanifest states are) both declared to be real or true.

COMMENTARY

David Bohm—a British physicist—used the evocative terms 'enfolded' and 'unfolded' to describe the two states of reality (it is rumored that he got this idea of unmanifest and manifest from discussions with Jiddu Krishnamurti). The analogy is pervasive in yoga philosophy where kundalini is said to be a form of 'coiled' material energy and is compared to a coiled snake. When this snake uncoils, then the energy is manifest. Yoga practitioners are therefore trying to uncoil this unmanifest form of energy present in every individual. The coiled snake analogy is also depicted in many ancient traditions where the coiling of the snake is replaced by the snake swallowing its head, and the snake is supposed to merge back into itself because it swallows itself completely.

The question is—since this energy is not visible in most people, how can we say that it even exists? Why even postulate the existence of this unmanifest energy? Shouldn't we not accept the reality of anything that we cannot observe? The answer to this question is that if we reject the unmanifest state, then we would be hard-pressed to explain its appearance. We would have to say that the manifestation must be because something existed somewhere else, and this preexisting thing is conserved, so when energy appears in one place, it must disappear in another place. This idea of conservation—when taken to its logical extreme in the origin of the universe—entails that an infinite amount of energy must be concentrated in a very small region of space. This enormous concentration of energy is then supposed to create a 'black hole' which sucks itself inward, and there is no reason for this 'black hole' to become the 'big bang'. So, the origin of the universe itself becomes a huge problem due to a singularity.

The contrary thesis is that everything preexists as a possibility. And these possibilities are 'enfolded' like a coiled snake. They are manifest when the snake 'unfolds'. Thus, the effect exists within the cause, and nothing that we see is newly created. It is simply becoming visible from a previous invisible state.

This brings us to the question of whether energy is conserved. The answer is yes and no. What do we mean by conservation? We mean that if some energy disappears here, then it must appear elsewhere. In short, energy conservation entails that energy is always manifest. But this is not true. Energy can become unmanifest or 'enfolded' and exist in the source in a 'coiled' form. When the energy becomes coiled, it is not observable, and yet it exists. There is infinite amount of energy in our bodies, but it exists in an enfolded state. The yogi tries to unfold this energy through a mystical process. But the Lord is the supreme mystic. He keeps the entire creation enfolded within, and then unfolds it by His will. Then, when He is bored of this creation, He enfolds it again within.

Therefore, the energy is conserved, but that conservation of energy is not according to classical physics—where energy is always manifest in one place or another, in one form or another. The conservation is rather quantum mechanical, where the energy becomes a possibility. In this state of possibility, infinite energy is present within the Lord, and this packing of energy doesn't create a 'black hole' or 'singularity'. The black hole conundrum arises in modern physics because we think that nature is without will. Therefore, if energy exists, then it must be emitted, and if it is not being emitted, then it must be because the gravitational pull must be preventing its escape. These ideas about black holes are false, and they arise because basic problems in quantum physics remain unresolved. For instance, we are unable to explain how a possibility is converted into a reality. In the case of these black holes regions of space that don't interact with us—i.e., they don't emit light to us, so we cannot see them, we just think that the reason they are not emitting light is because light is being sucked inward. But that is not true. The light is being selectively emitted to certain destinations, just not to us. This selection is due to choices and entitlements.

According to Vedic cosmology, the light of the sun is not received in the upper four planetary systems, the lower seven planetary systems, and the hellish planets. Therefore, the sun is also a black hole according to living entities in all these places, because they can never see the sun. But is the sun a black hole? No. It selectively emits the light to the three planetary systems. The other planets where the light of the sun doesn't reach have other sources of light, which will seem to be black holes to us. Since the parts where the sun's light doesn't reach are much bigger than the parts that we can see, therefore, the number of black holes are far more numerous than all the stars that we can see. All these objects in space keep the energy coiled and uncoil them upon will.

QUESTION

You have used many analogies to describe the unmanifest state—the seed from which the tree springs, the lake that gives rise to rivulets, the source of light that emanates the particles of light, the meanings that are expressed as words of speech through a speaker's mouth, or the snake that remains coiled and becomes uncoiled. Each analogy seems to capture the idea in a limited way, but they are also quite different in other ways. Which is the best analogy?

3.2.28 (347)

प्रकाशाश्रयवद्वा तेजस्त्वात्

prakāśāśrayavadvā tejastvāt

prakāśa-āśrayavat—like the shelter or the substrate of light; vā—moving from (the substrate); tejastvāt—from the light.

TRANSLATION

The analogy of the light separating from the substrate of light.

COMMENTARY

For nearly a century now, scientists have suspected that atomic theory has something to do with the nature of consciousness. This suspicion is confirmed here. Light is not itself consciousness, but it has many properties like that of consciousness. This also means that we should stop thinking of light in terms of material particles. One such idea is that light travels. According to this idea, since light travels, by the time it reaches us, it has become 'detached' from its source. Therefore, we cannot distinguish between sunlight, moonlight, or bulb light. We just know it as light, and the source of light is no longer knowable. But we also know from atomic theory that light is simply a state, not a particle. The particle is the sun, the moon, or the bulb. So, we cannot detach the state from the particle, and claim that light is traveling; we should say that the sun, the moon, or the bulb has a state that modifies the states of other particles. And the laws of this change must be based on the particle, rather than the state. Since all of matter is a state, the particle must be non-material, and to understand light as a state, we must understand how a non-material particle causes change. As we have discussed, the particle is the soul, and the cause is the desire and consequences of actions. So, unless we model the particle as something with desire and responsibility for its actions, we cannot understand the nature of light.

The analogies of the tree, the ocean, and the snake can also be interpreted physically, but the analogy of light cannot be interpreted in this way. For example, one can say that if the tree comes out of the seed, then the seed comes out of the tree. Therefore, everything created by the Lord must be equally capable of creation, which is false. Similarly, one can argue that the ocean is created only when the rivers flow into the ocean, but we can see that the rivers never come out of the ocean; therefore, the ocean is not the source; it is only the sink. Finally, we can say that the snake—even when coiled—always remains visible, and it occupies the same amount of space in the coiled and uncoiled states; hence, we cannot say that the uncoiled state is the manifestation of energy. Therefore, we must understand that many examples are given in the Vedic scriptures only as analogies. These analogies are useful to some extent, and not useful in other ways. In contrast, the example of light is not an analogy. If we study the nature of light, along with the source and sink of light, then it is not an analogy. It is rather the general template by which many other things can be understood. Hence, the sun is called Sūrya Nārāyana, and the sun-god has been worshipped in many religions. His creation is just like that of the Lord's creation.

QUESTION

What happens if someone wants to study light, without the source of light?

3.2.29 (348)

पूर्ववद्वा

pūrvavadvā

pūrvavat—as before; vā—alternatively.

TRANSLATION

Alternatively, as already discussed earlier.

COMMENTARY

The study of light alone is incomplete because light cannot be perceived unless there is an object that it illuminates, and the cause of that illumination cannot be explained unless there is a source. Therefore, impersonal doctrines that describe reality as merely a field of energy are incomplete. The complete theory of light requires a source and a destination. Since these destinations can be manifest from the source, and the light is itself manifest from the source, therefore, the source is by itself complete. Therefore, if we only study the source, then our theory is complete. But if we only study the objects manifest from the source or only the light that moves between the objects, then the theory is incomplete. All impersonalist claims that there is only light, and no source of light, or that light is itself its source, will forever remain incomplete.

In earlier discussions, we have seen that we can repeat the same question and if the context demands, a new or nuanced answer is generally given. However, if the answer is not new, it is not repeated. We just reference the earlier answer. This is often seen in mathematical proofs, when we reduce a new question to an older question, and then substitute the older question with the older answer. This substitution is not novelty. The novelty is that sometimes the same question can be answered differently based on the context. We have seen that novelty previously, and we are seeing the traditional approach here. Since sometimes questions can be answered in different ways, some of these questions may also be repeated—in anticipation of a new answer. That doesn't mean that the answer must be new; this sūtra refers to the older answer. The conclusion is that we must not speak unless we have something new to say.

This injunction also applies to the glorification of the Lord. While it seems that we are advised to chant the names of the Lord repeatedly, we are not repeating the same thing again and again. Every utterance of the name clears up some clutter from the past and therefore even for the neophyte, the repeated chanting is not the repetition of the same thing. As a devotee advances in spiritual life, every name has a unique meaning since different aspects of the Lord are realized through every utterance of the name. Therefore, Lord Chaitanya says: ānandāmbudhi-vardhanaṁ prati-padaṁ, which means that the ocean of bliss is expanding at every step. The impersonalist says that the soul is a drop and Brahman is the ocean, and that ocean is static. But according to Lord Chaitanya, the ocean is infinite, and it is constantly expanding. As a devotee advances in glorifying the Lord, every new glorification describes the Lord in a novel way. Therefore, the devotee doesn't become silent just because the whole truth has already been stated. He speaks because the same truth is constantly expanding, and his speaking is the expansion of an already infinite ocean. The impersonalist says that once you know the whole truth, there is nothing more to be said, and he advocates silence. But the devotee turns around this injunction and says: yes, it is already full, but it can be expanded even more.

QUESTION

If the study of light without the source of light is impossible, then why are so many people still wanting to obtain an understanding in this way?

3.2.30 (349)
प्रतषिधाच्च
pratiṣedhācca

pratiṣedhāt—due to forbidding; ca—as well.

TRANSLATION

Due to forbidding as well (we develop the desire for it).

COMMENTARY

Impersonalism is the forbidden fruit. But precisely because it is forbidden, we start desiring it. This is the rebellious nature of the soul: when something is forbidden, it becomes more attractive. The rebellious soul asks: Why has it been forbidden? Obviously, there must be something great about it, which is why we have been excluded from enjoying it. Thus, forbidding makes the fruit attractive. If the scriptures did not forbid something, then they would be accused of not giving the correct path. But if the scriptures forbid something, then they make it more attractive to the rebellious soul. Thus, we find atheists who love to interpret scientific theories as indicating a denial of God, without checking what the theory's limitations are. Impersonalist philosophers similarly like to interpret everything according to their goggles of impersonalism, whether it is true or not. In short, we seek the forbidden fruit, not because it has been proven to be true or right or good. We seek it simply because it has been forbidden.

Topic 7

QUESTION

If the soul is incomplete without the Lord, then doesn't this soul feel incomplete even as part of Brahman where the Lord is not fully understood?

3.2.31 (350)

परमतःसेतून्मानसंबन्धभेदव्यपदेशेभ्यः

paramataḥ setūnmānasaṃbandhabhedavyapadeśebhyaḥ

param—the Supreme Reality; ataḥ—therefore; setu-unmāna-saṃbandha-bheda-vyapadeśebhyaḥ—is described as the bridge between the standard (of measurement) and the different (individuals) through a relationship.

TRANSLATION

The Supreme Reality is therefore described as the bridge between the standard (of measurement) and the differences through a relationship.

COMMENTARY

Another example is given here to illustrate the incompleteness of the soul without the Lord. Suppose we say that an object is '5' without specifying the standard of measurement, then '5' is meaningless. This '5' becomes meaningful when the standard is specified—e.g., 5 kilograms, 5 meters, 5 minutes, etc. The number '5' is a quantity, but without the quality—i.e., kilogram, meter, or minute—it is meaningless. Furthermore, even to call something '5' we must know what '1' is. This one is the standard of measurement, the primary unit. And by this standard of measurement, we define both the quality and the quantity.

The Lord is the standard of measurement, which defines both the quality and the quantity. A meter for example is the definition of length as well as the measure of length. In relation to a meter, we can measure the different objects and order them. The standard of measurement—e.g., the meter—is the reference for everything else. So, based on this standard, if we say that something is half-meter, then the meter is implicit in this description. So, the meter is outside the individual thing being measured, but it is also inside the thing after the measurement, because the measurement embedded the meter in the thing. And this embedding of the meter in each thing is the relation to the meter. If we don't perform the measurement, both the quality and the quantity are unknown.

The individualist thinks that each person can become their own standard. That is, we are both the quality and the measure of everything. But this leads to a problem—Why should you be the standard? Why can't I be the standard? With the known problem of jealousy, we reject that anyone is the standard. But if there are many things, then we cannot live without a standard; we have to say something is bigger or smaller, higher or lower, etc. Therefore, it is not enough to say that nobody is a standard; we must also say that even these different things do not exist, because that removes the need for a standard.

Thus, after saying that nobody is a standard, we also reject the idea of a standard, collapse all the differences, and merge everything into a single undifferentiated identity since it removes the need for measurement. If we reject the differences between the individuals, then we get the 'infinite'. But infinite of what? Is it infinite meters, or infinite seconds, or infinite kilograms? The impersonalist has no answer to this problem, because to say that something is infinite kilograms, there must be something which is 1 kilogram, and that would be finite. To speak of this infinity, we must remove all qualities. So, we can say that Brahman is 'infinite', but it is not infinite kilograms, meters, or minutes. It is just a quantity and has no associated quality. And this makes it meaningless.

QUESTION

The example of measurement that you are giving here involves distinct objects—such as a kilogram and an apple. A materialist will say that these standards are arbitrary. For instance, it could also be a pound instead of a kilogram. And that would entail that anything can be a standard. Then, how does the Lord being called the standard of measurement address this issue?

3.2.32 (351)
सामान्यात्तु
sāmānyāttu

tu—but; sāmānyāt—on account of the merger (of the part in the whole).

TRANSLATION

But on account of the merger (of the part within the whole).

COMMENTARY

When we measure against a standard such as a kilogram, the kilogram is separate from the object being measured. This makes it possible to use arbitrary standards. However, this sūtra states that the standard of measurement is the whole, and the parts are measured against it. Of course, since the whole is successively divided into parts, there can be many standards that are bigger relative to the part. However, the Absolute Truth is the limit because it is only the whole and not the part of anything. So, even if we employ larger wholes to understand the parts, there is the whole truth which is itself Absolute.

This problem can further be understood if the whole is defined as 1, and everything else is a fraction of 1. The whole object is the first object. Then there are parts of this whole object, which are second, third, fourth, fifth, etc. We can divide the whole into parts, forming a tree structure, where the smallest part is a part of a larger part, which is part of an even larger part, which is part of the whole, etc. Since there are infinite such parts, in principle, the whole is 'infinite'. And because this whole is the first object, the whole is also '1'. In mathematical language, we can say that the Absolute Truth is cardinally infinite, and ordinally first. Since everything is inside the whole, therefore, we can also talk about the 'oneness' among the varied diversities. And yet this oneness doesn't take away the diversities, and the diversities never 'merge' into the oneness.

The diversities are always defined in relation to the whole. Since there is nothing other than the whole, the whole is the standard, but because the whole is 1, therefore, the standard is 1—not infinite. Since it is 1, we can conceive and perceive it. If this standard was infinite, then we could never know it. The standard is not without qualities; in fact, the standard is the fullness of knowledge, beauty, power, wealth, fame, and renunciation. And everything else has these qualities partially. So, when we divide the whole into parts, we are not cutting the whole *quantitatively*. We are rather saying: given that the whole knowledge is everything that can be known, what are the different departments of knowledge, that are parts of everything that can be known? The method of cutting the whole into parts is based on qualities, not quantities. Thus, for example, we don't say that physics is 1% of the whole knowledge. We rather say: physics is that part of knowledge that deals with the objectification of sense perception. The characterization of knowledge as 1% is meaningless, because another subject—e.g., economics—could also be 1%. If everything is divided into the smallest parts, then we can also count, and based on this counting we can derive quantities. Therefore, quantities are derivative of qualities. The qualities are primary and should be the basis of counting and numbering.

The impersonalist has the reverse viewpoint—drop all qualities, merge all quantities, and come up with infinity of nothing. If we multiply infinity with nothing, is it infinity or nothing? Nobody knows the answer, and the impersonalist rides on this confusion. The Buddhists say that infinity of nothing is nothing. And the impersonalist says that infinity of nothing is infinity. Thus, it is sometimes said that Advaita is Buddhism in a hidden form. It works off the same premises as Buddhism but arrives at a different conclusion. But the fact is that neither conclusion explains the world, although it is a grandiose philosophy. Such pretentious philosophies should be rejected by true seekers.

QUESTION

The measurement of the part against the whole seems quite strange. We measure a part against another part, but you are talking about a new type of measurement. How do we understand this type of measurement?

3.2.33 (352)

बुद्ध्यर्थःपादवत्

buddhyarthaḥ pādavat

buddhi—comprehension; arthaḥ—the meaning; pādavat—like parts.

TRANSLATION

It is possible to comprehend (if we see these) like parts of meaning.

COMMENTARY

We have noted this idea about the whole-part relation being between concepts many times earlier in the purports. This is the first sūtra that states this understanding explicitly. The reason is that we just noted that the soul is incomplete without the Lord, and this incompleteness was described as the standard. Now, if we think of wholes and parts physically, then we can have the whole as the standard, but we can also have the parts as the standards. A classic example of parts that become standards is that we define a standard of length as 'meter'—which is a part of the universe—and then we measure the expanse of the universe in terms of the meter. In the physical view of wholes and parts, either of these can be considered the standards. Greek philosopher Protagoras, in fact, came with up with the dictum that "man is the measure of all things". This claim by Protagoras counters the claim in the Bible: "God created man in His own image". Which of these two claims must be regarded as true? Is God a larger-than-life image of ourselves, or are we the smaller image of God?

These questions remain unanswerable due to the relativity of standards. But they become answerable when we consider the hierarchy of concepts. When you see a cow, there is no reason to postulate that it is also a mammal, unless you have seen horses, tigers, and dogs. Thus, our knowledge is limited by what we have seen. Conversely, if we haven't seen horses, tigers, and dogs, then the deeper level reality of a cow being a mammal will elude us. If instead we begin in the most abstract idea, then knowing that there is a cow entails that it is also a mammal. When you see a shade of red, you say it is part of the class of redness, it is part of a general class of colors, and it is a part of the general class of things that can be seen. In fact, it is impossible to understand a shade of red without understanding red, colors, and seeing. Therefore, in a physical conception of reality, anything can be a standard. However, in the semantic conception of reality, only the whole truth is the standard. Therefore, "God created man in His own image" can only be justified with a semantic viewpoint.

QUESTION

If the whole and the part are considered meanings, then, how do we understand the different locations that are part of the whole? Does it seem that the whole will become the origin, and the parts will be the individual locations? This seems like a strange notion of space in which everything is the origin, and the parts of this everything are different locations within this everything.

3.2.34 (353)

स्थानविशेषात् प्रकाशादिवत्

sthānaviśeṣāt prakāśādivat

sthānaviśeṣāt—from the differences of places; prakāśādivat—like light etc.

TRANSLATION

The different locations are like light (originating from the candle).

COMMENTARY

This sūtra again invokes the example of a candle and its light to explain the nature of space. This example has been quoted several times before but always in a new context. The latest context is that the whole and the part are described as meanings, and therefore, the light is like the partial meaning emanating out of the source, which is the original and complete meaning. Apart from the spiritual implications that we will discuss shortly, it also means that the source of light and the light emanating from that source are not physical things; they are symbols of ideas. Each light particle therefore is a symbol of a partial meaning. The light source is the symbol of the complete meaning. And the light particle is related to the other light particles through the differences in meaning.

Like a cow is defined by the idea 'cow', by the idea of 'mammal', and by distinction to tigers, similarly, each light particle—when understood as a symbol, is not an isolated or independent object. It is connected to the whole because the idea 'mammal' is immanent within the cow. It is also connected to the whole because it is defined by a distinction to tigers. Finally, every time we see other cows, they are connected to each other by a mutual distinction. This means that the connection comes to us in three ways— (1) by universals such as a mammal, (2) by individuals such as other cows, and (3) by contexts such as tigers.

Thus, we know the cow through two assertions (namely that it is a cow and a mammal), and two negations (that it is not a tiger, and not other cows). In modern science, we only know things through assertions and not negations. Furthermore, we only know things through one type of concept—e.g., a cow, and the hierarchy of concepts is discarded. Finally, even the concept of cow is discarded and only properties such as height, weight, color, etc. are employed. This is the current state of atomic theory, which tries to describe light in terms of physical properties, and neglects all kinds of concepts—cows, mammals, not tigers, and not other cows. This theory is well-known to be incomplete.

Once we understand the nature of light, then we can speak about its application to the nature of space. When light is identified as symbols of meaning, then the directions and locations in space are also meanings. We can call this a 'semantic space'. This space has a hierarchical structure, like a tree. As a result, the distinction between direction and location in this space is collapsed. Everything is also a unique *type* of thing. Thus, there are unique types of individuals, identified by their personality. There are unique types of bodies, identified by concepts. And there are unique types of roles, identified by their duties.

We sometimes distinguish between a dimension and a location due to the hierarchy—the higher node is the dimension, and the lower node is a value on that dimension. However, since the lower node is also a dimension relative to an even lower node, therefore, everything is both a value and dimension. Hence, we can say that a cow is a type of mammal, and Gir is a type of cow.

As we have discussed earlier, the dimension becomes a space, and the value becomes an object. Therefore, everything is both a space and an object. Things are objects relative to the 'larger' space, and they are spaces relative to smaller objects. 'Big' and 'small' are more abstract and more detailed concepts.

The origin of this light is abstract relative to all the symbols of light, and it contains all the symbols prior to their manifestation as a possibility. The origin is therefore just one point in the expanded space. The origin is also the entire space in an unmanifest form. Therefore, when the world expands from the Lord, the Lord seems to be one of the many individuals. But He is also the whole existence. When we think of the world physically, then the Lord cannot be a part of existence. But when the we think of the world semantically, then the whole truth can seem to be only one part of the existence. Similarly, the whole truth is also present in each of the parts. Thus, the light particles are in the candle, the candle is one of the light particles, and the candle is in all the light particles. Likewise, all the souls are in the Lord, the Lord is a soul, and the Lord is in all the souls. The materialists and the impersonalist philosophers cannot understand how the Lord is a soul, contains all souls, and exists in all souls. Therefore, they try to collapse all these things into a single undifferentiated 'field'.

QUESTION

Since the parts are emanating from the whole, how does this division of the whole into the parts occur? What is the cause of the division into parts?

3.2.35 (354)
उपपत्तेश्च
upapatteśca

upapatteḥ—due to reasoning or logical conclusion; ca—and.

TRANSLATION

And (the whole divides into parts) due to reasoning or logical conclusion.

COMMENTARY

The term *upapatti* is constituted of two roots—*upa* or secondary, and *pat* or falling. If we understand an inverted tree, then we can see that logical reasoning is the emergence of a branch (secondary) from the root, which is lower (fallen) than the root. In computing theory, reasoning is often identified as tree traversals. We represent knowledge in an inverted tree structure, and we traverse this tree—from root to leaves—to check the answer. Many theorem proving algorithms work in this way—they try to construct statements following a tree structure, and if the statement can be constructed, then it is proved.

The term *utapatti* is also constituted of two roots—*uta* or emergent, and *pat* or falling. Thus, *utapatti* refers to the creation or production, and *upapatti* refers to reasoning. The method of production is the method of reasoning. That is, in both cases, the emergent thing is lower than the source of the thing. Again, if we understand the inverted tree, then production means reasoning. Therefore, everything is created from the Absolute Truth by the process of reasoning, and this process operates by dividing the whole into parts, and then combining the various parts. During the annihilation of the material universe, these combinations are first destroyed, and the universe is reduced to the parts. Then these parts collapse back into the whole. While the universe exists, the parts exist as atoms (which are symbols) and these atoms combine in many ways. Thus, by the process of reasoning, the world is created, changed, and destroyed.

QUESTION

Our normal understanding of reasoning goes from premises to conclusions. But you refer to a model of reasoning in which the conclusion is the part and the premise is the whole, and reasoning goes from whole to part. How do we understand this model of reasoning, contrary to the other models?

3.2.36 (355)

तथान्यप्रतिषेधात्

tathānyapratiṣedhāt

tathā—similarly; anya-pratiṣedhāt—due to denial of other things.

TRANSLATION

(Just as the whole divides into parts) similarly, (the parts are created) by the denial of other things (i.e., the denial of certain parts of the whole).

COMMENTARY

In modern thinking, we start with some simple premises and use logic and reasoning to construct complexity. Thus, the axioms are simple, and the theorems are complex. But what are these simple axioms? The modern definition of 'simplest' is the smallest. It is an extension of physical thinking where big things are made from small things. In Vedic philosophy, the 'simplest' is the largest. For example, the simplest idea we can carry is that of *knowledge*. And yet, this idea contains everything that can ever be known. By this shift in the definition of 'simple', the model of reasoning changes. In modern thinking, we take the smallest axioms and construct larger propositions. In Vedic philosophy, we take the largest axioms, and divide them into smaller parts. This is not a physical division—we are not trying to break down the word 'knowledge' into individual letters. We are rather dividing the meaning knowledge into various types of knowledge. Thus, every branch of knowledge is produced by rejecting or negating some other part or aspect of the root of knowledge itself.

We have discussed this rejection before—a cow is not a tiger, it is not other cows, and the cow is never in two places at the same time. These negations are within the cow, and by these negations, the cow is connected to the tigers, to other cows, and to all the other locations where the cow is not present. All these are absent in a specific cow because the cow is *not* those things. And yet, because they are negated in a cow, they are present in the cow as negations.

These negations are called *abhāva* or non-existence in Nyāya. When we know that something is a cow, we know that it is not a tiger. Therefore, the non-existence is within the existence, but they are separate modes of existence. In modern science, we only consider the *bhāva* or existence and hence we think that everything exists independent of other things. But we cannot explain how by knowing something is X, we also know that it is not-not-X. This double negation is simply taken for granted in logic, but never explained in terms of the real world. Thus, logic remains separated from the material reality. If we try to reconcile logic with the real world, then the negation of tiger is in the cow. And the reason for that negation is that the cow is created from a mammal by obfuscating some aspects of mammals which are seen in other mammals.

The basic mechanism of reasoning in modern thinking is combining, joining, or mingling the atomic parts to create complex wholes. But the basic mechanism of reasoning in Vedic philosophy is dividing, splitting, and obfuscating the whole into atomic parts. Thus, the Vedic system of reasoning or logic—which is called *upapatti*—is completely different from the modern system.

QUESTION

When knowledge is created by the combination of atomic axioms, then knowledge becomes infinite, because there is no limit to how much these axioms can be combined. Therefore, many people argue that there is nothing called 'knowledge' because it is the set of all the provable theorems. And since this set is infinite, we cannot call any individual claim as 'knowledge'. How does that change if knowledge is defined as the division of the whole?

3.2.37 (356)

अनेन सर्वगतत्वमायामशब्दादिभ्यः

anena sarvagatatvamāyāmaśabdādibhyaḥ

anena—by this; sarvagatatvam—the all-pervasiveness; āyāma—the extent or measure; śabdādibhyaḥ—known from scriptural statements, etc.

TRANSLATION

By this (method of dividing the whole into parts), (knowledge) is both all-pervading (i.e., everything is knowledge) as well as measurable (because it was produced by subdivision); this is the understanding of the scriptures.

COMMENTARY

If we define the idea of 'color' as the set that contains all the individual shades, then unless all the shades have been collected, the set is incomplete and hence the definition of 'color' is incomplete. If the number of shades is infinite, then the set called 'color' can never be completed. And unless it has been completed, nothing in the set can be called 'color'. Since the shades are infinite, there can never be a definition of color, and unless we obtain that definition, we won't be able to identify the shades as types of colors and include them in a set.

This recursive dependence on the set and the member is solved only when we begin with meanings—i.e., we don't start with shades; we start with color. And we divide this color into parts—which can be as nuanced as we like. Even if the nuancing of the shades is left incomplete, the definition of color is still complete, and therefore even the coarse-grained shades can be considered colors.

Similarly, if we begin with knowledge, then everything produced by its subdivision is also knowledge. We may or may not know the smallest possible particles, but that isn't considered incomplete knowledge, because the method of constructing the knowledge is top-down rather than bottom-up. Thus, for example, the knowledge that there is an apple—although we don't see the atoms of the apple—can't be called an illusion. It is still knowledge, although more details about the apple can be known. The absence of these details doesn't make the knowledge of an apple an illusion. Similarly, even though we can divide the apple into smaller and smaller parts, thereby constructing an infinite number of knowledge propositions, the knowledge of 'apple' remains finite. Thus, the infinite division of the apple doesn't make the knowledge of the whole impossible. Rather, both the apple, and its atomic constituents, can be known, and by this knowing they form separate kinds of knowledge.

Topic 8

QUESTION

If knowledge is created by reasoning, then what about the results of our actions? The creation of knowledge is an effect, and the creation of the results of actions are the consequences. Are consequences also created by logical inference? If not, we would have two processes for effects and consequences.

3.2.38 (357)

फलमतःउपपत्तेः

phalamataḥ upapatteḥ

phalam—fruits (of actions); ataḥ—thus; upapatteḥ—due to reasoning.

TRANSLATION

Therefore, the fruits (of actions) are created due to reasoning.

COMMENTARY

Modern science recognizes the existence of a reaction that is equal and opposite to the action; the reaction always acts upon the cause. However, this reaction is identical to the transfer of energy—if you push a cart, the cart appears to push back; but this backward pressure is equal to the energy transferred. Modern science calls this a 'reaction' rather than an 'effect' because the term 'effect' is reserved for the changes caused to other objects. Thus, for example, if you get tired after working, then, science will call that a 'reaction' rather than an 'effect'. But these distinctions are based on the premise that the external action is the reason for an action, while the 'reaction' is simply a side effect. This is often a false premise; for example, if someone lifts weight to build their body, the goal of lifting weights is to build the body, not to lift the weights themselves. Therefore, to call the outcome of a stronger body a 'reaction' to weightlifting is somewhat counterintuitive. The stronger body should rather be called an effect, and the changes to the lifted weights should be considered a 'reaction'. In fact, it might be better to just call both these 'effects' produced by a transfer of energy, rather than calling one an 'effect' and the other a 'reaction'. Factually, both 'effect' and 'reaction' are created simultaneously and on different objects.

Once we set aside these 'reactions' as effects, then we can speak about consequences, which come in three varieties. First, every action leaves an imprint or memory in the actor; the collection of all these imprints is called *chitta*. Second, every action forms a new habit or destroys an existing habit; so, if you have done something once, it is more likely that you will perform that action again, and if that action was against your previously formed habits, then, it might alter the earlier habits; the collection of all the habits is called 'nature' or *guna* as it conditions us to behave in different ways. Third, all actions produce a moral consequence based on a person's role, duty, or responsibility. Note how each of these consequences hinges upon the fact that the actor is a conscious person. There would be no need for a memory imprint if the person wasn't conscious. Similarly, habits can be associated only with conscious persons. Finally, moral consequences are possible only when the actor has a choice and free will.

The habits, imprints, and consequences are different from the 'effect' and 'reaction', which can be described physically. These are described as meanings. The imprints are cognitive meanings or what we consider true and false, the habits are what we find good or bad, and the moral consequences are based on the judgments of right and wrong. Thus, the consequences must be distinguished from the physical 'effects' and 'reactions' as they are a causality based on meanings. When reasoning follows physical causality, then there are only effects from causes. But in semantic causality, there are consequences too. So, the creation of consequences is an intrinsic part of semantic reasoning.

Scientists have thought about perpetual motion machines—those which produce an endless cycle of cause and effect. However, if the causation only involves causes and effects, then such perpetual motion is impossible A self-perpetuating cycle of causation is produced due to consequences. Every consequence of an action becomes the seed for a new cause. The evolution of a soul through various bodies is one such self-perpetuating cycle and ending this self-perpetuating cycle of causation is the primary goal of liberation. The cycle can come to an end when consequences are not created. Thus, karma-yoga for instance focuses in the cessation of karma, dhyāna-yoga focuses on the cessation of all imprints on the chitta, and jñāna-yoga aims at the cessation of all habits. Each of these three forms of yoga take a soul to liberation. The process of bhakti-yoga, however, encourages the formation of divine impressions and habits, and when actions are performed due to love of God, there are no consequences. Thus, bhakti-yoga doesn't aim for liberation from activity, perception, and the body. It rather encourages this cycle arising out of the recollection of the Lord in the chitta, and the desires emanating from one's spiritual guna or qualities. This cycle is still considered liberation because there is no effect of karma.

QUESTION

If knowledge is created by reasoning, and the scriptures are considered knowledge, then does it follow that the scriptures are created logically?

3.2.39 (358)

श्रुतत्वाच्च

śrutatvācca

śrutatvāt—that which emerges from scriptures; ca—also.

TRANSLATION

That which emerges from scriptures too (utilizes logical reasoning).

COMMENTARY

One of the contentions of Mīmāṃsā philosophy is that the Vedic scriptures are logically necessary—like mathematical theorems derived from axioms. Many Mīmāṃsā philosophers believed that it wasn't God who spoke the scriptures; rather, just as the world is created logically, similarly, the scriptures are also created logically. The sages who codified these scriptures weren't, therefore, following the word of God (and some of them claimed that there is no God). It is rather that the scriptures are 'generated' by a logical process, and their meaning would be uncovered by the linguistic analysis of these texts. A parallel to this idea in modern times is the study of generative grammars which, given some alphabets and grammatical rules, can be used to produce sentences. The essence of knowledge was to obtain the generative rules. Since the world is symbolic meaning, therefore, it too can be generated using the same rules. And applying such generative rules would obtaining a result by our actions.

Thus, rituals were seen as generative actions, and the rules of these generations were obtained from the study of how the scriptures were generated. The theoretical study of scriptures led to the discovery of rules, and the practical use of rules in rituals and linguistic performances led to desired results.

This sūtra echoes the Mīmāṃsā contention that the Vedic scriptures are produced through a generative process. As we have discussed before, the world exists as a tree, which is generated from the root by the embedding of the three modes within each other. Knowledge is similarly also a tree, and it has been generated from the same root. In the previous sūtras, this generative process was described as logic, although not the logic of modern thinking because this logic has effects and consequences. This means that if we knew the generative process, then all the Vedic texts that were lost over time could be recreated. Any books that potentially have been modified can be corrected. And the truth of these books follows necessarily from the universality of the generative process. This is a purely linguistic method of confirming the truth of scriptures.

QUESTION

You said that knowledge is created logically, and then you said the Vedic scriptures are also generated logically. But these scriptures also prescribe the duties for the different classes of people. If the scriptures are logically necessary, does it mean that the social duties are also necessary in this way? Moral codes are generally considered normative rules—i.e., created as norms by society—rather than logically and rationally provable descriptive rules. But you seem to be saying that even the moral codes are logically necessary.

3.2.40 (359)
धर्मं जैमिनिःअत एव

dharmaṃ jaiminiḥ ata eva

dharmaṃ—the duties; jaiminiḥ—(sage) Jaimini; ata eva—in the same way.

TRANSLATION

The sage Jaimini opines that the duties (are necessary) in the same way.

COMMENTARY

This and the previous sūtras are connected as the explanation of scriptures, and the explanation of duties described in the scriptures. Jaimini, as we have seen, was the preeminent Mīmāṃsā philosopher. His opinion is cited in this regard as a follow-up to the previous sūtra by stating that the *dharma* is not a societal construct. The organization of society, the roles and duties of people in it, and the economic and political mechanisms are all logically necessary. In other words, there is no difference between natural laws and social laws. The laws of moral consequences and duties are therefore also natural laws.

The government in a country, for instance, has a head of state, a judiciary, a military etc. But these functions can be separated into different roles or combined into a single role. The duties of a role depend on whether these functions have been combined or separated. Hence, right and wrong is contextual, but not arbitrary. It can change with time, but it exists objectively at present. Each institutional structure brings an objective right and wrong, although we may not understand that objective duty, and misdemeanors lead to karma.

QUESTION

Earlier it was said that Bādarāyana is the author of Vedas. Now you are stating that these scriptures are produced through a process of logical derivation. How can we reconcile these two apparently contradictory contentions?

3.2.41 (360)
पूर्वं तु बादरायणःहेतुव्यपदेशात्

pūrvaṃ tu bādarāyaṇaḥ hetuvyapadeśāt

pūrvam—earlier; tu—but; bādarāyaṇaḥ—Bādarāyana; hetu-vyapadeśāt—on account of being declared to be the cause (of the scriptures).

TRANSLATION

Earlier it was said that Bādarāyana is declared the cause of Vedas, but (we also recognize the logically necessary status of the Vedic scriptures).

COMMENTARY

This sūtra states that there is no conflict in stating that the scriptures are logically necessary and that Bādarāyana is their author. Just like a human can prove mathematical theorems, similarly, Bādarāyana can be called the author of scriptures. However, the fact that a human proves a mathematical theorem doesn't make the truth of the theorem subject to that person's opinions. Thus, we speak about Pythagoras' theorem, because Pythagoras proved it. However, there is no contradiction in saying that Pythagoras is the author of the theorem and that the theorem is logically necessary. The fact is that someone else could have proved the same theorem, and it would be considered equally true.

This claim seems to contradict the Mīmāṃsā claim in which the scriptures are treated as a natural phenomenon and are hence considered authorless. But any such claim by Mīmāṃsā is rejected here. The knowledge is indeed necessary and independent of authors. However, knowledge can be codified into texts by an enlightened author. Therefore, Bādarāyana is said to be the Lord's empowered incarnation who codified the Vedas about 5000 years ago. However, the Vedas are also said to be spoken by Brahma, and the knowledge is said to be imparted by the Lord to Brahma. Thus, three contradictory doctrines of the origination of the scriptures—namely, divine origination, logical necessity, and historical authorship—are simultaneously accepted as being true.

This flies in the face of modern contentions that if scriptures are of divine origin, then no human could have written them. Or, that the truths of science are logically necessary and hence their existence contradicts divine authorship. The Lord is the source of the scriptures, but His process of creation is logical. The same logical process can also be used by humans. If the same process is followed, then humans can author scriptures on par with the Lord. Their historical appearance doesn't make them human creations, just like the historical appearance of Pythagoras doesn't make his theorem a human creation.

There is a lesson here for religions that claim divine origination, such as the revelation by an angel to an apostle, followed by a historical human authorship of revelations or conversations. The lesson is that the logical necessity associated with the claims in revelation or authorship cannot be rejected. When historical accuracies and divine revelations are challenged, it is not necessary to prove them. It is also possible to prove the logical necessity of the claims.

SECTION 3

Topic 1

QUESTION

Since Vedānta Sūtra is the conclusion of all Vedic knowledge, are the statements of Vedānta Sūtra also produced by the process of logical reasoning?

3.3.1 (361)

सर्ववेदान्तप्रत्ययम् चोदनाद्यविशेषात्

sarvavedāntapratyayam codanādyaviśeṣāt

sarva-vedānta-pratyayam—all Vedānta conclusions; codanādi—are rules etc.; aviśeṣāt—from the undifferentiated (or one without distinctions).

TRANSLATION

All Vedānta conclusions (subsidiary claims—*pratyaya*) are rules etc. produced from the undifferentiated (axiom—that which is without distinctions).

COMMENTARY

When reasoning combines axioms to produce a conclusion, then it requires more than one axiom. If these axioms were considered the primitive reality that precedes the manifested world, then this reality will have to be multiple axioms. However, when reasoning divides the axiom into parts, then it requires only one axiom, and this primitive reality is the Absolute Truth. This sūtra confirms that the primitive reality is the undifferentiated existence from which many kinds of differentiations are produced by a logical process. Earlier it has been said that Vedic texts, the duties and roles, and the cycle of self-propelled change are all produced by rules. This sūtra now extends this conclusion to the Vedānta Sūtra itself, noting that this text is *nyāya-prasthāna* or a logical treatise.

QUESTION

If all the texts are produced due to logical progression, then why are all the texts different? Shouldn't all these texts be uniform in their progression?

3.3.2 (362)

भेदान्नेति चेत् न एकस्यामपि

bhedānneti cet na ekasyāmapi

bhedāt—due to difference na—not; iti cet—if it be said; na—not so; ekasyāmapi—even in the same (text).

TRANSLATION

If it is said that (the texts) should not be different (due to logical progression) (then we say) not so (because) the one is also (the source of many).

COMMENTARY

A confusion arises due to the previous sūtra, where all texts—i.e., śrutī, smṛiti, and nyāya—are designated as logical treatises. These texts obviously follow different patterns, often have different descriptions, and don't seem to follow the same pattern in the Vedānta Sūtra. Then how can we call all of them logical progressions, when there are obvious differences between them?

The short answer is that there are many meanings of 'logical progression'. For instance, the Bhagavad-Gita describes a progression from jñāna-yoga to aśtānga-yoga, to karma-yoga to bhakti-yoga. A student approached a teacher and obtained knowledge—the method of jñāna-yoga. Then the student tried to realize this knowledge by meditation—the method of dhyāna-yoga. As portions of this truth were realized in meditation, one's life was transformed, and the realization had effects on all day-to-day activities—the method of karma-yoga. Finally, the nature of the self and its purpose of existence was realized—the method of bhakti-yoga. Therefore, there was a progression in the process, and the description in the Bhagavad-Gita reflects it; it is logical, although this 'logic' is based on ever-deepening nature of the soul's conditioning and the methods prescribed for the purification or removal of this conditioning.

Similarly, a pattern in the Purāṇa is the discussion of material nature, followed by the problem of birth, death, and suffering, the process by which liberation is attained, and the nature of the liberated state. The Tantra, similarly, discuss the nature of reality, followed by processes of practice that lead to liberation, and finally the result of these processes. The four Vedas follow a template in which reality is described in the Rig Veda, the rituals for attaining this reality are noted in the Yajur Veda, the deities to be worshipped through this ritual are described in the Sama Veda, and the methods of performing the rituals are present in the Atharva Veda. The Itihāsa follow a different template in which a hero is born among greatness, falls from grace, struggles during this fall, and then reclaims the position of greatness due to this struggle. The greatness at the beginning and the end might be different in many cases. In all these cases, an overview of the text may be provided in the beginning, along with the processes and the nature of reality in a summarized form, like an author captures the overview of the text in a preface or an introduction. However, this summary is succinct and is followed by a detailed recapitulation later.

The template for Vedānta Sūtra is quite different. It is a logical treatise because it follows the question-and-answer dialectical pattern of a debate, learning, and arriving at the complete knowledge. This template also exists in the Purāṇa, Tantra, and the Upaniśad as teacher-student conversations, but it is always a subsidiary pattern within the overall pattern of heroic transformation or the ordinary person who is not born a hero although takes the heroic path of spiritual practice anyway. The Vedānta Sūtra is unique in solely adhering to the dialectical pattern of logical process. However, every other scripture is also considered a logical treatise even though it follows different kinds of logical patterns. The point is that all Vedic scriptures follow a logical template, although the nature of these templates is different across different scriptures.

The simplest meaning of logical progression is a heroic storyline; another meaning is the journey of a non-hero who becomes a hero by undertaking the process of spiritual life, undergoes the tribulations of the process, and finally attains the perfection of life. Yet another meaning is the dialectical method of question and answer. And then there is a logical progression from the description of truth, followed by the righteous practices that result in the attainment of this reality, and the good that comes from its attainment. Sometimes, the righteous practices or dharma can be divided into an abstract description, followed by the details of the deities to be worshipped and their various qualities, followed by the detailed methods of performing the ritual. Thus, by 'logical treatise' we mean these templates of logical progression. There are many such templates, and all these templates can be considered 'logical progression'.

When the dialectics is emphasized, then the text is called nyāya-prasthāna. When the progression through a heroic cycle is emphasized, then the texts are called smṛiti. When the ordinary person becomes the hero through the practice of spiritual life, then the process is called śrutī. Thus, the Vedic texts are classified into three categories as śrutī, smṛiti, and nyāya. They all follow a logical progression, although, the patterns of this progression are quite different. Sometimes these templates are combined, although one template remains dominant. Therefore, 'logic' here is a general description of textual templates.

Once we note the existence of such varied templates, then we can also note that all these templates exemplify the question-and-answer template. The heroic character, for instance, is the premise; his fall from grace is the question; and the recovery into a state of greatness is the new conclusion. Similarly, the non-hero entangled in the material world can be the premise; following this, the process of becoming a hero is the question; and finally, the attainment of greatness is the new conclusion. Likewise, the description of reality is the premise; the method of attaining this reality is the question; and the results obtained by this attainment are the new conclusion. The elucidation of reality, though a succession of questions and answers, is yet another illustration of this pattern.

The previous sūtra said that the Vedānta Sūtra follows a logical pattern, and we have described this as the premise-problem-answer pattern. This sūtra now states that all other scriptures are only variations of this single pattern. In this pattern, we begin with a premise, we are then led to a question, problem, or contradiction, and the solution of this question, problem, or contradiction is a new premise. The sequence of premise-problem-answer forms a tripartite cycle. This cycle can be seen in the story of a hero. For example, their heroic status is the premise, the heroism being tested by difficulties is the question, and the reestablishment of the heroic status is the new conclusion. The journey of a non-hero can be a longer cycle, because accepting the premise that someone is a non-hero—e.g., entangled in the material world—can be long-drawn; similarly, the discovery of the processes by which the non-hero can become a hero can be even longer; finally, the implementation of these processes through practices can also be a long-drawn endeavor. Within this cycle, one might often go back to the question of whether he or she is a non-hero, what must be done to solve the problem, and how expediently must that method be implemented.

Some cycles—that involve short-term results, such as the results produced through a ritual—can be shorter. And the cycle of question-and-answer to attain knowledge is the shortest. Since this sūtra states that all these are variations of the same basic method of logical progression, we must understand that variety is produced by nesting of the shorter cycles inside the longer cycle. Thus, when a hero falls from grace, he might start learning the method of restoration of this greatness, and this process of learning can itself form a smaller cycle. Likewise, the implementation of this process to restore greatness can be another cycle. This sūtra claims that even the śrutī and smṛiti are outcomes of applying the same type of premise-question-answer cycle, although the pattern is not as obvious as in the case of Vedānta Sūtra. Therefore, the various scriptures are all produced logically, employing a common pattern of logical progression.

QUESTION

Even if we say that all these scriptures are logically necessary, and produced by the same method of logical progression, what is the need for so many scriptures? I can understand the necessity for Vedānta as the conclusion of all knowledge. But what about the many other scriptures which prescribe practices for the material world? Isn't the presence of so many scriptures a source of confusion, as they provide different instructions that seem conflicting?

3.3.3 (363)

स्वाध्यायस्य तथात्वेन हि समाचारेऽधिकाराच्च सववच्च तन्नियमः

svādhyāyasya tathātvena hi samācāre'dhikārācca savavacca tanniyamaḥ

svādhyāya—practice or the regular study; asya—of this (the scriptures); tathātvena—in accurate form, or just as they are, without concoction; iti—because; samācāre—in the action according to instruction; adhikārāt—due to qualification; ca—and; savavat—like liberated; ca—and; tanniyamaḥ—those rules.

TRANSLATION

The practice or regular study of these (scriptures) which is provided in accurate form (i.e., the scriptures are precise) (is suggested) because in the action according to the instruction (given in the scripture), due to the proper qualification, one becomes liberated (from material existence) and (from) those rules (of duty which have to be followed by everyone non-liberated).

COMMENTARY

When we say that scriptures are logically necessary, we create a problem—it seems that logical necessity implies that all scriptural injunctions are universally true. This universal truth would imply that the scriptural injunctions would apply even when one is liberated or transcendent to material nature. This notion of logical necessity is derived from the belief that whatever is logically true is true in all possible worlds. This sūtra, however, distinguishes between the injunctions of this world, and those that are transcendent to the world by saying that by following many injunctions one becomes free of these injunctions. There are certain scriptural injunctions whose purpose is to take a person to liberation whereupon the rules and regulations cease to be applicable. There are, however, other statements which apply even beyond the material world, which were noted in the previous sūtra where Vedānta was described as transcendental knowledge. The contention is that we must not equate the statements applicable to the material world with those that are transcendent. Instructions about the material world are like a ladder used to attain liberation. The ladder is useless after that. However, the statements about the transcendent reality are not a ladder, because they remain true and important forever.

QUESTION

If these diverse scriptures are not eternally relevant, then how can they be considered to lead one to eternal truth? Isn't there a fundamental contradiction between saying that some instructions are only contextually applicable, and yet following them leads one to the understanding of the universal truth?

3.3.4 (364)

दर्शयति च

darśayati ca

darśayati—sees (the eternal truth through all scriptures); ca—also.

TRANSLATION

(One can) also see (the eternal truth through the contextual statements).

COMMENTARY

All relative truths are produced by dividing the Absolute Truth. When they are so divided, the Absolute Truth also enters the relative truths in three ways. First, the Absolute Truth is present in the relative truth as the idea from which the relative truths are produced. For example, when you see a cow, you also see a mammal, an animal, and a living entity. Second, the Absolute Truth is present in each relative truth as the purpose of the relative truths' existence. The existence of diversity is not due to chance and it is not purposeless. Third, the Absolute Truth controls the working of the relative truths. The interaction of one relative truth with another is caused by the will of the Absolute Truth.

In modern science, we see one out of the three types of presences. For example, the laws of physics are applicable to diverse phenomena. We still cannot say that these phenomena manifested from a common source and that each phenomenon has a shared purpose—the other two kinds of innate presences. Nevertheless, by the applicability of natural laws to a wide range of phenomena, we say that the contextual truths also reveal the universal truth.

This is truer of the Absolute Truth where apart from control, the Absolute Truth is also present in everything as their purpose and the original concept. However, to the extent that everyone may not see how the Absolute Truth controls everything, is the source of everything, and is the purpose of everything, one might not see this innate presence. Then, it seems that the Absolute Truth must be different from all the relative truths. Such a claim is rejected here. The relative truths are not equated to the Absolute Truth, but the Absolute Truth can be known from the relative truths. Thus, for instance, a bicycle is not Newton's laws of motion, but Newton's laws of motion are innate in the bicycle. This sūtra similarly says that the Absolute Truth is present in everything, however, a deeper investigation may be needed to understand this presence.

Topic 2

QUESTION

So, you are saying that all these contextual methods of religious practice are also valid means for attaining the transcendental state beyond matter?

3.3.5 (365)
उपसंहारोऽर्थाभेदाद्विधिशेषवत्समाने च
upasaṃhāro'rthābhedādvidhiśeṣavatsamāne ca

upasaṃhāraḥ—the destruction of that which is secondary; arthābhedāt—due to the difference in the meaning; vidhiśeṣavat—like the subsidiary rites of a main sacrifice; samāne ca—are also merged (into the main sacrifice).

TRANSLATION

When all that is secondary (in a religion) is destroyed due to the differences of meaning or purpose (across these religions being destroyed), just like the subsidiary rites (of a main sacrifice) are also merged into the main sacrifice.

COMMENTARY

The basic paradigm for material life is selfishness, and the basic paradigm for spirituality is sacrifice. The sacrifice is also called a *yajñá*, and it has three components—*agni*, *soma*, and *vāyu*. The soma represents our pleasure, the agni is the purpose for which this pleasure is sacrificed, and vāyu is the process of sacrifice. Thus, yajñá means sacrifice of our pleasure (soma) for a higher purpose (agni) through a legitimate process (vāyu). In human life, we make many kinds of sacrifices—for our parents, children, community, society, and nation. These are also called yajñá, but they are not the supreme yajñá. The ultimate yajñá is when our happiness is sacrificed for the Lord. Everything has emanated from the Lord, and in a yajñá, those same things are put back into the Lord and used for His pleasure. A person worshipping a river, for example, takes the water of river and pours it back into the river, while chanting a mantra.

This idea is compared to the performance of elaborate yajñá in the Vedic system. There is a main yajñá which is performed at the beginning and at the end. Then there are also subsidiary yajñá which are performed in parallel to the main yajñá. When the subsidiary yajñá end, then the main yajñá is completed. In the same way, there are many duties and regulations which are subsidiary processes of the main process—i.e., the attainment of the Absolute Truth. If this main process is misunderstood, then the subsidiary processes seem contradictory. But if the main sacrifice is understood, then the other sacrifices are only seen as the subsidiary processes used in the service of the main sacrifice. This sūtra indicates that one must keep the main sacrifice—devotion to the Lord—as the primary sacrifice even while performing the subsidiary sacrifices.

Topic 3

QUESTION

However, if we say that there are many spiritual paths, then people believe that the practice of each path is itself the goal, and they get tied to the rules and regulations of that path and may sometimes fail to see the goal beyond the rules and regulations. How should one avoid incurring this kind of mistake?

3.3.6 (366)

अन्यथात्वं शब्दादिति चेत् न अविशेषात्

anyathātvaṃ śabdāditi cet na aviśeṣāt

anyathātvaṃ—there are other injunctions; śabdāt—from the scriptures; iti cet—if it be said; na—not so; aviśeṣāt—due to non-difference (of purpose).

TRANSLATION

If it is said that there are other injunctions from the scriptures, (then we say) not so, because of the non-difference (of the purpose in these injunctions).

COMMENTARY

The use of the term *aviśeṣāt* or non-difference is indicative of the whole-part relationship. The part is not separable from the whole, and yet, the part is not equal to the whole. Furthermore, the whole is always present in the part. Since the whole is present in the part, the parts cannot be whimsically rejected. Since the parts are not equal to the whole, the parts cannot be whimsically accepted. Thus, both blind acceptance and blind rejection are frowned upon.

If you want to travel to a destination, you might first walk to your car, then drive the car, then take a flight, then take a taxi, and finally walk to the destination. For each method of fulfilling the purpose—i.e., reaching the destination—you might follow different rules. For example, you must drive according to the rules of the road; you must pay for the flight and follow the regulations of sitting in an airplane; you pay the person who drives your taxi; etc. So, it seems like we are following different rules and regulations in each case. However, the ultimate regulation is that you must reach your destination. If you missed a flight, you could catch a bus or a train. A different set of rules may then apply, but those differences are immaterial because the main regulation of reaching the destination must be fulfilled. In the same way, the injunctions of scriptures are not false, but they are like the rules of driving on the road, flying in a commercial flight, or catching a taxi. The rules are not optional, but the method is itself optional. For instance, you might not use a flight; you can as well catch a train or a bus. However, if you use a flight (or a train or a bus) then you must follow the rules. Therefore, it is said that rules of day-to-day activity are necessary. But those day-to-day activities are themselves not necessary if the purpose of performing those activities is achieved in an alternative manner.

Each of the rules exists to achieve a purpose. The purpose of the rules of the road is that people must be safe. The purpose of paying a taxi driver is that the driver can continue driving. The trains must run on time so that people can reach their destination on time. But what is achieved by everyone being safe, the taxis running, or reaching the destination on time? All such rules are partially justifiable, however, the Absolute Truth justifies them completely. If the complete justification did not exist, then the partial justification would also not exist. The ultimate justification manifests into partial justifications, which then become the causes of the rules, which then seem diversified prescriptions. However, if we seek the justification underlying a justification, we will find that they are not self-justified—i.e., they are not self-evident principles. The Absolute Truth as the source of all happiness is hence the self-justified principle.

In the same way, the processes of karma-yoga, dhyāna-yoga, jñāna-yoga, and bhakti-yoga have different rules. The various types of yajñá also have different rules. These rules are not optional—if you are following that process. However, it is not necessary to follow any of these processes. These processes have a common purpose—namely, attaining devotion to the Lord. When the processes are followed, then their rules are justified by the goal to be attained—namely, devotion to the Lord. When the processes are not followed—because another process is more suitable for the goal—then the neglect of a process is also justified by the same principle, namely, devotion to the Lord. Therefore, the purpose justifies the rules when a process is followed, it justifies the selection of a process, and it justifies why any process even exists. As the innate justification of processes and rules, the purpose is non-different from the processes and rules—i.e., it is not identical, and yet not totally separable.

QUESTION

If we say that all the paths and injunctions have the same purpose, then doesn't it mean that all the paths will lead to the same destination and therefore no path can be considered superior or inferior to any of the other paths?

3.3.7 (367)
न वा प्रकरणभेदात् परोवरीयस्त्वादवित्
na vā prakaraṇabhedāt parovarīyastvādivat

na vā—rather not; prakaraṇa-bhedāt—on account of the difference in the context; parovarīyas—the greatest good; tvādivat—that which is like the source of everything (that has been manifest).

TRANSLATION

(We) rather not (claim that all the paths are equivalent) because of the difference in the activities and the context (of application). However, they are all manifest as diversities from the (purpose of delivering the) greatest good.

COMMENTARY

After rejecting the blind acceptance and blind rejection of all the paths, this sūtra clarifies that everything is not always good. They are all manifest from the purpose of delivering the greatest good, but they deliver that goodness depending on the context. This can be understood by comparing 'good' to 'health'. We say that health is good, but since everyone is diseased in a different way, health must be achieved in different ways. One suffering from cold must eat hot things to nullify the effects of cold. And one suffering from heat, must eat cool things to nullify the effects of heat. They are both aiming for health, but the methods of achieving this health depend on the illness that prevents health. A blind acceptance of these injunctions would mean that even a person suffering from heat would be given hot things, or one suffering from cold would be given cold things. Likewise, a blind rejection of the injunctions would mean that a person suffering from cold would not be given hot things, and a person suffering from heat would not be allowed cold things. Due to the contextuality, both blind acceptance and blind rejection are frowned upon. Furthermore, one must understand the purpose—e.g., the goal of health—to apply the contextual injunctions. Different injunctions apply to achieve the same goal in varied contexts.

Thus, the rituals, duties, roles, responsibilities, and practices are not the ends in themselves. They are methods to attain a goal, and while the goal remains unchanged, the methods can change, depending on the type of hurdle to be crossed before attaining the goal. Thus, marriage laws, the laws of property inheritance, the job duties of employment, etc. are highly contextual. For certain places, times, roles, and people, these injunctions are useful. But they are not universal truths. Hence, we can distinguish between the contextuality of ordinary religions and the final goal—i.e., the love of God—which they are expected to deliver. If the rules of social behavior are universalized, then contradictions between the different religions are created. But if we see their purpose—to elevate a different kind of person to the point of devotion to the Lord—then their unity is perceived. So, unity exists within the diversity as its purpose.

If you live next to a destination, then you can just walk to the destination. If you are little farther away, then you might take a taxi. If you are even farther away, you might use a train, followed by a taxi, followed by walking. And if you are very far, then you might use a flight before the other means of transport. Therefore, we cannot say that everyone must use a flight, let alone the same flight. Everyone need not use a train, let alone the same train. We might use different flights or no flights at all. We might use different trains, or no train at all. Thus, all these methods are optional. They are all created so that we can reach a destination, but the method may or may not be used by everyone.

QUESTION

The contextual application of injunctions makes the problem very hard, because we don't know which context requires which injunction. How can one know what is the right injunction to be applied in which specific context?

3.3.8 (368)

संज्ञातश्चेत् तदुक्तम् अस्ति तु तदपि

saṃjñātaścet taduktam asti tu tadapi

saṃjñātaḥ—by a complete and balanced knowledge; cet—if; tat—that; uktam—is said; asti—it is; tu—but; tat—that; api—even.

TRANSLATION

By a complete and balanced knowledge (of the context and the paths) if one says that (this path is the best), then it is (the path); but, even that (path) (must achieve the goal, and should not be accepted based on blind faith).

COMMENTARY

As the contextual application of injunctions is difficult, this sūtra advises two things. First, we must have a full understanding of the context, and the various possible paths. Without this understanding, one would be limited by their own knowledge, and prescribe only what they are familiar with, even though that path is not suitable for the present context. Second, even as one chooses this path, one must not abandon the sight of the goal. If the path is not achieving the goal, then one must reevaluate the path, and pick the path that will reach the goal. Therefore, even if one makes a mistake in selecting a path, continuous evaluation of the progress made because of following some injunctions cannot be abandoned. The paths can be changed provided some contextual injunction is not working appropriately to attain the goal. By employing these two methods—i.e., a full understanding of the context and the paths, and continually revising the path if it is not helping achieve the goal—one can find the contextually appropriate path that will attain the desired purpose.

Topic 4

QUESTION

But the problem of progress is itself very nebulous. How can one know that they are progressing in spiritual life if things keep changing all the time? Sometimes we think we have progressed, and at other times we think we haven't. So, how can a person know that there is indeed progress in life?

3.3.9 (369)

व्याप्तेश्च समञ्जसम्

vyāpteśca samañjasam

vyāpteḥ—the pervasiveness; ca—and; samañjasam—without conflict.

TRANSLATION

(By) the pervasiveness and overcoming the conflicts (in experience).

COMMENTARY

The problem of progress often comes up in science—how do we know that the newest theories of reality are advancing our understanding of nature? How do we know that science is progressing? The answer to that question is two-fold: consistency and completeness. Completeness means that the same theory can be applied to ever-increasing number of phenomena. Consistency means that as we try to explain a greater number of phenomena, our explanations are not mutually contradictory. Ultimately, both criteria point toward the unification of science. Consistency forces us to reconcile contradictory theories. And the result of this reconciliation is that a single theory explains everything. This means that we cannot blindly reconcile contradictory theories if the combined theory explains less than what the diversified theories explained earlier.

The same criteria are listed here for spiritual progress. In the beginning, we apply different injunctions for different problems, and these injunctions temporarily solve those different problems. But as one progresses, one uses the same injunction for every problem, and that injunction must solve all the problems. Therefore, if one is applying different injunctions in different situations, one must know that they haven't progressed. Only when the same injunction is being applied in all the contexts, can we say that we have indeed advanced.

A neophyte devotee, for instance, relies on many different injunctions for controlling the body, the mind, the intellect, the ego, and morality. They might practice regulations for a healthy living, exercise, and diet control. They might practice meditation to control the mind. They may read many books to train the intellect. They may practice methods of humility to control the ego. And they may follow the societal rules to remain moral. But as one progresses in devotion, there is only one injunction necessary—always remember the Lord, and never forget Him. To attain this goal, one engages in activities that increase the remembrance of the Lord and avoids those things that lead to forgetfulness of the Lord. Both sides of the requirement must be met because if one only tries to avoid those things that lead to forgetfulness, then by the rejection of all these activities one would be left with nothing. On the other hand, if one focuses on the engagement in the activities that lead to increased remembrance but doesn't give up the activities that lead to forgetfulness, then the effort of increasing the remembrance doesn't yield the desired results due to continual forgetfulness.

Every other rule pertaining to the body, the mind, the intellect, the ego, and morality is replaced by a single rule—always remember the Lord, and never forget Him. This rule is the universal theory that produces the benefits of the separate rules of body, mind, intellect, ego, and moral control. Thus, unification in our rules and theories is considered scientific progress as it delivers a greater amount of consistency and completeness: (1) consistency because the rules of the body aren't conflicting with the rules of the mind, etc. and (2) completeness because the same rule results in control of both the mind and the body.

In our day-to-day life we encounter many difficult situations. These difficulties hinder the practice of our chosen process. However, if one path is impossible, or very hard, we can choose another path—provided it leads to the same goal. Thus, every crisis can be converted into an opportunity—by changing the path. The scriptures state that devotion to the Lord can never be hindered in any situation. This means that every crisis also presents an opportunity, and difficulties are impetuses for us to choose a different path, but the devotion to the Lord is a goal that cannot be hindered by any problem.

Topic 5

QUESTION

Does this mean that one who is advanced in spiritual life has no need for the contextual rules and injunctions? That they can follow only the injunction that works in all these diverse contexts, and ignore the contextual rules?

3.3.10 (370)

सर्वाभेदादन्यत्रेमे

sarvābhedādanyatreme

sarvābhedāt—due to non-difference in all things; anyatra—in all the other places; ime—these (same rules and injunctions become applicable).

TRANSLATION

Due to the non-difference of all things (i.e., everything having the same purpose), in all the other places (situations) these (same rules and injunctions can be applied, and hence they are now treated as the universal truths).

COMMENTARY

Today we accept that laws of nature apply to all phenomena, but we do not accept that nature has a common purpose. Therefore, there is no guiding principle for choices. Everyone chooses based on their own interests. If choice is self-interested, then society cannot exist unless self-interest is subordinated to some laws that maximize collective interest. Since the laws that subordinate self-interest to collective interest are mostly man-made, therefore, we don't see the consequences of manipulating the laws. The rich and powerful can change the laws for their benefit, and their connivance would not affect them. In short, choices have consequences for the poor and destitute, but not for the rich and powerful. By replacing a divine purpose with self-interest, and then replacing morality with man-made laws, society becomes a slave to the rich and powerful. People could recognize God, and their choices would then be subordinated to this purpose and they would then be servants of God. But the rebellion in the soul against the service of God makes him the servant of ordinary people.

However, there is an alternative—the choices are free, and yet God is the universal governing principle for all 'good' choices. When this principle is discarded, only 'bad' choices are made. The universal governing principle for choices is also a universal law—i.e., it can be applied to all situations. This sūtra states that the satisfaction of the universal purpose is the governing law for all choices; this law replaces all contextually right laws. The universal truth is that essence which is visible in all phenomena. And the universal good is the person to be satisfied through all the phenomena. However, there is also contextuality of the right—the duties, or what needs to be done in a context (i.e., the specific actions or duties)—as they are not universally determined. Therefore, there is universal truth, universal good, and contextual right. The solution to this contextual right is obtained when we subordinate it to the universal good.

The previous sūtras stated that contextual injunctions should neither be accepted nor rejected blindly, which raises the question about how contextual choices must be made. The answer to that question was that the decision of right and wrong is dependent upon whether the goodness of purpose is achieved. Goodness was then defined as the universal guiding principle for choices. However, once this universality is obtained, then contextuality can be ignored.

Thus, the conversation has moved from universal truth, to contextual rightness, to universal good (rejecting contextual rightness). The arguments underlying this progress are complex, but the conclusion is quite simple—the Lord is the Supreme Truth and the Supreme Good. If we keep these two in mind, then the Supreme Right is automatically achieved, and we don't have to worry about what is right or wrong separately in each context. That eliminates the problem of diverse scriptures giving us diverse instructions for different contexts. The rejection of these contextual instructions is not absolute—they are useful because they take us to the point where the Supreme Truth is equated to the Supreme Good—i.e., the Absolute Truth is recognized as a *person*. If this goal is achieved, then it supersedes the contextual rightness. If this goal is not being achieved, then the purpose of contextual injunctions is unsatisfied. Therefore, the contextual injunctions are to take a person to the point of accepting the

Supreme Lord as the Supreme Good; after that, they are unnecessary.

Topic 6

QUESTION

People follow contextual rules of right and wrong, as it does them good—i.e., right action brings happiness, and wrong action brings unhappiness. You are saying that these right and wrong actions can be subordinated to the satisfaction of the Supreme Person. But that doesn't address the fundamental question about how each person becomes individually happy by their choices. Unless the question of individual happiness is addressed, isn't the doctrine of universal truth and universal good ultimately pointless for an individual?

3.3.11 (371)

आनन्दादयःप्रधानस्य

ānandādayaḥ pradhānasya

ānandādayaḥ—happiness etc.; pradhānasya—is the main goal.

TRANSLATION

The happiness (of each person) is the main goal.

COMMENTARY

In previous sūtras, we discussed the questions of universal truth, contextual right, and individual good. Since the contextual rightness presented grave problems—How do we decide what to do and when? —a guiding principle of universal goodness as proposed as the replacement for contextual right. However, now the principle of universal goodness conflicts with individual goodness: If we are always trying to satisfy the Supreme Person, then what about our happiness? Remember that the earlier criterion for deciding 'good' and 'bad' choices was their outcomes for the self—good is that which makes *us* happy, and bad is that which makes *us* unhappy. The new principle—of making God happy—may address the problem of contextual rightness, but does it address the question of individual happiness? This sūtra says that it does. The replacement of contextual right by universal goodness is not to take away individual goodness. In short, universal good produces both contextual rightness and individual goodness. Therefore, the individual good—i.e., our self-interest—is in the satisfaction of the Supreme Person. Serving the Supreme Person is not contrary to the idea of individual good, as it is also satisfied in the process. Thus, we can continue upholding the ideas of universal truth, contextual right, and individual good, and the principle of universal good can be used to determine what is contextual right, which then also achieves individual good. The pursuit of universal good doesn't contradict individual good, so everyone can employ this principle to decide what is right action to obtain happiness.

Happiness is obtained by the fulfillment of a purpose. The soul has an innate purpose, but it can also create alternative purposes. When those alternatives are created, the purpose is not always fulfilled because the soul doesn't have the power to always fulfill the purpose, and that creates unhappiness. However, when the innate purpose is accepted, then the power for its fulfillment comes from the Lord, and by fulfilling the purpose the soul becomes happy. The difference is simply that the soul can always use the Lord's power to satisfy the Lord, but he cannot always use the Lord's power to satisfy himself.

QUESTION

If individual good is indirectly achieved through the universal good, then why do we reject the notion of individual good—i.e., selfish happiness?

3.3.12 (372)

प्रयिशरिस्त्वाद्यप्राप्तिःउपचयापचयौ हि भेदे

priyaśirastvādyaprāptiḥ upacayāpacayau hi bhede

priyaśirastvādi—ultimate happiness etc. aprāptiḥ—is not obtained; upacaya—increase; apacaya—decrease; hi—because; bhede—due to difference.

TRANSLATION

Ultimate happiness (of each person) is not achieved (if we pursue individual happiness) because of the difference between increase and decrease (i.e., increasing one's happiness means decreasing someone else's happiness).

COMMENTARY

After subordinating individual good to the universal good, and then stating that individual good is achieved by the universal good, one can ask: If the individual good is anyway the guiding principle, then why not uphold it as a fundamental principle in itself? This sūtra answers: because if we pursue individual good, then increase in the happiness of one person entails the decrease in the happiness of another person. And if each person's happiness is alternately increasing and decreasing, then ultimate happiness is not achieved.

Thus, even though each person's happiness is the goal, this goal must be subordinated to the Supreme Person's happiness because only by subordinating individual happiness to the Supreme Person's happiness is everyone's happiness naturally achieved. Hence, individual and collective happiness are not contradictory, if individual happiness is subordinated to the happiness of the Lord. They are contradictory when individual happiness is placed above the Lord's happiness. The happiness of the Supreme Person is therefore the best self-interest of each person; the pursuit of individualistic and selfish happiness is contrary to the self-interest, as happiness and distress come alternately.

QUESTION

You are therefore saying that the happiness of the Supreme Person entails the happiness of all living entities? And, that by satisfying the Supreme

Person, every other individual (including the self) is also satisfied in the process?

3.3.13 (373)
इतरे त्वर्थसामान्यात्
itare tvarthasāmānyāt

itare—other; tu—but; arthasāmānyāt—due to identity of purpose.

TRANSLATION

(The happiness of) others is but identical to the purpose (of the self).

COMMENTARY

Some atheists argue that the practice of religion is also selfish because it only aims at one's own happiness. In fact, since in this pursuit of selfish happiness one may reject some social duties, therefore, others may be forced to suffer. Thus, individual happiness remains contrary to the happiness of others. And since this contradiction in seen in the spiritual pursuits, therefore, there is no difference with the other selfish activities where self-interest is supreme.

This sūtra dissolves the contradiction between self-interest, other-interest, and supreme-interest. When service to the Supreme Person is adopted as the fundamental principle, then whoever serves the Lord makes everyone else happy because the Lord is the complete truth, and His happiness is the complete happiness. When the complete is satisfied, then all the parts are satisfied. Therefore, service to the Lord is the source of service and happiness of everyone else. Even if the person serving the Lord is satisfied by his actions, this pleasure is not contrary to the pleasure of others. The self- and other-interests are contradictory when the supreme-interest is ignored. When a common purpose is established—i.e., the Lord is the supreme purpose—then harmony between the purposes of all living entities is established and contradictions between the diverse purposes of the different living entities are naturally dissolved.

The service to the Lord is, therefore, also the universal service principle. Of course, the selfish living entities may not agree; they may claim that while the Lord is being served, I'm not being served. But even as they pursue their own happiness, it comes at the cost of the happiness of others. And this cost entails that they too must pay the price for pursuing their happiness. But when the principle of selfishness is discarded, and the satisfaction of the Supreme Person is adopted as the fundamental principle, then everyone is automatically satisfied. The service to the other living entities is not necessarily service to the Lord, and since this service will always exclude some living entities, therefore, it becomes a selective service in which some individuals are benefitted while others are hurt. Universal happiness is achieved only when a common purpose is restored, and each person's activities fulfill this common purpose. If my self-interest is fulfilled by others' activities, then I'm pleased by the result just as the other person is pleased. Thus, service to the Supreme Person is happiness for everyone. Conversely, service to humanity, nature, animals, etc. is not ultimate happiness because each such service excludes some other living entities.

Topic 7

QUESTION

There are many people who may worship the Supreme Lord, not with the intention of pleasing Him, but with the goal of obtaining something from Him. Since this type of worship is selfish, and yet it is focused on the Lord, does such selfish meditation on the Lord also entail the happiness of everyone?

3.3.14 (374)
आध्यानाय प्रयोजनाभावात्
ādhyānāya prayojanābhāvāt

ādhyānāya—pensive and sorrowful meditation, or recollection with regret, hesitation, or dissatisfaction; prayojana-abhāvāt—due to missing the purpose.

TRANSLATION

Unhappy meditation (is rejected) due to missing the purpose.

COMMENTARY

In earlier chapters, the worship of demigods was rejected in favor of the Lord's worship—even if one is desirous of material enjoyments. Under such desire, a person begins meditation on the Lord in an unhappy state—" Lord, I don't have this or that, and I want you to give me what I want". This pensive, unhappy, dissatisfied, hesitant, and sorrowful mental state for meditation is rejected in this sūtra as being devoid of the main purpose. Since meditation is a means, and not the end, it doesn't constitute the happiness of the Lord. It is preferred over the worship of the demigods because one is asking the Supreme Person. However, since the meditator is asking for their happiness, rather than the happiness of the Supreme Person, this meditation is only a more advanced form of selfishness and not the principle of a shared purpose for everyone. This sūtra rejects such meditation as being the ultimate purpose of meditation.

QUESTION

But one might argue that such meditation is at least satisfying them, and since self-interest is ultimately their goal, their goals are being fulfilled. How can we convince someone that this self-interest is not the real purpose?

3.3.15 (375)
आत्मशब्दाच्च
ātmaśabdācca

ātmaśabdāt—on account of statements about the self; ca—also (rejected).

TRANSLATION

On account of statement about self (being the purpose) are also (rejected).

COMMENTARY

The previous sūtra stated that the Lord is not satisfied by selfish meditation. So, one might say: "At least, I will be satisfied by this meditation". And the response to that claim is: "Not necessarily". The Lord doesn't fulfill the material desires which the demigods cannot. He only grants what is within one's karma, just like the demigods. The worship of the Lord is still better because He can fulfill our desires in many departments—health, wealth, love, knowledge, etc. whereas each demigod can fulfill the desires in only one department.

Therefore, meditation on the Lord is better than the meditation on demigods because by this meditation one only needs to ask one source for everything. However, the results delivered by this meditation are also within one's karma. This karma is like money—it can be spent on whatever goods we want. If we have the money, but we are not getting the opportunity to buy the goods we want, then the worship of the demigods or the Lord can create the opportunity where we can spend our good karma in obtaining the desired goods. But this worship cannot deliver the goods beyond the deserved karma. Thus, it is incorrect to assume that by worshipping the Lord we can obtain whatever we want, and all our unhappiness would be overcome through such worship.

Since the previous sūtra spoke about unhappy meditation, and this sūtra talks about the self, it can also be translated as 'meditation on the self'. Since the previous sūtra rejected such meditation as delivering ultimate happiness, the 'meditation on the self' would also be considered rejected due to the use of the word *ca* or 'also'. While such a translation is possible, it breaks the logical continuity of the discussion, and hence we have preferred the alternative that 'statements about the self being happy by selfish meditation are rejected'.

Topic 8

QUESTION

In many places in the Vedic texts, self-interest is emphasized as the goal of life. For example, it is said that each person is suffering in this world, and they should aim for permanent happiness, which entails that the pursuit of one's happiness is the goal. How do we reconcile these statements with those you have made now—that the Supreme Person's happiness is the main goal?

3.3.16 (376)

आत्मगृहीतिरितरवत् उत्तरात्

ātmagṛhītiritaravat uttarāt

ātmagṛhīti—the self-interest; itaravat—as in other texts or in other places; uttarāt—on account of the subsequent qualification or clarification.

TRANSLATION

The statements about self-interest in other texts are modified or clarified in subsequent texts (by saying that the Supreme Person is the main interest).

COMMENTARY

A person absorbed in selfish pursuits is only motivated by self-interest. To motivate them, the problem of suffering is often brought up in all religions: that material existence brings the problem of repeated birth, death, old age, and disease. So, if we want to be free of these problems, then it is in our selfish interest to pursue a transcendental life which is eternal and free of suffering. Once the person is convinced that they must reject the pleasures of material existence, because they are always accompanied with suffering, then the preliminary background for subsequent discussion is set. Subsequently, however, the pursuit of individual happiness is modified or clarified: it is said that to obtain eternal happiness, one must satisfy the Supreme Person. This modification then shifts the focus from a selfish pursuit of happiness to a selfless devotion to the Lord. Of course, the devotion to the Lord could be prescribed upfront. But most people are not interested; they tend to question the existence of the soul and God, ask for many kinds of proofs, and wonder how this concerns them.

Some religious doctrines, such as Buddhism and Advaita, begin and end in the problem of suffering and how to overcome it. They remain selfish throughout: The spiritual aspirant only aims for their happiness, and not the happiness of the Lord. But they fail to realize that all happiness comes from the fulfilment of desires, and desires necessitate individuality. If individuality is lost, then desires are lost, and there is no happiness. Therefore, these are not spiritual doctrines because, although they lead to cessation of suffering, they do not lead to the creation of eternal pleasure. The pursuit of the cessation of suffering is selfish, and the pursuit of Lord's happiness is unselfish. If a person is in pain, then relief from suffering itself seems like happiness. But the cessation of suffering is not happiness. It just seems like happiness from a material viewpoint.

In so far as cessation of suffering is important, self-interest is emphasized. But in so far as genuine happiness is concerned, unselfish love is emphasized. Those engrossed in materialism can hardly see beyond the body; it is very hard for them to understand the existence of a transcendental body of the soul and the Lord, and loving relationships between them, a world where these loving pastimes are carried out, and how that world is also eternal and ever-expanding. For them, cessation from material miseries is prescribed as the starting point. However, as one progresses in this understanding, and can see the soul is different from the body, then he can also understand the form of the soul and the Lord, their non-difference, their loving relationships, and a transcendental world that exists beyond this world. Therefore, this sūtra states that after prescribing selfish cessation from suffering, the doctrine is revised later to speak about unselfish love of the Lord. This revision should not be viewed as a contradiction between doctrines, but as incremental progress in realization.

QUESTION

So, are you suggesting that the claims of impersonalism and personalism, or selfish spiritual liberation and the unselfish love of God, are not contradictory (although they are progressive) because both are stated in the scriptures?

3.3.17 (377)
अन्वयादिति चेत् स्यात् अवधारणात्
anvayāditi cet syāt avadhāraṇāt

anvayāt—due to contradiction; iti cet—if it be said; syāt—it is possible; avadhāraṇāt—on account of the differing conceptions (in scriptures).

TRANSLATION

If it is said that (confusion is imminent) due to contradictions (between earlier and later claims) (we say) it is possible due to different conceptions.

COMMENTARY

This sūtra acknowledges that confusion can result from the preliminary claims that one must aspire for freedom from material suffering, and the subsequent claims that one must aspire for eternal happiness by serving the Lord. There is also implicit acknowledgement that such confusions are common.

The Vedic system is a progressive path for self-realization. At the basic level, the rules of moral living are prescribed as the Varṇāśrama system of social organization—i.e., the right type of sociology, economics, and politics. At a more advanced level, the worship of the demigods is prescribed for fulfillment of desires. At an even more advanced level, the demigod worship is rejected, and the worship of the Supreme Lord is preferred even for those desirous of material happiness. Beyond such selfish and materialistic love of the Lord, there is the aspiration to be liberated from material existence and its imminent suffering. Beyond the state of liberation is the pursuit of eternal happiness by acquiring the qualities of the Lord, and living in the same place as the Lord, which is devoid of all suffering. And even beyond this desire to be happy is the pure unselfish love of God in which even the suffering is considered a pleasure if that pleases the Lord. The rules of social organization, the worship of demigods, or the worship of the Lord for material happiness are paths within the material world. The desire for liberation from suffering is the aspiration for Brahman. The aspiration for living in the proximity of the Lord, having the same type of form and qualities, and never entering the material world, is the life of Vaikuṇṭha. And the unselfish love of the Lord, in which the devotee is satisfied even in the material world if the Lord is pleased, is the life of Goloka.

These different descriptions can seem contradictory as they are described in different texts, and the resulting confusion is imminent. However, they can be understood as progressive stages of spiritual realization. Once this progression is grasped, then the apparent contradictions naturally disappear.

It was earlier stated that the nature of the Absolute Truth is only grasped by the study of diverse scriptures and reconciling their apparent contradictions. Those who take these contradictions on face value and reject one doctrine in preference for another—without understanding the progression—cannot be considered to have a full understanding. There are indeed contradictions between different levels of understanding, but these contradictions can be resolved if one understands that these are progressive levels of realization.

Topic 9

QUESTION

Does this entail that the scriptures should be understood in order of their progression, and see how later claims modify the previously made claims?

3.3.18 (378)

कार्याख्यानादपूर्वम्

kāryākhyānādapūrvam

kāryākhyānāt—from the descriptions of work; apūrvam—unprecedented.

TRANSLATION

From the unprecedented (i.e., not present in the previous texts) descriptions of actions (the successive processes of spiritual realizations are judged).

COMMENTARY

After acknowledging that scriptures can make conflicting claims, this sūtra says that the successive texts make novel claims, i.e., those not made earlier. In 3.3.16 (376) the term *uttarāt* or 'subsequently' was used about the modification of previous claims. In this sūtra, the term *apūrvam* or 'not previously' is used to refer to the novelty of the new claims. It might seem that these two are saying the same thing, but they are not. There is a subtle difference between 'successor' and 'not the predecessor'. Suppose you are tasked to sequence objects based on their colors—let's say from red to purple. This ordering produces a unique sequence only if there is one object for each color. If there are many objects with the same color, then there is no way to decide which of the many red objects should be ahead in a sequence. The same problem exists in the case of sentences. If we are ordering them by their meaning, then there is no way to decide which of the many sentences with identical meaning should be ahead of the others. With this understanding, we can now speak about the ordering of scriptures. The 'successor' indicates the next object or sentence. The term 'not the predecessor' means all the objects with the same color, or sentences with the same meaning, are not included. So, using 'successor' we get new objects or statements, and using 'not the predecessor' we exclude the same type of object or the statement with the same meaning. The 'successor' is the physical ordering of things and 'not the predecessor' is the semantic ordering of things.

In this case, we are speaking about the scriptures, which can be distinguished physically as different books and semantically as different doctrines. The term 'successor' indicates the order in which the texts have appeared, and it constitutes physical ordering. The term 'not the predecessor' indicates the progression in their meaning, and it constitutes semantic ordering. Thus, self-realization is emphasized in the four Vedas but in the Purāṇa, Tantra, and Itihāsa the devotion to the Lord is emphasized. But this sequence of texts is not the regression of meaning from greater to lesser perfection. It is rather the progression of meaning from lesser to greater perfection. Many people claim that the four Vedas are the superior original texts, and the later texts are the inferior modified texts. According to these claims, perfect knowledge came before it was diluted: the idea of the soul or the pursuit of self-realization was primordial perfect truth, and the idea of God or the pursuit of God-realization was added subsequently. This change was engendered by the problem that most people could not think of the self; they were used to thinking about something other than the self. Therefore, a Supreme Self was added to help them think of the self. The Supreme Self had the same properties as the self. However, it was more convenient to think about the self in this way, instead of self-realization.

If this doctrine of progression from superior to inferior is accepted, then the later texts would not be called *apūrvam*. The term *apūrvam* is never used derogatorily. It means novelty, newness, freshness, originality, etc. The order in the Vedic texts is therefore about progressive understanding rather than regression from perfection to imperfection. When the terms *uttarāt* and *apūrvam* are used in combination, there is a clear indication of a strict order—the previous is inferior and the subsequent is superior. It is not the other way around.

Topic 10

QUESTION

But you have earlier explained that manifestation progresses from the full truth to the partial truth. How can we now say that a more complete truth follows a partial truth? Your above statement implies that a preliminary truth about liberation is described initially followed by a more complete devotional truth. How do we reconcile the full to partial manifestation with the above idea that the partial truth is manifest before the full truth is later described?

3.3.19 (379)

समान एवञ्च अभेदात्

samāna evañca abhedāt

samāna—reconciliation; evam—like this; ca—also; abhedāt—on account of non-difference.

TRANSLATION

Reconciliation (among the diversities) like this (i.e., from preliminary to advanced) is also (possible) due to non-difference (between doctrines).

COMMENTARY

The Absolute Truth is described in three ways—as Brahman, Paramātma, and Bhagavān. As we have discussed, Bhagavān is the source of light, Brahman is the light, and the Paramātma is the representation of the source within each particle of light (identifying that this particle emerged from a source). Brahman is individual existence, Paramātma is the purpose of individual existence, and Bhagavān is the reference of that purpose. The purpose and reference are noted separately, because the purpose is in everyone, but the reference is common. In a different sense, Brahman is the diversity, Paramātma is the unity within the diversity, and Bhagavān is the diversity within the unity. Likewise, in a mathematical language, we can call these the set, the class, and the instance. Bhagavān is knowledge and the knower; the knower is a set, and knowledge is within that set. That set contains many knowers, which are called Brahman, or the many individuals. And when knowledge enters these partial knowers, the representation of knowledge is called Paramātma, or the class called knowledge.

Existence is preliminary understanding, the purpose of existence is more advanced, and the source of existence is the most advanced. If we complete the triad of understanding, it doesn't matter whether we begin in existence, proceed to purpose, and then identify the source, or we begin in the source, proceed to existence, and then identify the purpose of existence. The source also exists as the whole, and has a purpose, due to which the whole divides into parts. Likewise, we exist, we have a purpose, and as parts we have a source. So, the path that progresses from existence to purpose to source is not problematic just as the path from source to purpose to existence is the complete path.

The use of the term *ca* or 'also' indicates that the path from existence to purpose to source is also a legitimate path, after it was said that the path from the source to purpose to existence is the more perfect understanding. The reason is that in the pursuit of knowledge, we start from what is certain, and then proceed to what is uncertain. When we are pursuing knowledge, then our existence is certain, and the Lord's existence is uncertain. Therefore, we go from our existence to the existence of the Lord. However, when the Lord is creating knowledge, then His existence is certain, and the existence of other things is a possibility. Therefore, the Lord goes from His existence to the diversities manifested from His existence. Hence, there are two ways to look at the Veda—is this the pursuit of our knowledge, or the expression of Lord's knowledge?

The expression of the Lord's knowledge is given to Brahma, who then expresses this knowledge—primarily dividing it into four Vedas. The Veda is originally succinct, but it is then elaborated and expanded by Brahma. This knowledge is further expanded beyond the four Vedas by Bādarāyana, an empowered incarnation of Lord Viṣṇu. These expansions present the human quest. In short, it is assumed that the student is like a child, who needs to be taught the preliminary knowledge first, and advanced knowledge later. Therefore, the existence is followed by purpose, followed by the source. Therefore, even though the knowledge is divine—i.e., spoken by the Lord—its expression is meant for humanity, and therefore the order of expression is reversed.

This sūtra states that all these stages of knowledge are non-different. Just like the purpose is within the existence, and this internal purpose points to the external source, therefore, any detachment of the existence from the purpose and the source will always remain incomplete. Just like when we say, 'the sky is blue', there is a purpose—i.e., to describe the nature of the sky, and the word 'sky' refers to an object outside the sentence itself—similarly, the soul is also a sentence that has a meaning which refers to something other than the sentence. The purpose and the reference become important only when the sentence is understood semantically. If we look at the sentence physically, then we can see that the sentence exists, but we don't know its meaning—i.e., what it is stating, and the external object that is being referred to by the sentence. Brahman realization is the study of the soul as an existent. Paramātma realization is the study of the same soul as a sentence with meaning. And Bhagavān realization is the study of the same soul as the reference to the object being described.

Since each of them pertains to the study of the soul, therefore, they are non-different—the same reality is described in three successively more advanced ways. Hence, the Brahman understanding is not *wrong*—it is the existence of the soul. But it is incomplete because the sentence is treated like an object without a meaning. When the meaning and the reference of the meaning are realized, then the sentence is understood in a more complete manner. If we study the world as physical things, then the conclusion is that all this diversity springs from a single existent—Brahman. However, if we study the same diversity as distinct sentences, then the diversity leads us to meaning and reference. Unless a person is convinced that "I exist eternally", it is impossible to talk about the eternal meaning of their existence, and what this meaning refers to. So, even though the existence comes out of the source, the initial step for a spiritual aspirant is to understand that he is the soul before they understand God.

Topic 11

QUESTION

We have many times spoken about how everything expands from the whole, which then leads to the inverted tree model of reality in which the complete source must be understood before the parts are known. Now you are saying that knowledge can also be acquired from incomplete to complete—i.e., from minute details to the full truth. Can this be called a general method? Or is this method restricted only to the understanding of the Absolute Truth?

3.3.20 (380)

संबन्धादेवमन्यत्रापि

saṃbandhādevamanyatrāpi

saṃbandhāt—due to relation; evam—like this; anyatra—in other cases; api—also.

TRANSLATION

Since (the full-to-partial and partial-to-full) are like this (non-different) due to their relation (to the object of study), they can be used in other cases too.

COMMENTARY

Under a physical conception of the world, we think that the bigger truth is necessarily outside the partial truth—like a city is beyond the house, a country is beyond the city, etc. However, if the same reality is understood semantically, then even as the country is beyond the city, the nationality is embedded in each city, and the quality of that city is embedded in each house. Hence, people might say: "this looks like any American city", or "this looks just like a European town", or "this looks like an Indian village". The American, European, or Indian nature of something is a broader level reality, but it is also embedded in each part of that broader reality. Therefore, the study of a *broader* reality is also the study of a *deeper* reality. To know the broader reality, we don't necessarily have to go outward; we can also go deeper inward. Scientists today think that to know the full reality we must always look outward—through microscopes and telescopes. In the Vedic system, however, to know the full reality, we must withdraw the consciousness inward and look deeper within—beyond the bodily, mental, intellectual, egotistic, and moralistic coverings of the soul.

This process of spiritual realization is applicable to material study as well. For example, when you meet a person, you only see their skin color, body size, dress, and appearance. But you don't know anything about them—e.g., their family, occupation, friends, values, morals, etc. If you engage with them, then you can also know them 'deeply'—i.e., their family, upbringing, occupation, friends, values, and morals. All these are within the person, and yet not easily visible. To understand these deeper realities, we must ask different types of questions; if our quest is limited to their bodily appearance, then we will not discover the deeper nature of a person. Different realities are revealed only when different types of questions are asked. In the case of material study, the simplest question is: Does it exist? A more advanced question is: What is it? And an even more advanced question is: What can it be used to achieve? Thus, the method of knowing the self applies to the knowing of the world.

QUESTION

The impersonalist will say that the idea of 'deeper reality' is drawn from the study of matter, where there are many deeper levels of reality, beginning with the body. The soul is supposed to be the deepest level of reality. But you are insisting that there are deeper levels of understanding even in the soul. Why can't we say that there is just the soul, rather than levels in the soul?

3.3.21 (381)

न वा वशिेषात्

na vā viśeṣāt

na vā—rather not; viśeṣāt—on account of difference.

TRANSLATION

(We shall) rather not say (that the soul is one thing) due to the differences (between the many aspects of the understanding about the soul).

COMMENTARY

The impersonalist conception of the soul is that it exists, but is devoid of qualities; qualities, rather, are imputed upon the soul by matter. If these material qualities are removed, then the soul is itself without any qualities, and if there are no qualities, then there is no differentiation between souls. This conception of the soul is based on the physical view of things. When the same thing is understood as a symbol, then the symbol exists, the symbol has a meaning, and the symbol's meaning refers to something other than the symbol. We cannot equate the existence to the meaning or to the reference. So, the claim that the soul is without modes of understanding, and these modes are only added due to matter, is a flawed idea. The soul's understanding is also modal; existence, meaning, and reference are the three modes of the soul's understanding.

The term viśeṣāt can have many meanings: (1) differences, (2) qualities, (3) modalities, (4) individualities, etc. All these meanings when applied to the soul or God refute impersonalism. They are certainly observed in the case of matter. The difference between matter, soul, and God is that God is the reference to Himself, the soul can be reference to itself or to God, and matter is always a reference to something other than itself—either soul or God. The principle of symbolism is upheld in all three cases; they only differ in their references. There is hence a similarity between matter, soul, and God, and there is a difference. The similarity is that they are all symbols of meaning. The difference is that they have different references. The soul also has different references in the material world, in Brahman, and in the spiritual world (directed toward matter, directed toward self, and directed toward God). The impersonalist claims that Brahman is undivided, and matter is divided. But when the soul is undivided, then it has no individuality. Without individuality, there is no desire. And without the fulfillment of desire there is no happiness. The soul merely exists, but it doesn't know why it exists. This incomplete knowledge of the soul is not perfection.

QUESTION

When we have an ordinary experience, the existence, meaning, and reference are all equally present. In fact, it seems that we cannot even distinguish between these three things in experience because every experience has the notion of self-existence, the meaning of existence, and the thing being seen. So, is this tripartite distinction a theoretical one, or can it be observed as well?

3.3.22 (382)

दर्‌शयति च

darśayati ca

darśayati—experienced; ca—also.

TRANSLATION

(The distinction between existence, meaning, and reference) is also experienced (so, it is not merely a theoretical distinction between aspects).

COMMENTARY

Ordinary experiences generally come with existence (or self-experience), the meaning (or the purpose of one's existence), as well as the reference of this purpose (the external object by which our purpose is to be fulfilled). This might lead us to think that these are inseparable aspects of experience, and if they are inseparable, they cannot be considered as deeper realities; we must rather consider them as a single reality because they are experienced simultaneously. This sūtra states that each of the three can be separately experienced. Therefore, there is an experience in which we know "I exist" but we don't know the meaning of existence and the object that fulfills this existential meaning. Then there is an experience in which we experience both our existence and the meaning; this is when we decide that we are going to dedicate our life to some ideals, although we may not know how these ideals will be fulfilled. Then, we map this existential meaning to external objects or individuals that fulfill it. This is when we experience our existence, the existential ideal, and the object that fulfills this ideal. The successive experiences include the previous experiences, so there is an order or hierarchy between them. But since the experience progresses from existence to meaning to reference, we can see them separately. Therefore, the experience of Bhagavān is not contrary to the experience of Paramātma or Brahman; it includes it. Likewise, the Paramātma experience includes Brahman experience, but goes beyond it. Finally, the Brahman experience stands by itself, and may not include Paramātma or Bhagavān experiences. The possibility of this self-experience, however, doesn't preclude the other experiences; it is only a less inclusive experience of the self-existence alone.

Topic 12

QUESTION

If you accept that the existence of the self can be experienced even in material observations, then why do you say that separation from matter is required to know who we truly are? Aren't we seeing ourselves in every experience?

3.3.23 (383)
संभृतदिुयुव्याप्त्यपि चातः
saṃbhṛtidyuvyāptyapi cātaḥ

saṃbhṛtiḥ—possessed of; dyuvyāptiḥ—pervading the space; api—also; cātaḥ—and hence (we cannot consider this as the true nature of self).

TRANSLATION

Possessed of (this body and its connections) (we think of ourselves) as also pervading the space, and hence (this identity isn't the real identity of the soul).

COMMENTARY

Emotion, relation, and cognition exist in this world and use these to define our identity in relation to other people and things, the attributes of our body and its achievements, and the enjoyment of materialistic pleasures. Thus, we might consider ourselves rich because we own property, beautiful if we have an attractive body, famous if we are known by many people, powerful if this body controls the others, etc. Since all these are temporary, therefore, our identity is also temporary. But in the pursuit of this identity, we are distracted toward the external world. Spiritual life begins when the material connections are severed and only the relation to the self exists. Now, we are neither masters nor servants; we are neither enjoyers nor the enjoyed; we neither own anything nor are we owned. The self is defined not in relation to the world, but in relation to the self. Further progress involves the realization that the self is a part of the whole, that its purpose is defined by the whole, and its experiences must be directed toward the whole. Since this identity is permanent, therefore, it cannot be called an illusion. This sūtra states that the material notion of owning a body and its properties and by externalizing our consciousness into these objects we lose the real self of identity and self-existence. In fact, most us would consider ourselves diminished, and our identity lost, if these things were destroyed.

Topic 13

QUESTION

But as long as we are in the material world, we have to relate to this world through this body and so how can we give up these material identities?

3.3.24 (384)
पुरुषविद्यायामवि चेतरेषामनाम्नानात्
puruṣavidyāyāmiva cetareṣāmanāmnānāt

puruṣavidyāyām—the knowledge to become the master; iva—as if; ca—and; itareṣām—of the others; anām—the non-names; nānāt—from numerous.

TRANSLATION

From the numerous non-names (i.e., false designations of master etc.), the imaginary (as if) knowledge to become a master of the others (arises).

COMMENTARY

The previous sūtra stated that the real self-identity is unknown unless the association with the material world is discarded. So, a naïve interpretation of this claim can be that we must reject the material world, discard our roles and duties, and live in isolation. This sūtra, however, states that the real problem isn't those associations but the idea that we are the master of this body and everything associated with it. The term *eva* means 'certainly', and the term *iva* means 'as if' or 'just like'. The indication is that we are not truly masters, but we behave as if we are the masters. When this false sense of being the master is destroyed, then all the non-names (i.e., the false designations in relation to the world) are also destroyed. Therefore, we don't have to give up the roles and duties but must give up the idea that we are the masters of the world. Once this idea is given up, then we can use the roles and duties to serve the Lord.

Topic 14

QUESTION

Is this rejection of being a pretentious master like selflessness? Some people compare this idea to that of a hollow inside a coconut, stating that the self is viewed as nothing, although the body and its associations can continue?

3.3.25 (385)

वेधाद्यर्थभेदात्

vedhādyarthabhedāt

vedhādi—making a hole etc.; arthabhedāt—due to different meaning.

TRANSLATION

Making a hole etc. (is not accepted) due to a different meaning.

COMMENTARY

The cessation of false mastery doesn't entail the cessation of existence. A disease can be cured by killing the patient, but we don't consider that killing as a legitimate method of cure. In the same way, if we ceased to exist, then we will cease to be a master. But that is like killing the patient to cure the disease.

The real cure is not the cessation of existence, but the cessation of false mastery. It is achieved by the soul becoming a servant of the Lord. The advocates of voidism claim that if these material associations are given up, then the person ceases to be a father, mother, citizen, employee, etc. and if all such designations are removed, then we would not be left with any 'self'. Since all these designations are temporarily created due to association with material objects, therefore, the voidist claims that they are all false (which is correct). However, he also goes on to claim that there is really no self if all these designations are removed (which is incorrect). The notion of being a master is a false covering of the soul, but the existence of the soul is not itself false. This is borne by practical experience that even when a person gives up material identities, he doesn't cease to exist. Therefore, the meaning of giving up material identities is not to leave a 'hole' within, which would entail that there is no self. The idea is rather to remove the false attachments borne out of the idea of being a master.

Topic 15

QUESTION

But if all kinds of material attachments have been given up, and the associated identities are lost, then what type of identity can one claim to have?

3.3.26 (386)

हानौ तु उपायनशब्दशेषत्वात् कुशाच्छन्दस्तुत्युपगानवत् तदुक्तम्

hānau tu upāyanaśabdaśeṣatvāt kuśācchandaḥstutyupagānavat taduktam

hānau—a loss; tu—but; upāyana—engagement; śabdaśeṣatvāt—from being called the remainder; kuśā—a rope; cchandaḥ—verses; stuti—the prayers; upagānavat—just like singing as a subordinate; tat—that; uktam—is said.

TRANSLATION

There is a loss (of the material identity) but due to engagements (which cannot be destroyed), (the soul) is still said to remain; it is said that he is bound by the rope of verses like a servant singing the prayers to that (the Lord).

COMMENTARY

We can see a progression in these sūtras— (1) the soul carries false identities, (2) these false identities are destroyed when one gives up the idea of being a master, (3) however, the destruction of these identities doesn't leave a void, (4) because the soul is still bound to the Lord through devotional prayers.

The term *guna* or material modes are sometimes called a 'rope'. Similarly, the term *kuśā* also denotes a rope. The soul is never liberated from these bondages, and the idea of 'liberation' as being completely free is false. Only the nature of the rope is changed. If we say that the destruction of material identity destroys the soul (as the Buddhists claim) then this claim is rejected here. The soul is permanently bound to the Lord by prayer, and temporarily bound to the material body and its associations. When this temporary binding is removed, then the permanent binding remains. This permanent binding is the soul's identity. The soul is neither a standalone reality nor does it become non-existent by the destruction of the material identity. It rather regains its spiritual identity, that is defined as a 'rope' which binds the soul to the Lord devotionally.

Topic 16

QUESTION

When the material identities are destroyed, and the soul is situated only in relation to the Lord, what does he desire through that identity and relation?

3.3.27 (387)

सांपराये तर्तव्याभावात् तथा ह्यन्ये

sāṃparāye tartavyābhāvāt tathā hyanye

sāṃparāye—on the attainment of transcendence; tartavya-abhāvāt—from absence of desires; tathā—in the same way; hi—for; anye—others.

TRANSLATION

From the absence of (material) desires on the attainment of transcendence, in the way that (there are mundane achievements) for the others.

COMMENTARY

We desire achievements because we feel incomplete; achievements help us temporarily relieve the sense of incompleteness. We associate with the body, its relationships, and the material objects because they temporarily make us feel complete. And we pursue such objects, and become attached to them, because we seek to overcome the inner incompleteness by filling it with temporary distractions. When the soul has attained the devotion to the Lord, then his material aspirations—like those of the materially conditioned souls—are destroyed. Such a person has no material aspirations because he has no incompleteness.

QUESTION

Since such a person can still exist in the material world, what does he do? Does he reject the material relationships, or does he continue to accept them?

3.3.28 (388)

छन्दतःउभयावरिोधात्

chandataḥ ubhayāvirodhāt

chandataḥ—according to his liking; ubhaya-avirodhāt—due to there being no contradiction between the two (acceptance and rejection of the world).

TRANSLATION

(Such a person lives) according to his liking because there is no contradiction between the two (the acceptance and the rejection of the world).

COMMENTARY

The Vedic texts describe two contradictory paths; these are called *pravritti* or engagement, and *nivritti* or detachment. Transcendence can be obtained by either of these paths. The path of engagement requires a person to keep performing their prescribed duties but becoming detached from their results. The path of detachment requires a person to voluntarily severe the attachments by cutting of the activities themselves. As the saying goes: "out of sight, out of mind". The path of detachment pursues this ideology, and advocates cutting off the worldly attachments to take our mind off the world. The path of engagement, however, says that just because you live in a jungle doesn't mean you are not thinking about the city. Out of sight doesn't necessarily mean out of mind. The real goal is not to put things out of sight, but to take them out of our minds. In fact, a test of detachment is that these things exist in your sight, but you are not tempted by them. Engaging in the activities, but progressively developing the detachment is, therefore, a better path. Of course, one might suit a person better than others. But they have the same goal—detachment from the material desires, but they are attained in two different ways: renounce the actions or renounce the desire for the results of these actions. However, for one who has attained devotion to the Lord, the results of both paths are already achieved. So, he has no need to renounce the material world, because he has renounced the materialistic goals. And he has no need to engage with the world because he has no materialistic goals. Thus, even as engagement and renunciation are contradictory paths for ordinary people, for the devotee they are not contradictory. Therefore, he can renounce, or he can engage, according to his liking.

Topic 17

QUESTION

But he still must make some decisions—i.e., to accept or reject. Even if both acceptance and rejection are identical for him, he still must make some decisions. Without a purpose, how can decide what course of action to take?

3.3.29 (389)

गतेरर्थवत्त्वमुभयथा अन्यथा हि विरोधः

gaterarthavattvamubhayathā anyathā hi virodhaḥ

gateḥ—the actions; arthavattvam—by their utility; ubhayathā—in two ways; anyathā—otherwise; hi—certainly; virodhaḥ—a contradiction.

TRANSLATION

His actions (are determined) by their utility in two ways (i.e., useful and useless); otherwise, certainly (everything is) a contradiction (to his purpose).

COMMENTARY

The term *artha* denotes meaning or purpose. We normally measure the purpose in relation to our materialistic goals. But for the devotee, such goals are gone. However, the devotee still has goals—the pleasure of the Lord. Therefore, he decides whether something is useful or useless to the service of the Lord. Even if he has no selfish goals, he has the desire to please the Lord. So, the utility of the world is not lost; the utility is just measured in relation to the Lord. Everything else, which seems not useful to the service of the Lord, is considered a contradiction to the goal of pleasing the Lord and is therefore rejected.

QUESTION

But the purpose (of the Lord) may not always be satisfied in this world; there are so many hurdles to devotional service due to atheistic people. How can a devotee deal with such hurdles and difficulties in making choices?

3.3.30 (390)

उपपन्न्नःतल्लक्षणार्थोपलब्धेःलोकवत्

upapannaḥ tallakṣaṇārthopalabdheḥ lokavat

upapannaḥ—obtained; tat-lakṣaṇārtha-upalabdheḥ—as the symptoms of the achievement (of the purposes of the Lord); lokavat—just as in this world.

TRANSLATION

(Whatever is) obtained that has the symptoms of fulfilling (the purpose of the Lord) (is accepted) just as in this world (people take things good for them).

COMMENTARY

When a devotee is detached from materialistic goals and has developed devotional goals, he may decide to serve the Lord by engaging the material things into His service. But there are many practical difficulties—there is often resistance to such service by atheistic people and there are hardships in obtaining the resources for such service. When such difficulties arise, a devotee is inclined to ask: Is this hardship worth the effort, since results are hard to come by? Based on this hardship, should I continue to engage with the world, or renounce it? This sūtra answers this question. The devotee continues to serve the Lord in whatever way possible. Even if great results are not obtained, he accepts whatever results are obtained (or not obtained) with graciousness. He doesn't feel unhappy or bitter about the world being opposed to his devotional service. In short, effort continues to matter; the results thus obtained are immaterial.

Topic 18

QUESTION

Since you say that the devotee can accept or reject the prescribed duties, it seems that the rules of performing the duties in the scripture don't apply to him? Does this mean that he is contradicting the scriptural injunctions?

3.3.31 (391)

अनियमःसर्वासाम् अविरोधःशब्दानुमानाभ्याम्

aniyamaḥ sarvāsām avirodhaḥ śabdānumānābhyām

aniyamaḥ—there are no rules; sarvāsām—(applicable) to all; avirodhaḥ—non-contradiction; śabda-anumānābhyām—due to scripture or reasoning.

TRANSLATION

The rules that are applicable to everyone are not applicable to him; (by rejecting these rules) there is no contradiction to scripture or reasoning.

COMMENTARY

Rules are impersonal, and the Lord is a person. The person gives the rules for those who cannot see or understand the person, and by following those rules, we indirectly follow the person. However, if we can directly follow the person, then we would also fulfill the purpose for which those rules were given.

In the material world, however, the soul forgets the purpose of these rules as the satisfaction of the Lord. He just sees these impersonal rules and considers them to be meant for the satisfaction of the only person he knows—himself. As a result, he thinks that whenever he follows the rules, then he must also get something in return. For example, we pay our taxes so that the government will protect us from miscreants, or from unforeseen difficulties, in return. In short, there is a covenant between the lawgiver and the law-follower. In a primitive form, religion is such contracts between the Lord and His followers, and it is primitive because there is hardly any love; it is merely a contract between two parties. Thus, the devotion between the soul and God is deemphasized and the rules of the contract are emphasized; the followers of the religion also believe that by accepting these rules and regulations they are *entitled* to liberation. After all, that is the nature of the covenant—both parties are bound by it.

The advanced devotee of the Lord is, however, beyond such contractual obligations. He serves the Lord out of love. He doesn't need rules as contracts because he is not expecting anything in return. Thus, he is not bound by the contracts because a contract involves an entitlement, but the devotee has no entitlement. The devotee loves the Lord causelessly, not due to contractual reasons, and he becomes free from all such contractual laws. Instead, he binds the Lord by his causeless devotion: The Lord becomes dependent on the love of His devotee, but the devotee is not asking for anything in return from the Lord.

The religion of rules and regulations is primitive; it can make a person indirectly follow the Lord by making him follow the rules given by the Lord. Obedience to rules raises a person to the understanding of the Lord, provided one follows these rules as a matter of natural duty, and not because there is something expected in return. If rules are followed to get something in return, then the rules remain impersonal contracts, and the Lord is not understood. If the understanding of the Lord is obtained, then the rules cease to be meaningful. The devotee, upon a full understanding of the Lord, becomes the lawgiver and the Lord becomes the law-follower. Bound by the love of the devotee, the Lord becomes the devotee's servant, and their mutual affection grows incessantly.

Topic 19

QUESTION

Does this mean that the rules and regulations of the material world continue to apply to the person who hasn't developed the devotion to the Lord?

3.3.32 (392)

यावदधिकारमवस्थितिराधिकारिकाणाम्

yāvadadhikāramavasthitirādhikārikāṇām

yāvat-adhikāram—as long as one has the sense of rights; avasthitiḥ—(there is material) existence; ādhikārikāṇām—for those who feel righteous.

TRANSLATION

As long as one has the sense of rights, (there is material) existence for those who feel righteous (i.e., expect results in return for their religious duties).

COMMENTARY

All rules are meant to define the sense of right and wrong. But underlying all these rules is an expectation—if I do this correctly, then I will get this reward. Morality is based on this sense of right and wrong, and the laws of religion constitute morality. Morality is, however, not real religion. It is merely obedience to laws in return for something else. The followers of moral injunctions remain attached to the results, and they expect that the Lord must reciprocate with material benedictions, liberation, or protection, in return for the obedience to the laws. In short, the righteousness that we accept by obeying the moral injunctions is also applied back to the lawgiver, and one doesn't follow the laws because it pleases the Lord; one follows them because there is something in return. This contract constitutes the sense of righteousness. This sūtra states that as long as one has this sense of righteousness and expects reciprocation for following the laws, he remains bound by the laws. Righteousness is impersonal, and devotion is personal. We cannot love laws; we can follow them in return for something else. We can however love the Lord, who gives these laws.

Many people who follow religious practices become disenchanted quickly if they find that following the rules and regulations is not producing the expected results—i.e., material benedictions, liberation, or protection from suffering. They can't see the effects of karma, and how their suffering, entanglement, and vulnerability is caused by their own past actions. They may even blame the Lord for not reciprocating in accordance with their perceived covenants. This perceived breach of trust with the Lord then dissolves their obedience to the laws they were previously following. A new set of problems are now created, and the cycle of breaking the laws and bearing its consequences repeats.

Modern society is afflicted with the idea of rights. These began with the contracts between man and God, as Abrahamic religions taught covenants with God; they were extended to contracts between a citizen and their government; and slowly, all relationships—including marriages—became contracts. In every contract, there are rights and duties: You give something to get something in return. All relationships become business dealings, as everyone is calculating the profit and loss in a relationship, rather than loving each other. A slight reduction in a profit, or a slight increase in the loss, immediately leads to the disruption of the relationship. Thus, people have no patience and tolerance. The idea of contracts, covenants, and rights creates a society devoid of love. The other person is not a person; they are only the portals for giving and taking. The problem begins in a faulty conception of religion: If we cannot love God selflessly, then how can we love anyone else selflessly? If God is only following a contract, then how can every other relationship not also be contractual?

A religion of covenants is like a marriage bound by a prenuptial agreement. There is some love, but it is not irrevocable. Hence, this type of religion is considered imperfect. It is meant for those who find it hard to love God. If we maintain a sense of rights, then we must also be bound by duties. When we give up rights, then we also become free of duties. A perfect society can only exist if the living entities serve each other not because they are expecting something in return as determined by a covenant; rather, because they are bound by love.

Topic 20

QUESTION

If the soul is bound to the material world by his sense of righteousness and entitlement for actions, then how is the soul liberated from this existence?

3·3·33 (393)

अक्षरधियां त्ववरोधःसामान्यतद्भावाभ्यामौपसदवत् तदुक्तम्

akṣaradhiyāṃ tvavarodhaḥ sāmānyatadbhāvābhyāmaupasadavat taduktam

akṣaradhiyāṃ—surrendering to the infallible; tu—but; avarodhaḥ—without hurdles; sāmānya—due to similarity; tadbhāvābhyām—by being imbued with His nature; upasadavat—just like worship; tat—it; uktam—has been said.

TRANSLATION

Surrendering to the infallible but without the hurdles (of rules and regulations), due to the similarity (between the soul and the Lord) by being imbued with His nature (by constantly remembering Him), just like worshipping Him, (the transcendental existence is obtained); thus, it has been said.

COMMENTARY

The previous sūtra stated that one may follow the laws of God, but if he treats them as contractual laws, his material existence continues. Thus, a religion that teaches one to obey a contract with God doesn't lead to transcendence. It merely repeats the cycle of birth and death because we expect a return on our investment. If one desires to transcend, then one must give up the transactional mindset and surrender to the Lord. The rejection of rules and regulations is part of that surrender—we are not becoming immoral; we are rather rejecting the expectation of getting favorable returns for being moral. The Lord is not bound by laws of morality, because He doesn't act with return of expectations. When the soul acts in the same way, he also acquires the qualities of the Lord—i.e., freedom from the laws. This doesn't mean defiance to the Lord; it rather means serving the Lord without expecting anything in return. So, the transcendental state is beyond morality, not averse to morality. Under morality, we expect good things to come to us if we follow the rules and regulations. Giving up morality simply means discarding this expectation of returns. Rules and regulations may or may not be followed; since the desire of the soul has changed to please the Lord alone, such action has no consequences. Therefore, the sense of right and wrong ceases to exist, and consequently the laws of karma.

Topic 21

QUESTION

Isn't there anything else required for the attainment of transcendence?

3·3·34 (394)

इयदामननात्

iyadāmananāt

iyat—only so much; āmananāt—due to acceptance.

TRANSLATION

The acceptance of (surrender to the Lord) is enough (for transcendence).

COMMENTARY

The previous sūtra stated that by surrender to the Lord one can attain transcendence. The sūtra before that said that if the surrender is not accepted, then transcendence is not attained. Therefore, the previous two sūtras said that the surrender to the Lord is *necessary*. This sūtra states that surrender the Lord is *sufficient*. Generally, if there are many causes responsible for an effect, and each cause is necessary, then the absence of those causes will preempt the effect. By that calculation, the surrender to the Lord is necessary—so we can say that it is at least one of the causes of transcendence. But there is still a possibility that there are other causes because of which the surrender to the Lord may not be sufficient. This sūtra rejects the existence of any additional causes; it states that 'only so much'—i.e., the surrender to the Lord—is enough for transcendence. It follows that no other cause is required; however, this cause is necessary.

Topic 22

QUESTION

Why do you consider the surrender to the Lord as necessary and sufficient, when there are so many other legitimate paths described in the Vedic texts?

3·3·35 (395)
अन्तरा भूतग्रामवत्स्वात्मनः
antarā bhūtagrāmavatsvātmanaḥ

antarā—the innermost; bhūtagrāmavat—just like the first of the existents; svātmanaḥ—the meaning (or the mind) of the self (if the self is the body).

TRANSLATION

(The surrender to the Lord is necessary and sufficient because He) is the innermost reality, the first among all the other existents, and the meaning (or the mind) of the self (if the self is identified as the body of that mind).

COMMENTARY

As already discussed, the existence of the soul is an incomplete understanding. A more complete understanding is that this existence has a meaning or purpose. Just like the body exists, but the meaning of the existence is given by the mind, similarly, the soul is here compared to the body, whose meaning (i.e., the mind) is the Lord. The paths of spiritual realization—e.g., karma-yoga, jñāna-yoga, and dhyāna-yoga—are sometimes incompletely understood when they are expected only to deliver the liberation from material existence. Using these paths, the soul can become detached from the laws of material nature, but because it doesn't yet know the purpose of its existence, it likely falls again into the material world. Only when a transcendent purpose of existence is realized, then the soul doesn't fall (assuming it doesn't forget its innate purpose).

The existence of the soul is therefore like a symbol. Deeper than this existence is the meaning of existence. The existence and the meaning are inseparable in one sense—because the meaning is within the soul. And yet, the existence is not identical to the meaning—because we can know the existence and yet not know the meaning (although when we know the meaning, we also know the existence). Therefore, the meaning of existence goes beyond existence, and is considered more complete. We should not therefore think that self-realization is the end, if by this end, we simply know that the soul is different from the body. The greater self-realization is knowing the purpose of existence.

The comparison of the Lord to the mind is significant here because we are generally prepared to accept that the mind is different from the body. By calling the Lord the mind, the soul is now accepted as the body. Therefore, like a materially entangled person is considered inferior to one who is self-realized, similarly, the self-realized person is considered inferior to the Lord's devotee. This idea about the relation between the soul and the Lord is the basis of the Viśiṣṭādvaita doctrine in which the soul is the body of the Supreme Soul.

QUESTION

The distinction between the soul and the Lord was predicated upon the Lord being separate from the soul. Now you are saying that the Lord is like the mind of the body (of the soul) which means that since the mind is inside the body therefore there is no distinction between the soul and the Lord. So, rather than saying that the Lord is different from the soul, you are saying that these two are identical. Doesn't it contradict the previous statements on this?

3.3.36 (396)

अन्यथा भेदानुपपत्तरिति चेत् न उपदेशान्तरवत्

anyathā bhedānupapattiriti cet na upadeśāntaravat

anyathā—erroneously; bheda-anupapattiḥ—the distinction is not clearly understood; iti cet—if it be said; na—not so; upadeśānta—the final teaching; ravat—roaring or yelling (declaration with the greatest emphasis).

TRANSLATION

If it is said that (the Lord being the purpose of the soul) erroneously makes the distinction (between the soul and the Lord) unclear, (we say) not so; (the Lord being the purpose of the soul) is roaringly said to be the final teaching.

COMMENTARY

The distinction between the Lord and the soul has already been established as whole and part, and that distinction—or Dvaita—is not to be denied. However, if we keep this separation, then it is hard to explain why the soul must be devoted to the Lord. Of course, we can say that the soul is part of the Lord, but that begs the question: How can the soul go against the Lord if it were part of the Lord? Then again, if the Lord and the soul are truly separate, then how can the soul know the Lord, given the separation between the knower and the known? In Advaita philosophy, all illusions arise due to the knower-known distinction and certainty is established only regarding self-existence. This idea is also well-known in Western philosophy where Descartes noted that he can doubt everything but could not doubt his own existence, because the existence of that doubt necessitated the existence of the doubter. Therefore, the separation of the soul and Lord brings new problems of knowledge. This problem, however, disappears if we say that the Lord exists inside the soul as the purpose of his existence. In so far as we cannot doubt our existence, we can also perceive the purpose as a deeper reality. In this perception, we are not looking 'outside' to know the Lord. We are rather looking deeper inside. This internal looking doesn't mean that the Lord is not outside; it just means that the source from which everything emanates is also embedded in each thing as its purpose.

The Lord is both outside and inside the soul, and this creates contradictions only when we think of 'outside' and 'inside' physically. When the world is looked at semantically, these problems disappear. Just like mammal is the source of the idea of cow, and yet mammal is also present inside the cow, similarly, the Lord can be outside everything as their source, and inside everything as their purpose. If the Lord is only outside, then God-realization is necessarily different from self-realization. If the Lord is only inside, then self-realization is identical to God-realization. But if the Lord is both inside and outside, then self-realization is complete only with God-realization, and this self-realization doesn't make us God. This is the founding principle of non-difference.

The sūtra further states that this understanding of the Lord existing within the soul—after it has been said that He is outside the soul—is 'roaringly' asserted to be the final teaching. In short, this understanding is Vedānta. This sūtra is the basis of the Bhedābheda doctrine in which the Lord is both outside and inside the soul. This understanding proceeds through several stages. First, it is said that soul is different from God. Second, it is said that the soul is a property of God, like the body is a property of the soul. Third, it is said that God is captured in the soul and is hence bound by love within the soul. These successive viewpoints are not contradictory; they are rather the progression of the loving relation between the soul and the Lord. When the soul is averse to the Lord, then the two are separate. When the soul becomes devoted to the Lord, then he is a property of the Lord. But when this devotion toward the Lord gradually intensifies, then the Lord is bound and captured inside the soul. Finally, when the soul is overwhelmed by this love, then he acts just like the Lord, and the distinction between the soul and the Lord is dissolved for all practical purposes. Hence, the soul and the Lord are different, related as object and property, non-different from each other, and finally, they become identical.

Thus, all positions of Vedānta are true, but they are not simultaneously true. They are rather progressive statements about the devotion to the Lord. The identity between the soul and the Lord is the highest understanding, but this is not the impersonal unity devoid of individuality, love, and devotion.

Topic 23

QUESTION

If you call this the final understanding of Vedānta, does it apply only to the soul, or is it applicable even to the others—such as the relation between the Lord and the material nature, or between the soul and the material nature?

3·3·37 (397)

व्यतिहारःविशिषिन्तिहीतरवत्

vyatihāraḥ viśiṃṣanti hītaravat

vyatihāraḥ—reciprocity (of existence—whole in the part, part in the whole); viśiṃṣanti—distinct existence; hi—certainly; itaravat—just like the others.

TRANSLATION

The reciprocal distinct existence (of the whole within the part, and the part within the whole) is certainly (applicable) just like the other (doctrines).

COMMENTARY

The term *vyatihāraḥ* indicates alternation, reciprocity, or interchange. The term *viśiṃṣanti* indicates distinct or separated existence. This understanding is then applied to everything (not just the relation between the soul and the Lord). Just as the Lord and the soul are distinct existents, and yet, the Lord is inside the soul and the soul is inside the Lord, similarly, matter and the Lord are also distinct, and yet, matter is a part of the Lord and the Lord is within matter. When the soul exists in the material world, similarly, we can say that the soul is inside a material body (i.e., the soul is entangled within the material body), and the material body is inside the soul (as the soul's experience). If the body was merely a soul's experience—a position called Idealism in Western philosophy—then we could not say that the soul is entangled in matter; after all, the soul has full control over the material experience as it is within the soul. Conversely, if the soul was within the body, but the body wasn't within the soul—a position called Realism in Western philosophy—then we could not say that the soul is suffering due to its entanglement; after all, the body would only be a covering of the soul, and the soul and matter would be separate things.

To say that the soul is entangled in matter, we must accept that matter is distinct from the soul. And to say that the soul is suffering due to this entanglement, we must accept that the matter produces effects within the soul. Matter must enter the soul in order to create an experience. And yet, matter must be outside the soul for an objective external reality to exist and the material bondage—e.g., the laws of nature that force the soul—to be considered real.

We have discussed this problem earlier. When we have an experience, there is an objective external reality, and yet, there is a picture of that reality within the observer. The reality and its picture are physically distinct, but they are semantically identical. For instance, the external apple has taste, smell, color, shape, etc. and the internal apple also has those same properties. Due to this similarity, the external and the internal apples are identical (or can be identical if everything in the external apple becomes our conscious experience). And yet, the external apple will never be identical to the internal picture. The distinction between the external reality and the internal picture indicates that the soul and matter are physically distinct entities. And yet, during an experience, the apple enters the soul, and the soul enters the apple, and by this interchange or reciprocity, they become semantically identical. Therefore, even though the soul and the apple are physically distinct, they also become identical during an experience. If the experience ends, then they are individually separate.

Most people can accept the idea that the apple enters our mind, but they have a hard time accepting that the mind enters the apple. In short, they believe that we experience the world, but we are not bound by the world. So, the world is within us, but we are not within the world. Factually, there is no such experience. When you see an apple, you are not seeing the stars in the sky, hearing the people talking in the background, or aware of the pressure of the chair on your back. The exclusion of everything else means that we are in the apple, not anywhere else. But since we can focus on other things, therefore, we are outside everything. Therefore, the soul is different from the world because it can choose to experience different parts of the world or withdraw from all experiences. However, during an experience, the soul enters the perceived object. Hence, despite being separate from the world, the soul is bound by the world.

If the soul was always separate, then it could not experience anything, and duality of soul and matter leads to the mind-body problem in Western philosophy. If the soul is identical to the world, then we must at once experience everything in the world, which is again false. Therefore, we cannot assert duality, and we cannot assert identity. Now we say that the soul enters an object and becomes its part. The part is not identical to the whole, so identity is rejected. And the part is not separate from the whole, so duality is rejected. Our ability to focus on one thing means we are in that thing. Our ability to experience other things means they are all within us. And our ability to withdraw from all things implies that we are different from all things. Thus, various contradictory claims are made. They are all true, but not simultaneously true. They become true one after another as we (1) remain without experience, (2) get absorbed into one experience, and (3) change our experience from one thing to another.

The paradigm of reciprocity and interchange is applicable to all kinds of distinct realities—i.e., God, the soul, and matter—and their interrelations. The previous sūtra stated this idea in the context of the soul-God relation. And this sūtra advocates this reciprocal and interchange viewpoint along with others.

Topic 24

QUESTION

You have earlier described the Absolute Truth as comprised of masculine and feminine aspects. Now you are saying that each aspect is within the other aspect. How does this change the understanding of the Absolute Truth?

3.3.38 (398)

सैव हि सत्यादयः

saiva hi satyādayaḥ

sa eva—the same; hi—certainly; satyādayaḥ—the original truth.

TRANSLATION

The same (whole-part doctrine) certainly applies to the original truth.

COMMENTARY

In our earlier discussion, we noted how the Absolute Truth has masculine and feminine aspects—the masculine is the potential for desire, and the feminine is the potential to fulfill that desire. As potentials, the masculine and feminine are separate. However, this sūtra states that the masculine and feminine also enter each other and become inseparable from the other. As a result, two different entities—masculine and feminine—are both separate and inseparable. The same philosophy of mutual existence within each other is applicable.

The will is separate from power because the power may not be utilized by the will. When the power is used, the resulting effect is a combination of will and power, therefore, we say that they are inseparable. But this combination is also experienced, due to which the will enters power, and power enters will. In short, the combination of will and power is not a physical mixture of sugar and milk in which they remain separable. Conscious experience is the will entering power, and the power entering the will. For example, a powerful person may feel insecure and to reassure himself, he may look at the things that make him powerful. By absorbing himself in those things, he feels powerful. Then, when he feels this power, he is also tempted to use that power. Under this temptation, the will and power are separate. However, the power may be subordinated to the will—i.e., I will do what I want. Or, the will may be subordinated by the power—I will do what my power lets me do. When this dominant-subordinate relation is defined, then the will and the power combine to produce an effect. Finally, after the power is used to achieve the intended goals, then a sense of power enters the will as contentment and fulfillment. Thus, will and power are different, inseparable, will is within power, and power is within the will.

All these claims are true, but not simultaneously true. They become true one after another. When the Lord doesn't enjoy with His Śakti, the two are separate. When the Lord glances at His Śakti, He enters the Śakti, and feels powerful. This sense of power creates the temptation to enjoy, and the Lord combines with His Śakti to produce an effect. In this combination, however, the Lord may be dominant, or the Śakti may be dominant. Once that effect is achieved, the Śakti enters the Lord, and the Lord feels the contentment and fulfilment within. Depending on which aspect of this process we focus upon, we can say that the Lord and His Śakti are separate, inseparable, the Lord is within the Śakti, the Śakti is within the Lord, the Lord is superior, or the Śakti is superior. All such claims are potentially true always, but they are not simultaneously true.

Topic 25

QUESTION

You earlier said that in the material world, the Lord and His Śakti enter an unmanifest state during annihilation, and the world is again created when

the desire springs in the Lord. This desire also separates the Śakti from the Lord. But if they are merged in an unmanifest state, then what causes the desire?

3·3·39 (399)
कामादीतरत्र तत्र च आयतनादिभ्यः
kāmāditaratra tatra ca āyatanādibhyaḥ

kāmādi—the cause of desire; itaratra—in the other; tatra—thereafter; ca—also (the other into the cause); āyatana—the abode or resting place; ādibhyaḥ—the two causes (being the mutual resting places for the other cause).

TRANSLATION

The cause of desire (causes the desire) in the other; thereafter, also (the reverse happens). The two causes become the resting place for the other.

COMMENTARY

In the previous sūtra, we discussed how the feminine rests within the masculine as power, and He feels powerful. This is the unmanifest state of the material creation. However, it is also a contented and self-satisfied state. But sometimes, the self-satisfied state leads to a desire. What causes the desire?

The answer is that either the will or the power can produce the desire. Sometimes the feeling of being powerful creates a desire in the masculine. This is a common experience in all of us—when our body is strong, then desire is automatically produced in us. When the body becomes weak, then all desire vanishes. Thus, a healthy and strong person will develop many kinds of desires; and the same person, when sick will feel listless and devoid of all desires. Conversely, sometimes the desire is created first. This desire then agitates the power, and the person who was feeling rested earlier now feels powerful. Once this feeling of power is created in us, the will is also strengthened. Thus, through a mutual causation either will or power can be the other's cause.

The cause of desire is the *kāmādi*. The Lord is predominantly cause of desire in the material world, and His Sakti is predominantly the cause of desire in the spiritual world. This sūtra doesn't draw this distinction between the material and the spiritual worlds. It just says that the cause of desire evokes the desire in the other by entering the other. In this regard, we can note that there are different kinds of desires in the masculine and the feminine. The feminine desire is to be desired; the Lord's Śakti wants the Lord to be attracted toward Her. The masculine desire is not the desire to be desired, and so, the Lord is self-satisfied. However, He is still attracted to the Śakti not to feel attractive, but to fulfill the desire in His Śakti. Since the Lord is self-satisfied, therefore, He is said to be superior. But since the Śakti can cause Him to develop a desire, so She is said to be superior. The feminine is superior because She has the power to agitate the Lord. And the Lord is superior because She craves for His attention.

Even in this world, we see that women are attracted to confident and contented men. Women want to be desired and pursued by such confident men.

But they don't like the men who come off as being needy or dependent. So, there is a contradiction in a woman's desire—she wants to be pursued, but the pursuer should not be needy. In fact, the woman would like to think that the man is totally self-satisfied when it comes to other women, but she has the power to agitate even this self-satisfied man, so she must be very special. Therefore, women try to be attractive to agitate and tempt the confident and contented men, but they get angry if some needy man is attracted thereby.

In the same way, the Lord's Śakti is attracted to the Lord precisely because He is not attracted to anything—He is totally self-satisfied and contented. The Śakti wants the self-satisfied Lord to be agitated by the desire for Her. The Lord is not needy or dependent. But He enjoys being attractive to the devotee.

The feminine desire arises in a need, and the masculine desire arises in a want. In the material world, this need is perverted, and some women pursue men because they need the man's riches, power, influence, etc. But this is not the real need. The real need is to be wanted. Therefore, women who have material riches, power, and influence, still need a man to want them. This need to be wanted exists even in the spiritual world and characterizes the feminine. Similarly, even though the Lord is self-contented, He is also chivalrous. When He sees that a devotee needs Him, His chivalry creates a desire in Him. The impersonalist thinks that if the Lord has desire, then He must be needy. But the Lord is not needy, although He is chivalrous. If the devotee expresses neediness, then the Lord's chivalry creates a want in Him. But if the devotee turns away from the Lord, then the Lord remains self-satisfied. The Lord doesn't initiate the loving relationship with the devotee. He has no desire to dominate or control anybody else because He is self-satisfied. But if the devotee demonstrates a neediness and dependence on the Lord, then the Lord responds.

The difference between the feminine and the masculine is neediness and chivalry. The feminine need is to be wanted, and the masculine want is to be needed. This is seen in this world too, so, by the knowing of the nature of love between men and women, we can understand the Lord and His Śakti.

Topic 26

QUESTION

Your descriptions of the masculine and feminine aspects of the Absolute Truth are dangerously close to the materialistic ideas of sexuality. Isn't it risky to describe the Absolute Truth in this way because it can seem to justify the male-female attachment in this world, which then repeats the cycle of birth and death? How can we say that this understanding leads to transcendence?

3.3.40 (400)

आदरादलोपः

ādarādalopaḥ

ādarāt—due to respect; alopaḥ—there is no (need for) cessation.

TRANSLATION

Due to respect, there is no (need for) the cessation (of sexual desires).

COMMENTARY

There is a famous saying—Everything in this world is about sex, except sex itself; sex itself is about power. The foundation of material sex life is control, domination, and authority. All manifestations of this controlling mentality—such as those seen in politics, management, etc.—are modifications of the material sex desire. The controlling mindset is not the expression of confidence and self-satisfaction. It is rather the expression of neediness and dependency. The dominant person needs to be loved, but they express their need as domination, because they don't want to show that they are factually needy of others.

The sexual interaction between the Divine Couple is not based on domination; the feminine is self-sufficient, and yet She wants the masculine to desire Her. The masculine is self-satisfied, but due to that self-satisfaction He is also compassionate and loving. There is a subtle but important difference between the self-satisfied nature of the masculine, and the self-sufficient nature of the feminine. The self-satisfied person has the capacity for making everyone happy, and the self-sufficient person has the capacity for fulfilling their desires. The feminine cannot dominate the masculine because He is self-satisfied. And the masculine cannot dominate the feminine because She is self-sufficient. The central theme of materialistic sex life—i.e., domination—is, hence absent.

This separation between desire and power is crucial to the process of divine love. She is powerful, and He is desire. The feminine doesn't dominate the masculine because She wants the masculine to desire Her. The masculine is love, but He doesn't need to dominate anyone because He is self-satisfied. In fact, the self-satisfied nature of the masculine produces love in Him. Thus, there are two archetypes—the wanting to love, and the needing to be loved. Their interaction is based on love, rather than the desire to dominate or exert control.

In the material world, when men are dominant, they already have the power and riches to attract the women; the women are attracted to them because they are weak and seek a man to give them power. In short, men have both desire and power, while the women have desire, but no power. This results in the exploitation of women by the men. Conversely, when women are dominant, they already have the power and riches to attract the men; the men are attracted to them because they are weak, and they need the women to provide them power. In this case, women have both desire and power, and the men only have desire. This results in the exploitation of the men by the women.

The situation in the spiritual world is different. The feminine is already powerful; She doesn't need power from the masculine. But She wants to be desired and loved by the masculine. When She needs the masculine, She doesn't become powerless; but She wants the masculine's love. Likewise, the masculine is self-satisfied, and doesn't need anything from anyone else, including the power from the feminine. But when the feminine needs, He loves Her.

The comparisons between the loving affairs of the Divine Couple and mundane sex life are misplaced. In fact, if one understands the nature of their love, all materialistic sex desires are naturally destroyed. This sūtra states that there is ādara or 'respect' between the Divine Couple. This can be seen in contrast to the material sex life of domination where this mutual respect is missing. The feminine knows that the masculine is self-satisfied and doesn't need anyone; there is hence gratitude when the masculine desires Her. The masculine also knows that the feminine is self-sufficient and doesn't need anything from Him other than His love. He is honored to be desiring a self-sufficient person. This mutual respect and gratitude between the Divine Couple differentiates their loving dealings from those of the materialistic sex life of ordinary couples.

QUESTION

Even if we say that the loving affair between the Divine Couple is different from material sexuality, doesn't it still entail a sexual union between Them?

3.3.41 (401)

उपस्थितेऽतःतद्वचनात्

upasthite'taḥ tadvacanāt

upasthite—secondary presence; ataḥ—therefore; tat-vacanāt—from their words.

TRANSLATION

From their words (spoken by the source and comprehended by the other), therefore, a secondary presence (within each other).

COMMENTARY

Material ideas of sexuality involve physical intercourse between the masculine and the feminine. But such ideas of intercourse are rejected here. Earlier it was stated that the Lord impregnates the material energy simply by glancing at Her. When our senses perceive the object, there is an impression of the object in our senses, and an impression of the senses in the object. We normally understand that by seeing an object we get an impression of the object. But why should the observer be present in the observed reality? The reason is that before the knowledge from the object is transferred into the observer, the object must know which observer the knowledge must be sent to. This mutual identification of the source and destination of the knowledge is called 'entanglement' in atomic theory: Energy is transferred only when the destination is identified at the source. This identification is fixed by the senses entering the object to perceive them. Similarly, in this sūtra it is said that the sexual intercourse between the masculine and the feminine is just like the words being spoken. When the words are spoken, there is an impression of the meaning in the receiver, and an impression of the listener—to whom the meaning is intended—in the receiver. Therefore, words are not spoken without knowing the listener. We speak always keeping in mind the intended listener. Sometimes when we talk to ourselves, we may be the intended listener. Or, we may have the imaginary presence of someone else two whom we imagine to be talking. In either case, there is an intended listener. So, the listener is within the speaker before speaking, and the speaker is within the listener after speaking. The listener and speaker enter each other, but this doesn't constitute physical sexual intercourse.

The sexual intercourse between the Divine Couple is looking at each other, talking to each other, understanding each other, desiring each other, and giving something pleasing to each other. They enter each other because they are the source and destination of meaning, and this source and destination must be present within each other for any communication to occur between them.

Topic 27

QUESTION

But isn't it possible that the cause of desire isn't external; that the desire can also arise internally? Why do we say that the cause of desire injects a desire in the other, whereupon the result of the desire is fulfilled? Could we not also say that the desire arises automatically whereupon it is being fulfilled?

3.3.42 (402)

तन्नरि्धारणानयिमःतद्दृष्टेःपृथग्ध्यप्रतबिन्धःफलम्

tannirdhāraṇāniyamaḥ taddṛṣṭeḥ pṛthagdhyapratibandhaḥ phalam

tat-nirdhāraṇa-aniyamaḥ—no rule in deciding that (i.e., what comes first); tat-dṛṣṭeḥ—upon seeing that; pṛthak—separate (person); hi—certainly; apratibandhaḥ—no restriction; phalam—the effect (being the cause).

TRANSLATION

There is no rule in deciding that (which comes first); upon seeing that separate (person), certainly there is no restriction of the effect (being the cause).

COMMENTARY

When we look at the world, then the world can sometimes create a desire in us. Alternately, the desire can arise without an external provocation, and it can then be fulfilled by the world. Since both alternatives are possible, it is hard to say whether the world creates a desire in us and then fulfills it, or whether the desire arises first is then is fulfilled by it. The world can be the cause of the desire, and the desire can be the effect. Likewise, the desire can be the cause, and changes to the world can be the effect. Such alternatives cannot be fixed universally, but they are always fixed in a context. In the same way, the feminine can be the cause of instigating the masculine into a desire; in this case, She is the cause and the desire in Him is the effect. Conversely, the desire can arise automatically in the masculine, and She can be the effect that follows the cause—i.e., fulfills the desire. Due to this reciprocal model of causality, it is hard to say which comes first—the desire in the masculine or the power in the feminine. In between these two, there is no 'original cause'; they are hence said to be collectively understood as the Original Truth, not prior to one another.

Topic 28

QUESTION

But if the desire can arise in either masculine or feminine, why don't we say that these desires are selfish? That each side wants to satisfy themselves, and therefore, this interaction is just like the mundane worldly sexual activity?

3.3.43 (403)
प्रदानवदेव तदुक्तम्
pradānavadeva taduktam uktam

pradānavat—just like an offering; eva—certainly; tat–those; uktam—words (which are spoken, and then enter the listener).

TRANSLATION

(Because) those words (which are spoken and then enter the listener) are certainly like an offering (of a devout into the fire as in the case of a yajñá).

COMMENTARY

The process of yajñá is divided into three components—Soma or the offering, Agni or the fire, and Vayu or the process of offering. Soma indicates desire, pleasure, what we like, etc. Agni indicates the cause, reason, or purpose for which we sacrifice our desire, pleasure, or what we like. All of us make sacrifices to achieve something—e.g., you may work hard to earn some money, sacrificing your energy and personal time. To get something, we give away something. This is the principle of material exchange: The desire arises before the sacrifice is made. But in the process of love, which is also a yajñá, the sacrifice is made not to get anything, but simply to satisfy the receiver. The receiver also gives back, not to receive anything, but just to satisfy the giver. Thus, there are two kinds of sacrifices—in which one gives to receive, and the other in which one simply gives, without expectation of receiving anything. There is pleasure obtained in both cases, but the pleasure of selfish desire is generally unfulfilling because one provides only after calculating what they are going to receive.

Accordingly, there are two ways in which conversation can move. First, someone has a question, and they ask a question to get an answer. So, the questioner speaks first and demands an answer. The responder then provides an answer. Second, the questioner has a question but never asks. And yet, the responder simply answers the question by understanding that the questioner has a question that needs answering. Therefore, when desires are fulfilled after we ask, the process resembles a material transaction. However, when the desires are fulfilled even without asking, then the process is considered spiritual.

Thus, a first-class devotee is one who fulfills the Lord's desire without the Lord asking for it. The second-class devotee is one who fulfills the desire after it has been asked. And third-class devotee is one who counter questions, challenges, and demands an explanation—why should you desire this, and not that? How will I benefit from fulfilling your desire? Why should we not do this another way? Etc. If one asks submissively—e.g., Lord, I know you want something from me, but I'm not clear about it; can you please explain what I should be doing?—then he can be considered as good as a first-class devotee. Ultimately, such first-class devotees acquire a full understanding of the Lord, whereupon they don't even need to ask what the Lord wants. They automatically understand the desires in the Lord and fulfill them before He asks.

The Lord is also like that. He doesn't like asking anyone. Love is based on shyness—How can I demand? I'm already indebted by so many things I have received; how can I ask for more? Due to this shyness in the Lord, the conclusion of the scriptures—i.e., devotion to the Supreme Lord—is hidden from the non-devotees, because the Lord doesn't like to demand love from others. This conclusion is revealed only when someone asks: What is the greatest form of perfection? Such a seeker is a first-class devotee, although he may not know how to satisfy the Lord. The Lord then explains how He can be satisfied.

Topic 29

QUESTION

But we are talking about the Absolute Truth. If there is only shyness, then what about boldness? Is that considered to be absent in the Absolute Truth?

3.3.44 (404)

लिङ्गभूयस्त्वात् तद्धि बलीयःतदपि

liṅgabhūyastvāt taddhi balīyaḥ tadapi

liṅga-bhūyastvāt—because of presence of indicatory marks; tat—that (the Absolute Truth); hi—certainly; balīyaḥ—having boldness; tat—that; api—also.

TRANSLATION

That also; because of the presence of indicatory marks, that (the Absolute Truth) certainly (can be said to) possess boldness (not merely shyness).

COMMENTARY

Materialistic people are bold in asking for things but shy in giving back. The devotees are their opposite: There is shyness in asking, but boldness in giving. Due to this, the devotees give the Lord what He wants, even if He says: "Oh, it's not necessary". So, the combination of shyness in asking, and boldness in giving, constitutes a loving relation. The Lord is also shy in asking, but bold in giving. For a devotee, He gives without being asked, or even if the devotee says: "no I don't want". Thus, the devotee says to the Lord: "I don't want anything—not material prosperities, not respect and honor, not even liberation; I only want your loving devotion." And yet, the Lord gives to such a devotee everything—material prosperity, respect and honor, and liberation from the cycle of birth and death. The devotee out of shyness says: "I'm unqualified". This is not a fact, but it is also not pretentiousness. It is the genuine feeling in a devotee's heart, by which the devotee feels unqualified to serve the Lord, and yet, also feels gratitude at having obtained an opportunity to serve the Lord.

In the material world, boldness and humility are considered opposites. For example, most people think that talking politely is humility, and talking aggressively is boldness. But real boldness is giving up attachment to every material identity. And real humility is being ready to accept any kind of difficulty arising in the Lord's service. A devotee is both bold and humble—bold because he can leave this world even if there is happiness, and humble because he can stay in this world even if there are difficulties. The mundane visions of politeness and aggression are not the correct understandings of humility and boldness.

QUESTION

Several methods of spiritual advancement were mentioned earlier such as karma-yoga, jñāna-yoga, dhyāna-yoga, and bhakti-yoga (the performance of regulated devotional activities). The aim seems to be the combination of boldness in giving and shyness in asking. With this mood, can the other activities also be considered just like the loving relation within the Absolute Truth?

3·3·45 (405)

पूर्वविकल्पः प्रकरणात्स्यात्क्रिया मानसवत्

pūrvavikalpaḥ prakaraṇātsyātkriyā mānasavat

pūrva-vikalpaḥ—the earlier alternatives; prakaraṇāt—due to the context; syāt—may be; kriyā—a sacrifice; mānasavat—if they are the nature of the mind.

TRANSLATION

The earlier alternatives (which were prescribed) depending on the context (of a person), may be (considered) sacrifices if they are the nature of the mind.

COMMENTARY

The mind is responsible for understanding the meaning. This meaning comes in three forms— (1) universal, (2) contextual, and (3) individual. In different contexts, we might do different things, with different short-term goals. But there is a long-term goal or an overarching purpose. For example, we might get dressed, drive to work, attend meetings, do our assignments, etc. and each such activity involves a short-term goal, which are contextual goals. But there is also an overarching goal, namely, that we might want to earn money. We can call this the universal. But we can also ask: What do we do with this money? The answer is: We want to satisfy ourselves—the individual. Hence, there are contextual goals, universal goals, and individual goals. The context serves the universal, and the universal is pursued for the purposes of an individual.

In the same way, several contextual activities are prescribed for spiritual advancement—e.g., study scriptures, perform austerities, meditate on the Lord, and live a regulated life. The aim for all these contextual activities is a universal, which pervades throughout the activities—the idea of getting liberated from suffering and obtaining eternal happiness. But whose suffering and whose happiness? Generally, the answer is the individual self. Thus, contextual goals lead to the universal goal for happiness, but that universal is subordinate to an individual. The problem is simply in defining that individual person whose happiness is attained. We consider happiness as a universal goal, but we don't consider the person who embodies the universal happiness as the goal.

The true nature of the mind is that the universal is the knowledge of the Lord, the individual to be satisfied is the Lord, although the Lord can be satisfied differently in many contexts. If this mind is hidden, then a partial understanding of the universal is obtained. It is no longer the perfection of happiness but what I consider to be happiness. This partial understanding of happiness is then applied to the self—i.e., my happiness. And then all the contextual activities are tailored to selfish happiness. This is not the true nature of the mind. By the mind we can understand that happiness is a universal goal. But what is that type of happiness that exists in everyone must also be understood. If this happiness is understood, then the goal of happiness is the person who embodies this primordial notion of happiness, which pervades in everyone. If the mind is restricted in this understanding, then the universal is applied to the self.

There is hence a difference between *mānas* and *manas*—the former means 'mental', and the latter means 'mind'. The former represents the pure, primordial, and expansive mind, whereas the latter is the small and restricted mind. The great mind aims for the highest goal, the highest truth, and the highest relation. The limited mind seeks smaller goals, smaller truths, and smaller relationships. The minds of people in this world are mostly very small; they are not even interested in their spiritual well-being. They only care about the body. Somewhat more expansive is the mind that seeks liberation from the material suffering. And even more expansive is that mind which seeks to relate, to know, and to serve the Lord. This most expansive mind is the original mind, identified by *mānas*. The materialistic mind is produced by restricting the *mānas*.

QUESTION

You seem to be indicating that there are many kinds of minds. What do you mean by the great mind? How does it differ from the ordinary mind?

3.3.46 (406)
अतदिशाच्च
atideśācca

atideśāt—due to the reach to end of space; ca—also.

TRANSLATION

Due to the ability to reach to the end of space also (the mind is great).

COMMENTARY

The term *deśa* or space refers to the space of concepts or ideas. This space is very expansive, because it comprises all the concepts or ideas that can ever be understood. The soul has a position in this space which determines what we can understand. Things that are 'near' our mental state are cognized by us. Things are 'far' from our mental state cannot be understood by us. When a person has a small mind, there are things that he can and cannot understand. The person who has a great mind can reach to the limits of the space, which means that he can understand everything. Thus, there is nothing alien to him.

When one acquires devotion to the Lord, by understanding His nature, he also develops a very broad mind, that can comprehend any subject. People with a narrow mind can comprehend one subject—e.g., mathematics, physics, biology, economics, sociology, psychology, art, music, literature, etc. But the person with a broad mind can understand everything. People with a narrow mind can relate only to a specific culture, racial identification, social order, etc. But the person with a broad mind can relate to people in any culture, society, or racial denomination. Their ability to understand the expanses of space allows them to see the good and bad in everything. Hence, they can accept the goodness in any culture, just as they can reject the follies of any society. If they reject or criticize something in another culture, it is not because of malice toward others. However, those who have such attachments cannot appreciate their broadmindedness. They think that anyone offering criticism must be alien. For such people, whatever belongs to their culture is considered good, and whatever is alien to their culture is regarded as bad. They might blindly accept the follies in their culture as goodness, and think the goodness in the other cultures to be bad.

This sūtra says that a spiritually advanced person can go to the far ends of space. And by that reach, he doesn't consider himself to be restricted to a specific nation, society, or culture. This is the definition of broadmindedness.

QUESTION

Does this ability to know everything mean that they accept everything as the truth? Or, there is a difference between the meaning and the truth?

3.3.47 (407)
वदि्यैव तु नरि्धारणात्
vidyaiva tu nirdhāraṇāt

vidyā—knowing; eva—indeed; tu—but; nirdhāraṇāt—due to being fixed.

TRANSLATION

(They can) certainly know (everything) but (the perfect knowledge) is fixed (i.e., they don't accept everything known as the perfect knowledge).

COMMENTARY

Understanding everything doesn't mean accepting everything as true. The previous sūtra stated that the devotee of the Lord can understand everything. That doesn't mean he appreciates, likes, desires, or considers it true. He can distinguish between the diversities which are partially true, and the Absolute Truth, which is completely true. Even these partial truths have their purpose in the Lord. Therefore, the devotee can engage everything in the Lord's service. But in this engagement, he doesn't become attracted, attached, or bound to those partially true things, and doesn't become influenced by them. For example, a devotee can use wealth in the Lord's service, but he doesn't become attached to the wealth. Even though he may seem engaged in dealing with wealth, he is not like the ordinary person who is counting pennies. Likewise, a devotee can study many subject matters of the world and engage them in the Lord's service. But by this engagement he is not influenced by those ideas. He understands their place and role in knowledge, always accepting the Lord to be the Absolute Truth. Various fields of knowledge are contextually true, and hence they can be employed in different situations. This engagement with the world is said to be devotion if the mind is expanded in a way that even as everything is understood, only the Lord is accepted as the complete truth.

Ordinary people cannot distinguish between the engagement of the contextual knowledge in the Lord's service and the engagement with that knowledge. They think that everyone engaged with the worldly things, such as wealth and knowledge, must be just like the mundane people engaging with it. They urge others to reject these worldly diversities as they cannot see how the Absolute Truth exists within the diverse things. Their viewpoint amounts to the philosophy of māyāvāda in which the world is false, and transcendence is true.

QUESTION

The problem with diverse fields of knowledge is that they present different pictures of the world. Accordingly, those who think about these things with their minds also adopt these different viewpoints, which conflict with other views. Thus, it is said that philosophy cannot capture the whole truth. But you are saying that a broadminded person can understand things fully.

3.3.48 (408)

दर्शनाच्च

darśanācca

darśanāt—because the philosophy; ca—also (can be complete).

TRANSLATION

Because the philosophy can also (be complete) (therefore, we reject the idea that anything known by the mind must necessarily be incomplete).

COMMENTARY

The senses, the mind, and the intellect of this world are limited, and the sign of that limitation is that the whole truth cannot be understood. The impersonalist now attributes the problem to the existence of the senses, mind, intellect, itself, and claims that only when these are rejected is everything correctly known. This means that to attain transcendence, one must be devoid of perception, thought, judgment, etc. The devotees reject this conclusion. The material senses, mind, and intellect are certainly limited. But there are also pure senses, mind, and intellect which can see the whole truth. The material world can be characterized as the partial knowledge of parts. For example, we might look at a table—which is a part—and then know it partially (e.g., we may not know how the carpenter created it, where the wood for the table was sourced, etc.). The spiritual world is characterized either as the partial or the full knowledge of the whole. Even if a devotee knows the Lord incompletely, since the Lord is the whole truth, the devotee's knowledge is considered transcendence. Of course, the devotees who know the Lord well, also come close to knowing Him completely. There is no limit to our understanding of the Lord, and anyone can obtain a full understanding. Therefore, philosophy is also not limited. Our minds can, however, be limited if we remain unprepared to know the full truth. The shortfall in our mind and intellect cannot be imputed back to philosophy, i.e., just because our mind and intellect cannot grasp the whole truth, we cannot say that the problem lies with philosophy. That is a sour-grapes mentality in which when we fail to do something, we claim that it must be impossible. By pushing the problem elsewhere, we avoid the effort necessary for understanding. So, calling something unknowable is just a symptom of laziness and ineptitude, compounded with the arrogance that it could never be my shortcoming.

QUESTION

But many people cite scriptures (or the statements of those who are considered equivalent to the scriptures) that the full truth cannot be known through philosophy, although they accept that can be known by experience. What would you say in regard to such claims that are based on scriptures?

3.3.49 (409)

श्रुत्यादिबलीयस्त्वाच्च न बाधः

śrutyādibalīyastvācca na bādhaḥ

śrutyādi-balīyastvāt—on the strength of the scriptures etc. and others just like it; ca—also; na bādhaḥ—cannot be refuted, or there is no restriction.

TRANSLATION

On the strength of scriptures or others just like it also (the claim about philosophical knowledge being complete) cannot be refuted or isn't restricted.

COMMENTARY

In previous sūtras it was stated that those with the purified mind can know the full truth. This purification is achieved by devotion to the Lord because the basic impurity in the soul is self-centeredness and from that narrowing of the purpose of life from the Lord to the self. Further narrowness is subsequently produced—e.g., preoccupation with the body and its well-being. When the mind is narrowed in many ways, it is impossible to comprehend the full truth. And philosophizing then becomes useless because we are unable to think beyond our limited existence. But if the soul gives up the self-centered approach to life and becomes the Lord's devotee, then it is fully purified. Thereafter, there is no restriction to the philosophical understanding. Nevertheless, because many people engage in philosophy with a self-centered and restricted mind, the scriptures often state that one should give up philosophizing and become the Lord's devotee. It is true that an unpurified mind cannot grasp the whole truth, and without devotion the Lord cannot be known. However, it is incorrect to say that even a purified devotee also cannot explain the Absolute Truth. Those who cannot see the difference between the pure and the impure mind take such scriptural statements—that urge a person to only focus on devotion—as a universal rejection of the philosophical understanding. They claim that it is in principle impossible to state the nature of the Absolute Truth. They draw a false equivalence between a limited mind, which cannot understand the full truth to the mind of the devotee who can perceive and explain this truth.

This sūtra rejects the idea that the Absolute Truth cannot be explained philosophically. Even if there are statements in the scriptures, or by others whose words are considered equivalent to the scriptures, they are only meant to push a person toward purification of the mind before they attempt philosophy. Philosophizing without devotion can never be complete. But the converse is also true: Devotion without a philosophical understanding is incomplete. Therefore, those who claim to be devotees but cannot explain the nature of the Absolute Truth—citing the inability of philosophical expression to capture the nature of this truth—cannot be considered perfected devotees. The contradiction between devotion and philosophy exists only for the imperfect devotees. This contradiction is dissolved for the advanced devotee because for him everything that can be directly experienced can also be explained philosophically.

The supposed contradiction between faith in the Lord through devotion and the philosophical explanation through reason is at the root of many faults in religious practices today. Those who have no understanding of the Absolute Truth often feign devotion to the Lord. And because they claim that the Absolute Truth cannot be known by reason, there is no way to check their understanding. They pass on as perfect devotees while carrying numerous imperfections. They remain narrow-minded while talking about the Absolute Truth. Their followers also remain devoted to them fanatically because there is no way to know if the person is truly advanced as they keep appealing to their private experience without being able to explain this experience to anyone else. The genuine seekers should not be cheated by such pretentious spiritualists.

QUESTION

But there is a fundamental contention between devotion and knowledge. Those pursuing knowledge say that the devotees are unintelligent and emotional. And the devotees then cite scriptures and say that the Lord is known only through devotion. How do we reconcile this basic contradiction?

3.3.50 (410)

अनुबन्धादिभ्यःप्रज्ञान्तरपृथक्त्ववत् दृष्टश्च तदुक्तम्

anubandhādibhyaḥ prajñāntarapṛthaktvavat dṛṣṭaśca taduktam

anubandhādibhyaḥ—beginning with the subordinate binding (to the Lord); prajñāntara—knowledge appears within; pṛthaktvavat—as if they were different from each other; dṛṣṭaḥ—are seen; ca—and; tat-uktam—that (the understanding obtained by devotion) is then spoken (through philosophy).

TRANSLATION

Beginning with the subordinate binding (to the Lord), knowledge of the many seeming diversities (which are not truly separated) appears within as they are perceived (by direct experience). That (the understanding obtained by direct experience) is then spoken of (as the philosophical presentations).

COMMENTARY

After the previous sūtra rejected the claims of not being able to explain the Absolute Truth philosophically, this sūtra says that devotion to the Lord comes first. When someone becomes a devotee of the Lord, knowledge appears within as revelation. In this revelation, the diversity is only superficial because there is also a unity. The diverse views of the philosophers become incomplete parts of the whole truth. If this direct experience is obtained, the same understanding is then presented as philosophical conclusions to those who aren't yet devotees, who may not have obtained the inner revelation, or who may be baffled by the varieties of mutually contradictory philosophical positions. Therefore, the discovery of knowledge is through revelation. But that knowledge can be verified philosophically. Thus, one who knows the truth can use philosophy to explain the Absolute Truth, and others can learn the Absolute Truth from this expression of revelation. Since it is presented philosophically, the revelation can also be verified rationally. But if someone doesn't know, and doesn't obtain the knowledge through such revealed sources, and only searches for the truth by philosophical speculation, then knowledge can never be obtained. This is the difference between discovery and verification: Devotion is needed for discovery; philosophy for verification. However, since everything revealed can also be stated clearly and verified by reason, therefore, one must not blindly accept the claims about revelation unless they can also be verified rationally.

Scientists too have revelations: They get answers in dreams, or in spurts of insights that weren't preceded by a step-by-step process of reasoning. But such revelation isn't considered science unless it is explained through a logical argument. That logical argument may not be how they saw it initially. But it is necessary that all revelations must be formulated logically for it to be called science. A dream or hallucination is no less clear than the waking experience, and private revelations stand on par with such dreams and hallucinations. Just like we are convinced that we have a dream, but upon waking up we reason about it, and conclude that it was merely a dream. Similarly, if we want to be sure that a revelation is truth, rather than a dream or hallucination, it must be verifiable. This verification is not just important for others; it is equally important for each person who has this revelation to know that it wasn't a hallucination.

QUESTION

Many people claim that if they join a religious practice, and they follow the behaviors of devotees, then there is no need for philosophical understanding because a devotee automatically attains the Lord's abode. Then there are others who emphasize philosophy too much and are constantly engaged in debates with others, which may distract them from devotion. There are hence extremes of devotion without knowledge and knowledge without devotion.

3.3.51 (411)

न सामान्यादपि उपलब्धेःमृत्युवत् नहि लोकापत्तिः

na sāmānyādapi upalabdheḥ mṛtyuvat nahi lokāpattiḥ

na—not; sāmānyāt-api—despite the similarity; upalabdheḥ—is obtained; mṛtyuvat—upon death; na hi lokāpattiḥ—nor by worldly objections.

TRANSLATION

(Perfection) is not obtained, despite the similarity (of one's actions to those of the perfected souls) upon death (if they lack a perfect understanding). (Conversely, this understanding is) also not limited by the worldly objections.

COMMENTARY

Two extreme situations are discussed here. First, one may pursue some religious practices but not develop an understanding of the Absolute Truth. This sūtra states that although such people look like the pure devotees, the Lord's abode is not attained by them. Second, one may present this knowledge to others, but people may reject it. This sūtra states that such objections do not restrict a devotee's entry into the Lord's abode. These two extreme situations arise due to contradictory requirements. First, we say that something is not true if one claims to have divine experiences, but these cannot be explained rationally. Second, we say that even if we explain something rationally, many people may not accept it, either because they cannot understand it or because despite understanding it, they don't want to accept its truth. In the first case, a lot of people believe that a person is a devotee, but he is not. In the second case, a lot of people think that a person is not a devotee, but he is. Therefore, the criterion for entry into the Lord's abode is neither the superficial appearance of devotion (and the acceptance by many people), nor a superficial rejection of a devotee (by those who are not well-accepted by many—especially if they accept superficial devotees). Thus, popular consensus by many people is rejected as the qualification and popular rejection is not a disqualification. Not knowing and being popular is not qualifying and knowing but being unpopular is not disqualifying. On both sides, the sūtra rejects the opinion of the common ignorant people.

QUESTION

If popular opinion is rejected, then how does one know themselves to be advanced? Both direct experience and philosophical quests are being rejected as incomplete—direct experience because it could be a hallucination, and philosophical quest because it doesn't alone lead one to the complete truth.

3.3.52 (412)

परेण च शब्दस्य तादविध्यम् भूयस्त्वात्त्वनुबन्धः

pareṇa ca śabdasya tādvidhyam bhūyastvāttvanubandhaḥ

pareṇa—the transcendental experience; ca—and; śabdasya—of the scriptures; tādvidhyam—the knowledge of that (can be obtained); bhūyastvāt—from their existence; tu—only if; anubandhaḥ—there is a connection.

TRANSLATION

The transcendental experience and the knowledge of those scriptures (is obtained) only if a connection exists (between them).

COMMENTARY

Many people say that they have seen God. But if we ask them how God looks like, they tend to give descriptions that don't conform to the scriptures. Likewise, many people study the scriptures, but they cannot see God, reject God's existence, or don't understand them. This sūtra states that only when both are present—i.e., direct experience according to the tenets of the scriptures, and the profound understanding of the scripture due to direct experience—can we say that the person is a devotee. The scriptures are the descriptions of direct experience, but we cannot understand the scriptures unless we have the experience ourselves—how can you know the meaning of ginger, unless you have tasted ginger? Likewise, if we have an experience that doesn't conform to the descriptions in the scriptures, then it is not divine. Thus, experience is needed to understand scripture, and scriptures are needed to confirm the experience.

The process of spiritual advancement is progressive and iterative. One begins by studying scriptures, and if initial conviction is obtained through a rational understanding, then one molds their life according to their tenets. But since the scriptures are incompletely understood in the beginning, one follows them incompletely or incorrectly. Even with a limited understanding, however, one progresses and acquires experiences by which the scripture becomes clearer. With that clarity, one molds their life again—this time with a slightly better understanding of the scripture. And that remolding leads to a better experience, which leads to a deeper understanding, and the process repeats until one obtains the full understanding along with experiential confirmation.

Topic 30

QUESTION

Are such devotees—who have both divine experience as well as complete understanding of the scriptures—found in the material world? Most of the so-called religious people seem to lack either of the two, and often both.

3.3.53 (413)

एक आत्मनःशरीरे भावात्

eka ātmanaḥ śarīre bhāvāt

eka—some; ātmanaḥ—of the soul; śarīre—bodily; bhāvāt—from existence.

TRANSLATION

From the bodily existence of some souls (we can say it is possible).

COMMENTARY

The use of the term *eke* indicates that the perfected souls are rare. While many people practice religion, they either don't have any spiritual experience, or those who have some spiritual experience lack a perfect understanding of the scriptures. In fact, many who have had some religious or mystical experience consider that to be the ultimate truth; they distort the understanding of the scriptures to fit that experience, denying themselves the chance to obtain greater perfection, and misleading others into believing that their experience is the ultimate truth. A follower is limited by the guidance of a teacher. If the teacher is imperfect, then the student necessarily is limited by the teacher's perfection. Since the perfect teachers are very rare, finding such a teacher, and then learning from them, becomes the difficult prerogative of the student.

This is, however, not a denial of the existence of perfected souls. Perfect knowledge always exists, and perfected souls are always present. Such souls, however, may not always be popular. As noted in the earlier sūtra, many such souls with perfect realization are often rejected by society, because the society is not seeking such perfect knowledge. When this happens, then the Lord advents to make the perfect truth popular again. But even if the Lord hasn't appeared, and the truth is not popular, the truth always exists. If a seeker is sincere, then he can find such knowers of truth. Popularity of the truth is an extra facility provided by the Lord's appearance, and many people accept the truth simply because it is popular. However, if the truth is unpopular, then the seeker must make additional effort to find the teacher of the unpopular truth.

QUESTION

Why do you say that such devotees are rare? Isn't religion and transcendence meant for everyone? Why should it be hard if it is meant for everyone?

3.3.54 (414)
व्यतिरेकः तद्भावाभावित्वात् न तु उपलब्धिवत्
vyatirekaḥ tadbhāvābhāvitvāt na tu upalabdhivat

vyatirekaḥ—different; tadbhāva-abhāvitvāt—feeling the absence of that nature (the Absolute Truth); na—not; tu—but; upalabdhivat—as if obtained.

TRANSLATION

Understanding that the Lord is different from them, feeling His absence, but not (feeling His absence) as if (the Lord is) already obtained.

COMMENTARY

This sūtra describes why true devotees are rare. Generally, we suppose that if we are seeing something, then we cannot be separated from it. Conversely, if we are separated then we cannot see that thing. But the pure devotee lives in a paradoxical state—he constantly feels separated from the Lord, and due to that separation constantly thinks of the Lord. The example of an Indian bride is sometimes given to illustrate this point. She goes to her husband's house, but everyone seems strange. Meanwhile, the husband has left the house and gone to a far-off land on business. The wife behaves politely with her husband's family members, but in her heart, she constantly remembers her husband. The husband is at once present and absent. The material union is based on the body, and the spiritual union is based on the senses and the mind. In a dream, our senses and the mind can see things, even though the body cannot touch them. The devotee relies on this fact, and even when the body is separated, his senses and the mind are united with the Lord—just like a vision in a dream.

Now, the materialists like to say: If you are seeing God just like we see dreams, then God must be your hallucination. To this, the simple answer is that there is nothing wrong in having a hallucination if it lasts permanently and is always pleasing. What is so great about your impermanent and painful reality anyway? In fact, the definition of hallucination is that it appears and disappears, that it may sometimes be pleasing and sometimes be painful. By that definition of hallucination, the materialistic reality is a hallucination because it appears and disappears, and it is sometimes pleasing and sometimes painful. So, the materialist argument about hallucination works against the materialist.

Factually, the devotees don't consider the material world a hallucination. The waking experience involves the body, along with the senses and the mind. The dreaming experience only involves the senses and the mind. If we can see things that the body is not in contact with, then this reinforces the idea that the seer is different from the body. The materialist likes to think that there is no seer apart from the body, but he cannot explain the origin of dreams, where you can see things that have never been seen previously in this life. Since they were never seen before, therefore, they cannot be the resurrection of memory stored in the brain. It follows that our seeing is not limited to the body. Therefore, the dreaming experience is considered superior to the waking experience in Vedic philosophy because it leads to the view that there is more to our existence than the body. Now, the materialist says that these dreams are simply chemical activity in the brain, and you are not factually seeing anything. But if that is the case, then even the waking experience must only be chemical activity in the brain, and whatever you call reality is only your brain hallucination.

Since materialists like to claim that God's vision is a hallucination, as a counterargument, it is sometimes said that whatever mechanism makes God's experience a hallucination, also makes everything else you consider a reality a hallucination. Therefore, you cannot call God's experience a hallucination and claim a reality for everything else. What you call science, or measurement and observation, must also be hallucinations created by your brain chemicals.

Now, we must remember that this is not a factual acceptance of the world as a hallucination. It is simply a reductio ad absurdum demonstration of the fact that if you say that God's experience is a hallucination, then by extension every other experience also becomes a hallucination. If God doesn't exist due to hallucination, then matter also doesn't exist due to hallucination. If matter doesn't exist, then hallucination cannot be created out of thin air. Therefore, by claiming hallucination, the argument undercuts the existence of hallucination. The materialist argument can thus be silenced by this counterargument.

But the clever impersonalist exploits this line of argumentation. He says: We accept your suggestion that both the vision of God and the vision of the world are hallucinations. Since these are all hallucinations, therefore, only the observer is real, and the diversity of observers simply arises due to the difference of bodies, therefore, even this diversity must be unreal. This argument cannot be refuted based on evidence, because whatever evidence you provide against it would be termed a hallucination. Therefore, the correct response to such an argument is: What is wrong with hallucination if it is permanent and always pleasing? Isn't it true that by your doctrine of impersonal oneness you are trying to attain eternal happiness? From what you say, it seems that you must die to obtain that oneness, but the devotee can attain it right now.

Topic 31

QUESTION

Do such devotees ultimately give up the different branches of knowledge and practices for spiritual attainment, and focus only upon the Lord?

3·3·55 (415)

अङ्गावबद्धास्तु न शाखासु हि प्रतिवेदम्

aṅgāvabaddhāstu na śākhāsu hi prativedam

aṅgāvabaddhāḥ—as a part is tightly bound (to the next bigger part); tu—but; na—not; śākhāsu—in the branches; hi—because; prativedam—everything known must be known in relation or connection to the Absolute Truth.

TRANSLATION

Just as a part (e.g., a leaf) is tightly bound (to the next bigger part—e.g., a branch) but still not (bound) in the branches because ultimately everything must be known only in relation or connection to the Absolute Truth.

COMMENTARY

The devotion to the Supreme Lord is the root, while the various other processes of spiritual advancement are like branches of the tree. One begins with the branches, and slowly proceeds to the roots. However, this sūtra states that the devotee is connected to the branches and yet not connected. The connection to the branch is that the devotee doesn't give up the prescribed duties which are like contextual services to the Lord. And yet, He is not bound to these services, because the devotee's goal is ultimately to please the Lord. Thus, for instance, a scientist can keep doing science as their prescribed duty; but they are no longer bound by science, as their goal is to serve the Supreme Lord. Hence, the devotee doesn't renounce the activities that he is capable of through the body and mind, and yet, he doesn't remain attached to those activities.

The use of the term *prativedam* is illustrative; *prati* means 'mutual' or 'toward', and *vedam* means 'knowledge'. By knowing the Lord, we know ourselves, and by knowing ourselves fully, we know the Lord, because the Lord as the cause is present in the effect (the soul), and the soul as the effect emerges from the cause (the Lord). From the perspective of the soul, the term *prati* can indicate understanding the Lord as the soul is directed toward the Lord. Or, it can also mean mutual understanding—i.e., understanding the self along with the source of the self. The terms *anga* or 'parts' and śākhā or 'branches' further clarify this idea: the parts have emanated from the whole, so the whole is the cause and the parts are the effect. However, the whole is present in the part as the cause is present in the effect. Thus, by knowing the cause, we can know the effect. And by knowing the effect, we can know the cause. This is mutual knowledge. Nothing is completely known unless the complete is known.

QUESTION

But the different spiritual paths also required different kinds of practices. For example, the different branches of the Vedic system prescribe the chanting of different mantras. How can we say that in the practice of all these different paths, only the Absolute Truth is worshipped by these types of practices?

3.3.56 (416)

मन्त्रादिवद्वाऽविरोधः

mantrādivadvā'virodhaḥ

mantrādivat—like mantra etc.; vā—even; avirodhaḥ—is no contradiction.

TRANSLATION

Even if the (different) mantra (are chanted) there is no contradiction.

COMMENTARY

Every attribute can be applied to the Lord, but not to every other object. For example, if we say that the Lord is honest, then the claim is true. But even if we say that the Lord is a thief, the claim is true. If we say that the Lord is monogamous, it is true. But even if we say that the Lord is polygamous, it is true. If we say that the Lord is kind, then it is true. But even if we say that the Lord is cruel, it is considered true (the Vraja residents accuse the Lord of being cruel).

All these qualities—honest vs. dishonest, monogamous vs. polygamous, kind vs. cruel—are meanings. The object to which these properties are applied can be ordinary people, or the Supreme Lord. When most people chant mantras described in the different branches of the scriptures, they think that the mantras refer to different personalities, such as the Sun, Moon, stars, demigods, etc. This is not entirely false, because the meanings being attributed to such personalities are indeed their qualities. But this doesn't mean that the Lord is devoid of these qualities and the mantra cannot be applied to Him. For example, the Gayatri mantra states—"I worship that personality which illuminates the three worlds (*bhū, bhuvar* and *svarga*), one whose energy is seen in morning light, one who makes the demigods shine with splendor, and who is the cause, origin, and instigator of everything." The sun-god Sūrya is not mentioned, but because of the mention of 'morning light', most people tend to associate this mantra with Sūrya. However, one can even chant this mantra, pronouncing the same words and meanings, but with a different *reference*—the Supreme Lord, because He is indeed illuminating the entire world, is the cause of the entire world, and He is the powerful behind all the powerful. This is the fundamental property of the tree—the leaves are properties of the branches, the branches are properties of the trunk, and the trunk is a property of the root. Therefore, even the leaf can be called a property of the root, although there are branches in between.

In previous sūtras we saw how the Lord was said to be the origin of space, and since the entire space exists within Him, therefore, every point in space is a property of the origin and is defined in relation to that origin. This is the nature of the whole-part reality that the diverse locations in space are not separated from the origin, and yet, they are not identical to the origin. Like a property is different from an object, and yet the property is not separate from the object (you cannot separate the mass of a particle from the particle, and yet, the particle is not the mass), similarly, everything is a property of the Lord.

The difference is simply in the reference of meanings. The non-devotees think that they are praising different personalities by describing different qualities. And the devotee thinks that he is praising the Supreme Lord by describing the same qualities. The meanings are identical, but the reference is different. The impersonalist thinks that by using the term nirguna he is describing Brahman, which is devoid of qualities. But the devotee says that nirguna means one who is not bound by material nature, and that is the Supreme Lord. So, the impersonalist feels detachment by calling the Brahman nirguna. But the devotee feels ecstasy by praising the Lord as nirguna. For the impersonalist, if something is nirguna, then it cannot be saguna. But for the devotee, the Lord is also bound by the love of His devotees. So, He is free if someone tries to force Him. But He is bound if someone tries to love Him. These terms nirguna and saguna are not contradictory for the devotee. Therefore, the devotee can chant the mantra which uses the word nirguna just as He can chant the mantra that uses the word saguna. There is no fault in any mantra, if the reference is the Supreme Lord, rather than demigods, etc. This too is pure devotion to the Lord.

Topic 32

QUESTION

But even if many mantras can be attributed to the Lord, there are also many mantras which directly name the respective deities. How can we say that even such mantras don't need to be abandoned since you have previously said that the demigod worship must be abandoned for devotion to the Lord?

3.3.57 (417)

भूम्नःक्रतुवज्ज्यायस्त्वं तथा हि दर्शयति

bhūmnaḥ kratuvajjyāyastvaṃ tathā hi darśayati

bhūmnaḥ—generally; kratuvat—as in the case of sacrifice; jyāyastvaṃ—the most excellent; tathā—so; hi—certainly; darśayati—sees.

TRANSLATION

Generally, even in the case of sacrifices, the most excellent (is worshipped), so, certainly (the most excellent) is always seen (to be worshipped).

COMMENTARY

The demigod worship was previously rejected. But now a caveat is being added, namely, that when the Supreme Lord is worshipped, the worship of the demigods is like worshipping the root of the tree along with the branches and leaves. By implication, we can understand that the previous rejection was that of demigod worship alone. The key point is that no activity needs to be rejected (unless it is explicitly forbidden) if the Lord is added to that activity. It is a general practice that the demigods are never worshipped without the Lord. This general trend is called *bhūmnaḥ* or 'mostly' here. Thus, for instance, the Lord is offered flowers first, following which even the demigods are offered flowers.

When the demigods are thus worshipped along with the Lord, it is understood that the main person being worshipped is the Lord, and the others are secondary to Him. Because the Lord is present, it is understood that unless otherwise specified, everything said is about Him. Even if some things are not said about Him, by calling out others, they are only said after the Lord is worshipped.

Topic 33

QUESTION

The impersonalist also echoes a similar idea. Many of them say that whenever any demigod is worshipped, the Supreme Lord is worshipped. Therefore, these names of demigods are many ways to reference the same personality, and one can choose whatever name or mantra one wants to worship the Lord. Are you indicating a similar approach, or do you disagree with such a claim?

3.3.58 (418)

नाना शब्दादिभेदात्

nānā śabdādibhedāt

nānā—different; śabdādi-bhedāt—owing to difference of words etc.

TRANSLATION

(The demigods are) different, owing to the difference of words etc.

COMMENTARY

In the previous sūtra, the worship of demigods was endorsed provided they are always the secondary personalities being worshipped. This endorsement, however, doesn't equate to the claim that all these demigods are as good as the Supreme Lord, and there is no difference between their worships. This sūtra clearly states that the demigods are different from the Supreme Lord, otherwise, the names used to call them would be different. The names or words used to describe the demigods can denote three things—the role of a person, the qualities of a person, and the individual person. The qualities of the demigods can be applied to the Supreme Lord, and the Lord can also take the many positions occupied by the demigods. But the Supreme Lord doesn't become the same person as the demigods. The demigods are in a certain role, and have certain qualities, temporarily. The same qualities in the Lord are eternal, and if He wants, He can also accept the role eternally. Therefore, unless one claims that the Supreme Lord also has temporary qualities, any equivalence between the demigods and the Supreme Lord is false. An impersonalist, however, claims that the qualities in the Supreme Lord are products of material covering, which means that the Lord falls into matter and His qualities are not eternal. If one makes such a claim, then this sūtra states a clear difference between the two.

Topic 34

QUESTION

You have earlier said that the Lord can also be worshipped in the place of demigods, even for material gains. Now that you are saying that the demigods can be worshipped along with the Supreme Lord, were you indicating the worship of Supreme Lord alone, or the Supreme Lord with the demigods?

3.3.59 (419)
विकल्पःअविशिष्ट-फलत्वात्
vikalpaḥ aviśiṣṭa-phalatvāt

vikalpaḥ—alternative; aviśiṣṭa-phalatvāt—due to non-specific results.

TRANSLATION

(The Supreme Lord is) an alternative, due to non-specific results.

COMMENTARY

All our material results are given to us due to karma. However, since karma is like money, which can be spent in many ways, by performing the rites for demigods, one can find an alternative way of spending karma—different from what is currently being delivered or expected to be delivered. However, the Supreme Lord doesn't even entertain such requests, unlike the demigods. When a devotee asks the Lord for material benedictions, the Lord simply ignores it, and the results are delivered according to the direction of the demigods. Since the demigods are working according to the principles laid out by the Supreme Lord, the Lord doesn't interfere with their free will. After all, they too have the good karma to enjoy their freedom as they wish. If the Lord started interfering with every demigod's work, then those demigods won't be able to utilize their freedom. Therefore, the previous recommendations about worshipping the Supreme Lord for material gains were the worship of the demigods in the presence of the Supreme Lord. Such worship ensures that a person recognizes that even when the demigods are delivering the results, they are still subordinate to the Supreme Lord. Furthermore, this sūtra states that the Lord should be worshipped for "non-specific results". The indication is that the demigods give results in specific areas—e.g., wealth, health, family life, power, fame, beauty, etc. The Lord doesn't interfere with this working, but if one wanted something non-specific—i.e., which transcends the divisions of this material world—then only the Supreme Lord can deliver such results. Thus, the previous understanding of the demigod worship is nuanced by this sūtra, and the role of the Supreme Lord as the source of "non-specific results" is stated.

Topic 35

QUESTION

If the demigods are only delivering our karma, and the Supreme Lord doesn't interfere in this activity, then what is the use of worshipping the demigods? How can the demigods produce an outcome other than the destiny?

3.3.60 (420)

काम्यास्तु यथाकामं समुच्चीयेरन्न वा पूर्वहेत्वभावात्

kāmyāstu yathākāmaṃ samuccīyeranna vā pūrvahetvabhāvāt

kāmyāḥ—desires; tu—but; yathākāmaṃ—according to one's desire; samuccīyeran—one may (repurpose) the accumulated (karma) for oneself; na vā—or not; pūrva-hetu-abhāvāt—due to absence of previous reason.

TRANSLATION

(Karma is meant for fulfilling material) desires; but, (according to one's desire), one may (repurpose) the accumulated (karma) for oneself, or not; there is no predetermined result (i.e., the delivery of karma is not fixed).

COMMENTARY

Deserving is always relative to desiring. If we have performed good deeds, then the results of those deeds will be available to us as good results. However, the definition of that 'good' is up to us. For instance, if we enjoy a simple life, the good karma will be delivered as a life close to nature. If, on the other hand, we like an opulent life, then the result of the same karma can be delivered as material opulence. Karma simply means enjoyment or suffering but based on our nature—i.e., what we enjoy or suffer—karma can produce different outcomes. Thus, the total amount of good or bad things we encounter is fixed; they can, however, be delivered in different forms based on our proclivities.

This sūtra states according to one's desires, a person can repurpose their karma. For example, suppose you were born with the proclivity toward music, but over time, your nature has changed, and you are more interested in sport. Based on the proclivity at the time of birth, the delivery of karma was fixed—i.e., it will deliver the results in relation to music rather than sport. So, if one's proclivities have changed, the worship of demigods is meant to alter the delivery of good or bad results in relation to the new proclivity. If one has good karma, it can be revectored toward sport rather than music. Likewise, if one has bad karma, then the results will also be delivered in relation to the new proclivity. This is the extent of the demigod interference in our lives; they cannot increase or decrease the good and bad outcomes; however, they can revector the good and bad from one type of desire to another. Thus, it is appropriate to think of karma as money; based on the nature of birth, there is a pre-established destiny; however, this destiny can be altered if our desires change. Just like money can be spent for buying good food or good clothes, likewise, karma can also be spent in different ways. However, such changes need demigod intervention. Unlike money, which we can choose to spend whichever way we like, as regards karma, we need to seek the permission of the demigods prior.

Topic 36

QUESTION

You have indicated numerous paths so far. You earlier rejected demigod worship, but you have now allowed demigod worship, or the regular performance of ordinary duties as legitimates practices for spiritual enlightenment. Since there are many paths to develop devotion to the Lord, how does one decide the path? Are these paths to be considered mutually equivalent?

3.3.61 (421)

अङ्गेषु यथाश्रयभावः

aṅgeṣu yathāśrayabhāvaḥ

aṅgeṣu—regarding the many paths; yathā-śraya-bhāvaḥ—as one wants to take the shelter of a specific type (of path, one can do so).

TRANSLATION

Regarding the many paths, as one wants to take the shelter of a specific type (of path, one can do so).

COMMENTARY

There is a false conception among many people that each path leads to a different destination. This conception is based on the misunderstanding that the activities of these paths are themselves the goals. Factually, every path is meant to develop devotion to the Lord. For example, the path of jñāna-yoga is to develop knowledge of the Supreme Lord. The path of karma-yoga is meant to worship the Lord through one's prescribed duties. The purpose of aśtānga-yoga is to meditate upon the Lord's form in our heart. And the purpose of bhakti-yoga is to develop the devotion to the Lord through singing, dancing, offering, and worshiping the deity. In jñāna-yoga, we dovetail our intellect to the Lord. In karma-yoga, we serve the Lord through our senses. In aśtānga-yoga we devote our mind to the Lord. And in bhakti-yoga we dedicate our ego to the Lord. Each of these is a part of our material existence, and these parts can be offered to the Lord—by serving the Lord through our senses, mind, intellect, and the ego. Since the soul is associated with all these parts, therefore, the engagement of any part eventually leads to the engagement of the soul.

This sūtra states that one can choose the path one likes—according to their preference, proclivity, or desire. If the soul is being devoted to the Lord through the senses, mind, intellect, or the ego, the main purpose is being served. Thus, from the standpoint of purpose, all the paths are identical. And yet, since different parts of our existence are being devoted to the Lord, these paths are not equivalent. If the mind is controlled, then the senses are automatically controlled; therefore, devoting our mind to the Lord through aśtānga-yoga achieves the purpose of karma-yoga. Similarly, if the intellect is devoted to the Lord, then the mind is automatically devoted; therefore, the practice of jñāna-yoga achieves the results of both karma-yoga and aśtānga-yoga. Finally, if the ego is devoted to the Lord, then the results of all other yoga systems are achieved. Therefore, due to the hierarchy in these elements, some yoga systems are superior to others. But this 'superiority' is a material perspective. Ultimately, the soul is superior to all these elements, and the purpose of such engagements is the attainment of the soul's devotion to the Lord. Thus, there is no contradiction between different paths, some paths being superior to others, and all the paths having the same purpose. All such statements are true in different ways.

QUESTION

It is sometimes said that different methods should be applied based on one's progress. Is this approach of selecting a path also considered valid?

3.3.62 (422)

शषि्टेश्च

śiṣṭeśca

śiṣṭeḥ—from the remainder; ca—also.

TRANSLATION

From the remainder (i.e., after some progress is achieved, and other progress is remaining) also (we can decide the path useful for the remainder).

COMMENTARY

While each path can be employed to develop devotion to the Lord, each path is also specialized for different aspects of this devotion. For example, the first step in developing devotion to the Lord is detachment from the material world. If one is attached to the material world, then even spiritual activities are performed for materialistic purposes. Detachment is attained by karma-yoga; however, this detachment isn't positive knowledge about the self. Detachment simply indicates that I'm not this body, and the soul is separate from the body. This detachment from the body, and the eternity of the soul is an incomplete understanding. A more complete understanding is that my life also has a divine purpose. This purpose is understood by meditation on the Paramātma in the heart, through the process of aśtānga-yoga. With this meditation we understand that we are the parts and there is a whole, and the part must be devoted to the whole. However, the nature of the whole is still not understood. The process of jñāna-yoga is meant to bring a complete understanding of the whole, the different types of parts, and their interrelations. However, this only gives us a theoretical knowledge of the whole, not its direct experience. Therefore, the process of bhakti-yoga is recommended so that a spiritual aspirant can advance their experience from the self (in aśtānga-yoga) to the Absolute Truth.

Thus, different branches or spiritual practices can also be selected based on the current state of advancement in the spiritual aspirant, and what is remaining. If a person is not detached from material desires, he cannot meditate; even if he sits down to mediate, the mind wanders everywhere, and the meditation remains poor. But a person who has become detached from material desires can meditate on the Supreme Lord in the heart because the mind now becomes steady. By this meditation, he becomes convinced that perfection is not self-realization but dedicating the self to the Absolute Truth. Then he is qualified to pursue the knowledge of the Absolute Truth. If one is not convinced that the Absolute Truth is different from the self, and the self is part of that Absolute Truth, the pursuit of knowledge doesn't produce the desired result. It merely produces deviant, selfish, or voidistic philosophies. So, the appropriate time to pursue knowledge is when one knows that one is incomplete, and completeness is obtained by surrendering to the complete. Once knowledge of the complete is acquired, then one can pursue devotion. Unless one acquires a theoretical understanding of the Absolute Truth, the pursuit of devotion is trivialized as fanatic following rather than the experience of a scientifically known reality. Thus, acquisition of knowledge is the precursor to the practice of bhakti-yoga. In this way, there is also a progressive path toward spiritual attainment.

QUESTION

Some people say that all these paths can also be practiced in parallel. For example, as detachment progresses, one can meditate better. As meditation progresses, one can acquire better knowledge. And as knowledge is acquired, devotion in the Lord is reposed with conviction rather than fanatic belief. Do you think these paths can also be pursued in tandem and combination?

3.3.63 (423)

समाहारात्

samāhārāt

samāhārāt—due to the combined practice (perfection is attained).

TRANSLATION

Due to the combined practice (of many paths, perfection is attained).

COMMENTARY

Even though devotion to the Lord is the goal, the practice of this devotion remains incomplete unless the progress obtained by the other paths is also incorporated in the devotional practice. For instance, those who haven't acquired the detachment by the practice of karma-yoga assume that their service to the Lord must always produce the intended results. They don't realize that devotion is performing the activities for the Lord's pleasure, without expectation of a favorable outcome. Thus, sometimes a devotee may be appreciated for his work, and sometimes he may be criticized. The true devotee, who has developed detachment, remains equanimous in both cases. Those who haven't developed the detachment, on the other hand, are carried away by appreciation and become proud, and are easily demotivated or angry upon criticism. As their mind is overtaken by pride and frustration, the devotion to the Lord takes a backseat and pursuing fame and punishing critics becomes the main goal.

Similarly, those who haven't perfected their meditation, fail to understand that devotion is a mystical process by which the Lord becomes visible in the heart. They may be detached from materialistic engagements, but without the understanding of the mystical process, they remain focused upon the activities of their body. They may follow rules and regulations strictly, but they cannot experience the bliss in the heart. Since nobody can continue a process unless this bliss is experienced, most people attached to strict rules and regulations, but without a mystical experience, either fall back to enjoying mundane pleasures or sometimes even become angry opponents of the process itself.

Likewise, those who haven't developed a theoretical understanding of the Absolute Truth cannot understand how the name, form, and pastimes of the Lord are different from those in this world. They think that the body of the Lord is just like our body, rather than the form of knowledge. They cannot see that this form of knowledge contains the soul and is also contained in the soul. Even though they might do regulated practices, they remain influenced by many conflicting ideas—e.g., if the Lord is transcendent, then He cannot be immanent; if the Lord is kind, then He must not be cruel; if the Lord is masculine, then He cannot be feminine; if the Lord is omnipotent, then He cannot become subordinate to the devotee; if the Lord is different from the devotee, then He cannot act like the devotee; etc. Conditioned by all these contradictions, the person justifies his actions by one-sided arguments—i.e., those that consider one aspect of the contradictory feature of reality. This leads to needless arguments, in which a person is trapped in a false understanding and keeps doing misdeeds thinking that their one-sided understanding is indeed justified by the scriptures.

The process of devotion includes detachment, mysticism, and knowledge. Anyone who pursues devotion without bringing in these three components is likely to remain stuck in the stage from which progress is possible only by adding the missing ingredient. Therefore, devotion is not contradictory to detachment, mysticism, or knowledge. Those who claim such a contradiction haven't truly understood the nature of devotion. This sūtra states that these different processes can and should be combined. Whether we practice them alternately or include the benefits of the paths in the practice of devotion—i.e., cultivating detachment, mysticism, and knowledge—along with the devotion to the Lord is left to the individual person's judgment. But all of them are necessary.

QUESTION

But wasn't it said earlier that other than the devotion to the Lord, all other processes are conditioned by the modes of material nature? So, if one follows these other processes, then one also remains conditioned by the modes?

3.3.64 (424)

गुणसाधारण्यश्रुतेश्च

guṇasādhāraṇyaśruteśca

guṇa-sādhāraṇya-śruteḥ—the scriptural statements (about many paths) being conditioned by material modes, is an ordinary statement; ca—also.

TRANSLATION

The scriptural statements (about the many paths described in scriptures) being conditioned by material modes, is also an ordinary statement.

COMMENTARY

When scriptures advise a person to become detached, and act without desire for results, the likely outcome is that the renunciation of desires also leads to the dereliction of duties. The absence of desire for results makes a person ask: If I'm not expecting anything in return, then why should I do anything? This outcome is like that of a sad or frustrated person who can't get the results of their actions and rejects their duties under *tamo-guna*. Similarly, when scriptures advise a person to practice meditation and seek mystical experience beyond the waking and dreaming experiences, the likely outcome is that the person starts pursuing material power—bodily strength, mental or intellectual acuity, and mystic powers. The practice of meditation naturally makes a person inclined toward material enjoyment, much like a person who performs severe austerities under the mode of *rajo-guna* only to acquire greater power. Finally, when the scriptures say that one should acquire knowledge, the likely outcome is that a person gives up all consideration of mystical experience and a day-to-day confirmation of knowledge through bodily activity. Under the influence of *sattva-guna* the person gives up real and verifiable answers and becomes engrossed with theoretical speculation that cannot be practically realized.

We have also noted above that if someone practices devotion without detachment, mysticism, and knowledge, he is bewildered by success and failure, cannot find real happiness within, and remains confused by contradictions.

Thus, every spiritual pursuit can get riddled with negative outcomes, and therefore the ordinary statement is that all these processes are potentially imbued with the effect of the three modes of nature. However, we can also see that when these methods are combined, then they preserve the benefits of the other processes, and cancel out their negative effects. For instance, mystical experience cancels out the negative effects of detachment—one is not only detached from the day-to-day events but also attached to something beyond. The pursuit of knowledge cancels the materialistic tendencies of mystical pursuits, as one realizes that each individual person only knows the full truth partially, so mystical experience is always a partial understanding of the whole truth. Likewise, mystical experience also cancels out the negative effects of knowledge because one ensures that even if the full truth cannot be verified in a single experience, experience remains important to verify parts of those truth contextually. Finally, detachment cancels out the negative effects of knowledge because this knowledge should be universally applicable to all circumstances;

we cannot call something knowledge if it applies only to a few contextual scenarios.

Since knowledge, mysticism, and detachment have this tendency to cancel each other's negative effects, they can also be mutually contradictory. For example, if someone wants to pursue theoretical knowledge, without concern for the mystical or everyday confirmation of the knowledge, then the needs for practical and everyday confirmation will always distract them from the theoretical concerns of completeness, consistency, coherence, etc. Those pursuing mystical experiences will not be concerned about universal truth—if it gives them immense power to manipulate nature according to their will. And if someone acquired such power, their inclination toward detachment—which generally arises when one is frustrated by their efforts—would dramatically reduce. Therefore, we can see that there are natural conflicts between all these paths. And the conflicts between them entail that it is hard to combine them.

However, the devotion to the Lord reconciles these conflicts. Detachment arises because the goal is the pleasure of the Supreme Lord, not the outcomes in the material world. Detachment is not contrary to mystical experiences, as the devotee is ecstatic by this service. And the conflict between the universality of the Absolute Truth, and the contextuality of individual experience doesn't exist. Devotion selects the positives from each path and removes the conflicts by rejecting the negatives from each path, and thus combines them. Thus, detachment, mystical experience, complete knowledge, and devotion to the complete truth are simultaneously reconciled by the presence of devotion.

If the paths are kept separate, then they are individually incomplete and collectively contradictory. Thus, the general case is that of faults in each path (i.e., they are individually incomplete) and they are collectively flawed (because of contradictions between them). However, the special case is that if they are combined under devotion to the Lord, then both the incompleteness of the individual paths and the inconsistency between the paths is at once resolved. Therefore, in separated form, they seem conditioned by faults or the modes of material nature. But in combined form, they are free from all such faults.

QUESTION

The coexistence or combination of all the paths you are mentioning here doesn't seem to be mentioned by the scriptures, which only talk about the paths separately. How can we justify their combination based on scriptures?

3.3.65 (425)

न वा तत्सहभावाश्रुतेः

na vā tatsahabhāvāśruteḥ

na vā—rather not; tatsahabhāva-aśruteḥ—their coexistence not being mentioned by the scriptures (or not previously heard).

TRANSLATION

It is incorrect to say that the coexistence of that (the many paths) is not mentioned in the scriptures (as they are implicitly implied by the scripture).

COMMENTARY

A classic example of this coexistence is found in the Bhagavad-Gita, where Lord Kṛṣṇa describes karma-yoga, jñāna-yoga, dhyāna-yoga, and bhakti-yoga. Even as Arjuna rejects these paths due to their flaws and difficulties, since they are spoken by the Lord, they must be considered the perfect truth. It has been previously noted that scriptures are correctly understood only when the many seemingly contradictory statements are reconciled. This becomes even more important when such contradictions seem to exist within a single scripture, and the correct understanding of the scripture is that these are not contradictory. However, to the extent that spiritual life begins with detachment, then progresses into mystical experience of the self, then proceeds into a theoretical understanding of the Absolute Truth, and finally culminates into the devotion to the Absolute Truth, there is a progression from detachment to devotion. At each step in this progression, the pursuits of the past may seem incomplete or contradictory to the present pursuits. However, when the final goal of devotion to the Lord is achieved, then all these seeming contradictions are resolved. Since the final goal reconciles these contradictions, an avid practitioner must keep in mind that the rejection of a path is necessarily temporary and incomplete. Furthermore, progress means the simultaneous coexistence of all the paths.

QUESTION

If these paths must be reconciled because they are mentioned in the scriptures, doesn't it entail that the philosophical contradictions between the different paths—e.g., of engagement vs. renunciation—must be corrected?

3.3.65 (425)

दर्शनाच्च

darśanācca

darśanāt—from the philosophical systems; ca—also.

TRANSLATION

(The contradictions between paths must be reconciled) from philosophical systems as well (e.g., the systems of Yoga, Sāñkhya, Nyāya, Vaiśeṣika, Mīmāṃsā, and Vedānta, which are considered the six systems of philosophy).

COMMENTARY

In this sūtra, compared to the previous one, a distinction between scripture and philosophy is emphasized. After stating that there is no contradiction in the scripture, this sūtra states that any such contradiction in the philosophies must also not exist. Notably, these philosophical systems are based on Vedic texts, but the proponents of these systems have historically conflicted with each other. For example, many commentators in Vedānta reject the validity of other systems such as Sāñkhya, Yoga, and Vaiśeṣika. They might say that because Sāñkhya deals with the material categories, therefore, it has no reality, and only Brahman is real. Likewise, since Vaiśeṣika deals with the existence of atoms, and Brahman is undivided, therefore, any atomic division must be unreal. Finally, even the idea that there are separate ātmā and Paramātma, which then need to be united by Yoga, is flawed if these are factually not separated entities. Thus, in trying to establish the validity of a system of philosophy, the other systems are rejected, and this rejection of the other systems is forbidden here. Even as these systems can seem contradictory to many people, they are not contradictory. Their seeming contradiction is only a puzzle or paradox to be solved by the reader, by finding the understanding the reconciles all of them. The implication is that any understanding of Vedānta that rejects the truth of the other systems of philosophy can be immediately discarded. This is not to deny the presence of seeming contradictions, or even to gloss over these contradictions irrationally. It is only to assert that contradictions indicate the presence of a deeper truth that reconciles them. Unless they are reconciled, this deeper truth has not been described, and therefore their rejection or acceptance is superficial.

SECTION 4

Topic 1

QUESTION

It is sometimes said that of the four endeavors of man, only one (liberation) is transcendental. Therefore, it follows that many of the practices—such as the performance of duties—are not related to transcendence. If you say that all such practices can be spiritually elevating, doesn't it contradict this statement?

3.4.1 (426)

पुरुषार्थोऽतःशब्दादिति बादरायणः

puruṣārtho'taḥ śabdāditi bādarāyaṇaḥ

puruṣārthaḥ—the goal of life; ataḥ—therefore; śabdāt—from scriptures; iti—in this way; bādarāyaṇaḥ— Bādarāyana (who authored scriptures).

TRANSLATION

All the goals of life (dharma, artha, kāma, and moksha) are therefore (attained) from the scriptures, authored by Bādarāyana (i.e., the Vedic system).

COMMENTARY

The Vedic system describes four *puruṣārtha* or the purposes of life. These are called dharma or the performance of actions, artha or the obtainment of results, kāma or the fulfillment of desires, and moksha or liberation. All dharma involves a person's role, and these roles are relational. For example, you cannot be a father unless someone is a child; you cannot be a wife unless someone is a husband. This relational reality is called *sat* or awareness. It defines us by connecting us to something else. Similarly, while artha is sometimes translated as 'money', it includes every material object—house, car, land, cattle, jewelry, etc. Artha denotes 'meaning', and everything we find meaningful is artha. Artha springs from the *chit* of the soul; it includes both the things we find meaningful and the activities that give meaning to our life. Finally, *kāma* or the desire for pleasure springs from the ānanda of the soul. It includes selfish desires as well as selfless love; when a desire is fulfilled, we become happy. The simple sequence is that one performs the duties of one's role, obtains meaningful things, and enjoys with these things. While the roles, objects, and desires can seem mundane, there is a spiritual basis of these three aspects within the soul.

Unless one understands this spiritual basis of dharma, artha, and kāma, it is believed that these three are only for this world, and after these are renounced, then one attains moksha or liberation. Thus, moksha is incorrectly understood as freedom from roles or dharma, from cognition and activity, and from desires. But this is a wrong understanding. The *sat*, *chit*, and ānanda of the soul are eternal potentialities. They can remain in a dormant stage, but they can never be lost. Therefore, moksha or liberation means getting out of temporary roles, cognitions, activities, and desires, and being situated in eternal roles, cognitions, activities, and desires. This eternal dharma, artha, and kāma are obtained in relation to the Lord, when the soul is situated in a relationship to the Lord, sees the Lord and serves Him, and desires to make the Lord delighted. Liberation means the soul doesn't keep changing its dharma, artha, and kāma.

So, if we look at the puruṣārtha from a mundane perspective, then dharma, artha, and kāma must end with the material world, while moksha is a one-time achievement. But if we look at the same situation transcendentally, then moksha is a one-time achievement, but dharma, artha, and kāma are eternal.

The mundane view of puruṣārtha applies to all the spiritual paths, beginning with the pursuit of detachment through karma-yoga. Once we become detached from results, then we just keep performing our duties, but we are not interested in the pursuit of artha or results or selfish pleasure or kāma. But this is a limited understanding of puruṣārtha. The purpose of the soul doesn't end with liberation. Therefore, a more nuanced understanding of puruṣārtha is that everything continues beyond liberation, and this is possible only when we say that the pursuit of transcendental knowledge, love of the Lord, the vision of the Lord in the heart, and services to the Lord are not mundane puruṣārtha. When devotion is a legitimate kāma, then relation to the Lord is legitimate dharma, and the cognition and activities in that relation are legitimate artha. This transcendent relation, cognition, and emotion is itself the nature of mukti.

The combination of the multiple paths described earlier is meant for the attainment of this puruṣārtha even beyond the material world. If the broader view of paths is rejected, then many puruṣārtha (e.g., the pursuit of knowledge or the satisfaction of the Lord in this material world) would also be rejected.

This sūtra indicates that the combined practice of many paths is unique to the Vedic system because detachment, mystical experience, transcendental knowledge, and devotion are simultaneously pursued (or at least one after another). In other systems of religion, one or more of these are found missing. Thus, for instance, there are many mystical traditions that don't emphasize knowledge, devotion, or detachment; they only talk about mysticism. There are philosophical approaches which only speak about knowledge, but not about devotion or mystical experiences. Then there are methods of austerity which emphasize renunciation and may encourage devotion to the Lord, but there is little focus on philosophical understanding and mystical experiences. Therefore, the system propounded by Bādarāyana is unique in this respect.

QUESTION

You have mentioned that when the Lord is worshipped in any process,

that process—even though demigods may be worshipped alongside—is considered spiritual. What if the goal of the worshipper is not liberation, but simply material enjoyment? Will that still be considered the ultimate puruṣārtha?

3.4.2 (427)

शेषत्वात्पुरुषार्थवादो यथाऽन्येष्वितिजैमिनिः

śeṣatvātpuruṣārthavādo yathā'nyeṣviti jaiminiḥ

śeṣatvāt—from remainder; puruṣa-arthavādaḥ—are called selfish purposes of the enjoyers; yathā—just as; anyeṣu—in other cases; iti—thus; jaiminiḥ—(the individual worship of demigods as defined by) Jaimini (are not spiritual).

TRANSLATION

The remainder (of processes—which don't have transcendence as the goal) are called selfish purposes of the enjoyers, just as in other cases such as those described by Jaimini (e.g., the worship of demigods is not spiritual).

COMMENTARY

During the previous discussion on Jaimini's philosophy, the worship of demigods was decried. Subsequently, demigod worship was accepted if the Supreme Lord is worshipped as the superior personality. Now it is said that even the worship of the Lord along with the demigods is considered not the final goal (puruṣārtha) if the purpose of that worship is material enjoyment. If only the demigods are worshipped, then it is obvious that the person is interested only in material enjoyment, hence, it is easy to reject such worship. If only the Lord is worshipped, then there are several nuances. First, the Lord may be worshipped for obtaining material enjoyment, and not transcendence. Second, there may be some devotion for the Lord, mixed with the desire for enjoyment to be obtained through the demigods. Third, either the Lord alone or together with the demigods, may be worshipped to obtain liberation. It is understood that when the Lord is worshipped, then the soul is gradually purified of material desires. It is also understood that the demigods can assist the soul in the pursuit of liberation so that worship is not completely rejected. Ultimately, the main criterion is the intention of the worshipper. There are many methods for fulfilling each goal, but puruṣārtha is the goal, not the method of achieving it.

Thus, after clarifying many positions about who should and should not be worshipped, it is said that if the goal is not transcendence, then everything is considered material. This includes the worship of demigods in isolation (as given by Jaimini). However, the use of 'just as' indicates that even other methods where the Lord is worshipped for material gains are considered selfish endeavors. Since one can interpret the previously endorsed worship of demigods along with the Lord as a blanket acceptance of using worship for material ends, therefore, this sūtra rejects that conclusion by noting the importance of intention as the final determinant of whether something is considered a puruṣārtha.

QUESTION

But you previously also said that truth is obtained only by reconciling the diverse philosophical positions, and Mīmāṃsā is such a philosophical position. Doesn't the rejection of Jaimini contradict the previously stated position?

3.4.3 (428)
आचारदर्शनात्
ācāradarśanāt

ācāra—the established precedents (aiding dharma, artha, and kāma); darśanāt—from the six systems of philosophy (and may be incongruent).

TRANSLATION

The established precedents (aiding dharma, artha, and kāma) are from the six systems of philosophy or the visions of reality (and may be incongruent).

COMMENTARY

There is a fundamental difference between how philosophy is treated in the Western world, and how it was treated in the Vedic system. Everything in philosophy begins with some 'given'. The 'given' in Western philosophy is generally our experience, and the goal of philosophy is to explain this given. The 'given' in the Vedic system is the Vedic texts, and the goal of Vedic philosophy is to explain the Vedic texts. When we start explaining the 'given' we often limit ourselves to limited parts of the 'given'. For example, in science, we might explain the body, but not the mind. Or, we might explain physical motion but not how this motion is controlled by choices, why choices can be right and wrong, and how the morality of choice determines consequences. Due to the focus on limited parts of the 'given', a philosophical system can be incomplete. This is true for the Vedic philosophical systems as well. For instance, Sāñkhya focuses on the nature of matter, but has a limited focus on choices and their consequences. A more complete theory would have to add karma, which must then be followed by a doctrine of liberation, which then requires a description of the spiritual world, and finally the description of God who produced everything. At each successive step, new contradictions may be found in the philosophy.

The Vedic philosophical systems have divided these elements of a complete philosophy into several distinct aspects. For example, Sāñkhya describes matter as universals. Vaiśeṣika describes the individuals created from these universals. Yoga describes the nature of consciousness. Mīmāṃsā discusses the relation between choice and consequence. Nyāya identifies the principles of logical reasoning. There is always some overlap between these varied doctrines. But the differences of focus in them means that all possible details—which arise when we try to formulate a complete understanding—may not be present in them.

Thus, philosophies are often accused of incompleteness—some aspect of experience hasn't been explained. We might also find difficulties in reconciling different doctrines. When faced with these twin problems, philosophers often come up with new ideas or ways to reconcile these problems. But on what grounds can we accept one answer over another? The debate now moves away from the real problem, into the methods by which something is accepted true. The realist says—my solution solves a problem that you are unable to solve. The instrumentalist says—but we might be able to solve it in the future, and when I solve it, I will also provide the evidence for my chosen solution.

The real problem is that the realist should be able to explain and justify any claims of reality based on reason and experience, but they may not have the wherewithal for it. But instead of acknowledging the shortcoming, the argument is reversed, and the instrumentalist is accused of being biased toward observation and reason. That accusation leads to the counter-accusation of accepting the reality of things even when they cannot be observed or reasoned. The acrimonious debate then leads to both sides rejecting each other's views.

In one sense, the rejections are completely false. In another sense, the reasons for rejecting them are true, but these may not be the only reasons. There may exist reasons due to which the rejection can be rejected but the reason for the rejection can be accepted. The goal of philosophy is to identify the missing reasons, and their discovery improves our understanding because what wasn't known previously is now known. Until such additional reasons are found, the conflict between claims keeps simmering. Thus, this sūtra says that philosophies are the visions of the established knowledge. This is an indirect indication that reality is bigger than the vision, and the vision can be enhanced to completely describe the reality—whereupon these rejections will disappear.

QUESTION

If the philosophical systems are merely interpretations of the Vedic texts, then why can't we completely reject these interpretations, and just rely on the texts? What is the benefit of these interpretations if they are sometimes inconsistent with the texts? Doesn't this lead to many confusions for the aspirants?

3.4.4 (429)

तच्छ्रुतेः

tacchruteḥ

tat-sruteḥ—that the scriptures directly declare.

TRANSLATION

Those (philosophical systems of interpretation) are directly declared in the scriptures (so they are not arbitrary or whimsical creations).

COMMENTARY

Sāñkhya and Yoga are examples of philosophical systems directly mentioned in scriptures. Vedānta is seldom mentioned because it the conclusion of the Vedas. Mīmāṃsā, Nyāya, and Vaiśeṣika are not part of the Vedic texts, but they are mandatory additions because they deal with fundamental questions such as: What are the means to knowledge? How should a text be interpreted? What is language? How is it produced and how does it encode meanings? After we understand the meaning, how do we verify its truth? Even as the Vedic texts take epistemology, hermeneutics, and linguistics for granted, the questions are not less important, and they are examined by other philosophical systems.

For example, Vedic texts do not define the methods of knowledge such as pratyakśa (experience), anumāna (inference), śabda (revelation), upamāna (comparison), etc. But because these methods are used in the Vedic texts, questions naturally arise: How many methods must exist? Which method should be used when? Do these methods exhaust everything that can be known?

The key point is that the philosophical systems should not be whimsically rejected, because: (1) they are directly mentioned in the scriptures, (2) they are summaries of the scriptures, and (3) they explain the process of interpreting, verifying, reasoning, learning, judging, understanding, etc. The Vedic texts present knowledge, but the processes of understanding the texts are supplementary information. Just because linguistics, grammar, and logic are not explicitly discussed in the Vedic texts, doesn't mean they are human creations. They too are divine, but their nature is assumed without explanation in the texts.

Language and logic cannot be taught unless language and logic preexist within us in some primordial form. To learn a language, we must use a language; so, if there wasn't a language in us, then no other language can be learned. Likewise, to learn logic, we must use logic. If there were no logic within us, then we cannot be taught logic. So, language and logic are innate in all of us. Their presence is indicated using the term śabda-brahman, but the understanding of language and logic is as complex and involved as the collection of all the systems of philosophy. Every system of philosophy is nothing other than language and logic, and it is taught using the language and logic within us. This process is called 'purification'. The thing to be purified already exists, but it is imperfect, unclean, and contaminated. The external knowledge is not giving us anything new; it is cleaning up the thing that already exists within us.

QUESTION

But there are already so many Vedic texts, which are hard to reconcile. How does adding more philosophical systems to this not make the process of reconciliation worse? We are now expected to reconcile even more topics!

3.4.5 (430)

समन्वारम्भणात्

samanvārambhaṇāt

samanva—reconciliation; arambhanāt—for the reason for beginning.

TRANSLATION

(Philosophies exist) for the purpose of beginning the reconciliation.

COMMENTARY

The six philosophical systems extract all the fundamental ideas from the Vedic texts. Vedānta, for example, summarizes the relation between the whole and the part and describes matter and soul as the parts. The Yoga system discusses how the soul is entangled in matter and how it can be liberated from this entanglement. The Sāñkhya system describes the nature of matter, and how it creates both knowledge and illusion. The Mīmāṃsā system discusses the nature of knowledge, how it is embodied in texts, and how meaning must be extracted from the texts. And Nyāya discusses what types of proofs may be employed to know. Since words can represent God, soul, and matter, therefore, the entire system of whole-part relationships, how they are separate and inseparable, exists in language as well. Knowledge involves universals, but their expression creates the individuals. Vaiśeṣika is the study of how the universals become individuals; the individuals are not things but embodiments of meaning. How these individuals (matter and soul) evolve in a rational manner—e.g., that premises lead to questions, which then lead to answers, which then become the new premises; or that this succession of premises, questions, and answers forms an iterative, linear, and hierarchical structure—is the Nyāya system.

The collection of all these systems constitutes a 'science' that spans matter, soul, and God, as it covers all the fundamental topics of epistemology, ontology, hermeneutics, ethics, linguistics, logic, happiness, and transcendence. The comprehension of these topics, and their reconciliation, can be aided by the philosophical systems. This sūtra says that if one wants to understand the Vedic texts, then one can begin by understanding the philosophical systems. These systems are not added complexity; they are the means to understand it.

QUESTION

Does this philosophical understanding alone constitute the ultimate purpose of life? Or is this understand a preliminary step toward a practice?

3.4.6 (431)

तद्वतो विधानात्

tadvato vidhānāt

tadvataḥ—accordingly; vidhānāt—from the performances (or activities).

TRANSLATION

Accordingly (i.e., based upon the philosophical conclusions) from the performances (or activities) (i.e., knowledge must lead to changed behaviors).

COMMENTARY

Philosophy is of limited value if it doesn't translate into a change in our lives. Armchair speculation loses touch with reality, and the day-to-day concerns. One such disconnection is that philosophy may not tell us what to do in everyday life. This sūtra states that correct knowledge must lead to correct actions. If knowledge doesn't change our behavior, then it cannot lead to happiness, because happiness depends on the changes in our actions. Most modern pursuits of knowledge don't tell us what is right and wrong. Science can tell us how to make different things, but how do we use those things? When and where must they be used? Whether they should be used? And by whom? If knowledge is silent on behavior, then the advancement of the understanding of material nature can be very dangerous; it gives us powers but doesn't tell us how to use that power. Without guidance on the use of power, power is prone to be misused. And that misuse entangles the soul in suffering. Knowledge must make us happier. But if knowledge leads to increased suffering, then it doesn't fulfill the purpose for which we do everything—i.e., happiness.

QUESTION

But what if someone doesn't have the time, inclination, or the intelligence to pursue a philosophical understanding? How do they achieve the goal of life?

3.4.7 (432)

नियमाच्च

niyamācca

niyamāt—due to the prescribed rules; ca—also.

TRANSLATION

(Those who cannot follow philosophy can attain perfection) also by following the rules and regulations (of behavior that follow the philosophy).

COMMENTARY

Every religion prescribes rules on how to live life, although they may not explain why these rules are important. Without true knowledge, people are prone to invent new rules whimsically. And with such manufactured rules, whatever could have been achieved by following the rules borne out of a real philosophical understanding is also lost. In fact, religions start differentiating themselves based on these rules and regulations as 'divine revelation' without the ability to explain and justify why any such rules must be followed.

This sūtra states that those who cannot understand philosophy can also reap the benefits of philosophy by following the rules and regulations borne out of the philosophy. This doesn't mean that nobody needs to understand the rules. It just means some people can rely on the rules given by others—but those who give the rules must understand the reason why such rules are prescribed. In the Vedic system, only the Brahmana—i.e., the most intelligent and educated class of people—were involved in philosophical understanding. Everyone else simply followed the rules prescribed by the Brahmanas. The rules, however, were based on the understanding of matter, soul, and God. As the philosophical understanding declines—with the disappearance of the Brahmana—the rest of the population is simply left with rules and regulations. They cannot explain or justify why certain rules must be followed. And, over time, they discard the rules or invent new ones. Whatever benefits could have been achieved simply by following the previously devised rules (even without a philosophical understanding) now also disappears rapidly. Therefore, it is essential to establish the philosophical understanding before we formulate the rules. Although most people might simply follow the rules, if someone is intelligent enough to question why these rules are to be followed, there will be an explanation.

QUESTION

What if someone restricts themselves to philosophical understanding? Many philosophers are fond of hairsplitting irrelevant differences, arguing about nuances, which might sometimes create confusion rather than clarity.

3.4.8 (433)

अधिकोपदेशात्तु बादरायणस्यैवम् तद्दर्शनात्

adhikopadeśāttu bādarāyaṇasyaivam taddarśanāt

adhika-upadeśāt—from excessive teaching; tu—but; bādarāyaṇasya—of Badarayana's (view); evam—in this way; tat-darśanāt—from that vision.

TRANSLATION

But (the result) from excessive teaching of Bādarāyana's philosophy in this way (the result is same as that obtained) from that philosophy.

COMMENTARY

The study of scriptures is not considered different from the meditation on the Lord, the performance of mystical practices, or other such methods of spiritual advancement, because if properly performed, they deliver the same result. Thus, some people may focus more on deity worship, others may perform more meditation, while some others may study the scriptures more often. The key point is to devote our senses, mind, intellect, and consciousness to the Lord. Whichever that concentration is attained—through deity worship, by meditation, or by scriptural study—if the result is attained, then the processes by which they are attained are not considered superior or inferior. When our consciousness is focused on the Lord, then all perfection is already attained.

QUESTION

On the other hand, there can be people who aren't inclined to philosophy but may be interested in detachment, mystical experience, and devotion. If they attain these experiences and personality change, is philosophy still necessary for them? Or they also attain the results of philosophical understanding?

3·4·9 (434)
तुल्यं तु दर्शनम्
tulyaṃ tu darśanam

tulyam—equivalent; tu—but; darśanam—the philosophical conclusions.

TRANSLATION

(Those who obtain detachment, mystical experience, and devotion) are but equivalent to (those with the perfected) philosophical conclusions.

COMMENTARY

If you can see the sky, then you don't need a description of the sky. The description of the sky is needed to motivate one to see the sky—if they haven't seen it. Or, to tell them that once they see, they must know what demarcates the sky from a forest. If people don't know about the sky, then they will not be motivated to see the sky. Or, they might see a forest, and think that they are seeing the sky. But, for one who has seen the Absolute Truth, the preliminary steps of motivation and confirmation are already achieved. Therefore, theoretical knowledge is neither necessary nor sufficient. Not necessary because the vision of the Absolute Truth can be obtained through detachment, mystical experience, and devotion. And not sufficient because even those with theoretical knowledge may not obtain such vision. Nevertheless, to the extent that most people are not motivated without a theoretical description, and they may not know what to look for without such a description, these are important.

QUESTION

Then, can we say that knowledge is not universally required? That everyone doesn't need to know if they only follow the rules and regulations?

3·4·10 (435)
असार्वत्रिकी
asārvatrikī

asārvatrikī—not universally necessary.

TRANSLATION

(Knowledge is) not universally necessary.

COMMENTARY

The Vedic social system comprises four classes—Brahmana, Kshatriya, Vaisya, and Sudra. Out of these four classes, only the Brahmana are expected to be knowledgeable as they devise the rules and regulations for the other classes. The other three classes merely follow these regulations, without a profound philosophical understanding. Their relative ignorance about the philosophy, however, is not a hindrance to spiritual advancement, because all the four classes are treated as souls, equally qualified for spiritual pursuits. In fact, it is quite possible that those with philosophical knowledge don't put this knowledge into practice, while those without this philosophical knowledge are extremely diligent about the practice. Therefore, philosophical knowledge doesn't guarantee spiritual advancement, and philosophical ignorance doesn't deter one from spiritual advancement. This sūtra states that the acquisition of knowledge is not universally necessary. However, before one jumps to the conclusion that Brahmanas are not needed in society, we can note that if knowledge disappears in society, then rules and regulations become meaningless, over time they are altered whimsically, and the other three classes become incapable of spiritual pursuits. Therefore, the fact that a few Brahmanas pursue knowledge, while the rest of the population follows the rules enacted by them, doesn't undermine the importance of knowledge. The denial of universal necessity doesn't equate to universal non-necessity. It means some people must pursue knowledge.

There are two ways in which negations are employed, in relation to the term 'all'. When we say, 'not all', sometimes we mean 'none', and sometimes, the same 'not all' means 'some'. For example, one can claim that 'all men are handsome', and if this claim is denied, then there are two possible interpretations: (a) none of the men are handsome, and (b) some men are handsome. Factually, these are two different kinds of negations, but in current logic, we don't have the ability to make such distinctions. Therefore, the denial of 'all' is taken to be the acceptance of 'some'. Hence, if 'all men are handsome' is rejected, then it is accepted that 'some men are handsome'. But there is a problem. You could say 'energy is never conserved', and its rejection would mean 'energy is sometimes conserved'. By this rejection you will come to a partial truth. Conversely, if the claim that 'energy is always conserved' is denied, and we conclude that 'energy is sometimes conserved', then there is no difference between the denial of 'energy is never conserved' and 'energy is always conserved'. In both cases, 'all' and 'none' are replaced by 'some'. Therefore, these principles of reasoning cannot be applied universally and only context delineates what we mean.

QUESTION

Can someone even hope to know everything that is potentially knowable? The pursuit of complete knowledge seems very difficult due to numerous departments of knowing because one can only pursue few areas sufficiently.

3.4.11 (436)

वभिागःशतवत्

vibhāgaḥ śatavat

vibhāgaḥ—the divisions; śatavat—in the hundreds.

TRANSLATION

The divisions (of knowledge) are in the hundreds.

COMMENTARY

Knowing the whole truth isn't the same as knowing all the parts. This conception of knowledge arises when the whole is treated as the sum of the parts and the whole has no separate existence. But when we treat the whole semantically, this problem doesn't arise. Just like one can understand the meaning of 'mammal' by just understanding a few types of mammals—e.g., cows, dogs, cats, etc.—and doesn't need to know every type of mammal, similarly, it is not necessary to know every division of knowledge before the whole truth is understood. This is not a rejection of the other types of mammals, nor is it a claim that the meaning of 'mammal' could not be understood through other types (i.e., not cows, dogs, and cats). This sūtra says that it is impossible for anyone to know everything, without rejecting the existence of the complete knowledge.

Every division of knowledge involves different phenomena, which can be explained in many ways. If we use the phenomena to discover, compare, and then eliminate the explanations, then a very large number of divisions and a much larger number of phenomena will ensure that the perfect explanation—that applies to every division of knowledge—can never be found. However, if one accepts the explanation in the Vedic texts, then any division of knowledge can be used to verify the explanation. Since the whole truth can be verified through any division of knowledge, therefore, each such division serves as a perfect method for verification, and the result of that verification is perfect knowledge. But this perfect knowledge is not the complete verification of the truth across every possible domain of knowledge. In that sense, the knowledge can be complete, but the verification of that knowledge can be incomplete.

Verification of knowledge is an infinite process if we take the verification cognitively. However, if the application of knowledge leads to happiness, then that infinite process is shortened—we are convinced of its truth not because we verified it everywhere, but because it leads to perfect happiness right now. Thus, the classical method of epistemology—i.e., the discover by observation and experiment—is rejected in the Vedic system because you can never get perfect knowledge in a finite time. The verification of revealed knowledge is accepted as a valid method of convincing ourselves about its truth. However, for a persistent doubter, even this verification is infinite. Therefore, the ultimate solution is to obtain the happiness by the application of the knowledge.

This change in epistemology is wrought by the question: Why do we doubt? What gives rise to suspicion, that something may be wrong? And the answer is unhappiness. If we are unhappy, we are also suspicious. Suspicion can be partially overcome by verification. But it is completely rooted out only by happiness. Thus, it is said that all doubts are destroyed from the heart of a devotee when the happiness produced by the Lord's love is established. This means that the devotee hasn't verified the knowledge in every situation. But he is not suffering from the doubt to seek such verification. Simply by the perfection of happiness, he is convinced that the knowledge will always be true.

QUESTION

If you acknowledge that the divisions of knowledge are in the hundreds,

and therefore it is practically impossible for anyone to know everything, then what is the purpose of producing these diverse forms of knowledge? Wouldn't it be better to just have the conclusion without its diverse manifestations?

3.4.12 (437)
अध्ययनमात्रवतः
adhyayanamātravataḥ

adhyayana—the detailed study; mātravataḥ—as if only for that.

TRANSLATION

(The divisions of knowledge are) as if only for detailed study.

COMMENTARY

Knowing the truth is not the same as verifying the truth. For example, many people believe that atomic theory is true, but they have never seen atoms, and have never verified atomic theory. They rely on someone else's verification. And yet, the theory is available for everyone to verify—whether they choose to verify it is up to them. Now, if we eliminated the possibility of verification, then the theory's truth could still be upheld by a few people, but most people will reject the theory because it cannot be verified. In the same way, the Absolute Truth can be accepted on faith, without verification. Just like atomic theory is accepted by many on faith because they trust others who have verified it. This trust can, for instance, be reposed in a teacher. However, if everything simply depended on trust and faith, and the claims could not be verified, then most people would reject this knowledge. Therefore, the necessities of both faith and verification are rejected. The truth can be known by faith, so verification is not necessary. But that doesn't make faith necessary; the truth can also be verified, and faith is not necessary, provided someone wants the verification.

The meaning of this sūtra is that the many diverse branches of knowledge exist if one wants to verify. But since verification is not necessary, therefore, all these divisions are unnecessary. That, however, doesn't make faith in the Absolute Truth necessary, because verification of this truth is also possible. Those who are intelligent and inquisitive will want to verify the truth, and the many divisions of knowledge are open to them for verification. Those who are not intelligent or inquisitive, can accept the conclusion based on faith in the scripture, or based on the numerous verifications by the inquisitive people.

QUESTION

There is a view that says that all the diverse fields of knowledge are illusory because the ultimate truth is their unity. Therefore, we must reject these diversities as illusory forms of confusion, and only focus on the unity. You have also emphasized the unity earlier, as opposed to the diversity. So, the proponents of the unity take this emphasis further and reject the diversity.

3.4.13 (438)

न अविशेषात्

na aviśeṣāt

na—not; aviśeṣāt—the claim of unity (alone).

TRANSLATION

We reject the claim of unity alone (denying the reality of diversities).

COMMENTARY

The rejection of diversity, based on the supposed opposition to the unity, is based on a physical conception of reality. For example, a chair is the whole, and if you break it apart into legs, backrest, seat, etc. then none of them is the chair. Therefore, if we look at these individual parts, then we can never know the whole chair. To know the chair, we must stop looking at the parts—i.e., backrest, seat, and legs—and only by that rejection of the parts we will know the whole truth. The problem, however, is that if you reject all these parts, then you cannot verify if there is really a chair. You will just have the idea of a chair, with no verification if that idea is indeed real, true, or existent. Now, if we change our conception of reality from physical to semantic, then chair is present in every part of the chair, and yet the chair is beyond all these parts. The physical conception of whole and part says that the whole is transcendent to the parts. But the semantic conception of the whole and part allows the whole to both be transcendent and immanent. This semantic conception of reality is easily understood if we say that the Absolute Truth is not just a thing, but also a *theory*. For example, the laws of Newton's mechanics can be verified through a bicycle, hammer, billiard ball, steam engines, etc. So, these laws are governing all these diverse objects, and hence they are immanent in those objects. And yet, even if the bicycle is destroyed, the truth of Newton's mechanics is not; therefore, the laws are also transcendent. Furthermore, because Newton's laws can be verified through a bicycle, bicycles are *sufficient* for knowledge. And yet, since the laws can also be verified through locomotives, therefore, bicycles are not *necessary*. The whole exists in each part and is outside of the parts.

So, these claims about the rejection of the parts and acceptance of the whole are flawed; they are based on a physical conception of reality in which the whole is transcendent to the parts, so none of the parts can lead to the whole truth. There are many pseudo-spiritualists who decry the importance of diverse fields of knowledge, claiming that these don't lead one to the Absolute Truth. These people also suffer from the materialist and impersonalist ideas. They think that the Absolute Truth is like a table or chair, different from other things in this world. If we keep looking at the material things, then we can never know that transcendent object. They don't know that the Absolute Truth is like a theory—i.e., a semantic object—which is inside and outside of everything. Impersonalism and materialism are similar ideas, and people who reject materialism simply take to impersonalism without deepening their understanding.

QUESTION

Contrary to the view that diversity is an illusion, there is also a view that the unity of knowledge is impossible. Thus, many divisions of academia operate independently, and so great is their focus on the individual study, that they may sometimes even reject the possibility of Absolute Truth. They claim only the existence of piecemeal and fragmented knowledge. What would you say to such claims that oppose the unity by exemplifying the diversification?

3.4.14 (439)

स्तुतयेऽनुमतिर्वा

stutaye'numatirvā

stutaye—for the praising; anumatiḥ—permission; vā—alternatively.

TRANSLATION

Alternatively, for the praising (of diverse fields of knowledge), permission (to people who are interested in expanding the diverse fields of knowledge).

COMMENTARY

For many practical concerns, diverse fields of knowledge, such as economics, physics, mathematics, psychology, medicine, cosmology, etc. are often required. The rejection of these fields of knowledge as 'illusion' is not going to end their existence. Rather, most people will find alternative ideologies by which to practice these areas, if a consistent and coherent alternative understanding in the Absolute Truth isn't found. The search for such alternatives, in fact, is likely to yield a description of the world contrary to the Absolute Truth. This, as we can see, is the norm at the present in modern science, which professes itself as the main opponent of Western religions. On the other hand, if the Absolute Truth is seen as being manifest in all the diverse fields of knowledge, then not only can one advance in the understanding of the Absolute Truth through such diverse studies, but contradictions between the diverse fields, and the seeming contradictions between diversity and the unity, can also be dissolved. Moreover, not everybody is interested in the Absolute Truth alone. Many are simply curious about the workings of nature, the human mind, the material body, and so on. They can develop an interest in the Absolute Truth through the study of the diversities that leads to the unity. Thus, for (1) practical reasons of day-to-day living, (2) to prevent the emergence of conflicting alternative ideas that try to solve focused areas of problems in different ways, and (3) to get people interested in the Absolute Truth who are may not otherwise be so interested in religion, the diverse fields of knowledge are encouraged.

The Vedic system of medicine, called Ayurveda, for example, describes the body not as chemicals, but as three conflicting tendencies called kapha, pitta, and vāta. Health is defined as their 'balance' and sickness as their 'imbalance'. This sets the precedence for a broader understanding of nature as the three modes called sattva, rajas, and tamas, which are constantly conflicting and become dominant or subordinate. These dominant and subordinate structures entail that no position in the world is permanent. Therefore, we must balance these alternatives through choices, and every situation needs a different choice. The world cannot exist without such choices, and hence the soul is necessary. Since the soul can make mistakes in its choices, therefore, there must be laws of morality. But these moral laws themselves are contextual, so there must be an absolute principle by which we can make the correct choices. This absolute principle is devotion to the Lord. Therefore, we can see how the study of the body leads to the gradual understanding of conflict, choices, morality, and eventually God. In so far as health and medicine are common concerns for everyone, people will invent theories about health and the body. We can reject medicine as being irrelevant to transcendence, but we can also understand medicine compatible with the nature of transcendence. This doesn't make medicine the most important subject, but it remains another way for the doctors and the patients to develop the knowledge of Absolute Truth through medicine.

QUESTION

But isn't this diversity prone to some misuse for mundane purposes? For example, many people today use Yoga merely as bodily exercises. The purposes of controlling the mind and focusing it on the Paramātma doesn't exist. In the same way, medicine can be used simply for materialistic purposes. So, don't you consider these things as being prone to misuse by materialists?

3.4.15 (440)

कामकारेण चैके

kāmakāreṇa caike

kāmakāreṇa—for fulfilling the desires; ca—also; eke—sometimes.

TRANSLATION

(The diverse fields of knowledge) may also be sometimes used for fulfilling the (material) desires (and not merely for spiritual emancipation).

COMMENTARY

A hungry or a sick man cannot practice spirituality. A person who is constantly unhappy cannot understand philosophy or practice it. Even if people are well-fed and healthy, have peaceful lives and can practice devotion to the Lord, they are not yet advanced enough to do it all the time. The senses and the mind are very strong, and they drag a person toward their respective objects of enjoyment. If the senses and the mind are completely cut off from their objects, the result is not spiritual progress. Rather, one develops a sick body and mind, becomes unhappy, and eventually loses all interest in spiritual pursuits. Therefore, an intelligent person practices alternating enjoyment and renunciation. If this enjoyment doesn't result in sinful reactions, the practice of incremental enjoyment and renunciation isn't antithetical to the ultimate spiritual goals.

This sūtra uses *eke* or sometimes to affirm that knowledge cannot be used for limitless enjoyment. All enjoyment must be regulated. The two initial steps in the aśtānga-yoga system are *yama* and *niyama*. Yama is the end of sinful activities. Niyama is the regulated practice of various types of activities, including material enjoyments. Yama is things that should never be done, and niyama is those things which should be done regularly. Examples of niyama are eating on time and a fixed amount every day, sleeping for a few hours every day, restrictions on sex life, as well as practicing spiritual life for a fixed duration every day. If the life is regulated in this way, then this occasional enjoyment is not considered contrary to the spiritual goals. The problems arise when enjoyment violates yama (the sinful activities) and niyama (limitless enjoyment).

QUESTION

It is sometimes said that occasional enjoyments lead to the destruction of desires. But others also say that suppression of desire enhances these desires. Aren't these contradictory outcomes? How can both be considered true?

3.4.16 (441)

उपमर्दं च

upamardaṃ ca

upamardaṃ—destruction; ca—and.

TRANSLATION

(The occasional fulfillment of desires) also leads to destruction (of desires).

COMMENTARY

A common argument against restrictions on enjoyment is that when desires are regulated in this way, then the 'suppression' of desires enhances the desires, and the person is subsequently unable to control the desires. This argument confuses the 'regulation' of desires with their 'suppression'. Indeed, the senses and the mind are very strong, and given their previously formed habits of enjoyment, sudden cessation of all enjoyment will certainly lead to sudden indulgence. However, if one practices alternating indulgence and cessation, then the mind and the senses can be trained to form new habits. We must note that the senses and the mind are material. They don't 'need' enjoyment. The force of the senses and the mind exists only due to habit formation. Over numerous lifetimes, the soul has become accustomed to various types of enjoyments, and these habits and desires are therefore called our guna or 'nature'. It is not spiritual nature, but it exists as preformed habits. We cannot change our habits overnight. If we try to do so, the process will certainly be 'suppression', and since nature operates through alternating phases of dominance-subordination, a phase of suppression will certainly be followed by reckless indulgence. The correct process of changing the habits is forming new habits—gradually.

In fact, reckless indulgence doesn't lead to desire cessation. It rather forms new habits. The senses and the mind are not permanently satisfied if we do something excessively. Yes, we may get temporarily tired of a certain type of enjoyment, but in the process, we have formed a new habit of enjoyment. It will certainly return after a while, and the next indulgence will be bigger than the previous one, because new kinds of habits are being formed. Therefore, indulgence never leads to cessation of desires; it rather forms new habits. The process of change involves the formation of new habits, and that is possible only through gradual change. During this change, we should not suddenly stop all enjoyment. We should rather endeavor to reduce it gradually over time.

Of course, even if one stops all enjoyment suddenly, one is still forming a new habit. Yes, one may fall back into enjoyment after a while, but the old habit of renunciation will come back, and the next time one will be better equipped with renunciation. However, since the next indulgence also reinforces the old habits, the person—through alternating extreme renunciation and extreme indulgence—is now developing conflicting habits that move between the excesses. This is a painful path because sudden renunciation leads to a difficult time controlling the mind and the senses, and if one indulges again, he feels guilty about the enjoyment. Therefore, stopping indulgence suddenly is still progress, but it is not a recommended path due to resulting oscillations.

QUESTION

But you have said the desiring and enjoyment are fundamental properties of the soul, and hence they are eternal. It means the cessation of material enjoyment doesn't mean the end of the desires of enjoyment in the soul. So, there seems to be revectoring of desires from sense perception toward spiritual goals. How should we understand the gradual change in a person's desires?

3.4.17 (442)

ऊर्ध्वरेतस्सु च शब्दे हि

ūrdhvaretaḥsu ca śabde hi

ūrdhvaretaḥ su—the semen rises upward in them; ca—also; śabde—this is stated (by those practicing sense control and in yoga philosophy); hi—certainly.

TRANSLATION

Certainly, the semen also rises upward in them; such is the statement (of those who have practiced sense control and is noted in yoga philosophy).

COMMENTARY

The Ayurveda system of medicine describes the body as comprised of seven layers; the outermost layer is called the 'skin', and the innermost layer is called 'semen'. The 'skin' here doesn't mean the sense of touch; the sense of touch is a subtle material element that is beyond the gross body. By 'skin' we mean the gross material covering of the body. Within this skin is flesh, blood, bones, and within the bones lies the 'semen'. This 'semen' exists in both male and female bodies, and it should not be confused with the male procreative fluid. A more accurate understanding of this 'semen' is the potentiality from which the body is manifest. Modern science, for instance, speaks about the stem cells that exist within the bones, which can transform into any other type of cell, including skin, blood, flesh, and even the bones. The stem cells are the most primordial type of cells, and from these cells every other type of cell is formed. Therefore, the body in its more primitive form is these stem cells or 'semen'. The Ayurveda understanding of the body is that as one indulges in sense enjoyment, the 'semen' is gradually depleted. Thus, the body becomes tired, the bones feel weak, and the skin becomes shriveled, etc. On the other hand, if one refrains from sense pleasures, then the 'semen' gradually grows, and the result is stronger bones, better blood circulation, stronger body, shinier skin, etc.

Now, as the body is rejuvenated, there is greater tendency toward sense enjoyment. As we have discussed earlier, desire is stimulated by power, and power is used by desire. A stronger body naturally leads to more desires. And controlling these desires becomes harder. Thus, it is often seen that when someone renounces pleasure suddenly and prematurely, very soon the level of desires in the body increase significantly. One might then commit hedonistic acts which would have been unthinkable earlier. Under the influence of increasing power in the body, one might even display the adverse symptoms of power—e.g., cruelty, egotism, anger, etc. However, if one gets past such impulses through continued restraint, then the 'semen' in the body continues to grow, and makes the body, bones, blood, and the skin stronger and healthier.

In Freudian psychoanalysis there is a well-known process called 'sublimation' in which if our enjoying tendencies are suppressed in one avenue, then they automatically manifest in another avenue. Thus, for instance, Freud believed that sports, politics, and other passionate endeavors are simply sublimations of the sex desire. Freud, however, could not recognize how sublimation can also take one toward higher goals in life. He always thought that suppression of desire leads to sublimation, and this sublimation of the original desire in a convoluted form is the root cause of all the psychological illnesses.

The yogic understanding of sublimation, however, states that when the bodily strength is conserved by restraining from sense pleasure, then it initially seeks the previously dominant channels of enjoyment. So, the yogi is taught to be careful about these avenues of enjoyment. The goal is to keep shutting off the varied outlets of pleasure so that the energy can be continually sublimated. When all the mundane outlets of the energy have been shut off, then the same energy is sublimated toward spiritual goals. This sublimation of the energy toward higher purposes is called the 'rising of the semen'. We must not think of this process in physical terms—i.e., 'semen' is not rising like a liquid in a body. It is rising in the sense that the energy in the body changes form and different forms of energy are useful for different purposes. Modern science recognizes many forms of energy—kinetic, potential, thermal, etc. But in the Vedic system, this energy is typed—it can take innumerable forms. Thus, in one form, the energy is the passion and ability for music; in another form, the energy is the passion and ability for sports. The highest form of the energy ('height' indicating hierarchy of purposes) is spiritual activities. Thus, the 'rising' of the 'semen' is the change in the form of the material energy toward higher purposes.

The Śrīmad Bhāgavatam narrates the story of Hiraṇyakaśipu to illustrate this fact. He performed such severe austerities sitting in one place, that the ants had eaten away all the skin and flesh. And yet, he was alive because the 'semen' exists inside the bones, and the ants could not eat away the bones. The living force or the prāṇa exists in all the seven layers of the body, but even if the other layers are destroyed, the prāṇa continues to exist inside the bones. Thus, a person can continue living even if the only thing left in the body is bones. Śrīmad Bhāgavatam also gives the example of Maharshi Dadhīchi whose bones had become so strong due to austerities that they were the only material out of which the strongest weapon could be built for killing the demon Vṛtrāsura. Despite his immense power, he was compassionate and agreed to leave his body (actually, just the bones) for the preparation of the said weapon. This weapon came to be known as Vajra—the strongest owned by the demigod Indra.

The point is that the body is not just the skin, flesh, and bones; the deepest level of the body is the 'semen', and the body can remain alive even if the other layers are destroyed. The rising of the 'semen' is the transformation of this material reality into new forms suitable for the highest kinds of pursuits.

In an earlier sūtra it was said that material enjoyment is a necessity for most people. In a subsequent sūtra it was said that material enjoyment can be gradually reduced by regulated living. And this sūtra states that when this enjoyment is reduced, the energy is sublimated for higher purposes. Thus, a progressive path from the necessity of enjoyment, to occasional enjoyment, to the sublimation of one form of enjoyment into higher forms is understood.

Topic 2

QUESTION

But many people say that the reduction of material desires is only for those in the renounced order of life—also known as *sannyāsa*. For those in the family life there is no need for renunciation, and they can continue enjoying unlimitedly. What would be your response to this type of claim and argument?

3.4.18 (443)

परामर्शं जैमिनिरचोदना च अपवदति हि

parāmarśaṃ jaiminiracodanā ca apavadati hi

parāmarśaṃ—conclusion; jaiminiḥ—by Jaimini; acodanā—there are no restrictions; ca—and; apavadati hi—because it is certainly a bogus argument.

TRANSLATION

Such a conclusion is drawn by Jaimini; there are no restrictions (for practicing renunciation) and this is certainly a bogus argument.

COMMENTARY

Jaimini, and the Mīmāṃsā system, considered the performance of rituals as the essence of religion. Renunciation of material desires was possible, but it was only for those who had entered the sannyāsa stage of life. For the householders or grihastha, such renunciation was not accepted or recommended. Since people generally enter the sannyāsa stage very late in life, and by that time the body is already weakened, such renunciation by disability is not true renunciation. Even when the body is weakened, the desire to enjoy persists in the subconscious mind. Unless one has practiced renunciation throughout their life, the renunciation by disability doesn't help in spiritual advancement. Thus, we can see many old people being bedridden and unable to enjoy life. This bedridden state devoid of enjoyment cannot be considered renunciation. Therefore, the claim that renunciation is only for the old is called a bogus argument.

QUESTION

So, you are recommending the practice of desire control and renunciation throughout one's life, and all four stages of life must practice renunciation?

3.4.19 (444)

अनुष्ठेयं बादरायणःसाम्यश्रुतेःहि

anuṣṭheyaṃ bādarāyaṇaḥ sāmyaśruteḥ

anuṣṭheyam—should be practiced; bādarāyaṇaḥ—(so says) Bādarāyana; sāmya—uniformly (throughout life); śruteḥ—as the scripture enjoins.

TRANSLATION

(Renunciation and desire control) should be practiced, according to Bādarāyana, uniformly (throughout one's life) just as the scripture enjoins.

COMMENTARY

The practice of the āsrama system, comprising of four stages—called Brahmacharya, Grihastha, Vānaprastha, and Sannyāsa—is meant for inculcating gradual renunciation. In the Brahmacharya stage (that goes from 1-25 years) a student lives in a place offered by his teacher, begs for alms from householders, and eats after offering food to the teacher. In the Grihastha stage of life (from 25-50 years), one lives in their own house, but they donate a large fraction of their earning to the weaker sections of society, and whatever is left is enjoyed in a very regulated manner. In the Vānaprastha stage, men give up family life, and make a shelter in the forest, subsisting only on what nature provides, while women live with their children giving up the pleasures they enjoyed previously with their husbands. Finally, in the Sannyāsa stage, one gives up even the house in the forest, and simply travels from place to place—never staying in one place for more than 3 days—and subsisting on whatever they can get. Thus, out of the four stages, three stages—Brahmacharya, Vānaprastha, and Sannyāsa—explicitly forbid enjoyment, and the Grihastha stage is restricted enjoyment.

This sūtra states that one must uniformly practice sense control throughout their life. It is not possible to suddenly renounce everything in old age if one hasn't practiced renunciation throughout their life. The habits formed during childhood and early age, followed by continued practice of regulations, is the main practical recipe for a person to finally give up material desires.

QUESTION

But when a person is young, the senses and the body are strong, and the drive toward enjoyment is strong. This makes the sense control during youth very difficult. How can one practice renunciation if it is so difficult?

3.4.20 (445)

विधिर्वा धारणवत्

vidhirvā dhāraṇavat

vidhiḥ—injunctions (of regulated living that result in renunciation); vā—rather; dhāraṇavat—according to one's capacity to hold.

TRANSLATION

The injunctions (of regulated living that result in renunciation) must rather be applied according to one's capacity to hold (the difficulties of renunciation).

COMMENTARY

In earlier sūtras it was said that one should practice renunciation gradually. However, since every person may have achieved different levels of spiritual advancement in their previous lives, the recommendation is not for everyone to emulate the most renounced. Rather, one must understand their own capacity to renounce material pleasures, and then act accordingly. This is not a license for unlimited enjoyment. It is rather a statement about making progress from where one is presently situated—if one is deeply addicted to material pleasures, then the level of renunciation will naturally be lesser than one who has practiced such renunciation in the past and has progressed significantly. In short, the tendency to universalize rules and regulations must be avoided. These rules have a purpose—to elevate a person from their current state to a future better state. Habits are changed slowly, and one must consider the present habits and desires before undertaking ambitious steps in renunciation. Ambition and renunciation don't work together well. Some ambitious people take to harsh forms of renunciation hoping to emulate the most advanced personalities. However, that ambitious renunciation generally fails because ambition is used to suppress the desires for some time, but the desire is sublimated in other ways. Those sublimations of material desire then destroy the renunciation.

Topic 3

QUESTION

Since so many people have failed in renunciation, many people argue that those trying to renounce are simply doing it for obtaining praise. Sometimes it is also said those who have failed in life make a show of renunciation. And conversely, the renounced are also viewed as failures in life. What can we say to those arguments that renunciation is for show, or a sign of one's failure?

3.4.21 (446)

स्तुतिमात्रमुपादानादिति चेत् न अपूर्वत्वात्

stutimātramupādānāditi cet na apūrvatvāt

stutimātram—mere praise; upādānāt—due to appropriation; iti cet—it be said; na—not so; apūrvatvāt—on account of its incomparable nature.

TRANSLATION

If it is said that (renunciation is) merely for appropriating praise (from the gullible) (we say) not so because it is incomparable to (the enjoyment).

COMMENTARY

It is a common misconception that renunciation is another type of enjoyment. If someone has failed materially in life, then they take up renunciation to prove that they haven't truly failed. And because renounced people get a lot of respect from others, their actions are merely for appropriating praise. The flaw in this argument is that renunciation is progressive; one doesn't begin by renouncing some pleasures, and then fall back into those same pleasures. Those who do so, are certainly to be considered appropriating (false) praise. The intelligent people can see when someone pretends to be renounced only for getting more followers, wealth, power, fame, worship, etc. This is not renunciation; it is factually cheating and therefore worse than honest gratification. Real renunciation is described here as being incomparable to material enjoyment. In short, we cannot claim that renunciation is another type of enjoyment. This incomparable nature is seen due to progression. Just as a materialist becomes more and more attached to the enjoyment, similarly, the true renouncer becomes more and more detached from material enjoyment. The false renouncers remain attached to enjoyment, and sometimes, tend to enjoy—even pretending to be renounced—far more than those who claim not to be renounced.

The term *apūrva* has many other meanings, such as novelty, a new beginning, unprecedented, not done in the past, etc. All these meanings can be applied in this case if we understand that renunciation is progressive. It is not a temporary flash in the pan; it is rather a new beginning that progresses continually. It is not repetition of what one has done in the past; it is unprecedented. This doesn't mean that no renouncer appropriates praise. It only means that the definition of a renouncer is one who has arrived at an irrevocable point in their life; they are not renouncing as another way of extending enjoyment. They are renouncing because they have rejected the previous ways of their life.

QUESTION

From your answer it seems that you are implicitly accepting the possibility of false renunciation. If so, how can we know when it is false or true?

3.4.22 (447)

भावशब्दाच्च

bhāvaśabdācca

bhāva—the mood or intention; śabdāt—from the words; ca—also.

TRANSLATION

(Renunciation can be known) from the intention of the words as well.

COMMENTARY

Meanings are grasped in three stages—universal, contextual, and individual. By universal, we mean the dictionary meanings which are known to the speakers and listeners of a language. Typically, the same word has many meanings, and the context of speaking reduces the number of possibilities. For example, if someone says "no" to a proposal, then "no" has a universal meaning—i.e., the rejection of the proposal—but it also has a contextual meaning based on what was previously said (as it is the denial of what was previously said). However, even the context doesn't completely fix the meaning. After all, the word "no" may be uttered sarcastically, jokingly, or as a factual denial. Thus, to know the true meaning, one must delve into a person's intentions. The discovery of intentions requires us to broaden the context even further—we must know what a person believes in, their current and past goals, their habits (e.g., of lying or being sarcastic), etc.—which require knowing a person's true nature.

Linguists in the West have problems with the last two stages. They easily accept the stage of universal mapping of words to dictionary meanings. But they have difficulties in accepting how meanings are subject to context. Although many linguists now accept that context plays a huge role in deciphering meaning, the universalist nature of logic and mathematics ensures that this method is less understood and can never be automated into machines. Finally, practically everyone claims that a person's intentions can never be known. So, the conclusion is that the intended meanings can never be truly known.

But consider the case where a detective is trying to solve a serial murder. The first step is generally to find the murder weapon or methodology, because many things about the crime can be known from the way the murder was committed. But this is often not enough because the same methodology can be used on different victims. So, the detective also looks for patterns in the victims. This pattern then leads them to some understanding of the nature of the criminal, and why they might be committing these crimes. Then they use this pattern to look for potential persons who might commit such crimes, thereby widening their search through past events, crimes, even across locations and times. Thus, we can see that we go from physical evidence to the types of victims, to find the potential motives, and then use these motives to identify the criminal. So, the claim that motives can never be truly known is a false premise. Likewise, when it is hard to find the physical evidence, and the context cannot be broadened, many individuals are indicted simply if they are known to have motives, and there is a lot of circumstantial although inconclusive physical evidence.

So, the claim that we can never know the intentions underlying speech is false. Yes, it is possible that if we don't know enough about a person, we cannot understand the intended meaning. But this just means that we must broaden our understanding of the person by looking into their past behaviors. Sometimes, we might observe a person's body language, facial expressions, voice tones, and other things that indicate an emotional state. The point is that we always try to decipher a person's mental state as the explanation of their bodily actions. And we seek that explanation which spans their entire life holistically. The simplest explanation based on universal meanings, or even actions in a particular context, may conflict with those in other contexts. And this conflict is resolved by finding alternative explanations for events in other contexts.

This process of discovering the intentions is universal, and it applies to the detection of renunciation as well. A person may seem renounced in some cases but isn't renounced in other cases. The correct explanation is that which covers both scenarios, rather than one of them, and the context must be widened.

This method of deciphering the intention from empirical evidence is, however, not the only way. Those who have a developed mind, can directly perceive a person's mental state. This point was also made in an earlier sūtra in response to questions about how to know who a true devotee is. A preliminary response what that a devotee exhibits symptoms of bliss on their body. A deeper explanation, however, is that one must know their mental state. The difficulty in this mental perception is that it takes one to know one. You cannot identify a devotee by the mental perception process unless you are a devotee. Likewise, you cannot identify an evil person unless you are also evil. When something is alien to our nature, it doesn't fit into the 'molds' of our mind, and it goes unperceived. Our senses and the mind are like sockets of different shapes, into which objects of different shape fit. If the object and the mold are incompatible, then either the object is modified to fit the mold, or the mold is modified to fit the object, or they remain disconnected. Therefore, if we don't have the mold, we will either change the description of reality to fit what we understand, or we will change our molds of thinking to fit our mind to the external world, or we will simply say that the world cannot be understood using the present mind.

The advanced devotee—called an *uttama adhikārī*—sees everyone as a devotee because they have no other mental mold, and they cannot see evil. Likewise, a neophyte devotee—called a *kanistha adhikārī*—sees everyone else as a neophyte, because they have no other mental mold. In between these two, there is a class of people—called *madhyamā adhikārī*—who are pure, but they also carry the mental molds to perceive evil. Sometimes, the pure devotee learns these evil mental modes to discriminate between the good and the evil.

Given this problem of perception, in which you change your mind to understand the mental reality, other methods such as trying to find the best explanation of a broad set of action is employed. They are essential for those without mental perception, but unnecessary for those with mental perception. The same can be said of the renounced people as well. If one is truly renounced, he can see who is or is not renounced. But if one is not renounced, he might accept non-renounced as renounced, only to find later that perception was false. Such mistakes are detected over time as a person's nature is better understood.

Topic 4

QUESTION

But sometimes people say that a person is progressing in spiritual life, and since they haven't perfected it, they are sometimes renounced and sometimes indulgent. Such an argument begs for leniency against the practitioner by stating that they are not perfect, but they are much better than the others who seem much more indulgent. Should this claim be accepted as true or false?

3.4.23 (448)
पारप्लिवार्था इति चेत् न विशेषितत्वात्
pāriplavārthā iti cet na viśeṣitatvāt

pāriplavārthāḥ—the intention being unstable; iti cet—if it be said; na—not so; viśeṣita—their uniqueness; tvāt—from that (which is their worst state).

TRANSLATION

If it is said that the intention in a person is unstable (i.e., a person is sometimes good and sometimes bad, and hence we should average the two results), (we say) not so; their uniqueness is from that (which is their worst state).

COMMENTARY

If someone commits a murder, we don't say that this person only commits murder occasionally; most of the time he is not killing other people. Likewise, for a thief, we don't say that he only steals occasionally; the rest of the time he is an honest person. The same holds true for every other case. The true nature of a person is the worst thing he can do. The worst and best exists in us in a potential form. When the circumstances are ripe, some situations bring out the best in us, while others bring out the worst in us. Most of us will behave quite well if the circumstances are favorable to our desires. We are only tested by the unfavorable circumstances, which bring out the worst in us. Therefore, when the situation is good, a person's true nature remains unknown. It is known only when the situation worsens, that we see the bad qualities in a person, and that is their true nature. As a person advances in spiritual life, the cleaning of the mind happens from the grossest to the subtlest. This means that certain types of gross crimes—such a murder, violence, cheating etc.—will disappear first.

Over time, other subtle maladies such as anger, egotism, and sadness will also go away. The process of purification is not only that we stop performing certain actions, but we also wipe out the potentiality of that action ever in the future. If, for whatever reason, the actions are invisible, but the potentiality exists, then the lowest such type of potentiality defines the true nature of the person.

It is said that a chain is only as strong as its weakest link. The same is true of a person. He or she is only as good as their worst quality. The fact that these qualities may not always be visible to others doesn't make such people saints. Therefore, the argument that a person sometimes exhibits good qualities and sometimes exhibits bad qualities, and we should view the situation compassionately by erring on the side of the good rather than the bad is rejected.

Vedic texts are replete with narrations of demons like Hiraṇyakaśipu and Rāvana, who perform severe penances, obtain great mystical powers, and possess immense knowledge. But all these good qualities are immediately nullified by a single bad activity—namely the abduction of Mother Sita by Rāvana, or the torturing of Prahalad by Hiraṇyakaśipu. We do not praise the numerous good qualities in Hiraṇyakaśipu and Rāvana, even though their good qualities may be better than many others. A person's nature is judged by their worst quality because under appropriate circumstances that's all that we will see. The purport is that the renunciation must be judged by the worst indulgence. If one is capable of murder, although in a saint's dress, then he is a murderer.

QUESTION

Many people may not commit crimes but may incite others into the crimes. Should we consider them better than those who commit the crimes?

3.4.24 (449)

तथा चैकवाक्यतोपबन्धात्

tathā caikavākyatopabandhāt

tathā—similarly; ca—also; eka—occasionally; vākyataḥ—from the speaking; pabandhāt—(we know) being bound due to (their qualities).

TRANSLATION

(Just as those committing crimes are criminals), in the same way, also those who occasionally speak (incite others into crimes) are bound (by their qualities).

COMMENTARY

Those who incite, encourage, or demand others to commit sinful activities are not any better than those who follow these instructions. Thus, it is said that those who kill animals, transport the dead body, sell the meat, or cook it, are equally liable for the killing as the person who eats the meat. This is because if one of these steps did not occur, then the subsequent chain would collapse. Thus, for instance, if there is no demand for meat in a market, then the killing, transporting, selling, and cooking of meat will also end. Likewise, if the killing stops, then transportation, selling, cooking, and eating will also end. Therefore, everyone involved in the succession of such actions is equally implicated.

Topic 5

QUESTION

If everyone is equally implicated in a sequence of actions, doesn't it imply that they should be equally responsible and punishable for their actions?

3.4.25 (450)
अत एव चाग्नीन्धनाद्यनपेक्षा
ata eva cāgnīndhanādyanapekṣā

ata eva—therefore; ca—also; agni-indhanādi—fire and that which is lighted into fire, etc.; anapekṣā—should not be distinguished or compared.

TRANSLATION

Therefore, also there is no need to draw a distinction between whether the fire was caused by the initial spark of fire or by the wood that was ignited.

COMMENTARY

One can say that he only offered the initial spark of fire, and if the wood was not combustible then there would be no fire—thus trying to shift the blame to the combustible wood. This argument is rejected because the choice of the combustible wood was also made by the person who was offering the spark of fire. However, the responsibility is not taken away from the wood. Therefore, both the initial spark of fire and the combustible wood are equally responsible for the fire. Any attempt to move the responsibility from the spark to the wood, or from the wood to the spark, is rejected here. The purport is that since both parties are equally responsible, the resulting consequences are also equal.

Topic 6

QUESTION

If everyone is responsible for an action, doesn't it mean that even with good deeds, the good results of the deed must be received by all involved?

3.4.26 (451)
सर्वापेक्षा च यज्ञादिश्रुतेःअश्ववत्
sarvāpekṣā ca yajñādiśruteḥ, aśvavat

sarvāpekṣā—everyone's expectations; ca—also; yajñādi-śruteḥ—the scriptures state that the (benefit of) yajñá; aśvavat—just like the horse.

TRANSLATION

The scriptures state that a yajñá (or sacrifice) also fulfills everyone's expectations—even that of the horse (who may be sacrificed as part of the yajñá).

COMMENTARY

Just like the responsibility for a bad deed is shared by all those involved, similarly, the consequences of a good deed are also enjoyed by everyone involved. The example of the Ashvamedha yajñá is cited here, in which a horse is let loose by a king and wherever the horse goes, the king becomes the ruler of that land, unless the current ruler of that land holds the horse, fights with the king, and wins. At the end of the yajñá, the horse is sacrificed, but due to the participation in the yajñá, the horse ascends to heaven, while the king enjoys the kingdom. Thus, if the yajñá is performed according to prescribed rules and regulations, then, everyone benefits: the horse gets a better life, and the king rules over a much bigger kingdom. If, however, the yajñá is not performed according to the rules and regulations, then the king loses the battles, the horse is slaughtered for no good reason, and everybody loses in the process. This example is given to illustrate the fact that it is not just humans who share the consequences of good deeds, but even the animals are benefitted from it. The purport is that just as suffering is shared by the participants in a bad deed, similarly, the benefits are distributed among the those participating in a good deed.

QUESTION

We were speaking about renunciation, or detachment from the results of one's actions. But now we are saying that these actions bring good and bad results, and therefore one may be motivated by these results, which is then counterproductive to the goal of detachment. So, how can one perform the activities in a way that is renunciation of results, but not of the activities?

3.4.27 (452)

शमदमाद्युपेतःस्यात्तथा'पि तु
तद्वधिस्तदङ्गतया तेषामवश्यानुष्ठेयत्वात्

śamadamādyupetaḥ syāttathā'pi tu
tadvidhestadaṅgatayā teṣāmavaśyānuṣṭheyatvāt

śama—tranquility; damādi—self-control, etc.; upetaḥ—possessing; syāt—if; tathā api—even then; tu—but; tadvidheḥ—knowing that (the Absolute Truth); tadaṅgatayā—being a part (of the Absolute Truth); teṣām—those; avaśya—necessarily; anuṣṭheyatvāt—from being just like the performance.

TRANSLATION

Even if one possesses tranquility and self-control, one must submissively and necessarily become the performance (of the activity), knowing that (the Absolute Truth) and behaving just like the part (of that Absolute Truth).

COMMENTARY

There is a difference between doing an activity and becoming that activity. The term *anuṣṭheyatvāt* means that a person has become just like the activity. The use of 'just like' means that the person and the action are not identical. And yet, the person is so completely absorbed in the action, that the two have become non-different. But what does such a kind of non-difference mean?

When a materialistic person performs a yajñá, he offers something to the deity and expects something in return. But if a person becomes that activity, then the distinction between the person and the activity is dissolved. Then, the person offers himself to the worshipped deity. The deity is the agni, the worshipper is the soma, and the activity is the vāyu. There is a difference between the worshipper and the activity, but during the sacrifice, if the person offers himself, then the activity of offering and the object being offered are identical.

The earlier sūtras spoke about detachment and renunciation. But this sūtra states that this detachment is only the first step. The next step is that one offers himself because he is not expecting anything in return. When there is a desire from a yajñá, then there is a difference between the offering and the person making the offering. But if these desires are destroyed, then one surrenders oneself to the person being worshipped, and offers himself in the sacrifice.

Thus, the previous discussion about renunciation is now connected to the process of yajñá and is therefore equivalent to the process of yoga. In a yajñá, an offering is made. But in yoga, the self is offered. In a yajñá, there can be selfish expectations—I'm giving you this, so that you will give me that. But in yoga, there is no such expectation—I'm giving you myself, and since I have given myself to you, I have become your property; you can use me ask you like. If one is not detached from material enjoyment, then every offering is made with the expectation of a return, and even as one performs yajñá, one doesn't become that yajñá. When there is accompanying detachment, one offers oneself.

The results of good and bad actions are shared by the participants, if there is a difference between the activity and the person—i.e., when there is a desire to obtain something other than the performance of the activity itself. However, when this distinction is lost, then the results of good and bad actions disappear because one is no longer asking for results; one is offering oneself in the process, and the good and bad results are now owned by the person being worshipped.

The example of the whole and the part illustrates this idea. Suppose you hit someone using your hand. Then, you don't say: I did not hit you; it was only my hand. You own the responsibility of hitting, not the hand. In the same way, when the devotee offers himself to the Lord, and acts on the Lord's behalf, then the responsibility of the actions is not on the part; it rests with the whole. The Lord being absolute is not implicated by the actions—good or bad. Unlike the previous sūtras, which said that one will get good or bad results according to their actions, this sūtra says that if one offers oneself in the process, then the responsibility of the actions is no longer applicable to the actor. These actions are the responsibility of the Lord, and He is not implicated by the actions. Therefore, by offering oneself to the Lord, the soul is liberated from karma.

Topic 7

QUESTION

But if the killing of a horse is justified as part of the performance of yajñá, then many people extend this to say that we can kill the animals for our food, if this food is offered to the Lord. In fact, it is said that these animals have been given to us for our consumption by the Lord, and the Lord is therefore responsible for giving these animals for us, and He owns the result of the killing.

3.4.28 (453)

सर्वान्नानुमतिश्च प्राणात्यये तद्दर्शनात्

sarvānnānumatiśca prāṇātyaye taddarśanāt

sarva-anna-anumatiḥ—permission to take all sorts of food; prāṇātyaye—when life is jeopardized; tat-darśanāt—from that philosophy.

TRANSLATION

The permission to take all sorts of food (is granted) only when one's life is jeopardized; that is the philosophical conclusion (of the scriptures).

COMMENTARY

The basic principle of a yajñá or sacrifice is that something lower is sacrificed for something higher. Thus, a soldier may die defending a country, and that death is called a 'sacrifice'. But if the country could be defended by other peaceful means, then wars should not be waged, and soldiers should not be sacrificed unnecessarily. In short, when a sacrifice is to be performed, then we should also make endeavors to identify the lowest thing to be sacrificed.

When a horse was sacrificed in the Aśwamedha yajñá, the sacrifice was not merely for the satisfaction of the king's pride. Rather, a higher moral principle was be served by this yajñá, and only those kings who aimed to create a moral society by their rule would undertake such a sacrifice. The Brahmanas would perform this yajñá for the great kings, as a method to bring immoral rulers under the control of the moral ruler. The horse sacrifice was acceptable because the loss of the horse was smaller relative to the gains by this sacrifice. This wasn't indiscriminate killing of animals. It was a carefully considered bargain of identifying the least amount of loss for the greatest amount of gain. Thus, for example, a king would not indiscriminately kill the defeated rulers, if they accepted the rule of the superior king. The defeated king was only expected to present a token gift to the winning ruler, as a mark of acceptance of their superiority and authority. They did not lose their kingdom, or their position as the rulers. They, however, accepted the superiority of a more powerful ruler.

This general principle of sacrifices applies to our eating habits too. While eating, we sacrifice some life to sustain our life. However, this sacrifice is acceptable under two conditions—(a) our life must factually be superior to the lives of those whom we sacrifice, and (b) the least amount of sacrifice must be performed in the process. It is generally accepted that human life is superior to animal life, so animals can be sacrificed for human benefit. However, animal life is also superior to plant life. Therefore, by the principle of the least amount of sacrifice to obtain a gain, humans are allowed plant-based food, rather than meat. An exception is cow's milk, after the calf has had the mother's milk, and the cow still has surplus milk. In short, humans are not allowed to sacrifice a calf's hunger to satisfy their hunger. Even in the case of plants, the sacrifice must be minimized. For instance, trees cannot be cut indiscriminately, and firewood must come from the dried, fallen branches. Fruits can be plucked from trees because they are of no use to the tree. Grains can be used, after the harvest is ripe. It is said that jīvā jīvasya jīvanam, or life depends on other life. Therefore, some sacrifice is necessary. But this sacrifice must always be minimized.

This principle is enunciated in this sūtra by saying that animal food is allowed only when our life is in danger. If we cannot obtain plant-based food, and our life is in danger, then we can sacrifice animals (assuming our life is producing a greater good than the animal's life, which is implicitly presumed here). The principle of sacrificing something lower for something higher still holds true. This principle is only extended to meat-eating in rare cases.

QUESTION

You are saying that violence is not contrary to religious principles, and non-violence is not a universal principle. Rather, both violence and non-violence can be applied depending upon what is being gained and sacrificed?

3.4.29 (454)

अबाधाच्च

abādhācca

abādhāt—because of a non-contradiction or non-forbidding; ca—and.

TRANSLATION

Because of a non-contradiction or non-forbidding (both non-violence and killing can be employed, as they are a person's dharma in different cases).

COMMENTARY

The principle of dharma is identifying the best possible action under given circumstances. Sometimes violence is necessary, and at other times non-violence is required. If the greater good is served by violence, then violence is accepted. But if the greater good is served by non-violence, then non-violence is dharma. The soldier sacrifices his life for a greater good, and the soldier kills others for a greater good. The ruler must sometimes punish the criminals because that serves the greater good—the correct example is set for everyone. And the ruler must sometimes demonstrate kindness—because it teaches others to be kind. Cruelty and kindness are not universal principles; yajñá, which involves sacrificing something inferior for something superior, is the universal principle.

QUESTION

But we don't find such descriptions of violating moral principles in the śrutī. How can we justify such claims when they are absent in the śrutī?

3.4.30 (455)
अपि च स्मर्यते
api ca smaryate

api ca—moreover; smaryate—in the smritis.

TRANSLATION

Moreover, the smritis say (that a sacrifice for a higher gain is acceptable).

COMMENTARY

In this regard, there is a pertinent story from Rāmayana, where Lord Rāma asks his brother Lakshman to take Mother Sīta to the forest on a sightseeing trip, and then leaves Her in Sage Valmiki's aśrama. At the time of abandonment, Mother Sīta is pregnant with twins—Lava and Kuśa—who are then born in Sage Valmiki's aśrama. As the twins grow up, Sage Valmiki becomes their teacher, and under his tutelage, they become formidable warriors. One day while playing, they find a majestic horse running through the forest, and not knowing that the horse was sent by Lord Rāma to conquer other lands as part of an Aśvamedha yajñá, they capture the horse. The soldiers following the horse request the children to return the horse, but the twins refuse to do so. Eventually a battle starts, and Lava and Kuśa defeat every forthcoming warrior. Everyone is stunned that two five-year old boys have defeated an entire army. The word reaches Lord Rāma and He arrives on the battlefield to fight with the twins. But Sage Valmiki intervenes to stop the battle, informing the children that they are the sons of Lord Rāma, and the twins return to their father.

The story of their separation and union is tearful. But within it is a lesson about why Lord Rāma had abandoned Mother Sīta. The Rāmayana narrates the story that Lord Rāma abandoned Mother Sīta because He heard a washerman saying to his wife, that he is not like Lord Rāma to accept a woman after she was abducted by another man—a snide reference to Mother Sīta's abduction by Rāvana. Some people claim that Lord Rāma abandoned Mother Sīta because He was attached to His prestige and honor. The belief underlying such a claim is that since Mother Sīta was innocent, She should not have been abandoned. And by the principle of not punishing the innocent, Lord Rama must have turned a deaf ear to such false allegations. But the reasoning in the Rāmayana is different—Lord Rama sacrificed His and Mother Sīta's happiness for a greater cause of setting the right example through Their behaviors that promiscuity was unacceptable, even though in their specific case promiscuity did not exist.

There are examples in the smriti where the Lord Himself lies or urges others to lie for a greater good. For example, during the Mahabharata battle,

Lord Kṛṣṇa asked Yudhishthira to tell Dronāchārya that Aśvatthāmā had died (when Dronāchārya's son Aśvatthāmā hadn't died, although an elephant named Aśvatthāmā had been killed), so that he would drop his weapons out of grief for his son. Lord Kṛṣṇa also asked Arjuna to shoot arrows at Bhīśma while standing behind Shikhandī—who was a woman in his previous birth—because He knew that Bhīśma would not retaliate, and Arjuna will be able to shoot Bhīśma down. These things may sound unethical from our mundane perspective, but they are not. Dronāchārya and Bhīśma were such great warriors that they could never be defeated. Bhīśma had the boon of voluntary death, so he could never be killed unless he chose to leave his body voluntarily. And yet, defeating the side on which they were fighting on was the greater good.

We have earlier discussed how dharma is truthfulness, but these sūtras now reject that conclusion by stating that even lying is good when it serves the greater good. Thus, the understanding of dharma is gradually nuanced.

QUESTION

But isn't it likely that when the greater good is preferred as a higher principle, then everyone can claim some greater good and do whatever they want? Wouldn't the application of this principle lead to greater bad than good?

3.4.31 (456)

शब्दश्चातोऽकामकारे

śabdaścāto'kāmakāre

śabdaḥ—the scriptures; ca—and; a tu—but forbid; kāmakāre—acting according to one's wishful or whimsical desires.

TRANSLATION

And hence the scriptures forbid (applying the principles of greater good to sacrifice lesser good) by acting based on one's wishful or whimsical desires.

COMMENTARY

Even when the principles are described clearly, their application is not easily understood by everyone. For example, we discussed earlier how religions have been killing other people in the name of God's love. The same point is now made for the greater good—we cannot invent notions of good whimsically. Wars waged to spread democracy or capitalism are examples of such whims. Here is an indication that reading scriptures is not a substitute for intelligence on how to apply the scripture's injunctions. If that intelligence is missing, then scriptures are misinterpreted whimsically and used for selfish purposes.

Bad people misuse any good system to produce bad results. And a good person can use a bad system to produce the best results. The system is not always the cause of the good or the bad. Often, the people who use these systems are responsible for the good or bad results. When a system is put in the hands of an intelligent, well-meaning, and moral person, then the results are mostly good. When the same system is put in the hands of foolish, ill-meaning, or immoral people, then the results are mostly bad. Any system of principles, rules, and regulations is impersonal. We cannot encode principles, rules, and regulations in a machine and expect it to make the best decisions. An intelligent, moral, and well-meaning person is essential to use the system correctly.

Therefore, people who are foolish, ill-meaning, and immoral are forbidden from reading scriptures, because they misapply the scriptural principles. As these principles are misused, people blame the system, rather than the foolish, ill-willed, and immoral people employing it; the system is rejected, and all potential for goodness is destroyed. There is a real danger in the foolish, ill-willed, and immoral people ascending to any position of power and influence in a society—even when the society is structured according to a good system.

Modern democratic societies can already see such outcomes. The founding fathers of a nation may have been moral, intelligent, and well-meaning, and they might have created a system that can produce good outcomes. But when that system falls in the hands of foolish, ill-meaning, and immoral people, the results are always bad. Then people talk about changing the system—e.g., by creating new laws, structures, or regulations in society. But these new creations again fall into the hands of the foolish, ill-willed, and immoral people, and the changes to such laws, structure, and regulations don't create the desired outcomes. Hence, every society keeps trying to create the best system, rather than create the best people. They have imbibed the false idea that if the system was perfected, then the outcomes would naturally be good. In short, they think that a system of rules and regulations constitutes a machine that will coerce people to create good outcomes. They don't realize that the machine is controlled by immoral, foolish, and ill-willed people, who keep misusing the system.

Therefore, no amount of knowledge, education, or clarity in rules, and regulations can replace the judgments of a moral, well-meaning, and intelligent person. A system can be used to create more such moral, well-meaning, and intelligent people, only if the system is presently under such good people. If the system is under foolish, ill-meaning, and immoral people, we cannot expect the system to automatically produce a better future. Goodness doesn't begin in building a better system. It always begins in empowering better people.

The Vedic scriptures are eternal, and the knowledge in them is eternally true. But this eternal truth is visible, beneficial, and practically demonstrated only by the pure devotees of the Lord, who have the highest level of intelligence, the greatest understanding of the ultimate good, and the best ideas about when to apply which principle, for how long, and upon which people. Unfortunately, in the present age, every fool considers himself qualified to read the scriptures, understand their true meanings, and apply their principles. But the reality is that such fools drag themselves down, hurt other people by misapplying the scriptural principles, and bring a bad name to the system itself.

Topic 8

QUESTION

But since most people are prone to misinterpretation of the principles of

greater goodness, and are likely to misuse such principles toward selfish ends, what do we do? Obviously, we cannot stop reading the scriptures or trying to understand them. And we cannot just wait for the perfect people to arrive.

3.4.32 (457)
वहितित्वाच्चाश्रमकर्मापि
vihitatvāccāśramakarmāpi

vihitatvāt—since they are prescribed by the scriptures; ca—and; āśrama-karma—the duties of the āśrama (the four order of life—Brahmacharya, Grihastha, Vanaprastha, and Sannyasa); api—also.

TRANSLATION

And because the duties of the āśrama are prescribed in the scriptures (we can fall back upon them) also (in case of doubts about the greatest good).

COMMENTARY

We can now see how religion—which originates in the love of God, is then reduced to the moral values of excellence and virtue, which is again reduced to a sensible choice of sacrifice—eventually reduces to a system of rules and regulations. The reason is that people don't know how to love God. They are unable to grasp the nature of virtue. And they cannot even decide what should be sacrificed in order to enhance and preserve virtue. Given the free will to love God, pursue the moral virtues, or choose the sacrifice, most people simply misuse these higher principles of love, virtue, and sacrifice for selfish purposes. Then, the recommendation is to forget about the love of God, the pursuit of moral virtues, or even choosing the sacrifices. Simply follow some rules.

Once these higher principles are taken out of religion because their practitioners are foolish, ill-willed, and immoral, then nobody can understand why such rules and regulations were given anyway. With the loss of the underlying motivations—namely, that they were meant to produce a population that is loving, virtuous, and sacrificing—people start thinking that these rules and regulations are only the means for oppressing the common and innocent people. Now, even these rules are disregarded, and society descends into chaos.

This, by and large, is the fate of the Vedic system today. There are remnants of traditional Varṇāśrama system of social organization—i.e., the rules and regulations of classes—which is at present called the 'caste system'. Nobody understands that this system was rigidly enforced after people lost the ability to make good choices about what should be sacrificed and what should be preserved. This loss in judgment was preceded by the loss of virtue, and the loss of virtue was preceded by the loss of the love of God. Through such progressive decline, we are now left with a meaningless caste system, which is exploited by politicians as vote banks, and this system is now being slowly dismantled.

The people who criticize this system, however, aren't sacrificing, virtuous, or devotees of God. They can't even tolerate a regulated life. They like to have indiscriminate sexual partners, eat whatever can be digested, and fill their empty and meaningless lives with the fleeting pleasure of shiny things. And they consider this inconsequential existence better than one where one had the opportunity for gradual upliftment to the highest perfection of life. The wise man pays no heed to their criticism. The wise man tries to understand, revive, and practice those regulations that can lead one to the perfection of life.

QUESTION

But given that modern society is indeed declining and unable to follow the rules and regulations of the Varṇāśrama system, what can be done?

3·4·33 (458)
सहकारित्वेन च

sahakāritvena ca

sahakāritvena—by practicing mutual cooperation; ca—also.

TRANSLATION

By practicing mutual cooperation also (the society can be uplifted).

COMMENTARY

The Varṇāśrama system is hierarchical, with the Brahmanas, Kshatriyas, Vaisyas, and Sudra as the four classes. In the present age, there are hardly any Brahmanas—the well-intentioned, moral, and knowledgeable sages have been replaced by pseudo-intellectuals struggling to survive the academic system by publishing pretentious, unimaginative, and repetitious papers. There are hardly any Kshatriyas—the fearless leaders who make virtuous and bold decisions have been replaced by cowards who prefer self-preservation over change for good. There are hardly any Vaisyas—those who know that society's main wealth is land, forests, rivers, mountains, and domestic animals, have been replaced by bankers who create schemes of converting debts into assets for fleecing innocent investors. Society is now dominantly Sudras—the laborers toiling in factories and sweatshops to mass-produce goods without the artistry that was previously the hallmark of carpenters, weavers, potters, and jewelers.

The bankers and the politicians are the cheaters, and the academics and the workers are the cheated. When a bank fails, the politicians bail it out by levying extra taxes on the workers. Then, when the banks are doing well, the politicians allow the banks to charge high interest rates on the wealth that the toiling workers previously paid as taxes to bail out the banks. Meanwhile, the banks lend money to the politician's cronies, which are cycled back to the politicians to help them continue in power. Thus, the endless cycle of cheating continues.

When the Varṇāśrama system declines because the top three classes in the society are gone, and society is reduced to the battle between the cheaters and the cheated, then, there is no point in speaking about a class system. There is simply no morality, courage, or commonsense to understand the value of such a system, and there are also no people that belong to the higher classes. How can the Varṇāśrama system exist when the upper three classes are missing?

The best action is to first put an end to the dishonesty and corruption in society. This is possible if everyone acts cooperatively as a single class of people. Such a cooperative system is sometimes called 'socialist democracy' at present.

In a socialist democracy, the moneyed class is accountable to the courts of laws and investigative agencies that bring transparency; the courts of law and the investigative agencies are accountable to the politicians; and the politicians are accountable to the people. Any break in the chain of accountability destroys the socialist democracy. For example, if politicians manipulate people's opinion through propaganda about the false ideals of race, caste, creed, and nationality, then they are able to wrest control over the entire system of courts of laws, investigative agencies, banks, businesses, and the workers. The result is a totalitarian state which looks like hierarchical Varṇāśrama, because there is indeed a powerful ruler at the top, the military and courts below him, the banks below these, the moneyed class below these banks, and the workers below this moneyed class. But it is not righteous, truthful, and progressive. People may often love such a ruler because they hate everyone else more. And the rulers justify their authoritarian rule by appealing to the false ideals that brought them into power and use intimidation to silence those who question their actions.

Due to the structural similarity between authoritarian power structures and the traditional hierarchical societies based on morality and virtue, people often confuse one with the other. When faced with the problem of chaos in society, they support a dictator thinking that it is a replacement for Varṇāśrama.

This conclusion of substituting Varṇāśrama by an authoritarian rule is rejected in this sūtra. If a society cannot follow the rules and regulations of Varṇāśrama because there are no qualified Brahmanas, Kshatriyas, and Vaisyas, then the solution is cooperation, rather than authoritarian control.

What is the difference between cooperation and authoritarianism? In an authoritarian structure, the ruler is above the laws, and in a cooperative structure, the laws are above the ruler. But how you can put laws above the ruler, unless there is another ruler who enforces the laws? Therefore, cooperation simply means a system in which power is distributed over many ruling positions. Each such ruler in a distributed system is controlled by the other rulers in the system. The hierarchy of power is then replaced by the distribution of power.

In previous sūtras, we discussed how intelligent people can choose the sacrifice; in short, laws are not sacrosanct; the ultimate arbiter is the person. When this system fails, because everyone is not capable of making good choices, then the next system is Varṇāśrama, where some people are qualified to make good choices, and the choices of others are subordinated to their direction. Thus, the Brahmanas have the greatest freedom in the choice of what must be sacrificed; the Kshatriyas below them have a reduced choice, the Vaisyas have even lesser choices, and the Sudras have the least choice. When even this system fails, because there are no qualified Brahmana, Kshatriya, and Vaisya, then no ruler is above the rules, and the ruler has no choice for which rules to follow or disregard. In short, nobody is above the law, and nobody has the choice of which laws to apply in which situation. Whatever freedom of choice exists, only exists within the restrictions imposed by the law. But what happens if someone doesn't follow the law? That's when the system of checks and balances kicks in, and different divisions in a cooperative structure have the power to remove those not following the law. An authoritarian ruler is above all laws; he can define the laws for others, and choose which laws apply to him, and nobody has the power to remove him, although he can remove everybody. A ruler in a cooperative system is never above the law, all laws are defined through mutual approvals, the laws must always be applied (even if it doesn't make sense), and every ruler can be appointed and removed from their position of power.

Quite simply, a cooperative structure is the subordination of persons to an impersonal system of rules and regulations. The novelty is that the rules of governance are created by the rulers—not given by an external authority. In common language, this is called the rule of people, by the people, for the people. In every action, there are three causes—what, why, and how. The system of rules fixes how things must be done; every decision or action must follow a predefined procedure, so there is no choice of how things must be done. Similarly, the system of rules fixes why things should be done—no ruler has power to create the big-picture vision, although all the rulers can collectively create smaller and shorter-term goals permissible within the charter. Once the how and the why are fixed, the ruler is given the freedom to decide what must happen. However, this decision can be reversed by the other rulers. The meaning of cooperation is that they would not reverse each other whimsically and thereby paralyze the entire system of governance by undoing each other. But the power of undoing each other always exists in case it is ever needed.

Cooperation doesn't mean offering free advice to each other, which the receiver can ignore. That is called consulting. Cooperation is also not the joint ownership of the process and decision. That is called collaboration. Cooperation is specifically a distributed system of power in which everyone holds some power over the other, and this power is used to restrict and restrain them.

A system of cooperation is built on the premise that everyone is prone to mistakes, if not outright evil, but collectively they can counteract each other's errors. The Varṇāśrama system is built on the premise that a few people—i.e., the Brahmana—are never evil, and above almost all mistakes. The system in which everyone can choose the type of sacrifice can be made is built on the premise that nobody is evil, and nobody is likely to make many mistakes. Therefore, one can have an egalitarian society, a hierarchical society, or a society bound by rules. Everyone is free in an egalitarian society; some are freer than others in a hierarchical society; and nobody is free in a cooperative system. The progression in the discussion indicates the successive decline of freedom from an egalitarian system to a hierarchical system to now a cooperative system. This decline is necessary when most people are wicked, or prone to mistakes.

We might note that authoritarianism is not bad per se. It works perfectly if the leader is intelligent, well-intentioned, and moral because then he knows which scriptural injunctions to apply in which cases, to what extents, and to which people, in which places, and at what times. When the leaders lack these qualities, then they either universalize injunctions, or apply the wrong principle to a problem, or chose a principle based on their convenience at that time.

Their intentions may not always be bad; but the road to hell is paved with good intentions. Good intentions are only one of the three ingredients of good decision making; the other two are a superior intellect and moral courage. When leaders don't have these qualities, good intentions can produce bad results. Without these traits, power corrupts, and absolute power corrupts absolutely. The prescription is to replace a centralized power by a distributed system of power.

This is not an ideal system, by the way. The ideal system is being led by a perfect devotee of the Lord. If such a leader is absent, then the next best system is being guided by intelligent people who know how to apply scriptural injunctions in different situations—i.e., what to sacrifice and what to preserve under different circumstances—while preserving the goal. If intelligent people are not available, then one must adhere to the regulations of Varṇāśrama—e.g., people in the Sannyasa order must not handle money, manage property, or interact with women; their prerogative is traveling and teaching alone. If people are unable to even follow the principles of Varṇāśrama strictly, then the next best system is one based on the rule of law with many checks and balances. If these principles are disregarded, then we must know that the leaders have whimsically created their own system, which is not expected to work correctly.

QUESTION

Your prescriptions about the social order are fine, but how does living in a society relate to the attainment of spiritual enlightenment? How is one going to attain the divine love of God through such social rules and regulations?

3·4·34 (459)
सर्वथापि त एव उभयलिङ्गात्
sarvathāpi ta eva ubhayaliṅgāt

sarvathā api—in all the cases (described above); te eva—they must certainly; ubhaya-liṅgāt—(remain devoted) owing to the two-fold deities (i.e., the masculine and the feminine aspects of the Absolute Truth).

TRANSLATION

In all cases (described above—i.e., the distribution of power, the rules of Varṇāśrama, or an enlightened and judicious application of the principle of sacrifice), they must certainly (remain devoted) to the two-fold deities (i.e., the masculine and feminine aspects that together represent the Absolute Truth).

COMMENTARY

Religion is a private issue, but morality is a public issue. Religion is a private issue because the love of God cannot be forced on anybody. However, morality is a public issue because we can only live in a system governed by morals. We cannot live in a society if everyone lies. We cannot live in a society if everyone is selfish—e.g., nobody pays taxes. We cannot live in a society if everyone is inconsiderate of the others—e.g., people running off to courts for resolving minor disputes. And we cannot live in a society if nobody follows procedures—e.g., the rules of the road, garbage segregation, or the drawing of contracts. Therefore, morality is reduced to four publicly enforceable principles—truthfulness, austerity, compassion, and cleanliness. These are non-negotiable principles; their specific detailed implementation may change from one society to another, but no society can exist unless these principles are implemented and enforced. However, even as one follows these rules, one may choose to devote oneself to the Lord or may simply live by the moral code. Of course, the goal of life is not achieved if one only follows the moral codes of conduct. One must develop devotion to the Lord as well. However, these two are separate issues. Therefore, after dwelling on the moral conduct, this sūtra reiterates that morality is not enough; one must also become devoted to the two-fold deities.

This stance, however, leads to a big question. The humanists argue that society can be organized morally, without accepting soul and God. Does this mean that religion is so private, that it is totally unnecessary in defining the public conduct? The modern secular system of morality takes this stance.

But this stance is false because no social system can ever be perfected unless the people are perfect. And people cannot be perfected unless they have a higher purpose in life. The people will accept a higher purpose only when life doesn't end with death. Rather, whatever good or bad has been committed in this life must necessarily be enjoyed or suffered in another life. Since this oscillatory process of enjoying and suffering is dissatisfying, therefore, one must seek transcendence from this material existence, and that transcendence is the higher purpose. But that higher purpose necessitates devotion to God.

The humanist idea about an ideal society without God is a pipe dream because such idealism is possible only when people want to become ideal. Why would they want to be ideal unless there is an incentive attached to that perfection and a disincentive attached to the imperfection? Under a humanist conception, there is no life after death. Therefore, the rich and powerful are entitled to exploit, subjugate, and manipulate others—to maximize their happiness within this life. If they have very low risks of being punished for their actions, then why should they be truthful, compassionate, sacrificing, or agreeable?

Now the humanist invokes an evolutionary argument and says that every species wants to ensure its long-term collective survival, and altruistic behavior helps that collective survival, therefore, by the principle of evolution, altruism is nothing but the need for long-term collective survival. The problem with this argument is that it presupposes altruism to explain altruism. The claim about a species wanting its long-term collective survival is itself altruistic. So, that desire in us cannot be used to explain the emergence of altruism. We must rather ask: How did this altruism arise? For example, why should I care that the whole world will be dead after I'm dead—to act unselfishly in the first place?

The fact is that there can never be a moral society without a higher purpose in life and that higher purpose cannot exist without the realization of the soul and God. As a result, even if someone doesn't actively pursue devotion to God, they must have a conception of the soul and God to even behave morally.

When the notions of the soul and God are lost, then the sense of higher purpose in life is lost. Then everyone acts with their short-term goals of pleasure in mind, and disregard everyone else's interests. Society then descends into an immoral abyss. The result of rejecting the soul and God is the destruction of the social order. No atheistic society can survive for very long. All atheist, communist, humanist, and materialist societies shall die due to inner moral decline.

Communists know this, and the earlier communist regimes were predominantly authoritarian—altruism did not come naturally to people, and nobody wanted to think about the collective benefit of the society, which is why everyone who did not agree with the collective good over the individual good had to be slaughtered. After the collapse of inhumane communism, a new wave of 'humane' communists arose. This new version of communism says that social unity must be propped up by ideas like nationalism and racial identity. After all, for us to be altruistic, we must believe in a larger-than-life identity, and that identity can be a person's race and country. But even these 'humane' communists know that nationalism and social identity cannot produce cohesion. Therefore, this 'humane' communism is married to economic prosperity. Thus, in this new version of communism, social cohesion exists due to three reasons: (1) material prosperity, (2) racial identity, and (3) historical nationalism.

But here is the problem. The unity doesn't exist because of racial identity and historical nationalism. Those are simply tools of propaganda, which even the communists don't believe in; if they believed in this idea, then they would not marry individual prosperity with national and racial identity; they would have simply proceeded with the communist rule of a race with nationalistic ideals. The society under this type of communism is cohesive only because of economic prosperity. People believe that if they have lived in poverty for centuries, then any system that gives them a better life is acceptable. It has nothing to do with racial or nationalistic identity. In short, cohesion exists because there is collective prosperity, not because people are fundamentally altruistic.

Humanism is totally contradictory to the Vedic system. All unity comes when we serve the Lord. And we can live together even in difficult times because we have a higher purpose. Whether in happiness or distress, the devotees always pray to the Lord. They don't blame each other for their suffering. They blame themselves for their misdeeds which brought them to the current situation. When a spiritualist owns up the responsibility for his life and actions, then he asks: If I am responsible for my life, then why am I in this situation? Everyone else is shifting the blame to someone else, but they can't shift it forever. Someday, the blame will be shifted back to those shifting it to others.

QUESTION

But we find it very hard to combine social duties and spiritual pursuits. If we have spiritual pursuits, then we neglect our social duties. And if we follow the social duties, then the spiritual pursuits are almost always neglected. How can someone do both—i.e., social duties and spiritual pursuits in parallel?

3.4.35 (460)
अनभिभवं च दर्शयति
anabhibhavaṃ ca darśayati

anabhibhavaṃ—not overwhelmed; ca—and; darśayati—sees.

TRANSLATION

One who is not overwhelmed (by social duties) also sees (the Lord).

COMMENTARY

The previous sūtra said that one must be devoted to the two-fold deities even while performing their social duties. And this sūtra acknowledges the fact that either of these paths can be overwhelming. If one follows the spiritual path but neglects the social duties, then one might be ostracized from society, and lose their spiritual pursuits as well. On the other hand, one might perform their social duties diligently, but may largely neglect the spiritual goals. The result would be that one lives in a society but fails to achieve the goal of living. The recommendation is thus to not become overwhelmed with social duties.

Our social endeavors are overwhelming when we fear that not doing them will lead to a catastrophe. So, we keep devoting our time to social duties and neglect spiritual pursuits. But if we try to reduce our engagement in social duties then we will find that nothing catastrophic happens. Life just goes on as before, and people who were relying on us, learn to rely a little less. As they reduce their reliance on us, they also become less reliable, and then we are compelled to reduce our reliance on them. The trouble is that our distancing from others leads to others distancing from us, and we cannot tolerate that others are disengaging from us. Due to fear of abandonment, most people get sucked back into the engagement. But if we accept that something higher requires the sacrifice of something lower, then we gradually increase disengagement, which then creates the time for spiritual pursuits. I can say this from experience: I have devoted a lot of time to writing, which would have been impossible if I truly believed that my worldly disengagement would produce a catastrophe.

Topic 9

QUESTION

But what if someone is not able to reduce their social engagements, due to their specific circumstances, or due to the specific phase of life they are in? For example, students might have to spend a lot of time with their studies, and a mother may have to devote her entire day to taking care of children, or a man may have numerous responsibilities which he is unable to truly forego. How can they not be overwhelmed by their duties even as they keep doing them?

3.4.36 (461)

अन्तरा चापि तु तद्दृष्टेः

antarā cāpi tu taddṛṣṭeḥ

antarā—by the difference; ca—also; api tu—even though; taddṛṣṭeḥ—that can be realized or seen.

TRANSLATION

Even though (someone may not be able to disengage from social duties), simply by seeing the difference (between life and death) also that is seen.

COMMENTARY

One of the main causes of becoming overwhelmed is the (false) belief that the present situation will never end. A student feels that their education will never finish; there is always one subject after another and then the original subject comes back. A mother feels that her duties never seem to end; it is one chore after another, one duty after another, and then it starts all over again. A man overworked by numerous duties feels that life never seems to end; that he is running from one pillar to another, and then back to the same pillar again.

But all these things do end. Whatever seems overwhelming right now will fade away one day. Eventually, our parents will die, friends will abandon us, children will grow up to lead their own lives, and our colleagues will disappear. Ultimately, we will be left all alone, totally underwhelmed by the receding waves of the life's ocean, as the sun sets into the distant horizon. When one comes face to face with their loneliness, then all the overwhelming disappears. Everything seems meaningless and pointless, as it all just fades into oblivion.

This meditation is valuable since it forces us to think about death. Death is the final stop for everyone as far as this life is concerned. And at the point of death, we will be totally alone. Nobody is coming with you or for you. Every medal, award, or prize you have gotten in this life stops being yours. Since others only see the body, they won't even know that you got these medals once you enter the new body. Nobody would know you, or where you are going to go. You must walk alone into the next stage of your life. If life seems overwhelming right now, just imagine how underwhelming death would be.

We feel overwhelmed by our mundane duties because we cannot see the underwhelming nature of death. Therefore, anyone who feels that they cannot give up their duties to pursue spiritual life, must meditate upon death. Spiritual life may be imaginary for some people, but death is real for everyone.

QUESTION

You have previously asked me to meditate on the Paramātma in the heart, the Universal Form of the Lord, and the sound of the names of the Lord. Now you are asking me to meditate on death. How does that even make sense?

3.4.37 (462)

अपि च स्मर्यते

api ca smaryate

api ca—furthermore; smaryate—the smriti makes such recommendations.

TRANSLATION

The smriti also recommends (that we can meditate upon death).

COMMENTARY

This is the fourth and final occurrence of the sūtra—*api ca smaryate*. The previous three times, the same sūtra was used in 1.3.23 (86), 2.2.45 (216), and 3.4.30 (455). The repetitive use of sūtras is indicative of the fact that they are like the words 'yes' and 'no'. They don't have a context-independent meaning. Rather, only the context delineates what they mean. Therefore, if we have talked about the qualifications of guru previously, then this sentence means that smriti also describes the qualifications of a guru. If we have spoken about the regulative principles of society, then this sentence means that smriti also describes the regulative principles of society. If we have previously talked about life and death, then the smriti also describes the meditation upon life and death.

There are many lessons to be had here. First, four references to smriti, from a text which is understood as śrutī, means that the śrutī is not independent. Second, certain things like meditation on death are not found in śrutī, which describes the nature of Brahman; but they are found in smriti. Third, as we have discussed previously, Vedic texts have a progressive nature in which the higher truth is also described in the subsequent texts. Therefore, the relation between śrutī and smriti has the following three nuances—(1) sometimes śrutī refers to the smriti for additional details, (2) sometimes the śrutī refers to smriti to find those things that are not found in the śrutī, and (3) sometimes the śrutī refers to smriti to obtain a superior understanding that is absent from the śrutī.

Now, we can turn to the reference to smriti for the meditation on death. In the Bhagavad-Gita, Lord Kṛṣṇa makes two clear references to Himself as death.

Bhagavad-Gita 10.34:
mrtyuh sarva-haras caham
udbhavas ca bhavisyatam

I am all-devouring death, and I am the generator of all things yet to be.

Bhagavad-Gita 11.32:
kalo 'smi loka-ksaya-krt pravrddho
lokan samahartum iha pravrttah

Time I am, the destroyer of the worlds, and I have come to engage all people (i.e., I have come here to cause their deaths).

God is everything, but everything is not God. Similarly, God is death, but death is not God. To understand this, recall our familiar analogy of mammal and cow. The mammal is in each cow, but the mammal doesn't reduce to the cow. Likewise, Kṛṣṇa is in death, as the cause of death, but He is not death alone. He is also life. In fact, Kṛṣṇa is both life and death, which means that He is living, and all life is a manifestation of Kṛṣṇa. But He is also renounced from everything, and, by that renunciation, He causes everyone to be separated from their bodies and material attachments. The death of the body is not death of the soul. It is only the separation of the soul from the body, and this detachment is forced upon us by the Lord's will. If we become attached to the Lord, then this detachment is not forced. In short, if we are attached to the Lord, then He is also attached to us, and we don't see the renounced aspect of the Lord. But if we are detached from the Lord, then we sometimes see His renounced aspect.

Kṛṣṇa is the embodiment of six qualities—knowledge, beauty, power, wealth, fame, and renunciation. The devotees of the Lord see everything as the manifestation of the Lord's knowledge, beauty, power, wealth, and fame. They see Him in everything, as the source of everything, and as the controller of everything. The non-devotees, however, don't see the knowledge, beauty, power, wealth, and fame as emanating from the Lord, as the Lord being immanent in everything, and the Lord being the controller of all these things. They think that these qualities are their qualities, that they are knowledgeable, beautiful, powerful, famous, and wealthy. To alleviate that illusion, the Lord comes as death. "You think you are knowledgeable, beautiful, powerful, famous, and wealthy? All right, you are no more." Now you lose everything that you thought was yours before. And you restart the delusion of acquiring them again. Therefore, the Lord is also death. For those who cannot see the Lord as knowledge, beauty, power, wealth, and fame, the Lord shows Himself as forced renunciation.

If you are not sure that God exists, and the material engagements seem very real to you, then God can demonstrate to you His existence in the form of death. Hence, for those who are overly attached to material life, the meditation on death is recommended. It is not contrary to the meditation on the Paramātma, the Universal Form, or the meditation on the names of the Lord. The difference is that in these meditations, we see the Lord as knowledge, beauty, power, wealth, and fame, but while meditating on death we see Him as renunciation. Death is the most severe kind of renunciation, and God is renunciation itself. Therefore, the vision of death approximates the vision of renunciation itself. During this life, we might lose some money, some property, some friends, some family, etc. These are renunciations but they are partial. During death, we lose everything. Therefore, death is a more complete vision of renunciation. As sure as death and taxes. Since death is sure, therefore, the Lord is also sure.

QUESTION

But it is sometimes said that the soul doesn't have to leave the body. The soul rather ascends to the Lord's abode without any change in the body. Therefore, it seems that death is not always certain. How do we reconcile that?

3.4.38 (463)
वशिेषानुग्रहश्च
viśeṣānugrahaśca

viśeṣa-anugrahaḥ—the special benediction (of the Lord); ca—and.

TRANSLATION

And that (i.e., bypassing death) is a special benediction (of the Lord).

COMMENTARY

This body is not material. The purpose we use this body for is material. Matter and spirit are not different kinds of 'stuff'. Matter simply means the selfish use of the body, and spirit means the selfless use of the body. So long as we have selfish purposes, the purposes are always frustrated. And due to this frustration, we change our purpose. Then, as this purpose changes, we keep getting new bodies—to fulfill our new purpose. But if the purpose is fixed in a particular type of service of the Lord, then we don't need to renounce this body, because it fits our purpose. Hence, many devotees are elevated to the spiritual world in this body itself. That is because this body is not material or spiritual. It is an instrument and the instrument is neither good nor bad. The purpose for which the instrument is used is good or bad. So, if the devotee doesn't want to change the instrument, then there is no reason for the Lord to force separation from this instrument. That elevation with the body into the spiritual world is called a special benediction of the Lord in this sūtra. In short, this body is not temporary. It exists eternally, along with innumerably such eternally existing bodies. The body never changes; however, the soul changes the bodies.

When the soul has faulty purpose, then the Lord forces a change in the body. If the soul wants a different type of body to perform a different kind of service, then again, the Lord causes the change of the body. But if the soul doesn't want to change the body, and the purpose is not faulty, then the same body continues into the spiritual world. However, that body becomes eternal. This so-called disease, old age, and death are the soul moving from one body to another. There is an eternally healthy body, and there is an eternally sick body. But we don't have to go from sick to healthy and healthy to sick bodies. These changes are forced by the laws of nature and the Lord's will because we have faulty purposes. If the purpose is fixed, then the body is also fixed.

You don't use a hammer or a drill if you want to cut vegetables. In the same way, if your goal is fixed on some service, then the body doesn't change. The elevation with the same body—and bypassing death—is a clear refutation of impersonal doctrines about matter as illusion. Matter is not an illusion. It is an instrument. That instrument is always real, but the purpose is illusory. As this illusory purpose changes, the instrument to fulfill the purpose changes. But if the illusory purpose is destroyed, then the instrument is eternal anyway.

When the Lord appears in this world, He is not born into a new body. And when He disappears, then He doesn't die and get another body. These are false misconceptions propagated by the impersonalist to confuse people into thinking that enviousness and selfishness of the Lord can be spiritualized. So, the impersonalist says that the Lord is born, and He dies. When He is born, then He takes on a body. And then when He dies, He has no body. The fact is that the Lord has the same body always. And that is because the body is not material. One needs to know the science of matter, which the impersonalist doesn't. Without knowing this science, He creates a false theory of the soul. Hence, if matter is understood scientifically, then God's and the soul's bodies are also understood. And then we can know how matter is also eternal, just as the soul. However, the connection between the soul and matter is not eternal due to the faults in the soul's purposes. The Lord has no fault, so He has an eternal body. When the faults are corrected in the soul, the soul too has an eternal body.

QUESTION

But isn't it possible that certain purposes in the spiritual world cannot be fulfilled by the present body? Would we not need a different body for that?

3·4·39 (464)

अतस्त्वितरज्ज्यायो लिङ्गाच्च

atastvitarajjyāyo liṅgācca

ataḥ—therefore; tu—than; itarat—the other; jyāyoḥ—better; liṅgāt—from the body; ca—also.

TRANSLATION

Therefore, from the other (spiritual) body also better than (this body).

COMMENTARY

Even in this world, there are many kinds of bodies. Some bodies are better at swimming, some at flying, some at crawling, and others at walking. Some bodies have a better brain, other bodies have better hands and legs. Therefore, there is a superset of bodies found in the spiritual world, and a subset of that superset exists as the material world. As a result, in one sense, the material world is a part of the spiritual world, because the bodies here are a subset of the bodies in the spiritual world. In another sense, since the souls are rebellious to the Lord, the material world is said to be totally separate from the spiritual world. Being a part of the whole and being separate from the whole are different modes of describing the material world relative to the spiritual world.

Given the rebellion in the soul, most bodies in this world come with many limitations. Thus, most fish are unable to fly, and most birds are unable to swim. Even when some species can do both, their abilities are not on par with the best of the abilities in the other species. We also have two hands and two legs, which limit us to do only one or two things at one time. But in the Vedic scriptures, living beings with hundreds or thousands of hands are described. They can do hundreds of things simultaneously. This means that their bodies are superior to our bodies. But they are still called material—i.e., inferior bodies—because they are inferior to the best-in-class bodies with many more capabilities.

In this world, we get separate types of knives, but in the spiritual world, we can get many kinds of Swiss Army knives. Those are called 'superior' in this sūtra, after stating that the material body can also exist in the spiritual world. So, knives can go from this world to the spiritual world, and occasionally, some Swiss Army knife can be seen in this world. But mostly, the Swiss Army knives are found in the spiritual world, and hence, they are called 'superior'.

The superiority of the instrument is different from the superiority of the purpose for which the instrument is used. Since our purposes are inferior, we also generally get inferior instruments. But if the purpose is superior, then we can also obtain far superior instruments. With great power comes great responsibility. As we demonstrate responsibility, the power increases accordingly. Therefore, we get access to more powerful instruments by showing that we can handle the responsibility. If we cannot show that responsibility, then we lose the power. Therefore, most of the weak bodies are due to irresponsibility.

In this regard, the story of a mouse is narrated. A mouse approaches a saint and says: "I'm troubled by cats; they are trying to kill me; please help." So, the saint says: "OK, you become a cat." Then after some time, the cat comes to the saint says: "I'm troubled by dogs; they try to chase me away; please help me." So, the saint says: "OK, you become a dog." In this way, the saint gives him bigger and better bodies, until the body of a lion is obtained. Then the lion looks at the saint and says: "You appear to be quite tasty." And the saint then says: "Again become a mouse." So, this is the disease of the material world. We get some power, and we want more power. Then when we get enough power, we say: "God doesn't' exist". Then, God says: "Again become a mouse."

The bodies of the material world are limited because the moment one gets a more powerful body, he thinks he can challenge the Lord. Then the Lord makes him a mouse again. So, the progression to even better bodies is halted. But otherwise, all the bodies in the spiritual world can exist in this world.

Topic 10

QUESTION

You are saying that the body is not material, and the same body can exist in the spiritual world. You have also said that the devotion can exist in this world, and it exists in that world. So, if the intentions and the body are the same, the person's role must also be the same, because through that role one can fulfill their intentions using the body as an instrument. Then, if these things are the same, then why do we say that the spiritual world is different from the material world? How can the ingredients be the same and the result be any different?

3.4.40 (465)

तद्भूतस्य तु नातद्भावःजैमनिरपि नियिमातदरूपाभावेभ्यः

tadbhūtasya tu nātadbhāvaḥ jaiminerapi niyamātadrūpābhāvebhyaḥ

tadbhūtasya—on attaining that; tu—but; na—no; atadbhāvaḥ—ceasing from that; jaimineḥ—of Jaimini (is this opinion); api—also; niyama—rules; atadrūpa—not this form; abhāvebhyaḥ—due to the absence.

TRANSLATION

But on attaining that (a role in the spiritual world), there is no ceasing from that (the person's role); even Jaimini (thinks that) the rules (of this form) don't apply to the other form, due to the absence (of the rules and regulations).

COMMENTARY

The terms bhūta and bhāva cannot be applied to the body because it has already been established that the body can be the same in the spiritual and material worlds. Then what do bhūta and bhāva pertain to? They pertain to one's role, or the relationships to other souls. However, in these roles, the soul no longer has dharma or the rules and regulations that restrict one's activities.

A material society is characterized by rights and duties. Factually, nobody has any rights, other than what is given to them by their karma. But we all have a sense of entitlement to rights; when the entitlements are frustrated, we blame others and say—they did not perform their duties. We generally don't say that we did not have the karma to get our rights fulfilled. Now the question arises: When karma is finished, and we are not limited to the fulfillment of rights, do we still carry the sense of rights? That is, do we keep demanding others to do their duties? This sūtra rejects this conclusion. It says that there are no duties, which means that nobody is obligated to do anything for you. The next sūtra says that along with the dissolution of duties, even the rights are dissolved. So, these two sūtras are interconnected because rights and duties are two sides of the same coin—if someone else does their duty, then I fulfill my rights.

But doesn't this sound counterintuitive that the soul enters a perfect world, and still doesn't have any duties? Wouldn't this society collapse if everyone neglected their duties? This seems especially perplexing because the sūtra also states that having attained a role, nobody wants to give up that role. So, what is everybody going to do if not their duties according to their role?

The answer is that people do everything, but they are not required to do anything. The existence of rules means you are required to do something, and not doing it would invite a punishment, and doing it would invite a reward. But if we dissolve the duties, then doing the duty invites no reward, and not doing the duty invites no punishment. Freedom from karma means freedom from rewards and punishments. But that freedom is possible only when we are also free from the duties—i.e., the necessity to behave in a specific manner. Therefore, the dissolution of duties is identical to the dissolution of karma (i.e., reward and punishment), which is identical to the existence of freedom.

The spiritual world is like working in a voluntary organization. You do your work because you want to do it, not because you are required to do it. If you work, you are not paid for the service—the service is voluntary. And if you don't work, then you are not punished—the participation is also voluntary.

The only rule for working in a voluntary organization is that you don't prevent others from doing their work. You are welcome to assist or help them, and you are equally welcome to outdo whatever they are doing. In short, you can do the same work they are doing, although in a better way. Therefore, entry into the spiritual world doesn't mean an end to competition. The devotees of the Lord can compete, and they can serve each other. The service means that a soul will assist other devotees to do their service better. And competition means that a devotee will do better service than the others. But a devotee never says: "You cannot do this". Nor does a devotee hinder other devotees from doing what they can do, especially if they can do it better than themselves. When some devotee tries to hinder others from serving, this becomes a sign of envy.

To understand liberation, we must understand karma and dharma—namely that dharma is duties, and karma is rights. Freedom from karma means freedom from rights. But as soon as we stop having rights, we must stop demanding duties from others. Therefore, rights and duties are dissolved simultaneously. The soul obtains his freedom, and that freedom means that he now acts voluntarily. This voluntary action can be to serve other devotees, compete with other devotees, serve the Lord, or even compete with the Lord. The Lord is not averse to competition. He enjoys winning as much as He enjoys losing. Just like if a father and son play some sport, then the father enjoys winning, and the father enjoys losing to the son. In fact, the father enjoys losing more than winning. This is because of the affection between the father and the son. In the same way, the soul too must enjoy losing as much as he enjoys winning. If both situations are being enjoyed, then there is no envy, although there is competition. The moment one enjoys winning and doesn't enjoy losing, there is enviousness. Under that enviousness, one loses focus on what one can do to win and starts focusing on what one can do to prevent others from winning.

Everyone in the spiritual world is gracious— (1) they like serving each other rather than competing, (2) if they compete, they want others to win, and (3) even if they want to win, they are never unhappy losing. Serving the Lord, competing with the Lord, winning against the Lord, and losing against the Lord are all equally pleasurable. This is the symptom of lack of enviousness.

Therefore, carrots and sticks are useful only in this world to align the rebellious soul. But there is neither carrot nor stick in the spiritual world. And yet, everyone does everything according to their capacity and desire, voluntarily. This voluntary system of service doesn't conform to the authority structures of this world, the use of power to subjugate, control, reward, and punish. Therefore, it is important for spiritual leaders to understand when authority must be used to correct mistakes and purify the mischievous soul, and when the voluntary spirit must be encouraged to let the soul go free and do the best that one can. If the mischievous person goes free, then they create havoc. And if the solemn person is subjugated, then the potential for advancement is lost. Only one who has understood both material and spiritual worlds can act like this.

Topic 11

QUESTION

If there are no rules and regulations of duties, then what about the rights? Does it follow that even the rights are dissolved along with the duties? Doesn't the soul fall from the spiritual world without the rights and duties?

3.4.41 (466)

न च आधिकारिकमपि पतनानुमानात् तदयोगात्

na ca ādhikārikamapi patanānumānāt tadayogāt

na—not; ca—and; ādhikārikam—the sense of rights; api—even; patana-anumānāt—due to no reason for a fall; tadayogāt—because of union with that.

TRANSLATION

And nor is there any sense of rights; there is even no reason for a fall (due the non-fulfillment of rights), because of the union with that (the Lord).

COMMENTARY

In the purport to the previous sūtra we combined the discussion of both rights and duties, although the previous sūtra spoke about the dissolution of duties and this sūtra speaks about the dissolution of rights. When the duties are dissolved, then nobody is required to do anything. If they are not required to do anything, then nobody else can demand anything from them. All actions are voluntary. Therefore, there is no dharma (duties) and there is no karma (rights). Everything is driven by the soul's free will. However, this free will is purified, so one acts voluntarily. But even if one acts, they have no expectation of getting anything in return—i.e., gifts, rewards, remuneration, or recognition of their actions. And since there are no expectations, therefore, there are no rights.

In the material world, the preliminary teaching is responsibility—i.e., you do your duties, if you want your rights. The next better teaching is sacrifice—i.e., do your duties even if you are not getting anything in return. Once responsibility and sacrifice are perfected, then the next better teaching is that you don't have any duties—i.e., you can work voluntarily, or you can abandon all duties. However, since the soul has already perfected responsibility and sacrifice, he doesn't stop working, if he can work. He is just not obligated to work.

The pure devotees of the Lord understand this voluntary system of service, arising out of love. Love is not demanded, and even if love has been offered, there is no expectation of reciprocation. The only request is that the opportunity to love is not taken away. This means that the pure devotee of the Lord only asks the Lord to allow him to serve the Lord. He doesn't demand that the Lord loves Him back, and he is not disturbed even if the Lord doesn't love him back. When such voluntary love is established, the soul becomes totally free of the system of rights and duties of this world, and that is called liberation.

Therefore, by loving the Lord, liberation is automatically obtained, and there is no separate need for trying to become liberated before or after devotion to the Lord.

QUESTION

The freedom from rights and duties is also attained by the impersonalist who merges into Brahman, dissolves the separate identities and by the dissolution of separate identities, all the rights and duties are automatically dissolved. So, how is devotion to the Lord any better than impersonal liberation?

3.4.42 (467)

उपपूर्वमपि तु एके भावमशनवत् तदुक्तम्

upapūrvamapi tu eke bhāvamaśanavat taduktam

upapūrvam—the initial or first part; api tu—even though; eke—some; bhāvam—the existence; aśanavat—just like eating; tat—that; uktam—is said.

TRANSLATION

Even though the initial or first part of (the transcendental) existence (Brahman) is attained by some, it is called just like eating (without sharing).

COMMENTARY

When children grow up, sometimes they abandon their parents. They say: "It was your job to take care of me when I was a child. Now that I have grown up, I can do the job of taking care of myself. Hence, I don't need you anymore. Isn't it great that I'm no longer dependent upon your care?" The impersonalist has a similar stance. He was dependent on the Lord in the material world. The Lord provided the knowledge for his liberation, guided him to the correct spiritual master(s), and inspired him from within to pursue this path every time he fell away from the path. But having attained that position, he loses all gratitude for the Lord. He thinks that now that he has attained this position, he no longer needs the Lord. That is just like children who use their parents during childhood, obtain some education, get a job, and start living independently. Now, they think that they don't need the parents anymore, so they don't have to do anything for them. They don't realize that without their parents they would be nowhere. So, the person with such a selfish attitude is not considered the greatest. He may have become great by achieving liberation from the material world, but there are many levels of greatness. Having a high position is certainly great. But remembering where one came from, using whose help, appreciating their contribution to our greatness, and remaining indebted to them, is greater.

Topic 12

QUESTION

Does this mean that a liberated devotee abandons the rights and duties even within this world? How does he conduct himself upon liberation?

3·4·43 (468)

बहस्तिूभयथापि स्मृतेराचाराच्च

bahistūbhayathāpi smṛterācārācca

bahiḥ—outside; tu—but; bhayathā—just like a shining planet; api—even; smṛteḥ—from the smriti; ācārāt—from custom; ca—and.

TRANSLATION

The liberated soul acts outwardly just like a shining planet even though (this is not required of him) and acts according to smriti and custom.

COMMENTARY

The Bhagavad-Gita 3.21 states the following about a great person's actions:

yad yad ācarati śreṣṭhas
tat tad evetaro janaḥ
sa yat pramāṇaṁ kurute
lokas tad anuvartate

> Whatever action is performed by a great man, common men follow in his footsteps. And whatever standards he sets by exemplary acts, all the world pursues.

If a devotee abandons duties and rights, then this world will descend into chaos because the other people who do not understand the spirit of voluntary action would stop performing their duties. Hence it is said that the devotee acts outwardly like a shining planet or a great man in society, illuminating the world with knowledge and correct behavior according to the smriti and the established customs. The devotee follows the rules of whatever social system is best suited to the world at present. It may be a system of distributed power, a system of hierarchical power, or an egalitarian system of individual power. In either case, he is a shining planet—i.e., an exemplar of how people must conduct their lives. The devotee is not bound by any of these systems, and he has no preference for any of these. And yet, he tries to set an example for everyone.

Thus, advanced devotees are seen to support and exemplify all such systems alternately. Sometimes they let people decide the right action according to their judgment—illustrating the principle of individual power to decide what must be sacrificed and what must be preserved. Then sometimes they say that everyone must behave according to the principles of Varṇāśrama—implying that there are rules, but they are different for different classes of people, for different genders, and for those in different stages of life. Then sometimes they say that everyone must follow a common set of rules such as doing certain types of activities, at certain times, in a fixed predefined manner, and the performance of these duties must be monitored by a system of checks and balances. And then they sometimes say that a devotee is not bound by any rules or regulations. For most people, these diverse types of instructions can be very confusing. And some people then pick up whatever model that they find convenient.

But if we understand how all these systems are available, but they don't apply to everyone, then we can decide which system must be applied.

Topic 13

QUESTION

But what happens when an unqualified person imitates the actions of a liberated soul? Isn't there are difference between following and imitating?

3.4.44 (469)

स्वामिनिःफलश्रुतेरित्यात्रेयः

svāminaḥ, phalaśruterityātreyaḥ

svāminaḥ—the master, or the person making a choice; phala-śruteḥ—gets the results according to the injunctions of sruti; iti—thus; ātreyaḥ—Ātreya.

TRANSLATION

The master (or the person making a choice) gets the results according to the injunctions of the śrutī; thus, it has been stated by Ātreya.

COMMENTARY

Throughout the Vedānta Sūtra, we see many sages and great personalities being quoted. Then sometimes the pastimes of the Lord are cited and sometimes His words are cited. Sometimes logic and reason are employed. Sometimes practical experience is used. Sometimes one scripture refers to another and cites it as evidence. And in the previous sūtra, even worldly customs were referred to as exemplifying great behavior. Thus, we can see how what we call 'evidence' or pramāna, includes all these things. Sometimes it is what the Lord said. Sometimes it is how He acted. Sometimes it is based on what is stated in one scripture. But if something is not stated in some scripture, then we pick the reference from another scripture. Then sometimes it is the doctrine of one philosophical system. But sometimes these doctrines are overridden by another doctrine. And sometimes it is simply the opinion of a great personality.

Therefore, if anyone thinks that religion is a fixed set of rules, then they are mistaken. All these injunctions are true, but they are not simultaneously true. They don't apply to everyone, in all social roles, circumstances, places, or times. The advanced devotee doesn't depend on any of these things, but he uses all of them. Thus, a devotee may not necessarily cite scripture; he may also use reason and practical experience. Sometimes, he might use the established precedents of other great persons, and sometimes he might employ social customs. Finally, he is also totally free to state what is not present in any of these systems.

Therefore, when we study any of these statements or instructions, we must carefully resist the temptation to universalize them. The only universal statement is that the Absolute Truth is everything. But since everything is not the Absolute Truth, therefore, we must know the role, place, and time for everything. The problem is that most people think that if the Absolute Truth is everything, then everything is Absolute Truth. So, they take all these diverse injunctions and try to treat them as universal truths. They might cite some great personality, some scripture, some philosophical doctrine, or some social custom as evidence. But the existence of the evidence doesn't mean that it must be used here, now, for this person, in this specific circumstance, or this purpose.

As we have discussed, reality is modal, and these modes are always dominant and subordinate. This means that the number of universal truths is very limited. These include the claims that (1) God is the source of everything, (2) God is the purpose of everything, and (3) God is the controller of everything. Other than these three universal truths, all other claims are subject to time, place, person, role or situation, and purpose. One must know the modal nature of reality and what principle, instruction, or idea is dominant or subordinate in each situation. Unless this is known, everything else becomes a mistake.

A common mistake in this regard is blindly imitating the advanced soul. The previous sūtra said that the advanced devotee sets the example for the rest of the world, and *evetaro janah* is used to state how the common people can imitate the example set by a great person. But this sūtra rejects blind imitation and says that everyone gets the result according to the śrutī injunctions. The point is that we are not machines governed by rules and regulations. All these things are presented to broaden our mind, and familiarize us with the nature of truth, right, and good. But this familiarity is not a replacement for judgment and choice. What is choice? A choice is the decision about which principle is dominant or subordinate in a place, time, role, for a person, and a purpose. If we make mistakes in that judgment, then the consequences are ours.

Therefore, reading the scripture, the words and pastimes of the Lord, the instructions of great persons, and indulging in the use of reason and observation is essential to broaden our mind. But none of this produces a machine preprogrammed to follow the rules. When a person hasn't broadened their understanding, then obedience to some basic rules and regulation is better than speculating what the right choice is based upon incorrect or incomplete information. However, as one grows in their understanding, the role of choice and judgment increases. And ultimately, the soul is totally free to choose whatever he wants, subject to the condition that everyone is fully responsible for their choices.

The relation between choice and consequence means that there are contextual laws, and we are not totally free to do whatever we want. But since these laws are contextual, therefore, we must know the law in each situation. These laws are very easy in one sense—everything is produced by the domination of three modes. But it is also very hard because the dominant-subordinate structure changes in every situation. Therefore, one must first understand the philosophy of the modes, how they enter each other, to create numerous situations. Then we can study how great persons have acted in these situations. As this understanding is honed, we develop the ability to make good choices.

QUESTION

You seem to indicate that the situation or circumstance is not enough to decide what must be done. It is also a person's level of advancement that matters in such decisions. If that is the case, and we don't have a good understanding of our level of advancement, then how can we make good choices?

3.4.45 (470)

आर्त्विज्यमित्यौडुलोमिः तस्मै हि परिक्रीयते

ārtvijyamityauḍulomiḥ tasmai hi parikrīyate

ārtvijyam—the ritvik (priest or cleric); iti—thus; auḍulomiḥ—Audulomi; tasmai—for that; hi—because; parikrīyate—performs on one's behalf.

TRANSLATION

Therefore, Audulomi states that we can consult a ritvik (priest or cleric) for that (i.e., difficult decisions) because (they can make choices) on your behalf.

COMMENTARY

If we are confused about the correct choice in a specific place, time, role, etc., then we can consult a person who knows how to make good choices. This consultation is different from imitation. People often ask: "What would you have done in this situation?" This question assumes imitation; namely, if I do what the other person has done, then it must be good. The earlier sūtra endorsed such a position because it is better than speculating. But ultimately this question is flawed because (1) one may not have the ability to do what the great person has done, (2) the effect of that choice may be different on the person who is asking vs. the person who is telling, and (3) the tendency to universalize may lead to the wrong conclusion about how the present choice must be always applicable. Therefore, one should not ask: "What would you have done in this situation?" One should rather ask: "What should I do in this situation?"

Note the progression in these sūtras. Initially, it was said that one must follow the great person. Then it was said that you cannot blindly follow the great person because you are ultimately responsible for your choices. And now it is said that if you are confused about what should be done, then you can consult a great person. This progression is important because if clerics are always consulted, then two other conditions are not satisfied: (1) the clerics may simply be preaching without practicing it themselves, and (2) they don't know that advice is tailored to the spiritual level of a person, and the advisor is implicated in the consequences of advice. The progression indicates that only a great person must be consulted for advice. Then, mundane greatness is of no value; one must know how different people must act differently in different situations, and a wrong advice implicates the advisor in the consequences of the actions.

In modern times, there are numerous so-called gurus who keep advising people on different things. There are motivational gurus who tell you to be motivated, but they never put their motivation into practice to achieve anything great. There are business consultants who advise people on business, but they have never run a business themselves. And there are people who become gurus without ever studying under the tutelage of an enlightened guru. In this age, simply the ability to use flowery language is considered a mark of education. Such false advisors must be immediately rejected. Then, there may be many people who have achieved greatness, and we can listen to their ideas about how they overcame obstacles, but that doesn't tell us what we should do. These people come on television talk shows and create a fandom, but they don't benefit anyone, because their situations are quite different from our situations. Their advice is not completely useless, but it is always of limited value to us.

After we eliminate the advisors who don't follow their own advice and the advisors whose advice is inapplicable to us, then we can seek the enlightened person who can tell us what we must do. Such people were called Brahmanas earlier, and they had a superior position in society because everyone consulted them for their day-to-day decision making. They are called ritvik here, or a person who acts on your behalf. In short, you don't ask a ritvik: "What would you have done in this situation?" You ask: "What should I do in this situation?" and the ritvik will put himself in your shoes and act on your behalf. He will advise you as if he was in that situation, which means he must understand your specific role, ability, and situation, and then provide appropriate advice.

Again, in this modern age, there are people who "follow" other great people, but they never ask the right questions: "What should I do?" They just like to be associated to great people, as that makes them feel great. Sometimes, they may ask impersonal questions such as the meaning of this or that statement in a scripture, but not how that statement applies to their lives. They just collect theoretical and irrelevant facts and ideas, without changing their life. By not asking the right questions, they don't benefit from the greatness of others. They just feel satisfied that they are "in touch" with greatness, without trying to apply the principles of greatness in their lives, and themselves becoming great. A good teacher must also carefully avoid such false fandom. Therefore, there are basic qualification for both seekers and advisers. The adviser must be great, and spiritually enlightened, and the seeker must seek to apply that greatness in their life. If both these conditions are not met, then nothing great is achieved.

QUESTION

But we find it hard to even get the association of enlightened ritviks. What are the basic qualifications of a ritvik who can be consulted for advice?

3.4.46 (471)

शृुतेश्च

śruteśca

śruteḥ—about the śrutī; ca—and.

TRANSLATION

(The ritvik must) also (be knowledgeable) about the śrutī.

COMMENTARY

This sūtra clearly states that we must seek advice only from those who are well-versed in the śrutī, or that which is spoken by the Lord, heard and spoken by the great personalities, and understood under the tutelage of an enlightened spiritual master. A Brahmana is the knower of Brahman. A person wearing a Brahmanical thread is not a Brahmana or a ritvik. In India, at present, we can find many pandits who perform various kinds of rituals and ceremonies. They are well-versed in many mantras and rituals. But they don't know anything about the Absolute Truth. They don't know that the goal of life is transcending the material nature, and they are themselves often quite materialistic. If they are not broadminded, how can they put themselves in the shoes of others, and advise them on their activities? Unless they know that the rules and regulations are different for people in different stages of spiritual progress, and they are different for people in different situations, roles, places, and times, how can they tell someone else what they should be doing in their specific case?

Giving and taking advice is not free of the consequence of choices. Hence, a ritvik is implicated if they give the wrong advice. And a seeker is implicated in choosing a wrong ritvik. Therefore, seeking and offering advice are not without consequences, and both parties are equally responsible for making the right decisions. Therefore, the seekers must be careful about the advisor that they choose, and the advisors must be careful about which seekers they can advise. It is not at all improper for an advisor to decline to advise, either because he thinks that he doesn't understand the situation, or he doesn't believe that the seeker will follow the advice correctly, or even the sincerity of the seeker. Likewise, a seeker can reject an advisor if they are not qualified to advise.

This sūtra is a clear rejection of so-called clerics and priests. Many such clerics and priests are presently involved in sexual abuse, accumulation of wealth, the pursuit of political power, or the enlargement of an idiotic fandom. It is possible that a devotee might sometimes sacrifice some rule to fulfill a higher rule. But if lots of these rules are compromised, and the compromise is not for a higher principle, or it is claimed to be for a higher principle but such principles are not achieved by the compromises, then one must reject such clerics and priests. Such decisions cannot be universalized; but they must be judged.

Topic 14

QUESTION

But I am not even able to judge who truly knows the śrutī, and who doesn't. There are so many people who claim to know the myriad scriptures, but they may not always be the true knowers. There are also many contradictory religions which say different things. How do we identify the true knower?

3.4.47 (472)

सहकार्यन्तरविधिःपक्षेण तृतीयं तद्वतो विध्यादिवत्

sahakāryantaravidhiḥ pakṣeṇa tṛtīyaṃ tadvato vidhyādivat

sahakāryantaravidhiḥ—the differences in the rules or procedures of collective activity; pakṣeṇa—is a side or part; tṛtīyaṃ—a third one; tadvataḥ—just like; vidhyādivat—as in the case of the acquisition of knowledge etc.

TRANSLATION

The differences in the rules or procedures of collective activity are a third part (of the whole understanding), just like as in the case of the acquisition of knowledge, etc. (three parts are necessary to claim that one knows).

COMMENTARY

Scientific knowledge involves three parts or aspects—prediction, explanation, and justification. By prediction we mean the ability to say that "if you do this, then you will get this result". In modern science, this called state preparation and observation. Different religions or priests might tell people to do different things to get different results (or the same result). And these differences are often confusing. Therefore, prediction of outcomes based on our actions is considered an incomplete understanding. To make this knowledge more complete, we must seek an explanation of how a certain action leads to a specific result. For example, someone might say: The sun rises in the morning, which implies that if you observe the sky in the morning, then you will see the sun. But it is not enough to make that predictive claim. We must also explain how the sun appears in the morning and disappears in the night. Such explanations are constructed in modern science by speaking about the motion of the sun and the earth, postulating that motion is caused by a property called mass, which exerts a force on the earth due to the gravitational law. Such an explanation may sometimes contradict other explanations. For example, present gravitational theory is able to explain the motion of planets like earth, but it cannot explain the motion of galaxies (due to what is supposed to be dark matter) or the constantly increasing distance between the galaxies (due to what is supposed to be dark energy). But even assuming we obtained an explanation that doesn't suffer from all these discrepancies, we still cannot claim completely knowledge. This is because there may be alternative explanations that predict and explain the same phenomena. To be sure that our explanation is the best, we must also justify the explanation, or demonstrate that this is also the best explanation.

Therefore, knowledge progresses in three stages. At the first stage, we seek the consistency and completeness of predictions. This means that we can predict everything that will happen (completeness), and we will never predict anything that will not happen (consistency). At the second stage, we seek the consistency and completeness of explanations. This means that we can explain all the predictions (completeness), and no explanation of any prediction contradicts the explanations of other predictions (consistency). At the third stage, we seek the justification of these explanations. This is achieved if every explanation is found to be the best explanation (completeness), and the principles by which we consider one explanation the best explanation doesn't contradict the principles by which another explanation is judged to be the best (consistency).

Modern science is far from achieving these three goals. For instance, we don't have a theory that predicts everything that will happen, and everything that will not happen. There are theories that make predictions partially (e.g., the best current theory of matter—i.e., atomic theory—makes probabilistic predictions, but with a probability, something with a 50% probability may not happen for a hundred years, and then always happen for the next hundred years; therefore, you cannot say if it predicts what will happen and what will not happen). Then we have many theories which partially explain such partial predictions, but even these partial explanations are mutually incompatible with each other. For example, the prediction based on probabilities in atomic theory depends on the definition of an ensemble, but the same world can be divided into infinite number of ensembles, so the partial predictions have a partial explanation. Furthermore, the explanations of atomic theory involve non-locality, while the explanations of general relativity involve locality. Therefore, the explanations of partial predictions are both incomplete and inconsistent. Finally, even the partial explanations of partial predictions are partially justified by some chosen principle, but the justifying principles employed in one theory remain incompatible with the justifying principles in other theories. For example, the local explanation is justified by reduction, while the non-local explanation is justified by holism. Hence, even the justifications are incomplete and inconsistent.

This sūtra recommends a relentless pursuit for answers to determine if one truly knows. The true knower knows the relation between cause and effect. Such a true knower is also able to explain the reason why a cause becomes the effect. And finally, a true knower can justify this explanation as the best explanation. These explanations must expand horizontally—i.e., to diverse phenomena. And as we expand horizontally, we are also required to ascend vertically, because the explanation is deeper than the phenomenon, but the explanation is also a phenomenon explained by a deeper explanation. Thus, a diversifying tree-like hierarchy is constructed, in which every node in the tree is a prediction, an explanation, and a justification. Therefore, to convince oneself of whether one truly knows, one can employ a variety of tests of their knowledge. Also, we can learn the criterion for truly knowing, because unless one truly knows, he or she will always make bad decisions, which will then cause their suffering.

Most people believe that knowledge is only for some people. They don't understand that without knowledge, bad choices are made, and with bad choices one is entangled in misery. The panacea described here is that one can ask a true knower, which then leads to the problem of identifying the true knower, and that problem is not any easier than knowing oneself. Therefore, there is a progressive path in which one learns a few things from the teacher, applies and tests them, then learns more and applies and tests it again. To identify the teacher some guidelines are given, but they are not different from the guidelines of knowing oneself. However, since a teacher has better knowledge, he can teach the student the complete truth, through a gradual process.

QUESTION

If a teacher, guru, or ritvik has been found, and he is prepared to guide the seeker, then should the seeker always rely on the teacher's guidance or also develop the knowledge themselves to make the best decisions and choices?

3.4.48 (473)
कृत्स्नभावात्तु गृहिणोपसंहारः
kṛtsnabhāvāttu gṛhiṇopasaṃhāraḥ

kṛtsnabhāvāt—by attaining the whole truth; tu—verily; gṛhiṇā—those in the house; upasaṃhāraḥ—finish or destroy all that is secondary.

TRANSLATION

Verily, by a full understanding of the truth (of correct decision making), those living in the household can finish or destroy all that is secondary.

COMMENTARY

People living in households are pulled in many directions—earning a living, taking care of the family, maintaining the house, saving for the future, etc. A renounced person relinquishes all these responsibilities and has a much simpler focus on the ultimate aims of life. But a householder must juggle many different priorities. Unable to make the decisions, they might want a guru's advice on marriage, health, children, finances, etc. Gurus who have renounced the world may not be comfortable with such guidance, and it is sometimes not the best use of their stature. Thus, a householder can try to acquire the understanding by which they can make good choices and decisions themselves.

The fact is that everyone needs to learn the science of good decision-making. This is as true for householders as is for renounced people. And if one has learned this science, then one is automatically liberated. So, why wait for a stage of life to begin learning this science? Everyone can begin learning this science wherever they are. This sūtra states that if householders obtain a full understanding of the science of choices, then they can destroy all that is secondary, which means that they will be liberated from the difficulties of the world.

QUESTION

But we find that the knowers of truth do not easily disclose the truth to everyone. Meanwhile, those who don't know the truth tend to talk a lot. This creates confusion about the truth in the minds of most people because most people are attracted by the greatest amount of noise, rather than the truth.

3·4·49 (474)
मौनवदितरेषामप्युपदेशात्
maunavaditareṣāmapyupadeśāt

maunavat—just like one who is silent; itareṣām—to the others; api—even; upadeśāt—teach the others.

TRANSLATION

Even those who are just like silent, teach (the truth) to the others.

COMMENTARY

The truth is very subtle, because every type of contradictory claim is true, although these contradictions are not simultaneously true. When truth is impersonalized, then we think that something true must be true for all persons, at all places, and always. In the West, this impersonalized truth is called 'universal truth', and everyone seeking truth is conditioned by this impersonalism.

But if we say that truth is that which is true for everyone, everywhere, and always, then conflicting claims cannot exist. The need to overcome the contradictions in the truth now creates three kinds of approaches to knowledge. The nihilist says that all these contradictions must be dissolved to produce nothingness, because in nothingness there is no contradiction. The impersonalist says the truth is beyond these contradictions, but since all diversity is contradictory, therefore, we must remove such diversities to attain the truth. The materialist says that there are many contradictory propositions, but only one such proposition is true, and we must prove one of these propositions through reason and experiment. The problem is that the contradictions appear in different people, places, and times, so, the rejection of a contradiction means the rejection of half the people, places, and times. Now, these opposing sides engage in endless arguments and counterarguments, as each side dominates alternately, but they cannot exist without their opposite, so the contradiction never disappears.

The real knowers of the truth are aware that voidism, impersonalism, and materialism are not the answers to the problem of truth. But everyone seeking this truth comes to the true knower with the assumption that the truth must be found in one of these three approaches. Thus, if you say that something exists, then the nihilist has a problem—because he claims that nothing exists. Then, if you say that whatever exists is different from the other existing things, then the impersonalist has a problem—because he claims that only one thing exists. Then if you say that many existing things are mutually contradictory, then the materialist has a problem because he says that contradictions cannot exist. The nihilist and the impersonalist nod in vociferous agreement with the materialist, since they too don't want contradictions to exist, although the nihilist wants to dissolve everything, while the impersonalist wants to dissolve diversity.

The problem is that people have a preconceived notion of reality, and they want to fit the knowledge within that conception. The nihilist wants the conclusion to be nothingness; the impersonalist wants the conclusion to be the dissolution of diversity; and the materialist wants mutually consistent diversity. Arguing with a nihilist, an impersonalist, and a materialist becomes hard, not because they are right, but because they are always talking about a universal truth. The universal truth is impossible. But people think that the alternative to this universalism is relativism, so if we give up universalism then there is no truth. Thus, the relativist also jumps on to the bandwagon of criticism of truth.

To know the truth, we must know the following: (1) everything that is ever possible is eternally true, as a possibility, (2) these possibilities are mutually contradictory so all possibilities are collectively contradictory, but they are not seen simultaneously, and (3) one side of the contradiction manifests at one place, in one person, and at one time. Therefore, the Absolute Truth—as different from the universal truth—is a person who originally exists a possibility; He expands into many persons at different places and times, so the possibility becomes real, but this reality is not self-contradictory, because the contradiction is always in a different person, place, or time. In short, if we are prepared to discard our impersonalist ideas about 'universal truth', and can embrace a personalistic 'Absolute Truth', then knowledge is both consistent and complete.

One who is completely satisfied by knowing the truth has no necessity to tell anyone about this truth. But they impart this knowledge to the humble person. The sign of humility is not just the preparedness to accept a description of the truth within the nihilist, impersonalist, materialist, or relativist doctrines. The prior necessity is to discard all these models of truth themselves. If one is prepared to make this change, then real knowledge can also be obtained. Therefore, the fundamental criterion for someone to know is to be a devotee. They may not be pure devotees, but they must have some inkling of devotion. With an inkling of devotion, a pure devotee can make them perfect devotees, and with that perfection in devotion, one can also obtain perfect knowledge. There is, however, no scope for perfect knowledge within nihilism, impersonalism, materialism, or relativism—or even their parent doctrine of universalism.

Topic 15

QUESTION

Even if someone is prepared to teach, we find that the process of learning is very long. There are too many difficulties, and most people abandon the process because of these difficulties. Why is the understanding of truth so hard, if everyone is supposed to know this truth, and perfect their lives by it?

3.4.50 (475)

अनाविष्कुर्वन् अन्वयात्

anāviṣkurvan anvayāt

anāviṣkurvan—the activity of removing the poison; anvayāt—(establishes) from the connection (to the Absolute Truth).

TRANSLATION

The activity of removing the poison (automatically establishes) the connection (from the individual soul to the Supreme Lord—i.e., Absolute Truth).

COMMENTARY

We can see the progression through the last several sūtras. Initially, it was said that a cleric must be consulted—this seemed easy because we can just ask someone who knows. But the problem was: How do we identify such a person? So, then we discussed the qualifications of the cleric. But how many times can you ask someone? Every moment in our lives requires a choice or a decision. The practical difficulties in consulting someone at every moment led to the recommendation that we must develop this understanding ourselves. However, even to acquire this understanding we need a teacher. We are no longer talking about a cleric who will give us readymade answers to our questions. We are rather seeking a person who will teach us the truth by which we can decide ourselves. The problem is that the knowers don't reveal the complete knowledge easily. Therefore, it was said, they can reveal even though they mostly remain silent. But since they are generally silent, a person must exert on their own to extract the requisite knowledge from them. Now, we come to the problem of this sūtra, namely, that this process of extraction is long and hard. In response, this sūtra says that is hard because the poison is within us. When this poison is removed, then the knowledge is also automatically attained. Therefore, the hardship is not in the knowledge, but in the poison within.

What is that poison? As discussed in the previous sūtra, this poison takes many forms such as nihilism, impersonalism, materialism, and relativism. The process of freeing ourselves of this poison begins with the rejection of materialism—i.e., that we are only the body. If there is only the body, then there are no ideas, there can be no theories, and nothing can ever be known. The people who reject materialism, therefore sometimes argue for relativism—we have freedom, we can think and feel, but there is no universal truth; everyone must create their own truth. But relativism destroys society. Therefore, the person tired of relativism says that anything outside the self is an illusion, but since we are defined in relation to these things outside us, therefore, both the self and the other are illusions. Thus, arises the doctrine of nihilism. But calling the world and the self an illusion doesn't mitigate the suffering. Therefore, the person who rejected the self and the others, now says that the self and the other are identical. This is also the doctrine of impersonal unity or oneness. To attain this oneness, we must give up all desires and pleasures. By giving up material desires and pleasures, you can obtain freedom from suffering, but should freedom from suffering be also called happiness? Or, is happiness beyond the freedom from suffering? In short, suffering must be stopped, and happiness acquired?

The journey from materialism to relativism to nihilism to impersonalism is long and arduous because many types of poisons need to be removed. Once these poisons are removed, then the final step of knowing the Absolute Truth is very easy. In short, knowledge is not hard. What makes it hard is the poison within. Whenever truth is injected, it gets mixed up with the poison. The truth is then distorted, and often, parts of that truth are rejected. When these parts are rejected, then the truth gets weaker, and the poison gets stronger. To strengthen the truth, we must inject it again, to weaken the poison. So, the process is long because it necessitates a change in the person. Once that change has occurred, then knowledge is naturally obtained. Sri Chaitanya has termed this process as the 'cleansing of the mirror'. The soul is the mirror, but it is dirty. This dirt must be removed, and once it is removed, the reflection is clear. Therefore, knowing the truth is not constructing a picture of the truth piece by piece within a dirty mirror. The process is simply cleansing the mirror, removing the poison, purifying the mind and the senses, and destroying the infection.

This is a radical conception of knowledge in which the fault is not with the teacher, the books, or the philosophy. The fault is in the seeker. Most people have trouble grasping this idea, as they keep blaming the teacher, the books, or the philosophy—the teacher is not good enough, the books are contradictory, and the philosophy is hard. These conclusions are rejected in this sūtra.

In Western philosophy, there are three cardinal doctrines of the mind. The empiricists such as John Locke say that the mind is a blank slate. The idealists such as Immanuel Kant and Carl Jung say that the mind is preformed with all the ideals. And the psychoanalysts like Sigmund Freud say that the mind is forever dirty. If the mind is a blank slate, then there is no problem in knowing, because it is already clean. If the mind has all the ideals, then knowledge is simply knowing the ideals within. And if the mind is always dirty, then nothing can ever be known. Thus, Western philosophy closes all the doors to the purification of the mind—either the mind is blank, or the mind is already perfect, or the mind is forever dirty. In the first two cases, there is no need for purification. And in the third case, there is no possibility of purification. Therefore, people coming to Vedic philosophy from a Western perspective have a lot of trouble, because the basic premise is that you are dirty, and you must be cleaned, but nobody wants to accept that they are basically dirty and need cleansing.

Topic 16

QUESTION

The process of cleaning seems to be very hard, because the things that we are cleaning it with, may themselves be dirty. For example, if we say that we clean ourselves with knowledge, but all this knowledge is contaminated by the biases we already have, then this process of cleansing seems infinite. How can then we clean the mind before the perfection in knowledge is acquired?

3.4.51 (476)

अइहकिमप्यप्रस्तुतप्रतबिन्धे तददर्शनात्

aihikamapyaprastutapratibandhe taddarśanāt

aihikam—worldly; api—even; aprastuta-pratibandhe—in the unborn or the eternal restrictions; tat-darśanāt—from vision of that (the Lord) is obtained.

TRANSLATION

Even in this world, from the vision of that (the Lord) in the unborn or the eternal restrictions (i.e., the bounds of the Lord's love).

COMMENTARY

The term *prastuta* means that which has appeared, and when used alongside *aihikam*, which means worldly (or temporary), the meaning (by contrast) becomes that this world is temporary and the *aprastuta* must be eternal. We can also say that *aprastuta* is spiritual and *aikham* is material. In this case, this eternity and spirituality is combined with restrictions. Thus, we have come a full circle from the preceding sūtras where it was stated that the soul has no restrictions of rights and duties in the spiritual world. Before this sūtra, it was already confirmed that the body is not a restriction; it is merely an instrument for fulfilling the desire, and a different kind of body can be obtained to fulfill the desires. We even spoke about more capable bodies in the spiritual world. Therefore, after rejecting the body being a restriction, and then rejecting the restrictions of duties and rights, we are again speaking about restrictions.

What are these eternal restrictions? And why does the sūtra say that these restrictions can exist even in the material world? This restriction is not of a body or of duties and rights. These are the restrictions of love. They are eternally a possibility, and hence exist even in the material world. The love can manifest even while the soul is present in this world, so, the temporariness of this world doesn't impact the eternity of the love. Therefore, after saying the soul is free from rights and duties, this sūtra says that the soul is bound by love. In short, the Lord doesn't ask the soul to do anything, and the soul doesn't expect any reciprocation from the Lord. And yet, there is spontaneous activity. After stating, in the previous sūtra, that the soul must be purified, this sūtra says that if the loving devotion the Lord is established, then purification is automatic.

In short, the poisons of materialism, relativism, nihilism, and impersonalism are different manifestations of the deeper poison of the lack of love. If this love is not established, then the process of purification of the poison is very hard, because the poison simply changes different forms and one keeps moving from one kind of illusion to another. But if the love is established, then all kinds of poisons are destroyed, the soul is purified, and perfect knowledge is obtained. Therefore, the route to perfect knowledge is through devotion.

Topic 17

QUESTION

We have spoken about the difficulties in making the correct type of sacrifice; we have discussed the difficulties in Varṇāśrama; we have spoken about the challenges of a cooperative society; we discussed the difficulty in identifying the right teacher; we spoke about the difficulties in acquiring knowledge; and finally, we discussed the problems in removing the poisons in the soul. Is your final conclusion that devotion to the Lord solves all these problems?

3.4.52 (477)
एवं मुक्तफिलानियिमःतदवस्थावधृते
evaṃ muktiphalāniyamaḥ tadavasthāvadhṛte

evaṃ—in this way; muktiphala-aniyamaḥ—there is no rule that restricts the attainment of liberation; tat-avasthā-avadhṛte—that situation or position is devoid of all the faults (namely, the poisons mentioned previously).

TRANSLATION

In this way (by acquiring the devotion to the Lord), there is no rule that restricts the attainment of liberation, and that situation (of loving the Lord) devoid of all the faults (namely, the poisons that were discussed previously).

COMMENTARY

Love of the Lord is the solution to all problems of knowledge, social organization, and the unhappiness within. If this love is absent, then we struggle through a difficult process of identifying the correct decisions, and due to lack of knowledge, we seek teachers who might be misguided. If this love is absent, then social organization becomes impossible because there is no higher purpose that binds people together; people may stay together if their pleasure is being satisfied; however, any discrepancy in their selfish pleasures produces conflicts. Without this love, the soul constantly suffers from the fear of loss and eventually of death; with every loss comes loneliness, and death brings the ultimate separation from everyone and everything that made us feel secure. Therefore, even though happiness can be achieved through the progress in knowledge, better social organization, or worldly love, these methods of achieving happiness are themselves not guaranteed without the Lord's love. Hence, no method works without the Lord's devotion, and every method can work with the Lords' devotion. Therefore, devotion is not contrary to the pursuit of knowledge, better social organization, or worldly love. However, the individual pursuits of knowledge, social organization, and worldly love are inherently flawed.

Therefore, one must always begin in devotion to the Lord. This devotion may not be initially perfect. But it can be perfected through the gradual progression in knowledge, social organization, and loving relationships. All these things are meant to improve the devotion. However, if they are separated from this purpose, then they are individually and collectively frustrated.

Chapter 4

This is the shortest chapter in the text, and it discusses the nature of death, what happens after death, how a soul enters a spiritual abode, and how the experiences of the spiritual world are similar or different to those of this world.

Section 1: This section discusses the nature of death, what is lost at death and what is preserved at death. We all know that our material body and its associated things are lost at death. The mind and intellect are also destroyed at death and we need to learn everything again. However, this section describes how spiritual progress made during the present life is not lost upon death. This includes both the advancements obtained by spiritual knowledge and spiritual activities. However, if the soul is liberated by devotion to the Lord, then the pending karma, which would have otherwise been reaped in future lives is destroyed. Thus, the material suffering and enjoyment are destroyed upon liberation, but the partial spiritual progress made within a life is preserved.

Section 2: This section discusses the differences between the Sāñkhya and Yoga systems of practice. On one hand, it is said that the mind controls the senses, and the senses control the objects. On the other hand, it is said that the mind and sense control can also be obtained by controlling the prāṇa. However, the section then describes that by this mind and sense control, one enters the nihilistic state of balance that existed prior to the creation of the universe. The spiritual state beginning with Brahman is said to be beyond the nihilistic state. The section then describes how the liberated soul upon death reaches a specific abode of the Lord being guided by the light emanating from the abode. This idea is then generalized to say that even yogis ascending to higher planetary systems, and the soul going to lower and hellish planets are also similarly guided by the light. In short, depending upon a person's qualification, they can see only those planets and places which they deserve in the next life.

Section 3: This section discusses the nature of yajñá or sacrifice. An extensive discussion is undertaken about why these sacrifices are performed through fire, and not through air or water. The reasoning is that only the procedures of fire sacrifices are convenient—i.e., the mantras of the fire sacrifice are shorter and simpler—whereas the procedures of air and water sacrifices are much more complex. The section then says that fire was chosen as the method of sacrifices after careful consideration, which means that the rituals described in the four Vedas aren't the only types of sacrifices. The conditions under which other types of sacrifices (e.g., through water and air) can be performed are described.

Thus, the practicality of these sacrifices is taken into account, which underscores the fact that the Vedic knowledge is presented not just because it was imparted by the Lord, or is rationally understandable, or that it was converted in a textual form in a certain age, but also because it was practical. This practical knowledge is part of everything that is possible, some of which may be impractical. Thus, the pragmatic nature of the Vedic knowledge is established.

Section 4: This section discusses the state of pure devotion to the Lord. It is said the devotee has the body of pure cognition. Through this body, the soul has states of waking in which the devotee sees the Lord face-to-face, a body of dreaming through which the devotee sees the Lord through his imagination, and a body of deep sleep in which the devotee has a persona related to the Lord. The devotee is also said to feel separation from the Lord in the dreaming state, but this separation is not different from the union of the waking state. Finally, the section distinguishes the state of pure devotion from impersonalism, the idea that the soul merges into the Lord's body, that the soul is equivalent to the Lord, or that devotional experience is quite similar to the material illusions.

SECTION 1

Topic 1

QUESTION

It seems that whatever question I ask, you always come around to the same conclusion. It doesn't matter whether we discuss the nature of material reality, the structure of the universe, the nature of the body and mind, the question of right and wrong action, the process of social organization, the progression in knowledge, or the understanding of logic and meaning. You always give the same conclusion—namely, that the soul must be devoted to the Lord. Is it necessary to repeat this conclusion, even after we have already discussed it?

4.1.1 (478)

आवृत्तिःअसकृदुपदेशात्

āvṛttiḥ asakṛdupadeśāt

āvṛttiḥ—repetition; asakṛt—repeatedly; upadeśāt—from the teaching.

TRANSLATION

From the repeated teaching (of the ultimate conclusions in the scriptures).

COMMENTARY

In the beginning of Manu Samhita, which describes the rules for social order, Lord Viṣṇu is glorified as the creator of the world. In the beginning of Brihat Parāśara Hora, which describes the principles of astrology, Lord Viṣṇu is again glorified. Many Purāna, such as the Śrīmad Bhāgavatam, the Viṣṇu Purāna, and others, discuss the material creation, but describe Lord Viṣṇu to be its creator. In this way, personalism has been taught in every division of human knowledge which means that even if someone is studying non-transcendental topics, they are constantly reminded of the transcendental topic. Furthermore, as we have discussed, everything is inside the Lord, and the Lord is inside everything—as the original purpose. Therefore, we can study several subjects or topics, but before we start, we must ask ourselves: Why are we doing this? And the answer is the Lord. When we finish studying it, we need to summarize the subject, and we must then describe it as a branch of knowledge that describes one aspect of the Lord. And while we are studying it, we might often ask: How do we know? And the answer is that it was originally revealed by the Lord, subsequently accepted, understood, and tested by numerous others, and finally their understanding was sometimes weaved together with the Lord's instructions. Therefore, at the beginning, in the middle, and at the end, we always remember the Lord—as the purpose, as the cause, and the whole truth.

QUESTION

But how many times must this conclusion be repeated? Isn't it enough to say it once, and then focus our attention on the discussion or other things?

4.1.2 (479)

लिङ्गाच्च

liṅgācca

liṅgāt—from the indicatory marks; ca—also.

TRANSLATION

(We can judge) from the indicatory marks (of happiness) also.

COMMENTARY

There is no topic other than the Lord. He is the whole truth, He is the cause of the partial truth, and He is the purpose of all the partial truths. The conclusion of knowledge is therefore understood in three ways. First, we can say that there are diverse subjects, but what is the conclusion of studying all these subjects? In short, why should I study anything, instead of nothing? And the answer is that we want to know the Lord. Second, we can say that now that we know the conclusion, why should I study any of the detailed subjects or topics? And the answer is that the Lord has many aspects, and we are simply studying the aspects of His persona. Third, we can ask: But why should I study all these aspects? And the answer is that we serve the Lord through these aspects.

If we don't know the whole truth to begin with, then the diversities cannot be reconciled. But if we know the whole truth, but without the diversities, then the whole truth is impersonalized. Finally, if we know the whole and the part, but we don't engage the part in the service of the whole, then the parts are relativized. Hence, there is no knowledge without the Lord. Without the Lord, we can obtain numerous mutually contradictory theories that cannot be reconciled. Or, we can destroy all variety to say that it is an illusion. Or, we can conclude that all that I know is simply my experience, and has no objective existence. All these are different kinds of ignorance. Truth is where when we can find the consistent and complete knowledge, which is variegated, and it is real. That kind of truth is impossible unless we understand the nature of the Lord.

Ignorance and delusion appear in many forms. As a result, the truth is unknown, and whatever is known is misused. This sūtra says that to destroy the illusion and the misuse we must constantly repeat the understanding of the Lord as the origin, purpose, and controller of the world. He must be known at the beginning, in the middle, and at the end. Whatever else is known, remains incomplete or incorrect unless the Lord is known, and harmful unless it is used in the Lord's service. By listening to these descriptions repeatedly, we can destroy the many kinds of poisons that exist within us. Once these poisons are destroyed, the complete truth is known, and the person is completely satisfied. This satisfaction then develops into the love of the Lord. And due to that love, the symptoms of happiness appear in the body. These symptoms have been discussed earlier, and this sūtra simply says that we must go on listening to these descriptions until the symptoms of happiness appear in our body.

Topic 2

QUESTION

What is the effect of repeatedly hearing these descriptions of the Lord?

4.1.3 (480)

आत्मेति तूपगच्छन्ति ग्राहयन्ति च

ātmeti tūpagacchanti grāhayanti ca

ātmeti—as one's own; tu—but; upagacchanti—come near; grāhayanti—desire to perceive; ca—also.

TRANSLATION

(By repeatedly hearing these descriptions) one starts considering the Lord as their own, they come near, and they desire to perceive (the Lord) as well.

COMMENTARY

Three effects of listening to the descriptions of the Lord are described here. First, one starts considering the Lord as their own; this consideration is establishing the relation to the Lord. Just like we consider our father, mother, spouse, friend, or children our own, in the same way, the devotee starts considering that the Lord is one's own. The Lord is no longer an alien concept or someone who created the world, or merely as someone great. We know of many ideas, but we don't consider them our own. We know of many great people, who may have done great things, but we don't consider them our own. Without that attachment, such people, things, and ideas come into our consciousness and go out of it. With an attachment to the Lord, a personal relationship is created. Second, as this relation is created, then one comes close to the Lord. This closeness is knowing the nature of the Lord, such as what He likes and dislikes, how He looks like, how He interacts with His devotees, and so on. Third, despite this knowing, there is an ever-greater desire to know more. This is generally in contrast to our ordinary relationships. For example, we might consider our parents our own, and we might also know them, or be close to them. But we don't constantly desire to know them more; familiarity breeds contempt, and there is a limitation to how much one wants to know the other person. But there is no limit to this knowing in the case of the Lord. By knowing something about the Lord, the desire for knowing the Lord even more automatically increases.

Topic 3

QUESTION

But what is the difference between seeing the Lord, and hearing the various descriptions of the Lord? You have earlier said that these two things are identical as they have the same meaning. But now you are saying that by hearing about the Lord, there is progression to seeing the Lord. So, it seems that seeing the Lord is better than hearing. What is the difference in the two?

4.1.4 (481)

न प्रतीके न हि सः

na pratīke na hi saḥ

na—not; pratīke—in the symbol; na—not; hi—because; saḥ—he.

TRANSLATION

(The Lord is) no longer known in the symbols because He is not (a symbol).

COMMENTARY

When you read a travelogue, then you see the symbols of the experience of travel. The meaning or experience of the travel is present inside the travelogue as meaning; however, the travelogue is different from the travel. The difference is primarily that the travelogue doesn't capture all aspects of the travel. But if you undertake the travel, then you can experience all these details first-hand. Nevertheless, if you haven't traveled to a destination, then you might still read about the destination through a tourist guide, a tourism brochure, etc. The information in the brochure or the guide is incomplete, but it is not false.

In the same way, the scriptures are like tourist guides and travel brochures. They give information about the destination so that you might be attracted to go there. Once you develop attraction, then you obtain the wherewithal to travel. During this preparation, you keep imagining how good that destination would be, by recalling the pictures and descriptions of the destination from the travel brochures and guides. But, if the destination is great, then the experience of the place exceeds all the expectations set by the brochures and guides.

This analogy is employed in this sūtra by stating that the scriptures are symbols of reality. The symbols are true, in the sense that there is a real destination. But these symbols cannot capture that destination completely. They are provided to attract the potential aspirant, just like travel brochures are provided by travel agents. Once you reach that destination, you realize that everything in the brochure also exists in the destination, but everything in the destination isn't in the brochure; hence, the experience exceeds the brochure by far.

This is the meaning of saying that in the beginning, one only reads the brochures—i.e., the scriptures. But ultimately, one also travels. The brochure is true because everything in the brochure is in the destination. But the destination is greater than what is described in the brochure. Hence, the brochure is a symbol of the destination, but the Lord is the destination. Therefore, for the advanced devotee, He is not merely known by books; He is also experienced directly.

Topic 4

QUESTION

But we go to so many tourist places, we enjoy for some time, and then we come back. How is the spiritual world different from other tourist places?

4.1.5 (482)
ब्रह्मदृष्टिःउत्कर्षात्
brahmadṛṣṭiḥ utkarṣāt

brahmadṛṣṭiḥ—seeing the Lord; utkarṣāt—from growing attraction.

TRANSLATION

From the growing attraction upon seeing the Lord.

COMMENTARY

We go to many tourist places, do many touristy things, and then get bored. A tourist attraction may be quite enjoyable, but there are people living in that tourist destination who are not as excited to be in that destination. In fact, the people living in that tourist destination may want to go to other tourist destinations. This sūtra says that once you reach that destination, you never leave because the attraction keeps growing. Therefore, those who are already living in that destination are not looking to go to other tourist destinations. The attraction to the destination keeps growing, so alternative desires don't develop.

Knowing the Lord is not like knowing our relatives where the knowing stops at some time because we know everything there is to know, and when everything has been discovered, then, complacency sets in, and the attraction declines. We might still like our relatives, but we are not constantly eager to learn more about them. Hence, the early stages in a romantic relationship are quite exciting because we are learning new things about a new person. But after some time, everyone settles into their knowledge, and the excitement wanes. Now, people go to other tourist destinations to rekindle their romance, hoping that a new place will bring something new out of them and the others.

But the spiritual world is not like that. The Lord is infinite, and there are always new things to be known about the Lord. As we learn new things, we act in different ways. And this difference in action reveals another side of a person which was previously unknown. Similarly, as we know more, the Lord knows that we know more. Therefore, He too acts differently, and then He reveals something that was previously unknown. Therefore, attraction creates additional knowledge, additional knowledge creates novel actions, and that novel action then increases the attraction, and the cycle perpetuates endlessly.

The spiritual world is therefore like an ever-expanding tree. The Lord is the root of the tree, but every branch, twig, and leaf is present in the root. The soul is a leaf in this tree, but as the soul learns more about the Lord, and then due to this knowledge, the leaf expands—the root becomes a subbranch of the leaf as the knowledge acquired by the leaf. Then the Lord knows about this expanded leaf, and that expands Him. Thus, the devotee learns about the Lord, then the Lord knows that the devotee knows about Him, then the devotee knows that that the Lord knows that the devotee knows, and so on. The new knowledge produces new actions and so the novelty is never finished. Due to this expanding mutual knowledge, the soul expands inside the Lord, and the Lord expands inside the soul. And as we know more, we are also attracted even more.

Topic 5

QUESTION

You are saying that there is growing attraction between the soul and the Lord, but doesn't this attraction mean that ultimately the soul and the Lord will merge into a single entity? Just like we might say that two bodies with mass are attracted to each other, and due to this attraction, they come close to each other. Then as they come closer to each other, then, the attraction increases further. Due to this increased attraction, they must come even closer. So, the result of this mutually increasing attraction, and the decreasing distance between the attractor and the attracted, must be that they eventually collapse into a single object. And that object would not have the distinction between the two.

4.1.6 (483)

आदित्यादिमतयश्चाङ्गे उपपत्तेः

ādityādimatayaścāṅge upapatteḥ

ādityādi-matayaḥ—the ideas of the sun etc.; ca—also; aṅge—as a part or subordinate member; upapatteḥ—because of logical deduction.

TRANSLATION

The ideas of the sun etc. (i.e., the other planets) are also said to be the parts or subordinate members (of the Lord's body) and this is understood as logical deduction (namely, how the whole divides into the parts; the part is called *upa* and the part is considered lower relative to the whole which is called *patti*).

COMMENTARY

This sūtra refutes the black hole doctrine of love. According to this doctrine—espoused by the impersonalist—the soul and the Lord are attracted, and then they come closer to each other; as they come closer, the attraction increases and the distance decreases; eventually the soul collapses into the Lord.

This sūtra cites the example from Vedic cosmology, where the planets like the Sun and the Moon circumambulate the polestar, where Lord Viṣṇu resides. These planets are attracted to the Lord, and their circumambulation is caused by this attraction. However, these planets don't collapse into the polestar. Rather, the Sun and the other planets remain 'lower' than the polestar. These planets are said to be aspects or parts of Lord Viṣṇu, and the Lord is the whole. Therefore, by worshipping these planets, one worships some aspect of the Lord. The polestar denotes the cosmic ego, and the Lord is the soul of that ego.

The Sun, specifically, is said to be the representation of the Lord's intellect, while the Moon represents the mind. The other five planets, namely, Jupiter, Mercury, Mars, Venus, and Saturn are representations of the five elements. The polestar resides at the center of the Nakṣatra, which are initially divided into four parts—representing the four moral principles—and then are further divided into seven parts, thus creating the 28 Nakṣatra. Collectively, these 28 Nakṣatra represent morality. This morality then serves the ego or the polestar, as the Nakṣatra circumambulate the polestar. The intellect or the Sun then serves the morality. The moon then serves the Sun. Finally, the other five planets serve the Moon. This 'service' is described in Vedic cosmology as the control of one celestial entity over the other entities. Thus, for example, the polestar causes the rotation of the Nakṣatra. The Nakṣatra then 'drag' the Sun, the Sun 'drags' the Moon, and the Moon 'drags' the other planets. Due to this dragging, three primary kinds of calendars and times are recognized in cosmology.

The first time is attributed to the Nakṣatra movement and is called the sideral calendar. The second time is attributed to the Sun's motion and is called the solar calendar. The third time is due to the Moon's movement and is called the lunar calendar. Then, there are five other calendars called *vatsar*, *anuvatsar*, *parivatsar*, *samvatsar*, and *idavatsar*, and are attributed to the motion of the five planets. In this way, Vedic cosmology describes time through eight calendars. Only the first three calendars are well-known today. Cosmological texts give detailed calculations of how the Nakṣatra drag the Sun, and the Sun drags the Moon, which are then used to compute the time in Vedic cosmology. The calculation of the other five types of calendars is not found today, but these are noted in the Śrīmad Bhagavatam. As a result, the effect of one planet on the other planets—which forms the basis of astrology—is not fully understood today, although this understanding can be extrapolated with some effort.

Now, we can come to the main point of this sūtra, which is that attraction between the soul and the Lord is not physical. It is not like the gravitational force in which two bodies come closer, the attraction increases, which brings them even closer, and ultimately, they collapse into each other. The impersonalist uses these analogies because there are numerous Vedic texts which describe devotion to the Lord, and the impersonalist is unable to deny their existence. So, he coopts these texts, and says that even by devotion the soul merges into the Lord. In short, even when the Vedic texts describe devotion to the Lord, the impersonalist interprets them not as love, but as a vehicle to merger. For the impersonalist, if the final state is merger, then devotion can be accepted.

But this sūtra clearly refutes this identity by stating that the planets like the Sun and the Moon are aspects of the Lord, they remain lower than the Lord, and their attraction causes them to circumambulate the Lord, rather than collapse into the Lord. This whole-part doctrine is semantic. The hand is a property of the soul, the hand has expanded from the soul, and the hand serves the soul. The term *upapatti* is used to indicate logical deduction. We have discussed the nature of logical deduction earlier; *upa* means the part and *pat* means falling. The part falls out of the whole, like a leaf emerges from the root in an inverted tree. The separation of the part from the whole then creates an attraction between the whole and the part—the purpose of the part is the whole. Due to this attraction, the part serves the whole but doesn't merge into the whole.

Therefore, if physical analogies of attraction—e.g., gravitational force—are used, then the result is a black hole in which the soul and the Lord are merged, and the distinction between the two ceases to exist. But if semantic analogies of attraction—i.e., the whole is the purpose of the part—are used, then the result is constantly growing attraction, without the part collapsing into the whole.

Topic 6

QUESTION

Some people also say that the Paramātma is situated in the heart so that the soul can merge into the Paramātma, and this merger is called yoga. Just like if two numbers are added, then the result is a bigger number. Once these numbers have been added, then we cannot distinguish between the two numbers. In the same way, when the union between the soul and the Lord has occurred, then we must say that the soul has been added to God, and the result is a bigger quantity called Brahman. After this addition, we cannot separate them.

4.1.7 (484)

आसीनःसंभवात्

āsīnaḥ saṃbhavāt

āsīnaḥ—sitting; saṃbhavāt—due to the possibility (of soul's liberation).

TRANSLATION

Due to the possibility (of soul's liberation), (the Lord) is sitting (in the heart)

COMMENTARY

The impersonalist says that the Lord in the heart is also a finite entity because He has a form, and everything with a form is finite. However, after all the finite entities have been merged, then the result must be infinite. Therefore, yoga or union is like a mathematical addition of numbers in which small quantities are added to a larger quantity, and ultimately, we obtain infinity.

The quantitative idea of addition is again a physical idea. But according to the whole-part theory, the whole is 1, and everything else is a fraction of 1.

In this regard, we can note that numbers are used in two ways—cardinally and ordinally. Cardinally, numbers are one, two, three, etc. Ordinally, these numbers are first, second, third, etc. We do not start counting from infinity and then proceed backwards to 1. We rather count from 1. The number 1 divides into parts, which means that 1 is the root of the tree, and the fractions of the number 1 are the trunks, branches, and leaves of the tree. This is also how numbers are counted in a binary, ternary, or any other system of counting. The main problem is that to count something, we require a *base* of counting. For example, if the base is 10, then we divide the whole into 10 parts, not infinite parts. Then we divide each of these 10 parts into further 10 parts, not infinite parts. By the successive application of this division, infinite parts are created, but the sum of these parts is not infinite. The sum of all these parts is still 1. Once these parts have been created, we can say that the whole is the first part, then there are 10 subparts, each of which has 10 further subparts, and so on. The cardinality of the parts—i.e., the total number of parts—is infinite. This cardinality can also be numbered as the first, second, third, etc. part. But the whole is still 1.

The Param Brahman is the idea 1, and the Paramātma is the symbol of the idea 1. Just like you can represent the idea 1 infinite times by typing the numeral 1, similarly, the Param Brahman is the singular idea of 1, but the representations of this Param Brahman are infinite symbols of this idea. Nevertheless, because the numeral 1 represents the idea 1, therefore, in one sense, they are non-different, and yet in another sense, the numeral 1 is not identical to the idea 1.

Now we come to the main point of this sūtra, which is that the numeral 1 appears as the representation of the idea 1, so that we can understand the idea 1. If this numeral did not appear before us, then how will we grasp the idea? The impersonalist thinks that Brahman is physically infinite. Infinity cannot have a form, so Brahman must be formless. But this claim can be countered by saying that Brahman is the idea 1, and everything else is either a fraction of 1, or the representation of the idea 1, or even the representations of the fractions of 1. The fractions of 1 are the properties of the Lord, and the representations of 1 are the symbols of the whole. We cannot equate the representation of the fraction to the representation of the whole. For example, a table is the representation of the idea table, which is a part of the whole truth. The sound Kṛṣṇa is also a representation of the whole truth. That doesn't mean that the word 'table' and the word 'Kṛṣṇa' are equally limited because they are both parts. Yes, they are both parts, but one symbol means the whole, and the other symbol means the part. So, unless we distinguish these symbols by the meaning, we will simply see them as parts, and then apply physical analogies of whole and part.

The Paramātma is indeed a part of Param Brahman, but He is also a representation of the Param Brahman. Physically, He is a part, and semantically He is the whole. He appears before the soul—who is both physically and semantically a part—to enable the possibility of the part knowing the whole. This appearance of the Lord as His representation doesn't equate Him to the soul.

Therefore, when we speak about yoga, we must not talk about adding two numbers to get a bigger number. It is about recognizing how the soul is a small meaning, the Lord is the full meaning, and how the partial meaning has manifested from the whole meaning and hence must serve the full meaning.

The soul and the Lord exist in three modalities—universal, contextual, and the individual. The universal modality is the meaning—the Lord is the full meaning, and the soul is a partial meaning. The individual modality is that the Lord is a person, and the soul is a person. And the contextual modality is that this part is related to the whole, and the part gets its meaning in relation to the whole. We cannot call something the leg of a chair, unless we also say that there is a chair. The legness of the part is understood only in relation to the whole. Therefore, the chair must appear before the leg, for the leg to know that it is a leg. If the chair doesn't appear in this way, then how can the leg know what it is? But when the chair appears, it always appears as a symbol of the whole. In short, in each leg of the chair, the whole chair is immanent as a symbol. This symbol has the same meaning as the chair, but it is not equal to the chair.

Even when the soul merges into Brahman, it is like a fraction of 1 collapsing into 1. It doesn't mean that 1/100th now became 1. It means that 1/100th doesn't know that it is 1/100th. This ignorance is also called liberation, because at least the 1/100th is not thinking that it is separated from the 1. However, it is regarded inferior to the situation when 1/100th knows that it is 1/100th, doesn't consider itself separated from 1, and doesn't think itself to be identical to 1.

QUESTION

Are there other ways in which we can support the distinction between the soul and the Lord? How can we know that we are the parts and not the whole?

4.1.8 (485)

ध्यानाच्च

dhyānācca

dhyānāt—on account of meditation (implying that); ca—and.

TRANSLATION

And on account of meditation (implying that we are not the whole).

COMMENTARY

The impersonalist claims that meditation is temporary. We meditate on the Lord temporarily, which then increases our attraction to the Lord. Thereby we come closer to the Lord, which then increases the attraction further, until we collapse into the Lord. But the devotees say that meditation is eternal. The meaning in our mind may be the same as the Lord. But the individual who knows the meaning is always individual. Our attraction to the Lord is that we want to know Him. And the closeness to the Lord is that we know Him better. But regardless of how well we know Him, we don't become the Lord. Thus, attraction constantly increases, as does the proximity. But this proximity is not physical; it is semantic. We know the Lord; we do not become the Lord.

QUESTION

Then, why is it said that the soul is 'fixed' upon liberation? You are saying that the Sun is moving around the polestar, but it is said the soul is fixed. How can the idea of fixation be reconciled with the idea of motion and change?

4.1.9 (486)

अचलत्वं चापेक्ष्य

acalatvaṃ cāpekṣya

acalatvam—immobility; ca—also; apekṣya—is relative to.

TRANSLATION

Also, immobility (or fixedness) is in relation to (the Lord).

COMMENTARY

Many physical ideas are being refuted successively; now, it is the turn of refutating the physical idea of motion. This physical idea says that if you walk from one room to another in your house, then your position is not fixed. Therefore, if the devotee is active—i.e., moving around—then this motion cannot be called a fixed state. And if it is not fixed, then it is temporary. Whatever is temporary must also be false because truth is also eternal. Therefore, anything that is moving cannot be called the truth. The flaw in this claim is the equating of two different ideas, which seem almost identical, although they are not.

These two ideas are *motion* and *change*. In the material world, motion is almost always accompanied by a change. But in the spiritual world, motion exists without a change. Unless we distinguish between the two, it seems that every motion is also a change, and that change would entail temporariness. To understand the difference, let us discuss the Vedic description of motion.

Space in Vedic philosophy is semantic. In this space, different types of things are in their fixed position. There is hence a location for a type of object denoted by your house, and another location for the type of object denoted by your body. Therefore, both your body and the house are in fixed positions. The soul moves in this space—from one body to another. However, the body and the house do not move—since each body is at a fixed location in space.

Then why do we sometimes say that I am close to the house, and at other times say that I'm farther from the house? This sense of proximity and distance is created by an interaction between the body and the house. When the interaction between the house and the body becomes stronger, then the two seem to be close. But when the interaction is weakened, then the two seem farther. Thus, without moving from their position, the body and the house come closer and go farther, and this change in proximity and distance is called 'motion'.

Hence, there are two distinct ideas that seem to be similar, but they are not the same. The idea of *change* pertains to the soul moving across bodies, and the idea of *motion* pertains to the interaction between the bodies, which creates the sense of proximity and distance. Change is when the body feels stronger or weaker, you feel hungry or full, you feel energized or sick, etc. According to Vedic philosophy, all these bodies are eternally present; however, the soul moves from one body to another. Thus, the body is changing as you get older. But the body is also changing as you feel sick or healthy, hungry or full, energized or tired. Some of these changes are reversible and some of them are not. On the other hand, motion is when this body seems closer to a house. This proximity of the bodies can occur when the body is hungry or full, energized or tired, sick or healthy. Therefore, both change and motion are needed.

In the material world, both motion and change occur one after another, and sometimes change is the cause of motion and sometimes motion is the cause of change. For example, if your body changes from a satisfied to a hungry body (which is change) then you move to get something from the kitchen (which is motion). In this case, the motion is caused by change. Similarly, you might see something tasty because you have come close to it, and that encounter with food can make you hungry. In this case, coming close to food (i.e., motion) is the cause, and feeling hungry (i.e., change) is the effect. In general, most changes cause some motion, and most motions cause some change. Owing to this fact, in this world, the distinction between motion and change is collapsed, and we start describing even the change in the bodies as motion. For example, a scientist will say that your feeling of hunger is the motion of molecules.

Now imagine that you are have been eating, and the food is so tasty that you will like to keep eating. But you cannot because after some eating, the body becomes full. In short, your eating is motion, and the body changes due to this motion. But it would be nice if there was only motion and no change. In short, if you could keep eating the tasty food, and the body would never be full.

This imaginary situation becomes reality in the spiritual world. You can go on eating, but the body will never become full. You can stop eating, but the body is never hungry. You can work constantly, but the body is never tired. It is the same body always. It doesn't become old or young, fat or thin, hungry or satisfied, weak or strong. However, this fixed body keeps interacting with other bodies, and comes close to them or moves farther away from them. As a result, in the spiritual world, there is motion, but without any change. Since there is no change (of body), therefore, we can say that the position is fixed. But because there is motion (of body), hence, we can also say that there are activities.

Thus, change can exist without motion—e.g., you can lie in your bed the whole day, and you will still become hungry. And motion can exist without change—e.g., a devotee can keep working and never become tired. A yogi conquers the change in the body, and despite living for very long, his body remains young. He may also conquer hunger and sleep as these are changes to the body. Ultimately, some yogis can transfer themselves to higher planets in the same body. They have motion, but they don't have change. The problem of this world is change—i.e., that we are born, and we die: the body changes. The problem is not motion. Therefore, in the spiritual world, the devotees can serve the Lord without changing their body, and that motion doesn't entail any change.

The impersonalist is unable to distinguish between motion and change. He says: if you are moving, then you are changing, and whatever is changing is temporary, therefore, any activity performed in service of the Lord is temporary. Similarly, meditation on the Lord is also a mental state, so it is temporary. He doesn't realize that by this meditation or activity, the changes end.

Therefore, the fixedness of the spiritual world refers to the lack of change, not the absence of motion. In short, you have an eternal body, but that body keeps performing activities. This fixed body has a fixed location in space. It is a semantic object whose meaning determines the location in space. However, this body then interacts with other bodies, and the stronger interaction brings two bodies close, and the weaker interaction causes them to move apart. In short, the proximity and distance of motion are produced due to an interaction. The interaction is caused by our consciousness, under the control of desire. In the material world, this interaction is also produced due to karma; so sometimes, we are forced to suffer, even though we don't want to suffer. But in the spiritual world, the proximity and distance are produced because of one's desire. Hence, if a devotee desires to see the Lord, then the Lord is immediately there.

The Lord also has a fixed position in space—He is the origin of that space—and that origin is His body. And yet, He moves around, appears and disappears. By this motion, He doesn't change His body. It is simply motion, which is caused by His desire of interaction, which then creates proximity. Therefore, the proximity and distance are *effects* (of desire), rather than the *causes*.

Modern science inverts this idea and says if two things come close, then the force becomes greater, and then two objects interact strongly, and the result of that stronger interaction is faster motion. Thus, in the theory of gravitation, the force between two objects increases with decreasing distance, and with this increased force the speed of motion increases. Hence, the distance between two objects is the cause, the force between the objects is the effect, and the force makes the object move. In Vedic philosophy, the force of desire comes first. It then creates an interaction, which then reduces the distance, and that proximity then produces an experience. Therefore, we cannot ask: Can you show me God? This is because we are far from God. To see God, we must first come close to God. That proximity requires an interaction, which requires a desire. To see the Lord, we must develop a strong desire. That strong desire will produce an interaction with the Lord. That interaction will then reduce the distance to the Lord. And with that reduced distance we will see the Lord face to face.

If science adopts the semantic notion of space, then we will get two kinds of motion. First, there will be a motion of the soul across many bodies. Second, there will be stronger and weaker interaction between the bodies, which creates the experience of proximity and distance. In short, whatever science considers 'space' would no longer be a reality. It will simply be a phenomenal experience. The real space will be semantic in which the soul moves across bodies.

In summary, the devotee is fixed in relation to the Lord, but the devotee is also moving around the Lord. Likewise, the Lord is fixed in relation to the devotee, and yet, He moves around the devotee. This is the dance of the Lord with the devotee. But this dance is only motion; it is not a change of the body.

QUESTION

Does this mean that while meditating, we are factually close to the Lord? That we can see the Lord even in this body, as we develop a desire, which causes an interaction, which reduces the proximity and then creates a vision?

4.1.10 (487)

स्मरन्ति च

smaranti ca

smaranti—remembering (the Lord); ca—also (is a vision).

TRANSLATION

Remembering the Lord is also (the real experience of the Lord).

COMMENTARY

All materialistic theories of space are built upon our waking experience. But in Vedic philosophy, waking experience is understood based on the dreaming experience; the dreaming is understood based on the deep sleep; and the deep sleep is understood based on the transcendent state. Let's begin by understanding dreaming. While you are dreaming, your senses and the mind develop an interaction with a reality that is not interacting with the body. Since distance is created by an interaction, therefore, the reality you see in the dream is close to your senses and the mind, but far from the body. Factually, the body and the senses are equally far from the perceived object—during waking or dreaming. But during waking, the interaction is with the body, which then creates sensation and thoughts. And during dreaming, the interaction is with the senses and the mind. The effects of this interaction become visible in the body too—e.g., that your eyes might flutter during a dream—which means that the senses and the mind haven't left the body, and yet, you can see what the body can't.

If dreaming is understood, then the waking state is described in the same way. That is, whatever you are seeing, is not factually 'near' you. You have a human body, which has a type. And the computer, table, or chair, with which your body is currently interacting, have different types. The different meanings of the 'human', 'table', 'computer', and 'chair' etc. constitute their position in the space, and the distances in this space do not change over time. And yet, these distant objects interact, create proximity, and then perception. Hence, when you dream of a computer, the process is the same as when you see the computer while waking. Both are caused by an interaction. That interaction is caused by the combination of guna and karma. Therefore, sometimes you are forced to see certain things, and sometimes you see because of your desire.

The deep sleep state is the combination of the guna, karma, and chitta, which lie dormant, and they are activated in the dreaming and waking state. Within this dormant state, there are further subdivisions, and the dormant gets reactivated slowly. Therefore, sometimes, a distinction between a 'manifest' and 'about to manifest' is made. This 'about to manifest' sometimes creates dreams, so people can sometimes see the future, sometimes the past, and sometimes just their fantasies, which are neither in the past nor in the future. The past is seen due to the chitta, the future is seen due to karma, and the fantasies are seen due to guna. When none of these are seen, then the state is called deep sleep, in which the guna, karma, and the chitta simply exist dormant.

With this understanding, we can appreciate the nature of meditation on the Lord. It is a desire for the Lord, which creates an interaction, then reduces the distance, and then produces an experience. The process of seeing is the same in both cases. When we meditate, the distance between our senses and the Lord is immediately bridged, proximity is created, and the Lord is hence seen.

If we don't understand ordinary vision, then we also don't understand the vision of the Lord. But if science is advanced to explain ordinary vision, then the same science applies to the vision of the Lord. The difference is simply that to see the Lord, we would have to change our desires. In short, if we desire strongly, then that strong desire will create an immediate perception. Therefore, the devotee rejects all doctrines about liberation. He says: the main point is to see the Lord, and that seeing is available here and now. So, where is the problem if I'm entrapped in a temporary body if I can constantly see the Lord? The Lord that I see in my meditation is not different from the Lord that anyone else is seeing in the spiritual world. My experience cannot be called 'dreaming' while their experience is called 'waking'. They are factually the same experience.

Ultimately, the body doesn't see. The vision is due to the senses and the mind. In the spiritual world, the vision is created through the body, and in the material world, the vision is created directly through the senses and the mind. Thus, the Brahma Samhita says that with the eyes anointed by the mascara of love, the devotee constantly sees the Lord in the heart. Notably, this mascara is not applied to the gross bodily eyes. It is applied to the subtle senses.

The senses are comprised of three aspects—emotion, relation, and cognition. The emotion is the desire to see, which exists as lust in this world. The relation is the ability of the sense to connect to the object being seen. And the cognition is the ability to represent the object's meaning within the sense. Therefore, when we see, the senses 'go out' to the object of seeing, and then they 'bring back' the essence of the object and represent it within the sense. This going out and coming back is due to desire. Hence, if the desire exists, then the senses can go out to the Lord, and then they can bring back the Lord. In short, we have only one business—to develop the desire for the Lord. The rest is all the mechanics of perception. One can learn about the mechanics and develop the understanding of how the Lord can be seen. But even if one doesn't know anything about this mechanics, but simply has the desire, the Lord is still seen. Therefore, both devotees—those who know the mechanics and have the love, and those who don't know the mechanics but have the love—are on par. The mechanics is not important, but one who knows the mechanics can convince others about how the Lord is seen. Those who don't have the faith in the Lord, can also learn this mechanics before they develop devotion to the Lord.

Topic 7

QUESTION

You are saying that the Lord can be seen in any place, any time, in any body, and other than the desire for the Lord, there is no special qualification?

4.1.11 (488)

यत्रैकाग्रता तत्र अविशेषात्

yatraikāgratā tatra aviśeṣāt

yatra—wherever; ekāgratā—singular focus (of the mind); tatra—there; aviśeṣāt—from the absence of a specific quality.

TRANSLATION

Wherever there is singular focus (of the mind), there (the Lord can be seen), from the absence of a special quality (of the place, time, body, or the role).

COMMENTARY

As we have discussed, there are various types of bodies and roles in this world. Some bodies are superior, and some are inferior. Some roles are higher, and the other roles are inferior. Some places are considered holy, while other places are considered unholy. Some of the times (such as early morning) are considered superior to the other times (such as late nights). But all these are ultimately mundane considerations. They are applied when the mind is impure. Under this impurity, some places and some times are helpful in thinking about the Lord. When the body is unhealthy, then it is hard to concentrate the mind, therefore, a healthier body is considered superior. In some roles, we get a better opportunity to understand the Lord, as compared to other roles.

However, ultimately, there is no restriction of place, time, body, or role. The only thing that matters is desire. If the desire is there, then other things can assist, but they cannot prevent; wherever there is a will, there is a way. But when the desire is not there, then other things are not useful. One simply makes varieties of excuses, and the situation is used to justify the lack of desire.

Topic 8

QUESTION

But if the devotee reaches the spiritual world, and can see the Lord face to face, does the process of meditation or remembrance cease to be relevant?

4.1.12 (489)

आ प्रयाणात् तत्रापि हि दृष्टम्

ā prayāṇāt tatrāpi hi dṛṣṭam

ā prayāṇāt—till death; tatra—then; api—even; hi—certainly; dṛṣṭam—is seen.

TRANSLATION

Till death (the Lord is seen in meditation) then (when the devotee reaches the spiritual world) even (though the Lord can be seen face to face in the spiritual world) certainly (He is also) seen in (meditations).

COMMENTARY

For a devotee, the Lord is not simply cognitive perception. The Lord is also the purpose of existence. If you have a goal or a purpose, you keep imagining various possibilities, and your mind is engaged in these thoughts. These imaginations are created when the senses and the mind contact a possibility, which is then experienced. Since the possibility is eternal, therefore, the imagination is not unreal. But the imagination is created by the devotee's choice, rather than the Lord's choice. However, when the Lord is seen face to face, then the Lord fulfills that fantasy and imagination by His will. For example, the gopis of Vṛndāvana imagine how Kṛṣṇa will steal their butter. They imagine how Kṛṣṇa will eat a little and waste a lot. Then they imagine the ensuing argument with the thief and the complaint to the thief's mother. Then they imagine how the mother will scold the thief, and the thief will deny everything. Then they imagine that when the mother wants to punish the thief, they will placate the mother. This is, in one sense, a total fantasy. In this way, by imagination, the gopis are constantly thinking about Kṛṣṇa. But all this imagination also comes true when Kṛṣṇa does the very same things that the gopis have previously imagined. In short, what was fantasy previously, now becomes a reality. The fantasy is conjured by the devotee, and the fantasy is fulfilled by the Lord. Therefore, in one sense, there is a difference between fantasy and reality—because the devotee creates the fantasy, and the Lord fulfills the fantasy. But in another sense, there is no difference between fantasy and reality because the fantasy is always fulfilled, and when it is fulfilled, it is just like it was previously imagined.

The creation of all these fantasies is the meditation. And the fulfillment of these fantasies is the reality. Entry into the spiritual world doesn't mean an end to the meditation—or the creation of fantasies. Hence, even though the Lord can steal the butter of the gopis, and hence He can be seen doing all these things, the devotees are also constantly meditating on the Lord doing these things. Hence this sūtra says that meditation is not merely something we do in this world. In the spiritual world too, there is constant meditation. Hence, there is no contradiction between fantasies about the Lord, and the Lord's reality.

Topic 9

QUESTION

You said that the devotee reaches the spiritual world after death. But isn't it possible that the devotee had unfulfilled karma from previous lives

which must be suffered or enjoyed through subsequent births? How can the devotee reach the spiritual world upon death unless this karma has been finished?

4.1.13 (490)

तदधिगम उत्तरपूर्वाघयोरश्लेषविनाशौ तद्व्यपदेशात्

tadadhigama uttarapūrvāghayoraśleṣavināśau tadvyapadeśāt

tat-adhigame—in that attainment; uttara-pūrva-aghayoḥ—the subsequent sins that were previously created; aśleṣa-vināśau—the destruction of that which is clinging (to the soul); tat-vyapadeśāt—that is stated everywhere.

TRANSLATION

In that attainment (the continuous meditation on the Lord is), all the previously created sins that have to be subsequently (endured), and all that is clinging to the soul is destroyed; this is stated everywhere (in scriptures).

COMMENTARY

The soul exists in the world due to a causal body comprising three aspects, called guna, karma, and chitta. The guna is all the material desires, which exist as habits in us. When the devotee develops constant meditation on the Lord, these desires are destroyed. However, there are still impressions from the past in the chitta, and the karma accumulated in the previous births. The destruction of that which is clinging to the soul refers to the impressions of the chitta. And the destruction of the sins created in the past (to be endured in the future) refers to karma. Therefore, if the desires are destroyed, then impressions of the past, and the karma produced due to the actions from the past are also destroyed.

Karma is described in three ways—*sañcita*, *prārabdha*, and *kriyamāna*. The term kriyamāna refers to that karma which is acting right now. The term prārabdha refers to the karma that was fixed at the time of birth and must be endured in this life. And the term sañcita refers to the karma that would be reaped in the future lives. Upon death, the kriyamāna and the prārabdha are naturally destroyed, for everyone. However, for the devotees, even the sañcita is destroyed, if they have developed unceasing meditation on the Lord.

According to the rules of morality, everyone must suffer or enjoy the consequences of their previous actions. However, devotion to the Lord goes beyond ordinary morality, and this is indicated by the fact that karma is destroyed if devotion has been developed. In short, the basic principle of moral consequence—i.e., tit-for-tat—is not applied to the devotees. The purpose of morality is to bring the soul to devotion. And once that purpose is achieved, then the means to achieve that purpose are not necessary anymore. Of course, it is possible that karma is destroyed without a person becoming the Lord's devotee—e.g., in case of Brahman liberation. It is also possible that a devotee begins the process of devotion but can't perfect it. Such devotees need to take birth again, and karma acts upon them in a way to help them attain the devotional goal. Therefore, the true purpose of morality and karma is not the soul's punishment, because then a devotee could never circumvent their karma. The true purpose is to help them attain devotion, after which karma becomes unnecessary.

This is an important distinction between impersonal liberation and devotion to the Lord. The impersonalist can be liberated only when all the karma has been destroyed, and he is reborn until this karma has been destroyed. The devotee, however, doesn't have to wait for all the karma to be finished. As soon as perfect devotion to the Lord is attained, the karma of future lives is destroyed. This also means that even for a devotee the present life may not be pleasurable, due to the prārabdha which was fixed at the time of birth. Similarly, if someone hasn't perfected their devotion, then the sañcita will cause their rebirth.

Topic 10

QUESTION

A devotee may have developed affections to other devotees in this world during their presence. Are these affections are also destroyed upon death?

4.1.14 (491)

इतरस्याप्येवमसंश्लेषःपाते तु

itarasyāpyevamsaṃśleṣaḥ pāte tu

itarasya—other than this; api—even; evam—in this way; saṃśleṣaḥ—embracing or attachments; pāte—at death; tu—but.

TRANSLATION

Other than this (i.e., karma, guna, and chitta) (the spiritual) embracing or attachments are but (i.e., not destroyed) in this way even upon death.

COMMENTARY

Spiritual aspirants often take a spiritual initiation from a guru. The guru may subsequently leave the body, and by the argument of the previous sūtra, where all impressions of the past (in the chitta) or attachments and desires (i.e., guna) are destroyed, it may seem that the guru forgets about the disciple after he leaves this body. This sūtra rejects that conclusion and says that the spiritual embracing or attachments are not destroyed. But what is a spiritual attachment? And how does it differ from a material attachment? A devotee loves the Lord, and thereby he develops attachment to the others who love the Lord. Such love is spiritual. On the other hand, there may be other people that love us, or we may love them, but that love is not because of the common love of the Lord. When the affection between two persons is caused by their mutual love of the Lord, then this affection is not forgotten. However, a devotee is kind, and loves everyone—including trees, birds, and animals—but this affection is not spiritual because it is not born out of their mutual affection of the Lord. This affection, which might exist between a devotee and their family, friends, neighbors, etc. is limited to this life, and is lost upon death. Likewise, if a disciple is not sincere, then the guru may have some affection for the disciple in this life, but that affection is just like the love for other people not devoted to the Lord. Just as the other affections are lost upon death, similarly, the affection for the insincere disciple is also lost when the guru departs. The relation to the guru is eternal for the sincere disciple, and it is temporary for the insincere disciple.

All disciples must therefore become sincere to the Lord because the relation between the devotees is based upon their shared love of the Lord. It is sometimes incorrectly said that because a devotee is attached to the guru, who is then attached to the Lord, therefore, merely by attachment to the guru one becomes attached to the Lord. This idea is partly false. For example, if a disciple has personal affection for the guru, and renders him personal service, but neglects the guru's instructions on how to serve the Lord, then, such a disciple has affection for the guru, but no affection for the Lord. Such kinds of affections abound in this world—people love their spouses, children, country, and pets. But all these loving relations are not due to their mutual love of the Lord, and such loving relationships are destroyed upon death. In the same way, loving the guru's body or serving him personally, while neglecting the guru's instruction to serve the Lord is a mundane understanding of love. This idea of love equates the love between a guru and a disciple to that between two ordinary people. All such relationships of mundane affection are destroyed at death, according to this sutra. The enduring relationship instead is based on mutual love of the Lord.

The relationship between a guru and a disciple is also broken if the disciple doesn't respect the guru. Fault-finding, second-guessing, questioning of the judgments, or disobeying the instructions of the guru are all good grounds for the guru rejecting the disciple. While a magnanimous guru can tolerate many difficulties in teaching a disciple, as the guru endures these problems, the disciple develops a sense of false entitlement and that worsens his attitude. If the solution becomes a problem, then the solution must also be abandoned. Therefore, the correct approach is that the guru should abandon the disciple.

Topic 11

QUESTION

You said that the karma of the previous lives is destroyed for a devotee upon death. What about the karma of this life? A devotee may have performed some sinful actions before becoming a pure devotee. Are these actions from the present life also destroyed if one becomes a pure devotee of the Lord?

4.1.15 (492)
अनारब्धकार्ये एव तु पूर्वे तदवधेः
anārabdhakārye eva tu pūrve tadavadheḥ

anārabdha-kārye—the karma that has not yet begun to bear fruit; eva—certainly; tu—but; pūrve—previous; tadavadheḥ—limited to that duration.

TRANSLATION

Certainly, the karma that has not yet begun to bear fruit (is destroyed) but the previous (actions of this life) are limited to that duration (of life).

COMMENTARY

Many of us may have come to spiritual life without a full understanding of right and wrong, and we may have performed sinful activities during the performance of devotional practices. If a person becomes a pure devotee, then even this karma is destroyed. This means that upon leaving the body, all past obligations—from the previous lives and this life—are finished, and the soul may not take birth again. The condition is that one must be a pure devotee, which means constantly remembering the Lord, including and up to the point of death. As we have discussed earlier, death is a point of loss for most people, because they lose everything that they were previously attached to. However, for a devotee, death is a time of celebration since the laws that force a change of body—e.g., from childhood to youth to old age—don't apply after death.

Topic 12

QUESTION

What if someone has performed many actions for spiritual progress, but perfect devotion has not been attained? Are these actions also destroyed?

4.1.16 (493)
अग्निहोत्रादि तु तत्कार्यायैव तद्दर्शनात्
agnihotrādi tu tatkāryāyaiva taddarśanāt

agnihotrādi—the fire sacrifice etc.; tu—but; tat-kāryāya—actions for achieving that; eva—certainly; tat-darśanāt—from the understanding of that.

TRANSLATION

But (the progress made through) fire sacrifices, actions performed for achieving that, from the understanding of that, are certainly (not destroyed).

COMMENTARY

Whatever is done for material progress is always lost. For example, you may be wealthy in this life, but you may become poor in the next life. However, whatever is done for spiritual progress is never lost. Therefore, the level of progress attained in this life carries into the next life, and the subsequent progress begins from that level. Even in this life, every day's spiritual advancement begins from the advancement made on the previous day. If one realizes the gradual progression, then even without attaining the ultimate result, they also develop an unshakeable faith in the spiritual process. Through such realization, one can see a difference between material achievements which go up and down in this life, and spiritual achievements, which only increase with time.

Different people who come to spiritual life have different levels of conviction, attachment, and commitment. This difference can be attributed to the different levels of progress they have made in their previous lives. Thus, a child may be more advanced than an old man, and age is not a strict indicator of one's advancement. For example, Śukadeva Goswami was younger to his father and grandfather. However, he spoke on Śrīmad Bhagavatam, even as his father and grandfather listened in the audience. Therefore, from a social perspective, the elders are accorded respect. However, from a spiritual perspective, even a young person can be honored. Many people think that spiritual advancement is attained in old age, or that spiritual topics are for old people. But we see that some children are also attracted to spirituality from birth. Age only pertains to the body, but the soul is eternal, and its progression never diminishes.

QUESTION

But haven't you said that ultimately all these activities (like fire sacrifice) are not substitutes for devotion, thereby implying that they are somehow material? If the progress obtained by other material activities is lost, why is the progress obtained by actions other than Lord's devotion not lost at death?

4.1.17 (494)

अतोऽन्यापि ह्येकेषामुभयोः

ato'nyāpi hyekeṣāmubhayoḥ

ataḥ—therefore; anya—other; api—even; hi—indeed; ekeṣām—is one; ubhayoḥ—both.

TRANSLATION

Therefore, (the purpose) of all the other activities is indeed one (i.e., the progression in spiritual life) even both (i.e., also living a better material life).

COMMENTARY

If you drive a car, then the purpose of the car is to take you to some destination. However, for that purpose to be achieved, the car must be functional. Therefore, the maintenance of the car, and keeping it functional, also becomes a goal. However, the maintenance of the car is the secondary goal, and the achievement of the destination is the primary goal. But let's postulate that someone indeed has car maintenance as the primary goal. To keep the car working and shiny, they need money. If the car wasn't taking one to a goal, that money must come from somewhere else. Now, that something else, which is used to earn money, which is then used to maintain the car, becomes the secondary goal. Hence, there are always many goals, but these goals become primary and secondary, or as we have called them, dominant and subordinate.

Similar statements have been made in the past, so to understand why this statement is novel, we need to recall the previous discussion, and then contrast the present sūtra to the previous ones. All the confusion arises from the use of two approaches—one bottom-up and one top-down. In the final analysis, the world is top-down, with its root in the Lord. However, we can reach the Lord by following a bottom-up process. Thus, many seemingly contradictory statements are made. First, we can say that only devotion to the Lord is important, and everything else is unimportant. Second, we can say that all yoga processes and systems of knowledge are useful if they are pursued as secondary goals for the primary goal of devotion. Third, we can say that knowledge, work, and mystical experience are the primary goal, however, to perfect these goals, we must acquire devotion to the Lord since they are otherwise imperfect.

In the first case, we reject everything else at the outset and focus only on the devotion to the Lord. In the second case, we employ some of the other paths as tools to attain the final goal. And in the third case, we pursue the individual activities for their own sake, but after attaining a certain level, we realize that further perfection requires devotion to the Lord; then, devotion is used as a tool for perfecting the other activities, but further progression requires even more devotion; slowly, by this process, ultimately, devotion becomes unselfish.

The discussion in the previous sūtras pertained to the first two cases—outright rejection, or the acceptance as a secondary goal. Now, it is being said that even if you accept the other things as primary goals, you still need devotion to the Lord to perfect that goal, because otherwise it will always be imperfect.

To illustrate these three approaches, let's apply them to the discussion about the relation between religion and science. First, we can say that since science is the study of matter, and our goal is devotion, therefore, we should not bother with science. Second, we can say that scientific knowledge can help us achieve devotion to the Lord, so it is a good secondary goal for attaining a primary goal. Third, we can also say that science is the primary goal, and the scriptures are studied, or devotion is pursued, as a method to perfect science. In these approaches, the Lord is the only goal, the primary goal, and the secondary goal. But they are all accepted as legitimate processes because eventually they lead to the same conclusion, although the latter two systems are slower.

Thus, some devotees see a contradiction between religion and science, and they reject science. Some devotees don't see a contradiction and they recommend the use of science for the purposes of devotion. And some devotees see science itself as the goal, and religion as the vehicle to achieve the goal.

The previous sūtras accepted the first two methods, and this sūtra accepts even the third approach. Here it is said that when genuine progress is made by those who perform other activities (e.g., fire sacrifices) this effort is not lost and one keeps trying to perfect that process and eventually attains the devotion to the Lord. Hence, even philosophers and scientists can come to the point of loving the Lord, even if they are only interested in philosophy and science to begin with. Throughout this text, we have illustrated the reason for this attainment: all knowledge remains either inconsistent or incomplete until the Lord is understood, because only in the Lord the diversity and contradictions are reconciled. Hence, if a seeker sets out with the intention of knowing the truth, they are eventually led to devotion to the Lord. The problem is that most times philosophers and scientists are not interested in the truth. They are more interested in name, fame, power, wealth, and enjoyment, rather than the truth. Under these forces, the truth is suppressed or distorted, and over time, one suppression and distortion is replaced by another. Such a person hence goes in circles rather than progressing toward the Lord. Therefore, all scientific activity that claims atheism as the goal is lost over time, because it goes in circles. However, the agnostic, who is receptive toward the truth, can become a devotee.

If you are climbing a hill, then reaching a higher point includes reaching the lower point. But if you are going around in circles, then whatever was previously achieved is also lost. Therefore, the hierarchical path is progressive, and the circular path is a waste of time. In this sūtra, the many practices recommended in the scriptures that take us to a higher truth are acknowledged. They must, however, be distinguished from activities that take us in circles.

When people worship the demigods to obtain material benefits, they generally go in circles—some good karma is obtained, enjoyed, and then lost. But one can also worship the demigods and say—they give us only a certain type of happiness, and I must also know about the source of all happiness. When a person asks such a question, then he is gradually elevated to higher and higher planetary systems, until he reaches the place of the Lord, and realizes that He is the ultimate truth. The people who are progressively elevated from lower to higher planets must be distinguished from those who are elevated temporarily and then fall back to their previous state. The process of progressive elevation is partly material and partly spiritual. The higher level includes the lower level, so nothing is lost even as one progresses, but the ultimate truth is eventually attained. This sūtra says that the 'one' is attained and 'both' are attained.

We can attain the 'one' by exclusively focusing on the 'one'. We can attain the 'one' by using the 'other' as a tool or method employed to achieve the 'one'. And we can also attain the 'one' by focusing on the 'other' but accepting the 'one' as the guiding light to perfect the attainment of the 'other'. All these processes are accepted while rejecting the focus on 'other' without the 'one'.

Topic 13

QUESTION

It is much easier to understand the progression with knowledge because it is easier to see that knowledge exists in an inverted-tree-like structure. It is harder to see how different kinds of activities can also be called progressive. After all, all these actions are performed with our senses—e.g., hands. How do we say that some activity of the senses is superior to other such activities?

4.1.18 (495)
यदेव विद्ययेति हि
yadeva vidyayeti hi

yat-eva—as surely; vidyayā—with knowledge; iti—thus; hi—certainly.

TRANSLATION
As surely with knowledge, thus certainly (with the other activities).

COMMENTARY
The actions of our hands are not physical. They also have meanings. Thus, some movement is cooking, some movement is typing, and some movement is driving. But apart from these meanings, there are higher-level meanings in the mind. Just like the senses of knowledge perceive properties such as color, taste, smell, etc. and the mind perceives the meaning—e.g., that this thing is a table, or this word means something—similarly, the meaning associated with activity is associated with a purpose. When you read a book, you first get sensations, then you get a meaning, then you judge if this meaning is true or false, and then you try to get the purpose. However, when you perform the actions, then the activity is directly linked to a purpose, and other meanings are invoked to determine if the actions will achieve the purpose. For example, if you are driving a car, then you must know that turning the wheel clockwise will turn the car to the right, that this turning will take you closer to the destination, etc. But you will not do any of these things unless you have a purpose in mind. Therefore, action is considered superior to knowledge, because many people read books, but very few of these readers translate this knowledge into real activity.

In the Bhagavad-Gita, jnana-yoga is described as the first step to yoga. Following this there is dhyāna-yoga, or meditation which is generally performed for some time during a day. Karma-yoga is superior to both these methods because it is performed for most of the time. Thus, you might acquire some knowledge by reading a book, but it is generally hard to accept it, because the mind is uncontrolled. Then as the mind is controlled, the knowledge is accepted, and one decides to do something about what one has learnt. In short, activity is produced only after some conviction in its efficacy. On the other hand, it is possible to perform these activities mechanically without knowing their true meaning and purpose. For example, most people perform fire rituals without knowing what they are doing, and the results obtained thereby.

Thus, in one sense, activity is superior to knowledge, because one acts after a conviction. In another sense, one might act without an understanding, so activity is considered inferior to knowledge. Only the context decides what is superior. In the Bhagavad-Gita, Lord Kṛṣṇa imparts knowledge which then leads to activity—i.e., Arjuna fighting the battle. Therefore, the activity is a progression over knowledge. However, because many people on the same battlefield were fighting without this knowledge, their activities are inferior.

The Kauravās were fighting because they wanted to enjoy their kingdom. Bhīśma and Drona were fighting due to the obligation to the Kauravās. Many warriors on the side of Pāndavas were fighting to uphold goodness over evil.

And Arjuna was fighting simply because it was pleasing to the Lord. They have the same activity—i.e., fighting—but the underlying meanings are different. Hence, the same activity can be performed with different mental states. Likewise, different mental states can lead to different activities. For example, when Arjuna felt attached to his cousins and teachers, he refused to fight. Therefore, the same activity can be tied to different mental states, many activities can be tied to the same mental state, different mental states can result in different activities, and different mental states can also produce the same activity.

There is no hard and fast rule about whether an activity is higher or lower. But we can decide if the activity is superior or inferior based on the mental state. This allows us to say that the superiority or inferiority of both knowledge and action are based on the meaning. Once this equivalence is established, then there is no difference between knowledge and action. One may read a book and that reading is perfection if the knowledge is supreme. One may perform an action and that action is perfect if the person is thinking about the Lord.

Based on the mental state, we can determine if an action is superior or inferior. And this determination is based on the same principle by which we say that a book is superior or inferior. Therefore, if one performs a fire sacrifice with a higher meaning and purpose, then that activity is superior. Conversely, if one performs the same sacrifice without understanding the meaning or purpose, or the purpose is evil, then that same activity must be deemed inferior. Thus, by changing the meanings, we can progress by action, quite like knowledge.

Topic 14

QUESTION

But since these actions are performed with a goal or purpose in mind, isn't this activity considered selfish, and therefore, inferior to knowledge?

4.1.19 (496)

भोगेन त्वितिरे क्षपयित्वा संपदयते

bhogena tvitare kṣapayitvā saṃpadyate

bhogena—by enjoyment; tu—but; itare—of the other; kṣapayitvā—having exhausted; saṃpadyate—in the completion of the purpose of the activity.

TRANSLATION

But by the enjoyment of the (pleasure of) the other (the Lord), the results of the activity are destroyed (and) and completes the purpose of the activity.

COMMENTARY

The impersonalist believes that since purposeful activity leads to consequences, therefore, one must stop all activity. However, in this sūtra, this idea is rejected. The sūtra says that if we start enjoying the enjoyment of the Lord, then two things are attained— (1) we are enjoying and (2) there are no consequences. The impersonalist gets liberated—i.e., freed from the consequences—by sacrificing enjoyment. But the devotee destroys the consequences of actions without sacrificing the enjoyment. The distinction between mundane and spiritual activity is not in the activity; it is rather in the meaning of that activity. The mundane mind is occupied with the thoughts of impending selfish pleasure while the activity is performed. The spiritual mind is also occupied with the thoughts of the Lord's pleasure, and the thought also pleases the devotee.

We can call the pleasure obtained by pleasing the Lord selfish—after all, the devotee is enjoying. And we call this desire unselfish—because the devotee can also undergo bodily suffering if that pleases the Lord. The fact is that for a devotee, unselfishness dominates selfishness. In material life too, people proffer altruism because they know that if by their actions their relatives, friends, or countrymen are benefitted, then that benefit will also benefit them. So, they are not opposed to altruism, but the selfishness still dominates because the altruist will stop helping others if their happiness was sacrificed. Therefore, the material and the spiritual world are different because in the material world others are served as a byproduct of selfishness; but in the spiritual world, the individual happiness of a person is obtained as a byproduct of serving the Lord. If this inversion in causality is not understood, then we falsely equate lust with love. They are both desires, but the desire to love cannot be equated to lust.

SECTION 2

Topic 1

QUESTION

You are saying that there is no difference between knowledge and activity because underlying both is an intention or meaning in the mind, which determines whether the knowledge and activity are material or spiritual. How is this intention or meaning in the mind translated into a perceivable action?

4.2.1 (497)

वाङ्मनसि दर्शनाच्छब्दाच्च

vāṅmanasi darśanācchabdācca

vāk—speech; manasi—in mind; darśanāt—from being seen; ca—also; śabdāt—from scriptural statements; ca—and.

TRANSLATION

From the speech from scriptural statements also being seen in the mind.

COMMENTARY

Sāñkhya philosophy recognizes five senses of action, and speech is first. Therefore, while this sūtra describes the nature of speech, we can apply this to the actions of the other senses of action as well, by extending this example. This example is easily understood because we speak after a thought appears in the mind. The conversion of a thought into speech involves four components: (1) meaning, (2) language, (3) effort, and (4) speech. We know that the same meaning can be expressed using different word from different languages, and thus language plays a key role in converting the meaning into words. Similarly, while speaking, we need some power to transform thoughts into words.

The words we speak in a language exist in a shared space of that language. When someone learns a language, they become familiar with that space, or they enter that space. By 'space' I mean a collection of dimensions. Each dimension is a meaning or a universal, and that meaning or universal is given a name. For example, there are universals like cow and mammal. In English, these universals are called 'cow' and 'mammal' and in German 'kuh' and 'säugetier'. The words 'cow' and 'kuh' are the individual expressions of the same meaning.

Therefore, in one sense, the universal space is common for both languages. But when these universals are combined with the individual, a language-specific space of these universals is created. In this space, the meaning of each word is often defined by a contrast to other words in that language, which produces language-specific contextualized meanings, unique to a specific language.

The mind is a space in which (a) there are many dimensions of the universals, (b) these dimensions have different names, and (c) each dimension is related to some dimensions and not related to other dimensions. A thought in the mind is a linguistic object in this space. Just like when we place an object in a physical space, we describe it through coordinates such as {X, Y, Z} or {R, θ, φ} or {χ, ψ, ω} etc. In some cases, similar ideas have similar sounds across languages. In some cases, the same meaning is called by different sounds. And sometimes the different sounds also have different meanings. Once these dimensions are defined, then we create an object in this space using the same symbols. A thought is a linguistic encoding of meaning within the mind.

In Vedic philosophy, the sounds themselves have a meaning. For example, the sound 'Kṛṣṇa' means 'all attractive' and it doesn't matter what language you use, you can chant the name 'Kṛṣṇa' with the same effect. It may mean nothing in your language, but it has an objective meaning. This is because every meaning has an original name and a contextual relation to other names and meanings, which constitutes the original semantic space called śabda-brahman, whose dimensions are the letters of Sanskrit. These letters have three aspects—universal, individual, and contextual, or a meaning, a name, and a distinction to other meaning-names. We can create alternative languages by disconnecting these in their original form and connecting them in new ways. By this disconnection and connection, alternative languages are produced. However, there is never a situation in which we have pure meaning, without a name, and without a connection to other names and meanings, that contextualize the meaning.

Therefore, when this sūtra says that vāk or speech appears in the mind, it means that everyone thinks in some language. Thought is not pure meaning—i.e., something devoid of language. It is not pure speech—i.e., something devoid of meaning. It is the combination of a meaning, a name, and a relation.

Once the meaning appears in the mind, it expands further into two different, but related ways. These are called the expansions of knowledge and action. For example, you can use the word 'car' to describe a car, but if someone asks, "What you do mean by 'car'?" then you can explain the meaning in two ways. First, you can say that a car has this shape, size, color, etc. Second, you can say that it works in this way. Everything that looks like a car may not work like a car—i.e., move on a street. And everything that moves on a street may not be a car. Therefore, these two methods are employed to explain the meaning of 'car'. These explanations of the meaning are called its 'expansion'. Basically, the idea of car is expanded into something that we can perceive by our senses of knowledge, and something that can be used by our senses of action. Each such sense of knowledge or action is also a different space, and the mind combines these spaces to create a combined picture of the world we perceive and use.

The mind has a choice by which it creates dominant-subordinate structures. For example, sometimes we use the fact that people live in a building to say that the building is a house. At other times, we can consider the size of the building and say that it is bungalow. Then, we look at the garden around the house and say that it is a mansion. The choice of the mind is (a) how many facts it considers before formulating a meaning, and (b) which facts are given greater or lesser importance in formulating the meaning. Thus, if some facts are ignored, then the meaning is incomplete. And the dominant-subordinate structures create inconsistencies, which then result in a change in the selection or rejection of facts, followed by their reorganization in new dominant-subordinate structure.

The material mind either ignores some important facts or changes the dominant-subordinate structures to produce a false, wrong, or bad meaning. When the material mind expands into actions through the senses of action, then these incomplete, false, wrong, or bad meanings are expanded into improper actions. When the material mind uses the senses of knowledge to perceive, but ignores some facts, or organizes them incorrectly, then incorrect knowledge is produced. The spiritual mind, on the other hand, also neglects some facts and organizes the remaining facts with different priorities. And its action senses are also involved in converting this knowledge into activity. Hence, the false, bad, and wrong things must be filtered out, and whatever is remaining, can be organized with the purpose of serving the Lord. In short, the choice in the mind is used in many ways—initially to select facts, and then to organize the facts.

With this background, we can understand this sutra: It says that the mind is capable of perfect knowledge because the perfect knowledge of the scriptures can also appear in the mind. This 'appearance' is called darśan or seeing, and the term is also used for 'philosophy'. The Western idea of philosophy is 'love for wisdom', and it is practiced as speculation, question and answer, etc. In its best form, philosophy can be equated to anumāna, or thinking, imagination, and speculation. But the Vedic idea of philosophy 'vision' or 'seeing' in the mind. The entire universe, and even things beyond the universe, can be seen in the mind, and when the vision is true, right, and good, it is called darśana. The intellect decides if the vision is true; the ego determines if this is good; and the moral sense is responsible for deciding if the vision is righteous. These three instruments of judgment work along with the mind to determine darśana.

But besides this capacity for each mind to obtain the vision of that which is true, right, and good, there is another deeper meaning of darśana which is that it can appear in the mind *before* being expressed externally. A good example of such vision is that of Brahma who was given a darśana by the Lord in the mind by inspiring him to see the nature of the truth, right, and good. Brahma then expanded this into two things—the three Vedas called Rig, Sama, and Yajur represent the nature of truth, good, and right respectively, and form darśana. The fourth Veda called Atharva is the conversion of the truth, right, and good, into activities, which are described as ritualistic procedures. And the fifth Veda, which includes Purana, Itihasa, and Tantra, describe additional activities, pastimes, and procedures, by which common people can practice—and through that practice, understand—the nature of darśana or truth, right, and good.

Since the knowledge manifests from Brahma's mind due to the inspiration of the Paramātma in the heart, therefore, the knowledge subsequently encoded in the Vedas is transcendent, even though it is manifest as speech by Brahma (who is considered a soul—although an advanced and enlightened soul). It is however not considered Brahma's creation, because it is true, right, and good, and there is only one thing that is completely true, purely good, and perfectly right, and that thing is the Supreme Lord. All other things are partially true, partly good and bad, and partially righteous and unrighteous. Therefore, we can also say that darśana is nothing other the vision of the Lord in the mind. When the Lord appears in our mind, we can understand how He is the perfect truth, right, and good, then we have perfected our philosophical knowledge.

QUESTION

If the mind is spiritualized in this way, does it mean that the body is also spiritualized? What is the difference between spiritual and material bodies?

4.2.2 (498)

अत एव च सर्वाण्यनु

ata eva ca sarvāṇyanu

ataḥ eva—therefore certainly; ca—also; sarvāṇi—all (senses); anu—subordinates or servants (of the mind).

TRANSLATION

Therefore, certainly all (senses) are subordinate (to the mind) as well.

COMMENTARY

Since the mind can select or reject the data or actions of the senses, and organize this data and actions in different priorities, therefore, the mind is said to be controller of the senses. Accordingly, the senses are said to be the servants of the mind. Of course, the senses can sometimes make the mind their servant. At present, most people say that we have no free will, and we are dragged by the demands of the senses. This means that they haven't realized the ability in the mind to control the senses. If you don't use it, you lose it. Once the senses become dominant, they start dictating to the mind what is higher or lower priority. This situation is described in the Vedic texts as the condition of a husband who has ten wives, and each wife (i.e., the sense) drags the husband (i.e., the mind) in a different direction, asking the husband to do her bidding. As the husband tries to please one wife, the other wives demand attention. So, the husband runs from one wife to another, trying to please the unhappy wives.

Therefore, the first step in spiritual life is that the mind must obtain mastery over the senses. However, even if this mastery is obtained, one doesn't necessarily become perfect. One just becomes a better materialist. Perfection also requires that the mind uses its choice to select what is important and neglect what is unimportant, and then prioritize the more important things over the less important things. The spiritualist and the materialist are distinguished by the truthfulness, rightness, and goodness of their choices. Therefore, above the mind is the intellect to judge the truth, above the intellect is the ego to judge the goodness, and the above the ego is the moral sense to judge the rightness. Just like the senses are serving the mind, similarly, the mind serves the intellect, the intellect serves the ego, and the ego serves the moral sense. Perfection means that this hierarchy is collapsed. In short, the mind only thinks the truth, right, and good, so these separate instruments of judging are not required. And the difference between the mind and the senses is not required because the sense act as servants rather than masters, and voluntarily relinquish their priority to the other senses when required. Arbitration between the senses is necessary when the senses are in conflict; however, when there is cooperation, arbitration is not needed. Similarly, the distinction between the senses and the soul is dissolved because there is no difference between eternal happiness and sensual pleasure, between knowing the full truth and perceiving the immediate facts, between performing the duty or simply doing what one feels like doing.

The differences between the moral sense, ego, intellect, mind, senses, etc. in the material world, are byproducts of various types of conflicts. To overcome these conflicts, these entities exist in a hierarchy, and the higher entity controls the lower entity and here the mind's control over the senses is described.

In the spiritual world, the 'mind' is the soul; the soul's three aspects are the three faculties of judging truth, right, and good. Each of these three aspects has two further aspects called knowing and action. And each of these two aspects has five further aspects known as the senses of knowing and action. In the final analysis, there is no difference between the soul, the mind, and the senses. These are simply understood as the parts of the whole, and the parts sometimes serve the whole, and the whole sometimes serves the part. This 'service' is simply one part becoming dominant over the rest of the parts, and the other parts becoming subordinate. Then, the domination of the mind over the senses disappears in one way, but since the 'mind' is the soul, it also persists in another way.

Hence, the soul is the three aspects collectively. The moral sense, the ego, and the intellect are the three aspects of the soul. The two aspects of these three aspects are the senses of knowledge and action. And five aspects of each of these two aspects are the five senses of knowledge and action. Since we cannot separate these aspects, therefore, we cannot say that the soul is different from the ego, moral sense, intellect, mind, the ten senses, or the body. And yet, since we can distinguish between these aspects, therefore, the 24 elements of Sāñkhya exist even in the spiritual world, but they are not different from the soul.

In the Śrīmad Bhagavatam, Lord Viṣṇu is described to have 24 different forms. In these forms, different aspects of the Lord are permanently dominant and subordinate. They appear as different incarnations of Lord Viṣṇu, displaying different qualities. For example, the Aniruddha form of the Lord is called the representation of the mind; from a material perspective, the mind is subordinate to the intellect, ego, and the moral sense. But from a spiritual perspective, the mind is everything. Therefore, the Aniruddha, or Paramātma, is sometimes described subsequent to Vasudeva (the representation of the moral sense or *sat*), Saṅkarṣaṇa (the representation of the ego, or *ananda*), and Pradyumna (the representation of the intellect, or *chit*). At other times, the Paramātma is said to be the full representation of the Lord within the heart of a living entity.

These descriptions indicate that the 24 elements of Sāñkhya are not exclusively 'material' or separate from the study of the soul. They are also aspects of the soul, but when they become dominant or subordinate, different forms of the Lord are created. In fact, just as innumerable types of material bodies are created by the domination of these aspects, similarly, the Lord has innumerable forms. Finally, Lord Kṛṣṇa is described as the complete form in which any of these aspects can alternately become dominant or subordinate. In the Śrīmad Bhagavatam, therefore, He is described as the 25th form, and in Sāñkhya, the soul is said to be the 25th element. The 25th element is the balanced state of the 24 elements, which means that the other 24 forms are aspects of the complete form. Hence, the study of 24 elements is in one sense the study of matter. In another sense, it is the study of the soul. In another sense, it is the study of the many incarnations of the Lord. And finally, it is also the Absolute Truth.

The text has so far discussed so many topics, including the material elements. As we approach the conclusion of the text, it can seem surprising that the discussion of mind, senses, prāna, etc. are being revived. Indeed, a mundane reading of the text would imply that after discussing the soul and the Lord, we are again discussing matter. But we are not. We discussed the nature of matter earlier. In the beginning of this chapter, we discussed the body in the spiritual world, and how it acts in relation to the Lord. And what we are discussing now is the details about the spiritual body, and its similarity to the material body. The same words are employed in relation to both material and spiritual bodies, in relation to our body and the Lord's body. Hence, the discussion can be interpreted alternately as matter, soul, or the Lord. This is the power of the personal description; if we establish the principles, then we can scientifically study the soul and God, like we previously scientifically studied the nature of matter.

Topic 2

QUESTION

If the mind is superior to the senses, then how does the mind control the senses? And why are the senses sometimes said to control the mind?

4.2.3 (499)

तन्मनःप्राणे उत्तरात्

tanmanaḥ prāṇe uttarāt

tat—that; manaḥ—mind; prāṇe—in prāṇa; uttarāt—subsequently.

TRANSLATION

That mind is subsequently (or further) controlled by the prāṇa.

COMMENTARY

As we have discussed previously, prāṇa is the power of choice, and this choice is effected as the dominant-subordinate structures. We have also spoken about the power of choice in the mind, which also creates dominant-subordinate structures. Therefore, there are two different systems of control described in the Vedic texts. In the Sāñkhya system, the mind is controlled by the intellect, which is controlled by the ego, which is controlled by the moral sense, which is controlled by the soul. Therefore, if one has a strong sense of morality, then everything is subsequently controlled. In the Yoga system, all these elements of Sāñkhya are said to be controlled by the prāṇa. One method of controlling the prāṇa is the control of breath. And once the prāṇa is controlled, then everything else, including the senses, mind, intellect, ego, and the moral sense, are also controlled. These two systems seem to be contradictory, but they are not.

To resolve this contradiction, we can recall how the Absolute Truth is divided into masculine and feminine aspects; the masculine is the will and the feminine is the power to fulfill that will. The 24 elements of Sāñkhya are the expansions of power, and the prāṇa described in the Yoga system (which is also divided into many aspects) is the expansion of the will. Since power exists in the will, and the will exists in the power, a stark distinction between the two may not sometimes be made. But these can also be distinguished. We must also remember that the will can control the power, and the power can control the will. Therefore, in the Sāñkhya system, morality controls everything else, including prāṇa. But in the Yoga system, the prāṇa controls everything else.

To understand this mutual control, we can think of a machine which works if it is fed with power. The 24 elements of Sāñkhya are, in one sense, like different machines. As they are fed greater or lesser power, they become dominant or subordinate. Since 24 elements of Sāñkhya are expansions of power, and they can command the will, therefore, the body is able to control the soul—in the material world. But that doesn't mean that the soul cannot control the body by exercising its will over the power. When the power controls the will, then Prakriti is superior and Puruṣa (the soul) is inferior. But if the will of the Puruṣa gains control, then Puruṣa is superior and Prakriti is inferior. Since both can control each other, therefore, they can both be both superior and inferior, or neither is permanently superior or inferior. Thus, the Sāñkhya and Yoga systems are not contrary, even though they describe different methods of control. They are only differing emphases on the masculine or the feminine aspects.

In the Vaishnava texts, the Sāñkhya system is given greater emphasis, and in the Shakta texts, the Yoga system is given greater emphasis. Thus, the role of prāṇa is relatively obscure in the Vaishnava texts, and more pronounced in the Shakta texts. In the Upaniśad, there is an allegorical story about an argument between the different parts of the body. The mouth says that I swallow food, which is required for everyone else, so I'm superior. The hand says that I put the food in the mouth, so I'm superior. The stomach says that I digest everything from which the hand gets the power to put the food in the mouth, so I'm superior. In this way the argument goes on and remains inconclusive. Finally, the prāṇa says that each of the other parts are only involved in one aspect, however, I (the prāṇa) am involved in all the aspects. Therefore, I'm superior.

However, this story is incomplete, because the prāṇa is divided into many aspects. There are powers of ingestion, digestion, circulation, assimilation, and elimination. If we divide the prāṇa into many aspects, just like we divided the body into many parts, then, the superiority of the prāṇa cannot be established, just like the superiority of the other body parts could not be established.

Therefore, we must step away from notions of absolute superiority and inferiority and look at the problem from the perspective of masculine and feminine aspects. We have said that the soul comprises three aspects of relation, cognition, and emotion. But these aspects are also divided into will and power. The will aspect desires a relation, emotion, and cognition, and the power aspect fulfills that will. However, this description can lead to the mistaken idea that the power is inert, and the will is conscious. Hence, a nuanced understanding is that both masculine and feminine are persons, and they both have desire, will, or choice. However, these desires are different in the masculine and the feminine. As we have discussed earlier, the masculine is the want to be needed, and the feminine is the need to be wanted. Simplistically, the desires in the masculine and the feminine become different as wants and needs. This understanding helps us nuance our view of how the dominant-subordinate structures are created by choice—the choices are produced due to needs and wants.

There are many aspects of our material existence that exist as needs—e.g., sex drive, hunger, sleep, etc. There are also many aspects of our material existence that exist as wants—e.g., wealth, fame, power, etc. If one is struggling with needs, then the control of prāṇa through the Yoga process helps in conquering them. And if one is struggling with wants, then the control of the senses and the mind through the Sāñkhya understanding helps in conquering them.

Often if needs are unfulfilled, then they transform into wants. For example, unfulfilled sexuality, sleep deprivation, or unsatisfied hunger, can transform into the desire for power, fame, and wealth. Indeed, many spiritual aspirants who control eating, sleeping, and sex, maniacally pursue power, wealth, and fame. Similarly, sometimes if wants are unfulfilled, then they can transform into needs. For example, people failing to obtain wealth, power, and fame can develop insomnia, eating disorders, hypersexual behaviors, etc. Therefore, there are no hard and fast distinctions between Yoga and Sāñkhya, and both in combination or either of them alternately, can be employed by spiritual aspirants. As a result, Sāñkhya and Yoga systems have traditionally been seen sometimes as aspects of one system, and sometimes as two closely related systems.

Topic 3

QUESTION

You have earlier said that the prāṇa is Lord's energy and work according to His direction. You are now saying that the soul can also control the prāṇa. How do we reconcile these? Does prāṇa control the soul, or is controlled by it?

4.2.4 (500)

सोऽध्यक्षे तदुपगमादिभ्यः

so'dhyakṣe tadupagamādibhyaḥ

saḥ—that (prāṇa); adhyakṣe—in the ruler (i.e., the Lord); tat—that (the Lord); upagama—submissive approach; ādibhyaḥ—the cause of approach etc.

TRANSLATION

That (prāṇa—the feminine energy) in the ruler (i.e., the Lord—the masculine) is the cause of the submissive approach toward that (the Lord).

COMMENTARY

We earlier discussed how the Lord is the origin of space, the soul is different points in space, and the connection between the origin and the different points in space is described as prāṇa. The same point is now repeated, although now with the nuance that the soul can also approach the Lord through prāṇa.

The origin of space is the masculine form of the Absolute Truth. The expansion of space is the feminine form of the Absolute Truth. And the soul within that space is expanded from the masculine, present within the feminine. This has been previously described as the Lord injecting the soul as His 'seed' into the mother through His glance. The soul is therefore a child or a part of both the masculine and the feminine—the masculine is the father, and the feminine is the mother. The mother controls the father and is controlled by the father. The child can also control the mother, but not in the way the father does. But it doesn't mean that the child is powerless. The child also receives the power of the mother, provided it becomes submissive to both the father and the mother. This submission is described in this sūtra by using the word *upagama*. The term *gama* means going, and *upa* means as a subordinate part. If the soul is arrogant, then the prāṇa doesn't work. But if the soul is submissive, then the child can approach the mother to seek Her help, to approach the father. As we have discussed, the desires in the masculine and the feminine forms are like wants and needs. If a soul approaches the Lord with a want, then he acts like the masculine. The Lord may agree, as this is also considered devotion, although not on par as when the soul develops a need. When the desire in the soul is like a need, rather than a want, then the soul acts like the feminine. In short, now, the soul is more a mother's baby rather than the father's child. The mother now controls the baby and gives the baby the power to approach the Lord with devotion.

Effectively, there are two kinds of devotional desires—wants and needs. The soul who has renounced the false boldness of the material world which desires independence, and now agreed to surrender to the Lord as His servant, is considered great. However, there is still some boldness in the desire, by which the soul acts masculine. This masculinity is expressed in the fact that the soul is attracted to the Lord's six qualities of knowledge, beauty, power, wealth, fame, and renunciation, and behaves like the prince who sometimes wants to sit on the throne of the king—not to replace the king, but just to feel what the king feels being the king. We have discussed earlier how this devotion is described as the five kinds of liberation—having the same form as the Lord, living in the same place as the Lord, enjoying the same power as the Lord, living in proximity to the Lord, or believing that everything meant for the Lord is also meant for the soul. The affectionate child of a king considers himself just like the king, although there is no malice or competitiveness with the king.

But the devotion of wants is distinguished from the devotion of needs. The neediness is not like the aspiration for knowledge; it is instead like the necessity for food. The soul who has renounced the wants and developed the need for the Lord is considered greater, because the soul has greater dependence on the Lord, and the Lord enjoys His chivalrous nature of wanting to be needed even more. Under the neediness, the feminine aspect becomes predominant.

Under boldness, the prāṇa controls the senses and the body (i.e., the parts) and the wants in the mind, senses, and the body are fulfilled by the mind. Under shyness, the mind, senses, and the body become the controllers of prāṇa.

This basic difference appears even within this world in two types of meditation. In the first type of meditation, the meditator is advised to withdraw the senses within by controlling the mind, and to stop the flow of thoughts in the mind by focusing on the self. In the second type of meditation, the meditator is advised to let go of all the attempt to control the senses and the mind, and just observe; this 'observation' is called the 'mindfulness' of the aspirant, and involves letting go of one's tendency to control, and become a passive observer. This passive observation involves identifying oneself with prāṇa, which is attained if one simply focuses on the breath going inward and outward.

The practices of mindfulness are predominant in Buddhism and the practices of mind control are predominant in Yoga. While the mindful practice helps in cessation of thoughts, the Yoga system doesn't consider this cessation a spiritual state. It is rather a state devoid of material influences. Thus, superior than the state of material wants and needs is the state where one has no want or need—the state without wants is called Brahman, and the state without needs is called the state of nothingness. You might not be hungry right now, but you can become hungry after some time. Therefore, the cessation of needs is considered temporary relative to the cessation of wants by which one acquires a body. Once the body is acquired, then it also brings needs, and whatever started out as a project of fulfilling one's wants through the body, now becomes a project of fulfilling the body's needs. Thus, in the material world, the soul starts out with the masculine tendency to dominate but becomes the servant of the body. Therefore, freedom from wants—which led to the body—is considered superior to the freedom from needs. This superiority is predicated on the fact that if we gave up the body, then we will also be free from the needs of the body. So, by getting the state without the wants, we will also get the state devoid of the needs. Hence arise the nihilistic doctrine in which the soul is devoid of all needs, and the impersonal doctrine of Brahman in which the soul has no wants.

Superior to these is the state in which one wants the Lord. And even superior to that state is one in which one needs the Lord. As we have discussed before, Vaikuṇṭha is the realm of boldness, and Goloka is one of shyness.

Śrīla Rupa Goswami, in his Upadeśāmrta, describes six qualities of a guru, by which the guru has become free of needs—i.e., the necessity to serve the mind, the senses, and the body. The six minimum qualifications of a guru are—freedom from the urge to speak (i.e., the urges of the senses of action), the urges of the mind, the urges of anger (i.e., the ego), the urge for tasty food (i.e., the urges of the senses of knowledge), the urge for hunger, and the urge for sex (which are the two main urges of the body). This is the first state of the soul beyond the material world, although it is the nihilistic state aspired for by the Buddhists. Beyond this freedom from material needs is the freedom from material wants or Brahman. Thus, the guru may not be liberated but must be beyond this world. Such a guru can guide others in the material world because he is not controlled by the necessity to serve the body. But he may not be qualified to take the soul toward Brahman, the wanting, or the needing of the Lord.

Thus, we find many kinds of seemingly contradictory statements ranging from the claim that prāṇa is only a mechanical process that doesn't lead to perfection, to the claim that the surrendering to the Lord, and being governed by His will is the highest perfection for the soul. Accordingly, the Shakta system is sometimes considered lower than the Shaiva and Vaishnava system, and sometimes, the Shakta system of devotion to the feminine is called the highest system. The fact is that in the material world, surrendering to the material power is the lowest process, and in the spiritual world, this surrender is the highest goal. Previously, the process of prāṇa was considered but called inferior. Now, this process is being recommended, after the recommendation of mind control. Therefore, the superiority of this method is recognized after stating it is inferior. If one understands the contexts, then both statements are considered true.

QUESTION

You earlier said that the mind is the controller of the senses and the body. Now you are saying that the mind can be controlled by the prāṇa. Does this mean that the senses and the body can also be controlled by the prāṇa?

4.2.5 (501)

भूतेषु तच्छ्रुतेः

bhūteṣu tacchruteḥ

bhūteṣu—the elements; tat-śruteḥ—that is stated by the śrutī.

TRANSLATION

The (five) elements (are controlled by prāṇa); that is stated by the śrutī.

COMMENTARY

Most of us think that to push a table or a chair, we must use our hands. Then we also think that the movement of the hands is caused by the brain sending a signal to the hand. Finally, we say that the signal is the movement of molecules. But what causes the molecules to move from the brain to the hand?

In atomic theory, a molecule exists in a 'stationary state', and it jumps to another 'stationary state' although the cause of that jump is not known. In classical physics, motion was caused by a force, but in atomic theory, that force (e.g., electromagnetism) only produces a stationary state. Then, since the molecule jumps from one state to another, there are potentially many states to which it can conceivably jump, and the next state of the molecule cannot be predicted thus. Therefore, according to atomic theory: (1) we cannot explain how a signal is sent, or (2) even why the signal goes to the hand instead of the legs.

In Vedic philosophy, as we have discussed before, there is a difference between motion and change. When we perceive the world, and the world seems close to us, then, the proximity is caused by a stronger interaction between our body and the world; therefore, we can see things very far, without ever moving. Then, when we act, the action is manifest from the senses as a possibility (which was preexisting in the senses), and the senses don't change. Therefore, it is possible to perceive and act without bodily change, and all these perceptions and actions are motions and interactions of the body. If all activity was like this, then we would never get tired—e.g., by pushing a table. Since we do get tired in the material world, therefore, the body is changing. This change is described as the conservation of energy. For example, there is some energy in us, and when we push a table, the energy is transferred to the table (or to the floor as heat). We must regain the energy, and without its presence, the body feels tired.

As we have discussed earlier, motion doesn't require energy conservation, because there is no energy transferred, unless, of course, it is change rather than motion. When change occurs, then one body disappears and the other body appears, and to prevent the conclusion that something becomes nothing, and nothing becomes something, we use the principle of energy conservation.

Thus, energy conservation means something else in Vedic philosophy. It means that the total number of possibilities in the universe is fixed. However, these possibilities are sometimes manifest and sometimes unmanifest. When the world goes unmanifest, then, according to modern science, energy would not be conserved, but according to Vedic philosophy the energy would exist in a potential state. In terms of modern science, we could say that the kinetic, thermal, radiation, and every other kind of energy has become 'potential energy', but you cannot observe the effects of such potential energy. Therefore, strictly speaking, the energy conservation principle would be broken at that time. Likewise, during the creation of the universe, the scientific principle of energy conservation would be violated, since the unmanifest state is not superhot like the claim in big bang, and yet the universe is produced from the unmanifest state, which (according to modern science) would seem to be the creation of energy. Thus, the scientific principle of energy conservation is rejected in Vedic philosophy, although the material energy is said to be eternal. This eternity rests upon the principle that all the possibilities exist, even if we don't see them. Once the principle of energy conservation is clarified, then we can discuss prāṇa.

The first role of prāṇa is in creation, maintenance, and destruction. Creation means manifestation; destruction means unmanifestation; and maintenance is preventing the manifest to become unmanifest. The need for maintenance arises because there is a natural tendency in the material energy to become unmanifest. So, keeping it manifest—e.g., preventing the tables and chairs around you from disappearing automatically—requires prāṇa. Classical physics believes that the manifest state is natural, but in Vedic philosophy, it is unnatural. It is as if the material energy is a reluctant creator of the world, and She would rather wind up the worldly business as quickly as possible, if it is not needed. Thus, even if something has manifested, keeping it manifest is due to prāṇa.

The second role of prāṇa is called revelation and hiding. Hiding means that every time you act, you lose some ability—e.g., you now feel tired—and this ability is transferred to another object and place, which is called revelation. In short, unlike the previous case where a possibility is manifest into an observation, in this case, something that was previously possible, now becomes impossible, and what was previously impossible now becomes possible. This revelation and hiding creates the modern principle of energy conservation, because we say that energy (or the power to act) disappeared from here and appeared in another place. The energy conservation was 'local' in classical physics, but it is 'non-local' in atomic theory. In short, energy can disappear here, and appear anywhere else. The appearance and disappearance are also due to prāṇa.

In summary, in the former case, the possibility is fixed, and it becomes manifest and unmanifest; and in the latter case, the possibility itself appears and disappears (and subsequently, it can become manifest or unmanifest).

In atomic theory, these two ideas are described as the 'collapse' of a wavefunction (when a possibility becomes reality) and the 'evolution' of the wavefunction (when something impossible becomes possible or vice versa). In the material world, the wavefunction evolves, so this world is called temporary. In the spiritual world, the wavefunction doesn't evolve, so it is called permanent. In short, when you push a table in the material world, you get tired. But by pushing the table in the spiritual world, you don't get tired. The evolution of the wavefunction is called the change in the body in Vedic philosophy. This change exists in the material world but doesn't exist in the spiritual world. Thus, the body becomes weak and strong in this world, however, the body retains its strength in the spiritual world—whether it is working or not.

Therefore, the brain pushing a molecule, which then pushes your hand, which then pushes the table, and then causes you to feel tired, is the evolution or the change of the body. The soul moves from one body to another. And this evolution of the body is described here as the effect of the prāṇa on the five material elements. Once the body changes, there is ability to act, and that ability can then be used to perform some work. The problem is only that when you work, you also get tired. In short, in general, motion (or the collapse of the wavefunction) produces a change (the evolution of the wavefunction).

In modern atomic theory, this connection between motion and change isn't made. So, the theory says that the wavefunction evolves, and then collapses on a measurement. The problem is that a measurement involves the transfer of energy. So, when a measurement is performed, energy must leak out of the system, and that leak would cause the wavefunction to evolve again. By not making this connection between collapse and evolution, the problem of consciousness is restricted to the collapse—it is said that consciousness collapses the wavefunction, but the evolution of the wavefunction is deterministic. There is some truth to this idea: Even if you don't work, you will still feel hungry and tired after some time. So, there is indeed an evolution even without an energy transfer. But hunger and tiredness come faster when we work. Therefore, the evolution and collapse must also be connected within a scientific theory.

These ideas remain obscure even in Vedic philosophy, because of the use of the terms 'creation' and 'destruction' vs. 'revelation' and 'hiding' which seem to mean the same, and yet they are not the same. Due to revelation and hiding, the material universe appears and disappears, and we lose old bodies and gain new bodies. This process of change doesn't exist in the spiritual world. Therefore, prāṇa doesn't effect the five elements by making the body older or younger. It still effects the five elements by manifesting their abilities—e.g., if you taste an apple, the flavor is manifest upon the contact with the tongue. But even if you eat the apple, the apple is not diminished. Hence, eating doesn't make the body fat, and not eating doesn't make the body thin. In this world, it is said that "you can't eat your cake and have it too". That is true for this world. But in the spiritual world you can eat your cake, and you will still have it.

Thus, in the spiritual world, there is day and night, and yet, it is said that time doesn't exist. This creates much confusion in people's minds, because how can we have time and yet not have changes? The short answer is that time causes motion but doesn't cause change. In this world, motion and change are tightly interconnected, so we are unable to distinguish between them. But if the transmigration of the soul is understood, then we would have to distinguish between the motion of the body in this life, and the change of body across lives. Then we will understand that much of what we call motion is mixed up with change even in this life, so, the body is changing even now. Then we can understand how motion can exist without change, and that would mean that the soul can have a body, that it can talk and eat, and yet, everything is eternal. All these things can be understood scientifically so we don't have to rely on 'faith'. However, we must have the intelligence to understand a different science.

QUESTION

However, one might say that prāṇa is only manifest in the living body, and it is not always seen in the inanimate things. Therefore, the inanimate things must be moving without the prāṇa. And hence we should try to explain the working of the world without prāṇa, and then the body also without it.

4.2.6 (502)

नैकस्मिन् दर्शयतो हि

naikasmin darśayato hi

na—not; ekasmin—occasionally; darśayataḥ—perceives; hi—certainly.

TRANSLATION

(The prāṇa is) certainly not seen occasionally (i.e., it is always seen).

COMMENTARY

As we have discussed in the previous sūtra, many things happen in this world without our choice. For example, we get tired after working, although nobody chooses to feel tired. Hence, the materialist says that if these things are happening automatically, then even the body must not be working due to our choice. Since we just said that the body is controlled by prāṇa, and prāṇa can be controlled by a choice, but we simply cannot wish away tiredness, therefore, even the purported control of the mind through the prāṇa must be false. In short, the argument of the occasional presence of prāṇa leads to total denial. Therefore, whatever is not our choosing, must also be explained due to prāṇa.

We can see that machines can work automatically, but they can also be controlled by our will. Thus, you can switch on power to a fan, and you can switch off a running fan. Once the fan has been switched on, we are not making the fan rotate by our will; it is automatically rotating due to the energy flow. Similarly, the prāṇa can work automatically, and it can be controlled by our choices or free will. While we are asleep, we are not aware of breathing, blood circulation, or digestion. In fact, we are not aware of these things even while waking. Therefore, the prāṇa indeed works without a conscious intervention. The question is this—How do we intervene in this automated working of prāṇa?

The short answer is that nature works through the alternating patterns of dominant-subordinate structures. One mode becomes dominant for some time, while the other modes remain subordinate. However, in the material world, after some time, a conflict between the modes is produced and the resolution of that conflict is that the other modes must be allowed to become dominant. The alternating periods of mode domination produce what is called the 'balance' of the modes, and nature automatically creates balance. Thus, whatever seems important right now, will one day become subordinated and will remain there for some time. Then it will return to domination and the previously dominant modes will be subordinated. This process of mode alternation also happens in the spiritual world; however, the change is cooperative rather than competitive. In short, the modes don't compete for domination and lose the battle for domination to become subordinate. They relinquish their position naturally.

The cause of mode domination in the material world is prāṇa—the power of the mode to dominate is obtained due to prāṇa. This prāṇa in turn works under the control of time, which moves the power from one mode to another. Similarly, by controlling prāṇa, the effects of time can be reduced or stopped. This mutual control of time by prāṇa and prāṇa by time is understood as the will of Śiva and Śakti. Time is the cosmic will, and prāṇa is the cosmic power. This will and power are ultimately vested in Śiva and Śakti and are controlled by their desire. The difference is that time is the masculine desire of wants and prāṇa is the feminine desire of needs. Therefore, some alterations occur because they are wanted, and other changes happen because they are needed.

When the soul does not consciously intervene in the body's working, the body works automatically due to the desires of Śiva and Śakti. Just because we do not choose to become tired, doesn't mean that nature is mechanical. Nature is working due to desires, although these might not be our desires controlling nature. Due to the automated working, karma is automatically manifest as opportunities, and ability is gained or lost (e.g., we become tired) automatically. Within these abilities and opportunities, we can exercise our will as well.

All such classic claims of contradiction between choice and determinism are based on flawed concepts of causality, where matter is a reality rather than a possibility, where everyone has access to everything, and nobody's opportunities are restricted. Once abilities and opportunities are taken out of the equation, then choices lose meaning, because you cannot choose to exercise an ability within a given opportunity. So, the role of prāṇa is that we can control our desires by prāṇa, but nature and time control the ability and opportunity. If we don't exercise our choices, then the abilities and opportunities evolve automatically. But if we use our choices, then we can take advantage of the ability and opportunity. Therefore, the so-called determinism of nature is also due to prāṇa and time and ultimately desires, but that desire doesn't create determinism. It creates abilities and opportunities, that we can use by our prāṇa.

Topic 4

QUESTION

What state is attained by the complete control of the mind and prāṇa?

4.2.7 (503)

समाना चासृत्युपक्रमात् अमृतत्वं चानुपोष्य

samānā cāsṛtyupakramāt amṛtatvaṃ cānupoṣya

samānā—balanced; ca—and; ā sṛti-upakramāt—from which the creation begins; amṛtatvaṃ—immortality; ca—and; anupoṣya—not hungry.

TRANSLATION

(By the control of mind and prāṇa) one also attains the balanced state from which creation begins, which is immortal and not hungry.

COMMENTARY

In this sūtra, the nihilistic state of emancipation is described. The primordial state of matter is called pradhāna and it constitutes the balanced state of the three modes. In this balanced state, the dominant-subordinate structures of the modes don't exist. But when the soul is injected into pradhāna by the Lord's glance, then pradhāna creates prakriti in which the three modes are separated, and now they start producing dominant-subordinate structures, and pradhāna expands into a tree-like structure as the modes enter each other. This sūtra states that by controlling the mind and the prāṇa, this process can be reversed to the balanced state. The balancing means the absence of material cognition, emotion, and relation, and hence it is like a person in a dark room, with nothing to perceive, nothing to desire, and nothing to relate to. This is emancipation by the removal of everything other than the self, which means that there is self-awareness, but there is nothing else to be known. While the Buddhists aim for this state, their claim that it is nothingness is incorrect. The balancing pertains to the modes of matter, not to the modes in the soul. In short, even in the nihilistic state, the soul is not completely happy because there is a desire which is not being fulfilled due to lack of relation and cognition. The latter balancing is achieved in Brahman, when the desire is fulfilled by vectoring the desire to the self. Now, there is a self, there is a desire for self, a relation to the self, and the cognition of the self. Therefore, Brahman is superior to the nihilistic state because the nihilistic state is a dissatisfied state, but Brahman is satisfied.

Of course, even in self-awareness, the soul is not completely satisfied because the self is not the complete truth, and this incompleteness creates the desire to know something other than the self. Therefore, the soul can fall even from Brahman, although the possibility of a fall is reduced significantly.

The balanced state of the material modes is the *experience* of emptiness, not emptiness itself. It can be pleasurable relative to the material world, which is always conditioned by fear of three kinds—(1) the fear of loss, destruction, and death, (2) the anxiety that something bad will happen, within the anticipation of something good happening, and (3) the feeling of being oppressed by the world, even if one doesn't have the fear of death or the anxiety of something going wrong. A person who finds this world a burden wants to keep a distance from everything. That is achieved in nihilism. It is not the destruction of the self (although it is claimed to be so). It is also not the voiding of all experience—there is still awareness of the self. It is merely the voiding of the world.

The Buddhists claim that it voids the self because in self-awareness there is a difference and non-difference of the knower, known, and knowledge—all three are the self, and yet, they are different modes of the self. Factually, this is not a contradiction because one desires the self, focuses on the self, and then knows the self, alternately. Therefore, the denial by contradiction is also false. Similarly, the impersonalist claims that matter is inert, and Brahman is conscious, which is also false. Even to be self-conscious, one must desire the self; that desire requires a knower and it must be pointed toward a known. When the soul has dissolved its individuality, the knower and the known disappear, and hence, the knowledge of the self also disappears. It is merely existence without an awareness or experience. Therefore, if Brahman is defined as the dissolution of identity, then by definition, it must also entail the dissolution of self-awareness. Hence, there is a fundamental difference between the descriptions of Brahman in personalist and impersonalist philosophies. In the personalist philosophy, the soul is always an individual—even in Brahman—where he exists as self-awareness, but this self-awareness is free of the contradictions between the three aspects of the soul. The impersonalist instead says that there is no self, which means there should be no self-awareness. Therefore, if we follow the impersonal doctrine, then we can say that there is no self-awareness (which is false). Only when we say that the soul is eternally and individual can we say that the soul is self-awareness in Brahman. But this 'self' is incomplete, as it isn't aware of the whole truth (the Lord) and the other living entities (His parts). The "I" in Brahman is the balanced state of the soul's three modes, but this balance is temporary because the self is incomplete. Therefore, both nihilistic and impersonalist philosophies about the self are rejected compared to the devotion to the Lord, but they are superior to the material experience.

Topic 5

QUESTION

You have said that transcendence is spiritual experience. So, is the cessation of experience by mind and prāṇa control considered transcendence?

4.2.8 (504)

तदापीतेःसंसारव्यपदेशात्

tadāpīteḥ saṃsāravyapadeśāt

tat—that; ā apīteḥ—which has not entered (the supreme abode); saṃsāra-vyapadeśāt—from being described as the material world.

TRANSLATION

That which has not entered (the supreme abode) from being described as the material world (i.e., the experience of nothingness is not transcendence).

COMMENTARY

We have discussed how the soul can enter the spiritual world in the present body, therefore, the body is not material. Similarly, we have discussed how the spiritual world also has relationships, so these relationships are not material. The difference between material and spiritual is simply in the purpose in the soul. A fulfillment of selfish purpose and the selfish purpose that remains unfulfilled, are both considered material. The cessation of all purpose is better than selfish purpose, but it is still not considered spiritual. In this sūtra, the nihilistic state referred to by the previous sūtra is rejected as ultimate transcendence.

QUESTION

But you have said that the pradhāna is still beyond the material experience. So, it must be considered superior to material experience. In what way?

4.2.9 (505)

सूक्ष्मं प्रमाणतश्च तथोपलब्धेः

sūkṣmaṃ pramāṇataśca tathopalabdheḥ

sūkṣmaṃ—subtle; pramāṇataḥ—as greater proof or evidence; ca—also; tathā—thus or in the same way; upalabdheḥ—because it is experienced.

TRANSLATION

There is also greater proof of the subtle (i.e., the soul) thus obtained by the experience (of the absence of the worldly experience).

COMMENTARY

In Cartesian philosophy, the certainty of other facts is established based on the certainty of the self. Our thoughts, sensations, or judgments can be false or hallucinatory but the self that has these hallucinations cannot itself be a hallucination. If the self is known with certainty, then it is possible to distinguish between true and false—e.g., that which leads to the permanent happiness of the self is true and that which leads to unhappiness, or oscillates between happiness and distress, is false. The materialist claims that even the experience of the self is matter, which means happiness and distress are nothing other than material states. Since matter has no purpose, therefore, happiness cannot be a goal, and unhappiness is not unnatural. Hence, one cannot distinguish between truth and falsity, and the existence of matter cannot be established. Every method of science is therefore flawed because you have no way of knowing that your experiments are not hallucinations, that your theories are not false.

This sūtra states that as one controls the mind and prāṇa, he can see that the self exists even when the material experience doesn't. In the experience of nothingness, the self is not voided. Therefore, by such experience, one can confirm that the self is different from everything else—namely, that it is not the body, that it is not defined by relationships, and that it is not enjoyment, or suffering. This realization is valuable as a counterargument to materialism.

QUESTION

So, you are implying that the observer is different from matter because there is a state in which the observer exists without material experience?

4.2.10 (506)

नोपमर्देनातः

nopamardenātaḥ

na—not; upamardena—by the destruction; ataḥ—therefore.

TRANSLATION

Therefore, by the destruction (of the body) (the soul is) not (destroyed).

COMMENTARY

Many people argue: Can you prove the existence of the soul? A common argument cited in the support of the soul is transmigration to a different body. But the skeptic now asks: How do I know the same soul goes to another body? After all, we have no recollection or memory of past lives. Then, sometimes we can cite examples of how some people do recollect their past lives, especially if they have died in unnatural circumstances. However, even this doesn't satisfy the skeptic. He might say: these are possibly aberrations of the brain that creates a memory. So, this sūtra offers another method—you can control your mind and prāṇa and enter the emptiness state. In that state, there will be no thoughts, or sensations, or judgments. But you can still experience the self-existence. In short, if you cannot rely on external evidence, or doubt its existence, then make an effort and void the mind and senses by prāṇa control, and you can confirm that you are different from all that is being experienced. Of course, most skeptics don't have the motivation or even the resilience to pursue such a process. But the process is open to anyone who wants to obtain such an experience.

QUESTION

But how can we know that the experience of the self during the void and the experience of the self during ordinary experience are the same self?

4.2.11 (507)

अस्यैव च-उपपत्तेःएष ऊष्मा

asyaiva ca-upapatteḥ-eṣa ūṣmā

asya eva—certainly to this; ca—also; upapatteḥ—because of logical reasoning and conclusion; eṣaḥ—this; ūṣmā—heat.

TRANSLATION

Certainly, to this (the soul) also (attaches) this heat (i.e., the body) because of the logical conclusion (since it exists with and without experience).

COMMENTARY

The difference between the experience of the self during the experience of nothingness and the experience of the self during ordinary experience is "I" vs. "I am". By "I am" we mean three things— "I am this body and mind", "I am father and friend", and "I am happy or sad". During the experience of the void, the "I am" is destroyed because there is no cognition, emotion, and relation. But during worldly experience, the "I am" is defined through material cognition, emotion, and relation. Therefore, when the soul contacts matter, "I" expands into "I am". This expansion is based on two premises—(1) the soul and matter are separate existents, because the world can exist even when I don't exist (for the world), and (2) I can exist even if the world doesn't exist (for me). The interaction between the soul and matter creates an experience, and therefore, the experience is the conclusion obtained from the premises. If either of these two premises were false, then the conclusion would also become impossible.

As we have discussed earlier, premises don't lead to conclusions automatically. Rather, they first give rise to a question, and then, a conclusion is used to address the question. Therefore, if the soul's existence remains a premise and doesn't become a problem—e.g., you don't ask yourself: "Why do I exist?"—then there is no need for material contact. Similarly, if the existence of matter remains a possibility, and doesn't become a problem—e.g., "Why does matter exist?"—then even the material universe remains unmanifest. Our material experiences are the consequences of two premises converting into two problems. The soul develops the desire to enjoy the material energy, and the material energy develops the desire to control, manipulate, and delude the soul. Then, both these premises, which have now become problems, become the solution to each other's problems. The soul now tries to enjoy the material world, and the material energy enjoys the control, manipulation, and delusion of the soul.

Now, someone can say: How do we know that the "I am" in the world was previously the "I" outside the world? What is the evidence of the persistence of one's personal identity? Our sense of identity is founded on memory, and in the state of void, we will lose this memory, so we cannot recall the previous worldly experience, and without that recall, we cannot say that it is the same "I". The answer to that problem is that the absence of memory is not the only absence. The absence of the problem—which led to the contact—is the deeper absence. If we understand that the contact is caused by this problem, then the cessation of the problem is evidence enough that it is the same person. Therefore, the soul can know that it is the same individual within and without the body because the problems magnify in the body, and they are reduced without the body. Likewise, the problems of bodily experience change into the problems of existing without any experience. These problems existing within the soul, although their solution is in matter. By observing how one becomes happier without the bodily problems, and how suffers more due to the bodily problems, a person can know that the same soul exists within and without the body.

All of us have a desire for happiness because we have experienced happiness in the past. That recollection or memory of happiness is not due to the body but lies innate in the soul. As a result, everyone wants to live eternally, and happily. Where does that desire arise from? We don't see people living eternally and happily in this world. And yet, everyone is trying to be eternally happy. We don't accept unhappiness and suffering as a natural consequence of living. The reason for these discrepancies is that we don't completely rely on our material memories. We also rely on the spiritual memory of eternal happiness, which cannot be wiped out; we will never stop seeking eternal happiness.

Topic 6

QUESTION

But isn't it true that the soul forgets about the transcendental world when he enters the material world? If so, how can he remember the state without problems? And if he cannot remember, how can he establish continuity?

4.2.12 (508)

प्रतषिधादिति चेत् न शारीरात्

pratiṣedhāditi cet na śārīrāt

pratiṣedhāt—due to denial; iti cet—if it be said; na—not so; śārīrāt—due to the material body.

TRANSLATION

If it be said that the (memory of past lives or perfection) is denied in this body, (then we say) not so; it is (sometimes) due to the material body.

COMMENTARY

Many people say that we have no memory of the spiritual world. But then we can ask: Why are you trying to obtain happiness, order, righteousness, freedom, truthfulness, justice etc.? Shouldn't you be quite comfortable with suffering, chaos, deceit, injustice, bondage, and wrongs? What makes you aspire for perfection if you have no memory of perfection? If your experience is only about this world, and you have never seen perfection, why aren't you comfortable with it? The fact is that people aspire for perfection because they have seen perfection. This is especially true of the perfectionists. But even those who are not themselves perfect, or want to be perfect, still want others to be perfect. Every thief wants an honest accountant. Every cheater wants to receive a fair trial. Every murderer wants others to show him some mercy and kindness. So, whether we aspire to be perfect, or we expect others to be perfect, we have an inkling of perfection within us. That is the memory of past perfection.

The quest for perfection is the light in our life. However, in many people this light is dimmed, and they become lazy apologists for imperfection. They rationalize the imperfection in others, often simply to rationalize the imperfection in themselves. Until, of course, they face the sharp end of that imperfection in others directed toward them. Then, suddenly, their sense of perfection is revived, and indignation replaces complacency. Therefore, when a person suffers in their life, they develop a strong aspiration for perfection. Those who are relatively comfortable in their lives claim that there is no need for perfection, that perfection doesn't exist, or that we cannot define perfection because everyone has a different definition of perfection. The cure for this complacency is karma: when you suffer, then you will desire perfection. Then, you will dream of a world in which there was no crime, no pain, no injustices; a place where there is perfect love, freedom, and the opportunities to pursue happiness. How can this desire for perfection arise if there isn't a sense of perfection in us? Therefore, the dimming of the sense of perfection is not its complete elimination. It exists in everyone, but we think that we don't have to be perfect. But when we undergo suffering, then we realize that perfection is important even for us. In fact, one learns that their suffering is due to their imperfections, and the path of happiness is not in asking others to be perfect; it comes when we are perfect. The imperfect people will always exist; but we don't have to live with them.

QUESTION

But if everyone tends to forget the perfection upon the acquisition of the material body, then how can the recollection of perfection be revived?

4.2.13 (509)

स्पष्टो ह्येकेषाम्

spaṣṭo hyekeṣām

spaṣṭaḥ—clear; hi—certainly; ekeṣām—in some.

TRANSLATION

(The sense of perfection is) certainly clear in some (people).

COMMENTARY

The claim that the memory of perfection is lost when one enters the material body is rejected in this sūtra. It is certainly dimmed in most people and may be completely hidden in some. But there are also people in whom the desire for perfection, the understanding of perfection, and the method to attain that perfection is clear. Many people simply desire perfection but don't know what that perfection is, or how it may be attained. Some people desire perfection and know what that perfection is, but don't know how to achieve it. Finally, most people are simply lazy to even try to know perfection or try to achieve it.

Perfection means unity, but there are three levels of perfection; sometimes they are called perfect, more perfect, and most perfect. The impersonalist who aspires for Brahman says that unity is opposed to diversity, and hence, it is obtained when we reject diversity. The personalist who aspires for Vaikuṇṭha says that unity and diversity are not contradictory; the main problem is that people of this world are lazy, stupid, and inept, and they keep doing things that against their best interest. If only they became enlightened about our best interest, then everyone will do the right thing, and the suffering will end. The term kunṭha means lazy, stupid, and inept, and Vaikuṇṭha means freedom from stupidity, laziness, and ineptness. Śrīmad Bhagavatam 7.5.31 summarizes this idea:

na te viduḥ svārtha-gatiṁ hi viṣṇuṁ
durāśayā ye bahir-artha-māninaḥ
andhā yathāndhair upanīyamānās
te 'pīśa-tantryām uru-dāmni baddhāḥ

> They do not know that their selfish interest is certainly Viṣṇu. With false hopes, they consider the external world to be the meaning of life. Themselves blind and just like the blind (i.e., the leaders who are blind but pretend to be enlightened), they create false rules and regulations, even though they are bound due to the ropes created by the Lord.

So, the devotee who accepts diversity, and the laws created by the Lord, sees that his self-interest is in following these laws. He gives up all attempts to create new rules and regulations for people to become happy. He simply accepts the instructions of the Lord as the commandments to become happy.

Then, the personalist who aspires for Goloka says that even the selfish interest of our happiness is not perfect. Yes, it creates unity by accepting the Lord as an authority, but an even better perfection is if the Lord's happiness is the goal. Such a devotee pleases the Lord without desire for one's pleasure.

Accordingly, these three stages are called perfect, more perfect, and most perfect. This sūtra says that these ideas of perfection are not totally lost in this world. There are some people who have such varied ideas of perfection.

QUESTION

But in the present world, many of these ideas of perfection have been lost. How can we attain this perfection when we don't find such perfection?

4.2.14 (510)

स्मर्यते च

smaryate ca

smaryate—by remembering (the perfection); ca—also.

TRANSLATION

(Perfection can be attained) also by remembering (the perfection).

COMMENTARY

The knowledge of God exists because humanity desires perfection. However, the atheists claim that God is man's creation, and that they can create a perfect world through their rules and regulations. The result of atheism is that people with materialistic goals are produced. Once such goals are adopted as hallmarks of perfection, then lying, cheating, fighting, and killing become the means to attain such 'perfection'. Now, society descends into an abyss of imperfection but the rich and powerful, who haven't faced the sharp end of these imperfections themselves, continue pushing the false ideologies of perfection. Nature has a perfect arrangement to make them face the imperfections of the laws and regulations they have created. When one suffers endlessly, then one dreams of a perfect world again, free from such attempts at perfection.

This sūtra states that remembrance of the perfection leads one to perfection. How? If one thinks about perfection, their actions become perfect. And both due to the change in one's mind and in one's actions, the soul is transported to the world of perfection. Therefore, even if one is currently in an imperfect situation, one should constantly think about the perfect world. This thinking will make them perfect, and then transport them into a perfect world.

Topic 7

QUESTION

By thinking of perfection, does one reach the nihilistic state? Or does one go beyond the nihilistic state into the world that embodies the perfection?

4.2.15 (511)

तानि परे तथाह्याह

tāni pare tathāhyāha

tāni—those (thinking about perfection); pare—go beyond; tathā—in the same way (as those controlling the mind reach the nihilistic state); hi—certainly; āha—that is said.

TRANSLATION

Those (thinking about perfection) certainly go beyond (the nihilistic state) in the same way (as those controlling the mind and reach the nihilistic state); that is said (in the scriptures).

COMMENTARY

New bodies are acquired based on the mental state. Therefore, just as those controlling the mind and prāṇa stop the mind and end the sensations and thoughts, and hence reach the nihilistic state, similarly, those thinking about perfection engage the mind in this perfection and use the senses in the perception of perfection and perfect actions, and they reach the perfect world.

Many people performing meditation and controlling the body and the mind consider themselves superior to those who engage in the Lord's devotion. That conclusion is rejected here. If someone stops their mind, they reach the place devoid of all experience. But if someone engages their mind in thoughts about perfections, then they attain the Lord's abode which is the perfect place. Mind and sense control are harder because there is innate tendency in the soul to enjoy pleasure. Therefore, the control of mind and prāṇa is obtained with great difficulty, and yet, the result attained by this control is inferior to the result obtained by the devotees who constantly think about the Lord's pastimes.

Topic 8

QUESTION

What about those devotees who think about perfection in this world? Are they considered a part of the spiritual world or a part of the material world?

4.2.16 (512)

अवभिागःवचनात्

avibhāgaḥ vacanāt

avibhāgaḥ—non-difference; vacanāt—from the statements.

TRANSLATION

From the statements (those thinking about perfection in this world) are non-different (from those thinking of perfection in the spiritual world)

COMMENTARY

As we discussed earlier, the gopis in Vṛndāvana think about how Kṛṣṇa will steal their butter, which is their fantasy. But then Kṛṣṇa also fulfills their fantasy, and therefore, that fantasy is also reality. Similarly, the devotees in this world can also think about various kinds of pastimes with the Lord. Kṛṣṇa may not appear immediately to fulfill these fantasies, but the meditation upon the Lord is not false. Nevertheless, because there is a difference between the fantasy and its fulfillment, therefore, the term non-different is used in this sūtra.

The implication is that thoughts about the Lord may seem to be fantasy right now, but when the devotee reaches the Lord's abode, those fantasies become real. Sometimes, the Lord also comes to this world to fulfill our fantasies. Whatever can be imagined, exists as a possibility, as part of the Absolute Truth. We do not create anything; we only access what already exists. Since it exists eternally, therefore, it is real. And yet, when it manifests, it produces greater pleasure. Still, since the soul chooses from that which exists eternally, therefore, the soul is the cause of the manifestation, just as the Lord is the cause of the fulfillment. Even in the material world, if someone makes bad choices, they become responsible for those choices, even as the Lord fulfills their desires due to karma. Thus, the principle of desiring a possibility, and that desire getting fulfilled by the Lord is the same in this world and the spiritual world. The difference is that in this world, the choices are unmindful of the Lord, and hence they are material. But when the choices become mindful of the Lord, then they are spiritual. Since it is possible to make the same choices in material and spiritual worlds, therefore, the devotees in both places are non-different.

Topic 9

QUESTION

If devotees in the material world are non-different, but not identical, to those in the spiritual world, how do these devotees reach the spiritual world?

4.2.17 (513)

तदोकोऽग्रज्वलनं तत्प्रकाशितद्वारःविद्यासामर्थ्यात्
तच्छेषगत्यनुस्मृतियोगाच्च हार्दानुगृहीताःशताधिकया

tadoko'grajvalanaṃ tatprakāśitadvāraḥ vidyāsāmarthyāt
taccheṣagatyanusmṛtiyogācca hārdānugṛhītāḥ śatādhikayā

tat-okaḥ—that house; agra—foremost; jvalanam—illuminated; tat-prakāśita-dvāraḥ—the illuminated doors of that (illuminated house); vidyā-sāmarthyāt—according to the one's eligibility or understanding; tat-śeṣa-gati—moves toward upon the cessation of that (i.e., the body); anusmṛti-yogāt—based on the recollection of the union; ca—and; hārdānugṛhītāḥ—the heart being preoccupied or favored; śatādhikayā—that which is greater than hundred.

TRANSLATION

That house is the foremost illuminated; the doors (of the house) are illuminated; on the cessation of that (body) one moves toward (the house) based upon the recollection of the union according to one's eligibility or understanding (of the Lord). (The approach to the Lord's abode is possible if) the heart is preoccupied by that (pleasure) greater than hundreds (of material pleasures).

COMMENTARY

Many important points are made in this sūtra, which we should consider one by one. First, what do we mean by illumination? The material world is called 'darkness' because the real nature of things is hidden in this world. For example, you can see the body, but it is harder to know what someone is thinking, even harder to know what they believe in, even harder to understand their true intentions, and even harder to know their values. Since we cannot see all these things, therefore, people are able to cheat others by hiding their thoughts, beliefs, intentions, and values. The fundamental principle of a loving relationship is transparency. If we cannot be honest about who we are, then love may be based on deception, but it doesn't last. Therefore, illumination of the Lord's abode means that everyone knows everything about everyone. You cannot hide your true nature under a fancy suit or dress, pretending to be a devotee.

Second, there is a difference between the house and the door. Since we enter a house through the door, our true nature is discovered at the illuminated door. The owner of the house doesn't invite everyone in. Rather, He invites only those who meet the criteria for entering His abode. This means that every devotee cannot go to every abode. To go to an abode, one must have the qualifications necessary for the abode. The arriving devotee is therefore screened at the door to check if they are qualified to enter that specific abode, and the illumination of the door means that nothing can be hidden from the screening process. In short, you cannot simply enter an abode by faking your qualifications.

Third, the Lord has many residences, each suited for the devotees in different moods and understandings of the Lord. A devotee is guided toward that specific abode that matches their understanding, and this guidance is based upon what they have experienced during their meditation. This means that the person who has no understanding of the Lord cannot reach any abode. But even if a devotee has some understanding, he must go to the abode that matches that understanding. The Lord displays many kinds of pastimes with his devotees. In some pastimes, He is the master, in others, He also acts like a friend, child, parent, or lover. Each such form or aspect of the Lord requires a different understanding of the Lord. So, there is a desire in the devotee about where he wants to go, and there is screening about the devotee's qualifications. This indicates a process of mutual acceptance. The devotee may desire to enter the intimate pastimes of the Lord, but unless he is qualified, he is not allowed. Similarly, the devotee may be qualified for certain abodes, but he may prefer to go to another abode. The abode is decided by the desiring and the deserving.

Fourth, we cannot go to the Lord's house unless the heart is freed from mundane desires and has experienced a pleasure hundreds of times greater than material pleasure. Unless this pleasure has been experienced, one would naturally remain more attracted to the mundane pleasures of the world.

Thus, four methods of screening are described here. We cannot depart for the spiritual abode unless we have freedom from mundane desires—we will go to another body suited for mundane enjoyment based on these desires. If we depart for the Lord's abode, we must know which abode we are going to arrive at, and that is possible only if we have a specific attraction to a form of the Lord based on prior understanding. Once we arrive at this destination, we will be screened at the door to determine if we are indeed qualified to enter that abode. And once we enter, everyone can see what we are thinking, feeling, intending, etc. because nothing can be hidden from others in the Lord's abode.

These descriptions clearly indicate that one doesn't go the Lord's abode simply by joining an institution, accepting a guru for fashion, wearing a fancy dress that shows renunciation, or other ways in which people are deceived in this world. Rather, one must be completely purified of material desires, have the attraction for a form of the Lord, be qualified to serve that form of the Lord, and then act according to those requirements along with everyone else.

Topic 10

QUESTION

If the devotee has the attraction for a specific form of the Lord, and desires to enter that specific abode, how does he find that specific Lord's abode?

4.2.18 (514)

रश्म्यनुसारी

raśmyanusārī

raśmi-anusārī—following the rays of light.

TRANSLATION

(The soul goes to an abode of the Lord) by following the rays of light.

COMMENTARY

If you want to go to a destination, merely having the goal of reaching that destination is not enough. You must also have a map to the place and should be able to follow the route on the map for a destination. Vedic cosmology describes the maps of the material and spiritual worlds. But even if you have the map, you still need to see the road signs that guide you to the destination. This sūtra describes the road signs to reach the destination. If you are traveling on a highway, you will often see the signs that indicate the distance and direction to a destination. The road signs to a destination are called the 'rays of light' in this sūtra. In modern science, light only has a frequency and a quantity of energy. But, as we have discussed earlier, these particles of energy also have meanings. Therefore, light is not meaningless; it always carries a meaning. The previous sūtra spoke about the innumerable abodes of the Lord, where a devotee goes according to their desire and qualification. However, a devotee may be qualified to go to many abodes, and he must choose one of the many abodes.

This choice is facilitated by the abodes advertising their presence by the light emanating from that abode. Every planet and star in the material universe advertises their presence by a light with a unique type of meaning, and these meanings are studied in astrology as having different effects on our lives. In the same way, the different abodes of the Lord advertise their light. The devotee then follows the advertisement to its source, which is called 'following the rays of light' in this sūtra. Thereby, he reaches the abode through the light.

We have all seen shopping malls with many kinds of stores which advertise their presence by a shining sign. The spiritual world is also like a shopping mall. You enter a mall if you want the thing that the store advertises, and if you are qualified to pay for what the store advertises (as we discussed in the previous sūtra, the doors of the Lord's abode check a devotee's qualification, so window shopping is not allowed). Thus, the spiritual world affords infinite pleasures, and there is choice for the type of pleasure that the devotee desires. By following the light from an abode, a devotee reaches one of the Lord's abodes.

QUESTION

But what if the devotee doesn't know about many abodes of the Lord, and their differences? How will he decide under the ignorance of these abodes? Is the choice of the Lord's abode made randomly or even under ignorance?

4.2.19 (515)

नशिि नि इतचिेत् न सम्बन्धस्य यावद्देहभावत्विाद् दर्शयतचि

niśi na iti cet na sambandhasya yāvaddehabhāvitvād darśayati ca

niśi—the night or darkness; na—not; iti cet—if it be said; na—not; sambandhasya—according to the relationship; yāvat-deha-bhāvitvād—the type of body one has acquired; darśayati—(the soul is able to) see; ca—also.

TRANSLATION

If it be said (that the soul decides the abode) in darkness (we say) not so; whatever is not according to the relationship and unsuitable to the type of body one has acquired, is also not visible to the soul (for it to choose).

COMMENTARY

According to classical physics, light spreads uniformly in all directions, and therefore, we must receive light from every star and planet in the universe. However, according to atomic theory, light is only transmitted when the source and receiver are entangled. Thus, in classical physics, light is emitted as waves—and propagates equally in all directions. However, in atomic theory, light is emitted and absorbed as photons, which means that it is occasionally emitted and not to every destination. The contentious issue is whether can be emitted to every object in the universe (even occasionally). There are no good answers to this problem in atomic theory because we don't know how the source and the receiver of light are entangled. That explanation is provided in Vedic philosophy—we get to see something only if we have the requisite karma. Therefore, even in Vedic cosmology, the upper four planetary systems, the lower seven planetary systems, and the 28 hells are not visible to us. The influences on our life are controlled by the planets up till the polestar. Therefore, we can see things that are below the polestar—i.e., the parts of the zodiac (which cosmology calls 'galaxies') and the planets such as Mars, Venus, etc.

A similar principle is applied to the spiritual world in this sūtra by stating that not everyone sees every spiritual planet. Rather, these planets are seen according to one's relationship to the Lord, and the type of body one has. Notably, this means that not every type of body is found in every planet. The different relations and bodies constitute the devotee's 'deserving', and since the devotee deserves to enter these planets, therefore, the light from these planets reaches the devotee, to help him decide which planet he wants to go to. Hence, the decision is not totally random or blind. As we have said, the light has meaning, so one can obtain a description of the planet from the light. Therefore, the choices are informed, however, not every possibility is accessible for everyone.

Topic 11

QUESTION

Is this selective visibility of the Lord's abode unique to the spiritual world? Or can this also be applied to the transmigration in the material world?

4.2.20 (516)

अतश्चायनेऽपि दक्षिणे

ataścāyane'pi dakṣiṇe

ataḥ—from this (we can understand); cā—also; ayane—moving; api—even; dakṣiṇe—southern.

TRANSLATION

From this (we can) also (know) even the southern movement of the (sun).

COMMENTARY

In Vedic cosmology, the Sun goes around the Meru mountain, and the orbit of the Sun is slightly higher on one side, and slightly lower on another side. As the Sun moves in its orbit, it goes upward for six months, and then downward for the next six months. The phase of upward movement is called Uttarāyana or northward movement. And the phase of downward movement is called Dakśhināyana or southward movement. The living entities who die during the Uttarāyana movement, are said to move to higher planetary systems. And the living entities who die during the Dakśhināyana movement enter the lower planetary systems, including hells. The Mahabharata describes how Bhīśma fell to the ground due to Arjuna's arrows, during the Dakśhināyana phase. But he had his father's benediction to decide when he wanted die. So, he lay on a bed of arrows on the battlefield until the Sun turned toward Uttarāyana.

In the previous sūtra, it was said that the devotee ascending to the Lord's abode receives information only about those places that he is qualified to enter. This sūtra says that the same principle of selective visibility applies even to those leaving the body during the Dakśhināyana phase when the soul must enter the lower planetary systems according to his qualification for these planets. Similarly, from the narration about Bhīśma, we can understand that the heavenly planets become visible to a soul based on their qualification. In short, if you are not qualified, then you cannot even see the planet's existence.

QUESTION

But there are also many yogis who ascend to higher planetary systems in this universe. Is their destination also determined by their qualification?

4.2.21 (517)

योगिनःप्रति च स्मर्येते स्मार्ते चैते

yoginaḥ prati ca smaryete smārte caite

yoginaḥ prati—regarding the yogis; ca—and; smaryete—in the type of remembrance; smārte—in the ritualized activities; ca—also; ete—these.

TRANSLATION

And, regarding the yogis, (the destination depends upon) these—the type of remembrance (meditation) and the ritualized activities (fire sacrifices).

COMMENTARY

This sūtra clearly spells out the role of guna and karma in the acquisition of the next body. Guna represents what we desire, and this sūtra refers to the guna as the type of meditation one performs—whatever one is meditating upon is what they are desiring. Karma represents what we deserve, and this sūtra refers to karma by the kinds of ritualized activities one has performed, as they lead to good karma. To enter a material planet, one needs both—i.e., one must be qualified to enter, and one must desire to enter. This is one of the differences between good and bad karma—bad karma doesn't give us the choice of whether we want to suffer (i.e., the suffering is forced) but good karma gives us a choice about whether we want to enjoy. Therefore, a person with good karma can renounce pleasures, but the person with bad karma cannot renounce distress. Based on one's qualification, the relevant places of destination are visible, and among those that are visible, one can choose where one wants to go.

For the person going to one of the many lower planetary systems, more than one planet can be visible if they indeed deserve to enter them. However, for the hellish planets, typically only one planet would be visible, which means that one doesn't have a choice about how the suffering must be endured.

In the spiritual world, there is no karma. Therefore, the definition of qualification changes—the qualification is the devotee's mood. There is a subtle difference between mood and desire. For example, the desire can be to see the Lord as a father, mother, friend, servant, lover, etc. But the mood is whether one feels that kind of emotion to enter such a relationship. Desiring and feeling are subtle distinctions within the emotional state of a person. The qualification is whether a person feels the emotion appropriate for the desire. In short, *being* a friend is not a designation of a friend; rather, one must *feel* the friend's emotion.

This idea can be understood by looking at ordinary relationships. For example, a couple can get married, because they want to get married. But they may not feel attracted to each other, although they want to stay in the marriage. In this world, people look at various things before they get married—financial security, good looks, family status, etc. The Lord doesn't see any of these. However, He doesn't enter a relationship if there are only wants and no feelings. If someone cannot develop the feelings that make a good relationship, simply wanting to have such a relationship is not adequate. Therefore, the qualification is not karma. The qualification is the capacity to experience a type of feeling.

SECTION 3

Topic 1

QUESTION

How does the performance of fire sacrifices lead to good karma? The creation of good karma is understandable if we think about action and consequence. But it seems strange that fire sacrifices lead one to higher planets.

4.3.1 (518)
अर्चिरादिना तत्प्रथितेः
arcirādinā tatprathiteḥ

arciḥra—fire sacrifices; ādinā—eating, offering or etc.; tat-prathiteḥ—that (the Lord) is celebrated.

TRANSLATION

By offering fire sacrifices, that (the Lord) is celebrated (or worshipped).

COMMENTARY

In the Vedic system, fire sacrifices have been performed for ages as a system to worship the Lord, as well as the demigods. The sacrifice involves throwing grains such as rice into the fire. However, before the offering is made, the thing being offered is imbued with a meaning by the chanting of the mantra. For example, a worshipper takes a pinch of rice in their hand, chants a mantra to imbue that rice with a meaning, and then offers the rice into the fire. The rice is held in the hand from the beginning to the end of the mantra, and then, rice is offered into the fire by chanting *svāhā* which means "I give myself to you". What is being given is not the rice, but the rice as a symbol of meaning.

The fire can also represent the Lord, or one of the numerous demigods. Therefore, the fire also must be symbolized as the mouth of the Lord or one of the many demigods. This is also achieved by chanting mantras, after lighting the fire, to invite the Lord or the demigods to be present in the sacrifice as the fire. Thus, just as the rice becomes a symbol of meaning, similarly, the fire also symbolizes a personality, and both are achieved by the chanting of mantras.

The person making the offering is the subordinate principle, and the person to whom the offering is made is the dominant principle. The rice and the fire are just symbols of the person making the offering, and the person receiving the offering. Thus, by throwing rice into fire, essentially, the worshipper offers himself to the worshipper, although the offering is made through rice and fire. When a person becomes a devotee of the Lord, then he offers himself directly to the Lord. Now, rice and fire are not involved as intermediaries. Therefore, the process of devotional surrender and the process of a fire sacrifice are very similar in principles, however, they are implemented in different ways.

Topic 2

QUESTION

But why fire specifically? Could it not be water or air? Why isn't an offering made into water or air also considered the celebration of the Lord?

4.3.2 (519)
वायुमब्दात् अविशेषविशेषाभ्याम्
vāyumabdāt aviśeṣaviśeṣābhyām

vāyum—air; abdāt—from water; aviśeṣa-viśeṣābhyām—from the non-specific and specific.

TRANSLATION

From non-specific to specific, from air to water.

COMMENTARY

The use of fire in a sacrifice—as representing the mouth of the Lord—raises some questions: Why fire? What not air or water? After all, we could just throw the grains of rice in the wind or into a body or water, after symbolizing them as the mouths of the Lord through a mantra. If fire can be symbolized to be the Lord's mouth, by a mantra, then water and air could also be symbolized in the same way. Then why aren't systems of air or water sacrifices found in the scriptures? Why are sacrifices always performing using fire, and not air or water?

A similar question could also have been raised earlier when it was said that the devotee is guided to the Lord's abode through light. One might wonder: Why light? Or, why seeing? Could it not be sound, touch, taste, or smell? Any of these can carry the information from a source to a receiver. For example, one could say that the devotee can be pushed to the Lord's abode by the pressure of air on the skin. Similarly, a devotee could be guided to the Lord's abode by aroma. So, given these alternatives, what is so special about seeing?

This sūtra says that air and water are too non-specific and specific (respectively). What does this mean? We have discussed earlier about how the meaning in the mind expands from a subtle to a gross meaning. The subtle meaning is abstract, while the gross meaning is detailed. For example, the idea cow is abstract, and the shape of the cow is detailed. The successive perceptions of sound, touch, sight, taste, and smell add further details to the previous perception. Thus, sound contains touch, sight, taste, and smell in unmanifest form, but in touch sound is manifest, in sight, touch and sound are manifest, and so on. Accordingly, the air element is a non-specific or abstract representation of meaning, whereas the water element is a specific or a detailed representation of meaning. Since fire is between air and water, therefore, it is more specific than air, and less specific than water. The purport is that the fire element is an optimum representation of meaning—neither too detailed, nor too abstract.

We must note that since the grains and the fire are symbolized by mantras, therefore, a more abstract symbolizing would require the utterance of fewer sounds, but they would also be more difficult to pronounce. We can call this more 'compressed' encoding of meaning. Likewise, a more detailed symbolizing would require many more sounds, however, they would also be easily pronounceable. We can call this more 'expanded' meaning. As an analogy, scientific laws are expressed succinctly through formulae, but the full meanings of these formulae are harder to understand. Conversely, to explain these laws, we can employ long-form descriptions, which are also easier to understand.

The problem of semantic condensation leading to difficulty in uttering and understanding the sounds is seen while studying Vedic texts. The Sanskrit of the four Vedas is incredibly hard, and that is because it is incredibly condensed. Vedic mantras, for example, employ sounds like 'grim', 'shrim', 'klim', 'hrim', etc. and there is practically nobody who understands what these sounds mean. As a result, the popular phrase 'mumbo-jumbo' is used—somewhat appropriately. However, these are not meaningless sounds; they are just highly condensed meanings. Then, the Sanskrit of the sūtra-based texts, such as the six systems of philosophy (including the Vedānta Sūtra), has an intermediate level of difficulty. As we have seen, the meaning of each word depends on the context of what has and has not been previously said; the same sentence, therefore, has different meanings depending on the context. Finally, the Sanskrit of the Purāna and Itihāsa is the easiest; they are like long-form narrations where every word has a dictionary meaning, and the meaning changes only occasionally based on the context. Therefore, we can easily quote these texts while teaching others. The sūtras must be memorized and used as mathematical formulae, which can be understood, but the understanding is not for everyone. Finally, the Vedic mantras must be perfected by pronunciation, rhythm, and meter, and quite often, there is very little to comprehend regarding their meaning.

To return to the main point, once we understand the differences between abstract and detailed expressions, and the associated difficulties with more condensed (a minor error drastically changes the meaning) and the more expanded (they will necessitate very long performances), then we can see how something between the condensed and expanded methods would seem appropriate—it is easily remembered, uttered, less prone to mistakes, and not very long. This sūtra essentially says that the fire format of sacrifices is chosen over air or water sacrifices since that makes the sacrificial performance more convenient.

Topic 3

QUESTION

But you are implicitly accepting that even water and air could be used for sacrifices—even though the performance of such sacrifices would be harder?

4.3.3 (520)

तडितोऽधि वरुणः संबन्धात्

taḍito'dhi varuṇaḥ saṃbandhāt

taḍito—fire; adhi—after; varuṇaḥ—varuna; saṃbandhāt—due to the appropriateness.

TRANSLATION

After fire, varuna (water) (is accepted) due to the appropriateness.

COMMENTARY

In the previous sūtra, fire sacrifices were accepted due to their ease, however, others have not been rejected. Therefore, it is implicitly acknowledged that the mantras of the four Vedas could be different if they were to be used for air or water sacrifices. The four Vedas would be totally incomprehensible if the mantras were meant for air sacrifices, and they would be significantly longer if the mantras were meant for water sacrifices. This sūtra says that if one must perform other sacrifices, then the water sacrifices are more appropriate.

In short, instead of chanting mantras that are even more incomprehensible, it is preferred to chant mantras that are longer. This would naturally elongate the duration of the sacrifice. Similarly, the medium through which the offerings in the sacrifice reach their intended recipient would also change. Elements such as fire, water, and air have their own deities. In a fire sacrifice, the deity is called Agni (somewhat confusingly, the fire element is also called agni). In a water sacrifice, the deity is called Varuna (although in this case, the element is called apah or abda). Therefore, the previous sūtra could also be understood as referring to the demigod Agni, whereas this sūtra refers to the demigod Varuna.

Water sacrifices are not alien to Vedic culture, but their importance has been lesser. The offering to the forefathers, for example, is made in water, rather than in fire. Similarly, sometimes, the Sun is worshipped through water, rather than fire. Ultimately, these mediums of worship aren't very important. Greater importance is attached to the mantras, which are adapted for a medium.

Topic 4

QUESTION

Under what circumstances could one prefer an air sacrifice over the other forms of sacrifice (i.e., the water and fire sacrifices mentioned previously)?

4.3.4 (521)
आतिवाहिकाःतल्लिङ्गात्
ātivāhikāḥ tallingāt

ātivāhikāḥ—faster than vehicle; tat-lingāt—due to the symbols of that.

TRANSLATION

Due to the symbols of that (meaning) being faster than the vehicle.

COMMENTARY

All Vedic mantras follow a meter, which are categorized by the length of the meter. Thus, there are meters that are 12, 18, 24, 30, 36, 42, and 48 symbols long (each successive meter has 6 extra symbols than the previous one). The maximum size of the meters is said to be 72 symbols, so the total number of meters is sometimes accepted to be 12. The simplest meter is called *dvāśa-ākśhara* or 12 symbols long. For example, the mantra Om Namo Bhagavate Vāsudevāya is a 12-symbol mantra. The 12 phonemes in the above mantra are om-na-mo-bha-ga-va-te-va-su-de-va-ya, and since each symbol requires one unit of time, so, the 12 phonemes in the mantra require 12 units of time.

However, there can be some mantras in which the phonemes do not fit the individual units of time. An example would be a half-phoneme which requires half a symbol and therefore half the time needed for a regular phoneme. In such a case, two such half-phonemes could be combined to create a complex phoneme. But it is also possible that this half phoneme is followed by several full phonemes, and eventually a half-phoneme. If one looks at the wave patterns of mantras of such complex phonemes, then the pattern must change halfway through a time interval. This change can continue for several phonemes, until another half-phoneme is encountered, when the pattern returns to normal. To utter such a mantra, the tongue needs to change pattern halfway through the interval, utter each of the subsequent phonemes over two halves of two successive intervals, until the half-phoneme reverts the pattern back to normal. Due to the change of pattern halfway through the interval, twice the information must be encoded in that interval—once for each of the half-phonemes. This is when the symbol rate is seen to be twice as fast as the clock frequency.

When we encode information in any medium, the process is called modulating a carrier. The carrier has a constant frequency, and it is like the constant ticking clock in which you can insert one symbol per period. If the rate of transmitted symbols is slower than the carrier frequency, then a method called 'frequency modulation' is employed. If the rate of transmission is equal to the carrier frequency, then a method called 'amplitude modulation' is employed. And if the rate of transmission is greater than the carrier frequency, then a method called 'phase modulation' is employed. Phase modulation is basically changing a wave pattern within a single cycle of a wave. With advancing technology, modern circuits can fit anywhere between 2 to 64 symbols in a single cycle. For example, when 2 symbols are fit into a cycle, the method is called

BPSK (Binary Phase Shift Keying) and when 4 symbols are fit into a cycle, then then the method is called QPSK (Quad Phase Shift Keying). When 64 symbols are fit into a single cycle, then the method of modulation is called 64-PSK. In all such cases, the wave form changes pattern multiple times during a single time cycle.

While chanting mantras, the goal is not to increase the data rate of mantras, so greater speed isn't for faster chanting. It is needed due to complex sounds which constitute a single phoneme, and yet are not simple phonemes. When mantras use complex phonemes, then the symbol rate is greater than the carrier frequency, and this sūtra says that all sacrifices that require such mantras should be performed through the medium of air, rather than water or fire.

We can see from these sūtras why most Vedic rituals are forbidden in the present age—the rituals are long and complex, our pronunciations are imperfect, we are unable to keep time and the rhythm, and, of course, we don't understand the meaning. Hence, in this age, only the chanting of God's names is suggested. Some of these names also involve complex phonemes. For example, the sound Kṛṣṇa contains a complex phoneme—kṛṣ—in which kṛ and ṣ are half-phonemes—but there are no restrictions to the chanting of the sound Kṛṣṇa. Therefore, we can surmise that the recommendation of this sūtra is that the air is the preferred method for complex phonemes, not the only method.

QUESTION

If the methods of water and air are sometimes accepted, why are the number of sacrifices based on the water and the air methods so limited?

4.3.5 (522)

उभयव्यामोहात्तत्सिद्धेः

ubhayavyāmohāttatsiddheḥ

ubhaya—both; vyāmohāt—due to mental confusion; tat-siddheḥ—it is proven.

TRANSLATION

Both (the air and water methods) create mental confusion, it is proven.

COMMENTARY

The earlier sūtra indirectly implied that the sacrifices based on water and fire will be either too specific or too non-specific, and we discussed how they will either lead to very complex or very long pronunciations. If this wasn't clear enough, then this sūtra states explicitly that these methods lead to excessive mental confusion, and that has been established (perhaps by employing them). In short, the performance of fire sacrifices is not an accident, even though it sometimes seems mumbo-jumbo, and the method has been established after considering other methods, finding them too complex, and rejecting them.

QUESTION

You say that it has been proven, implying that other methods were employed, tested, and then rejected. But we don't find such descriptions in the śrutī. How should we understand their absence from these scriptures?

4.3.6 (523)
वैद्युतेनैव ततःतच्छ्रुतेः
vaidyutenaiva tataḥ tacchruteḥ

vaidyutena—certainly by the method of fire; eva—alone; tataḥ—thereafter; tat-śruteḥ—that (method) was presented as the śrutī.

TRANSLATION

(It was established) that by the method of fire alone (sacrifices should be performed) thereafter, that (the sacrifices) was presented as the śrutī.

COMMENTARY

In an earlier sūtra we discussed three claims about the origination of scriptures—(1) they were spoken by the Lord, (2) they were written at a specific time by an author, and (3) they can be rationally confirmed because they are logically expanded from the knowledge received from the Lord. Now, this sūtra adds a fourth method of experimental confirmation. It says that although the scriptures logically followed from the knowledge received by revelation, what we see as the śrutī isn't merely the revealed knowledge. Rather, that revealed knowledge was expanded into many forms (e.g., the rituals for water and air), then these methods were tested, and some of them were found to lead to mental confusion. Those methods were ignored, and only those that were found viable for the general population, and effective in producing the results, were presented as the śrutī. Again, the distinction between the śrutī and smriti can be dissolved through this distinction because the śrutī is not merely untested revelations. Rather, knowledge in a summarized form was revealed to Brahma, who then provided it to his sons, who then expanded this knowledge in many forms through logical inferences, tested the knowledge, and then presented the methods that work as the śrutī, while the other methods were discarded.

Topic 5

QUESTION

You are saying that the rituals were presented as śrutī after testing, and you have said that the śrutī is revealed knowledge. Generally, experimental methods are obtained after trial and error. But that doesn't square with the idea that the knowledge was also revealed. How do we reconcile these claims?

4.3.7 (524)

कार्यं बादरिःअस्य गत्युपपत्तेः

kāryaṃ bādariḥ asya gatyupapatteḥ

kāryaṃ—the rituals; bādariḥ—Bādari; asya—its; gati-upapatteḥ—the activities are produced by logical inference.

TRANSLATION

Bādari (says that) the activities in a ritual are obtained by logical reasoning.

COMMENTARY

When scientific knowledge is derived by trial-and-error, or speculation and experimentation, then we don't know upfront if a theory will work. Sometimes the theory works, and then we present it as truth. Sometimes, we find something working, and then we make a theory for it. But there is another approach for the formation of procedures and theories—we can start with the goal of what we want to achieve, find the position of that goal in the space of all possibilities, then compute the path to this destination in space, and finally convert this path into an activity and test whether it achieves the intended goals.

The problem today is that we don't know that there is a space in which all the possibilities exist eternally. We think that whatever we cannot see, also doesn't exist. So, we must first see its existence, and then we can form a theory about it. Or, whatever theory we formulate must be based on what we have already seen. Thus, all modern science is limited by what we can observe.

But the method of scriptures is not like that. It basically starts by asking: What are the different types of goals people might have? And, how can we achieve these goals? Then based on the knowledge of the Absolute Truth, they make logical inferences and identify the path from the present state to the goal, test that path as a procedure, and then describe it as a method of goal attainment. Thus, many scriptures provide detailed descriptions of reality, and other scriptures simply say that to attain this goal you must do this, live this kind of life, or perform these procedures. By producing a compendium of procedures—which are known as yajñá—the scriptures save people from the detailed investigation into the nature of reality before they fulfill their goals. However, since some people may be curious about how these procedures were arrived at, why they work, and what other procedures may be discovered using the same process through which the existing procedures were discovered, the scriptures also provide a detailed understanding of reality. Thus, the theoretical and practical aspects of the scriptures are interconnected. The practical aspects are for those who just want to attain some goals, without understanding the underlying details. They are like manuals to drive a car from one place to another. The theoretical aspects of the scriptures are the descriptions of a car's working.

This sūtra states that even the rituals were not derived by experimentation. Rather, one started out with a goal and found the method to achieve that goal. The goal-driven derivation is possible in a semantic reasoning system, so the term *upapatti* is used here. The difference is this. In an axiomatic reasoning system, we start with the premise and try to derive a theorem, but there is no way to determine if the method of proof is getting closer to a theorem or not. Therefore, the construction of a proof becomes a method by trial-and-error, and there are numerous conjectures in modern mathematics which remain unproven. However, in a semantic reasoning system, we start with the axiom, and we set the goal as the theorem's proof. And the system will then find the proof to the theorem automatically because it can determine if the proof is closer or farther from the theorem. In short, *upapatti* here means an automated theorem-proving system, in which the axioms are given, the theorem is the goal, and the proof is the path that connects the axioms to the goal. Once this proof is identified, then it can also be practically tested. The test would begin from the axioms, follow the path traced by the proof as a procedure, and finally construct the desired goal as the intended theorem. Thus, the methods of reason and experiment are identical—you can construct the desired object by a process, which you could theoretically derive earlier. Hence, there is no need to be amazed by such claims of deriving the rituals by logical inference. These things are imminently feasible in a semantic reasoning system—if the system is complete.

QUESTION

But how can we say that the theoretical methods of construction will produce the desired results? What seems to work on paper doesn't seem to always work in practice. Thus, we find that our plans often fail in practice, even though they seemed to be perfectly in order on paper. This is generally because in our planning we fail to foresee the situations that can thwart our plans. So, if you say that by knowing the procedure, we know the method of attainment, that seems to not take into account the many unforeseen causes of failure.

4.3.8 (525)

वशिेषतित्वाच्च

viśeṣitatvācca

viśeṣitatvāt—from being just like the specifics; ca—also.

TRANSLATION

Also, from being just like (we know) the specifics.

COMMENTARY

If you want to reach a destination by road, you might start out with a roadmap on how to reach that destination. However, at some point in your travel, you might find the road is blocked or under construction. Then you retrace your steps on the map and find the next best road. Similarly, the procedures given in scriptures may not always exactly match the most suitable path to a destination. In such a situation, one can abandon the path, and take another path that takes us to the destination. Therefore, the door is open to such modifications—provided the main road is inaccessible. However, generally, if the main road is open, we would not try to create a path just for the sake of it.

In the same way, the scriptures provide some roadmaps to the destination, but it would be incorrect to suppose that every type of hurdle is anticipated in the scriptures. When such hurdles are encountered, then adjustments can be made. These adjustments should, however, not violate the moral principles, unless there is no other way. Just as meat-eating is recommended when one is dying, and there is no alternative path, similarly, the principle of the least amount of sacrifice to deliver the greatest amount of benefit applies. This sūtra states that by studying the specifics of the situation, we can also adapt the procedures to attain the goal. Therefore, there is a recommended path, which should work in most cases. But if it is not, then changes are acceptable.

QUESTION

But doesn't it mean that people may change all Vedic procedures by citing the specifics of their situation? How does one guard against such changes?

4.3.9 (526)

सामीप्यात् तु तद्व्यपदेशः

sāmīpyāt tu tadvyapadeśaḥ

sāmīpyāt—due to nearness; tu—but; tat-vyapadeśaḥ—that is stated.

TRANSLATION

But it is stated that (the alternative paths are selected) by their nearness.

COMMENTARY

We have discussed how a path is determined by the proximity to the destination—i.e., the shorter path to destination is preferred. In this sūtra, another restriction is applied, namely, that the alternative path (if it must be chosen) must be near or close to the path described in the scriptures. For example, if you are traveling to a destination, and you find a blocked road, you don't go back to your home and start on a completely different path. You rather find the smallest deviation from the predetermined path to bypass the current hurdle. In the same way, the adjustment of paths doesn't entail the invention of arbitrary new paths. Rather, these adjustments are subject to (1) hurdles being encountered, (2) the smallest necessary adjustment from the path, and (3) the goal still being reachable by the new path. What is small is further determined semantically, rather than physically. For example, just because a road is blocked, we don't drive through someone's house, just because it seems to be the shortest path. We rather find the nearest legitimate path. In the same way, we should aim for the nearest path, but also a legitimate path. In short, we should minimize the changes to the path, and not violate moral principles in selecting paths.

QUESTION

If we are still not able to find the nearest path or smallest change to complete the sacrifice due to hurdles in its execution, what should a person do?

4.3.10 (527)

कार्यात्यये तदध्यक्षेण सहातःपरम् अभिधानात्

kāryātyaye tadadhyakṣeṇa sahātaḥ param abhidhānāt

kārye-atyaye—on the completion of the sacrifice; tat-adhyakṣeṇa saha—along with the ruler of that (sacrifice); ataḥ param—therefore the supreme (Lord); abhidhānāt—due to bringing in close connection.

TRANSLATION

(If the hurdles encountered during a sacrifice cannot be mitigated by the nearest adjustment, then path selection must be based on the criterion that) upon the completion of the sacrifice, along with the ruler of that (sacrifice—e.g., a demigod), even the supreme (Lord) (also) comes closer (to the worshipper).

COMMENTARY

The Lord is the remedy to all problems. He can correct every mistake, and He can make every imperfection perfect. Therefore, this sūtra says that if you are struggling to find the correct path under the present circumstances, then think about the Lord, and what will bring you closer to Him. This is again not an endorsement for wanton disregard for rules and regulations. It is permissible when the prescribed path is not working, and when there are no easy alternatives (because each alternative may not be very near to the original path).

QUESTION

But the śrutī doesn't permit one to change the procedures. They are meant to be strictly followed by the practitioners or they don't produce results.

4.3.11 (528)

स्मृतेश्च

smṛteśca

smṛteḥ—from the smriti; ca—also.

TRANSLATION

From the smriti also (we can understand how to adjust the regulations).

COMMENTARY

An illustrative example of the adjustment of the rules and regulations is provided in the story of Maharaja Ambarīṣa, as narrated in the Śrīmad Bhagavatam. Maharaja Ambarīṣa was fasting for Ekādaśi while Sage Durvāsā arrives at his palace. Maharaja Ambarīṣa invites the sage to accept food at his palace, and after accepting the invitation, the Sage goes for a bath in the river Yamuna. After the bath, Sage Durvāsā sits in meditation and time passes by. Since the time for breaking the Ekādaśi fast is about to pass, Maharaja Ambarīṣa faces a dilemma. Should he break the fast by eating something to preserve the vow of Ekādaśi? Or, should he not break the fast until the Sage Durvāsā has eaten? It was customary in Vedic culture to feed the guests before the host eats, which is good moral principle, but not on par with the Ekādaśi vow. The guru of Maharaja Ambarīṣa advises him to break the fast by drinking water.

When Sage Durvāsā returns from his bath, he realizes that Maharaja Ambarīṣa has already taken water, and he becomes very angry. Under this anger, Sage Durvāsā pulls a clutch of hair from his head and throws it on the ground to produce a demon which would kill Maharaja Ambarīṣa. However, Lord Viṣṇu sends His Sudarśana Chakra to protect Maharaja Ambarīṣa. The Chakra kills the demon, and then pursues Sage Durvāsā, who runs everywhere for shelter, but is unable to find protection. Finally, Sage Durvāsā goes to Lord Narayana for protection, but the Lord says that He is unable to protect someone who has offended the devotee. Then, Sage Durvāsā returns to Maharaja Ambarīṣa and begs for his forgiveness. Meanwhile, a year has elapsed, and Maharaja Ambarīṣa is still standing in the same place for Sage Durvāsā to return so he can feed him, surviving just by drinking water. Upon seeing the grievous condition of Sage Durvāsā, Maharaja Ambarīṣa prays to the Chakra to become peaceful. The Chakra then stops burning Sage Durvāsā, and the glories of the Lord's devotees are revealed. The main point is that even if ordinary people are offended by our actions, if the Lord is pleased, then these offences are disregarded. Therefore, the Lord's pleasure is the supremely beneficent goal of our lives.

QUESTION

But many people consider the rules of the śrutī to be higher than the descriptions in the smriti. They say that obedience to the rules and regulations is essential, and without such rules, the results of the sacrifice are not obtained. What should be the answer to these claims that contradict the smriti?

4.3.12 (529)
परं जैमनिर्मुख्यत्वात्
paraṃ jaiminiḥ mukhyatvāt

paraṃ—the Supreme Lord; jaiminiḥ—(says) Jaimini; mukhyatvāt—on account of that being the primary purpose (of the sacrifice).

TRANSLATION

(Even) Jaimini says that the Supreme Lord is the main purpose of the Vedic sacrifices (so who else is qualified to claim a higher position for rules?).

COMMENTARY

Many arguments about the temporarity of the Vedic rituals have been offered in the previous sūtras. First, it was said that these rituals have been derived from the Absolute Truth by logical inference. Second, it was said that in the process of derivation, many rituals were abandoned as they created mental confusion. Third, it was stated that often there are difficulties in following these procedures, and the procedures can therefore be adjusted if that brings the worshipper closer to the Lord, and examples from smriti can be used as affirmations of this principle. However, if someone still insists that the rules of śrutī must be upheld, then the sūtra cites the example of Jaimini—the foremost proponent of these rituals—and states that even he accepts the Lord to be the supreme.

The conclusion is that the rules and regulations are prescribed to help people if they want to achieve certain outcomes and to prevent people from behaving arbitrarily. But all such principles are subordinate to the Lord's pleasure. Whenever possible, these regulations must be strictly followed, and the least amount of deviation was prescribed earlier. But, ultimately, the only inviolable principle is that the Lord is satisfied by the performance of all such rules. When a religious practice blatantly disregards these regulations, then it falls victim to immorality. On the other hand, when a religion blindly follows these regulations, then it becomes fanatical and superstitious. Therefore, both blind obedience and blind disregard for these regulations are considered unacceptable.

QUESTION

Since you mention Jaimini, you are accepting the Mīmāṃsā philosophical system as a valid method of concluding the Lord being the supreme as well?

4.3.13 (530)

दर्शनाच्च

darśanācca

darśanāt—due to the philosophical systems; ca—also.

TRANSLATION

(The Lord can be accepted as the supreme purpose) due to the philosophical systems (demonstrating the purpose as the supreme) as well.

COMMENTARY

Matter can be controlled by choices, but choices need to be regulated. This regulation comes to us as rules of social order, the organization of objects into functional structures, and even the formation of institutions and societies. Apart from being good for life here, these regulations have a purpose—to become free of all regulations. When the soul is purified of material contaminations, then he learns how to use his freedom responsibly. The impersonalist says that we never get rid of rules of regulations unless we merge into Brahman. Therefore, the regulations of scriptures must be mandatorily followed. The personalist says that one is free of these regulations when one has learned to use their freedom responsibly. What is responsible use of freedom? It is the recognition that everything was created by the Lord and must be engaged in His service. When the soul acts responsibly, then the rules and regulations don't apply. As we have discussed earlier, even in this world, society can be egalitarian—i.e., everyone can act responsibly, without being bound by rules and regulations.

Since most people don't act responsibly in this way, therefore, a hierarchical system of organization is prescribed in which the responsible classes have greater freedom and the irresponsible classes have less freedom. But when society degrades to a point where nobody acts responsibly, then the hierarchy is flattened to a system in which nobody is free of rules and regulations.

Therefore, rules and regulations are not permanent; they are prescribed to bring a person to the point of responsible action. As one starts acting responsibly, the rules can be reduced, and ultimately, eliminated totally. The freedom from rules and regulations, rights and duties, rewards and punishments, is the highest goal of life. The rules are mandatory for the irresponsible people, but they are optional for the responsible people. The responsible people follow the rules not because they are bound by them, but because these rules get the best results. But when they do not get the best results, then they can be selectively applied, modified, or completely rejected. Thus, a philosopher should ask: What is the purpose of rules and regulations? Is it merely obedience to the rules? Or do we get out of the rules when we begin acting responsibly?

In Sāñkhya philosophy, the world comprises objects, rules, and purpose. The objects are organized by rules, and the rules are chosen by the purpose; the body is an object, the mind constitutes the rules, and the soul is the purpose. A more advanced understanding is that the purpose is in the soul, but the soul is not the purpose. Similarly, in Mīmāṃsā, the rules and regulations are meant to achieve a purpose—nobody accepts the idea that rules are self-justified.

QUESTION

Some people say that the fact that these can be adjusted based on time, place, and situation, means that such rituals and procedures are basically a method of entrapment to engage the mundane mind toward progressive activities, but ultimately, all such rituals must be considered delusional activities.

4.3.14 (531)

न च कार्ये प्रतपित्त्यभसिंधिः

na ca kārye pratipattyabhisaṃdhiḥ

na—not; ca—and; kārye—in the actions; pratipatti—the rules and regulations; abhisaṃdhiḥ—deliberately deceptive.

TRANSLATION

The rules and regulations in the actions are not deliberately deceptive.

COMMENTARY

The impersonalist oscillates between opposite extremes, trying to justify his untenable positions. At one end, he says that the rules must be strictly followed, and he criticizes devotees if they adjust the rules for serving the Lord. However, if someone asks them: If your rules are so sacrosanct, then why are they different from one scripture to another? Then, the impersonalist says that all the rules and regulations are yet another form of māyā or delusion. The central point of impersonalism is to deny the existence of an eternal purpose. Without a purpose, you must make opposite claims—(1) there are just rules without a purpose, or (2) if the rules are contradictory, then they must be illusory.

The devotee instead says that the contradictory rules are different prescriptions for different people. The man suffering from fever must apply a cold patch, and the man suffering from cold must apply a hot patch. The hot and cold is contextual, variable, and temporary; the goal is singular—good health. Therefore, there are no universal rules. However, there are good contextual rules—e.g., that cold needs a hot patch, and fever needs a cold patch. The rejection of universality of the rules is not the rejection of even the contextually good rules. Finally, as the context changes, even these contextual rules must be adapted. For example, someone suffering from both cold and fever needs to sit in a fresh, open, and airy atmosphere, because fresh air equally counteracts both cold and heat. The rigid application of rules won't produce health; and the rules and regulations are important only because they lead a person to health.

Therefore, both extremes of universally applying rules, and treating all rules as illusions, must be rejected. Universal acceptance and rejection must be replaced by a contextual acceptance and rejection, with the choice of the rule in each context driven by a singular purpose—the restoration of health.

Topic 6

QUESTION

So, do you recommend blind obedience and blind rejection of rules?

4.3.15 (532)

अप्रतीकालम्बनान्नयतीति बादरायणःउभयथाऽदोषात् तत्क्रतुश्च

apratīkālambanānnayatīti bādarāyaṇaḥ ubhayathā'doṣāt tatkratuśca

a pratīka-ālambanāt—by not taking shelter of symbols; nayati—the leader; iti bādarāyaṇaḥ—so says Bādarayana; ubhayathā—in both cases; adoṣāt—from absence of faults; tat-kratuḥ—does that (which pleases the Lord); ca—and.

TRANSLATION

Bādarayana says that the true leader by not taking shelter of symbols (i.e., the rules and regulations), in both cases (i.e., whether the rules are followed or not), due to having no fault does that (which pleases the Lord) also.

COMMENTARY

In every society today, there is a battle between those who demand more regulation, and those who demand less regulation. Those demanding more regulation say that the people are misbehaving, so they must be controlled by rules. And those demanding less rules say that when people are given freedom, the best results are produced. The devotee of the Lord rejects both extremes. He says that if one is devoted to the Lord, then whether the rules are followed, or they are rejected, there is no fault, because these rules are merely the symbols or representations of a higher purpose. If the purpose is fulfilled, then the rules and regulations are not themselves sacrosanct. This stage of devotion, however, is fully cognizant of the laws of moral action. If this principle is blindly imitated by an ordinary person, then they are implicated in the consequences of their actions, which causes them to suffer and enjoy. This is because an ordinary person whimsically picks whatever rules he likes and rejects whichever rules he doesn't. The sole criterion for deciding upon rules is his convenience. The devotee, however, picks the rules and regulations based on the Lord's pleasure.

QUESTION

To determine what will please the Lord requires a person to fully know the Lord. How can one decide what to do unless they know the Lord?

4.3.16 (533)

विशेषं च दर्शयति

viśeṣaṃ ca darśayati

viśeṣaṃ—the qualities (of the Lord); ca—also; darśayati—sees.

TRANSLATION

(The devotee) also sees the qualities (of the Lord).

COMMENTARY

This sūtra rejects the whimsical selection of rules and regulations by one who doesn't see the Lord or understands what pleases Him. An impersonalist subordinates our free will to rules and regulations. The anarchist subordinates the rules and regulations to our free will. But a devotee subordinates our free will to the Lord's free will. In short, the devotee learns to act just like the Lord would act in each situation. By acting just like the Lord, the devotee becomes non-different from the Lord. Since the Lord is not implicated by karma, similarly, the devotee is also not implicated by karma. But to act in this way, one must intimately know the Lord and ask: How will He act in this situation?

By this constant remembrance of the Lord and meditating upon Him to decide what we need to do, the devotee begins to see the Lord. Thus, by trying to act just like the Lord one gains an understanding of the Lord, and by this understanding, the he acts like the Lord even more. Thus, as soon as someone reposes their faith in the Lord, both their knowledge and actions improve—better actions lead to better knowledge, and better knowledge leads to better actions. This cyclic process of improvement is different from a blind acceptance and blind rejection of rules. It is about being non-different from the Lord.

SECTION 4

Topic 1

QUESTION

Does this mean that the Lord's devotees are authorized to create rules and regulations for society, even if they are different from the scriptures?

4.4.1 (534)

संपद्याविर्भावःस्वेनशब्दात्

saṃpadyāvirbhāvaḥ svenaśabdāt

saṃpadya—having attained; āvirbhāvaḥ—the manifestation of emotions (of the love of the Lord); svenaśabdāt—from that which is called his own.

TRANSLATION

(Those) having attained the manifestation of the emotional state (of the love of the Lord) from that which is called his own (personality) (are also qualified to propound rules and regulations for the general masses of people).

COMMENTARY

A devotee leads the world in three ways— (1) by explaining the nature of the Absolute Truth through scripture, reason, and observation, (2) by becoming the example and embodiment of this understanding, and (3) by propounding the rules and regulations for others who want to attain the same state. Many people may explain this understanding partially and imperfectly, and they are themselves not the perfect embodiments of this understanding. They are not considered qualified to prescribe the rules and regulations for the others.

Only one who has attained the emotional state of love of the Lord is described in this sūtra as being qualified to become leader, who can prescribe rules and regulations. Others are qualified to teach the understanding of the Absolute Truth, and practice this understanding themselves to become the perfect embodiments of the understanding. However, in general, they should refrain from trying to propound rules and regulations for others. This is mainly because there are innumerable injunctions about what must be done, and these injunctions apply to different people, places, times, and circumstances. Which rule and injunction applies to which person, in which place, time, and circumstance, needs a profound understanding of all four. When rules are misapplied or universalized, then the ultimate aim of achieving the Lord's love is missed, even if some temporary benefits may be attained by the application of rules.

The spiritual master is one who is expert in adjusting the injunctions for a person, in a time, place, or situation. And the qualification of the spiritual master is that he must have attained the emotional love of the Lord. Anyone else who pretends to be a spiritual master, and prescribes faulty rules and regulations, also becomes implicated in the consequences of such flawed rules.

QUESTION

Does this mean that one cannot understand the scriptures on their own, since they contain many contradictions applicable to people in different situations, and only a devotee of the Lord is qualified to decide what to apply?

4.4.2 (535)
मुक्तःप्रतिज्ञानात्
muktaḥ pratijñānāt

muktaḥ—liberated; pratijñānāt—from the promises (of this world).

TRANSLATION

One must be liberated from the promises (of the world).

COMMENTARY

The rulers of this world are themselves bound by rules. They may bend the rules of a nation or society to their wishes, but they cannot escape the laws of karma. The devotee is not bound by these laws; he is not even interested in obtaining power or mastery over material nature. He gives the rules and regulations for the benefit of people, so that they may attain a similarly liberated state. Therefore, he is also free from enviousness and fear—i.e., the worry that someone might attain the same position tomorrow as I have it today. Therefore, the regulations are not for subjugating people; they are for elevating them and bringing them to the point where all regulations cease to be meaningful.

QUESTION

This state of a person in which he is not bound by rules, but gives the rules for others, and yet follows the rules himself to set an example, seems contradictory. In one sense, the rules are rejected; in another sense, they are propounded; and in another sense, the propounder himself follows the rules that he has propounded. So, by following his rules, he seems to be bound by the rules he has propounded, which is contradictory to being free from all possible rules.

4.4.3 (536)
आत्मा प्रकरणात्
ātmā prakaraṇāt

ātmā—the self; prakaraṇāt—on account of the context.

TRANSLATION

The self (is only bound) by the context of its existence.

COMMENTARY

Being bound *by* circumstances is not the same as being bound *to* circumstances. Being bound to a circumstance is due to karma and being bound by circumstance is due to dharma. A liberated soul accepts the bounds imposed by circumstances as dharma, but he is not bound to the circumstance due to karma. Furthermore, the rules and regulations of this world are contextualized to a role, but not contextualized to the time, place, and person. For example, a court judge can render judgments on other people, but he is not allowed to change the rules based on different people. The previous judgments are used as precedents in courts to claim that if this was done to that person at a previous time and place, then the same principle must be reapplied now. In short, the rules and their applications tend to be universalized across times, places, and persons, and the freedom to contextualize these rules is taken away. The devotee is free from such universalization. Even when he breaks the principles that he himself upheld in other places, times, or toward people, he is not bound by karma. Thus, he identifies the best dharma for a place, time, and person.

Topic 2

QUESTION

Doesn't the definition of the dharma in relation to a context (or a socially constructed identity) entail that the self is not truly an individual entity?

4.4.4 (537)
अविभागेन दृष्टत्वात्
avibhāgena dṛṣṭatvāt

avibhāgena—non-different; dṛṣṭatvāt—from being seen like that.

TRANSLATION

(The self and the others) are non-different, from being seen like that.

COMMENTARY

Even when a soul is situated in a relation to others, the primary relation is to the Lord. In this relation, each part performs a different function; however, they serve a common goal. Just like the interest of the hand is not different from the interest of the legs, but the work of the hand is different from the work of the hands, similarly, each person is different and non-different. Due to the commonality of their interest, the individuals are non-different, but because they perform different functions, they are different. A materialist or an impersonalist predicates the difference between individuals based on their different bodies, but the devotee states that with the difference in bodies also comes an identification with the body as the purpose of existence. Thus, people develop a different purpose, which gives rise to competition and conflict in this world.

The materialist says that this competition must be regulated by rules, and the impersonalist says that the individuality must be dissolved. But the devotee says that the different bodies are not a problem—they are only instruments of capability. The rules and regulations are not fundamental—they are guidelines of how the instruments must be used. The differences of instruments and appropriate uses can be reconciled if the purpose is shared. Now, the common purpose becomes the identity and the bodily uniqueness becomes the difference. Since difference and identity exist simultaneously, therefore, each person is non-different from the other: the body is different, but the purpose is identical. Hence, the difference between the individuals need not be dissolved, and the differences need not lead to conflict. The reconciliation of the purpose is superior to materialist diversity and impersonalist unity. Since both principles of diversity and unity are rejected, therefore, 'non-difference' is used.

Topic 3

QUESTION

Isn't the principle of non-difference, by the attainment of common purpose, also seen in this world, when people gather in institutions and societies for a common purpose? If so, how is the devotee's non-difference better?

4.4.5 (538)

ब्राह्मेण जैमिनिःउपन्यासादिभ्यः

brāhmeṇa jaiminiḥ upanyāsādibhyaḥ

brāhmeṇa—those with the qualities of Brahman or Brahmanas; jaiminiḥ—(so says) Jaimini; upanyāsādibhyaḥ—on account of the narrations etc.

TRANSLATION

According to Jaimini (even in this world the dissolution of the difference between self-interest and other interest) is found in the Brahmanas (since the Brahmanas act in other's interest) according to narrations (about them).

COMMENTARY

A selfish person thinks that even if someone is helping them, it must be for their selfish reasons. Similarly, a selfish person thinks that if someone is criticizing them, then it must be due to their selfish reasons. These are the goggles through which most people see, and they classify others into selfish friends and selfish enemies. The advice of a selfish friend is distrusted, and the criticism of a selfish enemy is disregarded. Thus, people live within their bubbles of distrust and see the Brahmanas and devotees through the goggles of that distrust. If a Brahmana gives them advice, they don't think how it can benefit them, but how it must be benefitting the Brahmana to give such advice. If the Brahmana criticizes them, they don't think how they are hurting themselves, but why the Brahmana should hurt them. It is impossible to correct such misperceptions; the person with red goggles will see the world red. With such goggles, the cooperation of a Brahmana is equated to the sectarian alliances of selfish people, and their competition is equated to the drive for materialistic domination. Hence, mundane people cannot benefit from the advice and criticism of a Brahmana because they cannot distinguish them from the others. They are so comfortable living in the dark, that they consider any sign of light as an oncoming train.

Only when these goggles are removed, then one sees that some things are red, and some are not. But removing such goggles itself means progressing in realization. This sūtra says that it is possible to distinguish the Brahmanas from mundane cooperation and competition through some distinguishing marks. Two such qualities are the perfection of knowledge and renunciation.

QUESTION

But many qualities of the Brahmana are found in ordinary people. Many people may have some knowledge and renunciation. Then, what is the difference between the semi-knowledgeable and renounced vs. the devotees?

4.4.6 (539)

चितितन्मात्रेण तदात्मकत्वादित्यौडुलोमिः

cititanmātreṇa tadātmakatvādityauḍulomiḥ

citi-tanmātreṇa—the body of pure cognitive ability; tat-ātmakatvāt—because that being its true nature; iti—thus; auḍulomiḥ—Audulomi (states).

TRANSLATION

(The difference between the Brahmana and the liberated soul is that the liberated soul) exists in the body of pure cognitive ability because that is the soul's true nature; such is the (viewpoint or statement) of Audolomi.

COMMENTARY

The Brahmana is one who knows the difference between the soul and the body, and by that distinction, many types of material ignorance and attachments are destroyed. But the destruction of this ignorance and attachment is not the same as the acquisition of the Absolute Truth and attachment to it. Therefore, the Brahmana is superior to the materialist because the materialist doesn't know that he is different from the body. The devotee is also superior to the Brahmana because he not only rejects the material identity but also establishes the spiritual identity. In this spiritual identity, the soul has a body of pure cognition, which is different from the material body. This is indicated by the term *citi-tanmatrena* which means the pure quality of cognition. And this body is not different from the soul, which is indicated by saying that this body is ā*tmakatvāt*, which means the true nature of the self. The impersonalist argument is also refuted thereby because there is a body, and that body is the nature of the soul. As we have discussed before, the soul is the 'mind' with three aspects of cognition, relation, and emotion, and the senses are subdivisions of this mind. The parts are not separate from the whole, and yet, the parts are not the whole. Therefore, the soul has all the sensations, and yet, these senses are not separate from the soul. The Brahmana doesn't have such a fully developed body. He can see that he is different from the body, but he relies on the body for perception. The devotee has transcended this body and obtained another body. Thus, the devotees are superior to the Brahmanas, which are superior to the materialists. Meanwhile, the ideologies of impersonalism are false.

QUESTION

In the material world, we can understand that the soul has a body to perceive. But you are now saying that even in the liberated state, the soul has a body and various types of perceptions through the senses and the mind. Does this not create a contradiction between the bounded and liberated states?

4.4.7 (540)

एवमप्युपन्यासात् पूर्वभावादविरोधं बादरायणः

evamapyupanyāsāt pūrvabhāvādavirodhaṃ bādarāyaṇaḥ

evam—thus; api—even; upanyāsāt—on account of the narrations; pūrvabhāvāt—due to the former qualities existing; avirodhaṃ—there is no contradiction; bādarāyaṇaḥ—(so says) Bādarāyana.

TRANSLATION

Thus (with a pure cognition body), even (in the liberated state) according to the narrations (about the devotees), due to the previously existing qualities (of perception), Bādarāyana states that there is no contradiction (in this).

COMMENTARY

The impersonalist argument for the rejection of cognition arises from the fact that this cognition comprises of opposites such as hot vs. cold, bitter vs. sweet, big vs. small. Since these opposites cannot be reconciled, therefore, they cannot constitute Absolute Truth. And if this perception is not giving us the Absolute Truth, therefore, it must be an illusion. The mistake in this argument is that these opposites are simply potentialities, and they manifest one by one, at different places, in different relations, and with different persons. When they exist as potentials, the contradiction doesn't exist. When they are manifest, then, they are never manifest in the same place, time, person, and relation.

Therefore, the contradiction never arises. However, since these things exist in this world, so, the completeness of knowledge requires that they exist in the Absolute Truth as well. The impersonalist trades completeness for consistency and says that because there are contradictions, therefore, the Absolute Truth must be devoid of variety. But the devotees say that the Absolute Truth is not contradictory, despite manifesting all the contradictions. So, with the dissolution of the problem of contradictions, the argument for their reconciliation is unnecessary.

Thus, the devotee also has a body with all perceptive faculties, which then perceive contradictory qualities. These qualities are parts of the Absolute Truth, and the devotee sees the connection between these parts and the whole. Just like we might see two faces of a coin, and we know different aspects of the coin by this perception, similarly, the devotee perceives all these qualities and simply considers them different aspects of the Lord. Each aspect is known through a different desire, and a different relation, therefore, the Lord is never completely known. But this perspectival knowledge is not considered an illusion or ignorance, because we are not forbidden from experiencing other aspects. We just don't experience them simultaneously. And this lack of simultaneity arises due to the modal nature of reality. In short, modalities solve the problem of contradictions, while accommodating variety. The impersonalist solves the problem of contradictions by rejecting all variety. Therefore, the modal solution to the problem of contradictions is better than the impersonalist solution (in which all the variety exists in a balanced state of possibility).

Topic 4

QUESTION

You have described so many methods of spiritual attainment, but in each of these methods there are some difficulties. For example, there are difficulties in understanding the scriptures, in finding the right spiritual master, in performing the various processes for spiritual understanding, and in deciding the right course of action in each case. Therefore, none of the paths is trivially achieved. What is your recommendation in the face of such difficulties?

4.4.8 (541)

संकल्पादेव तु तच्छ्रुतेः

saṃkalpādeva tu tacchruteḥ

saṃkalpāt—through will; eva—only; tu—but; tat-śruteḥ—scriptures say.

TRANSLATION

But only by (a strong) will (is transcendence achieved); this is the verdict of the scriptures.

COMMENTARY

Any serious practitioner of spiritual life knows that the process is extremely difficult. There are many allurements of the world. There are uncontrolled desires. The mind and the body are not strong. It is not easy to understand the scriptures. The application of the scriptural principles is not easy. Meanwhile, the mind and the body are suffering in this world due to the previously produced karma. Under these situations, most people give up spiritual pursuits.

In the Bhagavad-Gita, Lord Kṛṣṇa states that out of thousands of men, one aims for perfection. Out of thousands of men aiming for perfection only one gets liberated. And out of thousands of such liberated souls, only one knows the Lord completely. If we take the lower end of these numbers, and if we say that there are about 7 billion people on this planet, then the best-case estimate would be less than 7 people on this planet would attain spiritual perfection.

A million out of a billion people take some interest in spirituality. While almost everyone has some religious affiliation, most of the people have no spiritual interest. A few million people in this world have some interest, and these people come from all walks of life, all religions, places, and social statues. When these million people endeavor for perfection, perhaps a thousand people get liberated. Thus, we can expect that a thousand souls on this planet will likely not be born again into a material body—most of them will dissolve their identity and enter Brahman, although they are likely to fall again into this world. Then, one out of the thousand liberated souls will obtain an understanding of the Lord. Such a soul will not return to the material world. Notably, this calculation applies only to humans, not to the other species like trees, plans, animals, birds, etc. If we count them too, then spiritual perfection is even rarer.

As a contrast, there are over 2000 billionaires in this world; so, it is a thousand times easier to become a billionaire than it is to attain spiritual perfection. Of course, a billionaire is created due to good karma. But spiritual perfection is not limited by karma; everyone can attain it. However, that doesn't mean that everyone will attain it. The requirement is simply a strong will. If this strong will exists, then the Lord directs the soul's actions from within the heart. But the Lord doesn't force anyone to do anything, and He doesn't interfere with a soul's free will. Therefore, if someone doesn't have a strong will to attain the spiritual perfection, then they will remain those who never tried seriously, or those who tried but failed, or those who tried and succeeded partially.

QUESTION

Why do you place such a great emphasis on the soul's free will? Can't the soul be pushed by others toward spiritual perfection? Aren't religious institutions trying to push many people toward such perfection in modern times?

4.4.9 (542)

अत एव चानन्याधिपतिः

ata eva cānanyādhipatiḥ

ata eva—for the same reason; ca—also; ananyādhipatiḥ—(the soul is said to be) without a ruler or lord (i.e., he is considered to be independent).

TRANSLATION

And for this very reason (of the free will being the most important), (the soul is said to be) without a ruler or a lord (i.e., he is considered free).

COMMENTARY

The injunctions of the scriptures are available to everyone, but they are not a substitute for effort. In modern times, people complain about lack of time, but it is not a lack of time; it is only a lack of will. Similarly, they say that it is hard to control the mind and the senses, but it is also a lack of will. Most people are afraid of failing, and hence they are afraid of trying. They are unable to take the hardship needed to attain the perfection of life, so they remain in the cycle of birth and death. Some people even complain that they have no free will—that they are controlled by the circumstances! All these are symptoms of tamo-guna under which a soul becomes conditioned to easy happiness, with the emphasis on 'easy'. As tamo-guna rises, charlatans appear to show people an easy path. Under rajo-guna, people endeavor, but only if results from their actions are seen. So, under rajo-guna people enthusiastically begin spiritual life, but if quick and immediate results are not obtained, then they go back to their earlier life as fast as they had come. Then, under the mode of sattva-guna, a person has the capacity to tolerate difficulties to obtain long-term gains. Therefore, if one begins spiritual life under sattva-guna, then they can sustain it over time.

Thus, a spiritual master doesn't just recommend a spiritual process, but also the method by which one can be elevated to sattva-guna. Methods of such elevation include giving up intoxication, meat-eating, illicit sex, and gambling, waking up early, maintaining routine, etc. These practices don't lead to spiritual advancement. However, they increase sattva-guna, which is necessary for one to persist in spiritual life. Many people think that these practices are themselves spiritual progress, but they are not. They are simply healthy, clean living, which is neither necessary nor sufficient for spiritual progress, but it is recommended to maintain sattva-guna. Once life is regulated in this way, then a person can perform spiritual activities, like chanting the Lord's names, worshipping the deity, meditating upon the Lord, and reading the scriptures. Under sattva-guna, one makes faster progress, because the mind has been regulated. The difficulty is that most people are so immersed in tamo-guna, that they don't want to change their lifestyle. Without developing sattva-guna, even if they read scriptures, they misunderstand everything. Even if they practice some meditation, their minds are constantly distracted. Since they don't make spiritual progress without sattva-guna, they blame the process and reject it quickly.

Therefore, this sūtra says that nobody can push you if you don't want to push yourself. As people are pushed, they become resentful. Even if a teacher tries to educate them, they argue with the teacher and blame the teacher for the difficulties. They resent the fact that knowledge is difficult, its application is even harder, and persisting on this path for a long time is the hardest.

Studies on sportspersons have shown that the most successful sportspersons aren't the most talented, the strongest, or those with the most resources. They rather have the quality of being able to get up after a fall and try again. This requires will. Thus, even material success comes to a person who endeavors consistently. The same principle applies to spiritual pursuits. The difference is that the spiritual pursuits are longer than material endeavors. Therefore, for a material endeavor, one must give up laziness and replace it with passion—i.e., the belief that by endeavoring one will get results. For spiritual pursuits, one must even give up passion, because the results are not immediate. The hare and the tortoise story is relevant in this context. The hare is passionate; he runs and then sleeps. The tortoise is persistent; he doesn't have the best resources, the greatest talent, or the most strength. But he persists and eventually wins. In the case of humans, persistence requires a high level of sattva-guna. Hence, the lazy people never get started in spiritual life, because they keep looking for excuses about how the hardship can be avoided by shifting the blame on something else. The passionate get started, but soon, they go back to sleep.

Many people make some effort initially, after which they settle into a comfort zone. They think: I'm making some effort, so that should be sufficient, right? Wrong. Effort means a constant striving toward greater perfection. When we settle into a comfort zone, that's where we remain. Spiritual progress is not measured by the quantitative output. It is measured by the qualitative change in a person. This change is in our control and cannot be forced by anyone. Therefore, the soul is lord and master of his destiny. It also means that the soul is alone in this journey—nobody is coming to save you unless you want to save yourself. Lordship comes with the responsibility for the right decisions.

Topic 5

QUESTION

But if someone doesn't have the strong will for spiritual perfection, how can they acquire it? How does one develop a stronger desire for perfection?

4.4.10 (543)

अभावं बादरिःआह ह्येवम्

abhāvaṃ bādariḥ āha hyevam

abhāvaṃ—absence; bādariḥ—Bādari; āha—says; hi—certainly; evam—in this way.

TRANSLATION

(The feeling) of absence; Bādari says that in this way (by feeling the absence) one certainly attains (a stronger desire).

COMMENTARY

The antidote to the comfort zone is the feeling of absence of the Lord. Most people who don't aspire for spiritual life don't feel this absence. They think:

My life is mostly okay; I have these things today, and I will have those things tomorrow, and in this way, I will live my life comfortably. This sense of comfort is the symptom of tamo-guna. One doesn't realize that the human life is obtained by great difficulty, and it is not to be wasted upon things that can be obtained in other lives too. The sense of comfort is produced by thinking that whatever exists with me presently is going to exist with me permanently. Thus, one might think that their wealth is going to grow, that their family will remain with them, etc. Hence, when someone loses their wealth, their loved ones abandon them in times of trouble, or they face other kinds of betrayals, then they realize the futility of the material life. Then they aspire for transcendence.

This aspiration is missing the perfection. In most people, it comes only when the material support system disappears, and one is left alone. In that state of loneliness, one cries for the Lord, and promises to never forget Him. But as soon as some comforts are obtained, one forgets the Lord immediately.

Therefore, mother Kunti prays to Lord Kṛṣṇa to keep sending her difficulties because under those difficulties the Lord is never forgotten. This sūtra says that one must replace their feeling of comfort by desperation, separation, and longing for the Lord. A strong will is not developed by the possibility of big achievements. Most people know that if they work hard then they might achieve great things. But they don't work hard. Why? Because they are comfortable in their present life. Those who are endeavoring (even under a mode of passion) have an inner burning desire; they think that the world is meaningless for them, and they must create some form of meaning to make their lives bearable. This kind of burning desire is necessary even for spiritual endeavors. Therefore, Lord Chaitanya states the following in the Śrī Śikṣāṣṭakam:

yugāyitaṁ nimeṣeṇa
cakṣuṣā prāvṛṣāyitam
śūnyāyitaṁ jagat sarvaṁ
govinda-viraheṇa me

"O Govinda! In your separation, each moment seems like a yuga. Tears are flooding my eyes like rain, and the whole world seems empty."

The philosophy of nihilism was earlier refuted in many ways. But in this sūtra, the philosophy of nihilism is also accepted. This nihilism is created by the feeling of separation from the Lord. The nihilist says that the world doesn't exist, that we are all alone in this world, or whatever exists is meaningless and we must give it meaning. The devotee accepts this ideology of meaninglessness without the Lord. His life is unbearable unless it is connected to the Lord's service. Such a devotee endeavors not because he wants to achieve anything. Rather, he endeavors simply to fill the emptiness created otherwise. When a devotee develops this constant sense of separation, then the Lord is immediately obtained. Therefore, the highest goal of life is to develop the sense of separation. It is a madness, but it is also the highest purpose of life. If this separation is established in the heart, then the Lord is not forgotten even for a moment.

The mode of sattva-guna also creates a comfort zone. It brings peace and tranquility in a person's life, and because the mind and the senses are no longer hassled toward futile pursuits, a person starts enjoying a life of peace. For this reason, sattva-guna is not considered a spiritual state. Rather, the state of desperation and emptiness is considered a spiritual state. But this desperation is not the pursuit of material gains; it is not the pseudo-happiness of laziness; and it is not the sense of comfort obtained under mental peace and tranquility. The spiritual journey is long because one must elevate themselves from laziness to passion, from passion to tranquility, and from tranquility to desperation.

Each stage of progression is hard, because the next step in spiritual progression is the very opposite of the previous step. Thus, the lazy person finds it hard to be passionate. A passionate person finds it hard to be tranquil. And the tranquil person finds it impossible to be desperate. Indeed, some people might equate tranquility with laziness, and passion with desperation. As a result, the devotees endeavoring for the Lord—because they find the world meaningless otherwise—are often equated to other passionate people, and the impersonalist says: Why don't you become more peaceful and tranquil? Why are you so agitated? Only someone who knows the full spectrum of progression realizes the difference between the states, and which state is higher than the others.

QUESTION

How do you characterize the feeling of absence of the Lord? What is the experience of meaninglessness, and what are the symptoms of this feeling?

4.4.11 (544)

भावं जैमिनिःविकिल्पामननात्

bhāvaṃ jaiminiḥ vikalpāmananāt

bhāvaṃ—the feeling (of absence); jaiminiḥ—Jaimini; vikalpa-āmananāt—due to (devoid) of alternatives, these do not enter the mind (as thoughts).

TRANSLATION

According to Jaimini, under the feeling (of absence), all the alternatives (of material enjoyment) do not enter the mind (and cannot be thought of).

COMMENTARY

The feeling of absence and meaninglessness is also experienced by a depressed person. Depression is the state of tamo-guna attained due to the failure of the attainment of rajo-guna. If we are frustrated in love, or other material achievements, then we fall into depression. In the depressed state, there is an active conflict between tamo-guna and rajo-guna. Anxiety is the preliminary stage of depression, and under anxiety, there is a paralysis caused by tamo-guna, and a hyperactivity caused by rajo-guna. As the condition progresses, one suddenly feels hungry and then loses appetite. The body gets stiff due to tamo-guna, and feverish due to rajo-guna, and both these conditions create pain. If one tries to cool the body, then stiffness increases; if one tries to heat the body, then the fever grows. Thus, the illness can be prolonged and incurable.

The way out of such a state is mild activity that produces small wins. Big things that require tremendous efforts, and the results which will arrive after a significant delay, cannot be performed during this state. Similarly, activities that don't produce a sense of achievement will push a person further back into depression. Hence, a person suffering from depression should not try to entertain themselves out of the problem, because there is no self-worth in it. Cooking a meal, cleaning the room, or paying bills, creates an immediate sense of accomplishment—i.e., it feeds the rajo-guna, and the sense of self-worth increases. Similarly, small activities, when no activity is being performed, also feeds rajo-guna. As rajo-guna becomes dominant, then tamo-guna is naturally subordinated, and the conflict between these modes subsides. One now becomes capable of doing bigger things. Such practical tips are often useful even for practicing devotees who may be struggling with various problems in their life.

These three modes exist even for advanced devotees. The devotee first feels separated from the Lord. To overcome this separation, the devotee performs activities satisfying to the Lord. Then by the achievement of results in such activities, the devotee feels satisfied. But this sense of satisfaction doesn't last. Rather, the sense of separation returns, the devotee acts for the pleasure of the Lord, and then again feels satisfied by the Lord's satisfaction. In this way, the modes keep cycling, and nothing other than the Lord is remembered.

QUESTION

When a devotee is imbued by this sense of separation from the Lord, then what does he do? What are his actions under the mental state of emptiness?

4.4.12 (545)
द्वादशाहवदुभयविधं बादरायणोऽतः
dvādaśāhavadubhayavidhaṃ bādarāyaṇo'taḥ

dvādaśāhavat—like the twelve-fold sacrifice; ubhayavidhaṃ—in two ways; bādarāyaṇaḥ—Bādarayana; ataḥ—therefore.

TRANSLATION

Therefore, Bādarayana says that (the devotees act) just like the twelve-fold sacrifice in two ways (i.e., serving the masculine and feminine forms).

COMMENTARY

During the reign of Svayambhuva Manu, there was no qualified person to become Indra, and therefore Lord Viṣṇu appeared as Indra, and He was then known as Yajna. He along with His wife—Lakshmi, who is called Dakśinā—had twelve sons named Tosha, Pratosha, Santosha, Bhadra, Sānti, Idaspati, Idhma, Kavi, Vibhu, Svahna, Sudeva, and Rocana. These twelve expansions represent the ten senses, the mind, and the ego. As we have noted earlier, our body comprises masculine and feminine aspects—the elements of Sāñkhya constitute the masculine aspect, and the prāṇa energizing the senses, mind, ego, etc. is the feminine aspect. In this sūtra, the term *dvādaśāhavat* or the twelve-fold sacrifice indicates the twelve parts of a sacrifice, and the term *ubhayavidhaṃ* or the two-fold practice, denotes the masculine and feminine aspects. They are a single family, but the parents are two-fold, and the children are twelve-fold. The constitute the entire perceptual apparatus of experience. The names of the children of Yajna and Dakśinā denote various kinds of happiness or satisfaction. Essentially, Yajna and Dakśinā unite to create happiness.

Now, this sūtra says that the devotees are just like the twelve-fold division of the two-fold practice. In short, they dedicate their mind, senses, and the ego to the Lord and His consort. Sometimes they want to serve the Lord, and sometimes they need the Lord. The sense of needing is the feeling of separation. The sense of wanting is the desire to serve. And the sense of satisfaction is the meeting of the want and the need—the Lord is obtained through His service. From this meeting, a new need is created, which then transforms into a want, which then meets the need, and the cycle repeats endlessly. Yajna is the person who is offered, Dakśinā is the offering for Yajna, and their union is the children. It is understandable if these things are not immediately clear. We can understand them to the extent that we can, and by experience it can become clearer.

QUESTION

You are saying that the devotee feels separated from the Lord. Then you are also saying that the devotee is united with the Lord. How do we reconcile this simultaneous separation and union? Doesn't it sound contradictory?

4.4.13 (546)
तन्वभावे सन्ध्यवत् उपपत्तेः
tanvabhāve sandhyavat upapatteḥ

tat-abhāve—in His absence; sandhyavat—just like union; upapatteḥ—it follows or is reasonable.

TRANSLATION

It follows that in His absence (one feels) also just like the union.

COMMENTARY

As we have discussed before, space is semantic, which means that there are three kinds of proximities and distance. The first type of proximity is similarity of meaning, and distance is dissimilarity of meaning. When this similarity is created, then the possibility of knowing the unknown is produced, and one becomes qualified to know. Once a person has become qualified, then he can interact with that reality and the qualification and capability to know is converted into an experience. Finally, the interaction to that reality is caused by our desire, and when the desire develops, then we are emotionally proximate.

Thus, everyone can experience the Lord through a desire, interaction, and qualification. In this sense, when these are present, the Lord is ever-present.

And yet, the difference is that when we see the Lord in this way, He is not visible to others, although the possibility of this interaction is eternal. Then again, when there is meeting, then the interaction is also visible to the others.

Hence, there is a difference between meeting and separation, and there is no difference between meeting and separation. Both meeting and separation are produced by the same process, although the separation creates private experience, and the meeting creates experience accessible even to others. Therefore, the term *sandhyavat* is used here, which means 'just like union'. It is not the same as meeting, and yet, it is not different from the meeting. The key point is that missing the Lord, finding the world empty, and then seeking the Lord, creates the same type of experience as when the Lord is face-to-face. It just remains our personal experience and is not known to the other devotees.

QUESTION

Then what happens if the soul reaches the spiritual world and finds the Lord face-to-face? How is that different from the experience of separation?

4.4.14 (547)
भावे जाग्रद्वत्
bhāve jāgradvat

bhāve—in attainment (of spiritual world); jāgrat-vat—just as in the waking state.

TRANSLATION

In the attainment (of the spiritual world, where the Lord is seen face-to-face), (the experience is) just like waking state (i.e., public experience).

COMMENTARY

This sūtra makes the distinction between the feelings of separation, and the meeting with the Lord face-to-face, even more explicit by comparing these two as dreaming and waking. During dreaming, we see a reality, which is eternally possible, but others don't see it. Then during waking, we can see the same reality, and others can see it too. From the perspective of an individual, there is no difference between waking and dreaming—everything that is experienced in a dream can also be experienced during waking, and vice versa. And yet, the dream experience is private, while the waking experience is public. Thus, while the devotee is in the material world, he experiences the Lord due to separation, but the experience is private, and it can be compared to dreaming. Then when the devotee reaches the spiritual world, the same experience becomes public.

Topic 6

QUESTION

But if you say that the devotee's experience is just like a dream, then

someone can say that it is not acceptable unless there is public evidence for it. I understand that God cannot be seen by everyone, but what is the evidence that the devotee is seeing the Lord? Can this seeing be known by the others?

4.4.15 (548)
प्रदीपवदावेशःतथा हि दर्शयति
pradīpavadāveśaḥ tathā hi darśayati

pradīpavat—like a lamp; āveśaḥ—seized by frenzy or imbued with the emotion; tathā—similarily; hi—certainly; darśayati—is seen.

TRANSLATION

Like a lamp (illuminates the world), similarly, imbued with the emotion (of the love of God), (the devotee) is certainly seen (to illuminate the world).

COMMENTARY

We previously discussed the argument from hallucination, which the impersonalist makes, and presented an argument against it: Even if the devotional experience is like a hallucination, what is wrong with that if it is permanent and blissful? This sūtra presents another argument against the claim of hallucination: we cannot see what the devotee sees, but we can find the evidence of that seeing, namely, that the devotee illuminates the world by his presence.

The material world is ignorance about the truth, right, and good. We don't see the truth because we think that matter is devoid of meaning; that is merely exists, but it doesn't tell us anything, it has no purpose, and it was produced randomly. With such ignorance, we are also unable to formulate consistent and complete theories about the world, but under ignorance we relegate the problem to the future. Then, as the meanings are taken out of reality, then the notions of right and good are either completely rejected or relativized to individuals. Thus, whatever an individual considers good, is good for him. And whatever a group of individuals consider right in a society is right for them. By disregarding the righteousness, people are entrapped in karma and they suffer endlessly, but they are unable to claim that pain and suffering is good.

The devotee alleviates this ignorance in many ways. First, he explains the nature of truth, right, and good. Second, he tells people how to elevate themselves to the truth, right, and good. Third, he demonstrates this elevated state through his own life. The explanation of truth, right, and good is the theory. The method of attaining this truth, right, and good, is the practice. And his life is the empirical evidence obtained by following the theory and practice.

An impersonalist is unable to explain even the nature of truth, right, and good. According to him, the self exists, but this existence has no meaning or purpose. This is like saying that the sentence "the sky is purple" exists, but we don't want to know if it is true, whether it should be spoken, and what happens when it is spoken. The materialist and impersonalist philosophies are nearly identical in the sense that both accept existence, although the former is existence with variety and the latter is existence without variety. That dissolution of variety doesn't constitute the answers to the questions of truth, right, and good. It is merely the dissolution of such questions themselves. Impersonalism is like a teacher shaming a student for asking good questions—because he doesn't know the answer. When this shame overwhelms the soul, he commits spiritual suicide. And by that suicide the questions of truth, right, and good cease.

Only a devotee has the answer to the questions of truth, right, and good. He also knows how to attain it, and he shows the perfection of such attainment in his life. Of course, the blind cannot see the light shining in their face.

QUESTION

You have described the waking and dreaming states of the devotee. What about the deep sleep state? Does that state also exist for the Lord's devotee?

4.4.16 (549)

स्वाप्ययसंपत्त्योरन्यतरापेक्षम् आविष्कृतं हि

svāpyayasaṃpattyoranyatarāpekṣam āviṣkṛtaṃ hi

svāpyaya—in deep sleep; saṃpattyoḥ—with the wealth of (absorption in the Lord); anyatara-apekṣam—any expectation or relativity; āviṣkṛtaṃ—covering being removed; hi—certainly.

TRANSLATION

In deep sleep, with the wealth of (absorption in the Lord), any expectation or relativity is certainly uncovered (i.e., the covering is removed).

COMMENTARY

The deep sleep state constitutes the personality or identity of the soul. We have discussed in the introduction how this personality is divided into five parts—(1) what I like, (2) what I can know, (3) what I can do, (4) where I exist, and (5) when I exist. Each such aspect of the personality also has a negative component—(1) what I dislike, (2) what I cannot know, (3) what I cannot do, (4) where I don't exist, and (5) when I don't exist. For a devotee, this personality changes into the following five aspects—(1) what the Lord likes, (2) what the Lord wants me to know, (3) what the Lord wants me to do, (4) where the Lord wants to me to stay, and (5) when the Lord wants me to stay. This is the wealth of absorption in the Lord. Then, with this wealth, all expectations of what I like or dislike, what I want to know or not know, what I want to do or not do, where I want to stay or not stay, and when I want to stay or not stay, are dissolved. Everything is reposed in the Lord's will. And with this reposing, the relativity of various opinions—i.e., that everyone wants something different—is dissolved. So, the wealth of the soul is not fame, power, money, knowledge, beauty, or renunciation. The real wealth is that the soul is surrendered to the Lord. This wealth is not separate from the self; it is also the soul's persona.

The dreaming state is manifest from the deep sleep state, which means that our persona creates the desires, fantasies, and apprehensions which are manifest in dreams. The same persona is then manifest during the waking stage. The difference is that the manifestation of the persona in dreams is conditioned by the senses, mind, intellect, ego, and moral sense, which have been developed in this life (although influenced by the unconscious of the past lives present as our persona). For example, humans will almost never see themselves as dogs or cats in a dream. Even if they have had other bodies in the past, they will always see themselves as what they are in the present life. If such identity is not yet developed, then there are no dreams. For example, newborn children have dreamless sleep because their senses are undeveloped, although they have an unmanifest persona. As a child grows up, the senses begin to develop, and babies begin to have dreams. In these dreams, they often move their body and make some sounds, which is an indication that the dream is mostly sensual. As the child develops further, the dreams have increasing mental component, and so you can try to interpret these dreams because now they have meanings. The dream experience, however, is not constrained by opportunity because you can go anywhere, see anything, and do anything. The waking experience is constrained by opportunities created by karma—you cannot go everywhere, cannot see everything, and cannot do everything. In summary, the dreams are the expression of the unconscious persona through the constraint of the present body, and the waking experience is the same unconscious persona constrained by the present body as well as the opportunities afforded to the body at a given time.

The devotee also has an unconscious persona which is manifest as dreams or remembrance of the Lord, and then waking or face-to-face encounters with the Lord. When the dreaming and waking don't exist, the persona still exists.

Topic 7

QUESTION

You have answered all my questions, but I want to discuss some alternative viewpoints. Can you clarify them for me? My first question is: You have accepted that an impersonalist state is also transcendental, although it is not the highest perfection. How is the impersonal liberation attained by someone?

4.4.17 (550)

जगद्व्यापारवर्जम् प्रकरणात् असंनिहितत्वाच्च

jagadvyāpāravarjam prakaraṇāt asaṃnihitatvācca

jagadvyāpāravarjam—rejecting the worldly business; prakaraṇāt—caused by different situations; asaṃnihitatvāt—due to as if not invested; ca—and.

TRANSLATION

By rejecting the worldly business that is produced by different situations, and (doing them) as if one is not invested (in the results of actions).

COMMENTARY

The soul's bond to the world is created by guna and karma. Guna means the desires and habits of enjoyment, and karma means the consequences of the actions produced due to these desires and habits of enjoyment. Accordingly, liberation from the material world is also obtained when both guna and karma are destroyed. In this sūtra, the method of destruction is explained as a two-fold process. First, the person rejects the businesses of this world in various types of situations. For example, such a person is not interested in solving the problems of world hunger, in creating a more prosperous or opulent society, or in educating people about the nature of this world. This is notable because many people aspiring for Brahman fall back into altruistic or charitable activities which are meant to improve a person's life in this world. Such activities are rejected in this world. Second, the person may perform some deeds for the bare sustenance, but even those actions are performed in a disinterested manner. Therefore, whether the results are obtained, the person remains equanimous. By the rejecting of all forms of worldly goodness, the person obtains freedom from guna, and by performing whatever little needs to be done with disinterest, he consumes the previously ordained good or bad karma, and doesn't create new karma. In short, utter disinterest is the recipe for getting to Brahman.

QUESTION

It is sometimes said that upon liberation, everyone becomes qualified to interact with the Lord, and then they have a direct interaction with the Lord. This seems contrary to the mood of shyness, but even in the mood of boldness, is the Lord known directly by everyone, or only by His intimate servants?

4.4.18 (551)

प्रत्यक्षोपदेशाददिति चेत् न आधिकारिकमण्डलस्थोक्तेः

pratyakṣopadeśāditi cet na ādhikārikamaṇḍalasthokteḥ

pratyakṣa-upadeśāt—from the teaching of direct experience; iti cet—if it be said; na—not; ādhikārika—qualified; maṇḍalastha—situated in a circle; ukteḥ—it is said;

TRANSLATION

If it be said that (the Lord is) directly perceived due to the teaching, (we say) not so; (He is known) only through those qualified to be situated in His circle; thus, it is said.

COMMENTARY

In many egalitarian religions, the equality of the soul is taught. It is said that the hierarchy of this world is an artificial creation, and this creation is exploited by the priests. Therefore, we must flatten society and treat everyone equally. This equality is supported on the principle of the souls being equal.

This sūtra however states that the Lord is supreme, and He has His inner circle of devotees. But this inner circle is also based on qualification. Therefore, the more qualified devotees know the Lord intimately, and the less qualified devotees know about the Lord through this inner circle. When a new devotee is introduced to this inner circle, it is through the recommendation of another devotee who is already in the inner circle of the Lord. Those in the inner circle make this introduction if they consider the devotee qualified to be in the Lord's inner circle. Therefore, the doctrine of equality is accepted in the sense that everyone can enter the Lord's inner circle. But it is also rejected on the principle that only those most qualified enter this circle, whereas the others know about the Lord through this inner circle. In short, the Lord doesn't immediately reveal Himself to everyone. He does, however, reveal Himself upon a pure devotee's recommendation. Therefore, it is said that the worship of the devotees is as good as the worship of the Lord because that mood of humility and graciousness is important to enter the inner circle of the Lord's personal devotees.

QUESTION

Some people say that the Lord has a form, but the soul becomes a part of the form and merges in the Lord. So, they don't deny that the Brahman has a form, but they reject the separation of the soul's identity from the Lord.

4.4.19 (552)
वकिारवर्ता च तथा हि स्थितिमाह

vikāravarti ca tathā hi sthitimāha

vikāra-avarti—that which is not covered by distortions; ca—and; tathā—in the same way; hi—certainly; sthitim—situated; āha—the scripture declares.

TRANSLATION

(Just as the Lord) is not covered by distortions, in the same way, (the devotee) is also certainly situated (free of distortions); thus, the scripture declares.

COMMENTARY

Impersonalism is not a new ideology; it is has existed for thousands of years, and it changes forms. In the simplest form, neither the soul nor God have any form; they are not even separate individuals. In a more sophisticated form, God has a form, but the soul is within God, so he is not recognized as a separate individual. In an even more sophisticated form, the soul and God are separate, but they are equivalent; just like a lamp can be used to light other lamps, but once they have been lit, all the lamps are considered equivalent; in the same way, this impersonalist argues that upon liberation we all become God.

In this sūtra, the second type of impersonalism is being refuted by saying that the soul indeed has a form separate from the Lord, but this form is not an illusory or distorted form. Illusion and distortion are almost identical ideas in Vedic philosophy because illusion is created from the Absolute Truth by distorting and hiding parts of the truth and presenting that distorted and partial truth as the whole truth. Therefore, that illusion is also real, and a part of God, but it is not the whole truth, because it was created by hiding other parts. Therefore, when the term *vikāra-avarti* is used, it means that the soul doesn't have the tendency to distort, and he is not covered by any distorted ideas.

The implication is that the separated existence of the soul from the Lord is not like the illusion found in this world in which each person considers themselves to be the center of the world and entitled to exploit other living entities. The knowledge of truth means that the Lord knows He is the Lord, and the soul knows that he is the soul. Thus, the cessation of illusion isn't the cessation of individuality. It is simply the end of the pretentious idea of being God.

QUESTION

Some people say that the Lord is only known through the scriptures, and every other method of knowing must be rejected. However, you have outlined other methods of knowing through reasoning and practical experience.

4.4.20 (553)

दर्शयतश्चैवं प्रत्यक्षानुमाने

darśayataścaivaṃ pratyakṣānumāne

darśayataḥ—sees; ca—also; evaṃ—thus; pratyakṣa-anumāne—in direct experience and inference.

TRANSLATION

(The devotees) thus also sees the Lord in direct experience and inference.

COMMENTARY

This is by far the main source of conflict between science and religion. The religious fanatic says that the words of scriptures cannot be understood by ordinary people and therefore they must be accepted based on faith. The scientific fanatic says that everything must be understood through *my* senses and rationality. Factually, both positions are wrong. The words of scriptures can be understood rationally and empirically, but it requires an advanced form of intelligence that goes beyond the measurement of instruments, and takes into account sense perception, thoughts in the mind, the judgment of truth, right, and good in the intellect, moral sense, and ego, followed by the understanding of the unconscious personality, then the soul which chooses this personality, and then the Lord who is the standard for judging the truth, right, and good. When the world is reduced to the numbers produced by measuring instruments, then both theoretical and empirical knowledge becomes severely incomplete. Thereafter, if the incomplete view is presented as the whole truth, then atheism is created. Similarly, if religions are unable to explain the details about perception, thinking, judging, choosing, and the ideal choices, then they become fanatic, and they attribute the absence of insight as the virtue of divine revelation.

This sūtra says that there is no contradiction between religion and science because the Lord is also understood through reason and experience. However, this is not a gratuitous license for speculation. Notably, modern science claims to employ the methods of reason and experience, but the main method of modern science is speculation. Thus, so many papers are published not because they are proven—rationally or empirically—but simply because they are *novel*. Keeping this in mind, we should not confuse reason and observation with speculation about truth. In short, the standards one applies to religion, namely that it should be rationally and empirically confirmed, must also be applied to science. The fact is that today these rigorous standards are only applied selectively. Thus, both science and religion indulge in reckless speculation, and speculating on truth has become the primary benchmark for an intellectual.

If speculation is rejected, and rigorous standards of reason and observation are applied, then, religion is not limited to the study of scriptures. Indeed, one of the measures of spiritual advancement is that a deep acquaintance with the truth enables a person to apply that truth in any context and field of study. Therefore, the proficient devotee can apply the understanding of truth without referencing the scriptures. This might seem ludicrous to novices in religion who want to see scriptural references for every type of claim. But as we have seen, the scriptures are so numerous and mutually contradictory, that without practical expertise we cannot apply them correctly. One who knows how to apply them doesn't check a book every time there is a decision to be made. He rather employs reason and experience to decide which injunction applies when. Thus, reason and experience are hallmarks of proficiency in scriptural knowledge, and those with such proficiency can also present an understanding of the Lord without referencing the scriptures—i.e., through reason and experience.

QUESTION

Some people say that once the soul enters the Lord's abode, and acquires a body just like Him, then the soul must be considered equivalent to God. Thus, in some religions, there are many souls, but they are also just like God.

4.4.21 (554)

भोगमात्रसाम्यलिङ्गाच्च

bhogamātrasāmyaliṅgācca

bhogamātra—only for enjoyment; sāmya—equality; liṅgāt—from the body; ca—also.

TRANSLATION

Also, from the body similar to the Lord, which is meant only for enjoyment.

COMMENTARY

Under *sārūpya mukti*, the liberated soul gets a body just like the Lord in the Vaikuṇṭha planets. Similarly, in other forms of liberation, a devotee might live in the same place as the Lord lives, have the same opulence as the Lord, or even enjoy all those things that the Lord enjoys. This, as we have discussed, is like a king's son sitting on the king's throne. The son considers the father's property his own and enjoys everything just like the father. But the son doesn't become the king thereby. In the same way, the Lord controls everything, and He delegates His power to the soul to let the soul experience His power. The Lord's graciousness should not however mean that the soul is factually the Lord.

For example, when you receive guests in your home, you welcome them in various ways, ask them to sit, while you run around to serve them. Does that mean that the guest is the host, and the host is the servant of the guest?

Many people understand the language of power, but they don't understand the language of love. In many religions, God is described as the most powerful person, thereby instilling fear of God in the soul. Once this fear is instilled, then love is deemphasized. So, people think that if they go to God's abode, then either they will merge with God, or if they are separate from God, then they must continue to fear His power. Since this fear is undesirable, therefore, the spiritualist tries to find ways to destroy the fear. But how can we give up fear of the most powerful person? It must be that we become as powerful as God. This type of contortionist thinking is the result of the doctrine that God is the most powerful, and the relation between the soul and God is based on His power. In short, if God was not powerful, then there would no reason to love Him.

This sūtra however says that the relation between soul and God is for enjoyment. The soul gets a body like the Lord so that he can see, touch, and hear the Lord. This similarity doesn't make the soul equivalent to the Lord.

QUESTION

Some people say that although the personal abode of the Lord exists, it is also as illusory as the material world because it has numerous qualities. For example, they might say that since the Lord is infinite, and yet He takes a finite form to enjoy with the devotee, therefore, this finitude is itself an illusion. But the Lord accepts this illusory state, which is inferior to the infinite state.

4.4.22 (555)

अनावृत्तिःशब्दात् अनावृत्तिःशब्दात्

anāvṛttiḥ śabdāt anāvṛttiḥ śabdāt

anāvṛttiḥ—no covering; śabdāt—due to scriptural declaration.

TRANSLATION

(There is) no covering (in the spiritual world) thus is stated in scriptures.

COMMENTARY

We have now come to the end of Vedānta Sūtra, and now we attack the central problem of why people think that the Lord doesn't have a form. The problem is that the whole seems to have the same size as the part. From a physical perspective, the Lord's abode is bigger than the Lord, and the Lord resides within the abode. Since the abode is bigger than the Lord, therefore, how can we say that the abode was previously a part of the Lord? Similarly, there are infinite other living entities who have the same size as the Lord, and some of them might even be taller or bigger than Him. So, how can these bigger bodies be said to be a part of the Lord? All doctrines of impersonalism begin from the problem of size, and how to fit the universe into a person. Since this problem cannot be solved in physical thinking, therefore, it is said that God is infinite, and whatever is infinite cannot have a form. Or, even if God has a form, the universe still cannot be a part of the Lord, because how can such a big universe be compressed into the body of a person who has the same size as us? Finally, if everything is accepted to be part of a person, then the universe is called a hallucination projected out of a person; the person is finite, the hallucination is infinite. In this way, many bad ideas are the result of physical thinking.

But none of these bad ideas work, and every time these ideas fail, we can try to patch them, or go back to the original problem of size, which arises from physical thinking. The solution to this problem is to give up physical thinking and adopt semantic thinking. The form of the Lord is not physical. He is rather the original idea of knowledge. This knowledge has many parts or aspects, which are parts of His body. When these parts are subdivided, the world is created, and this subdivision is called His expansion or renunciation. Each such expanded part was previously within the Lord, so these expansions are also His property; this is called His wealth. The Lord controls these expansions, so His control over the creation is called His power. Finally, the expansions are created due to a purpose of enjoyment, so the purpose exists in each part, and this presence of the whole in the part is called His fame that is all-pervasive.

The central problem in all religious philosophies is that they speak about God's wealth, power, fame, and beauty, but they don't speak about the origin of these things—knowledge. Once knowledge is ignored as the origin of everything else, then wealth, power, beauty, etc. are construed physically. Then we start thinking: How can all this wealth, power, beauty, and fame reside within a person, and be created from the person? In short, how can you fit the universe inside God's body? From this difficulty arises monotheism in which the world is created ex nihilo, impersonalism where God doesn't have a form, nihilism where nothing at all exists, and materialism where only matter exists. The idealists speak of knowledge, but that knowledge is without a knower or a known. Can we really say that knowledge exists when there is no knower? For that matter, how can knowledge be true, if it doesn't correspond to a known? Therefore, the existence of knowledge alone doesn't solve any real problem.

When we speak of semantic thinking, we are simply saying that wealth, power, beauty, and fame are manifestations of knowing, which exists in three aspects—knower, known, and knowledge—of the Supreme Person. When the Supreme Person knows Himself, then knowledge is manifest due to His knowing. This knowledge includes other knowers, knowns, and knowledge, as its parts. But, since everything arises from knowing, therefore everything is semantic. The beauty, power, wealth, fame, etc. should not be treated as substances, forces, shapes, and sizes. Semantic thinking means that the Absolute Truth is jñānam-advayam or non-dual knowing in which the knower, known, and knowledge have not been separated, the diversity has not been created, and whatever we call the manifest world rests within the Supreme Person.

Once this semantic thinking is adopted, then the Supreme Person is understood as the word 'universe' from which the universe has expanded. Once the universe expands, then the word 'universe' seems to be a part of the universe, and the impersonalist now says that the universe has covered the word 'universe' therefore the covering must be an illusion. However, the impersonalist doesn't say that although light expands from the Sun, therefore, the light must be a covering of the Sun, and therefore, the real Sun must be that which doesn't emit light. The problem is terminology. Is light the covering of the Sun—implying that the Sun is somehow constrained by the light? Or is light the expansion of the Sun—implying that the light was previously in the Sun? Clearly, the Sun is smaller than the space in which its light expands. So, why can't that be the basis of understanding why the Sun is finite, the light expands to a much larger space than the Sun, and yet, this light previously existed in the Sun?

The Gayatri mantra says—*Tat-Savitur Vareñyaṃ*—or the Sun is the husband of the light and is married to light. The light is a part of the Sun, the consort of the Sun, and yet different from the Sun. The same principle applies in this case. The Lord is the master of His creation since the creation is His energy; She was previously within the Lord, and now She has expanded from the Lord. This sūtra makes this point succinctly—there no covering because it is an expansion. If we change the word from 'covering' to 'expansion', then everything becomes clear, and the various kinds of bad contortionist ideas are also rebuffed.

Index

Made in the USA
Monee, IL
06 October 2023

44096544R00444